PROPERTY

ASPEN CASEBOOK SERIES

PROPERTY
Cases and Materials

Third Edition

JAMES CHARLES SMITH
John Byrd Martin Professor of Law
University of Georgia

EDWARD J. LARSON
Hugh & Hazel Darling Chair in Law
and University Professor of History
Pepperdine University

JOHN COPELAND NAGLE
John N. Matthews Professor
University of Notre Dame

JOHN A. KIDWELL
Late Professor of Law Emeritus
University of Wisconsin

 Wolters Kluwer
Law & Business

Published by Wolters Kluwer Law & Business in New York.
Wolters Kluwer Law & Business serves customers worldwide with CCH, Aspen Publishers, and Kluwer Law International products. (www.wolterskluwerlb.com)

To contact Customer Service, e-mail customer.service@wolterskluwer.com, call 1-800-234-1660, fax 1-800-901-9075, or mail correspondence to:

Wolters Kluwer Law & Business
Attn: Order Department
PO Box 990
Frederick, MD 21705

Printed in the United States of America.

1 2 3 4 5 6 7 8 9 0

ISBN 978-1-4548-2504-3

Library of Congress Cataloging-in-Publication Data

Smith, James Charles, 1952-
   Property: cases and materials/James Charles Smith, John Byrd Martin Professor of Law, University of Georgia; Edward J. Larson, Hugh & Hazel Darling Chair in Law and University Professor of History, Pepperdine University; John Copeland Nagle, John N. Matthews Professor University of Notre Dame; John A. Kidwell, Late Professor of Law Emeritus University of Wisconsin.
   — Third Edition.
      pages cm
   Includes index.
   ISBN 978-1-4548-2504-3
   1. Property — United States — Cases. 2. Real property — United States — Cases. I. Larson, Edward J. (Edward John) II. Nagle, John Copeland, 1960- III. Kidwell, John, 1945- IV. Title.
   KF560.P72 2013
   346.7304 — dc23
                                                                      2013011896

SUSTAINABLE FORESTRY INITIATIVE

Certified Sourcing
www.sfiprogram.org
SFI-01234

SFI label applies to the text stock

About Wolters Kluwer Law & Business

Wolters Kluwer Law & Business is a leading global provider of intelligent information and digital solutions for legal and business professionals in key specialty areas, and respected educational resources for professors and law students. Wolters Kluwer Law & Business connects legal and business professionals as well as those in the education market with timely, specialized authoritative content and information-enabled solutions to support success through productivity, accuracy and mobility.

Serving customers worldwide, Wolters Kluwer Law & Business products include those under the Aspen Publishers, CCH, Kluwer Law International, Loislaw, Best Case, ftwilliam.com and MediRegs family of products.

CCH products have been a trusted resource since 1913, and are highly regarded resources for legal, securities, antitrust and trade regulation, government contracting, banking, pension, payroll, employment and labor, and healthcare reimbursement and compliance professionals.

Aspen Publishers products provide essential information to attorneys, business professionals and law students. Written by preeminent authorities, the product line offers analytical and practical information in a range of specialty practice areas from securities law and intellectual property to mergers and acquisitions and pension/benefits. Aspen's trusted legal education resources provide professors and students with high-quality, up-to-date and effective resources for successful instruction and study in all areas of the law.

Kluwer Law International products provide the global business community with reliable international legal information in English. Legal practitioners, corporate counsel and business executives around the world rely on Kluwer Law journals, looseleafs, books, and electronic products for comprehensive information in many areas of international legal practice.

Loislaw is a comprehensive online legal research product providing legal content to law firm practitioners of various specializations. Loislaw provides attorneys with the ability to quickly and efficiently find the necessary legal information they need, when and where they need it, by facilitating access to primary law as well as state-specific law, records, forms and treatises.

Best Case Solutions is the leading bankruptcy software product to the bankruptcy industry. It provides software and workflow tools to flawlessly streamline petition preparation and the electronic filing process, while timely incorporating ever-changing court requirements.

ftwilliam.com offers employee benefits professionals the highest quality plan documents (retirement, welfare and non-qualified) and government forms (5500/PBGC, 1099 and IRS) software at highly competitive prices.

MediRegs products provide integrated health care compliance content and software solutions for professionals in healthcare, higher education and life sciences, including professionals in accounting, law and consulting.

Wolters Kluwer Law & Business, a division of Wolters Kluwer, is headquartered in New York. Wolters Kluwer is a market-leading global information services company focused on professionals.

In memory of John A. Kidwell (1945-2012), a remarkable teacher, co-author, and friend

John A. Kidwell

Summary of Contents

Contents

Preface

Our casebook takes a fresh approach to teaching property, one that combines a thorough overview of the traditional property law topics with an integrated approach to such subjects of current interest as intellectual property, rights in a person's persona, and property rights in living things. We are committed to giving our students a firm foundation in land-based property law, including such topics as present estates, future interests, concurrent ownership, private and public land-use regulation, takings, and landlord/tenant law, but recognize that people conceive of property more broadly than simply in terms of real property. Intellectual property offers a case in point: Information has economic value and may be protected by a property rights system. We believe that an in-depth and integrated treatment of intellectual property law promotes a broad understanding of the scope of property and exposes students to an area of law that is undergoing rapid changes.

Our pedagogical tools include principal cases, text, notes, problems, and excerpts from books, law review articles, and interdisciplinary sources. Where appropriate, we have included statutes, regulations, plans, and documents. We have used problems sparingly, where it strikes us as the best way to teach a particular topic. We have provided transitional and expository notes to facilitate student understanding and foster analysis of cases and materials. However, we have been careful to leave enough unsaid to preserve that "eureka!" moment when a student experiences an intellectual epiphany. To that end, we have edited many of our principal cases with a light hand.

We believe that the selection of cases is critical to the success of our teaching materials. If the facts aren't interesting and provocative, the case won't engage students and fuel class discussion. We have chosen cases that represent good facts and good law. We offer a mix of recent cases (*e.g., Elvis Presley International Memorial Foundation v. Crowell, Fair Housing Council v. Roomate.com,* and *Metro-Goldwyn-Mayer Studios, Inc. v. Grokster, Ltd.*) and classic cases (*e.g., Armory v. Delamarie, Dred Scott v. Sandford,* and *Village of Euclid v. Ambler Realty Co.*). We have a preference for selecting cases with concurring and dissenting opinions, and almost always we include a short excerpt from each dissent, believing that class discussion is enhanced if we expose students to contrasting points of view.

We have created this book to be modular by design so that those teachers who have only four or five credit hours with which to teach Property can choose to omit one or more chapters, without confounding their students with chapters that no longer makes sense. Each of our chapters can stand alone. (To use the Christmas lights analogy, our book is wired in parallel, not in a series, so that if one light goes off, the others will still shine.) We have tried to be as concise and succinct as possible, keeping chapters to a manageable length so that teachers can cover as much terrain as they need to without having to spend an inordinate amount of time pruning and splicing our book to fit their syllabus.

Throughout the experience of writing and editing, we have kept our focus on the broad question, "What is *property*, and why does that label matter?" We take up this theme in the first chapter and develop it throughout the book. We hope to provoke students to consider this fundamental question from multiple perspectives, seeing that property may be tangible (*e.g.*, as land) or intangible (*e.g.*, as information), and how property law intersects with other bodies of law, (*e.g.*, contracts). We take a broad view of property and pay substantial attention to new developments in property law. At the same time, our book provides a *balance*. We have furnished ample materials dealing with the major areas of land law and traditional personal property.

It is our goal that our students come away from our class with a clear and deep understanding of what encompasses property, and how and why the law has developed, and continues to develop, to delineate the rights and obligations of property holders. We sincerely hope that you enjoy these materials as much as we have in our teaching, and that your students, like ours, find them richly rewarding.

James Charles Smith
Edward J. Larson
John Copeland Nagle
John A. Kidwell

May 2013

Credits

The authors gratefully acknowledge the permissions granted to reproduce excerpts from, or illustrations of, the following materials.

Books and articles

Calabresi, Guido, & A Douglas Melamed, Property Rules, Liability Rules, and Inalienability: One View of the Cathedral, 85 Harvard L. Rev. 1089. Copyright © by The Harvard Law Review Association. Reprinted by permission of the authors.

Fox, Stephen, Shamrock Hilton, Handbook of Texas Online. Reprinted with permission from the Handbook of Texas Online, copyright © Texas State Historical Association, 1997-2004.

Hardin, Garrett, The Tragedy of the Commons. Reprinted with permission from 162 Science 1243-48. Copyright 1968 AAAS.

Heller, Michael, The Tragedy of the Anticommons: Property in Transition from Marx to Market, 111 Harvard L. Rev. 621. Copyright © by The Harvard Law Review Association. Reprinted by permission of the author.

Radin, Margaret Jane, Property and Personhood, 34 Stanford L. Rev. 957. Copyright © 1982 by Stanford Law Review. Reprinted with permission of Stanford Law Review in the format Textbook via Copyright Clearance Center.

Illustrations

Cooley, Thomas M., portrait by L.T., Ives (1885). Courtesy of the Michigan Supreme Court Historical Society.

Dred Scott photoprint (1857), available at the Prints and Photographs Online Catalog (PPOC) of the Library of Congress.

PROPERTY

1

The Emergence of Property Rights

This chapter introduces the idea of property by exploring how it has developed in two discrete modern contexts, the right of publicity and cultural property. First, we offer a few observations about the meaning of the term *property*. The next section of this chapter contains perspectives on property, which are useful to consider in connection with the materials in this chapter and throughout this entire book.

In the popular lay sense, property usually refers to tangible things. A person's property, we say, consists of her car, furniture, clothing, tools, and the like. Land ownership and intangible property, such as bank deposits, stocks, and bonds, are also often imagined as the ownership of *things*. In the study of law, the term *property* often is used in a legal sense different from the popular image as referring to a thing.

At one time, property was considered a thing subject to the complete control of its owner. This view is epitomized by a well-known passage from the *Commentaries* written by Sir William Blackstone, an eighteenth-century English barrister. Although Blackstone wrote his *Commentaries* as a guide for laymen, his work became famous as the premier English legal treatise, with countless British and American judges relying on his words as a definitive statement of the common law. With respect to property, he said:

> The third absolute right, inherent in every Englishman, is that of property, which consists in the free use, enjoyment, and disposal of all his acquisitions, without any control or diminution, save only by the laws of the land. . . .
>
> There is nothing which so generally strikes the imagination, and engages the affections of mankind, as the right of property; or that sole and despotic dominion which one man claims and exercises over the external things of the world, in total exclusion of the right of any other individual in the universe.

William Blackstone, *Commentaries on the Laws of England*, Book I at 134 & Book II at 2 (1766).

Modern definitions of property sometimes emphasize different aspects of property than Blackstone's definition. Consider the following two twentieth-century definitions of property.

> Introductory Note: The word "property" is used sometimes to denote the thing with respect to which legal relations between persons exist and sometimes to denote the

legal relations. The former of these two usages is illustrated in the expressions "the property abuts on the highway" and "the property was destroyed by fire." This usage does not occur in this Restatement. . . .

The word "property" is used in this Restatement to denote legal relations between persons with respect to a thing. The thing may be an object having physical existence or it may be any kind of an intangible such as a patent right or a chose in action. . . .

American Law Institute, *Restatement (First) of Property* (1936).

Now, at this point, it may be useful to summarize our analysis of property in terms of a simple label. Suppose we say, that is property to which the following label can be attached:

To the world:
Keep off X unless you have my permission, which I may grant or withhold.
Signed: Private Citizen
Endorsed: The state

Felix S. Cohen, *Dialogue on Private Property*, 9 Rutgers L. Rev. 357, 374 (1954).

Property today is often defined as a "bundle of rights" or, more vividly, as like "a 'bundle of sticks'—a collection of individual rights which, in certain combinations, constitute property." United States v. Craft, 535 U.S. 274, 278 (2002) (reprinted in Chapter 8). In *Craft*, Justice O'Connor credited Justice Cardozo with developing the "bundle of sticks" metaphor in his 1928 book *Paradoxes of Legal Science*, while others have emphasized the writings of Yale law professor Wesley Hohfeld in the prior decade. Indeed, the "bundle of sticks" metaphor can be traced to *Aesop's Fables*, albeit in a rather different context than property law.

The imagery of a bundle of sticks is meant to suggest that there are many distinct rights associated with property. Each right constitutes a single "stick" that is contained in the bundle. A property owner may hold all of those rights, or just some of them. Likewise, some of the sticks may be owned by one person, while other sticks are owned by another person. Or the government may own some of the sticks so that the private owner's rights to the property are less than absolute.

So which sticks comprise the total bundle of "property"? One list identifies a host of aspects of property ownership, including:

- The right to possess
- The right to use
- The right to manage
- The right to the income
- The right to consume
- The right to destroy
- The right to modify
- The right to alienate

Lawrence C. Becker, *The Moral Basis of Property Rights*, 22 Nomos 187, 190-91 (1980).

"Damn it, Wilbur, that's <u>our</u> bench!"

A. SEVERAL CLASSIC PERSPECTIVES ON PROPERTY

The idea of private property, in some form or another, is universal in all societies since the advent of recorded history. Yet is the institution of private property justifiable? If so, why? Since antiquity scholars have grappled with the broad questions of jurisprudence and moral philosophy raised by the attempt to support the institution of property and explain its limits. While it would be possible (and conceivably enlightening) to read hundreds of pages on this vast topic (easily lasting an entire law school course), for the time being we'll consider a thumbnail sketch of five leading perspectives or theories. These perspectives are, in some instances, cumulative rather than contradictory; they don't necessarily represent competing rationales. Later in the course we will consider some other ideas.

1. *Occupation.* This rationale, typically considered to be the earliest theory of private property, derives from Roman law. In the following excerpt, Sir Henry Maine describes the contours of the occupation theory and critiques it. A leading statesman and jurist of Victorian England, Maine served as a professor at Trinity College in Cambridge. He became prominent as a scholar of early legal systems, using comparative methods and integrating insights from the emerging social sciences of anthropology and economics. He spent most of the 1860s and '70s in India (then a British colony), where he organized the Indian legislature and designed the general plan for the Indian legal code.

■ HENRY MAINE, ANCIENT LAW
237-39, 243-44, 249-51 (Univ. of Ariz. Press 1986) (1861)

THE EARLY HISTORY OF PROPERTY

The Roman Institutional Treatises, after giving their definition of the various forms and modifications of ownership, proceed to discuss the Natural Modes of Acquiring Property. Those who are unfamiliar with the history of jurisprudence are not likely to look upon these "natural modes" of acquisition as possessing, at first sight, either much speculative or much practical interest. The wild animal which is snared or killed by the hunter, the soil which is added to our field by the imperceptible deposits of a river, the tree which strikes its roots into our ground, are each said by the Roman lawyers to be acquired by us *naturally*. . . .

It will be necessary for us to attend to one only among these "natural modes of acquisition," Occupation or Occupancy. Occupancy is the advisedly taking possession of that which at the moment is the property of no man, with the view (adds the technical definition) of acquiring property in it for yourself. The objects which the Roman lawyers called *res nullius*—things which have not or have never had an owner—can only be ascertained by enumerating them. Among things which *never had* an owner are wild animals, fishes, wild fowl, jewels disinterred for the first time, and land newly discovered or never before cultivated. Among things which *have not* an owner are moveables which have been abandoned, lands which have been deserted, and (an anomalous but most formidable item) the property of an enemy. In all these objects the full rights of dominion were acquired by the *Occupant*, who first took possession of them with the intention of keeping them as his own—an intention which, in certain cases, had to be manifested by specific acts. . . . The Roman principle of Occupancy, and the rules into which the jurisconsults expanded it, are the source of all modern International Law on the subject of Capture in War and of the acquisition of sovereign rights in newly discovered countries. They have also supplied a theory of the Origin of Property, which is at once the popular theory, and the theory which, in one form or another, is acquiesced in by the great majority of speculative jurists. . . .

. . . Occupancy is pre-eminently interesting on the score of the service it has been made to perform for speculative jurisprudence, in furnishing a supposed explanation of the origin of private property. It was once universally believed that the proceeding implied in Occupancy was identical with the process by which the earth and its fruits, which were at first in common, became the allowed property of individuals. The course of thought which led to this assumption is not difficult to understand, if we seize the shade of difference which separates the ancient from the modern conception of Natural Law. The Roman lawyers had laid down that Occupancy was one of the Natural modes of acquiring property, and they undoubtedly believed that, were mankind living under the institutions of Nature, Occupancy would be one of their practices. How far they persuaded themselves that such a condition of the race had ever existed, is a point, as I have already stated, which their language leaves in much uncertainty; but they certainly do seem to have made the conjecture, which has at all times possessed much plausibility, that the institution of property was not so old as the existence of mankind. Modern jurisprudence, accepting all their dogmas without reservation, went far beyond them in the eager curiosity with which it dwelt on the supposed state of Nature. Since then it had received the position that the earth and its fruits were once *res nullius*, and since its peculiar view of Nature led it to assume without hesitation that the human race had actually practised the Occupancy of *res nullius* long before the organisation of civil societies, the inference immediately suggested itself that Occupancy was the process by which the "no man's goods" of the primitive world became the private property of individuals in the world of history. . . .

Even were there no other objection to the descriptions of mankind in their natural state which we have been discussing, there is one particular in which they are fatally at variance with the authentic evidence possessed by us. It will be observed, that the acts and motives which these theories suppose are the acts and motives of Individuals. It is each Individual who for himself subscribes the Social Compact. It is some shifting sandbank in which the grains are Individual men, that according to the theory of Hobbes is hardened into the social rock by the wholesale discipline of force. It is an Individual who, in the picture drawn by Blackstone, "is in the occupation of a determined spot of ground for rest, for shade, or the like." The vice is one which necessarily afflicts all the theories descended from the Natural Law of the Romans, which differed principally from their Civil Law in the account which it took of Individuals, and which has rendered precisely its greatest service to civilisation in enfranchising the individual from the authority of archaic society. But Ancient Law, it must again be repeated, knows next to nothing of Individuals. It is concerned not with Individuals, but with Families, not with single human beings, but groups. Even when the law of the State has succeeded in permeating the small circles of kindred into which it had originally no means of penetrating, the view it takes of Individuals is curiously different from that taken by jurisprudence in its maturest stage. The life of each citizen is not regarded as limited by birth and death; it is but a continuation of the existence of his forefathers, and it will be prolonged in the existence of his descendants.

The Roman distinction between the Law of Persons and the Law of Things, which though extremely convenient is entirely artificial, has evidently done much to divert inquiry on the subject before us from the true direction. The lessons learned in discussing the Jus Personarum have been forgotten where the Jus Rerum is reached, and Property, Contract, and Delict, have been considered as if no hints concerning their original nature were to be gained from the facts ascertained respecting the original condition of Persons. The futility of this method would be manifest if a system of pure archaic law could be brought before us, and if the experiment could be tried of applying to it the Roman classifications. It would soon be seen that the separation of the Law of Persons from that of Things has no meaning in the infancy of law, that the rules belonging to the two departments are inextricably mingled together, and that the distinctions of the later jurists are appropriate only to the later jurisprudence. From what has been said in the earlier portions of this treatise, it will be gathered that there is a strong a priori improbability of our obtaining any clue to the early history of property, if we confine our notice to the proprietary rights of individuals. It is more than likely that joint ownership, and not separate ownership, is the really archaic institution, and that the forms of property which will afford us instruction will be those which are associated with the rights of families and of groups of kindred.

Question

Can you think of any modern situations in which a new claim to a property right could be rationalized as arising by virtue of occupation?

2. *Natural Law.* Many believe that private property is a natural right, immutable for all societies at all times. As is indicated by Maine, title by occupation can be justified by resort to natural law. Saint Thomas Aquinas occupies a central position in the history of natural law thinking. Living in Italy during the thirteenth century, he joined the Dominican Order and became highly prominent as a Christian theologian. His writings include Biblical commentaries, sermons, and philosophical works, the latter drawing extensively on Aristotle. His crowning achievement, the treatise *Summa Theologica*, is divided into three parts. Part 1 (God) argues that God is the universal first mover and first cause. Part 3 (Christ) explores the divine and human nature of Jesus. The following excerpt is from Part 2 (Ethics), in which Aquinas develops his system of ethics, whereby a person strives for the highest end, using the human abilities to reason and to act.

■ THOMAS AQUINAS, SUMMA THEOLOGICA
Ch. 2, Arts. 1 & 2 (Dominican trans. 1948) (1273)

. . . External things can be considered in two ways. First, as regards their nature, and this is not subject to the power of man but only to the power of God, Whose mere will all things obey. Secondly, as regards their use, and in this way man has a natural dominion over external things because, by his reason and will, he is able to use them for his own profit, as they were made on his account, for the imperfect is always for the sake of the perfect, as stated above. It is by this argument that the Philosopher [Aristotle] proves that the possession of external things is natural to man. Moreover, this natural dominion of man over other creatures, which is competent to man in respect to his reason, wherein God's image resides, is shown forth in man's creation by words: "Let us make man in Our image and likeness, and let him have dominion over the fishes of the sea," etc. Gen. 1:26. . . .

Two things are competent to man in respect of exterior things. One is the power to procure and dispense them, and in this regard it is lawful for man to possess property. Moreover, this is necessary to human life for three reasons. First, because every man is more careful to procure what is for himself alone than that which is common to many or to all, since each one would shirk the labor and leave to another that which concerns the community, as happens where there is a great number of servants. Secondly, because human affairs are conducted in more orderly fashion if each man is charged with taking care of some particular thing himself, whereas there would be confusion if everyone had to look after any one thing indeterminately. Thirdly, because a more peaceful state is ensured to man if each one is contented with his own. Hence it is to be observed that quarrels arise more frequently where there is no division of the things possessed.

The second thing that is competent to man with regard to external things is their use. In this respect man ought to possess external things, not as his own, but as common, so that, to wit, he is ready to communicate them to others in their need. Hence the Apostle says, "Charge the rich of this world . . . to give easily, to share," etc. 1 Tim. 6:17, 18. . . .

Questions

Is this justification for property inconsistent with the occupation theory? Does Aquinas offer a theological rationale for property rights?

3. *Labor.* Another perspective seeks to justify private property on the basis of the labor that produces it. John Locke, an English political philosopher who wrote at the end of the seventeenth century, is widely identified with the labor theory. He was not the first writer to advance the idea, but he succeeded in popularizing the theory. In his *Two Treatises of Government,* Locke attacks the doctrine of divine monarchy, arguing for a government founded on the contract or consent of the governed. He advocated limited government based on both the contract theory and citizens' property rights. Locke lived in Oxford for much of his life. Although he was trained in medicine, he never practiced on a regular basis, instead devoting himself to business, politics, government office, and writing. His publications heavily influenced the intellectual leaders of the American Revolution. Notice the natural law overtones in Locke's work.

■ JOHN LOCKE, TWO TREATISES OF GOVERNMENT
31-32, 35 (Peter Laslett 2d ed. 1967) (4th ed. 1713)

§27. Though the Earth, and all inferior Creatures be common to all Men, yet every Man has a *Property* in his own *Person.* This no Body has any Right to but himself. The *labour* of his Body, and the *work* of his Hands, we may say, are properly his. Whatsoever then he removes out of the State that Nature hath provided and left it in, he hath mixed his *labour* with, and joined to it something that is his own, and thereby makes it his *Property.* It being by him removed from the common state Nature placed it in, it hath by this *labour* something annexed to it, that excludes the common right of other Men: for this *labour* being the unquestionable Property of the Labourer, no Man but he can have a right to what that is once joined to, at least where there is enough, and as good left in common for others.

§28. He that is nourished by the acorns he picked up under an Oak, or the Apples he gathered from the Trees in the Wood, has certainly appropriated them to himself. No Body can deny but the nourishment is his. I ask then, when did they begin to be his? When he digested? Or when he ate? Or when he boiled? Or when he brought them home? Or when he picked them up? And 'tis plain, if the first gathering made them not his, nothing else could. That *labour* put a distinction between them and common. That added something to them more than Nature, the common Mother of all, had done; and so they became his private right. And will any one say he had no right to those Acorns or Apples he thus appropriated, because he had not the consent of all Mankind to make them his? Was it a Robbery thus to assume to himself what belonged to all in Common? If such a consent as that was necessary, Man had starved, notwithstanding the Plenty God had given him. We see in *Commons,* which remain so by Compact, that 'tis the taking any part of what is common, and removing it out of the state *Nature* leaves it in, which *begins the Property;* without which the Common is of no use. And the taking of this or that part, does not depend on the express consent of all the Commoners. Thus the Grass my Horse has bit; the Turfs my Servant has cut; and the Ore I have digged in any place where I have a right to them in common with others, become my *Property,* without the assignation or consent of any body. The *labour* that was mine, removing them out of that common state they were in, hath *fixed* my *Property* in them. . . .

§31. It will perhaps be objected to this, That if gathering the Acorns, or other Fruits of the Earth, &c. makes a right to them, then any one may *ingross* as much as he will. To which I Answer, Not so. The same Law of Nature, that does by this means give us Property, does also *bound* that *Property* too. "God has given us all things richly," 1 Tim. vi.12 is the Voice of Reason confirmed by Inspiration. But how far has he given it us? *To enjoy.* As much as any one can make use of to any advantage of life before it spoils; so much he may by his labour fix a Property in. Whatever is beyond this, is more than his share, and belongs to others. Nothing was made by God for Man to spoil or destroy. And thus considering the plenty of natural Provisions there was a long time in the World, and the few spenders, and to how small a part of that provision the industry of one Man could extend itself, and ingross it to the prejudice of others; especially keeping within the *bounds*, set by reason of what might serve for his *use*; there could be then little room for Quarrels or Contentions about Property so established.

§32. But the *chief matter of Property* being now not the Fruits of the Earth, and the Beasts that subsist on it, but the *Earth itself*, as that which takes in and carries with it all the rest: I think it is plain, that *Property* in that too is acquired as the former. *As much Land* as a Man Tills, Plants, Improves, Cultivates, and can use the Product of, so much is his *Property*. He by his *Labour* does, as it were, inclose it from the common. Nor will it invalidate his right to say, Every body else has an equal Title to it; and therefore he cannot appropriate, he cannot inclose, without the Consent of all his Fellow-Commoners, all Mankind. God, when he gave the World in common to all Mankind, commanded Man also to labour, and the penury of his Condition required it of him. God and his Reason commanded him to subdue the Earth, *i.e.* improve it for the benefit of Life, and therein lay out something upon it that was his own, his labour. He that in Obedience to this Command of God, subdued, tilled and sowed any part of it, thereby annexed to it something that was his *Property*, which another had no Title to, nor could without injury take from him. . . .

§35. 'Tis true, in *Land* that is *common* in *England*, or any other Country, where there is Plenty of People under Government, who have Money and Commerce, no one can inclose or appropriate any part, without the consent of all his Fellow-Commoners: Because this is left common by Compact, *i.e.* by the Law of the Land, which is not to be violated. And though it be Common, in respect of some Men, it is not so to all Mankind; but is the joint property of this Country, or this Parish. . . .

Question

Is this an alternative to the other theories advanced to this point, or an elaboration or extension of ideas implicit in the earlier theories?

4. *Utilitarianism.* Private property can be justified because it serves the function of maximizing the utility, or wealth, of individuals. Jeremy Bentham, an English philosopher, was a leading founder of utilitarianism — a theory seeking to posit the underlying structure of moral norms (ethics). Under his principle of utility, the rightness of every action depends solely upon its consequences: Does it produce pleasure or prevent pain? Not only was Bentham a prolific writer, he also campaigned tirelessly for legal, political, and social reforms. When he died in 1832, he left his large estate to University College, London, where pursuant to his instructions his mummified cadaver still resides. In the following excerpt, Bentham explains how the institution of property depends upon society's law.

■ JEREMY BENTHAM, THEORY OF LEGISLATION
68-69 (Oceana ed. 1975) (Richard Hildreth trans. 1864)

The better to understand the advantages of law, let us endeavor to form a clear idea of *property*. We shall see that there is no such thing as natural property, and that it is entirely the work of law.

Property is nothing but a basis of expectation; the expectation of deriving certain advantages from a thing which we are said to possess, in consequence of the relation in which we stand towards it.

There is no image, no painting, no visible trait, which can express the relation that constitutes property. It is not material, it is metaphysical; it is a mere conception of the mind.

To have a thing in our hands, to keep it, to make it, to sell it, to work it up into something else, to use it — none of these physical circumstances, nor all united, convey the idea of property. A piece of stuff which is actually in the Indies may belong to me, while the dress I wear may not. The aliment* which is incorporated into my very body may belong to another, to whom I am bound to account for it.

The idea of property consists in an established expectation; in the persuasion of being able to draw such or such an advantage from the thing possessed, according to the nature of the case. Now this expectation, this persuasion, can only be the work of law. I cannot count upon the enjoyment of that which guarantees it to me. It is law alone which permits me to forget my natural weakness. It is only through the protection of law that I am able to inclose a field, and to give myself up to its cultivation with the sure though distant hope of harvest.

But it may be asked, What is it that serves as a basis to law, upon which to begin operations, when it adopts objects which, under the name of property, it promises to protect? Have not men, in the primitive state, a *natural* expectation of enjoying certain things — an expectation drawn from sources anterior to law?

Yes. There have been from the beginning, and there always will be, circumstances in which a man may secure himself, by his own means, in the enjoyment of certain things. But the catalogue of these cases is very limited. The savage who has killed a deer may hope to keep it for himself, so long as his cave is undiscovered, so long as he watches to defend it, and is stronger than his rivals; but that is all. How miserable and precarious is such a possession! If we suppose the least agreement among savages to respect the acquisitions of each other, we see the introduction of a principle to which no name can be given but that of law. A feeble and momentary expectation may result from time to time from circumstances purely physical; but a strong and permanent expectation can result only from law. That which, in the natural state, was an almost invisible thread, in the social state becomes a cable.

Property and law are born together, and die together. Before laws were made there was no property; take away laws, and property ceases.

As regards property, security consists in receiving no check, no shock, no derangement to the expectation, founded on the laws, of enjoying such and such a portion of good. The legislator owes the greatest respect to this expectation which he has himself produced. When he does not contradict it, he does what is essential to the happiness of society; when he disturbs it, he always produces a proportionate sum of evil.

* [Food or nourishment. — EDS.]

5. *Constitutional Theory.* Given the number of modern American constitutional law cases that involve issues of individual property rights, it should not be surprising that delegates to the federal Constitutional Convention frequently discussed the government's role in creating or safeguarding property. Presumably, because the delegates shared a common understanding of real property, much of this discussion involved then controversial types of personal property such as intellectual property and human slavery, resulting in constitutional recognition of both (the former in Art. I, §8, the latter in Art. IV, §2 and elsewhere).

At the Constitutional Convention, the fundamental relationship between government and property was explored in the context of fixing the allocation of representatives among the states in the lower legislative body, the future House of Representatives. Some delegates favored allocating representation strictly on the basis of the relative population of the states. Others preferred an allocation based on some combination of the number of people and the value of property within the states. Both approaches necessarily raised the issue of whether to count slaves along with free persons in the population. The second approach raised the issue of whether slaves, the primary form of property wealth in the Southern states, should count as property. Ultimately, the delegates compromised between these two positions by allocating representation based on each state's free population plus three-fifths of its slave population. Art. I, §2, cl. 3. Among the delegates actively participating in this particular debate were two of the Convention's most brilliant and influential members, Gouverneur Morris, a future U.S. Senator, and James Wilson, a future U.S. Supreme Court justice. Others included General Charles C. Pinckney, a future Federalist Party nominee for president; William Johnson, a future U.S. Senator and president of what is now Columbia University; John Rutledge, a future U.S. Supreme Court justice; Pierce Butler, a future U.S. Senator; and George Mason, an early patriot leader who had written Virginia's bill of rights. The following selection comes from James Madison's notes of the Constitutional Convention covering the debate over a proposal to consider population and wealth in the allocation of representation.

■ THE RECORDS OF THE FEDERAL CONVENTION OF 1787
Vol. 1, 533-34, 580-81, 593-94, 603-06 (Max Farrand ed., Yale Univ. Press 1937)

Mr. Govr. Morris [of Pennsylvania] . . . thought property ought to be taken into the estimate as well as the number of inhabitants. Life and liberty were generally said to be of more value than property. An accurate view of the matter would nevertheless prove that property was the main object of society. The savage state was more favorable to liberty than the civilized; and sufficiently so to life. It was preferred by all men who had not acquired a taste for property; it was only renounced for the sake of property, which could only be secured by the restraints of regular government. . . . If property then was the main object of government, certainly it ought to be one measure of the influence due to those who were to be affected by the government. . . .

Mr. Rutledge [of South Carolina]. The gentleman last up had spoken some of his sentiments precisely. Property was certainly the principal object of society. If numbers should be made the rule of representation, the Atlantic states will be subjected to the [new states soon to be formed in the West]. . . .

Mr. Butler [of South Carolina] insisted that the labor of a slave in South Carolina was as productive and valuable as that of a freeman in Massachusetts . . . and that consequently an equal representation ought to be allowed for them in a government which was instituted principally for the protection of property, and was itself to be supported by property.

Mr. Mason [of Virginia] could not agree to the motion [to count slaves and freemen equally], notwithstanding it was favorable to Virginia, because he thought it unjust. It was certain that the slaves were valuable. . . . He could not, however, regard them as equal to freemen and could not vote for them as such. He added as worthy of remark, that the southern states have this peculiar species of property, over and above the other species of property common to all the states. . . .

Dr. Johnson [of Connecticut] thought that wealth and population were the true, equitable rule of representation; but he conceived that these two principles resolved themselves into one; population being the best measure of wealth. . . .

Mr. Govr. Morris [of Pennsylvania] . . . verily believed that the people of Pennsylvania will never agree to a representation of [slaves]. What can be desired by these [southern] states more than has been already proposed: That the legislature shall from time to time regulate representation according to population and wealth?

Gen. Pinckney [of South Carolina] desired that the rule of wealth should be ascertained and not left to the pleasure of the legislature; and that property in slaves should not be exposed to danger under a government instituted for the protection of property. . . .

Mr. Govr. Morris [of Pennsylvania] opposed the [motion to strike wealth] as leaving still an incoherence. If [slaves] were to be viewed as inhabitants and the revision was to proceed on the principle of numbers of inhabitants, they ought to be added in their entire number and not in the proportion of three to five. If as property, the word "wealth" was right, and striking it out would produce the very inconsistency which it was meant to get rid of. . . .

Mr. Wilson [of Pennsylvania] . . . could not agree that property was the sole or the primary object of government and society. The cultivation and improvement of the human mind was the most noble object. With respect to this object, as well as other personal rights, numbers were surely the natural and precise measure of representation. And with respect to property, they could not vary much from the precise measure.

6. *Economics.* Economic theories seek to explain, justify, and criticize rules of property law by using the methods and vocabulary of economics. In general, economics is an empirical social science, but it is strongly influenced by the ethical theory of utilitarianism. Thus, many people use economics in an attempt to achieve an objective or empirical approach to law and legal disputes. Like other disciplines, however, economics embraces a number of different schools of thought, all of which can be applied to the study of law. One can argue that economics is a methodology, rather than a substantive theory. The labor theory justifying property rights, in this sense, is an economic theory of property rights. Thus, there is no single "economic theory" of law. Rather, there are multiple approaches, some of which we'll consider later in this casebook. For right now, we'll just consider excerpts from classic books by Adam Smith, an eighteenth-century Scottish academician, and Karl Marx, a nineteenth-century German economist and revolutionary socialist. Smith became well known for his book, *The Theory of Moral Sentiments* (1759), but he became immortalized as the founder of capitalist economics when he published *The Wealth*

of Nations in 1776, at the beginning of the American Revolution and the outset of the Industrial Revolution. Marx, in contrast, became famous for the book that he wrote with fellow revolutionary Friedrich Engels, *The Communist Manifest* (1848), which denounced capitalism as a tool of the wealthy classes for the exploitation of labor.

Both Smith and Marx believed in a labor theory, but differed in its application and implications. *The Wealth of Nations* established Smith as the first important political economist and the founder of what we now call "classical economics." He argued that labor is the source of a nation's wealth and that the specialization of labor promotes the expansion of wealth. His advocacy of the "invisible hand" (people who pursue their self-interest unconsciously promote the public interest) continues to be a cornerstone in modern arguments in favor of free trade and limited government. While Smith promoted the idea of free and open markets, he was not an advocate of laissez-faire. *The Theory of Moral Sentiments* calls for a moral and ethical framework as a foundation for worthy market operations, necessarily provided for by government. In general, Smith believed in a natural right to property rooted in his labor theory of value. Protecting the fruits of one's labor as property served the instrumental ends of stabilizing civil society, creating incentives for work, and advancing the formation of capital. Marx believed that, by his time, capitalism had been captured by the owners of capital for their own benefit to the detriment of labor. This situation, he argued, produced internal tensions that would inevitably lead to the replacement of the capitalistic "dictatorship of the bourgeoisie" by a socialistic "dictatorship of the proletariat," or workers' state, that in turn would evolve into a classless society that he called communism.

■ ADAM SMITH, THE WEALTH OF NATIONS
8, 276-77, 400 (Univ. of Chicago Press 1976) (1776)

[The] division of labour, from which so many advantages are derived, is not originally the effect of any human wisdom, which foresees and intends that general opulence to which it gives occasion. It is the necessary, though very slow and gradual consequence of a certain propensity in human nature which has in view no such extensive utility; the propensity to truck, barter, and exchange one thing for another.

. . . It is common to all men, and to be found in no other race of animals, which seem to know neither this nor any other species of contracts. . . . [M]an has almost constant occasion for the help of his brethren, and it is in vain for him to expect it from their benevolence only. He will be more likely to prevail if he can interest their self-love in his favour, and show them that it is for their own advantage to do for him what he requires of them. Whoever offers to another a bargain of any kind, proposes to do this. . . . It is not from the benevolence of the butcher, the brewer, or the baker that we expect our dinner, but from their regard to their own interest. . . .

The whole annual produce of the land and labour of every country . . . naturally divides itself . . . into three parts; the rent of land, the wages of labour, and the profits of stock; and constitutes a revenue to three different orders of people; to those who live by rent, to those who live by wages, and to those who live by profit. These are the three great, original, and constituent orders of every civilised society, from whose revenue that of every other order is ultimately derived.

The interest of the first of those three great orders, it appears from what has been just now said, is strictly and inseparably connected with the general interest of the society. Whatever either promotes or obstructs the one, necessarily promotes or obstructs the other. When the public deliberates concerning any regulation of commerce or police, the proprietors of land never can mislead it, with a view to promote the interest of their own particular order; at least, if they have any tolerable knowledge of that interest. They are, indeed, too often defective in this tolerable knowledge. They are the only one of the three orders whose revenue costs them neither labour nor care, but comes to them, as it were, of its own accord, and independent of any plan or project of their own. . . .

The interest of the second order, that of those who live by wages, is as strictly connected with the interest of the society as that of the first. The wages of the labourer, it has already been shown, are never so high as when the demand for labour is continually rising, or when the quantity employed is every year increasing considerably. When this real wealth of the society becomes stationary, his wages are soon reduced to what is barely enough to enable him to bring up a family. . . .

His employers constitute the third order, that of those who live by profit. It is the stock that is employed for the sake of profit which puts into motion the greater part of the useful labour of every society. The plans and projects of the employers of stock regulate and direct all the most important operations of labour, and profit is the end proposed by all those plans and projects. But the rate of profit does not, like rent and wages, rise with the prosperity and fall with the declension of the society. On the contrary, it is naturally low in rich and high in poor countries, and it is always highest in the countries which are going fastest to ruin. The interest of this third order, therefore, has not the same connection with the general interest of the society as that of the other two. . . .

[The] annual revenue of every society is always precisely equal to the exchangeable value of the whole annual produce of its industry. . . . As every individual, therefore, endeavours as much as he can both to employ his capital in the support of domestic industry, and so to direct that industry that its produce may be of the greatest value; every individual necessarily labours to render the annual revenue of the society as great as he can. He generally, indeed, neither intends to promote the public interest, nor knows how much he is promoting it. By preferring the support of domestic to that of foreign industry, he intends only his own security; and by directing that industry in such a manner as its produce may be of the greatest value, he intends only his own gain, and he is in this, as in many other cases, led by an invisible hand to promote an end which was no part of his intention. Nor is it always the worse for the society that it was no part of it. By pursuing his own interest he frequently promotes that of the society more effectually than when he really intends to promote it. . . .

■ **KARL MARX & FRIEDRICH ENGELS, THE COMMUNIST MANIFESTO**
98-99 (Progress Publishers 1969) (1848)

The theoretical conclusions of the Communists are in no way based on ideas or principles that have been invented, or discovered, by this or that would-be universal reformer. They merely express, in general terms, actual relations springing from an existing class struggle, from a historical movement going on under our very eyes. The abolition of existing property relations is not at all a distinctive feature of communism. All property relations in the past have continually been subject to historical change consequent upon the change in historical conditions. The French Revolution, for example, abolished feudal property in favour of bourgeois property. The distinguishing feature of Communism is not the abolition of property generally, but the abolition of bourgeois property. But modern bourgeois private property is the final and most complete expression of the system of producing and appropriating products, that is based on class antagonisms, on the exploitation of the many by the few. In this sense, the theory of the Communists may be summed up in the single sentence: Abolition of private property.

We Communists have been reproached with the desire of abolishing the right of personally acquiring property as the fruit of a man's own labour, which property is alleged to be the groundwork of all personal freedom, activity and independence. Hard-won, self-acquired, self-earned property! Do you mean the property of petty artisan and of the small peasant, a form of property that preceded the bourgeois form? There is no need to abolish that; the development of industry has to a great extent already destroyed it, and is still destroying it daily. Or do you mean the modern bourgeois private property? But does wage-labour create any property for the labourer? Not a bit. It creates capital, *i.e.*, that kind of property which exploits wage-labour, and which cannot increase except upon condition of begetting a new supply of wage-labour for fresh exploitation. Property, in its present form, is based on the antagonism of capital and wage labour. Let us examine both sides of this antagonism.

To be a capitalist, is to have not only a purely personal, but a social *status* in production. Capital is a collective product, and only by the united action of many members, nay, in the last resort, only by the united action of all members of society, can it be set in motion. Capital is therefore not only personal; it is a social power. When, therefore, capital is converted into common property, into the property of all members of society, personal property is not thereby transformed into social property. It is only the social character of the property that is changed. It loses its class character.

Questions

Both Adam Smith and Karl Marx evaluate private property from the perspective of economic theory. How do their perspectives differ? Why do those differing perspectives lead to such dramatically different conclusions with respect to the protection or abolition of private property?

B. RIGHT OF PUBLICITY

We begin our study of particular forms of property by exploring what some believe to be a new form of private property, the right of publicity. There are several reasons we believe this is a useful starting point. First, a focal point of this book is the *creation* of property. Although the institution of private property is older than all records of human history, we should not see creation of property as a distant historical fact. It's a dynamic process, happening all the time, as communities adjust their property laws to respond to changing social, cultural, and technological circumstances. It's easy to see this by studying the right of publicity, a recently created type of property. You should realize that the direction of movement isn't always the creation of more property, even though that's the theme of the right of publicity. Sometimes claims previously recognized as property are taken away. Slavery as a form of property was widely recognized throughout the world prior to the twentieth century.

Second, the study of law includes not only learning rules, but also evaluation. This means examining the policies underlying those rules, and those that might underlie alternative rules. The publicity materials naturally invite focus on policy choices. It's easier to see this for a newer type of property, where we can readily imagine what differences it would make to refuse to recognize what we call a right of publicity.

Last, the *definition* of property matters a great deal. The question of the first magnitude is whether to recognize a claim as property. Even if a right is recognized, it isn't inevitable that it will be classed as property. It might, for example, be seen as a "personal" right protected by the law of torts. Although the answer, "yes" or "no," is highly important, it is not the ending point. How property is legally defined can be as important as the question of whether person X owns the property. Once we recognize a property right of publicity, we will see that there are a number of important subsidiary questions bearing on the definition of that right, that we must consider. Resolution of those subsidiary questions will be necessary to resolve disputes between competing claimants, thereby determining the "strength" of the property interest compared to the competing interests of other members of society.

■ STATE OF TENNESSEE EX REL. ELVIS PRESLEY INTERNATIONAL MEMORIAL FOUNDATION v. CROWELL
Court of Appeals of Tennessee, 1987
733 S.W.2d 89

KOCH, Judge. This appeal involves a dispute between two not-for-profit corporations concerning their respective rights to use Elvis Presley's name as part of their corporate names. The case began when one corporation filed an unfair competition action . . . to dissolve the other corporation [Elvis Presley Memorial Foundation, Inc.] and to prevent it from using Elvis Presley's name. Elvis Presley's estate intervened on behalf of the defendant corporation. It asserted that it had given the defendant corporation permission to use Elvis Presley's name and that it had not given similar permission to the plaintiff corporation.

The trial court determined that Elvis Presley's right to control his name and image descended to his estate at his death and that the Presley estate had the right to control the commercial exploitation of Elvis Presley's name and image. Thus, the trial court granted the defendant corporation's motion for summary judgment and dismissed the complaint.

The plaintiff corporation has appealed. . . .

Elvis Presley's career is without parallel in the entertainment industry. From his first hit record in 1954 until his death in 1977, he scaled the heights of fame and success that only a few have attained. His twenty-three year career as a recording star, concert entertainer and motion picture idol brought him international recognition and a devoted following in all parts of the nation and the world.

Elvis Presley was aware of this recognition and sought to capitalize on it during his lifetime. He and his business advisors entered into agreements granting exclusive commercial licenses throughout the world to use his name and likeness in connection with the marketing and sale of numerous consumer items. As early as 1956, Elvis Presley's name and likeness could be found on bubble gum cards, clothing, jewelry and numerous other items. The sale of Elvis Presley memorabilia has been described as the greatest barrage of merchandise ever aimed at the teenage set. It earned millions of dollars for Elvis Presley, his licensees and business associates.

Elvis Presley's death on August 16, 1977 did not decrease his popularity. If anything it preserved it. Now Elvis Presley is an entertainment legend, somewhat larger than life, whose memory is carefully preserved by his fans, the media and his estate.

The demand for Elvis Presley merchandise was likewise not diminished by his death. The older memorabilia are now collectors' items. New consumer items have been authorized and are now being sold. Elvis Presley Enterprises, Inc., a corporation formed by the Presley estate, has licensed seventy-six products bearing his name and likeness and still controls numerous trademark registrations and copyrights. Graceland, Elvis Presley's home in Memphis, is now a museum that attracts approximately 500,000 paying visitors a year. Elvis Presley Enterprises, Inc. also sells the right to use portions of Elvis Presley's filmed or televised performances. These marketing activities presently bring in approximately fifty million dollars each year and provide the Presley estate with approximately $4.6 million in annual revenue. The commercial exploitation of Elvis Presley's name and likeness continues to be a profitable enterprise. It is against this backdrop that this dispute between these two corporations arose.

A group of Elvis Presley fans . . . , calling themselves the Elvis Presley International Memorial Foundation, sought a charter as a Tennessee not-for-profit corporation. . . .

. . . [O]n February 26, 1981, the Secretary of State . . . issued a corporate charter to the Elvis Presley International Memorial Foundation (International Foundation).

Wall of Honor at Elvis Presley Memorial Trauma Center

The International Foundation raises funds by charging membership fees and dues and by sponsoring an annual banquet in Memphis. It uses its funds to support the trauma center of the new City of Memphis Hospital, which was named after Elvis Presley, and to provide an annual award of merit.

The Presley estate and Elvis Presley Enterprises, Inc. incorporated the Elvis Presley Memorial Foundation, Inc. (Foundation) as a Tennessee not-for-profit corporation on May 14, 1985. The Foundation is soliciting funds from the public to construct a fountain in the shopping center across the street from Elvis Presley's home. . . .

III. Elvis Presley's Right of Publicity

We are dealing in this case with an individual's right to capitalize upon the commercial exploitation of his name and likeness and to prevent others from doing so without his consent. This right, now commonly referred to as the right of publicity, is still evolving and is only now beginning to step out of the shadow of its more well known cousin, the right of privacy. . . .

A.

The right of privacy owes its origin to Samuel Warren's and Louis Brandeis' now famous 1890 law review article, Warren & Brandeis, *The Right to Privacy*, 4 Harv. L. Rev. 193 (1890). The authors were concerned with the media's intrusion into the affairs of private citizens and wrote this article to vindicate each individual's "right to be left alone." The privacy interest they sought to protect was far different from a celebrity's interest in controlling and exploiting the economic value of his name and likeness.

Writing in 1890, Warren and Brandeis could not have foreseen today's commercial exploitation of celebrities. They did not anticipate the changes that would be brought about by the growth of the advertising, motion picture, television and radio industries. American culture outgrew their concept of the right of privacy and soon began to push the common law to recognize and protect new and different rights and interests.

It would be difficult for any court today, especially one sitting in Music City U.S.A. practically in the shadow of the Grand Ole Opry, to be unaware of the manner in which celebrities exploit the public's recognition of their name and image. The stores selling Elvis Presley tee shirts, Hank Williams, Jr. bandannas or Barbara Mandrell satin jackets are not selling clothing as much as they are selling the celebrities themselves. We are asked to buy the shortening that makes Loretta Lynn's pie crusts flakier or to buy the same insurance that Tennessee Ernie Ford has or to eat the sausage that Jimmy Dean makes.

There are few everyday activities that have not been touched by celebrity merchandising. This, of course, should come as no surprise. Celebrity endorsements are extremely valuable in the promotion of goods and services. They increase audience appeal and thus make the commodity or service more sellable. These endorsements are of great economic value to celebrities and are now economic reality.

The first decision to recognize the right of publicity as a right independent from the right of privacy was Haelan Laboratories, Inc. v. Topps Chewing Gum, Inc., 202 F.2d 866 (2d Cir.), *cert. denied*, 346 U.S. 816 (1953). The United States Court of Appeals for the Second Circuit stated:

> This right might be called a "right of publicity." For it is common knowledge that many prominent persons (especially actors and ball-players), far from having their feelings bruised through public exposure of their likenesses, would feel sorely deprived if they no longer received money for authorizing advertisements, popularizing their countenances, displayed in newspapers, magazines, busses, trains and subways. This right of publicity would usually yield them no money unless it could be made the subject of an exclusive grant which barred any other advertiser from using their pictures.

Haelan Laboratories, Inc. v. Topps Chewing Gum, Inc., 202 F.2d 866, 868 (2d Cir. 1953).

The legal experts have consistently called for the recognition of the right of publicity as a separate and independent right. In 1977, the United States Supreme Court recognized that the right of publicity was distinct from the right of privacy. Zacchini v. Scripps-Howard Broadcasting Co., 433 U.S. 562, 571-74 (1977). Now, courts in other jurisdictions uniformly hold that the right of publicity should be considered as a freestanding right independent from the right of privacy. . . .

C.

The appellate courts of this State have had little experience with the right of publicity. The Tennessee Supreme Court has never recognized it as part of our common law or has never undertaken to define its scope. However, the recognition of individual property rights is deeply embedded in our jurisprudence. These rights are recognized in Article I, Section 8 of the Tennessee Constitution and have been called "absolute" by the Tennessee Supreme Court. Stratton Claimants v. Morris Claimants, 15 S.W. 87, 90 (Tenn. 1891). This Court has noted that the right of property "has taken deep root in this country and there is now no substantial dissent from it." Davis v. Mitchell, 178 S.W.2d 889, 910 (Tenn. App. 1943).

The concept of the right of property is multifaceted. It has been described as a bundle of rights or legally protected interests. These rights or interests include: (1) the right of possession, enjoyment and use; (2) the unrestricted right of disposition; and (3) the power of testimonial disposition.

In its broadest sense, property includes all rights that have value. It embodies all the interests a person has in land and chattels that are capable of being possessed and controlled to the exclusion of others. . . .

Our courts have recognized that a person's "business," a corporate name, a trade name and the good will of a business are species of intangible personal property.

Tennessee's common law thus embodies an expansive view of property. Unquestionably, a celebrity's right of publicity has value. It can be possessed and used. It can be assigned, and it can be the subject of a contract. Thus, there is ample basis for this Court to conclude that it is a species of intangible personal property.

D.

Today there is little dispute that a celebrity's right of publicity has economic value. Courts now agree that while a celebrity is alive, the right of publicity takes on many of the attributes of personal property. It can be possessed and controlled to the exclusion of others. Its economic benefits can be realized and enjoyed. It can also be the subject of a contract and can be assigned to others.

What remains to be decided by the courts in Tennessee is whether a celebrity's right of publicity is descendible at death under Tennessee law. Only the law of this State controls this question. The only reported opinion holding that Tennessee law does not recognize a *postmortem* right of publicity is Memphis Development Foundation v. Factors, Etc., Inc., 616 F.2d 956 (6th Cir.), *cert. denied*, 449 U.S. 953 (1980). We have carefully reviewed this opinion and have determined that it is based upon an incorrect construction of Tennessee law and is inconsistent with the better reasoned decisions in this field.

The United States Court of Appeals for the Sixth Circuit appears to believe that there is something inherently wrong with recognizing that the right of publicity is descendible. We do not share this bias. Like the Supreme Court of Georgia, we recognize that the "trend since the early common law has been to recognize survivability, notwithstanding the legal problems which may thereby arise." Martin Luther King Center for Social Change, Inc. v. American Heritage Products, Inc., 296 S.E.2d 697, 705 (Ga. 1982).

We have also concluded that recognizing that the right of publicity is descendible promotes several important policies that are deeply ingrained in Tennessee's jurisprudence. First, it is consistent with our recognition that an individual's right of testamentary distribution is an essential right. If a celebrity's right of publicity is treated as an intangible property right in life, it is no less a property right at death.

Second, it recognizes one of the basic principles of Anglo-American jurisprudence that "one may not reap where another has sown nor gather where another has strewn." M.M. Newcomer Co. v. Newcomer's New Store, 217 S.W. 822, 825 (Tenn. 1919). This unjust enrichment principle argues against granting a windfall to an advertiser who has no colorable claim to a celebrity's interest in the right of publicity.

Third, recognizing that the right of publicity is descendible is consistent with a celebrity's expectation that he is creating a valuable capital asset that will benefit his heirs and assigns after his death. It is now common for celebrities to include their interest in the exploitation of their right of publicity in their estate. While a celebrity's expectation that his heirs will benefit from his right of publicity might not, by itself, provide a basis to recognize that the right of publicity is descendible, it does recognize the effort and financial commitment celebrities make in their careers. This investment deserves no less recognition and protection than investments celebrities might make in the stock market or in other tangible assets.

Fourth, concluding that the right of publicity is descendible recognizes the value of the contract rights of persons who have acquired the right to use a celebrity's name and likeness. The value of this interest stems from its duration and its exclusivity. If a celebrity's name and likeness were to enter the public domain at death, the value of any existing contract made while the celebrity was alive would be greatly diminished.

Fifth, recognizing that the right of publicity can be descendible will further the public's interest in being free from deception with regard to the sponsorship, approval or certification of goods and services. Falsely claiming that a living celebrity endorses a product or service violates Tenn. Code Ann. §47-18-104(b)(2), (3) and (5). It should likewise be discouraged after a celebrity has died.

Finally, recognizing that the right of publicity can be descendible is consistent with the policy against unfair competition through the use of deceptively similar corporate names.

The legal literature has consistently argued that the right of publicity should be descendible. A majority of the courts considering this question agree. We find this authority convincing and consistent with Tennessee's common law and, therefore, conclude that Elvis Presley's right of publicity survived his death and remains enforceable by his estate and those holding licenses from the estate. . . .

IV. The Propriety of Granting a Summary Judgment

[Plaintiff claimed that even if Presley's right of publicity was descendible, the estate had unreasonably delayed in asserting its rights, and thus was barred from relief under the doctrine of laches. Holding there were material issues of fact bearing on laches, the court vacated the summary judgment and remanded for further proceedings.]

Notes and Questions

1. Does the right of publicity fit within any of the definitions of property in the first section of this chapter? Which if any of the theories of property discussed above justify the recognition of publicity as property?

2. The court in *Presley* emphasizes the economic value of the right to exploit a celebrity's fame. You should not conclude, however, that all valuable economic claims are property in our legal system. For example, in United States v. Willow River Power Co., 324 U.S. 499, 502 (1945), the government built a dam, raising the water level in a river and thereby reducing the value of a hydroelectric plant located upriver. The Court rejected the utility company's claim of a property right in the water level. "It is clear, of course, that a head of water has value and that the Company has an economic interest in keeping the St. Croix at the lower level. But not all economic interests are 'property rights'; only those economic advantages are 'rights' which have the law back of them, and only when they are so recognized may courts compel others to forbear from interfering with them or to compensate for their invasion."

3. Could the court have recognized publicity as a property right but held it was not descendible? Should the right of publicity be descendible? Andrew Jackson, the seventh President of the United States, was a Tennessee resident. Do his descendants own a right of publicity? Will Presley's estate own a right of publicity in the twenty-second century? The answers to the last two questions depend on state law, but probably not. Many states limit the length and reach back of postmortem rights of publicity by statute. For example, Tennessee limits the right to 10 years after death or for so long as it is in continued use, whichever is longer; Virginia limits it to 20 years; Florida to 40 years; Texas, Nevada, and Kentucky to 50 years; California to 70 years; and Washington to 75 years. Indiana recognizes the right of publicity for 100 years after the death of the personality and reaches backward for the full extent of those 100 years for persons who died before the law's enactment. Oklahoma also recognizes the right for 100 years but reaches back only 50 years.

4. Elvis Presley created a positive personality that has immense market value. Would the result of *Presley* be different if it involved someone who had created a notorious, but still marketable, personality? In 1970, the Illinois Supreme Court ruled that the infamous teenage thrill killer Nathan Leopold did not have a right of publicity (or privacy) against the author, publisher, producer, or distributor of the novel, play, and movie, *Compulsion*, based on his murder of Bobby Franks. That 1924 killing, committed by Leopold and his wealthy lover Richard Loeb, shocked the nation. "No right to privacy attached to matters associated with his participation in that completely publicized crime," the court wrote. Leopold v. Levin, 259 N.E.2d 250 (Ill. 1970). Earlier, a federal court reached a similar result under Illinois law in a case brought by descendents of Chicago mob boss Al Capone against the producers of *The Untouchables*, a television program that attributed fictional gangland crimes to Capone. Maritote v. Desilu Productions, Inc., 345 F.2d 418 (7th Cir.), *cert. denied*, 382 U.S. 883 (1965). Although these rulings can be seen as denying a right of publicity for criminal acts so as not to reward anti-social behavior, they both also involved the artistic use of a public personality, which raises issues of free expression discussed more fully below in *ETW Corporation*.

■ MARGARET JANE RADIN, PROPERTY AND PERSONHOOD
34 Stanford Law Review 957 (1982)

... [T]o achieve proper self-development — to be a person — an individual needs some control over resources in the external environment. The necessary assurances of control take the form of property right. Although explicit elaboration of this perspective is wanting in modern writing on property, the personhood perspective is often implicit in the connections that courts and commentators find between property and privacy or between property and liberty. ...

Almost any theory of private property rights can be referred to some notion of personhood. ... Conservatives rely on an absolute conception of property as sacred to personal autonomy. Communitarians believe that changing conceptions of property reflect and shape the changing nature of persons and communities. Welfare rights liberals find entitlement to a minimal level of resources necessary to the dignity of persons even when the entitlement must curtail the property rights of others. This article does not emphasize how the notion of personhood might figure in the most prevalent traditional lines of liberal property theory: the Lockean labor-desert theory, which focuses on individual autonomy, or the utilitarian theory, which focuses on welfare maximization.[3] It rather attempts to clarify a third strand of liberal property theory that focuses on personal embodiment or self-constitution in terms of "things." ...

Most people possess certain objects they feel are almost part of themselves. These objects are closely bound up with personhood because they are part of the way we constitute ourselves as continuing personal entities in the world. They may be as different as people are different, but some common examples might be a wedding ring, a portrait, an heirloom, or a house.

One may gauge the strength or significance of someone's relationship with an object by the kind of pain that would be occasioned by its loss. On this view, an object is closely related to one's personhood if its loss causes pain that cannot be relieved by the object's replacement. If so, that particular object is bound up with the holder. For instance, if a wedding ring is stolen from a jeweler, insurance proceeds can reimburse the jeweler, but if a wedding ring is stolen from a loving wearer, the price of a replacement will not restore the status quo — perhaps no amount of money can do so.

The opposite of holding an object that has become a part of oneself is holding an object that is perfectly replaceable with other goods of equal market value. One holds such an object for purely instrumental reasons. The archetype of such a good is, of course, money, which is almost always held only to buy other things. A dollar is worth no more than what one chooses to buy with it, and one dollar bill is as good as another. Other examples are the wedding ring in the hands of the jeweler, the automobile in the hands of the dealer, the land in the hands of the developer, or the apartment in the hands of the commercial landlord. I shall call these theoretical opposites — property that is bound up with a person and

---

3. The personality theory, the labor theory, and the utilitarian theory are respectively associated with Hegel, Locke, and Bentham. *See* G. Hegel, *Philosophy of Right* (T. Knox trans. 1821); J. Locke, *Second Treatise of Government* (New York 1952) (6th ed. London 1764); J. Bentham, *Theory of Legislation* (R. Hildreth trans. 1840) (1st ed. 1802). The sociobiological/psychological "territorial imperative" theory may be a fourth type stemming roughly from Darwin and Freud. ...

property that is held purely instrumentally—personal property and fungible property respectively. . . .

Once we admit that a person can be bound up with an external "thing" in some constitutive sense, we can argue that by virtue of this connection the person should be accorded broad liberty with respect to control over that "thing." But here liberty follows from property for personhood; personhood is the basic concept, not liberty. Of course, if liberty is viewed not as freedom from interference, or "negative freedom," but rather as some positive will that by acting on the external world is constitutive of the person, then liberty comes closer to capturing the idea of the self being intimately bound up with things in the external world.

It intuitively appears that there is such a thing as property for personhood because people become bound up with "things." But this intuitive view does not compel the conclusion that property for personhood deserves moral recognition or legal protection, because arguably there is bad as well as good in being bound up with external objects. If there is a traditional understanding that a well-developed person must invest herself to some extent in external objects, there is no less a traditional understanding that one should not invest oneself in the wrong way or to too great an extent in external objects. Property is damnation as well as salvation, object-fetishism as well as moral groundwork. In this view, the relationship between the shoe fetishist and his shoe will not be respected like that between the spouse and her wedding ring. At the extreme, anyone who lives only for material objects is considered not to be a well-developed person, but rather to be lacking some important attribute of humanity. . . .

. . . Locke says that "every Man has a Property in his own Person," from which it immediately follows that "[t]he Labour of his Body, and the Work of his hands . . . are properly his." If it makes sense to say that one owns one's body, then, on the embodiment theory of personhood, the body is quintessentially personal property because it is literally constitutive of one's personhood. If the body is property, then objectively it is property for personhood. This line of thinking leads to a property theory for the tort of assault and battery: Interference with my body is interference with my personal property. Certain external things, for example, the shirt off my back, may also be considered personal property if they are closely enough connected with the body.

The idea of property in one's body presents some interesting paradoxes. In some cases, bodily parts can become fungible commodities, just as other personal property can become fungible with a change in its relationship with the owner: Blood can be withdrawn and used in a transfusion; hair can be cut off and used by a wigmaker; organs can be transplanted. On the other hand, bodily parts may be too "personal" to be property at all. We have an intuition that property necessarily refers to something in the outside world, separate from oneself. Though the general idea of property for personhood means that the boundary between person and thing cannot be a bright line, still the idea of property seems to require some perceptible boundary, at least insofar as property requires the notion of thing, and the notion of thing requires separation from self. This intuition makes it seem appropriate to call parts of the body property only after they have been removed from the system. . . .

This view of personhood also gives us insight into why protecting people's "expectations" of continuing control over objects seems so important. If an object you now control is bound up in your future plans or in your anticipation of your future self, and it is partly these plans for your own continuity that make you a person, then your personhood depends on the realization of these expectations. This turn to expectations might seem to send property theory back toward Bentham, who declared that "the idea of property consists in an established expectation." But this justification for honoring expectations is far from Benthamite, because it applies only to personal property. In order to conclude that an object figuring into someone's expectations is personal, we must conclude both that the person is bound up with the object to a great enough extent, and that the relationship belongs to the class of "good" rather than "bad" object-relations. Hence we are forced to face the problem of fetishism, or "bad" object-relations. . . .

The personhood dichotomy comes about in the following way: A general justification of property entitlements in terms of their relationship to personhood could hold that the rights that come within the general justification form a continuum from fungible to personal. It then might hold that those rights near one end of the continuum — fungible property rights — can be overridden in some cases in which those near the other — personal property rights — cannot be. This is to argue not that fungible property rights are unrelated to personhood, but simply that distinctions are sometimes warranted depending upon the character or strength of the connection. Thus, the personhood perspective generates a hierarchy of entitlements: The more closely connected with personhood, the stronger the entitlement.

Does it make sense to speak of two levels of property, personal and fungible? I think the answer is yes in many situations, no in many others. Since the personhood perspective depends partly on the subjective nature of the relationships between person and thing, it makes more sense to think of a continuum that ranges from a thing indispensable to someone's being to a thing wholly interchangeable with money. Many relationships between persons and things will fall somewhere in the middle of this continuum. Perhaps the entrepreneur factory owner has ownership of a particular factory and its machines bound up with her being to some degree. If a dichotomy telescoping this continuum to two end points is to be useful, it must be because within a given social context certain types of person-thing relationships are understood to fall close to one end or the other of the continuum, so that decisionmakers within that social context can use the dichotomy as a guide to determine which property is worthier of protection. For example, in our social context a house that is owned by someone who resides there is generally understood to be toward the personal end of the continuum. There is both a positive sense that people are bound up with their homes and a normative sense that this is not fetishistic.

Just as Warren and Brandeis argued long ago that there was a right to privacy that had not yet been named, this article may be understood to argue that there is a right to personal property that should be recognized. Concomitantly, I have preliminarily argued that property rights that are not personal should not necessarily take precedence over stronger claims related to personhood. Our reverence for the sanctity of the home is rooted in the understanding that the home is inextricably part of the individual, the family, and the fabric of society. Where other kinds of object relations attain qualitatively similar individual and social importance, they should be treated similarly. . . .

■ MIDLER v. FORD MOTOR COMPANY
United States Court of Appeals for the Ninth Circuit, 1988
849 F.2d 460

*Bette Midler, Bradley Center,
Milwaukee, Nov. 1999*

NOONAN, Circuit Judge. This case centers on the protectibility of the voice of a celebrated chanteuse from commercial exploitation without her consent. Ford Motor Company and its advertising agency, Young & Rubicam, Inc., in 1985 advertised the Ford Lincoln Mercury with a series of nineteen 30 or 60 second television commercials in what the agency called "The Yuppie Campaign." The aim was to make an emotional connection with Yuppies, bringing back memories of when they were in college. Different popular songs of the seventies were sung on each commercial. The agency tried to get "the original people," that is, the singers who had popularized the songs, to sing them. Failing in that endeavor in ten cases the agency had the songs sung by "sound alikes." Bette Midler, the plaintiff and appellant here, was done by a sound-alike.

Midler is a nationally known actress and singer. She won a Grammy as early as 1973 as the Best New Artist of that year. Records made by her since then have gone Platinum and Gold. She was nominated in 1979 for an Academy award for Best Female Actress in *The Rose*, in which she portrayed a pop singer. *Newsweek* in its June 30, 1986 issue described her as an "outrageously original singer/comedian." *Time* hailed her in its March 2, 1987 issue as "a legend" and "the most dynamic and poignant singer-actress of her time." When Young & Rubicam was preparing the Yuppie Campaign it presented the commercial to its client by playing an edited version of Midler singing "Do You Want To Dance," taken from the 1973 Midler album, "The Divine Miss M." After the client accepted the idea and form of the commercial, the agency contacted Midler's manager, Jerry Edelstein. The conversation went as follows: "Hello, I am Craig Hazen from Young and Rubicam. I am calling you to find out if Bette Midler would be interested in doing . . . ?" Edelstein: "Is it a commercial?" "Yes." "We are not interested." Undeterred, Young & Rubicam sought out Ula Hedwig whom it knew to have been one of "the Harlettes," a backup singer for Midler for ten years. Hedwig was told by Young & Rubicam that "they wanted someone who could sound like Bette Midler's recording of [Do You Want To Dance]." She was asked to make a "demo" tape of the song if she was interested. She made an *a capella* demo and got the job.

At the direction of Young & Rubicam, Hedwig then made a record for the commercial. The Midler record of "Do You Want To Dance" was first played to her. She was told to "sound as much as possible like the Bette Midler record," leaving out only a few "aahs" unsuitable for the commercial. Hedwig imitated Midler to the best of her ability.

After the commercial was aired Midler was told by "a number of people" that it "sounded exactly" like her record of "Do You Want To Dance." Hedwig was told by "many personal friends" that they thought it was Midler singing the commercial. Ken Fritz, a personal manager in the entertainment business not associated with Midler, declares by affidavit that he heard the commercial on more than one occasion and thought Midler was doing the singing.

Neither the name nor the picture of Midler was used in the commercial; Young & Rubicam had a license from the copyright holder to use the song. At issue in this case is only the protection of Midler's voice. The district court described the defendants' conduct as that "of the average thief." They decided, "If we can't buy it, we'll take it." The court nonetheless believed there was no legal principle preventing imitation of Midler's voice and so gave summary judgment for the defendants. Midler appeals. . . .

Nancy Sinatra once sued Goodyear Tire and Rubber Company on the basis of an advertising campaign by Young & Rubicam featuring "These Boots Are Made For Walkin'," a song closely identified with her; the female singers of the commercial were alleged to have imitated her voice and style and to have dressed and looked like her. The basis of Nancy Sinatra's complaint was unfair competition; she claimed that the song and the arrangement had acquired "a secondary meaning" which, under California law, was protectible. This court noted that the defendants "had paid a very substantial sum to the copyright proprietor to obtain the license for the use of the song and all of its arrangements." To give Sinatra damages for their use of the song would clash with federal copyright law. Summary judgment for the defendants was affirmed. Sinatra v. Goodyear Tire & Rubber Co., 435 F.2d 711, 717-18 (9th Cir. 1970), *cert. denied*, 402 U.S. 906 (1971). If Midler were claiming a secondary meaning to "Do You Want To Dance" or seeking to prevent the defendants from using that song, she would fail like Sinatra. But that is not this case. Midler does not seek damages for Ford's use of "Do You Want To Dance," and thus her claim is not preempted by federal copyright law. Copyright protects "original works of authorship fixed in any tangible medium of expression." 17 U.S.C. §102(a). A voice is not copyrightable. The sounds are not "fixed." What is put forward as protectible here is more personal than any work of authorship. . . .

California Civil Code section 3344 is . . . of no aid to Midler. The statute affords damages to a person injured by another who uses the person's "name, voice, signature, photograph or likeness, in any manner." The defendants did not use Midler's name or anything else whose use is prohibited by the statute. The voice they used was Hedwig's, not hers. The term "likeness" refers to a visual image not a vocal imitation. The statute, however, does not preclude Midler from pursuing any cause of action she may have at common law; the statute itself implies that such common law causes of action do exist because it says its remedies are merely "cumulative." *Id.* §3344(g).

The companion statute protecting the use of a deceased person's name, voice, signature, photograph or likeness states that the rights it recognizes are "property rights." *Id.* §990(b). By analogy the common law rights are also property rights. Appropriation of such common law rights is a tort in California. Motschenbacher v. R.J. Reynolds Tobacco Co., 498 F.2d 821 (9th Cir. 1974). In that case what the defendants used in their television commercial for Winston cigarettes was a photograph of a famous professional racing driver's racing car. The number of the car was changed and a wing-like device known as a "spoiler" was attached to the car; the car's features of white pinpointing, an oval medallion, and solid red coloring were retained. The driver, Lothar Motschenbacher, was in the car but his features were not visible. Some persons, viewing the commercial, correctly inferred that the car was his and that he was in the car and was therefore endorsing the product. The defendants were held to have invaded a "proprietary interest" of Motschenbacher in his own identity. *Id.* at 825.

Midler's case is different from Motschenbacher's. He and his car were physically used by the tobacco company's ad; he made part of his living out of giving commercial endorsements. But, as Judge Koelsch expressed it in *Motschenbacher*, California will recognize an injury from "an appropriation of the attributes of one's identity." *Id.* at 824. It was irrelevant that Motschenbacher could not be identified in the ad. The ad suggested that it was he. The ad did so by emphasizing signs or symbols associated with him. In the same way the defendants here used an imitation to convey the impression that Midler was singing for them.

Why did the defendants ask Midler to sing if her voice was not of value to them? Why did they studiously acquire the services of a sound-alike and instruct her to imitate Midler if Midler's voice was not of value to them? What they sought was an attribute of Midler's identity. Its value was what the market would have paid for Midler to have sung the commercial in person.

A voice is more distinctive and more personal than the automobile accouterments protected in *Motschenbacher*. A voice is as distinctive and personal as a face. The human voice is one of the most palpable ways identity is manifested. We are all aware that a friend is at once known by a few words on the phone. At a philosophical level it has been observed that with the sound of a voice, "the other stands before me." D. Ihde, Listening and Voice 77 (1976). A fortiori, these observations hold true of singing, especially singing by a singer of renown. The singer manifests herself in the song. To impersonate her voice is to pirate her identity.

We need not and do not go so far as to hold that every imitation of a voice to advertise merchandise is actionable. We hold only that when a distinctive voice of a professional singer is widely known and is deliberately imitated in order to sell a product, the sellers have appropriated what is not theirs. . . .

Reversed and remanded for trial.

Notes and Questions

1. Bobby Freeman, San Francisco rhythm and blues artist, wrote and released the hit "Do You Wanna Dance" (also known as "Do You Want to Dance") in 1958. Since then, over 50 different performers have released covers, the best known being the Beach Boys, the Ramones, and Bette Midler.

Album cover *Do You Wanna Dance?*

2. Does Professor Radin's "personhood theory" of property support the recognition of publicity as property? Is Bette Midler's voice personhood property, or is it fungible, given her commercial use of her voice and Ula Hedwig's success in replication?

3. Radin's general argument is that claims to "personhood property" are more meritorious of legal protection than claims to fungible property. How does this play out

in the context of inheritance? Suppose Midler had died before production of the Lincoln Mercury commercial, and her estate sued Ford?

4. To what extent should Bette Midler have the right to prevent other singers from "covering" songs she recorded? Assume the subsequent performers have obtained all necessary licenses from the copyright holders. For example, can Midler stop Ula Hedwig from performing "Do You Want to Dance" at clubs and concerts? Is vocal similarity important? Would physical similarity (appearance and attire) between Midler and Hedwig matter?

5. How do decisions like *Presley* and *Midler* affect the behavior of advertising firms? Of companies that hire them? Of celebrities? Of producers of television shows and movies who hire actors? Do such decisions have an effect on the prices paid by consumers for the advertised goods?

6. The *Midler* court said the celebrity had no cause of action under California Civil Code §3344 because the defendant had not used her "name, voice, signature, photograph or likeness, in any manner." Is the court right in concluding that none of these elements of Midler's personality were used by the defendant? The court went on to say the celebrity has a common-law publicity right that's broader than the statutory right. Do you agree? It should be noted that the California statute does not require consent for every use of a celebrity's personality, but only for its use "on or in products, merchandise, or goods, or for purposes of advertising or selling, or soliciting purchases of, products, merchandise, goods or services." Further, the statute adds that "a use of a name, voice, signature, photograph, or likeness in connection with any news, public affairs, or sports broadcast or account, or any political campaign, shall not constitute a use for which consent is required." Cal. Civ. Code §3344. State and federal courts have also limited the statute to protect constitutional rights of free speech. Under the California statute, the right of publicity expires "70 years after the death of the deceased personality." Cal. Civ. Code §3344.1.

7. In 1998 the hip-hop music duo OutKast released an album, *Aquemini*, with a track entitled "Rosa Parks." The lyrics to "Rosa Parks," which some find vulgar, alluded to "moving to the back of the bus." It is clear that the Rosa Parks of the song title was the civil rights icon Rosa Parks whose 1955 act of civil disobedience on a Montgomery bus was a crucial moment in civil rights history. Rosa Parks sued OutKast and the record company on several theories, including a common law right of publicity theory. The district court granted summary judgment to the defendants on the ground that the first amendment protected their artistic expression. The Sixth Circuit reversed, finding a triable issue of fact as to whether the song title was "wholly unrelated" to the content of the song, and therefore a disguised commercial advertisement rather than protected expression. Parks v. LaFace Records, 329 F.3d 437 (6th Cir.), *cert. denied*, 540 U.S. 1074 (2003).

Some of the ideas in the following article have proven to be very influential. Which ones, do you think? What other ideas might Hardin's ideas serve to counterbalance? How do Hardin's observations affect a conception of property?

■ GARRETT HARDIN, THE TRAGEDY OF THE COMMONS
Reprinted with permission from 162 Science 1243-48. Copyright 1968 AAAS

. . . An implicit and almost universal assumption of discussions published in professional and semipopular scientific journals is that the problem under discussion has a technical solution. A technical solution may be defined as one that requires a change only in the techniques of the natural sciences, demanding little or nothing in the way of change in human values or ideas of morality.

. . . My thesis is that the "population problem," as conventionally conceived, [has no technical solution]. How it is conventionally conceived needs some comment. It is fair to say that most people who anguish over the population problem are trying to find a way to avoid the evils of overpopulation without relinquishing any of the privileges they now enjoy. They think that farming the seas or developing new strains of wheat will solve the problem — technologically. I try to show here that the solution they seek cannot be found. . . .

WHAT SHALL WE MAXIMIZE?

. . . A finite world can support only a finite population; therefore, population growth must eventually equal zero. (The case of perpetual wide fluctuations above and below zero is a trivial variant that need not be discussed.) When this condition is met, what will be the situation of mankind? Specifically, can Bentham's goal of "the greatest good for the greatest number" be realized?

No — for two reasons, each sufficient by itself. The first is a theoretical one. It is not mathematically possible to maximize for two (or more) variables at the same time. . . .

The second reason springs directly from biological facts. To live, any organism must have a source of energy (for example, food). This energy is utilized for two purposes: mere maintenance and work. For man maintenance of life requires about 1600 kilocalories a day ("maintenance calories"). Anything that he does over and above merely staying alive will be defined as work, and is supported by "work calories" which he takes in. Work calories are used not only for what we call work in common speech; they are also required for all forms of enjoyment, from swimming and automobile racing to playing music and writing poetry. If our goal is to maximize population it is obvious what we must do: We must make the work calories per person approach as close to zero as possible. No gourmet meals, no vacations, no sports, no music, no literature, no art. I think that everyone will grant, without argument or proof, that maximizing population does not maximize goods. Bentham's goal is impossible. . . .

The optimum population is, then, less than the maximum. The difficulty of defining the optimum is enormous; so far as I know, no one has seriously tackled this problem. . . .

We want the maximum good per person; but what is good? To one person it is wilderness, to another it is ski lodges for thousands. To one it is estuaries to nourish ducks for hunters to shoot; to another it is factory land. Comparing one good with another is, we usually say, impossible because goods are incommensurable. Incommensurables cannot be compared.

Theoretically this may be true; but in real life incommensurables are commensurable. Only a criterion of judgment and a system of weighting are needed. In nature the criterion is survival. Is it better for a species to be small and hideable, or large and powerful? Natural selection commensurates the incommensurables. The compromise achieved depends on a natural weighting of the values of the variables.

Man must imitate this process. There is no doubt that in fact he already does, but unconsciously. It is when the hidden decisions are made explicit that the arguments begin. The problem for the years ahead is to work out an acceptable theory of weighting. . . .

TRAGEDY OF FREEDOM IN A COMMONS

. . . The tragedy of the commons develops in this way. Picture a pasture open to all. It is to be expected that each herdsman will try to keep as many cattle as possible on the commons. Such an arrangement may work reasonably satisfactorily for centuries because tribal wars, poaching, and disease keep the numbers of both man and beast well below the carrying capacity of the land. Finally, however, comes the day of reckoning, that is, the day when the long-desired goal of social stability becomes a reality. At this point, the inherent logic of the commons remorselessly generates tragedy.

As a rational being, each herdsman seeks to maximize his gain. Explicitly or implicitly, more or less consciously, he asks, "What is the utility to me of adding one more animal to my herd?" This utility has one negative and one positive component.

1. The positive component is a function of the increment of one animal. Since the herdsman receives all the proceeds from the sale of the additional animal, the positive utility is nearly $+1$.
2. The negative component is a function of the additional overgrazing created by one more animal. Since, however, the effects of overgrazing are shared by all the herdsmen, the negative utility for any particular decision-making herdsman is only a fraction of -1.

Adding together the component partial utilities, the rational herdsman concludes that the only sensible course for him to pursue is to add another animal to his herd. And another. But this is the conclusion reached by each and every rational herdsman sharing a commons. Therein is the tragedy. Each man is locked into a system that compels him to increase his herd without limit—in a world that is limited. Ruin is the destination toward which all men rush, each pursuing his own best interest in a society that believes in the freedom of the commons. . . . The National Parks present another instance of the working out of the tragedy of the commons. At present, they are open to all, without limit. The parks themselves are limited in extent—there is only one Yosemite Valley—whereas population seems to grow without limit. The values that visitors seek in the parks are steadily eroded. Plainly, we must soon cease to treat the parks as commons or they will be of no value to anyone.

What shall we do? We have several options. We might sell them off as private property. We might keep them as public property, but allocate the right to enter them. The allocation might be on the basis of wealth, by the use of an auction system. It might be on the basis of merit, as defined by some agreed-upon standards. It might be by lottery. Or it might be on a first-come, first-served basis, administered to long queues. These, I think, are all objectionable. But we must choose—or acquiesce in the destruction of the commons that we call our National Parks.

POLLUTION

In a reverse way, the tragedy of the commons reappears in problems of pollution. Here it is not a question of taking something out of the commons, but of putting something in—sewage, or chemical, radioactive, and heat wastes into water; noxious and dangerous fumes into the air; and distracting and unpleasant advertising signs into the line of sight. . . .

The tragedy of the commons as a food basket is averted by private property, or something formally like it. But the air and waters surrounding us cannot readily be fenced, and so the tragedy of the commons as a cesspool must be prevented by different means, by coercive laws or taxing devices that make it cheaper for the polluter to treat his pollutants than to discharge them untreated. . . . The owner of a factory on the bank of a stream — whose property extends to the middle of the stream — often has difficulty seeing why it is not his natural right to muddy the waters flowing past his door. . . .

Freedom to Breed Is Intolerable

The tragedy of the commons is involved in population problems in another way. In a world governed solely by the principle of "dog eat dog" — if indeed there ever was such a world — how many children a family had would not be a matter of public concern. Parents who bred too exuberantly would leave fewer descendants, not more, because they would be unable to care adequately for their children. David Lack and others have found that such a negative feedback demonstrably controls the fecundity of birds. But men are not birds, and have not acted like them for millenniums, at least.

If each human family were dependent only on its own resources; if the children of improvident parents starved to death; if thus, overbreeding brought its own "punishment" to the germ line — then there would be no public interest in controlling the breeding of families. But our society is deeply committed to the welfare state, and hence is confronted with another aspect of the tragedy of the commons. . . .

Unfortunately this is just the course of action that is being pursued by the United Nations. In late 1967, some thirty nations agreed to the following: "The Universal Declaration of Human Rights describes the family as the natural and fundamental unit of society. It follows that any choice and decision with regard to the size of the family must irrevocably rest with the family itself, and cannot be made by anyone else." . . .

Conscience Is Self-Eliminating

It is a mistake to think that we can control the breeding of mankind in the long run by an appeal to conscience. Charles Galton Darwin made this point when he spoke on the centennial of the publication of his grandfather's great book. The argument is straightforward and Darwinian.

People vary. Confronted with appeals to limit breeding, some people will undoubtedly respond to the plea more than others. Those who have more children will produce a larger fraction of the next generation than those with more susceptible consciences. The differences will be accentuated, generation by generation. . . .

Pathogenic Effects of Conscience

The long-term disadvantage of an appeal to conscience should be enough to condemn it; but it has serious short-term disadvantages as well. If we ask a man who is exploiting a commons to desist "in the name of conscience," what are we saying to him? What does he hear? — not only at the moment but also in the wee small hours of the night when, half asleep, he remembers not merely the words we used but also the nonverbal communication cues we gave him unawares? Sooner or later, consciously or subconsciously, he senses that he has received two communications, and that they are contradictory: 1. (intended communication) "If you don't do as we ask, we will openly condemn you for not acting like a responsible citizen"; 2. (the unintended communication) "If you do behave as we ask, we will secretly condemn you for a simpleton who can be shamed into standing aside while the rest of us exploit the commons." . . .

For centuries it was assumed without proof that guilt was a valuable, perhaps even an indispensable, ingredient of the civilized life. Now, in this post-Freudian world, we doubt it. . . .

. . . The larger question we should ask is whether, as a matter of policy, we should ever encourage the use of a technique the tendency (if not the intention) of which is psychologically pathogenic. We hear much talk these days of responsible parenthood; the coupled words are incorporated into the titles of some organizations devoted to birth control. Some people have proposed massive propaganda campaigns to instill responsibility into the nation's (or the world's) breeders. But what is the meaning of the word *conscience*? When we use the word responsibility in the absence of substantial sanctions are we not trying to browbeat a free man in a commons into acting against his own interest? . . .

Mutual Coercion Mutually Agreed Upon

The social arrangements that produce responsibility are arrangements that create coercion, of some sort. Consider bank robbing. The man who takes money from a bank acts as if the bank were a commons. How do we prevent such action? Certainly not by trying to control his behavior solely by a verbal appeal to his sense of responsibility. Rather than rely on propaganda we . . . insist that a bank is not a commons; we seek the definite social arrangements that will keep it from becoming a commons. That we thereby infringe on the freedom of would-be robbers we neither deny nor regret. . . .

To say that we mutually agree to coercion is not to say that we are required to enjoy it, or even to pretend we enjoy it. Who enjoys taxes? We all grumble about them. But we accept compulsory taxes because we recognize that voluntary taxes would favor the conscienceless. We institute and (grumblingly) support taxes and other coercive devices to escape the horror of the commons.

An alternative to the commons need not be perfectly just to be preferable. With real estate and other material goods, the alternative we have chosen is the institution of private property coupled with legal inheritance. Is this system perfectly just? As a genetically trained biologist I deny that it is. It seems to me that, if there are to be differences in individual inheritance, legal possession should be perfectly correlated with biological inheritance — that those who are biologically more fit to be the custodians of property and power should legally inherit more. But genetic recombination continually makes a mockery of the doctrine of "like father, like son" implicit in our laws of legal inheritance. An idiot can inherit millions, and a trust fund can keep his estate intact. We must admit that our legal system of private property plus inheritance is unjust — but we put up with it because we are not convinced, at the moment, that anyone has invented a better system. . . .

Recognition of Necessity

Perhaps the simplest summary of this analysis of man's population problems is this: the commons, if justifiable at all, is justifiable only under conditions of low-population density. As the human population has increased, the commons has had to be abandoned in one aspect after another. . . .

Every new enclosure of the commons involves the infringement of somebody's personal liberty. Infringements made in the distant past are accepted because no contemporary complains of a loss. It is the newly proposed infringements that we vigorously oppose; cries of "rights" and "freedom" fill the air. But what does "freedom" mean? When men mutually agreed to pass laws against robbing, mankind became more free, not less so. . . .

[W]e must now [abandon] the commons in breeding. No technical solution can rescue us from the misery of overpopulation. Freedom to breed will bring ruin to all. At the moment, to avoid hard decisions many of us are tempted to propagandize for conscience and responsible parenthood. The temptation must be resisted, because an appeal to independently acting consciences selects for the disappearance of all conscience in the long run, and an increase in anxiety in the short. . . .

■ MICHAEL HELLER, THE TRAGEDY OF THE ANTICOMMONS: PROPERTY IN THE TRANSITION FROM MARX TO MARKETS
111 Harvard Law Review 621 (1998)

Socialist rule stifled markets and often left store shelves bare. One promise of the transition "from Marx to markets" was that new entrepreneurs would acquire the stores, create businesses, and fill the shelves. However, after several years of reform, storefronts often remained empty, while flimsy metal kiosks, stocked full of goods, mushroomed up on Moscow streets. Why did new merchants not come in from the cold?

. . . In a typical Moscow storefront, one owner may be endowed initially with the right to sell, another to receive sale revenue, and still others to lease, receive lease revenue, occupy, and determine use. Each owner can block the others from using the space as a storefront. No one can set up shop without collecting the consent of all of the other owners.

Empty Moscow storefronts are a stark example of anticommons property, a type of property regime that may result when initial endowments are created as disaggregated rights rather than as coherent bundles of rights in scarce resources. More generally, one can understand anticommons property as the mirror image of commons property. In a commons, by definition, multiple owners are each endowed with the privilege to use a given resource, and no one has the right to exclude another. . . .

In an anticommons, by my definition, multiple owners are each endowed with the right to exclude others from a scarce resource, and no one has an effective privilege of use. When there are too many owners holding rights of exclusion, the resource is prone to underuse—a tragedy of the anticommons. Legal and economic scholars have mostly overlooked this tragedy, but it can appear whenever governments create new property rights. [E]mpty Moscow storefronts [are] a canonical example of the tragedy of underuse. . . .

Komunalkas are [communal] apartments that have engendered a special loathing across the former Soviet Union, where they were prevalent. Komunalka performance also proves to be a fruitful example to contrast with storefront anticommons behavior. Many komunalkas were large prerevolutionary apartments, well-situated in downtown apartment buildings. At some points in Soviet history, several dozen people might have shared one komunalka, with each family, comprising up to three generations, assigned one room. Kitchen and bathroom facilities were shared. During privatization, tenants received some ownership rights in their room and, indirectly, the right to block others from using the whole apartment as a single-family or office space. In other words, each owner could keep any other owner from renting out the entire apartment in its most valuable market use. . . .

In the case of komunalkas, the apartment qua apartment remains empty so long as any room-owner can effectively veto use. If all the owners were to sell their rooms and leave the unit, the whole apartment could be marketed as a single piece of real estate. Entrepreneurs, often in partnership with one of the existing tenants, quickly discovered that the well-situated komunalkas could be converted to private property by exchanging the owners' rights to rooms for complete apartments on the city outskirts. To give a numerical example, in the case of some old, centrally located komunalkas in Moscow, the market value of the entire apartment might approach $500,000. Assume such a komunalka had four tenants, each occupying one room. Because of the discomforts and irritations of communal living, each of four communal rooms might have had a market value of only $25,000 if the rooms were kept in anticommons use, so that the whole apartment would have an anticommons value of $100,000. Converting the komunalka from anticommons to private property creates a $400,000 gain that the existing tenants and the bundler can divide after paying the transaction costs of conversion.

. . . [My] definition [of anticommons] departs from previous definitions along four dimensions: the universality of rights of exclusion, the implication of non-use as optimal, the formality of rights, and the scale of anticommons property.

First, because . . . others define an anticommons to include only situations in which everyone has a right to exclude, they have missed the existence of real-world anticommons property, in which a limited group of owners have rights of exclusion. . . . [My examples] demonstrate that non-use can occur even when a few actors have rights of exclusion in a resource that each wants to use.

Second, although perpetual non-use of property may be optimal in a few situations, there are more situations in which non-use exists but is not socially desirable. . . . [F]or most resources that people care about, some level of use is preferable to non-use, and an anticommons regime is a threat to, rather than the epitome of, optimal use.

Third, multiple rights of exclusion need not be formally granted through the legal system for anticommons property to emerge. For example, in the kiosk case in which state authority is quite weak, mafia groups hold informal rights of exclusion, which would-be kiosk owners must assemble to secure their space. . . .

Finally, anticommons property may occur at the level of a particular use of a scarce resource, rather than at the level of an entire property regime. For example, in a komunalka, an individual room may be held as private property, while the whole apartment is owned in anticommons form. It is sufficient to note that anticommons property in an object may appear at an efficient scale of use, without requiring that all possible uses of the object be characterized by anticommons ownership. . . .

■ ETW CORPORATION v. JIREH PUBLISHING, INC.

United States Court of Appeals for the Sixth Circuit, 2003
332 F.3d 915

GRAHAM, District Judge. Plaintiff-Appellant ETW Corporation ("ETW") is the licensing agent of Eldrick "Tiger" Woods ("Woods"), one of the world's most famous professional golfers. Woods, chairman of the board of ETW, has assigned to it the exclusive right to exploit his name, image, likeness, and signature, and all other publicity rights. . . .

Defendant-Appellee Jireh Publishing, Inc. ("Jireh") of Tuscaloosa, Alabama, is the publisher of artwork created by Rick Rush ("Rush"). Rush, who refers to himself as "America's sports artist," has created paintings of famous figures in sports and famous sports events. A few examples include Michael Jordan, Mark McGwire, Coach Paul "Bear" Bryant, the Pebble Beach Golf Tournament, and the America's Cup Yacht Race. Jireh has produced and successfully marketed limited edition art prints made from Rush's paintings.

In 1998, Rush created a painting entitled *The Masters of Augusta*, which commemorates Woods's victory at the Masters Tournament in Augusta, Georgia, in 1997. At that event, Woods became the youngest player ever to win the Masters Tournament, while setting a 72-hole record for the tournament and a record 12-stroke margin of victory. In the foreground of Rush's painting are three views of Woods in different poses. In the center, he is completing the swing of a golf club, and on each side he is crouching, lining up and/or observing the progress of a putt. To the left of Woods is his caddy, Mike "Fluff" Cowan, and to his right is his final round partner's caddy. Behind these figures is the Augusta National Clubhouse. In a blue background behind the clubhouse are likenesses of famous golfers of the past looking down on Woods. These include Arnold Palmer, Sam Snead, Ben Hogan, Walter Hagen, Bobby Jones, and Jack Nicklaus. Behind them is the Masters leader board. . . .

The Masters of Augusta by Rick Rush
Reprinted by permission. See www.RickRushArt.com.

ETW filed suit against Jireh on June 26, 1998, in the United States District Court for the Northern District of Ohio, alleging . . . violation of Woods's right of publicity under Ohio common law. Jireh counterclaimed, seeking a declaratory judgment that Rush's art prints are protected by the First Amendment. . . . Both parties moved for summary judgment.

The district court granted Jireh's motion for summary judgment and dismissed the case. See ETW Corp. v. Jireh Pub., Inc., 99 F. Supp. 2d 829 (N.D. Ohio 2000). ETW timely perfected an appeal to this court. . . .

D. RIGHT OF PUBLICITY CLAIM

ETW claims that Jireh's publication and marketing of prints of Rush's painting violates Woods's right of publicity. The right of publicity is an intellectual property right of recent origin which has been defined as the inherent right of every human being to control the commercial use of his or her identity. *See* McCarthy, The Rights of Publicity and Privacy §1:3 (2d ed. 2000). The right of publicity is a creature of state law and its violation gives rise to a cause of action for the commercial tort of unfair competition. *Id.* . . .

The Ohio Supreme Court recognized the right of publicity in 1976 in Zacchini v. Scripps-Howard Broadcasting Co., 351 N.E.2d 454 (1976). In *Zacchini,* which involved the videotaping and subsequent rebroadcast on a television news program of plaintiff's human cannonball act, the Ohio Supreme Court held that Zacchini's right of publicity was trumped by the First Amendment. On appeal, the Supreme Court of the United States reversed, holding that the First Amendment did not insulate defendant from liability for violating Zacchini's state law right of publicity where defendant published the plaintiff's entire act. *See* Zacchini v. Scripps-Howard Broadcasting Co., 433 U.S. 562 (1977). *Zacchini* is the only United States Supreme Court decision on the right of publicity. . . .

When the Ohio Supreme Court recognized the right of publicity, it relied heavily on the Restatement (Second) of Torts, §652. The court quoted the entire text of §652(C) of the Restatement, as well as comments a, b, c and d.

The Restatement originally treated the right of publicity as a branch of the right of privacy and included it in a chapter entitled "Invasion of Privacy." In 1995, the American Law Institute transferred its exposition of the right of publicity to the Restatement (Third) of Unfair Competition, Chapter 4, §46, in a chapter entitled "Appropriation of Trade Values." The current version of the Restatement (Third) of Unfair Competition defines the right of publicity as follows:

> Appropriation of the Commercial Value of a Person's Identity: The Right of Publicity. One who appropriates the commercial value of a person's identity by using without consent the person's name, likeness, or other indicia of identity for purposes of trade is subject to liability for the relief appropriate under the rules stated in §§48 and 49.

Id.

In §46, Comment c, *Rationale for Protection,* the authors of the Restatement suggest that courts may justifiably be reluctant to adopt a broad construction of the right.

> . . . The commercial value of a person's identity often results from success in endeavors such as entertainment or sports that offer their own substantial rewards. Any additional incentive attributable to the right of publicity may have only marginal

significance. In other cases the commercial value acquired by a person's identity is largely fortuitous or otherwise unrelated to any investment made by the individual, thus diminishing the weight of the property and unjust enrichment rationales for protection. In addition, the public interest in avoiding false suggestions of endorsement or sponsorship can be pursued through the cause of action for deceptive marketing. Thus, courts may be properly reluctant to adopt a broad construction of the publicity right. *See* §47.

In §47, Comment c, the authors of the Restatement note, "The right of publicity as recognized by statute and common law is fundamentally constrained by the public and constitutional interest in freedom of expression." In the same comment, the authors state that "the use of a person's identity primarily for the purpose of communicating information or expressing ideas is not generally actionable as a violation of the person's right of publicity." Various examples are given, including the use of the person's name or likeness in news reporting in newspapers and magazines. The Restatement recognizes that this limitation on the right is not confined to news reporting but extends to use in "entertainment and other creative works, including both fiction and non-fiction." *Id.* The authors list examples of protected uses of a celebrity's identity, likeness or image, including unauthorized print or broadcast biographies and novels, plays or motion pictures. *Id.* According to the Restatement, such uses are not protected, however, if the name or likeness is used solely to attract attention to a work that is not related to the identified person, and the privilege may be lost if the work contains substantial falsifications. *Id.*

We believe the courts of Ohio would follow the principles of the Restatement in defining the limits of the right of publicity. The Ohio Supreme Court's decision in *Zacchini* suggests that Ohio is inclined to give substantial weight to the public interest in freedom of expression when balancing it against the personal and proprietary interests recognized by the right of publicity. . . .

There is an inherent tension between the right of publicity and the right of freedom of expression under the First Amendment. This tension becomes particularly acute when the person seeking to enforce the right is a famous actor, athlete, politician, or otherwise famous person whose exploits, activities, accomplishments, and personal life are subject to constant scrutiny and comment in the public media. . . .

E. APPLICATION OF THE LAW TO THE EVIDENCE IN THIS CASE

. . . .

In regard to the Ohio law right of publicity claim, we conclude that Ohio would construe its right of publicity as suggested in the Restatement (Third) of Unfair Competition. . . . Under this rule, the substantiality and market effect of the use of the celebrity's image is analyzed in light of the informational and creative content of the defendant's use. Applying this rule, we conclude that Rush's work has substantial informational and creative content which outweighs any adverse effect on ETW's market and that Rush's work does not violate Woods's right of publicity. . . .

In balancing [the societal interest in free speech and "the shared communicative resources of our cultural domain"] against Woods's right of publicity, we note that Woods, like most sports and entertainment celebrities with commercially valuable identities, engages in an activity, professional golf, that in itself generates a significant amount of income which is unrelated to his right of publicity. Even in the absence of his right of publicity, he would still be able to reap substantial financial rewards from authorized appearances and endorsements. It is not at all clear that the appearance of Woods's likeness in artwork prints which display one of his major achievements will reduce the commercial value of his likeness.

While the right of publicity allows celebrities like Woods to enjoy the fruits of their labors, here Rush has added a significant creative component of his own to Woods's identity. Permitting Woods's right of publicity to trump Rush's right of freedom of expression would extinguish Rush's right to profit from his creative enterprise.

After balancing the societal and personal interests embodied in the First Amendment against Woods's property rights, we conclude that the effect of limiting Woods's right of publicity in this case is negligible and significantly outweighed by society's interest in freedom of artistic expression.

. . . Rush's work consists of a collage of images in addition to Woods's image which are combined to describe, in artistic form, a historic event in sports history and to convey a message about the significance of Woods's achievement in that event. Because Rush's work has substantial transformative elements, it is entitled to the full protection of the First Amendment. In this case, we find that Woods's right of publicity must yield to the First Amendment.

V. Conclusion

In accordance with the foregoing, the judgment of the District Court granting summary judgment to Jireh Publishing is affirmed.

CLAY, Circuit Judge, dissenting. . . .

[S]ince *Zacchini*, "the right of publicity has often been invoked in the context of commercial speech when the appropriation of a celebrity likeness creates a false and misleading impression that the celebrity is endorsing a product." Comedy III Productions v. Gary Saderup, Inc., 21 P.3d 797, 802 (Cal. 2001). "Because the First Amendment does not protect false and misleading commercial speech, and because even non-misleading commercial speech is generally subject to somewhat lesser First Amendment protection, the right of publicity often trumps the right of advertisers to make use of celebrity figures." *Id.* In this case, to the extent that the district court was correct in characterizing Defendant's prints as expressive works and not as commercial products, even though Defendant was selling the prints for financial gain, the issue becomes what degree of First Amendment protection should be afforded to Defendant's expressive work. . . .

In the instant case, where we are faced with an expressive work and the question of whether that work is protected under the First Amendment, the reasoning and transformative test set forth in *Comedy III* are in line with the Supreme Court's reasoning in *Zacchini* as well as in harmony with the goals of both the right to publicity and the First Amendment. Applying the test here, it is difficult to discern any appreciable transformative or creative contribution in Defendant's prints so as to entitle them to First Amendment protection. "A literal depiction of a celebrity, even if accomplished with great skill, may still be subject to a right of publicity challenge. The inquiry is in a sense more quantitative than qualitative, asking whether the literal and imitative or the creative elements predominate in the work." *Comedy III*, 21 P.3d at 809 (footnote omitted).

. . . Rush's print does not depict Woods in the same vein as the other golfers, such that the focus of the print is not the Masters Tournament or the other golfers who have won the prestigious green jacket award, but that of Woods holding his famous golf swing while at that tournament. Thus, although it is apparent that Rush is an adequately skilled artist, after viewing the prints in question it is also apparent that Rush's ability in this regard is "subordinated to the overall goal of creating literal, conventional depictions of [Tiger Woods] so as to exploit his . . . fame [such that Rush's] right of free expression is outweighed by [Woods'] right of publicity." *See id.* at 811.

In fact, the narrative that accompanies the prints expressly discusses Woods and his fame:

> But the center of their [other golfers'] gaze is 1997 winner Tiger Woods, here flanked by his caddie, "Fluff," and final round player partner's (Constantino Rocca) caddie on right, displaying that awesome swing that sends a golf ball straighter and truer than should be humanly possible. Only his uncanny putting ability serves to complete his dominating performance that lifts him alongside the Masters of Augusta.

Accordingly, contrary to the majority's conclusion otherwise, it is clear that the prints gain their commercial value by exploiting the fame and celebrity status that Woods has worked to achieve. Under such facts, the right of publicity is not outweighed by the right of free expression. . . .

Notes and Questions

1. What would it mean to treat the "right of publicity" as a commons, as defined by Garrett Hardin? What would it mean to treat the right as an anticommons, as defined by Michael Heller? Does *ETW Corporation* treat Tiger Woods' publicity rights as a commons or anticommons? Would either treatment (commons or anticommons) be appropriate? Would it result in tragedy?

2. How would the case be decided if the right of publicity was unaffected by the constraints of the First Amendment? We do not expect you to know about the contours of the First Amendment's freedom of speech, nor will we be teaching you that in a book about property law. But *ETW Corporation* shows how property law is affected by constitutional law. First Amendment arguments appear frequently in disputes about intellectual property law, where claims of personal property conflict with public desires for access to, say, copyrighted writings. The First Amendment also surfaces when the government seeks to regulate the use of land by entities engaged in protected speech, ranging from churches to adult bookstores. And the Fifth Amendment speaks of property in two important provisions: the guarantee that the government cannot deprive anyone of their property without due process of law, and the requirement that the government pay just compensation whenever it takes someone's property. We will consider what qualifies as "property" for those constitutional purposes at various points throughout our study of property law.

3. Why was this case brought in an Ohio federal court and decided under Ohio law? Elvis Presley lived in Tennessee and the dispute in *Presley* involved plaques and statutes in Tennessee, so it seems obvious that the case would be decided in Tennessee under Tennessee law. Similarly, Bette Midler lived in California and brought her case under California law. But neither Tiger Woods nor Rick Rush live in Ohio. Ohio was simply one of the many states where Rush was selling his painting of Woods at Augusta. Presumably, ETW Corporation chose to bring its lawsuit for Woods in

Ohio because, at the time, that state appeared to have a particularly expansive view of the rights of publicity. Even if Woods won, would Rush have been free to sell the painting in states with less expansive views of the rights of publicity?

4. In Shaw Family Archives Ltd. v. CMG Worldwide, Inc., 486 F. Supp. 2d 309 (S.D.N.Y. 2007), corporations purporting to hold Marilyn Monroe's postmortem right of publicity objected to T-shirts featuring pictures of the celebrated actress that were sold at a Target store in Indianapolis. These corporations, Marilyn Monroe LLC and CMG Worldwide, Inc., claimed that, although not expressly mentioned in the will of Monroe, the right had passed through the will's residuary clause to her two named residuary devisees, her acting coach and her psychiatrist. The court held that the devisees did not own and could not transfer Monroe's right of publicity because neither Indiana (where the shirt was sold), nor California (where Monroe died), nor New York (where her will was probated) recognized a right of publicity at the time of her death in 1962. "To this day, New York law does not recognize any common law right of publicity and limits its statutory publicity rights to living persons," the court noted. *Id.* at 314. By statute, California had created a descendible, posthumous right of publicity between the time of Monroe's death and the filing of the lawsuit but, in a parallel case involving Monroe's right of publicity, this law was held not to apply to the testamentary transfers of persons dying before its enactment. Milton H. Greene Archives, Inc. v. CMG Worldwide, Inc., 568 F. Supp. 2d 1152, 1156 (C.D. Cal. 2008). The *Shaw Family Archives* court made a similar finding regarding California law. 486 F. Supp. 2d at 315-16. In response to these two decisions, California enacted a new statute expressly designed "to abrogate" them by stating that the state's right of publicity did apply to predeceased persons and, in the absence of an express testamentary transfer, passed through the residual clause in the decedent's will. Cal. Civ. Code §3344.1. Monroe's estate still lost. In 2012, the Ninth Circuit Court of Appeals ruled, "Because Monroe died domiciled in New York, New York law applies to the question of whether Monroe LLC has the right to enforce Monroe's posthumous right of publicity. Because no such right exists under New York law, Monroe LLC did not inherit it through the residual clause of Monroe's will." Milton H. Greene Archives, Inc. v. Marilyn Monroe LLC, 692 F.3d 983 (9th Cir. 2012). The court noted that Monroe's posthumous right of publicity, if enforceable, would have considerable value but closed by quoting Monroe, "I knew I belonged to the Public and to the world, not because I was talented or even beautiful but because I had never belonged to anything or anyone else." *Id.* at 1000.

5. The corporations managing Marilyn Monroe's posthumous right of publicity presumably chose to bring their case in Indiana for T-shirts sold throughout the country because, at the time of the suit, Indiana had one of the most expansive statutes protecting rights of publicity. It provides that "a person may not use an aspect of a personality's right of publicity for a commercial purpose during the personality's lifetime or for one hundred years after the date of the personality's death without having obtained previous written consent" from the holder of the right of publicity. The statute defines a "right of publicity" as "a personality's property interest in the personality's name, voice, signature, photograph, image, likeness, distinctive appearance, gesture, or mannerisms" and a "personality" as any living or dead person whose rights of publicity have "commercial value, whether or not the person uses or authorizes the use of the person's rights of publicity for a commercial purpose during the person's lifetime." Ind. Code §32-36-1. These

statutory rights did not benefit Monroe's devisees, however, because Indiana follows the majority rule that the law of the testator's domicile controls all questions of a will's construction, including what property passes under the will. Shaw Family Archives v. CMG, 486 F. Supp. 2d at 314. "There are disputed issues of fact concerning whether Ms. Monroe was domiciled in New York or California at the time of her death," the court noted. "There is absolutely no doubt that she was *not* domiciled in Indiana. *Id.* at 315.

■ **WHITE v. SAMSUNG ELECTRONICS AMERICA, INC.**
   United States Court of Appeals for the Ninth Circuit, 1993
   989 F.2d 1512

[Plaintiff Vanna White was the long-time hostess of "Wheel of Fortune," a highly popular television game show. Samsung Electronics ran a series of advertisements, set in the twenty-first century, depicting items from popular culture juxtaposed with Samsung products; the suggestion was that Samsung products would endure. One of the ads featured a robot, dressed in a wig, gown, and jewelry, posed next to the easily recognizable Wheel and obviously intended to resemble White. White had not consented to the ad and sued, alleging (among other things) violations of her common law right of publicity. The district court dismissed this claim on summary judgment. The court of appeals reversed with respect to the right of publicity. Goodwin, C.J., wrote the majority opinion for the panel (published at 971 F.2d 1395), stating in part: "Television and other media create marketable celebrity identity value. Considerable energy and ingenuity are expended by those who have achieved celebrity value to exploit it for profit. The law protects the celebrity's sole right to exploit this value whether the celebrity has achieved her fame out of rare ability, dumb luck, or a combination thereof. We decline Samsung's invitation to permit the evisceration of the common law right of publicity through means as facile as those in this case" Samsung petitioned for an en banc rehearing, which the court rejected, with three judges dissenting.]

Kozinski, Circuit Judge, with whom Circuit Judges O'Scannlain and Kleinfeld join, dissenting from the order rejecting the suggestion for rehearing en banc. Saddam Hussein wants to keep advertisers from using his picture in unflattering contexts. Clint Eastwood doesn't want tabloids to write about him. Rudolf Valentino's heirs want to control his film biography. The Girl Scouts don't want their image soiled by association with certain activities. George Lucas wants to keep Strategic Defense Initiative fans from calling it "Star Wars." PepsiCo doesn't want singers to use the word "Pepsi" in their songs. Guy Lombardo wants an exclusive property right to ads that show big bands playing on New Year's Eve. Uri Geller thinks he should be paid for ads showing psychics bending metal through telekinesis. Paul Prudhomme, that household name, thinks the same about ads featuring corpulent bearded chefs. And scads of copyright holders see purple when their creations are made fun of.

Something very dangerous is going on here. Private property, including intellectual property, is essential to our way of life. It provides an incentive for investment and innovation; it stimulates the flourishing of our culture; it protects the moral entitlements of people to the fruits of their labors. But reducing too much to private property can be bad medicine. Private land, for instance, is far more useful if separated from other private land by public streets, roads and highways. Public parks, utility rights-of-way and sewers reduce the amount of land in private hands, but vastly enhance the value of the property that remains.

So too it is with intellectual property. Overprotecting intellectual property is as harmful as underprotecting it. Creativity is impossible without a rich public domain. Nothing today, likely nothing since we tamed fire, is genuinely new: Culture, like science and technology, grows by accretion, each new creator building on the works of those who came before. Overprotection stifles the very creative forces it's supposed to nurture.

The panel's opinion is a classic case of overprotection. Concerned about what it sees as a wrong done to Vanna White, the panel majority erects a property right of remarkable and dangerous breadth: Under the majority's opinion, it's now a tort for advertisers to *remind* the public of a celebrity. Not to use a celebrity's name, voice, signature or likeness; not to imply the celebrity endorses a product; but simply to evoke the celebrity's image in the public's mind. This Orwellian notion withdraws far more from the public domain than prudence and common sense allow. It conflicts with the Copyright Act and the Copyright Clause. It raises serious First Amendment problems. It's bad law, and it deserves a long, hard second look. . . .

But what does "evisceration" mean in intellectual property law? Intellectual property rights aren't like some constitutional rights, absolute guarantees protected against all kinds of interference, subtle as well as blatant. They cast no penumbras, emit no emanations: The very point of intellectual property laws is that they protect only against certain specific kinds of appropriation. I can't publish unauthorized copies of, say, *Presumed Innocent*; I can't make a movie out of it. But I'm perfectly free to write a book about an idealistic young prosecutor on trial for a crime he didn't commit. So what if I got the idea from *Presumed Innocent*? So what if it reminds readers of the original? Have I "eviscerated" Scott Turow's intellectual property rights? Certainly not. All creators draw in part on the work of those who came before, referring to it, building on it, poking fun at it; we call this creativity, not piracy.[15]

The majority isn't, in fact, preventing the "evisceration" of Vanna White's existing rights; it's creating a new and much broader property right, a right unknown in California law. It's replacing the existing balance between the interests of the celebrity and those of the public by a different balance, one substantially more favorable to the celebrity. Instead of having an exclusive right in her name, likeness, signature or voice, every famous person now has an exclusive right to *anything that reminds the viewer of her.* . . .

This is entirely the wrong place to strike the balance. Intellectual property rights aren't free: They're imposed at the expense of future creators and of the public at large. . . .

In the name of avoiding the "evisceration" of a celebrity's rights in her image, the majority diminishes the rights of copyright holders and the public at large. In the name of fostering creativity, the majority suppresses it. Vanna White and those like her have been given something they never had before, and they've been given it at our expense. I cannot agree.

---

15. In the words of Sir Isaac Newton, "if I have seen further it is by standing on [the shoulders] of Giants." *Letter to Robert Hooke*, Feb. 5, 1675/1676.

Newton himself may have borrowed this phrase from Bernard of Chartres, who said something similar in the early twelfth century. Bernard in turn may have snatched it from Priscian, a sixth century grammarian. *See* Lotus Dev. Corp. v. Paperback Software Int'l, 740 F. Supp. 37, 77 n.3 (D. Mass. 1990).

Appendix

Vanna White   **Samsung ad**

■   **EDWARD J. LARSON, MURDER WILL OUT: RETHINKING THE RIGHT OF PUBLICITY THROUGH ONE CLASSIC CASE**
62 Rutgers Law Review 131 (2009)

Since its first enunciation in the 1953 decision Haelen Laboratories, Inc. v. Topps Chewing Gum, Inc., the right of publicity has steadily expanded both in its reach and in the number of states that recognize it. Although some legal commentators continue to question whether it should even exist, the right of publicity was securely incorporated into the 1995 *Restatement (Third) of Unfair Competition* and appears entrenched in the law. . . . Hornbook definitions for the right of publicity still speak in terms of giving people the right to control the "commercial use" of their names and other aspects of their personas. Rather than clarify the extent of the right, such a definition has simply centered the confusion on what it means to use someone's identity commercially. . . .

The typical approach to this definitional conundrum has been to start with a broad no-commercial-use standard and then cabin it with exceptions to reach acceptable results in particular cases. In Leopold v. Levin, for example, citing Prosser's *Law of Torts* for authority, the court asserted that the right to privacy did not attach to matters associated with a "completely publicized crime." Of course it might seem strange to enable celebrated criminals or their heirs, through an expansive reading of right of publicity, to profit from or control uses of their criminal fame. As applied against Leopold or other celebrity criminals, however, this limitation is simply punitive and does not address the public-policy issues raised by limits on the expressive uses of celebrity persona generally. If it is important that writers, artists, and the public can draw on the identity of celebrities, then it should not matter whether those celebrities are sinners or saints. Indeed, the passages from

Prosser's *Law of Torts* cited in *Leopold* do not single out celebrity criminals for special treatment but rather assert that the same limits should apply to their rights of publicity as apply to those of other celebrities. . . .

To bring a semblance of order to limits in this field, commentators and courts have proposed or discussed various balancing tests for when the right of publicity gives way to the right of free expression. Two of these tests have attracted considerable recent attention among commentators and the courts. One test draws on the fair-use defense in copyright law generally. If a use would satisfy the fair-use test under copyright law, or some appropriately modified form of the fair-use test, then it would not violate the right of publicity either. Another test focuses on one element in the fair-use defense by looking at the extent of originality or "transformation" in the user's work. First articulating the test in a decision finding the unauthorized depicting of the classic comedy trio, the Three Stooges, on a T-shirt to violate the comedians' right of publicity, the California Supreme Court wrote: "We ask, in other words, whether a product containing a celebrity's likeness is so transformed that it has become primarily the defendant's own expression rather than the celebrity's likeness. And when we use the word 'expression,' we mean expression of something other than the likeness of the celebrity." If the unauthorized work does little more than reproduce a celebrity's identity for sale as commercial merchandise, then under this test it would violate the right of publicity.

Neither drawing on the fair use test nor applying the transformative use test has significantly clarified the murkier reaches of right-of-publicity law. Fair use is widely regarded as a vague and unpredictable aspect of copyright law devoid of bright line tests or simple standards and with no promise of any more precise application to the right of publicity. Further, its purpose in copyright law — the balancing of private incentives and public uses — is not necessarily applicable in the right of publicity context, where protecting private incentives may not be a major concern. Even in the copyright field, fair use is not the primary means of accommodating constitutional concerns.

Derived as it is from the fair-use doctrine, the transformative use test has attracted similar censure. Critics charge that it does not provide clear standards and leads to uncertain and potentially inconsistent results. Whereas one court held that an artist's drawing of the Three Stooges printed on T-shirts did not qualify as transformative, for example, another court claiming to apply the same test found that an artist's life-like drawing of Tiger Woods printed for mass distribution did qualify. Similarly, while the Supreme Court of California said it was "not difficult" to find transformation in a comic book depiction of the country-music Winter Brothers as the half-human and half-worm Autumn Brothers, a lower appellate court had found otherwise. Further, some critics question how the test would apply to writers and artists who seek fidelity to the original in their work. . . .

At least in part, uncertainty in the scope of the right of publicity arises from starting with the broad no-commercial-use standard and then trying to exclude uses that are protected for constitutional or policy reasons. . . . Courts could reduce the level of legal confusion and the resulting chill over uses of celebrity identities by defining the scope of the right of publicity in the affirmative rather than beginning with the no-commercial-use standard and then trying to cabin it with exceptions. Any such definition would begin with advertising. Thomas McCarthy, the author of the leading treatise in the field and proponent of a strong right of publicity, notes that "for all practical purposes, the only kind of speech impacted by the right of publicity is commercial speech — advertising, not news, not stories, not entertainment and not entertainment satire and parody—only advertising and other purely commercial uses." The unauthorized use of someone's identity in advertising or solicitation presents a classic case for liability. It can mislead the public into thinking that the person had endorsed the product or activity. It also potentially injures persons whose identities are exploited by invading their privacy, defaming their character, diminishing their ability to market their identity, and reducing their financial incentive to develop their identities. If, as McCarthy states, "[t]he vast majority" of right of publicity cases involve advertising, then they could be addressed simply by defining the right to bar the unauthorized use of a person's identity in advertising or solicitation. . . . This simple rule covers most cases, is easy to apply, and reflects current law.

Beyond advertising, however, the right of publicity becomes confused and problematic. One court held that an unauthorized poster of the recently deceased entertainer Elvis Presley bearing words "In Memoriam" violated the right to publicity, for example, while another court ruled that an unauthorized poster of comedian Pat Paulsen bearing the words "Paulsen for President" was protected expression. Similarly, one court held that the exploitation of a former hockey player's identity in a comic book violated the right of publicity while another court ruled that the use of a country-music duet's identity in a comic book did not. While the facts of these paired cases differed, they are close enough to leave commentators searching for a meaningful distinction. Further, one court used the transformative-use test to find that a sketch of the Three Stooges on a T-shirt violated the right of publicity while another court using the same test held that a life-like image of Tiger Woods in a large-run print was protected expression. All of these cases involved merchandise that expressed the ideas or thoughts of the creator, the consumer, or both. To differentiate them from commercial novels, plays, or movies privileges some more traditionally favored forms of expression over other less traditionally favored ones.

Rather than focus on the medium or type of expression, beyond advertising and solicitation, the right of publicity should only proscribe uses that primarily communicate endorsement. . . . Reasonable people could differ on individual cases, of course, but conveying a message of endorsement is the type of determination that users, consumers and jurors can more readily make than an abstract decision about whether a particular use is sufficiently expressive or transformative to merit constitutional protection. Importantly, while providing meaningful protection to publicity rights, it should not raise First Amendment concerns because people do not have a constitutional right falsely to communicate that someone has endorsed their product or activity.

Further, a no-endorsement test for merchandise and activities advances policy objectives underlying the right of publicity. One common justification for the right of publicity drawn from trademark law is to protect consumers from being misled about whether a trusted celebrity has endorsed a particular product or activity. This concern is triggered as much by a product that, by its design, name or nature, falsely implies a celebrity's endorsement as by an ad that falsely claims a celebrity's endorsement. Further, any unauthorized endorsement, whether claimed in an advertisement or implied by the product, poses similar risks of injury to the person whose identity has been exploited. Critics of a no-endorsement standard for the right of publicity typically argue that it does not go far enough to reach the uses of celebrities in advertising, rightly noting that merely including a celebrity in an ad can gain attention and boost sales even if the ad disclaims any endorsement. This criticism logically loses force, however, when a no-endorsement test only supplements a general no-advertising-use standard.

No standard defining the scope of the right of publicity is perfect, but a clear one is better than continuing the current legal confusion with the attendant chill on the exercise of both property rights and free expression. An advertising and endorsement (or A&E) test completely covers the common cases of celebrity advertising and reasonably addresses the problematic issue of celebrity-linked merchandise and activities. Some merchandise, including some falling within such traditionally protected categories of expression as books, movies or songs, could draw on a celebrity's identity purely for advertising purposes or to convey endorsement. This might include particular T-shirts, art prints, or posters. There could still be hard cases but the standard applied to them should be clear and understandable by users, consumers, jurors and celebrities. Is a person's identity being used in advertising (except in ads about a permitted use) or primarily to convey a message of endorsement? If not, the use passes muster. . . .

C. CULTURAL PROPERTY

Cultural property provides our second example of the emergence of property rights. According to the 1970 United Nations Educational, Scientific, and Cultural Organization (UNESCO) Convention, cultural property is "[p]roperty which, on religious or secular grounds, is specifically designated by each State as being of importance for archaeology, prehistory, literature, art or science." Typical types of cultural property include works of art, archaeological discoveries, historical buildings, traditional symbols, and native plants. Indigenous communities are especially likely to assert cultural property claims as they object to individual ownership of things that they insist belong to their entire community.

Unlike the right of publicity, claims of cultural property seek to limit the ability of individuals to assert property rights. The idea of "cultural" property posits that there are some objects that "belong" to the society as a whole. As such, they cannot be reduced to private ownership. Again unlike the right of publicity, cultural property claims have depended upon legislation, treaties, and other written legal instruments instead of upon the development of the common law. And the idea of cultural property remains less fully developed and less well defined than the right of publicity that is now recognized by the law.

Whether cultural property rights should continue to expand is still much debated. The representatives of cultures who fear the loss of special parts of the heritage are the most frequent champions of cultural property. But there are risks to that approach. Professor Michael Brown warns that "[i]f we turn culture into property, its uses will be defined and directed by law, the instrument by which states impose order on an untidy world. Culture stands to become the focus of litigation, legislation, and other forms of bureaucratic control." Michael F. Brown, *Who Owns Native Culture?* 8 (2003). Other scholars assert that cultural property is actually best protected by the ordinary rules of property law.

The following materials illustrate several kinds of disputes between public claims to culture and individual property rights. As you read the materials, consider whether cultural property satisfies any of the theories of property described in the first section of this chapter, and how property law may best respond to the concerns that animate claims of cultural property.

■ WILLCOX v. STROUP

United States Court of Appeals for the Fourth Circuit, 2006
467 F.3d 409, cert. denied, 550 U.S. 904 (2007)

WILKINSON, Circuit Judge. This case concerns the ownership of papers from the administrations of two governors of South Carolina during the Civil War. Debtor-plaintiff Thomas Law Willcox sued in United States Bankruptcy Court for a declaratory judgment that the papers were part of his estate. Defendant South Carolina contends that the papers are public property. The bankruptcy court held for the State. The district court reversed, holding that the State failed to establish that the papers constituted public property under South Carolina law of the Civil War era. Because the long possession of the papers by the Willcox family creates a presumption of ownership in their favor and the State has adduced insufficient evidence to defeat this presumption, we affirm.

I.

The debtor-plaintiff is Thomas Law Willcox ("Willcox"), a South Carolina resident whose family has lived in the state for many years. The defendants are Rodger Stroup, Director of the South Carolina Department of Archives and History, and the State of South Carolina (collectively "State"). . . .

At issue in this case are approximately 444 documents from the administrations of South Carolina Governors Francis Pickens (1860-62) and Milledge Bonham (1862-64). As the district court described them, "The Documents, which date from between December 1860 and August 1864, concern Confederate military reports, correspondence, and telegrams between various Confederate generals, officers, servicemen, and government officials, and related materials. The Documents also address a wide variety of official duties of the Governor during that time period. . . . [T]he court adopts the Bankruptcy Court's finding of fact that the Documents are properly described as Governor's records relating 'to matters of military significance, police powers, as well as to other duties of the Governors during the relevant time period.'" The collection has been appraised at $2.4 million.

Willcox found the papers in 1999 or 2000 in a shopping bag in a closet at his late stepmother's home. After finding the papers, Willcox sold a few of them to various individuals and gave two to his wife. In May 2004, Willcox scheduled an auction for August 7, 2004 to sell the remaining documents. The auctioneer publicized the upcoming sale and was contacted by defendant Stroup, who sought permission to microfilm the papers for the State Archives prior to auction. Willcox authorized the copying, and the papers were microfilmed. On the day before the auction, August 6, 2004, Stroup and the Attorney General's Office for the State of South Carolina obtained a temporary restraining order in state court enjoining the sale of the papers. . . .

Regarding the papers' history, the bankruptcy and district courts found, and we adopt, the following facts. The papers seem to have come into Willcox's family through his great-great-uncle, Confederate Major General Evander McIver Law, who most likely came into possession of them during the February 1865 attack on the South Carolina capital by Union General William Tecumseh Sherman. On February 15, 1865, in anticipation of imminent attack, Governor A.G. Magrath declared martial law in Columbia and appointed General Law the Provost Marshal of the city. On February 16, 1865, a large number of State archives and records were removed from Columbia for safekeeping. On February 17, 1865, General Law was relieved of his duties as Provost Marshal, and General Sherman took control of Columbia. The parties submit no direct evidence of how General Law came into possession of the papers, nor is there any suggestion that he did so illegally.

On February 16, 1896, General Law wrote a letter to a New York book dealer regarding the sale of some letters which, both parties agree, appear to belong to the collection at issue here. By the 1940s, Mrs. Annie J. Storm, the granddaughter of General Law, was in possession of the papers and attempted to sell them to both the University of North Carolina at Chapel Hill ("UNC") and the South Caroliniana Library of the University of South Carolina. Mrs. Storm described the documents as "original State House papers entrusted to [her] grandfather at the time of the surrender." No sale resulted, but the papers were placed on microfilm at the Southern Historical Collection at UNC.

No evidence has been submitted of the papers' movements between the time of the Storm correspondence and plaintiff Willcox's discovery more than fifty years later. The point for present purposes is simply that, while the precise route by which Civil War–era gubernatorial papers arrived in a shopping bag in Thomas Law Willcox's stepmother's closet remains a mystery, it appears that the papers have been in the possession of the Law and Willcox families for over one hundred and forty years. . . .

II.

The exceptional nature of the papers in dispute — their early vintage, their unknown history — presents issues distinct from those of the typical personal property case. Without the benefit of clear chain of title, evidence of original ownership, eyewitness testimony, and any number of documentary aids usually helpful in the determination of ownership, the court must utilize the legal tools that remain at its disposal. In this situation, tenets of the common law that usually remain in the background of ownership determinations come to the forefront, their logic and utility revealed anew.

That possession is nine-tenths of the law is a truism hardly bearing repetition. Statements to this effect have existed almost as long as the common law itself. *See* Oxford English Dictionary (draft rev. 2003) (citing a 1616 collection of adages for "Possession is nine points in the Law").

The importance of possession gave rise to the principle that "[p]ossession of property is indicia of ownership, and a rebuttable presumption exists that those in possession of property are rightly in possession." 73 C.J.S. *Property* §70 (2004). The common law has long recognized that "actual possession is, prima facie, evidence of a legal title in the possessor." William Blackstone, 2 *Commentaries* *196.

This presumption has been a feature of American law almost since its inception. "Undoubtedly," noted the Supreme Court, "if a person be found in possession . . . it is prima facie evidence of his ownership." Ricard v. Williams, 20 U.S. (7 Wheat.) 59, 105 (1822). . . .

The presumption of possession is not confined to the early nineteenth century, nor is it confined to examples of early Americana. Rather, it applies across the law of personal property. *See, e.g.,* Nesbitt v. Lewis, 517 S.E.2d 11, 14 (S.C. Ct. App. 1999) (ownership of dog); Hammond v. Halsey, 336 S.E.2d 495, 497 (S.C. Ct. App. 1985) (ownership of cannon); Clanton's Auto Auction Sales, Inc. v. Harvin, 120 S.E.2d

237, 239 (S.C. 1961) (ownership of automobile). The unusual circumstances of this case do, however, provide a notable illustration of why such a presumption exists in the first place.

First and foremost, the presumption operates to resolve otherwise impenetrable difficulties. Where neither party can establish title by a preponderance of the evidence, the presumption cuts the Gordian knot, determining ownership in favor of the possessor. This case shows the need for such a default rule. It presents questions the answers to which remain a mystery. Little is known of the papers' whereabouts, status, or movements from their creation to their acquisition by General Law. There is no evidence of how General Law acquired the papers. Not even the chain of possession within the Law and Willcox families has yet been determined with any certainty. In fact, in over one hundred and forty years of existence, these papers have apparently surfaced in the historical record only three times: in General Law's 1896 correspondence, in Annie Storm's 1940's correspondence, and in the current litigation.

This case thus poses questions which we are ill equipped to answer. Fortunately, however, the common law reveals its usefulness even in the acknowledgment of its limitations. The presumption of ownership from possession locates the parties' burdens. Where the party not in possession is able to establish superior title by satisfactory evidence, the presumption gives way in favor of this evidence. But where no such evidence is produced — where, as here, the events at issue are impossible to reconstruct — the presumption recognizes and averts the possibility of a court's presiding over a historical goose chase. *See* Richard A. Posner, *Economic Analysis of Law* 78 (6th ed. 2003).

Second, the presumption of ownership in the possessor promotes stability. "It is the policy and even the duty of the law, to have personal property vested as early as practicable." Collins v. Bankhead, 32 S.C.L. (1 Strob.) 25, 29 (S.C. Ct. App. 1846). The presumption of ownership from possession is one of an array of legal principles designed to this end. The presumption means that, absent proof to the contrary, settled distributions and expectations will continue undisturbed. Even where evidence overcomes the presumption, other principles work to protect settled expectations, including the statute of limitations, the doctrine of adverse possession, and equitable defenses such as laches, staleness, abandonment, and waiver.

Such principles, working in concert, favor status-quo distributions over great upsets in property rights. At the most basic level, this fosters "the policy of protecting the public peace against violence and disorder." *See* Sabariego v. Maverick, 124 U.S. 261, 297 (1888). In contemporary commercial society, it protects the expectations of those in possession, thus encouraging them to make improvements that increase social wealth. *See, e.g.*, Richard A. Posner, *Economic Analysis of Law* 80-84 (6th ed. 2003). Without rules such as the presumption of ownership, whether public or private, such valuable goals would give way to uncertainty.

In this case, the resulting confusion is not difficult to imagine. If the State were not required to defeat the presumption in order to gain title, a whole system of archival practice could be thrown into question. The State could claim ownership of other papers of Governors Pickens and Bonham held by the Library of Congress and Duke University, as well as papers of other South Carolina governors currently at institutions other than the State Archives. The result would be immense litigation over papers held by private owners, universities, historical societies, and federal depositories. It would upset settled archival arrangements and the expectations of institutions and historical scholars alike. Disregard of possession as presumptive evidence of ownership would throw the whole of this important area into turmoil.

Finally, while it has never been the practice of federal courts to ignore the law in favor of equitable considerations, it is worth noting that the employment of the presumption in this case in no way frustrates the public interest. Here, private possession does not shut the papers off from access by scholars or, indeed, by the interested public. They have been available for study for decades on microfilm at the University of North Carolina at Chapel Hill, and through the permission of plaintiff Willcox the South Carolina Department of Archives and History now also has a copy on microfilm. The papers are thus freely available for perusal and study regardless of who owns the originals. And, of course, if the State values possession of the original documents, it may acquire them on the open market.

In short, the common law, through the presumption of ownership in the possessor, resolves otherwise insoluble historical puzzles in favor of longstanding distributions and long-held expectations. Such a rule both protects the private interests of longtime possessors and increases social utility. Of course, this presumption will not always cut in one direction. In many instances, the State will possess the papers, and it will then be entitled to the strong presumption that the private party claims here. In this case, however, where the Law and Willcox families have been in possession for well over a century, the presumption favors plaintiff Willcox.

III.

Having recognized the presumption in favor of Willcox's ownership, the court must consider whether the State has rebutted this presumption. Under South Carolina law, the burden is on the party not in possession to prove title superior to that of the possessor. *See Hammond,* 336 S.E.2d at 497. In most cases, the party not in possession would attempt to meet its burden through factual evidence, such as evidence of title or of recent prior possession.

In this case, the State has been unable to provide such evidence. There is no documentary evidence of the State's title, nor is there evidence of its recent possession. While there is no suggestion that the Law and Willcox families are bona fide purchasers, since no purchase was involved, there is also no indication that they acquired the papers in bad faith. In any case, the State's burden may not be met by challenging the sufficiency of the possessor's title but only by proving the superior strength of its claim. *See id.*

Given the insufficient factual evidence, the State's remaining argument for ownership is that, under the law at the time of the documents' creation (1860-64) or their acquisition by General Law (1865), they were public property. South Carolina law of the relevant time period provides no basis for the State's claim of ownership.

A.

South Carolina case law does not suggest that such papers were public property during the Civil War era. Pinckney v. Henegan, 33 S.C.L. (2 Strob.) 250, 252 (S.C. App. L. 1848), merely stated that "[t]he public records in the Secretary of State's office do not belong to the Secretary; they are property of the State." The case did not refer to governors' papers or otherwise explain the nature of the records on file in the Secretary's office. It simply stated that public records are public property. This proposition does not elucidate the underlying question of what documents qualify as public records.

The other cases cited by the State were decided years after the time period in question. As such, they are of questionable relevance to the common law as it existed in the early 1860s. In addition, the cases all concern other types of records than papers of executive officials. Unlike deeds of property or birth and death certificates or creditors' liens, or bills of indictment, governors' records have both public and private aspects. Cases involving other types of records shed limited light on whether the gubernatorial papers in question were public property.

B.

South Carolina statutory law does not indicate that gubernatorial papers were public property at the relevant time. The State cites a 1719 statute addressing the preservation of public records and providing penalties for individuals who had "made away" with various records. *See* Act No. 405 of 1719, 3 S.C. Stat. at Large 98 (1838). The State also cites a 1789 act providing for the removal of public records to Columbia under the supervision of the governor. *See* Act No. 1448 of 1789, 5 S.C. Stat. at Large 102 (1839). Citation of such statutes, however, again begs the question of what documents were considered to be public records in the first place.

In addition, the State cites numerous nineteenth-century statutes, as well as the 1790 and 1861 Constitutions of South Carolina, which required the governor to submit various reports to the legislature. *See, e.g.,* S.C. Const. of 1790, art. II §12; S.C. Const. of 1861, art. II §12; Act No. 2886 of 1843, 11 S.C. Stat. at Large 270 (1873); Act No. 4567 of 1861, 13 S.C. Stat. at Large 4 (1875); Act No. 4700 of 1864, 13 S.C. Stat. at Large 199 (1875). While these requirements might make it necessary for the governor to keep accurate records, they are not relevant to the question of the ownership of such records, let alone gubernatorial papers more broadly.

The State also references two statutes passed after the events in question. First, an Act passed by the South Carolina legislature in December 1865 provided that future governors were to have a "suitable office" called the Executive Chamber, in which all papers associated with their administration were to be kept. *See* Act 4754 of 1865, 13 S.C. Stat. at Large 340 (1875). The Act also provided that the Secretary of State was to "collect, deposit and keep in Columbia all the books, records, and papers heretofore belonging [to the Executive Chamber]." *Id.* The passage of this law in December of 1865 strongly suggests that, prior to that time, such papers were *not* so regulated. In addition, the Act sheds no light on the question of what papers "heretofore" belonged to the Executive Chamber, and the State has provided no evidence that, prior to the passage of this Act, the papers at issue would have belonged to that category.

Second, the current South Carolina Public Records Act, S.C. Code Ann. §30-1-10 et seq. (1991 & Supp. 2005), provides for the maintenance of certain public records. This Act, which first appeared in the South Carolina Code of Laws in 1962, cannot possibly support the State's characterization of the law as it existed in the Civil War era. Whether the Act's definition of "public record" even now includes records of the governor's office is a question we need not address. *See* S.C. Code §§30-4-20(a), (c).

C.

Moreover, the nineteenth-century understanding of South Carolina common and statutory law appears to support this court's interpretation. While the State

Archives has at least some records of almost every South Carolina governor since 1860, of all the State's governors from the colonial period through 1866, the Archives contains the original papers of only one, Governor Edward Drayton (1800-02, 1808-10). Governor Drayton, in fact, complained to the legislature of the "careless" approach to state papers and proposed that the legislature pass a law requiring governors to maintain indexed journals for their successors. No such law was passed. Later governors continued to exercise control over their papers. A letter of May 11, 1883, from former Governor Magrath, governor at the time of Sherman's attack, to former Governor Bonham, some of whose papers are in dispute here, suggests that some of Governor Magrath's papers were returned to him by a later governor. The letter also states that Governor Pickens, the other governor whose papers are in dispute in this case, had many of his papers in his personal possession. This evidence suggests that governors of the Civil War era may have assumed private possession and control of gubernatorial papers.

Even in the twentieth century some South Carolina governors made donations of their papers more consistent with private than public ownership. Governor Strom Thurmond (1947-51) donated his papers to Clemson University. Governor Ernest F. Hollings (1959-1963) donated a portion of his papers to the University of South Carolina, as did Governor Robert McNair (1965-71). These donations suggest that even twentieth-century South Carolina governors have exercised a right of transfer over their papers, a right at the core of the bundle of rights known as property ownership.

In this respect, the practice in South Carolina accords with common law practice more generally. Presidential papers, for example, were considered private property from the time of George Washington, who following his second term removed his papers to Mount Vernon and bequeathed them in his will to his nephew, Supreme Court Justice Bushrod Washington. Jefferson, Madison, and Monroe also bequeathed their papers as private property by will. When Congress first provided public funding for presidential libraries, such libraries depended upon former presidents to deposit their papers voluntarily. *See* Presidential Libraries Act of 1955, Pub. L. No. 84-373, 69 Stat. 695 (codified as amended at 44 U.S.C. §2112 (2000)).

For Congress to change this private ownership regime required a law prospectively granting the United States "complete ownership, possession, and control" of official presidential records. *See* Presidential Records Act of 1978, 44 U.S.C. §2201 et seq. (2000) (implementing process for archiving records and making them publicly available as soon as possible, subject to exceptions for confidential and privileged materials). A previous law, the Presidential Records and Materials Preservation Act of 1974, Pub. L. 93-526, 88 Stat. 1695, which exerted federal control over former President Nixon's papers in the wake of the Watergate scandal, was determined to have effected a per se taking of President Nixon's property interest in his papers.

We conclude that the State has failed to establish that South Carolina law at the relevant time treated gubernatorial papers as public property. This conclusion leaves the State with no basis upon which to rebut the strong presumption of possession in the Law and Willcox families and no basis upon which to claim title superior to that of plaintiff Willcox. We note that the district court further held that "the State is barred from asserting an ownership interest in the Documents due to the running of the statute of limitations and staleness." While we have no reason to question this aspect of the district court's ruling, the State's failure to establish superior title renders it unnecessary to address it.

The judgment of the district court is hereby affirmed.

Notes and Questions

1. The South Carolina Department of Archives and History's website contains a page warning of the dangers of "the sale of historical public records through online and other auctions." *See* http://www.state.sc.us/scdah/DocumentSale.htm. The Department quotes a statement released by several national archives organizations that asserts that government records "represent the essential information by which all citizens may understand the consequences of decisions made by public agencies. They allow the governed to hold those who govern accountable. To that end, these documents should remain where they are available for public inspection. . . . Their disappearance into private hands deprives the public of access to important historical details concerning the development of property rights, taxation, judicial actions, and community growth, as well as the enduring impact of human beings upon their surrounding environments." *Id.* Or, in the words of a former South Carolina archivist, "You do not have a government, you do not have a democracy [without archives] which tell you what powers belong to the individuals, to the state, and to the federal government. The real function of the Archives is to be the repository of official government records. No archives, no state, no nation." *Id.* How do those interests compare to the policies favoring possession that are listed by the court? Are there other policies that support vesting ownership to the papers in the State?

2. The South Carolina Public Records Act provides the statutory basis for the preservation of government records in the state. The Act defines the term *public record* to include "all books, papers, maps, photographs, cards, tapes, recordings, or other documentary materials regardless of physical form or characteristics prepared, owned, used, in the possession of, or retained by a public body." S.C. Code §30-4-20(a). The court found it unnecessary to decide whether the gubernatorial papers were "public records" because they were prepared long before that statute took effect. But if the statute did apply, would it encompass the papers?

3. "One of the most counterintuitive facts of American history is that for nearly two hundred years presidential papers, including all those dealing with official business, were considered the private, personal property of the president." Joseph L. Sax, *Playing Darts with Rembrandt: Public and Private Rights in Cultural Treasures* 81 (1999). Professor Sax reports that "[l]arge amounts of material from the Grant, Harding, Pierce, Coolidge, and Arthur administrations were deliberately destroyed." *Id.* The Presidential Records Act makes such actions illegal with respect to all future presidents, but many other important papers lack similar protections. For example, Professor Sax notes that the papers of Supreme Court Justices and members of Congress "continue to be held as the private possessions of judicial and legislative officials, to be dealt with at their discretion." *Id.* at 93. Should Congress pass another records act to preserve such papers? Should it include the papers of every government employee?

4. One commentator has described cultural property as "another tragedy of the commons." Claudia Caruthers, Note, *International Cultural Property: Another Tragedy of the Commons*, 7 Pac. Rim L. & Pol'y J. 143 (1998). She explains that cultural property may become "so scarce that it possesses enough valuation to be the object of use claims under both the public domain and under private consumption," and

therefore "use of the resource and its commodification may become prey to the tragedy of the commons scenario." *Id.* at 164. But she adds that the existing regulatory regime "has the unintended consequence of promoting the black market" — *i.e.*, illegal transfers of property. *Id.* at 165. She thus recommends that cultural property should be inalienable. Would that solve her tragedy of the commons problem? Is that really the problem?

■ **CARTER v. HELMSLEY-SPEAR, INC.**
United States Court of Appeals for the Second Circuit, 1995
71 F.3d 77, cert. denied, 517 U.S. 1208 (1996)

CARDAMONE, Circuit Judge. Defendants 474431 Associates and Helmsley-Spear, Inc. (defendants or appellants), as the owner and managing agent respectively, of a commercial building in Queens, New York, appeal from an order of the United States District Court for the Southern District of New York (Edelstein, J.), entered on September 6, 1994 following a bench trial. The order granted plaintiffs, who are three artists, a permanent injunction that enjoined defendants from removing, modifying or destroying a work of visual art that had been installed in defendants' building by plaintiffs-artists commissioned by a former tenant to install the work. *See* Carter v. Helmsley-Spear, Inc., 861 F. Supp. 303 (S.D.N.Y. 1994). Defendants also appeal from the dismissal by the trial court of their counterclaim for waste. Plaintiffs cross-appeal from the dismissal of their cause of action for tortious interference with contractual relations and from the denial of their requests to complete the work and for an award of attorney's fees and costs.

On this appeal we deal with an Act of Congress that protects the rights of artists to preserve their works. One of America's most insightful thinkers observed that a country is not truly civilized "where the arts, such as they have, are all imported, having no indigenous life." 7 Works of Ralph Waldo Emerson, Society and Solitude, Chapt. II Civilization 34 (AMS ed. 1968). From such reflection it follows that American artists are to be encouraged by laws that protect their works. Although Congress in the statute before us did just that, it did not mandate the preservation of art at all costs and without due regard for the rights of others.

For the reasons that follow, we reverse and vacate the grant of injunctive relief to plaintiffs and affirm the dismissal by the district court of plaintiffs' other claims and its dismissal of defendants' counterclaim for waste.

BACKGROUND

. . . Defendant Helmsley-Spear, Inc. is the current managing agent of the property for Associates. . . .

Plaintiffs John Carter, John Swing and John Veronis (artists or plaintiffs) are professional sculptors who work together and are known collectively as the "Three-J's" or "Jx3." On December 16, 1991 SIG [a previous managing agent of the property] entered into a one-year agreement with the plaintiffs "engaging and hiring the Artists . . . to design, create and install sculpture and other permanent installations" in the building, primarily the lobby. Under the agreement plaintiffs had "full authority in design, color and style," and SIG retained authority to direct the location and installation of the artwork within the building. The artists were to retain

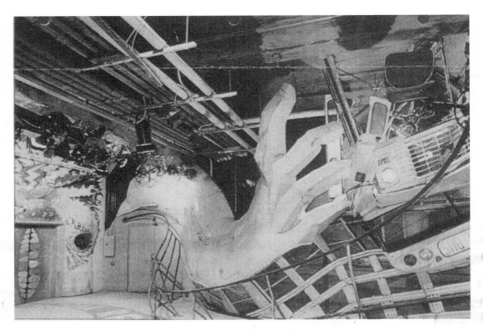

Three J's Sculpture in Building Lobby

copyrights to their work and SIG was to receive 50 percent of any proceeds from its exploitation. On January 20, 1993 SIG and the artists signed an agreement extending the duration of their commission for an additional year. [In] December 1993 [the parties] again extended the agreement.

The artwork that is the subject of this litigation is a very large "walk-through sculpture" occupying most, but not all, of the building's lobby. The artwork consists of a variety of sculptural elements constructed from recycled materials, much of it metal, affixed to the walls and ceiling, and a vast mosaic made from pieces of recycled glass embedded in the floor and walls. Elements of the work include a giant hand fashioned from an old school bus, a face made of automobile parts, and a number of interactive components. These assorted elements make up a theme relating to environmental concerns and the significance of recycling.

[In April 1994 defendant Associates acquired possession of the property] and defendant Helmsley-Spear, Inc. took over management of the property. Representatives of defendants informed the artists that they could no longer continue to install artwork at the property, and instead had to vacate the building. These representatives also made statements indicating that defendants intended to remove the artwork already in place in the building's lobby.

As a result of defendants' actions, artists commenced this litigation. . . .

I. ARTISTS' MORAL RIGHTS

A. History of Artists' Moral Rights

Because it was under the rubric of the Visual Artists Rights Act of 1990 that plaintiffs obtained injunctive relief in the district court, we must explore, at least in part, the contours of that Act. In doing so it is necessary to review briefly the concept of artists' moral rights and the history and development of those rights in American jurisprudence, which led up to passage of the statute we must now examine.

The term "moral rights" has its origins in the civil law and is a translation of the French *le droit moral*, which is meant to capture those rights of a spiritual, non-economic and personal nature. The rights spring from a belief that an artist in the process of creation injects his spirit into the work and that the artist's personality, as well as the integrity of the work, should therefore be protected and preserved. *See* Ralph E. Lerner & Judith Bresler, Art Law 417 (1989) (Art Law). Because they are personal to the artist, moral rights exist independently of an artist's copyright in his work. *See, e.g.*, 2 Nimmer on Copyright 8D-4 & n.2 (1994) (Nimmer).

While the rubric of moral rights encompasses many varieties of rights, two are protected in nearly every jurisdiction recognizing their existence: attribution and integrity. The right of attribution generally consists of the right of an artist to be recognized by name as the author of his work or to publish anonymously or pseudonymously, the right to prevent the author's work from being attributed to someone else, and to prevent the use of the author's name on works created by others, including distorted editions of the author's original work. The right of integrity allows the author to prevent any deforming or mutilating changes to his work, even after title in the work has been transferred.

In some jurisdictions the integrity right also protects artwork from destruction. Whether or not a work of art is protected from destruction represents a fundamentally different perception of the purpose of moral rights. If integrity is meant to stress the public interest in preserving a nation's culture, destruction is prohibited; if the right is meant to emphasize the author's personality, destruction is seen as less harmful than the continued display of deformed or mutilated work that misrepresents the artist and destruction may proceed. *See* Art Law at 421; *see also* 2 William F. Patry, Copyright Law and Practice 1044 n.128 (1994) (Copyright Law) (noting the different models but suggesting that "destruction of a work shows the utmost contempt for the artist's honor or reputation").

Although moral rights are well established in the civil law, they are of recent vintage in American jurisprudence. Federal and state courts typically recognized the existence of such rights in other nations, but rejected artists' attempts to inject them into U.S. law. *See, e.g.*, Vargas v. Esquire, Inc., 164 F.2d 522, 526 (7th Cir. 1947); Crimi v. Rutgers Presbyterian Church, 89 N.Y.S.2d 813, 816-18 (N.Y. Sup. Ct. 1949). Nonetheless, American courts have in varying degrees acknowledged the idea of moral rights, cloaking the concept in the guise of other legal theories, such as copyright, unfair competition, invasion of privacy, defamation, and breach of contract. . . .

Artists fared better in state legislatures than they generally had in courts. California was the first to take up the task of protecting artists with the passage in 1979 of the California Art Preservation Act, Cal. Civ. Code §987 et seq. (West 1982 & Supp. 1995), followed in 1983 by New York's enactment of the Artist's Authorship Rights Act, N.Y. Arts & Cult. Aff. Law §14.03 (McKinney Supp. 1995). Nine other states have also passed moral rights statutes, generally following either the California or New York models.

B. Visual Artists Rights Act of 1990

Although bills protecting artists' moral rights had first been introduced in Congress in 1979, they had drawn little support. The issue of federal protection of moral rights was a prominent hurdle in the debate over whether the United States should join the Berne Convention, the international agreement protecting literary and artistic works. . . . Congress passed the Berne Convention Implementation Act of 1988, Pub. L. No. 100-568, 102 Stat. 2853 (1988), and side-stepped the difficult question of protecting moral rights. . . . Two years later Congress enacted the Visual Artists Rights Act of 1990 (VARA or Act), Pub. L. No. 101-650 (tit. VI), 104 Stat. 5089, 5128-33 (1990). Construing this Act constitutes the subject of the present appeal. The Act

> protects both the reputations of certain visual artists and the works of art they create. It provides these artists with the rights of "attribution" and "integrity." . . .
>
> These rights are analogous to those protected by Article 6bis of the Berne Convention, which are commonly known as "moral rights." The theory of moral rights is that they result in a climate of artistic worth and honor that encourages the author in the arduous act of creation.

H.R. Rep. No. 514 at 5 (internal quote omitted). The Act brings to fruition Emerson's insightful observation.

Its principal provisions afford protection only to authors of works of visual art — a narrow class of art defined to include paintings, drawings, prints, sculptures, or photographs produced for exhibition purposes, existing in a single copy or limited edition of 200 copies or fewer. 17 U.S.C. §101 (Supp. III 1991). With numerous exceptions, VARA grants three rights: the right of attribution, the right of integrity and, in the case of works of visual art of "recognized stature," the right to prevent destruction. 17 U.S.C. §106A (Supp. III 1991). For works created on or after June 1, 1991 — the effective date of the Act — the rights provided for endure for the life of the author or, in the case of a joint work, the life of the last surviving author. The rights cannot be transferred, but may be waived by a writing signed by the author. Copyright registration is not required to bring an action for infringement of the rights granted under VARA, or to secure statutory damages and attorney's fees. 17 U.S.C. §§411, 412 (1988 & Supp. III 1991). All remedies available under copyright law, other than criminal remedies, are available in an action for infringement of moral rights. 17 U.S.C. §506 (1988 & Supp. III 1991). With this historical background in hand, we pass to the merits of the present litigation.

II. Work of Visual Art

Because VARA is relatively new, a fuller explication of it is helpful. In analyzing the Act, therefore, we will follow in order the definition set forth in §101, as did the district court when presiding over this litigation. The district court determined that the work of art installed in the lobby of Associates' building was a work of visual art as defined by VARA; that distortion, mutilation, or modification of the work would prejudice plaintiffs' honor and reputations; that the work was of recognized stature, thus protecting it from destruction (including removal that would result in destruction); and that Associates consented to or ratified the installation of the work in its building. The result was that defendants were enjoined from removing or otherwise altering the work during the lifetimes of the three artists.

[The court accepted the district court's factual finding that the work is a single piece of art, to be analyzed under VARA as a whole, rather than separate works to be considered individually.]

III. Work Made for Hire

Also excluded from the definition of a work of visual art is any work made for hire. 17 U.S.C. §101(B). A "work made for hire" is defined in the Copyright Act, in relevant part, as "a work prepared by an employee within the scope of his or her employment." *Id.* §101(1). Appellants maintain the work was made for hire and therefore is not a work of visual art under VARA. The district court held otherwise, finding that the plaintiffs were hired as independent contractors.

A. *Reid* Tests

The Copyright Act does not define the terms "employee" or "scope of employment." In Community for Creative Non-Violence v. Reid, 490 U.S. 730 (1989), the Supreme Court looked to the general common law of agency for guidance. It held that a multi-factor balancing test was required to determine if a work was produced for hire (by an employee) or was produced by an independent contractor. The Court elaborated 13 specific factors:

> the hiring party's right to control the manner and means by which the product is accomplished . . . the skill required; the source of the instrumentalities and tools; the location of the work; the duration of the relationship between the parties; whether the hiring party has the right to assign additional projects to the hired party; the extent of the hired party's discretion over when and how long to work; the method of payment; the hired party's role in hiring and paying assistants; whether the work is part of the regular business of the hiring party; whether the hiring party is in business; the provision of employee benefits; and the tax treatment of the hired party.

Reid, 490 U.S. at 751-52. . . .

[W]hile the existence of payroll formalities alone would not be controlling, in combination with other factors, it may lead to a conclusion that a given work is one made for hire. Such other factors include: plaintiffs under their contract could be and were in fact assigned projects in addition to the work in the lobby; they were paid a weekly salary for over two years for a contracted 40 hours of work per week; they were furnished many of the needed supplies necessary to create the work; and plaintiffs could not hire paid assistants without defendants' consent. These factors, properly considered and weighed with the employee benefits granted plaintiffs and the tax treatment accorded them, are more than sufficient to demonstrate that the artists were employees, and the sculpture is therefore a work made for hire as a matter of law. . . .

Notes and Questions

1. Who has the greatest interest in the contested sculpture: the Three-J's, Helmsley-Spear, the broader arts community, or someone else? Who has which property rights under VARA?

2. Like *Carter*, most VARA claims have failed to date. *See, e.g.,* Phillips v. Pembroke Real Estate, Inc., 459 F.3d 128 (1st Cir. 2006) (allowing the removal of a sculpture from a Boston park because VARA does not protect "site-specific art"); National Ass'n for Stock Car Auto Racing, Inc. v. Scharle, 184 Fed. Appx. 270 (3d Cir. 2006) (ruling that the drawings for a NASCAR trophy are not visual art under VARA); Pollara v. Seymour, 344 F.3d 265 (2d Cir. 2003) (finding that a banner

seeking greater legal representation for the poor fell within VARA's exception for
promotional materials); Martin v. City of Indianapolis, 192 F.3d 608 (7th Cir. 1999)
(holding that the city violated VARA when it demolished a large outdoor stainless
steel sculpture located in an urban renewal project); Nogueras v. Home Depot, 330
F. Supp. 2d 48 (D.P.R. 2004) (holding that VARA does not prohibit the unauthorized reproduction of a work to advertise brands of paint); Pollara v. Seymour, 206
F. Supp. 2d 333 (N.D.N.Y. 2002) (rejecting a VARA claim against the city's destruction of mural prepared for a legislative lobbying campaign because the mural was
not a "work of recognized stature" and it was a promotional material); Flack v.
Friends of Queen Catherine, Inc., 139 F. Supp. 2d 526 (S.D.N.Y. 2001) (denying
a motion to dismiss a VARA claim based on the "distorted" and "mutilated" modification of a sculpture of the namesake of the borough of Queens, but granting the
motion to dismiss claims against the city's throwing part of the sculpture into a
garbage dump and casting another part of the sculpture in bronze). Why has it
been so difficult to assert a successful VARA claim?

3. The right to destroy is typically viewed as one of the rights in the bundle that
constitutes property. But according to Lior Strahilvetz, "[c]onfronted with arguably
hard cases and high stakes, most American courts have rejected the notion that an
owner has the right to destroy that which is his." Lior Jacob Strahilvetz, *The Right to
Destroy*, 114 Yale L.J. 781, 784 (2005). Strahilvetz cites cases involving the refusal to
honor provisions in a will ordering the destruction of a house and a will providing
that a woman's diamonds and jewelry be placed in her casket, as well as statutes
prohibiting the destruction of historic buildings and rare wildlife. He also cites John
Locke's observation that "[n]othing was made by God for man to destroy." *Id.* at
789. Strahilvetz asserts, though, that the right to destroy promotes important expressive interests, spurs creative activity, and enhances social welfare. Should anyone
have the right to destroy the sculpture at issue in *Carter*? Should anyone be allowed
to destroy other types of cultural property?

Note on Law and Economics

Here we present some of the basic vocabulary from the discipline often dubbed
"law and economics." There are many different approaches taken by scholars who
explore the intersection of legal and economic analysis. Most law schools have one
or more courses devoted to the study of various aspects of this subject, and all
educated lawyers should have some degree of familiarity with economic models
and their vocabulary. This is because many judges and legal decision makers expect
legal reasoning to include economic and market references. We offer an introduction that should (we hope) prove unobjectionable to a broad range of readers.[1]
Your beginning study of law and economics does not necessarily have to take place

---

1. The "Chicago school" (so called because of the leading formative role, played by academics at
the University of Chicago in the 1960s, in articulating its premises) is one of the more influential, but also
controversial, camps in the world of law and economics. Judge (and Professor) Richard Posner, author of
the influential book *Economic Analysis of Law*, now in its sixth edition, is presently one leading spokesman
for the Chicago school tradition. Many analysts are critical of the market-oriented Chicago school
approach, asserting that its adherents exaggerate the extent to which real people are as rational as the
model suggests, or that they describe as objective and value-neutral choices that are subjective or value-
laden. We have no doubt that you will have many in-class and out-of-class discussions about law-and-
economics questions as you make your way through law school.

in the property course. Law and economics is an approach that can be brought to bear on all legal subject matters (though people differ as to the value of doing so). Nevertheless, property is a rich area in which to learn about law and economics, and there is a very substantial body of scholarship exploring the economic dimensions of property law. Our goal here is only to scratch the surface. It is, of course, up to your professor to decide the appropriate extent of emphasis on law and economics as you move through your own property course.

The starting points for understanding economics are the concepts of *scarcity* and *utility*. We live in a finite world; land, other physical resources, and time are all limited. The scarcer some sought-after thing becomes (arable land, food, clean water), the more likely it is that the community will recognize it as property. Utility is a measure of the value a person attaches to a particular good, service, or activity. It means the same thing here as it did earlier in this chapter, when we introduced the utilitarian theory of property law, connecting it to the work of Jeremy Bentham. Garrett Hardin was also talking about utility when he referred to and criticized Bentham's aphorism of the "greatest good for the greatest number" and when he spoke of seeking "the maximum good per person" (page 28, *supra*). Often the word *wealth* is used as a synonym for utility, but there is a danger of being misled by concentrating on the latter term. Considerations of utility often focus on economic values, but in most contexts, the term is not so limited. Utility embraces a person's pleasure or happiness, including noneconomic values such as personal security, the pursuit of hobbies during leisure time, and watching a sunset. Utility can be measured by examining the choices a person makes. In some settings, money can serve as a proxy for measuring utility. In market exchanges, the price paid for goods or services reveals the parties' preferences; economists identify this as a *revealed preference*. For a sale of goods, the buyer values the goods more than the price; conversely, the seller values the price more than the goods. Thus, each party to a voluntary exchange increases their utility.

The term *marginal utility* refers to the idea that a person's desire for particular goods or services often varies according to that person's existing ownership or consumption of the commodity in question. Usually, marginal utility declines as the person acquires more of the commodity. On a hot day after a workout at the park, an athlete may be willing to pay $3 for a bottle of Gatorade; perhaps a second bottle at the same price if he is really thirsty; but after buying one or several bottles, even though he has cash left he'll decide that he has had enough. He has declining marginal utility for Gatorade. (See graph below.) Likewise, if a person gets an offer to buy a beachfront condominium, he is more likely to be interested if he doesn't presently own one.

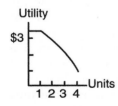

A key norm, explicit in utilitarian theory, is that utility is a good thing and thus people's utility ought to be maximized. The often-encountered phrases *utility maximization* and *wealth maximization* express this general idea, but with different nuances.[2] This norm leads directly to the touchstone of *efficiency*. A particular choice, state of affairs, or legal rule is said to be efficient if it maintains or increases utility. Conversely, a

---

2. Wealth is a narrower term than utility. Wealth limits the focus to economic values that are said to be quantifiable. Adopting the goal of maximizing wealth, rather than maximizing utility, narrows the investigation into the costs and benefits of an action. Chicago school practitioners generally seek to maximize wealth, believing the alternative of maximizing happiness or utility is too subjective because there is no reliable way to measure utility. From this perspective, in contrast to utility, wealth is often said to be measurable by a person's revealed preferences, as they engage in market transactions.

choice is *inefficient* if it reduces utility or prevents a gain in utility. Efficiency, in other words, means the maximizing of utility. By its nature, asking about efficiency involves choice — a comparison between at least two states. In the comparison process, we seek to determine which choice or legal rule is likely to produce the most efficient outcome. People, according to economists, constantly make decisions that impact their utility.

For example, consider Nova, who is out driving. Her car is dirty, and a clean car would make her happier. She's nearing a car wash facility, which charges $7. Is she going to pull in for a wash or drive on by? Her decision would be a "no brainer" (or costless) if the car wash was free and could be dispensed instantaneously. But instead Nova is in the real world. She is weighing a utility gain and a utility loss. Is the happiness provided by having a clean car worth more to her than the loss of $7 plus the delay of 10 minutes she must incur for the scrub and polish? This may depend on if she is already running late for an important appointment or if she is low on cash. In an instant she'll make a decision. She'll decide in a way that promotes her own self-interest. In doing so, she is assumed to act rationally and with good information.

Economists often make the assumption of *rationality* — persons in general try to maximize their own utility, by evaluating information that is available to them, as they go about their daily lives. In deciding whether to get a car wash, Nova will take the action that she believes will maximize her utility. She will respond to what Adam Smith calls self-interest, a force that free-market economists laud as promoting the communal good through the work of an "invisible hand" (page 12, *supra*). Closely related to rationality is the standard assumption of *consumer sovereignty* — each individual should be allowed to judge her own best interest (utility). It is up to Nova, and not the state or anyone else, to decide whether she is better off keeping her money and time or cleaning up her car. This idea of consumer sovereignty also relates to the idea of consumer choice and power in a competitive market. In a competitive market, sellers lack power, and must provide the goods and services demanded by consumers. In this way the markets protect consumers and give them sovereignty.

Economists employ various more precise definitions of efficiency, and two definitions merit special attention. Italian economist Vilfredo Pareto developed a concept now known as *Pareto efficiency*. A change in the status quo is Pareto efficient (also called *Pareto superior*) if it makes at least one person better off and no one worse off. If no Pareto-efficiency-enhancing changes are possible, then the situation is said to be *Pareto optimal*. Nova's exchange of money for a car wash is a Pareto-efficient move; the car wash company, like Nova, derives utility from the exchange, and (we assume) no third party will be adversely affected by the exchange. After the exchange, the situation is Pareto optimal if we posit that no further Pareto-efficient exchanges or moves are available to the two parties. Voluntary exchanges, such as Nova's purchase of a car wash, are one prime type of Pareto-optimizing move. A second prime type involves removal of legal rules that restrict persons and benefit no one. Imagine that a community named *Pleasantville* has a rule that prohibits pink houses. A new resident, Bud, wishes to paint his house pink (this would increase his utility), but cannot do so because of the rule. Assume that the "no pink house" rule benefits no one in Pleasantville. Based upon this assumption, the status quo is not Pareto efficient. Repeal of the rule would benefit Bud and harm no one because his neighbors are indifferent to color. This analysis leads to the normative conclusion that Pleasantville ought to repeal the rule. A legal prohibition, to be legitimate in a utility maximization analysis, must have some countervailing benefit to someone, to offset the cost imposed on the restricted persons. The following graph illustrates this example. Point A represents the status quo, with the rule in place. Bud and his neighbors have a certain amount of utility at the present time. Under our assumption, repeal of the rule benefits Bud and does not harm his neighbors. On the graph, the shift in utility produced by the repeal is represented by moving from Point A to Point B. Looking at the graph, more generally we can see that any move up or to the right of Point A is Pareto-optimizing. Moves outside of that quadrant (to the left or below Point A) are not Pareto-optimizing because they decrease the utility of Bud, his neighbors, or both.

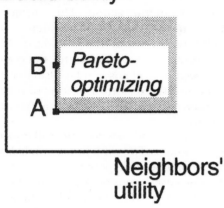

A different measure of efficiency was developed by two British economists, Nicholas Kaldor and John Hicks. A change produces *Kaldor-Hicks efficiency* if it increases society's aggregate utility. In other words, a change is efficient if the total gains exceed the total losses. There can be individuals who are made less well off by the new state of affairs, provided there is a net gain in utility after considering all affected members of society. Let's return to our no-pink-house example to consider Kaldor-Hicks efficiency. Under our original assumption, repeal benefits Bud and does not harm his neighbors. Repeal, which we previously said is Pareto efficient, is also Kaldor-Hicks efficient. It maximizes total societal utility by increasing Bud's utility without diminishing anyone else's.

This illustrates a truism. By definition, any change that is Pareto efficient is necessarily Kaldor-Hicks efficient. Now let's change our assumption. Bud's neighbors become conscious of color, and some are offended by the sight of pink houses in their community. Whether repeal, or another change to the no-pink-house rule, is Kaldor-Hicks efficient turns on the measurement of the costs and benefits. If Bud gains more utility from repeal than his neighbors lose, then repeal is efficient; otherwise it's inefficient. The following graph (see page 62) shows Kaldor-Hicks efficiency. Moves from Point A, the status quo, are Kaldor-Hicks efficient if they are to the right of a line passing through Point A with a slope of −1 (gains exceed losses). Thus, movement to Point C, as shown on the graph, is efficient because Bud's benefit from painting his house exceeds the costs to his neighbors. Moves to the left of that line are Kaldor-Hicks inefficient because losses exceed gains. It should be obvious that to engage in Kaldor-Hicks analysis, we have to come up with some method for quantifying gains and losses in utility. Measurement by some mechanism outside of the control of either party is needed. We cannot simply rely on Bud's assertion about how much he desires a pink house or his neighbors' claims as to how much it would hurt them to see it. In other words, if Bud and his neighbors argue as to whether Point C is to the left or right of the line shown on the graph, some process, such as submission to a third-party tribunal, is necessary to resolve the issue.

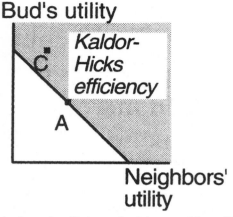

Bud's utility

Kaldor-Hicks efficiency

Neighbors' utility

Both definitions of efficiency cause us to focus on how a person's decision may affect other members of society. Those impacts are called *externalities.* The term *externality* implies self-interest of the actor — that the actor, in deciding whether to do something, will not consider the effects (costs imposed and benefits conferred) on others. *Negative externalities* refer to *costs* imposed on others by the action in question; *positive externalities* refer to *benefits* others would receive from the action. The problem with externalities is their tendency to induce inefficient decision making. The self-interested and rational actor will make decisions that seem efficient to her, but which are not efficient for the community. Garrett Hardin, in his excerpt (page 28, *supra*), explains how Herdsman will choose to add an extra animal to his herd, because the disastrous effects of overgrazing the commons are shared by all the other persons who herd animals, and thus are "negative externalities" as to Herdsman.

Suppose Bud has the right to paint his house pink, and that conduct will injure his neighbors in the use and enjoyment of their houses. The pink house will lower the resale value of all houses on the street by $1,000 because potential buyers tell realtors that they think the pink house is ugly. The costs imposed on the neighbors are negative externalities; Bud may fail to consider them when he decides whether to paint pink. The external costs may exceed the benefits to the actor, in which event the activity is inefficient and thus, according to this economic perspective, undesirable. In such a case, a legal rule or private covenant prohibiting pink houses, or regulating the color of homes in the development, may be beneficial.

Likewise, positive externalities may cause a person (a would-be actor) to abstain from taking efficient action. Imagine that a homeowner, Kasa, is thinking about putting in a beautiful rose garden in her side yard, right next to the boundary line, where now there is only scraggly grass. The next-door neighbor, Hania, would enjoy proximity to the garden as much as Kasa. This effect is a "positive externality." Suppose we quantify the utilities as follows. It will cost Kasa $500 in plants, supplies, and labor to put in the rose garden. She determines the value of the garden to her is $300, and thus she will not act. But the value of the garden to Hania is also $300. The Kaldor-Hicks efficient outcome is for Kasa to build the garden; there is a net gain of $100 when the costs and benefits to the two neighbors are aggregated. Still, Kasa is likely to choose not to put in the garden because she will not take account of the external benefit. She will be induced to act only if there is some mechanism that allows Kasa to capture at least $201 of value from Hania (which is less than that $300 value to Hania). Possible mechanisms could include a contract entered into by Kasa and Hania, or a homeowner's association that collects fees from all residents and pays those who put in rose gardens.

The following excerpt from a classic law review article does two things. First, it takes you further into the vocabulary of law and economics. Second, it develops the proposition that the law may choose to protect any right (including a property right) by what the authors term a property rule, a liability rule, or an inalienability rule.

■ **GUIDO CALABRESI & A. DOUGLAS MELAMED, PROPERTY RULES, LIABILITY RULES, AND INALIENABILITY: ONE VIEW OF THE CATHEDRAL**
85 Harvard Law Review 1089 (1972)

. . . The first issue which must be faced by any legal system is one we call the problem of "entitlement." Whenever a state is presented with the conflicting interests of two or more people, or two or more groups of people, it must decide which side to favor. Absent such a decision, access to goods, services, and life itself will be decided on the basis of "might makes right" — whoever is stronger or shrewder will win. Hence the fundamental thing that law does is to decide which of the conflicting parties will be entitled to prevail. The entitlement to make noise versus the entitlement to have silence, the entitlement to pollute versus the entitlement to breathe clean air, the entitlement to have children versus the entitlement to forbid them — these are the first order of legal decisions. . . .

The state not only has to decide whom to entitle, but it must also simultaneously make a series of equally difficult second order decisions. These decisions go to the manner in which entitlements are protected and to whether an individual is allowed to sell or trade the entitlement. In any given dispute, for example, the state must decide not only which side wins but also the kind of protection to grant. . . . We shall consider three types of entitlements — entitlements protected by property rules, entitlements protected by liability rules, and inalienable entitlements. . . .

An entitlement is protected by a property rule to the extent that someone who wishes to remove the entitlement from its holder must buy it from him in a voluntary transaction in which the value of the entitlement is agreed upon by the seller. It is the form of entitlement which gives rise to the least amount of state intervention: once the original entitlement is decided upon, the state does not try to decide its value. It lets each of the parties say how much the entitlement is worth to him, and gives the seller a veto if the buyer does not offer enough. . . .

Whenever someone may destroy the initial entitlement if he is willing to pay an objectively determined value for it, an entitlement is protected by a liability rule. This value may be what it is thought the original holder of the entitlement would have sold it for. But the holder's complaint that he would have demanded more will not avail him once the objectively determined value is set. Obviously, liability rules involve an additional stage of state intervention: not only are entitlements protected, but their transfer or destruction is allowed on the basis of a value determined by some organ of the state rather than by the parties themselves.

An entitlement is inalienable to the extent that its transfer is not permitted between a willing buyer and a willing seller. The state intervenes not only to determine who is initially entitled and to determine the compensation that must be paid if the entitlement is taken or destroyed, but also to forbid its sale under some or all circumstances. Inalienability rules are thus quite different from property and liability rules. Unlike those rules, rules of inalienability not only "protect" the entitlement; they may also be viewed as limiting or regulating the grant of the entitlement itself.

It should be clear that most entitlements to most goods are mixed. Taney's house may be protected by a property rule in situations where Marshall wishes to purchase it, by a liability rule where the government decides to take it by eminent domain, and by a rule of inalienability in situations where Taney is drunk or incompetent. . . .

II. THE SETTING OF ENTITLEMENTS

What are the reasons for deciding to entitle people to pollute or to entitle people to forbid pollution, to have children freely or to limit procreation, to own property or to share property? They can be grouped under three headings: economic efficiency, distributional preferences, and other justice considerations.

A. ECONOMIC EFFICIENCY

Perhaps the simplest reason for a particular entitlement is to minimize the administrative costs of enforcement. This was the reason Holmes gave for letting the costs lie where they fall in accidents unless some clear societal benefit is achieved by shifting them. . . .

[A]dministrative efficiency is just one aspect of the broader concept of economic efficiency. Economic efficiency asks that we choose the set of entitlements which would lead to that allocation of resources which could not be improved in the sense that a further change would not so improve the condition of those who gained by it that they could compensate those who lost from it and still be better off than before. This is often called Pareto optimality.[10] . . .

Recently it has been argued that on certain assumptions, usually termed the absence of transaction costs, Pareto optimality or economic efficiency will occur regardless of the initial entitlement.[12] For this to hold, "no transaction costs" must be understood extremely broadly as involving both perfect knowledge and the absence of any impediments or costs of negotiating. Negotiation costs include, for example, the cost of excluding would-be freeloaders from the fruits of market bargains.[13] In such a frictionless society, transactions would occur until no one could be made better off as a result of further transactions without making someone else worse off. . . .

Such a result would not mean, however, that the same allocation of resources would exist regardless of the initial set of entitlements. Taney's willingness to pay for the right to make noise may depend on how rich he is; Marshall's willingness to pay for silence may depend on his wealth. In a society which entitles Taney to make noise and which forces Marshall to buy silence from Taney, Taney is wealthier and Marshall poorer than each would be in a society which had the converse set of

---

10. . . . Most versions of Pareto optimality are based on the premise that individuals know best what is best for them. Hence they assume that to determine whether those who gain from a change could compensate those who lose, one must look to the values the individuals themselves give to the gains and losses. Economic efficiency may, however, present a broader notion which does not depend upon this individualistic premise. It may be that the state, for paternalistic reasons, is better able to determine whether the total gain of the winners is greater than the total loss of the losers.

12. This proposition was first established in Coase's classic article, *The Problem of Social Cost*, 3 J. Law & Econ. 1 (1960), and has been refined in subsequent literature. . . .

13. The freeloader is the person who refuses to be inoculated against smallpox because, given the fact that almost everyone else is inoculated, the risk of smallpox to him is less than the risk of harm from the inoculation. He is the person who refuses to pay for a common park, though he wants it, because he believes that others will put in enough money to make the park available to him. The costs of excluding the freeloader from the benefits for which he refused to pay may well be considerable as the two above examples should suggest. This is especially so since these costs may include the inefficiency of pricing a good, like the park once it exists, above its marginal cost in order to force the freeloader to disclose his true desire to use it — thus enabling us to charge him part of the cost of establishing it initially. . . .

entitlements. Depending on how Marshall's desire for silence and Taney's for noise vary with their wealth, an entitlement to noise will result in negotiations which will lead to a different quantum of noise than would an entitlement to silence. This variation in the quantity of noise and silence can be viewed as no more than an instance of the well accepted proposition that what is a Pareto optimal, or economically efficient, solution varies with the starting distribution of wealth. . . .

All this suggests why distributions of wealth may affect a society's choice of entitlements. It does not suggest why *economic efficiency* should affect the choice, if we assume an absence of any transaction costs. But no one makes an assumption of no transaction costs in practice. . . .

B. DISTRIBUTIONAL GOALS

. . . .

All societies have wealth distribution preferences. They are, nonetheless, harder to talk about than are efficiency goals. For efficiency goals can be discussed in terms of a general concept like Pareto optimality to which exceptions . . . can be noted. Distributional preferences, on the other hand, cannot usefully be discussed in a single conceptual framework. There are some fairly broadly accepted preferences — caste preferences in one society, more rather than less equality in another society. There are also preferences which are linked to dynamic efficiency concepts — producers ought to be rewarded since they will cause everyone to be better off in the end. Finally, there are a myriad of highly individualized preferences as to who should be richer and who poorer which need not have anything to do with either equality or efficiency — silence lovers should be richer than noise lovers because they are worthier.

Difficult as wealth distribution preferences are to analyze, it should be obvious that they play a crucial role in the setting of entitlements. For the placement of entitlements has a fundamental effect on a society's distribution of wealth. It is not enough, if a society wishes absolute equality, to start everyone off with the same amount of money. A financially egalitarian society which gives individuals the right to make noise immediately makes the would-be noisemaker richer than the silence loving hermit. Similarly, a society which entitles the person with brains to keep what his shrewdness gains him implies a different distribution of wealth from a society which demands from each according to his relative ability but gives to each according to his relative desire. One can go further and consider that a beautiful woman or handsome man is better off in a society which entitles individuals to bodily integrity than in one which gives everybody use of all the beauty available. . . .

C. OTHER JUSTICE REASONS

The final reasons for a society's choice of initial entitlements we termed "other justice reasons," and we may as well admit that it is hard to know what content can be poured into that term, at least given the very broad definitions of economic efficiency and distributional goals that we have used. Is there, in other words, a reason which would influence a society's choice of initial entitlements that cannot be comprehended in terms of efficiency and distribution? A couple of examples will indicate the problem.

Taney likes noise; Marshall likes silence. They are, let us assume, inevitably neighbors. Let us also assume there are no transaction costs which may impede negotiations between them. Let us assume finally that we do not know Taney's and Marshall's wealth or, indeed, anything else about them. Under these circumstances we know that Pareto optimality—economic efficiency—will be reached whether we choose an entitlement to make noise or to have silence. We also are indifferent, from a general wealth distribution point of view, as to what the initial entitlement is because we do not know whether it will lead to greater equality or inequality. This leaves us with only two reasons on which to base our choice of entitlement. The first is the relative worthiness of silence lovers and noise lovers. The second is the consistency of the choice, or its apparent consistency, with other entitlements in the society.

The first sounds appealing, and it sounds like justice. But it is hard to deal with. Why, unless our choice affects other people, should we prefer one to another?[30] To say that we wish, for instance, to make the silence lover relatively wealthier because we prefer silence is no answer, for that is simply a restatement of the question. Of course, if the choice does affect people other than Marshall and Taney, then we have a valid basis for decision. But the fact that such external effects are extremely common and greatly influence our choices does not help us much. It does suggest that the reaching of Pareto optimality is, in practice, a very complex matter precisely because of the existence of many external effects which markets find hard to deal with. . . .

Notes and Questions

1. If efficiency is a desired goal (as the economic model posits), then the law ought to promote the efficient use of resources. One basic way for the law to facilitate this is to allocate entitlements to persons who will use them efficiently. A famous proposition known as the *Coase Theorem*, discussed by Calabresi and Melamed in part IIA of their article, is a counter-argument. Chicago economist Ronald Coase explored the relationships among efficiency, externalities, and transaction costs. The Coase Theorem posits that, in the absence of transaction costs, parties will arrive at an efficient outcome, regardless of the legal rule's allocation of entitlements. Do you understand how this works? Consider Calabresi and Melamed's example of next-door neighbors Taney, the noise lover, and Marshall, the silence lover. Suppose the value to Taney of noise making is $120 and the value to Marshall of silence is $100. What is the efficient outcome, noise or silence? Under the Coase Theorem, will the neighbors achieve that efficient outcome if the legal rule is that Taney gets to make noise? If instead the legal rule regulates noise, and thus Marshall may demand silence? Does the choice of legal rule affect the distribution of wealth between Taney and Marshall?

2. The term *transaction costs* means all the costs associated with bargaining. If Taney and Marshall negotiate over the issue of noise, they each must devote time to the matter—that's a cost. Many other costs are possible. If they reach an agreement, they may have to (or want to) put that agreement in writing. Legal and expert fees can be a transaction cost because to reach some bargains, parties will hire lawyers and other experts to help them. Suppose that as between Taney and Marshall,

---

30. The usual answer is religious or transcendental reasons. But this answer presents problems. If it means that Chase, a third party, suffers if the noise-maker is preferred, because Chase's faith deems silence worthier than noise, then third parties are affected by the choice. Chase suffers; there is an external effect. But that possibility was excluded in our hypothetical. In practice such external effects, often called moralisms, are extremely common and greatly complicate the reaching of Pareto optimality. . . .

transaction costs for bargaining over the entitlement to noise or silence will be $15. How will that affect efficiency? What if their transaction costs are $25?

If Taney or Marshall is a *holdout*, that represents a transaction cost. Marshall might refuse to negotiate with Taney, either categorically or holding out for a better offer, which never comes. Can you see why that dynamic might be an insurmountable obstacle to attaining efficiency?

Calabresi and Melamed argue for a broad view of transaction costs, contending that the lack of perfect information and the possibility of freeloaders are transaction costs. As part of the bargaining process, Taney and Marshall may have to seek or confirm information. *Freeloaders* are persons who would be benefited by an exchange, but who refuse to pay a share of the cost. Assume that Taney and Marshall have other neighbors, who live close enough to hear noise if made by Taney. Can you explain how the neighbors might act as freeloaders?

3. The Coase Theorem's assumption of zero transaction costs is admittedly artificial. In the real world, there are always some transaction costs. It should be obvious that transaction costs are variable. Sometimes they will be great, presenting obstacles to efficiency-enhancing exchanges that cannot be overcome. Other times parties will incur the necessary transaction costs, and make exchanges that add to overall wealth. Often they vary according to the context. For the Taney and Marshall problem, do you think transaction costs will be higher or lower if they live on large lots in a rural area with no one else living near them, or if they live in close proximity to other neighbors? One value of the Coase Theorem is that it tells us when we should be more concerned about picking a legal rule that favors the efficient outcome. If transaction costs are predictably high, the parties will not be able to overcome the consequences of the law's inefficient original assignment of the entitlement. Moreover, the Coase Theorem provides an explanation of why it is in the public interest to fashion rules and processes that decrease, rather than add to, transaction costs.

■ UNITED STATES v. SCHULTZ
United States Court of Appeals for the Second Circuit, 2003
333 F.3d 393, cert. denied, 540 U.S. 1106 (2004)

MESKILL, Circuit Judge. Defendant-appellant Frederick Schultz (Schultz) appeals from a judgment of conviction. . . .

Schultz was a successful art dealer in New York City. On July 16, 2001, he was indicted on one count of conspiring to receive stolen Egyptian antiquities that had been transported in interstate and foreign commerce, in violation of 18 U.S.C. §371. The underlying substantive offense was violation of 18 U.S.C. §2315, the National Stolen Property Act (NSPA). . . .

The following facts were adduced at trial.

[Between 1991 and 1996, Schultz and Jonathan Parry purchased a number of Egyptian antiquities from individuals in Egypt. They brought the] Egyptian antiquities into America for resale, smuggling them out of Egypt disguised as cheap souvenirs, assigning a false provenance to them, and restoring them with 1920s techniques. [The antiquities included a sculpture of the head of Pharoah Amenhotep III, a sculpture of the daughter of Pharoah Ramses II, and a black top vase.] . . .

Throughout their partnership, Parry and Schultz communicated regularly; many of their letters were introduced in evidence by the government. Their letters indicate an awareness that there was a great legal risk in what they were doing. This awareness is reflected both in the content of the letters and in Parry's and Schultz's use of "veiled terms," code, or even languages other than English.

The jury found Schultz guilty on the sole count of the indictment, and on June 11, 2002, Schultz was sentenced principally to a term of 33 months' imprisonment. This appeal followed.

On appeal, the Court received three *amicus curiae* briefs. The National Association of Dealers in Ancient, Oriental & Primitive Art, Inc.; International Association of Professional Numismatists; The Art Dealers Association of America; The Antique Tribal Art Dealers Association; The Professional Numismatists Guild; and The American Society of Appraisers filed a brief in support of Schultz. An *ad hoc* group called Citizens for a Balanced Policy with Regard to the Importation of Cultural Property, made up of politicians, academics, and art collectors, also filed a brief in support of Schultz. These briefs argue primarily that allowing Schultz's conviction to stand would threaten the ability of legitimate American collectors and sellers of antiquities to do business. The Archaeological Institute of America; The American Anthropological Association; The Society for American Archaeology; The Society for Historical Archaeology; and the United States Committee for the International Council on Monuments and Sites filed a brief in support of the United States. This brief argues primarily that sustaining Schultz's conviction and applying the NSPA to cases such as this one will help to protect archaeological and cultural sites around the world.

DISCUSSION

I. APPLICATION OF THE NSPA TO CASES INVOLVING PATRIMONY LAWS

In order to preserve its cultural heritage, Egypt in 1983 enacted a "patrimony law" which declares all antiquities discovered after the enactment of the statute to be the property of the Egyptian government. The law provides for all antiquities privately owned prior to 1983 to be registered and recorded, and prohibits the removal of registered items from Egypt. The law makes private ownership or possession of antiquities found after 1983 illegal. Schultz's primary argument is that the NSPA does not apply to cases in which an object was "stolen" only in the sense that it was possessed or disposed of by an individual in violation of a national patrimony law, as opposed to "stolen" in the commonly used sense of the word, for instance, where an object is taken from a museum or a private collection. The government contends that the plain language of the NSPA indicates that the NSPA applies to any stolen property, regardless of the source of the true owner's title in the property. The question, in other words, is whether an object is "stolen" within the meaning of the NSPA if it is an antiquity which was found in Egypt after 1983 and retained by an individual (and, in this case, removed from Egypt) without the Egyptian government's consent.

The NSPA reads, in pertinent part, as follows:

> Whoever receives, possesses, conceals, stores, barters, sells, or disposes of any goods, wares, or merchandise, securities, or money of the value of $ 5,000 or more . . . which have crossed a State or United States boundary after being stolen, unlawfully converted, or taken, knowing the same to have been stolen, unlawfully converted, or taken . . . shall be fined under this title or imprisoned not more than ten years, or both.

18 U.S.C. §2315 (2000).

This statute is unambiguous. It applies to goods that are "stolen, unlawfully converted, or taken." Goods that belong to a person or entity and are taken from that person or entity without its consent are "stolen" in every sense of that word. See, e.g., Black's Law Dictionary 989-90 (6th ed. abr. 1991) (defining "stolen" as "acquired or possessed, as a result of some wrongful or dishonest act or taking, whereby a person willfully obtains or retains possession of property which belongs to another, without or beyond any permission given, and with the intent to deprive the owner of the benefit of ownership (or possession) permanently"); Webster's Third New International Dictionary 2248 (1971) (defining "stolen" as "obtained or accomplished by theft, stealth, or craft"). Accordingly, Schultz's actions violated the NSPA if the antiquities he conspired to receive in the United States belonged to someone who did not give consent for Schultz (or his agent) to take them. That "someone" is the nation of Egypt.

In 1983, Egypt enacted Law 117. The law, which is entitled "The Law on the Protection of Antiquities," reads, in pertinent part, as follows:

Article 1

An "Antiquity" is any movable or immovable property that is a product of any of the various civilizations or any of the arts, sciences, humanities and religions of the successive historical periods extending from prehistoric times down to a point one hundred years before the present, so long as it has either a value or importance archaeologically or historically that symbolizes one of the various civilizations that have been established in the land of Egypt or that has a historical relation to it, as well as human and animal remains from any such period. . . .

Article 6

All antiquities are considered to be public property — except for charitable and religious endowments. . . . It is impermissible to own, possess or dispose of antiquities except pursuant to the conditions set forth in this law and its implementing regulations.

Article 7

As of [1983], it is prohibited to trade in antiquities.

Article 8

With the exception of antiquities whose ownership or possession was already established [in 1983] or is established pursuant to [this law's] provisions, the possession of antiquities shall be prohibited as from [1983]. . . .

Schultz moved in the district court to dismiss the indictment on the ground that Law 117 did not vest true ownership rights in the Egyptian government, and, accordingly, the items he conspired to smuggle out of Egypt were not "stolen" within the meaning of the NSPA. In response to Schultz's motion, the district court conducted an evidentiary hearing [at which] two Egyptian officials testified as fact witnesses for the government: Dr. Gaballa Ali Gaballa and General Ali El Sobky.

Dr. Gaballa is Secretary General of Egypt's Supreme Council of Antiquities, which is a part of the Ministry of Culture. The Supreme Council employs more than 20,000 people. Dr. Gaballa was asked: "Who owns all newly discovered antiquities?" He responded: "The Egyptian government, of course." Dr. Gaballa clarified that people who owned antiquities prior to the adoption of Law 117 in 1983 are permitted to continue to possess the antiquities, but they may not transfer, dispose of, or relocate the antiquities without notifying the Egyptian government. Dr. Gaballa testified that pursuant to Law 117, when the Egyptian government learns that an antiquity has been discovered, agents of the government immediately take possession of the item. The item is then registered and given a number.

In response to questioning by the court, Dr. Gaballa asserted that there are no circumstances under which a person who finds an antiquity in Egypt may keep the antiquity legally. The person who found the antiquity is not compensated for the item, because it never belonged to the finder. The only time compensation is paid is when a person owns a plot of land on which an immovable structure is located, and the government takes possession of the entire plot of land in order to possess the structure; in such a case, only the value of the land itself, and not the value of the structure, is taken into account in determining the amount of payment. . . .

The government's second witness, General El Sobky, is the Director of Criminal Investigations for the Egyptian Antiquities Police. General El Sobky testified that his department, which employs more than 400 officers, regularly investigates and prosecutes people for violating Law 117. General El Sobky testified that most of the Law 117 investigations and prosecutions conducted by his department are of people who are trafficking in antiquities within Egypt, as opposed to exporting them out of Egypt. Furthermore, General El Sobky testified, even when a person is acquitted in such a prosecution, if the person is found to possess an antiquity, that antiquity is seized and retained by the government.

Schultz called one expert witness at the hearing, Khaled Abou El Fadl, a professor of Islamic and Middle Eastern law at the University of California — Los Angeles (UCLA) Law School. Professor Abou El Fadl opined that Law 117 was at times ambiguous and confusing. He further testified that the language of Law 117 did not make it clear whether the law "intended to keep the antiquities inside of Egypt or actually was asserting governmental ownership over the antiquities." Professor Abou El Fadl asserted that "nothing in Law 117 prevents the Antiquities Authority from leaving physical possession of even an antiquity discovered after 1983 in the hands of a private finder, so long as the private finder promptly notifies the Authority of his find."

On cross-examination, Professor Abou El Fadl stated that he had never practiced law in Egypt, nor was he licensed to practice law in Egypt. He testified that he had never read Law 117 prior to being requested to do so by Schultz's counsel, and that he had been unable to locate any treatises discussing Law 117.

Schultz contends that in spite of its plain language, Law 117 is not a "real" ownership law, and that Egypt does not truly claim ownership over all antiquities, but merely seeks to restrict their export. The district court disagreed, finding, based substantially on the testimony and other evidence presented at the hearing, that the plain language of Law 117 accurately reflects its purpose and effect: to vest absolute and true ownership of all antiquities found in Egypt after 1983 in the Egyptian government. . . .

Law 117 defines "antiquity" and prescribes the procedure to be followed by persons in possession of antiquities at the time the Law takes effect, and by persons who discover antiquities thereafter. It sets forth serious criminal penalties for the violation of its provisions. It provides for licensure of certain foreign archaeological missions, and for circumstances under which antiquities may be donated by the government to foreign museums in appreciation of those missions' work. The

Law's provisions are directed at activities within Egypt as well as export of antiquities out of Egypt. Law 117 makes it clear that the Egyptian government claims ownership of all antiquities found in Egypt after 1983, and the government's active enforcement of its ownership rights confirms the intent of the Law. Accordingly, we conclude that Law 117 is clear and unambiguous, and that the antiquities that were the subject of the conspiracy in this case were owned by the Egyptian government.

The question thus becomes whether Schultz's actions in conspiring to take antiquities owned by the Egyptian government pursuant to Law 117 out of Egypt violate the NSPA. Schultz argues that even if Law 117 does intend to vest true ownership of all antiquities with the Egyptian government, that sort of "ownership" should not be recognized by the United States for purposes of prosecution under the NSPA. . . .

Schultz contends that the adoption of the Convention on Cultural Property Implementation Act of 1983, 19 U.S.C. §§2601-2613 (CPIA), shows that Congress did not intend the NSPA to apply to objects such as the ones he conspired to bring to the United States. The CPIA implements a United Nations convention that was ratified by the United States in 1982, the purpose of which was to achieve "greater international cooperation towards preserving cultural treasures that not only are of importance to the nations whence they originate, but also to greater international understanding of our common heritage." S. Rep. No. 97-564, at 21 (1982).

The CPIA provides a mechanism for the American government to establish import restrictions on "cultural property" at the request of another signatory nation and after a determination by the President that (1) "the cultural patrimony of [the requesting nation] is in jeopardy from the pillage of archaeological or ethnological materials of [that nation]," (2) the requesting nation "has taken measures . . . to protect its cultural patrimony," (3) the import restrictions are necessary and would be effective in dealing with the problem, and (4) the restrictions are in the "general interest of the international community." 19 U.S.C. §2602(a)(1)(A)-(D) (2003).

Schultz argues that the CPIA was intended to be the only mechanism by which the United States government would deal with antiquities and other "cultural property" imported into the United States. However, nothing in the language of the CPIA supports that interpretation. . . .

The CPIA is an import law, not a criminal law; it is not codified in Title 18 ("Crimes and Criminal Procedure"), with the NSPA, but in Title 19 ("Customs Duties"). It may be true that there are cases in which a person will be violating both the CPIA and the NSPA when he imports an object into the United States. But it is not inappropriate for the same conduct to result in a person being subject to both civil penalties and criminal prosecution, and the potential overlap between the CPIA and the NSPA is no reason to limit the reach of the NSPA. . . .

In light of our own precedents and the plain language of the NSPA, we conclude that the NSPA applies to property that is stolen in violation of a foreign patrimony law. The CPIA is not the exclusive means of dealing with stolen artifacts and antiquities, and reading the NSPA to extend to such property does not conflict with United States policy. We believe that, when necessary, our courts are capable of evaluating foreign patrimony laws to determine whether their language and enforcement indicate that they are intended to assert true ownership of certain property, or merely to restrict the export of that property. . . .

Although we recognize the concerns raised by Schultz and the *amici* about the risks that this holding poses to dealers in foreign antiquities, we cannot imagine that it "creates an insurmountable barrier to the lawful importation of cultural property into the United States." Our holding does assuredly create a barrier to the importation of cultural property owned by a foreign government. We see no reason that property stolen from a foreign sovereign should be treated any differently from property stolen from a foreign museum or private home. The *mens rea* requirement of the NSPA will protect innocent art dealers who unwittingly receive stolen goods, while our appropriately broad reading of the NSPA will protect the property of sovereign nations. . . .

. . . Accordingly, the judgment of the district court is hereby affirmed.

Notes and Questions

1. Why were so many academics, art collectors, and politicians concerned about affirming Schultz's conviction? Why weren't they more sympathetic to the interests of the Egyptian government?

2. According to the State Department, "the difference between stolen and illicitly exported cultural property" is that "for an object to be considered stolen it must have an owner." http://exchanges.state.gov/culprop/faqs.html/. "Most art source countries have national laws that 1) vest ownership in the state of all cultural assets, known and unknown, above the ground and below the ground, thereby making the nation the owner; and 2) restrict the export of cultural objects except for temporary exhibition, research or conservation purposes." *Id.* Why doesn't the United States have such a law?

3. *Schultz* discusses the Convention on Cultural Property Implementation Act of 1983 (CPIA), which implements the 1970 UNESCO Convention on the Means of Prohibiting and Preventing the Illicit Import, Export and Transfer of Ownership of Cultural Property. The CPIA allows any signatories to the UNESCO convention to request that the United States impose import controls on certain cultural property. So far the United States has entered into such agreements with only 14 nations. *See* Chart of Current and Expired Import Restrictions under the Convention on Cultural Property Implementation Act, http://exchanges.state.gov/culprop/chart.html/. Many observers contend that the UNESCO framework for protecting cultural property has been a failure, though they recommend dramatically different solutions. Most scholars worry that the existing laws are insufficiently stringent, and they call for more nations to enforce more specific provisions. But Eric Posner insists that "cultural property is not different from property in general," and he claims "that the UNESCO convention likely has perverse effects and that the treatment of cultural property would improve, even during wartime, if the current regime of international regulation were abolished." Eric A. Posner, *The International Protection of Cultural Property: Some Skeptical Observations*. 8 Chi. J. Int'l L. 213, 215, 226 (2007).

4. Many museums in Europe and the United States possess objects that were recovered from archaeological expeditions in Egypt, Greece, and throughout the world within the past few centuries. Many of those host nations are now demanding the return of those objects as essential aspects of their cultural heritage. American courts have adjudicated litigation regarding such disputes. *See, e.g.,* Autocephalous Greek-Orthodox Church v. Goldberg & Feldman Fine Arts, Inc., 917 F.2d 278 (7th Cir. 1990) (ordering an Indiana art dealer to return four ancient Byzantine mosaics that had been removed from a church in Cyprus). Outside the courts, perhaps the most contested dispute concerns the Elgin Marbles, which "must

rank among the hottest cultural properties of all time." John Boardman, *The Elgin Marbles: Matters of Fact and Opinion*, 9 Int'l J. Cultural Prop. 233 (2000). The Elgin Marbles are a collection of marble sculptures taken from the Parthenon to London by Lord Elgin in 1806. Elgin has been accused of bribing the local authorities in order to obtain the sculptures. *See* William St. Clair, *Lord Elgin and His Marbles* (3d rev. ed. 1998). The Greek government sought the return of the sculptures in 1983, but the British government refused. The Greek claim rests on the obvious historic and cultural importance of the sculptures; the English position responds that "[t]he best interests of the marbles should be decisive," and the sculptures are best preserved and most readily accessible to the public at their current home in the British Museum.

5. The government is not always the protector of art. In March 2001, the Taliban government of Afghanistan ordered the destruction of two famous statues of Buddha that were carved into the side of a cliff near Bamiyan more than 1,500 years before. Mullah Muhammad Omar, the supreme leader of the Taliban, defended the decision as necessary to eliminate idols that were "gods of the infidels." *See* Barry Bearak, *Afghan Says Destruction of Buddhas Is Complete*, N.Y. Times, Mar. 12, 2001, at A4. One week later, a Taliban envoy offered a different explanation, blaming the decision on the government's "rage after a foreign delegation offered money to preserve the ancient works while a million Afghans faced starvation." *See* Barbara Crossette, *Taliban Explains Buddha Demolition*, N.Y. Times, Mar. 19, 2001, at A9. The Taliban destroyed the statues despite the outrage and pleas of the international community. It also destroyed countless Buddhist statuaries kept in the National Museum in Kabul. Later that year, an international military force led by the United States drove the Taliban from power because of its harboring of Osama bin Laden and the Al Qaeda terrorists involved in the September 11 attack on the World Trade Center and the Pentagon.

2

Personal Property

A. DISTINCTION BETWEEN REAL AND PERSONAL PROPERTY

In this chapter we address a number of topics concerning *personal property*. All property is either *personal property* or *real property*. The terms, which come to us from English common law, are historically based on the nature of the action available to protect the property. Real property (or "realty") referred to property for which the owner could obtain specific relief—the right to get the thing back from a wrongful possessor. Such an action is called an action *in rem*, or real action. Thus, "real property" means the owner is entitled to restitution of the thing from the wrongdoer. Due to the overwhelming social and economic importance of land in feudal England, real actions were confined largely to the recovery of freehold estates in land. For other property interests, such as actions to protect chattels, the owner had only "personal" actions to recover damages. Such property, protected by personal actions, was therefore called "personal property" or "personalty."

Today the historic distinction between real property and personal property, which looks to the type of judicial remedy available to the owner, is largely obsolete. Instead, under modern legal usage, real property generally consists of rights associated with land. Personal property, in contrast, generally consists of rights associated with movable things (chattels or goods) and intangible rights that are not associated with land. Nevertheless, there is still a primary relationship between property and remedy, although our vocabulary has evolved. Previously, the nature of the remedy determined whether property was real or personal. Now the nature of the remedy determines whether there is property at all. Property means you have the right to exclude other persons from a thing, whether land or personalty. To say you have the right to exclude others implies that a court will give you a remedy (specific relief or damages) if someone interferes with your right. Thus, the availability of a remedy is a necessary precondition for the existence of property. Generally but not always, a specific remedy such as an injunction is available.

■ BLACK HILLS INSTITUTE OF GEOLOGICAL RESEARCH v. SOUTH DAKOTA SCHOOL OF MINES AND TECHNOLOGY

United States Court of Appeals for the Eighth Circuit, 1993
12 F.3d 737, cert. denied, 513 U.S. 810 (1994)

MAGILL, Circuit Judge. Black Hills Institute of Geological Research and Black Hills Museum of Natural History Foundation (collectively, "Black Hills") appeal the district court's judgment in favor of the United States. The district court found that the United States holds title to a valuable Tyrannosaurus rex skeleton ("the fossil" or "Sue") in trust for Maurice Williams ("Williams"), an individual Indian who is the beneficial owner of trust land on which Black Hills discovered the fossil. . . . We affirm the district court's judgment that the United States holds trust title to the fossil . . . .

. . . The factual background is uncomplicated. Black Hills collects and restores fossils for display in museums. In August 1990, Black Hills was excavating fossils in western South Dakota. Sue Hendrickson, a researcher working on the project, discovered Sue on Williams' ranch while on break. Since 1969, the United States has held this ranch land in trust for the sole use and benefit of Williams, an Indian. Two days after the discovery, Black Hills scientists began excavating Sue, the most complete and valuable Tyrannosaurus rex skeleton known to man, from Williams' land. At some point during the excavation, Black Hills purported to purchase from Williams the right to excavate Sue for $5000. After excavation, Black Hills moved the ten tons of bones to Hill City, South Dakota, where scientists began the laborious process of restoring the fossil.

In May 1992, however, federal officers seized Sue and moved her to the South Dakota School of Mines and Technology. The United States attorney for South Dakota ordered the seizure on the ground that Black Hills' removal of Sue from Williams' land violated federal criminal statutes relating to federal lands. Black Hills then brought suit in district court [against the United States] to quiet title to Sue. . . .

We now reach the merits of the case. We must first decide precisely what issue is before us. Initially, Black Hills sued the government to quiet title to Sue. Black Hills' second amended complaint abandoned the quiet title action and sought an order requiring the government to return the fossil. Black Hills argues that the district court erred because it determined ownership, an issue Black Hills claims that it did not raise in the second amended complaint. According to Black Hills, the district court "only had jurisdiction to determine whether [Black Hills] or the Department of Justice was entitled to possession of the fossil."

In the second amended complaint, however, Black Hills stated that it "paid Williams $5000 in exchange for Sue. [Black Hills] scientists wrote a check to Williams on August 27, 1990, which he accepted and cashed in full payment for Sue." Thus, Black Hills alleged that it owned the fossil outright, not that it leased it or had some possessory interest that did not amount to full ownership. In light of this allegation, we can only construe its request that the district court order the "United States to return the fossil to [Black Hills]" as a claim for permanent possession of Sue. Determining whether Black Hills is entitled to permanent possession necessarily requires determining which party actually owns the fossil. Thus, we must determine whether the transaction between Williams and Black Hills transferred title of Sue to Black Hills.

The ownership issue depends on our construction of several statutes governing Indian trust land. Sue Hendrickson discovered the fossil on land to which the United States holds legal title in trust for Williams, an individual Indian. Under the [federal statutes the United States holds title to the land for Williams' benefit, with Williams having no power to sell or convey any part of the land. In contrast, Williams has the power to sell personal property.] . . .

Here, Black Hills claims that it purchased the right to excavate Sue from Williams for $5000. . . . All parties agree that the fossil is now personal property because it has been severed from the land. In Starr v. Campbell, 208 U.S. 527, 534 (1908), however, the Supreme Court held that timber from Indian trust land that the beneficial owner sold was subject to the trust patent's restraint on alienation even though the timber became personal property after the purchaser severed it from the land.

Thus, the relevant inquiry for purposes of assessing the validity of the transaction is whether the fossil was personal property or land before Black Hills excavated it. If it was land within the meaning of the relevant statutes and regulations, the transaction between Williams and Black Hills is void and the United States holds Sue in trust for Williams because the trust continued in Sue when she became personalty.

Whether the fossil was "land" within the meaning of both 25 U.S.C. §464 and 25 U.S.C. §483 is a matter of federal law. Because Congress has provided no definition of "land" applicable to these statutes, however, we may refer to state property law for guidance. South Dakota law denominates two classes of property: "[r]eal or immovable" property and "[p]ersonal or movable" property. S.D. Codified Laws Ann. §43-1-2. "Real or immovable property consists of: (1) Land; (2) That which is affixed to land; (3) That which is incidental or appurtenant to land; (4) That which is immovable by law. Every kind of property that is not real is personal." Id. §43-1-3. "Land," in turn, "is the solid material of the earth, whatever may be the ingredients of which it is composed, whether soil, rock, or other substance." Id. §43-1-4.

We hold that the fossil was "land" within the meaning of §464 and §483. Sue Hendrickson found the fossil embedded in the land. Under South Dakota law, the fossil was an "ingredient" comprising part of the "solid material of the earth." It was a component part of Williams' land, just like the soil, the rocks, and whatever other naturally-occurring materials make up the earth of the ranch. Black Hills makes several arguments to the contrary, none of which we find persuasive. That the fossil once was a dinosaur which walked on the surface of the earth and that part of the fossil was protruding from the ground when Hendrickson discovered it are irrelevant. The salient point is that the fossil had for millions of years been an "ingredient" of the earth that the United States holds in trust for Williams. The case very well might be different had someone found the fossil elsewhere and buried it in Williams' land or somehow inadvertently left it there. Here, however, a Tyrannosaurus rex died some 65 million years ago on what is now Indian trust land and its fossilized remains gradually became incorporated into that land. Although it is movable, personal property now, at the time Hendrickson discovered the fossil it was part of Williams' land and thus is subject to §464 and §483. As in Starr, 208 U.S. at 534, where an Indian sold timber constituting 15/16 of the value of the land, we would render the statutory restraint on alienation here essentially meaningless if Williams could transfer the right to excavate a priceless fossil derived from otherwise nondescript land without the Secretary's permission. Because he did not seek the Secretary's approval, we hold that Williams' attempted sale to Black Hills is void[5] and that the United States holds Sue in trust for Williams pursuant to the trust patent . . . .

Notes and Questions

1. The court in *Black Hills* states that "Williams' attempted sale to Black Hills is void and that the United States holds Sue in trust for Williams pursuant to the trust patent." What does this imply with respect to ownership of Sue after the trust expires in September 1994? Maurice Williams subsequently decided to sell Sue. At an auction held in 1997, the Field Museum of Natural History made the high bid, purchasing Sue for $8.36 million. Sue, the largest and most complete *T. rex* so far discovered, is on permanent display at the Field Museum in Chicago.

2. *Black Hills* demonstrates the idea that objects can move between the categories of realty and personalty. Crops, once real property, become personal property when harvested; likewise, minerals, oil and gas, and other natural resources upon severance from the land. Movement in the opposite direction is also very common. Goods are quintessential personal property, but often goods become associated with a particular parcel of land to such an extent that they are no longer goods but part of the real property. This transformation comes up in many different contexts and is highly important. The term *improvement* denotes the transformation. An improvement, such as a permanent building, a driveway, or a stone wall, is real property for all purposes, just like the underlying land. The building materials that compose the improvement, although once goods, have completely lost their identity as goods (personal property).

There is also a category of property that's between real property and personal property. Certain things have a substantial association with a specific parcel of land, but they're not so strongly associated with the land that they are considered real property for all purposes, like improvements. A large part of this category consists of *fixtures*—items that are attached to the land or a building. When an item is a fixture, it is legally part of the real property for at least some purposes.

3. Transformation issues are illustrated by examining the possible characterizations of mobile homes. When a mobile home is manufactured, it is unquestionably goods (personal property) at all times prior to delivery to the parcel of land where it is to be occupied. When placed on a lot and occupied, the mobile home may remain pure goods or may become a fixture or an improvement. The context in which the issue arises can have great significance. A particular mobile home can be personal property for one purpose, but the same home can be real property for another purpose. For example, a mobile home might be goods under Article 2 of the Uniform Commercial Code (UCC) for purposes of a sale, but might be taxed as real property by the local government.

4. Suppose the owner of a lot on which a mobile home is situated conveys the lot to a grantee, with no mention of the mobile home in the deed of conveyance and no

---

5. There is an ongoing dispute between Williams and Black Hills regarding this transaction. We intimate no opinion as to the remedies Black Hills may have under state law as to its $5000 payment to Williams. Moreover, because Black Hills does not argue that it acquired anything less than title to Sue, we need not decide whether Williams could have leased Sue or transferred other rights to Black Hills.

discussion of the issue between the parties. Should the grantor or the grantee then own the mobile home?

B. FINDERS

Lost and found property is not a major branch of the law. In terms of economic importance, it's not highly significant; most practicing attorneys will likely never encounter a lost property dispute. Yet for several reasons we think it's a good starting point for your study of personal property. First, everyone has had experience in losing and finding things, and thus has a basis for considering how the law should deal with disputes. Second, in contrast to most topics you study in the first year of law school, finders is a relatively small body of law, having relatively few reported cases and rules. This gives you the opportunity to master one topic in a short amount of time; although, you are likely to conclude, after reading the following materials, finders' rules and policies are more complicated than you originally thought. Third, we use finders' materials to introduce the key concepts of *title* and *possession*, which recur throughout all of property law, both personal and real.

■ **ARMORY v. DELAMIRIE**
Court of King's Bench, 1722
1 Strange 505, 93 Eng. Rep. 664

In Middlesex coram PRATT, Chief Justice. The plaintiff being a chimney sweeper's boy found a jewel and carried it to the defendant's shop (who was a goldsmith) to know what it was, and delivered it into the hands of the apprentice, who under pretence of weighing it, took out the stones, and calling to the master to let him know it came to three halfpence, the master offered the boy the money, who refused to take it, and insisted to have the thing again; whereupon the apprentice delivered him back the socket without the stones. And now in trover against the master these points were ruled: ⌐wrongful taking of personal property

1. That the finder of a jewel, though he does not by such finding acquire an absolute property or ownership, yet he has such a property as will enable him to keep it against all but the rightful owner, and consequently may maintain trover.

2. That the action well lay against the master, who gives a credit to his apprentice, and is answerable for his neglect.

3. As to the value of the jewel several of the trade were examined to prove what a jewel of the finest water that would fit the socket would be worth; and the Chief Justice directed the jury, that unless the defendant did produce the jewel, and shew it not to be of the finest water, they should presume the strongest against him, and make the value of the best jewels the measure of their damages: which they accordingly did.

Notes and Questions

1. Did the chimney sweeper's boy succeed in his action because he owned property, or did he own property because his action succeeded? Is the court's

statement that the finder has "a property" in the jewel a finding of fact or conclusion of law?

2. Why should the plaintiff prevail? Does the court give any reasons? Do any of the definitions of property or theories of property described in Chapter 1 support the court's decision? Could the court have ruled in favor of the defendant goldsmith?

3. Has the chimney sweeper's boy received the proper amount of damages? If he sold his rights in a voluntary market transaction, how much would an informed buyer pay?

4. What effect does the judgment against the goldsmith have on ownership of the jewel? What should happen if the person who lost the jewel subsequently brings an action against the boy or the goldsmith?

5. *Replevin.* The writ of replevin developed as an exception to the usual rule that an owner of converted chattels could sue only for damages. If a landlord wrongfully seized a tenant's chattels, replevin permitted a tenant to recover those specific chattels. Modern property law has expanded the scope of replevin, typically by statute, to permit an owner of a chattel to recover its possession from any wrongful possessor. If a plaintiff is permitted to sue in trover or replevin, how will she decide which action to bring?

6. *Conversion.* Under modern law, the action for conversion has largely replaced trover and replevin. In general, conversion is an act of dominion or control that is inconsistent with the owner's rights. Common examples are the defendant's wrongful taking, using, detaining, destroying, or selling the plaintiff's property.

■   **BRIDGES v. HAWKESWORTH**
Court of Queen's Bench, 1851
21 L.J.Q.B. 75, 91 Rev. Rep. 850

This was an appeal brought by the plaintiff from the Westminster County Court.

The plaintiff was a traveller for a large firm with which the defendant, who was a shopkeeper, had dealings. On one occasion (October 1847) the plaintiff, who had called at the defendant's on business, on leaving the defendant's shop noticed and picked up a small parcel which was lying on the shop floor. He immediately shewed it to the shopman, and on opening it found it contained bank notes to the value of 55£. The plaintiff told the defendant who came in that he had found a parcel of notes, and requested the defendant to keep them to deliver to the owner. The defendant advertised the finding of them in the newspapers, stating that they should be restored to the owner upon his properly describing them and paying the expenses. Three years having elapsed and no owner appearing to claim them, the plaintiff applied to the defendant for them, offering to pay the expense of the advertisements, and to indemnify the defendant against any claim in respect of them. The defendant refused to deliver them up, and the plaintiff consequently brought a plaint in the County Court of Westminster to recover the notes. The Judge decided that the defendant was entitled to keep them as against the plaintiff, and gave judgment for the defendant. . . .

PATTESON, Justice. The notes which are the subject of this action were evidently dropped by mere accident in the shop of the defendant by the owner of them. The facts do not warrant the supposition that they had been deposited there intentionally, nor has the case been at all put upon that ground. The plaintiff found them on the floor, they being manifestly lost by someone. The general right of the finder to any article which has been lost against all the world except the true owner was established in the case of Armory v. Delamirie, which has never been disputed. This right would clearly have accrued to the plaintiff had the notes been picked up by him outside the shop of the defendant. . . . The case, therefore, resolves itself into the single point, on which it appears that the learned Judge decided it: namely, whether the circumstance of the notes being found *inside* the defendant's shop, gives him, the defendant, the right to have them as against the plaintiff who found them. There is no authority to be found in our law directly in point. . . . It was well asked on the argument, if the defendant has the right, *when* did it accrue to him? If at all, it must have been antecedent to the finding by the plaintiff, for that finding could not give the defendant any right. If the notes had been accidentally kicked into the street, and then found by some one passing by, could it be contended that the defendant was entitled to them, from the mere fact of their having been originally dropped in his shop? If the discovery had not been communicated to the defendant, could the real owner have had any cause of action against him, because they were found in his house? Certainly not. The notes never were in the custody of the defendant, nor within the protection of his house before they were found, as they would have been had they been intentionally deposited there, and the defendant has come under no responsibility. . . . We find, therefore, no circumstances in this case to take it out of the general rule of law, that the finder of a lost article is entitled to it as against all parties except the real owner; and we think that rule must prevail, and that the learned Judge was mistaken in holding that the place in which they were found makes any legal difference. Our judgment therefore is, that the plaintiff is entitled to these notes as against the defendant, and that the judgment of the Court below must be reversed, and judgment given for the plaintiff for 50£. The plaintiff to have the costs of the appeal.

Judgment reversed.

■ SOUTH STAFFORDSHIRE WATER CO. v. SHARMAN

Queen's Bench Division, 1896
[1896] 2 Q.B. 44

Appeal from the decision of the county court of Staffordshire holden at Lichfield.

Under a conveyance dated January 6, 1872, from the mayor, aldermen, and citizens of the city of Lichfield, the plaintiffs were the owners in fee simple in possession of the land covered by the Minster Pool in that city.

In August, 1895, the plaintiffs employed the defendant, together with a number of other workmen, to clean out the pool. During the operation several articles of interest were found, and the defendant, while so employed, found in the mud at the bottom of the pool two gold rings. The plaintiffs demanded the rings; but he refused to deliver them up, and placed them in the hands of the police authorities, who, by advertisement and otherwise, endeavoured to find the owner of the rings. Ultimately, being unsuccessful in finding the real owner, the police authorities returned the rings to the defendant.

The plaintiffs then sued the defendant in detinue for the recovery of the rings. It was proved at the trial that there was no special contract between the plaintiffs and the defendant as to giving up any articles that might be found.

The county court judge gave judgment for the defendant, holding, on the authority of Armory v. Delamirie and Bridges v. Hawkesworth, that the defendant had a good title against all the world except the real owner. . . .

LORD RUSSELL OF KILLOWEN, Chief Justice. In my opinion, the county court judge was wrong, and his decision must be reversed and judgment entered for the plaintiffs. . . .

The plaintiffs are the freeholders of the locus in quo, and as such they have the right to forbid anybody coming on their land or in any way interfering with it. They had the right to say that their pool should be cleaned out in any way that they thought fit, and to direct what should be done with anything found in the pool in the course of such cleaning out. It is no doubt right, as the counsel for the defendant contended, to say that the plaintiffs must shew that they had actual control over the locus in quo and the things in it; but under the circumstances, can it be said that the Minster Pool and whatever might be in that pool were not under the control of the plaintiffs? In my opinion, they were. The case is like the case, of which several illustrations were put in the course of the argument, where an article is found on private property, although the owners of that property are ignorant that it is there. The principle on which this case must be decided, and the distinction which must be drawn between this case and that of Bridges v. Hawkesworth, is to be found in a passage in Pollock and Wright's *Essay on Possession in the Common Law*, p. 41: "The possession of land carries with it in general, by our law, possession of everything which is attached to or under that land, and, in the absence of a better title elsewhere, the right to possess it also. And it makes no difference that the possessor is not aware of the thing's existence. . . . It is free to any one who requires a specific intention as part of a de facto possession to treat this as a positive rule of law. But it seems preferable to say that the legal possession rests on a real de facto possession constituted by the occupier's general power and intent to exclude unauthorized interference."

That is the ground on which I prefer to base my judgment. There is a broad distinction between this case and those cited from Blackstone. Those were cases in which a thing was cast into a public place or into the sea — into a place, in fact, of which it could not be said that any one had a real de facto possession, or a general power and intent to exclude unauthorized interference.

The case of Bridges v. Hawkesworth stands by itself, and on special grounds; and on those grounds it seems to me that the decision in that case was right. Some one had accidentally dropped a bundle of bank-notes in a public shop. The shopkeeper did not know they had been dropped, and did not in any sense exercise control over them. The shop was open to the public, and they were invited to come there. A customer picked up the notes and gave them to the shopkeeper in order that he might advertise them. The owner of the notes was not found, and the finder then sought to recover them from the shopkeeper. It was held that he was entitled to do so, the ground of the decision being, as was pointed out by Patteson J., that the notes, being dropped in the public part of the shop, were never in the custody of the shopkeeper, or "within the protection of his house."

It is somewhat strange that there is no more direct authority on the question; but the general principle seems to me to be that where a person has possession of house or land, with a manifest intention to exercise control over it and the things which may be upon or in it, then, if something is found on that land, whether by an employee of the owner or by a stranger, the presumption is that the possession of that thing is in the owner of the locus in quo.

WILLS, Justice. I entirely agree; and I will only add that a contrary decision would, as I think, be a great and most unwise encouragement to dishonesty.

Appeal allowed; judgment for plaintiffs.

■ HANNAH v. PEEL
King's Bench Division, 1945
[1945] K.B. 509

BIRKETT, Justice. On December 13, 1938, the freehold of Gwernhaylod House, Overton-on-Dee, Shropshire, was conveyed to the defendant, Major Hugh Edward Ethelston Peel, who from that time to the end of 1940 never himself occupied the house and it remained unoccupied until October 5, 1939, when it was requisitioned, but after some months was released from requisition. Thereafter it remained unoccupied until July 18, 1940, when it was again requisitioned, the defendant being compensated by a payment at the rate of 250£ a year. In August, 1940, the plaintiff, Duncan Hannah, a lance-corporal, serving in a battery of the Royal Artillery, was stationed at the house and on the 21st of that month, when in a bedroom used as a sick-bay, he was adjusting the black-out curtains when his hand touched something on the top of a window-frame, loose in a crevice, which he thought was a piece of dirt or plaster. The plaintiff grasped it and dropped it on the outside window ledge. On the following morning he saw that it was a brooch covered with cobwebs and dirt. Later, he took it with him when he went home on leave and his wife having told him it might be of value, at the end of October, 1940, he informed his commanding officer of his find and, on his advice, handed it over to the police, receiving a receipt for it. In August, 1942, the owner not having been found the police handed the brooch to the defendant, who sold it in October, 1942, for 66£, to Messrs. Spink & Son, Ltd., of London, who resold it in the following month for 88£. There was no evidence that the defendant had any knowledge of the existence of the brooch before it was found by the plaintiff. The defendant had offered the plaintiff a reward for the brooch, but the plaintiff refused to accept this and maintained throughout his right to the possession of the brooch as against all persons other than the owner, who was unknown. By a letter, dated October 5, 1942, the plaintiff's solicitors demanded the return of the brooch from the defendant, but it was not returned and on October 21, 1943, the plaintiff issued his writ claiming the return of the brooch, or its value and damages for its detention. By his defence, the defendant claimed the brooch on the ground that he was the owner of Gwernhaylod House and in possession thereof. . . .

Bridges v. Hawkesworth has been the subject of considerable comment by textbook writers and, amongst others, by Mr. Justice Oliver Wendell Holmes [and] Sir Frederick Pollock. [They] agree that the case was rightly decided, but they differ as to the grounds on which it was decided and put forward grounds, none of which, so far as I can discover, were ever advanced by the judges who decided the case. Mr. Justice Oliver Wendell Holmes wrote (*The Common Law* (1881) at p. 222): "Common law judges and civilians would agree that the finder got possession first and so could keep it as against the shopkeeper. For the shop-keeper, not knowing of the thing, could not have the intent to appropriate it, and, having invited the public to his shop, he could not have the intent to exclude them from it." So he introduces the matter of two intents which are not referred to by the judges who heard the case. Sir Frederick Pollock, whilst he agreed with Mr. Justice Holmes that Bridges v. Hawkesworth was properly decided wrote (*Possession in the Common Law* (Pollock and Wright) at p. 39): "In such a case as Bridges v. Hawkesworth, where a parcel of banknotes was dropped on the floor in the part of a shop frequented by customers, it is impossible to say that the shopkeeper has any possession in fact. He does not expect objects of that kind to be on the floor of his shop, and some customer is more likely than the shopkeeper or his servant to see and take them up if they do come there." He emphasizes the lack of de facto control on the part of the shopkeeper. . . .

It has been said that [South Staffordshire Water Co. v. Sharman] establishes that if a man finds a thing as the servant or agent of another, he finds it not for himself, but for that other, and indeed that seems to afford a sufficient explanation of the case. The rings found at the bottom of the pool were not in the possession of the company, but it seems that though Sharman was the first to obtain possession of them, he obtained them for his employers and could claim no title for himself. . . .

It is fairly clear from the authorities that a man possesses everything which is attached to or under his land. Secondly, it would appear to be the law from the authorities I have cited, and particularly from Bridges v. Hawkesworth, that a man does not necessarily possess a thing which is lying unattached on the surface of his land even though the thing is not possessed by someone else. A difficulty however, arises, because the rule which governs things an occupier possesses as against those which he does not, has never been very clearly formulated in our law. He may possess everything on the land from which he intends to exclude others, if Mr. Justice Holmes is right; or he may possess those things of which he has a de facto control, if Sir Frederick Pollock is right. . . .

[The plaintiff's] conduct was commendable and meritorious. The defendant was never physically in possession of these premises at any time. It is clear that the brooch was never his, in the ordinary acceptation of the term, in that he had the prior possession. He had no knowledge of it, until it was brought to his notice by the finder. A discussion of the merits does not seem to help, but it is clear on the facts that the brooch was "lost" in the ordinary meaning of that word; that it was "found" by the plaintiff in the ordinary meaning of that word, that its true owner has never been found, that the defendant was the owner of the premises and had his notice drawn to this matter by the plaintiff, who found the brooch. In those circumstances I propose to follow the decision in Bridges v. Hawkesworth, and to give judgment in this case for the plaintiff for 66£. . . .

Notes and Questions

Would Major Peel have won the case if he had occupied the house before Corporal Hannah found the brooch? Should we view the house as constructively possessed by Major Peel? For both land and chattels, it is often said that property not actually possessed by anybody is *constructively possessed* by the person who has title thereto. For example, to sue for trespass to land the plaintiff must be in possession when the trespass began. But this does not bar an action by an owner of unoccupied land. "As to vacant land, in the absence of actual possession in anyone, complete and unrestricted title gives the owner constructive possession sufficient to maintain trespass without ever having had actual possession." Falejczyk v. Meo, 176 N.E.2d 10 (Ill. App. Ct. 1961).

■ **CORLISS v. WENNER**
Court of Appeals of Idaho, 2001
34 P.3d 1100

SCHWARTZMAN, Chief Judge. Gregory Corliss appeals from the district court's orders granting summary judgment in favor of Jann Wenner on the right to possess ninety-six gold coins unearthed by Anderson and Corliss on Wenner's property. . . . We affirm.

FACTUAL AND PROCEDURAL BACKGROUND

In the fall of 1996, Jann Wenner hired Anderson Asphalt Paving to construct a driveway on his ranch in Blaine County. Larry Anderson, the owner of Anderson Asphalt Paving, and his employee, Gregory Corliss, were excavating soil for the driveway when they unearthed a glass jar containing paper wrapped rolls of gold coins. Anderson and Corliss collected, cleaned, and inventoried the gold pieces dating from 1857 to 1914.[1] The coins themselves weighed about four pounds. Anderson and Corliss agreed to split the gold coins between themselves, with Anderson retaining possession of all the coins. At some point Anderson and Corliss argued over ownership of the coins and Anderson fired Corliss. Anderson later gave possession of the coins to Wenner in exchange for indemnification on any claim Corliss might have against him regarding the coins.

Corliss sued Anderson and Wenner for possession of some or all of the coins. Wenner, defending both himself and Anderson, filed a motion for summary judgment. The facts, except whether Corliss found all or just some of the gold coins without Anderson's help, are not in dispute. All parties agree that the coins were unearthed during excavation by Anderson and Corliss for a driveway on Wenner's ranch, that the coins had been protected in paper tube rolls and buried in a glass jar estimated to be about seventy years old. Following a hearing on Wenner's motion for summary judgment, the district court declined to grant the motion and allowed approximately five months for additional discovery. Six months later the court held a status conference at which counsel for Wenner and Anderson asked the court to rule on Wenner's motion and counsel for Corliss did not object. No new facts were offered.

The district court then entered a memorandum decision stating that the "finders keepers" rule of treasure trove had not been previously adopted in Idaho, that it was not a part of the common law of England incorporated into Idaho law at the time of statehood by statute, and that the coins, having been carefully concealed for safekeeping, fit within the legal classification of mislaid property, to which the right

---

1. Of the ninety-six coins gathered up by Anderson and Corliss, there were thirty-six five-dollar gold pieces with mint dates ranging from 1857 to 1909, twenty-two ten-dollar gold pieces dating from 1882 to 1910, and thirty-eight twenty-dollar gold pieces dating from 1870 to 1914. Corliss claimed the value of the coins was in excess of $30,000 and at oral argument offered a value of between $500,000 and $1,000,000. Counsel for Wenner countered that the value of the coins was between $25,000 and $30,000. There is no independent appraisal of the coins in the record.

of possession goes to the land owner. Alternatively, the court ruled that the coins, like the topsoil being excavated, were a part of the property owned by Wenner and that Anderson and Corliss were merely Wenner's employees. Corliss appeals.

LAW APPLICABLE TO DETERMINING THE RIGHTFUL POSSESSOR OF THE GOLD COINS

This is a case of first impression in Idaho, the central issue being the proper rule to apply in characterizing the gold coins found by Corliss and Anderson on Wenner's property. The major distinctions between characterizations of found property turn on questions of fact, *i.e.*, an analysis of the facts and circumstances in an effort to divine the intent of the true owner at the time he or she parted with the property. The material facts and circumstances surrounding the discovery of the gold coins are not in dispute. However, the characterization of that property, in light of these facts, is a question of law over which we exercise free review. With these principles in mind we now discuss, in turn, the choice of categories applicable to the district court's characterization of the gold coins found by Anderson and Corliss, recognizing that the choice of characterization of found property determines its rightful possessor as between the finder and landowner.

At common law all found property is generally categorized in one of five ways. Those categories are:

ABANDONED PROPERTY — that which the owner has discarded or voluntarily forsaken with the intention of terminating his ownership, but without vesting ownership in any other person;

LOST PROPERTY — that property which the owner has involuntarily and unintentionally parted with through neglect, carelessness, or inadvertence and does not know the whereabouts;

MISLAID PROPERTY — that which the owner has intentionally set down in a place where he can again resort to it, and then forgets where he put it;

TREASURE TROVE — a category exclusively for gold or silver in coin, plate, bullion, and sometimes its paper money equivalents, found concealed in the earth or in a house or other private place. Treasure trove carries with it the thought of antiquity, *i.e.*, that the treasure has been concealed for so long as to indicate that the owner is probably dead or unknown;

EMBEDDED PROPERTY — that personal property which has become a part of the natural earth, such as pottery, the sunken wreck of a steamship, or a rotted-away sack of gold-bearing quartz rock buried or partially buried in the ground.

Under these doctrines, the finder of lost or abandoned property and treasure trove acquires a right to possess the property against the entire world but the rightful owner regardless of the place of finding. The finder of mislaid property is required to turn it over to the owner of the premises who has the duty to safeguard the property for the true owner. Possession of embedded property goes to owner of the land on which the property was found.

One of the major distinctions between these various categories is that only lost property necessarily involves an element of involuntariness. The four remaining categories involve voluntary and intentional acts by the true owner in placing the property where another eventually finds it. However, treasure trove, despite not being lost or abandoned property, is treated as such in that the right to possession is recognized to be in the finder rather than the premises owner.

On appeal, Corliss argues that the district court should have interpreted the undisputed facts and circumstances surrounding of the placement of the coins in the ground to indicate that the gold coins were either lost, abandoned, or treasure trove. Wenner argues that the property was properly categorized as either embedded or mislaid property.

As with most accidentally discovered buried treasure, the history of the original ownership of the coins is shrouded in mystery and obscured by time. The coins had been wrapped in paper, like coins from a bank, and buried in a glass jar, apparently for safekeeping. Based on these circumstances, the district court determined that the coins were not abandoned because the condition in which the coins were found evidenced an intent to keep them safe, not an intent to voluntarily relinquish all possessory interest in them. The district court also implicitly rejected the notion that the coins were lost, noting that the coins were secreted with care in a specific place to protect them from the elements and from other people until such time as the original owner might return for them. There is no indication that the coins came to be buried through neglect, carelessness, or inadvertence. Accordingly, the district court properly concluded, as a matter of law, that the coins were neither lost nor abandoned.

The district court then determined that the modern trend favored characterizing the coins as property either embedded in the earth or mislaid—under which the right of possession goes to the landowner—rather than treasure trove—under which the right of possession goes to the finder. Although accepted by a number of states prior to 1950, the modern trend since then, as illustrated by decisions of the state and federal courts, is decidedly against recognizing the "finders keepers" rule of treasure trove.

Corliss argues that the district court erred in deciding that the law of treasure trove should not apply in Idaho. However, the doctrine of treasure trove has never been adopted in this state. Idaho Code §73-116 provides: "[t]he common law of England, so far as it is not repugnant to, or inconsistent with, the constitution or laws of the United States, in all cases not provided for in these compiled laws, is the rule of decision in all courts of this state." Nevertheless, the history of the "finders keepers" rule was not a part of the common law of England at the time the colonies gained their independence. Rather, the doctrine of treasure trove was created to determine a rightful possessor of buried Roman treasures discovered in feudal times. *See* Leeanna Izuel, *Property Owner's Constructive Possession of Treasure Trove: Rethinking the Finders Keepers Rule,* 38 U.C.L.A. L. Rev. 1659, 1666-67 (1991). And while the common law initially awarded the treasure to the finder, the crown, as early as the year 1130, exercised its royal prerogative to take such property for itself. *Id.* Only after the American colonies gained their independence from England did some states grant possession of treasure trove to the finder. *Id.* Thus, it does not appear that the "finders keepers" rule of treasure trove was a part of the common law of England as defined by Idaho Code §73-116. We hold that the district court correctly determined that I.C. §73-116 does not require the treasure trove doctrine to be adopted in Idaho.

Additionally, we conclude that the rule of treasure trove is of dubious heritage and misunderstood application, inconsistent with our values and traditions. The danger of adopting the doctrine of treasure trove is laid out in Morgan v. Wiser, 711 S.W.2d 220, 222-23 (Tenn. Ct. App. 1985) (gold coins found buried in an iron pot properly characterized as embedded property):

> [We] find the rule with respect to treasure-trove to be out of harmony with modern notions of fair play. The common-law rule of treasure-trove invites trespassers to roam

at large over the property of others with their metal detecting devices and to dig wherever such devices tell them property might be found. If the discovery happens to fit the definition of treasure-trove, the trespasser may claim it as his own. To paraphrase another court: The mind refuses consent to the proposition that one may go upon the lands of another and dig up and take away anything he discovers there which does not belong to the owner of the land. . . .

Land ownership includes control over crops on the land, buildings and appurtenances, soils, and minerals buried under those soils. The average Idaho landowner would expect to have a possessory interest in any object uncovered on his or her property. And certainly the notion that a trespassing treasure hunter, or a hired handyman or employee, could or might have greater possessory rights than a landowner in objects uncovered on his or her property runs counter to the reasonable expectations of present-day land ownership.[2]

There is no reason for a special rule for gold and silver coins, bullion, or plate as opposed to other property. Insofar as personal property (money and the like) buried or secreted on privately owned realty is concerned, the distinctions between treasure trove, lost property, and mislaid property are anachronistic and of little value. The principle point of such distinctions is the intent of the true owner which, absent some written declaration indicating such, is obscured in the mists of time and subject to a great deal of speculation.[3]

By holding that property classed as treasure trove (gold or silver coins, bullion, plate) in other jurisdictions is classed in Idaho as personal property embedded in the soil, subject to the same limitations as mislaid property, possession will be awarded to the owner of the soil as a matter of law. Thus, we craft a simple and reasonable solution to the problem, discourage trespass, and avoid the risk of speculating about the true owner's intent when attempting to infer such from the manner and circumstances in which an object is found. Additionally, the true owner,[4] if any, will have the opportunity to recover the property. . . .

■ MARK TWAIN, THE ADVENTURES OF TOM SAWYER
177-80 (1876)

There comes a time in every rightly constructed boy's life when he has a raging desire to go somewhere and dig for hidden treasure. This desire suddenly came upon Tom one day. He sallied out to find Joe Harper, but failed of success. Next he sought Ben Rogers; he had gone fishing. Presently he stumbled upon Huck Finn the Red-Handed. Huck would answer. Tom took him to a private place and opened the matter to him confidentially. Huck was willing. Huck was always willing to take a hand in any enterprise that offered entertainment and required no capital, for he had a troublesome superabundance of that sort of time which is *not* money.

"Where'll we dig?" said Huck.

---

2. We note that nothing would prevent a would-be treasure hunter or hired builder or excavator from contracting some type of arrangement where the right of possession is shared or purchased outright.

3. As one commentator has wryly noted, "The old rule of treasure trove may make good theater, but it's poor law, and its death can come none to soon." Richard B. Cunningham, *The Slow Death of the Treasure Trove*, Archaeology (Feb. 7, 2000).

4. We take no position as to whether a true owner would include testamentary or nontestamentary heirs.

"O, most anywhere."

"Why, is it hid all around?"

"No indeed it ain't. It's hid in mighty particular places, Huck — sometimes on islands, sometimes in rotten chests under the end of a limb of an old dead tree, just where the shadow falls at midnight; but mostly under the floor in ha'nted houses."

"Who hides it?"

"Why robbers, of course — who'd you reckon? Sunday-school sup'rintendents?" . . .

"But say — where you going to dig first?"

"Well, I don't know. S'pose we tackle that old dead-limb tree on the hill t'other side of Still-House branch?"

"I'm agreed."

So they got a crippled pick and a shovel, and set out on their three-mile tramp. They arrived hot and panting, and threw themselves down in the shade of a neighboring elm to rest and have a smoke.

"I like this," said Tom. "So do I." . . .

They worked and sweated for half an hour. No result. They toiled another half-hour. Still no result. Huck said:

"Do they always bury it as deep as this?"

"Sometimes — not always. Not generally. I reckon we haven't got the right place."

So they chose a new spot and began again. The labor dragged a little, but still they made progress. They pegged away in silence for some time. Finally Huck leaned on his shovel, swabbed the beaded drops from his brow with his sleeve, and said:

"Where you going to dig next, after we get this one?"

"I reckon maybe we'll tackle the old tree that's over yonder on Cardiff Hill back of the widow's."

"I reckon that'll be a good one. But won't the widow take it way from us, Tom? It's on her land."

"*She* take it away! Maybe she'd like to try it once. Whoever finds one of these hid treasures, it belongs to him. It don't make any difference whose land it's on." . . .

Notes and Questions

1. Is Tom Sawyer's explanation of treasure trove legally correct?

2. In England, since the twelfth century, treasure trove has belonged to the sovereign, not to the lucky finder. Under the common law, treasure trove was defined narrowly, requiring both a substantial percentage of gold or silver and a finding that the property was hidden for safekeeping, rather than lost or abandoned. Under modern practice, treasure trove goes to a British museum, which compensates the finder with a monetary award equal to its full market value. In Treasure Act 1996, Parliament significantly altered the law of treasure trove to expand museums' acquisition rights. Treasure trove is now defined to include all coins at least 300 years old with a minimum gold or silver content of 10 percent, or less if there are more than 10 coins. Other objects of archeological significance are also covered. All treasures are covered by the act's procedures, regardless of how they came to be buried in the ground.

3. Born in 1946, Jann Wenner, the defendant-appellee in *Corliss,* is the multi-millionaire co-founder of *Rolling Stone Magazine* whose publishing empire includes

the celebrity magazine *Us* and *Men's Journal*. As the editor of *Rolling Stone Magazine*, Wenner helped to launch the careers of writers Hunter S. Thompson and Tom Wolfe and photographer Annie Leibovitz. Wenner personally conducted some of *Rolling Stone*'s most significant interviews, including extended ones with John Lennon, Mick Jagger, Bob Dylan, and Eric Clapton. Wenner has also produced recordings and appeared in major motion pictures. In 2005, he was inducted into the Rock and Roll Hall of Fame and in 2006, had a surrogate son with his companion, fashion designer Matt Nye. Wenner uses the Idaho house as a vacation home.

4. The mislaid property doctrine, referred to in *Corliss*, is widely followed in the United States, but was never adopted by England. A true owner mislays property by intentionally putting it somewhere and forgetting to retrieve it; for example, a person who hangs her jacket on a restaurant's coat rack and leaves jacketless after a fine dinner. How do courts decide whether an item is lost or mislaid? What's the rationale for preferring the owner of the locus in quo over the finder of a mislaid item?

5. In footnote 4, the court in *Corliss* stated, "We take no position as to whether a true owner would include testamentary or nontestamentary heirs." Does this statement apply to lost, mislaid, and embedded property generally? What are the policy arguments for and against extending true ownership to testamentary or nontestamentary heirs?

6. *Unclaimed Property Acts.* Most states have statutes dealing with certain types of unclaimed personal property. The Uniform Unclaimed Property Act, revised in 1995 to replace prior versions promulgated in 1954 and 1981, provides for the state to take custody of certain intangible personal property held by banks and other companies. A state administrator collects property such as bank accounts, dividends, traveler's checks, unpaid wages, and the contents of safety deposit boxes that lie dormant for a specified time period (usually five years). If a search for the owner is unsuccessful, the state is authorized to sell the property other than money at a public sale. An owner who later appears has no claim to the sold property, but has a right of reimbursement from a state custodial account. The unclaimed property acts provide modest amounts of revenues for the states.

■ **COLUMBUS-AMERICA DISCOVERY GROUP v. ATLANTIC MUTUAL INSURANCE COMPANY**
United States Court of Appeals for the Fourth Circuit, 1992
974 F.2d 450, cert. denied, 507 U.S. 1000 (1993)

RUSSELL, Circuit Judge. "When Erasmus mused that '[a] common shipwreck is a source of consolation to all,' Adagia, IV.iii.9 (1508), he quite likely did not foresee inconcinnate free-for-alls among self-styled salvors." Martha's Vineyard Scuba HQ, Inc. v. The Unidentified, Wrecked and Abandoned Steam Vessel, 833 F.2d 1059, 1061 (1st Cir. 1987). Without doubt the Dutch scholar also could not imagine legal brawls involving self-styled "finders" from Ohio, British and American insurance underwriters, an heir to the Miller Brewing fortune, a Texas oil millionaire, an Ivy League university, and an Order of Catholic monks. Yet that is what this case involves, with the prize being up to one billion dollars in gold.

This gold was deposited on the ocean floor, 8,000 feet below the surface and 160 miles off the South Carolina coast, when the S.S. Central America sank in a hurricane on September 12, 1857. The precise whereabouts of the wreck remained unknown until 1988, when it was located by the Columbus-America Discovery Group ("Columbus-America"). This enterprise has since been recovering the gold, and last year it moved in federal district court to have itself declared the owner of the treasure. Into court to oppose this manoeuvre came British and American insurers who had originally underwritten the gold for its ocean voyage and then had to pay off over a million dollars in claims upon the disaster. Also attempting to get into the stew were three would-be intervenors who claimed that Columbus-America had used their computerized "treasure map" to locate the gold. The district court allowed the intervention, but it did not give the intervenors any time for discovery.

S.S. Central America

After a ten-day trial, the lower Court awarded Columbus-America the golden treasure in its entirety. It found that the underwriters had previously abandoned their ownership interests in the gold by deliberately destroying certain documentation. As for the intervenors, the Court held that there was no evidence showing that Columbus-America used their information in any way in locating the wreck.

Upon appeal, we find that the evidence was not sufficient to show that the underwriters affirmatively abandoned their interests in the gold. We also hold that once intervention was allowed, the district court abused its discretion by not affording the intervenors sufficient time for discovery. We therefore reverse the decision below and remand the case for further proceedings. . . .

Historically, courts have applied the maritime law of salvage when ships or their cargo have been recovered from the bottom of the sea by those other than their owners. Under this law, the original owners still retain their ownership interests in such property, although the salvors are entitled to a very liberal salvage award. Such awards often exceed the value of the services rendered, and if no owner should come forward to claim the property, the salvor is normally awarded its total value. . . .

A related legal doctrine is the common law of finds, which expresses "the ancient and honorable principle of 'finders, keepers.'" *Martha's Vineyard*, 833 F.2d at 1065. Traditionally, the law of finds was applied only to maritime property which had never been owned by anybody, such as ambergris, whales, and fish. 3A Benedict on Admiralty §158, at 11-15. A relatively recent trend in the law, though, has seen the law of finds applied to long lost and abandoned shipwrecks. *Id.* §158, at 11-16 to 11-18. . . .

Today, finds law is applied to previously owned sunken property only when that property has been abandoned by its previous owners. Abandonment in this sense means much more than merely leaving the property, for it has long been the law that "when articles are lost at sea the title of the owner in them remains." The Akaba, 54 F. 197, 200 (4th Cir. 1893); *see also* 3A *Benedict on Admiralty* §158, at 11-1 to 11-2. Once an article has been lost at sea, "lapse of time and nonuser are not sufficient, in and of themselves, to constitute an abandonment." Wiggins v. 1100 Tons, More or Less, of

Italian Marble, 186 F. Supp. 452, 456 (E.D. Va. 1960). In addition, there is no abandonment when one discovers sunken property and then, even after extensive efforts, is unable to locate its owner. Weber Marine, Inc. v. One Large Cast Steel Stockless Anchor and Four Shots of Anchor Chain, 478 F. Supp. 973, 975 (E.D. La. 1979).

B.

Gold from the S.S. Central America

Before addressing whether the district court correctly found that the insured shipments of gold were abandoned by the underwriters, several points should be noted. First, the Central America herself was self-insured, and successors in interest to the U.S. Mail and Steamship Company have made no attempt to claim an ownership interest in the wreck. Also, there appears to have been a fairly significant amount of passenger gold aboard, but this case, almost surprisingly, has failed to see descendants of any of the passengers attempt to gain a share of the treasure. Thus, an abandonment may be found, and Columbus-America may be declared the finder and sole owner, as to any recovered parts of the ship, all passenger possessions, and any cargo besides the insured shipments.

As for the insured gold, to "prima facially" prove their ownership interests at trial, the underwriters produced several original documents: entries from the Atlantic Mutual's Vessel Disasters Book concerning the disaster (one of which contained the scribbled notation, "estimated loss $150,000"); records of Board resolutions to pay claims; minutes from an underwriters' board meeting discussing the Central America; a study prepared by the New York Board of Underwriters regarding the disaster; and the salvage contract between the underwriters and Brutus de Villeroi. The insurers also produced a great many period newspaper articles. These discussed the amount of treasure on board; the insurers of this treasure and the amounts they insured; the willingness of the insurers to pay off claims; the general satisfaction the insureds received from having their claims promptly settled; and the salvage negotiations between the underwriters and the Boston Submarine Armor Company.

On appeal, Columbus-America exerts much effort in asserting that there exists insufficient evidence to prove that the underwriters who are now parties in this litigation actually insured and paid off claims upon the gold. The lower court, though, found prima facially that the underwriters did insure the treasure and that they received ownership interests in the gold once the claims were paid. Because of the extent of the catastrophe involved, and its feared repercussions in the American economy, newspapers around the country devoted much space and attention not only to the human aspects of the tragedy, but also the financial. Articles abounded on the quantity of gold aboard, its owners, and its insurers. Some of these articles do contradict others as to the exact amount certain underwriters insured. Still, we find that the district court did not err when it held that the underwriters who are now parties, or their predecessors in interests, paid off claims upon and became the owners of the commercial shipment of gold in 1857.

Despite finding that the underwriters owned the gold in 1857, the district court applied the law of finds and awarded Columbus-America the entire treasure. This was because at some point the insurers had abandoned their interests in the gold. On appeal, Columbus-America asserts that the lower court found an abandonment because of "20 distinct factors." It is clear, though, that the Court ruled as it did because of only two: the underwriters did nothing to recover the gold after 1858, and they supposedly destroyed all documentation they had regarding payment of claims for the gold.

During trial, the underwriters did not produce any of the original insurance contracts with the insureds, statements from shippers that goods were aboard, bills of lading, or canceled checks or receipts from paying off the claims. While such documents would have existed in 1857, none could be located in 1990. Thus, because an insurance executive testified that the usual practice today is for insurance companies to destroy worthless documents after five years, the district court found that the above documentation concerning the Central America must have been intentionally destroyed in the ordinary course of business. Such destruction, coupled with 130 years of nonuse, equalled, according to the Court, an abandonment. . . .

Contrary to the district court, we cannot find any evidence that the underwriters intentionally or deliberately destroyed any of their documents about the Central America. Instead, the only evidence we have is that after 134 years, such documents that may have once existed can no longer be located. With such a passing of time, it seems as, if not more, likely that the documents were lost or unintentionally destroyed, rather than being intentionally destroyed. . . .

In conclusion, when a previous owner claims long lost property that was involuntarily taken from his control, the law is hesitant to find an abandonment and such must be proved by clear and convincing evidence. Here, we are unable to find the requisite evidence that could lead a court to conclude that the underwriters affirmatively abandoned their interest in the gold. Thus, we hold that the lower court clearly erred when it found an abandonment and applied the law of finds. Accordingly, the case is remanded to the district court for further proceedings.

C.

On remand, the district court is to apply the law of salvage, and in so doing it must determine what percentage of the gold each underwriter insured. Equally, if not more, important, the Court must also determine the proper salvage award for Columbus-America. Although this is a decision that must be left to the lower court, we are hazarding but little to say that Columbus-America should, and will, receive by far the largest share of the treasure.

WIDENER, Circuit Judge, dissenting . . .

In my view, throughout its opinion, the majority has disregarded the rules set forth by the Supreme Court in Anderson v. City of Bessemer City, 470 U.S. 564 (1985). The majority, in contravention of the mandate that "where there are two permissible views of evidence, the factfinder's choice between them cannot be clearly erroneous," reverses the district court's factual finding as clearly erroneous simply because, in my opinion, "it would have decided the case differently." *Bessemer City*, 470 U.S. at 573-74. . . .

The majority's holding that "it seems as, if not more, likely that the documents were lost or unintentionally destroyed, rather than being intentionally destroyed," illustrates the majority's misconception of our role on appeal. It is not our role to decide a case on appeal based on which factual inference we would draw from the evidence. Rather we should only determine if the factual inferences drawn by the district court are supported by the evidence. In addition to the clear testimony of Atlantic Mutual's representative that the policies covering goods on the Central America were destroyed and that the bills of lading were probably destroyed, the evidence showed that not one of the numerous insurance companies involved in this litigation was able to produce any of the documents that would have to be produced prior to a claim being paid, and that the companies destroy documents on a routine basis. In my opinion, these facts fully support the inference drawn by the district court, but rejected by the majority, that the documents were intentionally destroyed. . . .

Notes and Questions

1. The court uses a standard definition of the term *abandonment,* the same one commonly employed for all goods, whether or not lost under water. Is the same standard appropriate? Should the outcome differ had the gold disappeared on land (perhaps due to robbery) and reappeared more than a century later?

2. Why did the court choose to follow the law of salvage rather than the law of finders? Should the law of finders replace the law of salvage as to shipwrecks and sunken treasures? Should the law of salvage replace the law of finders (every finder of lost property is entitled to a reasonable award from a true owner who asserts title)? A few states have finder reward statutes. For example, Alabama and Michigan provide for a "reasonable reward," and Iowa and Nebraska have statutes fixing a finder's reward at 10 percent. Is it good policy for a state to enact a finder's reward provision? If so, which approach is preferable? In the absence of a finder reward statute, may a court compensate the finder for her efforts?

3. On remand, the *Columbus-America* district court set the salvage award at 90 percent, relying upon the risks involved, the high expenditures for labor and equipment, and the long time for recovery operations. The court of appeals affirmed, concluding the award was not excessive. Columbus-America Discovery Group v. Atlantic Mut. Ins. Co., 56 F.3d 556 (4th Cir.), *cert. denied,* 516 U.S. 938 (1995).

4. When there are competing salvors or competing finders, who should prevail? In the context of shipwrecks, should the rule be:

   (a) the first person to discover the wreck?
   (b) the first person to give public notice of the discovery?
   (c) the first person to physically touch the wreck?
   (d) the first person to retrieve an object from the wreck and move it to the surface?
   (e) the first possessor of the wreck?
   (f) some other rule?

5. When there are successive finders, who should prevail? Suppose Adam finds a Rolex watch in a public park and loses it two weeks later at the beach, where Becky

finds it. Becky reports the loss to the police and advertises her find in the newspaper. Adam replies, requesting return of the watch. The true owner is still unknown. Must Becky comply?

In Clark v. Maloney, 3 Del. (3 Harr.) 68 (Super. Ct. 1840), plaintiff found 10 logs floating in Delaware Bay and moored them with ropes in the mouth of a creek. Subsequently, defendants found the logs adrift and floating up the creek. Plaintiff brought an action of trover. The court rejected the defendants' claim that "their title is as good as that of the plaintiff. . . . [T]he loss of a chattel does not change the right of property; and for the same reason that the original loss of these logs by the rightful owner, did not change his absolute property in them, but he might have maintained trover against the plaintiff upon refusal to deliver them, so the subsequent loss did not divest the special property of the plaintiff."

6. There is close affinity between finders' law and the *rule of capture*, discussed in the following case. Under the rule of capture, the first person to take possession of an unowned object becomes its owner. In Chapter 1, Henry Maine calls this idea "occupancy of *res nullius*," divided into two categories: things that never had an owner (such as wild animals) and things that once had an owner (such as abandoned goods). The most notable historic application of the rule of capture is in the province of wild animals. Property is awarded to the hunter who kills or mortally wounds an animal, or who captures that animal by depriving it of its liberty. The famous case cited in the following opinion at footnote 25, Pierson v. Post, is reproduced in Chapter 5 below. Decided by the New York Supreme Court in 1805 and frequently cited by subsequent courts, countless novice property law students have labored over "the fox case" (*Pierson*). As we'll see later in this course, courts have extended the rule of capture from its animal roots to resolve ownership disputes over other resources, such as water and oil and gas.

■ **POPOV v. HAYASHI**
Superior Court, San Francisco County, California, 2002
2002 WL 31833731

McCarthy, Judge. In 1927, Babe Ruth hit sixty home runs. That record stood for thirty four years until Roger Maris broke it in 1961 with sixty one home runs. Mark McGwire hit seventy in 1998. On October 7, 2001, at PacBell Park in San Francisco, Barry Bonds hit number seventy three. That accomplishment set a record which, in all probability, will remain unbroken for years into the future.

The event was widely anticipated and received a great deal of attention.

The ball that found itself at the receiving end of Mr. Bond's bat garnered some of that attention. Baseball fans in general, and especially people at the game, understood the importance of the ball. It was worth a great deal of money[1] and whoever caught it would bask, for a brief period of time, in the reflected fame of Mr. Bonds.

With that in mind, many people who attended the game came prepared for the possibility that a record setting ball would be hit in their direction. Among this group were plaintiff Alex Popov and defendant Patrick Hayashi. They were unacquainted at the time. Both men brought baseball gloves, which they anticipated using if the ball came within their reach.

---

1. It has been suggested that the ball might sell for something in excess of $1,000,000.

They, along with a number of others, positioned themselves in the arcade section of the ballpark. This is a standing room only area located near right field. It is in this general area that Barry Bonds hits the greatest number of home runs. The area was crowded with people on October 7, 2001 and access was restricted to those who held tickets for that section.

Barry Bonds came to bat in the first inning. With nobody on base and a full count, Bonds swung at a slow knuckleball. He connected. The ball sailed over the right-field fence and into the arcade. . . .

When the seventy-third home run ball went into the arcade, it landed in the upper portion of the webbing of a softball glove worn by Alex Popov. While the glove stopped the trajectory of the ball, it is not at all clear that the ball was secure. Popov had to reach for the ball and in doing so, may have lost his balance.

Even as the ball was going into his glove, a crowd of people began to engulf Mr. Popov. He was tackled and thrown to the ground while still in the process of attempting to complete the catch. Some people intentionally descended on him for the purpose of taking the ball away, while others were involuntarily forced to the ground by the momentum of the crowd.

Eventually, Mr. Popov was buried face down on the ground under several layers of people. At one point he had trouble breathing. Mr. Popov was grabbed, hit and kicked. People reached underneath him in the area of his glove. Neither the tape nor the testimony is sufficient to establish which individual members of the crowd were responsible for the assaults on Mr. Popov.

The videotape clearly establishes that this was an out of control mob, engaged in violent, illegal behavior. Although some witnesses testified in a manner inconsistent with this finding, their testimony is specifically rejected as being false on a material point.

Mr. Popov intended at all times to establish and maintain possession of the ball. At some point the ball left his glove and ended up on the ground. It is impossible to establish the exact point in time that this occurred or what caused it to occur.

Mr. Hayashi was standing near Mr. Popov when the ball came into the stands. He, like Mr. Popov, was involuntarily forced to the ground. He committed no wrongful act.[5] While on the ground he saw the loose ball. He picked it up, rose to his feet and put it in his pocket.

Although the crowd was still on top of Mr. Popov, security guards had begun the process of physically pulling people off. Some people resisted those efforts. One person argued with an official and another had to be pulled off by his hair.

Mr. Hayashi kept the ball hidden. He asked Mr. Keppel to point the camera at him. At first, Mr. Keppel did not comply and Mr. Hayashi continued to hide the ball. Finally after someone else in the crowd asked Mr. Keppel to point the camera at Mr. Hayashi, Mr. Keppel complied. It was only at that point that Mr. Hayashi held the ball in the air for others to see. Someone made a motion for the ball and Mr. Hayashi put it back in his glove. It is clear that Mr. Hayashi was concerned that someone would take the ball away from him and that he was unwilling to show it until he was on videotape. Although he testified to the contrary, that portion of his testimony is unconvincing.

---

5. Plaintiff argues that the Keppel tape shows Mr. Hayashi biting the leg of Brian Shepard. The tape does not support such a conclusion. The testimony which suggests that a bite occurred is equally unconvincing. In addition, there is insufficient evidence that Mr. Hayashi assaulted or attempted to take the ball away from Mr. Popov.

Mr. Popov eventually got up from the ground. He made several statements while he was on the ground and shortly after he got up which are consistent with his claim that he had achieved some level of control over the ball and that he intended to keep it. Those statements can be heard on the audio portion of the tape. When he saw that Mr. Hayashi had the ball he expressed relief and grabbed for it. Mr. Hayashi pulled the ball away.[6] Security guards then took Mr. Hayashi to a secure area of the stadium.

It is important to point out what the evidence did not and could not show. Neither the camera nor the percipient witnesses were able to establish whether Mr. Popov retained control of the ball as he descended into the crowd. Mr. Popov's testimony on this question is inconsistent on several important points, ambiguous on others and, on the whole, unconvincing. We do not know when or how Mr. Popov lost the ball.

Perhaps the most critical factual finding of all is one that cannot be made. We will never know if Mr. Popov would have been able to retain control of the ball had the crowd not interfered with his efforts to do so. Resolution of that question is the work of a psychic, not a judge.

LEGAL ANALYSIS

Plaintiff has pled causes of actions for conversion, trespass to chattel, injunctive relief and constructive trust.

Conversion is the wrongful exercise of dominion over the personal property of another. There must be actual interference with the plaintiff's dominion. Wrongful withholding of property can constitute actual interference even where the defendant lawfully acquired the property. If a person entitled to possession of personal property demands its return, the unjustified refusal to give the property back is conversion.

The act constituting conversion must be intentionally done. There is no requirement, however, that the defendant know that the property belongs to another or that the defendant intends to dispossess the true owner of its use and enjoyment. Wrongful purpose is not a component of conversion.

The injured party may elect to seek either specific recovery of the property or monetary damages.

Trespass to chattel, in contrast, exists where personal property has been damaged or where the defendant has interfered with the plaintiff's use of the property. Actual dispossession is not an element of the tort of trespass to chattel.

In the case at bar, Mr. Popov is not claiming that Mr. Hayashi damaged the ball or that he interfered with Mr. Popov's use and enjoyment of the ball. He claims instead that Mr. Hayashi intentionally took it from him and refused to give it back. There is no trespass to chattel. If there was a wrong at all, it is conversion.

Conversion does not exist, however, unless the baseball rightfully belongs to Mr. Popov. One who has neither title nor possession, nor any right to possession, cannot sue for conversion. The deciding question in this case then, is whether Mr. Popov achieved possession or the right to possession as he attempted to catch and hold on to the ball.

---

6. Defense counsel has attempted to characterize this encounter as one in which Mr. Popov congratulates Mr. Hayashi for getting the ball and offers him a high five. This is an argument that only a true advocate could embrace.

The parties have agreed to a starting point for the legal analysis. Prior to the time the ball was hit, it was possessed and owned by Major League Baseball. At the time it was hit it became intentionally abandoned property. The first person who came in possession of the ball became its new owner.

The parties fundamentally disagree about the definition of possession. In order to assist the court in resolving this disagreement, four distinguished law professors participated in a forum to discuss the legal definition of possession. The professors also disagreed.

The discussion was held during an official session of the court convened at The University of California, Hastings College of the Law. The session was attended by a number of students and professors including one first year property law class which used this case as vehicle to understand the law of possession. . . .

While there is a degree of ambiguity built into the term possession, that ambiguity exists for a purpose. Courts are often called upon to resolve conflicting claims of possession in the context of commercial disputes. A stable economic environment requires rules of conduct which are understandable and consistent with the fundamental customs and practices of the industry they regulate. Without that, rules will be difficult to enforce and economic instability will result. Because each industry has different customs and practices, a single definition of possession cannot be applied to different industries without creating havoc. . . .

We start with the observation that possession is a process which culminates in an event. The event is the moment in time that possession is achieved. The process includes the acts and thoughts of the would be possessor which lead up to the moment of possession.

The focus of the analysis in this case is not on the thoughts or intent of the actor. Mr. Popov has clearly evidenced an intent to possess the baseball and has communicated that intent to the world. The question is whether he did enough to reduce the ball to his exclusive dominion and control. Were his acts sufficient to create a legally cognizable interest in the ball?

Mr. Hayashi argues that possession does not occur until the fan has complete control of the ball. Professor Brian Gray, suggests the following definition "A person who catches a baseball that enters the stands is its owner. A ball is caught if the person has achieved complete control of the ball at the point in time that the momentum of the ball and the momentum of the fan while attempting to catch the ball ceases. A baseball, which is dislodged by incidental contact with an inanimate object or another person, before momentum has ceased, is not possessed. Incidental contact with another person is contact that is not intended by the other person. The first person to pick up a loose ball and secure it becomes its possessor."

Mr. Popov argues that this definition requires that a person seeking to establish possession must show unequivocal dominion and control, a standard rejected by several leading cases.[25] Instead, he offers the perspectives of Professor Bernhardt and Professor Paul Finkelman[26] who suggest that possession occurs when an

---

25. Pierson v. Post, 3 Cai. 175 (N.Y. Sup. Ct. 1805); Young v. Hitchens, 6 Q.B. 606 (1844); State v. Shaw, 65 N.E. 875 (Ohio 1902).

26. Professor Finkelman is the author of the definitive law review article on the central issue in this case. Paul Finkelman (Chapman Distinguished Professor of Law), *Fugitive Baseballs and Abandoned Property: Who Owns the Home Run Ball?*, 23 Cardozo L. Rev. 1609 (May 2002).

individual intends to take control of a ball and manifests that intent by stopping the forward momentum of the ball whether or not complete control is achieved.

Professors Finkelman and Bernhardt have correctly pointed out that some cases recognize possession even before absolute dominion and control is achieved. Those cases require the actor to be actively and ably engaged in efforts to establish complete control. Moreover, such efforts must be significant and they must be reasonably calculated to result in unequivocal dominion and control at some point in the near future.

This rule is applied in cases involving the hunting or fishing of wild animals or the salvage of sunken vessels. The hunting and fishing cases recognize that a mortally wounded animal may run for a distance before falling. The hunter acquires possession upon the act of wounding the animal not the eventual capture. Similarly, whalers acquire possession by landing a harpoon, not by subduing the animal.

In the salvage cases, an individual may take possession of a wreck by exerting as much control "as its nature and situation permit." Inadequate efforts, however, will not support a claim of possession. Thus, a "sailor cannot assert a claim merely by boarding a vessel and publishing a notice, unless such acts are coupled with a then present intention of conducting salvage operations, and he immediately thereafter proceeds with activity in the form of constructive steps to aid the distressed party."

These rules are contextual in nature. They are crafted in response to the unique nature of the conduct they seek to regulate. Moreover, they are influenced by the custom and practice of each industry. The reason that absolute dominion and control is not required to establish possession in the cases cited by Mr. Popov is that such a rule would be unworkable and unreasonable. The "nature and situation" of the property at issue does not immediately lend itself to unequivocal dominion and control. It is impossible to wrap one's arms around a whale, a fleeing fox or a sunken ship.

The opposite is true of a baseball hit into the stands of a stadium. Not only is it physically possible for a person to acquire unequivocal dominion and control of an abandoned baseball, but fans generally expect a claimant to have accomplished as much. The custom and practice of the stands creates a reasonable expectation that a person will achieve full control of a ball before claiming possession. There is no reason for the legal rule to be inconsistent with that expectation. Therefore Gray's Rule is adopted as the definition of possession in this case.

The central tenet of Gray's Rule is that the actor must retain control of the ball after incidental contact with people and things. Mr. Popov has not established by a preponderance of the evidence that he would have retained control of the ball after all momentum ceased and after any incidental contact with people or objects. Consequently, he did not achieve full possession.

That finding, however, does not resolve the case. The reason we do not know whether Mr. Popov would have retained control of the ball is not because of incidental contact. It is because he was attacked. His efforts to establish possession were interrupted by the collective assault of a band of wrongdoers.

A decision which ignored that fact would endorse the actions of the crowd by not repudiating them. Judicial rulings, particularly in cases that receive media attention, affect the way people conduct themselves. This case demands vindication of an important principle. We are a nation governed by law, not by brute force.

As a matter of fundamental fairness, Mr. Popov should have had the opportunity to try to complete his catch unimpeded by unlawful activity. To hold otherwise would be to allow the result in this case to be dictated by violence. That will not happen.

For these reasons, the analysis cannot stop with the valid observation that Mr. Popov has not proved full possession.

The legal question presented at this point is whether an action for conversion can proceed where the plaintiff has failed to establish possession or title. It can. An action for conversion may be brought where the plaintiff has title, possession or the right to possession.

Here Mr. Popov seeks, in effect, a declaratory judgment that he has either possession or the right to possession. In addition he seeks the remedies of injunctive relief and a constructive trust. These are all actions in equity. A court sitting in equity has the authority to fashion rules and remedies designed to achieve fundamental fairness.

Consistent with this principle, the court adopts the following rule. Where an actor undertakes significant but incomplete steps to achieve possession of a piece of abandoned personal property and the effort is interrupted by the unlawful acts of others, the actor has a legally cognizable pre-possessory interest in the property. That pre-possessory interest constitutes a qualified right to possession which can support a cause of action for conversion.

Possession can be likened to a journey down a path. Mr. Popov began his journey unimpeded. He was fast approaching a fork in the road. A turn in one direction would lead to possession of the ball — he would complete the catch. A turn in the other direction would result in a failure to achieve possession — he would drop the ball. Our problem is that before Mr. Popov got to the point where the road forked, he was set upon by a gang of bandits, who dislodged the ball from his grasp.

Recognition of a legally protected pre-possessory interest, vests Mr. Popov with a qualified right to possession and enables him to advance a legitimate claim to the baseball based on a conversion theory. Moreover it addresses the harm done by the unlawful actions of the crowd. It does not, however, address the interests of Mr. Hayashi. The court is required to balance the interests of all parties.

Mr. Hayashi was not a wrongdoer. He was a victim of the same bandits that attacked Mr. Popov. The difference is that he was able to extract himself from their assault and move to the side of the road. It was there that he discovered the loose ball. When he picked up and put it in his pocket he attained unequivocal dominion and control.

If Mr. Popov had achieved complete possession before Mr. Hayashi got the ball, those actions would not have divested Mr. Popov of any rights, nor would they have created any rights to which Mr. Hayashi could lay claim. Mr. Popov, however, was able to establish only a qualified pre-possessory interest in the ball. That interest does not establish a full right to possession that is protected from a subsequent legitimate claim.

On the other hand, while Mr. Hayashi appears on the surface to have done everything necessary to claim full possession of the ball, the ball itself is encumbered by the qualified pre-possessory interest of Mr. Popov. At the time Mr. Hayashi came into possession of the ball, it had, in effect, a cloud on its title.

An award of the ball to Mr. Popov would be unfair to Mr. Hayashi. It would be premised on the assumption that Mr. Popov would have caught the ball. That assumption is not supported by the facts. An award of the ball to Mr. Hayashi would unfairly penalize Mr. Popov. It would be based on the assumption that

Mr. Popov would have dropped the ball. That conclusion is also unsupported by the facts.

Both men have a superior claim to the ball as against all the world. Each man has a claim of equal dignity as to the other. We are, therefore, left with something of a dilemma.

Thankfully, there is a middle ground.

The concept of equitable division was fully explored in a law review article authored by Professor R.H. Helmholz in the December 1983 edition of the Fordham Law Review.[38] Professor Helmholz addressed the problems associated with rules governing finders of lost and mislaid property. For a variety of reasons not directly relevant to the issues raised in this case, Helmholz suggested employing the equitable remedy of division to resolve competing claims between finders of lost or mislaid property and the owners of land on which the property was found.

There is no reason, however, that the same remedy cannot be applied in a case such as this, where issues of property, tort and equity intersect.

The concept of equitable division has its roots in ancient Roman law. As Helmholz points out, it is useful in that it "provides an equitable way to resolve competing claims which are equally strong." Moreover, "[i]t comports with what one instinctively feels to be fair."[40]

Although there is no California case directly on point, Arnold v. Producers Fruit Company, 61 P. 283 (Cal. 1900), provides some insight. There, a number of different prune growers contracted with Producer's Fruit Company to dry and market their product. Producers did a bad job. They mixed fruit from many different growers together in a single bin and much of the fruit rotted because it was improperly treated.

When one of the plaintiffs offered proof that the fruit in general was rotten, Producers objected on the theory that the plaintiff could not prove that the prunes he contributed to the mix were the same prunes that rotted. The court concluded that it did not matter. After the mixing was done, each grower had an undivided interest in the whole, in proportion to the amount of fruit each had originally contributed.

The principle at work here is that where more than one party has a valid claim to a single piece of property, the court will recognize an undivided interest in the property in proportion to the strength of the claim.

Application of the principle of equitable division is illustrated in the case of Keron v. Cashman, 33 A. 1055 (N.J. Ch. 1896). In that case, five boys were walking home along a railroad track in the city of Elizabeth, New Jersey. The youngest of the boys came upon an old sock that was tied shut and contained something heavy. He picked it up and swung it. The oldest boy took it away from him and beat the others with it. The sock passes from boy to boy. Each controlled it for a short time. At some point in the course of play, the sock broke open and out spilled $775 as well as some rags, cloths and ribbons.

The court noted that possession requires both physical control and the intent to reduce the property to one's possession. Control and intent must be concurrent. None of the boys intended to take possession until it became apparent that the sock

---

38. Professor R.H. Helmholz, University of Chicago School of Law, *Equitable Division and the Law of Finders*, 52 Fordham L. Rev. 313 (1983). This article built on a student comment published in 1939. Comment, *Lost, Mislaid, and Abandoned Property*, 8 Fordham L. Rev. 222 (1939).

40. Helmholz, *supra* note 38, at 315.

contained money. Each boy had physical control of the sock at some point before that discovery was made.

Because none could present a superior claim of concurrent control and intent, the court held that each boy was entitled to an equal share of the money. Their legal claims to the property were of equal quality, therefore their entitlement to the property was also equal.

Here, the issue is not intent, or concurrence. Both men intended to possess the ball at the time they were in physical contact with it. The issue, instead, is the legal quality of the claim. With respect to that, neither can present a superior argument as against the other.

Mr. Hayashi's claim is compromised by Mr. Popov's pre-possessory interest. Mr. Popov cannot demonstrate full control. Albeit for different reasons, they stand before the court in exactly the same legal position as did the five boys. Their legal claims are of equal quality and they are equally entitled to the ball.

The court therefore declares that both plaintiff and defendant have an equal and undivided interest in the ball. Plaintiff's cause of action for conversion is sustained only as to his equal and undivided interest. In order to effectuate this ruling, the ball must be sold and the proceeds divided equally between the parties.

The parties are ordered to meet and confer forthwith before Judge Richard Kramer to come to an agreement as to how to implement this decision. If no decision is made by December 30, 2002, the parties are directed to appear before this court on that date at 9:00 A.M.

The court retains jurisdiction to issue orders consistent with this decision. The ball is to remain in the custody of the court until further order.

Notes and Questions

Popov and Hayashi declined to appeal Judge McCarthy's ruling. An auction held in New York City on June 25, 2003, televised live by ESPN, yielded a price of $450,000, far below the $3.2 million that the same collector paid in 1999 for the record seventieth home run ball hit by Mark McGwire. The story did not have a happy ending for everyone, though: Popov was sued by his attorney for $473,000 in legal fees.

C. BAILEES

Bailment is a common, everyday occurrence. A voluntary bailment is created whenever a person rents a car, checks luggage on an airline, takes clothes to the cleaners, borrows a book from a classmate, or leaves a pet with a friend during a trip. For many commercial transactions, the terms of the bailment are expressed in a writing, often in a standardized contract or in very small print on a receipt. Commercial bailments are typically characterized as bailments for the mutual benefit of the bailor and bailee, and are often called a bailment for hire. A bailee, like a finder, has a limited property right. In the following cases, notice the role played by the concept of possession.

■ BUENA VISTA LOAN & SAVINGS BANK v. BICKERSTAFF

Court of Appeals of Georgia, 1970
174 S.E.2d 219

This action is based on the alleged mysterious disappearance of $9,400 in cash from a safe deposit box which the plaintiff customer had rented from the defendant bank. The bank appeals from the denial of a summary judgment.

The evidence considered by the court on the motion for summary judgment consists of answers to interrogatories, depositions, and affidavits. Nothing in this evidence discloses any written agreement between the customer and the bank setting forth the terms and conditions under which the customer rented and used the safe deposit box.

The plaintiff's deposition shows that he rented the box about 1958 and received one key to the box. It was difficult to open the box with this key and he exchanged it at the bank for another key. He did not know what the bank did with the returned key. . . .

The plaintiff's deposition shows further that when he desired to gain access to the box he would give his key to a bank employee, who would use the key and a guard key retained by the bank to get the box and bring it to him. . . .

The president of the bank discloses in his deposition that there are two customer keys to each safe deposit box, and that both keys are given to the customer. He did not recall the exchange of keys as related by the plaintiff. If a customer lost a key in most instances the bank would simply replace the key by ordering another at the customer's expense. All employees except the janitor have access to the guard key. It is kept in a box together with the customer keys for unrented boxes. There are separate sections of boxes, and different guard keys are required. There are spare guard keys for each section stored in the same box with the customer keys. No record is made to identify which employee assists a customer. There is no system of dual control over the guard keys. . . . The president knew of the loss as reported by the customer, and knew of nothing to explain the loss. Questioning of employees had produced negative replies concerning the loss. All keys were tested and none of the keys kept in the vault would open the plaintiff's box. The depositions of two bank employees are in substantial accord with the testimony of the president as to the procedure followed.

The affidavit of an officer of a bank in an adjoining county in Georgia discloses that it is contrary to accepted practice in the banking industry to allow all employees to assist boxholders, to fail to maintain a rigorous indoctrination and training program for employees who assist boxholders, to fail to obtain a receipt for keys issued to a boxholder, or to allow the return of a customer key for indefinite retention and further availability. In his opinion the accepted practice if a boxholder loses a key is to have the lock changed, and to assign a new box to the renter as soon as possible, and the practice of merely having new keys cut and issued to the holder is disapproved. The guard key should not be left available to employees generally, but should be retained in the possession of a specially trained vault attendant, and under a system of dual control when locked in the vault so that the co-operation of two individuals is required to gain access to it. . . . If there is any doubt as to the proper method of handling a returned customer key it should be destroyed in the presence of witnesses. The affidavit of the president of another bank in Alabama is substantially to the same effect.

JORDAN, Presiding Judge. The plaintiff bases his claim primarily on the breach of a bailor-bailee relationship with the bank in respect to the alleged missing contents of the box, or, in the alternative, if the relationship is not that of a bailor-bailee, at least a duty on the part of the bank to exercise ordinary care to safeguard the contents of the box, contending that the evidence of negligence in this respect is sufficient to create a jury question.

The defendant relies on the decision in Tow v. Evans, 20 S.E.2d 922 (Ga. 1942), defining the relationship between the bank and a customer to whom it leases a safe deposit box in its vault as that of lessor and lessee giving the bank no dominion over certificates of stock placed therein by the lessee so as to enable a third party to reach such contents by statutory garnishment, and, viewing this relationship as merely one of landlord and tenant, contends that the bank incurs no liability by reason of the mysterious disappearance of the money. The bank argues further that even if the defendant was under a duty in some manner to protect the contents of the box, the evidence fails to disclose any breach that could be regarded as the proximate cause of the loss. . . .

We do not regard the mere labeling of the relationship in Tow v. Evans, *supra*, as that of lessor and lessee so as to prevent a third party from reaching the contents of a box by garnishment, as a holding which is dispositive of the relationship between the bank and a boxholder in respect to safeguarding the contents of the box and liability of the bank to the customer for a mysterious disappearance of the contents. . . .

. . . Had the customer merely delivered to the bank a locked container, which the bank undertook to safeguard for a fee, this court would have no difficulty in determining that a bailment existed, and that the bank was a depositary for hire. Had he delivered a sealed package of money, or property or securities, for the purpose of having the same safely kept, and the identical thing returned, it would be a special deposit, which is treated as a form of bailment.

The parties do not cite, and research fails to disclose any Georgia decision directly in point. The early case of Merchants' National Bank of Savannah v. Guilmartin, 15 S.E. 831 (Ga. 1892), recognizes a special deposit of securities for the accommodation of the customer, for which he received a receipt, as creating a gratuitous bailment, obligating the bank to exercise slight diligence, which could be met, in respect to a loss caused by the felonious appropriation by a cashier, "when it does its full duty in selecting a proper person, and in not disregarding indications of dishonesty which ought to arouse suspicion and investigation." When the same case was before the court again, 21 S.E. 55 at p.56, the court stated that nothing less than actual proof of the standard of diligence imposed on the bank would satisfy the requirement of the law. . . .

We view the relationship here created, as between the customer and the bank, as one of bailor and bailee, making the bank a depositary for hire under a duty to exercise ordinary care, the proof of which is cast upon the bank after proof of the fact of loss by the customer. This burden on the bailee is regarded as a presumption of negligence, *i.e.*, a rebuttable inference, thus placing on the bailee the affirmative duty of producing evidence of its diligence. Where some evidence of this nature is adduced in the trial of a case, whether the bailee has overcome the rebuttable inference would ordinarily be a matter for jury determination. . . . [T]he bank, as the movant for summary judgment, in order to prevail, has the greater burden of showing the absence of any genuine issue of fact as to a material matter and that as a matter of law it is entitled to judgment. . . . . What constitutes the exercise of ordinary care, or the lack of it, is ordinarily a jury question, and the evidence here, which discloses, among other things, practices which fall below acceptable standards in the industry, does not eliminate, as a permissible jury determination, that the failure to meet acceptable standards in the industry is a failure to exercise ordinary care which constitutes the proximate cause of the mysterious disappearance.

In view of the foregoing the trial court properly refused to grant a summary judgment for the bank.

Judgment affirmed.

Notes and Questions

1. In *Buena Vista*, what standard of care should apply to determine if the bank is liable for the loss of Bickerstaff's money? Consider a different type of transaction: If Maria borrows Bob's car to go shopping, what's the proper standard of care? The traditional rule places a bailment for the sole benefit of the bailee at the opposite end of the spectrum from a gratuitous bailment. Such a bailee is said to be under a duty to exercise extraordinary care, and thus liable even for slight negligence. Some courts reject the traditional three-tiered standard for a single more flexible one that tailors the duty of care to the circumstances. *E.g.*, Peet v. Roth Hotel Co., 253 N.W. 546 (Minn. 1934): "[T]he so-called distinctions between slight, ordinary, and gross negligence over which courts have perhaps quibbled for a hundred years, can furnish no assistance. . . . [O]rdinary care should be followed in every case without regard to former distinctions between slight, ordinary, and great care. . . . [The bailee's] liability, if any, is for negligence. In that field generally the legal norm is a care commensurate to the hazard, *i.e.*, the amount and kind of care that would be exercised by an ordinarily prudent person in the same or similar circumstances." The court found a bailment when the owner of a ring delivered it to a hotel cashier, to be picked up later by a jeweler for repair work, even though the cashier was unaware that the ring was very valuable. Bailment requires "mutual assent," but the mistake was not "of such character as to show no mutual assent and so no contract."

2. *Buena Vista* illustrates the role of presumptions in bailment cases. Bailors who return to find their bailed goods missing or damaged typically cannot determine what happened to them. Logically, bailees are in a better position than bailors to know or determine what happened to the bailed goods. It is in this context that presumptions operate. As in *Buena Vista*, courts generally rule that, once a bailor establishes that a bailment was created and that the bailee either failed to return the goods on proper demand or returned them in damaged condition, the burden of proof passes to the bailee to show that the goods were handled with due care. Negligence is presumed. If the bailee fails to rebut the presumption of negligence, the bailor can recover the full value of the bailed goods.

3. Is a bailment created when a car is parked in a commercial parking lot or garage? *See* Arguello v. Sunset Station, Inc., 252 P.3d 206 (Nev. 2011) (bailment created when car parked in valet parking lot; statute that relieves hotel of liability for theft or loss of property of patrons does not apply to motor vehicles); Waterton v. Linden Motor Inc., 810 N.Y.S.2d 319 (N.Y. City Civ. Ct. 2006) (no bailment when guest parks in below-ground hotel garage with no gate or other barrier controlling entry and retains keys); Allen v. Hyatt Regency-Nashville Hotel, 668 S.W.2d 286 (Tenn. 1984) (bailment created when driver who was not a hotel guest parked

car in an enclosed, indoor, commercial hotel garage that had an attendant controlling the exit and regular security personnel patrolling the premises).

Usually, the conclusion that no bailment was created means that the business is not liable for loss or damage to the owner's property. A few courts have skirted the bailment issue, permitting recovery on an implied contract theory. For example, in Parking Management, Inc. v. Gilder, 343 A.2d 51 (D.C. 1975), the customer parked in a garage space pointed out by an attendant. In front of a group of garage employees, the car owner put his girlfriend's cosmetic bag in the car's trunk. When he returned, he found his trunk lid damaged from being pried open. Although the trial court found a bailment existed, the appellate court refused to rule on the issue, recognizing that in prior cases it had held no bailment existed under similar circumstances. Nevertheless, the appellate court affirmed the trial court's judgment for plaintiff for damage to the car: "The car owner was entitled under the circumstances to expect that reasonable care would be utilized to prevent tampering with his auto. . . . [A]n operator [is] required to exercise reasonable care to avoid malicious mischief to, or theft of, vehicles parked in a commercial parking lot (a going concern), even though the arrangement was 'park and lock.'"

4. Many bailments for the mutual benefit of bailor and bailee are now covered by the UCC, rather than by common law principles. All states have adopted Article 2A, promulgated in 1987. The Article applies "to any transaction, regardless of form, that creates a lease." UCC §2A-102. The term *lease* is defined as "a transfer of the right of possession and use of goods for a term in return for consideration." UCC §2A-103(1)(j).

■ **SHAMROCK HILTON HOTEL v. CARANAS**
Court of Civil Appeals of Texas, 1972
488 S.W.2d 151

BARRON, Justice. This is an appeal in an alleged bailment case from a judgment non obstante veredicto in favor of plaintiffs below.

Plaintiffs, husband and wife, were lodging as paying guests at the Shamrock Hilton Hotel in Houston on the evening of September 4, 1966, when they took their dinner in the hotel restaurant. After completing the meal, Mr. and Mrs. Caranas, plaintiffs, departed the dining area leaving her purse behind. The purse was found by the hotel bus boy who, pursuant to the instructions of the hotel, dutifully delivered the forgotten item to the restaurant cashier, a Mrs. Luster. The testimony indicates that some short time thereafter the cashier gave the purse to a man other than Mr. Caranas who came to claim it. There is no testimony on the question of whether identification was sought by the cashier. The purse allegedly contained $5.00 in cash, some credit cards, and ten pieces of jewelry said to be worth $13,062. The misplacement of the purse was realized the following morning, at which time plaintiffs notified the hotel authorities of the loss.

Plaintiffs filed suit alleging negligent delivery of the purse to an unknown person and seeking a recovery for the value of the purse and its contents.

The trial was to a jury which found that the cashier was negligent in delivering the purse to someone other than plaintiffs, and that this negligence was a proximate cause of the loss of the purse. The jury further found that plaintiffs were negligent in leaving the purse containing the jewelry in the hotel dining room, and that this negligence was a proximate cause of the loss.

A motion for judgment n.o.v. and to disregard findings with respect to the findings that plaintiffs' negligence was a proximate cause of the loss of the purse and its contents was granted, and judgment was entered by the trial court for plaintiffs in the amount of $11,252.00 plus interest and costs. Shamrock Hilton Hotel and Hilton Hotels Corporation have perfected this appeal. . . .

Contrary to appellants' contention, we find that there was indeed a constructive bailment of the purse. The delivery and acceptance were evidenced in the acts of Mrs. Caranas' unintentionally leaving her purse behind in the hotel restaurant and the bus boy, a hotel employee, picking it up and taking it to the cashier who accepted the purse as a lost or misplaced item. The delivery need not be a knowingly intended act on the part of Mrs. Caranas if it is apparent that were she, the quasi or constructive bailor, aware of the circumstances (here the chattel's being misplaced) she would have desired the person finding the article to have kept it safely for its subsequent return to her. . . .

As stated above, the evidence conclusively showed facts from which there was

Shamrock Hilton

established a bailment with the Caranases as bailors and the hotel as bailee. The evidence also showed that the hotel, as bailee, had received Mrs. Caranas' purse and had not returned it on demand. Such evidence raised a presumption that the hotel had failed to exercise ordinary care in protecting the appellees' property. When the hotel failed to come forward with any evidence to the effect that it had exercised ordinary care, that the property had been stolen, or that the property had been lost, damaged or destroyed by fire or by an act of God, the appellees' proof ripened into proof by which the hotel's primary liability was established as a matter of law. Trammell v. Whitlock, 242 S.W.2d 157 (Tex. 1951). . . .

Further, this bailment was one for the mutual benefit of both parties. Appellees were paying guests in the hotel and in its dining room. Appellant hotel's practice of keeping patrons' lost personal items until they could be returned to their rightful owners, as reflected in the testimony, is certainly evidence of its being incidental to its business, as we would think it would be for almost any commercial enterprise which caters to the general public. Though no direct charge is made for this service there is indirect benefit to be had in the continued patronage of the hotel by customers who have lost chattels and who have been able to claim them from the management.

Having found this to have been a bailment for the mutual benefit of the parties, we hold that the appellants owed the appellees the duty of reasonable care in the return of the purse and jewelry, and the hotel is therefore liable for its ordinary negligence. Citizens' Nat. Bank v. Ratcliff & Lanier, 253 S.W. 253 (Tex. Comm'n App. 1923).

Appellants urge that if a bailment is found it existed only as to "the purse and the usual petty cash or credit cards found therein" and not to the jewelry of which the hotel had no actual notice. This exact question so far as we can determine has never been squarely put before the Texas Courts, but as appellants concede, the general rule in other jurisdictions is that a bailee is liable not only for lost property of which he has actual knowledge but also the property he could reasonably expect to find contained within the bailed property. . . .

We cannot say as a matter of law that there is no evidence upon which a jury could reasonably find that it was foreseeable that such jewelry might be found in a purse under such circumstances as here presented. It is known that people who are guests in hotels such as the Shamrock Hilton, a well-known Houston hotel, not infrequently bring such expensive jewelry with them, and it does not impress us as unreasonable under the circumstances that one person might have her jewelry in her purse either awaiting a present occasion to wear it or following reclaiming it from the hotel safe in anticipation of leaving the hotel. . . .

The judgment of the trial court is affirmed.

SAM D. JOHNSON (dissenting). If, as found by the majority, the evidence conclusively showed facts from which there was established a bailment, it is well to examine the relationship of the parties. Mrs. Caranas is characterized as a quasi or constructive bailor. The bailment is characterized as a mutual benefit and as a constructive bailment. If a bailment was created it was certainly unintentional. Mrs. Caranas had no intention of creating a bailment. The hotel had no such intention. Neither, in fact, for a considerable period of time knew of its existence.

This, for two reasons forming the basis of this dissent, is at least true of the jewelry allegedly contained in the purse. First, it seems to be conceded that the hotel had no actual notice of the existence of the jewelry in the purse and there is no authority in this state for the proposition that a bailee is liable for property he could reasonably expect to find contained in the bailed property. Secondly, even if the foregoing were true it does not occur to this writer that it is reasonable to expect a purse, inadvertently left under a chair in a hotel's restaurant and not even missed by the owner until the next day, might contain ten pieces of jewelry valued at $13,062. . . .

Notes and Questions

1. "The Shamrock Hotel, built in Houston between 1946 and 1949 by independent oilman Glenn H. McCarthy, was one of the most extravagantly mythologized symbols of Texas in the 1950s. . . . Edna Ferber transformed the Shamrock into the 'Conquistador' in her popular novel *Giant* (1952), and as such it was featured in the film *Giant* (1956), directed by George Stevens. . . . The pool measured 165 by 142 feet. It was repeatedly described as the largest outdoor pool in the world, so large that it could accommodate exhibition waterskiing. To celebrate the opening of the hotel, McCarthy brought in 175 film stars and executives from Los Angeles and journalists from across the country. The event, to which the public was invited, was so riotous that a live network radio broadcast by Dorothy Lamour had to be canceled. The notoriety of the Shamrock's opening reinforced the early 1950s image of Houston — and Texas — as a place that was larger than life, outrageously vulgar, yet oddly endearing. The conservative design of the hotel building and its opulent interiors elicited particularly caustic reactions, most famously from the

architect Frank Lloyd Wright, who toured the hotel shortly before its dedication. . . ."

". . . In 1985 the Shamrock property was sold by Hilton to the Texas Medical Center, [which] retained the garage building but in 1987 demolished the hotel, its lanai wing, and the swimming-pool gardens, replacing them with a surface parking lot. On St. Patrick's Day 1986, the fortieth anniversary of the ground-breaking, 3,000 people, including Glenn McCarthy, demonstrated at the hotel to protest its demolition. During its thirty-eight-year existence the Shamrock remained a powerful symbol of Houston. It passed from being a dubious emblem of Texan exaggeration to a place valued by Houstonians for its generous public spaces and its association with an expansive era in the city's history." Stephen Fox, *Handbook of Texas Online*, http://www.tsha.utexas.edu/handbook/online/articles/view/SS/ccs5.html.

2. Is bailment a creature of contract law or property law? Compare the following definitions:

(a) A bailment "involves a delivery of the thing bailed into the possession of the bailee, under a contract to return it to the owner according to the terms of the agreement." B.A. Ballou & Co. v. Citytrust, 591 A.2d 126 (Conn. 1991).

(b) "A bailment may be defined as the rightful possession of goods by one who is not the owner." Samuel Williston, *A Treatise on the Law of Contracts* §1030 (Walter Jaeger ed., 3d ed. 1967).

Does it matter whether a court follows a contract definition or a property definition of bailment? Did the *Shamrock Hilton* court pick either one?

3. Why did the majority in *Shamrock Hilton* reject the hotel's claim of *divisible bailment*—that the bailment covered the purse but not its contents? Consider Ampco Auto Parks, Inc. v. Williams, 517 S.W.2d 401 (Tex. Civ. App. 1974). Williams' car, stolen from a commercial parking lot, had in its trunk not only clothing but silver coins, pictures, "antique family heirlooms, jewelry, and a pre-Columbian bell (1000 B.C.)." Pleading negligence, Williams sought to recover the value of the trunk's contents. The court held for the parking operator, distinguishing *Shamrock Hilton* to find a divisible bailment. Williams "deliberately did not tell the AMPCO employees of the valuables contained in the trunk. . . . While it might be reasonably anticipated by an operator of a parking garage that the trunk of an automobile might contain the usual objects such as spare tires, jacks, etc., it is difficult to charge one with knowledge of such valuable and extraneous objects as were found in [Williams'] car."

4. A man who found a bag of valuable airplane tools in an airport parking lot transferred possession to his son. Several days later, the son gave the tools to a man who, claiming to be the true owner, described the contents of the bag. The son did not ask for any identification, and the transferee turned out to be an imposter, who was never apprehended. Two weeks later, the true owner reappeared and brought an action for conversion against father and son. Fisher v. Klingenberger, 576 N.Y.S.2d 476 (City Ct. 1991). The court considered the son's conduct to be negligent, but also observed: "[A]t common law . . . a finder was not liable, civilly or criminally, for keeping the property he had found against all false claims of ownership, or even against claims of ownership which the finder reasonably believed to be false. . . . Yet, at common law, if a possessor of goods, such as a finder, delivered

property to a third person whom he reasonably believed to be the true owner — but was mistaken as to that fact — he became liable to claims by the true owner, notwithstanding his delivery of the found property to a third person by honest mistake."

Could Mr. and Mrs. Caranas have brought their action on the theory of misdelivery? A Texas statute limits a hotel's liability for loss or damage to a guest's property to $50, unless the hotel is found negligent.

5. A New York case relieved an involuntary bailee from strict liability for misdelivery. In Cowen v. Pressprich, 192 N.Y.S. 242 (Sup. Ct. 1922), *rev'd*, 194 N.Y.S. 926 (App. Div. 1924), a securities broker, Cowen, mistakenly delivered a bearer bond to a customer who had asked for a different bond. The customer very quickly spotted the error, and opened a window to a small waiting room and called for Cowen's runner. A teenage boy, who turned out to be an imposter, accepted the bond. Cowen brought an action for conversion and did not plead negligence of the defendant. The Supreme Court, by 2 to 1, affirmed a judgment for the plaintiff: "A person who has been put, through no act or fault of his own, in such a situation as that in which the defendants were put upon the delivery to them of the wrong bond, has come to be known as 'involuntary bailee,' or bailee by casualty, or constructive or quasi bailee. . . . [T]he involuntary bailee, as long as his lack of volition continues, is not under the slightest duty to care for or guard the subject of the bailment, and cannot be held, in respect of custody, for what would even be the grossest negligence in the case of a voluntary bailment, but that, in case the involuntary bailee shall exercise any dominion over the thing so bailed, he becomes as responsible as if he were a voluntary bailee."

Judge Lehman, in a dissent adopted by the Appellate Division in a further appeal, stated: "[D]efendants were put in possession of the bond by mistake; they discovered the mistake promptly, and thereafter they committed no 'overt act' of interference with the bond except that they attempted to divest themselves of this possession by delivering the bond to a person whom they believed to be the messenger of the plaintiffs. . . . If in making an attempt to return the goods, which was lawful and proper in itself, the defendants used means which were not reasonable and proper, and as a result thereof the goods were lost or misdelivered, then the defendants would be liable for negligence or possibly for conversion, for every man is responsible for his own acts; but, if the defendants had a right to divest themselves of possession and attempt to return the goods, then, in the absence of some obligation resting upon contract to deliver the goods only to the true owner or upon his order, I do not see how the mere fact that through innocent mistake the defendants handed the bond to the wrong messenger could constitute a conversion."

The court in *Fisher* did not cite *Cowen*. Would holding Klingenberger liable for misdelivery, in the absence of negligence, be consistent with Judge Lehman's analysis?

6. Many states make it a crime for a finder to fail to take reasonable steps to return lost property to the owner. The Georgia statute is typical. "A person commits the offense of theft of lost or mislaid property when he comes into control of property that he knows or learns to have been lost or mislaid and appropriates the property to his own use without first taking reasonable measures to restore the property to the owner." Ga. Code §16-8-6.

D. BONA FIDE PURCHASERS

When property is transferred, the new owner typically receives the bundle of rights previously held by the transferor—no more, and no less. A person cannot convey better title than she has, courts often say. This basic tenet of property law is reflected by the Latin maxim, *nemo dat quod non habet* ("no one gives what he does not have"). This makes a good deal of intuitive sense: If you don't own it, you can't sell it. Thus a thief, who lacks title, is not able to pass title to a buyer, even if the buyer pays full value, acts in good faith, and has no reason to know of the seller's criminal conduct. The reason for this general rule is to protect the true owner by preserving her property rights, as against all subsequent transferees.

The doctrine of bona fide purchase is a limited exception to the *nemo dat* principle. Under certain circumstances, a person who qualifies as a bona fide purchaser (widely abbreviated as a "BFP") gets a better title than her seller had. BFPs get the title they bargained for, thereby promoting confidence in the market in which they purchased.

The BFP doctrine is aimed at the problem of ostensible ownership, in which a person (typically through some fault of the true owner) appears to own property that is actually owned by someone else. In connection with chattels, usually the ostensible owner has possession, and that possession enables the ostensible owner to mislead third parties as to title. Perhaps the ostensible ownership dimension of possession is part of the reason for the old saying that possession is nine-tenths of the law.

Although rooted in English common law and equity, the BFP doctrine is not a costless solution to the problem of ostensible ownership. There is, of course, a downside to protecting BFPs. In the prototype, there are three characters: the true owner, the holder who acquired the true owner's property, and the BFP who bought from the holder. Two persons are innocent (or relatively innocent) and one is entirely culpable. It is not possible completely to protect both the true owner and the BFP—there is only one piece of property at issue, and each claims to own all of it. Thus, when we choose to protect a BFP, the true owner is stripped of title and is relegated to a cause of action against the holder for the value of the property. When we protect the true owner and deny the BFP, the BFP will have a cause of action against the holder. Therefore, the dilemma is essentially to decide which of the two innocent parties should own the thing, and which should have the cause of action against the holder. While this might look good on paper, we should not feel comfortable believing that everyone is made whole. Even if money is as good as the property in question, the action against the holder is often worthless because after the deception is completed the holder may be hard to find and may lack discoverable assets with which to pay a judgment.

Example 1. Adam steals a television from a department store and sells it to Debby, a dealer in new and used televisions. Debby adds the stolen television to her inventory and sells it for $800 to Wiu, who has no reason to know he is buying stolen goods. The department store has the right to recover the television from Wiu.

Example 2. Isabel accidentally loses her purse containing considerable cash. Don finds the purse and uses the cash to buy a laptop computer at an electronics store. The sales clerk at the electronics store has no reason to know that the cash does not belong to Don. The electronics store has the right to keep the cash.

Example 3. Juan loans a bicycle to Zoey for use in Zoey's downtown document delivery service and allows Zoey to put a sign, "Zoey Delivers," on the side of the bike. Without Juan's knowledge or permission, Zoey then sells the bike to Bill, who reasonably believes that Zoey owns it. Bill can rightfully retain the bike.

Example 4. Isabel gives her diamond bracelet to Doug, a dealer in new and used jewelry, to sell on consignment, with Isabel to receive the sale price less Doug's 15 percent sales commission. Isabel and Doug orally agree that Doug will not sell the bracelet for less than $1,200. Without mentioning the minimum price, Doug sells the bracelet to Naomi for $900. Doug, who is insolvent, does not forward any money to Isabel, who claims she still owns the bracelet because the sale was unauthorized. Naomi successfully defends this claim because she qualifies as a BFP.

Although the BFP doctrine can apply in various settings, including in some cases of lost property and bailment, it usually arises in situations involving a fraudulent sale or consignment, where the true owner either intends to pass title to the holder (who acts in bad faith, such as by not paying in full or using a bad check) or entrusts the holder to sell the property on the owner's behalf. Where the transaction involves a purported sale or consignment to the holder, the doctrine of bona fide purchase is presently set forth in UCC §2-403, which is in force in all states. That section, which you should study carefully, provides as follows:

§2-403. Power to Transfer; Good Faith Purchase of Goods; "Entrusting"

(1) A purchaser of goods acquires all title which his transferor had or had power to transfer except that a purchaser of a limited interest acquires rights only to the extent of the interest purchased. A person with voidable title has power to transfer a good title to a good faith purchaser for value. When goods have been delivered under a transaction of purchase the purchaser has such power even though

a. the transferor was deceived as to the identity of the purchaser, or
b. the delivery was in exchange for a check which is later dishonored, or
c. it was agreed that the transaction was to be a "cash sale," or
d. the delivery was procured through fraud punishable as larcenous under the criminal law.

(2) Any entrusting of possession of goods to a merchant who deals in goods of that kind gives him power to transfer all rights of the entruster to a buyer in the ordinary course of business.

(3) "Entrusting" includes any delivery and any acquiescence in retention of possession regardless of any condition expressed between the parties to the delivery or acquiescence and regardless of whether the procurement of the entrusting or the possessor's disposition of the goods have been such as to be larcenous under the criminal law.

The following two decisions deal with two common BFP situations, fraudulent sales and consignments, both of which are now governed by the UCC. The first involves a holder who concealed his true identity, used a forged check, and obtained delivery of a car through punishable fraud. The second involves a transfer of a painting to a dishonest art dealer.

Trover: Finding

■ **CHARLES EVANS BMW, INC. v. WILLIAMS**
Court of Appeals of Georgia, 1990
395 S.E.2d 650

CARLEY, Chief Judge. The relevant facts in this trover action are as follows: Williams agreed to sell his car to an individual named Hodge and he accepted a cashier's check from Hodge as payment. With no indication on the certificate of title that Hodge was the purchaser, Williams signed the title in his capacity as seller and then delivered that document and the car to Hodge. The next day, Hodge, representing himself to be Williams, offered to sell the automobile to Charles Evans BMW, Inc. ("Evans BMW"). When a price was agreed upon, Hodge presented to Evans BMW the certificate of title bearing Williams' signature as seller and Evans BMW gave Hodge a check which named Williams as the payee. The check was cashed at a local bank when Hodge produced as identification a Kentucky driver's license bearing the same number of the Kentucky driver's license that had been issued to Williams. After the car had been purchased by Evans BMW from Hodge, Williams was notified that the cashier's check he had accepted from Hodge was a forgery. By the time that Evans BMW was made aware of the fact that it had not actually purchased the car from Williams but from Hodge representing himself to be Williams, it had already resold the car. At the direction of the local police authorities, however, the car and the certificate of title were returned to Evans BMW and the purchase price was refunded by Evans BMW. Thereafter, Evans BMW was further required to return the car to Williams. However, Evans BMW retained the certificate of title and initiated this trover action against Williams.

On these facts, cross-motions for summary judgment were filed. The trial court denied Evans BMW's motion for summary judgment and granted summary judgment in favor of Williams. It is from that order that Evans BMW brings this appeal.

1. . . . Williams was not deprived of his car by a physical taking of which he was unaware. The undisputed evidence of record shows that Williams *delivered his car under a transaction of purchase* procured by the perpetration of a criminal fraud whereby he was deceived as to the identity of the purchaser who gave him a check which was later dishonored. In these circumstances, Williams conveyed *voidable title* to Hodge and Hodge, having voidable rather than void title, had the power to transfer *good title* to a good faith purchaser for value. OCGA §11-2-403(1)

> empowers a purchaser with a voidable title to confer good title upon a good faith purchaser for value where the goods were procured through fraud punishable as larcenous under the criminal law. The distinction between *theft* and *fraud* in this context is found in the statutory definitions of "delivery" and "purchase." Delivery concerns a voluntary transfer of possession, [OCGA §11-1-201(14)], and purchase refers to a voluntary transaction creating an interest in property. [OCGA §11-1-201(32)]. In the present case, [Williams] voluntarily relinquished possession to [Hodge]. As one commentator has pointed out, "[a] thief who wrongfully takes goods is not a purchaser . . . but a swindler who fraudulently induces the victim to voluntarily deliver them is a purchaser. . . ." 2 W. Hawkland, Uniform Commercial Code Series, §2-4-303, pp. 606-07 (1982).

Jernigan v. Ham, 691 S.W.2d 553, 556 (Tenn. App. 1984) (emphasis in original).

2. It follows that, if Evans BMW was a good faith purchaser for value, it acquired good title to the car from Hodge.

"'Good faith' means honesty in fact in the conduct or transaction concerned." OCGA §11-1-201(19). "'Good faith' in the case of a merchant means honesty in fact and the observance of reasonable commercial standards of fair dealing in the trade." OCGA §11-2-103(1)(b). There is ample evidence of Evans BMW's "good faith" in its transaction with Hodge. Evans BMW's agent who actually negotiated the purchase neither knew nor had reason to know that Hodge's representations were false. When Evans BMW's agent noticed an error on the registration form, Hodge was told that he would have to obtain a corrected registration form from the county. When Hodge left and returned with the corrected form, this gave additional credence to his representations that he was Williams and the owner of the car. Hodge also presented a certificate of title which bore Williams' unforged signature as seller. The price that Evans BMW agreed to pay for the car was not nominal. Evans BMW gave Hodge a check made out to Williams and Hodge was successful in cashing that check by using a driver's license bearing the same number of the license that had actually been issued to Williams. Thus, Hodge's scheme to impersonate Williams not only duped Evans BMW, but was also successful against the county and the bank.

In opposition, there was no evidence to show that, in negotiating and consummating the purchase from Hodge, Evans BMW had been less than honest or had failed to observe reasonable commercial standards of fair dealing. Therefore, on the undisputed evidence of record, Evans BMW was, as a matter of law, a good faith purchaser for value when it bought the car from Hodge.

3. Williams urges that, even if Evans BMW was a good faith purchaser for value when it originally bought the car from Hodge, Evans BMW does not now occupy that status. The contention is that Evans BMW now claims title to the car, not from Hodge, but from the individual to whom Evans BMW eventually sold it. Since Evans BMW had actual knowledge of Hodge's fraud at the time that it returned the purchase price and accepted the car back from its purchaser, Williams urges that Evans BMW cannot now be considered to be a good faith purchaser for value.

The transaction whereby Evans BMW returned the purchase price and accepted the car back from its purchaser was not a repurchase of the car by Evans BMW. *See* OCGA §11-2-401(4). It was a rescission of appellant's sale of the car. Thus, even though appellant knew of Hodge's fraud at the time of rescission, it does not now occupy the status of a "bad faith" repurchaser from its purchaser. It reoccupies its original status as a "good faith" purchaser from Hodge.

4. Under the undisputed evidence of record, Evans BMW acquired good title to the car when it purchased it from Hodge and it retains that good title as against Williams who conveyed voidable title to Hodge. It follows that the trial court erred in granting Williams' motion for summary judgment and in denying summary judgment in favor of Evans BMW.

Judgment reversed.

Notes and Questions

1. Would Evans BMW still have won if it had not obtained the certificate of title endorsed by Williams? BFP disputes involving cars have an additional dimension. All states have some type of certificate of title act designed to establish ownership of motor vehicles. It is seldom clear how the certificate of title acts relate to the BFP rules of UCC §2-403. The Georgia certificate of title act is based on the Uniform Motor Vehicle Certificate of Title and Anti-Theft Act, which 10 states have enacted. Study the following provisions:

Code of Georgia §40-3-32. Transfer of vehicle generally

(a) If an owner transfers his interest in a vehicle other than by the creation of a security interest, he shall, at the time of delivery of the vehicle, execute an assignment and warranty of title to the transferee in the space provided therefor on the certificate of title or as the commissioner prescribes and cause the certificate and assignment to be delivered to the transferee. . . .

(b) Except as provided in Code Section 40-3-33 [special rules for vehicles held by dealers], the transferee, promptly after delivery to him of the vehicle and certificate of title, shall execute the application for a new certificate of title on the form the commissioner prescribes and cause the application and the certificate of title to be mailed or delivered to the commissioner or his appropriate authorized county tag agent together with the application for change of registration for the vehicle, so that the title application shall be received within 90 days from the date of the transfer of the vehicle. . . .

(d) Except as provided in Code Section 40-3-33 and as between the parties, a transfer by an owner is not effective until this Code section and Code Section 40-3-33 have been complied with; and no purchaser or transferee shall acquire any right, title, or interest in and to a vehicle purchased by him unless and until he shall obtain from the transferor the certificate of title thereto, duly transferred in accordance with this Code section.

2. Returning to the question asked above, assume you are representing Williams and he still has the certificate of title. What argument do you make based on the Georgia certificate of title act? How strong is your argument? What should happen if neither Williams nor Evans BMW presently has a certificate of title, and the old certificate endorsed by Williams is presently in the hands of the state commissioner, awaiting processing for the issuance of a new certificate to the new owner?

Courts have not arrived at a consensus with respect to how certificated motor vehicles should be treated under UCC §2-403. For example, in both NXCESS Motor Cars, Inc. v. JPMorgan Chase Bank, 317 S.W.3d 462 (Tex. Ct. App. 2010), and Toyota Motor Credit Corp. v. C.L. Hyman Auto Wholesale, Inc., 506 S.E.2d 14 (Va. 1998), a car owner fraudulently obtained a duplicate certificate of title that eliminated a reference to the financing bank's lien and then sold the car to an unsuspecting buyer. In the former case, the bank prevailed under §2-403 because the court held the seller had void title. In the latter case, the buyer prevailed under the certificate of title act, with the court concluding the seller had good title under §2-403.

3. The time it takes for a new car owner to obtain a new certificate of title varies widely. Depending upon the government office and its current backlog, the wait can range from several days up to four or five months. The owner generally cannot sell her car or use it as collateral for a loan until she gets the title. However, long processing times increase the risk of BFP claims; sometimes the owner can persuade a buyer or lender to go forward with a transaction prior to receipt of the title, especially if she displays a copy of her application for a certificate of title.

Electronic titles for cars, or e-titles, are beginning to replace traditional paper titles. As of 2012, 18 states use a system called Electronic Lien and Title (ELT), pioneered by California in 1989. So far e-titles supplement, but do not completely replace hard copy titles. An owner with an e-title can request a hard copy title, and in most states a hard copy title is still required for some transactions (for example, a sale to a buyer who isn't a car dealer). The trend is for states to mandate the use of

ELT titles by commercial lenders. By eliminating paper titles, the change is touted as having the advantages of saving time and expense and reducing the risk of fraudulent titles and fraudulent lien releases.

4. Land transactions also raise BFP problems. Like certificated motor vehicles, the law attempts to solve the problems of ostensible ownership by resort to a paper record, rather than by primary reliance on the assertions of a person who is in possession. For land, instead of a certificate of title, recording statutes provide for deeds and other instruments affecting title to be recorded in a county office, where they are available for inspection by would-be purchasers and other interested persons. We will study the recording statutes and the title search process later in Chapter 10. Because the issues concerning the bona fide purchase of chattels and the bona fide purchase of land have a number of similarities, it will pay dividends later on if you work hard to understand the materials in this section of this chapter.

■ **LINDHOLM v. BRANT**
Supreme Court of Connecticut, 2007
925 A.2d 1048

SULLIVAN, Justice. The plaintiff, Kerstin Lindholm, appeals from the judgment of the trial court in favor of the named defendant, Peter M. Brant, on the plaintiff's claim of conversion of a painting by Andy Warhol entitled "Red Elvis" (Red Elvis). The plaintiff claims on appeal that the trial court improperly determined that the defendant was a buyer in the ordinary course of business and, therefore, lawfully took all of the plaintiff's rights in Red Elvis pursuant to General Statutes §42a-2-403(2). We disagree and affirm the judgment of the trial court.

. . . The plaintiff was introduced to Anders Malmberg, a Swedish art dealer, in the late 1970's or early 1980's during the course of her marriage to Magnus Lindholm (Lindholm). Throughout the next thirty years, Malmberg served as an art advisor to both the plaintiff and Lindholm. In his capacity as an art dealer, Malmberg assisted the plaintiff in her purchase of two works of art, and assisted Lindholm in multiple purchases and sales of works of art. Malmberg handled all of the Lindholms' purchase and sale transactions for works of art.

In 1987, the plaintiff purchased Red Elvis from Malmberg for $300,000. . . .

In 1989, the plaintiff, with the assistance of Malmberg, loaned Red Elvis to the Museum of Modern Art in New York to be included in a Warhol exhibition. A label affixed to the painting indicated that it was owned by a "Private Collector" and had been loaned to the Museum of Modern Art "Courtesy Anders Malmberg." The defendant visited the exhibition, viewed Red Elvis and saw its label, thereby becoming aware that Malmberg was associated with Red Elvis and its owner.[4]

In 1996, the Guggenheim Museum (Guggenheim) decided to sponsor an exhibition of Warhol paintings that would travel to several European venues, ending in New York City during the summer of 2000. Vivien Greene, an assistant curator at the Guggenheim, prepared a list of Warhol works of art to be considered for inclusion in the exhibition. Red Elvis was one of the works of art on the list. . . .

Through the efforts of [Stellan Holm, a Swedish art dealer], who had contacted Malmberg, the plaintiff agreed to lend Red Elvis to the exhibition. . . . The

---

4. The defendant had purchased Red Elvis in or around 1969, when he was a young college student, and had owned the painting for a brief period of time.

defendant assisted the Guggenheim with the shipping arrangements for Red Elvis, which was sent from the United States to Europe in September, 1998. Accordingly, as of September, 1998, the defendant knew from Holm that the plaintiff owned Red Elvis and that it was on loan to the Guggenheim for a Warhol exhibition.

In 1998, Lindholm initiated divorce proceedings against the plaintiff in Connecticut. Because of a shortage of funds, the plaintiff enlisted Malmberg to assist her in selling certain works of art located in the Lindholms' residence in Greenwich. On November 16, 1999, the plaintiff and Malmberg entered into an agreement that designated Malmberg as the plaintiff's agent for the purpose of selling "'certain works.'" Although the agreement did not specify which artworks Malmberg was authorized to sell, the plaintiff had neither agreed to sell nor discussed with Malmberg or anyone else the possibility of selling Red Elvis. . . .

During this same time period, Holm, who had been working closely with the defendant in the purchase and sale of other Warhol works of art, advised the defendant, on the basis of a conversation with Malmberg, that Malmberg had purchased Red Elvis. Holm also asked whether the defendant would be interested in purchasing the painting if it became available for sale. Soon afterward, the defendant met with Holm and Malmberg at the defendant's residence. When Malmberg and Holm repeated that Malmberg had purchased Red Elvis from the plaintiff and asked whether the defendant would be interested in purchasing it, the defendant indicated that he would.

On or about February 2, 2000, the defendant agreed to pay Malmberg $2.9 million for Red Elvis. Malmberg gave the defendant an invoice for the $2.9 million sale, indicating that a $900,000 deposit would be required immediately and that the balance would be due by a certain date. Although the defendant wired the deposit money to Malmberg, he objected to paying the balance prior to delivery of the painting without first entering into a formal contract with Malmberg. The defendant retained counsel to draft a contract and to conduct the necessary lien searches to identify any claims that Lindholm, who was in the midst of a bitter divorce and was reputed to be litigious, might have to the painting. During the contract negotiations, the law firm that the defendant had retained conducted a lien search and an Art Loss Register[6] search relating to Red Elvis. Neither search revealed a claim or lien by Lindholm or any other individual. The defendant's counsel cautioned the defendant, however, that these searches only provided "minimal assurances" that Malmberg had good title to the painting.

The defendant and Malmberg exchanged numerous drafts of the contract during the negotiations, which were completed on March 20, 2000. Ultimately, Malmberg agreed to delay payment of the balance until the delivery of Red Elvis to a bonded warehouse in Denmark. . . .

The defendant also was concerned that, even though Holm had assured him that Malmberg was the current owner, Malmberg had not yet acquired title to the painting or that this transaction was going to be a "flip."[7] The defendant's counsel, in an effort to clarify whether Malmberg owned the painting, requested a copy of the invoice from the plaintiff to Malmberg. Malmberg denied this request on the

---

6. The Art Loss Register is a permanent international database of stolen and missing works of art recognized as the best mechanism for determining whether a piece of art is stolen.

7. "Flipping" is a term of art in the art industry that refers to a situation in which the purchaser of a painting immediately sells the painting for a higher price. The second purchase is often conditioned on the new owner's concealing the sale from the original owner. To prevent flipping, owners often will ask purchasers to agree not to resell the painting for a period of one year.

ground that such invoices are not normally and customarily disclosed in the context of an art transaction.

On February 17, 2000, during the contract negotiations between the defendant and Malmberg, the Guggenheim notified the plaintiff, as a lender to the Warhol exhibition, that the exhibition would be terminating prematurely. At that point, the plaintiff agreed, at the suggestion of Greene, to lend Red Elvis to the branch of the Guggenheim located in Bilbao, Spain. After Malmberg advised the plaintiff that Red Elvis would get better exposure at an exhibition at the Louisiana Museum in Copenhagen, Denmark, the plaintiff agreed to lend the painting to the Louisiana Museum. The plaintiff did not inform Greene that she had changed her mind about displaying the painting in Bilbao until Greene called her on March 17, 2000.

Also on March 17, 2000, the defendant spoke with Elissa Myerowitz, a registrar employed by the Guggenheim, to inquire when his Warhol works of art would be returned to him. The defendant also asked about the current status of Red Elvis. Myerowitz indicated that the painting was being returned to the plaintiff, who was listed as the lender on the loan forms. The defendant advised Myerowitz that the plaintiff no longer owned Red Elvis and that she should contact the new owner, Malmberg, because it was his understanding that Malmberg wanted Red Elvis to go to Denmark. The defendant believed that Red Elvis was going to be shipped to Denmark because, at that time in the negotiations, he had agreed to accept delivery there. Myerowitz then told Greene about her conversation with the defendant, after which Greene called the plaintiff. During this conversation, the plaintiff informed Greene that she had changed her mind and had decided to lend the painting to the Louisiana Museum. The plaintiff also informed Greene that Red Elvis should be released to Malmberg's custody because he was going to arrange for the shipment of the painting to Denmark. Greene advised the plaintiff that she would have to provide the Guggenheim with a letter authorizing the Guggenheim to release Red Elvis to Malmberg, which the plaintiff did on March 20, 2000. Greene then informed Myerowitz of the substance of Greene's conversation with the plaintiff, confirming that Red Elvis was to be released to Malmberg for shipment to the museum in Denmark. On March 21, 2000, the defendant called Myerowitz to inform her about the shipping arrangements to Denmark.

On April 12, 2000, after execution of the purchase contract, the defendant wired the remaining $2 million purchase price to Malmberg's bank account and took possession of Red Elvis. On April 27, 2000, the defendant had the painting insured and arranged to have it shipped from Denmark to the United States. The defendant then allowed Red Elvis to be shown in a traveling exhibition from May, 2000, through the end of 2002, doing nothing to conceal the fact that he believed that he owned the painting.

From March, 2000, until the fall of 2000, the plaintiff took no steps to verify that Red Elvis was on display at the Louisiana Museum but, instead, relied on Malmberg's representations that the painting was there. In the fall of 2000, Malmberg informed the plaintiff that Red Elvis had not arrived at the Louisiana Museum in time to be a part of the exhibition. . . .

In June, 2001, . . . the plaintiff read a magazine article that reported that the defendant had purchased Red Elvis from Malmberg. When the plaintiff telephoned Malmberg, he told her that the article was inaccurate and that the defendant actually had bought a different painting, which was referred to as Green Elvis.

On November 5, 2002, the plaintiff filed an amended complaint alleging, inter alia, conversion, conspiracy to commit fraud, statutory theft, and unjust enrichment against the defendant.[8] With respect to all counts, the defendant asserted the special defense that he was a buyer in the ordinary course of business pursuant to §42a-2-403(2), under which he took all of the plaintiff's rights to Red Elvis.

There is no dispute in the present case that the plaintiff's March 20, 2000 letter authorizing the Guggenheim to release Red Elvis to Malmberg constituted an entrustment under §42a-2-403(3), or that Malmberg, an art dealer, is a merchant dealing in "goods of that kind" — works of art — under §42a-2-403(2). Under the plain language of §42a-2-403(2) and (3), therefore, Malmberg, as a merchant dealing in art entrusted with the painting, had the power to transfer all the rights of the entruster to a buyer in the ordinary course of business.

A "'buyer in ordinary course of business'" is defined as "a person that buys goods in good faith, without knowledge that the sale violates the rights of another person in the goods, and in the ordinary course from a person . . . in the business of selling goods of that kind. A person buys goods in the ordinary course if the sale to the person comports with the usual or customary practices in the kind of business in which the seller is engaged or with the seller's own usual or customary practices. . . ." General Statutes §42a-1-201(9). . . .

We are required, therefore, to determine whether the defendant followed the usual or customary practices and observed reasonable commercial standards of fair dealing in the art industry in his dealings with Malmberg. [T]he defendant presented expert testimony that the vast majority of art transactions, in which the buyer has no reason for concern about the seller's ability to convey good title, are "completed on a handshake and an exchange of an invoice." It is not customary for sophisticated buyers and sellers to obtain a signed invoice from the original seller to the dealer prior to a transaction, nor is it an ordinary or customary practice to request the underlying invoice or corroborating information as to a dealer's authority to convey title. . . .

We are compelled to conclude, however, that the sale from Malmberg to the defendant was unlike the vast majority of art transactions. The defendant had good reason to be concerned that Lindholm might have claims to the painting. . . .

. . . [A] merchant buyer has a heightened duty of inquiry when a reasonable merchant would have doubts or questions regarding the seller's authority to sell. We further conclude that the steps that a merchant must take to conform to reasonable commercial standards before consummating a deal depend on all of the facts and circumstances surrounding the sale. In the present case, the defendant had concerns about Malmberg's ability to convey good title to Red Elvis because he believed that Lindholm might have had a claim to the painting. The defendant also was concerned that Malmberg had not yet acquired title to the painting or that the transaction might be a "flip."

Because of his concern that Lindholm might make a claim to Red Elvis, the defendant took the extraordinary step of hiring counsel to conduct an investigation and to negotiate a formal contract of sale on his behalf. He also insisted on and obtained a formal contract containing representations and warranties that Malmberg had title to the painting. In addition, during the course of the investigation, the defendant's counsel conducted both a lien search and an Art Loss Register

---

8. In January, 2003, the plaintiff filed a complaint in Sweden seeking to have Malmberg criminally prosecuted. In March, 2003, the Swedish court convicted Malmberg of gross fraud embezzlement and rendered judgment in favor of the plaintiff in the amount of $4.6 million. . . .

search that revealed no competing claims to Red Elvis. Although the defendant was cautioned that the searches provided only minimal assurance that Malmberg had good title to the painting, such searches typically are not conducted during the course of a normal art transaction and, therefore, provided the defendant with at least some assurance that Lindholm had no claims to the painting.

Moreover, the evidence was sufficient for the trial court reasonably to conclude that at all times during the transaction, both Malmberg and Holm had reputations as honest, reliable, and trustworthy art dealers. . . . The defendant had little reason to doubt Malmberg's claim that he was the owner of Red Elvis, and any doubts that he did have reasonably were allayed by relying on Holm's assurances that Malmberg had bought the painting from the plaintiff because she needed money due to her divorce. The defendant established at trial that it is customary to rely on the assurances of respected art dealers when conducting a transaction, and the defendant had no reason to depart from this practice. . . .

We recognize that the customary practice in the art industry of not requiring a merchant buyer to obtain documentary proof that the seller owns the work of art whenever there are reasonable doubts or questions regarding the seller's authority to sell imposes risks on persons who entrust art to an art dealer. Section 42a1-201(9) evinces a legislative desire, however, for courts to respect "the usual or customary practices in the kind of business in which the seller is engaged. . . ." We are not entitled to impose the type of business practices that we would prefer.

Moreover, the evidence presented at trial established that the reason that documentary proof of ownership customarily is not required is to protect the confidentiality of the owner and the buyer. Requiring a merchant buyer to obtain an invoice or other supporting documentation proving the seller's ownership would in every transaction destroy the privacy and confidentiality that buyers and sellers have come to desire and expect. . . .

[W]e conclude that the defendant was not required to contact directly the plaintiff or other parties who might have had knowledge concerning Red Elvis' title. . . .

The judgment is affirmed.

Notes and Questions

1. As between Kerstin Lindholm and Peter Brant, who was in a better position to avoid the loss occasioned by Malmberg's misconduct? The *Lindholm* court describes the practices generally followed in sale transactions for expensive artwork, and then observes, "We are not entitled to impose the type of business practices that we would prefer." Do you think those practices are reasonable? Did the UCC compel the court to defer to those practices?

2. The provenance of a painting is evidence of the history of its ownership and, for rare or valuable items whose ownership may be in dispute, can be important in establishing the validity of a sale. An active black market exists in looted and stolen art and artifacts. Dealers in rare books, valuable antiques, historical artifacts, or fine art are potentially liable for conducting or facilitating the purchase or sale of an item without having first investigated the provenance of the item and establishing, within reasonable commercial standards, that the transaction is duly authorized and lawful.

E. GIFTS

Gifts of property are familiar to everyone. Although laypersons usually don't consider the legal principles involved as they go about making and receiving gifts, there is an established body of law. All gifts are either testamentary (by will) or inter vivos (made by the donor during her lifetime). For an inter vivos gift of personal property, the law requires delivery of the subject matter to the donee. Ordinarily, delivery must be a physical transfer of possession. In the previous sections of this chapter, we've examined the legal concept of possession in the contexts of finders, bailees, and bona fide purchasers. Possession, thus, is a common link. As you study the following gift cases, consider the role played by possession, and how it compares to the role it plays in the other areas. What similarities and differences do you perceive?

■ **SIMPSON v. SIMPSON**
  District Court of Appeal of Florida, 1998
  723 So. 2d 326

GRIFFIN, Chief Judge. Appellant seeks review of an order of the probate court determining certain real and personal property to be exempt from the claims of creditors.

The decedent, Donald M. Simpson, died testate on March 29, 1997, leaving an estate valued at $172,854.04, including homestead property valued at $145,000. The entire estate was bequeathed to the decedent's only child, Terry A. Simpson, who was also appointed personal representative of the estate.

The appellant is Eleanor S. Simpson, the decedent's ex-wife (and Terry Simpson's mother). The nature of her claims against the estate are not significant for purposes of the appeal. . . .

In dispute below was the question whether the decedent's guns had been the subject of a gift to Terry, and, thus, were not part of the personal property of the estate. At the hearing, Terry testified:

> And the third area is that my dad had basically — he had some hunting weapons, some shotguns and rifles that he had — he no longer hunted, and the previous August when he and I were out on a fishing trip, he said: Well, I'd like to just give these to you. And so, he had given them to me, but I had not picked them up, had not made arrangements to transport them from his house, and I did not do that until after his death.

We conclude that this testimony is insufficient to establish the gift. This statement was allegedly made by the decedent to his son while the two of them were on a fishing trip in Montana approximately seven months before the decedent's death. The guns were located at the decedent's home in Orlando where they apparently remained from the time of decedent's return to his home after the Montana trip until he was hospitalized in March 1997. The decedent died on March 29, 1997. Apparently no action was taken concerning the guns prior to that time either by the elder or younger Simpson.

Appellee acknowledges that to establish an *inter vivos* gift, intent and delivery are necessary. Although there is equivocal evidence of intent, there is no evidence of delivery. Appellant urges that the guns "could have been" the subject of a "constructive" delivery but there is no evidence of constructive delivery. Accordingly, it was error to exclude the guns from the estate. . . .

Affirmed in part; Reversed in part.

DAUKSCH, Judge, dissenting. I respectfully dissent.

To me, the evidence of a gift of the guns was sufficient. No one disputes that the father gave the guns to his son; it is in the nature of human affairs that fathers hand their guns down to their sons. It is not in the nature of things that a mother would deny or interfere with this gesture between a father and son. The trial judge, like all fathers, knows this. It is not necessary that a donee of a gift move the gift from its storage place. *See* Barber v. Barber, 175 So. 713, 715 (Fla. 1937); In re Tardibone's Estate, 94 N.Y.S.2d 724, 726-27 (Sur. Ct. 1949); 38A C.J.S. Gifts §77 (1994).

■ GRUEN v. GRUEN

Court of Appeals of New York, 1986
496 N.E.2d 869

SIMONS, Judge. Plaintiff commenced this action seeking a declaration that he is the rightful owner of a painting which he alleges his father, now deceased, gave to him. He concedes that he has never had possession of the painting but asserts that his father made a valid gift of the title in 1963 reserving a life estate for himself. His father retained possession of the painting until he died in 1980. Defendant [Kemija Gruen], plaintiff's stepmother, has the painting now and has refused plaintiff's requests that she turn it over to him. She contends that the purported gift was testamentary in nature and invalid insofar as the formalities of a will were not met or, alternatively, that a donor may not make a valid inter vivos gift of a chattel and retain a life estate with a complete right of possession. Following a seven-day nonjury trial, Special Term found that plaintiff had failed to establish any of the elements of an inter vivos gift and that in any event an attempt by a donor to retain a present possessory life estate in a chattel invalidated a purported gift of it. The Appellate Division held that a valid gift may be made reserving a life estate and, finding the elements of a gift established in this case, it reversed and remitted the matter for a determination of value. That determination has now been made and defendant appeals directly to this court, pursuant to CPLR 5601(d), from the subsequent final judgment entered in Supreme Court awarding plaintiff $2,500,000 in damages representing the value of the painting, plus interest. We now affirm.

The subject of the dispute is a work entitled "Schloss Kammer am Attersee II" painted by a noted Austrian modernist, Gustav Klimt. It was purchased by plaintiff's father, Victor Gruen, in 1959 for $8,000. On April 1, 1963 the elder Gruen, a successful architect with offices and residences in both New York City and Los Angeles during most of the time involved in this action, wrote a letter to plaintiff, then an undergraduate student at Harvard, stating that he was giving him the Klimt painting for his birthday but that he wished to retain the possession of it for his lifetime. This letter is not in evidence, apparently because plaintiff destroyed it on instructions from his father. Two other letters were received, however, one dated May 22, 1963 and the other April 1, 1963. Both had been dictated by Victor Gruen and sent together to plaintiff on or about May 22, 1963. The letter dated May 22, 1963 reads as follows:

Dear Michael:

I wrote you at the time of your birthday about the gift of the painting by Klimt. Now my lawyer tells me that because of the existing tax laws, it was wrong to mention in that letter that I want to use the painting as long as I live. Though I still want to use it, this should not appear in the letter. I am enclosing, therefore, a new letter and I ask you to send the old one back to me so that it can be destroyed.

I know this is all very silly, but the lawyer and our accountant insist that they must have in their possession copies of a letter which will serve the purpose of making it possible for you, once I die, to get this picture without having to pay inheritance taxes on it.

Love,
s/Victor

Enclosed with this letter was a substitute gift letter, dated April 1, 1963, which stated:

Dear Michael:

The 21st birthday, being an important event in life, should be celebrated accordingly. I therefore wish to give you as a present the oil painting by Gustav Klimt of Schloss Kammer which now hangs in the New York living room. You know that Lazette and I bought it some 5 or 6 years ago, and you always told us how much you liked it.

Love,
s/Victor

Schloss Kammer am Attersee II

Plaintiff never took possession of the painting nor did he seek to do so. Except for a brief period between 1964 and 1965 when it was on loan to art exhibits and when restoration work was performed on it, the painting remained in his father's possession, moving with him from New York City to Beverly Hills and finally to Vienna, Austria, where Victor Gruen died on February 14, 1980. Following Victor's death plaintiff requested possession of the Klimt painting and when defendant refused, he commenced this action.

The issues framed for appeal are whether a valid inter vivos gift of a chattel may be made where the donor has reserved a life estate in the chattel and the donee never has had physical possession of it before the donor's death and, if it may, which factual findings on the elements of a valid inter vivos gift more nearly comport with the weight of the evidence in this case, those of Special Term or those of the Appellate Division. Resolution of the latter issue requires application of two general rules. First, to make a valid inter vivos gift there must exist the intent on the part of the donor to make a present transfer; delivery of the gift, either actual or constructive to the donee; and acceptance by the donee. Matter of Szabo, 176 N.E.2d 593, 595 (N.Y. 1961); Matter of Kelly, 33 N.E.2d 62, 67 (N.Y. 1941) (dissenting in part opn); Beaver v. Beaver, 22 N.E. 940, 941 (N.Y. 1889). Second, the proponent of a gift has the burden of proving each of these elements by clear and convincing evidence. Matter of Kelly, *supra* at 67-68.

DONATIVE INTENT

There is an important distinction between the intent with which an inter vivos gift is made and the intent to make a gift by will. An inter vivos gift requires that the donor intend to make an irrevocable present transfer of ownership; if the intention is to make a testamentary disposition effective only after death, the gift is invalid unless made by will. *See* McCarthy v. Pieret, 24 N.E.2d 102, 103 (N.Y. 1939); Gannon v. McGuire, 55 N.E. 7, 8 (N.Y. 1899).

Defendant contends that the trial court was correct in finding that Victor did not intend to transfer any present interest in the painting to plaintiff in 1963 but only expressed an intention that plaintiff was to get the painting upon his death. The evidence is all but conclusive, however, that Victor intended to transfer ownership of the painting to plaintiff in 1963 but to retain a life estate in it and that he did, therefore, effectively transfer a remainder interest in the painting to plaintiff at that time. Although the original letter was not in evidence, testimony of its contents was received along with the substitute gift letter and its covering letter dated May 22, 1963. The three letters should be considered together as a single instrument, *see* Matter of Brandreth, 62 N.E. 563, 564 (N.Y. 1902), and when they are they unambiguously establish that Victor Gruen intended to make a present gift of title to the painting at that time. But there was other evidence for after 1963 Victor made several statements orally and in writing indicating that he had previously given plaintiff the painting and that plaintiff owned it. Victor Gruen retained possession of the property, insured it, allowed others to exhibit it and made necessary repairs to it but those acts are not inconsistent with his retention of a life estate. Furthermore, whatever probative value could be attached to his statement that he had bequeathed the painting to his heirs, made 16 years later when he prepared an export license application so that he could take the painting out of Austria, is negated by the overwhelming evidence that he intended a present transfer of title in 1963. Victor's failure to file a gift tax return on the transaction was partially explained by allegedly erroneous legal advice he received, and while that omission sometimes may indicate that the donor had no intention of making a present gift, it does not necessarily do so and it is not dispositive in this case.

Defendant contends that even if a present gift was intended, Victor's reservation of a lifetime interest in the painting defeated it. She relies on a statement from Young v. Young, 80 N.Y. 422 (1880), that "'[a]ny gift of chattels which expressly reserves the use of the property to the donor for a certain period, or . . . as long as the donor shall live, is ineffectual.'" *Id.* at 436, quoting 2 Schouler, *Personal Property*, at 118. The statement was dictum, however, and the holding of the court was limited to a determination that an attempted gift of bonds in which the donor reserved the interest for life failed because there had been no delivery of the gift, either actual or constructive. *See id.* at 434. . . .

Defendant recognizes that a valid *inter vivos* gift of a remainder interest can be made not only of real property but also of such intangibles as stocks and bonds. Indeed, several of the cases she cites so hold. That being so, it is difficult to perceive any legal basis for the distinction she urges which would permit gifts of remainder interests in those properties but not of remainder interests in chattels such as the Klimt painting here. The only reason suggested is that the gift of a chattel must include a present right to possession. . . . Insofar as some of our cases purport to require that the donor intend to transfer both title and possession immediately to have a valid *inter vivos* gift, *see* Gannon v. McGuire, *supra* at 8; Young v. Young, *supra* at 430, they state the rule too broadly and confuse the effectiveness of a gift with the transfer of the possession of the subject of that gift. The correct test is "'whether the maker intended the [gift] to have *no effect* until after the maker's death, or whether he intended it to transfer *some present interest*.'" McCarthy v. Pieret, *supra* (emphasis added). As long as the evidence establishes an intent to make a present and irrevocable transfer of title or the right of ownership, there is a present transfer of some interest and the gift is effective immediately. . . .

Defendant suggests that allowing a donor to make a present gift of a remainder with the reservation of a life estate will lead courts to effectuate otherwise invalid testamentary dispositions of property. The two have entirely different characteristics, however, which make them distinguishable. Once the gift is made it is irrevocable and the donor is limited to the rights of a life tenant not an owner. Moreover, with the gift of a remainder title vests immediately in the donee and any possession is postponed until the donor's death whereas under a will neither title nor possession vests immediately. Finally, the postponement of enjoyment of the gift is produced by the express terms of the gift not by the nature of the instrument as it is with a will. *See* Robb v. Washington & Jefferson Coll., 78 N.E. 359, 361 (N.Y. 1906).

Delivery

In order to have a valid inter vivos gift, there must be a delivery of the gift, either by a physical delivery of the subject of the gift or a constructive or symbolic delivery such as by an instrument of gift, sufficient to divest the donor of dominion and control over the property. . . .

Defendant contends that when a tangible piece of personal property such as a painting is the subject of a gift, physical delivery of the painting itself is the best form of delivery and should be required. Here, of course, we have only delivery of Victor Gruen's letters which serve as instruments of gift. Defendant's statement of the rule as applied may be generally true, but it ignores the fact that what Victor Gruen gave plaintiff was not all rights to the Klimt painting, but only title to it with no right of possession until his death. Under these circumstances, it would be illogical for the law to require the donor to part with possession of the painting when that is exactly what he intends to retain.

Nor is there any reason to require a donor making a gift of a remainder interest in a chattel to physically deliver the chattel into the donee's hands only to have the donee redeliver it to the donor. As the facts of this case demonstrate, such a requirement could impose practical burdens on the parties to the gift while serving the delivery requirement poorly. Thus, in order to accomplish this type of delivery the parties would have been required to travel to New York for the symbolic transfer and redelivery of the Klimt painting which was hanging on the wall of Victor Gruen's Manhattan apartment. Defendant suggests that such a requirement would be stronger evidence of a completed gift, but in the absence of witnesses to the event or any written confirmation of the gift it would provide less protection against fraudulent claims than have the written instruments of gift delivered in this case.

ACCEPTANCE

Acceptance by the donee is essential to the validity of an inter vivos gift, but when a gift is of value to the donee, as it is here, the law will presume an acceptance on his part. Beaver v. Beaver, *supra* at 941. Plaintiff did not rely on this presumption alone but also presented clear and convincing proof of his acceptance of a remainder interest in the Klimt painting by evidence that he had made several contemporaneous statements acknowledging the gift to his friends and associates, even showing some of them his father's gift letter, and that he had retained both letters for over 17 years to verify the gift after his father died. . . .

Judgment appealed from and order of the Appellate Division brought up for review affirmed, with costs.

Notes and Questions

1. "A landscape by Gustav Klimt, the Viennese master, sold on October 9 for 14.5 million pounds at Christie's. Schloss Kammer am Attersee II had been expected to bring only about 6 million pounds, but an anonymous private collector bidding on the telephone was determined to fight off competition from a buyer in the room. Christie's described it as the most expensive work sold in London since 1988, a record price for Klimt and the most expensive work sold anywhere this year." Dalya Alberge, *Klimt Landscape Painting Sells for Record Price*, London Times, Oct. 10, 1997.

2. This case is your first introduction to the concept of the life estate, which divides ownership of property over time, between a present possessor (Victor, the life tenant) and the owner of a future interest (here a remainder owned by Michael). In Chapters 6 and 7, we will study life estates and remainders in detail. For now, it's important to understand that a future interest is conceptualized as presently owned, even though the owner's right to possession is deferred until the death of the life tenant. Thus, there is sharp distinction between a gift of a remainder, to take effect at the owner's death, and a promise to make a gift in the future, at the owner's death. The former is effective, the latter invalid.

3. Professor Philip Mechem identified three reasons why the law should insist upon delivery:

> In the first place, the delivery makes vivid and concrete to the donor the significance of the act he is doing. Anyone can realize the psychological difference between a man's saying he gives something, yet retaining it, and saying he gives it and seeing it pass irrevocably out of his control. The wrench of delivery, if the expression be understood and permissible, the little mental twinge at seeing his property pass from his hands into those of another, is an important element to the protection of the donor. If he is uncertain, if he hardly understands himself just what he means or (which is perhaps even more important) what he is understood to mean, he cannot fail to understand (and be understood) when he hands over the property. It gives him a *locus penitentiae*. It forces upon the most thoughtless and hasty at least a moment's acute consideration of the effects of what he is proposing to do. Where valuable property is being passed without consideration, perhaps in the agony of a dying moment, it does not seem unwise to insist upon this simple and automatic safeguard.
>
> Secondly, the act of manual tradition is as unequivocal to actual witnesses of the transaction as to the donor himself. Here normality is a big factor. What did the donor say? What did he mean? Perhaps he spoke under his breath, or was unable to speak clearly. Perhaps he hesitated and contradicted himself so that the outcome of his thought was not readily to be ascertained by witnesses in the flurry of the moment. If he hands

over the property, he has done an act that will settle many doubts, an act perhaps capable of more than one interpretation, yet readily and naturally susceptible of but one.

Thirdly, and lastly, the fact of delivery gives the donee, subsequently to the act, at least prima facie evidence in favor of the alleged gift. The law does not presume unlawful acts. Possession is ordinarily rightful. The evidence is of course at best presumptive, yet better than none. If the donee comes out of the sick room and says the bonds have been given to him he will be more credited, and more reasonably, if he has them in his possession. It is easier to fabricate a story than to abstract the property.

Philip Mechem, *The Requirement of Delivery in Gifts of Chattels and of Choses in Action Evidenced by Commercial Instruments*, 21 Ill. L. Rev. 341, 346-47 (1926). Has Victor Gruen felt the "wrench of delivery"? In *Simpson*, did Donald Simpson feel the "wrench of delivery"? Should this matter? Professor Mechem's second and third considerations bear upon evidence of donative intent. In your opinion, is there satisfactory evidence of Victor's intent? Of Donald's intent?

4. Suppose Victor didn't intend to give Michael a remainder interest in the Klimt painting, but he wanted to give him complete ownership in 1963. Could he accomplish this objective by means of a letter or another writing sent to Michael at Harvard?

5. Suppose Victor wanted to give Michael complete ownership at a time when both were present at the family home in New York City. Could they accomplish this objective without moving the painting out of Victor's home?

■   **IN RE ESTATE OF SMITH**
Superior Court of Pennsylvania, 1997
694 A.2d 1099

DEL SOLE, Judge. This is an appeal and cross-appeal from the decree of the Court of Common Pleas of Lehigh County, Orphans' Division, denying Appellant Jean Smith's and Cross-Appellant Willard Kressley's exceptions and entering a final decree in favor of Appellees. We affirm in part and reverse in part.

On May 7, 1994, Appellant's husband, Alfred E. Smith (Decedent), committed suicide in the basement of the couple's home. Prior to his suicide, Decedent took the following steps in an effort to attend to several of his personal affairs. On May 5, 1994, Decedent drafted four checks in various amounts to four individuals: Joy Youpa (Decedent's girlfriend), Carol Sandt (Ms. Youpa's sister), Barbara Kressley (Decedent's sister), and Diana Kressley (Decedent's niece). On May 6, 1994 Decedent prepared and executed a holographic will. The will contained the following contested provision: "I want Willard Kressley to have the option of buying my '66 Corvette from Jean [Appellant] for $12,000." Also on May 6, 1994, Decedent mailed the checks to his sister and niece accompanied with a suicide note.[1] On May 7, 1994,

---

1. The note stated:

I know this is a hell of a mess and I am truly sorry for the embarrassment, but I can't go on. I know there will be legal questions about the will, but they are my intentions. I know the estate taxes for the state could have been avoided, but I don't have time. *I'm sorry. I'm sorry. I'm sorry.*
   Good-bye
   Alfred
Barbara,
The checks are [to] use at your discretion.
   Alfred

before committing suicide, Decedent delivered the checks to his girlfriend and her sister by leaving the checks under a pizza box on their kitchen table. The two mailed checks and the note were received on May 9, 1994, two days after the suicide. Each of the recipients knew of Decedent's death at the time she cashed her check.

After Appellant, as administratrix of Decedent's estate, discovered that Decedent had written the four checks, she requested that the funds be returned by the recipients to the estate. The four recipients refused and Appellant commenced a civil action alleging conversion and seeking restitution. The civil action was transferred to Orphans' Court for disposition in connection with pending matters.

The court entered a decree holding that the four checks to the donees were valid gifts causa mortis and that Mr. Kressley was not entitled to the Corvette. Appellant and Cross-Appellant filed exceptions to the decree nisi which were denied. These appeals followed.

The issue presented by Appellant for our review is whether Decedent's death revoked gifts of checks which Decedent had written, but which were not negotiated until after his death. The lower court held that the gifts were not revoked because they were valid gifts causa mortis.

To establish a gift causa mortis, it must be shown that at the time of the alleged gift, the decedent intended to make a gift, the decedent apprehended death, the res of the intended gift was either actually or constructively delivered, and death actually occurred. In re Ream's Estate, 198 A.2d 556, 557 (Pa. 1964). It is not necessary that the donor expressly say he knows or believes he is dying, that may be inferred from the attendant circumstances. It will suffice if at the time the gift was made, the donor believed he was going to die, that he was likely to die soon; and death did actually ensue within a reasonable time thereafter. Titusville Trust Co. v. Johnson, 100 A.2d 93, 97 (Pa. 1953).

The facts of the instant case support a finding of a gift causa mortis. On May 5, 1994, Decedent wrote and executed the four checks to four separate individuals in various specific amounts. On May 6, 1994, Decedent mailed two of the checks, accompanied by a note of suicide. On May 7, 1994, Decedent physically delivered the other two checks, and then, sadly, took his own life. All of the requisite elements of a gift causa mortis have been established. Therefore, the lower court was correct in refusing to revoke the checks.[2] Next, Cross-Appellant Willard Kressley questions whether the lower court properly concluded that the portion of Decedent's holographic will granting Cross-Appellant the option to purchase Decedent's '66 Corvette at a reduced price was merely a request and not a mandatory obligation of Decedent's estate.

The lower court held that the language used in the holographic will regarding the disposition of the '66 Corvette rose only to a request and did not constitute a mandatory obligation upon the Estate Administratrix to give the property to Cross-Appellant.

However, our courts have held that the option to buy is a direct gift of the property itself, and such specific legatee must be made whole before the residue

---

2. We believe that by considering gifts made in contemplation of suicide to be gifts causa mortis, we further the public policy against suicide since the donor may retrieve the gifts if the suicide is not completed. As our courts have held, a gift causa mortis differs from other gifts only in that it is made when the donor believes he is about to die, and is revocable should he survive. Titusville Trust Co. v. Johnson, at 96. See In re Brown's Estate, 413 A.2d 1083 (Pa. 1980).

and remainder will be divided. *See* In re France's Estate, 43 A.2d 139 (Pa. 1945) (an option to buy corporate stock, given to testator's son by will, constituted a direct gift of the stock to the son, requiring that he be made whole before division of residue and remainder of testator's estate).

By using the particular language and placing the provision where he did, Decedent intended that Cross-Appellant's option be interpreted as a direct gift of the '66 Corvette before the residue and remainder of the estate was divided. The court lacked competent and adequate evidence to find otherwise. Therefore, we reverse the portion of the decree denying Cross-Appellant's exceptions regarding the disposition of Decedent's '66 Corvette.

Decree reversed in part and affirmed in part. Jurisdiction relinquished.

CIRILLO, President Judge Emeritus, concurring and dissenting. I agree that Mr. Kressley is entitled to receive the 1966 Corvette as a direct gift under the decedent's will. I vehemently disagree, however, with the majority's incomplete analysis and inaccurate conclusion that the decedent made valid *gifts causa mortis* of the four checks. . . .

A recitation of the details behind the death of the decedent is needed for a complete understanding of the lack of the proper donative intent for valid *gifts causa mortis*. On May 7, 1994, appellant's husband, Mr. Alfred E. Smith, committed suicide in the basement of their Allentown home. Decedent's expired body was found lying on a 3 × 6 foot piece of carpet, his head resting on a throw pillow.

Prior to his death, decedent wrote four checks to four different individuals in varying amounts. He left two of the checks on a kitchen table, under a pizza box, in the home of one of the donees. The remaining checks were mailed to the donees by the decedent. All four checks were dated May 5, 1994; two of the donees received their checks on May 7th, the remaining on May 10th. On May 9th, two donees cashed their checks, another donee cashed hers on May 10th and the last cashed her check on May 11th. Each recipient, at the time she cashed her check, knew that Mr. Smith had passed away. . . .

It is well established that a *gift causa mortis* is premised upon the fact that the donor/decedent *must* be making the gift while in his last illness or in "periculo mortis."[3] Michener v. Dale, 23 Pa. 59 (1854). Our supreme court has held that a conditional gift made by a soldier going off to war is not a valid *gift causa mortis*; such a donor is not "under apprehension of death." Linsenbigler v. Gourley, 56 Pa. 166 (1867). A gift while a donor is in full health has also been declared void for purposes of establishing a gift of bonds as *donatio causa mortis*. Stockham's Estate, 6 Dist. 196 (1897). It should be noted, however, that in order for a donor to be "in apprehension of death," one's illness need not be so extreme as in the case of proving an oral will made by a testator in his last sickness, before witnesses, and then later reduced to writing. *See* Stackhouse's Estate, 23 D. & C. 322 (1935) (even though decedent was optimistic concerning her recovery from illness at the time she gave a car as a gift to a donee, decedent did "act in apprehension of death" and gift was valid *donatio causa mortis* when donor died two days later); *see also* Lawrence v. Hartford Nat. Bank and Trust Co., 193 A.2d 506 (Conn. Super. 1963) (gift need not be made while decedent confined to bed; valid *gift causa mortis* made when 72-year-old woman, suffering a

---

3. This term is Latin for "in danger of death."

serious hip fracture, died after having surgery; surgery was made necessary by a present disease).

Because the intention to commit suicide may be readily abandoned at one's own will, courts from other jurisdictions have taken the position that the contemplated or intended suicide of a donor is not a "peril, ailment or disease" which can serve as the foundation of a *gift causa mortis*. 60 A.L.R.2d §2 at 577; *see also* Ray v. Leader Federal Savings & Loan Assoc., 292 S.W.2d 458, 467 (Tenn. App. 1953) ("[s]ickness, peril and danger, as used in definitions of donations *causa mortis* we believe to mean something other than a determination of an individual who is presumed to be well, physically and mentally, to take his life.").[4] *See also* 38 Am. Jur. 2d Gifts §10 (1968); Black's Law Dictionary 1286 (5th ed. 1979) (suicide is "[s]elf-destruction; the deliberate termination of one's existence."). Courts, therefore, have found that gifts made in contemplation of suicide are against public policy and should not be enforced. *See, e.g., Ray, supra.* . . .

Pennsylvania's policy of protecting human life is further evidenced by the criminalization of assisted suicide in our Criminal Code. *See* 18 Pa. C.S.A. §2505 (causing or aiding suicide). Unlike the majority, I find that it would be prudent to adopt the reasoning of other jurisdictions that render alleged *gifts causa mortis* void when they are made in contemplation of suicide. I find further support for adopting this view in light of the strict proof requirement promulgated by our highest state court in order to establish a valid *gift causa mortis*, as well as the disfavored disposition of property outside of a will. Such suicide gifts are not intended to be in apprehension of an impending illness; rather, they are completely voluntary, controlled by the will of the donor, and easily subject to change by the decision to not take one's own life.

In line with my conclusion, I cannot agree with the majority's convoluted reasoning, contained in a mere footnote, which states that: "We believe that by considering gifts made in contemplation of suicide to be *gifts causa mortis*, we further the public policy against suicide since the donor may retrieve the gifts if the suicide is not completed." By upholding and validating gifts made in contemplation of suicide, the majority rewards the donor and his or her donees for the intended and successful completion of a self-destructive act. Furthermore, in response to the majority's above-quoted language, I find that it is just as reasonable to conclude that a donor's intent to commit suicide while in the process of disposing of his or her property is as strong as, if not stronger than, his or her intent to retrieve and repossess the gifts upon a change in one's will to commit the act. The majority's holding cuts against the notion that courts prefer the reliable disposition of property through a will or by the well-expressed intentions in a living person's *inter vivos* transfer.

I, therefore, respectfully dissent.

---

4. I recognize that there are jurisdictions that would find that contemplation of suicide is sufficient for purposes of proving an element of a *gift causa mortis*. *See* Scherer v. Hyland, 380 A.2d 698 (N.J. 1977); *see also* Berl v. Rosenberg, 336 P.2d 975 (Cal. App. 1959) (public policy against suicide will not invalidate an otherwise valid *gift causa mortis*); In re Van Wormer's Estate, 238 N.W. 210 (Mich. 1931) (melancholia ending in suicide sufficient to sustain a *gift causa mortis*). These courts have focused on the fact that according to modern human psychological principles, the utter despair attendant upon one contemplating suicide may reasonably be viewed as even more imminent than a person struggling with a fatal physical illness. Such reasoning is attenuated, at best, in light of this Commonwealth's consistent views disfavoring suicide.

Notes an

1. According to a 1996 newspape
$26,000. The Corvette was worth $3?
went to his widow, Jean.

2. Why didn't Alfred Smith ma
donees? Does it matter under the fa

3. As dissenting judge Cirillo i
contemplating death by suicide r
tended to side with *Estate of Smit*
suicide context. Is the extension

4. Is it significant that Alfred
giving them cash? A number of c
until the bank pays the intendec
check is cashed, the money stays
690 (Va. 1994) (delivery of chec?
ability to stop payment means donc
might this rule promote? Is it sound.

■ LINDH v. SURMAN

Supreme Court of Pennsylvania, 1999
742 A.2d 643

NEWMAN, Justice. In this appeal, we are asked to decide whether a donee of an engagement ring must return the ring or its equivalent value when the donor breaks the engagement.

The facts of this case depict a tumultuous engagement between Rodger Lindh (Rodger), a divorced, middle-aged man, and Janis Surman (Janis), the object of Rodger's inconstant affections. In August of 1993, Rodger proposed marriage to Janis. To that purpose, he presented her with a diamond engagement ring that he purchased for $17,400. Rodger testified that the price was less than the ring's market value because he was a "good customer" of the jeweler's, having previously purchased a $4,000 ring for his ex-wife and other expensive jewelry for his children. Janis, who had never been married, accepted his marriage proposal and the ring. Discord developed in the relationship between Rodger and Janis, and in October of 1993 Rodger broke the engagement and asked for the return of the ring. At that time, Janis obliged and gave Rodger the ring. Rodger and Janis attempted to reconcile. They succeeded, and Rodger again proposed marriage, and offered the ring to Janis. For a second time, Janis accepted. In March of 1994, however, Rodger called off the engagement. He asked for the return of the ring, which Janis refused, and this litigation ensued.

Rodger filed a two-count complaint against Janis, seeking recovery of the ring or a judgment for its equivalent value. The case proceeded to arbitration, where a panel of arbitrators awarded judgment for Janis. Rodger appealed to the Court of Common Pleas of Allegheny County, where a brief non-jury trial resulted in a judgment in favor of Rodger in the amount of $21,200.[1] Janis appealed to the Superior Court, which affirmed the trial court in a 2-1 panel decision. Judge Ford Elliott,

---

1. The basis for the $21,200 award of the trial court was Rodger's testimony that this was the fair market value of the ring.

...eld that no-fault principles should control, and that the
...gardless of who broke the engagement, and irrespective of
...nalysis with the only principle on which all parties agree: that
...reats the giving of an engagement ring as a conditional gift. . . .
...rgues that the condition of the gift is acceptance of the proposal of
...n that acceptance of the proposal vests absolute title in the donee. This
...ntrary to Pennsylvania's view of the engagement ring situation. In Ruehl-
...nung, 98 Pa. Super. 535 (1930), the Superior Court provided what is still
...st thorough Pennsylvania appellate court analysis of the problem:

> It does not appear whether the engagement was broken by plaintiff or whether it was dissolved by mutual consent. It follows that in order to permit a recovery by plaintiff, it would be necessary to hold that the gifts were subject to the implied condition that they would be returned by the donee to the donor whenever the engagement was dissolved. Under such a rule *the marriage would be a necessary prerequisite* to the passing of an absolute title to a Christmas gift made in such circumstances. We are unwilling to go that far, *except as to the engagement ring.*

Id. at 540 (emphasis added). . . .

Janis' argument that Pennsylvania law does not permit the donor to recover the ring where the donor terminates the engagement has some basis in the few Pennsylvania authorities that have addressed the matter. . . .

This Court, however, has not decided the question of whether the donor is entitled to return of the ring where the donor admittedly ended the engagement. In the context of our conditional gift approach to engagement rings, the issue we must resolve is whether we will follow the fault-based theory, argued by Janis, or the no-fault rule advocated by Rodger. Under a fault-based analysis, return of the ring depends on an assessment of who broke the engagement, which necessarily entails a determination of why that person broke the engagement. A no-fault approach, however, involves no investigation into the motives or reasons for the cessation of the engagement and requires the return of the engagement ring simply upon the nonoccurrence of the marriage.

The rule concerning the return of a ring founded on fault principles has superficial appeal because, in the most outrageous instances of unfair behavior, it appeals to our sense of equity. Where one fiancee has truly "wronged" the other, depending on whether that person was the donor of the ring or the donee, justice appears to dictate that the wronged individual should be allowed to keep, or have the ring returned. However, the process of determining who is "wrong" and who is "right," when most modern relationships are complex circumstances, makes the fault-based approach less desirable. A thorough fault-based inquiry would not only end with the question of who terminated the engagement, but would also examine that person's reasons. In some instances the person who terminated the engagement may have been entirely justified in his or her actions. This kind of inquiry would invite the parties to stage the most bitter and unpleasant accusations against those whom they nearly made their spouse, and a court would have no clear guidance with regard to how to ascertain who was "at fault." . . .

A ring-return rule based on fault principles will inevitably invite acrimony and encourage parties to portray their ex-fiancees in the worst possible light, hoping to drag out the most favorable arguments to justify, or to attack, the termination of an engagement. Furthermore, it is unlikely that trial courts would be presented with situations where fault was clear and easily ascertained and, as noted earlier, determining what constitutes fault would result in a rule that would defy universal application. . . .

Having adopted this no-fault principle, we still must address the original argument that the donor should not get return of the ring when the donor terminates the engagement. Such a rule would be consonant with a no-fault approach, it is argued, because it need not look at the reasons for termination of the engagement; if there is proof that the donor ended the relationship, then he has frustrated the occurrence of the condition and cannot benefit from that. In other words, we are asked to adopt a no-fault approach that would always deny the donor return of the ring where the donor breaks the engagement.

We decline to adopt this modified no-fault position,[3] and hold that the donor is entitled to return of the ring even if the donor broke the engagement. We believe that the benefits from the certainty of our rule outweigh its negatives, and that a strict no-fault approach is less flawed than a fault-based theory or modified no-fault position.

We affirm the Order of the Superior Court.

CAPPY, Justice, dissenting, joined by Justices CASTILLE and SAYLOR. The majority advocates that a strict no-fault policy be applied to broken engagements. In endorsing this view, the majority argues that it is not only the modern trend but also the approach which will eliminate the inherent weaknesses of a fault-based analysis. According to the majority, by adopting a strict no-fault approach, we will remove from the courtroom the necessity of delving into the interpersonal dynamics of broken engagements in order to decide which party retains possession of the engagement ring. This view brings to mind the words of Thomas Campbell from *The Jilted Nymph:* "Better be courted and jilted than never be courted at all." . . .

The majority urges adoption of its position to relieve trial courts from having the onerous task of sifting through the debris of the broken engagement in order to ascertain who is truly at fault and if there lies a valid justification excusing fault. Could not this theory justifying the majority's decision be advanced in all other arenas that our trial courts must venture? Are broken engagements truly more disturbing than cases where we ask judges and juries to discern possible abuses in nursing homes, day care centers, dependency proceedings involving abused children, and criminal cases involving horrific, irrational injuries to innocent victims? The subject matter our able trial courts address on a daily basis is certainly of equal sordidness as any fact pattern they may need to address in a simple case of who broke the engagement and why. . . .

CASTILLE, Justice, dissenting, joined by Justices CAPPY and SAYLOR. . . . *The Restatement of Restitution,* §58 comment c, discusses the return of engagement rings and states that:

> Gifts made in the hope that a marriage or contract of marriage will result are not recoverable, in the absence of fraud. Gifts made in anticipation of marriage are not

---

3. The modified no-fault position is no more satisfactory than a strict no-fault system because it, too, would create an injustice whenever the donor who called off the wedding had compelling reasons to do so.

ordinarily expressed to be conditional and, although there is an engagement to marry, if the marriage fails to occur without the fault of the donee, normally the gift cannot be recovered. If, however, the donee obtained the gift fraudulently or if the gift was made for a purpose which could be obtained only by the marriage, a donor who is not himself at fault is entitled to restitution if the marriage does not take place, even if the gift was money. If there is an engagement to marry and the donee, having received the gift without fraud, later wrongfully breaks the promise of marriage, the donor is entitled to restitution if the gift is an engagement ring, a family heirloom or other similar thing intimately connected with the marriage, but not if the gift is one of money intended to be used by the donee before the marriage.

I believe that the Restatement approach is superior to the no-fault policy espoused by the majority because it allows equity its proper place in the outcome. . . .

■ ALBINGER v. HARRIS
Supreme Court of Montana, 2002
48 P.3d 711

Justice JAMES C. NELSON. Who owns a ring given in anticipation of marriage after the engagement is broken? Michelle L. Harris (Harris) appeals the disposition of an engagement ring by the Eighth Judicial District Court, Cascade County, Montana. . . .

Harris and [Michael] Albinger met in June 1995, and began a troubled relationship that endured for the next three years, spiked by alcohol abuse, emotional turmoil and violence. Albinger presented Harris with a diamond ring and diamond earrings on December 14, 1995. The ring was purchased for $29,000. Days after accepting the ring, Harris returned it to Albinger and traveled to Kentucky for the holidays. Albinger immediately sent the ring back to Harris by mail. The couple set a tentative wedding date of June 27, 1997, but plans to marry were put on hold as Harris and Albinger separated and reconciled several times. The ring was returned to or reclaimed by Albinger upon each separation, and was re-presented to Harris after each reconciliation.

Albinger and Harris lived together in Albinger's home from August 1995 until April 1998. During this time, Albinger conferred upon Harris a new Ford Mustang convertible, a horse and a dog, in addition to the earrings and ring. Harris gave Albinger a Winchester hunting rifle, a necklace and a number of other small gifts. Albinger received a substantial jury award for injuries sustained in a 1991 railroad accident. He paid all household expenses and neither party was gainfully employed during their cohabitation.

On the night of February 23, 1997, during one of the couple's many separations, Albinger broke into the house where Harris was staying. He stood over Harris' bed, threatened her with a knife and shouted, "I'm going to chop your finger off, you better get that ring off." After severely beating Harris with a railroad lantern, Albinger forcibly removed the ring and departed. Harris sued for personal injuries and the county attorney charged Albinger by information with aggravated burglary, felony assault, and partner and family member assault. The next month, after another reconciliation, Harris requested the county attorney drop all criminal charges in exchange for Albinger's promise to seek anger management counseling. . . .

The parties separated again in late April 1998. . . . The parties dispute who was responsible for the end of the relationship. No reconciliation followed, marriage plans evaporated and Harris refused to return the ring. . . .

On September 2, 1999, the District Court awarded the engagement ring or its reasonable value and court costs to Albinger [based upon the no-fault version of the "conditional gift" theory]. . . .

ABOLITION OF BREACH OF PROMISE ACTIONS

Historic breach of promise jurisprudence tended to view an engagement ring as either a pledge of personal property given to secure a marital promise or as consideration for the contract of marriage. *See* [Elaine Marie Tomko, Annotation, *Rights in Respect of Engagement and Courtship Presents when the Marriage Does Not Ensue* (1996),] 44 A.L.R. 5th 1, §§8 and 9. When a contract to marry was abrogated, the jilted lover could seek redress in a breach of promise action that sounded in contract law, but availed the plaintiff of tort damages. . . . The plaintiffs were almost invariably women seeking economic relief for themselves, compensation for pregnancy and material support for children of the relationship. Whatever "heart balm" was awarded to assuage lost love, ruined reputation or foreclosed opportunities to marry well "rest[ed] in the sound discretion of the jury." Section 8685, RCM (1935).

By the mid-1930's, several state legislatures questioned the efficacy of court "interference with domestic relations" and passed statutes barring actions for breach of promise to marry, alienation of affections, criminal conversation and other inappropriate conduct of the "private realm." *See* Rebecca Tushnet, *Rules of Engagement* (1998), 107 Yale Law Review 2583, 2586-91. . . .

In the wake of "anti-heart balm" statutes that barred breach of contract to marry actions, courts heard a plethora of legal theories designed to involve them in settling antenuptial property disputes while avoiding the language of contract law. The results were mixed. . . . Out of this legal morass, conditional gift analysis emerged as a popular way to resolve acrimonious engagement ring disputes. While some states pursue a fault-based determination for awarding the ring in equity, the modern wave aligns ring disposition with no-fault divorce property disposition and follows a bright-line rule of ring return.

ENGAGEMENT RING SYMBOLOGY

The custom of giving expensive engagement rings is largely a mid- to late-20th Century phenomenon. Margaret F. Brinig, *Rings and Promises* (1990), 6 J.L. Econ. & Org. 203, 209. Nineteenth Century etiquette books struggled to identify proper gifts between men and women. Viviana A. Ziegler, *The Social Meaning of Money* (1994). Expensive or excessively intimate gifts, such as jewelry or wearing apparel, were fit for a kept woman, or perhaps a man's wife, but not as tokens of respectable courtship. Ziegler, at 99. Upper class men and women occasionally exchanged diamond rings as gifts during the 19th Century. Ziegler, at 99. The six-prong gold or platinum setting holding a raised, brilliant-cut diamond, which has become the classic engagement ring style, was created by Tiffany's in the 1870s. Anne Ward et al., *Rings Through the Ages* (1981), at 198. DeBeers' launched its national advertising campaign in 1939 that promised: "A diamond is forever." Brinig, at 206. To cultivate a no-return custom in America, the cartel threatened to cut off supply to dealers who bought diamonds back from purchasers. Brinig, at 209. An interesting correlation exists between the mid-20th Century increase in demand for costly diamond engagement rings and the statutory changes by state legislatures to abolish the breach of promise action. Brinig, at 206. After the Second World War, expensive rings became not just symbols of love, but tangible economic commitments in themselves, and appear to have gained significance as other economic incidents of marriage were in flux. *See* Reva B. Siegel, *Modernization of Marital Status Law: Adjudicating Wives Rights to Earnings*, 1860-1930 (1994), 82 Geo. L.J. 2127, 2201-03. As courts closed to women seeking damages for breach of the promise to marry, the cost and the practice of giving engagement rings rose dramatically. Brinig, at 209. By the time Montana barred the breach of promise action [in 1963, §27-1-602, MCA], diamonds constituted over 80% of engagement ring sales. . . .

GENDER BIAS

Article II, Section 4 of the Montana Constitution recognizes and guarantees the individual dignity of each human being without regard to gender. . . .

The Montana Legislature made the social policy decision to relieve courts of the duty of regulating engagements by barring actions for breach of promise. While not explicitly denying access to the courts on the basis of gender, the "anti-heart balm" statutes closed courtrooms across the nation to female plaintiffs seeking damages for antenuptial pregnancy, ruined reputation, lost love and economic insecurity. . . .

Conditional gift theory applied exclusively to engagement ring cases carves an exception in the state's gift law for the benefit of predominately male plaintiffs. Montana's "anti-heart balm" statute bars all actions sounding in contract law that arise from mutual promise to marry, absent fraud or deceit, and bars all plaintiffs from recovering any share of expenses incurred in planning a canceled wedding. While antenuptial traditions vary by class, ethnicity, age and inclination, women often still assume the bulk of pre-wedding costs, such as non-returnable wedding gowns, moving costs, or non-refundable deposits for caterers, entertainment or reception halls. Consequently, the statutory "anti-heart balm" bar continues to have a disparate impact on women. If this Court were to fashion a special exception for engagement ring actions under gift law theories, we would perpetuate the gender bias attendant upon the Legislature's decision to remove from our courts all actions for breach of antenuptial promises. . . .

We reverse the District Court's conclusion of law and hold the engagement ring to be a gift given without implied or express condition. . . .

Justice TERRY N. TRIEWEILER concurring and dissenting. Gender discrimination is a bad thing. I am glad the majority is against it. However, I regret that the majority has taken this opportunity to declare their good intentions because gender equity has about as much to do with this case as banking law. Furthermore, the parties in the District Court will be as surprised to hear about the basis on which this appeal has been resolved as I was when I read the proposed opinion. Principles of gender equity were never argued or even raised by the parties at any stage in the proceeding. . . .

The precedent established by this case leads to all sorts of interesting possibilities. If we accept the majority's assumption that women are more likely to have to give back a conditional gift given in anticipation of marriage than men and that, therefore, traditional notions of gift law are no longer applicable because it is unfair, what should we do about maintenance? After all, don't men more often pay maintenance than women? Is that fair? What should we do about child support? Couldn't there be a statistical argument that men pay more child support than women? What should we do about paternity suits? Surely men are more frequently the defendants in paternity suits than women?

The simple fact is that if women are more likely to be the subject of an action to recover a conditional gift given in anticipation of a marriage which does not occur, it is because they are more frequently the recipient of the gift. Should we just prohibit gifts in anticipation of marriage altogether because men are more likely to have to pay for them? . . .

Before today, no court anywhere in the world has ever held that a conditional gift given in anticipation of marriage cannot be recovered if the condition on which it was given, the marriage, does not occur because to require its return would violate notions of gender fairness. . . .

Notes and Questions

1. The general rule at common law is that a gift must be irrevocable and unconditional. When a donor attempts to impose a condition, the typical outcome is that the condition is unenforceable. This is especially likely when the condition is oral, rather than written. Two exceptions to the prohibition on conditional gifts are the *gift causa mortis* doctrine and, in many states, engagement gifts. Suppose Mom transfers possession of a new Mustang convertible to her son, Alberto, a first-year law student. At the time, she tells Alberto, "The car is yours, but only if you pass all your first year courses." Alberto flunks out, so Mom demands the car, but Alberto won't return it. What result?

2. Suppose in Montana after *Albinger*, Alberto gives his bride-to-be (also a law student) an engagement ring, telling her when he hands it to her, "Of course, if we split up, you'll have to return the ring." With a wincing smile, she accepts the proposal; but, alas, the law school romance falls apart. Must she return the ring?

3. Most broken wedding engagements, unlike those in *Lindh* and *Albinger*, do not give rise to litigation. In those cases, what do you think happens with engagement presents? Does the groom or bride often seek legal advice before acting?

Are there widely shared social norms that influence behavior? Several etiquette books instruct the bride to return the ring, regardless of the reason for canceling the engagement (Emily Post, Amy Vanderbilt, Modern Bride *Guide to Etiquette*, Vogue's *Book of Etiquette*); in contrast, several online engagement etiquette sources counsel she can keep the ring if he broke the engagement. Do you expect that there might be regional or cultural differences in these informal norms? Should that matter? If there are generally accepted norms, should the courts defer to them?

3

Protecting Possession

This chapter explores the law's protection of a person's possession of property in a number of different contexts. The focal point is primarily but not exclusively real property. A key distinction is often made between *rightful possession* of land and *wrongful possession*. One might expect that the law would just protect rightful possession and punish wrongful possession. Although the law often does this — protect true owners and sanction wrongdoers — it's not so simple. Not only can it be very hard to distinguish rightful and wrongful possessors, but the law sometimes explicitly chooses to protect wrongdoers. This we'll see in the sections below dealing with possession and sovereignty, adverse possession, the *jus tertii* defense, and mistaken improvers.

A. POSSESSION AND SOVEREIGNTY

The puzzle of distinguishing rightful from wrongful possessors of land in America dates at least as far back as colonial times, when the first European settlers sought to displace the Native American occupants of land. What gave these new settlers the legal right to possess and own American land? Could they acquire it by purchase or treaty from the Native Americans, who had a fundamentally different concept of land ownership? Could they simply take it by force from its Native American occupants, and if so, how could the conflicting claims of various Europeans nations in the same American territory be reconciled? What role did "discovery" play in reconciling these conflicting European claims, and why should the first European discovery of a particular place matter when Native Americans had already found and taken possession of the entire continent? In considering these questions, ask yourself, if I "discover" your house for the first time while you are living in it, and can show that none of my friends even knew that your house existed prior to my "discovery" of it, should I own it? Would it matter if I could show that I and all my friends are from one ethnic, cultural, or religious group and that you and all your friends are from a different one? Would it matter if I could show that I could make better use of your house than you, or that I had more power than you? How do notions of national sovereignty impact these issues? The United States Supreme Court addressed such questions in 1823, and its still controversial answers stand at the foundation of American real property law.

■ JOHNSON v. M'INTOSH
Supreme Court of the United States, 1823
21 U.S. (8 Wheat.) 543

MARSHALL, Chief Justice. The plaintiffs in this cause claim the land, in their declaration mentioned, under two grants, purporting to be made, the first in 1773, and the last in 1775, by the chiefs of certain Indian tribes, constituting the Illinois and the Piankeshaw nations[. The defendant, M'Intosh, claimed the land under a grant from the United States made in 1819. The] question is, whether [plantiffs'] title can be recognized in the Courts of the United States?

The facts, as stated in the case agreed, show the authority of the chiefs who executed this conveyance, so far as it could be given by their own people; and likewise show, that the particular tribes for whom these chiefs acted were in rightful possession of the land they sold. The inquiry, therefore, is, in a great measure, confined to the power of Indians to give, and of private individuals to receive, a title which can be sustained in the Courts of this country.

As the right of society, to prescribe those rules by which property may be acquired and preserved is not, and cannot be drawn into question; as the title to lands, especially, is and must be admitted to depend entirely on the law of the nation in which they lie; it will be necessary, in pursuing this inquiry, to examine, not singly those principles of abstract justice, which the Creator of all things has impressed on the mind of his creature man, and which are admitted to regulate, in a great degree, the rights of civilized nations, whose perfect independence is acknowledged; but those principles also which our own government has adopted in the particular case, and given us as the rule for our decision.

On the discovery of this immense continent, the great nations of Europe were eager to appropriate to themselves so much of it as they could respectively acquire. Its vast extent offered an ample field to the ambition and enterprise of all; and the character and religion of its inhabitants afforded an apology for considering them as a people over whom the superior genius of Europe might claim an ascendancy. The potentates of the old world found no difficulty in convincing themselves that they made ample compensation to the inhabitants of the new, by bestowing on them civilization and Christianity, in exchange for unlimited independence. But, as they were all in pursuit of nearly the same object, it was necessary, in order to avoid conflicting settlements, and consequent war with each other, to establish a principle, which all should acknowledge as the law by which the right of acquisition, which they all asserted, should be regulated as between themselves. This principle was, that discovery gave title to the government by whose subjects, or by whose authority, it was made, against all other European governments, which title might be consummated by possession. . . .

While the different nations of Europe respected the right of the natives, as occupants, they asserted the ultimate dominion to be in themselves; and claimed and exercised, as a consequence of this ultimate dominion, a power to grant the soil, while yet in possession of the natives. These grants have been understood by all, to convey a title to the grantees, subject only to the Indian right of occupancy.

The history of America, from its discovery to the present day, proves, we think, the universal recognition of these principles. . . .

No one of the powers of Europe gave its full assent to this principle, more unequivocally than England. The documents upon this subject are ample and complete. So early as the year 1496, her monarch granted a commission to the

Cabots, to discover countries then unknown to *Christian people*, and to take possession of them in the name of the king of England. Two years afterwards, Cabot proceeded on this voyage, and discovered the continent of North America, along which he sailed as far south as Virginia. To this discovery the English trace their title.

In this first effort made by the English government to acquire territory on this continent, we perceive a complete recognition of the principle which has been mentioned. The right of discovery given by this commission, is confined to countries "then unknown to all Christian people;" and of these countries Cabot was empowered to take possession in the name of the king of England. Thus asserting a right to take possession, notwithstanding the occupancy of the natives, who were heathens, and, at the same time, admitting the prior title of any Christian people who may have made a previous discovery. . . .

Thus, all the nations of Europe, who have acquired territory on this continent, have asserted in themselves, and have recognized in others, the exclusive right of the discoverer to appropriate the lands occupied by the Indians. Have the American States rejected or adopted this principle?

By the treaty which concluded the war of our revolution, Great Britain relinquished all claim, not only to the government, but to the "propriety and territorial rights of the United States," whose boundaries were fixed in the second article. By this treaty, the powers of government, and the right to soil, which had previously been in Great Britain, passed definitively to these States. We had before taken possession of them, by declaring independence; but neither the declaration of independence, nor the treaty confirming it, could give us more than that which we before possessed, or to which Great Britain was before entitled. It has never been doubted, that either the United States, or the several States, had a clear title to all the lands within the boundary lines described in the treaty, subject only to the Indian right of occupancy, and that the exclusive power to extinguish that right, was vested in that government which might constitutionally exercise it. . . .

After these States became independent, a controversy subsisted between them and Spain respecting boundary. By the treaty of 1795, this controversy was adjusted, and Spain ceded to the United States the territory in question. This territory, though claimed by both nations, was chiefly in the actual occupation of Indians.

The magnificent purchase of Louisiana, was the purchase from France of a country almost entirely occupied by numerous tribes of Indians, who are in fact independent. Yet, any attempt of others to intrude into that country, would be considered as an aggression which would justify war.

Our late acquisitions from Spain are of the same character; and the negotiations which preceded those acquisitions, recognize and elucidate the principle which has been received as the foundation of all European title in America.

The United States, then, have unequivocally acceded to that great and broad rule by which its civilized inhabitants now hold this country. They hold, and assert in themselves, the title by which it was acquired. They maintain, as all others have maintained, that discovery gave an exclusive right to extinguish the Indian title of occupancy, either by purchase or by conquest; and gave also a right to such a degree of sovereignty, as the circumstances of the people would allow them to exercise. . . .

Although we do not mean to engage in the defense of those principles which Europeans have applied to Indian title, they may, we think, find some excuse, if not justification, in the character and habits of the people whose rights have been wrested from them. . . .

[T]he tribes of Indians inhabiting this country were fierce savages, whose occupation was war, and whose subsistence was drawn chiefly from the forest. To leave them in possession of their country, was to leave the country a wilderness; to govern them as a distinct people, was impossible, because they were as brave and as high spirited as they were fierce, and were ready to repel by arms every attempt on their independence.

What was the inevitable consequence of this state of things? The Europeans were under the necessity either of abandoning the country, and relinquishing their pompous claims to it, or of enforcing those claims by the sword, and by the adoption of principles adapted to the condition of a people with whom it was impossible to mix, and who could not be governed as a distinct society, or of remaining in their neighborhood, and exposing themselves and their families to the perpetual hazard of being massacred. . . .

However extravagant the pretension of converting the discovery of an inhabited country into conquest may appear; if the principle has been asserted in the first instance, and afterwards sustained; if a country has been acquired and held under it; if the property of the great mass of the community originates in it, it becomes the law of the land, and cannot be questioned. So, too, with respect to the concomitant principle, that the Indian inhabitants are to be considered merely as occupants, to be protected, indeed, while in peace, in the possession of their lands, but to be deemed incapable of transferring the absolute title to others. However this restriction may be opposed to natural right, and to the usages of civilized nations, yet, if it be indispensable to that system under which the country has been settled, and be adapted to the actual condition of the two people, it may, perhaps, be supported by reason, and certainly cannot be rejected by Courts of justice. . . .

After bestowing on this subject a degree of attention which was more required by the magnitude of the interest in litigation, and the able and elaborate arguments of the bar, than by its intrinsic difficulty, the Court is decidedly of opinion, that the plaintiffs do not exhibit a title which can be sustained in the Courts of the United States; and that there is no error in the judgment which was rendered against them in the District Court of Illinois.

Judgment affirmed, with costs.

Notes and Questions

1. If property consists of "a bundle of rights or legally protected interests," as was said above in the *Presley* case, page 18, according to Chief Justice Marshall in Johnson v. M'Intosh, what customary rights of land ownership were denied to the native occupants of American land after its discovery and conquest by Europeans? What customary rights of land ownership were at least in theory (if not always in practice) retained by Native Americans? How did the U.S. government go about dispossessing Native Americans of these remaining rights?

2. What did Chief Justice Marshall mean by his closing comment that the legal issues in Johnson v. M'Intosh were more interesting than difficult? Why are they interesting? Why does he assert that are they not intrinsically difficult as matters of law?

3. As Chief Justice Marshall suggested in his closing comment, the issues addressed in Johnson v. M'Intosh may seem like ancient history in the United States where land claims are virtually always decided within the framework of settled state

and national law. They still arise in various forms elsewhere. Consider the former Yugoslavia, for example, where new claims of national sovereignty in places like Bosnia and Kosovo led to the displacement of people from differing ethnic and religious groups during the 1990s. More recently, if a Sunni Iraqi "finds" a Shiite Iraqi's house in a Sunni neighborhood of Baghdad (or visa versa), can he possess it as his own? Where else are similar issues arising now?

4. To parse the High Court's words, in what ways did the "character and habits" of Native Americans lead Europeans to assert that European nations could claim American territory through some mix of discovery, conquest, and possession? What elements of the native people's character and habits mattered? Was it their "savage," allegedly uncivilized state? Was it that their "subsistence was drawn chiefly from the forest" so that "to leave them in possession of their country, was to leave the country a wilderness"? Was it their so-called heathen beliefs, such that, prior to its discovery by Europeans, their land was "unknown to Christian people"? Did it matter to the Spanish that the Aztecs and Incas lived in cities and cultivated crops when conquered in the 1500s or to the Americans that the Cherokee lived much like European Christians before being driven from Georgia over the Trail of Tears in 1838? Could similar arguments legitimize European colonization in Africa, Asia, Australia, and the Pacific Islands during the eighteenth and nineteenth centuries?

5. On August 2, 2007, in a widely publicized and carefully staged maneuver, Russia seemed to revive the doctrine of discovery by "claiming" some or all of the Arctic seafloor by having its sailors aboard a Russian submarine place a titanium Russian flag on the seabed at the North Pole. *See* Robert Miller, *Finders Keepers in the Arctic?*, L.A. Times, Aug. 6, 2007. Of course, Robert Peary claimed to have raised an American flag on the ice at the North Pole in 1909 and, three years later, Roald Amundsen did plant a Norwegian flag at the South Pole. These men and their companions are credited with "discovering" the earth's geographic poles. In 1958, the U.S. nuclear submarine *Nautilus* became the first seagoing vessel to cross the North Pole. Neither the United States nor Norway claim those polar regions on the basis of these acts. Legal commentators generally assert that international treaties such as the United Nations Convention on the Law of the Sea will control sovereignty over the Arctic seafloor much as the Antarctic Treaty System regulates international relations with respect to Antarctica. Why did Russia stage this act in 2007? As a legal matter, what difference could it make?

B. TRESPASS AND THE RIGHT TO EXCLUDE

The core of ownership of land is the right to exclusive possession. By the right to possession, we mean that the owner has the right to exclude others from the parcel in question. Private ownership of land, by definition, means that the land isn't a commons; it's not open to use by the public. Implicit in the right to exclude is the right to *include*. The owner has the general power to decide who may enter (and under what terms and conditions) and who may not. In our legal system, the cause of action for trespass to land defines the boundaries of the right to exclude. Indeed, if we define property as those rights that are protected by the state, the right to exclusive possession and the scope of the trespass action are opposite sides of one coin. A landowner has the right to exclusive possession to the extent, and only to the extent, that he can prevail in court based on the theory of trespass.

■ JACQUE v. STEENBERG HOMES, INC.
Supreme Court of Wisconsin, 1997
563 N.W.2d 154

BABLITCH, Justice. Steenberg Homes had a mobile home to deliver. Unfortunately for Harvey and Lois Jacque (the Jacques), the easiest route of delivery was across their land. Despite adamant protests by the Jacques, Steenberg plowed a path through the Jacques' snow-covered field and via that path, delivered the mobile home. Consequently, the Jacques sued Steenberg Homes for intentional trespass. At trial, Steenberg Homes conceded the intentional trespass, but argued that no compensatory damages had been proved, and that punitive damages could not be awarded without compensatory damages. Although the jury awarded the Jacques $1 in nominal damages and $100,000 in punitive damages, the circuit court set aside the jury's award of $100,000. The court of appeals affirmed, reluctantly concluding that it could not reinstate the punitive damages because it was bound by precedent establishing that an award of nominal damages will not sustain a punitive damage award. We conclude that when nominal damages are awarded for an intentional trespass to land, punitive damages may, in the discretion of the jury, be awarded. We further conclude that the $100,000 awarded by the jury is not excessive. Accordingly, we reverse and remand for reinstatement of the punitive damage award.

I.

. . . Plaintiffs, Lois and Harvey Jacque, are an elderly couple, now retired from farming, who own roughly 170 acres near Wilke's Lake in the town of Schleswig. The defendant, Steenberg Homes, Inc. (Steenberg), is in the business of selling mobile homes. In the fall of 1993, a neighbor of the Jacques purchased a mobile home from Steenberg. Delivery of the mobile home was included in the sales price.

Steenberg determined that the easiest route to deliver the mobile home was across the Jacques' land. Steenberg preferred transporting the home across the Jacques' land because the only alternative was a private road which was covered in up to seven feet of snow and contained a sharp curve which would require sets of "rollers" to be used when maneuvering the home around the curve. Steenberg asked the Jacques on several separate occasions whether it could move the home across the Jacques' farm field. The Jacques refused. The Jacques were sensitive about allowing others on their land because they had lost property valued at over $10,000 to other neighbors in an adverse possession action in the mid-1980's. Despite repeated refusals from the Jacques, Steenberg decided to sell the mobile home, which was to be used as a summer cottage, and delivered it on February 15, 1994.

On the morning of delivery, Mr. Jacque observed the mobile home parked on the corner of the town road adjacent to his property. He decided to find out where the movers planned to take the home. The movers, who were Steenberg employees, showed Mr. Jacque the path they planned to take with the mobile home to reach the neighbor's lot. The path cut across the Jacques' land. Mr. Jacque informed the movers that it was the Jacques' land they were planning to cross and that Steenberg did not have permission to cross their land. He told them that Steenberg had been refused permission to cross the Jacques' land.

One of Steenberg's employees called the assistant manager, who then came out to the Jacques' home. In the meantime, the Jacques called and asked some of their neighbors and the town chairman to come over immediately. Once everyone was present, the Jacques showed the assistant manager an aerial map and plat book of the township to prove their ownership of the land, and reiterated their demand that the home not be moved across their land.

At that point, the assistant manager asked Mr. Jacque how much money it would take to get permission. Mr. Jacque responded that it was not a question of money; the Jacques just did not want Steenberg to cross their land. Mr. Jacque testified that he told Steenberg to "[F]ollow the road, that is what the road is for." Steenberg employees left the meeting without permission to cross the land.

At trial, one of Steenberg's employees testified that, upon coming out of the Jacques' home, the assistant manager stated: "I don't give a — — what [Mr. Jacque] said, just get the home in there any way you can." The other Steenberg employee confirmed this testimony and further testified that the assistant manager told him to park the company truck in such a way that no one could get down the town road to see the route the employees were taking with the home. The assistant manager denied giving these instructions, and Steenberg argued that the road was blocked for safety reasons.

The employees, after beginning down the private road, ultimately used a "bobcat" to cut a path through the Jacques' snow-covered field and hauled the home across the Jacques' land to the neighbor's lot. One employee testified that upon returning to the office and informing the assistant manager that they had gone across the field, the assistant manager reacted by giggling and laughing. The other employee confirmed this testimony. The assistant manager disputed this testimony.

When a neighbor informed the Jacques that Steenberg had, in fact, moved the mobile home across the Jacques' land, Mr. Jacque called the Manitowoc County Sheriff's Department. After interviewing the parties and observing the scene, an officer from the sheriff's department issued a $30 citation to Steenberg's assistant manager. . . .

This case presents three issues: (1) whether an award of nominal damages for intentional trespass to land may support a punitive damage award and, if so; (2) whether the law should apply to Steenberg or should only be applied prospectively and, if we apply the law to Steenberg; (3) whether the $100,000 in punitive damages awarded by the jury is excessive. . . .

II.

. . . .

Steenberg argues that, as a matter of law, punitive damages could not be awarded by the jury because punitive damages must be supported by an award of compensatory damages and here the jury awarded only nominal and punitive damages. The Jacques contend that the rationale supporting the compensatory damage award requirement is inapposite when the wrongful act is an intentional trespass to land. . . .

The general rule was stated in Barnard v. Cohen, 162 N.W. 480 (Wis. 1917), where the question presented was: "In an action for libel, can there be a recovery of punitory damages if only nominal compensatory damages are found?" With the bare assertion that authority and better reason supported its conclusion, the *Barnard* court said no. *Id.* at 481. *Barnard* continues to state the general rule of punitive damages in Wisconsin. *See* Tucker v. Marcus, 418 N.W.2d 818, 823 (Wis. 1988). The rationale for the compensatory damage requirement is that if the individual cannot show actual harm, he or she has but a nominal interest, hence, society has little interest in having the unlawful, but otherwise harmless, conduct deterred, therefore, punitive damages are inappropriate. Maxwell v. Kennedy, 7 N.W. 657, 658-59 (Wis. 1880).

However, whether nominal damages can support a punitive damage award in the case of an intentional trespass to land has never been squarely addressed by this court. Nonetheless, Wisconsin law is not without reference to this situation. In 1854 the court established punitive damages, allowing the assessment of "damages as a punishment to the defendant for the purpose of making an example." McWilliams v. Bragg, 3 Wis. 424, 425(1854).[3] The *McWilliams* court related the facts and an illustrative tale from the English case of Merest v. Harvey, 128 Eng. Rep. 761 (C.P. 1814), to explain the rationale underlying punitive damages.

In *Merest*, a landowner was shooting birds in his field when he was approached by the local magistrate who wanted to hunt with him. Although the landowner refused, the magistrate proceeded to hunt. When the landowner continued to object, the magistrate threatened to have him jailed and dared him to file suit. Although little actual harm had been caused, the English court upheld damages of 500 pounds, explaining "in a case where a man disregards every principle which actuates the conduct of gentlemen, what is to restrain him except large damages?" *McWilliams*, 3 Wis. at 428.

To explain the need for punitive damages, even where actual harm is slight, *McWilliams* related the hypothetical tale from *Merest* of an intentional trespasser:

> Suppose a gentleman has a paved walk in his paddock, before his window, and that a man intrudes and walks up and down before the window of his house, and looks in while the owner is at dinner, is the trespasser permitted to say "here is a halfpenny for you which is the full extent of the mischief I have done." Would that be a compensation? I cannot say that it would be. . . .

Id. Thus, in the case establishing punitive damages in this state, this court recognized that in certain situations of trespass, the actual harm is not in the damage done to the land, which may be minimal, but in the loss of the individual's right to exclude others from his or her property, and the court implied that this right may be punished by a large damage award despite the lack of measurable harm.

Steenberg contends that the rule established in *Barnard* prohibits a punitive damage award, as a matter of law, unless the plaintiff also receives compensatory damages. . . . An examination of the individual interests invaded by an intentional trespass to land, and society's interests in preventing intentional trespass to land, leads us to the conclusion that the *Barnard* rule should not apply when the tort supporting the award is intentional trespass to land.

We turn first to the individual landowner's interest in protecting his or her land from trespass. The United States Supreme Court has recognized that the private landowner's right to exclude others from his or her land is "one of the most essential sticks in the bundle of rights that are commonly characterized as property." Dolan v. City of Tigard, 512 U.S. 374, 384 (1994). This court has long recognized "[e]very person's constitutional right to the exclusive enjoyment of his own property for any purpose which does not invade the rights of another person."

---

3. Because *McWilliams* was an action of trespass for assault and battery, we cite it not for its precedential value, but for its reasoning.

Diana Shooting Club v. Lamoreux, 89 N.W. 880, 886 (Wis. 1902) (holding that the victim of an intentional trespass should have been allowed to take judgment for nominal damages and costs). Thus, both this court and the Supreme Court recognize the individual's legal right to exclude others from private property.

Yet a right is hollow if the legal system provides insufficient means to protect it. Felix Cohen offers the following analysis summarizing the relationship between the individual and the state regarding property rights:

> [T]hat is property to which the following label can be attached:
> To the world:
> Keep off X unless you have my permission, which I may grant or withhold.
> Signed: Private Citizen
> Endorsed: The state

Felix S. Cohen, *Dialogue on Private Property*, 9 Rutgers Law Review 357, 374 (1954). Harvey and Lois Jacque have the right to tell Steenberg Homes and any other trespasser, "No, you cannot cross our land." But that right has no practical meaning unless protected by the State. And, as this court recognized as early as 1854, a "halfpenny" award does not constitute state protection.

The nature of the nominal damage award in an intentional trespass to land case further supports an exception to *Barnard*. Because a legal right is involved, the law recognizes that actual harm occurs in every trespass. The action for intentional trespass to land is directed at vindication of the legal right. W. Page Keeton, *Prosser and Keeton on Torts* §13 (5th ed. 1984). The law infers some damage from every direct entry upon the land of another. *Id.* The law recognizes actual harm in every trespass to land whether or not compensatory damages are awarded. *Id.* Thus, in the case of intentional trespass to land, the nominal damage award represents the recognition that, although immeasurable in mere dollars, actual harm has occurred.

The potential for harm resulting from intentional trespass also supports an exception to *Barnard*. A series of intentional trespasses, as the Jacques had the misfortune to discover in an unrelated action, can threaten the individual's very ownership of the land. The conduct of an intentional trespasser, if repeated, might ripen into prescription or adverse possession and, as a consequence, the individual landowner can lose his or her property rights to the trespasser. *See* Wis. Stat. §893.28.

. . . We turn next to society's interest in protecting private property from the intentional trespasser.

Society has an interest in punishing and deterring intentional trespassers beyond that of protecting the interests of the individual landowner. Society has an interest in preserving the integrity of the legal system. Private landowners should feel confident that wrongdoers who trespass upon their land will be appropriately punished. When landowners have confidence in the legal system, they are less likely to resort to "self-help" remedies. In *McWilliams*, the court recognized the importance of "'prevent[ing] the practice of dueling [by permitting] juries . . . to *punish* insult by exemplary damages.'" *McWilliams*, 3 Wis. at 428. Although dueling is rarely a modern form of self-help, one can easily imagine a frustrated landowner taking the law into his or her own hands when faced with a brazen trespasser, like Steenberg, who refuses to heed no trespass warnings.

People expect wrongdoers to be appropriately punished. Punitive damages have the effect of bringing to punishment types of conduct that, though oppressive and hurtful to the individual, almost invariably go unpunished by the public prosecutor. Kink v. Combs, 135 N.W.2d 789 (Wis. 1965). The $30 forfeiture was certainly not an appropriate punishment for Steenberg's egregious trespass in the eyes of the Jacques. It was more akin to *Merest*'s "halfpenny." If punitive damages are not allowed in a situation like this, what punishment will prohibit the intentional trespass to land? Moreover, what is to stop Steenberg Homes from concluding, in the future, that delivering its mobile homes via an intentional trespass and paying the resulting Class B forfeiture is not more profitable than obeying the law? . . .

In sum, as the court of appeals noted, the *Barnard* rule sends the wrong message to Steenberg Homes and any others who contemplate trespassing on the land of another. It implicitly tells them that they are free to go where they please, regardless of the landowner's wishes. As long as they cause no compensable harm, the only deterrent intentional trespassers face is the nominal damage award of $1, the modern equivalent of *Merest*'s halfpenny, and the possibility of a Class B forfeiture under Wis. Stat. §943.13. We conclude that both the private landowner and society have much more than a nominal interest in excluding others from private land. Intentional trespass to land causes actual harm to the individual, regardless of whether that harm can be measured in mere dollars. Consequently, the *Barnard* rationale will not support a refusal to allow punitive damages when the tort involved is an intentional trespass to land. Accordingly, assuming that the other requirements for punitive damages have been met, we hold that nominal damages may support a punitive damage award in an action for intentional trespass to land. . . .

In conclusion, we hold that when nominal damages are awarded for an intentional trespass to land, punitive damages may, in the discretion of the jury, be awarded. Our decision today shall apply to Steenberg Homes. Finally, we hold that the $100,000 punitive damages awarded by the jury is not excessive. Accordingly, we reverse and remand to the circuit court for reinstatement of the punitive damage award.

Notes and Questions

1. Did Steenberg's trespass cause any actual harm to the Jacques' real property? If so, what? If not, why should they recover anything in addition to nominal damages?

2. Suppose the court had decided to continue to follow the traditional rule that punitive damages are unavailable unless the plaintiff can prove actual compensatory damages. Can you think of a way to measure compensatory damages (not nominal or punitive damages) to be paid to the Jacques for what Steenberg did that does not depend upon physical injury to the field?

■ **ADAMS v. CLEVELAND-CLIFFS IRON COMPANY**
Court of Appeals of Michigan, 1999
602 N.W.2d 215

O'CONNELL, Judge. Defendants appeal as of right from a jury verdict awarding damages in trespass for invasions of plaintiffs' property by intrusions of dust, noise, and vibrations. The gravamen of this appeal presents the question whether Michigan recognizes a cause of action in trespass stemming from invasions of these intangible agents. No published decision of an appellate court of this state is directly on point. Because of the importance of this issue of first impression, we will expound on it in some detail. Following a recitation of facts, we will examine the origins of the doctrines of trespass to land and nuisance, observe recent developments of those doctrines in this and other jurisdictions, and then reaffirm for this state the traditional requirements for a cause of action in trespass.

We conclude that the law of trespass in Michigan does not cover airborne particulate, noise, or vibrations, and that a complaint alleging damages resulting from these irritants normally sounds instead in nuisance.

I. FACTS

Plaintiffs brought suit seeking damages in both trespass and nuisance, complaining of dust, noise, and vibrations emanating from the Empire Mine, which is operated by defendant Cleveland-Cliffs Iron Company and its subsidiary, defendant Empire Iron Mining Partnership.

The Empire Mine is one of the nation's largest mines, producing eight million tons of iron ore annually. The mine operates twenty-four hours a day, year round. At the time this action was commenced, all but three plaintiffs lived near the mine, in the village of Palmer in Marquette County. Cleveland-Cliffs, which also operates the nearby Tilden Mine, employs approximately 2,200 persons, making it the area's largest civilian employer.

The Empire Mine was originally dug in the 1870s, then expanded in the 1960s. A second pit was added in 1987, and a third in 1990-91.[2] The mine engages in blasting operations approximately three times a week, year round, and the extraction and processing of the iron ore generates a great deal of airborne dust. Plaintiffs complain that the blasting sends tremors through their property and that defendants' dust constantly accumulates inside and outside plaintiffs' homes. Plaintiffs assert that these emanations aggravate their need to clean and repaint their homes, replace carpets and drapes, repair cracks in all masonry, replace windows, and tend to cause plumbing leaks and broken sewer pipes.

According to the testimony, the dust from the mine is fine, gritty, oily, and difficult to clean. Some plaintiffs complained that they seldom opened their windows because of the dust, and virtually every plaintiff complained that the snow in Palmer tended to be gray or black. Evidence presented at trial indicates that the emissions from the mining operations have consistently remained within applicable air-quality standards and that the amount of particulate matter accumulating over Palmer each month amounts to less than the thickness of a sheet of paper, but that this amount is nonetheless four times greater than what normally settles onto surrounding communities.

In addition to concerns about the dust, many plaintiffs testified that the noise and vibrations from the blasts caused them to suffer shock, nervousness, and sleeplessness. Finally, several plaintiffs asserted that these conditions diminished the value of their homes, in some cases to the point of rendering them unmarketable.

---

2. With each expansion, surface material, also called "overburden," consisting of soil, subsoil, and rock was blasted loose then stockpiled at the edge of the mine property. As the mine was dug deeper, waste rock was likewise blasted loose and stockpiled. The resulting mass of overburden and waste rock is unsightly and so large that residents of Palmer have nicknamed it "Mt. Palmer" and say that it causes their town to have early sunsets.

Cliffs Michigan Mining Company's Empire Facility

At the close of proofs, the trial court instructed the jury concerning both trespass and nuisance. The jury found that three of the plaintiffs were not entitled to recover under either theory. Concerning the remaining fifty-two plaintiffs, however, the jury was unable to agree on a verdict regarding the nuisance claim, but returned a verdict in favor of these plaintiffs with regard to the trespass claim, awarding damages totaling $599,199. . . .

II. TRESPASS AND NUISANCE

The general concept of "property" comprises various rights — a "bundle of sticks," as it is often called — which is usually understood to include "[t]he exclusive right of possessing, enjoying, and disposing of a thing." Black's Law Dictionary (6th ed., 1990), p. 1216. As this latter characterization suggests, the right to exclude others from one's land and the right to quiet enjoyment of one's land have customarily been regarded as separate sticks in the bundle. Thus, possessory rights to real property include as distinct interests the right to exclude and the right to enjoy, violations of which give rise to the distinct causes of action respectively of trespass and nuisance. Prosser & Keeton, Torts (5th ed.), §87, p. 622.

A. HISTORICAL OVERVIEW

"At common law, trespass was a form of action brought to recover damages for any injury to one's person or property or relationship with another." Black's Law Dictionary (6th ed.), p. 1502. This broad usage of the term "trespass" then gave way to a narrower usage, referring to intrusions upon a person's "tangible property, real or personal." Prosser & Keeton, *supra* at §13, p. 67. Today, the general concept of "trespass" has been refined into several specific forms of trespass, see Black's Law Dictionary (6th ed.), pp. 1502-1504, and related doctrines known by various names.

Landowners seeking damages or equitable relief in response to violations of their possessory rights to land now generally proceed under the common-law derivatives of strict liability, negligence, nuisance, or trespass to land. It is the latter two products of this evolution from the general concept of trespass that are at issue in the present case.

"'[T]respass is an invasion of the plaintiff's interest in the exclusive possession of his land, while nuisance is an interference with his use and enjoyment of it.'" Hadfield v. Oakland Co. Drain Comm'r, 422 N.W.2d 205, 210 (Mich. 1988), quoting Prosser & Keeton, *supra* at §87, p. 622. Historically, "[e]very unauthorized intrusion upon the private premises of another is a trespass. . . ." Giddings v. Rogalewski, 158 N.W. 951, 953 (Mich. 1916). Because a trespass violated a landholder's right to exclude others from the premises, the landholder could recover at least nominal damages even in the absence of proof of any other injury. *Id.* Recovery for nuisance, however, traditionally required proof of actual and substantial injury. Further, the doctrine of nuisance customarily called for balancing the disturbance complained of against the social utility of its cause.

Traditionally, trespass required that the invasion of the land be direct or immediate and in the form of a physical, tangible object. *See, e.g.*, Williams v. Oeder, 659 N.E.2d 379, 382 n.2 (Ohio App. 1995) (noting then abandoning those traditional requirements); Davis v. Georgia-Pacific Corp., 445 P.2d 481, 483 (Or. 1968) (abandoning the traditional requirements); Norwood v. Eastern Oregon Land Co., 5 P.2d 1057, 1061 (Or. 1931), *modified*, 7 P.2d 996 (Or. 1932) (wrongful diversion of water onto another's land does not constitute trespass to land). Under these principles, recovery in trespass for dust, smoke, noise, and vibrations was generally unavailable because they were not considered tangible or because they came to the land via some intervening force such as wind or water. Instead, claims concerning these irritants were generally pursued under a nuisance theory.

B. RECENT TRENDS

Plaintiffs urge this Court to hold that they are entitled to recover in trespass for invasions of their premises by intangible things without regard for how these annoyances came to their land. Plaintiffs would have us follow the example of certain courts from other jurisdictions, which have eliminated the traditional requirements for trespass of a direct intrusion by a tangible object, directing the inquiry instead toward the nature of the interest harmed. These courts have permitted recovery in trespass for indirect, intangible invasions that nonetheless interfered with exclusive possessory interests in the land. *See* Mercer v. Rockwell Int'l Corp., 24 F. Supp. 2d 735, 743 (W.D. Ky. 1998) (allowing an action in "negligent trespass" concerning intrusions of invisible polychlorinated biphenyls [PCBs] that actually harm the property); Williams, *supra* (airborne particulate matter from a sand and gravel processing facility, an asphalt plant, and a concrete plant constituted trespass); Martin v. Reynolds Metals Co., 342 P.2d 790 (Or. 1959) (trespass may stem from fluoride compounds in the form of gases and particles). We agree with the characterization of cases of this sort found in Prosser & Keeton as being "in reality, examples of the tort of private nuisance or liability for harm resulting from negligence," not proper trespass cases. Prosser & Keeton, *supra* at §13, pp. 71-72 (concerning "decisions finding a trespass constituted by the entry of invisible gases and microscopic particles, but only if harm results"). Accordingly, we decline plaintiffs' invitation to strip the tort of trespass to land of its distinctive accouterments and commingle its identity with other causes of action.

As stated above, the traditional view of trespass required a direct entry onto the land by a tangible object. However, recent trends have led to an erosion of these requirements. Some courts have eliminated the requirement of a direct entry onto the land. *E.g.*, Bradley v. American Smelting & Refining Co., 709 P.2d 782, 787-88 (Wash. 1985); Borland v. Sanders Lead Co., Inc., 369 So. 2d 523, 527 (Ala. 1979). . . .

The courts that have deviated from the traditional requirements of trespass, however, have consequently found troublesome the traditional principle that at least nominal damages are presumed in cases of trespass. Thus, under the so-called modern view of trespass, in order to avoid subjecting manufacturing plants to potential liability to every landowner on whose parcel some incidental residue of industrial activity might come to rest, these courts have grafted onto the law of trespass a requirement of actual and substantial damages. Bradley, *supra* at 791; Borland, *supra* at 529. . . .

We do not welcome this redirection of trespass law toward nuisance law. The requirement that real and substantial damages be proved, and balanced against the usefulness of the offending activity, is appropriate where the issue is interference with one's use or enjoyment of one's land; applying it where a landowner has had to endure an unauthorized physical occupation of the landowner's land, however, offends traditional principles of ownership. The law should not require a property owner to justify exercising the right to exclude. To countenance the erosion of presumed damages in cases of trespass is to endanger the right of exclusion itself.

To summarize, the effects of recent trends in the law of trespass have included eliminating the requirements of a direct invasion by a tangible object, requiring proof of actual and substantial damages, and weighing the plaintiff's damages against the social utility of the operation causing them. This so-called "modern view of trespass" appears, with all its nuances and add-ons, merely to replicate traditional nuisance doctrine as recognized in Michigan. Indeed, the trends recognized or advanced by *Bradley, Borland, Martin,* and their kindred spirits have conflated nuisance with trespass to the point of rendering it difficult to delineate the difference between the two theories of recovery. . . .

III. Holding

Recovery for trespass to land in Michigan is available only upon proof of an unauthorized direct or immediate intrusion of a physical, tangible object onto land over which the plaintiff has a right of exclusive possession. Once such an intrusion is proved, the tort has been established, and the plaintiff is presumptively entitled to at least nominal damages. Where the possessor of land is menaced by noise, vibrations, or ambient dust, smoke, soot, or fumes, the possessory interest implicated is that of use and enjoyment, not exclusion, and the vehicle through which a plaintiff normally should seek a remedy is the doctrine of nuisance. To prevail in nuisance, a possessor of land must prove *significant harm* resulting from the defendant's *unreasonable interference* with the use or enjoyment of the property. Cloverleaf Car Co. v. Phillips Petroleum Co., 540 N.W.2d 297, 301-02 (Mich. App. 1995). Thus, in nuisance, the plaintiff must prove all damages, which may be awarded only to the extent that the defendant's conduct was "unreasonable" according to a public-policy assessment of its overall value. In the present case, because the intrusions of which plaintiffs complained were intangible things, the trial court erred in allowing the jury to award damages in trespass. Instead, any award of damages would have had to proceed from plaintiffs' alternative but (as yet) unsuccessful theory of nuisance.

As discussed above, we acknowledge that numerous courts in other jurisdictions have permitted the erosion of the traditional elements of the tort of trespass to land, directing their inquiry instead toward whether the invasion complained of interferes with the exclusive possession of the land generally without regard to whether the intrusion is direct or indirect, tangible or intangible. We prefer to retain the traditional elements, however, because they serve as gatekeepers — safeguarding genuine claims of trespass and keeping the line between the torts of trespass and nuisance from fading into a "wavering and uncertain" ambiguity. Further, retaining the distinction between the two theories of recovery limits the possibilities for dual liability stemming from the same conduct and results. *See* Reynolds, Distinguishing Trespass and Nuisance: A Journey Through a Shifting Borderland, 44 Okla. L.R. 227, 229 (1991).

The trial court's instruction regarding trespass, as set forth above, recognized a right to recover in trespass "if any damages were caused by the trespass" and that the agents potentially causing the damages included "emissions, dust, vibration, noise." Thus the trial court seems to have mirrored (and indeed gone beyond) the so-called modern view of trespass according to which intangible irritants could constitute trespass. This instruction thus erroneously conflated trespass with nuisance and produced the anomalous result that the jury failed to reach agreement on the nuisance claim while awarding damages for intrusions of intangible things pursuant to the trespass claim.

A. TANGIBLE

Because noise or vibrations are clearly not tangible objects, we hold that they cannot give rise to an action in trespass in this state.[12] We further hold that dust must generally be considered intangible and thus not actionable in trespass.

We realize, of course, that dust particles are tangible objects in a strict sense that they can be touched and are comprised of physical elements. However, we agree with those authorities that have recognized, for practical purposes, that dust, along with other forms of airborne particulate, does not normally present itself as a significant physical intrusion. *See* anno: Recovery in trespass for injury to land caused by airborne pollutants, 2 A.L.R.4th 1054, 1055 ("[t]raditionally, an invasion of the exclusive possession of land by intangible substances, such as an airborne pollutant, was usually held by the court not to constitute a trespass").

Dust particles do not normally occupy the land on which they settle in any meaningful sense; instead they simply become a part of the ambient circumstances of that space. If the quantity and character of the dust are such as to disturb the ambiance in ways that interfere substantially with the plaintiff's use and enjoyment of the land, then recovery in nuisance is possible.

---

12. This holds even if the noise or vibrations are so intense as to shatter all glass and fell all masonry or otherwise so persistent as to drive all persons from the premises. Although such hazards would indeed infringe on a landowner's possessory interest, it is the interest in use and enjoyment of the premises, not in exclusion from them, and therefore the cause of action lies not in trespass, but in nuisance or the related doctrines of negligence or strict liability.

B. DIRECT

"[S]ome courts have held that if an intervening force, such as wind or water, carries pollutants onto the plaintiff's land, then the entry is not 'direct.'" Williams, *supra* at 382 n.2. However, in order to avoid harsh results most courts have avoided an overly strict distinction between direct and indirect invasions, *see* Prosser & Keeton, *supra* at §13, pp. 68-69. Still, "[t]he differentiation between direct and indirect results may not be absolutely dead." *Id.* at 71.[13]

. . . We hold that the direct invasion requirement for an action in trespass to land is still alive in Michigan. The question then becomes, how strong must the connection between cause and effect be in order to satisfy this requirement?[14]

We agree with the Restatement view that "[i]t is enough that an act is done with knowledge that it will to a substantial certainty result in the entry of the foreign matter." 1 *Restatement of Torts*, 2d, §158, comment i, p. 279. Thus, a "direct or immediate" invasion for purposes of trespass is one that is accomplished by any means that the offender knew or reasonably should have known would result in the physical invasion of the plaintiff's land.[15] . . .

Reversed and remanded. We do not retain jurisdiction.

Notes and Questions

1. Based upon *Adams*, what are the key differences between trespass and nuisance? Is it easier for plaintiffs to win trespass cases or nuisance cases?

2. As the *Adams* court recognizes, a number of courts in other states have reformed trespass law by allowing recovery for airborne invasions of pollutants that are too small for the naked eye to see. What is the best reason for joining the trend? For resisting the trend, as *Adams* does?

3. There are other reasons, besides doctrinal differences, why it's sometimes necessary to distinguish trespass from other wrongs. For example, in McDowell v. State of Alaska, 957 P.2d 965 (Alaska 1998), underground petroleum leakage from a service station damaged plaintiffs' land. Plaintiffs brought three claims: trespass, negligence, and strict liability. The action was filed too late under the statute of limitations for negligence and strict liability (two years), but a six-year statute applied to trespass. In contrast to *Adams*, the *McDowell* court upheld plaintiffs' trespass claim, reasoning it alleged a "direct invasion" interfering with the "exclusive possession of their property."

---

13. *See also Reynolds, supra* at 228 ("the old element of trespass that prescribed a *direct* invasion of the plaintiff's interests still has significance" (emphasis in original)).

14. Because we conclude that no trespass existed in the present case because the intrusions at issue were not tangible things, we need not decide whether defendants caused those intrusions to enter plaintiffs' land by direct or immediate means for purposes of trespass law.

15. We note that the Restatement itself presents its rule as a departure from the traditional requirement of a direct or immediate invasion. 1 Restatement Torts, 2d, §158, comment i, pp. 278-279 ("it is not necessary that the foreign matter should be thrown directly and immediately upon the other's land"). We would, however, adopt the Restatement's formulation as a liberalization, not a rejection, of the strictest sense of the traditional requirement for a direct or immediate invasion. Accordingly, rather than reject this traditional requirement, we preserve this requirement as something akin to proximate cause, meaning "that which, in a natural and continuous sequence, unbroken by any efficient intervening cause, produces the injury and without which the accident could not have happened, if the injury be one which might be reasonably anticipated or foreseen." *Black's Law Dictionary* (6th ed.), p. 1225.

4. Suppose that you owned property next to a baseball field, and from time to time a long home-run ball would land on your property, occasionally damaging the siding on the house, breaking a window, or flattening garden plants. Trespass? Nuisance? See the English case of Miller v. Jackson, 1 Q.B. 966 (Court of Appeal 1977) for a delightful opinion by Lord Denning. (The case involved, of course, cricket and not baseball.)

5. Could you construct an argument, based on *Adams*, that the acts of *Jacque* Homes should not constitute trespass? Or, conversely, based on *Jacque*, that *Adams* is incorrectly decided?

■ **WATCHTOWER BIBLE AND TRACT SOCIETY OF NEW YORK, INC. v. VILLAGE OF STRATTON**
Supreme Court of the United States, 2002
536 U.S. 150

STEVENS, Justice. Petitioners contend that a village ordinance making it a misdemeanor to engage in door-to-door advocacy without first registering with the mayor and receiving a permit violates the First Amendment. Through this facial challenge, we consider the door-to-door canvassing regulation not only as it applies to religious proselytizing, but also to anonymous political speech and the distribution of handbills.

I.

Petitioner Watchtower Bible and Tract Society of New York, Inc., coordinates the preaching activities of Jehovah's Witnesses throughout the United States and publishes Bibles and religious periodicals that are widely distributed. Petitioner Wellsville, Ohio, Congregation of Jehovah's Witnesses, Inc., supervises the activities of approximately 59 members in a part of Ohio that includes the Village of Stratton (Village). Petitioners offer religious literature without cost to anyone interested in reading it. They allege that they do not solicit contributions or orders for the sale of merchandise or services, but they do accept donations. . . .

Section 116.01 [of the Village ordinance] prohibits "canvassers" and others from "going in and upon" private residential property for the purpose of promoting any "cause" without first having obtained a permit pursuant to §116.03. That section provides that any canvasser who intends to go on private property to promote a cause, must obtain a "Solicitation Permit" from the office of the mayor; there is no charge for the permit, and apparently one is issued routinely after an applicant fills out a fairly detailed "Solicitor's Registration Form." The canvasser is then authorized to go upon premises that he listed on the registration form, but he must carry the permit upon his person and exhibit it whenever requested to do so by a police officer or by a resident. . . .

A section of the ordinance that petitioners do not challenge establishes a procedure by which a resident may prohibit solicitation even by holders of permits. If the resident files a "No Solicitation Registration Form" with the mayor, and also posts a "No Solicitation" sign on his property, no uninvited canvassers may enter his property, unless they are specifically authorized to do so in the "No Solicitation Registration Form" itself. Only 32 of the Village's 278 residents filed such forms.

Each of the forms in the record contains a list of 19 suggested exceptions;[6] on one form, a resident checked 17 exceptions, thereby excluding only "Jehovah's Witnesses" and "Political Candidates" from the list of invited canvassers. Although Jehovah's Witnesses do not consider themselves to be "solicitors" because they make no charge for their literature or their teaching, leaders of the church testified at trial that they would honor "no solicitation" signs in the Village. They also explained at trial that they did not apply for a permit because they derive their authority to preach from Scripture. "For us to seek a permit from a municipality to preach we feel would almost be an insult to God." . . .

The District Court upheld most provisions of the ordinance as valid, content-neutral regulations that did not infringe on petitioners' First Amendment rights. The court did, however, require the Village to accept narrowing constructions of three provisions. First, the court viewed the requirement in §116.03(b)(5) that the applicant must list the specific address of each residence to be visited as potentially invalid, but cured by the Village's agreement to attach to the form a list of willing residents. 61 F. Supp. 2d 734, 737 (S.D. Ohio 1999). Second, it held that petitioners could comply with §116.03(b)(6) by merely stating their purpose as "the Jehovah's Witness ministry." *Id.* at 738. And third, it held that §116.05, which limited canvassing to the hours before 5 P.M., was invalid on its face and should be replaced with a provision referring to "reasonable hours of the day." *Id.* at 739. As so modified, the court held the ordinance constitutionally valid as applied to petitioners and dismissed the case.

The Court of Appeals for the Sixth Circuit affirmed. . . .

III.

The Village argues that three interests are served by its ordinance: the prevention of fraud, the prevention of crime, and the protection of residents' privacy. We have no difficulty concluding, in light of our precedent, that these are important interests that the Village may seek to safeguard through some form of regulation of solicitation activity. We must also look, however, to the amount of speech covered by

---

6. The suggested exceptions listed on the form are:

1. in Scouting Organizations
2. Camp Fire Girls
3. Children's Sports Organizations
4. Children's Solicitation for Supporting School Activities
5. Volunteer Fire Dept.
6. Jehovah's Witnesses
7. Political Candidates
8. Beauty Products Sales People
9. Watkins Sales
10. Christmas Carolers
11. Parcel Delivery
12. Little League
13. Trick or Treaters during Halloween Season
14. Police
15. Campaigners
16. Newspaper Carriers
17. Persons Affiliated with Stratton Church
18. Food Salesmen
19. Salespersons.

Apparently the ordinance would prohibit each of these 19 categories from canvassing unless expressly exempted.

the ordinance and whether there is an appropriate balance between the affected speech and the governmental interests that the ordinance purports to serve.

The text of the Village's ordinance prohibits "canvassers" from going on private property for the purpose of explaining or promoting any "cause," unless they receive a permit and the residents visited have not opted for a "no solicitation" sign. Had this provision been construed to apply only to commercial activities and the solicitation of funds, arguably the ordinance would have been tailored to the Village's interest in protecting the privacy of its residents and preventing fraud. Yet, even though the Village has explained that the ordinance was adopted to serve those interests, it has never contended that it should be so narrowly interpreted. To the contrary, the Village's administration of its ordinance unquestionably demonstrates that the provisions apply to a significant number of noncommercial "canvassers" promoting a wide variety of "causes." Indeed, on the "No Solicitation Forms" provided to the residents, the canvassers include "Camp Fire Girls," "Jehovah's Witnesses," "Political Candidates," "Trick or Treaters during Halloween Season," and "Persons Affiliated with Stratton Church." The ordinance unquestionably applies, not only to religious causes, but to political activity as well. It would seem to extend to "residents casually soliciting the votes of neighbors,"[12] or ringing doorbells to enlist support for employing a more efficient garbage collector.

The mere fact that the ordinance covers so much speech raises constitutional concerns. It is offensive — not only to the values protected by the First Amendment, but to the very notion of a free society — that in the context of everyday public discourse a citizen must first inform the government of her desire to speak to her neighbors and then obtain a permit to do so. Even if the issuance of permits by the mayor's office is a ministerial task that is performed promptly and at no cost to the applicant, a law requiring a permit to engage in such speech constitutes a dramatic departure from our national heritage and constitutional tradition. Three obvious examples illustrate the pernicious effect of such a permit requirement.

First, . . . there are a significant number of persons who support causes anonymously.[14] "The decision to favor anonymity may be motivated by fear of economic or official retaliation, by concern about social ostracism, or merely by a desire to preserve as much of one's privacy as possible." McIntyre v. Ohio Elections Comm'n, 514 U.S. 334, 341-342 (1995). The requirement that a canvasser must be identified in a permit application filed in the mayor's office and available for public inspection necessarily results in a surrender of that anonymity. Although it is true, as the Court of Appeals suggested, see 240 F.3d, at 563, that persons who are known to the resident reveal their allegiance to a group or cause when they present themselves at the front door to advocate an issue or to deliver a handbill, the Court of Appeals erred in concluding that the ordinance does not implicate anonymity interests. The Sixth Circuit's reasoning is undermined by our decision in Buckley v. American Constitutional Law Foundation, Inc., 525 U.S. 182 (1999). The badge requirement that we invalidated in *Buckley* applied to petition circulators seeking signatures in face-to-face interactions. The fact that circulators revealed their physical identities did not foreclose our consideration of the circulators' interest in maintaining their

---

12. Hynes [v. Mayor and Council of Oradell], 425 U.S. [610], at 620, n.4 [1976].

14. Although the Jehovah's Witnesses do not themselves object to a loss of anonymity, they bring this facial challenge in part on the basis of overbreadth. We may, therefore, consider the impact of this ordinance on the free speech rights of individuals who are deterred from speaking because the registration provision would require them to forgo their right to speak anonymously. See Broadrick v. Oklahoma, 413 U.S. 601, 612 (1973).

anonymity. In the Village, strangers to the resident certainly maintain their anonymity, and the ordinance may preclude such persons from canvassing for unpopular causes. Such preclusion may well be justified in some situations — for example, by the special state interest in protecting the integrity of a ballot-initiative process, *see ibid.*, or by the interest in preventing fraudulent commercial transactions. The Village ordinance, however, sweeps more broadly, covering unpopular causes unrelated to commercial transactions or to any special interest in protecting the electoral process.

Second, requiring a permit as a prior condition on the exercise of the right to speak imposes an objective burden on some speech of citizens holding religious or patriotic views. As our World War II–era cases dramatically demonstrate, there are a significant number of persons whose religious scruples will prevent them from applying for such a license. There are no doubt other patriotic citizens, who have such firm convictions about their constitutional right to engage in uninhibited debate in the context of door-to-door advocacy, that they would prefer silence to speech licensed by a petty official.

Third, there is a significant amount of spontaneous speech that is effectively banned by the ordinance. A person who made a decision on a holiday or a weekend to take an active part in a political campaign could not begin to pass out handbills until after he or she obtained the required permit. Even a spontaneous decision to go across the street and urge a neighbor to vote against the mayor could not lawfully be implemented without first obtaining the mayor's permission. . . .

The breadth and unprecedented nature of this regulation does not alone render the ordinance invalid. Also central to our conclusion that the ordinance does not pass First Amendment scrutiny is that it is not tailored to the Village's stated interests. Even if the interest in preventing fraud could adequately support the ordinance insofar as it applies to commercial transactions and the solicitation of funds, that interest provides no support for its application to petitioners, to political campaigns, or to enlisting support for unpopular causes. The Village, however, argues that the ordinance is nonetheless valid because it serves the two additional interests of protecting the privacy of the resident and the prevention of crime.

With respect to the former, it seems clear that §107 of the ordinance, which provides for the posting of "No Solicitation" signs and which is not challenged in this case, coupled with the resident's unquestioned right to refuse to engage in conversation with unwelcome visitors, provides ample protection for the unwilling listener. *Schaumburg,* 444 U.S., at 639, 1 ("[T]he provision permitting homeowners to bar solicitors from their property by posting [no solicitation] signs . . . suggest[s] the availability of less intrusive and more effective measures to protect privacy"). The annoyance caused by an uninvited knock on the front door is the same whether or not the visitor is armed with a permit.

With respect to the latter, it seems unlikely that the absence of a permit would preclude criminals from knocking on doors and engaging in conversations not covered by the ordinance. They might, for example, ask for directions or permission to use the telephone, or pose as surveyers or census takers. Or they might register under a false name with impunity because the ordinance contains no provision for verifying an applicant's identity or organizational credentials. Moreover, the Village did not assert an interest in crime prevention below, and there is an absence of any evidence of a special crime problem related to door-to-door solicitation in the record before us. . . .

The judgment of the Court of Appeals is reversed, and the case is remanded for further proceedings consistent with this opinion.

Justice BREYER, with whom Justice SOUTER and Justice GINSBURG join, concurring. While joining the Court's opinion, I write separately to note that the dissent's "crime prevention" justification for this ordinance is not a strong one. For one thing, there is no indication that the legislative body that passed the ordinance considered this justification. Stratton did not rely on the rationale in the courts below. . . .

Justice SCALIA, with whom Justice THOMAS joins, concurring in the judgment. I concur in the judgment, for many but not all of the reasons set forth in the opinion for the Court. I do not agree, for example, that one of the causes of the invalidity of Stratton's ordinance is that some people have a religious objection to applying for a permit, and others (posited by the Court) "have such firm convictions about their constitutional right to engage in uninhibited debate in the context of door-to-door advocacy, that they would prefer silence to speech licensed by a petty official." . . .

CHIEF JUSTICE REHNQUIST, dissenting. . . .

More than half a century ago we recognized that canvassers, "whether selling pots or distributing leaflets, may lessen the peaceful enjoyment of a home," and that "burglars frequently pose as canvassers, either in order that they may have a pretense to discover whether a house is empty and hence ripe for burglary, or for the purpose of spying out the premises in order that they may return later." Martin v. City of Struthers, 319 U.S. 141, 144 (1943). These problems continue to be associated with door-to-door canvassing, as are even graver ones.

A recent double murder in Hanover, New Hampshire, a town of approximately 7,500 that would appear tranquil to most Americans but would probably seem like a bustling town of Dartmouth College students to Stratton residents, illustrates these dangers. Two teenagers murdered a married couple of Dartmouth College professors, Half and Susanne Zantop, in the Zantops' home. Investigators have concluded, based on the confession of one of the teenagers, that the teenagers went door-to-door intent on stealing access numbers to bank debit cards and then killing their owners. *See Dartmouth Professors Called Random Targets*, Washington Post, Feb. 20, 2002, p. A2. Their *modus operandi* was to tell residents that they were conducting an environmental survey for school. They canvassed a few homes where no one answered. At another, the resident did not allow them in to conduct the "survey." They were allowed into the Zantop home. After conducting the phony environmental survey, they stabbed the Zantops to death. . . .

The double murder in Hanover described above is but one tragic example of the crime threat posed by door-to-door canvassing. Other recent examples include a man soliciting gardening jobs door-to-door who tied up and robbed elderly residents, *see* Van Derbken, *98-Year-Old Latest Victim in Series of Home Invasions*, San Francisco Chronicle, Sept. 13, 2000, p. A18, a door-to-door vacuum cleaner salesman who raped a woman, *see Employers Liable for Rape by Salesman*, Texas Lawyer, Jan. 11, 1999, p. 2, and a man going door-to-door purportedly on behalf of a church group who committed multiple sexual assaults, *see* Ingersoll, *Sex Crime Suspect Traveled with Church Group*, Wis. State Journal, Feb. 19, 2000, p. 1B. The Constitution does not require that Stratton first endure its own crime wave before it takes measures to prevent crime. . . .

The next question is whether the ordinance serves the important interests of protecting privacy and preventing fraud and crime. With respect to the interest in protecting privacy, the Court concludes that "[t]he annoyance caused by an uninvited knock on the front door is the same whether or not the visitor is armed with a permit." True, but that misses the key point: the permit requirement results in fewer uninvited knocks. Those who have complied with the permit requirement are less likely to visit residences with no trespassing signs, as it is much easier for the authorities to track them down. . . .

The ordinance prevents and detects serious crime by making it a crime not to register. Take the Hanover double murder discussed earlier. The murderers did not achieve their objective until they visited their fifth home over a period of seven months. If Hanover had a permit requirement, the teens may have been stopped before they achieved their objective. One of the residents they visited may have informed the police that there were two canvassers who lacked a permit. Such neighborly vigilance, though perhaps foreign to those residing in modern day cities, is not uncommon in small towns. Or the police on their own may have discovered that two canvassers were violating the ordinance. Apprehension for violating the permit requirement may well have frustrated the teenagers' objectives; it certainly would have assisted in solving the murders had the teenagers gone ahead with their plan.[3]

Notes and Questions

1. *Watchtower* on its surface is a First Amendment case, not a property case. You may be asking yourself why we put it in your property casebook. It's not a platform to get you to learn much about freedom of speech; due to its complexity that task must be reserved for your constitutional law course(s). For our purposes, *Watchtower* raises a basic question that transcends its First Amendment context: When and by what mechanisms should landowners be allowed to exclude, in advance, unannounced visitors?

The larger point is to see that property issues come up in many different legal settings. The meaning of property ownership is heavily shaped by the structure, norms, and rules of other legal subjects. The intersection between property and constitutional law is a prime example. This isn't the last time in this book that you'll encounter a case with constitutional dimensions.

2. We generally conceive of property rights as being defined by civil litigation. *Jacque* and *Adams* address the nature of a civil action of trespass. Yet in every state, trespass is also a crime. For many owners of the right to possess land (especially those who lack great wealth), the criminal law of trespass is much more important than the civil law of trespass. This is because when an owner orders someone to leave their property and that person refuses, the owner can call the police. When the police officer arrives, the typical outcome (assuming the officer believes the owner's story),

3. Indeed, an increased focus on apprehending criminals for "petty" offenses, such as not paying subway fares, is credited with the dramatic reduction in violent crimes in New York City during the last decade. *See, e.g.,* M. Gladwell, *The Tipping Point: How Little Things Can Make a Big Difference* (2000). If this works in New York City, surely it can work in a small village like Stratton.

is that the police orders the person to leave. Sometimes the officer makes an arrest, and sometimes the officer decides no warrant is necessary if the trespasser cooperates. Recall that in *Jacque,* the Wisconsin sheriff issued a criminal citation, for which Steenberg paid a modest $30 fine. In *Watchtower,* the Village made soliciting without a permit a criminal misdemeanor (in effect, criminal trespass).

Criminal trespass is defined more narrowly than civil trespass. Consider, for example, Texas Penal Code §30.05:

> *Criminal Trespass.* (a) A person commits an offense if he enters or remains on property, including an aircraft, of another without effective consent or he enters or remains in a building of another without effective consent and he:
>
>   (1) had notice that the entry was forbidden; or
>
>   (2) received notice to depart but failed to do so.
>
>   (b) For purposes of this section:
>
>   (1) "Entry" means the intrusion of the entire body. (2) "Notice" means:
>
>   (A) oral or written communication by the owner or someone with apparent authority to act for the owner;
>
>   (B) fencing or other enclosure obviously designed to exclude intruders or to contain livestock;
>
>   (C) a sign or signs posted on the property or at the entrance to the building, reasonably likely to come to the attention of intruders, indicating that entry is forbidden. . . .

3. All the justices in *Watchtower* assume that an individual Stratton homeowner, apart from the ordinance, has the right to exclude all solicitors (religious, political, or commercial) by posting a "No Trespassing" or "No Soliciting" sign. Are they right? Should this be the rule?

If every individual can exclude the petitioners by advance notice, why can't they do this collectively by legislation? Did they just write the ordinance incorrectly? Can you think of a different ordinance that meets the majority's objections and accomplishes the residents' apparent objectives?

4. To what extent can Jehovah's Witnesses present their message to strangers without entering private residential property? Should the availability of alternative avenues of communication affect the owner's right to exclude? Are speakers allowed to present information at shopping malls? In the town square? At places of work? Public parks? On the sidewalks? Increasingly during the past 20 years, more and more residential communities in the United States are "gated," with all streets and sidewalks private rather than public. A security system excludes everyone except residents and invited guests. Ownership of a home in a gated community safeguards residents' privacy and reduces the risk of crime, including fraud, far more effectively than the Stratton ordinance struck down by the Court. Should Jehovah's Witnesses have the right to enter gated communities to seek to communicate with residents?

■ SOTELO v. DIRECTREVENUE, LLC

United States District Court for the Northern District of Illinois, 2005
384 F. Supp. 2d 1219

GETTLEMAN, District Judge. Plaintiff Stephen Sotelo filed a five-count putative class action complaint against defendants DirectRevenue, LLC ("DR"),

DirectRevenue Holdings, LLC ("DR Holdings"), and BetterInternet LLC ("BI") (collectively, "Direct Revenue"), and Byron Udell & Associates, Inc., d/b/a Accu-Quote ("AccuQuote") and aQuantive, Inc. ("aQuantive"), alleging that, without his consent, defendants caused software known as "spyware"[1] ("Spyware") to be downloaded onto his personal computer. Plaintiff alleges that Spyware tracked plaintiff's Internet use, invaded his privacy, and caused substantial damage to his computer. Plaintiff asserts various claims under Illinois law: trespass to personal property (Count I); consumer fraud (Count II); unjust enrichment (Count III); negligence (Count IV); and computer tampering (Count V). Plaintiff seeks injunctive relief and compensatory damages. . . .

For the reasons discussed herein, defendants' motions [to dismiss] are denied in part and granted in part.

FACTS

. . . Defendant AccuQuote, an Illinois corporation with its principal place of business in Wheeling, Illinois, sells life insurance on the Internet. Defendant aQuantive is a publicly traded Washington corporation headquartered in Seattle, Washington, that is a marketing company that acts as an advertising agent for companies that advertise their products on the Internet . . . .

Plaintiff alleges that DirectRevenue deceptively downloaded Spyware, distributed by BI, on thousands of computers. Spyware allows DirectRevenue and companies that employ its services to track a computer user's web browsing behavior in order to deliver targeted advertisements to that computer. For example, if a computer with Spyware views music-related Internet sites, Spyware sends a signal of the computer user's activity back to DirectRevenue, which then targets the computer with advertisements from music-related companies that have paid for access to the computer via Spyware. DirectRevenue claims access to 12,000,000 computers in the United States, and has attracted national media attention and criticism for its alleged misconduct in gaining and maintaining such access.[3] According to plaintiff, aQuantive and AccuQuote, or someone on their behalf, used Spyware to send advertisements to the computers.

DirectRevenue "secretly installs" Spyware by bundling it with other legitimate software that is available "free" on the Internet, such as games. When the computer user downloads and installs a game, he or she simultaneously, but unwittingly, downloads Spyware. "The computer users do not consent, let alone have knowledge," that Spyware is being installed on their computers because DirectRevenue has "deceptively caused" Spyware to download without the users' consent or knowledge. DirectRevenue has an agreement governing Spyware called the "BetterInternet End User License Agreement" ("EULA") that purports to inform a consumer

---

1. Plaintiff defines spyware, also referred to as "adware," as "computer software downloaded to an end-user's computer over the Internet, without consent, that permits the company who downloaded the software (i.e., the spyware company) to track, profile, and analyze a computer user's behavior, for the purpose of sending him or her targeted advertising, which the spyware company can place for its clients."

3. Plaintiff includes excerpts of an article from the December 12, 2004, issue of *Newsweek*, stating, "Industry watchers familiar with [DirectRevenue] say it has stooped as low as any of its rivals in the practices it uses to distribute its software." The article also asserts, "Consumer advocates familiar with the company charge that DirectRevenue has engaged in an array of unethical practices: it secretly installs its software onto computers, designs its adware so that it reinstalls after users delete it and has changed its name so often that frustrated users can't find the company to complain."

that Spyware will be installed, computer use will be monitored, and the computer will receive targeted advertisements.

According to plaintiff, DirectRevenue installs Spyware in at least three different ways to avoid showing the EULA to computer users. First, for computers with Microsoft settings set to "low," Spyware automatically installs when a user downloads a free software program. These users are "never even shown the [EULA], told of its existence, or advised of the need for any sort of licensing." Second, computer users who have Microsoft Windows' Service Pack 2 (a security feature) installed on their computers receive a pop-up dialog box as the Spyware is being downloaded. The message in the dialogue box is an "unintelligible" incomplete sentence, refers only to "'the software,' rather than a bona fide program name," and asks the user to click "Install" or "Don't Install." There is no disclosure that the software being downloaded includes Spyware. There is a link to the EULA, but users are not asked to click on the link, advised of the availability of the EULA, or asked to agree to the EULA. Third, Internet users without Microsoft Windows Service Pack 2 are asked to agree to a "Consumer Policy Agreement," but not to the EULA, and there is no such policy available on DirectRevenue's website or elsewhere for computer users to review.

According to plaintiff, Spyware is designed to be difficult to remove from a computer once it is installed. DirectRevenue engages "in a uniformly deceptive course of conduct" to prevent users from removing Spyware after it is installed, including changing its name to prevent disgruntled computer users from complaining and altering the Spyware file names so that anti-Spyware programs and computer technicians cannot locate and remove it. DirectRevenue uses misleading aliases in an effort to deceive consumers including: BestOffers, BetterInternet, Ceres, LocalNRD, MSView, MultiMPP, MXTarget, OfferOptimizer, and Twaintec. The EULA, if users ever see it, directs users who want to remove Spyware from their computers to a website address, http://mypctuneup.com/contacts.php. However, at the time of the complaint, the link did not connect to a web page, and no such site could be found. If a user attempts to use the "add or remove programs" feature to remove the legitimate software to which Spyware was bundled, Spyware "unbundles" and remains on the computer.

Through Spyware, advertisers and advertising agents, including aQuantive and AccuQuote, have access to millions of computers for their targeted advertising. These advertisers, or companies they have hired to advertise on their behalf, bombard users' computers with ads that constantly "pop up" over whatever web page a user is viewing. The pop-up advertisements are sent in a manner that breaches the security of affected computers by bypassing commonly-used software designed to block pop-ups. Once an advertisement is sent, it generally remains on the computer screen until the computer user actually closes the advertisement. Even after closing the advertisement, however, it is sent over and over again, and users receive many advertisements repeatedly. According to plaintiff, "*Newsweek* reported that Direct Revenue may have as many as 1.5 billion advertising impressions (i.e., pop-ups) per month."

Plaintiff alleges that Spyware wreaks havoc on a computer and its user. Spyware destroys other software programs, and Spyware and the unsolicited advertisements that clog the screen cause computers to slow down, deplete Internet bandwidth and the computer's memory, and use pixels and screen-space on monitors. Productivity is decreased because hours are wasted attempting to remove Spyware from computers, closing recurring and frequent advertisements, and waiting for slowed machines. Users are forced to keep their slowed computers running longer, which uses more electricity, decreases the useful life of a computer, and forces the user to incur increased Internet access charges. It costs approximately $30 per year to purchase software to effectively remove Spyware and unwanted advertisements, and to guard against future infections. . . .

TRESPASS TO PERSONAL PROPERTY (COUNT I)

Count I asserts a claim for trespass to personal property/chattels against all defendants. Defendants argue in three separate motions to dismiss that Count I fails to state a claim upon which relief may be granted because plaintiff fails to plead causation and damages as required to state a trespass to personal property claim . . . .

AQuantive cites several cases that equate trespass to personal property with conversion, which has been addressed more frequently by modern courts. *See, e.g.*, Minuti v. Johnson, 2003 WL 260705, at *4 (N.D. Ill. Feb. 5, 2003) (equating the elements of trespass to chattels with conversion[8] where defendant maintained possession of property). AQuantive argues that plaintiff in the instant case fails to allege that he made any demand for or was refused the return of his property, which is an element of a conversion claim. The court agrees with plaintiff, however, that the two causes of action are distinct in cases such as this, where plaintiff does not allege his property is in defendant's possession or has been rendered entirely worthless, but rather that it was interfered with. *See* CompuServe Inc. v. Cyber Promotions, Inc., 962 F. Supp. 1015, 1022 (S.D. Ohio 1997) ("A plaintiff can sustain an action for trespass to chattels, as opposed to an action for conversion, without showing a substantial interference with its right to possession of that chattel."). The question, then, is whether plaintiff has sufficiently pled the elements of trespass to personal property.

In recent years, trespass to personal property, which had been largely relegated to a historical note in legal textbooks, has reemerged as a cause of action in Internet advertising and e-mail cases. A series of federal district court decisions, beginning with *CompuServe, Inc.*, has approved the use of trespass to personal property as a theory of liability for "spam e-mails" sent to an Internet service provider ("ISP") based upon evidence that the vast quantities of spam e-mail overburdened the ISP's own computer and made the entire computer system harder to use for computer users, the ISP's consumers. *E.g.*, America Online, Inc. v. IMS, 24 F. Supp. 2d 548 (E.D. Va. 1998); Hotmail Corp. v. Van$ Money Pie Inc., 1998 WL 388389 (N.D. Cal. Apr.16, 1998).

Although the above cases do not apply Illinois law, the law regarding trespass to personal property applied is substantially similar to that used in Illinois, and the courts' reasoning is applicable to the instant case. Defendants' attempt to distinguish these cases on the basis that the plaintiffs were ISP's, not individual computers users like plaintiff in the instant case, is unpersuasive. The elements of trespass to personal property — interference and damage ? do not hinge on the identity of the plaintiff, and the cause of action may be asserted by an individual computer user

---

8. The elements of a conversion claim are: (1) defendant's unauthorized and wrongful assumption of control; (2) plaintiff's right in the property; (3) plaintiff's right to immediate possession; and (4) plaintiff's demand for possession.

who alleges unauthorized electronic contact with his computer system that causes harm, such as Spyware . . . .

Plaintiff's allegations in the instant case reflect the frustration of many computer users, and are analogous to harms alleged by the ISP plaintiffs in the *CompuServe* line of cases. Simply put, plaintiff alleges that Spyware interfered with and damaged his personal property, namely his computer and his Internet connection, by overburdening their resources and diminishing their functioning. . . .

AccuQuote and aQuantive . . . argue that plaintiff fails to allege that they caused actual damage to his property. Several of the cases cited by aQuantive in support of this argument, however, are largely inapposite because they are summary judgment rulings. *See* Pearl Investments, LLC v. Standard I/O, Inc., 257 F. Supp. 2d 326, 354 (D. Me. 2003) (no evidence that defendant's unauthorized access to computer network impaired its condition, quality, or value); Intel Corp. v. Hamidi, 71 P.3d 296 (Cal. 2003) (no evidence that employee who sent six e-mail messages to several thousand employees over a two-year period impaired the system in any way). The only dismissal cited by aQuantive, DirecTV, Inc. v. Chin, 2003 WL 22102144, at *2 (W.D. Tex. Aug. 26, 2003), also cited by AccuQuote, is not binding on this court and is distinguishable. The *DirecTV* court dismissed the counter-plaintiff's trespass to chattels claim where he alleged generally that "on more than one occasion," he expended "time and resources" to delete pop-up advertisements from the counter-defendant, holding that the counter-plaintiff alleged "no facts" supporting damage. *Id.* In the instant case, by contrast, plaintiff has alleged that the advertisements caused significantly more injury than occasional wasted time and resources, as discussed above, and his pleading provides more specific details than the scant allegations in *DirecTV.*

AccuQuote and aQuantive also assert that because each individual advertisement can be closed by the computer user as it appears, they cannot cause any actionable injury. This argument ignores the reality of computer and Internet use, and plaintiff's allegation that part of the injury is the cumulative harm caused by the volume and frequency of the advertisements. The fact that a computer user has the ability to close each pop-up advertisement as it appears does not necessarily mitigate the damages alleged by plaintiff, which include wasted time, computer security breaches, lost productivity, and additional burdens on the computer's memory and display capabilities. Although plaintiff does not allege that AccuQuote and aQuantive are responsible for every pop-up advertisement that he has received, he alleges that they caused at least some of the estimated 1.5 billion advertising impressions generated by DirectRevenue per month, a portion of which were received by his computer. Indeed, AccuQuote admits that a marketing agency it employed placed what it describes as an "insignificant portion" of its advertisements through companies such as DirectRevenue. Questions of fact regarding how many, if any, of these advertisements caused the harms alleged by plaintiff are for a summary judgment motion or trial. At this stage in the litigation, plaintiff has sufficiently alleged that he was damaged by the alleged trespasses of AccuQuote and aQuantive on his computer.

Accordingly, the court denies the motions to dismiss Count I . . . .

[The court granted the motion to dismiss Count III (unjust enrichment) and denied the motions to dismiss the other counts alleging consumer fraud, negligence, and computer tampering.]

Notes and Questions

1. If Stephen Sotelo proves his allegations, what relief should he be entitled to? Do you find pop-up advertisements highly annoying? Are they a legitimate source of revenue for websites, the same as presenting commercials to TV viewers and radio listeners?

2. Since the 1997 *CompuServe* decision, spam e-mail has grown exponentially. Software developers have spent millions developing sophisticated spam filters, designed to keep spam out of users' mailboxes. Not surprisingly, spam senders are also clever people. As of today, the best spam filters are both under-inclusive and over-inclusive. They fail to block significant quantities of spam, and they filter out some e-mail messages (usually addressed to groups) that recipients want to receive. The technology "war" between spam senders and spam killers represents a market solution to the competing claims of spam advertisers, ISPs, and spam recipients. The *CompuServe* trespass decision, in contrast, is one type of regulatory approach, based on common law. Obviously, other types of regulatory approaches, including legislation, are possible. What type of approach is preferable?

3. How does the measure of damages for trespass to chattels compare to that awarded for trespass to land? For trespass to chattels, the owner traditionally recovers only for actual harm, typically measured by reduction in value, cost to repair, or loss in use. But a California court upheld a jury verdict for damages for mental suffering when the plaintiffs' dog, a miniature pinscher named Romeo, was struck with a bat by an irate neighbor. Plotnik v. Meihaus, 146 Cal. Rptr. 3d 585 (Ct. App. 2012) (plaintiffs also recovered for $2,600 veterinary bill to mend dog's leg).

C. ADVERSE POSSESSION

A person in wrongful possession of property is liable to the true owner. For land, the owner may bring a trespass action. For personal property, the owner may sue the converter in replevin or trover. All states have statutes of limitation, which require the owner to bring any such action within a specified period of time. The doctrine of adverse possession is based upon the running of that statute. It determines when the statute of limitations has expired, so that the owner is barred from filing an action; and it describes the status of property rights in the object after expiration of the statute. Land, instead of personal property, is the major setting for the law of adverse possession. The first five cases in this section address adverse possession of land, and the final case addresses personal property. While adverse possession of land generates a steady caseload for the courts, with thousands of reported opinions on the books, litigated cases involving personal property are rare. In many American states, there are no reported decisions at all.

One focal point of these materials is the relationship between adverse possession and the recording system for real property. Thus, it is important at the outset that you know something about the recording system (we explore the recording system in more detail in Chapter 10). All states maintain public records that reflect ownership claims to land. Every state has its own recording acts. These acts vary considerably from state to state, but they have a number of common features. The primary function of the recording system is title assurance. The recording system provides a method for determining who owns a tract of land — Blackacre, for example. The filed instruments are public records, which anyone may search and read. If *B* has contracted to buy Blackacre from *A*, typically *B* will not take *A*'s word that he in fact owns Blackacre, even if *A* is willing to give promises of good title (when set forth in a deed, such promises are called warranties). Instead, *B* will hire someone (usually an attorney or another title professional) to check the public records to confirm *A*'s claim of good title to Blackacre. The search may reveal any number of title defects: for example, outstanding mortgages or tax liens, easements, future interests such as rights of entry held by third parties; that third parties are cotenants; or in the worst case, that *A* has no record title at all.

As a system for title assurance, the protection afforded by recording acts is not foolproof. A strength of the recording system is that recording is cheap and easy; no public official needs to read and evaluate the legal significance of the instruments presented for recordation. This virtue, however, has spawned a major vice. Unlike the game Monopoly, where you either have the deed to Boardwalk or you don't, there is no single piece of paper or "deed" to Blackacre that is dispositive by itself. The entire set of recorded documents is only evidence of title — evidence that is often difficult for even the trained professional to assess. Due to a number of pitfalls in the system, the title searcher can obtain only probable answers as to the ownership of Blackacre. At best, this may be a high probability, but there will be a chance that other persons have valid claims to Blackacre even though their interests cannot be discovered by a competent title search.

With respect to the quality of the public records, adverse possession is a double-edged sword. Adverse possession strengthens record titles by barring potential claims of persons who are not in possession of a parcel of land after a specified period of time has elapsed, provided that certain conditions are met. By extinguishing old nonpossessory claims, this body of law helps to overcome some of the infirmities generated by our system of land transfer. The title-clearing function of adverse possession generally applies to entire parcels of land. Usually the litigants are the present possessor and claimants whose alleged interests lie somewhere back in the record chain of title.

The other edge of the sword impairs record titles in the context of neighboring landowners. Often neighbors encounter disputes as to the proper location of the boundary lines that separate their parcels. Boundary disputes may be of great economic significance to these neighbors, especially when one of them has made valuable improvements to the land under the erroneous belief of ownership. In this context, the law of adverse possession often modifies the true boundary line, reflected by deeds and other records, to conform to the parties' long-standing possession and use. You might ask yourself whether, on balance, adverse possession strengthens or weakens the recording system. How could one tell?

■ **TRAN v. MACHA**
Supreme Court of Texas, 2006
213 S.W.3d 913

PER CURIAM. Neighboring relatives shared the use of a driveway for many years, thinking it belonged to one of them when in fact it belonged to the other. The court of appeals held this mutual mistake and mutual use transferred title by adverse possession. We disagree, and thus reverse.

In the 1920s, land on what is now Case Street in the City of West University Place in Harris County was subdivided into lots 55 feet wide. But during construction in the 1930s and '40s, several houses were built on the mistaken assumption that the lots were only 50 feet wide. As a result, each house was increasingly shifted to the east side of its lot, until the house on Lot 5 was built next to that lot's eastern boundary with Lot 6. This case concerns a driveway built on a 20-foot strip of land just east of that boundary — a strip everyone assumed was on Lot 5, but was actually on Lot 6.

When Lillian Haliburton bought Lot 5 in 1970, Lot 6 was owned by her brother's family, the Buddes. For many years, both families used the driveway on the disputed strip. The driveway led to a garage built on both lots, which Haliburton used for parking and storage. Although Haliburton was no longer living at the time of trial, there was testimony that family members all presumed mistakenly that the driveway and garage belonged to her Lot 5.

In 1995, the Buddes sold Lot 6 to the defendants, Minh Thu Tran and Norman L. Roser. In 2001, Haliburton sold Lot 5 to the plaintiffs, William and Nita Macha, who already owned Lot 4 to the west. During the latter transaction, a survey revealed that the driveway was not a part of Lot 5, so the Machas secured a quitclaim deed conveying any interest Haliburton might have acquired in the strip by adverse possession. When Tran and Roser learned of the survey, they obtained a permit and erected a fence around the strip. This suit ensued.

A jury found the strip had passed by adverse possession to Haliburton, and thence to the Machas. The First Court of Appeals affirmed, holding in a divided opinion that Haliburton's use of the strip and everyone's mistaken belief that she owned it were legally sufficient evidence of adverse possession. *See* 176 S.W.3d 128 (Tex. App. — Houston [1st Dist.] 2004). We disagree.

Under Texas law, adverse possession requires "an actual and visible appropriation of real property, commenced and continued under a claim of right that is inconsistent with and is hostile to the claim of another person." Tex. Civ. Prac. & Rem. Code §16.021(1). The statute requires visible appropriation; mistaken beliefs about ownership do not transfer title until someone acts on them. Thus, there must be adverse *possession*, not just adverse *beliefs*.

The statute requires that such possession be "inconsistent with" and "hostile to" the claims of all others. Joint use is not enough, because "possession must be of such character as to indicate *unmistakably* an assertion of a claim of exclusive ownership in the occupant." Rhodes v. Cahill, 802 S.W.2d 643, 645 (Tex. 1990) (emphasis in original). Here, Haliburton shared use of the strip with the Buddes, so her use was not inconsistent with or hostile to their ownership.

The court of appeals held that Haliburton adversely possessed the strip by building a driveway and garage on it. But nothing in the record shows she did either. To the contrary, both were in place before she bought Lot 5, and nothing shows who built them or when. We agree that building a structure on property may be sufficient evidence of adverse possession. But the record here shows only that Haliburton *used* the driveway and garage, not that she *built* them.

The court of appeals also held that "adverse possession need not be intentional, so long as it is visible, open, and notorious." 176 S.W.3d at 133. It is true that "hostile" use does not require an intention to dispossess the rightful owner, or even know that there is one. But there must be an intention to claim property as one's own to the exclusion of all others; "[m]ere occupancy of land without any intention to appropriate it will not support the statute of limitations." Ellis v. Jansing, 620 S.W.2d 569, 571 (Tex. 1981). Here, there is no evidence Haliburton ever intended to exclude the Buddes, or that they used the driveway only with her express permission.

It may seem harsh that adverse possession rewards only those who believe "good fences make good neighbors,"[1] and not those who are happy to share. But the doctrine itself is a harsh one, taking real estate from a record owner without express consent or compensation. Before taking such a severe step, the law reasonably requires that the parties' intentions be very clear.

Accordingly, without hearing oral argument, we reverse the court of appeals' judgment and render judgment for the defendants.

■ HOWARD v. KUNTO

Court of Appeals of Washington, 1970
477 P.2d 210

PEARSON, Judge. Land surveying is an ancient art but not one free of the errors that often creep into the affairs of men. In this case, we are presented with the question of what happens when the descriptions in deeds do not fit the land the deed holders are occupying. Defendants appeal from a decree quieting title in the plaintiffs of a tract of land on the shore of Hood Canal in Mason County.

At least as long ago as 1932 the record tells us that one McCall resided in the house now occupied by the appellant-defendants, Kunto. McCall had a deed that described a 50-foot-wide parcel on the shore of Hood Canal. The error that brings this case before us is that 50 feet described in the deed is not the same 50 feet upon which McCall's house stood. Rather, the described land is an adjacent 50-foot lot directly west of that upon which the house stood. In other words, McCall's house stood on one lot and his deed described the adjacent lot.[2] Several property owners to the west of defendants, not parties to this action, are similarly situated.

Over the years since 1946, several conveyances occurred, using the same legal description and accompanied by a transfer of possession to the succeeding occupants. The Kuntos' immediate predecessors in interest, Millers, desired to build a dock. To this end, they had a survey performed which indicated that the deed description and the physical occupation were in conformity. Several boundary stakes were placed as a result of this survey and the dock was constructed, as well as other improvements. The house as well as the others in the area continued to be used as summer recreational retreats.

---

1. Robert Frost, North of Boston, *Mending Wall* (1915):

There where it is we do not need the wall.
He is all pine and I am apple orchard.
My apple trees will never get across
And eat the cones under his pines, I tell him.
He only says, "Good fences make good neighbors."

2. Defendant's deed and chain of title purported to convey "The West fifty (50) feet of the East two hundred (200) feet of Government Lot two (2), Section nineteen (19); and the West fifty (50) feet of the East two hundred (200) feet of Government Lot one (1), Section thirty (30); all in Township twenty-two (22), North, of Range two (2) West, W.M.; . . ." The land defendants and their predecessors occupied, according to the survey, was the "West 50 feet of the east 150 feet of Government Lot 2, in Section 19, Township 22 North, of Range 2 West of W.M. . . ."

The Kuntos then took possession of the disputed property under a deed from the Millers in 1959. In 1960 the respondent-plaintiffs, Howard, who held land east of that of the Kuntos, determined to convey an undivided one-half interest in their land to the Yearlys. To this end, they undertook to have a survey of the entire area made. After expending considerable effort, the surveyor retained by the Howards discovered that according to the government survey, the deed descriptions and the land occupancy of the parties did not coincide. Between the Howards and the Kuntos lay the Moyers' property. When the Howards' survey was completed, they discovered that they were the record owners of the land occupied by the Moyers and that the Moyers held record title to the land occupied by the Kuntos. Howard approached Moyer and in return for a conveyance of the land upon which the Moyers' house stood, Moyer conveyed to the Howards record title to the land upon which the Kunto house stood. Until plaintiffs Howard obtained the conveyance from Moyer in April, 1960, neither Moyer nor any of his predecessors ever asserted any right to ownership of the property actually being possessed by Kunto and his predecessors. This action was then instituted to quiet title in the Howards and Yearlys. The Kuntos appeal from a trial court decision granting this remedy.

At the time this action was commenced on August 19, 1960, defendants had been in occupance of the disputed property less than a year. The trial court's reason for denying their claim of adverse possession is succinctly stated in its memorandum opinion: "In this instance, defendants have failed to prove, by a preponderance of the evidence, a continuity of possession or estate to permit tacking of the adverse possession of defendants to the possession of their predecessors."

Finding of fact 6,[4] which is challenged by defendants, incorporates the above concept and additionally finds defendant's possession not to have been "continuous" because it involved only "summer occupancy."

Two issues are presented by this appeal:

(1) Is a claim of adverse possession defeated because the physical use of the premises is restricted to summer occupancy?

(2) May a person who receives record title to tract A under the mistaken belief that he has title to tract B (immediately contiguous to tract A) and who subsequently occupies tract B, for the purpose of establishing title to tract B by adverse possession, use the periods of possession of tract B by his immediate predecessors who also had record title to tract A?

In approaching both of these questions, we point out that the evidence, largely undisputed in any material sense, established that defendant or his immediate

---

4. "In the instant case the defendants' building was not simply over the line, but instead was built wholly upon the wrong piece of property, not the property of defendants, described in Paragraph Four (4) of the complaint herein, but on the property of plaintiffs, described in Paragraph Three of the complaint and herein. That the last three deeds in the chain of title, covering and embracing defendants' property, including defendants' deed, were executed in other states, specifically, California and Oregon. And there is no evidence of pointing out to the grantees in said three deeds, aforesaid, including defendants' deed, of any specific property, other than the property of defendants, described in their deed, and in Paragraph Four (4) of the complaint, and herein; nor of any immediate act of the grantees, including defendants, in said three (3) deeds, aforesaid, of taking possession of any property, other than described in said three (3) deeds, aforesaid; and the testimony of husband, defendant, was unequivocally that he had no intention of possessing or holding anything other than what the deed called for; and, that there is no showing of any continuous possession by defendants or their immediate predecessors in interest, since the evidence indicates the property was in the nature, for use, as a summer occupancy, and such occupancy and use was for rather limited periods of time during comparatively short portions of the year, and was far from continuous."

predecessors did occupy the premises, which we have called tract *B*, as though it was their own for far more than the 10 years as prescribed in RCW 4.16.020.[5] ...

We start with the oft-quoted rule that "to constitute adverse possession, there must be actual possession which is *uninterrupted*, open and notorious, hostile and exclusive, and under a *claim of right* made in good faith for the statutory period." Butler v. Anderson, 426 P.2d 467, 470 (Wash. 1967) (italics ours).

We reject the conclusion that summer occupancy only of a summer beach home destroys the continuity of possession required by the statute. It has become firmly established that the requisite possession requires such possession and dominion "as ordinarily marks the conduct of owners in general in holding, managing, and caring for property of like nature and condition." Whalen v. Smith, 167 N.W. 646, 647 (Iowa 1918).

We hold that occupancy of tract *B* during the summer months for more than the 10-year period by defendant and his predecessors, together with the continued existence of the improvements on the land and beach area, constituted "uninterrupted" possession within this rule. To hold otherwise is to completely ignore the nature and condition of the property. ...

We now reach the question of tacking. The precise issue before us is novel in that none of the property occupied by defendant or his predecessors coincided with the property described in their deeds, but was contiguous.

In the typical case, which has been subject to much litigation, the party seeking to establish title by adverse possession claims *more* land than that described in the deed. In such cases it is clear that tacking is permitted.

In Buchanan v. Cassell, 335 P.2d 600, 602 (Wash. 1959) the Supreme Court stated: "This state follows the rule that a purchaser may tack the adverse use of its predecessor in interest to that of his own where the land was intended to be included in the deed between them, but was mistakenly omitted from the description."

The general statement which appears in many of the cases is that tacking of adverse possession is permitted if the successive occupants are in "privity." *See* Faubion v. Elder, 301 P.2d 153 (Wash. 1956). The deed running between the parties purporting to transfer the land possessed traditionally furnishes the privity of estate which connects the possession of the successive occupants. Plaintiff contends, and the trial court ruled, that where the deed does not describe *any* of the land which was occupied, the actual transfer of possession is insufficient to establish privity.

To assess the cogency of this argument and ruling, we must turn to the historical reasons for requiring privity as a necessary prerequisite to tacking the possession of several occupants. Very few, if any, of the reasons appear in the cases, nor do the cases analyze the relationships that must exist between successive possessors for tacking to be allowed. *See* W. Stoebuck, *The Law of Adverse Possession in Washington* in 35 Wash. L. Rev. 53 (1960).

---

5. This statute provides:

4.16.020 *Actions to be commenced within ten years.* The period prescribed in RCW 4.16.010 for the commencement of actions shall be as follows:
   Within ten years:
   Actions for the recovery of real property, or for the recovery of the possession thereof; and no action shall be maintained for such recovery unless it appears that the plaintiff, his ancestor, predecessor or grantor was seized or possessed of the premises in question within ten years before the commencement of the action.

The requirement of privity had its roots in the notion that a succession of trespasses, even though there was no appreciable interval between them, should not, in equity, be allowed to defeat the record title. The "claim of right" . . . requirement of the statutes and cases was probably derived from the early American belief that the squatter should not be able to profit by his trespass.[6]

However, it appears to this court that there is a substantial difference between the squatter or trespasser and the property purchaser, who along with several of his neighbors, as a result of an inaccurate survey or subdivision, occupies and improves property exactly 50 feet to the east of that which a survey some 30 years later demonstrates that they in fact own. It seems to us that there is also a strong public policy favoring early certainty as to the location of land ownership which enters into a proper interpretation of privity.

On the irregular perimeters of Puget Sound, exact determination of land locations and boundaries is difficult and expensive. This difficulty is convincingly demonstrated in this case by the problems plaintiff's engineer encountered in attempting to locate the corners. It cannot be expected that every purchaser will or should engage a surveyor to ascertain that the beach home he is purchasing lies within the boundaries described in his deed. Such a practice is neither reasonable nor customary. Of course, 50-foot errors in descriptions are devastating where a group of adjacent owners each hold 50 feet of waterfront property.

The technical requirement of "privity" should not, we think, be used to upset the long periods of occupancy of those who in good faith received an erroneous deed description. Their "claim of right" is no less persuasive than the purchaser who believes he is purchasing *more* land than his deed described.

In the final analysis, however, we believe the requirement of "privity" is no more than judicial recognition of the need for some reasonable connection between successive occupants of real property so as to raise their claim of right above the status of the wrongdoer or the trespasser. We think such reasonable connection exists in this case.

Where, as here, several successive purchasers received record title to tract A under the mistaken belief that they were acquiring tract B, immediately contiguous thereto, and where possession of tract B is transferred and occupied in a continuous manner for more than 10 years by successive occupants, we hold there is sufficient privity of estate to permit tacking and thus establish adverse possession as a matter of law.

We see no reason in law or in equity for differentiating this case from Faubion v. Elder, 301 P.2d 153 (Wash. 1956), where the appellants were claiming *more* land than their deed described and where successive periods of occupation were allowed to be united to each other to make up the time of adverse holding. . . . This application of the privity requirement should particularly pertain where the holder of record title to tract B acquired the same with knowledge of the discrepancy.

Judgment is reversed with directions to dismiss plaintiffs' action and to enter a decree quieting defendants' title to the disputed tract of land in accordance with the prayer of their cross-complaint.

---

6. The English common law does not require privity as a prerequisite for tacking. *See* F. Clark, *Law of Surveying and Boundaries*, §561 (3d ed. 1959) at 568.

Notes and Questions

1. *Howard* gives a standard list of the ingredients for adverse possession. The claimant's possession must be:

(a)   actual;
(b)   uninterrupted (or continuous);
(c)   open and notorious (or visible);
(d)   hostile (or adverse);
(e)   exclusive; and
(f)   under claim of right made in good faith.

All states require the first five elements, although as *Howard* and subsequent cases illustrate, there can be significant differences as to their meaning. There is controversy as to the last element — that the possession must be under "claim of right" and asserted in good faith. This bears on whether the adverse possessor must have a particular state of mind, a topic we address beginning in the next case. Some states have additional requirements, such as "color of title" or payment of taxes on the land.

Take a close look at the Washington statute of limitations, reproduced in footnote 5 of the court's opinion. What is the relationship between the statute and the court's six requirements?

2. Are the courts that decided *Tran* and *Howard* more concerned with the behavior of the adverse possessor or the true owner? In both cases, have the adverse possessors earned title? Have the true owners slept on their rights?

3. In *Tran*, the court called the doctrine of adverse possession "a harsh one" because it takes "real estate from a record owner without express consent or compensation." Should the law allow the transfer of title to property via adverse possession? Should the adverse possessor have to pay for the property? A British landowner lost title to a neighbor who had grazed the land for over 12 years without the owner's permission. The owner challenged the decision under the European Convention on Human Rights, which provides: "Every natural or legal person is entitled to the peaceful enjoyment of his possessions. No one shall be deprived of his possessions except in the public interest and subject to the conditions provided for by law and by the general principles of international law." Art. 1 of Protocol No. 1. The European Court of Human Rights held that the United Kingdom's adverse possession statutes violated this provision, but on appeal the Grand Chamber of that court reversed by a vote of 10 to 7. The majority concluded that the law's impact was to "control the use of land" rather than to effect a deprivation of possessions, and that the law "pursued a legitimate aim in the general interest." J. A. Pye (Oxford) Ltd v. United Kingdom, Application No. 44302/02 (Aug. 30, 2007).

■ MANNILLO v. GORSKI

Supreme Court of New Jersey, 1969
255 A.2d 258

HANEMAN, Justice. Plaintiffs [Fred and Alice Mannillo] filed a complaint in the Chancery Division seeking a mandatory and prohibitory injunction against an alleged trespass upon their lands. Defendant [Margaret Gorski] counterclaimed for a declaratory judgment which would adjudicate that she had gained title to the disputed premises by adverse possession under N.J.S. 2A:14-6, N.J.S.A., which provides: "Every person having any right or title of entry into real estate shall make such entry within 20 years next after the accrual of such right or title of entry, or be barred therefrom thereafter." After plenary trial, judgment was entered for plaintiffs. Mannillo v. Gorski, 241 A.2d 276 (N.J. Ch. Div. 1968). . . .

. . . In 1946, defendant and her husband entered into possession of premises in Keansburg known as Lot No. 1007 in Block 42, under an agreement to purchase. Upon compliance with the terms of said agreement, the seller conveyed said lands to them on April 16, 1952. Defendant's husband thereafter died. The property consisted of a rectangular lot with a frontage of 25 feet and a depth of 100 feet. Plaintiffs are the owners of the adjacent Lot 1008 in Block 42 of like dimensions, to which they acquired title in 1953.

In the summer of 1946 Chester Gorski, one of the defendant's sons, made certain additions and changes to the defendant's house. He extended two rooms at the rear of the structure, enclosed a screened porch on the front, and put a concrete platform with steps on the west side thereof for use in connection with a side door. These steps were built to replace existing wooden steps. In addition, a concrete walk was installed from the steps to the end of the house. In 1953, defendant raised the house. In order to compensate for the resulting added height from the ground, she modified the design of the steps by extending them toward both the front and the rear of the property. She did not change their width.

Defendant admits that the steps and concrete walk encroach upon plaintiffs' lands to the extent of 15 inches. She contends, however, that she has title to said land by adverse possession. N.J.S.A. 2A:14-6, quoted above. Plaintiffs assert contrawise that defendant did not obtain title by adverse possession as her possession was not of the requisite hostile nature. They argue that to establish title by adverse possession, the entry into and continuance of possession must be accompanied by an intention to invade the rights of another in the lands, i.e., a knowing wrongful taking. They assert that, as defendant's encroachment was not accompanied by an intention to invade plaintiffs' rights in the land, but rather by the mistaken belief that she owned the land, and that therefore an essential requisite to establish title by adverse possession, i.e., an intentional tortious taking, is lacking.

The trial court concluded that defendant had clearly and convincingly proved that her possession of the 15-inch encroachment had existed for more than 20 years before the institution of this suit and that such possession was "exclusive, continuous, uninterrupted, visible, notorious and against the right and interest of the true owner." There is ample evidence to sustain this finding except as to its visible and notorious nature, of which more hereafter. However, the judge felt impelled by existing New Jersey case law, holding as argued by plaintiffs above, to deny defendant's claim and entered judgment for plaintiffs. 241 A.2d at 282. The first issue before this Court is, therefore, whether an entry and continuance of possession under the mistaken belief that the possessor has title to the lands involved, exhibits the requisite hostile possession to sustain the obtaining of title by adverse possession.

The first detailed statement and acceptance by our then highest court, of the principle that possession as an element of title by adverse possession cannot be bottomed on mistake, is found in Folkman v. Myers, 115 A. 615 (N.J. E. & A. 1921), which embraced and followed that thesis as expressed in Myers v. Folkman, 99 A. 97 (N.J. Sup. Ct. 1916). It is not at all clear that this was the common law of this

State prior to the latter case. An earlier opinion, Davock v. Nealon, 32 A. 675 (N.J. Sup. Ct. 1895), held for an adverse possessor who had entered under the mistaken belief that he had title without any discussion of his hostile intent. However, the court in Myers v. Folkman, *supra* at p. 98, distinguished *Davock* from the case then under consideration by referring to the fact that "Charles R. Myers *disclaims* any intent to claim what did not belong to him, and apparently never asserted a right to land outside the bounds of his title. . . ." (Emphasis supplied.) The factual distinction between the two cases, according to *Myers*, is that in the later case there was not only an entry by mistake but also an articulated disclaimer of an intent by the entrant to claim title to lands beyond his actual boundary. *Folkman*, although apparently relying on *Myers*, eliminated the requirement of that decision that there be expressed an affirmative disclaimer, and expanded the doctrine to exclude from the category of hostile possessors those whose entry and continued possession was under a mistaken belief that the lands taken were embraced within the description of the possessor's deed. In so doing, the former Court of Errors and Appeals aligned this State with that branch of a dichotomy which traces its genesis to Preble v. Maine Cent. R. Co., 27 A. 149 (Me. 1893) and has become known as the Maine doctrine. In *Preble*, the court said at 27 A. at p. 150:

> There is every presumption that the occupancy is in subordination to the true title, and, if the possession is claimed to be adverse, the act of the wrongdoer must be strictly construed, and the character of the possession clearly shown. Roberts v. Richards, 24 A. 425 (Me. 1891). "The intention of the possessor to claim adversely," says Mellen, C.J., in Ross v. Gould, 5 Me. 204 (1828), "is an essential ingredient in disseisin." And in Worcester v. Lord, 56 Me. 265 (1868) the court says: "To make a disseisin in fact, there must be an intention on the part of the party assuming possession to assert title in himself." Indeed, the authorities all agree that this intention of the occupant to claim the ownership of land not embraced in his title is a necessary element of adverse possession; and in case of occupancy by mistake beyond a line capable of being ascertained this intention to claim title to the extent of the occupancy must appear to be absolute, and not conditional; otherwise the possession will not be deemed adverse to the true owner. It must be an intention to claim title to all land within a certain boundary on the face of the earth, whether it shall eventually be found to be the correct one or not. If, for instance, one in ignorance of his actual boundaries takes and holds possession by mistake up to a certain fence beyond his limits, upon the claim and in the belief that it is the true line, with the intention to claim title, and thus, if necessary, to acquire "title by possession" up to that fence, such possession, having the requisite duration and continuity, will ripen into title. Hitchings v. Morrison, 72 Me. 331 (1881), is a pertinent illustration of this principle.
>
> If, on the other hand, a party through ignorance, inadvertence, or mistake occupies up to a given fence beyond his actual boundary, because he believes it to be the true line, but has no intention to claim title to that extent if it should be ascertained that the fence was on his neighbor's land, an indispensable element of adverse possession is wanting. In such a case the intent to claim title exists only upon the condition that the fence is on the true line. The intention is not absolute, but provisional, and the possession is not adverse.

This thesis, it is evident, rewards the possessor who entered with a premeditated and predesigned "hostility" — the intentional wrongdoer, and disfavors an honest, mistaken entrant. 3 American Law of Property (Casner ed. 1952), §104, pp. 773, 785; Bordwell, Disseisin and Adverse Possession, 33 Yale L.J. 1, 154 (1923).

The other branch of the dichotomy relies upon French v. Pearce, 8 Conn. 439 (Conn. 1831). The court said in *Pearce* on the question of the subjective hostility of a possessor, at pp. 442, 445-46:

> Into the recesses of his (the adverse claimant's) mind, his motives or purposes, his guilt or innocence, no enquiry is made. . . .
>   The very nature of the act (entry and possession) is an assertion of his own title, and the denial of the title of all others. It matters not that the possessor was mistaken, and had he been better informed, would not have entered on the land.

The Maine doctrine has been the subject of much criticism in requiring a knowing wrongful taking. The criticism of the Maine and the justification of the Connecticut branch of the dichotomy is well stated in 6 Powell, *Real Property* (1969) ¶1015, pp. 725-28:

> Do the facts of his possession, and of his conduct as if he were the owner, make immaterial his mistake, or does such a mistake prevent the existence of the prerequisite claim of right? The leading case holding the mistake to be of no importance was French v. Pearce, decided in Connecticut in 1831. . . . This viewpoint has gained increasingly widespread acceptance. The more subjectively oriented view regards the "mistake" as necessarily preventing the existence of the required claim of right. The leading case on this position is Preble v. Maine Central R.R., decided in 1893. This position is still followed in a few states. It has been strongly criticized as unsound historically, inexpedient practically, and as resulting in better treatment for a ruthless wrongdoer than for the honest landowner. . . . On the whole the law is simplified, in the direction of real justice, by a following of the Connecticut leadership on this point.

. . . Our Appellate Division in Predham v. Holfester, 108 A.2d 458 (N.J. App. Div. 1954) although acknowledging that the Maine doctrine had been severely criticized felt obliged because of *stare decisis* to adhere thereto.

We are in accord with the criticism of the Maine doctrine and favor the Connecticut doctrine for the above quoted reasons. As far as can be seen, overruling the former rule will not result in undermining any of the values which *stare decisis* is intended to foster. The theory of reliance, a cornerstone of *stare decisis*, is not here apt, as the problem is which of two mistaken parties is entitled to land. Realistically, the true owner does not rely upon entry of the possessor by mistake as a reason for not seeking to recover possession. Whether or not the entry is caused by mistake or intent, the same result eventuates — the true owner is ousted from possession. In either event his neglect to seek recovery of possession, within the requisite time, is in all probability the result of a lack of knowledge that he is being deprived of possession of lands to which he has title.

Accordingly, we discard the requirement that the entry and continued possession must be accompanied by a knowing intentional hostility and hold that any entry and possession for the required time which is exclusive, continuous, uninterrupted, visible and notorious, even though under mistaken claim of title, is sufficient to support a claim of title by adverse possession.

However, this conclusion is not dispositive of the matter *sub judice*. Of equal importance, under the present factual complex, is the question of whether defendant's acts meet the necessary standard of "open and notorious" possession. It must not be forgotten that the foundation of so-called "title by adverse possession" is the failure of the true owner to commence an action for the recovery of the land involved, within the period designated by the statute of limitations. The justifications for the doctrine are aptly stated in 4 Tiffany, Real Property (3d ed. 1939) §1134, p. 406 as follows:

> The desirability of fixing, by law, a definite period within which claims to land must be asserted has been generally recognized, among the practical considerations in favor of such a policy being the prevention of the making of illegal claims after the evidence necessary to defeat them has been lost, and the interest which the community as a whole has in the security of title. The moral justification of the policy lies in the consideration that one who has reason to know that land belonging to him is in the possession of another, and neglects, for a considerable period of time, to assert his right thereto, may properly be penalized by his preclusion from thereafter asserting such right. It is, apparently, by reason of the demerit of the true owner, rather than any supposed merit in the person who has acquired wrongful possession of the land, that this possession, if continued for the statutory period, operates to debar the former owner of all right to recover the land.

In order to afford the true owner the opportunity to learn of the adverse claim and to protect his rights by legal action within the time specified by the statute, the adverse possession must be visible and notorious. In 4 Tiffany, *supra* (Supp. 1969, at 291), the character of possession for that purpose, is stated to be as follows:

> . . . it must be public and based on physical facts, including known and visible lines and boundaries. Acts of dominion over the land must be so open and notorious as to put an ordinarily prudent person on notice that the land is in actual possession of another. Hence, title may never be acquired by mere possession, however long continued, which is surreptitious or secret or which is not such as will give unmistakable notice of the nature of the occupant's claim.

Generally, where possession of the land is clear and unequivocal and to such an extent as to be immediately visible, the owner may be presumed to have knowledge of the adverse occupancy. . . . However, when the encroachment of an adjoining owner is of a small area and the fact of an intrusion is not clearly and self-evidently apparent to the naked eye but requires an on-site survey for certain disclosure as in urban sections where the division line is only infrequently delineated by any monuments, natural or artificial, such a presumption is fallacious and unjustified. *See* concurring opinion of Judge (now Justice) Francis in Predham v. Holfester, 108 A.2d 458, 463-64 (N.J. App. Div. 1954). The precise location of the dividing line is then ordinarily unknown to either adjacent owner and there is nothing on the land itself to show by visual observation that a hedge, fence, wall or other structure encroaches on the neighboring land to a minor extent. Therefore, to permit a presumption of notice to arise in the case of minor border encroachments not exceeding several feet would fly in the face of reality and require the true owner to be on constant alert for possible small encroachments. The only method of certain determination would be by obtaining a survey each time the adjacent owner undertook any improvement at or near the boundary, and this would place an undue and inequitable burden upon the true owner. Accordingly we hereby hold that no presumption of knowledge arises from a minor encroachment along a common boundary. In such a case, only where the true owner has actual knowledge thereof may it be said that the possession is open and notorious.

It is conceivable that the application of the foregoing rule may in some cases result in undue hardship to the adverse possessor who under an innocent and mistaken belief of title has undertaken an extensive improvement which to some extent encroaches on an adjoining property. In that event . . . equity may furnish relief. Then, if the innocent trespasser of a small portion of land adjoining a boundary line cannot without great expense remove or eliminate the encroachment, or such removal or elimination is impractical or could be accomplished only with great hardship, the true owner may be forced to convey the land so occupied upon payment of the fair value thereof without regard to whether the true owner had notice of the encroachment at its inception. Of course, such a result should eventuate only under appropriate circumstances and where no serious damage would be done to the remaining land as, for instance, by rendering the balance of the parcel unusable or no longer capable of being built upon by reason of zoning or other restrictions.

We remand the case for trial of the issues (1) whether the true owner had actual knowledge of the encroachment, (2) if not, whether plaintiffs should be obliged to convey the disputed tract to defendant, and (3) if the answer to the latter question is in the affirmative, what consideration should be paid for the conveyance. The remand, of course, contemplates further discovery and a new pretrial.

Notes and Questions

1. A large majority of states, like New Jersey after *Mannillo*, embrace the Connecticut doctrine, rejecting the Maine doctrine. Even Maine has abandoned the rule; in 1993, the Maine legislature passed a statute (Me. Rev. Stat. tit. 14, §810-A), which reads:

> *Mistake of boundary line establishes hostility.* If a person takes possession of land by mistake as to the location of the true boundary line and possession of the land in dispute is open and notorious, under claim of right, and continuous for the statutory period, the hostile nature of the claim is established and no further evidence of the knowledge or intention of the person in possession is required.

2. The *Mannillo* court's definition of "open possession" as requiring the true owner's actual knowledge of a minor boundary encroachment is innovative. Courts in other states generally define openness without regard to the true owner's state of mind, focusing only upon whether the object itself or the entry is visible. For example, under this approach a subsurface trespass is usually held to be unopen. *See* the famous cave case, Marengo Cave Co. v. Ross, 10 N.E.2d 917 (Ind. 1937) (owner of cave entrance, who took possession of cave and operated it as tourist attraction for 46 years, cannot gain adverse possession title to portion of cave lying under neighbor's land). Is the *Mannillo* openness rule sound? On remand, at what point in time is the trial court supposed to assess actual knowledge, and who is the true owner whose state of mind is relevant?

■ **ITT RAYONIER, INC. v. BELL**
Supreme Court of Washington, 1989
774 P.2d 6

PEARSON, Justice. ITT Rayonier, Inc. (ITT), plaintiff, instituted this action to quiet title to property situated in Clallam County. In addition, ITT prayed for damages for trespass and for the ejectment of defendant Arthur Bell. Bell answered, alleging ITT was not entitled to judgment in its favor by reason of Bell's adverse possession of the property for a period greater than the statutory period of 10 years. Additionally, Bell counter-claimed against ITT praying for judgment quieting title in Bell. On July 8, 1986, the trial court entered partial summary judgment, quieting title in favor of ITT. The Court of Appeals affirmed. ITT Rayonier, Inc. v. Bell, 752 P.2d 398 (Wash. App. 1988).

FACTS

In 1972, Arthur Bell purchased a houseboat moored near the mouth of the Big River in Swan Bay on Lake Ozette. The property that is the subject of this action is directly adjacent to that moorage and was purchased by ITT in 1947. ITT, as owner of record, has paid the property taxes on the land in question continuously since its purchase. Bell admits that he never purchased any of the property involved in this action. Additionally, he concedes that he has never maintained any "No Trespassing" signs on the property, nor has he ever denoted any boundary with a fence or any other markers. A very rough approximation of the amount of land in question is one-half of an acre. Bell testified that he regularly occupies his houseboat in the spring, summer, and fall, and visits only occasionally during the winter months.

Bell testified that at the time he purchased the houseboat, he believed the adjacent land was owned by the State. When asked whether it was his understanding that other people could use the property, his response was, "[a]ctually when I — no, not really. When I was there they — I didn't think somebody was going to come up and go camping right there. But I suppose if they tried to, I wouldn't have said anything to them."

According to further deposition testimony of Bell, at the time he purchased the houseboat it had been moored in the same location since approximately 1962. The houseboat was moored to the land initially via a cable, and subsequently via a rope tied to two trees. The record reveals that only the following structures have been situated on the property in question for the full statutory period: a woodshed that existed prior to Bell's purchase of the houseboat, a woodshed he began building in 1978, an abandoned sauna that has existed since 1973, and the remains of an outhouse built by Bell in 1972 that has occupied numerous sites on the property.

Other than 6 weeks in the summer of 1973, when the houseboat was moored in Boot Bay, approximately 2 miles from the disputed property, the houseboat has at all times been situated adjacent to the property both Bell and ITT presently claim.

Bell's deposition testimony further reveals that he was away from the property during the 1974-75, 1975-76, and 1976-77 school years, while he was teaching school in Nanana, Alaska. During the first and third winters, he allowed friends to use the houseboat occasionally. During the 1975-76 school term, he rented the houseboat for $30 per month. Bell returned to Lake Ozette each of the three summers, personally occupying his houseboat during those months.

Bell's houseboat is not the only one in the area. Two families, the Klocks and the Olesens, have co-owned a houseboat for approximately 20 years that floats adjacent to both Bell's houseboat and the disputed property. Mr. Klock, in a sworn affidavit, stated:

> When using the houseboat, I and my family have used the adjacent land for the purpose of digging a hole for an outhouse and for other minimal uses. I do not own the land

next to my houseboat but have used it permissively over the last twenty years. Arthur Bell has never attempted to exclude us from using the property nor has he attempted to claim the property as his own.

In addition, Mr. Olesen swore to an identical statement.

Gerald Schaefer, an employee of ITT, stated in his sworn affidavit that ITT owns 383,000 acres in eight counties in Washington State. Often ITT is absent from its land for long periods of time:

> In its normal management of its land, Rayonier often will not visit or use its lands for long periods of time. After property has been logged and planted, it is common for Rayonier not to visit the property for 15 years, at which point precommercial thinning occurs. After precommercial thinning, property is often left 30 to 35 years before timber becomes commercial. It is virtually impossible to patrol all of Rayonier's lands that are not undergoing logging operations.

ANALYSIS

The doctrine of adverse possession arose at law, toward the aim of serving specific public policy concerns, "that title to land should not long be in doubt, that society will benefit from someone's making use of land the owner leaves idle, and that third persons who come to regard the occupant as owner may be protected." Stoebuck, *Adverse Possession in Washington,* 35 Wash. L. Rev. 53 (1960).

In order to establish a claim of adverse possession, there must be possession that is: (1) open and notorious, (2) actual and uninterrupted, (3) exclusive, and (4) hostile. Chaplin v. Sanders, 676 P.2d 431, 434 (Wash. 1984). Possession of the property with each of the necessary concurrent elements must exist for the statutorily prescribed period of 10 years. RCW 4.16.020. As the presumption of possession is in the holder of legal title, the party claiming to have adversely possessed the property has the burden of establishing the existence of each element. Skansi v. Novak, 146 P. 160, 162 (Wash. 1915), overruled on other grounds, Chaplin v. Sanders, *supra.*

EXCLUSIVE POSSESSION

We are asked whether summary judgment against the defendant was proper based on the defendant's failure to establish his exclusive possession of the disputed property for the statutory period. . . .

Relying upon the deposition testimony of Bell and the affidavits of Klock and Olesen, the trial court held Bell had failed to establish that his possession of the property was exclusive. The Court of Appeals affirmed, holding Bell's shared use of the property with the Klocks and Olesens was not possession in the nature one would expect from an owner, and thus the exclusivity requirement had not been met:

> While possession of property by a party seeking to establish ownership of it by adverse possession need not be absolutely exclusive, "the possession must be of a type that would be expected of an owner. . . ." Bell's possession of the subject property is not of the type one would expect of an owner. The intrusion onto the land by Klock and Olesen cannot be said to be merely casual. The evidence shows that they moored their houseboat near the same property for a longer period than did Bell. During this period,

they used the property in question along with Bell. Bell's acquiescence in their use of the land cannot be described to be simply the attitude of a good neighbor. It shows, rather, that there was a shared occupation of land. This does not constitute the exclusive use of land necessary for adverse possession and, in our judgment, reasonable persons could not conclude otherwise.

The Court of Appeals decision is in accord with another recent case from that court. In Thompson v. Schlittenhart, 734 P.2d 48 (Wash. App. 1987), the court held that the exclusivity element was lacking because the alleged adverse possessor had shared the use of the disputed area.

Nevertheless, by pointing to specific instances of his own use of the property, Bell attempts to establish his exclusive possession. Unfortunately, such an approach logically fails to negate instances of use by others. As this court has held, specific instances of property usage merely provide evidence of possession:

> Evidence of *use* is admissible because it is ordinarily an indication of *possession*. It is possession that is the ultimate fact to be ascertained. Exclusive dominion over land is the essence of possession, and it can exist in unused land if others have been excluded therefrom. A fence is the usual means relied upon to exclude strangers and establish the dominion and control characteristic of ownership.

Wood v. Nelson, 358 P.2d 312, 313-14 (Wash. 1961).

Possession itself is established only if it is of such a character as a true owner would make considering the nature and location of the land in question. Young v. Newbro, 200 P.2d 975, 977 (Wash. 1948), overruled on other grounds, Chaplin v. Sanders, *supra*. As quoted in Wood v. Nelson, *supra*, use alone does not necessarily constitute possession. The ultimate test is the exercise of dominion over the land in a manner consistent with actions a true owner would take. Thus, Bell's burden was to establish specific acts of use rising to the level of exclusive, legal possession. Unfortunately, while Bell recited certain improvements he had made in the property, he failed to state definitively the length of their existence. Thus, the record reflects that only a woodshed, a partially built and then abandoned sauna, and an outhouse have existed on the property for the full 10 year statutory period. As the Court of Appeals correctly held, Bell's shared and occasional use of the property simply did not rise to the level of exclusive possession indicative of a true owner for the full statutory period. Accordingly, we affirm the Court of Appeals.

Good Faith

Having affirmed the trial court's partial summary judgment against Bell, the Court of Appeals nevertheless provided an alternative ground for its decision:

> [A]nother element of adverse possession is that the party seeking to acquire title to land by adverse possession must possess the land under a good faith claim of right. Bell concedes that at no time, prior to the time he claims his possession of the property ripened into title, did he believe that he had title to this property or any claim of right to it. . . .
>
> . . . Holding in this case, as a matter of law, that Bell did not raise a genuine issue of fact on the question of his good faith claim of right to the property is, in our judgment, consistent with *Chaplin*.

This portion of the Court of Appeals decision is in error.

In Chaplin v. Sanders, 676 P.2d at 432-33, this court unanimously held that the adverse possessor's "subjective belief whether the land possessed is or is not his own and his intent to dispossess or not dispossess another are irrelevant to a finding of hostility." In so doing, this court expressly overruled cases dating back to 1896.

The Court of Appeals reasoned that the *Chaplin* decision did not specifically do away with the good faith element of adverse possession, and stated, "the question of whether or not one acts in good faith is a question that can only be answered by making a judgment about the actor's subjective belief." In a footnote, the court noted, "to conclude otherwise . . . we would be encouraging . . . 'squatting.'"

As stated, the doctrine of adverse possession was formulated at law to protect both those who knowingly appropriated the land of others, and those who honestly held the property in the belief that it was their own. 3 Am. Jur. 2d Adverse Possession §142 (1986). Twenty-four years before *Chaplin*, Professor Stoebuck suggested this court should return to the original formulation of the adverse possession doctrine:

> Perhaps the reader will agree that the law would have been clearer and in the long run more useful to the people if Washington had never gone into the "subjective intent" business at all. . . . [T]he common law of England seems to have . . . had no such element to adverse possession. Adverse possession revolves around the character of possession, and it is difficult to see why a man's secret thoughts should have anything to do with it. Maybe the idea originated in a confusion of permission or agreement between owner and possessor with unilateral intent in the possessor's mind. Whatever the reason, the court could yet perform a service by doing away with any requirement of subjective intent, negative or affirmative. Since a man cannot by thoughts alone put himself in adverse possession, why should he be able to think himself out of it?

Stoebuck, *Adverse Possession in Washington*, 35 Wash. L. Rev. 53, 80 (1960).

Today, we reaffirm our commitment to the rule enunciated in Chaplin v. Sanders, *supra*:

> The "hostility/claim of right" element of adverse possession requires only that the claimant treat the land as his own as against the world throughout the statutory period. The nature of his possession will be determined solely on the basis of the manner in which he treats the property. His subjective belief regarding his true interest in the land and his intent to dispossess or not dispossess another is irrelevant to this determination. Under this analysis, permission to occupy the land, given by the true title owner to the claimant or his predecessors in interest, will still operate to negate the element of hostility. The traditional presumptions still apply to the extent that they are not inconsistent with this ruling.

Chaplin v. Sanders, 676 P.2d at 436.

Accordingly, good faith no longer constitutes an element of adverse possession. Thus, we affirm the Court of Appeals on the basis of Bell's failure to establish exclusive possession, and reverse the Court of Appeals' alternative holding that Bell failed to establish a good faith claim to the property.

■ HALPERN v. LACY INVESTMENT CORPORATION
Supreme Court of Georgia, 1989
379 S.E.2d 519

GREGORY, Justice. Lacy, a corporation, is the titleholder of a parcel of land which [Shirley] Halpern claims to own by adverse possession [under O.C.G.A §44-5-170, which requires possession for a period of 20 years]. A jury found against Halpern's adverse possession claim and in favor of Lacy's counterclaims for damages for slander of title and trespass and for expenses of litigation. Halpern appeals from the judgment entered on the verdict.

The main issue on appeal is whether a *claim of right* must be made in *good faith* in order to satisfy the claim of right element of adverse possession or if the claim of right requirement is fully met by a showing only of *hostile* possession.

The parcel of land in question is located at the rear of Halpern's residential lot and is part of a large tract titled in Lacy's name. The Halpern lot was purchased in 1959 and a residence constructed on it in 1960. There was evidence that at the time of construction the Halperns realized they would like the parcel in question to be a part of their backyard. Mr. Halpern, who is now deceased, offered to purchase the parcel from Lacy's predecessor in title but he refused to sell. Knowing they did not own the parcel, the Halperns caused it to be bulldozed, cleared and included as part of their yard. They have used it ever since.

The trial court charged the jury that adverse possession or title by prescription has four requirements. One of those, he said, is that possession must be accompanied by a good faith claim of right. He went on to charge the jury that a good faith claim of right may be evidenced by acts or conduct relating to the property which are inconsistent with the true owner's title. He went even further to charge that a rebuttable presumption of a good faith claim of right may arise out of the dominion one exercises over the property. But he drew the line there and refused to give Halpern's request to charge that hostile possession *is* the legal equivalent of a claim of right. Halpern contends the charge and refusal to charge constitute error but we hold the trial court was correct.

Halpern relies on Ewing v. Tanner, 193 S.E. 243, 247 (Ga. 1937), a dispute over the ownership of personal property, where this court held that hostile possession and claim of right "are, for all practical purposes, legal equivalents." She also brings to our attention Chancey v. Georgia Power Company, 233 S.E.2d 365, 366 (Ga. 1977), where we wrote that a claim of right will be presumed from the assertion of dominion.

We hold that the correct rule is that one must enter upon the land claiming in good faith the right to do so. To enter upon the land without any honest claim of right to do so is but a trespass and can never ripen into prescriptive title. In the language used in Hannah v. Kenny, 83 S.E.2d 1, 5 (1954), such a person is called a "squatter." Here there was evidence that the Halperns knew the parcel of land was owned by another yet they simply took possession when their offer to purchase was declined. There was evidence to support a finding that this possession never changed its character.

One may maintain hostile possession of land in good faith. We construe that to be the meaning of *Ewing* in its assertion that hostile possession and claim of right are legal equivalents for all practical purposes. The holding is that most who have hostile possession of land do so with a good faith claim of right and therefore a jury or other factfinder may, in the absence of a contrary showing, infer from hostile possession that it is done in good faith that a claim of right exists. As the trial court instructed the jury, the requirement of good faith claim of right may be evidenced by acts in relation to the property inconsistent with the true owner's title. Hostile possession is such an act. *Ewing* will not be construed to hold that good faith is not required. A similar construction of *Chancey* is given.

[The court affirmed the award of attorneys' fees against Halpern.]

Judgment affirmed.

Notes and Questions

1. Would Mrs. Halpern have prevailed in Washington under the principles set forth in *ITT Rayonier?* Just as most courts refuse to look at the state of mind of the adverse possessor in the mistaken boundary context (preferring the Connecticut rule to the Maine rule), most courts refuse to ask whether the claimant was an intentional trespasser or a good faith trespasser.

2. Colorado and New York both amended their adverse possession statutes in 2008 to impose a good faith requirement, both in response to judicial decisions granting title to knowing trespassers. The New York statute now requires the adverse possessor to have a claim of right, defined as "a reasonable basis for the belief that the property belongs to the adverse possessor." N.Y. Real Prop. Acts. Law §501(3). Legislative history introduced with the new statute criticized existing law:

> The effect of cases like Walling v. Przybylo, 851 N.E.2d 1167 (N.Y. 2006), has been to encourage the offensive use of adverse possession. This legislation is all about good faith. A person who attempts to possess land that they know all too well does not belong to them should not be encouraged. If a person desires land, they can buy it. However, if they have a reasonable basis to believe that it is their land then that is exactly the good faith dispute over title to real property for which the adverse possession doctrine was established. Adverse possession should be used to settle good faith disputes over who owns land. It should not be a doctrine which can be used offensively to deprive a landowner of their real property. That only encourages mischief between neighbors and even between families.

The Colorado statute requires the possessor to have "a good faith belief" that she "was the actual owner of the property" and that "the belief was reasonable under the particular circumstances." The statute also requires a heightened evidentiary standard; to prevail, the claimant must "prove each element of the claim by clear and convincing evidence." Moreover, the statute grants the court discretion to order the true owner who loses damages based on the property value and any taxes and assessments paid by the true owner during the statutory period prior to the loss of title. Colo. Rev. Stat. §38-41-101(3), (5).

3. An additional element of adverse possession law is known as *color of title.* Color of title consists of a deed or other instrument that purports to transfer title to the adverse possessor. Color of title is not real title — if the claimant had real title, he wouldn't need to resort to adverse possession law. The deed or instrument constituting color of title is invalid or defective for some reason. Color of title serves two roles. First, in many states, a statute expressly requires color of title for certain adverse possession claims. Often the statute provides a shorter period of limitation for a claimant having color of title. Wisconsin, for example, reduces its 20-year period to 10 years if the claimant has color of title, and even reduces it further, to 7 years, if a claimant with color of title also pays real estate taxes on the land. Wis. Stat. §§893.25, 893.26, 893.27. A few states require color of title for all adverse possession claims.

Second, color of title enables the claimant to rely on the doctrine of *constructive adverse possession.* This means that if the claimant is in actual possession of only part of the land described in the colorable title, the claimant also gains title to the unoccupied portion. This is an exception to the normal rule that the adverse possessor can claim title only to portions of the true owner's land that he actually possesses. Here, due to having a colorable title, he is said to be in "constructive possession" of unoccupied portions.

May a claimant rely on color of title if he knows the writing is defective, and thus knows he is a trespasser? Many courts, even in states that generally reject a good faith requirement for adverse possession law, require subjective belief that the colorable title is valid. Can you explain why? In *Howard*, did the Kuntos have color of title? Did the claimants in the other three cases we've read have color of title?

4. By statute a number of states mandate that the adverse possessor, to gain title, must pay real estate taxes on the land while the limitation period is running. Some states require this of all claimants (California), and others require this for only certain cases (Minnesota — payment not required for adverse possession that establishes new boundary line between neighbors). What policy underlies the tax-payment requirement? Is it a proxy for good faith?

When a claimant is disqualified from using adverse possession law by a tax-payment requirement, the opportunity to resort to other theories becomes more important. In the context of neighboring landowners, the claimant could seek a *prescriptive easement* (easements are discussed in Chapter 11). Alternatively, the doctrine of *agreed boundaries* or the doctrine of *boundary by acquiescence* can readjust record boundary lines. Both doctrines, in contrast to adverse possession, proceed upon the theory of consent. Under agreed boundaries, an oral or informal agreement alters the boundary, provided the neighbors were uncertain as to the boundary's correct location or had a dispute. Boundary by acquiescence establishes a new boundary if the neighbors occupied up to a visible line, such as a fence, treating such line as their boundary for a lengthy period of time. *See* Zeglin v. Gahagen, 812 A.2d 558 (Pa. 2002) (privity of possession suffices for tacking to meet 21-year period for boundary by acquiescence, even though Pennsylvania requires deed privity for tacking for adverse possession).

■ **O'KEEFFE v. SNYDER**
Supreme Court of New Jersey, 1980
416 A.2d 862

POLLOCK, Justice. This is an appeal from an order of the Appellate Division granting summary judgment to plaintiff, Georgia O'Keeffe, against defendant, Barry Snyder, d/b/a Princeton Gallery of Fine Art, for replevin of three small pictures painted by O'Keeffe. In her complaint, filed in March, 1976, O'Keeffe alleged she was the owner of the paintings and that they were stolen from a New York art gallery in 1946. Snyder asserted he was a purchaser for value of the paintings, he had title by adverse possession, and O'Keeffe's action was barred by the expiration of the six-year period of limitations provided by N.J.S.A. 2A:14-1 pertaining to an action in replevin. Snyder impleaded third party defendant, Ulrich A. Frank, from whom Snyder purchased the paintings in 1975 for $35,000.

The trial court granted summary judgment for Snyder on the ground that O'Keeffe's action was barred because it was not commenced within six years of the alleged theft. The Appellate Division reversed and entered judgment for O'Keeffe. A majority of that court concluded that the paintings were stolen, the defenses of expiration of the statute of limitations and title by adverse possession were identical, and Snyder had not proved the elements of adverse possession.

Consequently, the majority ruled that O'Keeffe could still enforce her right to possession of the paintings. . . .

I.

The record, limited to pleadings, affidavits, answers to interrogatories, and depositions, is fraught with factual conflict. Apart from the creation of the paintings by O'Keeffe and their discovery in Snyder's gallery in 1976, the parties agree on little else.

O'Keeffe contended the paintings were stolen in 1946 from a gallery, An American Place. The gallery was operated by her late husband, the famous photographer Alfred Stieglitz.

An American Place was a cooperative undertaking of O'Keeffe and some other American artists identified by her as Marin, Hardin, Dove, Andema, and Stevens. In 1946, Stieglitz arranged an exhibit which included an O'Keeffe painting, identified as Cliffs. According to O'Keeffe, one day in March, 1946, she and Stieglitz discovered Cliffs was missing from the wall of the exhibit. O'Keeffe estimates the value of the painting at the time of the alleged theft to have been about $150.

About two weeks later, O'Keeffe noticed that two other paintings, Seaweed and Fragments, were missing from a storage room at An American Place. She did not tell anyone, even Stieglitz, about the missing paintings, since she did not want to upset him.

Before the date when O'Keeffe discovered the disappearance of Seaweed, she had already sold it (apparently for a string of amber beads) to a Mrs. Weiner, now deceased. Following the grant of the motion for summary judgment by the trial court in favor of Snyder, O'Keeffe submitted a release from the legatees of Mrs. Weiner purportedly assigning to O'Keeffe their interest in the sale.

O'Keeffe testified on depositions that at about the same time as the disappearance of her paintings, 12 or 13 miniature paintings by Marin also were stolen from An American Place. According to O'Keeffe, a man named Estrick took the Marin paintings and "maybe a few other things." Estrick distributed the Marin paintings to members of the theater world who, when confronted by Stieglitz, returned them. However, neither Stieglitz nor O'Keeffe confronted Estrick with the loss of any of the O'Keeffe paintings.

There was no evidence of a break and entry at An American Place on the dates when O'Keeffe discovered the disappearance of her paintings. Neither Stieglitz nor O'Keeffe reported them missing to the New York Police Department or any other law enforcement agency. Apparently the paintings were uninsured, and O'Keeffe did not seek reimbursement from an insurance company. Similarly, neither O'Keeffe nor Stieglitz advertised the loss of the paintings in Art News or any other publication. Nonetheless, they discussed it with associates in the art world and later O'Keeffe mentioned the loss to the director of the Art Institute of Chicago, but she did not ask him to do anything because "it wouldn't have been my way." O'Keeffe does not contend that Frank or Snyder had actual knowledge of the alleged theft.

Stieglitz died in the summer of 1946, and O'Keeffe explains she did not pursue her efforts to locate the paintings because she was settling his estate. In 1947, she retained the services of Doris Bry to help settle the estate. Bry urged O'Keeffe to report the loss of the paintings, but O'Keeffe declined because "they never got anything back by reporting it." Finally, in 1972, O'Keeffe authorized Bry to report the theft to the Art Dealers Association of America, Inc., which maintains for its members a registry of stolen paintings. The record does not indicate whether such a registry existed at the time the paintings disappeared.

In September, 1975, O'Keeffe learned that the paintings were in the Andrew Crispo Gallery in New York on consignment from Bernard Danenberg Galleries. On February 11, 1976, O'Keeffe discovered that Ulrich A. Frank had sold the paintings to Barry Snyder, d/b/a Princeton Gallery of Fine Art. She demanded their return and, following Snyder's refusal, instituted this action for replevin.

Frank traces his possession of the paintings to his father, Dr. Frank, who died in 1968. He claims there is a family relationship by marriage between his family and the Stieglitz family, a contention that O'Keeffe disputes. Frank does not know how his father acquired the paintings, but he recalls seeing them in his father's apartment in New Hampshire as early as 1941-1943, a period that precedes the alleged theft. Consequently, Frank's factual contentions are inconsistent with O'Keeffe's allegation of theft. Until 1965, Dr. Frank occasionally lent the paintings to Ulrich Frank. In 1965, Dr. and Mrs. Frank formally gave the paintings to Ulrich Frank, who kept them in his residences in Yardley, Pennsylvania and Princeton, New Jersey. In 1968, he exhibited anonymously Cliffs and Fragments in a one day art show in the Jewish Community Center in Trenton. All of these events precede O'Keeffe's listing of the paintings as stolen with the Art Dealers Association of America, Inc. in 1972.

Frank claims continuous possession of the paintings through his father for over thirty years and admits selling the paintings to Snyder. Snyder and Frank do not trace their provenance, or history of possession of the paintings, back to O'Keeffe.

As indicated, Snyder moved for summary judgment on the theory that O'Keeffe's action was barred by the statute of limitations and title had vested in Frank by adverse possession. For purposes of his motion, Snyder conceded that the paintings had been stolen. On her cross motion, O'Keeffe urged that the paintings were stolen, the statute of limitations had not run, and title to the paintings remained in her. . . .

III.

On the limited record before us, we cannot determine now who has title to the paintings. That determination will depend on the evidence adduced at trial. Nonetheless, we believe it may aid the trial court and the parties to resolve questions of law that may become relevant at trial.

Our decision begins with the principle that, generally speaking, if the paintings were stolen, the thief acquired no title and could not transfer good title to others regardless of their good faith and ignorance of the theft. . . . Proof of theft would advance O'Keeffe's right to possession of the paintings absent other considerations such as expiration of the statute of limitations.

Another issue that may become relevant at trial is whether Frank or his father acquired a "voidable title" to the paintings under N.J.S.A. 12A:2-403(1). That section, part of the Uniform Commercial Code (U.C.C.) does not change the basic principle that a mere possessor cannot transfer good title. 2 Anderson, Uniform Commercial Code (2d ed. 1971) §2-403:6 at 41 (*Anderson*). Nonetheless, the U.C.C. permits a person with voidable title to transfer good title to a good faith purchaser for value in certain circumstances. If the facts developed at trial merit application of that section, then Frank may have transferred good title to Snyder, thereby providing a defense to O'Keeffe's action. No party on this appeal has urged factual or legal contentions concerning the applicability of the U.C.C. Consequently, a more complete discussion of the U.C.C. would be premature, particularly in light of our decision to remand the matter for trial.

On this appeal, the critical legal question is when O'Keeffe's cause of action accrued. The fulcrum on which the outcome turns is the statute of limitations in N.J.S.A. 2A:14-1, which provides that an action for replevin of goods or chattels must be commenced within six years after the accrual of the cause of action.

The trial court found that O'Keeffe's cause of action accrued on the date of the alleged theft, March, 1946, and concluded that her action was barred. The Appellate Division found that an action might have accrued more than six years before the date of suit if possession by the defendant or his predecessors satisfied the elements of adverse possession. As indicated, the Appellate Division concluded that Snyder had not established those elements and that the O'Keeffe action was not barred by the statute of limitations. . . .

IV.

. . . The purpose of a statute of limitations is to "stimulate to activity and punish negligence" and "promote repose by giving security and stability to human affairs." Wood v. Carpenter, 101 U.S. 135, 139 (1879); Fernandi v. Strully, 173 A.2d 277 (N.J. 1961). A statute of limitations achieves those purposes by barring a cause of action after the statutory period. In certain instances, this Court has ruled that the literal language of a statute of limitations should yield to other considerations. . . .

To avoid harsh results from the mechanical application of the statute, the courts have developed a concept known as the discovery rule. Lopez v. Swyer, 300 A.2d 563 (N.J. 1973); Prosser, The Law of Torts (4th ed. 1971), §30 at 144-145; 51 Am. Jur. 2d, Limitation of Actions, §146 at 716. The discovery rule provides that, in an appropriate case, a cause of action will not accrue until the injured party discovers, or by exercise of reasonable diligence and intelligence should have discovered, facts which form the basis of a cause of action. The rule is essentially a principle of equity, the purpose of which is to mitigate unjust results that otherwise might flow from strict adherence to a rule of law. . . .

This Court first announced the discovery rule in Fernandi, supra. In Fernandi, a wing nut was left in a patient's abdomen following surgery and was not discovered for three years. The majority held that fairness and justice mandated that the statute of limitations should not have commenced running until the plaintiff knew or had reason to know of the presence of the foreign object in her body. The discovery rule has since been extended to other areas of medical malpractice. . . .

Increasing acceptance of the principle of the discovery rule has extended the doctrine to contexts unrelated to medical malpractice. See, e.g., Diamond v. New Jersey Bell Telephone Co., 242 A.2d 622 (N.J. 1968) (discovery rule applicable in negligent installation of an underground conduit causing flooding of plaintiff's property); New Mkt. Poultry Farms, Inc. v. Fellows, 241 A.2d 633 (N.J. 1968) (discovery rule applicable to negligently prepared survey discovered eleven years after the act). . . .

Similarly, we conclude that the discovery rule applies to an action for replevin of a painting under N.J.S.A. 2A:14-1. O'Keeffe's cause of action accrued when she first knew, or reasonably should have known through the exercise of due diligence, of the cause of action, including the identity of the possessor of the paintings.

See N. Ward, Adverse Possession of Loaned or Stolen Objects — Is Possession Still 9/10ths of the Law?, published in Legal Problems of Museum Administration (ALI-ABA 1980) at 89-90. . . .

In determining whether O'Keeffe is entitled to the benefit of the discovery rule, the trial court should consider, among others, the following issues: (1) whether O'Keeffe used due diligence to recover the paintings at the time of the alleged theft and thereafter; (2) whether at the time of the alleged theft there was an effective method, other than talking to her colleagues, for O'Keeffe to alert the art world; and (3) whether registering paintings with the Art Dealers Association of America, Inc. or any other organization would put a reasonably prudent purchaser of art on constructive notice that someone other than the possessor was the true owner.

V.

. . . To establish title by adverse possession to chattels, the rule of law has been that the possession must be hostile, actual, visible, exclusive, and continuous. Redmond v. New Jersey Historical Society, 28 A.2d 189 (N.J. E. & A. 1942); 54 C.J.S. *Limitations of Actions* §119 at 23. *Redmond* involved a portrait of Captain James Lawrence by Gilbert Stuart, which was bequeathed by its owner to her son with a provision that if he should die leaving no descendants, it should go to the New Jersey Historical Society. The owner died in 1887, when her son was 14, and her executors delivered the painting to the Historical Society. The painting remained in the possession of the Historical Society for over 50 years, until 1938, when the son died and his children, the legatees under his will, demanded its return. The Historical Society refused, and the legatees instituted a replevin action.

The Historical Society argued that the applicable statute of limitations, the predecessor of N.J.S.A. 2A:14-1, had run and that plaintiffs' action was barred. The Court of Errors and Appeals held that the doctrine of adverse possession applied to chattels as well as to real property, and that the statute of limitations would not begin to run against the true owner until possession became adverse. The Court found that the Historical Society had done nothing inconsistent with the theory that the painting was a "voluntary bailment or gratuitous loan" and had "utterly failed to prove that its possession of the portrait was 'adversary,' 'hostile.'" 28 A.2d at 195. The Court found further that the Historical Society had not asserted ownership until 1938, when it refused to deliver the painting to plaintiff, and that the statute did not begin to run until that date. Consequently, the Court ordered the painting to be returned to plaintiffs.

The only other New Jersey case applying adverse possession to chattels is Joseph v. Lesnevich, 153 A.2d 349 (N.J. App. Div. 1959). In *Lesnevich*, several negotiable bearer bonds were stolen from plaintiff in 1951. In October, 1951, Lesnevich received an envelope containing the bonds. On October 21, 1951, Lesnevich and his business partner pledged the bonds with a credit company. They failed to pay the loan secured by the bonds and requested the credit company to sell the bonds to pay the loan. On August 1, 1952, the president of the credit company purchased the bonds and sold them to his son. In 1958, within one day of the expiration of six years from the date of the purchase, the owner of the bonds sued the credit company and its president, among others, for conversion of the bonds. The Appellate Division found that the credit company and its president held the bonds "as openly and notoriously as the nature of the property would permit." *Lesnevich, supra,* at 357. The pledge of the bonds with the credit company was considered to be open possession.

As *Lesnevich* demonstrates, there is an inherent problem with many kinds of personal property that will raise questions whether their possession has been open, visible, and notorious. In *Lesnevich,* the court strained to conclude that in holding bonds as collateral, a credit company satisfied the requirement of open, visible, and notorious possession.

Other problems with the requirement of visible, open, and notorious possession readily come to mind. For example, if jewelry is stolen from a municipality in one county in New Jersey, it is unlikely that the owner would learn that someone is openly wearing that jewelry in another county or even in the same municipality. Open and visible possession of personal property, such as jewelry, may not be sufficient to put the original owner on actual or constructive notice of the identity of the possessor.

The problem is even more acute with works of art. Like many kinds of personal property, works of art are readily moved and easily concealed. O'Keeffe argues that nothing short of public display should be sufficient to alert the true owner and start the statute running. Although there is merit in that contention from the perspective of the original owner, the effect is to impose a heavy burden on the purchasers of paintings who wish to enjoy the paintings in the privacy of their homes.

In the present case, the trial court and Appellate Division concluded that the paintings, which allegedly had been kept in the private residences of the Frank family, had not been held visibly, openly, and notoriously. Notwithstanding that conclusion, the trial court ruled that the statute of limitations began to run at the time of the theft and had expired before the commencement of suit. The Appellate Division determined it was bound by the rules in *Redmond* and reversed the trial court on the theory that the defenses of adverse possession and expiration of the statute of limitations were identical. Nonetheless, for different reasons, the majority and dissenting judges in the Appellate Division acknowledged deficiencies in identifying the statute of limitations with adverse possession. The majority stated that, as a practical matter, requiring compliance with adverse possession would preclude barring stale claims and acquiring title to personal property. The dissenting judge feared that identifying the statutes of limitations with adverse possession would lead to a "handbook for larceny." The divergent conclusions of the lower courts suggest that the doctrine of adverse possession no longer provides a fair and reasonable means of resolving this kind of dispute.

The problem is serious. According to an affidavit submitted in this matter by the president of the International Foundation for Art Research, there has been an "explosion in art thefts" and there is a "worldwide phenomenon of art theft which has reached epidemic proportions."

The limited record before us provides a brief glimpse into the arcane world of sales of art, where paintings worth vast sums of money sometimes are bought without inquiry about their provenance. There does not appear to be a reasonably available method for an owner of art to record the ownership or theft of paintings. Similarly, there are no reasonable means readily available to a purchaser to ascertain the provenance of a painting. It may be time for the art world to establish a means by which a good faith purchaser may reasonably obtain the provenance of a painting. An efficient registry of original works of art might better serve the interests of artists, owners of art, and bona fide purchasers than the law of adverse possession with all of its uncertainties. L. DuBoff, The Deskbook of Art Law at 470-472

(Fed. Pub. Inc. 1977). Although we cannot mandate the initiation of a registration system, we can develop a rule for the commencement and running of the statute of limitations that is more responsive to the needs of the art world than the doctrine of adverse possession.

We are persuaded that the introduction of equitable considerations through the discovery rule provides a more satisfactory response than the doctrine of adverse possession. The discovery rule shifts the emphasis from the conduct of the possessor to the conduct of the owner. The focus of the inquiry will no longer be whether the possessor has met the tests of adverse possession, but whether the owner has acted with due diligence in pursuing his or her personal property.

For example, under the discovery rule, if an artist diligently seeks the recovery of a lost or stolen painting, but cannot find it or discover the identity of the possessor, the statute of limitations will not begin to run. The rule permits an artist who uses reasonable efforts to report, investigate, and recover a painting to preserve the rights of title and possession.

Properly interpreted, the discovery rule becomes a vehicle for transporting equitable considerations into the statute of limitations for replevin, N.J.S.A. 2A:14-1. In determining whether the discovery rule should apply, a court should identify, evaluate, and weigh the equitable claims of all parties. *Lopez, supra* at 567. If a chattel is concealed from the true owner, fairness compels tolling the statute during the period of concealment. That conclusion is consistent with tolling the statute of limitations in a medical malpractice action where the physician is guilty of fraudulent concealment.

It is consistent also with the law of replevin as it has developed apart from the discovery rule. In an action for replevin, the period of limitations ordinarily will run against the owner of lost or stolen property from the time of the wrongful taking, absent fraud or concealment. Where the chattel is fraudulently concealed, the general rule is that the statute is tolled.

A purchaser from a private party would be well-advised to inquire whether a work of art has been reported as lost or stolen. However, a bona fide purchaser who purchases in the ordinary course of business a painting entrusted to an art dealer should be able to acquire good title against the true owner. Under the U.C.C. entrusting possession of goods to a merchant who deals in that kind of goods gives the merchant the power to transfer all the rights of the entruster to a buyer in the ordinary course of business. N.J.S.A. 12A:2-403(2). In a transaction under that statute, a merchant may vest good title in the buyer as against the original owner. *See* Anderson, *supra*, §2-403:17 et seq. The interplay between the statute of limitations as modified by the discovery rule and the U.C.C. should encourage good faith purchases from legitimate art dealers and discourage trafficking in stolen art without frustrating an artist's ability to recover stolen art works.

The discovery rule will fulfill the purposes of a statute of limitations and accord greater protection to the innocent owner of personal property whose goods are lost or stolen. Accordingly, we overrule Redmond v. New Jersey Historical Society, *supra*, and Joseph v. Lesnevich, *supra*, to the extent that they hold that the doctrine of adverse possession applies to chattels.

By diligently pursuing their goods, owners may prevent the statute of limitations from running. The meaning of due diligence will vary with the facts of each case, including the nature and value of the personal property. For example, with respect to jewelry of moderate value, it may be sufficient if the owner reports the theft to the police. With respect to art work of greater value, it may be reasonable to expect an owner to do more. In practice, our ruling should contribute to more careful practices concerning the purchase of art.

The considerations are different with real estate, and there is no reason to disturb the application of the doctrine of adverse possession to real estate. Real estate is fixed and cannot be moved or concealed. The owner of real property knows or should know where his property is located and reasonably can be expected to be aware of open, notorious, visible, hostile, continuous acts of possession on it.

Our ruling not only changes the requirements for acquiring title to personal property after an alleged unlawful taking, but also shifts the burden of proof at trial. Under the doctrine of adverse possession, the burden is on the possessor to prove the elements of adverse possession. Wilomay Holding Co. v. Peninsula Land Co., 116 A.2d 484 (N.J. App. Div. 1955), *cert. den.*, 118 A.2d 128 (N.J. 1955). Under the discovery rule, the burden is on the owner as the one seeking the benefit of the rule to establish facts that would justify deferring the beginning of the period of limitations.

VI.

Read literally, the effect of the expiration of the statute of limitations under N.J.S.A. 2A:14-1 is to bar an action such as replevin. The statute does not speak of divesting the original owner of title. By its terms the statute cuts off the remedy, but not the right of title. Nonetheless, the effect of the expiration of the statute of limitations, albeit on the theory of adverse possession, has been not only to bar an action for possession, but also to vest title in the possessor. There is no reason to change that result although the discovery rule has replaced adverse possession. History, reason, and common sense support the conclusion that the expiration of the statute of limitations bars the remedy to recover possession and also vests title in the possessor. . . .

Before the expiration of the statute, the possessor has both the chattel and the right to keep it except as against the true owner. The only imperfection in the possessor's right to retain the chattel is the original owner's right to repossess it. Once that imperfection is removed, the possessor should have good title for all purposes. Ames, The Disseisin of Chattels, 3 Harv. L. Rev. 313, 321 (1890). As Dean Ames wrote: "An immortal right to bring an eternally prohibited action is a metaphysical subtlety that the present writer cannot pretend to understand." . . .

VII.

We next consider the effect of transfers of a chattel from one possessor to another during the period of limitation under the discovery rule. Under the discovery rule, the statute of limitations on an action for replevin begins to run when the owner knows or reasonably should know of his cause of action and the identity of the possessor of the chattel. Subsequent transfers of the chattel are part of the continuous dispossession of the chattel from the original owner. The important point is not that there has been a substitution of possessors, but that there has been a continuous dispossession of the former owner. . . .

For the purpose of evaluating the due diligence of an owner, the dispossession of his chattel is a continuum not susceptible to separation into distinct acts. Nonetheless, subsequent transfers of the chattel may affect the degree of difficulty encountered by a diligent owner seeking to recover his goods. To that extent, subsequent transfers and their potential for frustrating diligence are relevant in applying the discovery rule. An owner who diligently seeks his chattel should be entitled to the benefit of the discovery rule although it may have passed through many hands. Conversely an owner who sleeps on his rights may be denied the benefit of the discovery rule although the chattel may have been possessed by only one person.

We reject the alternative of treating subsequent transfers of a chattel as separate acts of conversion that would start the statute of limitations running anew. At common law, apart from the statute of limitations, a subsequent transfer of a converted chattel was considered to be a separate act of conversion. In his dissent, Justice Handler seeks to extend the rule so that it would apply even if the period of limitations had expired before the subsequent transfer. Nonetheless, the dissent does not cite any authority that supports the position that the statute of limitations should run anew on an act of conversion already barred by the statute of limitations. Adoption of that alternative would tend to undermine the purpose of the statute in quieting titles and protecting against stale claims. Brown, [*The Law of Personal Property* (3d ed. 1975)] §4.3 at 38.

The majority and better view is to permit tacking, the accumulation of consecutive periods of possession by parties in privity with each other. Lesnevich, *supra*. . . .

Treating subsequent transfers as separate acts of conversion could lead to absurd results. As explained by Dean Ames:

> The decisions in the case of chattels are few. As a matter of principle, it is submitted this rule of tacking is as applicable to chattels as to land. A denial of the right to tack would, furthermore, lead to this result. If a converter were to sell the chattel, five years after its conversion, to one ignorant of the seller's tort, the disposed owner's right to recover the chattel from the purchaser would continue five years longer than his right to recover from the converter would have lasted if there had been no sale. In other words, an innocent purchaser from a wrong-doer would be in a worse position than the wrong-doer himself, a conclusion as shocking in point of justice as it would be anomalous in law. (Ames, *supra* at 323, footnotes omitted)

It is more sensible to recognize that on expiration of the period of limitations, title passes from the former owner by operation of the statute. Needless uncertainty would result from starting the statute running anew merely because of a subsequent transfer. 3 *American Law of Property*, §15.16 at 837. It is not necessary to strain equitable principles, as suggested by the dissent, to arrive at a just and reasonable determination of the rights of the parties. The discovery rule permits an equitable accommodation of the rights of the parties without establishing a rule of law fraught with uncertainty. . . .

We reverse the judgment of the Appellate Division in favor of O'Keeffe and remand the matter for trial in accordance with this opinion.

SULLIVAN, Justice, dissenting. I do not see the need for a remand. . . .

In his affidavit filed in the cause, Snyder, although a professional art dealer, stated that he was unaware of the registry of stolen paintings maintained by the Association which showed the paintings as stolen at the time he purchased them. Although he paid $35,000 for them, Snyder made no attempt to authenticate the paintings or verify ownership — this in spite of the fact that Frank, who had acquired possession of them by gift from Dr. Frank, his late father, did not know how his father had come by the paintings.

Now that his motion for summary judgment has been lost, defendant Snyder suggests speculative possibilities that he says merit inquiry even though there is nothing in the record to support them. I see no substance in any of them, and a remand as prejudicial to plaintiff who is now more than 92 years of age.

She created these paintings. They were in her possession when they disappeared from her husband's art gallery in 1946. She did not learn of their whereabouts until late 1975 when they were offered for sale. She immediately started suit to recover them as soon as she was able to identify the person who had possession of them. Under these circumstances the six-year statute of limitations for bringing an action in replevin, N.J.S.A. 2A:14-1, was tolled and plaintiff, as the rightful owner, is entitled to a judgment in her favor. . . .

I would affirm the Appellate Division ruling in its entirety.

HANDLER, Justice, dissenting. The Court today rules that if a work of art has been stolen from an artist, the artist's right to recover his or her work from a subsequent possessor would be barred by the statute of limitations if the action were not brought within six years after the original theft. This can happen even though the artist may have been totally innocent and wholly ignorant of the identity of the thief or of any intervening receivers or possessors of the stolen art. The Court would grudgingly grant some measure of relief from this horrendous result and allow the artist to bring suit provided he or she can sustain the burden of proving "due diligence" in earlier attempting to retrieve the stolen artwork. No similar duty of diligence or vigilance, however, is placed upon the subsequent receiver or possessor, who, innocently or not, has actually trafficked in the stolen art. Despite ritualistic disavowals, the Court's holding does little to discourage art thievery. Rather, by making it relatively more easy for the receiver or possessor of an artwork with a "checkered background" to gain security and title than for the artist or true owner to reacquire it, it seems as though the Court surely will stimulate and legitimatize art thievery.

I believe that there is a much sounder approach in this sort of case than one that requires the parties to become enmeshed in duplicate or cumulative hearings that focus on the essentially collateral issues of the statute of limitations and its possible tolling by an extended application of the discovery doctrine. The better approach, I would suggest, is one that enables the parties to get to the merits of the controversy. It would recognize an artist's or owner's right to assert a claim against a newly-revealed receiver or possessor of stolen art as well as the correlative right of such a possessor to assert all equitable and legal defenses. This would enable the parties to concentrate directly upon entitlement to the artwork rather than entitlement to bring a lawsuit. By dealing with the merits of the claims instead of the right to sue, such an approach would be more conducive to reconciling the demands for individual justice with societal needs to discourage art thievery. In addition, such a rule would comport more closely with traditional common law values emphasizing the paramountcy of the rights of a true owner of chattels as against others whose possession is derived from theft. Simultaneously, it would acknowledge that the claims of the true owner as against subsequent converters may in appropriate circumstances be counterbalanced by equitable considerations. . . .

A fundamental miscalculation by the majority, however, is its assumption that [the] six-year limitations statute is applicable to O'Keeffe's claims. The statute of limitations defense was raised by defendant Snyder, but it is not available here because Snyder's acts of conversion — his purchase of the paintings from third-party defendant Frank and his refusal to return them to plaintiff O'Keeffe upon demand — constituted independent tortious acts each of which occurred well within six years of the commencement of plaintiff's lawsuit. Hence, there is no reason not to permit O'Keeffe's lawsuit and allow the parties to proceed to the heart of the controversy. . . .

There are several weaknesses in the Court's position. The most fundamental is the contention that O'Keeffe's claim against Snyder is "stale." . . . No persuasive reasons are advanced for the view that this notion of "stability," which would serve in many cases actually to legitimatize art theft, is more important than is the return of stolen unique, artistic creations to their creator or true owner when this is justified by equitable considerations. . . .

Notes and Questions

1. Despite the remand, no trial court proceedings occurred after the Supreme Court decision. O'Keeffe and Snyder settled their dispute, with one of the terms being that neither party would publicly disclose the settlement.

2. Does *Redmond*, discussed in the principal case, come out differently under the discovery rule than it did under the doctrine of adverse possession? What should happen when art is loaned to a museum for an indefinite period of time, sometimes called a "permanent loan"? Several courts have ordered the return of art to the owner's heirs after very long time periods. *See* Mucha v. King, 792 F.2d 602 (7th Cir. 1986) (artist's heirs entitled to recover painting that was in possession of museum, under consignment arrangement, for 59 years); In re Estate of McCagg, 450 A.2d 414 (D.C. Ct. App. 1982) (owner's heirs entitled to recover painting loaned to National Museum of American Art after 64 years).

In other contexts, there is authority for the proposition that when the parties fail to agree to the duration of a bailment, the bailor must request her property within a reasonable time. In Desiderio v. D'Ambrosio, 463 A.2d 986 (N.J. Super. Ct. 1983), a home seller and his buyer agreed that the seller could remove his three cast-iron statues from the property after the sale, when the seller completed building his new home. Seven years passed before the seller attempted to claim the statues. The court held for defendant in the seller's action for replevin and damages, distinguishing *Redmond*. "[H]ow long does a gratuitous bailment of indefinite term survive in the absence of any demand by the bailor and of any act by the bailee inconsistent with the bailor's title? . . . If the contract provides no specific time within which demand must be made, the limitation 'within a reasonable time' will be implied. . . . This court determines that plaintiff failed to make a demand for the property within a reasonable time of the bailment. . . . In the absence of special circumstances or a manifest contrary intention of the parties, the reasonable period was coterminous with the period within which an action for breach of the agreement might have been brought, here six years."

3. New York rejects the discovery rule, following a "demand and refusal" rule. Solomon R. Guggenheim Foundation v. Lubell, 569 N.E.2d 426 (N.Y. 1991): The Guggenheim Museum brought a replevin action for a gouache, painted by Marc Chagall, worth $200,000 against the Lubells, who purchased it from a Madison Avenue gallery in 1967 for $17,000. Apparently, a mailroom employee stole the painting from the Museum several years earlier. The Museum never notified any

law enforcement agency or any galleries, museums, or art associations of the theft, but it asserted "that this was a tactical decision based upon its belief that to publicize the theft would succeed only in driving the gouache further underground and greatly diminishing the possibility that it would ever be recovered."

The court denied defendants' statute of limitations defense, indicating that defendants might prevail under the affirmative defense of laches. To succeed under laches, defendants would have the burden of proving that plaintiff unreasonably delayed in bringing the replevin action, thereby causing prejudice to defendants. With respect to limitations, the court stated: "New York case law has long protected the right of the owner whose property has been stolen to recover that property, even if it is in the possession of a good-faith purchaser for value. There is a three-year Statute of Limitations for recovery of a chattel. The rule in this State is that a cause of action for replevin against the good-faith purchaser of a stolen chattel accrues when the true owner makes demand for return of the chattel and the person in possession of the chattel refuses to return it. Until demand is made and refused, possession of the stolen property by the good-faith purchaser for value is not considered wrongful. Although seemingly anomalous, a different rule applies when the stolen object is in the possession of the thief. In that situation, the Statute of Limitations runs from the time of the theft, even if the property owner was unaware of the theft at the time that it occurred."

The court recognized *O'Keeffe*'s discovery rule, but rejected it: "the demand and refusal rule . . . remains the law in New York and . . . there is no reason to obscure its straightforward protection of true owners by creating a duty of reasonable diligence. . . . Here, the parties hotly contest whether publicizing the theft would have turned up the gouache. According to the museum, some members of the art community believe that publicizing a theft exposes gaps in security and can lead to more thefts; the museum also argues that publicity often pushes a missing painting further underground. In light of the fact that members of the art community have apparently not reached a consensus on the best way to retrieve stolen art (*see* Burnham, *Art Theft: Its Scope, Its Impact and Its Control*), it would be particularly inappropriate for this Court to spell out arbitrary rules of conduct that all true owners of stolen art work would have to follow to the letter if they wanted to preserve their right to pursue a cause of action in replevin. All owners of stolen property should not be expected to behave in the same way and should not be held to a common standard. The value of the property stolen, the manner in which it was stolen, and the type of institution from which it was stolen will all necessarily affect the manner in which a true owner will search for missing property. We conclude that it would be difficult, if not impossible, to craft a reasonable diligence requirement that could take into account all of these variables and that would not unduly burden the true owner."

"Further, our decision today is in part influenced by our recognition that New York enjoys a worldwide reputation as a preeminent cultural center. To place the burden of locating stolen artwork on the true owner and to foreclose the rights of that owner to recover its property if the burden is not met would, we believe, encourage illicit trafficking in stolen art. Three years after the theft, any purchaser, good faith or not, would be able to hold onto stolen art work unless the true owner was able to establish that it had undertaken a reasonable search for the missing art. This shifting of the burden onto the wronged owner is inappropriate. In our opinion, the better rule gives the owner relatively greater protection and places the burden of investigating the provenance of a work of art on the potential purchaser."

4. In two passages of the majority opinion, the *O'Keeffe* court discusses BFP issues and UCC §2-403, a topic that we studied earlier in Chapter 2. What facts would Snyder have to prove to win as a BFP under §2-403? If the paintings were stolen, as O'Keeffe alleges, can there be a UCC defense based on voidable title or entrusting to a merchant?

D. *JUS TERTII* DEFENSE

A wrongful possessor of property, by definition, has a duty to the true owner or to one with better title to relinquish possession upon demand. If the property is goods rather than land, the wrongful possessor's duty is to respond in damages if the owner chooses trover. But does the wrongful possessor have any rights when third parties are involved, or is his wrongful possession legally unprotected? If *A* wrongfully takes *O*'s property, and then *B* wrongfully takes the property away from *A*, what should happen if *A* sues *B*? If *B* seeks to defend by pointing out *A*'s lack of ownership, *B* is said to raise a *jus tertii* defense.

■ ANDERSON v. GOULDBERG
Supreme Court of Minnesota, 1892
53 N.W. 636

Appeal by defendants, Hans J. Gouldberg and D.O. Anderson, from an order of the District Court of Isanti County, Lochren, J., made November 14, 1892, refusing a new trial.

This action was brought by the plaintiff, Sigfrid Anderson, against the defendants, partners as Gouldberg & Anderson, to recover the possession of ninety-three pine logs, marked L S X, or for the value thereof. Plaintiff claimed to have cut the logs on section 22, township 27, range 25, Isanti County, in the winter of 1889-1890, and to have hauled them to a mill on section 6, from which place defendants took them. The title to section 22 was in strangers, and plaintiff showed no authority from the owners to cut logs thereon. Defendants claimed that the logs were cut on section 26, in the adjoining township, on land belonging to the Ann River Logging Company, and that they took the logs by direction of the Logging Company, who were the owners. The court charged that even if plaintiff got possession of the logs as a trespasser, his title would be good as against any one except the real owner or some one who had authority from the owner to take them, and left the case to the jury on the question as to whether the logs were cut on the land of the Logging Company, and taken by defendants under its authority. The jury found a verdict for the plaintiff and assessed his damages at $153.45. From an order denying their motion for a new trial, defendants appeal.

MITCHELL, Justice. It is settled by the verdict of the jury that the logs in controversy were not cut upon the land of the defendants, and consequently that they were entire strangers to the property.

For the purposes of this appeal, we must also assume the fact to be (as there was evidence from which the jury might have so found) that the plaintiff obtained possession of the logs in the first instance by trespassing upon the land of some third party.

Therefore the only question is whether bare possession of property, though wrongfully obtained, is sufficient title to enable the party enjoying it to maintain replevin against a mere stranger, who takes it from him. We had supposed that this was settled in the affirmative as long ago, at least, as the early case of Armory v. Delamirie, 1 Strange 505 (1722), so often cited on that point.

When it is said that to maintain replevin the plaintiff's possession must have been lawful, it means merely that it must have been lawful as against the person who deprived him of it; and possession is good title against all the world except those having a better title.

Counsel says that possession only raises a presumption of title, which, however, may be rebutted. Rightly understood, this is correct; but counsel misapplies it. One who takes property from the possession of another can only rebut this presumption by showing a superior title in himself, or in some way connecting himself with one who has. One who has acquired the possession of property, whether by finding, bailment, or by mere tort, has a right to retain that possession as against a mere wrongdoer who is a stranger to the property. Any other rule would lead to an endless series of unlawful seizures and reprisals in every case where property had once passed out of the possession of the rightful owner.

Order affirmed.

■ **RUSSELL v. HILL**
   Supreme Court of North Carolina, 1900
   34 S.E. 640

MONTGOMERY, Justice. . . . In 1887, after entry and survey, F.H. Busbee, trustee, received a grant from the state for a tract of land in Swain county. Iowa McCoy made a subsequent entry and survey, and received a grant from the state for a part of the land embraced in the grant to Busbee, trustee. Busbee, trustee, was the owner of the land by virtue of his grant, which was properly registered, and registered before the entry, survey, and grant of Mrs. McCoy. Mrs. McCoy had no knowledge of Busbee's grant except the notice which the law implies from the fact of registration. Mrs. McCoy sold to the plaintiff certain timber standing on the land embraced in her grant, and the plaintiff cut the timber and carried the same in the shape of logs to the bank of Nantahala river, a floatable stream, for the purpose of floating them to the Asheville Furniture Company.

While the logs were lying on the river bank, the defendants, without any claim of right or title to them from Busbee, trustee, or from any one else, so far as the record shows, took possession of the logs without the consent of the plaintiff, and sold and delivered them to the Asheville Lumber Company for $686.84. The lumber company is insolvent.

The Court, upon the facts agreed, adjudged that the plaintiff could not recover, and rendered judgment accordingly.

We are of the opinion that there was no error in the ruling and judgment of the Court. Busbee, trustee, was the legal owner of the land. Mrs. McCoy was not in possession. If she had been in adverse possession, the title to the logs would have passed to the plaintiff, and he could have maintained this action; and Busbee would have been compelled to proceed against Mrs. McCoy for damages to the freehold. Brothers v. Hurdle, 32 N.C. 490 (1849); Ray v. Gardner, 82 N.C. 454 (1880).

The present action is in the nature of the old action of trover, and before the plaintiff could recover in an action of that nature he had to show both title and possession or the right of possession. . . . So, in the case before us, the title to the land from which the timber was cut is shown by the agreed state of facts to have been in Busbee, trustee, and not in the plaintiff, or Mrs. McCoy.

The same point arose in Barwick v. Barwick, 33 N.C. 80 (1850), and was decided in the same way. The court said: "But if it appears on the trial that the plaintiff, although in possession, is not in fact the owner, the presumption of title inferred from the possession is rebutted, and it would be manifestly wrong to allow the plaintiff to recover the value of the property; for the real owner may forthwith bring trover against the defendant, and force him to pay the value the second time. And the fact that he paid it in a former suit would be no defense . . . ; consequently trover can never be maintained unless a satisfaction of the judgment will have the effect of vesting a good title in the defendant, except where the property is restored and the conversion was temporary. Accordingly, it is well settled as the law of this State that to maintain trover the plaintiff must show title and the possession or a present right of possession." In the last-mentioned case the Court went on to say, in substance, that in some of the English books, and in some of the reports of our sister States, cases might be found to the contrary, but that those cases were all founded upon a misapprehension of the principle laid down in the case of Armory v. Delamirie, 1 St. 505 (1722). There, a chimney sweep found a lost jewel. He took it into his possession, as he had a right to do, and was the owner because of having it in possession unless the true owner should become known. That owner was not known, and it was properly decided that trover would lie in favor of the finder against the defendant, to whom he had handed it for inspection, and who refused to restore it. But the court said the case would have been very different if the owner had been known. . . .

Affirmed.

Douglas, Justice, dissents.

■ **TAPSCOTT v. COBBS**
Supreme Court of Appeals of Virginia, 1854
52 Va. 172

This was an action of ejectment in the Circuit court of Buckingham county, brought in February 1846, by the lessee of Elizabeth A. Cobbs and others against William H. Tapscott. Upon the trial the defendant demurred to the evidence. It appears that Thomas Anderson died in 1800, having made a will, by which he appointed several persons his executors, of whom John Harris, Robert Rives and Nathaniel Anderson qualified as such. By his will his executors were authorized to sell his real estate.

At the time of Thomas Anderson's death the land in controversy had been surveyed for him, and in 1802 a patent was issued therefor to Harris, Rives and N. Anderson as executors. Some time between the years 1820 and 1825, the executors [contracted to sell the land to Sarah Lewis for $217.50]. In a short time after her purchase she moved upon the land, built upon and improved it, and continued in possession until 1835, when she died. [Cobbs was one of Lewis' heirs. The three executors had previously died. From a separate lawsuit in 1826 brought by Thomas Anderson's devisees against Rives' estate, it appears Lewis did not pay the entire price. The commissioner in that suit settled the claim, stating: "The whole not yet collected, but Robert Rives assumes the liability."]

There is no evidence that the heirs of Mrs. Lewis were in possession of the land after her death, except as it may be inferred from the fact that she had been living upon the land from the time of her purchase until her death, and that she died upon it.

The proof was that [Tapscott] took possession of the land about the year 1842, without, so far as appears, any pretense of title. He made an entry with the surveyor of the county in December 1844, with a view to obtain a patent for it.

The court gave a judgment upon the demurrer for the plaintiffs, and Tapscott thereupon applied to this court for a *supersedeas*, which was allowed.

DANIEL, Justice. It is no doubt true, as a general rule, that the right of a plaintiff in ejectment to recover, rests on the strength of his own title, and is not established by the exhibition of defects in the title of the defendant, and that the defendant may maintain his defense by simply showing that the title is not in the plaintiff, but in some one else. And the rule is usually thus broadly stated by the authorities, without qualification. There are, however, exceptions to the rule as thus announced, as well established as the rule itself. As when the defendant has entered under the title of the plaintiff he cannot set up a title in a third person in contradiction to that under which he entered. Other instances might be cited in which it is equally as well settled that the defendant would be estopped from showing defects in the title of the plaintiff. In such cases, the plaintiff may, and often does recover, not by the exhibition of a title good in itself, but by showing that the relations between himself and the defendant are such that the latter cannot question it. The relation between the parties stands in the place of title; and though the title of the plaintiff is tainted with vices or defects that would prove fatal to his recovery in a controversy with any other defendant in peaceable possession, it is yet all sufficient in a litigation with one who entered into the possession under it, or otherwise stands so related to it that the law will not allow him to plead its defects in his defense.

Whether the case of an intrusion by a stranger without title, on a peaceable possession, is not one to meet the exigencies of which the courts will recognize a still further qualification or explanation of the rule requiring the plaintiff to recover only on the strength of his own title, is a question which, I believe, has not as yet been decided by this court. And it is somewhat remarkable that there are but few cases to be found in the English reporters in which the precise question has been decided or considered by the courts.

The cases of Read & Morpeth v. Erington, Croke Eliz. 321; Bateman v. Allen, *Ibid.* 437; and Allen v. Rivington, 2 Saund. R. 111, were each decided on special verdicts, in which the facts with respect to the title were stated. In each case it was shown that the plaintiff was in possession, and that the defendant entered without title or authority; and the court held that it was not necessary to decide upon the title of the plaintiff, and gave judgment for him. . . .

In 2 T. R. 749, we have nothing more than the syllabus of the case of Crisp v. Barber, in which it is said that a lease of a rectory-house, &c. by a rector, becomes void by 13th Eliz. ch. 20, by his nonresidence for eighty days, and that a stranger may take advantage of it. And that the lessee cannot maintain ejectment against a stranger who enters without any title whatever.

And in Graham v. Peat, 1 East's R. 244, in which, upon a like state of facts, arising under the same statute, the plaintiff brought trespass instead of ejectment, it was held that his possession was sufficient to maintain trespass against a wrong-doer, the chief justice, Lord Kenyon, remarking, that "if ejectment could not have been maintained, it was because that is a fictitious remedy founded upon title."

These two cases as reported may, perhaps, when taken in connection, be fairly regarded as holding that mere possession by the plaintiff will justify the action of trespass against an intruder, but is not sufficient to maintain ejectment. If so, they are in conflict with the earlier decisions before cited. . . . In this country the cases are numerous, and to some extent conflicting, yet I think that the larger number will be found to be in accordance with the earlier English decisions. I have found no case in which the question seems to have been more fully examined or maturely considered than in Sowder v. McMillan's heirs, 4 Dana's R. 456 (Ky. 1836). The views of the learned judge (Marshall) who delivered the opinion in which the whole court concurred, are rested on the authority of several cases in Kentucky, previously decided, on a series of decisions made by the Supreme court of New York, and on the three British cases of Bateman v. Allen, Allen v. Rivington, and Read & Morpeth v. Erington, before mentioned.

> These three cases (he says) establish unquestionably the right of the plaintiff to recover when it appears that he was in possession, and that the defendant entered upon and ousted his possession, without title or authority to enter; and prove that when the possession of the plaintiff and an entry upon it by the defendant are shown, the right of recovery cannot be resisted by showing that there is or may be an outstanding title in another; but only by showing that the defendant himself either has title or authority to enter under the title.
>
> It is a natural principle of justice, that he who is in possession has the right to maintain it, and if wrongfully expelled, to regain it by entry on the wrongdoer. When titles are acknowledged as separate and distinct from the possession, this right of maintaining and regaining the possession is, of course, subject to the exception that it cannot be exercised against the real owner, in competition with whose title it wholly fails. But surely it is not accordant with the principles of justice, that he who ousts a previous possession, should be permitted to defend his wrongful possession against the claim of restitution merely by showing that a stranger, and not the previous possessor whom he has ousted, was entitled to the possession. The law protects a peaceable possession against all except him who has the actual right to the possession, and no other can rightfully disturb or intrude upon it. While the peaceable possession continues, it is protected against a claimant in the action of ejectment, by permitting the defendant to show that a third person and not the claimant has the right. But if the claimant, instead of resorting to his action, attempts to gain the possession by entering upon and ousting the existing peaceable possession, he does not thereby acquire a rightful or a peaceable possession. The law does not protect him against the prior possessor. Neither does it indulge any presumption in his favor, nor permit him to gain any advantage by his own wrongful act.

To the same effect are the decisions in New Jersey, Connecticut, Vermont and Ohio. . . .

In Delaware, North Carolina, South Carolina, Indiana, and perhaps in other states of the Union, the opposite doctrine has been held.

In this state of the law, untrammeled as we are by any decisions of our own courts, I feel free to adopt that rule which seems to me best calculated to attain the ends of justice. The explanation of the law (as usually announced) given by Judge Marshall in the portions of his opinion which I have cited, seems to me to be founded on just and correct reasoning; and I am disposed to follow those decisions which uphold a peaceable possession for the protection as well of a plaintiff as of a defendant in ejectment, rather than those which invite disorderly scrambles for the possession, and clothe a mere trespasser with the means of maintaining his wrong, by showing defects, however slight, in the title of him on whose peaceable possession he has intruded without shadow of authority or title.

The authorities in support of the maintenance of ejectment upon the force of a mere prior possession, however, hold it essential that the prior possession must have been removed by the entry or intrusion of the defendant; and that the entry under which the defendant holds the possession must have been a trespass upon the prior possession. Sowder v. McMillan's heirs, 4 Dana's R. 456 (Ky. 1836). And it is also said that constructive possession is not sufficient to maintain trespass to real property; that actual possession is required, and hence that where the injury is done to an heir or devisee by an abator, before he has entered, he cannot maintain trespass until his re-entry. 2 Tucker's Comm. 191. An apparent difficulty, therefore, in the way of a recovery by the plaintiffs, arises from the absence of *positive* proof of their possession at the time of the defendant's entry. It is to be observed, however, that there is no proof to the contrary. Mrs. Lewis died in possession of the premises, and there is no proof that they were vacant at the time of the defendant's entry. And in Gilbert's Tenures 37, (in note) it is stated, as the law, that as the heir has the right to the hereditaments descending, the law presumes that he has the possession also. The presumption may indeed, like all other presumptions, be rebutted: but if the possession be not shown to be in another, the law concludes it to be in the heir.

The presumption is but a fair and reasonable one; and does, I think, arise here; and as the only evidence tending to show that the defendant sets up any pretense of right to the land, is the certificate of the surveyor of Buckingham, of an entry by the defendant, for the same, in his office, in December 1844; and his possession of the land must, according to the evidence, have commenced at least as early as some time in the year 1842; it seems to me that he must be regarded as standing in the attitude of a mere intruder on the possession of the plaintiffs.

Whether we might not in this case presume the whole of the purchase money to be paid, and regard the plaintiffs as having a perfect equitable title to the premises, and in that view as entitled to recover by force of such title; or whether we might not resort to the still further presumption in their favor, of a conveyance of the legal title, are questions which I have not thought it necessary to consider; the view, which I have already taken of the case, being sufficient, in my opinion, to justify us in affirming the judgment.

Judgment affirmed.

LEE, Justice, dissented.

Notes and Questions

1. For an action to recover possession of land, does *Tapscott* follow the rule and logic of *Anderson* or *Russell?* Or is it another position?

2. Should the *jus tertii* rule be the same for real property and personal property? Are there distinctions that could justify a state in following one rule for ejectment and another for conversion?

3. The *jus tertii* concept also comes up when the present possessor of property is not a wrongful possessor, but is in rightful possession without having title. This is why the courts in both *Anderson* and *Russell* evaluated as a precedent Armory v. Delamirie, the seminal finders' case reproduced in Chapter 2. A rightful possessor of goods is called a *bailee*, as we learned in Chapter 2. When a bailee under a voluntary bailment seeks relief against a third party, courts usually reject a *jus tertii* defense. In the leading case of *The Winkfield*, [1902] 42 (C.A.), a collision at sea destroyed a substantial amount of mail. The British Postmaster General sued for damages. The trial court disallowed part of the claim on the basis that the Postmaster General, under the doctrine of sovereign immunity, was not liable to the owners of the lost mail. On appeal, the court reversed, saying: "As between bailee and stranger, possession gives title — that is, not a limited interest, but absolute and complete ownership, and he is entitled to receive back a complete equivalent for the whole loss or deterioration of the thing itself. As between bailor and bailee the real interests of each must be inquired into, and, as the bailee has to account for the thing bailed, so he must account for that which has become its equivalent and now represents it. What he has received above his own interest he has received to the use of his bailor. The wrongdoer, having once paid full damages to the bailee, has an answer to any action by the bailor." When the bailee, rather than litigate, settles the claim against the wrongdoer, the bailor may likewise be barred. Ray Brown, *The Law of Personal Property* 314 (Walter Raushenbush ed., 3d ed. 1975).

4. The prevailing core of *jus tertii* — that a mere possessor may recover from a wrongdoer as if he were the true owner — is sometimes expressed as the *doctrine of relativity of title*. Laypersons generally think about title to property as absolute; a person either has title to a particular property, or he doesn't. The law, however, generally treats title as a relative concept. A claimant, A, may have better title to an asset than B; but B has better title than C; and C has better title than D. A particular litigation that adjudicates title only tells you whether plaintiff's title is better than defendant's, or vice versa. In the future, both parties may learn that a non-litigant has better title than either party.

5. Few recent cases discuss the *jus tertii* defense. One exception, in the context of intellectual property, is Diarama Trading Co. v. J. Walter Thompson U.S.A., Inc, 2005 U.S. Dist. LEXIS 19496 (S.D.N.Y. 2005), in which two diamond trading companies disputed the right to use the acronym "DTC." Diarama, an American company, obtained the trademark rights to "DTC" in 1999, but four international companies claimed that they could use "DTC" thanks to their longstanding relationship with De Beers Consolidated Mines, Ltd., a leading South African diamond mining company that had used "DTC" in various ways for more than half a century. The court said that the four international companies "are essentially raising the *jus tertii* defense to trademark infringement; that is, they are relying on the allegedly superior trademark rights of a third party to establish their own priority of use over Diarama's rights in the 'DTC' mark." The court then observed, "the *jus tertii* defense is severely disfavored by the federal courts, which have only entertained it where the defendant invoking it makes a 'showing of privity or successor-in-interest status with respect to such [superior trademark] rights.'" (citation omitted). The court found that the four international companies satisfied that demanding standard by

presenting evidence of the earlier use of "DTC" by De Beers and the relationship between the companies and De Beers.

E. MISTAKEN IMPROVERS

As a general rule, the true owner of a chattel who is out of possession retains his property rights, regardless of subsequent transfers of the chattel and regardless of how subsequent possessors deal with the chattel. Earlier we saw two exceptions to the general principle: the running of the statute of limitations, under adverse possession or the discovery rule, and the doctrine of bona fide purchase. A third exception is the principle of mistaken improvement, sometimes called the doctrine of title by accession, in which a person adds value to a chattel without the owner's consent. The added value stems either from the performance of labor, the attachment or addition of other chattels, or both. As illustrated by the last case in this section, comparable issues arise when a person improves someone else's land or building without their consent.

■ **WETHERBEE v. GREEN**
Supreme Court of Michigan, 1871
22 Mich. 311

This was an action of replevin, brought by George Green, Charles H. Camp and George Brooks, in the circuit court for the county of Bay, against George Wetherbee, for one hundred and fifty-eight thousand black ash barrel-hoops . . . [At trial] the jury found for plaintiffs. The judgment entered upon the verdict comes into this court by writ of error.

COOLEY, Justice . . . Wetherbee claimed . . . that replevin could not be maintained for the hoops, because he had cut the timber in good faith, relying upon a permission which he supposed proceeded from the parties having lawful right to give it, and had, by the expenditure of his labor and money, converted the trees into chattels immensely more valuable than they were as they stood in the forest, and thereby he had made such chattels his own. And he offered to show that the standing timber was worth twenty-five dollars only, while the hoops replevied were shown by the evidence to be worth near seven hundred dollars. . . . The evidence offered to establish these facts was rejected by the court, and the plaintiffs obtained judgment.

The principal question which, from this statement, appears to be presented by the record, may be stated thus: Has a party who has taken the property of another in good faith, and in reliance upon a supposed right, without intention to commit wrong, and by the expenditure of his money or labor, worked upon it so great a transformation as that which this timber underwent in being transformed from standing trees into hoops, acquired such a property therein that it cannot be followed into his hands and reclaimed by the owner of the trees in its improved condition?

The objections to allowing the owner of the trees to reclaim the property under such circumstances are, that it visits the involuntary wrong-doer too severely for his unintentional trespass, and at the same time compensates the owner beyond all reason for the injury he has sustained. In the redress of private injuries the law aims not so much to punish the wrong-doer as to compensate the sufferer for his injuries; and the cases in which it goes farther and inflicts punitory or vindictive penalties are those in which the wrong-doer has committed the wrong recklessly, willfully, or maliciously, and under circumstances presenting elements of aggrava-tion. Where vicious motive or reckless disregard of right are not involved, to inflict upon a person who has taken the property of another, a penalty equal to twenty or thirty times its value, and to compensate the owner in a proportion equally enor-mous, is so opposed to all legal idea of justice and right and to the rules which regulate the recovery of damages generally, that if permitted by the law at all, it must stand out as an anomaly and must rest upon peculiar reasons.

As a general rule, one whose property has been appropriated by another without authority has a right to follow it and recover the possession from any one who may have received it; and if, in the meantime, it has been increased in value by the addition of labor or money, the owner may, nevertheless, reclaim it, provided there has been no destruction of substantial identity. So far the authorities are agreed. A man cannot generally be deprived of his property except by his own voluntary act or by operation of law; and if unauthorized parties have bestowed expense or labor upon it that fact cannot constitute a bar to his reclaiming it, so long as identification is not impracticable. But there must, nevertheless, in reason be some limit to the right to follow and reclaim materials which have undergone a process of manufacture. Mr. Justice Blackstone lays down the rule very broadly, that if a thing is changed into a different species, as by making wine out of another's grapes, oil from his olives, or bread from his wheat, the product belongs to the new operator, who is only to make satisfaction to the former proprietor for the materials converted: 2 Bl. Com., 404. We do not understand this to be disputed as a general proposition, though there are some authorities which hold that, in the case of a willful appropriation, no extent of conversion can give to the willful trespasser a title to the property so long as the original materials can be traced in the improved article. The distinction thus made between the case of an appropriation in good faith and one based on intentional wrong, appears to have come from the civil law, which would not suffer a party to acquire a title by accession, founded on his own act, unless he had taken the materials in ignorance of the true owner, and given them a form which precluded their being restored to their original condition: 2 Kent, 363. While many cases have followed the rule as broadly stated by Blackstone, others have adopted the severe rule of the civil law where the conversion was in willful disregard of right. The New York cases of Betts v. Lee, 5 Johns. 348 (N.Y. Sup. 1810); Curtis v. Groat, 6 Johns. 168 (N.Y. 1810); and Chandler v. Edson, 9 Johns. 362 (N.Y. Sup. 1812), were all cases where the willful trespasser was held to have acquired no property by a very radical conversion. . . .

The cases of confusion of goods are closely analogous. It has always been held that he who, without fraud, intentional wrong, or reckless disregard of the rights of others, mingled his goods with those of another person, in such manner that they could not be distinguished, should, nevertheless, be protected in his ownership so far as the circumstances would permit. The question of motive here becomes of the highest importance; for, as Chancellor Kent says, if the commingling of property "was willfully made without mutual consent, . . . the common law gave the entire property, without any account, to him whose property was originally invaded, and its distinct character destroyed." Popham's Rep. 38, Pl. 2. If *A* will willfully intermix his corn or hay with that of *B*, or casts his gold into another's crucible, so that it becomes impossible to distinguish what belonged to *A* from what belonged to *B*, the whole belongs to *B*. . . . But this rule only applies to wrongful or fraudulent intermixtures. There may be an intentional intermingling and yet no wrong intended; as where a man mixes two parcels together, supposing both to be his own; or, that he was about to mingle his with his neighbor's, by agreement, and mistakes the parcel. In such cases, which may be deemed accidental intermixtures, it would be unreasonable and unjust that he should lose his own or be obliged to take and pay for his neighbor's, as he would have been under the civil law. . . . In many cases there will be difficulty in determining precisely how he can be protected with due regard to the rights of the other party; but it is clear that the law will not forfeit his property in consequence of the accident or inadvertence, unless a just measure of redress to the other party renders it inevitable. Story on Bailm., §40; Sedg. on Dams., 483.

The important question on this branch of the case appears to us to be, whether standing trees, when cut and manufactured into hoops, are to be regarded as so far changed in character that their identity can be said to be destroyed within the meaning of the authorities. And as we enter upon a discussion of this question, it is evident at once, that it is difficult, if not impossible, to discover any invariable and satisfactory test which can be applied to all the cases which arise in such infinite variety. "If grain be taken and made into malt, or money taken and made into a cup, or timber taken and made into a house, it is held in the old English law that the property is so altered as to change the title: Bro. Tit. Property, Pl. 23"; 2 Kent, 363. But cloth made into garments, leather into shoes, trees hewn or sawed into timber, and iron made into bars, it is said may be reclaimed by the owner in their new and original shape. Some of the cases place the right of the former owner to take the thing in its altered condition upon the question whether its identity could be made out by the senses. Year Book 5, H. 7, fo. 15, Pl. 6; 4 Denio, 335, note. But this is obviously a very unsatisfactory test, and in many cases would wholly defeat the purpose which the law has in view in recognizing a change of title in any of these cases. That purpose is not to establish any arbitrary distinctions, based upon mere physical reasons, but to adjust the redress afforded to the one party and the penalty inflicted upon the other, as near as circumstances will permit, to the rules of substantial justice.

It may often happen that no difficulty will be experienced in determining the identity of a piece of timber which has been taken and built into a house; but no one disputes that the right of the original owner is gone in such a case. A particular piece of wood might perhaps be traced without trouble into a church organ, or other equally valuable article; but no one would defend a rule of law which, because the identity could be determined by the senses, would permit the owner of the wood to appropriate a musical instrument, a hundred or a thousand times the value of his original materials, when the party who, under like circumstances, has doubled the value of another man's corn by converting it into malt, is permitted to retain it, and held liable for the original value only. Such distinctions in the law would be without reason, and could not be tolerated. When the right to the improved article is the point in issue, the question, how much the property or labor of each has contributed to make it what it is, must always be one of first importance. The owner of a beam built into the house of another loses his property in it, because the beam is insignificant in value or importance as compared to that to which it has become attached, and the musical instrument belongs to the maker rather than to the man whose timber was used in making it, — not because the timber cannot be identified, but because in bringing it to its present condition the value of the labor has swallowed up and rendered insignificant the value of the original materials. The labor, in the case of the musical instrument, is just as much the principal thing as the house is in the other case instanced; the timber appropriated is in each case comparatively unimportant.

No test which satisfies the reason of the law can be applied in the adjustment of questions of title to chattels by accession, unless it keeps in view the circumstances of relative values. When we bear in mind the fact that what the law aims at is the accomplishment of substantial equity, we shall readily perceive that the fact of the value of the materials having been increased a hundred fold, is of more importance in the adjustment than any chemical change or mechanical transformation, which, however radical, neither is expensive to the party making it, nor adds materially to the value. There may be complete changes with so little improvement in value, that there could be no hardship in giving the owner of the original materials the improved article; but in the present case, where the defendant's labor — if he shall succeed in sustaining his offer of testimony — will appear to have given the timber in its present condition nearly all its value, all the grounds of equity exist which influence the courts in recognizing a change of title under any circumstances.

We are of opinion that the court erred in rejecting the testimony offered. The defendant, we think, had a right to show that he had the proper authority to do so; and if he should succeed in making that showing, he was entitled to have the jury instructed that the title to the timber was changed by a substantial change of identity, and that the remedy of the plaintiff was an action to recover damages for the unintentional trespass. . . .

For the reasons given the judgment must be reversed, with costs, and a new trial ordered.

Notes and Questions

1. Suppose Wally buys $25 worth of silk from a thief in Hong Kong and ships it to New York at his own expense and risk, where the silk is worth $700. Can the true owner replevy the silk in New York?

2. If Green brings an action for damages against Wetherbee, how should damages be measured? Suppose we can identify the following components for the value of the hoops:

$ 25	Value of standing timber
75	Cost of cutting & removing timber
500	Expenses of making hoops (labor, materials, overhead)
100	Profit
$700	Value of hoops

3. *Confusion of goods*, discussed by the court in *Wetherbee*, results when fungible property of two or more owners is commingled. Because the original property is not separately identifiable, usually each person owns an undivided share of the whole based upon the respective quantities contributed. What should happen if there is no solid evidence of how much each person contributed to the common mass? During the Civil War, the Union Army seized large quantities of Mississippi cotton from a number of owners. Much of the cotton the Army used, and much of the rest was stolen, lost, or destroyed. After the surrender of Vicksburg, the remaining cotton was intermingled and stored in a common mass. Treasury agents sold the cotton,

holding the proceeds for the benefit of the former owners. Tracing original ownership into the common mass was not possible due to the lack of records. The government resisted paying the owners on the ground that none of them could prove title to a definite amount of cotton. The U.S. Supreme Court, however, ordered payment, giving each owner a percentage of the fund equal to the proportion that his number of captured bales of cotton bore to the total number of captured bales. Intermingled Cotton Cases, 92 U.S. 651 (1875).

4. Imagine that Owner authorizes Garage to repair his car and then fails to pay Garage's bill. Is Garage entitled to keep the car until Owner pays the bill? What if the car is subject to a security interest in favor of Bank, which financed Owner's purchase of the car? We have two victims of Owner; whose interests prevail? The inadequacy of the common law solutions to such problems led to the creation of "mechanics lien" statutes (*e.g.*, Wis. Stat. §779.41) in all states. Such statutes grant the Garage a lien, which allows it to retain the goods until payment is made, and they address priority among competing claimants such as Garage and Bank.

■ **ISLE ROYALE MINING COMPANY v. HERTIN**
Supreme Court of Michigan, 1877
37 Mich. 332

COOLEY, Chief Justice. The parties to this suit were owners of adjoining tracts of timbered lands. In the winter of 1873-4 defendants in error, who were plaintiffs in the court below, in consequence of a mistake respecting the actual location, went upon the lands of the mining company and cut a quantity of cord wood, which they hauled and piled on the bank of Portage Lake. The next spring the wood was taken possession of by the mining company, and disposed of for its own purposes. The wood on the bank of the lake was worth $2.87-1/2 per cord, and the value of the labor expended by plaintiffs in cutting and placing it there was $1.87-1/2 per cord. It was not clearly shown that the mining company had knowledge of the cutting and hauling by the plaintiffs while it was in progress. After the mining company had taken possession of the wood, plaintiffs brought this suit. The declaration contains two special counts, the first of which appears to be a count in trover for the conversion of the wood. The second is as follows:

> And for that whereas also, the said plaintiff, Michael Hertin, was in the year 1874 and 1875, the owner in fee simple of certain lands in said county of Houghton, adjoining the lands of the said defendant, and the said plaintiffs were, during the years last aforesaid, engaged as co-partners in cutting, hauling and selling wood from said lands of said Michael Hertin, and by mistake entered upon the lands of the said defendant, which lands adjoined the lands of the said plaintiff, Michael Hertin, and under the belief that said lands were the lands of the said plaintiff, Michael Hertin, cut and carried away therefrom a large amount of wood, to-wit: one thousand cords, and piled the same upon the shore of Portage Lake, in said county of Houghton, and incurred great expense, and paid, laid out and expended a large amount of money in and about cutting and splitting, hauling and piling said wood, to-wit: the sum of two thousand dollars, and afterwards, to-wit: on the first day of June, A.D. 1875, in the county of Houghton aforesaid, the said defendant, with force and arms, and without any notice to or consent of said plaintiffs, seized the said wood and took the same from their possession and kept, used and disposed of the same for its own use and purposes, and the said plaintiffs aver that the labor so as aforesaid done and performed by them,

and the expense so as aforesaid incurred, laid out and expended by them in cutting, splitting, hauling and piling said wood, amounting as aforesaid to the value of two thousand dollars, increased the value of said wood ten times and constituted the chief value thereof, by reason whereof the said defendant then and there became liable to pay to the said plaintiff, the value of the labor so as aforesaid expended by them upon said wood and the expense so as aforesaid incurred, laid out and expended by them in cutting, splitting, hauling and piling said wood, to-wit: on the same day and year last aforesaid and at the place aforesaid, undertook, and then and there faithfully promised the said plaintiffs to pay unto the said plaintiffs the said sum of two thousand dollars, and the interest thereon.

The circuit judge instructed the jury as follows: "If you find that the plaintiffs cut the wood from defendant's land by mistake and without any willful negligence or wrong, I then charge you that the plaintiffs are entitled to recover from the defendant the reasonable cost of cutting, hauling and piling the same." This presents the only question it is necessary to consider on this record. The jury returned a verdict for the plaintiffs.

Some facts appear by the record which might perhaps have warranted the circuit judge in submitting to the jury the question whether the proper authorities of the mining company were not aware that the wood was being cut by the plaintiffs under an honest mistake as to their rights, and were not placed by that knowledge under obligation to notify the plaintiffs of their error. But as the case was put to the jury, the question presented by the record is a narrow question of law, which may be stated as follows: whether, where one in an honest mistake regarding his rights in good faith performs labor on the property of another, the benefit of which is appropriated by the owner, the person performing such labor is not entitled to be compensated therefor to the extent of the benefit received by the owner therefrom? The affirmative of this proposition the plaintiffs undertook to support, having first laid the foundation for it by showing the cutting of the wood under an honest mistake as to the location of their land, the taking possession of the wood afterwards by the mining company, and its value in the condition in which it then was and where it was, as compared with its value standing in the woods.

We understand it to be admitted by the plaintiffs that no authority can be found in support of the proposition thus stated. It is conceded that at the common law when one thus goes upon the land of another on an assumption of ownership, though in perfect good faith and under honest mistake as to his rights, he may be held responsible as a trespasser. His good faith does not excuse him from the payment of damages, the law requiring him at his peril to ascertain what his rights are, and not to invade the possession, actual or constructive, of another. If he cannot thus protect himself from the payment of damages, still less, it would seem, can he establish in himself any affirmative rights, based upon his unlawful, though unintentional encroachment upon the rights of another. Such is unquestionably the rule of the common law, and such it is admitted to be.

It is said, however, that an exception to this rule is admitted under certain circumstances, and that a trespasser is even permitted to make title in himself to the property of another, where in good faith he has expended his own labor upon it, under circumstances which would render it grossly unjust to permit the other party to appropriate the benefit of such labor. The doctrine here invoked is the familiar one of title by accession, and though it is not claimed that the present case is strictly within it, it is insisted that it is within its equity, and that there would be no departure from settled principles in giving these plaintiffs the benefit of it.

The doctrine of title by accession is in the common law as old as the law itself, and was previously known in other systems. Its general principles may therefore be assumed to be well settled. A willful trespasser who expends his money or labor upon the property of another, no matter to what extent, will acquire no property therein, but the owner may reclaim it so long as its identity is not changed by conversion into some new product. Indeed some authorities hold that it may be followed even after its identity is lost in a new product; that grapes may be reclaimed after they have been converted into wine, and grain in the form of distilled liquors. . . . And while other authorities refuse to go so far, it is on all hands conceded that where the appropriation of the property of another was accidental or through mistake of fact, and labor has in good faith been expended upon it which destroys its identity, or converts it into something substantially different, and the value of the original article is insignificant as compared with the value of the new product, the title to the property in its converted form must be held to pass to the person by whose labor in good faith the change has been wrought, the original owner being permitted, as his remedy, to recover the value of the article as it was before the conversion. This is a thoroughly equitable doctrine, and its aim is so to adjust the rights of the parties as to save both, if possible, or as nearly as possible, from any loss. But where the identity of the original article is susceptible of being traced, the idea of a change in the property is never admitted, unless the value of that which has been expended upon it is sufficiently great, as compared with the original value, to render the injustice of permitting its appropriation by the original owner so gross and palpable as to be apparent at the first blush. Perhaps no case has gone further than Wetherbee v. Green, 22 Mich. 311 (1871), in which it was held that one who, by unintentional trespass, had taken from the land of another young trees of the value of $25, and converted them into hoops worth $700, had thereby made them his own, though the identity of trees and hoops was perfectly capable of being traced and established.

But there is no such disparity in value between the standing trees and the cord wood in this case as was found to exist between the trees and the hoops in Wetherbee v. Green. The trees are not only susceptible of being traced and identified in the wood, but the difference in value between the two is not so great but that it is conceivable the owner may have preferred the trees standing to the wood cut. The cord wood has a higher market value, but the owner may have chosen not to cut it, expecting to make some other use of the trees than for fuel, or anticipating a considerable rise in value if they were allowed to grow. It cannot be assumed as a rule that a man prefers his trees cut into cord wood rather than left standing, and if his right to leave them uncut is interfered with even by mistake, it is manifestly just that the consequences should fall upon the person committing the mistake, and not upon him. Nothing could more encourage carelessness than the acceptance of the principle that one who by mistake performs labor upon the property of another should lose nothing by his error, but should have a claim upon the owner for remuneration. Why should one be vigilant and careful of the rights of others if such were the law? Whether mistaken or not is all the same to him, for in either case he has employment and received his remuneration; while the inconveniences, if any, are left to rest with the innocent owner. Such a doctrine offers a premium to heedlessness and blunders, and a temptation by false evidence to give an intentional trespass the appearance of an innocent mistake.

A case could seldom arise in which the claim to compensation could be more favorably presented by the facts than it is in this; since it is highly probable that the defendant would suffer neither hardship nor inconvenience if compelled to pay the plaintiffs for their labor. But a general principle is to be tested, not by its operation in an individual case, but by its general workings. If a mechanic employed to alter over one man's dwelling house, shall by mistake go to another which happens to be unoccupied, and before his mistake is discovered, at a large expenditure of labor shall thoroughly overhaul and change it, will it be said that the owner, who did not desire his house disturbed, must either abandon it altogether, or if he takes possession, must pay for labor expended upon it which he neither contracted for, desired nor consented to? And if so, what bounds can be prescribed to which the application of this doctrine can be limited? The man who by mistake carries off the property of another will next be demanding payment for the transportation; and the only person reasonably secure against demands he has never assented to create, will be the person who, possessing nothing, is thereby protected against any thing being accidentally improved by another at his cost and to his ruin.

The judgment of the circuit court must be reversed, with costs, and a new trial ordered.

Notes and Questions

Justice Thomas M. Cooley

1. Cooley Law School, located in Lansing, Michigan, bears the name of Justice Thomas M. Cooley (1824-1898), author of the *Wetherbee* and *Isle Royale* opinions. While sitting on the state supreme court, he served as professor of law and American history at the University of Michigan. He joined the law faculty when the school opened in 1859 and became its second dean, teaching property and other courses. Cooley soon gained a national reputation for his opinions and his literary writings, the best known being his treatise on constitutional limitations. Two years after retiring from the bench in 1885, President Grover Cleveland appointed Cooley as the first chairman of the new Interstate Commerce Commission.

2. Are *Wetherbee* and *Isle Royale* consistent? Are you persuaded by Justice Cooley's distinguishing of *Wetherbee*? Are the two cases explainable on the basis of the culpability of the wrongdoer's conduct? Should the law protect a mistaken improver or a confuser of goods if that person acted negligently, recklessly, intentionally, or with fraud? In Somers v. Kane, 210 N.W. 287 (Minn. 1926), Kane rightfully took possession of some abandoned logs, but he wrongfully took Somers' logs and mixed them with the abandoned logs. The trial court awarded all the logs to Somers based on a jury finding that Kane acted with fraud. The supreme court reversed, relying on Justice Cooley's treatise on torts: "The logs of the plaintiff could not be identified,

log for log, after their mingling with those of the defendants, but their relative amount and value could be found with approximate correctness. The law intends compensation for wrong done, and not a penalty. . . . In 1 *Cooley on Torts* (3d ed.) 68, the doctrine which appeals to us as sound and supported by the authorities is stated as follows: 'Even if the commingling were malicious or fraudulent, a rule which would take from the wrongdoer the whole, when to restore the other his proportion would do him full justice, would be a rule wholly out of harmony with the general rules of civil remedy, not only because it would award to one party a redress beyond his loss, but also because it would compel the other party to pay, not damages, but a penalty.'"

3. After being cited by only a handful of courts during the twentieth century, *Wetherbee* has reappeared in a distinctly twenty-first century context. In Robert B. v. Susan B., 135 Cal. Rptr. 2d 785 (Cal. Ct. App. 2003), Susan visited a fertility clinic to receive an embryo produced from anonymously donated ova and sperm. Meanwhile, Robert and his wife Denise visited the same clinic so that Robert's sperm could be used to fertilize the eggs of an anonymous donor, to be implanted into Denise. The agreement with the donor specified that Robert and Denise would be the parents of any children produced from the embryos. The clinic mistakenly implanted one of their embryos into Susan, who then gave birth to a baby boy. In Robert's ensuring paternity action, the trial court awarded temporary custody to Susan and temporary visitation rights to Robert, but it denied Denise's claim that she was the "intended" mother of the boy. The court of appeals affirmed. In particular, the court "reject[ed] Denise's comparison to a plot of land or the timber growing on it. Wetherbee v. Green (1871), 22 Mich. 311. This is a parentage action, not a replevin proceeding." Does that explanation suffice to distinguish the attempted analogy to the law of accession? Compare that response to the conclusion of Professor Alice Noble-Allgire: "when a gestational mother has produced a child from another woman's genetic material, one reasonably could conclude that the gestational mother's labor and materials made a significantly greater contribution to the final product than the genetic mother's egg production. Accordingly, the gestational mother would likely prevail under the accessions doctrine in the unlikely event that a court accepts a pure property rights analysis for claims concerning children." Alice M. Noble-Allgire, *Switched at the Fertility Clinic: Determining Maternal Rights When a Child Is Born from Stolen or Misdelivered Genetic Material*, 64 Mo. L. Rev. 517 (1999).

To what extent should the principles of accession law apply to disputes concerning intangible property? Consider one possible application. A company who owns a "trade secret" has the right to prevent its employees from disclosing the secret to competitors (as discussed in Chapter 4). When an employee with knowledge of a trade secret changes jobs, under certain conditions disclosure or use of that trade secret may be inevitable—the problem is known as "inevitable misappropriation." Courts have struggled to resolve the competing interests of former employer, new employer, and employee. Mr. Koh argues that current approaches focus too narrowly on just the former employer's ownership of the trade secret. He prefers an approach that treats the situation as an accession, the transformed property consisting of the trade secret, the employee's human capital, and the employee's fundamental rights to work and choose her employment. Jay L. Koh, *From Hoops to Hard Drives: An Accession Law Approach to the Inevitable Misappropriation of Trade Secrets*, 48 Am. U. L. Rev. 271 (1998).

■ HARDY v. BURROUGHS

Supreme Court of Michigan, 1930
232 N.W. 200

CLARK, Justice. The trial court on motion declined to dismiss the bill of complaint and defendants have appealed. The allegations of the bill, here taken as true, are that plaintiffs [Walter Hardy and his partner] constructed on lot 234 of Carton Park in Flint a dwelling house, that the lot is owned by defendants Burroughs, subject to outstanding land contract in defendants Tanhersley, that plaintiffs so constructed by mistake, that defendants Tanhersley have taken possession of the house and occupy it, that defendants decline to make any adjustment with plaintiffs, and that the value of the house is $1,250.

No fraud is alleged, nor is there allegation of any conduct on the part of defendants to constitute estoppel, such as standing by and knowingly permitting plaintiffs to put up the house on the wrong lot.

It is not contended there can be recovery at law, Isle Royale Mining Co. v. Hertin, 37 Mich. 332 (1877), and, this not being ejectment, the statute providing of compensation for improvements (section 13211, 3 Comp. Laws 1915) is not applicable. Lemerand v. Railroad Co., 75 N.W. 763 (Mich. 1898). If the owners had invoked the aid of the court of equity in the premises as against the builders as defendants, the court might require the owners to compensate the builders on the maxim "that he who seeks equity must do equity." Rzeppa v. Seymour, 203 N.W. 62 (Mich. 1925). Abundant authority sanctions the exercise of the jurisdiction in such cases in favor of defendants or as auxiliary to some other relief properly cognizable in equity. Union Hall Association v. Morrison, 39 Md. 281 (1874). The question is, May the plaintiffs, the builders, sustain the bill as plaintiffs, except upon some ground of fraud or estoppel growing out of the conduct of the owners of the land, which, as has been said, is not in the case? On this question the authorities are divided. In 31 C.J. p. 315, it is said: "According to some authorities a bona fide occupant's right, in equity, to compensation for his improvements applies to him as defendant only, and does not give him the right to recover the value of his improvements after eviction by a direct affirmative suit against the owner of the property, although he made them innocently or through mistake, unless the owner of the land has been guilty of fraud, or of acquiescence after knowledge of his legal rights, or unless the parties have agreed upon compensation for the improvements. But according to other authorities, where an occupant in good faith has made improvements and has been evicted by the true owner, he may sue in equity for the value of his improvements without reference to any fraud or other misconduct on the part of the true owner."

In 14 R.C.L. p. 18, the weight of authority is recognized as in accord with the rule first stated in the above quotation. But the author of a note in 53 L.R.A. pp. 337, 339, after reviewing cases on both sides, aptly concludes: "And it would, indeed, seem strange that a state of facts which will furnish a perfect affirmative defense in an equity action should not constitute a cause of action, when necessary, in a suit in equity. In other words, that accident shall determine the assertion of what is a conceded equitable right."

The better reasoning is that plaintiffs may maintain this bill. It is not equitable on the facts here before us that defendants profit by plaintiffs' innocent mistake, that defendants take all and plaintiffs nothing. The fact that defendants need no relief and therefore seek none ought not to bar plaintiffs' right to relief in equity. It

[handwritten margin note: Authorities Divided]

was said by Judge Story in Bright v. Boyd, 1 Story's Rep. 478 (C.C. Me. 1841): "To me it seems manifestly unjust and inequitable, thus to appropriate to one man the property and money of another, who is in no default. The argument, I am aware, is, that the moment the house is built, it belongs to the owner of the land by mere operation of law; and that he may certainly possess and enjoy his own. But this is merely stating the technical rule of law, by which the true owner seeks to hold, what, in a just sense, he never had the slightest title to, that is, the house. It is not answering the objection; but merely and dryly stating, that the law so holds. But, then, admitting this to be so, does it not furnish a strong ground why equity should interpose, and grant relief?" . . .

If, upon the hearing, plaintiffs make a case for equitable relief, it will be proper to offer to defendants by decree the privilege of taking the improvements at the fair value found by the court, or to release to plaintiffs upon their paying the fair value of the lot found by the court, and this within a reasonable time limited by decree. If defendants decline or neglect to comply therewith, conveyance to plaintiffs upon payment made may be decreed. . . .

Affirmed. Costs to plaintiffs.

Notes and Questions

1. Was the lot in *Hardy* worth more or less than the house? Do the relative values matter?

2. Does it solve the problem in *Hardy* if the mistaken improver removes the house and restores the surface? Should the landowner have the right to insist on removal? Should the builder have the right to insist on removal? In Producers Lumber & Supply Co. v. Olney Bldg. Co., 333 S.W.2d 619 (Tex. Civ. App. 1960), Olney Building Company, a subdivider, mistakenly built a house on a lot it had sold two years earlier to Producers for $1,428. After the dwelling was almost completed, a title search revealed the problem. The parties briefly tried to negotiate a settlement, with Producers asking $3,700 for the lot. When no agreement was reached, Olney sent bulldozers to demolish the house. Producers sued for damages. The jury found Olney had built the house in good faith, but had destroyed it maliciously. Producers recovered $5,000 for the value of the house, $600 for site restoration, and $300 for exemplary damages. While under Texas law Olney would have had the right to reimbursement for the value of the house or the right to buy the lot, the court stated: "Under no circumstances is an improver authorized to go upon the land of another, without his knowledge or consent, and demolish the improvements that he has through mistake placed thereon, and if he does so he commits waste and can be required to pay the landowner for such waste." Judge Barrow dissented on the basis that the house belonged to Olney, not Producers, and Olney had the right to remove the house, even if it was necessary to tear it down in order to do so. He thought Producers should have recovered only $900. "There is no sound reason to exact of [Olney] additional punitive damages in the sum of $5,000 and make the donation to [Producers], as chastisement for [Olney's] alleged uncleanliness of hands, after full restitution has been made in awarding to [Producers] all damages which the jury found it suffered, as well as the exemplary damages found by the jury."

3. The court mentioned that Hardy had no statutory right to compensation for improvements because the action was not in ejectment. Most states have statutes,

often called "betterment" acts, that give certain improvers the right to offset the value of improvements against liability for rents and profits and the right to counterclaim for excess value. Georgia's betterment act is typical:

> In all actions for the recovery of land, the defendant who has a bona fide possession of the land under adverse claim of title may set off the value of all permanent improvements placed on the land in good faith by himself or other bona fide claimants under whom he claims. If the legal title to the land is found to be in the plaintiff and if the value of such improvements at the time of trial exceeds the mesne profits, the jury may render a verdict in favor of the plaintiff for the land and in favor of the defendant for the amount of the excess of the value of the improvements over the mesne profits.

Ga. Code §44-11-9(a). The landowner has the choice of recovering the land and paying for the improvements, or selling the land to the improver for an amount equal to its unimproved value. *Id.* §44-11-9(b), (c).

F. VERTICAL LIMITS

■ UNITED STATES v. CAUSBY
Supreme Court of the United States, 1946
328 U.S. 256

DOUGLAS, Justice. This is a case of first impression. The problem presented is whether respondents' property was taken within the meaning of the Fifth Amendment by frequent and regular flights of army and navy aircraft over respondents' land at low altitudes. The Court of Claims held that there was a taking and entered judgment for respondent, one judge dissenting. 60 F. Supp. 751. The case is here on a petition for a writ of certiorari which we granted because of the importance of the question presented.

Respondents own 2.8 acres near an airport outside of Greensboro, North Carolina. It has on it a dwelling house, and also various outbuildings which were mainly used for raising chickens. The end of the airport's northwest-southeast runway is 2,220 feet from respondents' barn and 2,275 feet from their house. The path of glide to this runway passes directly over the property—which is 100 feet wide and 1,200 feet long. The 30 to 1 safe glide angle[1] approved by the Civil Aeronautics Authority passes over this property at 83 feet, which is 67 feet above the house, 63 feet above the barn and 18 feet above the highest tree.[3] The use by the United States of this airport is pursuant to a lease executed in May, 1942, for a term commencing June 1, 1942 and ending June 30, 1942, with a provision for renewals until June 30, 1967, or six months after the end of the national emergency, whichever is the earlier.

Various aircraft of the United States use this airport—bombers, transports and fighters. The direction of the prevailing wind determines when a particular runway is used. The northwest-southeast runway in question is used about four per cent of the time in taking off and about seven per cent of the time in landing. Since the

---

1. A 30 to 1 glide angle means one foot of elevation or descent for every 30 feet of horizontal distance.

3. The house is approximately 16 feet high, the barn 20 feet, and the tallest tree 65 feet.

United States began operations in May, 1942, its four-motored heavy bombers, other planes of the heavier type, and its fighter planes have frequently passed over respondents' land and buildings in considerable numbers and rather close together. They come close enough at times to appear barely to miss the tops of the trees and at times so close to the tops of the trees as to blow the old leaves off. The noise is startling. And at night the glare from the planes brightly lights up the place. As a result of the noise, respondents had to give up their chicken business. As many as six to ten of their chickens were killed in one day by flying into the walls from fright. The total chickens lost in that manner was about 150. Production also fell off. The result was the destruction of the use of the property as a commercial chicken farm. Respondents are frequently deprived of their sleep and the family has become nervous and frightened. Although there have been no airplane accidents on respondents' property, there have been several accidents near the airport and close to respondents' place. These are the essential facts found by the Court of Claims. On the basis of these facts, it found that respondents' property had depreciated in value. It held that the United States had taken an easement over the property on June 1, 1942, and that the value of the property destroyed and the easement taken was $2,000.

I.

The United States relies on the Air Commerce Act of 1926, 44 Stat. 568, 49 U.S.C. §171, as amended by the Civil Aeronautics Act of 1938, 52 Stat. 973, 49 U.S.C. §401. Under those statutes the United States has "complete and exclusive national sovereignty in the air space" over this country. 49 U.S.C. §176(a). They grant any citizen of the United States "a public right of freedom of transit in air commerce[4] through the navigable air space of the United States." 49 U.S.C. §403. And "navigable air space" is defined as "airspace above the minimum safe altitudes of flight prescribed by the Civil Aeronautics Authority." 49 U.S.C. §180. And it is provided that "such navigable airspace shall be subject to a public right of freedom of interstate and foreign air navigation." *Id.* It is, therefore, argued that since these flights were within the minimum safe altitudes of flight which had been prescribed, they were an exercise of the declared right of travel through the airspace. The United States concludes that when flights are made within the navigable airspace without any physical invasion of the property of the landowners, there has been no taking of property. It says that at most there was merely incidental damage occurring as a consequence of authorized air navigation. It also argues that the landowner does not own superadjacent airspace which he has not subjected to possession by the erection of structures or other occupancy. Moreover, it is argued that even if the United States took airspace owned by respondents, no compensable damage was shown. Any damages are said to be merely consequential for which no compensation may be obtained under the Fifth Amendment.

It is ancient doctrine that at common law ownership of the land extended to the periphery of the universe — *Cujus est solum ejus est usque ad coelum.*[5] But that doctrine has no place in the modern world. The air is a public highway, as Congress has

---

4. "Air commerce" is defined as including "any operation or navigation of aircraft which directly affects, or which may endanger safety in, interstate, overseas, or foreign air commerce." 49 U.S.C. §401(3).

5. 1 Coke, *Institutes* (19th ed. 1832) ch. 1, §1(4a); 2 Blackstone, *Commentaries* (Lewis ed. 1902) p. 18; 3 Kent, *Commentaries* (Gould ed. 1896) p. 621.

declared. Were that not true, every transcontinental flight would subject the operator to countless trespass suits. Common sense revolts at the idea. To recognize such private claims to the airspace would clog these highways, seriously interfere with their control and development in the public interest, and transfer into private ownership that to which only the public has a just claim.

But that general principle does not control the present case. For the United States conceded on oral argument that if the flights over respondents' property rendered it uninhabitable, there would be a taking compensable under the Fifth Amendment. It is the owner's loss, not the taker's gain, which is the measure of the value of the property taken. United States v. Miller, 317 U.S. 369 (1943). Market value fairly determined is the normal measure of the recovery. *Id.* And that value may reflect the use to which the land could readily be converted, as well as the existing use. United States v. Powelson, 319 U.S. 266, 275 (1943), and cases cited. If, by reason of the frequency and altitude of the flights, respondents could not use this land for any purpose, their loss would be complete.[6] It would be as complete as if the United States had entered upon the surface of the land and taken exclusive possession of it.

We agree that in those circumstances there would be a taking. Though it would be only an easement of flight which was taken, that easement, if permanent and not merely temporary, normally would be the equivalent of a fee interest. It would be a definite exercise of complete dominion and control over the surface of the land. The fact that the planes never touched the surface would be as irrelevant as the absence in this day of the feudal livery of seisin on the transfer of real estate. The owner's right to possess and exploit the land — that is to say, his beneficial ownership of it — would be destroyed. It would not be a case of incidental damages arising from a legalized nuisance such as was involved in Richards v. Washington Terminal Co., 233 U.S. 546 (1914). In that case, property owners whose lands adjoined a railroad line were denied recovery for damages resulting from the noise, vibrations, smoke and the like, incidental to the operations of the trains. In the supposed case, the line of flight is over the land. And the land is appropriated as directly and completely as if it were used for the runways themselves.

There is no material difference between the supposed case and the present one, except that here enjoyment and use of the land are not completely destroyed. But that does not seem to us to be controlling. The path of glide for airplanes might reduce a valuable factory site to grazing land, an orchard to a vegetable patch, a residential section to a wheat field. Some value would remain. But the use of the airspace immediately above the land would limit the utility of the land and cause a diminution in its value. That was the philosophy of Portsmouth Harbor Land & Hotel Co. v. United States, 260 U.S. 327 (1922). In that case the petition alleged that the United States erected a fort on nearby land, established a battery and a fire control station there, and fired guns over petitioner's land. The Court, speaking through Mr. Justice Holmes, reversed the Court of Claims which dismissed the petition on a demurrer, holding that "the specific facts set forth would warrant a finding that a servitude has been imposed."[8] 260 U.S. at page 330.

---

6. The destruction of all uses of the property by flooding has been held to constitute a taking. Pumpelly v. Green Bay Co., 13 Wall. 166 (1871); United States v. Lynah, 188 U.S. 445 (1903); United States v. Welch, 217 U.S. 333 (1910).

8. On remand the allegations in the petition were found not to be supported by the facts. 64 Ct. Cl. 572 (1928).

The fact that the path of glide taken by the planes was that approved by the Civil Aeronautics Authority does not change the result. The navigable airspace which Congress has placed in the public domain is "airspace above the minimum safe altitudes of flight prescribed by the Civil Aeronautics Authority." 49 U.S.C. §180. If that agency prescribed 83 feet as the minimum safe altitude, then we would have presented the question of the validity of the regulation. But nothing of the sort has been done. The path of glide governs the method of operating — of landing or taking off. The altitude required for that operation is not the minimum safe altitude of flight which is the downward reach of the navigable airspace. The minimum prescribed by the authority is 500 feet during the day and 1000 feet at night for air carriers (Civil Air Regulations, Pt. 61, §§61.7400, 61.7401, Code Fed. Reg. Cum. Supp., Tit. 14, ch. 1) and from 300 to 1000 feet for other aircraft depending on the type of plane and the character of the terrain. *Id.*, Pt. 60, §§60.350-60.3505, Fed. Reg. Cum. Supp., *supra.* Hence, the flights in question were not within the navigable airspace which Congress placed within the public domain. If any airspace needed for landing or taking off were included, flights which were so close to the land as to render it uninhabitable would be immune. But the United States concedes, as we have said, that in that event there would be a taking. Thus, it is apparent that the path of glide is not the minimum safe altitude of flight within the meaning of the statute. The Civil Aeronautics Authority has, of course, the power to prescribe air traffic rules. But Congress has defined navigable airspace only in terms of one of them — the minimum safe altitudes of flight.

We have said that the airspace is a public highway. Yet it is obvious that if the landowner is to have full enjoyment of the land, he must have exclusive control of the immediate reaches of the enveloping atmosphere. Otherwise buildings could not be erected, trees could not be planted, and even fences could not be run. The principle is recognized when the law gives a remedy in case overhanging structures are erected on adjoining land.[9] The landowner owns at least as much of the space above the ground as he can occupy or use in connection with the land. *See* Hinman v. Pacific Air Transport, 84 F.2d 755 (9th Cir. 1936). The fact that he does not occupy it in a physical sense — by the erection of buildings and the like — is not material. As we have said, the flight of airplanes, which skim the surface but do not touch it, is as much an appropriation of the use of the land as a more conventional entry upon it. We would not doubt that if the United States erected an elevated railway over respondents' land at the precise altitude where its planes now fly, there would be a partial taking, even though none of the supports of the structure rested on the land.[10] The reason is that there would be an intrusion so immediate and direct as to subtract from the owner's full enjoyment of the property and to limit his exploitation of it. While the owner does not in any physical manner occupy that stratum of

9. *Baten's Case*, 9 Coke R. 53b (1611); Meyer v. Metzler, 51 Cal. 142 (1875); Codman v. Evans, 89 Mass. 431 (1863); Harrington v. McCarthy, 48 N.E. 278 (Mass. 1897). *See* Ball, *The Vertical Extent of Ownership in Land*, 76 U. Pa. L. Rev. 631, 658-671.

10. It was held in Butler v. Frontier Telephone Co., 79 N.E. 716 (N.Y. 1906), that ejectment would lie where a telephone wire was strung across the plaintiff's property, even though it did not touch the soil. The court stated page 718: ". . . an owner is entitled to the absolute and undisturbed possession of every part of his premises, including the space above, as much as a mine beneath. If the wire had been a huge cable, several inches thick and but a foot above the ground, there would have been a difference in degree, but not in principle. Expand the wire into a beam supported by posts standing upon abutting lots without touching the surface of plaintiff's land, and the difference would still be one of degree only. Enlarge the beam into a bridge, and yet space only would be occupied. Erect a house upon the bridge, and the air above the surface of the land would alone be disturbed."

airspace or make use of it in the conventional sense, he does use it in somewhat the same sense that space left between buildings for the purpose of light and air is used. The superadjacent airspace at this low altitude is so close to the land that continuous invasions of it affect the use of the surface of the land itself. We think that the landowner, as an incident to his ownership, has a claim to it and that invasions of it are in the same category as invasions of the surface.

In this case, as in Portsmouth Harbor Land & Hotel Co. v. United States, *supra*, the damages were not merely consequential. They were the product of a direct invasion of respondents' domain. As stated in United States v. Cress, 243 U.S. 316, 328, ". . . it is the character of the invasion, not the amount of damage resulting from it, so long as the damage is substantial, that determines the question whether it is a taking."

We said in United States v. Powelson, *supra*, 319 U.S. at page 279, that while the meaning of "property" as used in the Fifth Amendment was a federal question, "it will normally obtain its content by reference to local law." If we look to North Carolina law, we reach the same result. Sovereignty in the airspace rests in the State "except where granted to and assumed by the United States." Gen. Stats. 1943, §63-11. The flight of aircraft is lawful "unless at such a low altitude as to interfere with the then existing use to which the land or water, or the space over the land or water, is put by the owner, or unless so conducted as to be imminently dangerous to persons or property lawfully on the land or water beneath." *Id.*, §63-13. Subject to that right of flight, "ownership of the space above the lands and waters of this State is declared to be vested in the several owners of the surface beneath." *Id.* §63-12. Our holding that there was an invasion of respondents' property is thus not inconsistent with the local law governing a landowner's claim to the immediate reaches of the superadjacent airspace.

The airplane is part of the modern environment of life, and the inconveniences which it causes are normally not compensable under the Fifth Amendment. The airspace, apart from the immediate reaches above the land, is part of the public domain. We need not determine at this time what those precise limits are. Flights over private land are not a taking, unless they are so low and so frequent as to be a direct and immediate interference with the enjoyment and use of the land. We need not speculate on that phase of the present case. For the findings of the Court of Claims plainly establish that there was a diminution in value of the property and that the frequent, low-level flights were the direct and immediate cause. We agree with the Court of Claims that a servitude has been imposed upon the land. . . .

III.

The Court of Claims held, as we have noted, that an easement was taken. But the findings of fact contain no precise description as to its nature. It is not described in terms of frequency of flight, permissible altitude, or type of airplane. Nor is there a finding as to whether the easement taken was temporary or permanent. Yet an accurate description of the property taken is essential, since that interest vests in the United States. . . .

Since on this record it is not clear whether the easement taken is a permanent or a temporary one, it would be premature for us to consider whether the amount of the award made by the Court of Claims was proper.

The judgment is reversed and the cause is remanded to the Court of Claims so that it may make the necessary findings in conformity with this opinion.

BLACK, Justice, dissenting, joined by Justice BURTON. . . .

It is inconceivable to me that the Constitution guarantees that the airspace of this Nation needed for air navigation, is owned by the particular persons who happen to own the land beneath to the same degree as they own the surface below.[3] No rigid Constitutional rule, in my judgment, commands that the air must be considered as marked off into separate compartments by imaginary metes and bounds in order to synchronize air ownership with land ownership. I think that the Constitution entrusts Congress with full power to control all navigable airspace. Congress has already acted under that power. It has by statute, 44 Stat. 568, 52 Stat. 973, provided that "the United States of America is . . . to possess and exercise complete and exclusive national sovereignty in the air space (over) the United States." This was done under the assumption that the Commerce Clause of the Constitution gave Congress the same plenary power to control navigable airspace as its plenary power over navigable waters. . . .

No greater confusion could be brought about in the coming age of air transportation than that which would result were courts by Constitutional interpretation to hamper Congress in its efforts to keep the air free. Old concepts of private ownership of land should not be introduced into the field of air regulation. I have no doubt that Congress will, if not handicapped by judicial interpretations of the Constitution, preserve the freedom of the air, and at the same time, satisfy the just claims of aggrieved persons. The noise of newer, larger, and more powerful planes may grow louder and louder and disturb people more and more. But the solution of the problems precipitated by these technological advances and new ways of living cannot come about through the application of rigid Constitutional restraints formulated and enforced by the courts. What adjustments may have to be made, only the future can reveal. It seems certain, however, the courts do not possess the techniques or the personnel to consider and act upon the complex combinations of factors entering into the problems. The contribution of courts must be made through the awarding of damages for injuries suffered from the flying of planes, or by the granting of injunctions to prohibit their flying. When these two simple remedial devices are elevated to a Constitutional level under the Fifth Amendment, as the Court today seems to have done, they can stand as obstacles to better adapted techniques that might be offered by experienced experts and accepted by Congress. Today's opinion is, I fear, an opening wedge for an unwarranted judicial interference with the power of Congress to develop solutions for new and vital and national problems. In my opinion this case should be reversed on the ground that there has been no "taking" in the Constitutional sense.

Notes and Questions

1. Early law equated ownership of land with dominion and control over the land surface. Prior to the Industrial Revolution, there was no practical reason to consider whether ownership extended far below or above the surface. The common law's

---

3. The House in its report on the Air Commerce Act of 1926 stated: "The public right of flight in the navigable air space owes its source to the same constitutional basis which, under decisions of the Supreme Court, has given rise to a public easement of navigation in the navigable waters of the United States, regardless of the ownership of adjacent or subjacent soil." House Report No. 572, 69th Congress, First Session, page 10.

invention of the *ad coelum* doctrine helped to move legal thought away from the conception of land as a flat, two-dimensional surface. Instead, the doctrine visualizes ownership as tri-dimensional and not dependent upon the presence of physical materials. An owner can sell trees, topsoil, rock, and minerals, and still own land, even if it's only a hole in the ground. Land ownership means dominion and control over a container — specified, identifiable geometrical space — which may or may not contain matter (apart from air) at any point in time.

As *Causby* indicates, twentieth-century air travel strained the notion that ownership *to the sky* had no finite limitation, and thus conferred ownership *of the sky*. Unless modified, the *ad coelum* doctrine would cripple air travel by allowing private landowners to bring trespass actions based on overflights. The *ad coelum* doctrine gave way, but there is no modern consensus as to the precise nature of its reform. There are at least three theories of airspace ownership that accommodate aviation:

In the first theory, the *ad coelum* doctrine is retained as a general matter, but aircraft are privileged to enter airspace. The first Restatement of Torts adopted this theory, subjecting the privilege to the conditions that the flight be conducted "(a) for the purpose of travel through the air space or for any other legitimate purpose, (b) in a reasonable manner, (c) at such a height as not to interfere unreasonably with the possessor's enjoyment of the surface of the earth and the air space above it, and (d) in conformity with such regulations of the State and federal aeronautical authorities as are in force." Restatement of Torts §194 (1934); *see id.* §159 ("an unprivileged intrusion in the space above the surface of the earth, at whatever height above the ground, is a trespass").

In the second theory, the *ad coelum* doctrine is retained, but ownership ceases at a certain height. That height may be fixed at the minimum altitudes mandated by federal law for aircraft, or the height ceiling may vary according to the owner's use of the property. Whether the height ceiling is fixed or variable, this theory preserves the core idea of the *ad coelum* doctrine that to own land is to own a container (three-dimensional space). This theory differs from the first theory in that proper overflights do not enter privately owned airspace. Rather, they take place beyond the vertical boundary of the tract of land.

In the third theory, the *ad coelum* doctrine is rejected, with land ownership defined as owning the surface plus an ancillary right to use airspace. Ownership does not consist of exclusive possession of space above the ground. The ancillary right to use airspace in connection with the surface is dormant until the owner adds improvements that subject that airspace to his control.

2. The second *Restatement of Torts* dropped its commitment to the *ad coelum* doctrine modified by a privilege, as described in Note 1, and substituted the following approach (*Restatement of Torts* (Second) §159 (1966)):

> (1) Except as stated in Subsection (2), a trespass may be committed on, beneath, or above the surface of the earth.
> (2) Flight by aircraft in the air space above the land of another is a trespass if, but only if,
>> (a) it enters into the immediate reaches of the air space next to the land, and
>> (b) it interferes substantially with the other's use and enjoyment of his land.
> Caveat: The Institute expresses no opinion as to whether the rule stated in Subsection (2) is to be applied to the flight of space rockets, satellites, missiles, and similar objects. . . .

Comment f. . . . Illustrations:

1. A erects a house on the border of his land. The eaves of the roof overhang B's land. A is a trespasser.

2. A strings a telephone wire across a corner of B's land. Although no telephone poles are placed on B's land, this is a trespass.

3. A extends his arm over the boundary fence between A's land and B's land. A is a trespasser.

4. A, while hunting birds on a public pond, fires a shot across B's land close to the surface. The shot does not come to rest on B's land, but falls into another public body of water on the other side of it. A is a trespasser.

3. In 1958, 12 years after the *Causby* decision, Congress redefined navigable airspace to include the glide paths "needed to ensure safety in the takeoff and landing of aircraft." 49 U.S.C. §40102(30). Should this legislation alter the outcome in *Causby* on the theory that low-altitude overflights incident to takeoffs and landings are no longer trespasses? No, according to Griggs v. Allegheny County, 369 U.S. 84 (1962) (per Douglas, with Black and Frankfurter, dissenting).

Despite Justice Black's call for a legislative solution, Congress never established a statutory mechanism to compensate landowners negatively impacted by airport development. Takings principles, applied by federal and state courts, continue to define the competing claims to entitlement. For example, the owner of a landfill one-half mile from Austin's new airport, which opened in 1999 on the site of Bergstrom Air Force Base, brought a takings claim. Overflights necessitated restrictions on landfill operations, causing a $2.95 million reduction in the fair market value of the property. The owner obtained a jury verdict for that amount, but the state supreme court reversed, distinguishing *Causby*. The court stated that the harm to the landfill was indirect and that "a landowner must show that the overflight effects impacted the land directly, immediately, and substantially so that the property was unusable for its intended purpose." City of Austin v. Travis County Landfill Co., 73 S.W.3d 234 (Tex.), *cert. denied*, 537 U.S. 950 (2002).

■ **SOUTHWEST WEATHER RESEARCH, INC. v. ROUNSAVILLE**
Court of Civil Appeals of Texas, 1958
320 S.W.2d 211, aff'd, 327 S.W.2d 417 (Tex. 1959)

PER CURIAM. This is an appeal from an injunction issued by the Eighty-third District Court, Jeff Davis County, Texas, which said injunction commands the appellants "to refrain from seeding the clouds by artificial nucleation or otherwise and from in any other manner or way interfering with the clouds and the natural condition of the air, sky, atmosphere and air space over plaintiffs' lands and in the area of plaintiffs' lands to in any manner, degree or way affect, control or modify the weather condition on or about said lands, pending final hearing and determination of this cause; and from further flying over the above-described lands of plaintiffs and discharging any chemicals or other matter or material into the clouds over said lands." Appellees are ranchmen residing in West Texas counties, and appellants are owners and operators of certain airplanes and equipment generally used in what they call a "weather modification program," and those who contracted and arranged for their services.

It is not disputed that appellants did operate their airplanes at various times over portions of lands belonging to the appellees, for the purpose of and while engaged in what is commonly called "cloud seeding." Appellants do not deny having done this, and testified through the president of the company that the operation would continue unless restrained. He stated, "We seeded the clouds to attempt to suppress the hail." The controversy is really over appellants' right to seed clouds or otherwise modify weather conditions over appellees' property; the manner of so doing; and the effects resulting therefrom. Appellants stoutly maintain that they can treat clouds in such manner as will prevent the clouds from precipitating hail, and that such operation does not and cannot decrease either the present or ultimate rainfall from any cloud or clouds so treated. Appellants were hired on a hail suppression program by a large number of farmers in and around Fort Stockton and other areas generally east, or easterly, of Jeff Davis County. It was developed that the farmers' land was frequently ravaged by damaging hail storms, which appellants claim originated in and over the Davis Mountains in the Jeff Davis County area.

The appellees' testimony, on the other hand, which was elicited from several witnesses, was to the effect that this program of cloud seeding destroyed potential rain clouds over their property.

The trial court, in granting the temporary injunction, found as a matter of fact that appellants were engaging in day-to-day flying airplanes over appellees' lands and into the clouds over appellees' lands, and expelling a foreign substance into the clouds above appellees' lands in such a manner that there was a change in the contents of the clouds, causing them to be dissipated and scattered, with the result that the clouds over plaintiffs' lands were prevented from following their natural and usual course of developing rain upon and over and near plaintiffs' lands, thereby resulting in retarded rainfall upon plaintiffs' properties. The court further held that such was injurious to appellees and was in interference of their property rights, and would cause irreparable damage if not restrained. . . .

So, summing up the fact situation or the evidence that was before the trial court, we find that the three appellees and other witnesses testified that they had visually observed the destruction of potential rain clouds over their own property by the equipment of the appellants. They testified that they had seen this happen more than once. The experts differed sharply in the probable effect of a hail suppression program accomplished by the cloud seeding methods used here. The trial court apparently, as reflected by his findings included in the judgment, believed the testimony of the lay witnesses and that part of the expert testimony in harmony with his judgment. This he had a right to do as the trier of facts. . . .

Now we must turn to the objections of the appellants, who protest the issuance of the injunction on the grounds, generally, that appellants had every right to do what they were doing in order to protect their crops from hail, and that the facts or credible evidence did not justify the issuance of the injunction. Appellants maintain that appellees have no right to prevent them from flying over appellees' lands; that no one owns the clouds unless it be the State, and that the trial court was without legal right to restrain appellants from pursuing a lawful occupation; also, that the injunction is too broad in its terms.

First of all, it must be noted that, here, we do not have any governmental agency, State or Federal, and find no legislative regulation. This is exclusively a dispute between private interests. It has been said there is no precedent and no legal justification for the trial court's action. It has long been understood that equity was created for the man who had a right without a remedy, and, as later modified, without an adequate remedy. Appellees urge here that the owner of land also owns in connection therewith certain so-called "natural rights" and cites us the following quotation from Spann v. City of Dallas, 235 S.W. 513, 514 (Tex. 1921), in which Chief Justice Nelson Phillips states:

> Property in a thing consists not merely in its ownership and possession, but in the unrestricted right of use, enjoyment and disposal. Anything which destroys any of these elements of property, to that extent destroys the property itself. The substantial value of property lies in its use. If the right of use be denied, the value of the property is annihilated and ownership is rendered a barren right. . . .

In Volume 34, Marquette Law Review, at Page 275, this is said:

> Considering the property right of every man to the use and enjoyment of his land, and considering the profound effect which natural rainfall has upon the realization of this right, it would appear that the benefits of natural rainfall should come within the scope of judicial protection, and a duty should be imposed on adjoining landowners not to interfere therewith.

In the Stanford Law Review, November 1948, Volume 1, in an article entitled, *Who Owns the Clouds?*, the following statements occur:

> The landowner does have rights in the water in clouds, however. The basis for these rights is the common-law doctrine of natural rights. Literally, the term "natural rights" is well chosen; these rights protect the landowner's use of his land in its natural condition. . . .

All forms of natural precipitation should be elements of the natural condition of the land. Precipitation, like air, oxygen, sunlight, and the soil itself, is an essential to many reasonable uses of the land. The plant and animal life on the land are both ultimately dependant upon rainfall. To the extent that rain is important to the use of land, the landowner should be entitled to the natural rainfall.

In California Law Review, December 1957, Volume 45, No. 5, in an article, *Weather Modification*, are found the following statements:

> What are the rights of the landowner or public body to natural rainfall? It has been suggested that the right to receive rainfall is one of those "natural rights" which is inherent in the full use of land from the fact of its natural contact with moisture in the air. . . . Any use of such air or space by others which is injurious to his land, or which constitutes an actual interference with his possession or his beneficial use thereof, would be a trespass for which he would have remedy. . . .

Appellees call our attention to various authorities that hold that, although the old *ad coelum* doctrine has given way to the reality of present-day conditions, an unreasonable and improper use of the air space over the owner's land can constitute a trespass: Guith v. Consumers Power Co., 36 F. Supp. 21 (E.D. Mich. 1940); *Restatement of the Law of Torts*, paragraph 194 etc.; United States v. Causby, 328 U.S. 256 (1946). Other cases are cited, also, and apparently hold that the landowner, while not owning or controlling the entire air space above his property, is entitled to protection against improper or unreasonable use thereof or entrance thereon.

We believe that under our system of government the landowner is entitled to such precipitation as Nature deigns to bestow. We believe that the landowner is entitled, therefore and thereby, to such rainfall as may come from clouds over his own property that Nature, in her caprice, may provide. It follows, therefore, that this enjoyment of or entitlement to the benefits of Nature should be protected by the courts if interfered with improperly and unlawfully. It must be noted that defendant's planes were based at Fort Stockton, in Pecos County, and had to fly many miles to seed clouds over defendants' lands in Jeff Davis County. We do not mean to say or imply at this time or under the conditions present in this particular case that the landowner has a right to prevent or control weather modification over land not his own. We do not pass upon that point here, and we do not intend any implication to that effect.

There is ample evidence here to sustain the fact findings of the trial court that clouds were destroyed over property of appellees by operations of the appellants. The trial court chose to believe the evidence to that effect, and we hold there was ample evidence to support him in so holding and finding. We further hold that the trial court was justified in restraining appellants from modifying or attempting to modify any clouds or weather over or in the air space over lands of the appellees.

However, we do find that the temporary injunction granted by the trial court was too broad in its terms, in that it purports to restrain appellants from any activity with reference to land in the area of "plaintiffs' lands." The trial court's injunction is, therefore, modified so as to restrain appellants from the activities therein described only as they apply to the lands of appellees. . . .

Notes and Questions

1. What theory of airspace ownership does the court in *Southwest Weather Research* adopt? How does it compare to Justice Douglas' theory in *Causby*?

2. Weather modification companies are employed for several different purposes: to cause or increase precipitation, to suppress hail, or to modify violent storms. Although there is a lack of consensus among scientists as to the effectiveness of their efforts, weather modification efforts have continued since the 1950s, especially in the Western states. Eighteen states, including Texas, regulate weather modification by statute. The federal Weather Modification Reporting Act, enacted in 1971, requires weather modifiers to notify the Secretary of Commerce before undertaking activities and to file follow-up reports. The state and federal statutes do not address the issues raised in *Southwest Weather Research*—landowners' rights to atmospheric waters and to object to overflights—and case law is limited and inconclusive.

3. Climate change lies at the other end of the spectrum from *Southwest Weather Research*, where the context is man-made weather change that is localized and temporary. Climate change presents major challenges for people in all nations, which many expect to take on critical importance in the coming years as temperatures swell, polar ice melts, sea levels rise, and extreme weather events become more frequent. While the study of climate change cuts across many disciplines, connections to property rights are obvious. They include regulation of property that produces greenhouse gases (for example, buildings and automobiles); the disappearance and change in boundaries of coastal land, and some islands entirely; alterations in land uses and values caused by changes in temperature, rainfall, and

the availability of fresh water, especially affecting agriculture; and rights associated with modern weather modification programs that might mitigate climate changes.

■ EDWARDS v. SIMS
Court of Appeals of Kentucky, 1929
24 S.W.2d 619

STANLEY, Commissioner. This case presents a novel question.*

[L.P. Edwards discovered a cave under land belonging to him and his wife, Sally Edwards. The entrance to the cave is on the Edwards land. Edwards named it the "Great Onyx Cave," no doubt because of the rock crystal formations within it which are known as onyx. This cave is located in the cavernous area of Kentucky, and is only about three miles distant from the world-famous Mammoth Cave. Its proximity to Mammoth Cave, which for many years has had an international reputation as an underground wonder, as well as its beautiful formations, led Edwards to embark upon a program of advertising and exploitation for the purpose of bringing visitors to his cave. Circulars were printed and distributed, signs were erected along the roads, persons employed and stationed along the highways to solicit the patronage of passing travelers, and thus the fame of the Great Onyx Cave spread from year to year, until eventually, and before the beginning of the present litigation, it was a well-known and well-patronized cave. Edwards built a hotel near the mouth of the cave to care for travelers. He improved and widened the footpaths and avenues in the cave, and ultimately secured a stream of tourists who paid entrance fees sufficient not only to cover the cost of operation, but also to yield a substantial revenue in addition thereto. The authorities in charge of the development of the Mammoth Cave area as a national park undertook to secure the Great Onyx Cave through condemnation proceedings, and in that suit the value of the cave was fixed by a jury at $396,000. In April, 1928, F.P. Lee, an adjoining landowner, filed this suit against Edwards and the heirs of Sally Edwards, claiming a portion of the cave was under his land, and praying for damages, for an accounting of the profits which resulted from the operation of the cave, and for an injunction prohibiting Edwards and his associates from further trespassing upon or exhibiting any part of the cave under Lee's land. At the inception of this litigation, Lee undertook to procure a survey of the cave in order that it might be determined what portion of it was on his land. The chancellor ordered that a survey be made, and Edwards prosecuted an appeal from that order to this court. The appeal was dismissed because it was not from a final judgment. Edwards v. Lee, 19 S.W.2d 992 (Ky. 1929).]

Following that decision, this original proceeding was filed in this court by the appellants in that case (who were defendants below) against Hon. N.P. Sims, judge of the Edmonson circuit court, seeking a writ of prohibition to prevent him enforcing the order and punishing the petitioners for contempt for any disobedience of it. It is alleged by the petitioners that the lower court was without jurisdiction or authority to make the order, and that their cave property and their right of possession and privacy will be wrongfully and illegally invaded, and that they will be greatly and irreparably injured and damaged without having an adequate remedy, since the damage will have been suffered before there can be an adjudication of their rights

*The following paragraph is from Edwards v. Lee's Adm'r, 96 S.W.2d 1028 (Ky. 1936).

1917 postcard published by Great Onyx Cave Hotel (L.P. Edwards proprietor)

on a final appeal. It will thus be seen that there are submitted the two grounds upon which this court will prohibit inferior courts from proceeding, under the provisions of section 110 of the Constitution, namely: (1) Where it is a matter in which it has no jurisdiction and there is no remedy through appeal, and (2) where the court possesses jurisdiction but is exercising or about to exercise its power erroneously, and which would result in great injustice and irreparable injury to the applicant, and there is no adequate remedy by appeal or otherwise. Duffin v. Field, Judge, 271 S.W. 596 (Ky. 1925).

There is no question as to the jurisdiction of the parties and the subject-matter. It is only whether the court is proceeding erroneously within its jurisdiction in entering and enforcing the order directing the survey of the subterranean premises of the petitioners. There is but little authority of particular and special application to caves and cave rights. In few places, if any, can be found similar works of nature of such grandeur and of such unique and marvelous character as to give to caves a commercial value sufficient to cause litigation as those peculiar to Edmonson and other counties in Kentucky. The reader will find of interest the address on "The Legal Story of Mammoth Cave" by Hon. John B. Rodes, of Bowling Green, before the 1929 Session of the Kentucky State Bar Association, published in its proceedings. In Cox v. Colossal Cavern Co., 276 S.W. 540 (Ky. 1925), the subject of cave rights was considered, and this court held there may be a severance of the estate in the property, that is, that one may own the surface and another the cave rights, the conditions being quite similar to but not exactly like those of mineral lands. But there is no such severance involved in this case, as it appears that the defendants are the owners of the land and have in it an absolute right.

Cujus est solum, ejus est usque ad coelum ad infernos (to whomsoever the soil belongs, he owns also to the sky and to the depths), is an old maxim and rule. It is that the owner of realty, unless there has been a division of the estate, is entitled to the free and unfettered control of his own land above, upon, and beneath the surface. So whatever is in a direct line between the surface of the land and the center of the earth belongs to the owner of the surface. Ordinarily that ownership cannot be interfered with or infringed by third persons. 17 C.J. 391; Langhorne v. Turman, 133 S.W. 1008 (Ky. 1911). There are, however, certain limitations on the right of enjoyment of possession of all property, such as its use to the detriment or interference with a neighbor and burdens which it must bear in common with property of a like kind. 22 R.C.L. 77.

With this doctrine of ownership in mind, we approach the question as to whether a court of equity has a transcendent power to invade that right through its agents for the purpose of ascertaining the truth of a matter before it, which fact thus disclosed will determine certainly whether or not the owner is trespassing upon his neighbor's property. Our attention has not been called to any domestic case, nor have we found one, in which the question was determined either directly or by analogy. It seems to the court, however, that there can be little differentiation, so far as the matter now before us is concerned, between caves and mines. And as declared in 40 C.J. 947: "A court of equity, however, has the inherent power, independent of statute, to compel a mine owner to permit an inspection of his works at the suit of a party who can show reasonable ground for suspicion that his lands are being trespassed upon through them, and may issue an injunction to permit such inspection."

There is some limitation upon this inherent power, such as that the person applying for such an inspection must show a bona fide claim and allege facts showing a necessity for the inspection and examination of the adverse party's property; and, of course, the party whose property is to be inspected must have had an opportunity to be heard in relation thereto. In the instant case it appears that these conditions were met. . . .

We can see no difference in principle between the invasion of a mine on adjoining property to ascertain whether or not the minerals are being extracted from under the applicant's property and an inspection of this respondent's property through his cave to ascertain whether or not he is trespassing under this applicant's property.

It appears that before making this order the court had before him surveys of the surface of both properties and the conflicting opinions of witnesses as to whether or not the Great Onyx Cave extended under the surface of the plaintiff's land. This opinion evidence was of comparatively little value, and as the chancellor (now respondent) suggested, the controversy can be quickly and accurately settled by surveying the cave; and "if defendants are correct in their contention this survey will establish it beyond all doubt and their title to this cave will be forever quieted. If the survey shows the Great Onyx Cave extends under the lands of plaintiffs, defendants should be glad to know this fact and should be just as glad to cease trespassing upon plaintiff's lands, if they are in fact doing so." The peculiar nature of these conditions, it seems to us, makes it imperative and necessary in the administration of justice that the survey should have been ordered and should be made.

If it appears that the circuit court is not exceeding its jurisdiction or proceeding erroneously, the claim of irreparable injury need not be given consideration. It is only when the inferior court is acting erroneously, *and* great or irreparable damage will result, *and* there is no adequate remedy by appeal, that a writ of prohibition will issue restraining the other tribunal, as held by authorities cited above.

The writ of prohibition is therefore denied.

Whole court sitting.

Logan, Justice (dissenting). The majority opinion allows that to be done which will prove of incalculable injury to Edwards without benefiting Lee, who is asking that this injury be done. I must dissent from the majority opinion, confessing that I may not be able to show, by any legal precedent, that the opinion is wrong, yet having an abiding faith in my own judgment that it is wrong.

It deprives Edwards of rights which are valuable, and perhaps destroys the value of his property, upon the motion of one who may have no interest in that which it takes away, and who could not subject it to his dominion or make any use of it, if he should establish that which he seeks to establish in the new suit wherein the survey is sought.

It sounds well in the majority opinion to tritely say that he who owns the surface of real estate, without reservation, owns from the center of the earth to the outmost sentinel of the solar system. The age-old statement, adhered to in the majority opinion as the law, in truth and fact, is not true now and never has been. I can subscribe to no doctrine which makes the owner of the surface also the owner of the atmosphere filling illimitable space. Neither can I subscribe to the doctrine that he who owns the surface is also the owner of the vacant spaces in the bowels of the earth.

The rule should be that he who owns the surface is the owner of everything that may be taken from the earth and used for his profit or happiness. Anything which he may take is thereby subjected to his dominion, and it may be well said that it belongs to him. I concede the soundness of that rule, which is supported by the cases cited in the majority opinion; but they have no application to the question before the court in this case. They relate mainly to mining rights; that is, to substances under the surface which the owner may subject to his dominion. But no man can bring up from the depths of the earth the Stygian darkness and make it serve his purposes; neither can he subject to his dominion the bottom of the ways in the caves on which visitors tread, and for these reasons the owner of the surface has no right in such a cave which the law should, or can, protect because he has nothing of value therein, unless, perchance, he owns an entrance into it and has subjected the subterranean passages to his dominion.

A cave or cavern should belong absolutely to him who owns its entrance, and this ownership should extend even to its utmost reaches if he has explored and connected these reaches with the entrance. When the surface owner has discovered a cave and prepared it for purposes of exhibition, no one ought to be allowed to disturb him in his dominion over that which he has conquered and subjected to his uses.

It is well enough to hang to our theories and ideas, but when there is an effort to apply old principles to present-day conditions, and they will not fit, then it becomes necessary for a readjustment, and principles and facts as they exist in this age must be made conformable. For these reasons the old sophistry that the owner of the surface of land is the owner of everything from zenith to nadir must be reformed, and the reason why a reformation is necessary is because the theory was never true in the past, but no occasion arose that required the testing of it. Man had no dominion over the air until recently, and, prior to his conquering the air, no one had any occasion to question the claim of the surface owner that the air above him was subject to his dominion. Naturally the air above him should be subject to his dominion in so far as the use of the space is necessary for his proper enjoyment of the surface, but further than that he has no right in it separate from that of the public at large. The true principle should be announced to the effect that a man who owns the surface, without reservation, owns not only the land itself, but everything upon, above, or under it which he may use for his profit or pleasure, and which he may subject to his dominion and control. But further than this his ownership cannot extend. It should not be held that he owns that which he cannot use and which is of no benefit to him, and which may be of benefit to others.

Shall a man be allowed to stop airplanes flying above his land because he owns the surface? He cannot subject the atmosphere through which they fly to his profit or pleasure; therefore, so long as airplanes do not injure him, or interfere with the use of his property, he should be helpless to prevent their flying above his dominion. Should the waves that transmit intelligible sound through the atmosphere be allowed to pass over the lands of surface-owners? If they take nothing from him and in no way interfere with his profit or pleasure, he should be powerless to prevent their passage.

If it be a trespass to enter on the premises of the landowner, ownership meaning what the majority opinion holds that it means, the aviator who flies over the land of one who owns the surface, without his consent, is guilty of a trespass as defined by the common law and is subject to fine or imprisonment, or both, in the discretion of a jury.

If he who owns the surface does not own and control the atmosphere above him, he does not own and control vacuity beneath the surface. He owns everything beneath the surface that he can subject to his profit or pleasure, but he owns nothing more. Therefore, let it be written that a man who owns land does, in truth and in fact, own everything from zenith to nadir, but only for the use that he can make of it for his profit or pleasure. He owns nothing which he cannot subject to his dominion.

In the light of these unannounced principles which ought to be the law in this modern age, let us give thought to the petitioner Edwards, his rights and his predicament, if that is done to him which the circuit judge has directed to be done. Edwards owns this cave through right of discovery, exploration, development, advertising, exhibition, and conquest. Men fought their way through the eternal darkness, into the mysterious and abysmal depths of the bowels of a groaning world to discover the theretofore unseen splendors of unknown natural scenic wonders. They were conquerors of fear, although now and then one of them, as did Floyd Collins, paid with his life, for his hardihood in adventuring into the regions where Charon with his boat had never before seen any but the spirits of the departed. They let themselves down by flimsy ropes into pits that seemed bottomless; they clung to scanty handholds as they skirted the brinks of precipices while the flickering flare of their flaming flambeaux disclosed no bottom to the yawning gulf beneath them; they waded through rushing torrents, not knowing what awaited them on the farther side; they climbed slippery steeps to find other levels; they wounded their bodies on stalagmites and stalactites and other curious and weird formations; they found chambers, star-studded and filled with scintillating light reflected by a phantasmagoria revealing fancied phantoms, and tapestry woven by the toiling gods in the dominion of Erebus; hunger and thirst, danger and deprivation could not stop them. Through days, weeks, months, and years—ever linking chamber with chamber, disclosing an underground land of enchantment, they continued their explorations; through the years they toiled connecting these wonders with the outside world through the entrance on the land of Edwards which he had discovered; through the years they toiled finding safe ways for those who might come to view what they had found and placed their seal upon. They knew nothing, and cared less, of who owned the surface above; they were in another world where no law forbade their footsteps. They created an underground kingdom where Gulliver's people may have lived or where Ayesha may have found the revolving column of fire in which to bathe meant eternal youth.

When the wonders were unfolded and the ways were made safe, then Edwards patiently, and again through the years, commenced the advertisement of his cave. First came one to see, then another, then two together, then small groups, then small crowds, then large crowds, and then the multitudes. Edwards had seen his faith justified. The cave was his because he had made it what it was, and without what he had done it was nothing of value. The value is not in the black vacuum that the uninitiated call a cave. That which Edwards owns is something intangible and indefinable. It is his vision translated into a reality.

Then came the horse leach's daughters crying: "Give me," "give me." Then came the "surface men" crying, "I think this cave may run under my lands." They do not know they only "guess," but they seek to discover the secrets of Edwards so that they may harass him and take from his that which he has made his own. They have come to a court of equity and have asked that Edwards be forced to open his doors and his ways to them so that they may go in and despoil him; that they may lay his secrets bare so that others may follow their example and dig into the wonders which Edwards has made his own. What may be the result if they stop his ways? They destroy the cave, because those who visit it are they who give it value, and none will visit it when the ways are barred so that it may not be exhibited as a whole.

It may be that the law is as stated in the majority opinion of the court, but equity, according to my judgment, should not destroy that which belongs to one man when he at whose behest the destruction is visited, although with some legal right, is not benefited thereby. Any ruling by a court which brings great and irreparable injury to a party is erroneous.

For these reasons I dissent from the majority opinion.

Notes and Questions

1. After the court denied the writ of prohibition, the chancellor granted an injunction against further trespasses by Edwards. He found "there was 6,449.88 feet of said cave exhibited to the public during 1923 to 1930, inclusive, and that 2,048.60 feet of said footage was under Lee's lands." Edwards v. Lee's Administrator, 96 S.W.2d 1028, 1029 (Ky. 1936). He awarded Lee one-third of Edwards' net proceeds, which totalled $76,943.90 for the years involved. On appeal, Edwards argued that the plaintiffs "had simply a hole in the ground, about 360 feet below the surface, which they could not use and which they could not even enter except by going through the mouth of the cave on Edwards' property, [and Lee's] property has not in any way been injured by the use to which it has been put by appellants, and since this is fundamentally an action for damages arising from trespass, the recovery must be limited to the damages suffered by appellees (in other words, nominal damages) and cannot properly be measured by the benefits accruing to the trespasser from his wrongful use of the property." The court, however, agreed with Lee and affirmed the chancellor's decision. "In substance [Lee's] action is ex contractu and not, as appellants contend, simply an action for damages arising from a tort. Ordinarily, the measure of recovery in assumpsit for the taking and selling of personal property is the value received by the wrongdoer. . . . The philosophy . . . is that a wrongdoer shall not be permitted to make a profit from his own wrong."

2. What do you think of the strategy used by Edwards' lawyer? Was it smart to sue Judge Sims? Were there any alternatives?

3. The dissenter, Marvel Mills Logan, was a native of Edmonson County, the location of the Great Onyx Cave. He relinquished his seat on the court of appeals (then the name of Kentucky's highest court) in 1931, after he was elected to the U.S. Senate as a Democrat, where he served until his death in 1939. Under Justice Logan's theory, why does Edwards own all of the cave? Did he own the cave before he opened it as a tourist attraction? Before he discovered it?

4

Intellectual Property

"Intellectual property law" is a phrase used to name, collectively, the laws of patents, copyrights, trademarks, trade secrets, and (by some) the right of publicity. It is a phrase of convenience rather than a term of art; the precise boundaries of the term are neither agreed upon nor crucial. The laws governing patents, copyrights, and trademarks were all well established before the term *intellectual property* ("IP") came into common usage. These various laws serve to advance and protect *different* interests. In fact these interests are sufficiently different that many question whether the common attributes justify the use of a single collective name. People (and even some lawyers) commonly misuse the terminology of intellectual property law. To get started, we offer the following sketch of the most familiar members of the IP troupe. Caveat: Each of these paragraphs is subject to some exception, or qualification.

Patents are granted by the U.S. Patent and Trademark Office, after a review of the application of an inventor. The applicant has the burden of showing that the claimed invention is new, non-obvious, and useful. The patent confers 20 years of exclusive rights in the claimed subject matter. The 20-year term runs from the date of the application for the patent. Patents can be obtained to protect diverse technologies. One could obtain a patent for a new machine, or a new chemical compound, or a new way to make an old compound. Patent law is exclusively the province of the federal government under a grant of authority in the Constitution; states are not permitted to issue patents, nor are state courts allowed to adjudicate cases of patent infringement.

Copyrights arise when works of authorship are captured in permanent form. Since 1978 the copyright vests automatically; no affirmative steps need be taken by the author. The subject matter includes not only books, but songs, sculpture, computer programs, motion pictures and works of architecture. Like patents, copyrights are exclusively the province of federal law. Copyrights now last for much longer than previously; today, in most cases, they endure for the life of the author plus 70 years. Registration of a claim to copyright in the U.S. Copyright Office, though often advantageous, is not essential. Some critics of the copyright law believe that copyright protection is both excessively broad, and unnecessarily long. You might ask yourself how long should a copyright last? What arguments support a long (or short) term?

Trademarks are commonly included as a species of intellectual property, but have quite a different rationale, and arise differently than either patents or copyrights. The words EXXON, and KODAK, are examples of trademarks. The reason

233

for protecting trademarks is *not* to promote investment in their creation, but rather to protect consumers from being deceived as to the origin of goods bearing the marks. Trademark rights develop as consumers associate the marks on the goods with a single source. Notwithstanding that trademark law has relatively little in common with patents and copyrights, the practice persists of calling trademark law a species of intellectual property, if only because the same lawyers who do patent and copyright work also often advise on trademark questions, and the same federal agency that issues patents handles the registration process for trademarks. But state law creates trademark rights as well, and so trademark law is both state and federal law. As we will see, the breadth of protection for trademarks has increased with the development of the law of trademark dilution.

Trade secret law is state law that confers on those who manage to keep valuable information to themselves the competitive advantage of exclusive access to that information. The (supposedly) secret formula for Coca Cola is often cited as an example of a trade secret.[1] Trade secret law is arguably tort law, rather than property law, but since the subject matter of the secret can be identical to the subject matter of a patent or copyright its designation as intellectual property is not surprising. Trade secrets last for as long as the secrecy is maintained.

Right of publicity law is a relatively recent development and serves to protect the interests of celebrities in controlling the exploitation of their names and likenesses. It is generally regarded as a spinoff from the right of privacy; the right of privacy itself is a legal newcomer, generally understood as a twentieth-century development. The right of publicity is a creature of state law, and its contours are still developing. It is covered in Chapter 1 of this book.

Misappropriation is a kind of unfair competition claim that had its genesis in the INS v. AP case, included in this chapter. The core of the claim is an assertion of inappropriate borrowing of the fruits of another's investment.

This chapter is intended to introduce the vocabulary and major ideas of the law of intellectual property. The chapter is so short that it hardly qualifies even as an introduction, let alone a survey. A widely available law school casebook supplement devotes 370 pages just to the texts of the *statutes* that constitute the federal patent, copyright, and trademark laws. Single-spaced. Thousands of additional pages of judicial opinions and commentary have been written to clarify or explain the meaning of the words of those statutes. Additional pages are needed to represent state laws bearing on the same or related subjects. The goals of this chapter, then, are modest and include:

a. giving a better appreciation of the significance of labeling something as "property" and the ramifications of using that label rather than tort or contract, as the heading under which to consider an issue;

b. providing, by means of reading a small number of important cases, a high-altitude glimpse of the landscape of a part of the law that has become increasingly important;

---

1. *See* Mark Pendergrast, *For God, Country and Coca Cola: The Unauthorized History of the Great American Soft Drink Company and the Company That Makes It* (Collier Books 1993), which purports to contain the original formula.

c. offering an opportunity to understand some of the major ideas shaping patent, copyright, and trademark law.

As you read the cases that follow ask yourself in each instance whether the interest protected has the characteristics that justify characterizing it as "property" and next, whether the label matters. Some of the cases explicitly consider the question, while others deal with it only implicitly. In at least one case the question was whether to extend legal protection to something previously thought to be excluded, and in another whether to render unprotectible something that previously had been widely thought to be protectible.

The materials are presented in substantially chronological order, rather than organized by subject matter, which would be the more conventional choice. This was done for several reasons. First, some of the cases are usefully considered in the context of more than one of the conventional headings; a single case may raise trademark and copyright issues. Second, the policies that are at stake cut across all of the subject matters. And third, the chronological ordering allows you to more explicitly consider the possibility of large scale movements, over time, across the subject matters that comprise the law of intellectual property.

A. THE HISTORICAL FOUNDATIONS OF INTELLECTUAL PROPERTY LAW

THE CONSTITUTION (1789)

The idea of using grants of exclusive rights to reward innovators is an old one. In the late fifteenth century Venice enacted an ordinance that looked very like a patent statute; it granted exclusive rights to "every person who shall build any new and ingenious device in this city."[2] The English Parliament passed an early copyright statute, the Statute of Anne, in 1710. And so it was understood by the eighteenth century that both patents and copyrights were socially desirable because potential inventors and authors, unless rewarded, would underinvest in inventing and writing. The drafters of the U.S. Constitution expressly acknowledged this, and sought to provide an incentive mechanism by including in the U.S. Constitution Article 1, Section 8, which provides:

> The Congress shall have power . . . To promote the Progress of Science and useful Arts, by securing for limited Times to Authors and Inventors the exclusive Right to their respective Writings and Discoveries.

Congress acted promptly to exercise this power, enacting the first federal patent law in 1790. Patentable subject matter was defined in the early statute as including "any useful art, machine, manufacture or composition of matter, or any new and useful improvement [thereon]." These remain the principal categories of patentable subject matter even today.[3] Relatively quickly the courts and the Congress began

---

2. Giulio Mandlich, *Venetian Patents* (1450-1550), 30 J. Pat. & Trademark Off. Soc'y 166, 177 (1948).
3. "Art" meant process or method and the 1952 re-draft of the patent statute substituted the words "process or method" for the word "art."

to work out the substantive requirements, which evolved into the now-familiar requirements that to be patentable an innovation, in addition to falling within a specified subject matter category, be novel, useful, and non-obvious. Thomas Jefferson is conventionally credited with playing a very important role in the creation of the patent system, including implementing it as part of his duties as Secretary of State.[4]

Congress acted with equal dispatch in passing the first copyright law, also in 1790. Initially the subject matter of copyright was relatively narrow. The first copyright statute protected only "maps, charts and books." Subsequent amendments during the nineteenth and twentieth centuries broadened the subject matter to include nearly every form in which information can be expressed. While always justified on the ground that, without protection, there would be insufficient investment in creating the works, the extension of copyright protection also served to advance someone's private interests. The *breadth* of protection was increased at the same time that new kinds of subject matter were brought within copyright's protection.

Patents and copyrights, by conferring exclusive rights in a work, provide rewards proportional to the value of that work. By exploiting exclusive rights in patentable and copyrightable subject matter, creators can (they hope) charge amounts sufficient to recapture their capital investment plus make a profit; this is in many ways comparable to granting farmers the exclusive rights to harvest crops that have required labor to plant and tend. It is important to realize, however, that there are at least two importantly different ways to justify the same structure of incentives/rewards.

The first justification is the essentially utilitarian justification which urges that we give authors or inventors an incentive *just large enough* to encourage them to engage in the socially useful creative or innovative work we (the society) want them to do. The second justification is that the authors or inventors are naturally and inherently entitled to the value of their creative or innovative work. Thomas Jefferson wrote of these conflicting rationales in an oft-quoted 1813 letter.

It has been pretended by some, (and in England especially,) that inventors have a natural and exclusive right to their inventions, and not merely for their own lives, but inheritable to their heirs. But while it is a moot question whether the origin of any kind of property is derived from nature at all, it would be singular to admit a natural and even an hereditary right to inventors. It is agreed by those who have seriously considered the subject, that no individual has, of natural right, a separate property in an acre of land, for instance. By a universal law, indeed, whatever, whether fixed or movable, belongs to all men equally and in common, is the property for the moment of him who occupies it, but when he relinquishes the occupation, the property goes with it. Stable ownership is the gift of social law, and is given late in the progress of society. It would be curious then, if an idea, the fugitive fermentation of an individual brain, could, of natural right, be claimed in exclusive and stable property. If nature has made any one thing less susceptible than all others of exclusive property, it is the action of the thinking power called an idea, which an individual may exclusively possess as long as he keeps it to himself; but the moment it is divulged, it forces itself into the possession of every one, and the receiver cannot dispossess himself of it. Its peculiar character, too, is that no one possesses the less, because every other possesses the whole

---

4. Recent scholarship argues that Jefferson's role may have been exaggerated by earlier writers. *See* Edward C. Walterscheid, *Patents and the Jeffersonian Mythology*, 29 J. Marshall L. Rev. 269 (1995).

of it. He who receives an idea from me, receives instruction himself without lessening mine; as he who lights his taper at mine, receives light without darkening me. That ideas should freely spread from one to another over the globe, for the moral and mutual instruction of man, and improvement of his condition, seems to have been peculiarly and benevolently designed by nature, when she made them, like fire, expansible over all space, without lessening their density in any point, and like the air in which we breathe, move, and have our physical being, incapable of confinement or exclusive appropriation. Inventions then cannot, in nature, be a subject of property. Society may give an exclusive right to the profits arising from them, as an encouragement to men to pursue ideas which may produce utility, but this may or may not be done, according to the will and convenience of society, without claim or complaint from anybody.[5]

In many instances, it may not be necessary to distinguish between these two theories; both theories might justify a claim, or neither. But in other situations, as we will see, it may be crucial to decide whether to give the innovator only the portion of those fruits that are believed necessary to induce the public benefit, or, alternatively, all of the fruits of the exploitation of the work. These competing rationales are often called, respectively, the "public benefits" and the "natural rights" justifications.

There is, in fact, a third possible explanation for some rules, which is that a particular rule advances the interests of some individual or group with political or economic power. This third explanation is generally not advanced as a rationale itself, but rather the interested party defends the (self-interested) assertion in terms of some broader principle. It is often useful to see who is supporting a rule; this may sometimes more readily explain it than would any recourse to abstract principle.

A recent Supreme Court case required the Court to revisit these fundamental questions. The term of copyright had grown successively longer since the enactment of the first copyright statute, which provided for a term of 14 years, renewable for another 14 years if the author survived the first term. In 1978, the term for most works was extended to "life of the author plus 50 years." In 1998, Congress passed the Copyright Term Extension Act (CTEA), which extended the term of all copyrights by 20 additional years. This extension applied not only to works created after 1998, but also to those works that were already subject to one of a variety of terms as specified by the pre-1998 law. Plaintiffs who wished to publish works that would have entered the public domain but for the CTEA sued, arguing that the CTEA was unconstitutional. In Eldred v. Ashcroft, 537 U.S. 186 (2003), the Supreme Court affirmed the constitutionality of the extension (while appearing to admit that the extension might have been unwise as a matter of policy). The Court relied heavily on the fact that Congress had extended the term of existing copyrights in the past, as well as on a well-established tradition of deference to Congress. The Court ruled that the long term did not violate the limited-terms requirement of the Constitution, and was not an irrational exercise of congressional authority. Both the majority and dissent were acutely aware of the historical context within which they wrote; Madison and Jefferson are cited several times by both majority and dissenters.

Justices Stevens and Breyer dissented. Their dissents both distinguish the cases cited by the majority of the Court, and urge that, however difficult it may be to draw

---

5. *Letter to Isaac McPherson* (Aug. 13, 1813), reprinted in 13 *The Writings of Thomas Jefferson* (Andrew A. Lipscomb et al. eds., 1903) at 333-34.

the line establishing the outer boundary of congressional power, this enactment goes over the line. Justice Breyer wrote:

> The Constitution's Copyright Clause grants Congress the power to "*promote* the *Progress* of Science . . . by securing for *limited* Times to *Authors* . . . the exclusive Right to their respective Writings." Art. I, §8, cl. 8 (emphasis added). The statute before us, the 1998 Sonny Bono Copyright Term Extension Act, extends the term of most existing copyrights to 95 years and that of many new copyrights to 70 years after the author's death. The economic effect of this 20-year extension — the longest blanket extension since the Nation's founding — is to make the copyright term not limited, but virtually perpetual. Its primary legal effect is to grant the extended term not to authors, but to their heirs, estates, or corporate successors. And most importantly, its practical effect is not to promote, but to inhibit, the progress of "Science" — by which word the Framers meant learning or knowledge, E. Walterscheid, The Nature of the Intellectual Property Clause: A Study in Historical Perspective 125-126 (2002). . . .
>
> Thus, I would find that the statute lacks the constitutionally necessary rational support (1) if the significant benefits that it bestows are private, not public; (2) if it threatens seriously to undermine the expressive values that the Copyright Clause embodies; and (3) if it cannot find justification in any significant Clause-related objective. Where, after examination of the statute, it becomes difficult, if not impossible, even to dispute these characterizations, Congress' "choice is clearly wrong." Helvering v. Davis, 301 U.S. 619, 640 (1937). . . .
>
> This statute will cause serious expression-related harm. It will likely restrict traditional dissemination of copyrighted works. It will likely inhibit new forms of dissemination through the use of new technology. It threatens to interfere with efforts to preserve our Nation's historical and cultural heritage and efforts to use that heritage, say, to educate our Nation's children. It is easy to understand how the statute might benefit the private financial interests of corporations or heirs who own existing copyrights. But I cannot find any constitutionally legitimate, copyright-related way in which the statute will benefit the public. Indeed, in respect to existing works, the serious public harm and the virtually nonexistent public benefit could not be more clear.
>
> I have set forth the analysis upon which I rest these judgments. This analysis leads inexorably to the conclusion that the statute cannot be understood rationally to advance a constitutionally legitimate interest. The statute falls outside the scope of legislative power that the Copyright Clause, read in light of the First Amendment, grants to Congress. I would hold the statute unconstitutional. I respectfully dissent.

Note that the preceding paragraphs have addressed patents, and copyrights, but not trademarks. Merchants have placed marks on their goods, to indicate origin, for hundreds of years. Trademark law, like federal patent and copyright law, was also developing during the nineteenth century, but as part of the common law of torts — especially the tort of deceit. In 1870, the Congress passed the first federal act which provided for the registration of trademarks. But this law proved to be short-lived because in 1879 in the Trademark Cases, 100 U.S. 82 (1879), the Supreme Court ruled that law unconstitutional. The Court rejected the claim that the law was authorized under the patent and copyright clause of the Constitution, ruling instead that any power Congress had to register trademarks must be found in the Commerce Clause. It was not until 1905 that Congress acted to exercise its authority under the Commerce Clause and even then the exercise of power was very limited, by today's standards. The modern federal law of trademarks did not arise until 1946 with the enactment of the Trademark Act of 1946, popularly known as the Lanham Act. The Lanham Act has been amended many times since it was enacted. The federal act, which in its earliest form was primarily seen as providing for the federal registration of rights created under state law, is increasingly understood as the primary locus of substantive trademark law. It authorizes suits to protect both registered and unregistered marks. Suits under the Lanham Act can be brought in either state or federal courts.

As you read the following seminal copyright case, ask yourself which of the alternative theories of intellectual property protection it relies on. Would Jefferson have approved, or disapproved, of the Court's decision?

■ BAKER v. SELDEN

Supreme Court of the United States, 1879
101 U.S. 99

BRADLEY, Justice. Charles Selden, the testator of the complainant in this case, in the year 1859 took the requisite steps for obtaining the copyright of a book, entitled "Selden's Condensed Ledger, or Book-keeping Simplified," the object of which was to exhibit and explain a peculiar system of book-keeping. In 1860 and 1861, he took the copyright of several other books, containing additions to and improvements upon the said system. The bill of complaint was filed against the defendant, Baker, for an alleged infringement of these copyrights. The latter, in his answer, denied that Selden was the author or designer of the books, and denied the infringement charged, and contends on the argument that the matter alleged to be infringed is not a lawful subject of copyright.

The parties went into proofs, and the various books of the complainant, as well as those sold and used by the defendant, were exhibited before the examiner, and witnesses were examined to both sides. A decree was rendered for the complainant, and the defendant appealed.

The book or series of books of which the complainant claims the copyright consists of an introductory essay explaining the system of book-keeping referred to, to which are annexed certain forms or blanks, consisting of ruled lines, and headings, illustrating the system and showing how it is to be used and carried out in practice. This system effects the same results as book-keeping by double entry; but, by a peculiar arrangement of columns and headings, presents the entire operation, of a day, a week, or a month, on a single page, or on two pages facing each other, in an account-book. The defendant uses a similar plan so far as results are concerned; but makes a different arrangement of the columns, and uses different headings. If the complainant's testator had the exclusive right to the use of the system explained in his book, it would be difficult to contend that the defendant does not infringe it, notwithstanding the difference in his form of arrangement; but if it be assumed that the system is open to public use, it seems to be equally difficult to contend that the books made and sold by the defendant are a violation of the copyright of the complainant's book considered merely as a book explanatory of the system. Where the truths of a science or the methods of an art are the common property of the whole world, any author has the right to express the one, or explain and use the other, in his own way. As an author, Selden explained the system in a particular way. It may be conceded that Baker makes and uses account-books arranged on substantially the same system; but the proof fails to show that he has violated the copyright of Selden's book, regarding the latter merely as an explanatory work; or that he has infringed Selden's right in any way, unless the latter became entitled to an exclusive right in the system.

The evidence of the complainant is principally directed to the object of showing that Baker uses the same system as that which is explained and illustrated in Selden's books. It becomes important, therefore, to determine whether, in obtaining the copyright of his books, he secured the exclusive right to the use of the system or method of book-keeping which the said books are intended to illustrate and explain. It is contended that he has secured such exclusive right, because no one can use the system without using substantially the same ruled lines and headings which he has appended to his books in illustration of it. In other words, it is contended that the ruled lines and headings, given to illustrate the system, are a part of the book, and, as such, are secured by the copyright; and that no one can make or use similar ruled lines and headings, or ruled lines and headings made and arranged on substantially the same system, without violating the copyright. And this is really the question to be decided in this case. Stated in another form, the question is, whether the exclusive property in a system of book-keeping can be claimed, under the law of copyright, by means of a book in which that system is explained? The complainant's bill, and the case made under it, are based on the hypothesis that it can be. . . .

There is no doubt that a work on the subject of book-keeping, though only explanatory of well-known systems, may be the subject of a copyright; but, then, it is claimed only as a book. Such a book may be explanatory either of old systems, or of an entirely new system; and, considered as a book, as the work of an author, conveying information on the subject of book-keeping, and containing detailed explanations of the art, it may be a very valuable acquisition to the practical knowledge of the community. But there is a clear distinction between the book, as such, and the art which it is intended to illustrate. The mere statement of the proposition is so evident, that it requires hardly any argument to support it. The same distinction may be predicated of every other art as well as that of book-keeping. A treatise on the composition and use of medicines, be they old or new; on the construction and use of ploughs, or watches, or churns; or on the mixture and application of colors for painting or dyeing; or on the mode of drawing lines to produce the effect of perspective, — would be the subject of copyright; but no one would contend that the copyright of the treatise would give the exclusive right to the art or manufacture described therein. The copyright of the book, if not pirated from other works, would be valid without regard to the novelty, or want of novelty, of its subject-matter. The novelty of the art or thing described or explained has nothing to do with the validity of the copyright. To give to the author of the book an exclusive property in the art described therein, when no examination of its novelty has ever been officially made, would be a surprise and a fraud upon the public. That is the province of letters-patent, not of copyright. The claim to an invention or discovery of an art or manufacture must be subjected to the examination of the Patent Office before an exclusive right therein can be obtained; and it can only be secured by a patent from the government.

The difference between the two things, letters-patent and copyright, may be illustrated by reference to the subjects just enumerated. Take the case of medicines. Certain mixtures are found to be of great value in the healing art. If the discoverer writes and publishes a book on the subject (as regular physicians generally do), he gains no exclusive right to the manufacture and sale of the medicine; he gives that to the public. If he desires to acquire such exclusive right, he must obtain a patent for the mixture as a new art, manufacture, or composition of matter. He may copyright his book, if he pleases; but that only secures to him the exclusive right of printing and publishing his book. So of all other inventions or discoveries. . . .

The copyright of a work on mathematical science cannot give to the author an exclusive right to the methods of operation which he propounds, or to the diagrams which he employs to explain them, so as to prevent an engineer from using them whenever occasion requires. The very object of publishing a book on science or the useful arts is to communicate to the world the useful knowledge which it contains. But this object would be frustrated if the knowledge could not be used without incurring the guilt of piracy of the book. And where the art it teaches cannot be used without employing the methods and diagrams used to illustrate the book, or such as are similar to them, such methods and diagrams are to be considered as necessary incidents to the art, and given therewith to the public; not given for the purpose of publication in other works explanatory of the art, but for the purpose of practical application.

Of course, these observations are not intended to apply to ornamental designs, or pictorial illustrations addressed to the taste. Of these it may be said, that their form is their essence, and their object, the production of pleasure in their contemplation. This is their final end. They are as much the product of genius and the result of composition, as are the lines of the poet or the historian's periods. On the other hand, the teachings of science and the rules and methods of useful art have their final end in application and use; and this application and use are what the public derive from the publication of a book which teaches them. But as embodied and taught in a literary composition or book, their essence consists only in their statement. This alone is what is secured by the copyright. The use by another of the same methods of statement, whether in words or illustrations, in a book published for teaching the art, would undoubtedly be an infringement of the copyright.

Recurring to the case before us, we observe that Charles Selden, by his books, explained and described a peculiar system of book-keeping, and illustrated his method by means of ruled lines and blank columns, with proper headings on a page, or on successive pages. Now, whilst no one has a right to print or publish his book, or any material part thereof, as a book intended to convey instruction in the art, any person may practice and use the art itself which he has described and illustrated therein. The use of the art is a totally different thing from a publication of the book explaining it. The copyright of a book on book-keeping cannot secure the exclusive right to make, sell, and use account-books prepared upon the plan set forth in such book. Whether the art might or might not have been patented, is a question which is not before us. It was not patented, and is open and free to the use of the public. And, of course, in using the art, the ruled lines and headings of accounts must necessarily be used as incident to it.

The plausibility of the claim put forward by the complainant in this case arises from a confusion of ideas produced by the peculiar nature of the art described in the books which have been made the subject of copyright. In describing the art, the illustrations and diagrams employed happen to correspond more closely than usual with the actual work performed by the operator who uses the art. Those illustrations and diagrams consist of ruled lines and headings of accounts; and it is similar ruled lines and headings of accounts which, in the application of the art, the book-keeper makes with his pen, or the stationer with his press; whilst in most other cases the

CONDENSED LEDGER.

Bro't Forw'd.		ON TIME.		DATE:				DISTRIBU- TION.		TOTAL.		BALANCE.	
DR.	CR.	DR.	CR.	DR.	CR.	SUNDRIES to SUNDRIES		DR.	CR.	DR.	CR.	DR.	CR.
						CASH.							
						DR.	CR.						
						$	$						
						Carried Forward....							

One of Selden's Ledger Forms

diagrams and illustrations can only be represented in concrete forms of wood, metal, stone, or some other physical embodiment. But the principle is the same in all. The description of the art in a book, though entitled to the benefit of copyright, lays no foundation for an exclusive claim to the art itself. The object of the one is explanation; the object of the other is use. The former may be secured by copyright. The latter can only be secured, if it can be secured at all, by letters-patent. . . .

[The Court's discussion of two cases is omitted.]

Another case, that of Page v. Wisden (20 L.T.N.S. 435), which came before Vice-Chancellor Malins in 1869, has some resemblance to the present. There a copyright was claimed in a cricket scoring-sheet, and the Vice-Chancellor held that it was not a fit subject for copyright, partly because it was not new, but also because "to say that a particular mode of ruling a book constituted an object for a copyright is absurd."

These cases, if not precisely in point, come near to the matter in hand, and, in our view, corroborate the general proposition which we have laid down.

In Drury v. Ewing, 7 F. Cas. 1113 (C.C.S.D. Ohio 1862), which is much relied on by the complainant, a copyright was claimed in a chart of patterns for cutting dresses and basques for ladies, and coats, jackets, &c., for boys. It is obvious that such designs could only be printed and published for information, and not for use in themselves. Their practical use could only be exemplified in cloth on the tailor's board and under his shears; in other words, by the application of a mechanical operation to the cutting of cloth in certain patterns and forms. Surely the exclusive right to this practical use was not reserved to the publisher by his copyright of the chart. Without undertaking to say whether we should or should not concur in the decision in that case, we think it cannot control the present.

The conclusion to which we have come is, that blank account books are not the subject of copyright; and that the mere copyright of Selden's book did not confer upon him the exclusive right to make and use account-books, ruled and arranged as designated by him and described and illustrated in said book.

The decree of the Circuit Court must be reversed, and the cause remanded with instructions to dismiss the complainant's bill; and it is [s]o ordered.

Notes and Questions

1. Had Selden created an improved book-keeping system? Was that a socially useful thing to do? What does Baker v. Selden say about Selden's ability to capture the benefit of that investment, and insight? Why shouldn't the law protect that which is at the heart of the author/innovator's contribution? Wasn't Baker enriching himself by taking advantage of work done by Selden? Isn't that unjust?

2. Baker v. Selden has proven to be an enormously important decision. What is the precise holding of Baker v. Selden? That the book and forms were copyrightable and copyrighted, but not infringed? Or that the book, excluding the part of the book consisting of the forms, was eligible for copyright? (See the next to the last sentence in the opinion.) You should know that, more than 100 years after the case was decided, there is still significant disagreement about its exact meaning. This case is important because of its early articulation of the idea/expression dichotomy. But some have argued that it is also a case about a second distinction: the distinction between an art or practice, and the description of that art or practice. One distinction? Or two?

3. Note that Congress has codified the idea/expression dichotomy in §102(b) of the current copyright statute. 17 U.S.C. §102(b): "In no case does copyright protection for an original work of authorship extend to any idea, procedure, process, system, method of operation, concept, principle, or discovery, regardless of the form in which it is described, explained, illustrated, or embodied in such work." What do you think of the drafting of §102(b)? Is it preferable to use four verbs that mean nearly the same thing, but whose use suggests they might mean something different, or to use one verb and hope those applying it would see that it extended to its synonyms as well? Why do lawyers seem so fond of the multiple-verb form?

4. Baker v. Selden's importance, alluded to in Note 2, is obviously not because of its most narrow holding — that "blank account-books are not the subject of copyright." The importance of the case is to be found in its establishment of the

principle that copyright protection is limited to the protection of the expression of the idea, and doesn't extend to the idea itself. The implications of this proposition are not so easily imagined on first reading, but extend well beyond the question of whether, and to what extent, blank forms for recording information may be the subject of copyright. Some of the most contentious and important copyright cases seeking to apply the distinction between the unprotectible art, and the protectible description of the art, concern computer software. *See, e.g.*, Apple Computer, Inc. v. Franklin Computer Corp., 714 F.2d 1240 (3d Cir. 1983), *cert. dismissed*, 464 U.S. 1033 (1984).

The potency of Baker v. Selden is underscored by Lotus Development Corp. v. Borland International, Inc., 799 F. Supp. 203 (D. Mass. 1992), *rev'd*, 49 F.3d 807 (1st Cir. 1995), *aff'd by an equally divided Court*, 516 U.S. 233 (1996). Lotus was the developer of Lotus 1-2-3, the first widely adopted spreadsheet program for personal computers. Borland, a Lotus competitor, worked for nearly three years to develop a program to compete with Lotus 1-2-3, and in 1987 released Quattro and Quattro Pro. To compete effectively in a market comprised of users who were familiar and comfortable with the Lotus 1-2-3 menu structures and commands, Borland included in Quattro programs a "Lotus Emulation Interface," which was admittedly a copy of the Lotus 1-2-3 menu tree. Lotus sued, asserting that its menu structure was copyrightable expression, and that Borland's copying represented infringement. The trial court ruled in favor of Lotus on the question of the copyrightability of the menu structure on the ground that "[a] very satisfactory spreadsheet menu tree can be constructed using different commands and a different command structure from those of Lotus 1-2-3. In fact, Borland has constructed just such an alternate tree for use in Quattro Pro's native mode." 799 F. Supp. at 217.

Borland argued, on appeal, that the case was controlled by Baker v. Selden, urging that "[t]he facts of Baker v. Selden, and even the arguments advanced by the parties in that case, are identical to those in this case. The only difference is that the 'user interface' of Selden's system was implemented by pen and paper rather than by computer." 49 F.3d at 814.

While the First Circuit said that it didn't find the analogy to be as close as Borland's argument suggested, it did go on to rule that the Lotus menu command hierarchy was uncopyrightable because it constituted Lotus 1-2-3's "method of operation" and that §102(b), the statutory embodiment of the policy of Baker v. Selden, expressly denied copyright to methods of operation.

> That the Lotus menu command hierarchy is a "method of operation" becomes clearer when one considers program compatibility. Under Lotus's theory, if a user uses several different programs, he or she must learn how to perform the same operation in a different way for each program used. For example, if the user wanted the computer to print material, then the user would have to learn not just one method of operating the computer such that it prints, but many different methods. We find this absurd. The fact that there may be many different ways to operate a computer program, or even many different ways to operate a computer program using a set of hierarchically arranged command terms, does not make the actual method of operation chosen copyrightable; it still functions as a method for operating the computer and as such is uncopyrightable. (49 F.3d at 817-18)

The Supreme Court granted certiorari, but deadlocked 4 to 4. This affirmed the First Circuit decision, but with no definitive resolution of the issue, given the lack of a Supreme Court opinion. It is also worth noting that Circuit Judge Boudin, concurring, would have found the menu structure copyrightable, but would have concluded that Borland's borrowing was privileged under the doctrine of "fair use."

What would be the result, in the world of software development, of a clear rule confirming the Borland position? The Lotus position? If you were in Congress, and the issue were presented to you for a vote, which choice would you make, and why?

The next reading introduces the requirements for obtaining a patent. But before reading the case, ask yourself what the requirements *should be* for obtaining a patent, given the reasons that justify having a patent system. *Warning*: The case is somewhat less explicit about what is required than some other cases you've read; it takes some things for granted. This means you may have to work a bit harder to identify the legal standard that the Court is seeking to apply.

■ THE BARBED WIRE PATENT
Supreme Court of the United States, 1892 143 U.S. 275

This was a bill in equity for the infringement of letters patent No. 157,124, issued to Joseph F. Glidden, November 24, 1874, for an "Improvement in Wire Fences." In his specification the patentee stated that "this invention has relation to means for preventing cattle from breaking through wire fences; and it consists in combining, with the twisted fence-wires, a short transverse wire, coiled or bent at its central portion about one of the wire strands of the twist, with its free ends projecting in opposite directions." . . .

. . . The following drawings accompanied the specification:

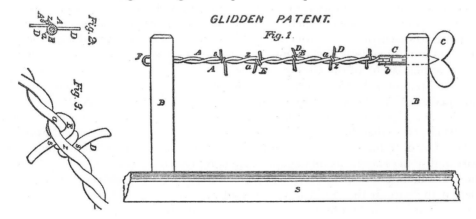

[The plaintiff, Washburn & Moen Manufacturing Co., acquired the patent by assignment. The defendants were Beat'Em All Barbed-Wire Co. and other fence sellers.]

BROWN, Justice. No serious question is or can be made regarding the infringement in this suit, the defendants relying solely upon the want of novelty. To

determine satisfactorily the question whether there is involved in this device sufficient novelty to support a patent, it is necessary to consider somewhat at length the
progress which had been made in constructing barbed wire fences prior to the issue
of this patent, as it appears both from the face of the prior patents themselves and
from the oral evidence introduced by the defendants tending to show an unpatented use of such device before the application was made in this case.

(1) The use of wire fences, composed either of a single wire, or of two or more
wires twisted together, antedates by many years the barbed feature of such fences.
But, either by reason of their comparative invisibility or their weakness, they proved
an insufficient protection against cattle, and fell largely into disuse. Something was
needed, not so much to strengthen them, as to deter cattle from encountering them
or testing their strength. Natural hedges of thorn, which in effect contain the
principle of the barbed wire, have been employed both in this country and in
England from time immemorial. Fences of other materials and various forms had
been armed with pickets, spurs, iron points, spikes, sharp stones, or bits of broken
glass inserted in plaster, but prior to 1867 no one seems to have conceived the idea
of arming wire fences with a similar protecting device. In July of that year, however,
one William D. Hunt took out a patent for arming the wires with a series of small
spur-wheels, their spurs being sharpened so as to prick readily. These wheels were
provided with openings at their centers through which the wire passed, fitting it
loosely so that the wheel would revolve easily upon it. . . . This was obviously a crude
and unsatisfactory device, and never seems to have gone into general use. . . .

In the same year . . . Lucien B. Smith took out a patent for a wire fence, having
spools of iron or wood strung upon it, each spool being perforated and provided
with four spurs projecting radially from them, and so arranged that they would
revolve, while they were held in place lengthwise of the wires by slight bends or
deflections in the wires at a distance of two or three feet apart, forming short straight
lengths of about four inches, upon which the spools were hung. This patent
contained the first suggestion of a barb proper, though in a very imperfect form;
but it embodied an idea of which the public was not slow to avail itself, and gave an
impetus to succeeding inventors, which finally resulted in the barbed fence now in
use. Though valuable as illustrating the state of the art, it will scarcely be claimed to
be an anticipation* of the Glidden device.

The patent of February 11, 1868, to Michael Kelly indicated a decided step in
advance of its predecessors, consisting as it did of small flat pieces of iron or
steel . . . each provided with a hole corresponding with the size of the wire, though
a little larger, so that they could be introduced easily upon the wire, either by proper
machinery or by hand. "These pieces," says the patentee, "after being strung on the
wire at distances about six inches apart, are compressed laterally upon the wire by a
blow of a hammer, or otherwise, so as to flatten the hole *e*, and also correspondingly
flatten the wire at the point where this adjunct is to stand. I term these pieces
'thorns'; and it will be observed that each presents two sharp points. . . . The wire
thus provided with the sharp points or thorns serves in the ordinary manner, with
the addition of possessing an offensive character, which will soon teach cattle to
respect it and not attempt to force it." Figure 2 of this patent, a representation of
which is here given, undoubtedly contained the idea subsequently developed by
Glidden, but there was apparently no method of holding the barb in place, save by a

---

* ["Anticipation" is a term of art in patent law. Prior art "anticipates" only if it is essentially identical
to the claimed invention. This is explored in more detail in Note 3 following the opinion. — Eds.]

blow of a hammer — at least such seems to have been the opinion of the patentee at the time the patent was originally issued. . . .

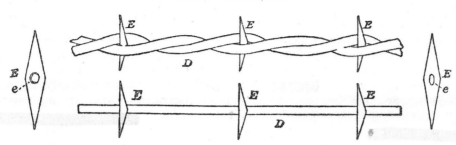

KELLY PATENT.

From this review of the state of the art at the time the patent in suit was issued it is evident that Glidden can neither claim broadly the use of the plain or the twisted wire, nor the sharp thorns or barbs, nor indeed the combination of the two as they appear in the Kelly patent. It does not follow, however, that he did not make a most valuable contribution to the art of wire fencing in the introduction of the coiled barb, in combination with the twisted wire, by which it is clamped and held in position. By this device the barb was prevented from turning or moving laterally and was held rigidly in place. If this be also true of the device shown in Figure 2 of the Kelly patent of February 11, 1868, the immobility of the barb in that patent is due to the aid of a blow struck by a hammer, since the mere fact that the barbs were strung upon the wires would not of itself prevent a movement within certain limits unless they were held fast by compression. . . . The vital difference in the two patents is in the shape of the barb itself. In one case a flat bit of metal is used of an elongated diamond shape, through which a hole is pierced, by means of which it is strung upon the wire, requiring something more than the aid of a second wire twisted upon the first to render it immovable. In the other the barb is a piece of wire coiled about one of the fence wires, and held rigidly in place by the twisting of another wire about the first.

It is true that the affixing of barbs to a fence-wire does not apparently give a wide scope to the ingenuity of the inventor; but from the crude device of Hunt to the perfected wire of Glidden, each patent has marked a step in the progress in the art. The difference between the Kelly fence and the Glidden fence is not a radical one, but slight as it may seem to be, it was apparently this which made the barbed-wire fence a practical and commercial success. The inventions of Hunt and Smith appear to be scarcely more than tentative, and never to have gone into general use. The sales of the Kelly patent never seem to have exceeded 3000 tons per annum, while plaintiff's manufacture and sales of the Glidden device (substituting a sharp barb for a blunt one) rose rapidly from 50 tons in 1874 to 44,000 tons in 1886, while those of its licensees in 1887 reached the enormous amount of 173,000 tons. Indeed, one who has travelled upon the western plains of this continent cannot have failed to notice the very large amount of territory enclosed by these fences which otherwise, owing to the great scarcity of wood, would have to be left unprotected.

Under such circumstances courts have not been reluctant to sustain a patent to the man who has taken the final step which has turned a failure into a success. In the law of patents it is the last step that wins. It may be strange that, considering the important results obtained by Kelly in his patent, it did not occur to him to substitute a coiled wire in place of the diamond shape prong, but evidently it did not; and to the man to whom it did ought not to be denied the quality of inventor. There are many instances in the reported decisions of this court where a monopoly has been sustained in favor of the last of a series of inventors, all of whom were groping to attain a certain result, which only the last one of the number seemed able to grasp. . . .

(2) Thus far we have considered, as bearing upon the state of the art, devices, the character, construction and scope of which were exactly defined in the specifications and drawings of actual patents, the only question presented being the proper interpretation of such patents, and the bounds they had set to the ingenuity of succeeding inventors. We have now to deal with certain unpatented devices, claimed to be complete anticipations of this patent, the existence and use of which are proven only by oral testimony. In view of the unsatisfactory character of such testimony, arising from the forgetfulness of witnesses, their liability to mistakes, their proneness to recollect things as the party calling them would have them recollect them, aside from the temptation to actual perjury, courts have . . . imposed upon defendants the burden of proving such devices . . . beyond a reasonable doubt. Witnesses whose memories are prodded by the eagerness of interested parties to elicit testimony favorable to themselves are not usually to be depended upon for accurate information. The very fact, which courts as well as the public have not failed to recognize, that almost every important patent, from the cotton gin of Whitney to the one under consideration, has been attacked by the testimony of witnesses who imagined they had made similar discoveries long before the patentee had claimed to have invented his device, has tended to throw a certain amount of discredit upon all that class of evidence, and to demand that it be subjected to the closest scrutiny. . . .

The testimony of the defendant tended to show the existence, public exhibition and use of a number of fences prior to the date of the application in this case; but what is known as the Morley fence is supported by the largest amount of evidence, and was the one the learned District Judge who heard this case in the court below held to have been an anticipation of this patent. 33 Fed. Rep. 261.

A panel of this fence appears to have been exhibited at a county fair in Delaware County, Iowa, at Delhi, in 1858 and 1859. It appears that Morley owned lands in Delaware County; that his family lived in Pennsylvania; that for a number of years, from 1858 to 1864, he spent a portion of his time in Iowa, living alone or boarding with his neighbors; that he was not of entirely sound mind; and that he died in an insane asylum in Pennsylvania in 1867, after a year's immurement. . . . The testimony of the defendants tended to show . . . that . . . Morley came to the house of one Dubois, a farmer living in Delaware County, having with him a piece of fence-wire, which had short pieces of wire wound around it; that Morley remained with him that night; that the next day he saw a panel of fence on the fair ground exhibited by Morley, made by stretching wires from a tree or post to another post; and that the wire so used was the same or similar to that previously shown him by Morley. . . . One Potter testified that he attended the fair and saw Morley there; that he exhibited a panel of fence made of wires strung between a tree and a post, with barbs made of short wires twisted around the plain wire; that Morley gave him a piece of the wire with barbs on it; that he took it home with him; that he and his wife talked about it and its effect upon stock; that he had the specimen of the wire in his summer kitchen for a year or more, and then put it in an old trunk in which he kept various relics and keepsakes; that it had remained there, and was there still; and then, on request of defendants' counsel, witness went to his home, brought the specimen of wire before the notary, and made it an exhibit in the case. . . .

In all some twenty-four witnesses were sworn on behalf of the defendants to the existence of the Delhi fair fence. According to the recollection of some of the witnesses it was made of three or four strands of single wire, on which the barbs were fastened, the wires being attached at their ends to posts in the ground, or to a post and a tree; and that the top wire had barbs on it formed of short pieces of wire wrapped around it, some say once, others twice, and still others three times. The other two or three strands of single wire were without barbs. Beneath the top barbed wire was a board to attract the attention of the cattle, either secured to the posts or suspended by a wire from the top wire strand. This fence was put up on the second day of the fair and exhibited one day, as it appears the fair continued but two days. No one seems to know what became of the panel, nor of the barbed wire upon it; it was never seen after the fair, beyond the single piece produced by the witness Potter. . . .

It further appeared that in 1866 Morley took out a patent for a triangular cattle pen, built of posts and boards supported upon wheels, so constructed that it could be moved by the animal inside of it. Some seven or eight witnesses testified that at different times when they saw this machine it had on it one or more strands of fence-wire with barbs or prickers on them, put on in the same manner as were the barbs on the Delhi fair exhibit, and the whole strung on the top of the posts above the boards. . . .

Upon the other hand, plaintiff met this testimony with that of a large number of witnesses who had seen these fences and also the cattle pen, and who testified that there was no barbed wire connected with them. . . .

Even conceding that Morley did exhibit a wire fence armed with barbs at the Delhi County fair, we do not think the testimony connected with this fence makes out a case of prior use of the device patented by Glidden, for the following reasons: *First*, while the fence may have been armed with barbs, there is very little, if anything, to show that it was constructed according to the design of the Glidden fence. Indeed, after the lapse of twenty-five years it would, in the nature of things, be highly improbable that any witness who saw this fence for the single day it was exhibited there would be able to describe it accurately. *Second*, if Morley had regarded this fence as of any value he would have applied for a patent upon it, since he did in fact obtain a patent for his travelling pen, which appears to have been a comparatively worthless contrivance. If this pen had been armed with a barbed wire it is somewhat singular that no allusion was made to it in the drawings or specification. *Third*, the testimony of Potter, that he preserved a piece of wire given to him by Morley in a trunk containing some old relics for over twenty-five years, is not only contradicted by his son, who was familiar with the trunk, had examined its contents, and testified that he had never seen the wire there, but is improbable upon its face. *Fourth*, if any experiments were made by Morley in this direction they were evidently looked upon by him and by the public as of no practical value, and were subsequently abandoned and the fences lost.

While we think the testimony goes far to establish the fact that Morley exhibited a wire fence at this fair, and perhaps also used it upon his farm at about the date claimed, we are far from being satisfied that it was the Glidden device, or so near an approximation to it as to justify us in holding that it was an anticipation.

[The Court then discusses the insufficiency of evidence as to other fences, alleged by the defendants to have anticipated Glidden's.]

There was a vast amount of testimony of similar character tending to show the use of coiled barbs upon fence-wires, which it would serve no good purpose to discuss in detail. There was evidently prior to Glidden's application more or less experimenting in a rude way in and about Delaware County, upon the subject of barbed wires as applied to wire fences, and we think it is quite probable that coiled barbs were affixed to single wires before the Glidden application was made. We are not satisfied, however, that he was not the originator of the combination claimed by him of the coiled barb, locked and held in place by the intertwisted wire. . . . [I]t was Glidden, beyond question, who first published this device; put it upon record; made use of it for a practical purpose; and gave it to the public, by which it was eagerly seized upon, and spread until there is scarcely a cattle-raising district in the world in which it is not extensively employed. Under these circumstances, we think the doubts we entertain concerning the actual inventor of this device should be resolved in favor of the patentee.

The decree of the Circuit Court will, therefore, be reversed, and the case remanded with instructions to enter a decree for the plaintiff for an accounting, and for further proceedings in conformity with this opinion.

FIELD, Justice, dissented, upon the ground that there was no novelty in the invention.

Notes and Questions

1. Many would assert that the novelty requirement is the most self-evident of the substantive requirements of a patent system. Why might this be so? Why shouldn't Glidden prevail if he simply proves that he was the first to seek a patent on the improved barbed wire?

2. What problems do you see in determining the meaning of a requirement that requires "novelty" as a requirement of patentability? Is novelty a simple matter? (At about the same time as the decision in the *Barbed Wire Patent* case, a leading treatise writer on patent law devoted 155 pages to the topic.)

3. In its opinion the Court discusses earlier wire fence construction that, though somewhat similar to Glidden's, did not "anticipate" the Glidden invention. "Anticipate" is a term of art in patent law. In order for a device in the prior art to anticipate, and so defeat novelty, the prior art reference needs to contain each and every element of the invention claimed by the patent applicant. The degree of similarity required must be essentially complete. If an applicant for a patent is claiming "a device consisting of parts *A*, *B* and *C*" and the prior art contains two devices, one consisting of an *A* and a *B*, and another consisting of parts *A*, *C*, and *D*, neither of the prior art references anticipates the claimed device, and it is not permissible to combine them.

4. The novelty requirement, introduced so early in the requirements for patentability, is presently largely embodied in §102(a) of the patent statute (35 U.S.C. §102), which provides:

§102. Conditions for Patentability; Novelty
    (a) A person shall be entitled to a patent unless —
    (1) the claimed invention was patented, described in a printed publication, or in public use, on sale, or otherwise available to the public before the effective filing date of the claimed invention; . . .

You should try to deconstruct §102(a). How many rules does it contain? Which of its aspects does the Court in the *Barbed Wire Patent* case address?

Congress revised the statutory novelty requirement as part of the America Invents Act of 2011, which became effective on March 16, 2013. The America Invents Act makes a number of important changes to patent law and the patent issuance process. The most sweeping change is to transform the United States from a "first to invent" to a "first to file" system, which conforms U.S. law to the standard presently followed by virtually all other countries. Under the new law, the first inventor to file, subject to a grace period, is entitled to a patent regardless of another's prior invention. How does replacement of the historic "first to invent" system with the "first to file" system affect patent infringement litigation in situations like that presented by the *Barbed Wire Patent* case? In that case, would the plaintiff or the defendants be more likely to prevail? Will it be easier or harder for courts to reach decisions?

5. What substantive requirements, in addition to novelty, do you believe would be either necessary or appropriate with respect to the issue of patentability? In Hotchkiss v. Greenwood, 52 U.S. (11 How.) 248 (1850), the Court formulated a condition for patentability that went beyond mere novelty. The case involved a patent on the mere substitution of materials for the manufacture of doorknobs (porcelain or clay for wood or metal). The Court, in finding the patent invalid, said:

> Unless more ingenuity and skill . . . were required . . . than were possessed by an ordinary mechanic acquainted with the business, there was an absence of that degree of skill and ingenuity which constitute essential elements of every invention. In other words, the improvement is the work of the skillful mechanic, not that of the inventor. (52 U.S. at 267)

This judicial gloss on the patent statute remained uncodified until 1952. It is now, in a substantially unchanged form, found in §103.

> §103. Conditions for Patentability; Non-obvious Subject Matter
>
> A patent may not be obtained though the invention is not identically disclosed or described as set forth in section 102 of this title, if the differences between the subject matter sought to be patented and the prior art are such that the subject matter as a whole would have been obvious at the time the invention was made to a person having ordinary skill in the art to which said subject matter pertains. Patentability shall not be negatived by the manner in which the invention was made.

In Graham v. John Deere Co., 383 U.S. 1 (1966), the first important interpretation of the 1952 statute, the Supreme Court noted:

> The section is cast in relatively unambiguous terms. Patentability is to depend, in addition to novelty and utility, upon the "non-obvious" nature of the "subject matter sought to be patented" to a person having ordinary skill in the pertinent art.
>
> The first sentence of this section is strongly reminiscent of the language in *Hotchkiss*. Both formulations place emphasis on the pertinent art existing at the time the invention was made and both are implicitly tied to advances in that art. The major distinction is that Congress has emphasized "non-obviousness" as the operative test of the section, rather than the less definite "invention" language of *Hotchkiss* that Congress thought had led to "a large variety" of expressions in decisions and writings. In the title itself the Congress used the phrase "Conditions for patentability; *non-obvious*

subject matter" (italics added), thus focusing upon "non-obviousness" rather than "invention." The Senate and House Reports, S. Rep. No. 1979, 82d Cong., 2d Sess. (1952); H. R. Rep. No. 1923, 82d Cong., 2d Sess. (1952), reflect this emphasis in these terms:

> "Section 103, for the first time in our statute, provides a condition which exists in the law and has existed for more than 100 years, but only by reason of decisions of the courts. An invention which has been made, and which is new in the sense that the same thing has not been made before, may still not be patentable if the difference between the new thing and what was known before is not considered sufficiently great to warrant a patent. That has been expressed in a large variety of ways in decisions of the courts and in writings. Section 103 states this requirement in the title. It refers to the difference between the subject matter sought to be patented and the prior art, meaning what was known before as described in section 102. If this difference is such that the subject matter as a whole would have been obvious at the time to a person skilled in the art, then the subject matter cannot be patented."

The Court, in *Graham,* also endorsed the use of the so-called sub-tests of invention.

> While the ultimate question of patent validity is one of law, the §103 condition, which is but one of three conditions, each of which must be satisfied, lends itself to several basic factual inquiries. Under §103, the scope and content of the prior art are to be determined; differences between the prior art and the claims at issue are to be ascertained; and the level of ordinary skill in the pertinent art resolved. Against this background, the obviousness or nonobviousness of the subject matter is determined. Such secondary considerations as commercial success, long felt but unsolved needs, failure of others, etc., might be utilized to give light to the circumstances surrounding the origin of the subject matter sought to be patented. As indicia of obviousness or nonobviousness, these inquiries may have relevancy.

Could the defendants in the *Barbed Wire Patent* case have sought to defeat the patent on the ground now embodied in §103? How would Glidden have argued, in response?

6. How reliable do you expect the patent office and the courts are when applying the patentability criteria? The criteria themselves are complex and subtle. The patent office, confronted with an application, must apply the patentability criteria in light of information about relevant prior art. A patent examiner, who works within a particular range of subject matter, must supplement her training by finding and relying on information in the patent office files. The examiner must also rely on the information provided by the patent applicant. All of this information may be incomplete. Even though the applicant has a duty of candor in dealing with the patent office, and must disclose known prior art, the applicant doesn't have perfect knowledge. Patent examiners face an increasing number of patent applications, and are under significant pressure to keep up; on average they have only about 18 hours to invest in evaluating the patent, and conducting the back and forth negotiations with the applicant. The examiner may yield, and issue a patent, rather than pursue doubts about patentability. The result is that as many as half the patents issued, and subsequently litigated, are ultimately found to be invalid. (Remember, an issued patent is only *presumably* valid. It can be held invalid in subsequent litigation, either because of newly discovered prior art, not available to the examiner, or because the examiner is found to have made a mistake in issuing the patent.)

How well do we want our patent-issuing process to work? Some argue that we should hire more patent examiners, and do a more rigorous job of evaluating patent applications, so that we can avoid issuing invalid patents. Others argue that this would be a waste of time. Most of the extra effort would inevitably be invested in evaluating applications on what turned out to be unimportant applications. Most patents turn out not to be valuable in any event; probably only 15 percent of patents are licensed or litigated. Even though they may be valid, in the sense that they meet the standards of patentability, most patents don't represent advances embraced by the market. There is an old adage that if you invent a better mousetrap, the world will beat a path to your doorstep. But that mousetrap needs to be better (and probably significantly better) and not merely patentable. Better to wait to see which patents turn out to be actually worth something, and then re-examine their validity either in the Patent and Trademark Office, or in court. *See* Mark A. Lemley, *Rational Ignorance at the Patent Office*, 95 Nw. U. L. Rev. 1495 (2001).

The next case explores important tenets of the law of trademarks and unfair competition.

■ HANOVER STAR MILLING COMPANY v. METCALF
Supreme Court of the United States, 1916
240 U.S. 403

PITNEY, Justice. [Two cases, both involving Hanover Star Milling Company and the "Tea Rose" trademark, were consolidated on appeal. In the first case (#23), Hanover Star Milling brought an action against Metcalf for trademark infringement and unfair competition based upon Metcalf's sales of flour in Alabama. In 1885, Hanover had begun manufacturing and selling "Tea Rose" flour in Illinois, using a wrapping with the words "Tea Rose" and a distinctive design containing three roses imprinted upon labels attached to sacks and barrels. In 1900, Hanover began selling substantial amounts of "Tea Rose" flour in Alabama and other southeastern states. Later Metcalf, an Alabama merchant, began selling flour labeled as "Tea Rose" but which was manufactured by the Steeleville Milling Company of Illinois. Hanover sued Metcalf and won an injunction preventing Metcalf from selling flour with the "Tea Rose" trademark in Alabama, but the Fifth Circuit reversed. The Court, in a part of this opinion that is omitted, remanded case #23 for further proceedings.

In the second case (#30), Allen & Wheeler Company brought a trademark infringement action *against* Hanover Star Milling Company. In 1872, Allen & Wheeler, an Ohio flour manufacturer, had begun using the words "Tea Rose" to identify one of its brands of flour. Allen & Wheeler did not sell or advertise "Tea Rose" flour in Alabama or the other southeastern states. Instead, it sold flour under the brands "Eldean Patent" and "Trojan Special" in Alabama and Georgia. Nevertheless, the district court enjoined Hanover from selling flour with the "Tea Rose" trademark in all markets. The Seventh Circuit reversed.]

It should be added that, so far as appears, none of the parties here concerned has registered the trademark under any act of Congress or under the law of any State. Nor does it appear that in any of the States in question there exists any peculiar local rule, arising from statute or decision. Hence, the cases must be decided according to common-law principles of general application. . . .

It will be convenient to dispose first of No. 30. . . . The decision of the Court of Appeals for the Seventh Circuit in favor of the Hanover Company and against the Allen & Wheeler Company was rested upon the ground that although the adoption of the Tea Rose mark by the latter antedated that of the Hanover Company, its [Allen & Wheeler's] only trade, so far as shown, was in territory north of the Ohio River, while the Hanover Company had adopted "Tea Rose" as its mark in perfect good faith, with no knowledge that anybody else was using or had used those words in such a connection, and during many years it had built up and extended its trade in the southeastern territory, comprising Georgia, Florida, Alabama, and Mississippi, so that in the flour trade in that territory the mark "Tea Rose" had come to mean the Hanover Company's flour, and nothing else. The court held in effect that the right to protection in the exclusive use of a trademark extends only to those markets where the trader's goods have become known and identified by his use of the mark; and because of the non-occupancy by the Allen & Wheeler Company of the southeastern markets it had no ground for relief in equity. Let us test this by reference to general principles.

The redress that is accorded in trademark cases is based upon the party's right to be protected in the good-will of a trade or business. The primary and proper function of a trade-mark is to identify the origin or ownership of the article to which it is affixed. Where a party has been in the habit of labeling his goods with a distinctive mark, so that purchasers recognize goods thus marked as being of his production, others are debarred from applying the same mark to goods of the same description, because to do so would in effect represent their goods to be of his production and would tend to deprive him of the profit he might make through the sale of the goods which the purchaser intended to buy. Courts afford redress or relief upon the ground that a party has a valuable interest in the good-will of his trade or business, and in the trade-marks adopted to maintain and extend it. The essence of the wrong consists in the sale of the goods of one manufacturer or vendor for those of another.

This essential element is the same in trade-mark cases as in cases of unfair competition unaccompanied with trade-mark infringement. In fact, the common law of trade-marks is but a part of the broader law of unfair competition.

Common-law trade-marks, and the right to their exclusive use, are of course to be classed among property rights, *Trade-mark Cases*, 100 U.S. 82, 92, 93 (1879); but only in the sense that a man's right to the continued enjoyment of his trade reputation and the good-will that flows from it, free from unwarranted interference by others, is a property right, for the protection of which a trade-mark is an instrumentality. As was said in the same case (p. 94), the right grows out of use, not mere adoption. In the English courts it often has been said that there is no property whatever in a trade-mark, as such. Per Lord Langdale, M. R., in Perry v. Truefitt, 6 Beav. 73 (1842). But since in the same cases the courts recognized the right of the party to the exclusive use of marks adopted to indicate goods of his manufacture, upon the ground that "A man is not to sell his own goods under the pretense that they are the goods of another man; he cannot be permitted to practise such a deception, nor to use the means which contribute to that end. He cannot therefore be allowed to use names, marks, letters, or other *indicia*, by which he may induce purchasers to believe, that the goods which he is selling are the manufacture of another person" (6 Beav. 73); it is plain that in denying the right of property in a trade-mark it was intended only to deny such property right except as appurtenant to an established business or trade in connection with which the mark is used. This is evident from the expressions used in these and other English cases. Thus, in Ainsworth v. Walmsley, L.R. 1 Eq. Cas. 518, 524, Vice Chancellor Sir Wm. Page Wood said: "This court has taken upon itself to protect a man in the use of a certain trade-mark as applied to a particular description of article. He has no property in that mark *per se*, any more than in any other fanciful denomination he may assume for his own private use, otherwise than with reference to his trade. If he does not carry on a trade in iron, but carries on a trade in linen, and stamps a lion on his linen, another person may stamp a lion on iron; but when he has appropriated a mark to a particular species of goods, and caused his goods to circulate with this mark upon them, the court has said that no one shall be at liberty to defraud that man by using that mark, and passing off goods of his manufacture as being the goods of the owner of that mark."

In short, the trade-mark is treated as merely a protection for the good-will, and not the subject of property except in connection with an existing business. The same rule prevails generally in this country, and is recognized in the decisions of this court already cited.

Expressions are found in many of the cases to the effect that the exclusive right to the use of a trade-mark is founded on priority of appropriation. Thus, in Canal Co. v. Clark, 13 Wall. 311, 323 (1871), reference is made to "the first appropriator"; in McLean v. Fleming, 96 U.S. 245, 251 (1877), to "the person who first adopted the stamp"; Manufacturing Co. v. Trainer, 101 U.S. 51, 53 (1879), the expression is "any symbol or device, not previously appropriated, which will distinguish," etc. But these expressions are to be understood in their application to the facts of the cases decided. In the ordinary case of parties competing under the same mark in the same market, it is correct to say that prior appropriation settles the question. But where two parties independently are employing the same mark upon goods of the same class, but in separate markets wholly remote the one from the other, the question of prior appropriation is legally insignificant, unless at least it appear that the second adopter has selected the mark with some design inimical to the interests of the first user, such as to take the benefit of the reputation of his goods, to forestall the extension of his trade, or the like. . . .

. . . Allowing to the Allen & Wheeler firm and corporation the utmost that the proofs disclose in their favor, they have confined their use of the "Tea Rose" trade-mark to a limited territory, leaving the south-eastern States untouched. Even if they did not know — and it does not appear that they did know — that the Hanover Company was doing so, they must be held to have taken the risk that some innocent party might, during their forty years of inactivity, hit upon the same mark and expend money and effort in building up a trade in flour under it. If, during the long period that has elapsed since the last specified sale of Allen & Wheeler "Tea Rose" — this was "in the later 70's" — that flour has been sold in other parts of the United States, excluding the south-eastern States, no clearer evidence of abandonment by non-user of trade-mark rights in the latter field could reasonably be asked for. And when it appears, as it does, that the Hanover Company in good faith and without notice of the Allen & Wheeler mark has expended much money and effort in building up its trade in the south-eastern market, so that "Tea Rose" there means Hanover Company's flour and nothing else, the Allen & Wheeler Company is estopped to assert trade-mark infringement as to that territory.

The extent and character of that territory, and its remoteness from that in which the Allen & Wheeler mark is known, are circumstances to be considered. Alabama alone — to say nothing of the other states in question — has an area of over

50,000 square miles, and by the census of 1910 contained a population of more than 2,000,000. Its most northerly point is more than 250 miles south of Cincinnati, which is the nearest point at which sales of Allen & Wheeler "Tea Rose" are shown to have been made, and these at a time antedating by approximately forty years the commencement of the present controversy. We are not dealing with a case where the junior appropriation of a trademark in occupying territory that would probably be reached by the prior user in the natural expansion of his trade, and need pass no judgment upon such a case. Under the circumstances that are here presented, to permit the Allen & Wheeler Company to use the mark in Alabama, to the exclusion of the Hanover Company, would take the trade and good-will of the latter company—built up at much expense and without notice of the former's rights—and confer it upon the former, to the complete perversion of the proper theory of trade-mark rights. . . .

[The Court found certain conflicts and inadequacies in the record for case No. 23.]

It results that the decree under review in No. 23 should be reversed, and the cause remanded for further proceedings in accordance with this opinion, and that the decree in No. 30 should be affirmed.

HOLMES, Justice, concurring. I am disposed to agree that the decree dismissing the bill of the Hanover Star Milling Company should be reversed and that the decree denying a preliminary injunction to the Allen & Wheeler Company should be affirmed, and I agree in the main with the reasoning of the court, so far as it goes. But I think it necessary to go farther even on the assumption that we are dealing with the question of trademarks in the several states only so far as commerce among the states is not concerned. The question before us, on that assumption, is a question of state law, since the rights that we are considering are conferred by the sovereignty of the state in which they are acquired. This seems to be too obvious to need the citation of authority, but it is a necessary corollary of the *Trade-Mark Cases*, 100 U.S. 82 (1879). Those cases decided that Congress cannot deal with trademarks as used in commerce wholly between citizens of the same state. It follows that the states can deal with them, as in fact they sometimes do by statute (Mass. Rev. Laws, chap. 72, §§2, 3), and when not by statute by their common law.

As the common law of the several states has the same origin for the most part, and as their law concerning trademarks and unfair competition is the same in its general features, it is natural and very generally correct to say that trademarks acknowledge no territorial limits. But it never should be forgotten, and in this case it is important to remember, that when a trademark started in one state is recognized in another it is by the authority of a new sovereignty that gives its sanction to the right. The new sovereignty is not a passive figurehead. It creates the right within its jurisdiction, and what it creates it may condition, as by requiring the mark to be recorded, or it may deny. The question, then, is what is the common law of Alabama in cases like these. It appears to me that if a mark previously unknown in that state has been used and given a reputation there, the state well may say that those who have spent their money innocently in giving it its local value are not to be defeated by proof that others have used the mark earlier in another jurisdiction more or less remote. Until I am compelled to adopt a different view I shall assume that that is the common law of the state. . . . Those who have used the mark within the state are those who will be defrauded if another can come in and reap the reward of their efforts on the strength of a use elsewhere over which Alabama has no control. . . .

Notes and Questions

1. The Court discusses the relationship between trademark infringement and unfair competition. The difference is difficult to explain. Most now regard trademark infringement as a type of unfair competition. In this case, Hanover Star Milling alleged that Metcalf was selling flour so marked and advertised as to deliberately mislead the public into believing it was the Hanover product. Such behavior would constitute unfair competition even if it didn't involve, under the usages of the day, trademark infringement.

2. So, is a trademark right a property right, or not? What difference does it make? Given what you know now, would you class trademark rights along with copyrights and patents? How are they similar? How different?

3. The terminology of unfair competition law is a mess. Trademark law is generally understood to be a species of the genus unfair competition. But, as McCarthy observed in his multi-volume treatise on the subject, "One has only to read a few judicial opinions to recognize the semantic quagmire that awaits the lawyer or judge who attempts to give a precise definition to that evasive concept called 'unfair competition.'" 1 *McCarthy on Trademarks and Unfair Competition* §1.9 (1998). We add this comment only to alert you to the terminological complexity, and confusion, associated with the topic. Many have sought to create a coherent set of categories and associated names; the principal problem is not so much with the consistency of any particular system, but rather with the fact that there is little consensus about which vocabulary to use. The *Restatement of Unfair Competition* (1993) is one recent effort to create order. Perhaps lawyers will begin to rely on its conventions. This will be helpful for the future, perhaps, but so long as we have to read the old cases, we risk being confused. The following taxonomy might be helpful, so long as you know that there are many who would find it either incomplete, or would object to some of the categorizations. This chapter will include an introduction to some of the varieties of unfair competition; we have marked those for your reference.

Unfair competition consists of:

1. Trade identity unfair competition. This may involve:
   a. Trademark infringement (See Hanover Star Milling Company v. Metcalf, *supra*)
   b. Copying trade names, labels, commercial dress (See Kellogg Co. v. National Biscuit Co., *infra*)
   c. Dilution of trademarks (See Jordache Enterprises, Inc. v. Hogg Wyld, Ltd., *infra*)
   d. Use of confusingly similar business and professional names
   e. Use of confusingly similar titles of literary works
2. Unfair trade practices
   a. Antitrust violations
   b. False and deceptive advertising
   c. Trade disparagement
   d. Trade secret theft (See E.I. DuPont DeNemours & Co. v. Christopher, *infra*)
   e. Misrepresentation
   f. Bait and switch selling practices
   g. Filing groundless lawsuits or claims as a competitive weapon
   h. Harassing the customers of another

3. Other
   a. Violation of the right of publicity? (See cases in Chapter 1)
   b. Misappropriation? (See International News Service v. Associated Press, *infra*)

This next case is undoubtedly a leading case in the history of intellectual property. It has had an unusual history, however, and remains controversial. It has much to teach us as a matter of policy, history, and rhetoric.

■ INTERNATIONAL NEWS SERVICE v. ASSOCIATED PRESS
Supreme Court of the United States, 1918
248 U.S. 215

PITNEY, Justice. The parties are competitors in the gathering and distribution of news and its publication for profit in newspapers throughout the United States. The Associated Press, which was complainant in the District Court, is a cooperative organization, . . . its members being individuals who are either proprietors or representatives of about 950 daily newspapers published in all parts of the United States. . . . Complainant gathers . . . news and intelligence of current and recent events of interest to newspaper readers and distributes it daily to its members for publication in their newspapers. The cost of the service, amounting approximately to $3,500,000 per annum, is assessed upon the members and becomes a part of their costs of operation, to be recouped, presumably with profit, through the publication of their several newspapers. Under complainant's by-laws each member agrees . . . that no member shall furnish or permit anyone in his employ or connected with his newspaper to furnish any of complainant's news in advance of publication to any person not a member. And each member is required to gather the local news of his district and supply it to the Associated Press and to no one else.

Defendant is a corporation . . . whose business is the gathering and selling of news to its customers and clients, consisting of newspapers published throughout the United States, under contracts by which they pay certain amounts at stated times for defendant's service. It has wide-spread news-gathering agencies; the cost of its operations amounts, it is said, to more than $2,000,000 per annum; and it serves about 400 newspapers located in the various cities of the United States and abroad, a few of which are represented, also, in the membership of the Associated Press.

The parties are in the keenest competition between themselves in the distribution of news throughout the United States; and so, as a rule, are the newspapers that they serve, in their several districts. . . .

The bill was filed to restrain the pirating of complainant's news by defendant in three ways: First, by bribing employees of newspapers published by complainant's members to furnish Associated Press news to defendant before publication, for transmission by telegraph and telephone to defendant's clients for publication by them; Second, by inducing Associated Press members to violate its by-laws and permit defendant to obtain news before publication; and Third, by copying news from bulletin boards and from early editions of complainant's newspapers and selling this, either bodily or after rewriting it, to defendant's customers.

The District Court . . . granted a preliminary injunction under the first and second heads; but refused at that stage to restrain the systematic practice . . . of taking news bodily from the bulletin boards and early editions of complainant's newspapers and selling it as its own. The court expressed itself as satisfied that this practice amounted to unfair trade, but . . . considered that the allowance of an injunction should await the outcome of an appeal. . . . [T]he Circuit Court of Appeals sustained the injunction order and modified it and remanded the cause with directions to issue an injunction also against any bodily taking of the words or substance of complainant's news until its commercial value as news had passed away. 245 Fed. Rep. 244, 253. . . .

The only matter that has been argued before us is whether defendant may lawfully be restrained from appropriating news taken from bulletins issued by complainant or any of its members, or from newspapers published by them, for the purpose of selling it to defendant's clients. Complainant asserts that defendant's admitted course of conduct in this regard both violates complainant's property right in the news and constitutes unfair competition in business. . . . As presented in argument, these questions are: 1. Whether there is any property in news; 2. Whether, if there be property in news collected for the purpose of being published, it survives the instant of its publication in the first newspaper to which it is communicated by the news-gatherer; and 3. Whether defendant's admitted course of conduct in appropriating for commercial use matter taken from bulletins or early editions of Associated Press publications constitutes unfair competition in trade.

The federal jurisdiction was invoked because of diversity of citizenship, not upon the ground that the suit arose under the copyright or other laws of the United States. Complainant's news matter is not copyrighted. It is said that it could not, in practice, be copyrighted, because of the large number of dispatches that are sent daily; and, according to complainant's contention, news is not within the operation of the copyright act.* Defendant, while apparently conceding this, nevertheless invokes the analogies of the law of literary property and copyright, insisting as its principal contention that, assuming complainant has a right of property in its news, it can be maintained (unless the copyright act be complied with) only by being kept secret and confidential, and that upon the publication with complainant's consent of uncopyrighted news by any of complainant's members in a newspaper or upon a bulletin board, the right of property is lost, and the subsequent use of the news by the public or by defendant for any purpose whatever becomes lawful. . . .

In considering the general question of property in news matter, it is necessary to recognize its dual character, distinguishing between the substance of the information and the particular form or collocation of words in which the writer has communicated it.

No doubt news articles often possess a literary quality, and are the subject of literary property at the common law; nor do we question that such an article, as a literary production, is the subject of copyright by the terms of the act as it now stands. In an early case at the circuit Mr. Justice Thompson held in effect that a newspaper was not within the protection of the copyright acts of 1790 and 1802.

---

* [Even though it may have been impractical or inconvenient to claim copyright in news stories in 1918, that is not as true today, given changes in the federal copyright statute that have eased the burdens of copyright formalities. — Eds.]

Clayton v. Stone, 5 F. Cas. 999 (S.D.N.Y. 1829) (No. 2872). But the present act is broader; it provides that the works for which copyright may be secured shall include "all the writings of an author," and specifically mentions "periodicals, including newspapers." Act of March 4, 1909, c. 320, §§4 and 5, 35 Stat. 1075, 1076. . . .

But the news element—the information respecting current events contained in the literary production—is not the creation of the writer, but is a report of matters that ordinarily are *publici juris*; it is the history of the day. It is not to be supposed that the framers of the Constitution, when they empowered Congress "to promote the progress of science and useful arts, by securing for limited times to authors and inventors the exclusive right to their respective writings and discoveries" (Const., Art. I, §8, par. 8), intended to confer upon one who might happen to be the first to report a historic event the exclusive right for any period to spread the knowledge of it.

We need spend no time, however, upon the general question of property in news matter at common law, or the application of the copyright act, since it seems to us the case must turn upon the question of unfair competition in business. And, in our opinion, this does not depend upon any general right of property analogous to the common-law right of the proprietor of an unpublished work to prevent its publication without his consent; nor is it foreclosed by showing that the benefits of the copyright act have been waived. We are dealing here not with restrictions upon publication but with the very facilities and processes of publication. The peculiar value of news is in the spreading of it while it is fresh; and it is evident that a valuable property interest in the news, as news, cannot be maintained by keeping it secret. Besides, except for matters improperly disclosed, or published in breach of trust or confidence, or in violation of law, none of which is involved in this branch of the case, the news of current events may be regarded as common property. What we are concerned with is the business of making it known to the world, in which both parties to the present suit are engaged. That business consists in maintaining a prompt, sure, steady, and reliable service designed to place the daily events of the world at the breakfast table of the millions at a price that, while of trifling moment to each reader, is sufficient in the aggregate to afford compensation for the cost of gathering and distributing it, with the added profit so necessary as an incentive to effective action in the commercial world. The service thus performed for newspaper readers is not only innocent but extremely useful in itself, and indubitably constitutes a legitimate business. The parties are competitors in this field; and, on fundamental principles, applicable here as elsewhere, when the rights or privileges of the one are liable to conflict with those of the other, each party is under a duty so to conduct its own business as not unnecessarily or unfairly to injure that of the other. Hitchman Coal & Coke Co. v. Mitchell, 245 U.S. 229, 254 (1917).

Obviously, the question of what is unfair competition in business must be determined with particular reference to the character and circumstances of the business. The question here is not so much the rights of either party as against the public but their rights as between themselves. *See* Morison v. Moat, 9 Hare, 241, 258, 68 Eng. Rep. 492 (Ch. 1851). And although we may and do assume that neither party has any remaining property interest as against the public in uncopyrighted news matter after the moment of its first publication, it by no means follows that there is no remaining property interest in it as between themselves. For, to both of them alike, news matter, however little susceptible of ownership or dominion in the absolute sense, is stock in trade, to be gathered at the cost of enterprise, organization, skill, labor, and money, and to be distributed and sold to those who will pay money for it, as for any other merchandise. Regarding the news, therefore, as but the material out of which both parties are seeking to make profits at the same time and in the same field, we hardly can fail to recognize that for this purpose, and as between them, it must be regarded as *quasi* property, irrespective of the rights of either as against the public.

In order to sustain the jurisdiction of equity over the controversy, we need not affirm any general and absolute property in the news as such. . . .

The question, whether one who has gathered general information or news at pains and expense for the purpose of subsequent publication through the press has such an interest in its publication as may be protected from interference, has been raised many times, although never, perhaps, in the precise form in which it is now presented.

Board of Trade v. Christie Grain & Stock Co., 198 U.S. 236, 250 (1905), related to the distribution of quotations of prices on dealings upon a board of trade, which were collected by plaintiff and communicated on confidential terms to numerous persons under a contract not to make them public. This court held that, apart from certain special objections that were overruled, plaintiff's collection of quotations was entitled to the protection of the law; that, like a trade secret, plaintiff might keep to itself the work done at its expense, and did not lose its right by communicating the result to persons, even if many, in confidential relations to itself, under a contract not to make it public; and that strangers should be restrained from getting at the knowledge by inducing a breach of trust. . . .

The peculiar features of the case arise from the fact that, while novelty and freshness form so important an element in the success of the business, the very processes of distribution and publication necessarily occupy a good deal of time. Complainant's service, as well as defendant's, is a daily service to daily newspapers; most of the foreign news reaches this country at the Atlantic seaboard, principally at the City of New York, and because of this, and of time differentials due to the earth's rotation, the distribution of news matter throughout the country is principally from east to west; and, since in speed the telegraph and telephone easily outstrip the rotation of the earth, it is a simple matter for defendant to take complainant's news from bulletins or early editions of complainant's members in the eastern cities and at the mere cost of telegraphic transmission cause it to be published in western papers issued at least as early as those served by complainant. Besides this, and irrespective of time differentials, irregularities in telegraphic transmission on different lines, and the normal consumption of time in printing and distributing the newspaper, result in permitting pirated news to be placed in the hands of defendant's readers sometimes simultaneously with the service of competing Associated Press papers, occasionally even earlier.

Defendant insists that when, with the sanction and approval of complainant, and as the result of the use of its news for the very purpose for which it is distributed, a portion of complainant's members communicate it to the general public by posting it upon bulletin boards so that all may read, or by issuing it to newspapers and distributing it indiscriminately, complainant no longer has the right to control the use to be made of it; that when it thus reaches the light of day it becomes the common possession of all to whom it is accessible; and that any purchaser of a newspaper has the right to communicate the intelligence which it contains to anybody and for any purpose, even for the purpose of selling it for profit to newspapers published for profit in competition with complainant's members.

The fault in the reasoning lies in applying as a test the right of the complainant as against the public, instead of considering the rights of complainant and defendant, competitors in business, as between themselves. The right of the purchaser of a single newspaper to spread knowledge of its contents gratuitously, for any legitimate purpose not unreasonably interfering with complainant's right to make merchandise of it, may be admitted; but to transmit that news for commercial use, in competition with complainant—which is what defendant has done and seeks to justify—is a very different matter. In doing this defendant, by its very act, admits that it is taking material that has been acquired by complainant as the result of organization and the expenditure of labor, skill, and money, and which is salable by complainant for money, and that defendant in appropriating it and selling it as its own is endeavoring to reap where it has not sown, and by disposing of it to newspapers that are competitors of complainant's members is appropriating to itself the harvest of those who have sown. Stripped of all disguises, the process amounts to an unauthorized interference with the normal operation of complainant's legitimate business precisely at the point where the profit is to be reaped, in order to divert a material portion of the profit from those who have earned it to those who have not; with special advantage to defendant in the competition because of the fact that it is not burdened with any part of the expense of gathering the news. The transaction speaks for itself, and a court of equity ought not to hesitate long in characterizing it as unfair competition in business.

The underlying principle is much the same as that which lies at the base of the equitable theory of consideration in the law of trusts—that he who has fairly paid the price should have the beneficial use of the property. Pom. Eq. Jur., §981. It is no answer to say that complainant spends its money for that which is too fugitive or evanescent to be the subject of property. That might, and for the purposes of the discussion we are assuming that it would, furnish an answer in a common-law controversy. But in a court of equity, where the question is one of unfair competition, if that which complainant has acquired fairly at substantial cost may be sold fairly at substantial profit, a competitor who is misappropriating it for the purpose of disposing of it to his own profit and to the disadvantage of complainant cannot be heard to say that it is too fugitive or evanescent to be regarded as property. It has all the attributes of property necessary for determining that a misappropriation of it by a competitor is unfair competition because contrary to good conscience.

The contention that the news is abandoned to the public for all purposes when published in the first newspaper is untenable. Abandonment is a question of intent, and the entire organization of the Associated Press negatives such a purpose. The cost of the service would be prohibited if the reward were to be so limited. No single newspaper, no small group of newspapers, could sustain the expenditure. Indeed, it is one of the most obvious results of defendant's theory that, by permitting indiscriminate publication by anybody and everybody for purposes of profit in competition with the news-gatherer, it would render publication profitless, or so little profitable as in effect to cut off the service by rendering the cost prohibitive in comparison with the return. . . .

It is said that the elements of unfair competition are lacking because there is no attempt by defendant to palm off its goods as those of the complainant, characteristic of the most familiar, if not the most typical, cases of unfair competition. Howe Scale Co. v. Wyckoff, Seamans & Benedict, 198 U.S. 118, 140 (1905). But we cannot concede that the right to equitable relief is confined to that class of cases. In the present case the fraud upon complainant's rights is more direct and obvious.

Regarding news matter as the mere material from which these two competing parties are endeavoring to make money, and treating it, therefore, as *quasi* property for the purposes of their business because they are both selling it as such, defendant's conduct differs from the ordinary case of unfair competition in trade principally in this that, instead of selling its own goods as those of complainant, it substitutes misappropriation in the place of misrepresentation, and sells complainant's goods as its own.

Besides the misappropriation, there are elements of imitation, of false pretense, in defendant's practices. The device of rewriting complainant's news articles, frequently resorted to, carries its own comment. The habitual failure to give credit to complainant for that which is taken is significant. Indeed, the entire system of appropriating complainant's news and transmitting it as a commercial product to defendant's clients and patrons amounts to a false representation to them and to their newspaper readers that the news transmitted is the result of defendant's own investigation in the field. But these elements, although accentuating the wrong, are not the essence of it. It is something more than the advantage of celebrity of which complainant is being deprived.

The doctrine of unclean hands is invoked as a bar to relief; it being insisted that defendant's practices against which complainant seeks an injunction are not different from the practice attributed to complainant, of utilizing defendant's news published by its subscribers. At this point it becomes necessary to consider a distinction . . . between two kinds of use that may be made by one news agency of news taken from the bulletins and newspapers of the other. The first is the bodily appropriation of a statement of fact or a news article, with or without rewriting, but without independent investigation or other expense. . . . The other use is to take the news of a rival agency as a "tip" to be investigated, and if verified by independent investigation the news thus gathered is sold. This practice complainant admits that it has pursued and still is willing that defendant shall employ. . . .

The decree of the Circuit Court of Appeals will be affirmed.

HOLMES, Justice, concurring, joined by Justice MCKENNA. When an uncopyrighted combination of words is published there is no general right to forbid other people repeating them — in other words there is no property in the combination or in the thoughts or facts that the words express. Property, a creation of law, does not arise from value, although exchangeable — a matter of fact. Many exchangeable values may be destroyed intentionally without compensation. Property depends upon exclusion by law from interference, and a person is not excluded from using any combination of words merely because someone has used it before, even if it took labor and genius to make it. If a given person is to be prohibited from making the use of words that his neighbors are free to make some other ground must be found. One such ground is vaguely expressed in the phrase unfair trade. This means that the words are repeated by a competitor in business in such a way as to convey a misrepresentation that materially injures the person who first used them, by appropriating credit of some kind which the first user has earned. The ordinary case is a representation by device, appearance, or other indirection that the defendant's goods come from the plaintiff. But the only reason why it is actionable to make such a representation is that it tends to give the defendant an advantage in his competition with the plaintiff and that it is thought undesirable that an advantage should be gained in that way. Apart from that the defendant may use such unpatented devices and uncopyrighted combinations of words as he likes. The ordinary case, I say, is palming off the defendant's product as the plaintiff's, but the same evil may follow from the opposite falsehood — from saying, whether in words or by implication, that the plaintiff's product is the defendant's, and that, it seems to me, is what has happened here.

Fresh news is got only by enterprise and expense. To produce such news as it is produced by the defendant represents by implication that it has been acquired by the defendant's enterprise and at its expense. When it comes from one of the great news-collecting agencies like the Associated Press, the source generally is indicated, plainly importing that credit; and that such a representation is implied may be inferred with some confidence from the unwillingness of the defendant to give the credit and tell the truth. If the plaintiff produces the news at the same time that the defendant does, the defendant's presentation impliedly denies to the plaintiff the credit of collecting the facts and assumes that credit to the defendant. If the plaintiff is later in western cities it naturally will be supposed to have obtained its information from the defendant. The falsehood is a little more subtle, the injury a little more indirect, than in ordinary cases of unfair trade, but I think that the principle that condemns the one condemns the other. It is a question of how strong an infusion of fraud is necessary to turn a flavor into a poison. The dose seems to me strong enough here to need a remedy from the law. But as, in my view, the only ground of complaint that can be recognized without legislation is the implied misstatement, it can be corrected by stating the truth; and a suitable acknowledgment of the source is all that the plaintiff can require. I think that within the limits recognized by the decision of the Court the defendant should be enjoined from publishing news obtained from the Associated Press for _____ hours after publication by the plaintiff unless it gives express credit to the Associated Press; the number of hours and the form of acknowledgment to be settled by the District Court.

BRANDEIS, Justice, dissenting. . . .

News is a report of recent occurrences. The business of the news agency is to gather systematically knowledge of such occurrences of interest and to distribute reports thereof. The Associated Press contended that knowledge so acquired is property, because it costs money and labor to produce and because it has value for which those who have it not are ready to pay; that it remains property and is entitled to protection as long as it has commercial value as news; and that to protect it effectively the defendant must be enjoined from making, or causing to be made, any gainful use of it while it retains such value. An essential element of individual property is the legal right to exclude others from enjoying it. If the property is private, the right of exclusion may be absolute; if the property is affected with a public interest, the right of exclusion is qualified. But the fact that a product of the mind has cost its producer money and labor, and has a value for which others are willing to pay, is not sufficient to ensure to it this legal attribute of property. The general rule of law is, that the noblest of human productions — knowledge, truths ascertained, conceptions, and ideas — become, after voluntary communication to others, free as the air to common use. . . .

First: Plaintiff's principal reliance was upon the "ticker" cases; but they do not support its contention. The leading cases on this subject rest the grant of relief, not upon the existence of a general property right in news, but upon the breach of a contract or trust concerning the use of news communicated; and that element is lacking here. . . .

Second: Plaintiff also relied upon the cases which hold that the common-law right of the producer to prohibit copying is not lost by the private circulation of a literary composition, the delivery of lecture, the exhibition of a painting, or the performance of a dramatic or musical composition. These cases rest upon the ground that the common law recognizes such productions as property which, despite restricted communication, continues until there is a dedication to the public under the copyright statutes or otherwise. But they are inapplicable for two reasons. (1) At common law, as under the copyright acts, intellectual productions are entitled to such protection only if there is underneath something evincing the mind of a creator or originator, however modest the requirement. The mere record of isolated happenings, whether in words or by photographs not involving artistic skill, are denied such protection. (2) At common law, as under the copyright acts, the element in intellectual productions which secures such protection is not the knowledge, truths, ideas, or emotions which the composition expresses, but the form or sequence in which they are expressed; that is, "some new collocation of visible or audible points, — of lines, colors, sounds, or words." *See* White-Smith Music Co. v. Apollo Co., 209 U.S. 1, 19 (1908). An author's theories, suggestions, and speculations, or the systems, plans, methods, and arrangements of an originator, derive no such protection from the statutory copyright of the book in which they are set forth, Baker v. Selden, 101 U.S. 99 (1879); and they are likewise denied such protection at common law.

That news is not property in the strict sense is illustrated by the case of Sports and General Press Agency, Ltd., v. "Our Dogs" Publishing Co., Ltd., [1916] 2 K.B. 880, where the plaintiff, the assignee of the right to photograph the exhibits at a dog show, was refused an injunction against defendant who had also taken pictures of the show and was publishing them. The court said that, except in so far as the possession of the land occupied by the show enabled the proprietors to exclude people or permit them on condition that they agree not to take photographs (which condition was not imposed in that case), the proprietors had no exclusive right to photograph the show and could therefore grant no such right. And, it was further stated that, at any rate, no matter what conditions might be imposed upon those entering the grounds, if the defendant had been on top of a house or in some position where he could photograph the show without interfering with the physical property of the plaintiff, the plaintiff would have no right to stop him. If, when the plaintiff creates the event recorded, he is not entitled to the exclusive first publication of the news (in that case a photograph) of the event, no reason can be shown why he should be accorded such protection as to events which he simply records and transmits to other parts of the world, though with great expenditure of time and money.

Third: If news be treated as possessing the characteristics not of a trade secret, but of literary property, then the earliest issue of a paper of general circulation or the earliest public posting of a bulletin which embodies such news would, under the established rules governing literary property, operate as a publication, and all property in the news would then cease. Resisting this conclusion, plaintiff relied upon the cases which hold that uncopyrighted intellectual and artistic property survives private circulation or a restricted publication; and it contended that in each issue of each paper, a restriction is to be implied, that the news shall not be used gainfully in competition with the Associated Press or any of its members. There is no basis for such an implication. But it is, also, well settled that where the publication is in fact a general one — even express words of restriction upon use are inoperative. In other words, a general publication is effective to dedicate literary property to the public, regardless of the actual intent of its owner.

Fourth: Plaintiff further contended that defendant's practice constitutes unfair competition, because there is "appropriation without cost to itself of values created by" the plaintiff; and it is upon this ground that the decision of this court appears to be based. To appropriate and use for profit, knowledge and ideas produced by other men, without making compensation or even acknowledgment, may be inconsistent with a finer sense of propriety; but, with the exceptions indicated above, the law has heretofore sanctioned the practice. Thus it was held that one may ordinarily make and sell anything in any form, may copy with exactness that which another has produced, or may otherwise use his ideas without his consent and without the payment of compensation, and yet not inflict a legal injury; and that ordinarily one is at perfect liberty to find out, if he can by lawful means, trade secrets of another, however valuable, and then use the knowledge so acquired gainfully, although it cost the original owner much in effort and in money to collect or produce.

Such taking and gainful use of a product of another which, for reasons of public policy, the law has refused to endow with the attributes of property, does not become unlawful because the product happens to have been taken from a rival and is used in competition with him. The unfairness in competition which hitherto has been recognized by the law as a basis for relief, lay in the manner or means of conducting the business; and the manner or means held legally unfair, involves either fraud or force or the doing of acts otherwise prohibited by law. In the "passing off" cases (the typical and most common case of unfair competition), the wrong consists in fraudulently representing by word or act that defendant's goods are those of plaintiff. *See* Hanover Milling Co. v. Metcalf, 240 U.S. 403, 412-413 (1916). In the other cases, the diversion of trade was effected through physical or moral coercion, or by inducing breaches of contract or of trust or by enticing away employees. In some others, called cases of simulated competition, relief was granted because defendant's purpose was unlawful; namely, not competition but deliberate and wanton destruction of plaintiff's business.

That competition is not unfair in a legal sense, merely because the profits gained are unearned, even if made at the expense of a rival, is shown by many cases besides those referred to above. He who follows the pioneer into a new market, or who engages in the manufacture of an article newly introduced by another, seeks profits due largely to the labor and expense of the first adventurer; but the law sanctions, indeed encourages, the pursuit. . . .

The means by which the International News Service obtains news gathered by the Associated Press is also clearly unobjectionable. It is taken from papers bought in the open market or from bulletins publicly posted. No breach of contract such as the court considered to exist in Hitchman Coal & Coke Co. v. Mitchell, 245 U.S. 229, 254 (1917); or of trust such as was present in Morison v. Moat, 9 Hare 241, 68 Eng. Rep. 492 (Ch. 1851); and neither fraud nor force, is involved. . . .

It is also suggested, that the fact that defendant does not refer to the Associated Press as the source of the news may furnish a basis for the relief. But the defendant and its subscribers, unlike members of the Associated Press, were under no contractual obligation to disclose the source of the news; and there is no rule of law requiring acknowledgment to be made where uncopyrighted matter is reproduced. . . .

Fifth: . . .

The rule for which the plaintiff contends would effect an important extension of property rights and a corresponding curtailment of the free use of knowledge and of ideas; and the facts of this case admonish us of the danger involved in recognizing such a property right in news, without imposing upon news-gatherers corresponding obligations. A large majority of the newspapers and perhaps half the newspaper readers of the United States are dependent for their news of general interest upon agencies other than the Associated Press. The channel through which about 400 of these papers received, as the plaintiff alleges, "a large amount of news relating to the European war of the greatest importance and of intense interest to the newspaper reading public" was suddenly closed. The closing to the International News Service of these channels for foreign news (if they were closed) was due not to unwillingness on its part to pay the cost of collecting the news, but to the prohibitions imposed by foreign governments upon its securing news from their respective countries and from using cable or telegraph lines running therefrom. For aught that appears, this prohibition may have been wholly undeserved; and at all events the 400 papers and their readers may be assumed to have been innocent. For aught that appears, the International News Service may have sought then to secure temporarily by arrangement with the Associated Press the latter's foreign news service. For aught that appears, all of the 400 subscribers of the International News Service would gladly have then become members of the Associated Press, if they could have secured election thereto. It is possible, also, that a large part of the readers of these papers were so situated that they could not secure prompt access to papers served by the Associated Press. The prohibition of the foreign governments might as well have been extended to the channels through which news was supplied to the more than a thousand other daily papers in the United States not served by the Associated Press; and a large part of their readers may also be so located that they cannot procure prompt access to papers served by the Associated Press. . . .

Courts are ill-equipped to make the investigations which should precede a determination of the limitations which should be set upon any property right in news or of the circumstances under which news gathered by a private agency should be deemed affected with a public interest. Courts would be powerless to prescribe the detailed regulations essential to full enjoyment of the rights conferred or to introduce the machinery required for enforcement of such regulations. Considerations such as these should lead us to decline to establish a new rule of law in the effort to redress a newly-disclosed wrong, although the propriety of some remedy appears to be clear.

Notes and Questions

1. Why couldn't the plaintiff in this case simply sue for copyright infringement? This might be a good time to note that early versions of the copyright law required that authors take a number of steps in order to claim a copyright in a work. These steps included strict compliance with notice and registration requirements. But these formal requirements for the preservation to a claim to copyright eroded substantially as copyright law developed.

The 1909 statute required the copyright owner to place an appropriate copyright notice on the work when it was published in order to claim a federal copyright. After 1978, a federal copyright claim arose when the work was "fixed in a tangible medium" but might be lost if the work was published without a suitably inscribed notice *and* the omission was not cured within five years. In 1989, even this relatively forgiving formal requirement was eliminated. Neither registration nor putting a copyright notice on the work is now required (although there are some reasons to continue to do both).

2. Does Pitney, in the majority opinion, recognize a "property right" in the news? Is such a finding a *sine qua non* for a victory for the plaintiff? Note that in both this case, and in *Hanover Star Milling*, the Court relies on a notion of a right that is property-like, but not quite the genuine article. This suggests something does flow from the label the Court is reluctant to apply.

3. In Brandeis' dissenting opinion, he observes: "And, it was further stated that, at any rate, no matter what conditions might be imposed upon those entering the grounds, if the defendant had been on top of a house or in some position where he could photograph the show without interfering with the physical property of the plaintiff, the plaintiff would have no right to stop him." Would Justice Pitney, author of the Court's opinion, have conceded this? What about an aerial photograph?

4. The following passage contains the lines that are probably the most frequently quoted. Why might that be so?

> [D]efendant, by its very act, admits that it is taking material that has been acquired by complainant as the result of organization and the expenditure of labor, skill, and money, and which is salable by complainant for money, and that defendant in appropriating it and selling it as its own is endeavoring to reap where it has not sown, and by disposing of it to newspapers that are competitors of complainant's members is appropriating to itself the harvest of those who have sown. . . . [Defendant seeks] to divert a material portion of the profit from those who have earned it to those who have not. . . .

What is the source of the rhetorical power of this language? Is it a legal standard? Note the sentence at the end of the same paragraph:

> The transaction speaks for itself, and a court of equity ought not to hesitate long in characterizing it as unfair competition in business.

What does "the transaction speaks for itself" mean? Later in the opinion, the Court observes: "The device of rewriting complainant's news articles, frequently resorted to, carries its own comment." Do these observations mean that the legal significance is so obvious that there is no reason to offer an analysis? Or is it a rhetorical trick offered to conceal the difficulty of offering a clear explanation?

5. The "holding" of the case can be expressed in a variety of ways, ranging from broad to narrow. Which of the following do you believe best represents the rule of the case? What can be said for each?

(a) One cannot reap where one has not sown;

(b) One cannot take advantage of the investment of another;

(c) A competitor may not take advantage of the investment of another;

(d) A competitor may not take advantage of the investment of another in those cases in which the activity of the competitor borrowed from is socially important, and might not occur if the borrowing is allowed to continue;

(e) Equitable relief (but not, perhaps, damages) should be available in the situation described in d.;

(f) The equitable restrictions contemplated in e. should be minimally burdensome, and should be narrowly crafted so that the socially desirable activity will occur; and

(g) News-gathering organizations cannot take advantage of the effects of the earth's rotation, combined with the use of the efforts of their competitors, to gain a competitive cost advantage.

6. What would have been the consequences of allowing INS to continue to copy the news from the AP dispatches, papers, and bulletin boards?

(a) to AP (and member newspapers);
(b) to members of the public on
  (1) the East Coast and
  (2) the West Coast?

Are these effects, in economic terms, distributional effects, or efficiency effects?

7. Intellectual property protection is often justified on the ground that, absent protection, the desired investment in socially desirable innovation would not occur. Is that the rationale of the *INS* case? Is that rationale the same as one based in seeking to avoid "unjust enrichment"?

8. Which of the three opinions would you join? What are the weaknesses and strengths of the various opinions which are material to your choice?

B. INTELLECTUAL PROPERTY LAW MATURES

The next case provides an opportunity to observe the interaction of rule and policy, as well as to develop an appreciation of how some of the category boundaries may relate to one another. What is the relationship between patents, and trademarks, and protection for the physical characteristics of products that might serve to signify origin?

■ **KELLOGG CO. v. NATIONAL BISCUIT CO.**
Supreme Court of the United States, 1938
305 U.S. 111

BRANDEIS, Justice. This suit was brought in the federal court for Delaware by National Biscuit Company against Kellogg Company to enjoin alleged unfair competition by the manufacture and sale of the breakfast food commonly known as shredded wheat. The competition was alleged to be unfair mainly because Kellogg Company uses, like the plaintiff, the name shredded wheat and, like the plaintiff, produces its biscuit in pillow-shaped form.

Shredded wheat is a product composed of whole wheat which has been boiled, partially dried, then drawn or pressed out into thin shreds and baked. The shredded wheat biscuit generally known is pillow-shaped in form. It was introduced in 1893 by Henry D. Perky, of Colorado; and he was connected until his death in 1908 with companies formed to make and market the article. Commercial success was not attained until the Natural Food Company built, in 1901, a large factory at Niagara

Falls, New York. . . . [I]ts business and goodwill were acquired by National Biscuit Company.

Kellogg Company has been in the business of manufacturing breakfast food cereals since its organization in 1905. For a period commencing in 1912 and ending in 1919 it made a product whose form was somewhat like the product in question, but whose manufacture was different, the wheat being reduced to a dough before being pressed into shreds. For a short period in 1922 it manufactured the article in question. In 1927, it resumed manufacturing the product. . . .

[Litigation began in 1928 when National Biscuit Co. sued two dealers in Kellogg biscuits. The litigation took many twists and turns until, finally, in 1938 the Circuit Court of Appeals directed the District Court to enter an injunction against Kellogg Company. The order enjoined Kellogg:] "(1) from the use of the name 'Shredded Wheat' as its trade name, (2) from advertising or offering for sale its product in the form and shape of plaintiff's biscuit, and (3) from doing either."

Kellogg Company then filed a petition for a writ of certiorari. . . .

The plaintiff concedes that it does not possess the exclusive right to make shredded wheat. But it claims the exclusive right to the trade name "Shredded Wheat" and the exclusive right to make shredded wheat biscuits pillow-shaped. It charges that the defendant, by using the name and shape, and otherwise, is passing off, or enabling others to pass off, Kellogg goods for those of the plaintiff. Kellogg Company denies that the plaintiff is entitled to the exclusive use of the name or of the pillow-shape; denies any passing off; asserts that it has used every reasonable effort to distinguish its produce from that of the plaintiff; and contends that in honestly competing for a part of the market for shredded wheat it is exercising the common right freely to manufacture and sell an article of commerce unprotected by patent.

First. The plaintiff has no exclusive right to the use of the term "Shredded Wheat" as a trade name. For that is the generic term of the article, which describes with a fair degree of accuracy, and is the term by which the biscuit in pillow-shaped form is generally known by the public. Since the term is generic, the original maker of the product acquired no exclusive right to use it. As Kellogg Company had the right to make the article, it had, also, the right to use the term by which the public knows it. Ever since 1894 the article has been known to the public as shredded wheat. For many years, there was no attempt to use the term "Shredded Wheat" as a trade-mark. When in 1905 plaintiff's predecessor, Natural Food Company, applied for registration of the words "Shredded Whole Wheat" as a trade-mark . . . William E. Williams gave notice of opposition. Upon the hearing it appeared that Williams had, as early as 1894, built a machine for making shredded wheat, and that he made and sold its product as "Shredded Whole Wheat." The Commissioner of Patents refused registration. The Court of Appeals of the District of Columbia affirmed his decision. . . .

Moreover, the name "Shredded Wheat," as well as the product, the process and the machinery employed in making it, has been dedicated to the public. The basic patent for the product and for the process of making it, and many other patents for special machinery to be used in making the article, issued to Perky. In those patents the term "shredded" is repeatedly used as descriptive of the product. The basic patent expired October 15, 1912; the others soon after. Since during the life of the patents "Shredded Wheat" was the general designation of the patented product, there passed to the public upon the expiration of the patent, not only the right to make the article as it was made during the patent period, but also the right to apply thereto the name by which it had become known. As was said in Singer Mfg. Co. v. June Mfg. Co., 163 U.S. 169, 185 (1896):

> It equally follows from the cessation of the monopoly and the falling of the patented device into the domain of things public that along with the public ownership of the device there must also necessarily pass to the public the generic designation of the thing which has arisen during the monopoly. . . .
>
> To say otherwise would be to hold that, although the public had acquired the device covered by the patent, yet the owner of the patent or the manufacturer of the patented thing had retained the designated name which was essentially necessary to vest the public with the full enjoyment of that which had become theirs by the disappearance of the monopoly.

It is contended that the plaintiff has the exclusive right to the name "Shredded Wheat," because those words acquired the "secondary meaning" of shredded wheat made at Niagara Falls by the plaintiff's predecessor. There is no basis here for applying the doctrine of secondary meaning. The evidence shows only that due to the long period in which the plaintiff or its predecessor was the only manufacturer of the product, many people have come to associate the product, and as a consequence the name by which the product is generally known, with the plaintiff's factory at Niagara Falls. But to establish a trade name in the term "shredded wheat" the plaintiff must show more than a subordinate meaning which applies to it. It must show that the primary significance of the term in the minds of the consuming public is not the product but the producer. This it has not done. The showing which it has made does not entitle it to the exclusive use of the term shredded wheat but merely entitles it to require that the defendant use reasonable care to inform the public of the source of its product. . . .

Second. The plaintiff has not the exclusive right to sell shredded wheat in the form of a pillow-shaped biscuit — the form in which the article became known to the public. That is the form in which shredded wheat was made under the basic patent. The patented machines used were designed to produce only the pillow-shaped biscuits. And a design patent was taken out to cover the pillow-shaped form.[4] Hence, upon expiration of the patents the form, as well as the name, was dedicated to the public. . . .

Where an article may be manufactured by all, a particular manufacturer can no more assert exclusive rights in a form in which the public has become accustomed to see the article and which, in the minds of the public, is primarily associated with the article rather than a particular producer, than it can in the case of a name with similar connections in the public mind. Kellogg Company was free to use the pillow-shaped form, subject only to the obligation to identify its product lest it be mistaken for that of the plaintiff.

Third. The question remains whether Kellogg Company in exercising its right to use the name "Shredded Wheat" and the pillow-shaped biscuit, is doing so fairly. Fairness requires that it be done in a manner which reasonably distinguishes its product from that of plaintiff.

---

4. The design patent would have expired by limitations in 1909. In 1908 it was declared invalid by a district judge on the ground that the design had been in public use for more than two years prior to the application for the patent and theretofore had already been dedicated to the public. Natural Foods Co. v. Bulkley, No. 28,530 (N.D. Ill. East. Div. 1908).

Each company sells its biscuits only in cartons. The standard Kellogg carton contains fifteen biscuits; the plaintiff's twelve. The Kellogg cartons are distinctive. They do not resemble those used by the plaintiff either in size, form, or color. And the difference in the labels is striking. The Kellogg cartons bear in bold script the names "Kellogg's Whole Wheat Biscuit" or "Kellogg's Shredded Whole Wheat Biscuit" so sized and spaced as to strike the eye as being a Kellogg product. It is true that on some of its cartons it had a picture of two shredded wheat biscuits in a bowl of milk which was quite similar to one of the plaintiff's registered trade-marks. But the name Kellogg was so prominent on all of the defendant's cartons as to minimize the possibility of confusion.

Some hotels, restaurants, and lunchrooms serve biscuits not in cartons, and guests so served may conceivably suppose that a Kellogg biscuit served is one of the plaintiff's make. But no person familiar with plaintiff's product would be misled. The Kellogg biscuit is about two-thirds the size of plaintiff's; and differs from it in appearance. Moreover, the field in which deception could be practiced is negligibly small. Only 2½ per cent of the Kellogg biscuits are sold to hotels, restaurants and lunchrooms. Of those so sold 98 per cent are sold in individual cartons containing two biscuits. These cartons are distinctive and bear prominently the Kellogg name. To put upon the individual biscuit some mark which would identify it as the Kellogg product is not commercially possible. Relatively few biscuits will be removed from the individual cartons before they reach the consumer. The obligation resting upon Kellogg Company is not to insure that every purchaser will know it to be the maker but to use every reasonable means to prevent confusion.

It is urged that all possibility of deception or confusion would be removed if Kellogg Company should refrain from using the name "Shredded Wheat" and adopt some form other than the pillow-shape. But the name and form are integral parts of the goodwill of the article. To share fully in the goodwill, it must use the name and the pillow-shape. And in the goodwill Kellogg Company is as free to share as the plaintiff. *Compare* William R. Warner & Co. v. Eli Lilly & Co., 265 U.S. 526, 528, 530. Moreover, the pillow-shape must be used for another reason. The evidence is persuasive that this form is functional — that the cost of the biscuit would be increased and its high quality lessened if some other form were substituted for the pillow-shape.

Kellogg Company is undoubtedly sharing in the goodwill of the article known as "Shredded Wheat"; and thus is sharing in a market which was created by the skill and judgment of plaintiff's predecessor and has been widely extended by vast expenditures in advertising persistently made. But that is not unfair. Sharing in the goodwill of an article unprotected by patent or trade-mark is the exercise of a right possessed by all — and in the free exercise of which the consuming public is deeply interested. There is no evidence of passing off or deception on the part of the Kellogg Company; and it has taken every reasonable precaution to prevent confusion or the practice of deception in the sale of its product. . . .

Decrees reversed with direction to dismiss the bill.

Justice MCREYNOLDS and Justice BUTLER are of opinion that the decree of the Circuit Court of Appeals is correct and should be affirmed. To them it seems sufficiently clear that the Kellogg Company is fraudulently seeking to appropriate to itself the benefits of a goodwill built up at great cost by the respondent and its predecessors.

Notes and Questions

1. The case mentions a "design patent." A design patent (as opposed to a utility patent) is a right to exclude others from manufacturing or selling an article of manufacture embodying a claimed ornamental feature. In order to obtain a design patent, requirements of novelty and non-obviousness, paralleling the requirements for utility patents, must be met — except that it must be alleged that the patented ornamental feature has no utilitarian advantage, or to put it another way, is purely ornamental. One of the authors of this text believes that the risks of anti-competitive uses of design patents make their social value questionable.

2. What relief did National Biscuit want? Would it ever be appropriate for a producer to have the right to exclude others from selling products that were shaped, or colored, just like those of the producer? Suppose I was a baker. Could I gain registration of the mark "White Bread"? What about "Health Bread"? What if I baked my bread so that each slice was in approximately the shape of the state of Georgia — could a competitor mimic me?

3. Is National Biscuit claiming the right to the exclusive right to the words "shredded wheat"? Or the exclusive right to make such biscuits in a particular shape? Or both? What is the difference between the two claims? Is there a different rationale for each?

The classical marks are symbols or words. But the reason that we prohibit others from simulating them on competing goods is to avoid confusing the public as to the source of goods. Are symbols or words the only ways in which consumers can identify sources? Of course we know that they are not. Sometimes consumers identify the source of a product by recognizing that all products of a certain shape come from a particular maker. If I give you a piece of chocolate candy in the shape of a truncated pyramid, you know it is a piece of CHUNKY brand candy. Similarly, we can often identify products by means of their packaging. At a time when soft drinks were sold primarily in bottles, most major purveyors of these products had a bottle that was distinctive, which served to identify the producer, whether or not the bottle bore any kind of label. Customers could have told you, with eyes closed, whether they had a Coca-Cola, or Pepsi-Cola, or Crush soft drink in their hands. Courts recognized the source-identifying potential of product shape and packaging, and acted to grant protection. The shape of the product or configuration of packaging was called the product's "trade dress." Trademark protection can be extended to trade dress.

Are there special problems associated with protecting trade dress, and treating product shape or packaging as we treat symbols or words? What does the *Kellogg* case suggest about this question?

4. Did the Court hold that once a utility patent expires the patentee can never make a trademark-like claim to the exclusive use of the source-identifying function of the shape of products made using the patented machine? What could justify such a rule?

5. National Biscuit makes an argument based on the trademark concept of "secondary meaning." Some explanation might be helpful. Trademark law generally prohibits conferring trademark status on words which are either generic or descriptive. Generic words can *never* become trademarks. Descriptive words can IF they come to be used in a source-signifying way rather than a descriptive way. Imagine that I begin to sell a product bearing the label "REFRESHING LEMONADE." "Refreshing" is a word that could easily be understood as describing the

characteristics of the lemonade. But if I sell the product for some time, and adopt "REFRESHING" as my trademark, and if the public comes to associate the word "refreshing" as applied to lemonade as telling them the source of the lemonade, rather than merely one of its characteristics, then I will be able to assert trademark rights in REFRESHING, for a lemonade product. "Refreshing" will have developed secondary meaning as to lemonade. Competitors, by the way, would remain free to use the word "refreshing" to describe the characteristics of their lemonade, as in "We think that you will find Ocean Breeze lemonade to be a refreshing way to end a summer afternoon."

■ E.I. DuPONT DeNEMOURS & COMPANY v. CHRISTOPHER
United States Court of Appeals for the Fifth Circuit, 1970
431 F.2d 1012, cert. denied, 400 U.S. 1024 (1971)

GOLDBERG, Circuit Judge. This is a case of industrial espionage in which an airplane is the cloak and a camera the dagger. The defendants-appellants, Rolfe and Gary Christopher, are photographers in Beaumont, Texas. The Christophers were hired by an unknown third party to take aerial photographs of new construction at the Beaumont plant of E.I. DuPont DeNemours & Company. Sixteen photographs of the DuPont facility were taken from the air on March 19, 1969, and these photographs were later developed and delivered to the third party.

DuPont employees apparently noticed the airplane on March 19 and immediately began an investigation to determine why the craft was circling over the plant. By that afternoon the investigation had disclosed that the craft was involved in a photographic expedition and that the Christophers were the photographers. DuPont contacted the Christophers that same afternoon and asked them to reveal the name of the person or corporation requesting the photographs. The Christophers refused to disclose this information, giving as their reason the client's desire to remain anonymous.

Having reached a dead end in the investigation, DuPont subsequently filed suit against the Christophers, alleging that the Christophers had wrongfully obtained photographs revealing DuPont's trade secrets which they then sold to the undisclosed third party. DuPont contended that it had developed a highly secret but unpatented process for producing methanol, a process which gave DuPont a competitive advantage over other producers. This process, DuPont alleged, was a trade secret developed after much expensive and time-consuming research, and a secret which the company had taken special precautions to safeguard. The area photographed by the Christophers was the plant designed to produce methanol by this secret process, and because the plant was still under construction parts of the process were exposed to view from directly above the construction area. Photographs of that area, DuPont alleged, would enable a skilled person to deduce the secret process for making methanol. DuPont thus contended that the Christophers had wrongfully appropriated DuPont trade secrets by taking the photographs and delivering them to the undisclosed third party. In its suit DuPont asked for damages to cover the loss it had already sustained as a result of the wrongful disclosure of the trade secret and sought temporary and permanent injunctions prohibiting any further circulation of the photographs already taken and prohibiting any additional photographing of the methanol plant.

The Christophers answered with motions to dismiss for lack of jurisdiction and failure to state a claim upon which relief could be granted. Depositions were taken during which the Christophers again refused to disclose the name of the person to whom they had delivered the photographs. DuPont then filed a motion to compel an answer to this question and all related questions.

On June 5, 1969, the trial court . . . granted the Christophers' motion for an interlocutory appeal under 28 U.S.C.A. §1292(b) to allow the Christophers to obtain immediate appellate review of the court's finding that DuPont had stated a claim upon which relief could be granted. Agreeing with the trial court's determination that DuPont had stated a valid claim, we affirm the decision of that court.

. . . The only question involved in this interlocutory appeal is whether DuPont has asserted a claim upon which relief can be granted. The Christophers argued both at trial and before this court that they committed no "actionable wrong" in photographing the DuPont facility and passing these photographs on to their client because they conducted all of their activities in public airspace, violated no government aviation standard, did not breach any confidential relation, and did not engage in any fraudulent or illegal conduct. In short, the Christophers argue that for an appropriation of trade secrets to be wrongful there must be a trespass, other illegal conduct, or breach of a confidential relationship. We disagree.

It is true, as the Christophers assert, that the previous trade secret cases have contained one or more of these elements. However, we do not think that the Texas courts would limit the trade secret protection exclusively to these elements. On the contrary, in Hyde Corporation v. Huffines, 314 S.W.2d 763 (1958), the Texas Supreme Court specifically adopted the rule found in the *Restatement of Torts* §757 (1939) which provides:

> One who discloses or uses another's trade secret, without a privilege to do so, is liable to the other if (a) he discovered the secret by improper means, or (b) his disclosure or use constitutes a breach of confidence reposed in him by the other in disclosing the secret to him. . . .

Thus, although the previous cases have dealt with a breach of a confidential relationship, a trespass, or other illegal conduct, the rule is much broader than the cases heretofore encountered. Not limiting itself to specific wrongs, Texas adopted subsection (a) of the Restatement which recognizes a cause of action for the discovery of a trade secret by any "improper" means.

The defendants, however, read Furr's Inc. v. United Specialty Advertising Co., 338 S.W.2d 762 (Tex. Civ. App. 1960), *writ ref'd n.r.e.*, as limiting the Texas rule to breach of a confidential relationship. The court in *Furr's* did make the statement that "the use of someone else's idea is not automatically a violation of the law. It must be something that meets the requirements of a 'trade secret' *and has been obtained through a breach of confidence* in order to entitle the injured party to damages and/or injunction." *Id.* at 766 (emphasis added). We think, however, that the exclusive rule which defendants have extracted from this statement is unwarranted. In the first place, in *Furr's* the court specifically found that there was no trade secret involved because the entire advertising scheme claimed to be the trade secret had been completely divulged to the public. Secondly, the court found that the plaintiff in the course of selling the scheme to the defendant had voluntarily divulged the entire scheme. Thus the court was dealing only with a possible breach of confidence concerning a properly discovered secret; there was never a question of any impropriety in the discovery or any other improper conduct on the part of the defendant. The court merely held that under those circumstances the defendant had not acted improperly if no breach of confidence occurred. We do not read *Furr's* as limiting the trade secret protection to a breach of confidential relationship when the facts of the case do raise the issue of some other wrongful conduct on the part of one discovering the trade secrets of another. If breach of confidence were meant to encompass the entire panoply of commercial improprieties, subsection (a) of the Restatement would be either surplusage or persiflage, an interpretation abhorrent to the traditional precision of the Restatement. We therefore find meaning in sub-section (a) and think that the Texas Supreme Court clearly indicated by its adoption that there is a cause of action for the discovery of a trade secret by any "improper means." Hyde Corporation v. Huffines, *supra.*

The question remaining, therefore, is whether aerial photography of plant construction is an improper means of obtaining another's trade secret. We conclude that it is and that the Texas courts would so hold. The Supreme Court of that state has declared that "the undoubted tendency of the law has been to recognize and enforce higher standards of commercial morality in the business world." Hyde Corporation v. Huffines, *supra,* 314 S.W.2d at 773. That court has quoted with approval articles indicating that the *proper* means of gaining possession of a competitor's secret process is "through inspection and analysis" of the product in order to create a duplicate. K & G Tool & Service Co. v. G & G Fishing Tool Service, 314 S.W.2d 782, 783, 788 (1958). . . .

We think, therefore, that the Texas rule is clear. One may use his competitor's secret process if he discovers the process by reverse engineering applied to the finished product; one may use a competitor's process if he discovers it by his own independent research; but one may not avoid these labors by taking the process from the discoverer without his permission at a time when he is taking reasonable precautions to maintain its secrecy. To obtain knowledge of a process without spending the time and money to discover it independently is *improper* unless the holder voluntarily discloses it or fails to take reasonable precautions to ensure its secrecy.

In the instant case the Christophers deliberately flew over the DuPont plant to get pictures of a process which DuPont had attempted to keep secret. The Christophers delivered their pictures to a third party who was certainly aware of the means by which they had been acquired and who may be planning to use the information contained therein to manufacture methanol by the DuPont process. The third party has a right to use this process only if he obtains this knowledge through his own research efforts, but thus far all information indicates that the third party has gained this knowledge solely by taking it from DuPont at a time when DuPont was making reasonable efforts to preserve its secrecy. In such a situation DuPont has a valid cause of action to prohibit the Christophers from improperly discovering its trade secret and to prohibit the undisclosed third party from using the improperly obtained information.

We note that this view is in perfect accord with the position taken by the authors of the Restatement. In commenting on improper means of discovery the savants of the Restatement said:

f. *Improper means of discovery.* The discovery of another's trade secret by improper means subjects the actor to liability independently of the harm to the interest in the secret. Thus, if one uses physical force to take a secret formula from another's pocket, or breaks into another's office to steal the formula, his conduct is wrongful and subjects him to liability apart from the rule stated in this Section. Such conduct is also an improper means of procuring the secret under this rule. But means may be improper under this rule even though they do not cause any other harm than that to the interest in the trade secret. Examples of such means are fraudulent misrepresentations to induce disclosure, tapping of telephone wires, eavesdropping or other espionage. A complete catalogue of improper means is not possible. In general they are means which fall below the generally accepted standards of commercial morality and reasonable conduct.

Restatement of Torts §757, comment f at 10 (1939).

In taking this position we realize that industrial espionage of the sort here perpetrated has become a popular sport in some segments of our industrial community. However, our devotion to freewheeling industrial competition must not force us into accepting the law of the jungle as the standard of morality expected in our commercial relations. Our tolerance of the espionage game must cease when the protections required to prevent another's spying cost so much that the spirit of inventiveness is dampened. Commercial privacy must be protected from espionage which could not have been reasonably anticipated or prevented. We do not mean to imply, however, that everything not in plain view is within the protected vale, nor that all information obtained through every extra optical extension is forbidden. Indeed, for our industrial competition to remain healthy there must be breathing room for observing a competing industrialist. A competitor can and must shop his competition for pricing and examine his products for quality, components, and methods of manufacture. Perhaps ordinary fences and roofs must be built to shut out incursive eyes, but we need not require the discoverer of a trade secret to guard against the unanticipated, the undetectable, or the unpreventable methods of espionage now available.

In the instant case DuPont was in the midst of constructing a plant. Although after construction the finished plant would have protected much of the process from view, during the period of construction the trade secret was exposed to view from the air. To require DuPont to put a roof over the unfinished plant to guard its secret would impose an enormous expense to prevent nothing more than a school boy's trick. We introduce here no new or radical ethic since our ethos has never given moral sanction to piracy. The market place must not deviate far from our mores. We should not require a person or corporation to take unreasonable precautions to prevent another from doing that which he ought not do in the first place. Reasonable precautions against predatory eyes we may require, but an impenetrable fortress is an unreasonable requirement, and we are not disposed to burden industrial inventors with such a duty in order to protect the fruits of their efforts. "Improper" will always be a word of many nuances, determined by time, place, and circumstances. We therefore need not proclaim a catalogue of commercial improprieties. Clearly, however, one of its commandments does say "thou shall not appropriate a trade secret through deviousness under circumstances in which countervailing defenses are not reasonably available."

Having concluded that aerial photography, from whatever altitude, is an improper method of discovering the trade secrets exposed during construction of the DuPont plant, we need not worry about whether the flight pattern chosen by the Christophers violated any federal aviation regulations. Regardless of whether the flight was legal or illegal in that sense, the espionage was an improper means of discovering DuPont's trade secret.

The decision of the trial court is affirmed and the case remanded to that court for proceedings on the merits.

Notes and Questions

1. Should we describe DuPont's interest in being protected by competitor-inspired aerial photography as a "property" interest? What would Justice Pitney (author of the majority opinion in INS v. AP) have said? Justice Brandeis dissented in that case; what would he have said? Note especially Brandeis' discussion of Sports and General Press Agency, Ltd. v. Our Dogs Publishing Co., Ltd.

2. What are the interests that the law of trade secrets seeks to protect? Are they the same as those of patent law? Is there an overlap? You should know that in 1974 the Supreme Court ruled in Kewanee Oil v. Bicron Corp., 416 U.S. 470 (1974), that trade secret law was not preempted by the federal patent scheme. Lower courts had split over the question of whether an earlier Supreme Court case, Sears, Roebuck & Co. v. Stiffel Co., 376 U.S. 225 (1964), eliminated all state laws that sought to protect technologies that were patentable subject matter, on the ground that this constituted an interference with the federal scheme.

Why isn't the overflight of the airplane a trespass to the property of the plaintiff? What about *cujus est solum ejus est usque ad coelum* (Whose is the soil, his it is up to the sky), as discussed in Chapter 3?

3. The law of trade secrets developed as common law doctrine. It became a candidate for statutory codification as the advantages of developing a more uniform standard, from state to state, became apparent. The National Commissioners on Uniform State Laws developed a Uniform Law that has been adopted, albeit with some modifications, in many states.

C. INTELLECTUAL PROPERTY IN THE TWENTY-FIRST CENTURY

■ JORDACHE ENTERPRISES, INC. v. HOGG WYLD, LTD.
United States Court of Appeals for the Tenth Circuit, 1987
828 F.2d 1482

TACHA, Circuit Judge. This case, a trademark infringement action brought against a manufacturer that identifies its blue jeans for larger women with a smiling pig and the word "Lardashe" on the seat of the pants, reminds us that "you can't make a silk purse out of a sow's ear."

Appellant Jordache Enterprises, Inc., alleges error in a district court decision finding no likelihood of confusion between the Jordache and Lardashe trademarks and finding no violation of New Mexico's antidilution statute. We affirm.

Appellant . . . is the fourth largest blue jeans manufacturer in the United States. It produces and markets all types of apparel for men, women, and children, the principal product being designer blue jeans. Most items are identified by one of appellant's several registered trademarks, including the word "Jordache" printed in block letters, the word "Jordache" printed in block letters and superimposed over a drawing of a horse's head, and a drawing of a horse's head alone. . . .

In 1984, appellees Marsha Stafford and Susan Duran formed Hogg Wyld, Ltd., now Oink, Inc., for the purpose of marketing designer blue jeans for larger women. In an operation conducted out of their homes in New Mexico, the two women designed a product, selected a manufacturer, and ultimately sold over 1,000 pairs of jeans. Sales were limited to specialty shops in several southwestern states and to acquaintances or others who heard of the product. The women have not directly advertised their jeans, although several retailers have done so.

The name of the Oink, Inc. blue jeans gave rise to this suit. Names suggested at one time or another for the jeans by Stafford, Duran, or others, included . . . "Vidal Sowsoon," and "Calvin Swine." Other names and marks were suggested as a take-off on Stafford's childhood nickname, "lardass." This nickname inspired ideas such as "Wiseashe" with a picture of an owl, "Dumbashe" with a picture of a donkey, "Horsesashe" with a picture of a horse, and "Helium Ash" with a picture of a balloon. The women decided to name their jeans "Lardashe."

. . . Jordache brought suit against Stafford, Duran, and their corporation, alleging trademark infringement in violation of the Lanham Trade-Mark Act, 15 U.S.C. §§1051-1127, the New Mexico Trademark Act, N.M. Stat. §§57-3-1 to -14 (1987), and common law. The district court, after a three-day bench trial, held that no trademark infringement had occurred on any of the alternative claims. *Jordache Enters. v. Hogg Wyld, Ltd.*, 625 F. Supp. 48 (D.N.M. 1985). Jordache now appeals to this court.

I.

The Lanham Act prohibits the unauthorized use of a reproduction, copy, or imitation of a registered trademark in a way that "is likely to cause confusion" with the registered mark. 15 U.S.C. §1114(1)(a); *see also* 15 U.S.C. §1125(a) (similar test for infringement of an unregistered trademark by a junior user). "Confusion occurs when consumers make an incorrect mental association between the involved commercial products or their producers." *San Francisco Arts & Athletics, Inc. v. United States Olympic Comm.*, 483 U.S. 522 (1987) (Brennan, J., dissenting). This court has identified several factors, originally set forth in *Restatement of Torts* §729 (1938), that are relevant to whether there is a likelihood of confusion between two marks:

(a) the degree of similarity between the designation and the trade-mark or trade name in
    (i)   appearance;
    (ii) pronunciation of the words used;
    (iii) verbal translation of the pictures or designs involved;
    (iv) suggestion;
(b) the intent of the actor in adopting the designation;
(c) the relation in use and manner of marketing between the goods or services marketed by the actor and those marketed by the other;
(d) the degree of care likely to be exercised by purchasers.

. . . The district court examined these factors and concluded that there is no likelihood of confusion between the Jordache trademark and the Lardashe trademark. 625 F. Supp. at 53-54. Likelihood of confusion is a question of fact that we review under the clearly erroneous standard. Appellant contends that the district court erred as a matter of law in its consideration of several of the factors and that, in any event, the court's findings are clearly erroneous.

A.

The similarity between the marks in appearance, pronunciation of the words used, translation of the designs used, and suggestion or meaning is the first factor to consider in determining whether there is a likelihood of confusion. The district court found that the Jordache mark and the Lardashe mark are not confusingly similar. Appellant argues that the court employed an improper legal construction of "suggestion" or "meaning" in reaching this result. Even if we were to reject this argument, appellant would have us hold the finding of no similarity to be clearly erroneous. . . .

Our review of the evidence shows that the marks, and their suggested images, are obviously different. Many of the Jordache jeans are identified by a small brown patch with the word "Jordache" written in white in block letters with a gold horse's head superimposed over the lettering. In other instances, the patch is white with blue block lettering and no horse. Sometimes "Jordache" is written in script or only the horse's head is used. In contrast, the Lardashe jeans have a large, brightly colored pig head and two hooves, giving the appearance that a pig is peering over the back pocket. The word "Lardashe" is written in script beneath the pig's head, below which is an upside down embroidered heart. See appendix. We agree with the district court that the "striking, brightly colored, and far from subtle" pig design is "humorous, or 'cute,' or facetious." 625 F. Supp. At 53. Thus, while the similarity of the words used in the mark would support an inference of likelihood of confusion, we agree with the district court's finding that the striking dissimilarities in the designs used in the marks greatly outweigh any similarities.

B.

The intent of a party in selecting a trademark is another factor in determining whether there is a likelihood of confusion. The district court found the appellees' "intent was to employ a name that, to some extent, parodied or played upon the established trademark Jordache"; appellees "did not intend to 'palm off' their jeans as Jordache jeans; that is, to confuse the public into believing it was buying a Jordache product." *Id.* at 52. Appellants contend the court erred in its analysis of intent and the relevance of parody. . . .

In one sense, a parody is an attempt "to derive benefit from the reputation" of the owner of the mark, Sicilia Di R. Biebow & Co. v. Cox, 732 F.2d 417, 431 (5th Cir. 1984), if only because no parody could be made without the initial mark. The benefit to the one making the parody, however, arises from the humorous association, not from public confusion as to the source of the marks. A parody relies upon a difference from the original mark, presumably a humorous difference, in order to produce its desired effect.

"Now everything is funny as long as it is happening to somebody Else, but when it happens to you, why it seems to lose some of its Humor, and if it keeps on happening, why the entire laughter kinder Fades out of it." W. Rogers, *Warning to Jokers: Lay Off the Prince*, in *The Illiterate Digest*, I-3 *The Writings of Will Rogers* 75 (1974). The same is true in trademark law. As McCarthy writes, "No one likes to be the butt of a joke, not even a trademark. But the requirement of trademark law is that a likely confusion of source, sponsorship or affiliation must be proven, which is not the same thing as a 'right' not to be made fun of." 2 J. McCarthy, *Trademarks and Unfair Competition* §31:38 at 670 (2d ed. 1984). . . .

Our single concern here, however, is whether an intent to parody an existing trademark supports an inference of a likelihood of confusion under the reasoning that one who chooses a mark similar to an existing mark intends to confuse the public. We hold that it does not. An intent to parody is not an intent to confuse the public. . . .

[The court concluded that other trial court findings that went to other factors to be considered in determining whether there was a likelihood of confusion were "not clearly erroneous."]

The district court weighed all of the factors and concluded there is no likelihood of confusion between the Lardashe mark and the Jordache marks. We have examined the record, including the testimony of Becky Ingram concerning industry confusion and all of the other evidence appellant contends the district court overlooked. We hold the district court's finding of no likelihood of confusion is not clearly erroneous.

II.

Jordache also raises a claim under New Mexico's antidilution statute which provides: "Likelihood of injury to business reputation or of dilution of the distinctive quality of a trademark or trade name . . . is a ground for injunctive relief notwithstanding the absence of competition between the parties or the absence of confusion as to the source of goods or services." N.M. Stat. §57-3-10 (1987).

No state court in New Mexico has interpreted this statute. We are thus presented with a question of law regarding what interpretation the New Mexico courts would adopt for this statute.

It has been widely observed that many courts have been hostile to state antidilution statutes. . . . The decisions holding that antidilution statutes do not apply to competitive products are an indication of this hostility. . . . As the district court noted, "The paradigmatic dilution case involves the situation where the same or very similar marks are being used on vastly different products. Examples might include BEEFEATER used for a restaurant; DIOR used for a cleaning establishment; BACARDI used for jewelry; PLAYBOY used for auto repair." 625 F. Supp. at 56 (citation omitted). Indeed, the first exposition of the dilution doctrine stated the real injury in dilution cases "is the gradual whittling away or dispersion of the identity and hold upon the public mind of the mark or name by its use upon *non-competing* goods." Schechter, *The Rational Basis of Trademark Protection*, 40 Harv. L. Rev. 813, 825 (1927) (emphasis added).

The district court in this case recognized that other courts have limited antidilution statutes to cases involving noncompeting products, but the district court did not so limit the New Mexico statute. Given the plain language of the statute that relief is available "notwithstanding the absence of competition between the parties," we agree the statute cannot be limited to cases involving noncompeting products. "Had the [legislature] intended to make the absence of competition a prerequisite to . . . relief, it could easily have done so." Lesportsac, Inc. v. K Mart Corp., 617 F. Supp. 316, 319 (E.D.N.Y. 1985). We will not ignore the clear words of the New Mexico legislature.

There are three grounds under which an owner of a distinctive trademark may obtain relief under an antidilution statute. Relief may be granted if:

[T]here is a likelihood of dilution due to (1) injury to the value of the mark caused by actual or potential confusion, (2) diminution in the uniqueness and individuality of the mark, or (3) injury resulting from use of the mark in a manner that tarnishes or appropriates the goodwill and reputation associated with plaintiff's mark.

L.L. Bean, Inc. v. Drake Publishers, Inc., 811 F.2d 26, 30 (1st Cir.), *cert. denied,* 483 U.S. 1013 (1987). Dilution, like likelihood of confusion, is a question of fact that we review under the clearly erroneous standard.

The first ground merely repeats the likelihood of confusion test for relief under the Lanham Act. We have held there is no likelihood of confusion between the Lardashe and the Jordache trademarks. Therefore, there is no dilution of Jordache's marks in this sense.

Dilution of a trademark can also occur if the challenged mark blurs the mental image conveyed by the original mark. The statutorily protected distinctive quality of a trademark is diluted as the mark's propensity to bring to mind a particular product or source is weakened. Stop the Olympic Prison v. United States Olympic Comm., 489 F. Supp. 1112, 1123 (S.D.N.Y. 1980). As the distinctive quality disappears, the trademark becomes generic and loses its legal protection.

In the present case, the district court found that "[b]ecause of the parody aspect of Lardashe, it is not likely that public identification of JORDACHE with the plaintiff will be eroded; indeed, parody tends to increase public identification of a plaintiff's mark with the plaintiff."625 F. Supp. at 57. The court further found that "[u]nder all the circumstances, the continued existence of LARDASHE jeans simply will not cause JORDACHE to lose its distinctiveness as a strong trademark for jeans and other apparel." *Id.* We hold these findings are not clearly erroneous.

The third element of dilution law is tarnishment. A mark can be tarnished if it is used in an unwholesome context. Precisely what suffices as an unwholesome context is not immediately evident. *Compare* Toho Co. v. Sears, Roebuck & Co., 645 F.2d 788, 793 (9th Cir. 1981) (use of "Bagzilla" mark on garbage bags not "unsavory or degrading"); Tetley, Inc. v. Topps Chewing Gum, Inc., 556 F. Supp. 785, 794 (E.D.N.Y. 1983) ("Petley Flea Bags" does not tarnish "Tetley Tea Bags"); Girl Scouts of United States v. Personality Posters Mfg., 304 F. Supp. 1228, 1233-34 (S.D.N.Y. 1969) (use of "Be Prepared" slogan on poster portraying a pregnant girl in a Girl Scout uniform does not injure the Girl Scouts), *with* Dallas Cowboys Cheerleaders, Inc. v. Pussycat Cinema, Ltd., 604 F.2d 200, 205 (2d Cir. 1979) (use of Dallas Cowboys Cheerleaders uniforms in "sexually depraved" movie improperly injures plaintiff's business reputation); Original Appalachian Artworks, Inc. v. Topps Chewing Gum, Inc., 642 F. Supp. 1031, 1039-40 (N.D. Ga. 1986) (use of "Garbage Pail Kids" on various products sufficient evidence of tarnishment to support a preliminary injunction); Coca-Cola Co. v. Gemini Rising, Inc., 346 F. Supp. 1183, 1189 (E.D.N.Y. 1972) (use of Coca-Cola design in "Enjoy Cocaine" poster improper tarnishment). The district court found that while LARDASHE "might be considered to be in poor taste by some consumers . . . it is not likely to create in the mind of consumers a particularly unwholesome, unsavory, or degrading association with plaintiff's name and marks." 625 F. Supp. at 57. We have examined the record, including the marks in question, and we conclude that the district court's finding is not clearly erroneous.

Appellant contends that tarnishment can also occur in another manner that was not discussed by the district court. A few cases have held a trademark was tarnished by "use in a context which, while not inherently 'unwholesome', is out-of-keeping with plaintiff's high-quality image." 2 J. McCarthy, *Trademark and Unfair Competition Law* §24:13(E) at 222 and cases cited therein (2d ed. 1984). According to appellant, these cases require a finding of tarnishment here because of the alleged disparity in quality between Lardashe jeans and Jordache jeans.

This argument presumes that the public will associate the manufacturer of Lardashe jeans with the manufacturer of Jordache jeans, thereby causing damage to the high quality image of Jordache. Because we find that the Lardashe mark was an intentional parody of the Jordache mark, we assume that the public will to some extent associate the two marks. To be actionable, however, the association of the two marks must tarnish or appropriate the good will and reputation of the owner of the mark. If the public associates the two marks for parody purposes only and does not associate the two sources of the products, appellant suffers no actionable injury. Indeed, a manufacturer of a high quality product will typically benefit if its competitors are marketing a poor quality product at similar prices — *unless* the public associates the manufacturer of the poor quality product with the manufacturer of the high quality product. *See id.* at 5-31 ("A trademark owner should not be made to tolerate an unknown quality level for products, whether similar or not, *if they would likely be associated with his business.*") (emphasis added). Thus, the actionable association of marks is limited to an association of the source of the marks. Association of marks for parody purposes without corresponding association of manufacturers does not tarnish or appropriate the good will of the manufacturer of the high quality similar product.

The New Mexico statute plainly states that an actionable dilution of a trademark can occur despite the absence of competition between the parties and despite the absence of confusion as to the source of the products. But the statute also provides that relief is available only if there is some likelihood of injury to business reputation or of dilution of the distinctive quality of the trademark. There can be no likelihood of either injury if the public does not associate a product bearing one trademark with the manufacturer of a product bearing a different trademark.

The cases finding a trademark had been tarnished even though there was no unwholesome context all involve the use of identical, or almost identical, trade names on different products. *See* Steinway & Sons v. Robert Demars & Friends, 210 U.S.P.Q. 954 (C.D. Cal. 1981) (Steinway pianos and Stein-Way clip-on beverage can handles); Cartier, Inc. v. Three Sheaves Co., Inc., 465 F. Supp. 123 (S.D.N.Y. 1979) (Cartier jewelry, china, and silver and Cattier cosmetics and toiletries); Carling Brewing Co. v. Philip Morris Inc., 297 F. Supp. 1330 (N.D. Ga. 1968) (Black Label beer and Black Label cigarettes); Tiffany & Co. v. Boston Club, Inc., 231 F. Supp. 836 (D. Mass. 1964) (Tiffany jewelry, china, silverware, and glassware and Tiffany's Restaurant and Lounge); *see also* Yale Elec. Corp. v. Robertson, 26 F.2d 972, 974 (2d Cir. 1928) (Hand, L., J.) (Yale locks and Yale flashlights). In each of these cases the public could readily associate one product with the manufacturer of the other product on the assumption that the manufacturer is in the business of producing two separate and distinct products. This is not the case here. It is unlikely that the public would assume that the same manufacturer would use quite different marks on substantially the same product. While we do not hold that this type of tarnishment is established only where the Lanham Act likelihood of confusion test has been satisfied, the antidilution statute does require some showing that the public will associate both products with the same manufacturer. Our review of the record convinces us that the public will not associate Lardashe jeans with the appellant or, if they do, they will only make the association because of the parody and not because they believe Jordache Enterprises, Inc. manufactures Lardashe jeans. Therefore, there is no likelihood of an injury to appellant, and its dilution claim must fail.

III.

"'If it had grown up,' she said to herself, 'it would have been a dreadfully ugly child; but it makes rather a handsome pig, I think.'" L. Carroll, *Alice's Adventures in Wonderland* 78-79 (1892).

The judgment of the district court is affirmed.

Appendix

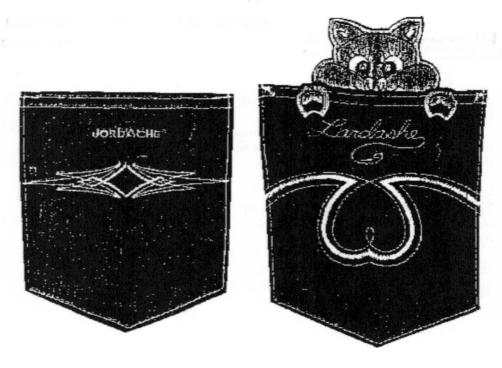

Notes and Questions

1. What do you understand is required for a trademark owner to prevail in an action for trademark infringement? What injury is at the heart of such a claim? It is often asserted that trademark law is fundamentally a consumer protection law, only incidentally advancing the interests of trademark owners. Make sure you understand how this might be so.

2. The *Jordache* case introduces an alternative theory that can be asserted by trademark owners — dilution. What is the nature of a dilution claim? How does it differ from an infringement claim? Why might the development of protection against dilution be controversial?

3. Do you find the mark created by Marsha Stafford and Susan Duvan to be offensive? Should that be a factor in the case? Though the case doesn't indicate that they sought to register the mark under the federal Lanham Act, had they sought registration they might have confronted a challenge under 15 U.S.C. §1052. It provides:

> No trademark by which the goods of the applicant may be distinguished from the goods of others shall be refused registration on the principal register on account of its nature unless it —
>
> > (a) consists of or comprises immoral, deceptive, or scandalous matter; or matter which may disparage . . . persons, living or dead, institutions, beliefs, or national symbols, or bring them into contempt or disrepute; . . .

Section 1052 deals with registrability. It does not prohibit *use* of a mark. Probably the most notable recent challenge to the registrability of a mark on grounds that a mark violates the requirements of §1052(a) is Harjo v. Pro-Football, Inc., 50 U.S.P.Q.2d 1705 (TTAB 1999). In *Harjo*, the plaintiffs challenged the registrability of the trademark REDSKINS as applied to the Washington Redskins football team. The Trademark Trial and Appeal Board (TTAB) ordered the cancellation of the mark, but in Pro-Football, Inc. v. Harjo, 2003 U.S. Dist. LEXIS 17180 (D.D.C. Sept. 30, 2003), the D.C. Circuit Court ruled that there was insufficient evidence to support some of the TTAB findings and entered summary judgment for the football club owners.

■ FEIST PUBLICATIONS, INC. v. RURAL TELEPHONE SERVICE CO.

Supreme Court of the United States, 1991
499 U.S. 340

O'Connor, Justice. This case requires us to clarify the extent of copyright protection available to telephone directory white pages.

Rural Telephone Service Company, Inc., is a certified public utility that provides telephone service to several communities in northwest Kansas. It is subject to a state regulation that requires all telephone companies operating in Kansas to issue annually an updated telephone directory. Accordingly, as a condition of its monopoly franchise, Rural publishes a typical telephone directory, consisting of white pages and yellow pages. . . . Rural distributes its directory free of charge to its subscribers, but earns revenue by selling yellow pages advertisements.

Feist Publications, Inc., is a publishing company that specializes in area-wide telephone directories. Unlike a typical directory, which covers only a particular calling area, Feist's area-wide directories cover a much larger geographical range, reducing the need to call directory assistance or consult multiple directories. The Feist directory that is the subject of this litigation covers 11 different telephone service areas in 15 counties and contains 46,878 white pages listings — compared to Rural's approximately 7,700 listings. Like Rural's directory, Feist's is distributed free of charge and includes both white pages and yellow pages. Feist and Rural compete vigorously for yellow pages advertising.

As the sole provider of telephone service in its service area, Rural obtains subscriber information quite easily. Persons desiring telephone service must apply to Rural and provide their names and addresses; Rural then assigns them a telephone number. Feist is not a telephone company, let alone one with monopoly status, and therefore lacks independent access to any subscriber information. To obtain white pages listings for its area-wide directory, Feist approached each of the 11 telephone companies operating in northwest Kansas and offered to pay for the right to use its white pages listings.

Of the 11 telephone companies, only Rural refused to license its listings to Feist. Rural's refusal created a problem for Feist, as omitting these listings would have left a gaping hole in its area-wide directory, rendering it less attractive to potential yellow pages advertisers. In a decision subsequent to that which we review here, the District Court determined that this was precisely the reason Rural refused to license its listings. The refusal was motivated by an unlawful purpose "to extend its monopoly in telephone service to a monopoly in yellow pages advertising." Rural Telephone Service Co. v. Feist Publications, Inc., 737 F. Supp. 610, 622 (Kan. 1990).

Unable to license Rural's white pages listings, Feist used them without Rural's consent. Feist began by removing several thousand listings that fell outside the geographic range of its area-wide directory, then hired personnel to investigate the 4,935 that remained. These employees verified the data reported by Rural and sought to obtain additional information. As a result, a typical Feist listing includes the individual's street address; most of Rural's listings do not. Notwithstanding these additions, however, 1,309 of the 46,878 listings in Feist's 1983 directory were identical to listings in Rural's 1982-1983 white pages. App. 54 (¶15-16), 57. Four of these were fictitious listings that Rural had inserted into its directory to detect copying.

Rural sued for copyright infringement in the District Court for the District of Kansas taking the position that Feist, in compiling its own directory, could not use the information contained in Rural's white pages. Rural asserted that Feist's employees were obliged to travel door-to-door or conduct a telephone survey to discover the same information for themselves. Feist responded that such efforts were economically impractical and, in any event, unnecessary because the information copied was beyond the scope of copyright protection. The District Court granted summary judgment to Rural, explaining that "courts have consistently held that telephone directories are copyrightable" and citing a string of lower court decisions. 663 F. Supp. 214, 218 (1987). In an unpublished opinion, the Court of Appeals for the Tenth Circuit affirmed. . . .

II.

A.

This case concerns the interaction of two well-established propositions. The first is that facts are not copyrightable; the other, that compilations of facts generally are. Each of these propositions possesses an impeccable pedigree. That there can be no valid copyright in facts is universally understood. The most fundamental axiom of copyright law is that "no author may copyright his ideas or the facts he narrates." Harper & Row Publishers, Inc. v. Nation Enterprises, 471 U.S. 539, 556 (1985). Rural wisely concedes this point, noting in its brief that "facts and discoveries, of course, are not themselves subject to copyright protection." Brief for Respondent 24. At the same time, however, it is beyond dispute that compilations of facts are within the subject matter of copyright. Compilations were expressly mentioned in the Copyright Act of 1909, and again in the Copyright Act of 1976.

There is an undeniable tension between these two propositions. Many compilations consist of nothing but raw data — *i.e.*, wholly factual information not accompanied by any original written expression. On what basis may one claim a copyright in such a work? Common sense tells us that 100 uncopyrightable facts do not magically change their status when gathered together in one place. Yet copyright law seems to contemplate that compilations that consist exclusively of facts are potentially within its scope.

The key to resolving the tension lies in understanding why facts are not copyrightable. The *sine qua non* of copyright is originality. To qualify for copyright protection, a work must be original to the author. *See Harper & Row, supra,* at 547-549. Original, as the term is used in copyright, means only that the work was independently created by the author (as opposed to copied from other works), and that it possesses at least some minimal degree of creativity. 1 M. Nimmer & D. Nimmer, *Copyright* §§2.01[A], [B] (1990) (hereinafter Nimmer). To be sure, the requisite level of creativity is extremely low; even a slight amount will suffice. The vast majority of works make the grade quite easily, as they possess some creative spark, "no matter how crude, humble or obvious" it might be. *Id.*, §1.08[C][1]. Originality does not signify novelty; a work may be original even though it closely resembles other works so long as the similarity is fortuitous, not the result of copying. To illustrate, assume that two poets, each ignorant of the other, compose identical poems. Neither work is novel, yet both are original and, hence, copyrightable. *See* Sheldon v. Metro-Goldwyn Pictures Corp., 81 F.2d 49, 54 (2d Cir. 1936).

Originality is a constitutional requirement. The source of Congress' power to enact copyright laws is Article I, §8, cl. 8, of the Constitution, which authorizes Congress to "secure for limited Times to Authors . . . the exclusive Right to their respective Writings." In two decisions from the late 19th century — *The Trade-Mark Cases*, 100 U.S. 82 (1879); and Burrow-Giles Lithographic Co. v. Sarony, 111 U.S. 53 (1884) — this Court defined the crucial terms "authors" and "writings." In so doing, the Court made it unmistakably clear that these terms presuppose a degree of originality.

In *The Trade-Mark Cases*, the Court addressed the constitutional scope of "writings." For a particular work to be classified "under the head of writings of authors," the Court determined, "originality is required." 100 U.S. at 94. The Court explained that originality requires independent creation plus a modicum of creativity: "While the word *writings* may be liberally construed, as it has been, to include original designs for engraving, prints, etc., it is only such as are *original*, and are founded in the creative powers of the mind. The writings which are to be protected are *the fruits of intellectual labor*, embodied in the form of books, prints, engravings, and the like." *Ibid.* (emphasis in original).

In *Burrow-Giles*, the Court distilled the same requirement from the Constitution's use of the word "authors." The Court defined "author," in a constitutional sense, to mean "he to whom anything owes its origin; originator; maker." 111 U.S. at 58. As in *The Trade-Mark Cases*, the Court emphasized the creative component of originality. It described copyright as being limited to "original intellectual conceptions of the author," *id.*, and stressed the importance of requiring an author who accuses another of infringement to prove "the existence of those facts of originality, of intellectual production, of thought, and conception." *Id.* at 59-60.

The originality requirement articulated in *The Trade-Mark Cases* and *Burrow-Giles* remains the touchstone of copyright protection today. . . . Leading scholars agree on this point. As one pair of commentators succinctly puts it: "The originality requirement is *constitutionally mandated* for all works." Patterson & Joyce, *Monopolizing the Law: The Scope of Copyright Protection for Law Reports and Statutory Compilations*, 36 UCLA L. Rev. 719, 763, n.155 (1989) (emphasis in original) (hereinafter Patterson & Joyce). . . .

It is this bedrock principle of copyright that mandates the law's seemingly disparate treatment of facts and factual compilations. "No one may claim originality as to facts." Nimmer §2.11[A], p. 2-157. This is because facts do not owe their origin to an act of authorship. The distinction is one between creation and discovery: The first person to find and report a particular fact has not created the fact; he or she has merely discovered its existence. . . . Census takers, for example, do not "create" the population figures that emerge from their efforts; in a sense, they copy these figures from the world around them. . . . Census data therefore do not trigger copyright because these data are not "original" in the constitutional sense. . . .

Factual compilations, on the other hand, may possess the requisite originality. The compilation author typically chooses which facts to include, in what order to place them, and how to arrange the collected data so that they may be used effectively by readers. These choices as to selection and arrangement, so long as they are made independently by the compiler and entail a minimal degree of creativity, are sufficiently original that Congress may protect such compilations through the copyright laws. Nimmer §§2.11[D], 3.03. Thus, even a directory that contains absolutely no protectible written expression, only facts, meets the constitutional minimum for copyright protection if it features an original selection or arrangement. *See Harper & Row*, 471 U.S. at 547. *Accord*, Nimmer §3.03.

This protection is subject to an important limitation. The mere fact that a work is copyrighted does not mean that every element of the work may be protected. Originality remains the *sine qua non* of copyright; accordingly, copyright protection may extend only to those components of a work that are original to the author. Patterson & Joyce 800-802; Ginsburg, *Creation and Commercial Value: Copyright Protection of Works of Information*, 90 Colum. L. Rev. 1865, 1868, and n.12 (1990) (hereinafter Ginsburg). Thus, if the compilation author clothes facts with an original collocation of words, he or she may be able to claim a copyright in this written expression. Others may copy the underlying facts from the publication, but not the precise words used to present them. In *Harper & Row*, for example, we explained that President Ford could not prevent others from copying bare historical facts from his autobiography, *see* 471 U.S. at 556-557, but that he could prevent others from copying his "subjective descriptions and portraits of public figures." *Id.* at 563. Where the compilation author adds no written expression but rather lets the facts speak for themselves, the expressive element is more elusive. The only conceivable expression is the manner in which the compiler has selected and arranged the facts. Thus, if the selection and arrangement are original, these elements of the work are eligible for copyright protection. . . .

This inevitably means that the copyright in a factual compilation is thin. Notwithstanding a valid copyright, a subsequent compiler remains free to use the facts contained in another's publication to aid in preparing a competing work, so long as the competing work does not feature the same selection and arrangement. As one commentator explains it: "No matter how much original authorship the work displays, the facts and ideas it exposes are free for the taking. . . . The very same facts and ideas may be divorced from the context imposed by the author, and restated or reshuffled by second comers, even if the author was the first to discover the facts or to propose the ideas." Ginsburg 1868.

It may seem unfair that much of the fruit of the compiler's labor may be used by others without compensation. As Justice Brennan has correctly observed, however, this is not "some unforeseen byproduct of a statutory scheme." *Harper & Row*, 471 U.S. at 589 (dissenting opinion). It is, rather, "the essence of copyright," *ibid.*, and a constitutional requirement. The primary objective of copyright is not to reward the labor of authors, but "to promote the Progress of Science and useful Arts." Art. I, §8, cl. 8. *Accord*, Twentieth Century Music Corp. v. Aiken, 422 U.S. 151, 156 (1975). To this end, copyright assures authors the right to their original expression, but encourages others to build freely upon the ideas and information conveyed by a work. *Harper & Row, supra*, at 556-557. This principle, known as the idea/expression or fact/expression dichotomy, applies to all works of authorship. As applied to a factual compilation, assuming the absence of original written expression, only the compiler's selection and arrangement may be protected; the raw facts may be copied at will. This result is neither unfair nor unfortunate. It is the means by which copyright advances the progress of science and art.

This Court has long recognized that the fact/expression dichotomy limits severely the scope of protection in fact-based works. More than a century ago, the Court observed: "The very object of publishing a book on science or the useful arts is to communicate to the world the useful knowledge which it contains. But this object would be frustrated if the knowledge could not be used without incurring the guilt of piracy of the book." Baker v. Selden, 101 U.S. 99, 103 (1879). We reiterated this point in *Harper & Row*.

> No author may copyright facts or ideas. The copyright is limited to those aspects of the work — termed "expression" — that display the stamp of the author's originality.
>
> Copyright does not prevent subsequent users from copying from a prior author's work those constituent elements that are not original — for example . . . facts, or materials in the public domain — as long as such use does not unfairly appropriate the author's original contributions. (471 U.S. at 547-548 (citation omitted).)

This, then, resolves the doctrinal tension: Copyright treats facts and factual compilations in a wholly consistent manner. Facts, whether alone or as part of a compilation, are not original and therefore may not be copyrighted. A factual compilation is eligible for copyright if it features an original selection or arrangement of facts, but the copyright is limited to the particular selection or arrangement. In no event may copyright extend to the facts themselves.

B.

As we have explained, originality is a constitutionally mandated prerequisite for copyright protection. The Court's decisions announcing this rule predate the Copyright Act of 1909, but ambiguous language in the 1909 Act caused some lower courts temporarily to lose sight of this requirement.

The 1909 Act embodied the originality requirement, but not as clearly as it might have. *See* Nimmer §2.01. The subject matter of copyright was set out in §§3 and 4 of the Act. Section 4 stated that copyright was available to "all the writings of an author." 35 Stat. 1076. By using the words "writings" and "author" — the same words used in Article I, §8, of the Constitution and defined by the Court in *The*

Trade-Mark Cases and *Burrow-Giles* — the statute necessarily incorporated the originality requirement articulated in the Court's decisions. It did so implicitly, however, thereby leaving room for error.

Section 3 was similarly ambiguous. It stated that the copyright in a work protected only "the copyrightable component parts of the work." It thus stated an important copyright principle, but failed to identify the specific characteristic — originality — that determined which component parts of a work were copyrightable and which were not.

Most courts construed the 1909 Act correctly, notwithstanding the less-than-perfect statutory language. They understood from this Court's decisions that there could be no copyright without originality. . . .

But some courts misunderstood the statute. *See, e.g.*, Leon v. Pacific Telephone & Telegraph Co., 91 F.2d 484 (9th Cir. 1937); Jeweler's Circular Publishing Co. v. Keystone Publishing Co., 281 F. 83 (2d Cir. 1922). These courts ignored §§3 and 4, focusing their attention instead on §5 of the Act. Section 5, however, was purely technical in nature: It provided that a person seeking to register a work should indicate on the application the type of work, and it listed 14 categories under which the work might fall. One of these categories was "books, including composite and cyclopaedic works, directories, gazetteers, and other compilations." §5(a). Section 5 did not purport to say that all compilations were automatically copyrightable. Indeed, it expressly disclaimed any such function, pointing out that "the subject-matter of copyright is defined in section four." Nevertheless, the fact that factual compilations were mentioned specifically in §5 led some courts to infer erroneously that directories and the like were copyrightable *per se*, "without any further or precise showing of original — personal — authorship." Ginsburg 1895.

Making matters worse, these courts developed a new theory to justify the protection of factual compilations. Known alternatively as "sweat of the brow" or "industrious collection," the underlying notion was that copyright was a reward for the hard work that went into compiling facts. The classic formulation of the doctrine appeared in *Jeweler's Circular Publishing Co.*, 281 F. at 88:

> The right to copyright a book upon which one has expended labor in its preparation does not depend upon whether the materials which he has collected consist or not of matters which are publici juris, or whether such materials show literary skill *or originality*, either in thought or in language, or anything more than industrious collection. The man who goes through the streets of a town and puts down the names of each of the inhabitants, with their occupations and their street number, acquires material of which he is the author (emphasis added).

The "sweat of the brow" doctrine had numerous flaws, the most glaring being that it extended copyright protection in a compilation beyond selection and arrangement — the compiler's original contributions — to the facts themselves. Under the doctrine, the only defense to infringement was independent creation. A subsequent compiler was "not entitled to take one word of information previously published," but rather had to "independently work out the matter for himself, so as to arrive at the same result from the same common sources of information." *Id.* at 88-89 (internal quotations omitted). "Sweat of the brow" courts thereby eschewed the most fundamental axiom of copyright law — that no one may copyright facts or ideas. *See* Miller v. Universal City Studios, Inc., 650 F.2d 1365, 1372 (5th Cir. 1981) (criticizing "sweat of the brow" courts because "ensuring that later writers obtain the facts independently . . . is precisely the scope of protection given . . . copyrighted matter, and the law is clear that facts are not entitled to such protection").

Decisions of this Court applying the 1909 Act make clear that the statute did not permit the "sweat of the brow" approach. The best example is International News Service v. Associated Press, 248 U.S. 215 (1918). In that decision, the Court stated unambiguously that the 1909 Act conferred copyright protection only on those elements of a work that were original to the author. International News Service had conceded taking news reported by Associated Press and publishing it in its own newspapers. Recognizing that §5 of the Act specifically mentioned "'periodicals, including newspapers,'" §5(b), the Court acknowledged that news articles were copyrightable. *Id.* at 234. It flatly rejected, however, the notion that the copyright in an article extended to the factual information it contained: "The news element — the information respecting current events contained in the literary production — is not the creation of the writer, but is a report of matters that ordinarily are *publici juris*; it is the history of the day." *Ibid.*

Without a doubt, the "sweat of the brow" doctrine flouted basic copyright principles. . . . "Protection for the fruits of such research . . . may in certain circumstances be available under a theory of unfair competition. But to accord copyright protection on this basis alone distorts basic copyright principles in that it creates a monopoly in public domain materials without the necessary justification of protecting and encouraging the creation of 'writings' by 'authors.'" Nimmer §3.04, p. 3-23.

c.

[The Court recapitulated the legislative history of the copyright statute revision which it believed disavowed the "sweat of the brow" theory. It found additional support in the statutory language itself.]

The definition of "compilation" is found in §101 of the 1976 Act. It defines a "compilation" in the copyright sense as "a work formed by the collection and assembling of preexisting materials or of data *that* are selected, coordinated, or arranged *in such a way that* the resulting work as a whole constitutes an original work of authorship" (emphasis added).

The purpose of the statutory definition is to emphasize that collections of facts are not copyrightable per se. It conveys this message through its tripartite structure, as emphasized above by the italics. The statute identifies three distinct elements and requires each to be met for a work to qualify as a copyrightable compilation: (1) the collection and assembly of pre-existing material, facts, or data; (2) the selection, coordination, or arrangement of those materials; and (3) the creation, by virtue of the particular selection, coordination, or arrangement, of an "original" work of authorship. "This tripartite conjunctive structure is self-evident, and should be assumed to 'accurately express the legislative purpose.'" Patry, *Copyright in Compilations of Facts (or Why the "White Pages" Are Not Copyrightable)*, 12 Com. & Law 37, 51 (Dec. 1990) (hereinafter Patry), quoting Mills Music, Inc. v. Snyder, 469 U.S. 153, 164 (1985).

At first glance, the first requirement does not seem to tell us much. It merely describes what one normally thinks of as a compilation — a collection of pre-existing material, facts, or data. What makes it significant is that it is not the *sole* requirement. It is not enough for copyright purposes that an author collects and assembles facts. To satisfy the statutory definition, the work must get over two additional hurdles. In this way, the plain language indicates that not every collection of facts receives copyright protection. Otherwise, there would be a period after "data."

The third requirement is also illuminating. It emphasizes that a compilation, like any other work, is copyrightable only if it satisfies the originality requirement ("an *original* work of authorship"). Although §102 states plainly that the originality requirement applies to all works, the point was emphasized with regard to compilations to ensure that courts would not repeat the mistake of the "sweat of the brow" courts by concluding that fact-based works are treated differently and measured by some other standard. As Congress explained it, the goal was to "make plain that the criteria of copyrightable subject matter stated in section 102 apply with full force to works . . . containing preexisting material." H.R. Rep., at 57; S. Rep., at 55.

The key to the statutory definition is the second requirement. It instructs courts that, in determining whether a fact-based work is an original work of authorship, they should focus on the manner in which the collected facts have been selected, coordinated, and arranged. This is a straightforward application of the originality requirement. Facts are never original, so the compilation author can claim originality, if at all, only in the way the facts are presented. To that end, the statute dictates that the principal focus should be on whether the selection, coordination, and arrangement are sufficiently original to merit protection.

Not every selection, coordination, or arrangement will pass muster. This is plain from the statute. It states that, to merit protection, the facts must be selected, coordinated, or arranged "in such a way" as to render the work as a whole original. This implies that some "ways" will trigger copyright, but that others will not. *See* Patry 57 & n.76. Otherwise, the phrase "in such a way" is meaningless and Congress should have defined "compilation" simply as "a work formed by the collection and assembly of preexisting materials or data that are selected, coordinated, or arranged." That Congress did not do so is dispositive. In accordance with "the established principle that a court should give effect, if possible, to every clause and word of a statute," Moskal v. United States, 498 U.S. 103, 109-110 (1990) (internal quotation marks omitted), we conclude that the statute envisions that there will be some fact-based works in which the selection, coordination, and arrangement are not sufficiently original to trigger copyright protection.

As discussed earlier, however, the originality requirement is not particularly stringent. A compiler may settle upon a selection or arrangement that others have used; novelty is not required. Originality requires only that the author make the selection or arrangement independently (*i.e.*, without copying that selection or arrangement from another work), and that it display some minimal level of creativity. Presumably, the vast majority of compilations will pass this test, but not all will. There remains a narrow category of works in which the creative spark is utterly lacking or so trivial as to be virtually nonexistent. *See generally* Bleistein v. Donaldson Lithographing Co., 188 U.S. 239, 251 (1903) (referring to "the narrowest and most obvious limits"). Such works are incapable of sustaining a valid copyright. Nimmer §2.01[B].

Even if a work qualifies as a copyrightable compilation, it receives only limited protection. This is the point of §103 of the Act. Section 103 explains that "the subject matter of copyright . . . includes compilations,"§103(a), but that copyright protects only the author's original contributions—not the facts or information conveyed:

> The copyright in a compilation . . . extends only to the material contributed by the author of such work, as distinguished from the preexisting material employed in the work, and does not imply any exclusive right in the preexisting material. (§103(b).)

As §103 makes clear, copyright is not a tool by which a compilation author may keep others from using the facts or data he or she has collected. "The most important point here is one that is commonly misunderstood today: copyright . . . has no effect one way or the other on the copyright or public domain status of the preexisting material." H.R. Rep., at 57; S. Rep., at 55. The 1909 Act did not require, as "sweat of the brow" courts mistakenly assumed, that each subsequent compiler must start from scratch and is precluded from relying on research undertaken by another. *See, e.g.,* Jeweler's Circular Publishing Co., 281 F. at 88-89. Rather, the facts contained in existing works may be freely copied because copyright protects only the elements that owe their origin to the compiler — the selection, coordination, and arrangement of facts.

In summary, the 1976 revisions to the Copyright Act leave no doubt that originality, not "sweat of the brow," is the touchstone of copyright protection in directories and other fact-based works. Nor is there any doubt that the same was true under the 1909 Act. The 1976 revisions were a direct response to the Copyright Office's concern that many lower courts had misconstrued this basic principle, and Congress emphasized repeatedly that the purpose of the revisions was to clarify, not change, existing law. The revisions explain with painstaking clarity that copyright requires originality, §102(a); that facts are never original, §102(b); that the copyright in a compilation does not extend to the facts it contains, §103(b); and that a compilation is copyrightable only to the extent that it features an original selection, coordination, or arrangement, §101. . . .

III.

There is no doubt that Feist took from the white pages of Rural's directory a substantial amount of factual information. At a minimum, Feist copied the names, towns, and telephone numbers of 1,309 of Rural's subscribers. Not all copying, however, is copyright infringement. To establish infringement, two elements must be proven: (1) ownership of a valid copyright, and (2) copying of constituent elements of the work that are original. *See Harper & Row,* 471 U.S. at 548. The first element is not at issue here; Feist appears to concede that Rural's directory, considered as a whole, is subject to a valid copyright because it contains some foreword text, as well as original material in its yellow pages advertisements. *See* Brief for Petitioner 18; Pet. for Cert. 9.

The question is whether Rural has proved the second element. In other words, did Feist, by taking 1,309 names, towns, and telephone numbers from Rural's white pages, copy anything that was "original" to Rural? Certainly, the raw data does not satisfy the originality requirement. Rural may have been the first to discover and report the names, towns, and telephone numbers of its subscribers, but this data does not "'owe its origin'" to Rural. *Burrow-Giles,* 111 U.S. at 58. Rather, these bits of information are uncopyrightable facts; they existed before Rural reported them and would have continued to exist if Rural had never published a telephone directory. The originality requirement "rules out protecting . . . names, addresses, and telephone numbers of which the plaintiff by no stretch of the imagination could be called the author." Patterson & Joyce 776.

Rural essentially concedes the point by referring to the names, towns, and telephone numbers as "preexisting material." Brief for Respondent 17. Section

103(b) states explicitly that the copyright in a compilation does not extend to "the preexisting material employed in the work."

The question that remains is whether Rural selected, coordinated, or arranged these uncopyrightable facts in an original way. As mentioned, originality is not a stringent standard; it does not require that facts be presented in an innovative or surprising way. It is equally true, however, that the selection and arrangement of facts cannot be so mechanical or routine as to require no creativity whatsoever. The standard of originality is low, but it does exist. . . .

The selection, coordination, and arrangement of Rural's white pages do not satisfy the minimum constitutional standards for copyright protection. As mentioned at the outset, Rural's white pages are entirely typical. Persons desiring telephone service in Rural's service area fill out an application and Rural issues them a telephone number. In preparing its white pages, Rural simply takes the data provided by its subscribers and lists it alphabetically by surname. The end product is a garden-variety white pages directory, devoid of even the slightest trace of creativity.

Rural's selection of listings could not be more obvious: It publishes the most basic information — name, town, and telephone number — about each person who applies to it for telephone service. This is "selection" of a sort, but it lacks the modicum of creativity necessary to transform mere selection into copyrightable expression. Rural expended sufficient effort to make the white pages directory useful, but insufficient creativity to make it original.

We note in passing that the selection featured in Rural's white pages may also fail the originality requirement for another reason. Feist points out that Rural did not truly "select" to publish the names and telephone numbers of its subscribers; rather, it was required to do so by the Kansas Corporation Commission as part of its monopoly franchise. *See* 737 F. Supp. at 612. Accordingly, one could plausibly conclude that this selection was dictated by state law, not by Rural.

Nor can Rural claim originality in its coordination and arrangement of facts. The white pages do nothing more than list Rural's subscribers in alphabetical order. This arrangement may, technically speaking, owe its origin to Rural; no one disputes that Rural undertook the task of alphabetizing the names itself. But there is nothing remotely creative about arranging names alphabetically in a white pages directory. It is an age-old practice, firmly rooted in tradition and so commonplace that it has come to be expected as a matter of course. *See* Brief for Information Industry Association et al. as *Amici Curiae* 10 (alphabetical arrangement "is universally observed in directories published by local exchange telephone companies"). It is not only unoriginal, it is practically inevitable. This time-honored tradition does not possess the minimal creative spark required by the Copyright Act and the Constitution. . . .

Because Rural's white pages lack the requisite originality, Feist's use of the listings cannot constitute infringement. This decision should not be construed as demeaning Rural's efforts in compiling its directory, but rather as making clear that copyright rewards originality, not effort. As this Court noted more than a century ago, "'great praise may be due to the plaintiffs for their industry and enterprise in publishing this paper, yet the law does not contemplate their being rewarded in this way.'" Baker v. Selden, 101 U.S. at 105.

The judgment of the Court of Appeals is reversed.

Notes and Questions

1. What was the status of the copyrightability of telephone white pages before *Feist*? What was the rationale for such protection, insofar as originality was concerned? Was it originality in the selection and organization or originality in the "sweat of the brow" of the author?

2. In her opinion, Justice O'Connor says that "Common sense tells us that 100 uncopyrightable facts do not magically change their status when gathered together in one place." What does that sentence mean? Is copyright doctrine a matter of "common sense"? Is it the case that their status does not in fact change, because common sense tells us so, or that their status *does* change, notwithstanding that this may be contrary to common sense? Since the opinion is intended, to some extent at least, to be a persuasive and argumentative document, you should be aware of the fact that there was a great deal of judicial authority for the copyrightability of white pages, tables of random numbers, and other compilations that would never have been described as in any sense imaginative or creative. The courts had been living with, and applying, a body of rules that seemed to violate Justice O'Connor's principle of "common sense" for many years.

3. Justice O'Connor also says that, "The key to resolving the tension lies in understanding why facts are not copyrightable." She then goes on to suggest that it is lack of *originality* that is the key to their non-copyrightability. Is there another possibility? Is there another case that you have read, which could provide support for the view that isolated facts are uncopyrightable?

4. Even if originality is constitutionally compelled, does that mean that originality must have a certain content, and that originality cannot be found in compilations distinguished by the amount of labor invested in them? Couldn't we have two kinds of originality: inspiration dependent, and perspiration dependent?

5. The legislative history of the 1976 Copyright Revision Acts suggests that §102 was intended to "... incorporate without change the standard of originality established by the courts under the present [1909] copyright statute." Weren't *Leon* and the other directory cases the body of case law sought to be embodied in the originality standard, especially in 1976?

6. Assuming it could be done in a constitutional way, should the practical effect of *Feist* be reversed by legislation? What is the effect of *Feist* on the protectibility of databases? What kinds of databases are the most socially valuable? The kind in which the data have been pre-selected, and pre-arranged? Or the kind in which the user selects and arranges data drawn from a large, unorganized, but reliable compilation?

7. How would Justice Pitney have decided *Feist*? Could Rural Telephone have brought a misappropriation claim against Feist? (Such a claim might be invalid because at least some misappropriation claims are preempted under §301 of the Copyright Act.)

Technological change that involves the storage, transmission, or modification of information places stress on the law of intellectual property. How many such changes can you name that took place during the twentieth century?

In the late 1970s, Detroit completed a major downtown redevelopment project that included public spaces that featured fountains. The city council, as part of this project, drafted and enacted rules governing the uses of the public spaces — regulating skateboarding, bicycling, etc. A manager urged that the rules include a prohibition on fishing in the fountains. When someone reminded him that there were no fish in the fountains, he replied, somewhat indignantly, "What if someone *put* some fish in the fountains, and then started fishing for them? How would you stop them?"

Amusing? Perhaps. But of what relevance? Simply this: At about the same time that the Detroit city council was struggling with whether to prohibit fishing in fountains that contained no fish, Congress was seeking to remodel copyright law. There were thorny issues to be addressed. And they understood that things changed, and so they sought to deal, as well as they could, both with the issues that were present, and with those they could imagine — the issues that they sensed were just over the horizon, but on their way. But it was much easier for the Detroit city council to imagine fish being added to the fountains (and many would have said more likely) than it was for the Congress of 1976 to imagine that within 30 years teenagers would carry a device smaller than a deck of playing cards that could contain thousands of songs, or that one could sit at a coffee shop and download, over a wireless connection, a motion picture. And so it is not surprising that they left unaddressed the question of how to deal with these issues.

The next case is one of the fish that have been added to the fountain. The development of the Internet, by the way, is only the most recent technological development that has created uncertainty in the field of intellectual property. Some of these uncertainties are more serious than others. Some can be solved by judicial decision — others seem to require legislative action. You might challenge yourself to think about how the following technologies "stressed" IP law, and why: photography, motion pictures, radio, television, cable television, satellite television, the photocopy machine, computers, high-speed computers, inexpensive storage media for digital information, and most recently the Internet.

Ask yourself, after you have read the case, how the Internet and its related technologies challenge the assumptions that underlie copyright law. Some have gone so far as to assert that those changes are so profound that existing copyright is thoroughly inadequate. Some then argue that copyright should be substantially strengthened, whereas others argue that copyright law is either irrelevant, or should be weakened since it is largely unnecessary or counterproductive.

■ **METRO-GOLDWYN-MAYER STUDIOS, INC. v. GROKSTER, LTD.**
Supreme Court of the United States, 2005
545 U.S. 913

SOUTER, Justice. The question is under what circumstances the distributor of a product capable of both lawful and unlawful use is liable for acts of copyright infringement by third parties using the product. We hold that one who distributes a device with the object of promoting its use to infringe copyright, as shown by clear expression or other affirmative steps taken to foster infringement, is liable for the resulting acts of infringement by third parties.

I

A

Respondents, Grokster, Ltd., and StreamCast Networks, Inc., defendants in the trial court, distribute free software products that allow computer users to share electronic files through peer-to-peer networks, so called because users' computers communicate directly with each other, not through central servers. The advantage of peer-to-peer networks over information networks of other types shows up in their substantial and growing popularity. Because they need no central computer server to mediate the exchange of information or files among users, the high-bandwidth communications capacity for a server may be dispensed with, and the need for costly server storage space is eliminated. Since copies of a file (particularly a popular one) are available on many users' computers, file requests and retrievals may be faster than on other types of networks, and since file exchanges do not travel through a server, communications can take place between any computers that remain connected to the network without risk that a glitch in the server will disable the network in its entirety. Given these benefits in security, cost, and efficiency, peer-to-peer networks are employed to store and distribute electronic files by universities, government agencies, corporations, and libraries, among others.

Other users of peer-to-peer networks include individual recipients of Grokster's and StreamCast's software, and although the networks that they enjoy through using the software can be used to share any type of digital file, they have prominently employed those networks in sharing copyrighted music and video files without authorization. A group of copyright holders (MGM for short, but including motion picture studios, recording companies, songwriters, and music publishers) sued Grokster and StreamCast for their users' copyright infringements. . . .

Discovery during the litigation revealed the way the software worked, the business aims of each defendant company, and the predilections of the users. Grokster's eponymous software employs what is known as FastTrack technology, a protocol developed by others and licensed to Grokster. StreamCast distributes a very similar product except that its software, called Morpheus, relies on what is known as Gnutella technology. A user who downloads and installs either software possesses the protocol to send requests for files directly to the computers of others using software compatible with FastTrack or Gnutella. . . .

. . . Grokster and StreamCast use no servers to intercept the content of the search requests or to mediate the file transfers conducted by users of the software, there being no central point through which the substance of the communications passes in either direction.

Although Grokster and StreamCast do not therefore know when particular files are copied, a few searches using their software would show what is available on the networks the software reaches. MGM commissioned a statistician to conduct a systematic search, and his study showed that nearly 90% of the files available for download on the FastTrack system were copyrighted works. Grokster and Stream-Cast dispute this figure, raising methodological problems and arguing that free copying even of copyrighted works may be authorized by the rightholders. They also argue that potential noninfringing uses of their software are significant in kind, even if infrequent in practice. Some musical performers, for example, have gained new audiences by distributing their copyrighted works for free across peer-to-peer networks, and some distributors of unprotected content have used peer-to-peer networks to disseminate files, Shakespeare being an example. Indeed, StreamCast has given Morpheus users the opportunity to download the briefs in this very case, though their popularity has not been quantified.

As for quantification, the parties' anecdotal and statistical evidence entered thus far to show the content available on the FastTrack and Gnutella networks does not say much about which files are actually downloaded by users, and no one can say how often the software is used to obtain copies of unprotected material. But MGM's evidence gives reason to think that the vast majority of users' downloads are acts of infringement, and because well over 100 million copies of the software in question are known to have been downloaded, and billions of files are shared across the FastTrack and Gnutella networks each month, the probable scope of copyright infringement is staggering. . . .

Grokster and StreamCast are not, however, merely passive recipients of information about infringing use. The record is replete with evidence that from the moment Grokster and StreamCast began to distribute their free software, each one clearly voiced the objective that recipients use it to download copyrighted works, and each took active steps to encourage infringement.

[The Court then summarized efforts by Streamcast and Grokster to capture the market of Napster users after a court of appeals held that Napster's file-sharing service constituted copyright infringement.]

In addition to this evidence of express promotion, marketing, and intent to promote further, the business models employed by Grokster and StreamCast confirm that their principal object was use of their software to download copyrighted works. Grokster and StreamCast receive no revenue from users, who obtain the software itself for nothing. Instead, both companies generate income by selling advertising space, and they stream the advertising to Grokster and Morpheus users while they are employing the programs. As the number of users of each program increases, advertising opportunities become worth more. . . .

Finally, there is no evidence that either company made an effort to filter copyrighted material from users' downloads or otherwise impede the sharing of copyrighted files. Although Grokster appears to have sent e-mails warning users about infringing content when it received threatening notice from the copyright holders, it never blocked anyone from continuing to use its software to share copyrighted files. Joint Appendix 75-76. StreamCast not only rejected another company's offer of help to monitor infringement, *id.* at 928-929, but blocked the Internet Protocol addresses of entities it believed were trying to engage in such monitoring on its networks, *id.* at 917-922.

B

After discovery, the parties on each side of the case cross-moved for summary judgment. The District Court limited its consideration to the asserted liability of Grokster and StreamCast for distributing the current versions of their software, leaving aside whether either was liable "for damages arising from *past* versions of their software, or from other past activities." 259 F. Supp. 2d 1029, 1033 (C.D. Cal. 2003). The District Court held that those who used the Grokster and Morpheus software to download copyrighted media files directly infringed MGM's copyrights, a conclusion not contested on appeal, but the court nonetheless granted summary judgment in favor of Grokster and StreamCast as to any liability arising from distribution of the then current versions of their software. . . .

The Court of Appeals affirmed. 380 F.3d 1154 (9th Cir. 2004). In the court's analysis, a defendant was liable as a contributory infringer when it had knowledge of direct infringement and materially contributed to the infringement. But the court read Sony Corp. of America v. Universal City Studios, Inc., 464 U.S. 417 (1984), as holding that distribution of a commercial product capable of substantial non-infringing uses could not give rise to contributory liability for infringement unless the distributor had actual knowledge of specific instances of infringement and failed to act on that knowledge. . . .

II

A

MGM and many of the *amici* fault the Court of Appeals' holding for upsetting a sound balance between the respective values of supporting creative pursuits through copyright protection and promoting innovation in new communication technologies by limiting the incidence of liability for copyright infringement. The more artistic protection is favored, the more technological innovation may be discouraged; the administration of copyright law is an exercise in managing the trade-off. *See* Sony Corp. v. Universal City Studios, *supra* at 442.

The tension between the two values is the subject of this case, with its claim that digital distribution of copyrighted material threatens copyright holders as never before, because every copy is identical to the original, copying is easy, and many people (especially the young) use file-sharing software to download copyrighted works. . . . As the case has been presented to us, these fears are said to be offset by the different concern that imposing liability, not only on infringers but on distributors of software based on its potential for unlawful use, could limit further development of beneficial technologies. *See, e.g.*, Lemley & Reese, *Reducing Digital Copyright Infringement Without Restricting Innovation*, 56 Stan. L. Rev. 1345, 1386-1390 (2004); Brief for Innovation Scholars and Economists as *Amici Curiae* 15-20; Brief for Emerging Technology Companies as *Amici Curiae* 19-25; Brief for Intel Corporation as *Amicus Curiae* 20-22.

The argument for imposing indirect liability in this case is, however, a powerful one, given the number of infringing downloads that occur every day using Stream-Cast's and Grokster's software. When a widely shared service or product is used to commit infringement, it may be impossible to enforce rights in the protected work effectively against all direct infringers, the only practical alternative being to go against the distributor of the copying device for secondary liability on a theory of contributory or vicarious infringement.

One infringes contributorily by intentionally inducing or encouraging direct infringement, *see* Gershwin Pub. Corp. v. Columbia Artists Management, Inc., 443 F.2d 1159, 1162 (2d Cir. 1971), and infringes vicariously by profiting from direct infringement while declining to exercise a right to stop or limit it, Shapiro, Bernstein & Co. v. H. L. Green Co., 316 F.2d 304, 307 (2d Cir. 1963).[9] . . .

---

9. We stated in Sony Corp. v. Universal City Studios that "the lines between direct infringement, contributory infringement and vicarious liability are not clearly drawn. . . . [R]easoned analysis of [the *Sony* plaintiffs' contributory infringement claim] necessarily entails consideration of arguments and case law which may also be forwarded under the other labels, and indeed the parties . . . rely upon such arguments and authority in support of their respective positions on the issue of contributory infringement." 464 U.S. at 435 n.17. In the present case MGM has argued a vicarious liability theory, which allows imposition of liability when the defendant profits directly from the infringement and has a right and ability to supervise the direct infringer, even if the defendant initially lacks knowledge of the infringement. Because we resolve the case based on an inducement theory, there is no need to analyze separately MGM's vicarious liability theory.

B

Despite the currency of these principles of secondary liability, this Court has dealt with secondary copyright infringement in only one recent case, and because MGM has tailored its principal claim to our opinion there, a look at our earlier holding is in order. In Sony Corp. v. Universal City Studios, *supra*, this Court addressed a claim that secondary liability for infringement can arise from the very distribution of a commercial product. There, the product, novel at the time, was what we know today as the videocassette recorder or VCR. Copyright holders sued Sony as the manufacturer, claiming it was contributorily liable for infringement that occurred when VCR owners taped copyrighted programs because it supplied the means used to infringe, and it had constructive knowledge that infringement would occur. At the trial on the merits, the evidence showed that the principal use of the VCR was for "time-shifting," or taping a program for later viewing at a more convenient time, which the Court found to be a fair, not an infringing, use. 464 U.S. at 423-424. . . .

On those facts, with no evidence of stated or indicated intent to promote infringing uses, the only conceivable basis for imposing liability was on a theory of contributory infringement arising from its sale of VCRs to consumers with knowledge that some would use them to infringe. But because the VCR was "capable of commercially significant noninfringing uses," we held the manufacturer could not be faulted solely on the basis of its distribution. *Id.* at 442.

This analysis reflected patent law's traditional staple article of commerce doctrine, now codified, that distribution of a component of a patented device will not violate the patent if it is suitable for use in other ways. 35 U.S.C. §271(c). . . .

In sum, where an article is "good for nothing else" but infringement, Canda v. Michigan Malleable Iron Co., 124 F. 486, 489 (6th Cir. 1903), there is no legitimate public interest in its unlicensed availability, and there is no injustice in presuming or imputing an intent to infringe. Conversely, the doctrine absolves the equivocal conduct of selling an item with substantial lawful as well as unlawful uses, and limits liability to instances of more acute fault than the mere understanding that some of one's products will be misused. It leaves breathing room for innovation and a vigorous commerce. *See* Sony Corp. v. Universal City Studios, 464 U.S. at 442.

The parties and many of the *amici* in this case think the key to resolving it is the *Sony* rule and, in particular, what it means for a product to be "capable of commercially significant noninfringing uses." Sony Corp. v. Universal City Studios, *supra* at 442. MGM advances the argument that granting summary judgment to Grokster and StreamCast as to their current activities gave too much weight to the value of innovative technology, and too little to the copyrights infringed by users of their software, given that 90% of works available on one of the networks was shown to be copyrighted. Assuming the remaining 10% to be its noninfringing use, MGM says this should not qualify as "substantial," and the Court should quantify *Sony* to the extent of holding that a product used "principally" for infringement does not qualify. . . .

We agree with MGM that the Court of Appeals misapplied *Sony*, which it read as limiting secondary liability quite beyond the circumstances to which the case applied. *Sony* barred secondary liability based on presuming or imputing intent to cause infringement solely from the design or distribution of a product capable of substantial lawful use, which the distributor knows is in fact used for infringement. The Ninth Circuit has read *Sony*'s limitation to mean that whenever a product is capable of substantial lawful use, the producer can never be held contributorily liable for third parties' infringing use of it; it read the rule as being this broad, even when an actual purpose to cause infringing use is shown by evidence independent of design and distribution of the product, unless the distributors had "specific knowledge of infringement at a time at which they contributed to the infringement, and failed to act upon that information." 380 F.3d at 1162. . . .

C

Sony's rule limits imputing culpable intent as a matter of law from the characteristics or uses of a distributed product. But nothing in *Sony* requires courts to ignore evidence of intent if there is such evidence, and the case was never meant to foreclose rules of fault-based liability derived from the common law. . . .

The classic case of direct evidence of unlawful purpose occurs when one induces commission of infringement by another, or "entices or persuades another" to infringe, *Black's Law Dictionary* 790 (8th ed. 2004), as by advertising. . . .

For the same reasons that *Sony* took the staple-article doctrine of patent law as a model for its copyright safe-harbor rule, the inducement rule, too, is a sensible one for copyright. We adopt it here, holding that one who distributes a device with the object of promoting its use to infringe copyright, as shown by clear expression or other affirmative steps taken to foster infringement, is liable for the resulting acts of infringement by third parties. We are, of course, mindful of the need to keep from trenching on regular commerce or discouraging the development of technologies with lawful and unlawful potential. Accordingly, just as *Sony* did not find intentional inducement despite the knowledge of the VCR manufacturer that its device could be used to infringe, 464 U.S. at 439 n.19, mere knowledge of infringing potential or of actual infringing uses would not be enough here to subject a distributor to liability. Nor would ordinary acts incident to product distribution, such as offering customers technical support or product updates, support liability in themselves. The inducement rule, instead, premises liability on purposeful, culpable expression and conduct, and thus does nothing to compromise legitimate commerce or discourage innovation having a lawful promise. . . .

In sum, this case is significantly different from *Sony* and reliance on that case to rule in favor of StreamCast and Grokster was error. *Sony* dealt with a claim of liability based solely on distributing a product with alternative lawful and unlawful uses, with knowledge that some users would follow the unlawful course. The case struck a balance between the interests of protection and innovation by holding that the product's capability of substantial lawful employment should bar the imputation of fault and consequent secondary liability for the unlawful acts of others.

MGM's evidence in this case most obviously addresses a different basis of liability for distributing a product open to alternative uses. Here, evidence of the distributors' words and deeds going beyond distribution as such shows a purpose to cause and profit from third-party acts of copyright infringement. If liability for inducing infringement is ultimately found, it will not be on the basis of presuming or imputing fault, but from inferring a patently illegal objective from statements and actions showing what that objective was.

There is substantial evidence in MGM's favor on all elements of inducement, and summary judgment in favor of Grokster and StreamCast was error. On remand, reconsideration of MGM's motion for summary judgment will be in order.

The judgment of the Court of Appeals is vacated, and the case is remanded for further proceedings consistent with this opinion.

[Concurring opinions of Justices GINSBURG and BREYER are omitted.]

Notes and Questions

1. If you were in Congress, would you vote to embody the *Grokster* outcome in an amendment to the copyright statute or reject *Grokster* in favor of some other rule?

2. How successfully has the Court distinguished the *Sony* case? Was *Sony* wrongly decided? How much vitality is left in the *Sony* decision?

3. Are there instances of contributory infringement in trademark law? What, for example?

Note on Intellectual Property in a Global Context

The previous pages of this chapter have focused on the intellectual property laws of the United States. Every country in the world has its own intellectual property laws. Generally these laws have no extraterritorial effect. A patent issued in the United States confers no rights in Brazil or South Africa, for example. A U.S. inventor who wants patent protection in Brazil must seek a Brazilian patent.

Before the end of the nineteenth century, however, it was appreciated there were some reasons to harmonize these various laws and to create administrative procedures to make it easier for inventors and authors to protect their inventions and writings outside their own countries. Steps in this direction were taken by means of international treaties and conventions. The first such treaties contained simple non-discrimination provisions: signatories to the treaty agreed not to discriminate against non-citizens when it came to IP claims. For example, signatories to the Paris Convention of 1894 agreed to treat the nationals of other signatories to the Convention no worse than they treated their own nationals insofar as patent law was concerned.

The next step consisted of treaties in which signatory countries promised that their national laws would contain certain minimum protections. Over time with the globalization of markets, pressure has increased to include more and more countries in these international regimes and to raise minimum standards.

But is a strong regime of intellectual property laws best for all countries? For all citizens? The creation of international agreements on IP involves balancing economic and ethical principles. Some advocates of the interests of less wealthy nations argue that economic development and well-being are not well served by expansive and extensive restrictions on the flow of ideas and information. Widely divergent cultures may also make different value judgments about the goals they wish to achieve.

It is obvious that countries that produce an immense amount of IP-protectible material in the form of media and patentable inventions have an economic interest in strong laws establishing legal rights of authors and inventors, whereas it is in the economic interest of countries with lower rates of IP production to avoid establishing high barriers to the dissemination of information. Simply put, legal rights for authors and inventors create additional wealth for the rights owners, but reduce the wealth of those who do not enjoy access to the works due to their protected status.

Historically, this dynamic resulted in countries offering differential protections for domestic and foreign intellectual property. Countries often safeguarded the economic interests of their own authors and inventors, but allowed the pirating of imported works. During the late nineteenth and early twentieth centuries, a series of treaties and agreements resulted in a much more symmetrical treatment of protected works, at least among the wealthier nations. Later less industrialized nations such as China and India became signatories, but they failed to adopt meaningful enforcement mechanisms, so within their borders the rules had few practical consequences.

An important recent development is the introduction of TRIPS (Agreement on Trade-Related Aspects of Intellectual Property Rights) as part of the WTO (World Trade Organization). TRIPS creates a set of IP-law standards that all participating nations must meet or exceed. The relationship with the WTO means that compliance and enforcement is connected to a broader system of trade, with potential sanctions for noncompliance. This has created strong incentives for nations to implement and adhere to the standards of wealthy trading partners such as the United States. In practice, this results in substantial expansion of authors' and inventors' rights in less wealthy countries, and creates new classes of IP-protected works. Governments generally assess the costs of international trade penalties as outweighing the benefits of permitting relatively free use of imported protected works.

The tension between economic interests and social ethics is keenly felt in the realm of medicine. Drugs are considered to be patentable inventions, but given the wide disparities of capital and basic health between nations, many consider it unethical to allow drug companies to maintain a patent-based monopoly on production and charge whatever the market will bear for drugs with substantial lifesaving benefits in nations with little capital wealth to purchase them. The general principle that saving lives is more important than protecting intellectual property has fairly wide support, but practical issues of cost, technology of production, and politics complicate any attempt to implement a system that seeks to balance economic and ethical issues to maximize utility. The question decision makers are faced with is "What is the most efficient way to produce and distribute lifesaving medicines without disrupting the economic and legal systems on which drug research and development depend?" This is an area of rapid change and evolution in trade agreements and international law.

A related issue involves competing claims over the use of traditional knowledge, or art. A drug derived from research into traditional native medicine may be granted a patent by a country with no access to information about the prior art of a tribal culture on the other side of the world. Advocates for indigenous peoples have called for the extension of IP protection for traditional knowledge, with commercialization allowed only by licensing from the indigenous community.

Another concern of those who question the benefits of strong IP protection in less wealthy nations is the erosion of fair-use rights for educational and personal, non-commercial uses of information. The TRIPS regulations do include limited acknowledgment of fair-use rights, but critics claim they are not extensive enough for the educational needs of the population. Access to textbooks and other materials is less available in the poorest parts of the world where greater education may have a strongly beneficial impact, and some social-justice advocates believe the consent requirements for redistribution in TRIPS are too onerous for these situations. Again, setting policies requires deciding between different models of optimal outcomes. Is the goal to provide the maximum incentive for producing new knowledge, or to enable as many people as possible to have access to knowledge? Should there be different IP rules for wealthy, and poor, countries?

As more information shifts to digital form, questions of fair use and redistribution become more vexing. Fair use standards have special implications in the case of digital reproduction. Technology that falls under the heading of DRM (Digital Rights/Restrictions Management) uses encryption preemptively to control access to and reproduction of information. This renders fair use technically impossible, thus displacing the fair-use balancing mechanisms of IP law. Fair-use privileges set forth in statutes and international agreements are less meaningful because the controllers of DRM "keys" may set whatever policies they wish to control copying. This represents an historic shift of power to owners of information because they are no longer dependent on any external enforcement mechanism, or statute. In effect, a DRM-ed file makes and enforces its own laws. In the context of international trade, DRM technology makes it harder for a country to adapt IP protections to its local culture and economy.

Economic issues also come into play in the establishment and enforcement of systems of international IP harmonization. Administering a copyrights and patents registry is expensive, and costs rise if the registry needs to be coordinated with external entities. Enforcement costs are also substantial. Some argue that the costs associated with asserting privileges in the face of a threat by a wealthy rights-owner are so high that many with a legal right to borrow cannot meaningfully assert those privileges. So far the economic benefits of freer trade have proven sufficient to induce less wealthy countries to adopt, in principle, the extensive set of IP rights that are standard in the United States and Europe. Implementation and enforcement, however, lag considerably. The tension between providing appropriate incentives to authors and inventors on the one hand, and denying poor countries access to inventions and information on the other, poses long-term challenges to policy makers.

5

Property in Living Things

People own both living and non-living things. For the most part, the theories and rules presented in preceding chapters governing the ownership of non-living things also apply to living things and will not be restated here. Living plants (such as standing timber) are usually attached to real property and treated as part of the underlaying real estate for property-law purposes. Once severed from the land, plants and plant products (such as logs) simply become personal property, and are treated as such by the law. Domesticated animals, except for added restrictions designed to keep them under control and protect them from undue suffering, are also treated like personal property. Although owners may attach emotional significance to their animals, so far as the law is concerned, people own their pets and farmers own their livestock much as they own their other goods. As the following two cases illustrate, however, live wild animals pose greater complexities than either plants or domesticated animals because they are neither attached to the land nor clearly subject to anyone's ownership or control (at least unless and until someone captures or kills them).

A. ANIMALS AND OTHER ORGANISMS

■ PIERSON v. POST

Supreme Court of New York, 1805
3 Cai. R. 175, 2 Am. Dec. 264

This was an action of trespass on the case commenced in a justice's court, by the present defendant [Lodowick Post] against the now plaintiff [Jesse Pierson].

The declaration stated that Post, being in possession of certain dogs and hounds under his command, did, "upon a certain wild and uninhabited, unpossessed and waste land, called the beach, find and start one of those noxious beasts called a fox," and whilst there hunting, chasing and pursuing the same with his dogs and hounds, and when in view thereof, Pierson, well knowing the fox was so hunted and pursued, did, in the sight of Post, to prevent his catching the same, kill and carry it off. A verdict having been rendered for plaintiff below, the defendant there sued out a *certiorari*, and now assigned for error, that the declaration and the matters therein contained were not sufficient in law to maintain an action.

305

TOMPKINS, Judge. . . .

The question submitted by the counsel in this cause for our determination is, whether Lodowick Post, by the pursuit with his hounds in the manner alleged in his declaration, acquired such a right to, or property in, the fox as will sustain an action against Pierson for killing and taking him away?

The cause was argued with much ability by the counsel on both sides, and presents for our decision a novel and nice question. It is admitted that a fox is an animal *ferae naturae*, and that property in such animals is acquired by occupancy only. These admissions narrow the discussion to the simple question of what acts amount to occupancy, applied to acquiring right to wild animals.

If we have recourse to the ancient writers upon general principles of law, the judgment below is obviously erroneous. Justinian's Institutes (lib. 2, tit. 1, sec. 13), and Fleta (lib. 3, ch. 2, p. 175), adopt the principle, that pursuit alone vests no property or right in the huntsman; and that even pursuit, accompanied with wounding, is equally ineffectual for that purpose, unless the animal be actually taken. The same principle is recognized by Bracton (lib. 2, ch. 1, p. 8).

Puffendorf (lib. 4, ch. 6, sec. 2 and 10) defines occupancy of beasts *ferae naturae*, to be the actual corporeal possession of them, and Bynkershock is cited as coinciding in this definition. It is indeed with hesitation that Puffendorf affirms that a wild beast mortally wounded or greatly maimed, cannot be fairly intercepted by another, whilst the pursuit of the person inflicting the wound continues. The foregoing authorities are decisive to show that mere pursuit gave Post no legal right to the fox, but that he became the property of Pierson, who intercepted and killed him.

It, therefore, only remains to inquire whether there are any contrary principles or authorities, to be found in other books, which ought to induce a different decision. Most of the cases which have occurred in England, relating to property in wild animals, have either been discussed and decided upon the principles of their positive statute regulations, or have arisen between the huntsman and the owner of the land upon which beasts *ferae naturae* have been apprehended; the former claiming them by title of occupancy, and the latter *ratione soli*. Little satisfactory aid can, therefore, be derived from the English reporters.

Barbeyrac, in his notes on Puffendorf, does not accede to the definition of occupancy by the latter, but on the contrary, affirms that actual bodily seizure is not, in all cases, necessary to constitute possession of wild animals. He does not, however, describe the acts which, according to his ideas, will amount to an appropriation of such animals to private use, so as to exclude the claims of all other persons, by title of occupancy, to the same animals; and he is far from averring that pursuit alone is sufficient for that purpose. To a certain extent, and as far as Barbeyrac appears to me to go, his objections to Puffendorf's definition of occupancy are reasonable and correct. That is to say, that actual bodily seizure is not indispensable to acquire right to, or possession of, wild beasts; but that, on the contrary, the mortal wounding of such beasts, by one not abandoning his pursuit, may, with the utmost propriety, be deemed possession of him; since thereby the pursuer manifests an unequivocal intention of appropriating the animal to his individual use, has deprived him of his natural liberty, and brought him within his certain control. So, also, encompassing and securing such animals with nets and toils, or otherwise intercepting them in such a manner as to deprive them of their natural liberty, and render escape impossible, may justly be deemed to give possession of them to those persons who, by their industry and labor, have used such means of apprehending them. . . .

We are more readily inclined to confine possession or occupancy of beasts *ferae naturae*, within the limits prescribed by the learned authors above cited, for the sake of certainty, and preserving peace and order in society. If the first seeing, starting or pursuing such animals, without having so wounded, circumvented or ensnared them, so as to deprive them of their natural liberty, and subject them to the control of their pursuer, should afford the basis of actions against others for intercepting and killing them, it would prove a fertile source of quarrels and litigation.

However uncourteous or unkind the conduct of Pierson towards Post, in this instance, may have been, yet this act was productive of no injury or damage for which a legal remedy can be applied. We are of the opinion the judgment below was erroneous, and ought to be reversed.

LIVINGSTON, Judge [dissenting]. . . .

This is a knotty point, and should have been submitted to the arbitration of sportsmen, without poring over Justinian, Fleta, Bracton, Puffendorf, Locke, Barbeyrac, or Blackstone, all of whom have been cited; they would have had no difficulty in coming to a prompt and correct conclusion. In a court thus constituted, the skin and carcass of poor Reynard would have been properly disposed of, and a precedent set, interfering with no usage or custom which the experience of ages has sanctioned, and which must be so well known to every votary of Diana. But the parties have referred the question to our judgment, and we must dispose of it as well as we can, from the partial lights we possess, leaving to a higher tribunal the correction of any mistake which we may be so unfortunate as to make. By the pleadings it is admitted that a fox is a "wild and noxious beast." . . . His depredations on farmers and on barnyards, have not been forgotten; and to put him to death wherever found, is allowed to be meritorious, and of public benefit. Hence it follows, that our decision should have in view the greatest possible encouragement to the destruction of an animal, so cunning and ruthless in his career. But who would keep a pack of hounds; or what gentleman, at the sound of the horn, and at peep of day, would mount his steed, and for hours together, "*sub jove frigido*," or a vertical sun, pursue the windings of his wily quadruped, if, just as night came on, and his stratagems and strength were nearly exhausted, a saucy intruder, who had not shared in the honors or labors of the chase, were permitted to come in at the death, and bear away in triumph the object of pursuit? Whatever Justinian may have thought of the matter, it must be recollected that his code was compiled many hundred years ago, and it would be very hard indeed, at the distance of so many centuries, not to have a right to establish a rule for ourselves. In his day, we read of no order of men who made it a business, in the language of the declaration in this cause, "with hounds and dogs to find, start, pursue, hunt, and chase," these animals, and that, too, without any other motive than the preservation of Roman poultry; if this diversion had been then in fashion, the lawyers who composed his institutes, would have taken care not to pass it by, without suitable encouragement. . . .

It may be expected, however, by the learned counsel, that more particular notice be taken of their authorities. I have examined them all, and feel great difficulty in determining, whether to acquire dominion over a thing, before in common, it be sufficient that we barely see it, or know where it is, or wish for it, or make a declaration of our will respecting it; or whether, in the case of wild beasts, setting a trap, or lying in wait, or starting, or pursuing, be enough; or if an actual wounding, or killing, or bodily tact and occupation be necessary. Writers on general law, who have favored us with their speculations on these points, differ on them all; but, great as is the diversity of sentiment among them, some conclusion must be adopted on the question immediately before us. . . .

Now, as we are without any municipal regulations of our own, . . . we are at liberty to adopt one of the provisions just cited, which comports also with the learned conclusion of Barbeyrac, that property in animals *ferae naturae* may be acquired without bodily touch or manucaption, provided the pursuer be within reach, or have a reasonable prospect (which certainly exited here) of taking what he has thus discovered an intention of converting to his own use.

When we reflect also that the interest of our husbandmen, the most useful of men in any community, will be advanced by the destruction of a beast so pernicious and incorrigible, we cannot greatly err in saying that a pursuit like the present, through waste and unoccupied lands, and which must inevitably and speedily have terminated in corporeal possession, or bodily seisin, confers such a right to the object of it, as to make anyone a wrong-doer who shall interfere and shoulder the soil. The justice's judgment ought, therefore, in my opinion, to be affirmed.

Notes and Questions

1. How did the court characterize the actions of fox killer Jesse Pierson? According to the court, who owned the dead fox, Pierson or Lodowick Post, the pursuer? Did it matter that the fox was killed on unowned property? In general, should it matter if the hunter is trespassing on another person's real property when a wild animal is killed or captured? Should it matter if the hunter holds a hunting license from the state? Should it matter if the animal is not a legal game animal or not hunted in season? Typically, trespassers and illegal hunters have no right to keep the animals they kill or capture.

2. Pierson v. Post involved the then popular "sport" of fox hunting. As a 200-year-old decision in which the judges were treating a somewhat frivolous lawsuit with mock solemnity, the opinions are filled with outmoded terminology and references to obscure Roman and English legal authorities and scholars. Modern readers should not stumble on these references. They could be enjoyed as judicial humor. Justinian's Institutes, for example, was a compilation of ancient Roman law. Most of the other references are to medieval or early modern English legal scholars. The judges in this case were of some note. The author of the majority opinion, Daniel Tompkins, served as the governor of New York from 1807 to 1817 and as vice president of the United States from 1817 to 1825. The dissenting judge, H. Brockholst Livingston, served as a United States Supreme Court justice from 1806 to 1823.

For an examination of the historical setting of the *Pierson* controversy, see Bethany R. Berger, *It's Not About the Fox: The Untold History of* Pierson v. Post, 55 Duke L.J. 1089 (2006). Professor Berger concludes that the litigation reflected conflict over "land use and control of this Long Island community in the face of the rapid changes occurring in the decades after the Revolutionary War. . . . [C]ommunity rights to [the land where the fox was killed were] simultaneously claimed by the colonial settlers, the English crown, the Dutch government, the Shinnecock tribe, the Pequot and Narragansett tribes, the original settlers, the later town residents, and the State of New York. . . . Lodowick Post's declaration that he started the fox on 'unpossessed and waste land'" was questionable. In fact, Pierson "had a particular claim to the land on which the fox was caught."

3. This decision addresses the question: Who owns wild animals? There are several plausible answers. A state could claim to own all wild animals within its boundaries as its sovereign right. Landowners could claim to own all wild animals on their property. Alternatively, is it plausible that animals are unowned so long as they are living in their natural state? What are the policy and practical implications of each view for people and for wild animals?

4. By statute, most American states claim to own all wild animals within their borders. A Wyoming statute is typical. Passed in the mid-twentieth century, it declares that "all wildlife in Wyoming is the property of the state." Wyo. Stat. §23-1-103. Under its statutory regime, Wyoming claims to own wild animals within its boundaries "for the common benefit and interest of all its citizens." What does this mean? As a practical matter, how would this differ from Wyoming owning those animals as their guardian or for their benefit and interest? Which is the appropriate role for a state? In either instance, on what basis should the state authorize hunting? Could the state ban hunting altogether? Do the owners of real property have any greater property right to hunt animals on their own land than on public land? As the owner of animals "for the common benefit and interest of all its citizens," should the state be liable when those animals injure someone or someone's property?

5. If the state owns wild animals either by statute or by sovereign right, do its agents have the right to enter private property for purposes such as counting, inspecting, tending, and protecting its animals? Should the state be able to prohibit landowners from destroying or modifying habitats necessary for the well-being of the animals? Should the state be able to prohibit its citizens from capturing and domesticating wild animals? Does the state lose ownership over formerly wild animals that have been domesticated?

6. Who is liable if a wild animal damages property or injures someone? In 2007, while visiting her daughter's suburban Savannah home, Gwyneth Williams was killed and partially eaten by a wild alligator. Williams' estate and family sued the homeowners association that owned the lagoon where the attack happened. Asserting the doctrine that a landowner is not responsible for harm caused by a free wild animal on the owner's land (the doctrine of animals *ferae naturae*), the homeowners association filed a motion for summary judgment. After the trial court denied the motion and an appellate court affirmed, in 2012 the Georgia Supreme Court reversed in a 4-3 decision that granted the association's motion for summary judgment. In a narrow opinion that did not reach the doctrine of animals *ferae naturae*, the majority wrote that testimony indicated Williams was aware that alligators lived in the lagoon but chose to walk near it, "either knowingly assuming the risks of walking in areas inhabited by wild alligators or failed to exercise ordinary care by doing so." Landings Association v. Williams, 728 S.E.2d 577 (Ga. 2012).

■ BILIDA v. McCLEOD

United States Court of Appeals for the First Circuit, 2000
211 F.3d 166

BOUDIN, Circuit Judge. The sad history of this section 1983 case began in or around 1988 when Claire Bilida rescued an orphaned raccoon thereafter named "Mia." Bilida and her family raised the raccoon as a pet and kept her in a cage attached to the back of the family's home in Warwick, Rhode Island. Mia lived there for seven years until she was seized and destroyed in August 1995 by the Rhode

Island Department of Environmental Management ("the Department") in the episode that provoked this suit for violation of Bilida's constitutional rights.

On August 8, 1995, a Warwick police officer named Kenneth Brierly entered Bilida's backyard in response to a security alarm signal. While investigating the alarm, which proved to be false, Brierly saw Mia in her cage. Uncertain whether possession of the raccoon was legal, he called Nora Legault, the city's animal control officer, and then left the premises. A half hour or so later, Legault and Brierly returned to find Bilida at home. Legault asked Bilida for her permit from the Department,

Mia

which is required under Rhode Island law for possession of raccoons and certain other animal species.[1]

Bilida told Legault that she had a permit but then was unable to produce one. Legault and Brierly departed and Legault returned to her office, called the Department, and discovered that Bilida did not have a permit. The Department then sent two of its officers (Jeffrey Belmonte and Sheila DiSarro) to Bilida's home where the officers — who had no warrant — entered Bilida's gated backyard and seized Mia after a struggle with Bilida. DiSarro then issued Bilida a summons for illegally possessing a raccoon but (according to Bilida) the officers promised her that Mia would not be killed.

Having taken the raccoon, the officers then consulted with the deputy chief of the Department, Thomas Greene, and he in turn contacted Susan Littlefield, the state's public health veterinarian. Littlefield, after learning that Mia had been hand fed by Bilida, told Greene that according to the state's rabies protocol, Mia had to be euthanized and tested for rabies. The protocol, which was adopted in response to a supposed epidemic of raccoon rabies moving up the east coast in the early 1990s, calls for animals in certain high risk "target species" to be tested for rabies (which requires killing the animal) under specified circumstances.[2] With no further word to Bilida, Mia was then shot, tested, and found to have no rabies infection.

Bilida was prosecuted in state court for the misdemeanor offense of possessing the raccoon without a permit. In the state proceeding, Bilida obtained an evidentiary hearing on whether the final warrantless entry onto her property and seizure of the raccoon violated the Fourth Amendment made applicable to the states through the Fourteenth Amendment. The state court judge found that the officers had acted in good faith but also concluded that they had violated the Fourth Amendment

---

1. A statutory provision enacted in 1971 prohibits possession without a permit of certain wild animals, including the family to which raccoons belong. R.I. Gen. Laws §4-18-3 (1998); *see also id.* §20-16-5 (1997). The current relevant regulations are in R.I. Code R. 12 080 043.

2. R.I. Rabies Control Board, *Rules & Regulations Governing Rabies Control Within the State of Rhode Island* §§2.00(b), 7.01 (rev. ed. Nov. 1994). Whether the nature of Bilida's exposure to Mia required euthanizing the raccoon is not entirely clear from the language of the protocol; it refers *inter alia* to cases of possible exposure "via . . . saliva . . . and . . . [a] pre-existing break in the skin. . . ." There is no indication whether Bilida's feeding or handling of Mia resulted in such exposure.

because no exigent circumstances justified the warrantless entry and seizure of the already caged animal. Following the suppression order, the state abandoned the prosecution of Bilida.

Bilida filed her own complaint in the federal district court, naming as defendants the director of the Department [Andrew McCleod], deputy chief Greene, the two officers who had made the seizure (Belmonte and DiSarro), veterinarian Littlefield (later dismissed by consent), and the State of Rhode Island. She asserted federal claims under 42 U.S.C. §1983 for violations of her constitutional rights of "privacy," due process, and protection against unreasonable search and seizure. The complaint sought a declaration that Bilida's rights had been violated, punitive damages, and other unspecified relief.

In a thoughtful opinion, the district court granted the defendants' motion for summary judgment, holding that no federal right of privacy was violated; that the warrantless search and seizure were justified by the "plain view" exception to the warrant requirement; and that Bilida had no property interest in Mia to trigger a right to due process pertaining to Mia's treatment. Bilida v. McCleod, 41 F. Supp. 2d 142 (D.R.I. 1999). The district court dismissed the state claims without prejudice. On this appeal, Bilida's main arguments are that preclusion doctrine required a finding that the search and seizure were illegal and that in any event the district court erred in its legal rulings on the plain view and property issues. [The court's analysis and denial of Bilida's non-property claims are omitted.] . . .

In this court, Bilida's other substantive federal claim is that the seizure and destruction of Mia violated Bilida's due process rights (the complainant's generalized "privacy" claim has not been pursued on this appeal). Bilida's brief presents a short argument as to why Bilida should be regarded as having a sufficient property interest in the raccoon to entitle her to due process and she suggests that at the very least she was entitled to some kind of notice and a hearing before Mia was destroyed.

While the state might have more to say in its favor in a full-scale trial, it is not apparent why Mia should have been destroyed without providing Bilida an opportunity to object and obtain some kind of administrative review or judicial intervention. Seemingly, no state law required Mia's immediate destruction, and an administrative policy — even if one applied here, see note 2, above — can always be waived or modified. There is no indication of a genuine emergency, such as the biting of a child by an apparently rabid dog. And Bilida says she was told that Mia would not be killed.

Nevertheless, the due process clause protects "property" interests; and while the notion of property interest has been stretched quite far in certain contexts, it depends importantly on what interests are recognized under state law. *See* Board of Regents v. Roth, 408 U.S. 564, 577 (1972); Marrero-Garcia v. Irizarry, 33 F.3d 117, 121 (1st Cir. 1994). Citing these cases, the district court ruled that "even where additional process might be laudable," the court could not "create constitutional protection for objects that the state has declared illegal to possess." 41 F. Supp. 2d at 151.

A number of cases hold, as the district court did here, that a claimant has no property interest in "per se contraband," *i.e.*, something that it is illegal merely to possess. *E.g.*, Boggs v. Rubin, 161 F.3d 37, 40 (D.C. Cir. 1998), *cert. denied*, 528 U.S. 811 (1999). Because a raccoon taken from the wild cannot lawfully be possessed in Rhode Island without a permit, the district court deemed Mia to fall into the same category. With little enthusiasm, we agree with the district court that state law undermines Bilida's claim of the required property interest.

Under Rhode Island law, "wild game within a state belongs to the people in their collective sovereign capacity" and is not subject to "private ownership except in so far as the people may elect to make it so." State v. Kofines, 80 A. 432, 440 (R.I. 1911). State law makes illegal possession of raccoons taken from the wild without a permit issued by the Department. *See* note 1, above. This amounts to saying that, under state law, Mia could not be reduced to private ownership and lawfully possessed as property without a permit. Needless to say, this would be a different case if Bilida did have a permit, but she no longer claims ever to have had one. [The court's discussion and denial of individual liability for the government actors are omitted.]. . .

Thus, we can conceive of no purpose for remanding this matter for further proceedings in federal court, although Bilida is entirely free to pursue her pendant state claims in state court. It need hardly be said that this outcome is not an endorsement of the state's procedures for treatment of pet raccoons.

Affirmed.

Notes and Questions

1. A Providence, Rhode Island, newspaper, the *Journal-Bulletin*, offered numerous reports on the ill-fated saga of Mia's stay with the Bilidas. Mia, according to Claire Bilida, "came when I whistled. She was litter-box trained. When I told her to go to bed, she would. And she loved it when you scratched her shoulder blades. She just scrunched up and whistled." Mia enjoyed her own plastic swimming pool and was best friends with the family's dog. After Mia's death, Bilida wrote, "I lost the most treasured animal, the brightest spot in my life." Bilida spoke at a public hearing opposing the Department's actions "[w]earing a huge 'Remember Mia' badge emblazoned with the animal's wistful face." The episode was also the "catalyst" for Bilida's unsuccessful 1996 run for a seat in the state legislature as a candidate of the Cool Moose Party. "The government is too involved in people's lives," she explained, "and people are not involved enough in the government."

2. Under traditional common law, as described above in Pierson v. Post, a person acquires a property interest in a wild animal by killing, capturing, or otherwise possessing it. Under the common law, would Claire Bilida have a property interest in Mia? If so, when was this property interest acquired? Why did this common law standard not apply in this case? Under Rhode Island law, who owns wild game within the state? By statute or case law, most states prohibit individuals from killing, capturing, or possessing wild animals without a permit. Suppose an automobile driver in Rhode Island accidentally hits and kills a deer; who owns the carcass?

3. The law in every state treats domesticated animals, including pets, differently from wild animals. Subject to certain restrictions, the law everywhere allows people to own certain domesticated animals as their personal property. If a domesticated animal gives birth, its owner also owns its offspring as his personal property. Why are domesticated animals treated differently than wild animals? Do people own their pets in the same way that they own other personal property? Should they?

Rhode Island's view of pets had begun to change even before the First Circuit ruled in *Bilida*. In 2001, it became the first state to enact a statute recognizing individuals as "guardians" of their companion animals. In doing so, Rhode Island joined cities such as Boulder, West Hollywood, and Berkeley, which had enacted similar laws. Under Rhode Island law, a "guardian" is "a person who possesses, has title to or an interest in, harbors or has control, custody or possession of an animal and who is responsible for an animal's safety and well-being." R.I. Gen. Laws §4-1-1(a)(4). Guardians have "the same rights and responsibilities of an owner, and both terms shall be used interchangeably." *Id.* The purpose of the statute, then, is to "elevate public perception of pets from property to that of 'individuals with needs and interests of their own.'" Laurie Fulkerson, *2001 Legislative Review*, 8 Animal L. 259, 265 (2002).

Professor Miranda McGowan insists, "Those of us who have pets may even be deeply offended at the idea that Fluffy is legally considered to be personal property—a mere chattel." Miranda Oshige McGowan, *Property's Portrait of a Lady*, 85 Minn. L. Rev. 1037, 1103 (2001). She explains:

> Pets are our family members. Some people take their pets on vacation with them, and some people's relationships with their pets are better than, and outlast, their marriages. Pets make our lives better — pet owners are reportedly happier than people who don't own pets. People buy their pets holiday presents, and as a nation we spend twenty-one billion dollars per year on things for our pets. There is a whole tranche [slice] of law dealing with the enforceability of wills and trusts benefitting pets. Fala sits proudly next to his master in the Roosevelt memorial. Nixon's little dog, Checkers, saved his career (for a while at least); more people bought Millie's book than voted for the first George Bush; and Socks was, by far, the most popular Clinton. . . . When our pets die, we mourn. When it is due to someone else's negligence, some of us sue. Recognizing the deep bond people have with their pets, several states have allowed plaintiffs to recover damages for emotional distress to compensate for a pet's wrongful death, making an exception to the general rule of no emotional distress damages for harm to personal property.

Id. at 1103-04. More generally, some animal rights activists are seeking to change the historic view of animals as property. According to one proponent, science has established that "humans are just like another animal in the evolutionary chain and humans are much like other animals — there are no clear distinguishing characteristics, only differences in the degree to which animals and humans have certain characteristics." Thomas G. Kelch, *Toward a Non-Property Status for Animals*, 6 N.Y.U. Envtl. L.J. 531, 558 (1998). Does the treatment of animals as property or not depend upon one's view of their similarities to humans? Many animals communicate, feel pain and pleasure, and recognize others. Some have large brains, exhibit consciousness, and display considerable intelligence — probably more than young human children and some mentally challenged humans. Should these factors matter in determining the relative rights of various types of animals? What is the legal basis for human domination over other animals? A pioneering book raising these issues is Peter Singer, *Animal Liberation: A New Ethics for our Treatment of Animals* (1975).

4. Federal statutes and some state statutes restrict the sale and, in some instances, the ownership of certain animal parts, such as ivory, some furs, and anything related to migratory birds or endangered species. For example, the federal law relating to eagles makes it a crime, subject to criminal and civil penalties, for anyone without a permit to "take, possess, sell, purchase, barter, offer to sell, purchase or barter, transport, export or import, at any time or in any manner, any bald eagle commonly known as the American eagle, or any golden eagle, alive or dead, or any part, nest, or egg thereof of the foregoing eagles." 16 U.S.C.

§668. Suppose a hunter finds the carcass of a dead bald eagle; may the hunter lawfully take possession of the eagle's feathers or talons as artifacts? *See* United States v. Hatzel, 385 F. Supp. 1311 (W.D. Mo. 1974) (yes). If the hunter may keep the feathers or talons, can he sell them? *See* Andrus v. Allard, 444 U.S. 51 (1979) (holding that eagle parts legally owned before passage of the statute cannot be sold). Similar questions have arisen under the federal Endangered Species Act. *See, e.g.,* United States v. Winnie, 97 F.3d 975 (7th Cir. 1996) (upholding the conviction of a hunter who mounted the skin and skull of a cheetah that he killed while on a safari in Africa on his basement wall); United States v. Billie, 667 F. Supp. 1485 (S.D. Fla. 1987) (rejecting a religious freedom defense asserted by a Seminole leader who killed and possessed a Florida panther). *See generally* John Copeland Nagle & J.B. Ruhl, *The Law of Biodiversity and Ecosystem Management* 227-45 (2002) (detailing the ESA's prohibition on the possession of protected species).

■ PIONEER HI-BRED INTERNATIONAL, INC. v. HOLDEN FOUNDATION SEEDS, INC.

United States District Court for the Southern District of Iowa,
1987 WL 341211, aff'd, 35 F.3d 1226 (8th Cir. 1994)

O'BRIEN, District Judge. This matter came on for trial before the Court at Des Moines, Iowa, consuming approximately 26 trial days with intermittent recesses. This case was bifurcated by this Court and, thus, this trial relates to the issue of liability only. All issues not resolved by this opinion will be determined at a later date.

The Court has concluded that Pioneer Hi-Bred International, Inc. (Pioneer) should prevail in this litigation on the issue of liability. . . .

BACKGROUND

The hybrid seed corn industry is segmented; the Plaintiff Pioneer furnishes a prime example of an integrated type of company. Pioneer has its own breeding program, develops its own seed stocks, creates its own parent corn, produces the hybrid seed, and contends that it maintains complete ownership over all of these operations until the ownership of that hybrid is ultimately transferred to the farmer. Plaintiff contends that until said sale and transfer takes place, the ownership of the material at all times remains in Pioneer. There are other integrated companies in the industry similar to Pioneer.

Another segment of the industry consists of foundation seed companies such as Holden Foundation Seeds, Inc. (Holden) and the hybrid seed companies that purchase parent seed from them.[3] The hybrid seed companies plant the seed purchased from the foundation companies, do the necessary detasseling, roguing and harvesting to produce hybrid seed, condition the harvested seed, and then size, bag, and sell the hybrid seed to the farmer. These hybrid corn companies compete

---

3. Foundation seed companies do not sell hybrid seed corn to farmers; they sell inbred lines to their customers (seed corn companies) who produce hybrid seed corn for sale to farmers. In the mid-1980s, Holden was selling to about 200 such companies each year.

    Hybrid: an offspring of two plants of different races, breeds, varieties, or species; in corn, hybrid seed are commonly produced by crossing two different inbred lines.

    Inbred lines: In corn, inbred lines are lines developed by self pollination and selection until the line is relatively homozygous (true breeding).

directly with Pioneer at the retail level. The ability of these companies to successfully compete is dependent on many factors, but without parent material from which competitive hybrids can be produced, such companies cannot remain competitive. Ronald Holden testified that Holden supplies the parent seed for 30% to 40% of the hybrid seed corn sold in the United States each year. . . .

In order to create a hybrid seed, a company typically plants four to six rows of a particular parent referred to as a female, and alongside of it two rows of a parent referred to as a male. All plants in the female rows are detassled so that no pollen from those plants can fertilize the silks on those same plants.

Seed fields are usually planted in isolation from other corn. Thus, the only pollen that can fertilize the female rows is from the male rows planted alongside. The seed on the ears in the female rows is the F_1 hybrid seed. The male rows self pollinate, have no value in the further breeding process, and are either chopped out or harvested separately and fed to livestock or commingled with other corn at elevators.

The parent or inbred material may often have rather small — even deformed — ears. However, when one such parent is crossed with another parent as above described, the result of mixing the genes is such that if the proper parents are selected, the resulting hybrid seed produces a splendid crop, *i.e.*, a large ear, a higher yield, and other sought-after characteristics.

To put it another way, if an inbred line — called *A* — with small stalks, small ears and low yield, is crossed with itself or another inbred line essentially the same as *A*, all you are going to get are plants that are small, have small ears and low yield. Similarly, an inbred line called *B*, crossed with itself or a similar inbred line will produce only plants much like those of inbred line *B*. However, if you crossed inbred line *A* with inbred line *B* each with small stalks, small ears and low yield, sometimes if you have the right cross, the hybrid of inbred *A* times inbred *B* will produce plants of great vigor, good ears and outstanding yield. This phenomenon is called hybrid vigor. . . .

The main controversy is . . . whether or not Holden wrongfully acquired and appropriated the seed of Pioneer's H3H and/or H43SZ7 and used it to produce and market Holden inbred lines designated LH38, LH39 and LH40. Holden claims that they independently developed their LH38, LH39 and LH40 lines without taking anything from Pioneer and without using anything that belonged to Pioneer. Holden claims that its inbreds LH38, LH39 and LH40 have as their male parent Holden's inbred L120. Pioneer claims that Holden has no records of any nature or description which would show where they got L120, and Pioneer further claims that L120 is a Pioneer line or was derived from a Pioneer line. Over the course of this litigation, the parties were attempting to persuade the Court in relation to the above premises. . . .

Holden's nursery books[9] have very detailed records of what lines were planted and what crosses were made for twenty years or more prior to trial. This is standard operating procedure for any corn breeder. Originally, Holden said these nursery books would clearly show the L120 story; however, a change in position occurred here also. The changes were revealed by Holden after they were required to produce additional documents and records. Originally . . . Holden contended that L120 was

---

9. Nursery books are precise books kept by corn breeders showing specifically what line of corn is growing in each row of a field so that the geneology can be readily traced back.

selected from the Oh43Ht program after five to seven backcrosses.[22] . . . When the Court required defendants to produce all pages from the nursery books prior to 1972 that made reference to Oh43Ht, the defendants were forced to change their position because the pages produced show that the only Oh43Ht material in existence at the end of 1972 contained a minimum of eleven backcrosses to Oh43.

The Court deems it very significant that not a single L number (the alleged life blood of Holden Foundation Seeds, Inc. that separated it from the other foundation houses) can be traced to a row in a Holden field in a preceding generation. It is unimaginable that Holden would go to all the work necessary to maintain detailed and documented nursery records that allow every line of Oh43Ht, a public line, to be traced for six years without a break through winter and summer nurseries, and yet would not record the far more meaningful records of source rows or comparable identifying designations or descriptions of their breeder's work while conducting several years of simultaneous line development work in hopes of developing a successful new line. This glaring, poorly explained and consistent failure to record source designations for every L line used by Holden is hard to accept as continuing oversight. It is even more unlikely to be a conscious omission in any legitimate corn program. Further, it is hard to reconcile with the breeder's other careful records of breeding relating to far less meaningful nursery activity.

Another glaring shortcoming in Holden's case is the fact that though it holds onto many kinds of corn seeds for its reserve, it "inadvertently" threw away the last of the L120 seed it had. This is surprising since L120 is the keystone to their great new corn lines. . . . Holden's explanations as to how and why it was discarded are not persuasive. Its presence would have been most valuable evidence, if in fact it did not come from Pioneer's parent seed, by clearly demonstrating in growouts, electrophoresis and/or chromatography tests that it was in fact not identical, or close to Pioneer's seed. . . .

Roland Holden is the original founder of Holden Foundation Seeds. He retired about 1972. He testified at the trial. Mr. Holden told of looking for Pioneer line parent seed over a number of years. He had the male of Pioneer 3588. He got it while searching through a "friendly" farmer's[27] field of Pioneer corn. [He testified as follows:]

> I found Pioneer's 3588, a male in a field of hybrid corn. It's easy to find a female parent. It's hard to find a male parent, but I did it. . . . I also had Pioneer's 3709 line and a Pioneer female parent. I would go out in late October or November and pick up Pioneer corn. I'd pick up both male and female parents. The male comes off in a field in shell form and spills easier than the ear corn. . . . It would have come out of a Pioneer production field where inbreds were used to make hybrids. I would go to a Pioneer field at times near my home. It was close to a lake where I hunted game. I'd make 12 to 14 trips each fall to that area. I've been doing it for years. Lately I go a little less. . . . I had the male parent of Pioneer's 3588, 3780 and 3709. . . .

. . . While Pioneer has not specifically shown that any of these activities on Roland Holden's part were the exact source of Holden's having Pioneer's lines,

---

22. If L120, as claimed, was backcrossed with Oh43 five to seven times, the mathematical probabilities are that it would be 96% to 99% the same as Oh43 and would not be any new "find" to base a new Holden line on.

27. A nearby farmer who had purchased Pioneer seed and was growing it. According to Roland Holden, this farmer knew what he was doing.

it is very clear that for a number of years, Roland Holden was doing anything he could to try to find out more about and grow Pioneer lines. . . .

Various kinds of scientific tests produced some of the most important evidence concerning the lineage of Holden's LH38, LH39 and LH40 lines. [Pioneer agreed to these pre-trial tests comparing the genetic make-up and grow-out of its lines with those of Holden. The court describes these scientific tests and their result in great detail leading to the following conclusion:] There is no question but that Pioneer came out of the various tests in an impressive fashion. They took risky positions prior to the tests and the results soundly support them.

All that would have been necessary to torpedo Pioneer's contentions would have been for the electrophoresis (test) at one of the 34 loci not to have "fit" the claim that L120 was in fact Pioneer's H3H or H43SZ7. They all "fit." Pioneer could not have known of this "fit" ahead of time. . . .

In the same way, chromatography could easily have conclusively disproved Pioneer's claims. If the chromatographic combinations using L120 did not fit the Pioneer contentions, Pioneer's claims would have been seriously refuted. In each combination in which Pioneer's H4SZ7 or H3H were substituted for L120 the results were convincingly in support of Pioneer's contentions.

In the growout of 1984,[57] the results could have easily disproved Pioneer's contentions; however, in each combination in which Pioneer's H3H or H43SZ7 was substituted for "L120" in the LH38, LH39 or LH40 pedigrees, the results were persuasively favorable to Pioneer's position, and another chance to torpedo Pioneer's claims evaporated.

As mentioned above, Pioneer gambled. If it was not correct, it would have to dismiss. The tests *each* support Pioneer and persuade the Court that while it is not clear how Holden got the Pioneer male parent seed, it had it and used it. . . .

TRADE SECRETS

The proof required to establish a trade secret claim in Iowa is measured by the preponderance of the evidence standard. In Basic Chemicals, Inc. v. Benson, 251 N.W.2d 220, 226 (Iowa 1977), the court set forth the essential elements of a trade secrets claim. "The generally recognized prerequisites for a claim for relief based upon the appropriation of a trade secret are (1) *existence of a trade secret,* (2) *acquisition of the secret as a result of a confidential relationship,* and (3) *unauthorized use of a secret.*"

In the *Basic Chemicals* case, the Iowa Supreme Court adopted the *Restatement of Torts* §757 definitions of a "trade secret" and "secrecy":

> *Definition of trade secret.* A trade secret may consist of any formula, pattern, device or compilation of information which is used in one's business and which gives him an opportunity to obtain an advantage over competitors who do not know or use it. It may be a formula or a chemical compound, a process of manufacturing, treating or preserving materials, a pattern for a machine or other device, or a list of customers. . . .
>
> *Secrecy.* The subject matter of a trade secret must be secret. Matters of public knowledge or general knowledge in an industry cannot be appropriated by one as his secret. . . . An exact definition of a trade secret is not possible. Some factors to be

---

57. A "growout" is nothing more than a planned planting of certain lines to observe the growth and compare the results.

considered in determining whether given information is one's trade secret are: (1) the extent to which the information is known outside of his business; (2) the extent to which it is known by employees and others involved in his business; (3) the extent of measures taken by him to guard the secrecy of the information; (4) the value of the information to him and to his competitors; (5) the amount of effort or money expended by him in developing the information; (6) the ease or difficulty with which the information could be properly acquired or duplicated by others.

Accordingly, the provisions of the Restatement appear to be the appropriate starting point for the resolution of a trade secret controversy. . . .

In light of the totality of the circumstances, the Court holds that the genetic messages of H3H and H43SZ7 are "trade secrets." The genetic message of these lines of corn which Pioneer spent a great amount of money and effort developing is akin to a secret formula. This valuable formula did not exist outside of Pioneer's fields and the fields of its contractors and could only be duplicated with a great deal of effort and some luck. Furthermore, the evidence revealed that Pioneer took all reasonable precautions to protect the secrecy of the genetic message of these lines.

In the case at bar, the *Basic Chemicals* second prerequisite — "that the acquisition of the secret must be as a result of a confidential relationship" — is not present. There is no such relationship between Pioneer and Holden. However, this Court is persuaded that, under the Restatement §757, which the *Basic Chemicals* case also embraced, the "confidential relationship" requirement is not an absolute requirement or element in the proof of misappropriation of a trade secret. While the facts in the usual case present a "confidential relationship" situation, such as an employee changing companies and taking trade secrets with him, the real key is whether the defendant discovered the secret by improper means. [For support, the court cites and quotes from the case of E.I. duPont deNemours & Co. v. Christopher, 431 F.2d 1012, 1014 (5th Cir. 1970).]

This more liberal view of the tort of misappropriation of trade secrets is consistent with two policies — (1) maintenance of commercial morality, and (2) the encouragement of research and innovation — which have been identified by the Supreme Court as underlying trade secret protection. Kewanee Oil Co. v. Bicron Corp., 416 U.S. 470, 481-82 (1974). . . .

The practical impact of accepting these precedents in relation to this case is that this Court is persuaded that Pioneer's H3H and/or Pioneer's H43SZ7 have been used by the Defendant Holden. The Court further finds that Pioneer has met its burden regarding misappropriation. Since it has met this burden, Holden has the burden of showing that H3H and/or H43SZ7 were lawfully acquired. The Court finds that Holden has failed to meet that burden and has further failed to show that it has developed its inbred lines LH38, LH39 and LH40 independently of Pioneer's H3H and/or H43SZ7. . . .

CONVERSION

Plaintiff's pendent common law tort theories include the tort of conversion. Specifically, Pioneer alleges that Holden converted to its own use Pioneer's line H3H or its recurrent parent, H43SZ7.

"Conversion is the act of wrongful control or dominion over chattels in derogation of another's possessory right thereto." Welke v. The City of Davenport, 309 N.W.2d 450, 451 (Iowa 1981).

Any conversion here would not be the usually understood conversion: "He took my plow and I want it back." Pioneer's chattel is not an ear of corn or a bushel of it. It contends that Holden converted the "genetic qualities or genetic message" contained inside a kernel of H3H or H43SZ7 corn.

Can conversion be maintained for such a taking?

The answer to this novel question of law depends upon whether "the genetic qualities or genetic message" of H3H or H43SZ7 is "property" which is protected by the law of conversion under Iowa law. The Iowa courts have not ruled on whether a particular combination of genes will be viewed under the law as property. Also, this Court found no decision where the Iowa courts ruled on a closely analogous issue. Accordingly, this Court must determine what the Iowa Supreme Court would probably hold were it called upon to decide the issue.

The Iowa Supreme Court has used the term "personal property" when describing the subject matter of conversion. It has defined the term personal property very broadly in another context to include "everything which is the subject of ownership and is not classified as real estate." Gingerich v. Protein Blenders, Inc., 95 N.W.2d 522, 524 (Iowa 1959).

Furthermore, case law from other jurisdictions indicates that intangible personal property can be converted. First, in a case involving rights under a patent, the Michigan Court of Appeals in Miracle Boot Puller Co., Ltd. v. Plastray Corp., 225 N.W.2d 800, 804 (Mich. Ct. App. 1975), held as follows: "The mold being a specifiable, physical chattel can be the subject of conversion; likewise, intangible personal property can also be the subject of conversion. As such, the intangible right to benefit from a patent right can be converted."

Second, in Schnucks Twenty-five, Inc. v. Bettendorf, 595 S.W.2d 279, 284 (Mo. Ct. App. 1979), a seller of a business who later breached a covenant not to compete under the same name could be sued for converting the trade name. Third, in National Surety Corp. v. Applied Systems, Inc., 418 So. 2d 847, 849-50 (Ala. 1982), a computer program could be the subject of a conversion suit, even if computer tapes themselves were not converted, because as the Alabama court reasoned, a criminal statute punished the theft of intangible personal property and it would only be consistent to make intangible personal property the subject of conversion. . . .

This Court is persuaded that the fact that Holden changed the "genetic qualities or genetic message" contained in H3H after acquiring but before putting it on the market does not preclude liability for a claim of conversion. *See Restatement (Second) of Torts* §226.

In light of the foregoing authority, the Court could easily rule that the genetic message of H3H or H43SZ7 is "property" which is protected by the tort of conversion under Iowa law. However, when dealing with novel questions of Iowa law, this Court is very concerned about the possibility of establishing broad legal precedents which could lead to undesirable and unintended results in future cases. After its review of the rules of law and the concepts relating to conversion and trade secrets, the Court is convinced that the law of trade secrets provides a better fit for the facts of this case. . . .

Consequently, the Court concludes as a matter of law that, under the narrow facts of this case, the conversion claim is an alternative to the trade secrets claim and need be decided only if the plaintiff does not prevail on its trade secrets claim. Notwithstanding this legal conclusion, the Court will decide the conversion claim so that there is a full record for appeal. Under the analysis adopted by this Court, the alternative ruling will become important only if the finding for Pioneer on the trade secrets claim is reversed.

If Pioneer's interest in the genetic message is not ultimately protected by the law of trade secrets, the Court rules as a matter of law that Pioneer's interest in the genetic message is "property" which is protected by the law of conversion. Furthermore, the Court finds that Holden asserted wrongful control over the genetic message of H3H and that such control detracted from Pioneer's ability to control how its property was used. . . .

Notes and Questions

1. Despite the complex science involved in the generation of new plant and animal strains by cross-breeding or genetic manipulation, the underlying facts in this case are straightforward. Hybrid plants can be produced by pollinating one inbred strain by another inbred strain. In the case of corn, this can produce more productive, marketable plants. Pioneer argued that Holden unlawfully acquired the "genetic message" from one or more of Pioneer's inbred strains and used it to produce marketable hybrid strains. In the first (and so far only) case of its kind, Pioneer charged that this unauthorized appropriation of a genetic message constituted conversion of Pioneer's property interest in the inbred strain's genome. In the alternative, Pioneer argued that appropriating the genetic message constituted an appropriation of its trade secret in the inbred strain's genetic information. Chapter 4 contains an introduction to the law of trade secrets and reproduces the *DuPont* case relied on by the court in *Pioneer Hi-Bred*. Once it determined that Holden had somehow unlawfully obtained the genetic message of Pioneer's H3H or H43SZ7 stain and used it to generate its highly profitable LH38, LH39, and LH40 hi-bred lines, the court in *Pioneer Hi-Bred* accepted both of Pioneer's claims but gave preference to the trade secret claim because the Iowa state courts had never applied the law of conversion to a genetic message. Would Holden's actions still constitute conversion if Pioneer had not maintained sufficient secrecy surrounding its inbred strains to qualify for trade secret protection, or if Holden had somehow innocently obtained the genetic message?

2. The decision in *Pioneer Hi-Bred* followed the landmark U.S. Supreme Court decision in Diamond v. Chakrabarty, 447 U.S. 303 (1980), which held for the first time that genetically modified living organisms were patentable intellectual property. The patentability of living organisms was an open question in 1980, when the *Chakrabarty* case was decided. Although the Court ruled in favor of patentability by a 5-4 margin over a strong dissent, once decided, there has been no turning back. Although *Chakrabarty* involved a genetically modified bacterium, the Court's logic was not limited to micro-organisms. Higher and more complex genetically modified organisms, including corn, were soon patented. Is there any legal distinction between patenting micro-organisms and patenting higher plants and animals? What about patenting genetically modified people? In *Chakrabarty*, the opponents of patent protection for genetically modified organisms argued that living things were so different from non-living things that standard patent law (enacted with non-living things in mind) should not cover living things without express congressional assent.

B. HUMAN LIFE

The following Supreme Court decision is the most famous (and infamous) property law ruling in American history. It was an evil decision, if ever there was one, and led the United States down the path toward the Civil War, in which more Americans died than in all other wars combined. The Court's ruling was overruled on the battlefield and by constitutional amendment. It should not be studied for its holding, but rather as an illustration of how property law can be used and abused. The decision deals directly with the issue at hand of property interests in human life. It may make you uncomfortable; it should make you angry.

■ **DRED SCOTT v. SANDFORD**
Supreme Court of the United States, 1857
60 U.S. (19 Howard) 393

This case [was filed on the basis of diversity jurisdiction and] was brought up, by writ of error, from the Circuit Court of the United States for the district of Missouri. . . .

The counsel then filed the following agreed statement of facts, viz:

In the year 1834, the plaintiff was a negro slave belonging to Dr. Emerson, who was a surgeon in the army of the United States. In that year, 1834, said Dr. Emerson took the plaintiff from the State of Missouri [whose law authorized human slavery] to the military post at Rock Island, in the State of Illinois [whose law did not authorize slavery], and held him there as a slave until the month of April or May, 1836. At the time last mentioned, said Dr. Emerson removed the plaintiff from said military post at Rock Island to the military post at Fort Snelling, situate on the west bank of the Mississippi River, in the territory known as Upper Louisiana [now Minnesota, where the law did not allow slavery]. . . . Said Dr. Emerson held the plaintiff in slavery at said Fort Snelling, from said last-mentioned date until the year 1838. . . .

In the year 1838, said Dr. Emerson removed the plaintiff . . . from said Fort Snelling to the State of Missouri, where they have ever since resided. . . .

It is agreed that Dred Scott brought suit for his freedom [on the basis of his former residency in a free state and territory] in the [state] court of St. Louis county; that there was a verdict and judgment in his favor; that on a writ of error to the [Missouri] Supreme Court, the judgment below was reversed, and the same remanded to the [state] court, where it has been continued to await the decision of this case [begun in federal court and appealed to the U.S. Supreme Court regarding the plaintiff's status as citizen or property under the U.S. Constitution]. . . .

TANEY, Chief Justice. . . .

The question is simply this: Can a negro, whose ancestors were imported into this country, and sold as slaves, become a member of the political community formed and brought into existence by the Constitution of the United

Dred Scott

States, and as such become entitled to all the rights, and privileges, and immunities, guaranteed by that instrument to the citizen? . . .

It is true, every person, and every class and description of persons, who were at the time of the adoption of the Constitution recognized as citizens in the several States, became also citizens of this new political body; but none other; it was formed by them, and for them and their posterity, but for no one else. . . .

It becomes necessary, therefore, to determine who were citizens of the several States when the Constitution was adopted. And in order to do this, we must recur to the Governments and institutions of the thirteen colonies, when they separated from Great Britain and formed new sovereignties, and took their places in the family of independent nations. We must inquire who, at that time, were recognized as the people or citizens of a State, whose rights and liberties had been outraged by the English Government; and who declared their independence, and assumed the powers of Government to defend their rights by force of arms.

In the opinion of the court, the legislation and histories of the times, and the language used in the Declaration of Independence, show, that neither the class or persons who had been imported as slaves, nor their descendants, whether they had become free or not, were then acknowledged as a part of the people, nor intended to be included in the general words used in that memorable instrument. . . .

They had for more than a century before been regarded as beings of an inferior order, and altogether unfit to associate with the white race, either in social or political relations; and so far inferior, that they had no rights which the white man was bound to respect; and that the negro might justly and lawfully be reduced to slavery for his benefit. He was bought and sold, and treated as an ordinary article of merchandise and traffic, whenever a profit could be made by it. This opinion was at that time fixed and universal in the civilized portion of the white race. . . .

And in no nation was this opinion more firmly fixed or more uniformly acted upon than by the English Government and English people. They not only seized them on the coast of Africa, and sold them or held them in slavery for their own use; but they took them as ordinary articles of merchandise to every country where they could make a profit on them, and were far more extensively engaged in this commerce than any other nation in the world.

The opinion thus entertained and acted upon in England was naturally impressed upon the colonies they founded on this side of the Atlantic. And, accordingly, a negro of the African race was regarded by them as an article of property, and held, and bought and sold as such, in every one of the thirteen colonies which united in the Declaration of Independence, and afterwards formed the Constitution of the United States. . . .

Upon the whole, therefore, it is the judgment of this court, that it appears by the record before us that the plaintiff in error is not a citizen of Missouri, in the sense in which that word is used in the Constitution; and that the Circuit Court of the United States, for that reason, had no jurisdiction in the case, and could give no judgment in it. Its judgment for the defendant must, consequently, be reversed, and a mandate issued, directing the suit to be dismissed for want of jurisdiction. . . .

DANIEL, Justice [concurring]. . . .
Now, the following are truths which a knowledge of the history of the world, and particularly of that of our own country, compels us to know — that the African negro race never have been acknowledged as belonging to the family of nations; that as amongst them there never has been known or recognized by the inhabitants of

other countries anything partaking of the character of nationality, or civil or political polity; that this race has been by all the nations of Europe regarded as subjects of capture or purchase; as subjects of commerce or traffic; and that the introduction of that race into every section of this country was not as members of civil or political society, but as slaves, as *property* in the strictest sense of the term. . . .

It may be assumed as a postulate, that to a slave, as such, there appertains and can appertain no relation, civil or political, with the State or the Government. He is himself strictly *property*, to be used in subserviency to the interests, the convenience, or the will, of his owner; and to suppose, with respect to the former, the existence of any privilege or discretion, or of any obligation to others incompatible with the magisterial rights just defined, would be by implication, if not directly, to deny the relation of master and slave, since none can possess and enjoy, as his own, that which another has a paramount right and power to withhold. Hence it follows, necessarily, that a slave, the *peculium* or property of a master, and possessing within himself no civil nor political rights or capacities, cannot be a CITIZEN. For who, it may be asked, is a citizen? What do the character and *status* of citizen import? Without fear of contradiction, it does not import the condition of being private property, the subject of individual power and ownership. . . .

McLean, Justice, dissenting. . . .

In the argument, it was said that a colored citizen would not be an agreeable member of society. This is more a matter of taste than of law. Several of the States have admitted persons of color to the right of suffrage, and in this view have recognized them as citizens; and this has been done in the slave as well as the free States. . . .

In the great and leading case of Prigg v. Pennsylvania, 41 U.S. 539 (16 Pet.) 539, 594 (1842), this court says that, by the general law of nations, no nation is bound to recognize the state of slavery, as found within its territorial dominions, where it is in opposition to its own policy and institutions, in favor of the subjects of other nations where slavery is organized. If it does it, it is as a matter of comity, and not as a matter of international right. The state of slavery is deemed to be a mere municipal regulation, founded upon and limited to the range of the territorial laws. . . .

We need not refer to the mercenary spirit which introduced the infamous traffic in slaves, to show the degradation of negro slavery in our country. This system was imposed upon our colonial settlements by the mother country, and it is due to truth to say that the commercial colonies and States were chiefly engaged in the traffic. But we know as a historical fact, that James Madison, that great and good man, a leading member in the Federal Convention, was solicitous to guard the language of that instrument so as not to convey the idea that there could be property in man. . . .

Many of the States, on the adoption of the Constitution, or shortly afterward, took measures to abolish slavery within their respective jurisdictions; and it is a well-known fact that a belief was cherished by the leading men, South as well as North, that the institution of slavery would gradually decline, until it would become extinct. The increased value of slave labor, in the culture of cotton and sugar, prevented the realization of this expectation. Like all other communities and States, the South were influenced by what they considered to be their own interests.

But if we are to turn our attention to the dark ages of the world, why confine our view to colored slavery? On the same principles, white men were made slaves. All slavery has its origin in power, and is against right. . . .

CURTIS, Justice, dissenting. . . .

Slavery, being contrary to natural right, is created only by municipal law. This is not only plain in itself, and agreed by all writers on the subject, but is inferable from the Constitution, and has been explicitly declared by this court. The Constitution refers to slaves as "persons held to service in one State, under the laws thereof." Nothing can more clearly describe a *status* created by municipal law. In Prigg v. Pennsylvania (10 Pet. 611), this court said: "The state of slavery is deemed to be a mere municipal regulation, founded on and limited to the range of territorial laws." . . .

And not only must the *status* of slavery be created and measured by municipal law, but the rights, powers, and obligations, which grow out of that *status*, must be defined, protected, and enforced, by such laws. . . .

Is it conceivable that the Constitution has conferred the right on every citizen to become a resident on the territory of the United States with his slaves, and there to hold them as such, but has neither made nor provided for any municipal regulations which are essential to the existence of slavery?

Is it not more rational to conclude that they who framed and adopted the Constitution were aware that persons held to service under the laws of a State are property only to the extent and under the conditions fixed by those laws; that they must cease to be available as property, when their owners voluntarily place them permanently within another jurisdiction, where no municipal laws on the subject of slavery exist? . . .

Notes and Questions

1. This decision, along with many other decisions in this casebook, depends on the definition of property and property rights; sometimes the boundary of that definition is the subject of a court's discussion, and in other cases the boundary is assumed. In the first three opinions in the chapter, courts asserted or assumed that various wild or domesticated animals were the property of an individual or the state. In *Dred Scott*, the majority asserted that African-American slaves were property of their European American owners. To reach this result, Chief Justice Roger B. Taney and Justice Peter V. Daniel argued that, in Justice Daniel's words, members of "the African negro race never have been acknowledged as belonging to the family of nations," and thus are "subjects of capture or purchase" much like wild animals. In the majority's view, traditional common law principles like those described in Pierson v. Post for wild animals would also apply to Africans. The minority, represented here in the dissenting opinions of Justices John McLean and Benjamin R. Curtis, took the view (as espoused by John Locke and some other English and American legal philosophers) that slavery was an unnatural state for any human being, including an African. Justice McLean quotes the earlier Supreme Court decision in Prigg v. Pennsylvania for the proposition that, "by the general law of nations, no nation is bound to recognize the state of slavery." In reasoning lifted directly from Locke, Justice Curtis adds that slavery is "contrary to natural right." For these dissenters, people become property only by virtue of the positive law of a state or nation, not by virtue of natural law, the general law of nations, or the common law of property. Why would these two views lead to different results when applied to a situation as presented here, where a slave was voluntarily taken by his owner from a slave state to a free state or territory?

2. In 1857, when *Dred Scott* was decided, European Americans were deeply divided over the issue of slavery. Half of the states did not permit human slavery; half of the states allowed it. Further, federal law barred slavery in most of the territories, which then made up much of the western two-thirds of the continental United States. Americans opposed either to slavery or to the extension of slavery into free states and territories feared that this ruling was part of a larger scheme by the pro-slavery majority on the U.S. Supreme Court to extend slavery into all federal territories or, perhaps, even into free states. At the time, this fear was most famously articulated by the great Illinois trial lawyer Abraham Lincoln in his 1857 "A House Divided" speech to the Illinois legislature, an address that helped catapult him to the White House in the next presidential election. In that speech, Lincoln outlined the Supreme Court's apparent scheme and his proposed response to it as follows:

The *working* points of that machinery are:

First, that no negro slave, imported as such from Africa, and no descendants of such slave can ever be a *citizen* of any State, in the sense of that term as used in the Constitution of the United States.

This point is made in order to deprive the negro, in every possible event, of the benefit of that provision of the United States Constitution, which declares that — "the citizens of each State shall be entitled to all privileges and immunities of citizens in the Several States."

Secondly, that "subject to the Constitution of the United States," neither *Congress* nor a *Territorial Legislature* can exclude slavery from any United States Territory.

The point is made in order that individual men may *fill up* the territories with slaves, without danger of losing them as property, and thus enhance the chances of *permanency* to the institution through all the future.

Thirdly, that whether the holding of a negro in actual slavery in a free State, makes him free, as against the holder, the United States courts will not decide, but will leave to be decided by the courts of any slave State the negro may be forced into by the master.

This point is made, not to be pressed *immediately;* but, if acquiesced in for a while, and apparently *indorsed* by the people at an election, *then* to sustain the logical conclusion that what Dred Scott's master might lawfully do with Dred Scott, in the free State of Illinois, every other master may lawfully do with any other *one* or one *thousand* slaves, in Illinois, or in any other free State. . . .

While the opinion of the Court, by Chief Justice Taney, in the *Dred Scott* case, and the separate opinions of all the concurring Judges, expressly declare that the Constitution of the United States neither permits Congress nor a territorial legislature to exclude slavery from any United States territory, they all *omit* to declare whether or not the same Constitution permits a state, or the people of a State, to exclude it. . . .

Welcome or unwelcome, such decision *is* probably coming, and will soon be upon us, unless the power of the present political dynasty shall be met and overthrown. We shall *lie down* pleasantly dreaming that the people of *Missouri* are on the verge of making their State *free;* and we shall *awake to* the *reality*, instead, that the *Supreme* Court has made *Illinois* a slave State.

To meet and overthrow the power of that dynasty, is the work now before all those who would prevent that consummation.

What is Lincoln's remedy to *Dred Scott?* In response to *Dred Scott*, what is he urging that people opposed to slavery or the extension of slavery do? Is this an appropriate response for partisans opposed to Court rulings? When Lincoln became president and the Civil War began, some Southern justices resigned from the U.S. Supreme Court. Chief Justice Taney died soon thereafter. President Lincoln filled these vacancies with justices committed to overruling *Dred Scott*, including the appointment of a leading abolitionist politician and lawyer, Salmon Chase, as Chief Justice.

3. After four years of Civil War, Lincoln's 1863 emancipation of the slaves in rebel-held territory, and the subduing of most pro-slavery Southern states by the Union army, slavery was ended everywhere in the United States by the ratification of the Thirteenth Amendment to the United States Constitution in 1865. It provides:

> Neither slavery nor involuntary servitude, except as a punishment for crime whereof the party shall have been duly convicted, shall exist within the United States, or any place subject to their jurisdiction.

The Fourteenth Amendment was ratified three years later. The all-important first section of this amendment states:

> All persons born or naturalized in the United States, and subject to the jurisdiction thereof, are citizens of the United States and of the state wherein they reside. No state shall make or enforce any law which shall abridge the privileges or immunities of citizens of the United States; nor shall any state deprive any person of life, liberty, or property, without due process of law; nor deny to any person within its jurisdiction the equal protection of the laws.

How do these two amendments effectively overrule the *Dred Scott* decision? How do they impact American property law?

4. Despite the promise of the Thirteenth and Fourteenth Amendments, legalized slavery in the American South simply gave way to a legalized system of apartheid enforced through statutes providing for racial segregation in public facilities (such as schools and parks) and Jim Crow laws facilitating the exclusion of African Americans from private places of public accommodation (such as restaurants, theaters, and buses). Judicially enforced racial covenants kept African Americans out of white neighborhoods in the North as well as the South. Much as before the Civil War, property law continued to be the principal means of racial restriction. Founded in 1940 under the leadership of future Supreme Court Justice Thurgood Marshall, the NAACP Legal Defense Fund used the Fourteenth Amendment to challenge laws supporting apartheid, leading to Brown v. Board of Education, 347 U.S. 483 (1954), which finally overturned laws mandating separate schools for Blacks and Whites but had little practical effect in ending racial segregation in public education. Real progress in racial integration came only after coordinated campaigns of non-violent civil disobedience to segregation laws, such as those led by Martin Luther King, Jr., in Birmingham, Alabama, during 1963, culminated in the enactment and enforcement of meaningful federal civil rights statutes. Responding to his critics from his jail cell in Birmingham, King explained the need for civil disobedience to unjust property laws in terms that echoed the dissenting opinions in *Dred Scott* and the writings of Lincoln and other legal theorists:

> You express a great deal of anxiety over our willingness to break laws. This is certainly a legitimate concern. Since we so diligently urge people to obey the Supreme Court's decision of 1954 outlawing segregation in public schools, at first glance it may seem rather paradoxical for us consciously to break laws. One may well ask: "How can you advocate breaking some laws and obeying others?" The answer lies in the fact that there are two types of laws: just and unjust. I would be the first to advocate obeying just laws. One has not only a legal but a moral responsibility to obey just laws. Conversely, one has

a moral responsibility to disobey unjust laws. I would agree with St. Augustine that "an unjust law is not law at all."

Now, what is the difference between the two? How does one determine whether a law is just or unjust? A just law is a man-made code that squares with the moral law or the law of God. An unjust law is a code that is out of harmony with moral law. To put it in the terms of St. Thomas Aquinas: An unjust law is a human law that is not rooted in eternal law and natural law. Any law that uplifts human personality is just. Any law that degrades human personality is unjust. All segregation statutes are unjust because segregation distorts the soul and damages the personality. It gives the segregator a false sense of superiority and the segregated a false sense of inferiority. Segregation, to use the terminology of the Jewish philosopher Martin Buber, substitutes an "I-it" relationship for an "I-thou" relationship and ends up relegating persons to the status of things.

Martin Luther King, Jr., *Why We Can't Wait* 70-71 (Signet Classics 2000). How did segregation statutes use property law for an unjust end? What property rights were restricted by laws that excluded African Americans from access to public or private facilities and the ownership of certain property? In the foregoing book dealing with the Birmingham civil-rights campaign, King argues that "the nation must not only radically readjust its attitude toward the Negro in the compelling present, but must incorporate in its planning some compensatory consideration for the handicaps he has inherited from the past." *Id.* at 124. What forms of affirmative action in property law are appropriate?

■ **GREENBERG v. MIAMI CHILDREN'S HOSPITAL RESEARCH INSTITUTE**
United States District Court for the Southern District of Florida, 2003
264 F. Supp. 2d 1064

MORENO, District Judge. This case presents an unfortunate legal dilemma set against the backdrop of a historic breakthrough in the treatment of a previously intractable genetic disorder. Both parties in this case were jointly engaged in a noble and dogged pursuit to detect and find a cure for a fatal genetic disorder called Canavan disease, a rare genetic disease that occurs most frequently in Ashkenazi Jewish families.

Plaintiffs, a group of individuals and non-profit institutions, are attempting to assert legal rights against Defendant researcher and his research institution's commercialization of the fruits of their Canavan disease research. Before the Court is Defendants' Motions to Dismiss pursuant to Fed. R. Civ. P. 12(b)(6) for failure to state a claim upon which relief may be granted. Because the Court finds that Plaintiffs have failed to allege sufficient facts as to all their claims except unjust enrichment, the motions are granted in part. . . .

The Complaint alleges a tale of a successful research collaboration gone sour. In 1987, Canavan disease still remained a mystery — there was no way to identify who was a carrier of the disease, nor was there a way to identify a fetus with Canavan disease. Plaintiff Daniel Greenberg approached Dr. Matalon, a research physician who was then affiliated with the University of Illinois at Chicago for assistance. Greenberg requested Matalon's involvement in discovering the genes that were ostensibly responsible for this fatal disease, so that tests could be administered to determine carriers and allow for prenatal testing for the disease.

At the outset of the collaboration, Greenberg and the Chicago Chapter of the National Tay-Sachs and Allied Disease Association, Inc. ("NTSAD") located other Canavan families and convinced them to provide tissue (such as blood, urine, and autopsy samples), financial support, and aid in identifying the location of Canavan families internationally. The other individual Plaintiffs began supplying Matalon with the same types of information and samples beginning in the late 1980s. Greenberg and NTSAD also created a confidential database and compilation — the Canavan registry — with epidemiological, medical and other information about the families.

Defendant Matalon became associated in 1990 with Defendants Miami Children's Hospital Research Institute, Inc. ("MCHRI") and Variety Children's Hospital d/b/a Miami Children's Hospital ("MCH"). Defendant Matalon continued his relationship with the Plaintiffs after his move, accepting more tissue and blood samples as well as financial support.

The individual Plaintiffs allege that they provided Matalon with these samples and confidential information "with the understanding and expectations that such samples and information would be used for the specific purpose of researching Canavan disease and identifying mutations in the Canavan disease which could lead to carrier detection within their families and benefit the population at large." Plaintiffs further allege that it was their "understanding that any carrier and prenatal testing developed in connection with the research for which they were providing essential support would be provided on an affordable and accessible basis, and that Matalon's research would remain in the public domain to promote the discovery of more effective prevention techniques and treatments and, eventually, to effectuate a cure for Canavan disease." This understanding stemmed from their "experience in community testing for Tay-Sachs disease, another deadly genetic disease that occurs most frequently in families of Ashkenazi Jewish descent."

There was a breakthrough in the research in 1993. Using Plaintiffs' blood and tissue samples, familial pedigree information, contacts, and financial support, Matalon and his research team successfully isolated the gene responsible for Canavan disease. After this key advancement, Plaintiffs allege that they continued to provide Matalon with more tissue and blood in order to learn more about the disease and its precursor gene.

In September 1994, unbeknownst to Plaintiffs, a patent application was submitted for the genetic sequence that Defendants had identified. This application was granted in October 1997, and Dr. Matalon was listed as an inventor on the gene patent and related applications for the Canavan disease, Patent No. 5,679,635 (the "Patent"). Through patenting, Defendants acquired the ability to restrict any activity related to the Canavan disease gene, including without limitation: carrier and prenatal testing, gene therapy and other treatments for Canavan disease and research involving the gene and its mutations.

Although the Patent was issued in October 1997, Plaintiffs allege that they did not learn of it until November 1998, when MCH revealed their intention to limit Canavan disease testing through a campaign of restrictive licensing of the Patent. Specifically, on November 12, 1998, Plaintiffs allege that Defendants MCH and MCHRI began to "threaten" the centers that offered Canavan testing with possible enforcement actions regarding the recently-issued patent. Defendant MCH also began restricting public accessibility through negotiating exclusive licensing agreements and charging royalty fees.

Plaintiffs allege that at no time were they informed that Defendants intended to seek a patent on the research. Nor were they told of Defendants' intentions to commercialize the fruits of the research and to restrict access to Canavan disease testing.

Based on these facts, Plaintiffs filed a six-count complaint on October 30, 2000, against Defendants asserting the following causes of action: (1) lack of informed consent; (2) breach of fiduciary duty; (3) unjust enrichment; (4) fraudulent concealment; (5) conversion; and (6) misappropriation of trade secrets.

[The court granted Defendants' motion with respect to counts 1, 2, 4, and 6; and denied Defendants' motion with respect to count 3. With respect to Plaintiffs' claim of conversion, the court wrote:]

The Plaintiffs allege in Count V of their Complaint that they had a property interest in their body tissue and genetic information, and that they owned the Canavan registry in Illinois which contained contact information, pedigree information and family information for Canavan families worldwide. They claim that MCH and Matalon converted the names on the register and the genetic information by utilizing them for the hospitals' "exclusive economic benefit." The Court disagrees and declines to find a property interest for the body tissue and genetic information voluntarily given to Defendants. These were donations to research without any contemporaneous expectations of return of the body tissue and genetic samples, and thus conversion does not lie as a cause of action.

In Florida, the tort of "conversion is an unauthorized act which deprives another of his property permanently or for an indefinite time." Nat'l Union Fire Ins. Co. of Penn. v. Carob. Aviation, Inc., 759 F.2d 873, 878 (11th Cir. 1985). Using property given for one purpose for another purpose constitutes conversion.

First, Plaintiffs have no cognizable property interest in body tissue and genetic matter donated for research under a theory of conversion. This case is similar to Moore v. Regents of the University of California, 793 P.2d 479, 488 (Cal. 1990), where the Court declined to extend liability under a theory of conversion to misuse of a person's excised biological materials. The plaintiff in *Moore* alleged that he had retained a property right in excised bodily material used in research, and therefore retained some control over the results of that research. The California Supreme Court, however, disagreed and held that the use of the results of medical research inconsistent with the wishes of the donor was not conversion, because the donor had no property interest at stake after the donation was made. The Court also recognized that the patented result of research is "both factually and legally distinct" from excised material used in the research. *Id.* at 492.

Second, limits to the property rights that attach to body tissue have been recognized in Florida state courts. For example, in State v. Powell, 497 So. 2d 1188 (Fla. 1986), the Florida Supreme Court refused to recognize a property right in the body of another after death. Similarly, the property right in blood and tissue samples also evaporates once the sample is voluntarily given to a third party.

Plaintiffs rely on Pioneer Hi-Bred v. Holden Foundation, 1987 WL 341211 (S.D. Iowa, Oct. 30, 1987), *aff'd*, 35 F.3d 1226 (8th Cir. 1994), for their assertion that genetic information itself can constitute property for the purposes of the tort of conversion. In that case, the Court held that a corn seed's property interest in the genetic message contained in a corn seed variety is property protected by the laws of conversion. Plaintiffs argue that giving permission for one purpose (gene discovery) does not mean they agreed to other uses (gene patenting and commercialization). Yet, the *Pioneer* court recognized that, "where information is gathered and arranged at some cost and sold as a commodity on the market, it is properly protected as property." This seemingly provides more support for property rights inherent in Defendants' research rather than the donations of Plaintiffs' DNA. Finally, Plaintiffs cite a litany of cases in other jurisdictions that have recognized that body tissue can be property in some circumstances. *See, e.g.,* Brotherton v. Cleveland, 923 F.2d 477, 482 (6th Cir. 1991) (aggregate of rights existing in body tissue is similar to property rights); York v. Jones, 717 F. Supp. 421, 425 (E.D. Va. 1989) (couple granted property rights in their frozen embryos). These cases, however, do not involve voluntary donations to medical research. . . .

The Court finds that Florida statutory and common law do not provide a remedy for Plaintiffs' donations of body tissue and blood samples under a theory of conversion liability. Indeed, the Complaint does not allege that the Defendants used the genetic material for any purpose *but* medical research. Plaintiffs claim that the *fruits* of the research, namely the patented material, was commercialized. This is an important distinction and another step in the chain of attenuation that renders conversion liability inapplicable to the facts as alleged. If adopted, the expansive theory championed by Plaintiffs would cripple medical research as it would bestow a continuing right for donors to possess the results of any research conducted by the hospital. At the core, these were donations to research without any contemporaneous expectations of return. Consequently, the Plaintiffs have failed to state a claim upon which relief may be granted on this issue. Accordingly, this claim is dismissed.

Notes and Questions

1. Florida state law outlaws the sale of any human organ or tissue. Fla. Stat. §873.01. This provision follows the Uniform Anatomical Gift Act, enacted in most states. Further, federal law makes it "unlawful for any person to knowingly acquire, receive, or otherwise transfer any human organ for valuable consideration for use in human transplantation if the transfer affects interstate commerce." 42 U.S.C. §274e. Sales for other purposes (such as research and education) are not prohibited. At the same time, many states and the federal government have statutes and programs designed to encourage the donation of human tissue and organs for transplantation. One such state law is described in Newman v. Sathyavaglswaran, the final case in this chapter. Why does the government encourage the donation of human organs but outlaw their sale? Which approach (donation or sale) is likely to generate a greater supply of human organs for transplantation? Which approach is likely to generate a more equitable distribution of available organs? Should the same rules apply for indispensable organs, such as the heart, which can only be donated after the donor's death, and for dispensable organs, such as one kidney, which can be donated during the donor's life? The Florida statute expressly covers both hearts and kidneys. Fla. Stat. §873.01(3)(a).

2. Typically, the government permits persons to sell their replaceable body products, such as hair, plasma, sperm, and eggs. Indeed, student newspapers at elite colleges and universities frequently include ads offering payment for

"donated" eggs. One such ad in the May 9, 2012, issue of the Williams College *Record* stated,

Why are these replaceable body products treated differently in this respect than human organs and tissue—especially when some organs (such as the liver, if only part is removed) and tissue regenerate? Suppose that a beauty salon operator collected and sold the clipped hair of his patrons, without their consent, to shampoo, wig, and doll manufacturers. Would those patrons have a valid claim for conversion? How would their claim differ from those of Daniel Greenberg?

3. Laws against the sale of organs and body parts for transplantation do not apply in the *Greenberg* case because tissue from individual plaintiffs was used for research, not for transplantation. No federal or Florida state law expressly prohibits the sale of human organs or tissue for medical research. The Uniform Anatomical Gift Act (as enacted in Florida) confers limited property rights upon patients to determine how their excised organs and tissue are used. In particular, the Act requires that, before excised materials are used for transplantation, consent must be obtained from the donor or, if the donor is deceased, from the donor's next of kin. Fla. Stat. §765.512. In effect, this Act recognizes that persons have at least a limited legal right to "exclude others" from using their excised material — a matter that is explored more fully below in *Newman*.

4. One count of the plaintiffs' complaint in *Greenberg* survived the defendants' motion to dismiss for failure to state a claim upon which relief could be granted. That count charged that the defendants were unjustly enriched by using the patent to collect licensing fees. Under Florida law, the elements of a claim for unjust enrichment are (1) the plaintiff conferred a benefit on the defendant, who had knowledge of the benefit; (2) the defendant voluntarily accepted and retained the benefit; and (3) under the circumstances it would be inequitable for the defendant to retain the benefit without paying for it. Under the facts as stated in the opinion, who should prevail under this count? What added facts would support a ruling for the plaintiffs? The case settled without a trial on this count.

5. In 2002, DNA Copyright Institute, a California corporation, began offering the commercial service of copyrighting a person's DNA by filing their DNA code with the U.S. Copyright Office. The company is no longer in business. Would such copyright protection have helped the plaintiffs in this case? Although written and computer codes enjoy copyright protection, there is no binding legal authority for the proposition that DNA codes may be copyrighted, especially since individuals are not generally viewed as the "author" of their own DNA. Philip Cohen, *Born to Make You Happy*, New Scientist, April 25, 2001, at 12.

■   **KURCHNER v. STATE FARM FIRE & CASUALTY CO.**
District Court of Appeal of Florida, 2003
858 So. 2d 1220

RAMIREZ, Judge. Harry and Suzanne Kurchner appeal from an adverse summary judgment. Because we do not construe State Farm's insurance policy to provide coverage, we affirm.

Harry Kurchner is a recipient of cancer chemotherapy treatment. Prior to undergoing chemotherapy treatment, he and his wife, Suzanne Kurchner, decided to cryopreserve[1] Harry's sperm with South Florida Institute for Reproductive Medicine ("SFIRM"). Cryopreservation offered the Kurchners an opportunity to have children in the future should Harry's chemotherapy treatment make him sterile. Harry subsequently deposited five sperm samples with SFIRM. SFIRM was to store the sperm samples separately in tanks maintained with alarms which were to set off when the cooling apparatuses of the tanks failed. SFIRM instead stored all of the samples together and the samples were destroyed when the storage tank's cooling apparatus failed. Harry eventually became sterile as a result of his chemotherapy treatment.

The Kurchners filed suit against SFIRM seeking damages arising from the destruction of Harry's cryopreserved sperm. Appellee State Farm Fire and Casualty Co. provided SFIRM with Comprehensive Business Liability insurance. When State Farm denied coverage and refused to defend it, SFIRM filed a declaratory relief action contending that State Farm had a duty to defend and indemnify SFIRM. The Kurchners and SFIRM entered into a settlement agreement in which the Kurchners assumed SFIRM's rights.

The State Farm policy, under section II — Comprehensive Business Liability, provides coverage for "bodily injury, property damage, personal injury or advertising injury." The Definitions section of the policy defines "bodily injury" as "bodily injury, sickness or disease sustained by a person, including death resulting from the bodily injury, sickness or disease at any time." Coverage would otherwise be excluded, under section II(d) — Comprehensive Business Liability — for property damage that is "personal property in the care, custody or control of any insured."

Both sides moved for summary judgment. The trial court entered judgment in State Farm's favor finding that the "sperm outside of the body is property and is not a part of the body" and concluding that there was no "bodily injury" under State Farm's policy. We agree.

Terms utilized in insurance policies are given their plain and unambiguous meaning. . . .

The Kurchners argue that State Farm's coverage for damages to "bodily injury" includes Harry's sperm as a part of his body according to the definition of "bodily" defined as "of or pertaining to the body." If we were to agree with the Kurchners that the policy provides coverage, we must first agree with the proposition that sperm removed from a body constitutes a "bodily injury" sustained "by a person." This creates an issue of first impression in Florida and comes to this Court under the most unfortunate of circumstances for the Kurchners. Cases from other jurisdictions, Florida Statutes, and the common understanding of the relevant terms demonstrate, however, that cells removed from a body no longer constitute

---

1. This is a procedure through which tissues or organs can be preserved at extreme low temperatures.

part of the body and instead constitute property whose destruction is not considered bodily injury.

Florida Statutes that govern the donation and disposition of sperm recognize that sperm removed from the body becomes property. For example, section 742.14, Florida Statutes (2002), provides that "[o]nly reasonable compensation directly related to the donation of eggs, sperm, and preembryos shall be permitted." Section 742.17, Florida Statutes (2002), recognizes that control over the disposition of eggs, sperm, and preembryos may be governed by a written agreement.

Cases from other jurisdictions hold that preserved sperm or eggs constitute personal property. In Hecht v. Superior Court, 16 Cal. App. 4th 836, 20 Cal. Rptr. 2d 275, 283 (1993), the court held that a deceased sperm donor had an interest in his sperm which fell within the broad definition of "property" under the state's probate code. The court in Moore v. Regents of University of California, 793 P.2d 479 (Cal. 1990), likewise treated excised cells as "property" for purposes of a conversion action, but did not agree for policy reasons to extend the conversion liability to cover the unauthorized use of such cells. . . .

Affirmed.

Notes and Questions

1. Was Harry Kurchner's sperm still property when it was within his body? Suppose his sperm wasn't destroyed, and it was used to impregnate his wife. Would the embryo be "property"?

2. A line of cases deals with the status of frozen embryos. Typically, the dispute arises after a couple contracts with a reproductive medical center, which facilitates the production and storage of embryos but then the couple divorces before implantation takes place. Although the fact patterns vary, in most cases the woman wants possession and control of the embryo, but the man does not want to become a biological father. The emerging rule holds that courts honor a preexisting written contract governing the disposition of the frozen embryos, but that either party can rescind the agreement if he or she has a change of mind and now desires to prevent implantation. For a discussion of the current state of the law in the context of a divorce case in a community property state, see Roman v. Roman, 193 S.W.3d 40 (Tex. Ct. App. 2006).

3. Neil Armstrong, the first man to walk on the moon, left a barbershop after a haircut at Marx's Barber Shop in Lebanon, Ohio. To his surprise, the barber sold the cuttings, for $3,000, to a collector. The collector, according to Guinness World Records, has the largest collection of hair from historical celebrities, including samples from Abraham Lincoln, Marilyn Monroe, Albert Einstein, Napoleon, and others. Armstrong threatened to sue if Marx did not get the hair back and return it. The collector refused to return Armstrong's hair, but litigation was avoided. Armstrong and Marx agreed that Marx would donate $3,000 (the sales proceeds) to a charity of Armstrong's choosing. What should have been the result had this gone to court? Terry Kinney, *Neil Armstrong Threatens to Sue Barber Who Sold Hair*, Akron Beacon Journal, June 1, 2005. Apparently to avoid something similar happening to her, the pop star Madonna employs a "sterilization team" to remove all traces of her hair, skin, and saliva from her dressing room after a performance. *It Must Be True*, The Week, July 6-13, 2012, at 12.

■ **NEWMAN v. SATHYAVAGLSWARAN**
United States Court of Appeals for the Ninth Circuit, 2002
287 F.3d 786, cert. denied, 537 U.S. 1029

FISHER, Circuit Judge. Parents, whose deceased children's corneas were removed by the Los Angeles County Coroner's office without notice or consent, brought this 42 U.S.C. §1983 action alleging a taking of their property without due process of law. The complaint was dismissed by the district court for a failure to state a claim upon which relief could be granted. We must decide whether the longstanding recognition in the law of California, paralleled by our national common law, that next of kin have the exclusive right to possess the bodies of their deceased family members creates a property interest, the deprivation of which must be accorded due process of law under the Fourteenth Amendment of the United States Constitution. We hold that it does. The parents were not required to exhaust post-deprivation procedures prior to bringing this suit. Thus, we hold that they properly stated a claim under §1983.

I. FACTUAL AND PROCEDURAL BACKGROUND

. . . Robert Newman and Barbara Obarski (the parents) each had children, Richard Newman and Kenneth Obarski respectively, who died in Los Angeles County in October 1997. Following their deaths, the Office of the Coroner for the County of Los Angeles (the coroner) obtained possession of the bodies of the children and, under procedures adopted pursuant to California Government Code §27491.47 as it then existed, removed the corneas from those bodies without the knowledge of the parents and without an attempt to notify them and request consent. The parents became aware of the coroner's actions in September 1999 and subsequently filed this §1983 action alleging a deprivation of their property without due process of law in violation of the Fourteenth Amendment. . . .

II. PROPERTY INTERESTS IN DEAD BODIES

The Fourteenth Amendment prohibits states from "depriv[ing] any person of life, liberty, or property, without due process of law." U.S. Const. amend. XIV, §1. At the threshold, a claim under §1983 for an unconstitutional deprivation of property must show (1) a deprivation (2) of property (3) under color of state law. If these elements are met, the question becomes whether the state afforded constitutionally adequate process for the deprivation. Here, it is uncontested that the coroner's action was a deprivation under color of state law. The coroner argues, however, that the dismissal of the parents' complaint was proper because they could not have a property interest in their children's corneas. . . . Thus, the first step of our analysis is to analyze the history of rules and understandings of our nation with respect to the possession and protection of the bodies of the dead.

A. HISTORY OF COMMON LAW INTERESTS IN DEAD BODIES

Duties to protect the dignity of the human body after its death are deeply rooted in our nation's history. In a valuable history of the subject, the Supreme Court of Rhode Island recounted:

> By the civil law of ancient Rome, the charge of burial was first upon the person to whom it was delegated by the deceased; second, upon the *scripti haeredes* (to whom the property was given), and if none, then upon the *haeredes legitimi* or *cognati* in order. . . . The

heirs might be compelled to comply with the provisions of the will in regard to burial. And the Pontifical College had the power of providing for the burial of those who had no place of burial in their own right.

Pierce v. Proprietors of Swan Point Cemetery, 10 R.I. 227, 235-36 (1872) (citations omitted). . . .

The Roman practice of including duties to protect the body of the dead in civil law had no parallel in the early English common law because burials were matters of ecclesiastical cognizance. Thus, Blackstone explained that "though the heir has a property [interest] in the monuments and escutcheons of his ancestors, yet he has none in their bodies or ashes; nor can he bring any suit or action against such as indecently, at least, if not injuriously, violate and disturb their remains, when dead and buried." Bessemer Land & Improvement Co. v. Jenkins, 18 So. 565, 567 (1895) (quoting 1 Bl. Comm. 429). . . .

Many early American courts adopted Blackstone's description of the common law, holding that "a dead body is not the subject of property right." *Bessemer Land*, 18 So. at 567. The duty to protect the body by providing a burial was often described as flowing from the "universal . . . right of sepulture," rather than from a concept of property law. Wynkoop v. Wynkoop, 42 Pa. 293, 300-01 (1862). As cases involving unauthorized mutilation and disposition of bodies increased toward the end of the 19th century, paralleling the rise in demand for human cadavers in medical science and use of cremation as an alternative to burial, *see* In re Johnson's Estate, 7 N.Y.S.2d at 85-86 (describing "an outpouring" of such cases), courts began to recognize an exclusive right of the next of kin to possess and control the disposition of the bodies of their dead relatives, the violation of which was actionable at law. Thus, in holding that a city council could not "seize upon existing private burial grounds, make them public, and exclude the proprietors from their management," the Supreme Court of Indiana commented that "the burial of the dead can [not] . . . be taken out of the hands of the relatives thereof" because "we lay down the proposition, that the bodies of the dead belong to the surviving relations, in the order of inheritance, as property, and that they have the right to dispose of them as such, within restrictions analogous to those by which the disposition of other property may be regulated." Bogert v. City of Indianapolis, 13 Ind. 134, 136, 138 (1859). Over a decade later, the Rhode Island Supreme Court . . . described the nation's common law as bestowing upon next of kin "a duty [towards the dead], and we may also say a right, to protect from violation; and a duty on the part of others to abstain from violation"; a dead body "may therefore be considered as a sort of *quasi* property." *Pierce*, 10 R.I. at 238.

B. INTEREST IN DEAD BODIES IN CALIFORNIA LAW

In 1872, the same year *Pierce* was decided, California enacted Penal Code §292, imposing a legal duty on next of kin to bury the deceased. In 1899, the California Supreme Court held that duty required recognition of exclusive rights of possession, control and disposition vesting in those with the duty. O'Donnell v. Slack, 55 P. 906, 907 (Cal. 1899). These rights, it explained, were by law "protected, and for a violation of which [next of kin] are entitled to indemnification." *Id.* . . . Following *O'Donnell* and *Pierce*, California courts commonly use the term "quasi property" to describe the rights of next of kin to the body of the deceased. . . .

In 1931, the exclusive rights of possession, control and disposition of the corpse recognized in *O'Donnell*, together with the duty previously contained in Penal Code

§292, were codified in Health and Safety Code §7100.[7] California has at all times recognized these rights as exclusive of others.

C. THE RIGHT TO TRANSFER BODY PARTS

The first successful transplantation of a kidney in 1954 led to an expansion of the rights of next of kin to the bodies of the dead. In 1968, the National Conference of Commissioners on Uniform State Laws approved the Uniform Anatomical Gift Act (UAGA), adopted by California the same year, which grants next of kin the right to transfer the parts of bodies in their possession to others for medical or research purposes. Cal. Health & Safety Code §7150 et seq. The right to transfer is limited. The California UAGA prohibits any person from "knowingly, for valuable consideration, purchas[ing] or sell[ing] a part for transplantation, therapy, or reconditioning, if removal of the part is intended to occur after the death of the decedent," Cal. Health & Safety Code §7155, as does federal law, 42 U.S.C. §274e (prohibiting the "transfer [of] any human organ for valuable consideration").

In the 1970s and 1980s, medical science improvements and the related demand for transplant organs prompted governments to search for new ways to increase the supply of organs for donation. Many perceived as a hindrance to the supply of needed organs the rule implicit in the UAGA that donations could be effected only if consent was received from the decedent or next of kin. In response, some states passed "presumed consent" laws that allow the taking and transfer of body parts by a coroner without the consent of next of kin as long as no objection to the removal is known. California Government Code §27491.47, enacted in 1983, was such a law.

III. DUE PROCESS ANALYSIS

"[T]o provide California non-profit eye banks with an adequate supply of corneal tissue," S. Com. Rep. SB 21 (Cal. 1983), §27491.47(a) authorized the coroner to "remove and release or authorize the removal and release of corneal eye tissue from a body within the coroner's custody" without any effort to notify and obtain the consent of next of kin "if . . . [t]he coroner has no knowledge of objection to the removal." The law also provided that the coroner or any person acting upon his request "shall [not] incur civil liability for such removal in an action brought by any person who did not object prior to the removal . . . nor be subject to criminal prosecution." §27491.47(b).

In analyzing whether the implementation of that law by the coroner deprived the parents of property, we define property as "the group of rights inhering in the citizen's relation to the physical thing, as the right to possess, use and dispose of

---

7. At the time relevant to this case, the statute read:

The right to control the disposition of the remains of a deceased person, unless other directions have been given by the decedent, vests in, and the duty of interment and the liability for the reasonable cost of interment of such remains devolves upon the following in the order named:
a. The surviving spouse.
b. The surviving child or children of the decedent.
c. The surviving parent or parents of the decedent.
d. The person or persons respectively in the next degrees of kindred in the order named by the laws of California as entitled to succeed to the estate of the decedent.
e. The public administrator when the deceased has sufficient assets.

Id. (amended 1999).

it. . . . In other words, it deals with what lawyers term the individual's 'interest' in the thing in question." United States v. General Motors Corp., 323 U.S. 373, 378 (1945); *accord* Phillips v. Washington Legal Found., 524 U.S. 156 (1998). . . . Our holding is not affected by California's labeling of the interests of the next of kin as "quasi property," a term with little meaningful legal significance.[13] . . .

Because the property interests of next of kin to dead bodies are firmly entrenched in the "background principles of property law," based on values and understandings contained in our legal history dating from the Roman Empire, California may not be free to alter them with exceptions that lack "a firm basis in traditional property principles." *Phillips*, 524 U.S. at 165-68. . . .

We need not, however, decide whether California has transgressed basic property principles with enactment of §27491.47 because that statute did not extinguish California's legal recognition of the property interests of the parents to the corneas of their deceased children. It allowed the removal of corneas only if "the coroner has no knowledge of objection," a provision that implicitly acknowledges the ongoing property interests of next of kin.

The effect of §27491.47 was to remove a procedure — notice and request for consent prior to the deprivation — and a remedy — the opportunity to seek redress for the deprivation in California's courts. A state may not evade due process analysis by defining "'[p]roperty' . . . by the procedures provided for its deprivation." Cleveland Bd. of Educ. v. Loudermill, 470 U.S. 532, 541 (1985). "While the legislature may elect not to confer a property interest . . . it may not constitutionally authorize the deprivation of such an interest, once conferred, without appropriate procedural safeguards." *Id.* With §27491.47, California eliminated procedural safeguards but retained the interest.

When the coroner removed the corneas from the bodies of the parents' deceased children and transferred them to others, the parents could no longer possess, control, dispose or prevent the violation of those parts of their children's bodies. To borrow a metaphor used when the government physically occupies property, the coroner did not merely "take a single 'strand' from the 'bundle' of property rights: it chop[ped] through the bundle, taking a slice of every strand." Loretto v. Teleprompter Manhattan CATV Corp., 458 U.S. 419, 435 (1982). This was a deprivation of the most certain variety.

At bottom, "[p]roperty rights serve human values. They are recognized to that end, and are limited by it." State v. Shack, 277 A.2d 369, 372 (1971). The property rights that California affords to next of kin to the body of their deceased relatives serve the premium value our society has historically placed on protecting the dignity of the human body in its final disposition. California infringed the dignity of the bodies of the children when it extracted the corneas from those bodies without the consent of the parents. The process of law was due the parents for this deprivation of their rights. . . .

---

13. The Supreme Court has used the term to identify a property interest only once. In International News Service v. Associated Press, 248 U.S. 215, 236-242 (1918), the majority held that news "must be regarded as quasi property," the taking of which without consent constitutes the basis for an unfair competition action. The Court's label did not affect the holding of the case. There is no entry for "quasi property" in *Black's Law Dictionary* (6th ed. 1990) or *Ballantine's Law Dictionary* (3d ed. 1969), although each contains entries for "quasi contract." The only examples of "quasi property" listed under the entry in Words and Phrases are news, citing *International News Service*, and dead bodies. 35A *Words and Phrases* 487 (1965); *see id.* (2000 cumulative supp.).

We do not hold that California lacks significant interests in obtaining corneas or other organs of the deceased in order to contribute to the lives of the living. Courts are required to evaluate carefully the state's interests in deciding what process must be due the holders of property interests for their deprivation. An interest so central to the state's core police powers as improving the health of its citizens is certainly one that must be considered seriously in determining what process the parents were due. But our Constitution requires the government to assert its interests and subject them to scrutiny when it invades the rights of its subjects.[17] Accordingly, we reverse the district court's dismissal of the parents' complaint and remand for proceedings in which the government's justification for its deprivation of parents' interests may be fully aired and appropriately scrutinized.

The dismissal of the parents' §1983 claim is reversed and remanded for further proceedings.

FERNANDEZ, Judge, dissenting. . . . [A]ny civilized state desires that the bodies of its deceased members be disposed of in an appropriate way, on grounds of decency, consideration for others, and pragmatism. And it should be done with reasonable haste and without undue acrimony. California's statutory scheme reflects all of that. It decidedly does not confer a property right upon anyone. Assuming that a decedent has not made his own arrangements for disposal of his own earthly remains, the state makes sure that somebody else will both do so and pay for it. To that end, California has provided that "[t]he right to control the disposition of the remains of a deceased person . . . vests in, and the duty of disposition and the liability for the reasonable cost of disposition of the remains devolves upon," a list of individuals. Cal. Health & Safety Code §7100(a). Thus, this so-called right is actually in the nature of a duty and expense designed to assure that the remains will not simply be left about, but will be quickly interred. And the state has created something like a table of intestate succession for the purpose of assuring that the right and duty land firmly on a defined group. First comes the person who has a power of attorney for health care. Cal. Health & Safety Code §7100(a)(1). Then comes the spouse. *Id.* at (a)(2). Then adult children, then parents, then next of kin. *Id.* at (a)(3)-(5). At the end is the public administrator, but he only gets the so-called right if there are "sufficient assets" to allow him to discharge his duty. *Id.* at (a)(6). This somewhat remarkable list surely shows just how peculiar it is to dub what we are dealing with a constitutionally protected property right. Is not it interesting that the holder of a power of attorney comes before the closest relatives, and equally interesting to see that the public administrator may wind up with the "right"? Or is it essentially a duty? . . .

Nobody who has had the misfortune of having his loved ones die can fail to be moved by the prospect that somebody else will treat the loved one's former earthly vessel with disrespect. That feeling does not, however, demonstrate that California has conferred a constitutionally protected property right upon family members. In fact, it has not; it has merely given them enough of a right to allow them to fulfill their duty, and it has limited that in a number of ways. One of those ways has to do

17. It has been said in another context that establishing "a culture of justification — a culture in which every exercise of power is expected to be justified" — lies at the heart of the establishment of constitutional bills of rights. Etienne Mureinik, *A Bridge to Where? Introducing the Interim Bill of Rights,* 10 S. Afr. J. Hum. Rts. 31, 32 (1994).

with corneal tissue. As to that, the duty may not devolve, and concomitantly the right will be neither necessary nor constitutionally protected.

Thus, I respectfully dissent.

Notes and Questions

1. As the *Newman* court notes, the term *quasi property* is commonly applied to the interest of the next of kin in a decedent's body and was used by the U.S. Supreme Court to characterize the interest of a news service in the news that it had collected. International News Service v. Associated Press, 248 U.S. 215 (1918) (reproduced in Chapter 4 of this casebook). For property law purposes, in what ways are dead bodies like the news? In what ways are they not like other types of real or personal property?

2. In the United States, the formal legal proposition that certain specified individuals have a quasi-property interest in the dead bodies of others dates from the late nineteenth century. Before that time, relatives, friends, and public or church officials typically buried the dead; and the law did not interfere. As cremation became a popular alternative to burial and demand rose for bodies to be used in medical research, the law evolved to deal with disputes over who controlled the body of a decedent. California law, as set forth in *Newman,* is typical of the state statutory and common law that developed on this matter throughout the United States. Under such law, in what sense does the next of kin "own" the body of a decedent? What may the next of kin do with the body and its organs? Would it be legal under California law for the next of kin simply to keep the body, such as (to use an extreme example from a movie based in California) Norman Bates did with his mother's body in *Psycho?* Are the only legal options burial, cremation, and donation for medical research or transplantation? What about natural-history museums — should they be allowed to retain and display mummified remains of ancient Egyptians and early Native Americans over the objections of modern Egyptians and Native Americans?

3. A 2012 ad in the *San Francisco Examiner* offers "cryomation" as another option for disposing of human bodies. Billed as "The Greenest Way to Go," cryomation uses liquid nitrogen to chill the body to such low temperatures that it dissolves into a freeze-dried power that, unlike the ashes produced by cremation, retains the body's carbon. Cryomation allegedly reduces the deceased's "carbon footprint" by 75 percent over cremation. Paul Larson, *Evolving Technology Impacts the Way We Deal with Death,* San Francisco Examiner, Apr. 19, 2012, at 20.

4. In a highly publicized legal dispute, the children of baseball legend Ted Williams feuded over what to do with the slugger's body. Williams, who many regard as the greatest hitter in baseball history, was declared legally dead on July 5, 2002, at the age of 83. Citing his will, Williams' oldest child, Bobby-Jo Williams Ferrell, wanted to have Williams' body cremated. Citing a later written document, Williams' other two children, John Henry Williams and Claudia Williams, wanted to have Williams' body cryogenically preserved for possible later revitalization. John Henry Williams had the body flown from Florida, where Ted Williams resided, to the Arizona facilities of the Alcor Life Extension Foundation, one of two institutions in the United States that cryogenically preserve bodies at very low temperatures. There, Ted Williams' body was cryogenically preserved. Alcor charges $150,000 to preserve an entire body and $80,000 to preserve a severed head. Cryogenic supporters claim properly preserved bodies and heads might one day be thawed and

brought back to life, though most medical and scientific experts doubt it could ever be done. As of July 2007, there were 77 persons in "cryonic suspension" in Alcor's facilities and at least 827 people had completed their financial and legal arrangements for cryopreservation. The Alcor web page, http://www.alcor.org, includes the following questions and answers about the processes:

Q: What is cryonics?

A: Cryonics (from Greek *kryos* meaning *icy cold*) is the low-temperature preservation of humans who can no longer be sustained by contemporary medicine, in the expectation they can be healed and resuscitated in the future using more advanced medical technologies. Cryopreservation of people is not reversible with current technology. . . .

Q: Has anyone ever been revived?

A: No adult human has ever been revived from temperatures far below freezing. Cryonics patients are cared for in the expectation that future technology, especially molecular nanotechnology, will be available to reverse damage associated with the cryonics process.

Q: Aren't cryonics patients dead?

A: Law requires cryonics patients to be legally dead, but this does not mean they are biologically dead. Under ideal conditions, cryonics can begin moments after the heart stops beating. Blood circulation and breathing are then artificially restored, keeping cells of the brain and the rest of the body biologically alive during the early stages of the procedure. The blood chemistry and blood gases (oxygen, carbon dioxide, pH) of a cryonics patient receiving good cardiopulmonary support are similar to those of a legally living person. Cryonics patients are therefore legally dead, but biologically alive, depending on how rapidly procedures are begun after the heart stops. . . .

Bobby-Jo Williams Ferrell filed suit in Florida state court to have her father's body cremated. Her two siblings opposed her request. The three children are Ted Williams' next of kin. Assuming that the applicable state law is similar to that described in *Newman*, which side should win the lawsuit? Suppose the three children simply disagreed on whether Williams' body should be buried or cremated; should that dispute be resolved in the same manner? Would the outcome be different if all three children agreed that Ted Williams' body should be cryogenically preserved but his will said that he wanted his body cremated? In December 2002, Ferrell and her siblings settled their lawsuit, without a court ruling on these questions. In exchange for dropping the suit, she received her one-third share of a $645,000 insurance policy immediately, 10 years earlier than originally scheduled.

6

Present Estates

A. INTRODUCTION

What is the legal basis for land ownership? Who originally owned the land? Who would own a given parcel of land if its present owners died without devising it to anyone? In England, after the Norman Conquest of 1066, the monarchy developed a complex (and self-serving) scheme of land ownership under which the monarch claimed to own the land. Other people were her tenants. It was a hierarchical system — a form of feudalism — with those in possession (or "seisin") of individual parcels of real estate holding those parcels as tenants of those above them in a pyramidal series of tenancies culminating in the monarch at its apex. During the seventeenth and eighteenth centuries, English settlers carried this system of land ownership to the British North American colonies, which would become the United States. It never fully took root in such a vast territory where seemingly limitless land appeared to lie beyond the western frontier. In the American Revolution of 1776-83, every state renounced the monarchy and its feudal system of land ownership. The states or "the people" — rather than the monarch — became sovereign. Nevertheless, elements of the old English system of real property ownership survived in the American states, both in substantive concepts and the terminology of property law. Learning that medieval terminology is a part of understanding the substance of modern American property law.

The Anglo-American system of land ownership is a remarkably intricate and (in some ways) beautiful creation. Like a work of fine art, it is an artificial human composition that imposes a reality on a space and, by doing so, gives that space meaning to us. It is a historical system developed by courts and legislatures over the centuries to serve evolving human needs. Although it is a logical system, it must be learned in order to be used and appreciated. One of its chief characteristics is that it is not only a spatial system (carving land ownership into geographical units), but it is also a temporal system (carving it over time). It recognizes both present estates and future interests in identifiable tracts of land. The owner of a present estate in land either actually possesses that land or has the present right to possess it. The owner of a future interest in land will or may have the right to possess that land in the future. This chapter deals with present estates; the next chapter deals with future interests.

Traditional English property law recognized four (and only four) basic types of present estates in land: the fee simple, the fee tail, the life estate, and the leasehold. The first three of these are called freehold estates because their tenants are "seized" of the land; the fourth is called a non-freehold estate because the landlord has seisin. The fee simple takes four forms: the fee simple absolute, the fee simple subject to condition subsequent, the fee simple determinable, and the fee simple subject to executory limitation. The fee tail is no longer used and will be only briefly noted in this chapter. The life estate takes two forms: an estate measured by the duration of the life of the owner of the tenancy, and an estate measured by the life of a third party. The leasehold takes four forms: the term of years, the periodic tenancy, the tenancy at will, and the tenancy at sufferance. These are the only kinds of present estates that exist; new kinds are not allowed. Each of them has a precise legal meaning. If the author of a deed or a will uses language that fails clearly to create one of these recognized estates, courts will interpret it as creating one of them and deal with the property accordingly. This can create traps for the unwary and disappointments for the ill-advised. With proper legal counsel, however, modern landowners can use these few types and form of estates to create a multitude of serviceable arrangements. The leasehold, in particular, has become a key feature of modern American property law, and is the subject of a subsequent chapter. The present chapter deals principally with four forms of the fee simple and the life estate. That will be enough.

■ IN RE O'CONNOR'S ESTATE
Supreme Court of Nebraska, 1934
252 N.W. 826

YEAGER, District Judge. This is an appeal by the state of Nebraska from the judgment of the district court for Adams county, Nebraska, in which county the estate of John O'Connor was probated. The estate escheated to the state of Nebraska for want of heirs. The county of Adams contends that the state is liable for the payment of an inheritance tax. This is the only question in the case. The county of Adams was successful in the action in district court and the state of Nebraska has appealed to this court.

It appears that this case must be determined on the true meaning of the term "escheat." In early England or during the feudal period, escheat meant the falling back or reversion of lands to the lord of the fee upon the failure of heirs capable of inheritance under the original grant. In both England and the United States now, by escheat is meant the lapsing or reverting to the crown or the state as the original and ultimate proprietor of real estate, by reason of a failure of persons legally entitled to hold the same.

Clearly the theory of the law in the United States, then, is that first and originally the state was the proprietor of all real property and last and ultimately will be its proprietor, and what is commonly termed ownership is in fact but tenancy, whose continuance is contingent upon legally recognized rights of tenure, transfer, and of succession in use and occupancy. When this tenancy expires or is exhausted by reason of the failure of the state or the law to recognize any person or persons in whom such tenancy can be continued, then the real estate reverts to and falls back upon its original and ultimate proprietor, or, in other words, escheats to the state.

This state has never departed from the accepted meaning and interpretation of escheat in the United States. In our first Constitution (Const. 1866, art. VI, sec. 3) it was provided: "All lands, the title to which shall fail from defect of heirs, shall revert or escheat to the people." This provision is no longer to be found in our Constitution, but in section 7, art. VII, escheat is recognized. Though the above quoted provision has been taken out of the Constitution, it has never been removed from the statutes, where it has remained unchanged since 1875. Section 76-501, Comp. St. 1929, being the provision referred to, is as follows: "Upon failure of heirs the title shall vest at once in the state, without an inquest or other proceedings in the nature of office found." It then becomes apparent that in this state by "escheat" is meant a reversion of title to the state upon failure of heirs.

Section 6622, Rev. St. 1913, contained the law providing for taxes upon inheritances. On account of its length we will not quote it here, but an analysis of its provisions clearly shows that what was intended was a tax upon a right of succession to property by inheritance, will, or by transfer made in contemplation of death, which is clearly distinguishable from a reversion, which can only take place where the title holder dies without will, without heirs, and without having made a transfer of the property in contemplation of death. . . .

. . . The judgment of the district court is reversed and the action dismissed.

Notes and Questions

1. This case involves *real property*, which traditionally means land and things that are permanent, fixed, and immovable attachments to land, such as buildings, timber, and mineral rights. All other property is personal property. This definition reflects the origins of property law terminology in medieval England, where land was the basis of wealth. In what way is land more "real" than a car or even a copyright? When does a trailer home become real property?

2. The *estate* of John O'Connor at issue in this case consisted of all the real and personal property in which O'Connor had a right or interest at the time of his death. In this sense, the word *estate* simply means what a person owns at any given time — it need not be grand or lordly; it can be quite modest. A person's house is his castle, no matter how humble. An *estate in land* constitutes a person's right or interest in a particular parcel of real property (or real estate). Derived from the medieval English term for status, the word *estate* harkens back to feudal times when a person's social standing came from the property that he or she owned. As such, it too reflects the feudal origins of the modern American system of property ownership. In twenty-first-century America, to what extent is one's status still measured by one's estate?

3. John O'Connor had no *heirs*. This term has a precise meaning at law. One's *heirs* are determined only at one's death. They are the relatives designated by state statute to receive a dead person's (or *decedent's*) property in the event that he dies without a valid will (or *intestate*). In every state, one's heirs are one's spouse and children (or their descendants). If no spouse or direct descendants survive the decedent, then (depending on state law) the decedent's heirs may include his or her parents, brothers and sisters (or their descendants), or uncles and aunts (or their descendants), typically in that order of priority. In feudal England, if someone died without heirs, his or her real estate *escheated* to the monarch or feudal lord. After all, the decedent was only a *tenant* on the land and owed service or other obligations to his feudal lord. Even though no American state retains the medieval system of estate *tenure* — opting instead for modern concepts of land ownership — they all maintain that when someone dies intestate and without heirs, his or her real estate escheats to the state. Why does real estate escheat to the state rather than to the United States? How is escheat different from inheritance?

4. Even though John O'Connor faced the prospect of dying without heirs, he need not have let his estate escheat to the state. He could have *conveyed* his real property by sale or gift at any time before he died. In either case, the transfer is called a *conveyance* and typically it is done by a written *deed*. Alternatively, he could have executed a valid *will* designating who or what entities would receive his estate upon his death. Those receiving real property under a *will* are called *devisees* (not heirs). Those receiving personal property (or a *legacy* or *bequest*) under a will are called *legatees* (again, not heirs). People typically use a *will* to *devise* real property and to *bequeath* personal property to specific family members, close friends, and valued institutions (such as churches, charitable organization, and law schools). Heirs only receive the property of a decedent that is not otherwise *devised* or *bequeathed*, which includes all the property for decedents dying intestate, though they are still called heirs even if they receive nothing. A decedent dies *testate* if he has a valid will. Most people die intestate. Why? When John O'Connor died, was there a transfer of his property to the State of Nebraska?

5. There may have been a good reason why John O'Connor chose to die without a will or an acknowledged heir, but no one will ever know. He was a reclusive shoemaker who moved to Adams County, Nebraska, claiming to have only 25¢ to his name. He never married and kept to himself. He died in 1913 possessing several farms, business buildings, mortgages, stocks, bonds, and bank accounts worth over $100,000, which was a significant estate at the time. During his lifetime, rumors spread that he had been part of the Jesse James gang, been a gold miner who had robbed and killed his partner, been an embezzler, or otherwise illegally gained his wealth. No one knew where he got his money but no one ever proved that he gained it wrongfully. When he died, over 100 people came forward claiming that they were his heirs at law or beneficiaries under his purported wills. None of these claims were proven, though by the time all of the resulting litigation was resolved, Adams County calculated that it had expended over $10,000 in jury fees alone. Throughout the period of this litigation, O'Connor's body remained unburied so that court officials could check it for identifying marks cited by claimants. On one occasion, for example, examiners

Photo of JOHN O'CONNOR
The Hastings recluse, taken 2½ years after death and 5 days before burial. Funeral was held at
LIVINGSTON BROS. CHAPEL HOME
HASTINGS, NEBR.
SEE OTHER SIDE

cut open one leg to see if it had ever been broken as one purported heir claimed. When O'Connor's body was finally buried in 1916, over 400 people attended the funeral service but only one person sent flowers. Bill Sole, *Who Was John O'Connor?*, Adams County Hist. News, June 1980, at 3-6.

6. The only known picture of O'Connor was taken over two years after he died, when two local undertakers — Albert and Walter Livingston — propped O'Connor's tuxedoed corpse between them for a photograph (reproduced at left). They used the picture in a card advertising their funeral parlor. Thinking back to the discussion in Chapter 1 of the right of publicity, should the Livingston brothers have obtained permission to use O'Connor's image in their advertising and, if so, who could give it after O'Connor's death?

7. In designating various persons for property law purposes, certain terms apply to groups of relatives. A person's lineal descendants — including children, grand-children, great-grandchildren, and so on down the line — are called his or her *issue*. They (along with one's spouse) come first under state statutes governing intestate inheritance. A person's lineal forebears — including parents, grandparents, great-grandparents, and so on up the line — are called his or her *ancestors*. They come second under state intestacy statutes. All other relatives — including brothers and sisters, uncles and aunts, nieces and nephews, and cousins — are called *collaterals*. State intestacy statutes differ on the treatment of collaterals, and whether remote collaterals are heirs at all. Why would a state cut off remote collaterals from inherit-ing property as heirs?

B. FEE SIMPLE ABSOLUTE

The fee simple absolute (usually just called "the fee simple") is the estate that most people associate with land ownership. It is the most "complete" estate in that it carries the greatest rights and has the fewest limits. The owner can keep it, convey it to another by sale or gift, or devise it by will. If not conveyed prior to death or devised by will, it passes to the owner's heirs. The fee simple absolute does not impose any conditions on how the owner uses the land. His ownership is "absolute" so far as the law allows. The traditional language for creating a fee simple absolute in a deed or will was "*O* to *A* and his [or her] heirs," where *O* symbolizes the grantor and *A* symbolizes the grantee. Following conventional practice, throughout this chapter we will use *O* to mean a grantor and *A* to mean a grantee. In this particular example, the words "to *A*" are called *words of purchase* and indicate who is receiving the estate. The words "and his [or her] heirs" are *words of limitation* or *words of inheritance*, and simply mean that the estate is inheritable by *A*'s heirs — that is, that it is a fee simple absolute rather than a life estate. They do not give *A*'s heirs any interest in the estate whatsoever except for the mere right to inherit it *if A* dies intestate while still owning it in fee simple absolute. Because the fee simple absolute has become the common form of complete land ownership, courts now generally recognize that it is created by the simple language "*O* to *A*," even without appending the words "and his [or her] heirs." Confusion can still arise when other words are included in a deed or will, as the following case illustrates.

■ ROBERTS v. RHODES

Supreme Court of Kansas, 1982
643 P.2d 116

FROMME, Justice. . . . The case concerns title to two small adjacent tracts of land deeded to a school more than 70 years ago to be used for school purposes but without reversion or other language of limitation in the deeds. The district court held that when these tracts were no longer used for school purposes, the tracts reverted to the heirs and assigns of the original grantors. On appeal the Court of Appeals reversed the decision of the district court and held the deeds conveyed fee simple title to the school district.

The school district sold the land in 1971. The defendants Rhodes acquired the tracts by mesne conveyances from the school district. The plaintiffs Roberts claim title to these tracts by deed from the heirs of the original grantors and by reversion, since the land is no longer used for school purposes. We will now look at the wording in the original deeds [made in 1902 and 1908]:

> ... D. W. Smith and Margaret Smith, husband and wife, ... "in consideration of the sum of One Dollar ($1.00), the receipt of which is hereby acknowledged, do by these presents, remise, release and quitclaim unto [School District No. 35 of Montgomery County, Kansas, its] *heirs and assigns,* all the following described Real Estate ... *it being understood that this grant is made only for school or cemetery purposes."* ... Emphasis supplied.

... As may be noted, the two deeds contain the ordinary verbiage of a quitclaim deed except for the following additional phrases:

> 1. ... [It] being understood that this grant is made only for school or cemetery purposes.
> 2. ... It being understood that this grant is made for school and cemetery purposes only.

Under the agreed statement of facts, the two tracts of land were accepted and used for school purposes for over sixty years. They were not used for cemetery purposes. The understanding that the grant was made "for school *or* cemetery purposes" in the first deed, and "for school *and* cemetery purposes" in the second deed was clearly expressed. However, the grants were used for school purposes. A school district is not legally authorized to operate a cemetery. The difficulty in construing the deeds arises from a failure of the parties to provide for what should happen to the land after it has been used for school purposes for sixty years and then is no longer needed for such purpose. In the case of the second deed, which provided the tract was to be used for school *and* cemetery purposes, there was no provision for reversion in case the tract was not used for cemetery purposes. Usually, if it is intended to limit the estate granted, some form of limitation over is required.

The general rule for creation of an estate in fee simple determinable is set forth in the *Restatement of Property* §44, p. 121 (1936) as follows:

> An estate in fee simple determinable is created by any limitation which, in an otherwise effective conveyance of land,
> (a) creates an estate in fee simple; and
> (b) provides that the estate shall automatically expire upon the occurrence of a stated event.

The difficulty here is that neither deed made provision for the estate to revert or terminate on the occurrence of any stated events.

The statutory direction as to what interest generally should pass by conveyance is set out in K.S.A. 58-2202 as follows:

> The term "heirs," or other words of inheritance, shall not be necessary to create or convey an estate in fee simple; and every conveyance of real estate shall pass all the estate of the grantor therein, unless the intent to pass a less estate shall expressly appear or be necessarily implied in the terms of the grant.

Where in the present conveyances to the school district can you find an intent to pass a less estate than one in fee simple? The conveyances run to heirs and assigns of the school district. It is true that it was understood by the parties that the grants were made for school purposes. It is also true that for over sixty years it was used for school purposes. The understanding under which these grants were made was fulfilled. In the absence of an intent to limit the title shown in the conveyance, either expressly or by necessary implication, the grantors pass all the interest they own in the real estate. The statute 58-2202 merely expresses the following accepted rules of real estate law. Forfeitures are not favored in the law. The general rule is well settled that the mere expression that property is to be used for a particular purpose will not in and of itself suffice to turn a fee simple into a determinable fee.

As pointed out in the Restatement, courts have in some cases recognized a special limitation on the interest conveyed which may cause the created interest to automatically expire upon the occurrence of a stated event. Words which are recognized as sufficient to express such automatic expiration include "until," "so long as," or "during," or those conveyances which contain a provision that "upon the happening of a stated event the land is to revert to the grantor." *Restatement of Property* §44, comment 1, p. 128. The conveyances in our present case contained none of these words limiting the period or term for which the grant was made.

It appears safe to say as a general rule the mere statement of the purposes of a conveyance will not limit the extent of the grant. . . .

The early Kansas case of Curtis v. Board of Education, 23 P. 98 (Kan. 1890), follows the general rule. The grantor conveyed property to School District No. 45 by warranty deed containing the provision "for the erection of a school-house thereon, and for no other purposes." *Id.* at 99. When this deed was challenged by the original grantor, this court as constituted in 1890 held an absolute estate in fee simple passed to the school district. *Curtis* has been followed by this court and remains the law in Kansas.

In Trego County v. Hays, 145 P. 847 (Kan. 1915), the deed there in controversy recited a part of the consideration to be "that the said county erect a building and maintain a county high school therein or revert to the original owner." *Id.* at 848. A building was erected at a cost of $28,000 in which a high school was maintained for several years. It was held that the school was established and maintained in good faith as a permanent institution. The condition for "permanent" location of a school was held to have been complied with by its maintenance for a reasonable period (11 years) and the grantors had no longer any interest in the property conveyed. . . .

In cases where the deed for school purposes contains a reversion clause providing that when the premises "shall fail to be used for school purposes" they should revert to the grantor, the grantors or their successors generally are held to be the owners on the discontinuance and abandonment of the tract for school purposes. Thompson v. Godfrey, 379 P.2d 269 (Kan. 1963); Rose v. School District No. 94, 179 P.2d 181 (Kan. 1947).

However, in Rose v. School District No. 94, when the original deed conveyed the premises on an express provision for reverter in event the premises are abandoned for school purposes, it was held the land reverted but the buildings never became a part of the real estate. In such case the buildings remained the property of the school district which retained the right to sell the same subject to removal by a purchaser. . . .

After considering all the foregoing cases and authorities we conclude under the facts and circumstances of this case a quitclaim deed from the owner of property to a named school district by which a small tract of land is remised, released and quitclaimed to the school district, its heirs, and assigns, by metes and bounds description, "it being understood that this grant is made only for school or cemetery purposes" and, without reversion or other language of limitation used, conveys fee simple title when the land has been accepted and used by the grantee for school purposes for more than sixty years.

Accordingly the judgment of the district court is reversed and the case is remanded with directions to enter judgment for the defendants. The judgment of the Court of Appeals is affirmed.

SCHROEDER, Chief Justice, and HERD, Justice, dissent.

Notes and Questions

1. The original deed in this case is from the Smiths, as grantors, to the School District and its heirs and *assigns*, as grantee. As noted above, this is standard language for creating a fee simple. Of course, a school district, as a government entity rather than a living person, could never have heirs. It could have assigns, however, which simply means anyone to whom it conveys the property. In this case, the defendant Rhodes was the School District's assigns. As noted in the decision, the terms "and heirs" or "its heirs and assigns," when used in this context, are "words of limitation" or "words of inheritance." The language, "unto School District No. 35 of Montgomery County, Kansas," constitutes "words of *purchase*." "Words of purchase" identify the grantee, and it does not matter whether the grantee acquires the estate by sale or by gift. As used in property law, purchase means the acquisition of real estate by any means except by inheritance. Although the deeds refer to consideration of one dollar, this is boilerplate language commonly used in deed forms. One cannot tell from the opinion whether the Smiths gave the tracts to the School District or sold them for their fair market value or for a lower price. Should the amount of consideration paid affect the interpretation of the deed as to the quality of the estate conveyed?

2. The Smiths *quitclaimed* two tracts to the School District. They did so by a quitclaim deed. Such a deed sometimes is used to convey property where there is doubt as to the validity of the grantor's title or authority to covey the tract. It also commonly is used in gift deeds where the grantor does not want to assume any further obligation with regard to the property. A quitclaim deed operates as a release that conveys the grantor's entire title, interest, or claim in the property to the grantee, but without warranting that such title is valid. Where the grantor is willing to assure the validity of his or her title, or the grantee insists on such an assurance, then the parties execute a *warranty* deed. By a warranty deed, a grantor promises to warrant and defend the grantee's title and possession of the estate against all legal challenges arising under the deed. Why might the Smiths have used a quitclaim deed to convey their two tracts to the School Board?

3. In *Roberts*, the court invokes widely accepted *rules of construction* (or interpretation) to resolve the meaning of an ambiguous deed. Courts generally proceed in this fashion when confronted with ambiguity, and doing so on a consistent basis helps to assure predictability and consistency in the law. For example, the court states, "Forfeitures are not favored in the law." It also quotes from a state statute: "Every conveyance of real estate shall pass all the estate of the grantor therein, unless the intent to pass a less estate shall expressly appear or be necessarily implied in the terms of the grant." It adds, "It appears safe to say as a general rule that mere

statement of the purposes of a conveyance will not limit the extent of the grant." Where the grantor of real estate held it in fee simple absolute prior to conveying it to a grantee, these well-established rules of construction support a holding that, unless the deed clearly states or implies otherwise, the grantor conveyed his entire interest in the property. Although the law recognizes defeasible fee estates, it clearly favors the fee simple absolute. Why?

4. Even though the fee simple absolute carries the greatest rights and has the fewest limitations of any estate in land known to the law, it is not limitless. As discussed in other chapters of this book, the rights of any landowner to use and enjoy her property is limited by the rights of others under nuisance law and by the police powers of the state. Further, a fee simple absolute (like other estates) may be encumbered by an easement, real covenant, equitable servitude, mortgage, or other interest in the property held by others. Nevertheless, the fee simple absolute provides the essential baseline of complete property ownership under modern American law.

5. Suppose that *O* holds a fee simple absolute interest in a parcel of real estate called Blackacre. Suppose further that *O* conveys Blackacre "to *A* and his heirs." If *A* has adult children who are his most likely heirs, could he sell Blackacre without obtaining their consent? Could *A* devise Blackacre to someone other than his heirs? If *A* dies intestate without a spouse or any children, would Blackacre escheat to the state?

C. FEE SIMPLE DEFEASIBLE

Some people like to retain an element of control over things even after they part with them. This can happen in the context of broken personal relationships, often with unfortunate consequences; it happens in the case of land sales as well, sometimes with unforeseen results. A homeowner may want his house to remain someone's home, for example, or a retiring farmer may want her farm to become a permanent park. Alternatively, a property owner might be willing to donate her land for building a neighborhood school but want the option of regaining the land if the school is ever closed. Certainly, the property owners in *Roberts* indicated concern that their land be used as a school or cemetery, but they did not express their concern in a way that made it legally binding on later landowners. The common law did develop estates that carried such limits or conditions, however. They are called "defeasible estates," and remain widely used today.

Three types of defeasible estates exist — each of which will or may terminate upon the happening of a future event: the fee simple subject to condition subsequent, the fee simple determinable, and the fee simple subject to executory limitation. As the preceding decisions suggest, the law does not favor any limits or conditions on estates, in part because they restrict the present use and future development of land. Although no precise language is required to create a defeasible estate (such as one for school purposes or another as a memorial hospital), the deed or will conveying or devising the property must clearly express such an intent — and certain time-honored language is helpful toward that end. This language differs depending on the type of defeasible estate desired. The following three cases deal with disputed but ultimately successful efforts to create defeasible estates, one of each type. As such, these cases illustrate how such estates can be created and operate. If the deed or will had been clearer at the outset, however, perhaps a lawsuit could have been avoided.

(handwritten: On Call!)

■ LAWYERS TRUST COMPANY v. CITY OF HOUSTON

Supreme Court of Texas, 1962
359 S.W.2d 887

(handwritten margin note: W.T. Carter Lumber & Building Co)

SMITH, Justice. This is a trespass to try title suit [filed against the City of Houston and R.N. Ferguson. The trial court granted judgment for plaintiff, but the Court of Civil Appeals reversed]. On the 12th day of August, 1926, W. T. Carter Lumber & Building Company executed an instrument [that] plotted . . . several tracts . . . into lots and blocks, to be known as "Garden Villas." The instrument, subject to certain reservations, dedicated unto the public certain described portions of such tracts for park and other purposes [as follows]:

(handwritten margin note: Portions of the land for parks)

> If, on or after the expiration of twenty-five (25) years from date hereof, any tract or tracts dedicated for parks, civic centers, schools or community places as shown on said plat, cease to be used for the purpose or purposes indicated thereon, the fee title to any such tract or tracts shall vest and be in W. T. Carter Lumber & Building Company. . . .

(handwritten margin note: 25 years -> any of that land not being used for said purpose reverts back to Building Co.)

. . . The land involved here was designated on the map or plat as Park No. 1 and was used by the public for park purposes from the date of dedication through the year 1944. The city limits of Houston were extended in 1949 so as to include Park No. 1.

The record shows that sometime in the middle 1930's Mr. Ferguson was placed on the park property as an employee of the W. T. Carter Lumber & Building Company. The reason for this was that the residents of Garden Villas were complaining that the park was being used for improper purposes. As an accommodation to the public, Mr. Ferguson was placed on the property partly to police the same. In this connection, we point out that at no time after the execution of the deed of dedication was W. T. Carter Lumber & Building Company under a duty to furnish police protection to the public.

In 1947 the W. T. Carter Lumber & Building Company conveyed to the Carter Investment Company all of its rights to the property. Thereafter, in 1957, the Carter Investment Company conveyed to the Lawyers Trust Company its interest in the property. Although Ferguson continued to live on the property from 1947 until the time of his death in 1959, he was never at any time an employee of either the Carter Investment Company or the Lawyers Trust Company.

(handwritten margin note: fee Simple Determinable)

Park No. 1 tract, taken from existing Garden Villas Park, Nov. 2007

Lawyers Trust Company contends that a [fee simple determinable] was created by the deed of dedication and that consequently upon cessation of use of the property for park purposes on and after August 12, 1951, the estate created by the deed of dedication automatically terminated. . . .

The City contends that the language of the deed of dedication conclusively shows that a condition subsequent was created, but that a forfeiture resulting from the breach of the condition subsequent was waived. . . .

It is a cardinal rule in determining from the language of deeds whether [a fee simple determinable] or a condition subsequent was intended by the parties that the instrument as a whole must be considered. Stevens v. Galveston H. & S. A. Ry., 212 S.W. 639 (Tex. Comm. App. 1919). The pertinent provision of the deed before us begins with the word "if," a word of art which traditionally has been held to create a condition subsequent. By this we do not mean that by use of the word "if" a condition subsequent is created as a matter of law. We mention it merely as one portion of the deed which must be considered and given effect. It is a rather strong indication that the parties intended a condition subsequent. However, we do not treat its import as conclusive. When we turn to other language in the deed of dedication, we find that provision that the property "shall vest and be in" the grantor in the event the property is not used for its designated purpose. The quoted language seems to provide that the estate will terminate automatically and that it will revest immediately upon the occurrence of the stated contingency. It seems to foreclose the necessity of a re-entry on the part of the grantor in order to terminate the estate. This unmistakably indicates a [fee simple determinable]. But, here again, such indication is not conclusive. Similar language in other conveyances of this character has not been held to be prohibitive of the creation of a condition subsequent. Stevens, supra.

It is well settled that when there is doubt from the entire language of the instrument whether its fair construction imports a [fee simple determinable] or a condition subsequent the doubt must be resolved in favor of the latter as being in a sense less onerous upon the grantee in that, under such a construction, the estate does not terminate automatically with the occurrence of the stated contingency, but only after re-entry or its equivalent is made by the grantor. Stevens, supra.

. . . Therefore, in accordance with the above-mentioned constructional preference, we are led to the conclusion that a condition subsequent was created by the terms of the deed.

The Court of Civil Appeals has held that "the evidence is without dispute that the property had ceased to be used for park purposes since about 1944." The City does not contend that the property was used for park purposes at any time after 1944.

Although we do not agree with Lawyers Trust in its contention that the language of the deed of dedication created a [fee simple determinable] and that the fee simple title automatically vested in W. T. Carter Lumber & Building Company, we do agree that as of August 12, 1951, the Carter Investment Company, the then owner of the title, had the right of re-entry by virtue of the broken condition, and that right was acquired by the Lawyers Trust Company by virtue of the deed to it as grantee executed in October, 1957 by the Carter Investment Company. This right of re-entry was properly exercised by Lawyers Trust by the filing of this suit in 1959. Therefore, Lawyers Trust is entitled to recover the title to Park No. 1, the property involved in this suit, unless we conclude to sustain in City in either of its contentions of waiver and estoppel or that because of the acts and conduct of Ferguson it was excused from using the park after the condition had been broken. We do not agree with either contention.

With regard to the latter of these two contentions, it should be remembered that at no time after the execution of its deed of dedication until August 12, 1951, did the Carter Lumber & Building Company have any right or duty to put Mr. Ferguson, or anyone else, on the park property. They had by their deed of dedication divested themselves of any possessory interest. Consequently, Mr. Ferguson was at best a tenant at sufferance and as such could have been removed at any time by proper proceedings instituted by the county or city authorities. . . .

On the question of waiver, the City argues the delay of seven and one-half years before suit was filed effected a waiver of the right of re-entry. In effect, the City is saying that a grantor may lose his right to claim a forfeiture for breach of a condition subsequent merely because of lapse of time between the breach of a condition subsequent and the time of re-entry. . . .

A waiver of a breach of a condition subsequent may be presumed after a reasonable lapse of time has occurred without any assertion of right by the grantor under the condition. But . . . it is incumbent upon the grantee to allege and prove such lapse of time. Waiver is a question of fact, and whether in any particular case there is a waiver is a matter of intention on the part of the grantor, to be ascertained from his acts and all the attendant circumstances of the case. Waiver of the right to claim a forfeiture has not been established as a matter of law. Granting, without deciding, that the evidence in the present case presented an issue of fact on the question of whether the grantor waived his right to claim a forfeiture, the issue was the City's issue and it waived the issue by failing to request and obtain a submission of it to the jury.

It is true that delay in exercising the right of re-entry coupled with proof that the grantee was misled by such delay and as a result changed his position by making improvements on the property or investing money in it, then it can be said that the grantor has waived his right of re-entry and is estopped from asserting his claim of the right of forfeiture. There is no evidence of any act on the part of the grantor or its grantees, Carter Investment Company and Lawyers Trust, which could be calculated to mislead the City, nor is there any evidence that the City has changed its position on the strength of the failure to file suit prior to February, 1959. . . .

The judgment of the Court of Civil Appeals is reversed and that of the trial court is affirmed.

Handwritten margin note: Waiver is a question of fact & City waived the issue by failing to submit to a jury.

Notes and Questions

1. The court in *Lawyers Trust* found that the language of the original grant created a fee simple subject to *condition subsequent*, which some courts call a *fee simple on condition subsequent*. Like the fee simple absolute, a fee simple subject to condition subsequent can last indefinitely. Unlike the fee simple absolute, its continuance is tied to a condition subsequent (or condition that may arise later). The triggering condition may involve the performance or failure to perform a particular act (such as using land for park purposes) or the occurrence of a future event. If the condition is triggered, then the grantor has the right to terminate the estate. The grantor's future interest is called a *right of entry* or sometimes, as in *Lawyers Trust*, a *right of re-entry*. If the right is not exercised or enforced, the estate continues uninterrupted. The estate does not end automatically upon the triggering of the condition. Although in most states a right of entry may be conveyed or devised to someone else after it exists, it must be created initially in the grantor (or, if by a will, in the grantor's estate). Why does the court describe a fee simple subject to condition subsequent as less onerous than a defeasible fee simple that ends automatically upon the happening of a triggering limitation? Which type of estate is less likely

to terminate? Because courts view the fee simple subject to condition subsequent as less onerous than the fee simple determinable (where the estate ends automatically upon the triggering of the limitation), when in doubt as to which of these two estates is created by a deed or will, they favor the former. This is a standard rule of construction. Of course, as noted earlier, courts favor the fee simple absolute over any type of defeasible fee.

2. Although the *Lawyers Trust* court ultimately held that the language in the grant created a fee simple subject to condition subsequent, this conclusion was far from obvious. The court's goal is to find the original intent of the parties. To avoid any doubt, the will or deed simply could have stated that it created a fee simple subject to condition subsequent, and then identified the condition. Most commonly, the intent to create a fee simple subject to condition subsequent is expressed by inserting explicit language of condition in the deed as an afterthought, such as by qualifying the grant with words like "but if," "provided that," "on condition that," or "however." The quoted provision in the *Lawyers Trust* deed does this, tersely and somewhat elliptically, by beginning a new sentence in the deed with the word "If." The provision then creates ambiguity when it goes on to provide that if any tract "cease to be used" for park purposes "the fee title . . . shall vest and be in [the grantor]." Faced with this ambiguity, the court invokes the rule of construction stated in Note 1 to conclude that the grant creates a fee simple subject to condition subsequent rather than a fee simple determinable.

■ MAYOR AND CITY COUNCIL OF OCEAN CITY v. TABER
Court of Appeals of Maryland, 1977
367 A.2d 1233

ORTH, Judge. This appeal concerns the ownership of an improved lot of ground at the northwest corner of Atlantic Avenue and Caroline Street in Ocean City, Maryland, which was occupied and used by the United States of America as a Life Saving Station for almost a hundred years. At the hub of the controversy is whether the United States acquired title in fee simple absolute through adverse possession or lost all its right, title, interest and estate in the property by realization of a possibility of reverter.

The relevant record title to the property devolves through three conveyances: 1) a deed dated 28 July 1876 from Stephen Taber and wife to Hillary R. Pitts, Benjamin Jones Taylor and George W. Purnell, Trustees (the Trustees) . . . (the 1876 deed); 2) a deed dated 11 September 1878 from the Trustees to the United States of America . . . (the 1878 deed); 3) a deed dated 23 June 1967 from the United States of America to the Mayor and City Council of Ocean City . . . (the 1967 deed). . . .

On 15 January 1869 Stephen Taber and Hepburn S. Benson obtained a patent from the State of Maryland. The patent . . . gave Taber and Benson "The Lady's Resort to the Ocean," a 280 acre tract of land along the Atlantic Ocean in Worcester County. Taber acquired Benson's interest by deed dated 9 October 1871. . . .

Stephen Taber created Ocean City, "desirous," as he explained in the 1876 deed, "of conforming to the views and general public sentiment of the people of Worcester and the adjacent counties in their desire to establish a place as a sea-side Summer Resort and the promotion of the growth of the same." Fifty acres of "The Lady's Resort to the Sea," with his acquiescence and approval, were "laid off into a town, with lots, streets and avenues, as is called and known as Ocean City," and he granted the fifty acres to the Trustees by the deed of 1876, appending a plat of the proposed town. The terms of the trust were set out in the habendum clause. The Trustees were to hold the property

> upon trust, that they or their successors shall convey the same, with as little delay as practicable, at the expense of the grantee or grantees named in the deeds in lots as they are described on said plate and according to their numbers; to such persons as draw the same at a distribution of said lots, made by the Stockholders of the Atlantic Hotel Company at the Atlantic Hotel at Ocean City on the thirty first day of August Eighteen Hundred and Seventy Five. And if there are any lots remaining which are not drawn at the aforesaid distribution, then and in that event, the said trustees or their successors are hereby authorized and empowered to sell and convey the same to such persons as they think proper or to make any other disposition of said lots they think proper and appropriate the proceeds thereof in such manner as they shall deem most advantageous to the interest of said Ocean City.

> . . . .

The deed of 1878 conveyed a part of lot no. 3 to the United States of America. . . . The deed declared that lot no. 3 had not been drawn in the distribution and that a part thereof had been sold to the United States by the Trustees for the sum of one dollar. . . . The habendum clause reads:

> to have and to hold the said lot of land and privileges, unto the United States from this date for the purpose aforesaid. And it is further stipulated, that when the United States shall fail to use the said Life Saving Station, the land hereby conveyed for the purpose aforesaid, shall, without any legal proceedings, suit or otherwise, revert to the said Trustees, their successors and assigns, absolutely, and they shall be entitled to re-enter upon and take possession thereof free from all encumbrances of every nature or kind.

The deed was signed and acknowledged by the Trustees and signed by the Secretary of the Treasury.

The 1967 deed was designated a "Quitclaim Deed." The United States of America was "Grantor," and the Mayor and City Council of Ocean City, Maryland, was "Grantee." . . . The deed expressly declared that it was "executed and delivered to the Grantee without representations, warranties or covenants, either express or implied." . . .

Postcard of the Ocean City Life Saving Station

On 17 July 1973 an equity action for a declaratory judgment was instituted in the Circuit Court for Worcester County by Thomas T. Taber, Jr., *et alii* (appellees) against the Mayor and City Council of Ocean City (appellant), *et alii.* [The Circuit Court granted summary judgment for appellees.] . . .

Appellant would have the 1878 deed be ineffective. Thus, it reasons, the United States, and appellant through privity of estate, would have acquired legal title to the property by adverse possession.

The 1878 deed, on its face, was a valid conveyance by the Trustees to the United States of an estate in fee simple determinable of a part of lot no. 3. It would be ineffective only if the Trustees had no power to make the conveyance. . . .

The 1878 deed conveyed an estate in fee simple determinable. Such an estate has been long recognized in Maryland. The estate is discussed in 1 H. T. Tiffany, *The Law of Real Property* §220 (3rd ed. B. Jones 1939):

> An estate in fee simple determinable, sometimes referred to as a base or a qualified fee, is created by any limitation which, in an otherwise effective conveyance of land, creates an estate in fee simple and provides that the estate shall automatically expire upon the occurrence of a stated event. . . .
>
> If one who has an estate in fee simple creates a determinable fee in favor of another, he has thereafter merely a possibility of re-acquiring the land by reason of the occurrence of the contingency named or indicated, this possibility being known as a possibility of reverter.
>
> . . . .

What the United States acquired in the property was a determinable fee and nothing more. Of course, the United States had the power to convey what it owned. . . . This it did by the 1967 deed, which remised, released and forever quitclaimed any and all right, title and interest which it had and on an "as is, where is" basis. The United States expressly made no warranties or covenants with reference to the property. The most that appellant acquired from the United States [from] the 1967 deed was a determinable fee, subject to the liability to termination set out in the 1878 deed. The trial judge "specifically" found that the 1967 deed established "the fact that the United States of America, as of that date, did 'fail to use the said Life Saving Station.'" This finding was not clearly erroneous. Maryland Rule 886. It is ironic that evidence of the occurrence of the event terminating the estate was supplied by delivery of the 1967 deed conveying the determinable fee. The estate in fee simple determinable having terminated, the property reverted, and appellant was left with no right, title, interest or estate whatsoever. . . .

Appellant's . . . adverse possession [claim is] predicated upon the 1876 deed being void and the 1878 deed being ineffective. As we have found that both stood valid as far as the subject property was concerned, the possession of the United States was not hostile to the true owner, and it occupied the property, not under color of title, but under good legal title. . . .

We note that, as the 1878 deed was in full force and effect, the statutory period for adverse possession would not start to run until 23 June 1967, the date of the occurrence of the event terminating the estate of fee simple determinable as found by the trial judge. . . .

Appellant asks if the appellees are "estopped from asserting a claim to the premises under the theories of estoppel, waiver or laches?" In the circumstances, it is patent that they are not. . . . It was not necessary for appellees to assert a claim to the fee simple absolute estate or to take any other positive action. They acquired a fee simple absolute estate by the realization of the possibility of reverter.

Judgment affirmed; costs to be paid by appellant.

Notes and Questions

1. The court in *Ocean City* found that the language of the 1878 deed created a fee simple *determinable.* Like the fee simple subject to condition subsequent, the fee simple determinable can last indefinitely. Also like the fee simple subject to condition subsequent, its continuance is tied to the performance of, or failure to perform, a particular act (such as using the property as a Life Saving Station) or the occurrence of a future event (such as closing the Life Saving Station) — called a *limitation.* A fee simple determinable differs from a fee simple subject to condition subsequent in one key respect. If the limitation is triggered, then an estate in fee simple determinable automatically ends without any action by the grantor or any other person. The retained future interest is called a *possibility of reverter.* As between a fee simple determinable and a fee simple subject to condition subsequent, why might a grantor prefer the former? Why might a grantee prefer the latter?

2. The *granting* clause of the 1878 deed conveys a part of lot no. 3 to the United States "for the purpose of a Life Saving Station. . . ." As the court in *Roberts* held, such language standing alone, although suggestive of a defeasible fee, usually is insufficient to create one. In this case, however, the ambiguity in the granting clause (which normally would be construed in favor of a fee simple absolute) is resolved by language in the *habendum* clause. A deed typically has both a granting clause, which describes the estate being created and the property being conveyed, and a habendum clause, which more specifically defines the extent of the grantee's estate. A standard habendum clause (like the one in this case) begins with the phrase "to have and to hold." Most commonly, the intent to create a fee simple determinable is expressed in a granting clause by describing the triggering act or event as a temporal limit on the estate's duration, such as by using words like "so long as," "during," "while," or "until." For example, to create a fee simple determinable, the granting clause of the deed in *Roberts* could have conveyed the tract "to the school district so long as used for school or cemetery purposes." Note that the limitation is stated as part of the description of *A*'s estate without any intervening punctuation mark. Such phrasing is not necessary to create a fee simple determinable, but it helps to communicate the intention of creating one. In *Ocean City*, this temporal limitation is expressed by the habendum clause stating that "when the United States shall fail to use the said Life Saving Station, the land hereby conveyed for the purpose aforesaid, shall, without any legal proceedings, suit or otherwise, revert to the [grantors], their successors and assigns, absolutely. . . ." A cautious drafter could have expressed the limitation in both clauses, and specifically have stated that the deed created a fee simple determinable.

3. This case involves one of the country's earliest planned beachfront vacation communities, Ocean City, Maryland. The deed in question dates from the late nineteenth century, when Americans in large numbers first began swimming in the ocean for recreational purposes. To accommodate the new sport, the federal government (which had long been active in ocean rescue) began building and staffing lifesaving stations at popular beaches, a service now more commonly provided by state and local governments. The developers of Ocean City probably donated the prime waterfront lot to the federal government. Why would they choose to do this? Is it reasonable to assume that this conveyance would only be for so long as the government maintained a lifesaving station on the lot? Given this

temporal limitation, when the United States stopped maintaining lifesaving stations, why did it convey its interest in the lot by a quitclaim deed rather than by a warranty deed? Suppose the United States had conveyed the lot to Ocean City for use as a municipal life saving station; would the lot have automatically reverted to the grantees?

■ **CITY OF PALM SPRINGS v. LIVING DESERT RESERVE**
Court of Appeals of California, 1999
82 Cal. Rptr. 2d 859

McKINSTER, Justice. Not infrequently, wealthy individuals, intending both to promote the common weal and to memorialize themselves, give property to a city on the condition that it be used in perpetuity for some specified purpose. With disturbing regularity, however, the city soon tires of using the donated property for the purpose to which it agreed when it accepted the gift, and instead seeks to convert the property to some other use. In this case, for instance, the City of Palm Springs ("City") built a golf course on 30 acres of donated property which it had accepted in 1986 on the express condition that it be used in perpetuity as a desert wildlife preserve. The trial court reluctantly approved. We reverse.

FACTUAL AND PROCEDURAL BACKGROUND

In June of 1986, . . . the McCallum Desert Foundation ("Foundation") . . . executed a grant deed ("Deed"), conveying 30 acres of land ("Land") to the City. The Deed provides:

> THIS DEED IS MADE AND ACCEPTED ON THE EXPRESS CONDITION that the land hereby conveyed be used solely as the site of the McCALLUM DESERT PRESERVE AND EQUESTRIAN CENTER, and that grantee, its successors or assigns shall forever use the land and premises for the purpose of maintaining a public park for the exposition of desert fauna and flora, named as the McCALLUM DESERT PRESERVE AND EQUESTRIAN CENTER. In the event that the property is not used solely and perpetually as the site of the McCALLUM DESERT PRESERVE AND EQUESTRIAN CENTER, then the interest in the land and premises herein conveyed shall pass to the Living Desert Reserve, Palm Desert, California, and grantee shall forfeit all rights thereto.

The City expressly accepted the grant in October of 1986. Less than three years later, however, the City decided that it would rather build a golf course on the Land. Believing that the golf course would be inconsistent with the condition in the Deed, the City asked the Living Desert for permission to buy other property for use as a preserve instead of the Land. Those negotiations continued periodically without success. The City's final offer was made in November of 1992, when it offered to buy the Living Desert's reversionary interest in the Land for $200,000 and threatened to take the interest by eminent domain if the Living Desert did not agree.

After the Living Desert declined that offer, the City adopted a resolution of necessity by which it found that the public health, safety and welfare required the acquisition of the Living Desert's reversionary interest in the

Land for the purpose of expanding the City's municipal golf course. In March of 1993, the City filed a complaint in eminent domain by which it sought to do so. . . .

. . . Living Desert cross-complained against the City to quiet title to the Land. It alleged that, as a result of the City's breach of the conditions and the notice of that breach, the fee-simple interest of the City in the Land had reverted to the Living Desert. . . .

At the beginning of trial, the City moved for judgment on the pleadings. The trial court granted the motion as to the cross-complaint, finding that the interest of the Living Desert is measured as of the date the complaint in eminent domain was filed, that as of that date the City had not yet changed the use of the Land or otherwise violated the Deed, and that the Living Desert therefore owned only a reversionary interest, not the fee title to the Land. . . . Following an evidentiary bench trial, the trial court issued a statement of decision in which it ruled that the reversionary interest was not a compensable interest and hence no payment was due to the Living Desert, and entered judgment in favor of the City. The Living Desert appeals. The Attorney General of the State of California appears as an amicus curiae. . . .

Challenging the assumptions under which the case was tried below, the Attorney General contends that the Foundation gave the Land to the City in a charitable trust, not in fee simple subject to a condition subsequent, that the effect of the judgment was to terminate that trust, and that therefore the judgment must be reversed because the trial court lacked subject matter jurisdiction to terminate a charitable trust. In its reply brief, the Living Desert adopts the Attorney General's argument as an alternative analysis.

Discussion

The Attorney General raises a fundamental issue: What is the nature of the interests created by the Deed? The Deed obviously does not convey the Land to the City in fee simple absolute. But was the Land given to the City in trust, or in fee simple subject to a condition subsequent?

"A charitable trust is a fiduciary relationship with respect to property arising as a result of a manifestation of an intention to create it, and subjecting the person by whom the property is held to equitable duties to deal with the property for a charitable purpose." Rest. 2d, Trusts, §348, p. 210. The elements essential to its creation are a proper manifestation by the settlor of an intention to create a trust, a trust res, and a charitable purpose promoting the welfare of mankind or the public at large, of a community, or of some other class of persons which is indefinite as to numbers and individual identities.

The legal title of the res or corpus of any trust is held by the trustee, but the beneficiaries own the equitable estate or beneficial interest. In the event of a breach of duty by the trustee of a private trust, the beneficiaries may sue the trustee for damages and for an equitable decree enforcing the trust. But because a charitable trust has an indefinite class of beneficiaries, standing to enforce the trust is generally limited to the Attorney General as the representative of the public.

"However, a gift may have a charitable purpose and yet not constitute a charitable trust." Schaeffer v. Newberry, 50 N.W.2d 477, 480 (Minn. 1951). Rather than create a trust, the owner of property may transfer it to another on the condition that if the latter should fail to perform a specified act the transferee's interest shall be forfeited either to the transferor or to a designated third party. "In such a case the interest of the transferee is subject to a condition subsequent[4] and is not held in trust." Rest. 2d, Trusts, §11, com. a, p. 32.

A gift of property in fee subject to a condition subsequent differs from a gift of that same property in trust in at least two ways. First, the transferee of a conditional gift receives both legal and equitable title to the property. Unless and until the transferee breaches the conditions imposed by the transferor, he or she is in the same position as an owner in fee simple absolute. Second, the transferee has no enforceable duties. The breach of condition may result in the termination of the transferee's interest, but it does not subject the transferee to actions for damages or to enforce the condition.

"Whether a trust or a condition is created depends upon the manifested intention of the transferor; the mere fact that the word 'condition' is used does not necessarily indicate that a condition and not a trust is intended." Rest. 2d, Trusts, §11, com. c, pp. 32-33. Trusts can be created by words of condition. Property given "upon condition" that it be applied to certain charitable purposes is especially likely to be construed as having been given in a charitable trust. The question in each case is whether (1) the donor intended to provide that if the property were not used for the designated charitable purposes it should revert either to the donor's estate or to a contingent donee, or (2) the donor intended to impose an enforceable obligation on the donees to devote it to those purposes.

The Deed expressly states the Foundation's intent that, in the event of a breach of the condition, the transferee (City) shall forfeit its interest in favor of a third party (the Living Desert). Accordingly, the Deed must be construed as granting to the City a fee simple subject to a condition subsequent, and assigning to the Living Desert a power of termination. . . .

The general rule in California is that, when a condemnor takes property the ownership of which is split into an estate in fee simple subject to a condition subsequent and a power of termination, the owner of the future interest is not entitled to any compensation unless the condition has been breached as of the date of valuation. If no such breach has yet occurred, then the possibility of a reversion is too remote and speculative to be valued, and the reversionary interest is deemed to be valueless for purposes of condemnation.

However, the general rule denying compensation to the holder of the reversionary interest applies only "in the absence of exceptional circumstances. . . ." People ex rel. Dept. of Public Works v. City of Fresno, 26 Cal. Rptr. 853, 862 (Cal. App. 1962). One of the exceptions is that the reversionary interest is compensable if the reversion would have been likely to occur within a reasonably short time. . . .

Although we have found no California case involving similar facts, the Supreme Court of Texas has addressed that precise issue on a substantially identical factual

---

4. Under the common law, there were [three] types of defeasible estates: a fee simple determinable, the reversionary interest of which was the possibility of reverter; a fee simple subject to a condition subsequent, the reversionary interest of which was the right of re-entry[; and a fee simple subject to an executory limitation, the reversionary interest of which was the executory interest]. The distinctions between these [three] defeasible estates were statutorily abolished [in California] by the adoption of Civil Code section 885.020 in 1982. All defeasible fees are now known as fees simple subject to a condition subsequent, and all executory interests reserved by the grantor after granting such fees are known as powers of termination.

record. . . . The Texas Supreme Court held that when the purpose of taking the future interest was to permit the holder of the present interest to use the property in a manner which violates the conditions under which the present interest was given to the condemner, the violation of those conditions is imminent and the taking is compensable. The court explained that any other result would be contrary to public policy. "To allow a governmental entity, as grantee in a gift deed, to condemn the grantor's reversionary interest by paying only nominal damages would have a negative impact on gifts of real property to charities and governmental entities. It would discourage these types of gifts in the future. This is not in the best interests of the citizens of this State." Leeco Gas & Oil Co. v. Nueces County, 736 S.W.2d 629, 631 (Tex. 1987). . . . That policy of enforcing the donor's charitable intent . . . is totally inconsistent with a rule which would permit a public entity receiving a conditional gift to destroy the condition through condemnation without compensation to the holder of the reversionary interest. . . .

Had the condition been violated before the City commenced its condemnation action, the measure of compensation payable to the Living Desert would have been the fair market value of an estate in fee simple absolute. The violation here had not yet occurred when this action was filed but was reasonably imminent. . . . Under that circumstance, the trial court should apply the same measure of compensation to determine the value of Living Desert's power of termination, *i.e.*, 100 percent of the value of the unrestricted fee in the Land. . . .

DISPOSITION

That portion of the judgment ruling in favor of the City on the Living Desert's cross-complaint to quiet title is affirmed. That portion ruling in favor of the City on its complaint in eminent domain is reversed, and the trial court is directed that the Living Desert's power of termination is compensable. The matter is remanded to the trial court to determine the compensation due, in accordance with the views expressed in this opinion. The Living Desert Reserve shall recover its costs on appeal.

Notes and Questions

1. As noted in the court's footnote above, the state of California has, by statute, merged the three traditional common law defeasible estates into one, and called it the fee simple subject to condition subsequent. What public policy does this merger serve? Under the common law in most states, the deed in *Palm Springs* (as interpreted by the court) would create a fee simple *subject to executory limitation*. Like the other defeasible fee simple estates, the fee simple subject to executory limitation can last indefinitely. Also like them, its continuance is tied to the performance of a particular act (such as using the property as a desert preserve) or the occurrence of a future event (such as converting the desert preserve into a watered golf course). Like the fee simple determinable, if the triggering act or event occurs, then the estate automatically terminates. Unlike the fee simple determinable, however, the triggering event operates to cut short the preceding estate, rather than follow its natural expiration. If the event takes place, then the present estate shifts from the initial grantee (or her heirs or assigns) to a designated alternative grantee (or her heirs or assigns) — in this case, from the city to Living Desert Reserve. At the outset,

the alternative grantee is said to hold an *executory interest,* which becomes a possessory estate if the triggering event occurs. Why might some grantors of a determinable fee prefer having the property shift to a particular third party rather than having it revert to themselves or their heirs? In this context, for example, consider situations like this case, where the grantor wants the property permanently maintained as a desert preserve.

2. No particular language is required to create a fee simple subject to executory limitation. In this case, the deed uses conditional language like that found in a deed creating a fee simple subject to condition subsequent, but adds that, if the condition is triggered, then the property passes to an alternative grantee. (Note the words "express condition" and "in the event that.") Classic language of this type might read, "to *A* and her heirs, but if the property is no longer used as a desert park, to *B* and her heirs." Unlike a fee simple subject to condition subsequent, however, the transfer happens automatically. Under the common law, it was not permitted to create a defeasible estate (akin to the fee simple subject to condition subsequent) where the elective right of entry or power of termination was held from its inception by a third party. Of course, as this case states, that is permitted in California under the statutory reform merging the three traditional defeasible fee simple estates into a single fee simple subject to condition subsequent.

3. In this case, the city threatened to use its power of *eminent domain* to *condemn* the Living Desert's executory interest in the property. Using its eminent domain authority, a government or governmental entity may force a private landowner to sell her property to it for a public purpose. The government must pay fair market value for the property. The process is called *condemnation.* It happens everywhere — though the process varies to some extent from state to state. Complications can arise when the condemned property has multiple owners, such as in this case where there is both a present estate (the city's defeasible fee simple) and a future interest (the Living Desert's executory interest). In theory, each owner should receive the fair market value of her estate or interest, with the total compensation for all equal to the value of the fee simple absolute. Consider a hypothetical case: *A* holds property in fee simple determinable so long as it is used for residential purposes; *O* holds the possibility of reverter in fee simple absolute. The state condemns the property to build a road. *A* could receive whatever amount of money the property would command on the open market as a residence. *O* could receive any added amount that the property would command on the open market for unlimited uses. In California and some other states, the future interests associated with determinable estates are deemed to be too remote to have any value — at least until the future interest is triggered. Is this reasoning justified? Even if such a result is fair in the hypothetical case, why would it be unfair in *Palm Springs*? Eminent domain is discussed more fully in Chapter 14.

4. This case raises the issue of property held in *charitable trust.* The Attorney General argues that the grantor transferred the property to the city in trust as a public desert preserve and equestrian center. Under such an interpretation of the deed, the city would hold legal title to the property, but it would be obligated to manage it for public benefit within the terms of the trust. Because such a trust is designed to benefit a class of individuals or the public generally, it is called a charitable trust. A charitable trust differs from a *private trust* in that its beneficiaries are uncertain and it typically is enforced by some public officer, such as the Attorney General in this case. Although a grantor may offer, and the trustee may accept, property in trust — the deed must express such an intent. Without clear language,

courts will not assume limits on the grantee's ownership of property. The deed in this case says nothing explicit about conveying the property in trust or creating a charitable trust. Its phrasing suggests a fee simple subject to executory limitation. We deal with trusts more in Swanson v. Swanson, in Chapter 7.

D. FEE TAIL

The fee tail is a relic of medieval English property law that has no practical significance today. At most, modern American property lawyers only need to know the term and the words used to create one in case they ever appear in a deed or will, or to understand a current statute that abolishes the fee tail. Dynastic-minded medieval landowners created the fee tail as a means to ensure that estates would stay within families, and not be sold or lost by later descendants. If *O* conveys land in fee tail to *A*, then at *A*'s death the land passes directly to his issue (or next lineal descendants). Those descendants then hold the land in fee tail for their issue, and so on until the line dies out, at which time the land reverts to *O* or *O*'s heirs in fee simple absolute. The classic language for creating a fee tail was, "*O* to *A* and the heirs of his body." Although suited to medieval England, the fee tail severely restricted the sale and development of land. It never found favor in America, and gradually disappeared from use in the states where it once existed. In most American states, the words that in medieval England would have created a fee tail now create a fee simple absolute. A few states preserve the fee tail for a single generation, creating in effect a life estate in the initial grantee, but if that grantee has issue, then they receive the estate in fee simple absolute. A few other states preserve the fee tail in form but allow the grantee (or any subsequent tenant in tail) to convert it into a fee simple absolute. Today, landowners wishing to convey only lifetime use or possession of property typically create a life estate.

E. LIFE ESTATE

The life estate is the oldest surviving form of property ownership in the Anglo-American legal system. Although it is no longer the most common form of land ownership, it remains widely used because it still serves people's needs. This requires some explanation. Most often, when people transfer property, they do so "forever" in fee simple absolute. (Defeasible fee simple estates are comparatively rare and the fee tail estate is obsolete.) Yet no individual grantee, devisee, or heir actually owns property forever. At most, people own property for a lifetime — and doing so is their immediate concern. Holding property in fee simple absolute allows its owner to convey it freely or pass it to her devisees or heirs, but often this is a secondary concern to lifetime possession and use. Further, some dynastic-minded grantors want control over who receives their property in future generations. For example, the family matriarch may want her children to receive the proceeds from certain income-producing property during their lives, but want the property itself preserved for her grandchildren. Alternatively, a husband may want his second wife to remain in the family home after his death, but then have the house go to the children of his first marriage after her death. The desire to impose such lifetime limits on property is common, particularly for intra-family transfers. A life estate can help realize them. Most life estates are created by gift, devise, or bequest — few people buy (or sell) life estates. Often, life estates are held in trust, with trustees managing the property for beneficiaries who receive the income from it for life. In the United States, property worth hundreds of billions of dollars currently is held in trusts for life — making the life estate a vibrant feature of modern American property law. With or without a trust, as the following cases illustrate, tensions can arise between the life tenant and those holding a future interest in the property.

■ **WHITE v. BROWN**
Supreme Court of Tennessee, 1977
559 S.W.2d 938

BROCK, Justice. This is a suit for the construction of a will. The Chancellor held that the will passed a life estate, but not the remainder, in certain realty, leaving the remainder to pass by inheritance to the testatrix's heirs at law. The Court of Appeals affirmed.

Mrs. Jessie Lide died on February 15, 1973, leaving a holographic will which, in its entirety, reads as follows:

> April 19, 1972
> I, Jessie Lide, being in sound mind declare this to be my last will and testament. I appoint my niece Sandra White Perry to be the executrix of my estate. I wish Evelyn White to have my home to live in and *not* to be *sold*.
> I also leave my personal property to Sandra White Perry. My house is <u>not</u> to be <u>sold</u>.
>   Jessie Lide
>   [Underscoring by testatrix]

Mrs. Lide was a widow and had no children. Although she had nine brothers and sisters, only two sisters residing in Ohio survived her. These two sisters quitclaimed any interest they might have in the residence to Mrs. White. The nieces and nephews of the testatrix, her heirs at law, are defendants in this action.

Mrs. White, her husband, who was the testatrix's brother, and her daughter, Sandra White Perry, lived with Mrs. Lide as a family for some twenty-five years. After Sandra married in 1969 and Mrs. White's husband died in 1971, Evelyn White continued to live with Mrs. Lide until Mrs. Lide's death in 1973 at age 88.

Mrs. White, joined by her daughter as executrix, filed this action to obtain construction of the will, alleging that she is vested with a fee simple title to the home. The defendants contend that the will conveyed only a life estate to Mrs. White, leaving the remainder to go to them under our laws of intestate succession. The Chancellor held that the will unambiguously conveyed only a life interest in the home to Mrs. White and refused to consider extrinsic evidence concerning Mrs. Lide's relationship with her surviving relatives. Due to the debilitated condition of the property and in accordance with the desire of all parties, the Chancellor ordered the property sold with the proceeds distributed in designated shares among the beneficiaries.

I.

Our cases have repeatedly acknowledged that the intention of the testator is to be ascertained from the language of the entire instrument when read in the light of surrounding circumstances. But, the practical difficulty in this case, as in so many other cases involving wills drafted by lay persons, is that the words chosen by the testatrix are not specific enough to clearly state her intent. Thus, in our opinion, it is not clear whether Mrs. Lide intended to convey a life estate in the home to Mrs. White, leaving the remainder interest to descend by operation of law, or a fee interest with a restraint on alienation. Moreover, the will might even be read as conveying a fee interest subject to a condition subsequent (Mrs. White's failure to live in the home).

In such ambiguous cases it is obvious that rules of construction, always yielding to the cardinal rule of the testator's intent, must be employed as auxiliary aids in the courts' endeavor to ascertain the testator's intent.

In 1851 our General Assembly enacted two such statutes of construction, thereby creating a statutory presumption against partial intestacy.

Chapter 33 of the Public Acts of 1851 (now codified as T.C.A. §§64-101 and 64-501) reversed the common law presumption[1] that a life estate was intended unless the intent to pass a fee simple was clearly expressed in the instrument. T.C.A. §64-501 provides: "Every grant or devise of real estate, or any interest therein, shall pass all the estate or interest of the grantor or devisor, unless the intent to pass a less estate or interest shall appear by express terms, or be necessarily implied in the terms of the instrument."

Chapter 180, Section 2 of the Public Acts of 1851 (now codified as T.C.A. §32-301) was specifically directed to the operation of a devise. In relevant part, T.C.A. §32-301 provides: "A will . . . shall convey all the real estate belonging to [the testator] or in which he had any interest at his decease, unless a contrary intention appear by its words and context."

Thus, under our law, unless the "words and context" of Mrs. Lide's will clearly evidence her intention to convey only a life estate to Mrs. White, the will should be construed as passing the home to Mrs. White in fee. "If the expression in the will is doubtful, the doubt is resolved against the limitation and in favor of the absolute estate." Meacham v. Graham, 39 S.W. 12, 15 (Tenn. 1897). . . .

II.

Thus, if the sole question for our determination were whether the will's conveyance of the home to Mrs. White "to live in" gave her a life interest or a fee in the home, a conclusion favoring the absolute estate would be clearly required. The question, however, is complicated somewhat by the caveat contained in the will that the home is "not to be sold" — a restriction conflicting with the free alienation of property, one of the most significant incidents of fee ownership. We must determine, therefore, whether Mrs. Lide's will, when taken as a whole, clearly evidences her intent to convey only a life estate in her home to Mrs. White.

---

1. Because the feudal lord granted land solely as compensation for personal services, the grant was for no longer than the life of the grantee. Later the grant was extended to the sons and other issue of the grantee under the designation of "heirs." Heirs were thus entitled to stand in the place of their ancestor after his death if mentioned in the grant — but only if specifically mentioned. Thereafter, the word "heirs," when used in a conveyance to a man "and his heirs," came to include collateral as well as lineal heirs, ultimately indicating that such grantee took an estate which would pass to his heirs or the heirs of anyone to whom he aliened it. That is, "heirs" ceased to be a word of purchase and became a word of limitation. I Tiffany, *Real Property* §28 (3d ed. 1939).

Under ordinary circumstances a person makes a will to dispose of his or her entire estate. If, therefore, a will is susceptible of two constructions, by one of which the testator disposes of the whole of his estate and by the other of which he disposes of only a part of his estate, dying intestate as to the remainder, this Court has always preferred that construction which disposes of the whole of the testator's estate if that construction is reasonable and consistent with the general scope and provisions of the will. A construction which results in partial intestacy will not be adopted unless such intention clearly appears. It has been said that the courts will prefer any reasonable construction or any construction which does not do violence to a testator's language, to a construction which results in partial intestacy. . . .

In our opinion, testatrix's apparent testamentary restraint on the alienation of the home devised to Mrs. White does not evidence such a clear intent to pass only a life estate as is sufficient to overcome the law's strong presumption that a fee simple interest was conveyed.

Accordingly, we conclude that Mrs. Lide's will passed a fee simple absolute in the home to Mrs. White. Her attempted restraint on alienation must be declared void as inconsistent with the incidents and nature of the estate devised and contrary to public policy.

The decrees of the Court of Appeals and the trial court are reversed and the cause is remanded to the chancery court for such further proceedings as may be necessary, consistent with this opinion. Costs are taxed against appellees.

HARBISON, Justice, dissenting. With deference to the views of the majority, and recognizing the principles of law contained in the majority opinion, I am unable to agree that the language of the will of Mrs. Lide did or was intended to convey a fee simple interest in her residence to her sister-in-law, Mrs. Evelyn White.

The testatrix expressed the wish that Mrs. White was "to have my home to live in and *not* to be *sold*." The emphasis is that of the testatrix, and her desire that Mrs. White was not to have an unlimited estate in the property was reiterated in the last sentence of the will, to wit: "My house is not to be sold." . . .

The will does not seem to me to be particularly ambiguous, and like the Chancellor and the Court of Appeals, I am of the opinion that the testatrix gave Mrs. White a life estate only, and that upon the death of Mrs. White the remainder will pass to the heirs at law of the testatrix. . . . [T]he testatrix knew how to make an outright gift, if desired. She left all of her personal property to her niece without restraint or limitation. As to her sister-in-law, however, she merely wished the latter have her house "to live in," and expressly withheld from her any power of sale.

The majority opinion holds that the testatrix violated a rule of law by attempting to restrict the power of the donee to dispose of the real estate. Only by thus striking a portion of the will, and holding it inoperative, is the conclusion reached that an unlimited estate resulted.

In my opinion, this interpretation conflicts more greatly with the apparent intention of the testatrix than did the conclusion of the courts below, limiting the gift to Mrs. White to a life estate. I have serious doubt that the testatrix intended to create any illegal restraint on alienation or to violate any other rules of law. It seems to me that she rather emphatically intended to provide that her sister-in-law was not to be able to sell the house during the lifetime of the latter — a result which is both legal and consistent with the creation of a life estate.

In my opinion the judgment of the courts below was correct and I would affirm.

Notes and Questions

1. As its name implies, a life estate lasts only so long as the grantee (or *life tenant*) lives. Upon the life tenant's death, the property automatically *reverts* to the original grantor or shifts to a designated successor grantee (traditionally called a *remainderman*). Thus, every life estate is paired with a future interest — either a *reversion* in the grantor or a *remainder* in a successor grantee. Textbook language for creating the former type of life estate is "*O* to *A* for life." Textbook language for creating the latter type of life estate is "*O* to *A* for life, then to *B* and her heirs." Life tenants possess their property until their death, but they cannot pass it to their devisees or heirs. They may convey the property during their lifetime, but their grantee will only possess it so long as the original life tenant lives. When a life estate is transferred to another, it is called a life estate *pur autre vie*, from old French words meaning "for another's life." An estate *pur autre vie* can also be created directly at the inception, without a subsequent transfer: for example, "*O* to *A* for the life of *B*." Why would anyone want a life estate measured on someone else's life?

2. The lawsuit in *White* arose over ambiguous language in Jessie Lide's will. In construing Lide's will, the *White* court stressed that its ultimate object was to carry out the testator's intent. Of course, courts construing the meaning of ambiguous deeds also seek to effectuate the parties' intent — but there are at least two parties to a deed, the grantor and the grantee, and they may have conflicting intents (certainly, they have conflicting interests). A will has but one testator, which simplifies the process of resolving intent and, as a practical matter, makes that intent all the more determinative. Nevertheless, as the court notes, the testator's intent can still be elusive. If Jessie Lide had written, "I wish Evelyn White to have my home for life," then the will clearly would have devised a life estate. Ambiguity comes from her use of the words "to live in" rather than "for life." What is the difference?

3. In this case, as in *Roberts*, the court invoked generally accepted rules of construction favoring the fee simple absolute over lesser estates. When in doubt, a will or deed is presumed to devise or convey the largest possible estate — in this case, a fee simple absolute rather than a life estate. Further, in construing a will, it is presumed that the testator intends to devise or bequeath all of her property. Are these presumptions valid? In this case, if Jessie Lide only devised a life estate in her home to Evelyn White, then she would have died intestate with respect to the reversion or remainder interest in her real property.

4. According to the court, the emphatic provision in Jessie Lide's will that her home is "*not* to be *sold*" raised a separate issue from that of whether the will created a fee simple absolute or a life estate. It is in the very nature of an estate held in fee simple absolute that it can be transferred by its owner. Courts disfavor *restraints on alienation* because they make property unmarketable and hinder its exploitation. Restraints on alienation take many forms. Some are partial in that they discourage or delay the transfer of property, such as by requiring prior approval or limiting the pool of buyers. Others are absolute in that they prohibit its transfer altogether. The restriction in *White* is an absolute *disabling restraint* because it bars the grantee from selling her interest in the property. Disabling and other absolute restraints placed on fee simple property are void. Courts differ concerning the treatment of partial restraints placed on fee simple property and on absolute or partial restraints placed on lesser estates, depending on their reasonableness in a given situation. As the dissenting judge stated, the restraint in *White* might not be incompatible with a life

estate. Under the common law, a life tenant of property must preserve it for those who hold the reversion or remainder interest. Typically, a life tenant can convey her life interest in property, however, and thereby pass along the duty of preserving it to her grantee. Most courts hold that an absolute disabling restraint on a life estate is void. Is the restraint in Lide's will persuasive evidence that she intended to create a life estate?

■ **WILLIAMS v. ESTATE OF WILLIAMS**
Supreme Court of Tennessee, 1993
865 S.W.2d 3

REID, Chief Justice. This suit seeks the construction of the last will and testament of G. A. Williams, deceased, and the declaration of the rights of the parties in a tract of land described in the will. . . .

The only facts alleged are that G. A. Williams died on November 17, 1944, the instrument attached to the complaint is a copy of his last will and testament, the farm mentioned in the will is located in McMinn County, and, inferentially, the farm was owned by the testator at the time of his death. . . . The testator was survived by nine children, including the three daughters named in the will. The plaintiff, Ethel Williams, who was 92 years of age when the complaint was filed, is the only survivor of the three children named in the will. The defendant Etta Tallent is the only other surviving child of the testator, and the other defendants are lineal descendants of the testator. Ethel Williams has maintained possession of the farm since the death of the testator, jointly with Ida Williams and Mallie Williams until their deaths. Apparently none of the three named daughters ever married, though that fact does not affirmatively appear.

The will is as follows:

I, G.A. WILLIAMS, being of sound mind make this my last will and Testament: At my death I want Ida Williams, Mallie Williams, and Ethel Williams, three of my daughters to have my home farm where I now live, consisting of one hundred and eighty-eight acres, to have and to hold during their lives, and not to be sold during their lifetime. If any of them marry their interest ceases and the ones that remain single have full control of same. I am making this will because they have stayed at home and taken care of the home and cared for their mother during her sickness, and I do not want them sold out of a home. If any one tries to contest this will I want them debarred from any interest in my estate. /s/ G.A. Williams, July the 18, 1933.

The [answer] alleged that the interest received by Ethel Williams was a life estate under the will or, in the alternative, a life estate under the will and a "remainder interest" by intestate succession. The latter disposition was adopted by the Chancellor initially, but on rehearing was abandoned for the finding that the devise of a life estate without limitation over indicated an intention that the named daughters have the property in fee simple, which is the position asserted by Ethel Williams on appeal.

The Court of Appeals affirmed the holding of the trial court. It held, on the authority of White v. Brown, 559 S.W.2d 938 (Tenn. 1977), that each named daughter owned a one-third undivided interest in fee simple. The record does not support that decision.

The function of a suit to construe a will is to ascertain and effect the intention of the testator. The determinative intention is the predominant purpose expressed by the testator in the will. . . .

In the case before the Court, the predominant intention of the testator is clear. Each of the testator's three daughters who had "stayed home" was to have the farm jointly with the other two daughters, so long as they were living and unmarried, as a residence and for their support; after the death or marriage of any of the three daughters, the remaining two daughters would hold jointly until the marriage or death of another; and the remaining unmarried daughter was to hold until she married or died. The statements that the farm was "not to be sold during their lifetime" and "I do not want them sold out of a home" emphasized and re-enforced the predominant intention that each of the three daughters have a residence and support during her life or until she should marry. The testator's statement that he was favoring those children above the others because they had "stayed at home and taken care of . . . their mother" implicitly recognized that each had foregone the opportunity to become self-supporting or be supported by a husband, and limiting the duration of the devise to such time as a daughter should marry, indicates that the devise was intended to be a substitute for support that might otherwise have been available.

The intention of the testator was not to make an absolute gift to all or either of the daughters. The first statement in the will limits the devise "during their lives." The next statement limits the devise to the duration of their unmarried state. The testator devised to the daughters an interest not readily alienable and one that could not be defeated by a suit for partition or sale for partition. His reason for selecting the estate devised is indicated by the statements "not to be sold during their lifetime" and "I do not want them sold out of a home." Upon the death or marriage of the named daughters, the testator's purpose as to them would have been accomplished and the testator's heirs would inherit the property by intestate succession.

The testator recognized that his other heirs would acquire some interest in the property upon his death. The primary emphasis was that the daughters' limited interests not be disturbed by the owners of the interest not devised to the daughters. The severity of his admonition is shown by the provision that any person who should "contest" the will would be "debarred" from any interest, not just in the farm but in his estate.

This case is not controlled by White v. Brown, relied upon by the Court of Appeals. In that case, the following provision was found to constitute the devise of a fee simple: ". . . I wish Evelyn White to have my home to live in and *not* to be *sold*. I also leave my personal property to Sandra White Perry. My house is not to be sold." 559 S.W.2d at 938. The majority in *White* based its decision on that portion of what is now T.C.A. §32-3-101 (1984), which provides: "A will . . . shall convey all the real estate belonging to [the testator], or in which he had any interest at his decease, unless a contrary intention appear by its words in context." However, in language applicable to the case before the Court, Justice Harbison, dissenting, stated:

> I have serious doubt that the testatrix intended to create any illegal restraint on alienation or to violate any other rules of law. It seems to me that she rather emphatically intended to provide that her sister-in-law was not to be able to sell the house during the lifetime of the latter — a result which is both legal and consistent with the creation of a life estate.

Id. at 942. That statute does not control the disposition in the case before the Court because, as discussed above, a contrary intention appears from the will. The provision that each daughter's interest would terminate upon her marriage, as well as upon her death, is a further indication that the testator did not intend for the named daughters to have an absolute estate in the farm. . . . Consequently, the estate devised to the named daughters was less than a fee simple.

Upon the death of the testator, each named daughter held a life estate, defeasible . . . upon her marriage. Each daughter also had an executory interest in each of the other two daughters' one-third interest, which would vest in her possession if the other life tenant should die or marry while she remained unmarried. The heirs-at-law of the testator held a reversion in fee simple, subject to the . . . life estates and the executory interests in the named daughters, which reversion would vest in possession, at the latest, upon the death of the survivor of the named daughters.

The judgment of the Court of Appeals is reversed, and the case is remanded for further proceedings.

Notes and Questions

1. Fortuitously, both *White* and *Williams* were decided by the Tennessee Supreme Court. In *White*, the court found that the phrase "to live in" created a fee simple absolute. In *Williams*, it found that the phrase "to have and to hold during their lives" created a life estate. What is the difference between these two phrases?

2. Every life estate must be paired with a reversion or remainder. What future interest is the life estate in *Williams* paired with? This is tricky. When there are multiple life tenants, there are three possibilities as to what happens when one life tenant dies:

- Life estate lasts until the last life tenant dies; the share of each survivor increasing by means of a remainder.
- Life estate lasts until the last life tenant dies; the share of the deceased life tenant passing through her estate.
- An estate for joint lives; the life estate ending when the first life tenant dies.

Which of the three possibilities did the will in *Williams* create? Absent language specifying otherwise, the first of these options is generally favored because it passes the greatest interest to the life tenant. Applied in this case, each of the three unmarried, stay-at-home sisters held a one-third life estate in the family farm. Each of these life estates was paired with a mix of remainders and reversions. Assuming that none of them ever married, when the first sister died, her one-third life estate triggered a remainder *for life* in her two surviving sisters. Thereafter, each of these two sisters held a one-half life estate in the family farm. When the second sister died, her one-half life estate triggered a remainder for life in the last surviving sister, Ethel Williams. Thereafter, Ethel held the entire life estate in the family farm. When Ethel dies, the property will revert to G. A. Williams' estate and thus pass to his heirs. Do you understand why? Who are G. A.'s heirs?

3. The genius of the Anglo-American system of present estates and future interests lies in its functional complexity. There are only a few types of present

estates and future interests, but they can be combined in a rich variety of ways, as exemplified by this case. G. A. Williams' will provided that each sister's interest would terminate upon her marriage (as well as upon her death) in which event her interest would automatically shift to her surviving, unmarried sisters. Thus, under the will, each sister held her life estate in the family farm subject to executory limitation and each of them also held an executory interest for life in the life estates of her two sisters. Defeasible limitations do not only apply to the fee simple, but can be appended to life and leasehold estates as well.

4. The present estates and future interests in *Williams* are further complicated by the fact that, under the will, G. A. Williams' farm would automatically revert to G. A.'s estate (and therefore to G. A.'s heirs) upon the marriage (as well as the death) of all of the three stay-at-home sisters. Because this reversion could occur before the normal end of the life estate, the three sisters hold a defeasible life estate (which is also, and separately, subject to executory limitations). Do you understand why? G. A. Williams may not have known that he created such a complex array of estates and interests with his brief, four-sentence-long will — but that appears to have been his intent. The court was able to carry out G. A.'s apparent intent by using a combination of traditional present estates and future interests.

5. The *Williams* court states that none of the three stay-at-home sisters ever married. Restraints on marriage are a common type of conditional gift, usually imposed by men and directed to women. Probably, they are employed less today than they once were. Suppose Ethel or one of her sisters had wanted to marry. Is it proper that she would lose her interest in the farm? Modern law sometimes invalidates marriage restraints. *Restatement (Second) of Property, Donative Transfers* §6.1 (1983), provides:

> (1) Except as stated in subsection (2), an otherwise effective restriction in a donative transfer which is designed to prevent the acquisition or retention of an interest in property by the transferee in the event of any first marriage of the transferee is invalid. If the restriction is invalid, the donative transfer takes effect as though the restriction had not been imposed.
>
> (2) If the dominant motive of the transferor is to provide support until marriage, the restraint is normally valid.

The comment to the Restatement section explains:

> [A marriage restraint imposes] an economic sanction . . . upon the transferee in the form of a penalty for failure to comply with the wishes of the transferor. . . . The invalidation stated in this section results from the unwillingness to penalize the transferee for the transferee's failure to respect the socially undesirable attempt of the transferor to use a disposition of property as a means of coercing abstention from marriage. This antisocial character is absent only when the dominant motive of the transferor is found to have been the provision of support until marriage. Under such circumstances, the exception stated in subsection (2) applies to validate the restraint.

When it comes to remarriages, the Restatement is more lenient. Conditions imposed on the donor's widow or widower are per se valid, regardless of motive. *Id.* §6.3. Why should this be? Conditions imposed by other donors on remarriage are valid if reasonable under all the circumstances. *Id.*

■ MATTESON v. WALSH

Appeals Court of Massachusetts, 2011
947 N.E.2d 44

FECTEAU, Justice. This is a cross appeal from a Superior Court judgment that entered following a bench trial on an action for waste to real property in the town of Chatham (town). The plaintiff, Elizabeth Gay Matteson, brought this action as a holder of a remainder interest against her brother, Robert L. Walsh, a life tenant. The judge concluded that Walsh's failure to pay the property taxes constituted waste, essentially because his failure to do so endangered the remaindermen's interest. The judge also determined that substantial deterioration of the property had occurred by Walsh's neglect of the property amounting to waste and injuring the remainder interest, and causing Matteson to make substantial payments to repair. The total monetary award to Matteson was about $65,000 (to reimburse her for approximately $12,000 in real estate taxes she paid plus approximately $53,000 in repair costs). The judge terminated Walsh's life estate and entered an order that title was to be held by Matteson, Walsh, and their sister Catherine T. Baisly as tenants in common. We affirm in part and reverse in part.

BACKGROUND

The judge found the following facts, which neither party disputes as plainly wrong. The property was inherited by Dorothy G. Walsh, the testator and the parties' mother in 1961; she devised it in her 1977 will to Walsh, as life tenant, and thereafter to Matteson, Baisly, and the heirs of Walsh.[2] The mother died in 1987, and Walsh, who had already been living on the property since 1962, continued to reside there. The property has been in the Walsh family for several generations, is slightly less than one-half acre, and is improved by three buildings: a home, first constructed in 1858, as well as a summer cottage and an unattached garage, both built in approximately 1900. The home contains two "apartments," with Walsh living on the first floor and the other rented out on a year-round basis; the cottage is also rented out on a seasonal basis. Walsh collected and kept all the rents.

Commencing in about 2004, for reasons unexplained, Walsh simply stopped paying taxes and water bills, resulting in the town's issuance of a notice of tax-taking in 2005. He also stopped maintaining the residences, and they fell into disrepair. Upon learning of the notice of tax-taking, Matteson and Baisly stepped in and paid the delinquent 2004 and 2005 taxes of approximately $8,000, $6,000 of which Walsh repaid. Walsh, however, failed to pay taxes for the next three years, and Matteson again satisfied those taxes in an amount of about $13,000. Walsh did not reimburse her for any of these subsequent payments. Matteson also paid the water bills,[3] and she hired a "fix it up" man to repair the premises, which were apparently in

---

2. The first clause of the simple, three-clause will of Dorothy Walsh states:

I devise my house at 61 School Street, Chatham, Barnstable County, Massachusetts, to my son, ROBERT L. WALSH, for his life provided he survives me for thirty (30) days, and in the event he does not so survive me or at his death, the remainder is to be divided in three (3) equal shares between the heirs of the said ROBERT L. WALSH, ELIZABETH G. MATTESON of Old Queen Anne Road, Chatham, Barnstable County, Massachusetts, and CATHERINE T. BAISLY of Morris Island Road, Chatham, Barnstable County, Massachusetts, or their heirs by right of representation.

3. The judge did not find that Walsh's nonpayment of water and insurance bills constituted waste. Matteson does not appeal from that portion of the judge's decision.

considerable distress.[4] The total cost for these repairs came to about $120,000. Residing at the premises, Walsh was aware of these ongoing repairs and he made no objection, did not order the repair man to leave, and did not reimburse Matteson. Eventually, Matteson brought this action against Walsh for waste.

The judge found that Walsh had committed waste with respect to the nonpayment of taxes resulting in a tax-taking by the town and that Walsh had committed waste with respect to the deterioration of the buildings. While he did not itemize the particular aspects of the disrepair that he held to have constituted "substantial injury," the judge stated that his finding was made after review of all the evidence, which included the testimony of Walsh, Matteson, and Matteson's carpenter, and documentary evidence that included photographs and itemized bills paid by Matteson; the judge found that approximately $53,000 of the $120,000 paid by Matteson was necessary for repair of the property. Implicit in this finding was

that the amount ordered to be repaid by Walsh was for the repair of substantial structural items, many of which Walsh himself had listed on a maintenance priority list that he gave to Matteson indicating that repairs were needed soon or as soon as possible. The evidence showed that there were many parts of all three buildings that were open to the weather and not watertight, resulting in structural rot.

Walsh Family Home Prior to Repairs in 2006

DISCUSSION

1. Waste

Matteson brought this action against Walsh pursuant to the provisions of G.L. c. 242, §1, which states, in relevant part, that "[i]f a tenant in dower, by the curtesy, for life or for years commits or suffers waste on the land so held, the person having the next immediate estate of inheritance may have an action of waste against such tenant to recover the place wasted and the amount of the damage." Waste has been defined as "an unreasonable or improper use, abuse, mismanagement, or omission of duty touching real estate by one rightfully in possession, which results in its substantial injury." Delano v. Smith, 92 N.E. 500, 501 (Mass. 1910). In *Delano*, the court further defined waste as "the violation of an obligation to treat the premises in such manner that no harm be done to them and that the estate may revert to those having an underlying interest undeteriorated by any wilful or negligent act." Referring to its historical application, the *Delano* court noted "waste" frequently was used "in an agricultural sense, where it means a damaging use not in accordance with good husbandry. . . . It generally consists in some definite physical injury. This is shown by reference to the earlier definitions, as for instance that of Blackstone, who calls it a 'spoil or destruction in houses, gardens, trees and other corporeal

---

4. The work for which Matteson paid also consisted of external repair of the grounds, referred to as landscaping; the judge did not find that such constituted waste.

hereditaments.'" *Id.* Walsh argues that his actions in failing to pay taxes and in failing to maintain the buildings does not amount to waste resulting in substantial injury to the interest of the remainder. We disagree.

a. Taxes

Walsh committed waste by failing to pay the taxes on the property, which resulted in a taking by the town. Walsh contends that a life tenant may not be held liable for waste for "merely" failing to pay property taxes, at least where, as in this case, the property has not actually been taken and sold. This is incorrect.

The town in fact issued a notice of taking. It is true that the town never actually seized the property and sold it; however, implicit in the judge's findings was that this step was not taken due only to Matteson having stepped in, paying the taxes then overdue, and satisfying that debt. . . . Permitting the real estate taxes assessed to the property to remain unpaid to the point that the taxing authority records a tax-taking amounts to waste.

b. Damage to property

Walsh committed waste by failing to maintain the property. . . .

While there appears to be no evidence that Walsh affirmatively destroyed or removed anything from the property, the judge found a degree of neglect that amounted to severe and substantial deterioration against the right of the remainder interest that amounts to waste. The judge determined that about half of Matteson's repair expenses constituted damages for waste. The judge's decision to award Matteson damages representing approximately $53,000 for the amount of significant structural repair necessitated by Walsh's neglect, and to reimburse Matteson for her payment of taxes was likewise amply supported by the evidence and within the authority of the governing statute.

2. Relief

Matteson complains in her cross appeal that the judge erred by granting Walsh a fee interest in common after having ordered divestment of his life interest. . . . Matteson's essential argument is that because the devising instrument specifies that [Matteson, Baisly, and] Walsh's "heirs" are to take upon termination of Walsh's life estate, and because Walsh has no "heirs" other than his two sisters, the fee interest should now pass to Matteson and Baisly, alone, as tenants in common. Walsh, unsurprisingly, contends that the judge's ruling was correct in this respect. . . .

The judge's decision to grant Walsh a one-third undivided interest in the property in common with his sisters under the will] is . . . incorrect and cannot stand. The property passes instead to the holders of the remainder interest following termination of the life estate. Nor can Walsh be granted an interest under the remainder interest as a place-holder for his heirs, as yet unascertained, contrary to his contention and the ruling by the judge.

Such contention involves the issue as to what point in time Walsh's heirs are to be ascertained. . . . It appears that one reason the judge granted a remainder interest to Walsh was that his heirs could not be ascertained until his death. Historically, heirs were determined at the date of death of either the testator or the life tenant, depending on the governing life. In this case, the governing life would be that of Robert Walsh. However, . . . a change in the rule was effectuated, for instruments created after January 1, 1965, such as the will at issue here, by virtue of G.L. c. 184, §6A, inserted by St. 1964, c. 307, §1, which states:

> In a limitation of real or personal property to a class described as the "heirs" or "next of kin" of a person, or described by words of similar import, to take effect in enjoyment upon the happening of an event within the period of the rule against perpetuities, the class shall, unless a contrary intention appears by the instrument creating such limitation, be determined as if such person died at the time of the happening of the event.

This statute has been interpreted to have created a presumption that heirs are to be determined as of the date of distribution, unless contra-indicated by the governing document. *See* 2 Belknap, *Newhall's Settlement of Estates and Fiduciary Law in Massachusetts* §33.57, at 433 (5th ed. 1997). Therefore, given the divestment of the life estate by the judge by operation of G.L. c. 242, §1, under which the remainder interests are to "recover the place wasted," and by operation of G.L. c. 184, §6A, such a judgment (the grant of recovery of the real property by the remainder interests) results in the vesting of the remainder interest as it is an "event" that terminates the life estate. Accordingly, "distribution" is required as of the date of such recovery. This outcome is consistent with the general rule of law that favors vested over contingent interests. Thus, according to this latter statute, the remainder interests must be determined as of the date of recovery under c. 242, §1, the statute of waste.

We also note from the record that Matteson and Baisly appear to be Walsh's only heirs, but as there was no definitive finding that such was the case as of the date of the termination of Walsh's life estate, a remand is necessary to ascertain the heirs in whom the remainder interests have vested.

So much of the judgment that grants an interest in common in the property at issue to Walsh is to be vacated; that portion of the judgment that grants a one-third undivided interest in the property in common to each of Matteson and Baisly is affirmed. The case is remanded for further proceedings consistent with this opinion, to identify the "heirs of Robert Walsh," and to grant such heirs an interest in the remaining one-third of the property.

Notes and Questions

1. Even though no one owns property for longer than a lifetime, fee-simple owners have an economic interest in preserving and protecting their property because they can convey or devise it to others beyond their lifetimes. In short, they can reap its future value through a present sale. Life tenants, in contrast, cannot sell the future value of the property beyond their own life expectancy. Thus, they have no innate economic interest in preserving the property beyond their lifetimes and may have an economic interest in affirmatively stripping it of value. The resulting acts or failures to act, while reasonable for the life tenant, may unreasonably harm the holders of the remainder interest. Common law judges developed the *doctrine of waste* to address this situation. For example, a life tenant may have an economic incentive to strip forest land of its valuable timber without replanting it or remove and sell valuable copper pipes from a building and replace them with inexpensive and inferior steel ones. If unreasonable, such acts, which substantially reduce the value of the underlying property, can constitute *voluntary (or affirmative)*

waste. Similarly, life tenants — particularly as they get older like Robert Walsh in this case — have less economic incentive in preserving the value of the property and may allow buildings to deteriorate without performing normal maintenance. If substantial and unreasonable, as it was in Walsh's case, such failures to act can constitute *permissive waste.*

The doctrine of waste can apply wherever the ownership of property is split either between owners in rightful possession (here a life tenant) and holders of future interests (here remainderpersons) or among multiple owners in shared current possession. Whether by affirmative acts or failing to take reasonable care, it is *waste* for one owner in rightful possession to reduce substantially the value of property for its other present or future owners. As *Matteson* suggests, what constitutes waste is highly fact-dependent — both on the acts and the relationship of the parties. The doctrine of waste empowers the holder of a reversion or remainder interest in property or the co-owner of property to force a present possessor of the property to preserve its capital value intact. The remedies for waste vary, but can include an injunction, monetary damages, and forfeiture of the property. The common law doctrine of waste developed in the context of life estates, but (with statutory modification in many states) applies to leasehold estates as well. It never applies to property held in fee simple absolute. Waste applies to defeasible fee simple estates differently, taking account of the probability that the future interest will not become possessory.

2. In *Matteson*, the court ruled that failure to pay property taxes to the point that taxing authorities took steps to seize the property constituted waste. Why would the imminent threat of seizure be required to turn nonpayment of property taxes into waste? Would the failure to pay these taxes constitute voluntary or permissive waste? Similarly, addressing Walsh's failure to maintain the buildings, the court ruled that only neglect that resulted in structural damage constituted waste. Walsh's sister, Matteson, paid more than twice this amount for property repairs. Why would only neglect resulting in structural damage constitute waste? Why did Walsh's non-payment of water bills, which Matteson paid on his behalf, not constitute waste? The court awarded both monetary damages for the amounts expended to combat waste and ended the life estate. Thus, Matteson received both monetary damages and, along with her sister, title to the property. Was this fair or was Matteson doubly compensated?

3. In this case, Dorothy Walsh devised the remainder interest in the property to Matteson, Baisly, and the heirs of Robert Walsh. She obviously assumed that the remainder interest would pass only after the life estate ended upon Robert's death. In fact, because Robert committed waste, it ended prior to his death. Perceiving that Dorothy wanted to divide the future interest among her three children or their heirs, the trial court awarded a one-third fee-simple interest in the property to each sibling. Why did the appellate court reverse this ruling and award each sister a one-half interest in the property, with nothing to their brother? Would the result have been different if Robert had children?

4. Claims of waste often grow out of family disputes, which resulted in *Matteson* after a parent devised a life estate in family real estate to one child with the remainder to be split among all the children or their descendants when the benefitted child died. Such arrangements can work well when the siblings get along. It can be a recipe for bitterness, recriminations, and even lawsuits when the siblings or their children turn against each other or some of them feel slighted. In preparing wills or deeds involving life estates, should lawyers warn their clients about such risks?

F. LEASEHOLD ESTATES

Leaseholds comprise a final type of present, possessory estates in land. Because of their widespread current use and their departure from their common law roots, leasehold estates merit a separate chapter in any survey of modern American property law. We address this topic at length in Chapter 9. In the present context, it is helpful to introduce the basic kinds of leaseholds. Historically, the most important kind of leasehold was the "term of years," which runs for a specific period of time, such as for six months, five years, or (surprisingly often) 99 years. Any period of time can be specified, even 999 years. Classic language for creating a term of years lease is, "to A for ____ years (or months)." Absent contrary language in the lease, a tenant under a term of years can freely convey or devise his leasehold interest during its term for the balance of its term. Another common kind of leasehold estate is the "periodic tenancy," which typically is stated to run "from month-to-month" (as in many apartment leases) or "from year-to-year" (as in some commercial and residential leases). Periodic tenancies continue for succeeding periods until terminated by either the landlord or tenant. Two other types of leaseholds are recognized by the law. A "tenancy at will" has no fixed duration: It can be terminated "at will" by either the landlord or the tenant. A "tenancy at sufferance" exists when a tenant remains in possession of leased property after the end of the lease. Like a fee simple or life estate, a leasehold estate may be made defeasible by adding the appropriate words of limitation, such as "so long as used as a school" or "provided that it is used as a school." Leasehold tenants are subject to the doctrine of waste.

7
Future Interests

A future interest in property is a legally recognized, presently existing right to the future possession of property. It is not a mere hope or expectancy such as a son may hold in someday receiving the property now owned in fee simple absolute by his parents. The owner of a future interest holds present property rights that are enforceable in court. Some future interests are certain to materialize into present estates: For example, a reversion or remainder is certain to become possessory by someone at the end of a life estate. Other future interests may or may not materialize into present estates: For example, a possibility of reverter, right of entry, or executory interest only becomes possessory upon the happening of a triggering event. Under traditional English common law, all of these five types of future interests — which remain the only types recognized at law — were inheritable; reversions and some remainders were devisable and alienable as well. Under modern practice in most American states, all five types of future interests are freely transferable by sale, gift, will, and inheritance.

If the fee simple absolute estate (as the most complete form of land ownership) is equated to a pie, then other present estates and future interests can be seen as pieces of that pie — some larger and some smaller. For any particular parcel of real property, the pieces must add up to one whole pie. A present life estate combines with future reversion or remainder interests to comprise a whole, for example, as do a fee simple determinable and a possibility of reverter. The following chart lists seven present estates and links them with future interests retained by the grantor or transferred to a second grantee.

Present Estate	Future Interest in Grantor		Future Interest in 2nd Grantee
Fee simple absolute	None		None
Fee simple subject to condition subsequent	Right of entry		None
Fee simple determinable	Possibility of reverter		None
Fee simple subject to executory limitation	None		Executory interest
Fee tail	Reversion	and/or	Remainder
Life estate	Reversion	and/or	Remainder
Leasehold	Reversion	and/or	Remainder

The preceding chapter presented these present estates and introduced their associated future interests. This chapter examines these future interests and the rules of law and construction applicable to them. Together, present estates and future interests supply the essential foundation of modern American real property law.

A. REVERSION AND REMAINDER

A reversion is the name for the future interest left over after the holder of a greater estate in real property (such as a fee simple absolute) transfers a lesser estate in the property that is certain to end (such as a life estate or a term of years) without specifying in the deed or will who is to receive that future interest. For a deed, the reversion remains in the grantor; for a will, it remains in the successor in interest of the testator. Where *O* owns property in fee simple, for example, the simple language, "to *A* for life," creates a reversion. In contrast, if the deed or will creating such a lesser estate specifies some second grantee who is to receive the leftover future interest, then that interest is called a remainder. Classic language for creating a remainder is "to *A* for life, then to *B* and her heirs." Reversions and remainders follow estates that end naturally, and it is said that they "wait patiently" until the underlying present estate terminates. For example, neither a reversion nor a remainder can interrupt a life estate by causing it to end earlier than it otherwise would. When a reversion or remainder is transferred, it retains the same name after the transfer. Thus, if a grantor later conveys a reversion interest to a second grantee, it is still called a reversion — not a remainder. Although the basic concept of reversions and remainders is straightforward, the following three cases illustrate the complications that can arise in their use.

■ ABO PETROLEUM CORPORATION v. AMSTUTZ
Supreme Court of New Mexico, 1979
600 P.2d 278

PAYNE, Justice. This action was brought in the District Court of Eddy County by Abo Petroleum and others against the children of Beulah Turknett Jones and Ruby Turknett Jones to quiet title to certain property in Eddy County. Both sides moved for summary judgment. The district court granted Abo's motion, denied the children's motion, and entered a partial final judgment in favor of Abo. The children appealed, and we reverse the district court.

James and Amanda Turknett, the parents of Beulah and Ruby, owned in fee simple the disputed property in this case. In February 1908, by separate instruments entitled "conditional deeds," the parents conveyed life estates in two separate parcels, one each to Beulah and Ruby. Each deed provided that the property would remain the daughter's

> during her natural life, . . . and at her death to revert, vest in, and become the property absolute of her heir or heirs, meaning her children if she have any at her death, but if she die without an heir or heirs, then and in that event this said property and real estate shall vest in and become the property of [her] estate . . . to be distributed as provided by law. . . .

At the time of the delivery of the deed, neither daughter was married, nor were any children born to either daughter for several years thereafter.

In 1911, the parents gave another deed to Beulah, which covered the same land conveyed in 1908. This deed purported to convey "absolute title to the grantee. . . ." In 1916, the parents executed yet another deed to Beulah, granting a portion of the property included in her two previous deeds. A second deed was also executed to Ruby, which provided that it was a "correction deed" for the 1908 deed.

After all the deeds from the parents had been executed, Beulah had three children and Ruby had four children. These children are the appellants herein.

Subsequent to the execution of these deeds, Beulah and Ruby attempted to convey fee simple interests in the property to the predecessors of Abo. The children of Beulah and Ruby contend that the 1908 deeds gave their parents life estates in the property, and that Beulah and Ruby could only have conveyed life estates to the predecessors in interest of Abo. Abo argues that the 1911 and 1916 deeds vested Beulah and Ruby with fee simple title, and that such title was conveyed to Abo's predecessors in interest, thereby giving Abo fee simple title to the property.

We begin our inquiry by examining the nature of the estates James and Amanda Turknett conveyed in the 1908 deeds.

First, the deeds gave each of the daughters property "during her natural life." As Abo apparently concedes, these words conveyed only a life estate.

Second, each deed provided that upon the daughter's death, the property would pass to her "heir or heirs," which was specifically defined as "her children if she have any at her death." Because it was impossible at the time of the original conveyance to determine whether the daughters would have children, or whether any of their children would survive them, the deeds created contingent remainders in the daughters' children, which could not vest until the death of the daughter holding the life estate.

Third, each deed provided that if the contingent remainder failed, the property would become part of the daughter's estate, and pass "as provided by law at the time of her death." The effect of this language would be to pass the property to the heirs of the daughter upon the failure of the first contingent remainder. Because one's heirs are not ascertainable until death, the grant over to the daughter's estate created a second, or alternative, contingent remainder.

The only issues that remain are whether the parents retained any interest, whether by their subsequent deeds to their daughters they conveyed any interest that remained, and whether those conveyances destroyed the contingent remainders in the children.

The grantor-parents divested themselves of the life estate and contingent remainder interests in the property upon delivery of the first deed. Because both remainders are contingent however, the parents retained a reversionary interest in the property.

Abo's position is that by the subsequent conveyances to the daughters, the parents' reversionary interest merged with the daughters' life estates, thus destroying the contingent remainders in the daughters' children and giving the daughters fee simple title to the property. This contention presents a question which this Court has not previously addressed — whether the doctrine of the destructibility of contingent remainders is applicable in New Mexico.

This doctrine, which originated in England in the Sixteenth Century, was based upon the feudal concept that seisin of land could never be in abeyance. From that principle, the rule developed that if the prior estate terminated before the occurrence of the contingency, the contingent remainder was destroyed for lack of a supporting freehold estate. [O]ne instance in which this could happen occurred when the supporting life estate merged with the reversionary interest. . . .

The doctrine of destructibility of contingent remainders has been almost universally regarded to be obsolete by legislatures, courts and legal writers. It has been renounced by virtually all jurisdictions in the United States, either by statute or judicial decision, and was abandoned in the country of its origin over a century ago. . . .

The only tenable argument in support of the doctrine is that it promotes the alienability of land. It does so, however, only arbitrarily, and oftentimes by defeating the intent of the grantor. Land often carries burdens with it, but courts do not arbitrarily cut off those burdens merely in order to make land more alienable.

Because the doctrine of destructibility of contingent remainders is but a relic of the feudal past, which has no justification or support in modern society, we decline to apply it in New Mexico. . . .

We hold that the conveyances of the property to the daughters did not destroy the contingent remainders in the daughters' children. The daughters acquired no more interest in the property by virtue of the later deeds than they had been granted in the original deeds. Any conveyance by them could transfer only the interest they had originally acquired, even if it purported to convey a fee simple.

The summary judgment and partial final judgment entered in favor of Abo are reversed, and the cause is remanded for further proceedings consistent with this opinion.

Notes and Questions

1. Remainders are either *vested* or *contingent*. A vested remainder is one that is held by an ascertained person and that will become possessory upon the natural termination of the preceding estate. For example, a deed "from O to A for life, then to B and her heirs," creates a vested remainder in B. B may die or convey the remainder before A dies, and thus never personally possess the property, but the property certainly will pass to B or B's heirs or assigns upon A's death, and that is enough to vest the remainder in B. In contrast, a contingent remainder is held by an unascertained person or subject to a condition precedent other than the natural termination of the preceding estate. For example, a deed "from O to A for life, then to B if B is then alive," creates a contingent remainder in B. If B dies before A, the remainder will vanish and the property will revert to O or O's heirs or assigns upon A's death.

In *Abo*, the court interpreted each of the two 1908 deeds as creating a life estate in one of the Turknett daughters with an initial contingent remainder in "her children if she have any at her death." Any such conveyance to a described group is called a *class gift*. Do you understand why these class gifts are contingent? When would they vest? Neither daughter had any children in 1908, but subsequently both of them did. Suppose that each of the 1908 deeds instead gave the initial remainder simply to the daughter's "children if she have any." Would these class gifts be vested or contingent at the time of their creation? If contingent, when would they vest and in whom would they vest? So long as it is not subject to a condition precedent, a remainder in a class of persons (such as B's children) vests as soon as any member of that class is ascertained but, so long as additional members can be added to the class (such as by *B* having more children), it is characterized as a *vested remainder subject to open* or (from the perspective of vested class members) a *vested remainder subject to partial divestment or defeasance.*

2. By definition, contingent remainders can fail. Therefore, grantors who write contingent remainders into their deeds or wills often add *alternative* contingent remainders as well. For example, a deed "from *O* to *A* for life, then to *B* if *B* is then alive, but if *B* does not survive *A*, then to *C*," creates an alternative contingent remainder in *C* that would become a vested remainder if *B* dies before *A*. *B* dying before *A* is a condition precedent to *C* obtaining the property. In *Abo*, the court interpreted each of the 1908 deeds as creating an alternative contingent remainder in the heirs of the daughter holding the underlining life estate. Do you understand why these alternative remainders are contingent? When would they vest? Remember, a person's heirs are not ascertained until his death.

3. The contingent reminders in either 1908 deed could fail if Beulah or Ruby Turknett die without living children or other heirs. In that event, the property of that sister would revert to her parents (as grantors) or their successors in interest. Thus, the parents retained a reversion in both properties. When the parents later conveyed to Beulah whatever interest they still had in her property they triggered an old English rule of property law. Under the *doctrine of merger*, a possessory or vested life estate merges into the next vested future interest in fee simple (whether a reversion or a vested remainder) when both are held by the same person (unless they were created in the same document). When this happens, under the *doctrine of the destructibility of contingent remainders*, any intervening contingent remainders are destroyed. This results from the destructibility doctrine's general mandate that any contingent remainder is destroyed if it is still contingent when the prior estate ends (whether by merger or otherwise). Applied to the facts in *Abo*, this would destroy the contingent remainders of Beulah's children and heirs, and give Beulah the property in fee simple absolute. The destructibility doctrine makes property more marketable, but it often does so at the expense of the grantor's original intent. In most American states, the destructibility doctrine (and many other traditional English rules of property law) either has been abolished or was never recognized. Does the *Abo* court abolish or simply not recognize the doctrine? Does it make any difference? When the appellants in a later New Mexico case argued that *Abo* simply abolished the doctrine, so that it still applied to a pre-*Abo* deed, the state supreme court declared, "[W]e specifically hold that the doctrine is not now and has never been the law in New Mexico." Johnson v. Amstutz, 678 P.2d 1169 (N.M. 1984).

■ **SWANSON v. SWANSON**
Supreme Court of Georgia, 1999
514 S.E.2d 822

FLETCHER, Presiding Justice. The issue in this appeal is whether Laura C. "Peggy" Swanson inherits from her deceased husband Bennie Swanson the remainder interests he had in trusts created by his father. Because Bennie Swanson's remainder interests vested before his death and conditions subsequent contained in the trust provisions did not occur before the life beneficiary of the trusts died, Bennie's vested remainder was not defeased and instead passed according to the terms of his will. Therefore, we reverse.

When George Swanson died testate in 1970 he was survived by his wife Gertrude Swanson and his nine children. George's will created two trusts in which Gertrude had a life estate with the remainder left to the nine children, who were all named in the will. Bennie Swanson was one of these children. Bennie died testate prior to Gertrude. He had no children, but was survived by his wife Peggy Swanson, who is the sole beneficiary under his will. After Gertrude's death, Peggy Swanson and other relatives of George and Gertrude brought this action seeking a declaration of their rights under the trusts. The trial court granted summary judgment against Peggy on her claim that she was entitled to Bennie's remainder interests in the trusts. Peggy appeals and six of George and Gertrude's children are appellees.

To distinguish between vested remainders and contingent remainders, a court must determine whether at the time the instrument takes effect there is "a person who in his own right, or as a part of his estate, would take all of this property if [the life estate] ended now."[1] If there is such a person, then the remainder is vested subject to partial or complete defeasance.[2] If no such person is identifiable, then the remainder is subject to a condition precedent and is a contingent remainder. . . .

THE ITEM IV TRUST

The Item IV Trust provided that,

[t]he corpus of this trust shall be disposed of according to the directions of my wife, Gertrude Swanson, either given by her appointment during her lifetime or by will upon her death. If she fails to make such disposition, then and in that event, the corpus of this trust, upon her death, shall pass to my nine children, hereinabove named, to be divided among them in equal shares, share and share alike. If any of my children should not be in life at the time of death of my said wife, the share of such deceased child shall go to his or her surviving children, per stirpes.

Following George's death, there were immediately identifiable persons who would take if the life estate ended: George's nine children. Therefore, each child had a vested remainder interest. Additionally, there were two conditions subsequent attached to the vested remainder. These conditions, which could bring about total defeasance of the vested remainder, were: (1) Gertrude's exercise of her power of appointment;[8] and (2) a child predeceasing Gertrude, but leaving children who survived Gertrude.[9] Neither of these conditions occurred prior to the termination of Gertrude's life estate. She did not exercise her power of appointment and although Bennie died before Gertrude, he left no children who survived Gertrude. . . . [T]herefore, Bennie's interest remained fully vested and passed under his will. . . .

---

1. Richard R. Powell, *Powell on Real Property* §20.04[2] (1998).

2. *Id.* §20.04[2]. Vested remainders may also be indefeasibly vested. A different analysis applies in determining whether a remainder is indefeasibly vested. Remainders subject to partial defeasance are also referred to as vested subject to open.

8. Exercise of a power of appointment is viewed as operating as a condition subsequent on the remainder in default of appointment.

9. Whether this condition or the condition in the Item V Trust required the child of a remainder beneficiary to survive the life tenant is not an issue in this case as Bennie had no children surviving him.

THE ITEM V TRUST

The Item V Trust provided that "the remaining assets of this trust shall be divided into nine equal shares, one share for each of my surviving children or for the then surviving issue of each deceased child of ours." As with the Item IV Trust, there were immediately identifiable persons who would take if the life estate ended: the surviving children. OCGA §44-6-66 directs that we construe words of survivorship to refer to the death of the testator in order to vest remainders. . . . In light of the strong preference in this state for construing conditions as subsequent, we will not construe the mere adjective "surviving" as a condition precedent.

There was one condition subsequent attached that could have caused a total defeasement of the vested remainder in each of George's children: the child predeceasing Gertrude, but leaving children who survived Gertrude. Although Bennie died prior to Gertrude, he had no children and, therefore, just as with the Item IV Trust, Bennie's vested remainder was not defeased and his one-ninth interest flowed into his estate.

In conclusion, we hold that Bennie Swanson's one-ninth interest in the trusts passes to his wife, his sole heir and beneficiary under his will because (1) his remainder was vested; (2) no condition subsequent occurred prior to the termination of the life estate; (3) there is no language in the will that plainly manifests a contrary intent; and (4) this construction is supported by case law and the applicable common law principles.

Judgment reversed.

SEARS, Justice, dissenting [joined by CHIEF JUSTICE BENHAM and Justice HINES]. I disagree with the majority's conclusion that the appellant, Peggy Swanson, is entitled to the remainder interests of Bennie Swanson, her deceased husband, in the two trusts created by Bennie's father. Even assuming Bennie had a vested interest in the trusts, I conclude that the trusts contained a condition subsequent that required Bennie to survive the life tenant to maintain his right to the property. Because he did not do so, he was divested of any interest he had in the property, and Peggy therefore has no interests in the trusts. For these reasons, I respectfully dissent. . . .

I turn first to the Item IV Trust. Our decision in Lemmons v. Lawson, 468 S.E.2d 749 (Ga. 1996), is illustrative of the proper construction to give this trust. In *Lemmons*, the relevant part of the will provided that "upon the death of my wife [the life beneficiary]," the estate was to pass to the testator's three sisters-in-law. The will then provided that in the event that one or more of the sisters-in-law were not in life, their shares would go elsewhere. We held that "the phrase 'upon the death of my wife,'" combined with the direction that "'in the event that [a certain sister-in-law] is not in life,'" her share would be directed elsewhere, indicated that the testator "contemplated that the remaindermen survive the testator's wife in order to receive an interest." *Lemmons*, 468 S.E.2d at 751 (brackets in original). . . .

In the present case, the Item IV Trust contains an identical testamentary pattern as that in *Lemmons*, and I conclude that it demonstrates the same testamentary intent as that found in *Lemmons*. . . . In this regard, both the trust in *Lemmons* and the two trusts in this case provide that upon the death of the life tenant, the trust assets will pass to the named remaindermen. Further, the trusts in both cases provide that if the remaindermen do not survive the life tenant, then the property will pass to a substitute beneficiary. Thus, if *Lemmons* contained a condition of survivorship as a condition subsequent, the present case does also.

As for the Item V Trust, I also conclude that it expresses an intent that the remaindermen survive to the time of distribution. It provides that upon the death of the testator's wife, the corpus shall be paid to his "surviving children" or to the "then surviving issue of each deceased child." Item V then provides that the corpus "shall be paid over" to the foregoing named beneficiaries. The use of the phrases "surviving children" and "then surviving issue of each deceased child" indicates both that the testator desired that the beneficiaries survive the testator's wife and that "his property pass within [his] bloodline" rather than be "diverted to others." Lamb v. NationsBank, 507 S.E.2d 457, 460 (Ga. 1998). Moreover, the fact that the testator also provided that the corpus should be "paid over" to the beneficiaries indicates that the testator contemplated that the beneficiaries would be living at the time of the distribution. . . .

For these reasons, I conclude that both the Item IV and V Trusts provide that a vested remainderman's interest may be divested by the condition subsequent of failing to survive the life tenant. Because Bennie Swanson did not survive his mother, I conclude that his wife is not entitled to a share of the trusts in question. Accordingly, I respectfully dissent.

Notes and Questions

1. This case deals with a common situation in *trust* law. In his will, George Swanson devises a lifetime interest in the bulk of his sizable estate to his wife, Gertrude. Rather than give her this property outright, however, he devises it to her in trust. In doing so, he utilizes a venerable feature of Anglo-American property law: the trust. Under a trust, one or more persons or entities (called *trustees*) own property on behalf of another person or persons (called *beneficiaries*). The property (sometimes called the trust's *corpus* or *res*) may be real, as in a house and land, or personal, such as stocks and bonds, or both. The trustees are the legal owners of the property, but must manage it exclusively in the best interests of the beneficiaries and ultimately must convey it to them. The beneficiaries are the equitable owners of the property. Thus, any one item of trust property has two types of owners — one at law and one in equity. In this case, the trustee may be an institution or an individual; the beneficiaries are Gertrude (who received income from the trust during her life) and her children and their descendants, devisees, or heirs (who received the corpus of the trust following her death).

There are many reasons why property is conveyed to trustees rather than directly to beneficiaries. In some cases, the beneficiaries are minors, who are legally barred from controlling property. In other cases, they may be either unable to manage the property or not as able to do so as the trustees. Many times, multiple beneficiaries of a single trust have conflicting interests, such as perhaps in the case of a beloved surviving spouse of a testator's second marriage and the equally beloved children of the testator's first marriage. Often, the object of a trust is to protect the beneficiaries from themselves or each other. Within broad fiduciary limits designed to protect beneficiaries, a trust's creator enjoys wide discretion in crafting the trust to serve her purposes. The specific terms of a trust typically are set forth in a written trust agreement. Those terms may authorize the trustees to buy or sell trust property. The trust agreement may also authorize or entitle the beneficiaries to receive payments from the trust's income or principal at regular intervals or as needed. The trust may last for a definite or indefinite period, ranging from a short time to several generations. The particular features of any given trust depend on the terms of the trust agreement and the discretion given to the trustees. In part because of its extreme malleability, the trust has become an increasingly valuable tool of property control and ownership. Today, more Americans hold more property in trust than ever before. Why might George Swanson devise property to Gertrude in trust rather than devise it to her outright?

2. In *Swanson*, the majority and the dissent agree that (under the will) Bennie Swanson received a vested remainder *subject to defeasance*, better known as a vested remainder *subject to divestment*. Such a future interest is vested because it is held by an ascertained person and not subject to a condition precedent in order to become possessory. It is subject to a condition subsequent, however, that may prevent it from ever becoming possessory. For example, a conveyance "to A for life, then to B, but if B divorces A, then to C" gives B a vested remainder, but it is subject to divestment before B takes possession — do you see how? In *Swanson*, everyone agrees that Bennie could be divested of his remainder interest in the Item IV Trust by his mother. Further, he surely would be divested of his interests in both trusts if he died before his mother but left descendants who outlived her. The majority and dissenting justices disagree only about whether, under the terms of the will, Bennie (and his heirs or assigns) would be divested of his interests under the trusts simply by pre-deceasing his mother. For the Item V Trust, this answer turns on whether the court interprets the term "surviving children" to mean that, to take under the trust, a child must survive the testator or survive the life tenant. For the Item IV Trust, this answer turns on whether the court interprets the will to impose a like condition. Do you see why? Both approaches are plausible, and either would be legally enforceable. The testator should have expressed his intent more clearly.

3. In all likelihood, George Swanson created two trusts (rather than one) in his will for estate-tax reasons. At one time, the federal estate-tax deduction for property passing to a surviving spouse only applied to the devise of a life estate if the spouse held a general *power of appointment* over the property. Such a power enables a life tenant to convey the property in fee simple absolute, and thereby bust the lifetime limits on it. Where a life tenant holds a power of appointment but does not exercise it, however, the property passes to the designated holder of the remainder interest. Under an estate tax regime that provides a marital deduction to life estates only if they carry a power of appointment, some wealthy couples would divide the incidence of the graduated federal estate tax between their estates by passing some of their assets through a trust that would be subject to the marital deduction, and therefore exempt from estate tax until the second spouse died (the Item IV Trust in this case), and some of their assets through a trust creating only a life estate in the spouse, which would be subject to estate tax upon the first spouse's death (the Item V Trust here).

■ BAKER v. WEEDON

Supreme Court of Mississippi, 1972
262 So. 2d 641

PATTERSON, Justice. This is an appeal from a decree of the Chancery Court of Alcorn County. It directs a sale of land affected by a life estate and future interests with provision for the investment of the proceeds. The interest therefrom is to be paid to the life tenant for her maintenance. We reverse and remand.

John Harrison Weedon was born in High Point, North Carolina. He lived throughout the South and was married twice prior to establishing his final residence in Alcorn County. His first marriage to Lula Edwards resulted in two siblings, Mrs. Florence Weedon Baker and Mrs. Delette Weedon Jones. Mrs. Baker was the mother of three children, Henry Baker, Sarah Baker Lyman and Louise Virginia Baker Heck, the appellants herein. Mrs. Delette Weedon Jones adopted a daughter, Dorothy Jean Jones, who has not been heard from for a number of years and whose whereabouts are presently unknown.

John Weedon was next married to Ella Howell and to this union there was born one child, Rachel. Both Ella and Rachel are now deceased.

Subsequent to these marriages John Weedon bought Oakland Farm in 1905 and engaged himself in its operation. In 1915 John, who was then 55 years of age, married Anna Plaxico, 17 years of age. This marriage, though resulting in no children, was a compatible relationship. John and Anna worked side by side in farming this 152.95-acre tract of land in Alcorn County. There can be no doubt that Anna's contribution to the development and existence of Oakland Farm was significant. The record discloses that during the monetarily difficult years following World War I she hoed, picked cotton and milked an average of fifteen cows per day to protect the farm from financial ruin.

While the relationship of John and Anna was close and amiable, that between John and his daughters of his first marriage was distant and strained. He had no contact with Florence, who was reared by Mr. Weedon's sister in North Carolina, during the seventeen years preceding his death. An even more unfortunate relationship existed between John and his second daughter, Delette Weedon Jones. She is portrayed by the record as being a nomadic person who only contacted her father for money, threatening on several occasions to bring suit against him.

With an obvious intent to exclude his daughters and provide for his wife Anna, John executed his last will and testament in 1925. It provided in part:

> Second; I give and bequeath to my beloved wife, Anna Plaxico Weedon all of my property both real, personal and mixed during her natural life and upon her death to her children, if she has any, and in the event she dies without issue then at the death of my wife Anna Plaxico Weedon I give, bequeath and devise all of my property to my grandchildren, each grandchild sharing equally with the other. . . .

Subsequent to John Weedon's death in 1932 and the probate of his will, Anna continued to live on Oakland Farm. In 1933 Anna, who had been urged by John to remarry in the event of his death, wed J. E. Myers. This union lasted some twenty years and produced no offspring which might terminate the contingent remainder [given to] Weedon's grandchildren by the will.

There was no contact between Anna and John Weedon's children or grandchildren from 1932 until 1964. Anna ceased to operate the farm in 1955 due to her age and it has been rented since that time. Anna's only income is $1000 annually from the farm rental, $300 per year from sign rental and $50 per month by way of social security payments. Without contradiction Anna's income is presently insufficient and places a severe burden upon her ability to live comfortably in view of her age and the infirmities therefrom.

In 1964 the growth of the city of Corinth was approaching Oakland Farm. A right-of-way through the property was sought by the Mississippi State Highway Department for the construction of U.S. Highway 45 bypass. The highway department located Florence Baker's three children, the contingent remaindermen by the will of John Weedon, to negotiate with them for the purchase of the right-of-way. Dorothy Jean Jones, the adopted daughter of Delette Weedon Jones, was not located and due to the long passage of years, is presumably dead. A decree pro confesso was entered against her.

Until the notice afforded by the highway department the grandchildren were unaware of their possible inheritance. Henry Baker, a native of New Jersey, journeyed to Mississippi to supervise their interests. He appears, as was true of the other grandchildren, to have been totally sympathetic to the conditions surrounding Anna's existence as a life tenant. A settlement of $20,000 was completed for the right-of-way bypass of which Anna received $7,500 with which to construct a new home. It is significant that all legal and administrative fees were deducted from the shares of the three grandchildren and not taxed to the life tenant. A contract was executed in 1970 for the sale of soil from the property for $2,500. Anna received $1,000 of this sum which went toward completion of payments for the home.

There was substantial evidence introduced to indicate the value of the property is appreciating significantly with the nearing completion of U.S. Highway 45 bypass plus the growth of the city of Corinth. While the commercial value of the property is appreciating, it is notable that the rental value for agricultural purposes is not. It is apparent that the land can bring no more for agricultural rental purposes than the $1,000 per year now received.

The value of the property for commercial purposes at the time of trial was $168,500. Its estimated value within the ensuing four years is placed at $336,000, reflecting the great influence of the interstate construction upon the land. Mr. Baker, for himself and other remaindermen, appears to have made numerous honest and sincere efforts to sell the property at a favorable price. However, his endeavors have been hindered by the slowness of the construction of the bypass.

Anna, the life tenant and appellee here, is 73 years of age and although now living in a new home, has brought this suit due to her economic distress. She prays that the property, less the house site, be sold by a commissioner and that the proceeds be invested to provide her with an adequate income resulting from interest on the trust investment. She prays also that the sale and investment management be under the direction of the chancery court.

The chancellor granted the relief prayed by Anna under the theory of economic waste. His opinion reflects:

> ... The change of the economy in this area, the change in farming conditions, the equipment required for farming, and the age of this complainant leaves the real estate where it is to all intents and purposes unproductive when viewed in light of its capacity and that a continuing use under the present conditions would result in economic waste. ...

This Court has long recognized that chancery courts do have jurisdiction to order the sale of land for the prevention of waste. Kelly v. Neville, 101 So. 565 (Miss. 1924). In Riley v. Norfleet, 148 So. 777, 781 (Miss. 1933), Justice Cook, speaking for the Court and citing *Kelly, supra*, stated:

> ... The power of a court of equity on a plenary bill, with adversary interest properly represented, to sell contingent remainders in land, under some circumstances, though

the contingent remaindermen are not then ascertained or in being, as, for instance, to preserve the estate from complete or partial destruction, is well established.

While Mississippi and most jurisdictions recognize the inherent power of a court of equity to direct a judicial sale of land which is subject to a future interest, nevertheless the scope of this power has not been clearly defined. It is difficult to determine the facts and circumstances which will merit such a sale.

It is apparent that there must be "necessity" before the chancery court can order a judicial sale. It is also beyond cavil that the power should be exercised with caution and only when the need is evident. Lambdin v. Lambdin, 48 So. 2d 341 (Miss. 1950). These cases, *Kelly*, *Riley* and *Lambdin*, *supra*, are all illustrative of situations where the freehold estate was deteriorating and the income therefrom was insufficient to pay taxes and maintain the property. In each of these this Court approved a judicial sale to preserve and maintain the estate. The appellants argue, therefore, that since Oakland Farm is not deteriorating and since there is sufficient income from rental to pay taxes, a judicial sale by direction of the court was not proper.

The unusual circumstances of this case persuade us to the contrary. We are of the opinion that deterioration and waste of the property is not the exclusive and ultimate test to be used in determining whether a sale of land affected by future interest is proper, but also that consideration should be given to the question of whether a sale is necessary for the best interest of all the parties, that is, the life tenant and the contingent remaindermen. . . .

Our decision to reverse the chancellor and remand the case for his further consideration is couched in our belief that the best interest of all the parties would not be served by a judicial sale of the entirety of the property at this time. While true that such a sale would provide immediate relief to the life tenant who is worthy of this aid in equity, admitted by the remaindermen, it would nevertheless under the circumstances before us cause great financial loss to the remaindermen.

We therefore reverse and remand this cause to the chancery court, which shall have continuing jurisdiction thereof, for determination upon motion of the life tenant, if she so desires, for relief by way of sale of a part of the burdened land sufficient to provide for her reasonable needs from interest derived from the investment of the proceeds. The sale, however, is to be made only in the event the parties cannot unite to hypothecate the land for sufficient funds for the life tenant's reasonable needs. . . .

Notes and Questions

1. Suppose Anna Plaxico had a child who predeceased her. Who, under John Weedon's will, would be entitled to Oakland Farm upon Anna's death? If Anna had a child, would that child's remainder interest in the farm be vested or contingent? Why? Under the will, who would receive the farm upon Anna's death if she never had any children? At the time of the court's decision in 1972, Anna had never had any children and she was 73 years old: Is the remainder interest in the farm of John Weedon's grandchildren vested or contingent? Why? Is there anything that Anna can do in 1972 to deprive John Weedon's grandchildren (or their successors in interest) of the farm?

2. In 1964, Anna Plaxico and John Weedon's grandchildren jointly agreed to sell a portion of Oakland Farm to the state for $20,000. They split the money, with three-eighths of it going to Anna and five-eighths of it going to the grandchildren. In 1970, they split the proceeds from the sale of soil from the farm in roughly the same ratio: two-fifths for Anna and three-fifths for the grandchildren. Why did they split the proceeds in this manner? If John Weedon had regularly sold soil from the farm prior to devising the life estate to Anna, could Anna have continued to do so without the removal constituting unlawful waste?

If the state had judicially condemned a portion of the farm for highway use in 1964 (rather than having negotiated a sale price for it), the court probably would have handled the proceeds in one of two ways. It might have put the entire amount in trust, with the interest paid to Anna for her life and the principal distributed to the grandchildren upon her death. Alternatively, it could have determined the present fair market value of Anna's life estate in the condemned portion. Anna would then receive that amount immediately, with the balance of the proceeds paid to the grandchildren at the same time. Which option a court chooses depends on the needs and interests of the parties and the approach favored in its particular state. Both approaches are quite common. Computer software is available to compute the present value of any life estate, factoring in the property's fair market value and the life tenant's age.

3. We introduced the doctrine of waste in the discussion of Matteson v. Walsh in Chapter 6. In that case, property rights in a house were split between a brother, who held a life estate, and his sisters and heirs, who held the remainder. The *Matteson* court found that neglect using "severe and obstantial deterioration" would constitute permissive waste but lesser neglect or damage would not. In *Baker*, property rights in Oakland Farm are split between John Weedon's widow, who holds a life estate, and Weedon's grandchildren by a prior marriage, who hold contingent remainders. The *Baker* court concluded that, on the one hand, it may be permissive waste to the life tenant not to cash in on at least some of the farm's appreciated value but, on the other hand, it would be affirmative waste to the grandchildren to cash out entirely before a foreseeable further jump in the farm's value. If it has *equity* powers, a court can craft remedies that serve the best interests of all the parties. What remedy would best serve Anna Plaxico's interests in this case? What remedy would best serve the grandchildren's interests? What remedy balances those competing interests? *Baker* illustrates the conflict that can arise between parties holding present estates and future interests in the same property. Suppose you had been John Weedon's attorney: Could you have suggested alternative ways to devise Oakwood Farm so as to minimize these foreseeable future conflicts between John's devisees?

B. RIGHT OF ENTRY AND POSSIBILITY OF REVERTER

Rights of entry and possibilities of reverter are future interests retained by grantors who create fees simple subject to condition subsequent and fees simple determinable, respectively. Unlike a life estate or a term of years leasehold, a fee simple subject to condition subsequent and a fee simple determinable may last forever. Unlike a fee simple absolute, however, these two types of defeasible estates may terminate by their own terms. The holder of a right of entry or a possibility of reverter has current, legally recognized property rights, but they are considerably less extensive than those possessed by the holder of a reversion or remainder interest. Under English common law, for example, the holder of a right of entry or a possibility of reverter could not convey or devise that interest (except by way of release to the fee owner), but it was inheritable by his heirs. Most American states now freely permit the conveyance and devise of all future interests. Further, when the state condemns a defeasible fee, traditionally the holder of a right of entry or possibility of reverter receives nothing. In addition, the doctrine of waste rarely applies to defeasible estates. The following cases illustrate some of these traditional rules, and how they are beginning to change.

■ **MAHRENHOLZ v. COUNTY BOARD OF SCHOOL TRUSTEES**
Appellate Court of Illinois, 1981
417 N.E.2d 138

JONES, Justice. This case involves an action to quiet title to real property located in Lawrence County, Illinois. Its resolution depends on the judicial construction of language in a conveyance of that property. This case is before us on the pleadings, plantiffs' third amended complaint having been dismissed by a final order. The pertinent facts are taken from the pleadings.

On March 18, 1941, W. E. and Jennie Hutton executed a warranty deed in which they conveyed certain land, to be known here as the Hutton School grounds, to the trustees of School District No. 1, the predecessors of the defendants in this action. The deed provided that "this land to be used for school purpose only; otherwise to revert to Grantors herein." W. E. Hutton died intestate on July 18, 1951, and Jennie Hutton died intestate on February 18, 1969. The Huttons left as their only legal heir their son Harry E. Hutton.

The property conveyed by the Huttons became the site of the Hutton School. Community Unit School District No. 20 succeeded to the grantee of the deed and held classes in the building constructed upon the land until May 30, 1973. After that date, children were transported to classes held at other facilities operated by the District. The District has used the property since then for storage purposes only.

[In July 1941, the Huttons executed a deed purporting to convey their reversionary interest in the Hutton School grounds to Earl and Madeline Jacqmain. On October 9, 1959, the Jacqmains transferred this interest the plaintiffs, Herbert and Betty Mahrenholz.]

On May 7, 1977, Harry E. Hutton, son and sole heir of W. E. and Jennie Hutton, conveyed to the plaintiffs all of his interest in the Hutton School land. This document was filed in the recorder's office of Lawrence County on September 7, 1977. On September 6, 1977, Harry Hutton disclaimed his interest in the property in favor of the defendants. . . . The disclaimer was filed in the recorder's office of Lawrence County on October 4, 1977. . . .

The parties appear to be in agreement that the 1941 deed from the Huttons [to the school district] conveyed a defeasible fee simple estate to the grantee, and gave rise to a future interest in the grantors, and that it did not convey a fee simple absolute, subject to a covenant. The fact that provision was made for forfeiture of the estate conveyed should the land cease to be used for school purposes suggests that this view is correct.

The future interest remaining in this grantor or his estate can only be a possibility of reverter or a right of re-entry for condition broken. As neither interest may be transferred by will nor by inter vivos conveyance [under Illinois law], and as the land was being used for school purposes in 1959 when the Jacqmains transferred their interest in the school property to the plaintiffs, the trial court correctly ruled that the plaintiffs could not have acquired any interest in that property from the Jacqmains by the deed of October 9, 1959.

Consequently this court must determine whether the plaintiffs could have acquired an interest in the Hutton School grounds from Harry Hutton. The resolution of this issue depends on the construction of the language of the 1941 deed of the Huttons to the school district. As urged by the defendants, and as the trial court found, that deed conveyed a fee simple subject to a condition subsequent, followed by a right of re-entry for condition broken. As argued by the plaintiffs, on the other hand, the deed conveyed a fee simple determinable followed by a possibility of reverter. In either case, the grantor and his heirs retain an interest in the property which may become possessory if the [limitation] is broken. We emphasize here that although [Illinois law] provides that rights of re-entry for condition broken and possibilities of reverter are neither alienable nor devisable, they are inheritable. The type of interest held governs the mode of reinvestment with title if reinvestment is to occur. If the grantor had a possibility of reverter, he or his heirs become the owner of the property by operation of law as soon as the condition is broken. If he has a right of re-entry for condition broken, he or his heirs become the owner of the property only after they act to retake the property.

It is alleged, and we must accept, that classes were last held in the Hutton School in 1973. Harry Hutton, sole heir of the grantors, did not act to legally retake the premises but instead conveyed his interest in that land to the plaintiffs in 1977. If Harry Hutton had only a naked right of re-entry for condition broken, then he could not be the owner of that property until he had legally re-entered the land. Since he took no steps for a legal re-entry, he had only a right of re-entry in 1977, and that right cannot be conveyed inter vivos. On the other hand, if Harry Hutton had a possibility of reverter in the property, then he owned the school property as soon as it ceased to be used for school purposes. Therefore, assuming (1) that cessation of classes constitutes "abandonment of school purposes" on the land, (2) that the conveyance from Harry Hutton to the plaintiffs was legally correct, and (3) that the conveyance was not pre-empted by Hutton's disclaimer in favor of the school district, the plaintiffs could have acquired an interest in the Hutton School grounds if Harry Hutton had inherited a possibility of reverter from his parents.

The difference between a fee simple determinable (or determinable fee) and a fee simple subject to a condition subsequent, is solely a matter of judicial interpretation of the words of a grant. . . .

A fee simple determinable may be thought of as a limited grant, while a fee simple subject to a condition subsequent is an absolute grant to which a condition is appended. In other words, a grantor should give a fee simple determinable if he intends to give property for so long as it is needed for the purposes for which it is given and no longer, but he should employ a fee simple subject to a condition subsequent if he intends to compel compliance with a condition by penalty of a forfeiture. . . .

[T]he Huttons would have created a fee simple determinable if they had allowed the school district to retain the property so long as or while it was used for school purposes, or until it ceased to be so used. Similarly, a fee simple subject to a condition subsequent would have arisen had the Huttons given the land upon condition that or provided that it be used for school purposes. In the 1941 deed, though the Huttons gave the land "to be used for school purpose only, otherwise to revert to Grantors herein," no words of temporal limitation, or terms of express condition, were used in the grant.

The plaintiffs argue that the word "only" should be construed as a limitation rather than a condition. The defendants respond that where ambiguous language is used in a deed, the courts of Illinois have expressed a constructional preference for a fee simple subject to a condition subsequent. Both sides refer us to cases involving deeds which contain language analogous to the 1941 grant in this case.

We believe that a close analysis of the wording of the original grant shows that the grantors intended to create a fee simple determinable followed by a possibility of reverter. Here, the use of the word "only" immediately following the grant "for school purpose" demonstrates that the Huttons wanted to give the land to the school district only as long as it was needed and no longer. The language "this land to be used for school purpose only" is an example of a grant which contains a limitation within the granting clause. It suggests a limited grant, rather than a full grant subject to a condition, and thus, both theoretically and linguistically, gives rise to a fee simple determinable.

The second relevant clause furnishes plaintiffs' position with additional support. It cannot be argued that the phrase "otherwise to revert to grantors herein" is inconsistent with a fee simple subject to a condition subsequent. Nor does the word "revert" automatically create a possibility of reverter. But, in combination with the preceding phrase, the provisions by which possession is returned to the grantors seem to trigger a mandatory return rather than a permissive return because it is not stated that the grantor "may" re-enter the land.

The terms used in the [March] 1941 deed, although imprecise, were designed to allow the property to be used for a single purpose, namely, for "school purpose." The Huttons intended to have the land back if it were ever used otherwise. Upon a grant of exclusive use followed by an express provision for reverter when that use ceases, courts and commentators have agreed that a fee simple determinable, rather than a fee simple subject to a condition subsequent, is created. . . .

We hold, therefore, that the 1941 deed from W. E. and Jennie Hutton to the Trustees of School District No. 1 created a fee simple determinable in the trustees followed by a possibility of reverter in the Huttons and their heirs. Accordingly, the trial court erred in dismissing plaintiffs' third amended complaint which followed its holding that the plaintiffs could not have acquired any interest in the Hutton School property from Harry Hutton. We must therefore reverse and remand this cause to the trial court for further proceedings.

We refrain from deciding . . . whether the defendants have ceased to use the Hutton School grounds for "school purposes."

Notes and Questions

1. What is a "school purpose"? Does the use of property for storage by a school district constitute a "school purpose"? If W. E. and Jennie Hutton wanted the property to be used for a community school in their vicinity, should they have written a more specific limitation into the deed?

2. Given the constructional preference for finding a fee simple subject to condition subsequent over a fee simple determinable (discussed earlier in *Lawyer's Trust*), why does the *Mahrenholz* court find that the language in the 1941 deed

creates a fee simple determinable? If the court instead had found that the deed created a fee simple subject to condition subsequent, who would have the right to possess the property at the time of the court's 1981 decision? Assuming that the school district was in rightful possession of the property in 1981 and Harry Hutton retained a right of entry, if the district had breached the "school purpose" condition in 1973 by closing Hutton School, could Harry Hutton still exercise his right of entry in 1981? Although the common law does not place any time limits on exercising a right of entry, several American states do so. Some of these statutes limit the duration of rights of entry and possibilities of reverter to a certain number of years from the date of their initial creation. *E.g.*, Fla. Stat. Ann. §689.18 (21 years). Others require that they be exercised or enforced within a certain number of years after the condition or limitation was breached. *E.g.*, 735 Ill. Comp. Stat. 5/13-102 & 103 (seven years). Still others require that holders of rights of entry or possibilities of reverter periodically file in the local land records a declaration of their continuing intent to enforce the condition or limitation. *E.g.*, Iowa Code §614.24. The court also may use its equity powers to impose limits on the duration of rights of entry and possibilities of reverter and to require that rights be enforced in a timely fashion. For example, in *Lawyer's Trust*, reprinted in Chapter 6, the Texas Supreme Court stated, "It is true that delay in exercising the right of re-entry coupled with proof that the grantee was misled by such delay and as a result changed his position by making improvements on the property or investing money in it, then it can be said that the grantor has waived his right of re-entry." These statutory and judicial limitations typically apply to the enforcement of executory interests as well.

3. Under Illinois law as interpreted in *Mahrenholz*, if closing the school breached the "school purpose" limitation in the 1941 deed, who owned the Hutton School grounds following the court's 1981 decision? Why? Would Harry Hutton's May 1977 conveyance to Herbert and Betty Mahrenholz have any effect? Would Hutton's September 1977 disclaimer in favor of the School District have any effect? At the time of the *Mahrenholz* decision, Illinois retained the traditional common law restriction against the conveyance of rights of entry and possibilities of reverter. If these future interests were freely alienable in Illinois, as they are in most states, who would have held the possibility of reverter when the school was closed in 1973 and (if the closing of the school violated the deed's "school purpose" limitation) who would have then owned the Hutton School grounds?

4. The *Mahrenholz* court uses the term *right of re-entry*, which is synonymous with *right of entry*, which is more often used. Some courts and some legal commentators call the future interest retained by the grantor of a fee simple subject to condition subsequent a *power of termination*.

■ **FOWLER v. LAC MINERALS (USA), LLC**
United States Court of Appeals for the Eighth Circuit, 2012
694 F.3d 930

GRUENDER, Circuit Judge. LAC Minerals (USA), LLC ("LAC") and Robert Fowler are bound by an agreement relating to 944 acres of property once targeted for mining development. Fowler filed suit, arguing that the agreement required LAC to assign to Fowler certain portions of the property no longer needed for mining operations. . . .

I. Background

Fowler's predecessor-in-interest, Viable Resources, Inc. ("Viable"), and LAC's predecessor company, St. Joe American Corporation, entered into a joint venture agreement in 1984 with the goal of developing certain mining prospects in Lawrence County, South Dakota. As part of the joint venture, in 1985 Viable deeded 90 mining claims involving approximately 944 acres of land to LAC. In the deed, Viable reserved a right "to obtain a reconveyance in the property . . . as specified in" an amended joint venture agreement. The parties agree that a 1988 Restated Joint Venture Agreement ("RJVA") superseded the amended joint venture agreement referenced in the deed and that the RJVA is the controlling agreement. The parties also agree that the right to obtain a reconveyance referred to in the deed is defined in section 4.3 of the RJVA, which reads as follows:

> *Release of Property*: During the course of the conduct of mineral exploration under this Agreement the Manager [LAC] may in its sole discretion determine that certain portions of the Property have little potential for containing minerals of economic value or will not be required for mineral development or mining facilities. Upon annual review the Manager may eliminate such portions of the Property from the terms of this Agreement, and in such event [LAC] will reassign any such portions to Viable.

Section 2.1 of the RJVA establishes a minimum term of fifty years for the agreement, subject to extension under certain conditions. In 1992, however, state mining regulators issued a "stop order" for all mining operations on the property because of problems with acid drainage. There is no dispute that, as a result of the "stop order," no mineral exploration has occurred since 1993. . . .

Fowler, one of the original organizers of Viable, succeeded to Viable's rights in the property in November 1999. On October 11, 2001, Fowler formally requested the release of land not being used for mining purposes. Over the next several years, LAC sent occasional communications indicating that it was in the process of determining which portions of the 944 acres could be released, but it never made such a determination. In 2008, Fowler sued (1) for a declaratory judgment that LAC was obligated to reassign any portion of the property that became unneeded for mining or reclamation efforts, (2) for specific performance of that obligation with respect to portions currently not needed, and (3) to quiet title for such portions. LAC counterclaimed for a declaratory judgment that it owned the 944 acres "absolutely . . . as against Fowler and all persons claiming under him" and to quiet title "against all claims of Fowler and all persons claiming under him."

On cross motions for summary judgment, the district court concluded that LAC held the property in fee simple subject to a condition subsequent requiring it "to reassign the property back to" Fowler "when the mining deed's purposes are exhausted." After an ensuing bench trial, the district court found that the transfer of Viable's reversionary rights to Fowler was not precluded by S.D.C.L. §43-4-3, which states that "[a] mere right of reentry, or of repossession for breach of a condition subsequent, cannot be transferred to anyone except the owner of the property affected thereby," because the deeds and RJVA established a covenant running with the land, rather than a "mere" right of reentry. . . .

LAC now appeals, arguing that the district court erred in holding that Fowler retains an interest in the land. In support, it contends that (i) section 4.3 of the RJVA did not create a condition subsequent, but rather a contractual covenant for which damages would be the only remedy for breach; [and] (ii) even if the RJVA did create a condition subsequent in favor of Viable, Viable was precluded from transferring its associated rights by S.D.C.L. §43-4-3. . . .

II. DISCUSSION

. . . .

LAC first asserts that section 4.3 of the RJVA establishes a contractual covenant, rather than a condition subsequent. "The chief distinction between a condition subsequent and a covenant pertains to the remedy in the event of a breach, which in the former subjects the estate to a forfeiture and in the latter is merely a ground for recovery of damages." Rowbotham v. Jackson, 5 N.W.2d 36, 37 (S.D. 1942). "Whether a clause shall be construed to be a condition subsequent or [a] covenant must depend upon the contract or circumstances and the intention of the party creating the estate." *Id.* "Forfeitures and condition subsequent not being favored in law, a deed will not be construed to create a conditional estate unless the language used unequivocally indicates an intention . . . to that effect." DeHaven v. Hall, 753 N.W.2d 429, 435 (S.D. 2008).

In this case, the deed specifically refers to a "right to obtain a *reconveyance* in the property . . . as specified in" the parties' agreement (emphasis added). In turn, the referenced agreement states that, should certain specified events occur with respect to any portion of the property, LAC "will *reassign* any such portions to Viable" (emphasis added). This express language unequivocally establishes the grantor's right to reacquire the relevant portions of the deeded estate upon occurrence of the stated conditions. *Cf. DeHaven*, 753 N.W.2d at 436-37 (finding a deed established a covenant that was susceptible to a remedy only of damages, rather than a condition subsequent to be remedied by reversion to the grantors, where the deed stated a duty to maintain the granted easement but included "no language that expressly or implicitly provides that the easement will be forfeited if [the grantees] fail to maintain it"). As a result, we agree with the district court that the deed here establishes a condition subsequent, rather than a covenant.

In opposition, LAC argues that section 4.3 cannot create a condition subsequent because it gives the grantor no power to terminate the estate. "A conveyance that creates a fee simple estate subject to a condition subsequent provides the grantor, heirs, and successors a *power to terminate* upon the happening of the stated event, *i.e.*, when a condition is broken." Swaby v. N. Hills Reg'l R.R. Auth., 769 N.W.2d 798, 808 (S.D. 2009). LAC contends that it, rather than Viable, enjoyed sole power to terminate the estate because section 4.3 gives LAC "sole *discretion* [to] determine that certain portions of the Property" will not be needed for mining purposes and states that LAC "*may* eliminate such portions of the Property from the terms of this Agreement" (emphases added). To be sure, LAC is vested with broad discretion in determining which portions of the property are unneeded for mining operations and eliminating those portions from the scope of its mining management. However, this determination constitutes the condition subsequent itself, not the resulting power to terminate. If, for whatever reason, the determination and elimination decisions are made, section 4.3 states that "in such event [LAC] *will reassign* any such portions to" the grantor (emphasis added). Because the grantor has the power to terminate by demanding reassignment if the condition subsequent comes to pass, the basic structure of a condition subsequent is satisfied, regardless of the degree of LAC's control over the condition subsequent.

LAC next asserts that Viable was precluded from transferring its rights associ-ated with the condition subsequent by S.D.C.L. §43-4-3. Section 43-4-3 prohibits the assignment to a third party of a grantor's right of reentry or repossession unless the original instrument contemplated such assignments or otherwise indicated an intent for the restriction to run with the land. *See Rowbotham*, 5 N.W.2d at 37-38 (holding that an identically worded predecessor statute prohibited the assignment of a grantor's rights under a reverter clause where the "reverter language used in the deed . . . runs to [the grantors] personally, and not to their assigns"). Here, we agree with the district court that the RJVA expressly contemplated the assignment of Viable's right of repossession under section 4.3. In particular, section 11.1 of the RJVA expressly authorizes each party to assign "its rights in the Agreement" to any affiliate of that party, without restriction. LAC identifies no provision of the deed or the RJVA that would suggest Viable's reversionary rights under section 4.3 were somehow excluded from the general assignment provisions of section 11.1. Because the plain language of the parties' agreement establishes Viable's right to make certain assignments, Viable held more than a "mere" right of repossession, see S.D.C.L. §43-4-3. Thus, the transfer of Viable's right of repossession to Fowler was not precluded by statute. . . .

For the foregoing reasons, we affirm the district court's judgment that Fowler retains a reversionary interest in the land.

Notes and Questions

1. Prior cases in this book including *Mahrenholz* announce a constructional preference for a fee simple subject to condition subsequent over a fee simple deter-minable. Does the *Fowler* court need to apply such a preference to conclude that the deed created a fee simple subject to condition subsequent? Look carefully at the language of the *Fowler* deed and related Release of Property, particularly the phrase stating that LAC "will reassign" the non-mineral portions of the property. Should that language create a fee simple determinable? What language in the deed leads the court to characterize the estate as a fee simple subject to a condition subsequent? Are you able to rewrite the deed so the court would call it a fee simple determinable? If the *Fowler* deed had created a fee simple determinable, would LAC Minerals have a claim to the title under the doctrine of adverse possession, at least if South Dakota's adverse-possession period had been satisfied? In answering this question, please consider all the elements of adverse possession as set forth in the *Howard* and *ITT Rayonier* opinions in Chapter 3. In particular, would LAC's possession of the land following the end of the fee simple determinable have been hostile and under a claim of right made in good faith?

2. In this case, Fowler argues that the deed creates a fee simple subject to a condition subsequent. LAC counters that it creates a fee simple absolute subject to a covenant. As noted in the opinion, since forfeitures are not favored at law, courts will only construe deeds to create defeasible fees (rather than fee simple absolutes) when the language is clear. What makes the language clear in this case? Do you see why the distinction is important to the case's outcome? The different construc-tions lead to different remedies. Under the law of property, if the condition of a fee simple subject to a condition subsequent is triggered, then the holder of the future interest may re-enter and claim the property itself. Under the law of contracts, if the

covenant of a fee simple absolute subject to a covenant is breached, then the injured party may obtain damages or injunctive relief, but not the property itself.

3. Traditional common law prohibits the conveyance of rights of entry except to the owner of the fee simple. As noted in *Fowler*, South Dakota has modified this rule to allow transfer when the original deed authorizes or anticipates transfer. South Dakota's modification of the common law rule became an issue in this case because Fowler received the right of entry by assignment from Viable and is seeking to enforce it against LAC. If the common law restriction on transfer still applied in South Dakota, only Viable could enforce the right of entry. LAC invokes the restriction on transferring rights of entry in an attempt to defeat Fowler's claim. Why does Fowler prevail on this issue?

C. EXECUTORY INTEREST

An executory interest is a future interest created in an alternative grantee that divests (or cuts short) a present estate before its natural end. Like a possibility of reverter, but unlike a right of entry, an executory interest becomes possessory automatically upon the happening of a triggering condition or limitation. Executory interests are of two basic types. The first type of executory interest can divest the grantor in the future — this is called a springing executory interest because it springs out from the grantor. Such an executory interest would be created in *A* by a deed "from *O* to *A* when she marries." The second type of executory interest can divest an initial grantee of her present estate — this is called a shifting executory interest because it shifts the estate from an initial grantee to an alternative one. Such an executory interest would be created in *B* by a deed "from *O* to *A*, but if the property is no longer used as a library, then to *B*." The holder of an executory interest has current, legally recognized property rights akin to those possessed by the holder of a possibility of reverter or a right of entry. As the following case illustrates, however, executory interests are subject to special limitations.

■ **WASHINGTON STATE GRANGE v. BRANDT**
Court of Appeals of Washington, 2006
148 P.3d 1069

Dwyer, Judge. . . . In 1911, Henry and Elizabeth Shields conveyed by deed a parcel of land, approximately 70 feet by 70 feet, from the southeast corner of their property to the Orchard Grange. The Orchard Grange then constructed a building on the property. . . .

In 1950, Raymond and Margaret Gorze, successors to the Shields, conveyed a second parcel to the Orchard Grange by statutory warranty deed. This parcel, approximately two acres in size, borders the 1911 deed parcel on that parcel's north and west boundaries. The parcel was deeded from a larger tract of land owned by the Gorzes.

In pertinent part, the 1950 statutory warranty deed reads:

The GRANTORS Margaret Gorze and R.A. Gorze, wife and husband for and in consideration of One Dollar, ($1.00) in hand paid, conveys and warrants to Orchard Grange # 346, the following described real estate . . . :

... ALSO *the land herein deeded reverts back to original plot in event it is no longer used for Grange purposes.*

Clerk's Papers (CP) at 179 (emphasis added). The 1950 deed parcel was used by the Orchard Grange solely for parking and vehicular access.

In 2004, the Orchard Grange dissolved and the 1950 deed parcel ceased to be used for "Grange purposes," *i.e.*, parking and vehicular access. Subsequently, the Orchard Grange's interest in both the 1911 deed parcel and the 1950 deed parcel succeeded to the Washington State Grange.

In 1961, the Gorzes conveyed a rectangular 0.63-acre parcel on the northwest side of their 86-acre property to Margaret Gorze's parents, Phil and Elaine Shintaffer. This property shares no boundaries with either the 1911 deed parcel or the 1950 deed parcel. The parcel conveyed in 1961 is currently owned by the John May Living Trust.

In 1964, the Gorzes entered into a real estate contract with [Robert and Myrna Brandt] for the sale of the remainder of the Gorzes' property, approximately 85 acres. This real estate contract was fulfilled and, in 1984, a statutory warranty deed was conveyed to the Brandts.

In 2005, the Brandts discovered a legal description error in the 1984 deed by which, they claim, the Gorzes mistakenly failed to convey to them a tract of land which included the 1950 deed parcel. On March 4, 2005, the Brandts obtained a quitclaim deed from Kathleen Warren, the personal representative of Margaret Gorze's estate, which purported to correct the legal description error. As a result of this conveyance, the Brandts claim that they acquired the Gorzes' reversionary interest in the 1950 deed parcel.[5]

On May 18, 2005, the Grange filed this action against the Brandts seeking to quiet title in the Grange to the property conveyed by the 1950 statutory warranty deed. The trial court granted summary judgment to the Grange, holding that the 1950 deed's reversionary clause was void in its entirety by application of the rule against perpetuities, and that the effect of the void clause was to leave the Grange, as successor to the Orchard Grange, a fee simple absolute interest in the subject property. . . .

. . . The Brandts argue that the trial court erroneously applied the rule to entirely invalidate the reversionary clause. The Brandts insist that the limiting language in the deed cut short the Orchard Grange's estate and reserved a future interest exclusively in the Gorzes by either: (1) a possibility of a reverter or (2) a right of entry.[7]

___

5. Whether Warren intended to transfer the Gorzes' reversionary interest in the 1950 deed parcel to the Brandts was not resolved in the trial court. In a declaration filed with the trial court, Warren stated that it was "never my intention to quit claim to Robert J. Brandt and Myrna L. Brandt any interest the Estate of Margaret Jane Gorze may have had, if any, in the property described in the 1950 deed from [the Gorzes] to the Orchard Grange # 346." . . .

7. The right of entry is the future estate that follows a present estate upon condition subsequent. *Restatement of Property* §24 (1936). The following words are usually held to create conditions subsequent: "upon condition that," and "provided that." *Id.* §45, cmt. j. In cases where the language is ambiguous, Washington courts have a preference for a fee on a condition subsequent rather than a fee simple determinable, because of the latter's automatic forfeiture. However, in this case, the deed language is clearly durational ("in event it is no longer used for") as opposed to conditional ("on condition that," "provided that"). Because there is no ambiguity in the language used, the interest conveyed in the deed was a determinable interest, not an interest subject to a condition subsequent. Therefore, the future interest conveyed in the 1950 deed was not a right of entry.

The rule against perpetuities provides that "no interest is good unless it must vest, if at all, not later than twenty-one years after some life in being at the creation of the interest." John Chipman Gray, *The Rule Against Perpetuities* §201 (Roland Gray, 4th ed. 1942). The purpose of the rule is to prevent the fettering of the marketability of property over long periods of time by indirect restraints upon its alienation.

The rule against perpetuities has its origin in English common law. When Washington was granted statehood, English common law became the rule of decision in all Washington courts. Since then, the rule against perpetuities has been in force and has been applied to invalidate future interests, which, by possibility, may not become vested within a life or lives in being at the time of the grant and twenty-one years thereafter.

The rule against perpetuities is not a rule of construction. Instead, it is a positive mandate of law to be applied irrespective of the intent of the grantor. In order to determine whether a conveyed interest violates the rule, a court first must construe the language of the conveyance in precisely the same manner as if there were no rule against perpetuities, and then "apply the rule rigorously, in complete disregard of the wishes or intention of the [grantor]." Betchard v. Iverson, 212 P.2d 783, 786 (Wash. 1949).

The rule against perpetuities operates against those future interests that are not vested at the time of the conveyance. An executory interest is a future interest that is not vested at the time of its creation. By definition, an executory interest is an estate that, upon the happening of a stated event, is automatically divested in favor of a third person transferee as opposed to the grantor.

In the reversionary clause at issue, the future interest was to be retained in the "original plot." However, real property cannot own an interest in real property. County School Bd. v. Dowell, 58 S.E.2d 38 (Va. 1950). It can only be that, upon termination of the determinable fee, the property was to pass to the "then owner" of the "original plot." Thus, the Orchard Grange acquired an interest properly denominated as a "fee simple subject to an executory interest" in the "then owner" of the "original plot."

When an interest is certain to either vest or fail before the twenty-first anniversary of the death of a particular person, that person is deemed a measuring life for the interest. Generally, an executory interest without a measuring life must be certain to vest or fail within 21 years of the grant or it violates the rule against perpetuities and must be stricken.

The reversionary language in the 1950 deed contains no reference to an ascertainable measuring life. Thus, the executory interest in the "then" owner or owners of the "original plot" violates the rule against perpetuities because of the possibility that the interest of the unidentified "then" owner or owners of the "original plot" would not vest within twenty-one years of the grant.[10] Consequently, the executory interest in the "then" owner or owners of the "original plot" must be stricken. . . .

Generally, where an executory interest is void because of the rule against perpetuities, the preceding interest becomes a fee simple absolute. *Restatement of Property* §229. However, where a fee simple determinable is followed by an invalid

---

10. Indeed, the Orchard Grange could have continued to use the land "for Grange purposes" in perpetuity. *See, e.g.*, City of Klamath Falls v. Bell, 490 P.2d 515 (Or. App. 1971) (Conveyance to city for "so long as" it used land for a library granted city a fee simple determinable interest. City could have used land for a library in perpetuity. Subsequent executory interest was therefore void as violative of rule against perpetuities.).

executory interest, only the executory interest is stricken, not the determinability. *Id.* Thus, the fee remains determinable and a possibility of reverter vests in the grantor by operation of law.

After striking the invalid executory interest, the language "reverts back" followed by the phrase "in event it is no longer used for Grange purposes" created a determinable fee simple with a possibility of reverter in the Gorzes, as grantors. . . . When the 1950 deed parcel ceased to be used for "Grange purposes," the land reverted to the Gorzes. Accordingly, after applying the rule against perpetuities to invalidate the executory interest, which was invalid from its inception, the interest effectively granted to the Orchard Grange was one in fee simple determinable with a possibility of reverter that vested exclusively in the Gorzes and their heirs or assigns.

The Brandts contend that the trial court erred in quieting title in the Washington State Grange because the Orchard Grange, at most, had only a determinable fee estate that expired when the land ceased to be used for Grange purposes. The Brandts further claim that, upon the termination of the Orchard Grange's estate, the possibility of reverter vested in the Brandts, as a result of being transferred to the Brandts from the Gorzes via the 1984 statutory warranty deed or the 2005 quitclaim deed.

"The owner of any reversionary interest in land has the power . . . to transfer his interest or any part thereof." *Restatement of Property* §159(1). . . .

However, a possibility of reverter does not run with the land; it vests solely in the grantor and the grantor's heirs or assigns. *Restatement of Property* §154, cmt. g. In other words, a possibility of reverter remains solely in the grantor unless the reverter interest is expressly transferred to a third party.

The possibility of reverter arising from the 1950 deed vested exclusively in the Gorzes, as the grantors, not in the land the Gorzes eventually sold to the Brandts or the Shintaffers. Thus, the only means by which the Brandts could have acquired the possibility of reverter is if they received the reverter interest from the Gorzes by either purchase or devise. However, the Gorzes did not transfer their reverter interest to the Brandts by the 1984 deed. That deed merely fulfilled the real estate contract between the Gorzes and the Brandts involving the transfer of the Gorzes' real property. It neither expressly nor impliedly transferred any future reversionary interest held by the Gorzes.

The Brandts contend, however, that even if they did not acquire the Gorzes' reversionary interest via the 1984 deed, the 2005 quitclaim deed passed all of the Gorzes' interest in the property, including the reverter interest in the 1950 deed parcel, to the Brandts. The trial court did not resolve the factual dispute which arose as a result of this claim being raised below. Instead, the court reached its decision to quiet title in the Grange simply by reviewing the "four corners" of the 1950 deed.

The estate of Margaret Gorze is not a party to this action. We cannot determine the interest, if any, held by the estate in the real property at issue. The record before us is not sufficiently developed for us to make such a determination. In the absence of such a determination, however, it is not possible to resolve the Brandts' claim to title. . . .

Accordingly, the trial court's order of summary judgment quieting title in the Grange is reversed and the cause is remanded for further proceedings consistent with this opinion.

Notes and Questions

1. By the 1950 deed at issue in *Washington State Grange*, the Gorzes conveyed their property with the stipulation that "the land herein deeded reverts back to original plot in event it is no longer used for Grange purposes." Disregarding the problem with the rule against perpetuities, what type of present estate did this deed create? What type of future interest did it create in the owners of the "original plot"? If an executory interest, would it be springing or shifting?

2. Would it make any difference to the outcome of this case if the Gorzes instead deeded the land "to Orchard Grange, but if the land is no longer used for Grange purposes, then to the owners of the original plot"? What type of estate would this alternative language create? What type of future interest would it create in the owners of the original plot? If an executory interest, would it be springing or shifting?

3. Suppose the Gorzes had deeded the land "to Orchard Grange if and when Grantee constructs a building on it." Who would hold the right to possess the land until the Grange completed a building? If the Gorzes, what type of present estate would they hold? What type of future interest would this language create? If an executory interest, would it be springing or shifting?

4. The court in *Washington State Grange* refers to the generally accepted rule that, in interpreting deeds, courts limit their review to the "four corners" of the deed itself. In contrast, in decisions involving testamentary transfers such as White v. Brown and Williams v. Estate of Williams, courts freely look beyond the will to other evidence of the testators' intent. In investigating questions of intent, why should courts treat deeds differently from wills?

5. Executory interests were void under early English common law. First authorized at law by the Statute of Uses, which was enacted by the English Parliament in 1535, executory interests quickly became an integral feature of Anglo-American property law, and remain so to this day. Once executory interests were authorized, they were treated by English courts much like contingent remainders in that they could be devised or inherited, but could not be conveyed during the holder's lifetime. They are now freely conveyable in most states.

6. Unlike rights of entry and possibilities of reverter, executory interests are subject to the rule against perpetuities. In a state like Washington that permits the conveyance of existing future interests, the Gorzes could have avoided the rule by creating the limitation as a possibility of reverter. Then they could have subsequently conveyed to whomever they liked. The future interest would remain a possibility of reverter even after it was conveyed, and thus exempt from the rule against perpetuities. This alternative route to the desired result illustrates the formal, sometimes arbitrary impact of the rule against perpetuities, and why it is important for property lawyers to understand it. As one traditional English rule of property law that still has vital significance in many American states, we examine the rule against perpetuities at length in the next section.

D. RULE AGAINST PERPETUITIES

In the previous decision, we encountered the rule against perpetuities for the first time in this casebook. The *Washington State Grange* court quotes Professor John Chipman Gray's classic statement of the rule. Gray's 27 words succinctly set forth the rule's essence. As a beginning property-law student, you should understand their meaning. As property-law professors, we can recite them from memory. Like other traditional English rules of property law, the rule against perpetuities was designed to promote the marketability and development of present estates and limit the dead-hand control of grantors over future interests. Indeed, it remains successful enough in doing so that most American states retain it in some modified form despite having abolished many other formal rules of English property law.

The traditional rule against perpetuities imposes a maximum time limit on the potential duration of every contingent remainder, vested remainder subject to open, and executory interest to which it applies. Under the rule, none of these future interests can possibly last longer than 21 years beyond the death of the last relevant person alive at the time of its creation. Each of them must certainly vest, close, become possessory, or fail within this period; if not, then (under the traditional rule) it is void from the moment of its creation. For example, a grantor may convey property "to his children for life, then to their children who reach the age 21." This ties up the property during the lives of the grantor's children and the legal minority of their children, but no longer. For a contrasting example, a grantor may not convey property "to his children for life, then to their children for life, then to their children for life, and so on ad infinitum," creating something akin to a fee tail in the property. Such a conveyance could tie up the property indefinitely because there is little market for a life estate *pur autre vie* and limited incentive for anyone to develop such an estate. These are but two straightforward examples of how the rule works: Its applications are many and varied. As with any formal property rule, the rule against perpetuities occasionally entraps unwary grantors and often can be evaded by clever drafting. It has bedeviled law students and bemused law professors for generations. The preceding decision and the two that follow illustrate its reach and application in typical, modern situations.

■   **WARREN v. ALBRECHT**
    Appellate Court of Illinois, 1991
    571 N.E.2d 1179

HOWERTON, Justice. This appeal from an action to quiet title to land in Madison County involves the common law rule against perpetuities. James W. McGaughey devised land as follows:

> . . . The above described real estate is given, devised and bequeathed [to] the said John Warren . . . for and during his natural life, and at his death to . . . his then living child or children, or survivors thereof, and in the event there be no descendents of said child or children, then to his sisters, viz: Emma B. Warren and Goldy Maude Warren, for the sole use and benefit forever, share and share alike, subject to the following conditions, viz: That in the event of the death of either of said sisters and leaving no child or children, or descendants of said child or children, then to the survivor, and if neither of said sister [is] living, then to my legal heirs at law, as per the laws of descent, share and share alike and for their sole use and benefit forever.

James W. McGaughey died in 1943. John Warren, his two sons, Donald and Ronald Warren, and his two sisters, Emma B. Warren (Oliver) and Goldy Maude Warren (Albrecht), are living.

In 1987, John Warren's sons, Donald and Ronald Warren, quitclaimed their interest in the land to their father.

In 1988, John Warren, plaintiff, brought an action to quiet title claiming that James W. McGaughey's devise violated the common law rule against perpetuities. Both plaintiff and defendants filed motions for summary judgment. The circuit court granted defendants summary judgment. John Warren appealed.

The rule against perpetuities is a common law rule directed toward the remoteness of vesting. Its ultimate purpose is to prevent the "clogging of titles beyond reasonable limits in time by contingent interests, and to keep land freely alienable in the market places." R. Boyer, *Survey of the Law of Property* 158 (3d ed. 1981). The rule provides:

> No interest is good unless it must vest, if at all, not later than twenty-one years after some life in being at the creation of the interest.

Gray, *The Rule Against Perpetuities* §201, at 191 (4th ed. 1942).

If, by any possibility, an interest cannot vest or fail within the 21-year limit, then the devise is void for remoteness. Interests subject to the rule are contingent remainders, executory interests (or devises), options to purchase land not incident to a lease for years, and powers of appointment. Interests not subject to the rule are present interests in possession, reversions, vested remainders, possibilities of reverter, powers of termination, charitable trusts, and resulting trusts.

Determining into which of these interests this case falls involves a three-step process. First, the language of the devise is explained. Secondly, the status of title is identified. Thirdly, the rule is applied.

In examining the language of the devise, the primary objective is to give effect to the testator's intent by giving the testator's words their plain and ordinary meaning. Here, the language is plain. John Warren was to enjoy the property . . . for his life. At John Warren's death, his children were to take the property, and if any of those children predeceased him, the surviving children were to take the property; if no children or descendants survived John Warren, the estate was to go to John Warren's sisters, Emma and Goldy. If either Emma or Goldy died prior to taking, the survivor was to take; if both died prior to taking, the property would go to the testator's heirs at law. . . .

Here, John Warren was given a life estate. His child or children were given a contingent remainder in fee simple. The descendants of his children were given an alternative contingent remainder in fee simple. Emma and Goldy were also given an alternative contingent remainder in fee simple. James W. McGaughey's heirs at law were not determined until his death, but after his death in 1943 they also possessed an alternative contingent remainder in fee simple.

Lastly, we apply the rule. In his complaint, John Warren claimed that the language — "and in the event there be no descendents of said child or children, then to his sisters" — violated the rule because John Warren's children could be divested longer than 21 years after his death if his children were to die leaving no descendants. To determine if his analysis is correct, we first ask what interest is involved. Here, the children have an alternative contingent remainder in fee simple. A contingent remainder exists if there is a condition precedent to vesting. Here, the condition is that the children survive their father. Applying the rule, we note that once John Warren dies, the interest must necessarily vest or fail. John Warren will either have children survive him, or he won't. Therefore, the devise to his children does not violate the rule. Warren argues that after the estate vests in his child or children, it can be divested if his child or children died without descendants. We disagree.

We believe that a plain reading of the devise indicates that the estate vests at the time of John Warren's death. The language in the fifth paragraph of decedent's will, in our opinion, clearly expresses his purpose. If John Warren's children survive, the estate vests in them. If the children are not alive at John's death, the estate vests in their survivors. If at the time of John's death there are no children or descendants, the estate vests in John's sisters. If the sisters or their children do not survive John's death, then John's heirs at law take the estate. The decedent provided for various alternatives, but, in any event, the estate vests at the life tenant's death. The rule against perpetuities does not apply to vested interests. . . .

The trial court was correct in its granting of defendant's motion for summary judgment, holding the devise did not violate the rule against perpetuities.

Notes and Questions

1. The *Warren* court speaks of "a plain reading of the devise," but the will's language is far from plain. The court interprets the above-quoted language as follows: The devise grants a life estate to John Warren. Upon his death, the property goes to his then-living children. If any child predeceases John, then that child's share goes to her then-living descendants. Nothing goes to children or descendants who are not alive when John dies, which makes their remainders contingent upon them surviving John. At the latest, when will all of these remainders either vest or fail? Is this within the perpetuities period? If all these contingent remainders fail, then (upon John's death) the property goes to John's then-living sisters. If either sister predeceases John, then her share goes to her then-living descendants. Nothing goes to sisters or their descendants who are not alive when John dies, which makes their remainders doubly contingent — not only on them surviving John, but also on all of John's descendants predeceasing him. At the latest, when will all of these remainders either vest or fail? Is this within the perpetuities period? If all of the contingencies fail, then (upon John's death) the property goes to the testator's heirs. Do the testator's heirs hold a remainder or a reversion? At the latest, when will it vest or fail? Is this within the perpetuities period?

2. As stated by the court, under the common law rule against perpetuities, "No interest is good unless it must vest, if at all, not later than twenty-one years after some life in being at the creation of the interest." A "life in being" must be a *validating* or *measuring life*, which is a life of someone alive when the interest was created whose life will determine whether and when the interest will vest or fail. In *Warren*, the validating life is that of John Warren. All of the contingent interest must either vest or fail upon his death. Do you understand why? This satisfies the rule against perpetuities, with 21 years to spare.

3. John Warren initiated this lawsuit to void the future interests of his sisters in the property, and thereby quiet title in himself. He argued that the phrase in the devise reading, "in the event there be no descendants of said child or children, then to his sisters," violates the rule against perpetuities. Do you see how this phrase, read alone, could violate the rule by giving to the sisters (and their descendants) an executory interest in the property? At the latest, when could it happen that John's children had no descendants? Could this occur more than 21 years after

John's death? If the court reads the failure of John's line as a condition subsequent triggering an executory interest in the sisters and their descendants, then (under the rule against perpetuities) that future interest would be void from the outset. The rest of the devise would survive, and John (and his descendants) would have the property.

4. The common law rule against perpetuities should be understood as a rule of logical proof. Any contingent remainder or other future interest subject to the rule must surely vest, fail, or otherwise resolve within the perpetuities period. If this cannot be proven to a logical certainty, then the interest is void from the outset. At least four issues commonly confuse lawyers and law students in the rule's netherworld. First, in computing the perpetuities period for a devise, the clock begins to run when the testator dies, not when the will is signed. Second, a child is considered alive (and therefore "a life in being") from the moment of conception (so long as that child is later born alive); and for a child conceived before (but born after) the death of the person who serves as the validating life, 21 years and 10 months (rather than 21 years) is tagged onto the validating life to cover the child's potential time *in utero*. Third, in applying the rule, all living persons are considered capable of having children, no matter the person's age or physical condition. For example, a conveyance "to A for life, then to A's children who reach age 25," is void even if A is age 80 and all of A's children are over age 25. A could have another child and this child might not reach age 25 within 21 years of A's death. Fourth, any person alive at the creation of a future interest could later marry someone who was not born before its creation. Thus, for example, a conveyance "to A for life, then to O's surviving spouse for life, then to O's then-living children," is void even if O is 80 and O's current spouse is alive. If O later remarried someone not alive at the time of the conveyance (say when O is 99 and the new spouse is 19), there would be no validating life against which to measure when the contingent interest of O's children would vest.

5. There is an exception for charitable gifts and devises; the rule against perpetuities does not apply where both the present estate and the future interest are initially held by charitable organizations. Thus, for example, a grantor could give land "to the Sierra Club so long as the land remains a wildlife preserve, then to the Nature Conservatory." This executory interest is valid even though it could remain open beyond the perpetuities period. What public policy justifies an exemption from the rule for charitable gifts and devises?

■ UNITED VIRGINIA BANK/CITIZENS & MARINE v. UNION OIL COMPANY OF CALIFORNIA
Supreme Court of Virginia, 1973
197 S.E.2d 174

CARRICO, Justice. The question for decision in this appeal is whether the provisions of a land option agreement violate the rule against perpetuities. For reasons to be later discussed, we hold that the rule is violated.

The question arose in a declaratory judgment proceeding brought by United Virginia Bank/Citizens & Marine (hereafter, the Bank), executor and trustee under the last will and testament of William Jonathan Abbitt, deceased, against Union Oil Company of California and Sanford & Charles, Inc. (hereafter, Sanford). The Bank sought a declaration that an option agreement entered into by Abbitt during his lifetime was void and unenforceable on the ground it was in violation of the rule against perpetuities. The trial court held that the agreement was valid and enforce-able, and the Bank appeals.

The agreement in question was entered into on April 7, 1966, between Abbitt and Union Oil Company of California. It was later assigned by Union Oil to Sanford, the active appellee here. It granted the optionee the right and option to purchase a parcel of land 200 feet by 200 feet at the northwest corner of an intersection to be formed by two highways, "Boxley Boulevard Extension and new U.S. 60," proposed to be constructed in the city of Newport News. The option was granted for a period of 120 days. However, the agreement provided as follows:

> It is expressly understood that the 120 days option period shall begin at the time the City of Newport News, Virginia acquires the right of way of Boxley Boulevard Extension and new U.S. 60.

It is this provision which is the focal point of the controversy between the parties, the Bank contending that it results in a violation of the rule against perpe-tuities and Sanford insisting that it does not. Resolution of the controversy requires an examination of the status of "Boxley Boulevard Extension and new U.S. 60" at the time the option agreement was executed. . . .

The Bank contends that the provisions of the agreement in question, making exercise of the option contingent upon acquisition by the city of the rights-of-way of the proposed highways, violates the rule against perpetuities. The Bank says that on April 7, 1966, the date the agreement was executed, "it was not known when, if ever, the City would acquire the rights-of-way for either of [the] proposed thorough-fares." Therefore, the Bank argues, there was "every possibility" that the option might not expire within the period prescribed by the rule against perpetuities.

Sanford contends, on the other hand, that since the proposed highways were shown on the major thoroughfare plan and were contemplated to be completed at the latest by January, 1987, or within 21 years from April 7, 1966, the date of the option agreement, the limitation created by the agreement did not violate the rule against perpetuities. . . .

A preliminary matter requires attention. We must determine what period is to be employed in testing the validity of the limitation created by the option agreement under consideration. Ordinarily, the rule against perpetuities is expressed in terms of the necessity of an interest vesting within a period measured by a life or lives in being plus 21 years and 10 months. But here, the optionee is a corporate, not a human, entity, and the parties have not contracted with reference to a life or lives in being, but rather with reference to an event contemplated to occur sometime in the future. In such circumstances, a gross term of 21 years is the determinative period.

As applied to an option agreement, the rule against perpetuities requires that the option must be exercised, if at all, within the period fixed by the rule. If there exists at the time the agreement is entered into, a possibility that exercise of the option might be postponed beyond the prescribed period, the agreement is invalid because it is in violation of the rule.

The question becomes, therefore, whether there existed at the time the option agreement was entered into in this case a possibility that exercise of the option might be postponed beyond a period of 21 years from the date of the agreement.

Turning to the option agreement itself, it is clear that the parties intended that the optionee would exercise the option, if at all, only upon occurrence of the specific contingency set up in the agreement, that is, the acquisition by the city of the rights-of-way of the proposed highways. It is equally as clear, from the agreement and the surrounding circumstances, that on the date the agreement was executed there existed the distinct possibility that the specified contingency might not occur until after expiration of a period of 21 years from the date of the agreement.

Sanford argues, however, that it was "the dominant intent" of the parties to the option agreement that the city would acquire the rights-of-way in question, if at all, within a reasonable time and that such time "under the circumstances of this case is less than 21 years." This being true, Sanford asserts, we should exercise the *cy pres* power of the judiciary and imply into the terms of the option agreement a provision that the contingency of the city's acquisition of the rights-of-way would occur within a reasonable time not more than 21 years from the date of the agreement. This, Sanford concludes, would effectuate the intention of the parties and avoid a construction of the agreement which would violate the rule against perpetuities.

The answer to this argument is three-fold. In the first place, "the dominant intent" Sanford refers to does not appear from the option agreement itself or from any other source. Secondly, the asserted intent relates to acts which parties other than those privy to the agreement must perform to bring about occurrence of the agreed contingency. So whatever may have been the intent of the contracting parties, it is of little moment. Lastly, assuming, without deciding, that the power of *cy pres* is otherwise available in a case such as this, it may not be employed in Virginia as a vehicle to alter an agreement so as to evade the rule against perpetuities. . . .

Sanford next urges us to adopt the "wait and see" doctrine which has been legislatively enacted into the law of several states and judicially applied in others. Under this doctrine, the rule against perpetuities is determined to have been violated or not by taking into consideration events which occur after the period fixed by the rule has commenced. If, upon a later look, the event upon which an interest was made contingent is found to have occurred and the interest has vested or has become certain to vest within the period fixed by the rule, the rule is held not to have been violated. . . . But . . . the established rule in Virginia, to which we adhere, is that a perpetuities problem may not be solved by resort to what occurs after commencement of the period fixed by the rule. . . .

For the reasons assigned, we hold the option agreement of April 7, 1966, in violation of the rule against perpetuities and, therefore, invalid and unenforceable. Accordingly, the judgment of the trial court will be reversed and final judgment will be entered here declaring the agreement void.

Notes and Questions

1. In some states, the rule against perpetuities applies to *options to purchase* and *rights of first refusal* in addition to contingent remainders, vested remainders subject to open, and executory interests. An option to purchase gives its holder an enforceable right to buy a particular piece of property at an ascertained price for a specific length of time, and thus is akin to a future interest. A right of first refusal gives its holder an enforceable right to buy a particular piece of property at the price offered by others. The rationale for these various applications of the rule is similar. Contingencies restrain the marketability and development of property, so the rule limits their duration. As in the foregoing case, options to purchase often involve commercial transactions between corporations, which (of course) are not living

beings. Without a human validating life to add into the equation, the perpetuities period is a flat 21 years. A perpetuities problem can arise when an option to purchase is tied to the happening of an event (such as road construction) rather than to a date or time period. If the event could happen after the perpetuities period, then the option is void — as it was in *United Virginia Bank*. As applied to a specific option to purchase, does application of the rule against perpetuities advance the original intentions of the parties? If not, why would one party (usually the optionor) later invoke the rule to void the transaction? Is this fair to the other party? Whose interest does the rule serve?

2. Because of the harsh, inflexible impact of the rule against perpetuities in some cases, courts and legislatures have sought to soften its application. In some states, courts possess the authority to reform future interests so as to bring them within the perpetuities period. This authority is called *cy pres*, which means "as near as possible." The object is to carry out the intentions of the parties "as near as possible" under the rule. In the foregoing case, for example, the optionee urged the court to imply that the option to purchase could last no longer than 21 years. Despite the popularity of the *cy pres* among property-law academics, most states do not recognize the doctrine. Where it is recognized, however, it applies to all future interests subject to the rule.

3. In *United Virginia Bank*, the optionee also urged the court to adopt a *wait-and-see* approach to the common law rule against perpetuities. Under this approach, as adopted by the courts of some states, contingent future interests remain valid throughout the perpetuities period, and are voided only if the contingency is not resolved by the end of period. Would taking a wait-and-see approach to the rule have saved the option to purchase in *United Virginia Bank*? How long would the parties wait to see if the city acquired the two roadways?

4. The most popular variant of the wait-and-see approach to the rule against perpetuities appears in the Uniform Statutory Rule Against Perpetuities (USRAP), which (since its promulgation in 1986) has been enacted into law by a majority of state legislatures. Under USRAP, contingent future interests are valid for either the common law perpetuities period or 90 years, whichever is longer. Thereafter, courts are empowered to reform the interest so as to bring it within this extended perpetuities period. Further, USRAP exempts options to purchase and other commercial transactions from all perpetuities limits. Since the foregoing decision in *United Virginia Bank*, Virginia adopted USRAP. How would the case be decided under USRAP? Not surprisingly, a few states that initially adopted USRAP later abolished the rule against perpetuities altogether or at least as applied to perpetual trusts. Some other states have skipped the intermediate step by simply abolishing the rule against perpetuities. As a result, the rule against perpetuities now survives in its traditional form only in Alabama, Arkansas, Wyoming, and the District of Columbia. The variations of it elsewhere are legion.

E. RULES OF CONSTRUCTION AND RULES OF LAW

Rules of construction are flexible guidelines used by courts to interpret ambiguous deeds and wills. As decisions in this chapter and the preceding one illustrate, the estates system is littered with such rules. For example, as the *Roberts* court declares, when forced to interpret language that could create either a fee simple absolute or a fee simple defeasible, courts favor the former. As the *Lawyer's Trust Company* court adds, as between a fee simple determinable and a fee simple subject to condition subsequent, courts favor the latter. Such rules of construction promote consistency and predictability in property law, but they are not iron-clad doctrines that judges must follow in the face of a common-sense reading of the document or clear evidence of the parties' intent. In *Swanson*, for example, the court invokes the standard rule of construction that words of survivorship in a grant refer to surviving the grantor, not another grantee. In *Harris Trust*, reprinted below, a different court declines to apply that same rule. In both cases, the result seems just. In this sense, rules of construction are tools used by courts, not binding constraints on them. As such, they remain a vital feature of modern American property law.

Rules of law, in contrast, are inflexible constraints on how grantors and grantees can convey and hold property. Once a mainstay of the traditional English estates system, such rules have encountered resistance in American courts and legislatures. In *Abo*, for example, the New Mexico Supreme Court rejects the doctrine of the destructibility of contingent remainders as "but a relic of the feudal past, which has no justification or support in modern society." In the following decision, the Illinois Supreme Court similarly dismisses the historic doctrine of worthier title. Of all the traditional English rules of law that once controlled various conveyances, only the rule against perpetuities remains a significant factor in modern property law — and even it has been reformed or abolished in a majority of American states. We will have to wait and see if any of the traditional English rules of property law survive much into the twenty-first century.

■ HARRIS TRUST AND SAVINGS BANK v. BEACH

Supreme Court of Illinois, 1987
513 N.E.2d 833

SIMON, Justice. . . .

In this case Harris Trust and Savings Bank, Robert Hixon Glore and William Gray III, trustees of two trusts, sought instructions from the circuit court of Cook County regarding to whom and in what manner the trusts should be distributed. The central controversy is over the proper construction of the remainder over to the heirs following the death of a life tenant: specifically, the question is whether the settlor intended that his heirs be ascertained at his death, or whether he desired that they be determined after the death of his wife, who was the life tenant.

. . . Frank P. Hixon and Alice Green entered into an antenuptial agreement dated March 30, 1921, and following that, they were married. The agreement created a trust consisting of 200 shares of preferred stock of Pioneer Investment Company, a Hixon family holding company. The trust provided that Alice was to receive the net income of the trust for life. . . . In exchange for the provisions made for her in the trust, Alice surrendered any interest, including dower, which she might have had in Hixon's estate. If Hixon survived Alice, the trust property was to be reconveyed to him. If Alice survived Hixon, the trust provided that on her death "the balance of said trust fund shall be divided among the heirs of the party of the first part [Hixon], share and share alike."

On May 31, 1926, Hixon created a second trust to provide for Alice. The principal of this trust consisted of 300 shares of stock of Pioneer Investment Company. This trust provided that Alice was to receive the income from the principal for life and upon her death "this trust shall terminate, and the trust fund shall be distributed equally among my [Hixon's] heirs." . . .

Hixon died in 1931, when he was 69 years old. He was survived by Alice, who was then 49, by Dorothy and Ellen, who were then 38 and 36, respectively, and by his grandchildren, Frances Glore Beach, Charles F. Glore, Jr., and Robert Hixon Glore, who were then minors.

Alice lived for 51 more years. Both the 1921 and the 1926 trusts continued for her benefit until she died in February 1982. At that time, Hixon's then living descendants were his grandchildren, Frances Glore Beach and Robert Hixon Glore (the grandchildren), and the children of his deceased grandchild, Charles F. Glore, Jr. — Charles F. Glore III, Sallie Glore Farlow, and Edward R. Glore (the great-grandchildren). The parties agree that both the 1921 and the 1926 trust should be distributed in the same manner.

If Hixon's heirs are those surviving at his death, the trust estates will pass under the wills of his two daughters, Ellen H. Glore and Dorothy H. Clark, who both died in 1973. Ellen had three children. One child, as noted above — Charles F. Glore, Jr. — is deceased and survived by three children, Hixon's great-grandchildren. Ellen's other two children — the grandchildren Robert and Frances — are living and are parties to this suit. Dorothy had no children. The devisees under her will are defendants California Institute of Technology, Santa Barbara Foundation, Santa Barbara Cottage Hospital and the Kansas Endowment Association (collectively the charities), and her husband Alfred. Alfred is deceased and his portion of the assets would be distributed to his devisees, Frederick Acker, as special trustee under the will of Charles F. Glore, Jr., and Robert Hixon Glore. On the other hand, if the heirs are determined at the time of Alice's death, the trust estates will be divided among Hixon's now-living descendants — the two grandchildren and three great-grandchildren.

The four charities assert that the heirs should be those heirs alive at Hixon's death; this determination would include them since they were devisees under Dorothy's will. The grandchildren and the great-grandchildren argue that the heirs should be those who were surviving at Alice's death, but they disagree over whether the trusts should be divided *per stirpes* (by each share) or *per capita* (by each head). . . .

I.

The word "heirs" refers to "those persons appointed by the law to inherit an estate in case of intestacy." Le Sourd v. Leinweber 105 N.E.2d 722, 724 (Ill. 1952). When used in its technical sense, the testator's or settlor's heirs are, of course, determined at the time of his death. This court, however, has never adopted the technical meaning of the word "heirs" as a rule of law. We have observed that "'heirs' when used in a will does not necessarily have a fixed meaning. It may mean children or, where there are no children, it may mean some other class of heirs . . . if the context of the entire will *plainly shows* such to have been the intention of the testator." Stites v. Gray, 123 N.E.2d 483, 486 (Ill. 1955) (emphasis added). A determination of the class of heirs, therefore, is governed by the settlor's or testator's intention rather than by a fixed rule of law. The rule in Illinois, however, has been that, unless the settlor's intention to the contrary is "plainly shown" in the trust document, courts will rely upon the technical meaning of the term "heirs" by applying it as a rule of construction. The charities are, therefore, correct in their observation that presently our rule of construction requires us to determine heirs at the settlor's death unless the trust or will provides clear evidence to the contrary. The initial question we must address is whether we should continue to adhere to this standard of proof.

The charities contend that this high degree of proof is necessary to rebut the rule of construction because of the policy favoring early vesting of remainders. . . . However, they overlook that two eminent scholars in the field of Illinois future interest law revised their views regarding the policy in favor of early vesting. In the supplement to their treatise entitled the *Illinois Law of Future Interests,* Carey and Schuyler observe that "it was the rule regarding the destructibility of contingent remainders that caused courts to favor the early vesting of estates. . . . But now, in this state and in many others, there is no rule of destructibility. If the original reason for favoring early vesting is gone, why continue to favor it?" H. Carey and D. Schuyler, *Illinois Law of Future Interests* 190 (Cum. Pocket Part 1954).

Briefly stated, the destruction of contingent remainders was an archaic device which frequently frustrated grantors' intentions by prematurely defeating an interest subject to a condition. By vesting remainders as quickly as possible the drastic effects of destructibility "could be contained by a rule of construction which resulted in declaring that future interests were vested and hence indestructible." H. Carey and D. Schuyler, *Illinois Law of Future Interests* 190 (Cum. Pocket Part 1954). Our legislature abolished destructibility . . . in 1921. However, despite the passage of this statute, vesting remainders as quickly as possible was such an imbedded rule of construction that in many cases courts continued to adhere to it without question and regardless of the consequences. . . .

We agree with Professors Carey and Schuyler that early vesting of remainders should no longer be followed in this State without question. Early vesting is an axiom which must not get in the way when a contrary intent is demonstrated by a preponderance of the evidence. Requiring *clear and convincing* evidence or a *plain showing* to rebut the presumption in favor of the technical meaning of the term "heirs," has its roots in the maxim favoring early vesting of remainders. Frequently this policy, as is the case here (where trust property would pass from the settlor's family), frustrates what the ordinary settlor would have intended. We hold that because the primary reason for early vesting is no longer as important as it formerly was, proof by the preponderance of the evidence that the settlor, testator, or donor intended to use the term "heirs" in its nontechnical sense is sufficient to delay the vesting of a gift to a time other than at the grantor's death.

The result of delaying a gift to the heirs is not dramatic. The fear that a contingent remainder could be prematurely destroyed no longer exists. Further, should a predeceased member of the class be excluded from the gift, the result is not drastic. If the predeceased "heir" leaves issue, as is the case here, the settlor's own blood still enjoys the gift. If, on the other hand, a predeceased member fails to leave issue, as also occurred here, the gift is prevented from falling into the hands of strangers. In sum, by altering the degree of proof necessary to delay the vesting of a gift to the heirs, we do no harm. Instead, we further the ordinary grantor's intent, which is exactly what a proper rule of construction ought to do. Consequently, in this case we must determine which parties have offered the preponderant proof as to Hixon's intent — the charities or the grandchildren and great-grandchildren.

Hixon's trusts, as the charities stress, do not explicitly state the point at which his heirs should be determined. The 1921 trust provides that the "balance of said trust fund shall be divided among the heirs," and the 1926 trust states that "the trust shall be distributed equally among my [Hixon's] heirs." When the trusts are considered as a whole, however, it becomes apparent that the documents revolve totally around Alice's life and death; Hixon's life and death play only secondary roles. As the grandchildren and great-grandchildren note, the trusts were created for Alice's benefit in exchange for her rights to dower or any other portion of Hixon's estate. The trusts were intended to last throughout her life, and depending upon when she died, the trust principal would either revert to Hixon or be distributed to his heirs. Alice's central role in the trust is indicative of Hixon's intent to make her and not himself the point of reference for determining the heirs. . . . Viewing all of these indications with respect to Hixon's intent together, we conclude that the preponderant proof favors the position of the grandchildren and great-grandchildren and Hixon's heirs should therefore be determined at Alice's death.

II.

Because we have concluded that it was Hixon's intention that the heirs were to be ascertained at Alice's death, the doctrine of worthier title is not applicable. The doctrine, which was developed in medieval England but abolished there in 1833, voids a gift to the grantor's heirs. It was premised on the notion that it was worthier to take by descent than by devise. The doctrine was incorporated into American common law, but in Illinois our legislature abolished it in 1955.

In Illinois, the doctrine applies only where the devisees would take exactly the same estate by devise as they would by descent. It "is not applicable where there is a difference in kind or quality of the estate or property to be passed under the devise from that which would descend under the statute [the laws of descent and distribution]." McNeilly v. Wylie, 59 N.E.2d 811, 812 (Ill. 1945). Therefore, under Illinois law the doctrine is not likely to operate when the heirs are determined after the termination of a life estate; when vesting is postponed the devisees rarely receive either the same amount or the same estate as they would had their gift taken effect at the testator's death.

Having already concluded that Hixon's heirs are to be determined at Alice's and not at Hixon's death, those who would take Hixon's estate under the laws of descent and distribution had Hixon died intestate — Alice and the two daughters — are not the same as those who will take after Alice's death — the grandchildren and great-grandchildren. As a result, the doctrine is not relevant and therefore we need not reach the other issues briefed before this court: whether the doctrine is a rule of construction or rule of law and whether the doctrine is an anachronism which should be abandoned in the case of trusts established in Illinois prior to our 1955 statutory abolition of the doctrine.

III.

The final question is whether the gift to the grandchildren and great-grandchildren should be distributed *per stirpes* or *per capita.* The great-grandchildren contend that because Hixon used the words "share and share alike" and instructed the trustees to distribute the gift "equally," the gift must be divided on a *per capita* basis. The great-grandchildren accurately observe that, "When the words 'equally,' 'equal among,' 'share and share alike,' or other similar words, are used to indicate an equal division among a class, the persons among whom the division is to be made are usually held to take per capita unless a contrary intention is discoverable from the will." Dollander v. Dhaemers, 130 N.E. 705, 706 (Ill. 1921). However, "it is worthy of remark that the leading cases which sustain a distribution per capita intimate that a very small indication of intent to the contrary would change the rule." *Id.* at 707, quoting Eyer v. Beck, 38 N.W. 20, 21 (Mich. 1888). When a testator leaves his estate to his or her heirs, courts generally conclude that the testator intended the gift to be distributed in accordance with laws of descent and distribution which provide for a *per stirpes* distribution. Under these circumstances we have stated that "a gift to issue 'equally' and 'share and share alike' does not require that each of such issue shall have an equal share with the other; that the mandate is satisfied if the issue of equal degree taking *per stirpes* share equally." Condee v. Trout, 39 N.E.2d 350, 352 (Ill. 1942).

In the present case, Hixon left the remainder in the trust principal to his heirs. That he provided for his heirs to share equally in that gift fails to rebut the presumption in favor of a *per stirpes* distribution; the gift to the class of heirs is a sufficient indication that Hixon intended the remainder to be divided in accordance with the laws of descent and distribution. . . .

We conclude that the remainder in the heirs should be distributed *per stirpes* with the three great-grandchildren each taking one-ninth of the estate and the two grandchildren each taking one-third. . . .

Notes and Questions

1. As the *Harris Trust* court notes, furthering "the ordinary grantor's intent . . . is exactly what a proper rule of construction ought to do." Because rules of construction evolved to address ambiguities arising in normal cases, their application can become problematic in abnormal ones. In *Harris Trust,* for example, the grantor created two typical marital trusts designed to provide income to his second wife for life, with the remainder to his "heirs," who would most likely be the two adult children from his first marriage. The trust corpus consisted of stock in the family business, which normally would remain within the family. Then the abnormal happened. The second wife outlived both children and one grandchild, with one of the deceased children having devised a portion of her estate outside the family. After considering rules of construction favoring the early vesting of contingent remainders and giving words their technical meaning, the court rejects their application in this case. Do you see why? Did the court's ruling advance the grantor's intent? Would following the standard rules of construction in this case have frustrated his intent?

2. The *Harris Trust* court distinguishes flexible rules of construction from fixed rules of law. If triggered, a rule of law applies whether or not it advances the intentions of the parties. Harris' descendants raise one such rule in this case, the *doctrine of worthier title.* Under that doctrine, if a living grantor (Frank Hixon in this case) uses one instrument to create a limited estate in a grantee (his wife, here) and a remainder or executory interest in his own heirs, then the future interest becomes a reversion in the grantor. How would the doctrine help Harris' descendants if the court had given a technical reading to the word "heirs"? The doctrine of worthier title has been abolished in many states, but the conveyance at issue in *Harris Trust* occurred before the doctrine was abolished in Illinois—so it might have applied. The court avoids deciding whether to abandon the doctrine retroactively by not

giving the technical meaning to the word "heirs." Do you see how this avoids the issue?

3. Another rule of law, the *rule in Shelley's case,* is closely related to the doctrine of worthier title. Under the rule in Shelley's case, if any deed or will purports to create a life estate in a grantee with a remainder in the grantee's heirs, then the remainder in the grantee's heirs becomes a remainder in the grantee. So long as there is no intervening vested remainder, the doctrine of merger then unites the grantee's life estate with her vested remainder into a single present estate. The rule in Shelley's case has been abolished in all but eight states, though it still has retroactive effect in other states.

4. Frank Hixon's two trusts create further ambiguity by saying that the corpus is to be divided or distributed "equally" among Hixon's heirs, "share and share alike." This ambiguity would not matter if all of Hixon's heirs (for purposes of the distribution) were of the same class or level (such as all children or grandchildren). As it turned out, however, Hixon's heirs include two grandchildren and three great-grandchildren of a deceased grandchild. If the court distributed the corpus equally among these five heirs, each would get one-fifth. This is called a *per capita* distribution. When a grantor gives property to his heirs, however, courts typically assume that the intention is for it to pass *per stirpes,* with equal shares going down each line of descent. Applied to Hixon's heirs, the two living grandchildren would get one-third each, and the three children of the deceased grandchild would share the final third, or one-ninth each. As the court notes, the standard rule of construction holds that a gift or devise to one's "heirs" or "issue" passes *per stirpes* unless some contrary intent is stated. Should Hixon's use of the words "equally" and "share and share alike" have overcome this otherwise reasonable presumption? Grantors and testators commonly avoid this ambiguity by simply stating in the deed or will whether heirs or issue are to receive property *per capita* or *per stirpes.*

8

Concurrent Ownership

Any of the estates in land, present or future, may be owned by one individual person or by multiple persons. When an estate is owned by more than one person, the owners are called *cotenants*. Modern law allows three types of cotenancy and nine mostly Western states recognize community property between spouses.

The two most common types of cotenancy are joint tenancy and tenancy in common. A *joint tenancy* grants each cotenant a right of survivorship. When a joint tenant dies, that tenant's interest expires, which means the property is then owned by the surviving joint tenant or tenants. A joint tenant's interest is neither inheritable nor devisable and all joint tenants must have equal interests in the property. A joint tenancy is ordinarily used only among related parties or between unmarried partners as a land ownership and estate planning device. It's a substitute for devising property by will.

A *tenancy in common* differs from a joint tenancy in that the cotenants have no right of survivorship and do not necessarily own equal interests in the property. Each tenant's interest is freely inheritable and devisable. This type of cotenancy is commonly used by business partners and friends who own real estate together. If a deed or will does not specify what form of cotenancy is being created, traditional common law presumed a joint tenancy, but modern law presumes a tenancy in common.

Both joint tenants and tenants in common can convey their interest to another person. When a tenant in common makes a conveyance, the grantee becomes a new tenant in common. When a joint tenant makes a conveyance, the grantee becomes a tenant in common, *not* a new joint tenant. Under modern practice in all 50 states, any joint tenant or tenant in common may obtain a judicial *partition* (or legal division) of the cotenancy, with each of the former cotenants receiving their appropriate share of the whole.

The least common type of cotenancy is *tenancy by the entirety* (sometimes called *tenancy by the entireties*), which is recognized in less than half of the states and seldom used in many of them. Only married couples can hold property in this form of cotenancy, except in Hawaii, where same-sex couples can hold property as tenants by the entirety if they register as "reciprocal beneficiaries" under a statute passed in 1997. Haw. Rev. Stat. §509-2. With tenancy by the entirety, there is a right of survivorship, just as for joint tenancy; but there is no right to partition, and conveyances by a single spouse are generally ineffective. The tenancy by the entirety represents a form of judgment proofing. Often a tenancy by the entirety shields the property from attachment or execution by a creditor of just one spouse.

The final modern form of shared ownership is *community property*, which came to the United States from the Spanish civil code and survives primarily in states that once were ruled by Spain, such as Texas and California. Unless some other form of ownership is established, each item of real and personal property held by married persons in these states is presumed to be owned 50-50 by the two spouses. Because these two forms of ownership overlap, states that recognize community property do not permit tenancy by the entirety.

A. COTENANTS

1. *Right to Shared Possession*

■ GEORGIA v. RANDOLPH
Supreme Court of the United States, 2006
547 U.S. 103

SOUTER, Justice. The Fourth Amendment recognizes a valid warrantless entry and search of premises when police obtain the voluntary consent of an occupant who shares, or is reasonably believed to share, authority over the area in common with a co-occupant who later objects to the use of evidence so obtained. Illinois v. Rodriguez, 497 U.S. 177 (1990); United States v. Matlock, 415 U.S. 164 (1974). The question here is whether such an evidentiary seizure is likewise lawful with the permission of one occupant when the other, who later seeks to suppress the evidence, is present at the scene and expressly refuses to consent. We hold that, in the circumstances here at issue, a physically present co-occupant's stated refusal to permit entry prevails, rendering the warrantless search unreasonable and invalid as to him.

I.

Respondent Scott Randolph and his wife, Janet, separated in late May 2001, when she left the marital residence in Americus, Georgia, and went to stay with her parents in Canada, taking their son and some belongings. In July, she returned to the Americus house with the child, though the record does not reveal whether her object was reconciliation or retrieval of remaining possessions.

On the morning of July 6, she complained to the police that after a domestic dispute her husband took their son away, and when officers reached the house she told them that her husband was a cocaine user whose habit had caused financial troubles. She mentioned the marital problems and said that she and their son had only recently returned after a stay of several weeks with her parents. Shortly after the police arrived, Scott Randolph returned and explained that he had removed the child to a neighbor's house out of concern that his wife might take the boy out of the country again; he denied cocaine use, and countered that it was in fact his wife who abused drugs and alcohol.

One of the officers, Sergeant Murray, went with Janet Randolph to reclaim the child, and when they returned she not only renewed her complaints about her husband's drug use, but also volunteered that there were "'items of drug evidence'" in the house. Brief for Petitioner 3. Sergeant Murray asked Scott Randolph for permission to search the house, which he unequivocally refused.

The sergeant turned to Janet Randolph for consent to search, which she readily gave. She led the officer upstairs to a bedroom that she identified as Scott's, where the sergeant noticed a section of a drinking straw with a powdery residue he suspected was cocaine. He then left the house to get an evidence bag from his car and to call the district attorney's office, which instructed him to stop the search and apply for a warrant. When Sergeant Murray returned to the house, Janet Randolph withdrew her consent. The police took the straw to the police station, along with the Randolphs. After getting a search warrant, they returned to the house and seized further evidence of drug use, on the basis of which Scott Randolph was indicted for possession of cocaine.

He moved to suppress the evidence, as products of a warrantless search of his house unauthorized by his wife's consent over his express refusal. The trial court denied the motion, ruling that Janet Randolph had common authority to consent to the search.

The Court of Appeals of Georgia reversed, and was itself sustained by the State Supreme Court, principally on the ground that "the consent to conduct a warrantless search of a residence given by one occupant is not valid in the face of the refusal of another occupant who is physically present at the scene to permit a warrantless search." 604 S.E.2d 835, 836 (Ga. 2004). . . .

We granted certiorari to resolve a split of authority on whether one occupant may give law enforcement effective consent to search shared premises, as against a co-tenant who is present and states a refusal to permit the search. . . .

II.

To the Fourth Amendment rule ordinarily prohibiting the warrantless entry of a person's house as unreasonable *per se*, one "jealously and carefully drawn" exception, Jones v. United States, 357 U.S. 493, 499 (1958), recognizes the validity of searches with the voluntary consent of an individual possessing authority, *Rodriguez*, 497 U.S. at 181. That person might be the householder against whom evidence is sought, or a fellow occupant who shares common authority over property, when the suspect is absent, *Matlock, supra* at 170, and the exception for consent extends even to entries and searches with the permission of a co-occupant whom the police reasonably, but erroneously, believe to possess shared authority as an occupant, *Rodriguez, supra* at 186. None of our co-occupant consent-to-search cases, however, has presented the further fact of a second occupant physically present and refusing permission to search, and later moving to suppress evidence so obtained. The significance of such a refusal turns on the underpinnings of the co-occupant consent rule, as recognized since *Matlock*.

A.

The defendant in that case was arrested in the yard of a house where he lived with a Mrs. Graff and several of her relatives, and was detained in a squad car parked nearby. When the police went to the door, Mrs. Graff admitted them and consented to a search of the house. 415 U.S. at 166. In resolving the defendant's objection to use of the evidence taken in the warrantless search, we said that "the consent of one who possesses common authority over premises or effects is valid as against the absent, nonconsenting person with whom that authority is shared." *Id.* at 170. Consistent with our prior understanding that Fourth Amendment rights are not limited by the law of property, we explained that the third party's "common authority" is not synonymous with a technical property interest:

> The authority which justified the third-party consent does not rest upon the law of property, with its attendant historical and legal refinement, but rests rather on mutual use of the property by persons generally having joint access or control for most purposes, so that it is reasonable to recognize that any of the co-inhabitants has the right to permit the inspection in his own right and that the others have assumed the risk that one of their number might permit the common area to be searched.

Id. at 171 n.7. The common authority that counts under the Fourth Amendment may thus be broader than the rights accorded by property law, *see Rodriguez, supra* at 181-182 (consent is sufficient when given by a person who reasonably appears to have common authority but who, in fact, has no property interest in the premises searched), although its limits, too, reflect specialized tenancy arrangements apparent to the police, *see* Chapman v. United States, 365 U.S. 610 (1961) (landlord could not consent to search of tenant's home).

The constant element in assessing Fourth Amendment reasonableness in the consent cases, then, is the great significance given to widely shared social expectations, which are naturally enough influenced by the law of property, but not controlled by its rules. *Matlock* accordingly not only holds that a solitary co-inhabitant may sometimes consent to a search of shared premises, but stands for the proposition that the reasonableness of such a search is in significant part a function of commonly held understanding about the authority that co-inhabitants may exercise in ways that affect each other's interests.

B.

Matlock's example of common understanding is readily apparent. When someone comes to the door of a domestic dwelling with a baby at her hip, as Mrs. Graff did, she shows that she belongs there, and that fact standing alone is enough to tell a law enforcement officer or any other visitor that if she occupies the place along with others, she probably lives there subject to the assumption tenants usually make about their common authority when they share quarters. They understand that any one of them may admit visitors, with the consequence that a guest obnoxious to one may nevertheless be admitted in his absence by another. As *Matlock* put it, shared tenancy is understood to include an "assumption of risk," on which police officers are entitled to rely, and although some group living together might make an exceptional arrangement that no one could admit a guest without the agreement of all, the chance of such an eccentric scheme is too remote to expect visitors to investigate a particular household's rules before accepting an invitation to come in. So, *Matlock* relied on what was usual and placed no burden on the police to eliminate the possibility of atypical arrangements, in the absence of reason to doubt that the regular scheme was in place.

It is also easy to imagine different facts on which, if known, no common authority could sensibly be suspected. A person on the scene who identifies himself, say, as a landlord or a hotel manager calls up no customary understanding of authority to admit guests without the consent of the current occupant. . . . In these circumstances, neither state-law property rights, nor common contractual arrangements, nor any other source points to a common understanding of authority to admit third parties generally without the consent of a person occupying the premises. . . .

C.

Although we have not dealt directly with the reasonableness of police entry in reliance on consent by one occupant subject to immediate challenge by another, we took a step toward the issue in an earlier case dealing with the Fourth Amendment rights of a social guest arrested at premises the police entered without a warrant or the benefit of any exception to the warrant requirement. Minnesota v. Olson, 495 U.S. 91 (1990), held that overnight houseguests have a legitimate expectation of privacy in their temporary quarters because "it is unlikely that [the host] will admit someone who wants to see or meet with the guest over the objection of the guest," *id.* at 99. If that customary expectation of courtesy or deference is a foundation of Fourth Amendment rights of a houseguest, it presumably should follow that an inhabitant of shared premises may claim at least as much, and it turns out that the co-inhabitant naturally has an even stronger claim.

To begin with, it is fair to say that a caller standing at the door of shared premises would have no confidence that one occupant's invitation was a sufficiently good reason to enter when a fellow tenant stood there saying, "stay out." Without some very good reason, no sensible person would go inside under those conditions. Fear for the safety of the occupant issuing the invitation, or of someone else inside, would be thought to justify entry, but the justification then would be the personal risk, the threats to life or limb, not the disputed invitation.

The visitor's reticence without some such good reason would show not timidity but a realization that when people living together disagree over the use of their common quarters, a resolution must come through voluntary accommodation, not by appeals to authority. Unless the people living together fall within some recognized hierarchy, like a household of parent and child or barracks housing military personnel of different grades, there is no societal understanding of superior and inferior, a fact reflected in a standard formulation of domestic property law, that "[e]ach cotenant . . . has the right to use and enjoy the entire property as if he or she were the sole owner, limited only by the same right in the other cotenants." 7 R. Powell, *Powell on Real Property* §50.03[1], p. 50-14 (M. Wolf gen. ed. 2005). The want of any recognized superior authority among disagreeing tenants is also reflected in the law's response when the disagreements cannot be resolved. The law does not ask who has the better side of the conflict; it simply provides a right to any co-tenant, even the most unreasonable, to obtain a decree partitioning the property (when the relationship is one of co-ownership) and terminating the relationship. And while a decree of partition is not the answer to disagreement among rental tenants, this situation resembles co-ownership in lacking the benefit of any understanding that one or the other rental co-tenant has a superior claim to control the use of the quarters they occupy together. In sum, there is no common understanding that one co-tenant generally has a right or authority to prevail over the express wishes of another, whether the issue is the color of the curtains or invitations to outsiders.

D.

Since the co-tenant wishing to open the door to a third party has no recognized authority in law or social practice to prevail over a present and objecting co-tenant, his disputed invitation, without more, gives a police officer no better claim to reasonableness in entering than the officer would have in the absence of any consent at all. Accordingly, in the balancing of competing individual and governmental interests entailed by the bar to unreasonable searches, the cooperative occupant's invitation adds nothing to the government's side to counter the force of an object-ing individual's claim to security against the government's intrusion into his dwelling place. . . .

III.

This case invites a straightforward application of the rule that a physically pres-ent inhabitant's express refusal of consent to a police search is dispositive as to him, regardless of the consent of a fellow occupant. Scott Randolph's refusal is clear, and nothing in the record justifies the search on grounds independent of Janet Ran-dolph's consent. The State does not argue that she gave any indication to the police of a need for protection inside the house that might have justified entry into the portion of the premises where the police found the powdery straw (which, if lawfully seized, could have been used when attempting to establish probable cause for the warrant issued later). Nor does the State claim that the entry and search should be upheld under the rubric of exigent circumstances, owing to some apprehension by the police officers that Scott Randolph would destroy evidence of drug use before any warrant could be obtained.

The judgment of the Supreme Court of Georgia is therefore affirmed.

Justice BREYER, concurring. If Fourth Amendment law forced us to choose between two bright-line rules, (1) a rule that always found one tenant's consent sufficient to justify a search without a warrant and (2) a rule that never did, I believe we should choose the first. That is because, as the Chief Justice's dissent points out, a rule permitting such searches can serve important law enforcement needs (for example, in domestic abuse cases) and the consenting party's joint tenancy diminishes the objecting party's reasonable expectation of privacy.

But the Fourth Amendment does not insist upon bright-line rules. Rather, it recognizes that no single set of legal rules can capture the ever changing complexity of human life. It consequently uses the general terms "unreasonable searches and seizures." And this Court has continuously emphasized that "[r]easonable-ness . . . is measured . . . by examining the totality of the circumstances." Ohio v. Robinette, 519 U.S. 33, 39 (1996). . . .

Chief Justice ROBERTS, with whom Justice SCALIA joins, dissenting. The Court creates constitutional law by surmising what is typical when a social guest encounters an entirely atypical situation. The rule the majority fashions does not implement the high office of the Fourth Amendment to protect privacy, but instead provides pro-tection on a random and happenstance basis, protecting, for example, a co-occu-pant who happens to be at the front door when the other occupant consents to a search, but not one napping or watching television in the next room. And the cost of affording such random protection is great, as demonstrated by the recurring cases in which abused spouses seek to authorize police entry into a home they share with a nonconsenting abuser.

The correct approach to the question presented is clearly mapped out in our precedents: The Fourth Amendment protects privacy. If an individual shares infor-mation, papers, *or places* with another, he assumes the risk that the other person will in turn share access to that information or those papers *or places* with the government. . . .

. . . Just as Mrs. Randolph could walk upstairs, come down, and turn her husband's cocaine straw over to the police, she can consent to police entry and search of what is, after all, her home, too. . . .

[Concurring opinion by Justice STEVENS and dissenting opinions by Justices SCALIA and THOMAS are omitted. Justice ALITO did not participate.]

Notes and Questions

1. *Randolph* deals with the intersection of criminal law and property law. The police might have sought a warrant to search the Randolphs' house, but that would have occasioned delay and required a showing of "probable cause" to a judge or magistrate. There are a number of instances in which the police may conduct a search without first obtaining a search warrant. A search by consent is one such instance. In most cases when the search reveals evidence of a crime, the consenting party becomes the defendant in the criminal prosecution; but in some cases, like *Randolph*, a third party has given the consent. The rules governing the validity of third-party consent are complex. Our purpose here is not to study search and seizure law in any significant way — that task must be left to a course in criminal procedure. The point here is for you to see how property rights can affect criminal law issues, and vice versa. Notice that the *Randolph* Court determines the legality of the search not by direct examination of the Fourth Amendment prohibition of "unreasonable searches and seizures," but by exploring the nature of the cotenancy relationship as defined by widely shared social expectations and property law.

2. Did the police unlawfully invade Scott Randolph's privacy notwithstanding his wife's consent to the search of their house? Should it matter that Janet and Scott Randolph were estranged and that the police officers could reasonably suspect that Janet would benefit from her husband's arrest and conviction? Might the officers' expectations be different if Janet and Scott Randolph were happily married? Further, should it make any difference which spouse owned or rented their residence or if they owned or rented it together? What if they were simply two unmarried and unattached people renting a residence together or if they were business partners who co-owned or co-leased an office or other commercial premises — should different rules apply? What if Scott was Janet's guest, or her minor son?

3. Criminal conduct of one cotenant can affect the property rights of another cotenant due to the application of *forfeiture laws*. Federal statutes provide for civil or criminal forfeiture of property used in a wide range of illegal activities, the most prominent being drug trafficking. The drug statutes provide an exception to forfeiture for the property interest of an "innocent owner," but it is often difficult for a co-owner to prove innocence. State statutes also provide for forfeiture of property in connection with certain crimes, sometimes without an innocent owner defense. For example, in Bennis v. Michigan, 516 U.S. 442 (1996), a husband was convicted of gross indecency for having sex with a prostitute in a car parked on a public street. His wife, co-owner of the car with her wayward husband, did not know, at the time, of his wrongdoing. The State declared the car forfeited under its public nuisance statute, refusing to recognize or pay for her one-half interest. By a 5-4 vote, the Supreme Court rejected her claim that Michigan's failure to provide an innocent-owner defense violated the Due Process Clause or the Takings Clause. Should forfeiture

laws be curtailed or expanded, or do they presently strike the right balance between law enforcement objectives and the protection of private property?

4. At common law, all cotenants have the right to possess the entire premises and have the right to transfer their possessory rights, by lease or license, to other persons. Yet the Court refuses to apply those rules in this particular context of police searches. Can you think of other situations in which these broad propositions ought to bend when cotenants' interests or desires conflict?

■ **BARROW v. BARROW**
Supreme Court of Florida, 1988
527 So. 2d 1373

OVERTON, Justice. This is a petition to review Barrow v. Barrow, 505 So. 2d 506 (Fla. 2d DCA 1987), in which the district court held that in partition actions the rules regarding notice of ouster from a former marital home must be applied differently for cotenants who are former spouses than for other cotenants. The circumstances involve a claim for rental value from a former spouse in possession. The district court relied on its prior decision of Adkins v. Edwards, 317 So. 2d 770 (Fla. 2d DCA 1975). . . . We find the rules of the law governing partition should be the same for former spouses as for other cotenants, but conclude the respondent is entitled under an established exception to set off her claim for reasonable rental value against a claim for maintenance or improvement expenses.

. . . [P]etitioner, James Barrow, owned title to and built a residence on four and one-half acres of land prior to his marriage to the respondent, Donna Barrow. This property became their residence for the ten years they were married. In a dissolution proceeding, the final judgment awarded an undivided one-half interest in the property as alimony to Donna Barrow. The final judgment made no provision for possession by either party and made no direction regarding the sale or disposition of the property.

Donna Barrow moved her family to Idaho immediately after separating from the petitioner. Several years later, she initiated this proceeding with a complaint seeking partition of the former marital home. James Barrow counterclaimed for one-half the amounts expended by him for taxes, insurance, and other services necessary to maintain and improve the property. Donna Barrow responded by seeking one-half the fair rental value for the period James Barrow had occupied the home after the parties' dissolution. Before the trial court, James Barrow asserted that his former wife did not object to his sole occupancy; that she was not excluded from the premises; that he did not hold the premises adversely or hostilely to her title: and that he had never refused her access to the property. Donna Barrow responded that James Barrow had occupied the home throughout the dissolution proceedings; that he had changed the locks on the doors; that he had obtained a new telephone number; and that he had declined to respond to her letters.

In considering Donna Barrow's claim that she was entitled to fair rental value of the property, the trial court concluded that the Second District's decision in *Adkins* required approval of her claim. The trial court found Donna Barrow entitled to $8,254.50, a sum representing one-half of the determined fair rental value of the property for the period beginning August 5, 1983, the date of entry of the final judgment of dissolution of marriage, and ending January 15, 1986, the date of the nonjury trial in this partition proceeding, and further found James Barrow entitled to $2,591, a sum representing one-half the property taxes and insurance premiums. The trial court considered the claim of the respondent as an independent claim and not solely as a setoff. The record establishes that the trial judge based his ruling on the Second District's decision in *Adkins*, even though he apparently did not agree with it. His comments at the end of the testimony and arguments of counsel were as follows:

> THE COURT: You have one tenant moving out of the state and leaving and the other one is staying in the house. You do not have any demand for rent. You do not have any demand for possession. You have nothing. You have just apparently a voluntary relinquishment on the part of the wife.
>
> It strikes me that there a something a little inequitable about the idea that the other co-tenant is liable for rent, even though he does not know — he or she — that that claim is being made or going to be made and not knowing it does not have any way to exercise a judgment as to whether he wants to stay on or not, particularly in the case — you do not have a mortgage — particularly in the case where you have a large mortgage.
>
> The person staying on there did not have the idea that there was going to be — unless you imply it in law that they have that claim.
>
> I personally would think that the law should have something to do with making a demand for it, but perhaps if the cases do not, they do not.

On appeal, the district court, in a simple three-line opinion, stated its affirmance was on the authority of *Adkins*. . . .

[W]e find it appropriate to review the applicable case law beginning with our decision in Coggan v. Coggan, 239 So. 2d 17 (Fla. 1970). In *Coggan*, a former wife of a doctor brought an action against her former husband for partition of his office building and for an accounting of one-half the rental value. The building had been jointly owned by the parties until their divorce, at which time they became tenants in common. Nothing was stated in the decree or by agreement as to its use and possession, and the former husband continued in possession, paying the taxes, making necessary repairs, and exercising complete control over the property. *Id.* at 18. On appeal, the district court recognized the common law rule that, when one tenant in common has exclusive possession of the lands and uses those lands for his own benefit but does not receive rents or profits therefrom, he is not liable or accountable to his cotenant not in possession unless he holds adversely or as a result of ouster or the equivalent thereof. Coggan v. Coggan, 230 So. 2d 34, 36 (Fla. 2d DCA 1969), *aff'd in part, quashed in part*, 239 So. 2d 17 (Fla. 1970). In *Coggan*, the evidence at trial revealed that the doctor had always considered himself the sole owner of the property and believed his former wife had no rights therein; however, there was no evidence that he had ever expressed that attitude to her or that she was cognizant of his claim. The district court found that under these circumstances the husband's actions were the equivalent of an ouster and granted the former wife's claim for rents. 230 So. 2d at 36. Upon review by this Court, we quashed that holding and stated:

> The possession of a tenant in common is presumed to be the possession of all cotenants until the one in possession brings home to the other the knowledge that he claims the exclusive right or title. . . .
>
> *There can be no holding adversely or ouster or its equivalent, by one cotenant unless such holding is manifested or communicated to the other.* Where a tenant out of possession claims an accounting of a tenant in possession, he must show that the tenant in possession is holding the exclusive possession of the property adversely or holding the exclusive

possession as a result of ouster or the equivalent thereof. This possession must be attended with such circumstances as to evince a claim of the exclusive right or title by the tenant in possession imparted to the tenant out of possession.

239 So. 2d at 19 (emphasis added). . . .

In Adkins v. Edwards, 317 So. 2d 770 (Fla. 2d DCA 1975), the Second District Court of Appeal . . . distinguished our *Coggan* decision, reasoning that the nature of the properties involved in *Coggan* was such that joint occupancy by the cotenants was not effectively precluded. The *Adkins* court held:

> In cases like this there frequently exists an aura of hostility and awkwardness not necessarily common to cotenancy of lands or other properties held for commercial purposes. While *neither of the parties contended that he or she was ousted from possession*, it is unrealistic to believe that parties who could not get along living together while they were married would be expected to enjoy common usage of the former marital home after their divorce.

Id. at 771 (emphasis added). . . .

The reasoning of the district court in *Adkins* is clearly contrary to the rule initially approved by this Court in 1875 in Bird v. Bird, 15 Fla. 424 (1875). In *Bird*, we held that when one cotenant has exclusive possession of lands owned as a tenant in common with another, and uses those lands for his own benefit and does not receive rents or profits therefrom, such cotenant is not liable or accountable to his cotenant out of possession unless such cotenant in exclusive possession holds adversely or as a result of ouster or the equivalent therefore. We explained what ouster meant in Stokely v. Conner, 68 So. 452 (Fla. 1915), where we stated that

> a tenant in common, to show an ouster of his cotenant, must show acts of possession inconsistent with, and exclusive of, the rights of such cotenant, and such as would amount to an ouster between landlord and tenant, and knowledge on the part of his cotenant of his claim of exclusive ownership. He has the right to assume that the possession of his cotenant is his possession, until informed to the contrary, either by express notice, or by acts and declarations that may be equivalent to notice. Exclusive possession by one tenant in common, and receipt of the rents and profits of the common land, for a great length of time, is not sufficient to create a legal presumption of the actual ouster of a cotenant.

Id. at 159. We stated in *Coggan* that "[t]here can be no holding adversely or ouster or its equivalent, by one cotenant unless such holding is manifested or communicated to the other." 239 So. 2d at 19. In the instant case, as reflected by the trial judge's findings, there was no communication by the cotenant in possession to the cotenant out of possession that the former was holding the property exclusively and adversely to the latter. We reaffirm our decision in *Coggan*.

Under these facts, we first reaffirm the necessity for communication mandated by the common law rule. Accepting the district court's holding would result in significant changes not only in the law of partition, but also in the law of adverse possession, because it would start the time for adverse possession running with a former spouse's occupancy of the former marital home when he or she is a cotenant. We reject respondent's argument that we should overrule the common law principles of partition and make an exception with regard to the communication requirement for former spouses who hold former marital property as cotenants. To hold that the occupation by one cotenant of the former marital home presumptively ousts the other former spouse cotenant would only create additional legal problems for parties to dissolution proceedings.

Second, we find that there is an existing applicable exception which was not discussed in . . . *Adkins*. . . . It also was not discussed in *Coggan* or *Bird* because it was not applicable. It is an established principle of law that when a cotenant in possession seeks contribution for amounts expended in the improvement or preservation of the property, his claim may be offset by the value of his or her use of the property which has exceeded his or her proportionate share of ownership. A general statement concerning this exception is contained in 51 A.L.R.2d 388 entitled "Accountability of cotenants for rents and profits or use and occupation." It states

> Nevertheless where one owner has enjoyed the occupancy and in any way seeks the assistance of a court in obtaining contribution from others in respect of improvements or protective expenditures made, he is ordinarily charged, *by way of offset,* with the reasonable value of his occupancy in excess of his proportionate share, *even though he would not otherwise be liable,* and similar adjustments are commonly made in partition suits generally.

Annotation, 51 A.L.R.2d 388, 395 (1957) (emphasis added). . . .

It is clear that, under this exception, Donna Barrow is entitled to claim the reasonable rental value solely as an offset against the claim of the cotenant, James Barrow, for the costs of maintaining the property. Here, Donna Barrow's claim for the rental value is limited to $2,591, the amount of James Barrow's claim, since the rental value exceeds his claim.

In conclusion, we hold: (1) the possession of a tenant in common is presumed to be the possession of all tenants until the one in possession communicates to the other the knowledge that he or she claims the exclusive right or title and there can be no holding adversely or ouster by the cotenant in possession unless the adverse holding is communicated to the other; (2) where one cotenant has exclusive possession of lands and uses the lands for his or her own benefit and does not receive rents or profits therefrom, such a cotenant is not liable or accountable to the cotenant out of possession unless he or she holds adversely or as a result of ouster or its equivalent; and (3) when a cotenant in possession seeks contribution for amounts expended in the improvement or preservation of the property, that claim may be offset by cotenants out of possession by the reasonable rental value of the use of the property by the cotenant in possession to the extent it has exceeded his or her proportionate share of ownership.

Finally, we note that animosity can exist between other family members or former business partners holding property as cotenants as can exist between former spouses. To avoid subsequent litigation between former spouses, we emphasize that it is in the best interests of all parties that property dispositions in matrimonial matters be concluded, if at all possible, in the dissolution proceedings, including a determination, if possible, of possession of any property held in a cotenancy.

Accordingly, we quash the decision of the district court and disapprove the reasoning in *Adkins*. . . . We direct the Second District Court of Appeal to remand this cause to the trial court for further proceedings consistent with this opinion.

It is so ordered.

Notes and Questions

1. The rules discussed in *Barrow* date back to the Statute of Anne, passed by the English Parliament in 1705. The statute provided, "Actions of Account shall and may be brought . . . by one Joint-tenant, and Tenant in Common, his Executors and Administrators, against the other . . . for receiving more than comes to his just share or Proportion, and against the Executor and Administrator of such Joint-tenant, or Tenant in Common." Prior to this statute, a cotenant had no liability to the other owners for any benefits received from the property, including rents and profits paid by third parties, provided the cotenant had not agreed to act as agent for the other owners. The Statute of Anne became part of the common law in most U.S. states. English courts interpreted the statute to require an accounting only if the cotenant in possession obtained rents and profits from third parties, continuing to allow a cotenant personally to enjoy sole possession with no duty to account. Most U.S. courts, like *Barrow*, hold likewise; but in a minority of states, a cotenant in sole possession has a duty to account to the other owners, regardless of ouster.

2. In *Barrow*, James claimed the right to reimbursement for one-half of what he expended for property taxes, insurance premiums, improvements, and repairs (maintenance). Generally, a cotenant who pays more than her share of *necessary payments* has the right to contribution — the other cotenant(s) must pay their share upon demand. The paying cotenant can bring an action for contribution against the other owners. Traditionally, the law has recognized as "necessary" only the payment of property taxes, mortgage loans, and other debts that are liens on the property. Nonpayment of such items is likely to result in loss of the property for all the cotenants; if the obligation is not paid, the creditor has the right to foreclose on the property.

Traditionally, a cotenant who makes or pays for improvements and repairs does not have a right to contribution, in the absence of a promise by the other cotenants to share the cost. Due to history and logic, a distinction is made between improvements and repairs. Improvements are seen as optional; if no one makes them, the property still retains its value, but the failure to make needed repairs can cause further deterioration of the existing improvements, and thus loss of value. At English common law, a cotenant could request that other cotenants share the cost of making necessary repairs to a house or mill. If they refused, she could bring a writ of repairs (*writ de reparatione facienda*), pursuant to which the repairs were made under direction of the court with all cotenants contributing to the cost. Several U.S. states today have broadened this ancient form of relief, allowing a cotenant to pay for repairs and obtain contribution prior to going to court, provided that she notifies the other cotenants of the need for repairs before acting and the repairs are reasonably necessary. In many states today, the law on this point is unclear because there are no reported modern cases outside of the context of partition or an accounting for rents and profits.

The law might treat a cotenant who makes improvements and repairs on her own and lacks a right to contribution as a volunteer with no opportunity to recover all of the cost. However, the paying cotenant gets some protection. She can recover for the value she has contributed under three circumstances: in a partition in kind, in a partition by sale, and in an accounting for rents and profits. With a partition by kind, the court assigns to the paying cotenant the portion of the property she has improved or repaired when this can be done without prejudice to the other cotenants. In the latter two circumstances, the paying cotenant has the burden of proving the extent to which her expenditures generated sales proceeds, rents, or profits. In Graham v. Inlow, 790 S.W.2d 428 (Ark. 1990), the trial court awarded an extra $70,000 of the proceeds of a partition by sale to a cotenant who renovated barns and other buildings. The court observed, "because tenants in common might be improved out of their property, the cotenant can only receive the enhancement value of the improvement to the property. . . . The proper measurement is the difference between the value of the land without the improvements and the value of the land with the improvements in their then condition." The court disallowed the award due to inadequate evidence in the record as to the difference in value.

■ ARK LAND COMPANY v. HARPER

Supreme Court of Appeals of West Virginia, 2004
599 S.E.2d 754

DAVIS, Justice. This is an appeal by Rhonda Gail Harper, Edward Caudill, Rose M. Thompson, Edith D. Kitchen, Therman R. Caudill, John A. Caudill, Jr., Tammy Willis, and Lucille M. Miller (hereinafter collectively identified as the "Caudill heirs"), appellants/defendants below, from an order of the Circuit Court of Lincoln County. The circuit court's order authorized a partition and sale of real property jointly owned by the Caudill heirs and Ark Land Company (hereinafter referred to as "Ark Land"), appellee/plaintiff below. Here, the Caudill heirs contend that the legal precedents of this Court warrant partitioning the property in kind, not a sale. After a careful review of the briefs and record in this case, we agree with the Caudill heirs and reverse the circuit court.

I. FACTUAL AND PROCEDURAL HISTORY

This is a dispute involving approximately 75 acres of land situate in Lincoln County, West Virginia. The record indicates that "the Caudill family has owned the land for nearly 100 years." The property "consists of a farmhouse, constructed around 1920, several small barns, and a garden." Prior to 2001, the property was owned exclusively by the Caudill family. However, in 2001 Ark Land acquired a 67.5% undivided interest in the land by purchasing the property interests of several Caudill family members. Ark Land attempted to purchase the remaining property interests held by the Caudill heirs, but they refused to sell. Ark Land sought to purchase all of the property for the express purpose of extracting coal by surface mining.

After the Caudill heirs refused to sell their interest in the land, Ark Land filed a complaint in the Circuit Court of Lincoln County in October of 2001. Ark Land filed the complaint seeking to have the land partitioned and sold. The circuit court appointed three commissioners, pursuant to W. Va. Code §37-4-3, to conduct an evidentiary hearing. The commissioners subsequently filed a report on August 19, 2002, wherein they concluded that the property could not be conveniently partitioned in kind.

The Caudill heirs objected to the report filed by the commissioners. The circuit court held a *de novo* review that involved testimony from lay and expert witnesses. On

October 30, 2002, the circuit court entered an order directing the partition and sale of the property. . . . From this ruling the Caudill heirs appealed.

III. Discussion

The dispositive issue is whether the evidence supported the circuit court's conclusion that the property could not be conveniently partitioned in kind, thus warranting a partition by sale. During the proceeding before the circuit court, the Caudill heirs presented expert testimony by Gary F. Acord, a mining engineer. Mr. Acord testified that the property could be partitioned in kind. Specifically, Mr. Acord testified that lands surrounding the family home did not have coal deposits and could therefore be partitioned from the remaining lands. On the other hand, Ark Land presented expert testimony which indicated that such a partition would entail several million dollars in additional costs in order to mine for coal.

We note at the outset that "[p]artition means the division of the land held in cotenancy into the cotenants' respective fractional shares. If the land cannot be fairly divided, then the entire estate may be sold and the proceeds appropriately divided." 7 *Powell on Real Property* §50.07[1] (2004). It has been observed that, "[i]n the United States, partition was established by statute in each of the individual states. Unlike the partition in kind which existed under early common law, the forced judicial sale was an American innovation." Phyliss Craig-Taylor, *Through a Colored Looking Glass: A View of Judicial Partition, Family Land Loss, and Rule Setting*, 78 Wash. U. L.Q. 737, 752 (2000). . . .

Partition by sale, when it is not voluntary by all parties, can be a harsh result for the cotenant(s) who opposes the sale. This is because "[a] particular piece of real estate cannot be replaced by any sum of money, however large; and one who wants a particular estate for a specific use, if deprived of his rights, cannot be said to receive an exact equivalent or complete indemnity by the payment of a sum of money." Wight v. Ingram-Day Lumber Co., 17 So. 2d 196, 198 (Miss. 1944). Consequently, "[p]artition in kind . . . is the preferred method of partition because it leaves cotenants holding the same estates as before and does not force a sale on unwilling cotenants." *Powell* §50.07[4][a]. The laws in all jurisdictions "appear to reflect this longstanding principle by providing a presumption of severance of common ownership in real property by partition in-kind." Craig-Taylor, 78 Wash. U. L.Q. at 753. . . .

In Consolidated Gas Supply Corp. v. Riley, 247 S.E.2d 712, 713 (W. Va. 1978), this Court set out the following standard of proof that must be established to overcome the presumption of partition in kind:

> By virtue of W. Va. Code §37-4-3, a party desiring to compel partition through sale is required to demonstrate (1) that the property cannot be conveniently partitioned in kind, (2) that the interests of one or more of the parties will be promoted by the sale, and (3) that the interests of the other parties will not be prejudiced by the sale.[6]

---

6. The relevant part of W. Va. Code §37-4-3 reads as follows:

When partition cannot be conveniently made, the entire subject may be allotted to any party or parties who will accept it, and pay therefor to the other party or parties such sum of money as his or their interest therein may entitle him or them to; *or in any case in which partition cannot be conveniently made, if the interests of one or more of those who are entitled to the subject, or its proceeds, will be promoted by a sale of the entire subject, or allotment of part and sale of the residue, and the interest of the other person or persons so entitled will not be prejudiced thereby*, the court . . . may order such sale (emphasis added).

In its lengthy order requiring partition and sale, the circuit court addressed each of the three factors in *Consolidated Gas Supply Corp.* as follows:

(14) That upon the Court's review and consideration of the entire record, even after the [Caudill heirs'] expert witness testified, the Court has determined that it is clearly evident that the subject property's nature, character, and amount are such that it cannot be conveniently, (that is "practically or justly") partitioned, or divided by allotment among its owners. Moreover, it is just and necessary to conclude that such a proposal as has been made by the [Caudill heirs], that of allotting the manor house and the surrounding "bottom land" unto the [Caudill heirs], cannot be affected without undeniably prejudicing [Ark Land's] interests, in violation of the mandatory provisions of Code §37-4-3; and,

(15) That while its uniform topography superficially suggests a division-in-kind, as proposed by Mr. Acord, the access road, the bottom lands and the relatively flat home site is, in fact, integral to establishing the fair market value of the subject property in its entirety, as its highest and best use as mining property, as shown by the uncontroverted testimony of [Ark Land's] experts Mr. Morgan and Mr. Terry; and,

(16) That from a review of the Commissioners' Report, it indicates that sale of the subject property will promote the interests of [Ark Land], "but may prejudice the best interest of the [Caudill heirs]." Obviously, from the legal principles and the reviewing standards set out above, the "best interests" of either party is not the standard upon which the Court must determine these issues. In that respect, it is undisputed that the remaining heirs, that are [the Caudill heirs] herein, do not wish to sell, or have the Court sell, their interests in the subject property, solely due to their sincere sentiment for it as the family's "home place." Other family members, however, did not feel the same way. Given the equally undisputed testimony of [Ark Land's] experts, it is just and reasonable for the Court to conclude that the interests of all the subject property's owners will not be financially prejudiced, but will be financially promoted, by sale of the subject property and distribution among them of the proceeds, according to their respective interests. The subject property's value as coal mining property, its uncontroverted highest and best use, would be substantially impaired by severing the family's "home place" and allotting it to them separately. Again, the evidence is not only a preponderance, but unrebutted, that Mr. Acord's proposal would greatly diminish the value of the subject property. Accordingly, the Court does hereby conclude as a matter of law that the subject property should be sold as a whole in its entirety, and that it cannot be partitioned in kind by allotment of part and a sale of the residue.

We are troubled by the circuit court's conclusion that partition by sale was necessary because the economic value of the property would be less if partitioned in kind. We have long held that the economic value of property *may* be a factor to consider in determining whether to partition in kind or to force a sale.

Whether the aggregate value of the several parcels into which the whole premises must be divided will, when distributed among, and held in severalty by, the different parties, be materially less than the value of the same property if owned by one person, is a fair test by which to determine whether the interests of the parties will be promoted by a sale.

Croston v. Male, 49 S.E. 136, 136 (W. Va. 1904). However, our cases *do not* support the conclusion that economic value of property is the exclusive test for determining whether to partition in kind or to partition by sale. In fact, we explicitly stated in Hale v. Thacker, 12 S.E.2d 524, 526 (W. Va. 1940), "that many considerations, other than monetary, attach to the ownership of land, and courts should be, and always have been, slow to take away from owners of real estate their common-law right to have the same set aside to them in kind." . . .

In view of the prior decisions of this Court, as well as the decisions from other jurisdictions, we now make clear and hold that, in a partition proceeding in which a party opposes the sale of property, the economic value of the property is not the exclusive test for deciding whether to partition in kind or by sale. Evidence of long-standing ownership, coupled with sentimental or emotional interests in the property, may also be considered in deciding whether the interests of the party opposing the sale will be prejudiced by the property's sale. This latter factor should ordinarily control when it is shown that the property can be partitioned in kind, though it may entail some economic inconvenience to the party seeking a sale.

In the instant case, the Caudill heirs were not concerned with the monetary value of the property. Their exclusive interest was grounded in the longstanding family ownership of the property and their emotional desire to keep their ancestral family home within the family.[7] It is quite clear that this emotional interest would be prejudiced through a sale of the property.

The expert for the Caudill heirs testified that the ancestral family home could be partitioned from the property in such away as to not deprive Ark Land of any coal. The circuit court summarily and erroneously dismissed this uncontradicted fact because of the increased costs that Ark Land would incur as a result of a partition in kind. In view of our holding, the additional economic burden that would be imposed on Ark Land, as a result of partitioning in kind, is not determinative under the facts of this case.

. . . The facts in this case reveal that, prior to 2001, Ark Land had no ownership interest in the property. Conversely, for nearly 100 years the Caudill heirs and their ancestors owned the property and used it for residential purposes.[8] In 2001 Ark Land purchased ownership rights in the property from some Caudill family members. When the Caudill heirs refused to sell their ownership rights, Ark Land immediately sought to force a judicial sale of the property. In doing this, Ark Land established that its proposed use of the property, surface coal mining, gave greater value to the property. This showing is self-serving. In most instances, when a commercial entity purchases property because it believes it can make money from a specific use of the property, that property will increase in value based upon the expectations of the commercial entity. This self-created enhancement in the value of property cannot be the determinative factor in forcing a pre-existing co-owner to give up his/her rights in property. To have such a rule would permit commercial entities to always "evict" pre-existing co-owners, because a commercial entity's interest in property will invariably increase its value. *See* Butte Creek Island Ranch v. Crim, 186 Cal. Rptr. 252 (Ct. App. 1982) ("Plaintiff . . . sought a forced sale of the land in order to acquire defendant's interest which he did not desire to sell. This is nothing short of the private condemnation of private land for private purposes, a result which is abhorrent to the rights of defendant as a freeholder.").

7. The circuit court's order suggests that, because some family members sold their interest in the property, no real interest in maintaining the family home existed. While it may be true that the family members who sold their interest in the property did not have any emotional attachment to the family home, this fact cannot be dispositively attributed to the Caudill heirs. The interest of the Caudill heirs cannot be nullified or tossed aside, simply because other family members do not share the same sentiments for the family home.

8. No one lives permanently at the family home. However, the family home is used on weekends and for special family events by the Caudill heirs.

We are very sensitive to the fact that Ark Land will incur greater costs in conducting its business on the property as a result of partitioning in kind. However, Ark Land voluntarily took an economical gamble that it would be able to get all of the Caudill family members to sell their interests in the property. Ark Land's gamble failed. The Caudill heirs refused to sell their interests. The fact that Ark Land miscalculated on its ability to acquire outright all interests in the property cannot form the basis for depriving the Caudill heirs of their emotional interests in maintaining their ancestral family home. The additional cost to Ark Land that will result from a partitioning in kind simply does not impose the type of injurious inconvenience that would justify stripping the Caudill heirs of the emotional interest they have in preserving their ancestral family home. . . .

IV. CONCLUSION

In view of the foregoing, we find that the circuit court erred in determining that the property could not be partitioned in kind. We, therefore, reverse the circuit court's order requiring sale of the property. This case is remanded with directions to the circuit court to enter an order requiring the property to be partitioned in kind, consistent with the report and testimony of the Caudill heirs' mining engineer expert, Gary F. Acord.

MAYNARD, Chief Justice, concurring in part and dissenting in part. I concur with the new law created by the majority in this case. That is to say, I agree that evidence of longstanding ownership along with sentimental or emotional attachment to property are factors that should be considered and, in some instances, control the decision of whether to partition in kind or sale jointly-owned property which is the subject of a partition proceeding.

I dissent in this case, however, because I do not believe that evidence to support the application of those factors was presented here. In that regard, the record shows that none of the appellants have resided at the subject property for years. At most, the property has been used for weekend retreats. While this may have been the family "homeplace," a majority of the family has already sold their interests in the property to the appellee. Only a minority of the family members, the appellants, have refused to do so. I believe that the sporadic use of the property by the appellants in this case does not outweigh the economic inconvenience that the appellee will suffer as a result of this property being partitioned in kind.

I am also troubled by the majority's decision that this property should be partitioned in kind instead of being sold because I don't believe that such would have been the case were this property going to be put to some use other than coal mining. For instance, I think the majority's decision would have been different if this property was going to be used in the construction of a four-lane highway. Under those circumstances, I believe the majority would have concluded that such economic activity takes precedence over any long-term use or sentimental attachment to the property on the part of the appellants. In my opinion, coal mining is an equally important economic activity. This decision destroys the value of this land as coal mining property because the appellee would incur several million dollars in additional costs to continue its mining operations. As a result of the majority's decision in this case, many innocent coal miners will be out of work. . . .

Notes and Questions

1. The *Ark Land* court focuses on the distinction between *partition in kind* and *partition by sale*. Every cotenant (except a tenant by the entirety) has the right to a partition, but not necessarily the type of partition that she prefers. The previous case, *Barrow*, resulted in a partition by sale, with the parties' arguments centering on whether adjustments should be made in splitting the sales proceeds. Normally, a court-ordered sale is a public sale by auction. This may result in a sale to an outsider, but often the high bidder is one of the existing cotenants. Thus, partition by sale often functions as a court-supervised buyout procedure. Instead of an auction sale, however, a court may specify another method for sale if allowed by the local partition statute. *See* Cox v. Cox, 71 P.3d 1028 (Idaho 2003) (affirming judgment requiring sale by listing of house with real estate broker; under Idaho statutes, cotenant does not have right to insist on sale at auction).

What if James or Donna Barrow had asked for a partition in kind of the residence? Would that be appropriate? The West Virginia partition statute discussed in *Ark Land* reflects the preference, followed in all states, for partition in kind. If any cotenant asks for partition in kind, the court should grant that remedy if it can fairly divide the property. Why should the law prefer partition in kind to partition by sale?

2. Cotenants may restrict or modify their rights to partition by written agreement. Courts, however, often refuse to enforce such agreements if they are unlimited in time or have other provisions that appear unreasonable. Judicial overriding of the parties' contract is usually explained on the basis that broad agreements not to partition amount to improper "restraints on alienation." (Recall that in Chapter 6, in connection with White v. Brown, we discussed the doctrine against restraints on alienation.) In Schultheis v. Schultheis, 675 P.2d 634 (Wash. Ct. App. 1984), parents conveyed farmland to their six children. Each cotenant agreed not to sell an interest outside the family for 10 years and never to seek partition, with the agreements to run with the land. Thirteen years later, four children sought partition. In many states, the agreement to bar partition forever would be void. The court, however, affirmed the trial court's decision to set a reasonable time limit. Nevertheless, the partition seekers won because the trial court set the time limit as the first to occur of the parents' death or 10 years after execution of the agreement.

3. Many courts, unlike the court in *Ark Land*, have developed a bright-line rule that orders a partition by sale if the fair market value of the entire property exceeds the aggregated fair market values of the sub-parcels that would result from a partition in kind. Other courts primarily consider economic factors, giving little weight to noneconomic interests of family members. The partition rules have a greater impact on landowners of modest means, who are more likely to hold property in cotenancy and to transfer property by intestate succession to relatives. Wealthier landowners are more likely to transfer property to a trust or an entity such as a corporation, to engage in estate planning, and if the property is held in cotenancy to change the default partition rules by express agreement.

The Uniform Partition of Heirs Property Act, promulgated in 2010 and since adopted by Georgia and Nevada, establishes remedies for use in partition actions involving "heirs property," defined as real property held by tenants in common, a minimum percentage of which are relatives, who have not entered into an express agreement regulating partition of the property. The Act protects family-member owners by requiring judicially supervised valuation of the property, by granting to cotenants who did not request partition the right to buy out the shares of the cotenants who requested partition, and if sale is necessary by providing regulations that seek to ensure that cotenants receive adequate compensation. Normally, a sale must be made on the open market using the services of a real estate broker.

2. Joint Tenancy

■ JAMES v. TAYLOR

Court of Appeals of Arkansas, 1998
969 S.W.2d 672

PITTMAN, Judge. The issue in this case is whether a deed from the late Eura Mae Redmon to her three children, W.C. Sewell, Billy Sewell, and appellee Melba Taylor, was a conveyance to them as tenants in common or as joint tenants with the right of survivorship. . . .

The deed in question was executed by Mrs. Redmon on January 14, 1993. The conveyance was made to the three grantees "jointly and severally, and unto their heirs, assigns and successors forever," with the grantor retaining a life estate. W.C. Sewell and Billy Sewell died on November 18, 1993, and May 11, 1995, respectively. Mrs. Redmon died on February 17, 1997. Shortly thereafter, appellee filed a complaint in White County Chancery Court seeking a declaration that her mother had intended to convey the property to the grantees as joint tenants, thereby making appellee, by virtue of her brothers' deaths, sole owner of the property. Appellants, who are descendants of W.C. and Billy Sewell, opposed the complaint on the ground that the deed created a tenancy in common among the grantees.

The case went to trial, and the chancellor, upon hearing extrinsic evidence of Mrs. Redmon's intent, found that she meant to convey the property to her children as joint tenants with the right of survivorship. He thereby quieted title to the property in appellee. It is from that order that this appeal has been brought.

Appellants and appellee agree that the term "jointly and severally" as used to describe an estate in property is ambiguous. However, they disagree over the rule of construction to be applied in the face of such ambiguity. Appellants contend that, under Arkansas law, a deed to two or more persons presumptively creates a tenancy in common unless the deed expressly creates a joint tenancy. They cite Ark. Code Ann. §18-12-603 (1987), which reads as follows: "Every interest in real estate granted or devised to two (2) or more persons, other than executors and trustees as such, shall be in tenancy in common unless expressly declared in the grant or devise to be a joint tenancy." According to appellants, the very existence of an ambiguity within the deed means that, under the statute, a tenancy in common has been created. Appellee, on the other hand, points to the well-established rule that, when faced with an ambiguity in a deed, the trial court may determine the intent of the grantor by looking to extraneous circumstances to decide what was really intended by the language in the deed. *See* Wynn v. Sklar & Phillips Oil Co., 493 S.W.2d 439 (Ark. 1973). Because, appellee argues, the chancellor in this case had strong evidence before him that Mrs. Redmon intended to create a joint tenancy in her children, his finding should not be overturned unless clearly erroneous.

The extrinsic evidence considered by the chancellor in this case weighs in favor of appellee. That evidence consisted of appellee's testimony that her mother had informed her attorney that she wanted the deed drafted so that, if one of her children died, the property would belong to the other two children, and so on; that shortly after the death of W.C. Sewell, Mrs. Redmon executed a new will leaving her property to Billy Sewell and appellee and leaving nothing to W.C.'s children; that Mrs. Redmon had set up bank accounts payable upon her death to her children, and, after W.C. and Billy died, deleted their names leaving the name of the surviving child; and that Mrs. Redmon was upset before her death upon learning that there was a problem with the deed. However, we hold that the considerations expressed in Ark. Code Ann. §18-12-603 override the rule of construction urged by appellee.

Section 18-12-603 is a statute like one of many throughout the country. At common law, joint tenancy was favored and, where possible, that estate was held to exist. However, in Arkansas, and in many other states, statutes have been adopted which presumptively construe an instrument to create a tenancy in common rather than a joint tenancy. These statutes do not prohibit joint tenancies but merely provide for a construction against a joint tenancy if the intention to create it is not clear. A statute such as section 18-12-603 is not an expression of a public policy against joint tenancies but is merely a choice by the legislature of a rule of construction that selects one of two possible interpretations of a provision otherwise ambiguous.

Ordinarily, a statute such as section 18-12-603 does not require the actual use of the words "joint tenancy." For example, Wood v. Wood, 571 S.W.2d 84 (Ark. 1978), involved a conveyance to "Boyd E. Wood and Murtha A. Wood, husband and wife, as tenants by entirety." In fact, the grantees were not legally married, and no entireties estate was created. However, our supreme court held that the conveyance satisfied the requirements of the statute necessary to create a joint tenancy because it was clear that the grantor intended to convey a survivorship estate. Survivorship is the distinctive characteristic of a joint tenancy. Where, from the four corners of an instrument, a court can interpret the intention of the grantor or testator as creating a survivorship estate, the court will deem the estate to be a joint tenancy with the right of survivorship.

Nothing appears from the four corners of the deed in this case to indicate Mrs. Redmon's intent to convey a survivorship interest, unless that intention is to be found in the term "jointly and severally." Appellants do not cite, nor have we discovered through our own research, any Arkansas case in which a grant of ownership was made to two or more parties "jointly and severally." As the chancellor noted below, "jointly and severally" are words of tort, not property. They have no meaning in the world of estates. In the context of an ownership interest, such a term is a legal anomaly; several ownership is, by definition, a denial of joint ownership. . . .

In Montgomery v. Clarkson, 585 S.W.2d 483 (Mo. 1979), property was deeded to two grantees "jointly." The Missouri court, relying on a statute virtually identical to ours, held that a joint tenancy was not created by the use of such language. . . . The holding in *Montgomery* is in accord with the rule that a conveyance to grantees "jointly" does not create a joint tenancy.

If use of the word "jointly" is not sufficient to create a joint tenancy, the term "jointly and severally," with its elusive connotation, cannot do so either. Further, Arkansas recognizes that the practice of divining the intent of a grantor or testator is subject to the qualification that such practice must not conflict with settled principles of law and rules of property. *See* Smith v. Wright, 779 S.W.2d 177 (Ark. 1989) (a rule of property law should be applied whenever the language of the conveyance fits under the rule, without regard to the conveyor's intention).

Appellee argues that, given the deed's ambiguity, our focus should be on the intent of the grantor as gleaned not only from the instrument itself but from the extrinsic evidence presented at trial. However, evidence of the grantor's intention cannot prevail over the statute. To allow that would be to render section 18-12-603 meaningless.

Based upon the foregoing, we hold that the deed in this case did not create a joint tenancy in the grantees. The language of the deed is insufficient to overcome the statutory presumption of a tenancy in common. . . .

Reversed and remanded.

Notes and Questions

1. Most states have statutes that modify the joint tenancy estate as recognized by common law. Very often those statutes reverse the common law presumption in favor of joint tenancy, replacing it with a presumption in favor of a tenancy in common. Several states passed statutes prohibiting joint tenancies altogether. The Georgia experience is typical. Legislation passed in 1828 provided:

> when two or more persons shall hold and possess any estate of lands in joint tenancy, in this State, and one or more of said joint tenants may depart this life during the existence of said estate, the title or interest of the deceased joint tenant, in said estate, shall not go and become the property of the surviving joint tenant or tenants, as under the English law, but . . . the same shall be distributed as all other estates, under the existing laws of this State.

A statute enacted in 1854 extended the ban to joint estates in personal property. Notwithstanding these acts, Georgia courts recognized survivorship rights that were expressly created, reasoning that the devisees or grantees held either joint life estates, followed by a contingent remainder in fee, or defeasible fees. In 1976, the Georgia legislature lifted its prohibition, substituting the following rules codified in Ga. Code Ann. §44-6-190:

> *How joint tenancy with survivorship created; severance.* Deeds and other instruments of title, including any instrument in which one person conveys to himself and one or more other persons, any instrument in which two or more persons convey to themselves or to themselves and another or others, and wills, taking effect after January 1, 1977, may create a joint interest with survivorship in two or more persons. Any instrument of title in favor of two or more persons shall be construed to create interests in common without survivorship between or among the owners unless the instrument expressly refers to the takers as "joint tenants," "joint tenants and not as tenants in common," or "joint tenants with survivorship" or as taking "jointly with survivorship." Any instrument using one of the forms of expression referred to in the preceding sentence or language essentially the same as one of these forms of expression shall create a joint tenancy estate or interest that may be severed as to the interest of any owner by the recording of an instrument which results in his lifetime transfer of all or a part of his interest; provided, however, that, if all persons owning joint tenant interests in a property join in the same recorded lifetime transfer, no severance shall occur.

2. As the last note indicates, there are alternative ways to create survivorship rights, including a conveyance of joint life estates followed by contingent

remainders. Suppose you were representing a client who wanted to create survivorship rights, and state law allows a joint tenancy in fee simple. What factors would you consider in deciding whether to employ a joint tenancy, life estates followed by remainders, a will, or something else?

3. Well-drafted instruments that convey property to more than one grantee use language that specifies, with no possible ambiguity, the type of cotenancy that is being created. The Georgia statute quoted in Note 1 states that certain phrases will suffice to create a joint tenancy, and then indicates that other language that is "essentially the same" also works. In a number of states, less guidance is given. For example, the Arkansas statute construed in *James* presumes a tenancy in common unless language "expressly declares" a joint tenancy. In Chapter 7, we discussed the distinction between rules of construction and rules of law. The court in *James* faced arguments as to whether the joint tenancy statute set forth a rule of construction or a rule of property law. How did the court decide this issue, and why? How does this decision bear on the admissibility of extrinsic evidence that shows the grantor, Mrs. Redmon, intended to create a joint tenancy?

■ **JACKSON v. O'CONNELL**
Supreme Court of Illinois, 1961
177 N.E.2d 194

KLINGBIEL, Justice. This appeal from a decree for partition entered by the circuit court of Cook County presents the question whether a conveyance by one of three joint tenants of real estate to another of the joint tenants destroyed the joint tenancy in its entirety or merely severed the joint tenancy with respect to the undivided third interest so conveyed, leaving the joint tenancy in force and effect as to the remaining two-thirds interest.

. . . The various parcels of real estate in question are situated in Cook County and were formerly owned by Neil P. Duffy. The latter died testate in 1936 and by his will he devised the properties to his three sisters, Nellie Duffy, Anna Duffy, and Katherine O'Connell, as joint tenants. Thereafter Nellie Duffy, a spinster, by quitclaim deed dated July 21, 1948, conveyed and quitclaimed all her interest in the properties to Anna Duffy. The deed was in statutory form. It was duly delivered and recorded. Nellie Duffy died in 1949.

Some eight years later, in May 1957, Anna Duffy died testate. By her will she devised whatever interest she had in the real estate in question to four nieces, Beatrice Jackson, Eileen O'Barski, Catherine Young and Margaret Miller, plaintiffs herein.

Following the death of Anna Duffy, the plaintiffs commenced this suit against Katherine O'Connell (hereafter referred to as the defendant) and others to partition the real estate. Their suit is predicated on the theory that Nellie Duffy's quitclaim deed, dated July 21, 1948, to Anna Duffy severed in its entirety the joint tenancies existing between Nellie Duffy, Anna Duffy, and the defendant; that as a result, Anna Duffy became the owner of an undivided two-thirds interest and defendant an undivided one-third interest in the various parcels of real estate, as tenants in common; that plaintiffs, as successors in interest to Anna Duffy, accordingly each own an undivided one-sixth and defendant an undivided one-third interest as tenants in common. The defendant answered and filed a counterclaim on the theory that Nellie Duffy's quitclaim deed of July 21, 1948, to Anna Duffy severed the joint tenancies only so far as the grantor's one-third interest was concerned; that the joint tenancies between Anna Duffy and defendant continued in full force and effect as to the remaining two-thirds; that upon Anna Duffy's death in 1957, defendant succeeded to that two-thirds interest as surviving joint tenant; and that plaintiffs are each entitled to a one-twelfth interest only, as devisees of the one-third interest which passed to Anna Duffy by reason of Nellie Duffy's quitclaim deed.

The cause was referred to a master who found the interests in accordance with defendant's contentions. The decree for partition appealed from confirmed the master's conclusions.

At the hearing before the master, plaintiffs adduced over defendant's objection testimony of the attorney who had drawn Nellie Duffy's quitclaim deed for the purpose of showing that the grantor intended the deed to operate as a complete severance of the joint tenancy and that the attorney's advice was that the deed would have that legal effect. Such testimony cannot control the effect of the deed upon the joint tenancy but that issue must be determined as a matter of law. The deed was unambiguous and its legal effect cannot be changed by parol evidence that it was intended to have a legal operation different from that which would be imported by its terms.

The problem then resolves itself down to the effect of Nellie Duffy's quitclaim deed upon the joint tenancy as a matter of law. The question appears to be one of first impression in Illinois.

The estate of joint tenancy comes down to us from the early English law and while the rules applicable to it have been modified in some particulars by statute in Illinois, most of the principles governing joint tenancies today are those which existed at common law. For example, it has been held from the earliest times that four coexisting unities are necessary and requisite to the creation and continuance of a joint tenancy; namely, unity of interest, unity of title, unity of time, and unity of possession. Any act of a joint tenant which destroys any of these unities operates as a severance of the joint tenancy and extinguishes the right of survivorship.

It appears to have been well settled at common law that where there were three joint tenants, and one conveyed his interest to a third party, the joint tenancy was only severed as to the part conveyed; the third party grantee became a tenant in common with the other two joint tenants, but the latter still held the remaining two-thirds as joint tenants with right of survivorship therein. Counsel for plaintiffs argue that the rule should not apply where the conveyance is to a fellow joint tenant; that in such a case the interest of the grantee becomes different in quantity from that of the remaining joint tenant; that the unity of interest is destroyed and a severance of the entire joint tenancy necessarily results. . . .

Blackstone, after pointing out that a joint tenancy may be terminated by destroying the unity of interest, adds the following qualification: "Yet, if one of three joint-tenants aliens his share, the two remaining tenants still hold their parts by joint-tenancy and survivorship; and if one of three joint-tenants release his share to one of his companions, though the joint-tenancy is destroyed with regard to that part, yet the two remaining parts are still held in jointure; for they still preserve their original constituent unities." 2 *Blackstone's Commentaries*, (*186), Lewis's ed. p. 653. . . .

Modern-day writers support the same view. . . .

With respect to the contention that Nellie Duffy's quitclaim deed destroyed the joint tenancies in their entirety because as a result of that deed the undivided interests of the grantee, Anna Duffy, and the defendant in the various properties were rendered unequal, it is to be noted that their interests in the undivided two-thirds, which formed the subject matter of the joint tenancies here in question, remained the same. It is settled in Illinois that a valid joint tenancy may exist in an undivided interest. Klouda v. Pechousek, 110 N.E.2d 258 (Ill. 1953). The requisite unity of interest is satisfied in such a case if it exists with respect to the undivided interest which forms the subject matter of the joint tenancy. . . .

It is contended that error was committed in the exclusion of testimony offered to show Anna Duffy's understanding of the legal effect of the quitclaim deed. This testimony was properly excluded for reasons previously stated.

The decree of the circuit court of Cook County was right and is affirmed.

■ **DUNCAN v. VASSAUR**
Supreme Court of Oklahoma, 1976
550 P.2d 929

DAVISON, Justice. The real estate involved herein are lots 20, 21, 22, 23 and 24, Block 16, in Checote Addition to the City of Okmulgee, Oklahoma. This property was owned by Edgar Vassaur, Jr., prior to his marriage to Betty E. Vassaur and was by him conveyed to Edgar Vassaur, Jr. and Betty E. Vassaur as joint tenants by Warranty Deed dated June 30, 1969, and remained in joint tenancy when on August 9, 1971, the wife, Betty Elaine Vassaur, shot and killed her husband.

On September 30, 1971, after she had been charged with first degree manslaughter for killing her husband, Betty E. Vassaur, as a widow, conveyed the involved property to her father, William M. Duncan, the appellee.

Edgar Vassaur, Sr., is the administrator of his deceased son's estate. As such he claimed ownership of one-half of the property . . . . [This claim was] asserted in an answer and cross petition filed by the administrator in the action to quiet the title to the realty brought by Duncan against the estate. Duncan interposed a demurrer to the answer and cross petition and moved for judgment on the pleadings. The trial judge sustained the demurrer, dismissed the cross petition and granted Duncan's motion for judgment on the pleadings.

At issue here is the interpretation and applicability of the Oklahoma "slayer statute," 84 O.S. 1971 §231, which provided in parts here pertinent as follows:

> No person who is convicted of murder or manslaughter in the first degree under the laws of this State . . . of having taken . . . the life of another, shall inherit from such person, or receive any interest in the estate of the decedent, or take by devise or legacy, or descent or distribution, from him or her, any portion of his or her estate. . . .

. . . .

The question before us has been the subject for determination by a number of states with a number of different and contrary views, such as: (1) Some jurisdictions hold that the murderer is deprived of the entire interest except for a life interest in one-half. (2) The murderer is entitled to keep all the property. (3) The murderer holds upon a constructive trust to the extent of the computed value of one-half of the property as of the date of the victim's death for the period of the victim's expectancy. (4) The murderer is chargeable as constructive trustee of the entire property for the benefit of his victim's estate. (5) The murderer is chargeable as constructive trustee of one-half of the property for the benefit of the victim's estate. (6) By the murder, the joint tenancy has separated and terminated and one-half of the property should go to the heirs of the deceased (murdered person) and the other one-half to the murderer, or to his heirs, when deceased. . . .

[T]he most equitable solution of the question is to hold that by the murder, the joint tenancy is separated and terminated and one-half of the property should go to the heirs of the deceased husband (murdered person) and the other one-half to the murderer, wife, or to her heirs, when deceased. By such holding, the joint tenancy is changed to a tenancy in common. We so hold.

In adopting the above theory, we are guided by [the Oklahoma "slayer statute"] and by several cases from other jurisdictions.

In the case of Bradley v. Fox, 129 N.E.2d 699, 706 (Ill. 1955), the following language was used:

> It is our conclusion that Fox by his felonious act, destroyed all rights of survivorship and lawfully retained only the title to his undivided one-half interest in the property in dispute as a tenant in common with the heir-at-law of Matilda Fox, deceased. . . .
>
> In so construing the rights of the parties to deny a murderer the fruits of his crime, this court is functioning, not as a "theological institution," as suggested in the Ohio case cited by defendants, but as a tribunal dedicated to the adjudication of law, for effecting justice is not a novel role for the courts, nor one transcending the sphere of other institutions.

. . . .

Lastly, it will be noted in plaintiff's petition that it was not claimed that plaintiff was an innocent purchaser for value, without notice of the fact that his grantor, Betty E. Vassaur, had been charged with murdering her husband at the time of the execution and delivery of the deed to him.

It is inconceivable that plaintiff did not know of the fact that his daughter had murdered her husband on August 9, 1971, when on the 30th day of September, 1971, he received the deed in question. However, the plaintiff should be given an opportunity to prove that he was a bona fide innocent purchaser for a valuable consideration and that he was without knowledge that his grantor, daughter, had murdered her husband at the time of the execution and delivery of the deed.

It follows that the judgment must be reversed and the cause remanded with directions to set aside the judgment of dismissal and in the absence of proper proof of plaintiff being an innocent purchaser for a valuable consideration and without knowledge that his daughter had murdered her husband at the time of the execution and delivery of the deed, then in that event, the trial court is directed to enter judgment in favor of the defendant, administrator as follows: That one-half of the property should go to the plaintiff and the other one-half to the administrator of the deceased to be distributed to the heirs of the deceased. . . . It is so ordered.

Notes and Questions

1. Both *Jackson* and *Duncan* deal with the issue of *severance*. What conduct of one or more joint tenants will terminate that relationship, causing a shift to a tenancy in

common? As *Jackson* indicates, a joint tenant's conveyance of her entire ownership interest severs the joint tenancy as to the conveyed share. One fertile ground for controversy is a transfer by one joint tenant of a lesser interest. Courts usually resolve the issue by trying to decide whether the transfer has destroyed any of the four unities. *See* Biggers v. Crook, 656 S.E.2d 835 (Ga. 2008) (deed to secure debt given by one joint tenant, which functions as a mortgage under Georgia law, is not severance because purpose is to grant lender a "security lien"); Alexander v. Boyer, 253 A.2d 369 (Md. 1969) (lease by one joint tenant is severance because it destroys unities of interest and possession). Judicial results are inconsistent; in some states, mortgages sever joint tenancies and leases do not.

2. In Hood v. Vandevender, 661 So. 2d 198 (Miss. 1995), Linda and her husband Chrysler took title to a house as joint tenants. One year later Linda killed Chrysler and pled guilty to manslaughter, receiving a 20-year suspended sentence. Linda defaulted in paying a mortgage loan on the property, and in a foreclosure proceeding Chrysler's estate claimed a share of the property under a slayer statute providing: "If any person wilfully cause or procure the death of another in any way, he shall not inherit the property, real or personal, of such other; but the same shall descend as if the person so causing or procuring the death had predeceased the person whose death he perpetrated." Miss. Code §91-1-25. The court held for Linda, explaining: "[N]ot only is evidence of a manslaughter conviction or plea not conclusive, it is only slight evidence of willfulness, and evidence only that a killing occurred. Here the only evidence on the issue is that Linda admitted that she had been charged with murder and pled guilty to manslaughter. She received a 20 year suspended sentence. . . . There are several manslaughter statutes in this state, some of which do not require willfulness. . . . The burden of proof is upon the estate to show that the normal operation of the joint estate, survivorship, should not obtain."

3. Are the policies any different when the victim is a tenant by the entirety rather than a joint tenant? In Hicks v. Boshears, 846 S.W.2d 812 (Tenn. 1993), Boshears feloniously killed his wife. The Boshears' children sued their father to establish ownership of land held by their parents as tenants by the entirety. Reversing its precedent from 1906, the court held: "[T]he tenancy by the entirety is converted into a tenancy in common by the defendant's act in feloniously killing the other tenant. . . . This conclusion accommodates the two historic legal principles at issue: the equitable maxim that one should not be allowed to profit by wrongdoing, codified in the statutory prohibition against a killer taking or inheriting property from his victim, and the ownership of property as tenants by the entirety. . . . This interpretation does not, as contended by the defendant, violate Article 1, Section 12 of the state constitution by allowing a forfeiture of vested interest in land. . . . [T]he defendant's interest in the property at the time of the murder was not a fee simple estate. He has no constitutional right to have the tenancy by the entirety converted into a fee simple by his felonious act. . . . The interest that he already possessed, an undivided interest in the property equally shared with his wife, is preserved and converted into a non-contingent estate."

4. Courts often reach similar results when personal property is held in joint tenancy. In In re Estate of Fiore, 476 N.E.2d 1093 (Ohio App. 1984), Charles pled no contest to the charge of murdering Leonard. They had owned a savings account as joint tenants. An Ohio statute provided: "No person who is convicted of or pleads guilty to [murder in the first or second degree] shall in any way benefit by the death. All property of the decedent, and all money, insurance proceeds, or other property

or benefits payable or distributable in respect of the decedent's death, shall pass or be paid or distributed as if the guilty person had predeceased the decedent." Relying on this statute, Leonard's estate received the entire balance of the joint and survivorship account.

B. MARITAL PROPERTY

In some fundamental ways, the law views a married couple as a single unit. In the realm of property law, this has resulted in marital property taking on certain aspects of cotenancy, with the spouses serving as the cotenants. The resulting legal issues fall within the following three major functional areas:

- Management and control of property during the marriage;
- Property rights when the marriage terminates by divorce;
- Property rights of a surviving spouse when the marriage terminates by the death of one partner.

These three areas are properly seen as distinct, with a number of discrete rules that apply only in one setting. They are not wholly autonomous, however, and can be impacted by choices made by the spouses themselves. For example, a couple's choice about the form in which to hold property impacts management and control rights. If one spouse alone takes title to an asset, that spouse normally has the sole right to manage that item, though states may limit a spouse's ability to hold property separately. Conversely, a choice to hold the asset in some form of concurrent ownership ordinarily carries with it shared management rights. That same choice as to ownership form alters survivorship rights. For example, a decision to hold property in tenancy by the entirety, analyzed in the next case, grants the spouses a particular set of coequal management rights and specifies an indestructible survivorship right.

1. Tenancy by the Entirety

■ **UNITED STATES v. CRAFT**
Supreme Court of the United States, 2002
535 U.S. 274

O'CONNOR, Justice. This case raises the question whether a tenant by the entirety possesses "property" or "rights to property" to which a federal tax lien may attach. 26 U.S.C. §6321. Relying on the state law fiction that a tenant by the entirety has no separate interest in entireties property, the United States Court of Appeals for the Sixth Circuit held that such property is exempt from the tax lien. We conclude that, despite the fiction, each tenant possesses individual rights in the estate sufficient to constitute "property" or "rights to property" for the purposes of the lien, and reverse the judgment of the Court of Appeals.

I.

In 1988, the Internal Revenue Service (IRS) assessed $482,446 in unpaid income tax liabilities against Don Craft, the husband of respondent Sandra

L. Craft, for failure to file federal income tax returns for the years 1979 through 1986. When he failed to pay, a federal tax lien attached to "all property and rights to property, whether real or personal, belonging to" him. 26 U.S.C. §6321.

At the time the lien attached, respondent and her husband owned a piece of real property in Grand Rapids, Michigan, as tenants by the entirety. After notice of the lien was filed, they jointly executed a quitclaim deed purporting to transfer the husband's interest in the property to respondent for one dollar. When respondent attempted to sell the property a few years later, a title search revealed the lien. The IRS agreed to release the lien and allow the sale with the stipulation that half of the net proceeds be held in escrow pending determination of the Government's interest in the property.

Respondent brought this action to quiet title to the escrowed proceeds. The Government claimed that its lien had attached to the husband's interest in the tenancy by the entirety. It further asserted that the transfer of the property to respondent was invalid as a fraud on creditors. . . .

[T]he District Court concluded that where, as here, state law makes property exempt from the claims of creditors, no fraudulent conveyance can occur. It found, however, that respondent's husband's use of nonexempt funds to pay the mortgage on the entireties property, which placed them beyond the reach of creditors, constituted a fraudulent act under state law, and the court awarded the IRS a share of the proceeds of the sale of the property equal to that amount. [The Court of Appeals affirmed.]

II.

Whether the interests of respondent's husband in the property he held as a tenant by the entirety constitutes "property and rights to property" for the purposes of the federal tax lien statute, 26 U.S.C. §6321, is ultimately a question of federal law. The answer to this federal question, however, largely depends upon state law. . . .

A common idiom describes property as a "bundle of sticks" — a collection of individual rights which, in certain combinations, constitute property. *See* B. Cardozo, *Paradoxes of Legal Science* 129 (1928) (reprint 2000). State law determines only which sticks are in a person's bundle. Whether those sticks qualify as "property" for purposes of the federal tax lien statute is a question of federal law.

In looking to state law, we must be careful to consider the substance of the rights state law provides, not merely the labels the State gives these rights or the conclusions it draws from them. Such state law labels are irrelevant to the federal question of which bundles of rights constitute property that may be attached by a federal tax lien. In Drye v. United States, 528 U.S. 49 (1999), we considered a situation where state law allowed an heir subject to a federal tax lien to disclaim his interest in the estate. The state law also provided that such a disclaimer would "creat[e] the legal fiction" that the heir had predeceased the decedent and would correspondingly be deemed to have had no property interest in the estate. *Id.* at 53. We unanimously held that this state law fiction did not control the federal question and looked instead to the realities of the heir's interest. We concluded that, despite the State's characterization, the heir possessed a "right to property" in the estate — the right to accept the inheritance or pass it along to another — to which the federal lien could attach. *Id.* at 59-61.

III.

We turn first to the question of what rights respondent's husband had in the entireties property by virtue of state law. In order to understand these rights, the tenancy by the entirety must first be placed in some context.

English common law provided three legal structures for the concurrent ownership of property that have survived into modern times: tenancy in common, joint tenancy, and tenancy by the entirety. The tenancy in common is now the most common form of concurrent ownership. The common law characterized tenants in common as each owning a separate fractional share in undivided property. Tenants in common may each unilaterally alienate their shares through sale or gift or place encumbrances upon these shares. They also have the power to pass these shares to their heirs upon death. Tenants in common have many other rights in the property, including the right to use the property, to exclude third parties from it, and to receive a portion of any income produced from it.

Joint tenancies were the predominant form of concurrent ownership at common law, and still persist in some States today. The common law characterized each joint tenant as possessing the entire estate, rather than a fractional share: "Joint-tenants have one and the same interest . . . held by one and the same undivided possession." 2 W. Blackstone, *Commentaries on the Laws of England* 180 (1766). Joint tenants possess many of the rights enjoyed by tenants in common: the right to use, to exclude, and to enjoy a share of the property's income. The main difference between a joint tenancy and a tenancy in common is that a joint tenant also has a right of automatic inheritance known as "survivorship." Upon the death of one joint tenant, that tenant's share in the property does not pass through will or the rules of intestate succession; rather, the remaining tenant or tenants automatically inherit it. Joint tenants' right to alienate their individual shares is also somewhat different. In order for one tenant to alienate his or her individual interest in the tenancy, the estate must first be severed — that is, converted to a tenancy in common with each tenant possessing an equal fractional share. Most States allowing joint tenancies facilitate alienation, however, by allowing severance to automatically accompany a conveyance of that interest or any other overt act indicating an intent to sever.

A tenancy by the entirety is a unique sort of concurrent ownership that can only exist between married persons. Because of the common-law fiction that the husband and wife were one person at law (that person, practically speaking, was the husband, *see* J. Cribbet et al., *Cases and Materials on Property* 329 (6th ed. 1990)), Blackstone did not characterize the tenancy by the entirety as a form of concurrent ownership at all. Instead, he thought that entireties property was a form of single ownership by the marital unity. Orth, *Tenancy by the Entirety: The Strange Career of the Common-Law Marital Estate*, 1997 B.Y.U. L. Rev. 35, 38-39. Neither spouse was considered to own any individual interest in the estate; rather, it belonged to the couple.

Like joint tenants, tenants by the entirety enjoy the right of survivorship. Also like a joint tenancy, unilateral alienation of a spouse's interest in entireties property is typically not possible without severance. Unlike joint tenancies, however, tenancies by the entirety cannot easily be severed unilaterally. Typically, severance requires the consent of both spouses, or the ending of the marriage in divorce. At common law, all of the other rights associated with the entireties property belonged to the husband: as the head of the household, he could control the use of the property and the exclusion of others from it and enjoy all of the income produced from it. The husband's control of the property was so extensive that, despite the rules on alienation, the common law eventually provided that he could unilaterally alienate entireties property without severance subject only to the wife's survivorship interest.

With the passage of the Married Women's Property Acts in the late 19th century granting women distinct rights with respect to marital property, most States either abolished the tenancy by the entirety or altered it significantly. Michigan's version of the estate is typical of the modern tenancy by the entirety. Following Blackstone, Michigan characterizes its tenancy by the entirety as creating no individual rights whatsoever: "It is well settled under the law of this state that one tenant by the entirety has no interest separable from that of the other. . . . Each is vested with an entire title." Long v. Earle, 269 N.W. 577, 581 (Mich. 1936). And yet, in Michigan, each tenant by the entirety possesses the right of survivorship. Each spouse — the wife as well as the husband — may also use the property, exclude third parties from it, and receive an equal share of the income produced by it. Neither spouse may unilaterally alienate or encumber the property, although this may be accomplished with mutual consent. Divorce ends the tenancy by the entirety, generally giving each spouse an equal interest in the property as a tenant in common, unless the divorce decree specifies otherwise.

In determining whether respondent's husband possessed "property" or "rights to property" within the meaning of 26 U.S.C. §6321, we look to the individual rights created by these state law rules. According to Michigan law, respondent's husband had, among other rights, the following rights with respect to the entireties property: the right to use the property, the right to exclude third parties from it, the right to a share of income produced from it, the right of survivorship, the right to become a tenant in common with equal shares upon divorce, the right to sell the property with the respondent's consent and to receive half the proceeds from such a sale, the right to place an encumbrance on the property with the respondent's consent, and the right to block respondent from selling or encumbering the property unilaterally.

IV.

We turn now to the federal question of whether the rights Michigan law granted to respondent's husband as a tenant by the entirety qualify as "property" or "rights to property" under §6321. The statutory language authorizing the tax lien "is broad and reveals on its face that Congress meant to reach every interest in property that a taxpayer might have." United States v. National Bank of Commerce, 472 U.S. 713, 719-20 (1985). "Stronger language could hardly have been selected to reveal a purpose to assure the collection of taxes." Glass City Bank v. United States, 326 U.S. 265, 267 (1945). We conclude that the husband's rights in the entireties property fall within this broad statutory language.

Michigan law grants a tenant by the entirety some of the most essential property rights: the right to use the property, to receive income produced by it, and to exclude others from it. These rights alone may be sufficient to subject the husband's interest in the entireties property to the federal tax lien. They gave him a substantial degree of control over the entireties property, and, as we noted in *Drye*, "in determining whether a federal taxpayer's state-law rights constitute 'property' or 'rights to property,' [t]he important consideration is the breadth of the control the [taxpayer] could exercise over the property." 528 U.S. at 61.

The husband's rights in the estate, however, went beyond use, exclusion, and income. He also possessed the right to alienate (or otherwise encumber) the property with the consent of respondent, his wife. It is true, as respondent notes, that he lacked the right to unilaterally alienate the property, a right that is often in the bundle of property rights. There is no reason to believe, however, that this one stick — the right of unilateral alienation — is essential to the category of "property." . . .

This Court has already stated that federal tax liens may attach to property that cannot be unilaterally alienated. In United States v. Rodgers, 461 U.S. 677 (1983), we considered the Federal Government's power to foreclose homestead property attached by a federal tax lien. Texas law provided that "'the owner or claimant of the property claimed as homestead [may not], if married, sell or abandon the homestead without the consent of the other spouse.'" *Id.* at 684-85, quoting Tex. Const., Art. 16, §50. We nonetheless stated that "[i]n the homestead context . . . , there is no doubt . . . that not only do both spouses (rather than neither) have an independent interest in the homestead property, but that a federal tax lien can at least attach to each of those interests." 461 U.S. at 703 n.31.

Excluding property from a federal tax lien simply because the taxpayer does not have the power to unilaterally alienate it would, moreover, exempt a rather large amount of what is commonly thought of as property. It would exempt not only the type of property discussed in *Rodgers,* but also some community property. Community property states often provide that real community property cannot be alienated without the consent of both spouses. Accordingly, the fact that respondent's husband could not unilaterally alienate the property does not preclude him from possessing "property and rights to property" for the purposes of §6321.

Respondent's husband also possessed the right of survivorship — the right to automatically inherit the whole of the estate should his wife predecease him. Respondent argues that this interest was merely an expectancy, which we suggested in *Drye* would not constitute "property" for the purposes of a federal tax lien. 528 U.S. at 60 n.7 ("[We do not mean to suggest] that an expectancy that has pecuniary value . . . would fall within §6321 prior to the time it ripens into a present estate"). *Drye* did not decide this question, however, nor do we need to do so here. As we have discussed above, a number of the sticks in respondent's husband's bundle were presently existing. It is therefore not necessary to decide whether the right to survivorship alone would qualify as "property" or "rights to property" under §6321.

That the rights of respondent's husband in the entireties property constitute "property" or "rights to property" "belonging to" him is further underscored by the fact that, if the conclusion were otherwise, the entireties property would belong to no one for the purposes of §6321. Respondent had no more interest in the property than her husband; if neither of them had a property interest in the entireties property, who did? This result not only seems absurd, but would also allow spouses to shield their property from federal taxation by classifying it as entireties property, facilitating abuse of the federal tax system. Johnson, *After* Drye: *The Likely Attachment of the Federal Tax Lien to Tenancy-by-the-Entireties Interests,* 75 Ind. L.J. 1163, 1171 (2000). . . .

We therefore conclude that respondent's husband's interest in the entireties property constituted "property" or "rights to property" for the purposes of the federal tax lien statute. We recognize that Michigan makes a different choice with respect to state law creditors. . . . But that by no means dictates our choice.

The interpretation of 26 U.S.C. §6321 is a federal question, and in answering that question we are in no way bound by state courts' answers to similar questions involving state law. . . .

V.

We express no view as to the proper valuation of respondent's husband's interest in the entireties property, leaving this for the Sixth Circuit to determine on remand. We note, however, that insofar as the amount is dependent upon whether the 1989 conveyance was fraudulent, this case is somewhat anomalous. The Sixth Circuit affirmed the District Court's judgment that this conveyance was not fraudulent, and the Government has not sought certiorari review of that determination. Since the District Court's judgment was based on the notion that, because the federal tax lien could not attach to the property, transferring it could not constitute an attempt to evade the Government creditor, 65 F. Supp. 2d at 657-59, in future cases, the fraudulent conveyance question will no doubt be answered differently.

The judgment of the United States Court of Appeals for the Sixth Circuit is accordingly reversed, and the case is remanded for proceedings consistent with this opinion.

Justice SCALIA, with whom Justice THOMAS joins, dissenting. . . .

I write separately to observe that the Court nullifies (insofar as federal taxes are concerned, at least) a form of property ownership that was of particular benefit to the stay-at-home spouse or mother. She is overwhelmingly likely to be the survivor that obtains title to the unencumbered property; and she (as opposed to her business-world husband) is overwhelmingly unlikely to be the source of the individual indebtedness against which a tenancy by the entirety protects. It is regrettable that the Court has eliminated a large part of this traditional protection retained by many States.

Justice THOMAS, with whom Justices STEVENS and SCALIA join, dissenting. . . .

. . . As the Court recognizes, pursuant to Michigan law, as under English common law, property held as a tenancy by the entirety does not belong to either spouse, but to a single entity composed of the married persons. . . .

The Court does not dispute this characterization of Michigan's law with respect to the essential attributes of the tenancy by the entirety estate. However, relying on Drye v. United States, 528 U.S. 49, 59 (1999), . . . the Court suggests that Michigan's definition of the tenancy by the entirety estate should be overlooked because federal tax law is not controlled by state legal fictions concerning property ownership. But the Court misapprehends the application of *Drye* to this case.

Drye . . . was concerned not with whether state law recognized "property" as belonging to the taxpayer in the first place, but rather with whether state laws could disclaim or exempt such property from federal tax liability after the property interest was created. *Drye* held only that a state-law disclaimer could not retroactively undo a vested right in an estate that the taxpayer already held, and that a federal lien therefore attached to the taxpayer's interest in the estate. 528 U.S. at 61 (recognizing that a disclaimer does not restore the *status quo ante* because the heir "determines who will receive the property — himself if he does not disclaim, a known other if he does"). . . .

Extending this Court's "state law fiction" jurisprudence to determine whether property or rights to property *exist* under state law in the first place works a sea change in the role States have traditionally played in "creating and defining" property interests. By erasing the careful line between state laws that purport to disclaim or exempt property interests after the fact, which the federal tax lien does not respect, and state laws' definition of property and property rights, which the federal tax lien does respect, the Court does not follow *Drye*, but rather creates a new federal common law of property. This contravenes the previously settled rule that the definition and scope of property is left to the States. . . .

Notes and Questions

1. The tenancy by the entirety issues raised by *Craft* fall within the larger context of debt collection. When can a creditor take the property of a debtor, without the debtor's consent, to compel payment? Stating it another way, what property (if any) should be exempt from debt collection measures such as attachment of a lien, levy, execution, or garnishment? In most states, homestead laws exempt a person's principal residence, and similar exemptions apply to a person's personal effects (such as clothing) and tools of a trade. Federal law also protects certain property from creditors' claims; for example, creditors generally cannot garnish social security benefits or pension payments. In addition, bankruptcy law significantly restricts the ability of creditors to reach property. When a debtor files a bankruptcy petition, all creditors must immediately suspend all debt collection efforts, and the debtor will often obtain bankruptcy relief that protects some of her property rights.

A property owner generally cannot make her property exempt from creditors' claims simply by declaring it shall be exempt. Tenancy by the entirety functions as an exception to this principle when husband and wife own the property, their state recognizes the form, and they choose the form. Is this justified?

2. In all states, spouses who decide to own property together have a number of choices they can make as to form of ownership. Don and Sandra Craft could have held the Grand Rapids property as tenants in common or as joint tenants. Had they picked either of these two types of cotenancy, what would be the respective rights of Don, Sandra, and the United States upon the filing of the federal tax lien? Suppose they formed a corporation or a partnership, in which they owned equal interests, and conveyed the property to that entity. Then what impact would the tax lien have?

3. After *Craft*, what would happen in Michigan if one spouse commits a tort, the victim obtains a judgment, and seeks to satisfy the judgment by obtaining a judgment lien against property held in tenancy by the entirety? Will that creditor be in the same position as the United States with respect to its tax lien?

4. Suppose Husband and Wife own property as tenants by the entirety, and the United States files a tax lien for unpaid taxes owed solely by Wife. Unlike the facts in *Craft*, neither spouse makes or attempts to make a conveyance. Can the United States at this point in time assert any rights to the property? What happens if Wife dies after filing of the lien while the tenancy is still in place? If Husband dies?

5. In all states recognizing tenancy by the entirety, spouses can elect to own real property in that form. There is a split of authority among those states as to whether they may also hold personal property as tenants by the entirety. Michigan is one of the states that restricts this tenancy to real property. In a state that allows a tenancy by the entirety in personal property, what should happen when a creditor has a claim

against one spouse and both spouses sell real property held in a tenancy by the entirety? May the spouses claim they hold the purchase price as tenants by the entirety, thus defeating the creditor's attempt to levy on the money?

6. At English common law, a conveyance of land to a married couple necessarily created a tenancy by the entirety. A couple could not own as joint tenants or tenants in common. Thus, the instrument did not have to employ any particular language to create that estate. Today, in American states that recognize the tenancy by the entirety, a couple may choose that form or joint tenancy or tenancy in common. In drafting their instrument, the parties should clearly specify the desired type of ownership. When intent isn't clearly stated, most such states presume a tenancy by the entirety. In several states, the normal presumption of tenancy in common applies. In states presuming a tenancy by the entirety, what language is sufficient to overcome that presumption? In Pattelli v. Bell, 721 N.Y.S.2d 734 (Sup. Ct. 2001), a grantor conveyed real property to herself, her son-in-law, and daughter, using the words, "to Helen Brostrom, Charles T. Bell and Barbara Bell, his wife, as joint tenants with the right of survivorship." Rejecting the argument that each grantee owned one-third as a joint tenant, the court held: "The language in the granting clause setting forth 'Charles T. Bell and Barbara Bell, his wife' created a tenancy-by-the-entirety because there is no language to the contrary. For a conveyance to a husband and wife to create a tenancy other than one by the entirety, there must be specific language stating otherwise, which the 1989 deed's granting clause does not so contain. If, on the other hand, the granting clause stated that they were to take 'as joint tenants with right of survivorship, among all of said individuals,' then a three-way joint tenancy would have been created giving the word 'all' significance."

In states that recognize tenancy by the entirety for personal property, courts must resolve similar issues in determining intent. In Beal Bank, SSB v. Almand & Assocs., 780 So. 2d 45 (Fla. 2001), the court prevented creditors of husbands from garnishing bank accounts held by husbands with their wives. The court held that a rebuttable presumption of a tenancy by the entireties arises if the requisite unities are present and the signature card for the bank account does not specifically disclaim ownership by the entireties. It observed: "the legitimate expectations of the parties regarding an account jointly held by them as a married couple should be no different than a home jointly owned by them as a married couple. The time has come for us to recognize that more confusion and less predictability in the law exists because of our Court's failure to recognize a presumption in favor of a tenancy by the entireties arising from joint ownership of bank accounts by husband and wife. Because this issue involves one arising from this State's common law and because the refusal to extend a presumption to personal property was a product of this Court's jurisprudence, we conclude that it is appropriate for us to recede from our prior case law." Subsequently, Florida lower courts and bankruptcy courts have wrestled with the issue whether *Beal Bank* creates a presumption for all personal property or just for bank accounts.

2. Death

Under traditional Anglo-American common law, a surviving spouse was entitled to a *legal life estate* in real estate owned by the deceased during marriage, with a surviving wife's estate known as *dower* and a surviving husband's estate as *curtesy*. All but four states (Arkansas, Kentucky, Michigan, and Ohio) have replaced dower and curtesy with an elective or *forced share* specified by statute. Under these laws, the surviving spouse is entitled to a percentage of the deceased spouse's estate, typically one-third or one-half. If the decedent's will is less generous to the survivor, that spouse has the right to disaffirm the will and take the mandated share. The forced share treats real property and personal property alike, and does not give the survivor rights in property conveyed by the spouse before death.

One weakness of the traditional forced share statute is that it operates independently of assets transferred by the decedent outside of probate. Many decedents leave behind significant non-probate assets, including life insurance proceeds, retirement benefits, and joint tenancy property. Depending upon whether such assets go to the surviving spouse or to other persons, the forced share may give the survivor too much or too little property. The Uniform Probate Code (UPC) resolves this problem by defining an "augmented estate," which includes non-probate assets. Under the UPC, the survivor is guaranteed a percentage of the augmented estate, which increases based upon the length of the marriage. UPC §2-202. For marriages of at least 15 years, the survivor takes 50 percent. UPC §2-203. Prenuptial agreements may allow spouses to "contract out" of forced share rules, subject to limitations of the laws of particular states.

3. *Divorce*

Who gets what upon divorce is one of the most emotional areas of property law. The source of the emotion is not so much intrinsic interest in the governing legal theories or rules; rather, the emotion stems from the intensely personal interests involved and the popular fascination with celebrity divorces. The tabloids and reality television shows pay great attention to divorces of the rich and famous, responding to their customers' appetites for stories filled with avarice and deceit — and perhaps pain and suffering. Although many divorces are settled amicably, many others are passionately contested. In most divorces there are a number of issues to resolve in addition to property rights; but in every divorce, there is property to divide, even if division proves noncontroversial.

A thumbnail sketch of divorce law should help you to understand the context of the next two cases. In the United States, traditional (historical) divorce law bears little resemblance to the modern regime. Two major reforms — no-fault divorce and the equitable division of property — have worked a fundamental change in divorce law. Both represent a drastic change from prior law. Under traditional divorce law, a husband or wife who sought a divorce had to bring judicial action to establish "grounds" for divorce. What grounds were sufficient depended upon state law, and they varied considerably from state to state. Usually, the plaintiff spouse had to prove major wrongdoing by the defendant, such as adultery, bigamy, desertion, or physical abuse. In New York, the sole ground for divorce was adultery. In the event of a contest, divorce could be hard to get. When both spouses wanted a divorce, they usually succeeded, in spite of the law, by collusively presenting perjured testimony. Residents of states where divorces were hard to obtain traveled to states with liberal divorce laws to dissolve their marriages. Nevada became the nation's divorce capital during the middle part of the twentieth century.

Beginning in the 1960s, state legislatures reformed their divorce statutes to eliminate the need to establish grounds for a divorce. Courts are now authorized to grant divorces, without identifying fault or grounds, by making a general finding such as "irreconcilable differences" or "marital discord." Judicial action is still required — it's still easier to get married than to get divorced. But a consequence of the reform is that if one spouse wants a divorce and files an action, that action will succeed even if the other spouse (the defendant) wants the marriage to continue. In effect, this has led to a system in which any spouse has a "legal right" to a divorce. When states moved to a "no fault" system, divorces generally became faster and less expensive. During the same time period when the no-fault reform swept the nation, U.S. divorce rates rose dramatically. Presently, roughly one-half of U.S. marriages end in divorce. Did the "no-fault" reform cause the divorce rate to accelerate? Often law responds to social change rather than inducing that change, and the former is the more likely explanation in this context. Major economic and cultural changes took place from the 1950s to the 1970s, as the "baby boomer" generation married and raised families. More husbands and wives came to view divorce as preferable to continuing in a marriage relationship perceived to be flawed or less than ideal. Divorce became socially acceptable, rather than stigmatizing. Nevertheless, even if legislative adoption of the no-fault system did not cause the groundswell of divorces, it certainly facilitated that phenomenon.

The second major divorce reform was the adoption of equitable division of property, which replaced a separate title system. Under traditional divorce law, property was divided by the relatively simple process of deciding who owned what, and confirming that ownership. For assets for which there was documentary evidence of title, such as land, automobiles, and stocks, this was relatively easy. For assets typically lacking such evidence, such as household furniture and other goods, conflicting claims were harder to resolve. The court divided the assets into three groups: first, things owned solely by husband; second, things owned solely by wife; and third, things they owned together (as cotenants in so-called common law property states or community property in those states recognizing that concept — we'll study community property later in this chapter). Assets in the third category were divided, with each spouse keeping whatever share they already owned, and with provision for partition or sale when appropriate. Divorce, therefore, was designed not to effect a change in property rights. The property division provision of a decree was designed to maintain the preexisting ownership of assets. Upon divorce, each spouse was supposed to own exactly what he and she owned while they were married. When the separate title system appeared inequitable, the alimony system came into play. If a poorer spouse (usually the wife) needed economic support after divorce, the court set an amount of alimony, payable periodically. Alimony is conceptualized not as a claim on the wealthier spouse's property, but as a personal obligation of that spouse. The justification for alimony is the recipient's need; it is not that the recipient "owns" a right to collect money because the payor left the marriage with greater wealth or earning potential. In many states today, the term *maintenance* has replaced *alimony*, with no change in the underlying concept.

During the same time period that legislatures embraced "no-fault" divorce, they replaced the separate title method of dividing property with equitable division of property. The new system is straightforward, at least on the surface. In almost all states, all property owned by either spouse is classified as "separate property" or "marital property." Separate property consists of property acquired by a spouse prior to the marriage and gifts (including inheritances and devises) made specifically to that spouse during the marriage. Everything else, including income earned by either spouse during the marriage, is marital property. In most states, the divorce court must give each spouse all of that person's separate property, although in a few states the divorce court has the power to divide even separate property between the parties. Courts tend to have more discretion in the allocation of marital property. In some states, a 50-50 split is favored (though not mandatory). In other states, courts commonly consider various factors, including need, length of the marriage, and contributions by each spouse, in allocating marital property between the divorcing spouses.

■ O'BRIEN v. O'BRIEN

Court of Appeals of New York, 1985
489 N.E.2d 712

SIMONS, Judge. In this divorce action, the parties' only asset of any consequence is the husband's newly acquired license to practice medicine. The principal issue presented is whether that license, acquired during their marriage, is marital property subject to equitable distribution under Domestic Relations Law §236(B)(5). Supreme Court held that it was and accordingly made a distributive award in defendant's favor.[1] It also granted defendant maintenance arrears, expert witness fees and attorneys' fees. On appeal to the Appellate Division, a majority of that court held that plaintiff's medical license is not marital property and that defendant was not entitled to an award for the expert witness fees. . . .

We now hold that plaintiff's medical license constitutes "marital property" within the meaning of Domestic Relations Law §236(B)(1)(c) and that it is therefore subject to equitable distribution pursuant to subdivision 5 of that part. That being so, the Appellate Division erred in denying a fee, as a matter of law, to defendant's expert witness who evaluated the license.

I.

Plaintiff [Michael O'Brien] and defendant [Loretta O'Brien] married on April 3, 1971. At the time both were employed as teachers at the same private school. Defendant had a bachelor's degree and a temporary teaching certificate but required 18 months of postgraduate classes at an approximate cost of $3,000, excluding living expenses, to obtain permanent certification in New York. She claimed, and the trial court found, that she had relinquished the opportunity to obtain permanent certification while plaintiff pursued his education. At the time of the marriage, plaintiff had completed only three and one-half years of college but shortly afterward he returned to school at night to earn his bachelor's degree and to complete sufficient premedical courses to enter medical school. In September 1973 the parties moved to Guadalajara, Mexico, where plaintiff became a full-time medical student. While he pursued his studies defendant held several teaching and tutorial positions and contributed her earnings to their joint expenses. The parties returned to New York in December 1976 so that plaintiff could complete the last two semesters of medical school and internship training here. After they returned, defendant resumed her former teaching position and she remained in it at the time this action was commenced. Plaintiff was licensed to practice medicine in

---

1. The action was originally instituted by plaintiff husband and defendant wife asserted a counterclaim in her answer. Subsequently, the husband withdrew his complaint and reply to the counterclaim and the wife received an uncontested divorce.

October 1980. He commenced this action for divorce two months later. At the time of trial, he was a resident in general surgery.

During the marriage both parties contributed to paying the living and educational expenses and they received additional help from both of their families. They disagreed on the amounts of their respective contributions but it is undisputed that in addition to performing household work and managing the family finances defendant was gainfully employed throughout the marriage, that she contributed all of her earnings to their living and educational expenses and that her financial contributions exceeded those of plaintiff. The trial court found that she had contributed 76% of the parties' income exclusive of a $10,000 student loan obtained by defendant. Finding that plaintiff's medical degree and license are marital property, the court received evidence of its value and ordered a distributive award to defendant.

Defendant presented expert testimony that the present value of plaintiff's medical license was $472,000. Her expert testified that he arrived at this figure by comparing the average income of a college graduate and that of a general surgeon between 1985, when plaintiff's residency would end, and 2012, when he would reach age 65. After considering Federal income taxes, an inflation rate of 10% and a real interest rate of 3% he capitalized the difference in average earnings and reduced the amount to present value. He also gave his opinion that the present value of defendant's contribution to plaintiff's medical education was $103,390. Plaintiff offered no expert testimony on the subject.

The court, after considering the life-style that plaintiff would enjoy from the enhanced earning potential his medical license would bring and defendant's contributions and efforts toward attainment of it, made a distributive award to her of $188,800, representing 40% of the value of the license, and ordered it paid in 11 annual installments of various amounts beginning November 1, 1982 and ending November 1, 1992. The court also directed plaintiff to maintain a life insurance policy on his life for defendant's benefit for the unpaid balance of the award and it ordered plaintiff to pay defendant's counsel fees of $7,000 and her expert witness fee of $1,000. It did not award defendant maintenance. . . .

II.

The Equitable Distribution Law contemplates only two classes of property: marital property and separate property. Domestic Relations Law §236(B)(1)(c), (d). The former, which is subject to equitable distribution, is defined broadly as "all property acquired by either or both spouses during the marriage and before the execution of a separation agreement or the commencement of a matrimonial action, *regardless of the form in which title is held*." Domestic Relations Law §236(B)(1)(c) (emphasis added); *see* §236(B)(5)(b), (c). Plaintiff does not contend that his license is excluded from distribution because it is separate property; rather, he claims that it is not property at all but represents a personal attainment in acquiring knowledge. He rests his argument on decisions in similar cases from other jurisdictions and on his view that a license does not satisfy common-law concepts of property. Neither contention is controlling because decisions in other States rely principally on their own statutes, and the legislative history underlying them, and because the New York Legislature deliberately went beyond traditional property concepts when it formulated the Equitable Distribution Law. *See generally*, 2 Foster-Freed-Brandes, *Law and the Family — New York* ch. 33, at 917 et seq. (1985

Cum. Supp.). Instead, our statute recognizes that spouses have an equitable claim to things of value arising out of the marital relationship and classifies them as subject to distribution by focusing on the marital status of the parties at the time of acquisition. Those things acquired during marriage and subject to distribution have been classified as "marital property" although, as one commentator has observed, they hardly fall within the traditional property concepts because there is no common-law property interest remotely resembling marital property. "It is a statutory creature, is of no meaning whatsoever during the normal course of a marriage and arises full-grown, like Athena, upon the signing of a separation agreement or the commencement of a matrimonial action. [Thus] [i]t is hardly surprising, and not at all relevant, that traditional common law property concepts do not fit in parsing the meaning of 'marital property.'" Florescue, "*Market Value,*" *Professional Licenses and Marital Property: A Dilemma in Search of a Horn,* 1982 N.Y. St. Bar Assn. Fam. L. Rev. 13. Having classified the "property" subject to distribution, the Legislature did not attempt to go further and define it but left it to the courts to determine what interests come within the terms of section 236(B)(1)(c).

We made such a determination in Majauskas v. Majauskas, 463 N.E.2d 15 (N.Y. 1984), holding there that vested but unmatured pension rights are marital property subject to equitable distribution. Because pension benefits are not specifically identified as marital property in the statute, we looked to the express reference to pension rights contained in section 236(B)(5)(d)(4), which deals with equitable distribution of marital property, to other provisions of the equitable distribution statute and to the legislative intent behind its enactment to determine whether pension rights are marital property or separate property. A similar analysis is appropriate here and leads to the conclusion that marital property encompasses a license to practice medicine to the extent that the license is acquired during marriage.

Section 236 provides that in making an equitable distribution of marital property, "the court shall consider: . . . (6) any equitable claim to, interest in, or direct or indirect contribution made to the acquisition of such marital property by the party not having title, including joint efforts or expenditures and contributions and services as a spouse, parent, wage earner and homemaker, and *to the career or career potential* of the other party [and] . . . (9) the impossibility or difficulty of evaluating any component asset or any interest in a business, corporation or *profession.*" Domestic Relations Law §236(B)(5)(d)(6), (9) (emphasis added). Where equitable distribution of marital property is appropriate but "the distribution of an interest in a business, corporation or *profession* would be contrary to law" the court shall make a distributive award in lieu of an actual distribution of the property. Domestic Relations Law §236(B)(5)(e) (emphasis added). The words mean exactly what they say: that an interest in a profession or professional career potential is marital property which may be represented by direct or indirect contributions of the non-title-holding spouse, including financial contributions and nonfinancial contributions made by caring for the home and family.

The history which preceded enactment of the statute confirms this interpretation. Reform of section 236 was advocated because experience had proven that application of the traditional common-law title theory of property had caused inequities upon dissolution of a marriage. The Legislature replaced the existing system with equitable distribution of marital property, an entirely new theory which considered all the circumstances of the case and of the respective parties to the marriage. Equitable distribution was based on the premise that a marriage is, among other things, an economic partnership to which both parties contribute as spouse, parent, wage earner or homemaker. Consistent with this purpose, and implicit in the statutory scheme as a whole, is the view that upon dissolution of the marriage there should be a winding up of the parties' economic affairs and a severance of their economic ties by an equitable distribution of the marital assets. Thus, the concept of alimony, which often served as a means of lifetime support and dependence for one spouse upon the other long after the marriage was over, was replaced with the concept of maintenance which seeks to allow "the recipient spouse an opportunity to achieve [economic] independence." Assembly Memorandum, 1980 N.Y. Legis. Ann. at 130.

The determination that a professional license is marital property is also consistent with the conceptual base upon which the statute rests. As this case demonstrates, few undertakings during a marriage better qualify as the type of joint effort that the statute's economic partnership theory is intended to address than contributions toward one spouse's acquisition of a professional license. Working spouses are often required to contribute substantial income as wage earners, sacrifice their own educational or career goals and opportunities for child rearing, perform the bulk of household duties and responsibilities and forego the acquisition of marital assets that could have been accumulated if the professional spouse had been employed rather than occupied with the study and training necessary to acquire a professional license. In this case, nearly all of the parties' nine-year marriage was devoted to the acquisition of plaintiff's medical license and defendant played a major role in that project. She worked continuously during the marriage and contributed all of her earnings to their joint effort, she sacrificed her own educational and career opportunities, and she traveled with plaintiff to Mexico for three and one-half years while he attended medical school there. The Legislature has decided, by its explicit reference in the statute to the contributions of one spouse to the other's profession or career, *see* Domestic Relations Law §236(B)(5)(d)(6), (9); (e), that these contributions represent investments in the economic partnership of the marriage and that the product of the parties' joint efforts, the professional license, should be considered marital property.

The majority at the Appellate Division held that the cited statutory provisions do not refer to the license held by a professional who has yet to establish a practice but only to a ongoing professional practice. *See, e.g.,* Arvantides v. Arvantides, 478 N.E.2d 199 (N.Y. 1985). There is no reason in law or logic to restrict the plain language of the statute to existing practices, however, for it is of little consequence in making an award of marital property, except for the purpose of evaluation, whether the professional spouse has already established a practice or whether he or she has yet to do so. An established practice merely represents the exercise of the privileges conferred upon the professional spouse by the license and the income flowing from that practice represents the receipt of the enhanced earning capacity that licensure allows. That being so, it would be unfair not to consider the license a marital asset.

Plaintiff's principal argument, adopted by the majority below, is that a professional license is not marital property because it does not fit within the traditional view of property as something which has an exchange value on the open market and is capable of sale, assignment or transfer. The position does not withstand analysis for at least two reasons. First, as we have observed, it ignores the fact that whether a professional license constitutes marital property is to be judged by the language of the statute which created this new species of property previously unknown at common law or under prior statutes. Thus, whether the license fits within traditional property concepts is of no consequence. Second, it is an over-statement to assert that a professional license could not be considered property even outside the context of section 236(B). A professional license is a valuable property right, reflected in the money, effort and lost opportunity for employment expended in its acquisition, and also in the enhanced earning capacity it affords its holder, which may not be revoked without due process of law. *See* Matter of Bender v. Board of Regents, 30 N.Y.S.2d 779, 784 (App. Div. 1941). That a professional license has no market value is irrelevant. Obviously, a license may not be alienated as may other property and for that reason the working spouse's interest in it is limited. The Legislature has recognized that limitation, however, and has provided for an award in lieu of its actual distribution. *See* Domestic Relations Law §236(B)(5)(e).

Plaintiff also contends that alternative remedies should be employed, such as an award of rehabilitative maintenance or reimbursement for direct financial con-tributions. . . . It is sufficient to observe that normally a working spouse should not be restricted to that relief because to do so frustrates the purposes underlying the Equitable Distribution Law. Limiting a working spouse to a maintenance award, either general or rehabilitative, not only is contrary to the economic partnership concept underlying the statute but also retains the uncertain and inequitable eco-nomic ties of dependence that the Legislature sought to extinguish by equitable distribution. Maintenance is subject to termination upon the recipient's remarriage and a working spouse may never receive adequate consideration for his or her contribution and may even be penalized for the decision to remarry if that is the only method of compensating the contribution. . . .

Turning to the question of valuation, it has been suggested that even if a professional license is considered marital property, the working spouse is entitled only to reimbursement of his or her direct financial contributions. *See* Note, *Equitable Distribution of Degrees and Licenses: Two Theories Toward Compensating Spousal Contributions*, 49 Brooklyn L. Rev. 301, 317-22 (1983). By parity of reasoning, a spouse's down payment on real estate or contribution to the purchase of securities would be limited to the money contributed, without any remuneration for any incremental value in the asset because of price appreciation. Such a result is completely at odds with the statute's requirement that the court give full consid-eration to both direct and indirect contributions "made to the acquisition of such marital property by the party not having title, including joint *efforts* or expendi-tures and *contributions and services as a spouse, parent,* wage earner *and homemaker."* Domestic Relations Law §236(B)(5)(d)(6) (emphasis added). If the license is marital property, then the working spouse is entitled to an equitable portion of it, not a return of funds advanced. Its value is the enhanced earning capacity it affords the holder and although fixing the present value of that enhanced earning capacity may present problems, the problems are not insurmountable. Certainly they are no more difficult than computing tort damages for wrongful death or diminished earning capacity resulting from injury and they differ only in degree from the problems presented when valuing a professional practice for purposes of a distributive award, something the courts have not hesitated to do. The trial court retains the flexibility and discretion to structure the distributive award equitably, taking into consideration factors such as the working spouse's need for immediate payment, the licensed spouse's current ability to pay and the income tax consequences of prolonging the period of payment and, once it has received evidence of the present value of the license and the working spouse's contributions toward its acquisition and considered the remaining factors mandated by the statute, it may then make an appropriate distribution of the marital property including a distributive award for the professional license if such an award is warranted. . . .

III.

. . . Plaintiff also contends that the trial court erred in excluding evidence of defendant's marital fault on the question of equitable distribution. Arguably, the court may consider marital fault under factor 10, "any other factor which the court shall expressly find to be just and proper." Domestic Relations Law §236(B)(5)(d)(10). Except in egregious cases which shock the conscience of the court, however, it is not a "just and proper" factor for consideration in the equitable distribution of marital property. Blickstein v. Blickstein, 472 N.Y.S.2d 110, 113-14 (App. Div. 1984), *appeal dismissed*, 484 N.E.2d 1058 (N.Y. 1984). That is so because marital fault is inconsistent with the underlying assumption that a marriage is in part an economic partnership and upon its dissolution the parties are entitled to a fair share of the marital estate, because fault will usually be difficult to assign and because introduction of the issue may involve the courts in time-consuming procedural maneuvers relating to collateral issues. We have no occasion to consider the wife's fault in this action because there is no suggestion that she was guilty of fault sufficient to shock the conscience. . . .

Accordingly, in view of our holding that plaintiff's license to practice medicine is marital property, the order of the Appellate Division should be modified, with costs to defendant, by reinstating the judgment and the case remitted to the Appellate Division. . . .

MEYER, Judge. I concur in Judge Simons' opinion but write separately to point up for consideration by the Legislature the potential for unfairness involved in distributive awards based upon a license of a professional still in training.

An equity court normally has power to "'change its decrees where there has been a change of circumstances.'" People v. Scanlon, 184 N.E.2d 302, 303 (N.Y. 1962). The implication of Domestic Relations Law §236(B)(9)(b), which deals with modification of an order or decree as to maintenance or child support, is, however, that a distributive award pursuant to section §236(B)(5)(e), once made, is not subject to change. Yet a professional in training who is not finally committed to a career choice when the distributive award is made may be locked into a particular kind of practice simply because the monetary obligations imposed by the distributive award made on the basis of the trial judge's conclusion (prophecy may be a better word) as to what the career choice will be leaves him or her no alternative.

The present case points up the problem. A medical license is but a step toward the practice ultimately engaged in by its holder, which follows after internship, residency and, for particular specialties, board certification. Here it is undisputed that plaintiff was in a residency for general surgery at the time of the trial, but had the previous year done a residency in internal medicine. Defendant's expert based his opinion on the difference between the average income of a general surgeon and that of a college graduate of plaintiff's age and life expectancy, which the trial judge utilized, impliedly finding that plaintiff would engage in a surgical practice despite plaintiff's testimony that he was dissatisfied with the general surgery program he was in and was attempting to return to the internal medicine training he had been in the previous year. The trial judge had the right, of course, to discredit that testimony, but the point is that equitable distribution was not intended to permit a judge to make a career decision for a licensed spouse still in training. Yet the degree of speculation involved in the award made is emphasized by the testimony of the expert on which it was based. Asked whether his assumptions and calculations were in any way speculative, he replied: "Yes. They're speculative to the extent of, will Dr. O'Brien practice medicine? Will Dr. O'Brien earn more or less than the average surgeon earns? Will Dr. O'Brien live to age sixty-five? Will Dr. O'Brien have a heart attack or will he be injured in an automobile accident? Will he be disabled? I mean, there is a degree of speculation. That speculative aspect is no more to be taken into account, cannot be taken into account, and it's a question, again, Mr. Emanuelli, not for the expert but for the courts to decide. It's not my function nor could it be." . . .

Notes and Questions

1. New York courts subsequently extended *O'Brien* to situations in which the enhanced earning potential is not reflected by a piece of paper, such as a license to practice medicine or a professional degree. The best known case is Elkus v. Elkus, 572 N.Y.S.2d 901 (App. Div. 1991), which involved the divorce of the famous mezzo-soprano opera star Frederica von Stade. Because her husband assisted in the development of her career and cared for their children, the court ruled that he owned a share of her post-divorce earnings as "celebrity goodwill."

2. Do you understand the *O'Brien* court's distinction between the division of marital property and maintenance (formerly known as alimony)? Suppose just about the time of the divorce, Loretta won a major jackpot in the state lottery. What effect should this happy event have on her property claim to Michael's medical license? On her maintenance award, had she obtained one?

3. The *O'Brien* holding remains a minority rule. Most courts have rejected the proposition that enhanced earning potential, developed while the couple is married, represents marital property, whether or not the enhanced earning potential is reflected by a professional degree. A large number of those courts, however, have provided the non-career spouse with a measure of protection, accepting one of the two alternatives discussed in *O'Brien*. The spouse is entitled to either (1) reimbursement of her financial contributions, with appropriate interest, or (2) a special type of alimony, known as "rehabilitative maintenance," which pays educational or job-related expenses for the non-career spouse to enhance her earning potential. Would either of these alternatives fairly compensate Loretta O'Brien? The right of a divorced spouse to get maintenance or reimbursement is *not* conceptualized as property rights. Why not? Couldn't they be considered to be "property," without changing the nature of the entitlement? Reimbursement would be like protecting the victim of a contract breach with reliance damages, rather than expectation damages. Doesn't rehabilitative maintenance seek to compensate the non-career spouse by measuring her opportunity costs, forgone when the couple decided to concentrate their efforts on the career advancement of the other spouse?

4. Community Property

In nine states, the institution of *community property* defines marital property. The community property system differs markedly from the common law system, which originated in England and evolved in America. The common law system starts from the premise of *separate title*—each spouse holds a separate title or ownership to property. At common law individual ownership is the norm; cotenancies are not implied from the fact of marriage. The modern common law marital property rights system has kept separate title as its underlying base, with modifications designed to protect the non-owner. Thus, a wealthier spouse may owe the other spouse a duty of support. A surviving spouse has the right to inherit a share of the deceased spouse's estate. And if the marriage ends in divorce, each spouse has a claim to an equitable or in some cases equal share of the "marital property," which redistributes property owned by the wealthier spouse to the poorer spouse.

In contrast, community property starts from the premise that the marriage is a unity or at least an *economic partnership.* Accumulations of wealth belong to the couple together. All income earned during marriage belongs to both partners, regardless of which spouse is employed or receives the income. As the map at the bottom of this page shows, the community property states all lie west of the Mississippi River, with the exception of Wisconsin, which became a community property state in 1986 by adopting the Uniform Marital Property Act. Community property has its historical roots in the civil law. While European nations colonized the Americas, France and Spain had community property systems, which they imposed upon their colonies. Louisiana, unlike other states, has a civil-law jurisprudence. Consequently, its community property system derives largely from French law. Areas like Texas and California, once ruled by Spain and Mexico, became common law jurisdictions as a general matter after U.S. statehood, but they retained community property as their marital property regime. Other Western states that have community property either have a Spanish background (Arizona, New Mexico, Nevada), or their territorial governments (pre-statehood) looked to California as a model for their legal system (Idaho and Washington).

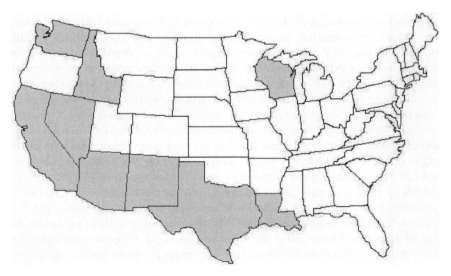

Nine Community Property States

In all nine states, spouses are allowed to own *separate property*, which consists of all premarital property (property owned by husband or wife at the time they married) untainted by postmarital additions, gifts (inter vivos and testamentary) made solely to one spouse, and inheritances of one spouse. There is a strong presumption that all property owned by either spouse during marriage is community property. A person who claims a particular asset is separate property has the burden proving it has an untainted separate source. Moreover, proceeds of community property are community property. The manner in which the couple holds title doesn't matter. It doesn't matter if one spouse alone holds record title; if it has a community source it is community property. (Wisconsin follows this distinction between community and separate property, but uses different vocabulary; the uniform act calls them "marital property" and "individual property.")

The basic idea of modern community property is easy to understand, and your first impression might be that community property is simple and easy to administer. For a number of reasons, this is not the case. Indeed, it is precisely because of its complexity that community property creates so much business for attorneys. Any lawyer practicing law in a community property state needs to know how the system works in that state, and because of this, it is a favorite topic on bar exams in those states. The system's complexity stems both from historical change and from diversity among the states. First, community property, like the common law and all legal systems, is not static. It has evolved over time, starting from a European medieval system that did not treat husband and wife equally. These pre-modern systems used the "community" concept only as a means to define the wife's claim to property when the marriage ended by death, dissolution, or divorce: During marriage, the husband controlled it. Equality in management and control evolved over time. In California, full equality dates to a 1927 statute, which defined the wife's interest as "present, existing and equal"; and in some other states, equality was not achieved until the 1970s. Community property, like other bodies of law, continues to evolve today.

Second, regarding many fundamental issues of community property law, the states have adopted different rules. Important differences include the following:

- What is the status of income generated by separate property while the couple is married? Suppose Husband owns Blackacre, which is rented to tenants and Wife owns shares of stock and receives dividends. In Idaho, Louisiana, and Texas, the rents and dividends are community property, but in the other states, income from separate property remains separate.

- How is community property divided if the couple divorces? California, New Mexico, and Louisiana mandate an *equal division*, but the other states allow the court to make an *equitable division* of community property, much like divorce courts in common law states can make an equitable division of marital property.

- Can the couple voluntarily agree to change separate property into community property, or community property into separate property? Such a change is known as "transmuting" the property. Some states prohibit such changes even by mutual agreement of the parties, some allow it by written agreements, and some allow it by either written or oral agreements.

- Who can convey title to community property? Suppose Wife uses money she has earned while married to buy Blackacre and takes title in her name alone. Without Husband's consent, she then sells Blackacre to Buyer, who is unaware that Blackacre is community property. In some states, Buyer qualifies as a bona fide purchaser (BFP) based upon payment of value and lack of actual knowledge, but other states protect Husband if Buyer has inquiry notice that he bought Blackacre from a married woman.

- Who can make a gift of community property? Some states (Texas) allow one spouse acting alone to make reasonable gifts, but other states (California and Washington) allow the non-generous spouse to set aside any gift of community property.
- Can a debt incurred by one spouse be classified as a "community debt" for which both spouses are liable? In most states, the community property system has no effect on liabilities, but Louisiana recognizes community debts, which are payable out of community assets. A few states, including Washington, also recognize community debts, but to a lesser extent than Louisiana.
- Who succeeds to community property upon the death of a spouse? In all states, each spouse has testamentary capacity to devise his or her one-half of the community property. But if a spouse dies intestate, in some states the decedent's children or descendants take the decedent's one-half (Arizona, Louisiana, Texas, Wisconsin). In other states, community property has a survivorship aspect—the one-half goes to the widow or widower in the absence of a will.

The nine community property states contain over one quarter of the entire U.S. population, but community property has an impact on more Americans than even this fraction suggests. Americans are highly mobile, and many couples reside in more than one state during their lifetime. The marital property rights of "migrating couples" are complicated. Any couple that has ever had a domicile in a community property state is subject to that state's regime with respect to property they acquired while domiciled there. The baseline rule is that characterization of property does not change upon relocation. Thus, a couple that lives in Texas for 10 years, and then lives in Florida for the next 10 years, is subject to both states' marital property regimes. Assets that were originally Texas community property retain that character, whether or not they are transported to Florida. Income earned after the change in domicile is not community property; it is subject to the Florida system of marital property rights. Proceeds of Texas community property, however, remain Texas community property, even though acquired after they moved to Florida. Tracing assets, of course, is often hard to do, especially if cash from savings and cash from present earnings are commingled. Most migrating couples, not surprisingly, do not consider the effects relocation will have on their property rights. Depending upon the degree to which the relevant states allow couples to transmute (change) the character of their assets, couples that do appreciate the significance of the different regimes have the ability to "opt out" of the baseline choice-of-law rules.

As a practical matter, these differences have the greatest impact at the time of divorce. At that point a court must identify and divide the couple's community property and separate property. As stated above, the starting point is a presumption that all property titled in either spouse is part of the community estate and (depending on the state) subject to equal or equitable division. A spouse who claims that something is separate property must be able to track the property, through time, to its source. In some states, separate property retains its separate character so long as it can be tracked back to a separate source. In other states, separate property must not only have had a separate source but must have remained untainted by the addition of any community assets. The following examples illustrate these differences:

Example 1: At the time of his marriage, Juan had a bank account in his own name containing $100,000. While married, he continues to deposit his earnings into this bank account, which grows to $150,000 by the time of his divorce. During the entire time of his marriage, Juan can show that his bank account never dropped below $100,000. In some community property states, $100,000 in this bank account would remain Juan's separate property and the added $50,000 would be community property. In other community property states, the entire $150,000 would be community property because it was tainted by the addition of commingled community assets.

Example 2: Same facts as Example 1 except the amount in the account steadily dropped during marriage to $50,000 despite the addition by Juan or his wife of some community earnings to it. So long as Juan can show that the balance in his account never dropped below $50,000 during his marriage, in some community property states the remaining $50,000 (as a relic of his premarital $100,000) would be his separate property; in other such states, the entire $50,000 would be community property due to the tainting of commingled community assets.

Example 3: At the time of her marriage, Isabella owned a house that she retains following their marriage. During their marriage, both spouses contribute to the mortgage payments and cost of improvements on the house from current earnings. In some community property states, the house remains Isabella's separate property, with her husband having only a community property interest in the cost of mortgage principal payments and improvements paid for with community assets. In other community property states, the entire house has become community property through the addition to it of community assets in the form of mortgage principal payments or improvements.

The characterization of property as separate or community does not necessarily resolve which spouse gets it upon divorce. Indeed, the rules for allocating property between the two spouses differ in the various community property states (just as they do in common law states). As noted above, in some states, divorce courts must equally divide community assets with no leeway for judicially mandated interspousal property transfers. For example, in California each spouse must receive all of his or her separate property. California also mandates an equal division of community property between the spouses. In other states, a court is allowed to make an equitable division of community property, which may diverge from a 50-50 split. Notice that the Texas court in *Osuna*, reproduced below, calls this the "up for grabs" rule. This creates a system that functions much like those employed in common law states, where the court makes an "equitable distribution" of "marital property." Texas and several other states also grant the divorce court some degree of power to award one spouse's separate property to the other spouse. Although the community property model is theoretically inconsistent with post-divorce support obligations, some of the community property states including California allow for the grant of alimony (or maintenance). The following cases introduce some of these complexities, but law students in a community property state should supplement this coverage with an upper level course in community property law:

■ IN RE MARRIAGE OF HORN
Court of Appeal of California, 1986
226 Cal. Rptr. 666

WORK, Associate Justice. Robert Horn appeals a judgment awarding Cyndee L. Horn a community interest in his severance pay received from the National Football League.

I.

The parties married on June 8, 1974, and separated on January 25, 1983. Robert was employed as a professional football player from 1976 to 1984, playing with the National Football League during the 1976 through 1983 seasons and with the New Jersey Generals of the United States Football League during the 1984 season. After the 1984 season, he was released from the Generals, and at the time of trial (Aug. 1984), was unemployed.

In 1982, the National Football League Players Association (Union) and the management of the National Football League (NFL) added a "severance pay" provision to their collective bargaining agreement (CBA) which provides that any player credited with two or more seasons with the NFL is entitled to receive a lump sum of severance pay, computed on how many seasons played with the NFL. . . .

The CBA also contains a retirement plan provision and a termination pay provision.[3] Robert is eligible for a lump sum severance payment of $100,000, based on his eight seasons with the NFL.[4]

II.

In In re Marriage of Skaden, 566 P.2d 249 (Cal. 1977), the California Supreme Court found termination benefits to be community property. *Skaden* involved termination pay payable to an insurance sales agent under an employment agreement, which provided for the benefits after two or more years of employment, based on percentages of net premiums collected within a five-year period after termination on policies credited to the agent's account. Payments were to be made on an installment basis. . . .

Skaden rejected the argument the payments were "consideration for termination" because nothing in the agreement so suggested, and since termination could be involuntary (*i.e.*, upon death or the company's notice, rather than the agent's notice). . . . *Skaden* concluded the benefits were, like pension benefits, "a form of deferred compensation for services rendered," noting the right to the benefits were

---

3. The CBA refers to the "Bert Bell NFL Player Retirement Plan and Trust Agreement," which is not included in the record on appeal. The parties agreed to transfer the NFL retirement benefit to Robert as part of the division of community property. . . .

4. In Robert's brief to the trial court, he stated he could receive the $100,000 in April 1985, if he does not return to professional football and applies for the payment by the first game of the 1984-1985 season.

"derived from the terms of the employment contract" and became vested after two years of employment. *Id.* at 252-53.

In contrast, In re Marriage of Flockhart, 173 Cal. Rptr. 818 (Cal. App. 1981), In re Marriage of Wright, 189 Cal. Rptr. 336 (Cal. App. 1983), and recently, In re Marriage of Kuzmiak, 222 Cal. Rptr. 644 (Cal. App. 1986), found various types of termination pay to be separate property.

Flockhart involved "weekly lay-off" benefits paid by the United States to an employee adversely affected by the government's expansion of Redwood National Park. *Flockhart* equated the benefits to disability and workers' compensation benefits given, because of an employee's *status* as a disabled person, to presently compensate for loss of earnings, not to compensate for services previously rendered. The undisputed purpose of the Redwood Employee Protection Program was to replace lost income, the payments were reduced by present earnings, and the payments were not received because of any contractual agreement, but because of the employee's status as an "affected employee." In re Marriage of Flockhart, *supra* at 819-20. . . .

Wright considered employee termination pay as a voluntary payment by the employer, and not as part of the employment contract. The employer, a hospital administrator, testified he paid the money because he recognized the employee would have difficulty securing further employment because the employee's father-in-law (the hospital chaplain) and the employee's wife had threatened to ruin him financially, professionally, and personally. The benefits were considered analogous to those in *Flockhart* and the disability benefits cases, noting that in the latter the compensation is for future loss of earnings even if the right to the payments accrued during the marriage. . . .

Kuzmiak involved military separation pay to personnel discharged because they fail to be promoted, and based on the number of years served and annual salary. The legislative history of 10 United States Code section 1174, states: "The separation pay is a contingency payment for an officer who is career committed but to whom a full military career may be denied. It is designed to encourage him to pursue his service ambition, knowing that if he is denied a full career under the competitive system, he can count on an adequate readjustment pay to ease his reentry into civilian life." In re Marriage of Kuzmiak, *supra* at 646. . . .

III.

The issue here is whether the NFL severance pay is in the *Skaden* category of deferred compensation for past services, or as Robert asserts, the *Flockhart-Wright-Kuzmiak* category of present compensation for loss of earnings. The trial court stated: "In the instant case obviously the pay was for services previously rendered. He would be paid one amount if he was there for two years. . . . I think it was 10,000 for two years and if he remained eight years or more he would receive 100 or 110,000 so obviously the pay that he was to receive was to be based on past services rendered as distinguished from that portion of the collective bargaining agreement which provided for half a month's pay or whatever it is at the termination of employment."

We agree with the trial court's conclusion, but disagree with its reasoning that merely because the severance pay is tied to number of years of employment the pay is *obviously* for services previously rendered. In *Kuzmiak*, for example, the military separation pay was based on the number of years served, and yet the pay was found to be separate property. We must evaluate the character of the pay by looking at all relevant circumstances.

IV.

The severance pay here contains the following characteristics: (a) it is derived from a contract right; (b) it is based on the number of seasons worked; (c) it must be paid back to the NFL if the player returns to professional football within one year of receipt; (d) it will be paid back to him when he again leaves football, but no additional amount will have accrued for the seasons worked after his return; (e) it is given to the player's stated beneficiary or estate if he dies; (f) it is received in a lump sum after a certain period of time has passed following the player's notification to the club of his intent to permanently retire from professional football.

At a minimum, Robert will receive a lump sum of $100,000 severance pay based on his eight seasons with the NFL. During all eight seasons, he was married and was accruing the right to severance pay. He has earned an absolute right to the payment, which he will receive after he permanently leaves football.

There are no absolute rights to receive severance pay in the *Flockhart-Wright-Kuzmiak* line of cases or the disability cases.

In each of those cases, the payments are received *only if* a loss of work is forced upon an employee. None of those cases involve a contractual right to a payment, which arises after a certain number of years of employment and which will definitely be paid in the future. . . .

V.

At trial, Robert attempted to present the testimony of a Union negotiator that severance pay was designed to assist the player in the transition period after he leaves football. The trial court disallowed the testimony on the basis of the parol evidence rule and irrelevancy.

We agree the testimony should have been admitted. . . . However, we find the error harmless because admission of the testimony would not have resulted in a different outcome. People v. Watson, 299 P.2d 243, 254 (Cal. 1956).

Assuming the negotiator testimony would have established the severance pay was designed to assist the player in the transition period after he leaves football, this does not necessarily lead to the conclusion the pay was compensation for present loss of earnings rather than deferred compensation, for purposes of characterizing the property under community property law. Even were the pay designed to support the player after leaving football, the objective characteristics of the severance pay (*i.e.*, the player has an absolute right to the pay which accrues during his seasons of employment, regardless of whether or not he is ever involuntarily forced to leave football) establish its character as deferred compensation for services previously rendered. Even retirement pay is designed to provide support to employees after their careers are ended and they are no longer earning money, In re Marriage of Stenquist, 582 P.2d 96, 101 (Cal. 1978), yet this factor does not result in a separate property characterization of retirement pay. . . .

Similarly, even though the NFL severance pay may be generally designed to support players in their transition after football, like retirement pay, it is pay that the player earns the absolute right to receive because of the seasons he has played regardless of whether he experiences any involuntary loss of earnings. Indeed, even if he dies before it is received and never experiences a transition period, his beneficiary or estate receives the pay. We conclude the severance pay is deferred compensation for services previously rendered and thus community property.

The judgment is affirmed.

Notes and Questions

1. Bob Horn, middle linebacker from Oregon State, was a fourth round draft choice of the San Diego Chargers, where he played from 1976 to 1981. The next two seasons he played for the San Francisco 49ers.

2. A core principle is that income earned during the marriage is community property, but income earned after the marriage ends is separate property. How should retirement plans be treated when a retired worker receives payments after the marriage ends? Early cases often classified retirement benefits as separate property, treating them as post-marriage earnings, or as a replacement for post-marriage earnings. All community property states now reject this approach. Instead, retirement plans are treated as community property to the extent they represent income that was earned during marriage. This is true whether the employer makes contributions to the plan, the worker makes contributions, or both contribute. Characterization is easiest when the worker is married for the entire time period of employment. Then the entire pension or other retirement benefit is community property. When employment predates the marriage, or continues after termination of the marriage by divorce or death of the non-employee, then an allocation is necessary. The portion of the benefit attributable to premarital or postmarital work is separate property.

As *Horn* indicates, some types of post-employment benefits are not deemed to be community property even though the benefit is attributable to work performed earlier, while the couple was married. Disability pensions and workers' compensation payments, which the court mentions, are prime examples. Is this exclusion from community property justified? What if a worker's post-marriage disability payments are due to a disability insurance policy, which the worker purchased using earned income to pay the premiums?

The *Horn* court regards severance pay (sometimes called termination pay or separation pay) as occupying a middle ground between normal retirement benefits and disability/workers' compensation payments. Depending upon its particular characteristics, it may be community property or separate property. Do you think Robert Horn's severance pay from the National Football League is more like a disability payment or regular retirement pay? Should it matter whether football injuries caused him to retire?

3. Although *Horn* explores severance pay in the context of community property, similar outcomes are often achieved in common law marital property regimes in the context of divorce, although the path of analysis differs. Cyndee Horn prevailed because she owned an equal share in Robert's severance payment rights, a community asset, from the moment he obtained those rights. Had they lived in a common law state, Robert would be the sole owner of his right to future receipt of severance pay while the marriage lasted, subject, however, to a caveat. If the marriage happens to end in divorce, the court, as we learned earlier in this chapter, can make an equitable division of all marital property. Retirement benefits are generally classified as marital property, with the same special problems raised by disability benefits,

severance payments, and the like. This reform in common law states makes them more like community property states, but without expressly repudiating the separate title tradition.

4. Suppose Robert Horn had died, still married, before he received his $100,000 severance payment, and that his will devised all of his property to a charity. Does Cyndee have a claim to all or any part of the severance payment? Does it matter whether they were domiciled in California or in a common law marital property state?

■ **OSUNA v. QUINTANA**
   Court of Appeals of Texas, 1999
   993 S.W.2d 201

RODRIGUEZ, Justice. This is an appeal from a decree of divorce in which appellee Socorro Quintana was awarded a $460,000 joint and several liability judgment against her husband, Jose Quintana, and his mistress, appellant Esther Osuna. . . .

Jose and Socorro were married in Mexico in 1958. In 1971, Jose met Esther and commenced an affair with her that continued to the time of trial. In 1983, while still married to Socorro, Jose participated in a ceremonial marriage with Esther. In 1984, their first child was born. After that time, Jose supported Esther and the child, plus two more children he had with her.

During the 1970's and 1980's Jose earned a very high income through the operation of his Texas business, Farm Supply House, Inc. Jose had sole management and control of this company and the income it generated. He also owned and controlled other businesses, including a ranch in California, the Quintana Horse Ranch in Seguin, Texas, where he bred, stabled, and trained horses, five restaurants, a packing plant, and two boutiques in California called Osuna's. Socorro had no involvement in or knowledge of the management of these businesses.

In September 1985, Jose purchased a house [at Hidden View] for Esther and the children. As a down payment on the house, Jose paid $164,465.32 drawn on the Quintana Horse Ranch business account. In October, he paid $20,992.51 to furnish the house. These funds also came from the Quintana Horse Ranch business account. Over the next seven years, Jose made the monthly $1800 mortgage payment on the house. In November 1994, Esther paid $83,000 to refinance the Hidden View house. The record is not clear what precipitated the action, but it is apparent that sometime after 1994, the house was foreclosed upon, resulting in a surplus of $26,400. Chicago Title Company interpleaded this money into the registry of the Court.

In 1985, Jose purchased two Mercedes Benz automobiles for $12,500 each. Approximately five years later, he sold one of the automobiles to Esther for $5,000, but continued to drive the car. In 1994, shortly before Socorro filed for divorce, Jose purchased Esther a new Dodge minivan for which he paid approximately $17,000 in cash.

The court granted the divorce, and awarded to Socorro the house in which she resided, the $26,400 in the court's registry, the 1985 Mercedes Benz, and the 1994 Dodge minivan. The court also awarded Socorro a joint and several liability judgment in the amount of $460,000, representing money that Jose had allegedly given to Esther during 1994 in fraud of the community estate.

Both Esther and Jose properly perfected an appeal. . . .

In issue number one, Esther complains the trial court erred in awarding a $460,000 judgment against her in favor of Socorro. The judgment represents three deposits of $140,000, $215,000 and $105,000 that Jose allegedly made for Esther's benefit into accounts at NationsBank and Groos Bank. . . .

Esther contends there was no evidence the deposits made to her constituted a fraud on the community. We disagree. Socorro's cause of action for fraudulent transfer is based on the fiduciary relationship that exists between a husband and a wife as to the community property controlled by each spouse. The breach of a legal or equitable duty which violates the fiduciary relationship existing between spouses is termed "fraud on the community," a judicially created concept based on the theory of constructive fraud.

That Jose provided Esther the funds for the $140,000 and $215,000 deposits was not controverted. This money rightfully belonged to Jose and Socorro's community estate. [There was no evidence that Jose provided the funds for the $105,000 deposit, and therefore the trial court erred in finding the $105,000 represented community funds.] . . .

The case of Roberson v. Roberson, 420 S.W.2d 495 (Tex. Civ. App. — Houston [14th Dist.] 1967, no writ), is directly on point. In *Roberson*, the parties were married in 1947. In early 1960, Dr. Roberson, the husband, filed for divorce, which was denied in June 1961. After the Texas court denied his divorce, Dr. Roberson went to Juarez, Mexico and obtained a Mexican divorce without Elsie Roberson's knowledge. He then married Marinelle Pullen in September 1961, and represented her to be his lawful wife. They lived together at least until July, 1964.

When Elsie learned of this purported marriage, she filed suit against Dr. Roberson for declaratory judgment to establish that the marriage to Marinelle was invalid and void. The trial court entered judgment on December 23, 1963, declaring that the Mexican divorce was void; that Marinelle's marriage was void and of no effect, and that Elsie was the lawful wife of Dr. Roberson.

Elsie then filed for divorce, which was granted. She was awarded, *inter alia*, $10,000 as a reimbursement for gifts made in fraud of her community interest. . . .

In the present case, the facts are much more egregious. Jose and Esther carried on their relationship for more than twenty-three years, during which time Jose fathered three children by Esther. Jose gave Esther more than $164,000 as a down payment on the Hidden View house, and made the monthly mortgage payment on the house for over seven years. The evidence showed that in 1994 alone Jose gave to Esther at least $355,000, which was deposited into accounts in her name. As noted by the *Roberson* court:

> It is so repugnant to our sense of justice that this court will never sanction the proposition that a husband may desert his lawful wife, and while living in adultery with another woman, donate to the latter as a gift his wife's interest in the property owned by them in common. . . .

Roberson, 420 S.W.2d at 502.

Esther claims there is no evidence that she committed a fraud on the community. Again, we disagree. A third person who knowingly participates in the breach of a fiduciary duty may also be liable for that fraud. Esther testified she knew as early as 1984 that Jose was married, yet she continued to accept money and gifts from him after that date. Moreover, a conveyance or disposition of the community property may be a legal fraud even though there is an absence of intent.

Relying on Carnes v. Meador, 533 S.W.2d 365 (Tex. Civ. App. — Dallas 1975, writ ref'd n.r.e.), Esther also contends the court erred in entering a joint and several judgment against her because Socorro must first look to Jose to satisfy any judgment. In *Carnes*, the Dallas Court of Appeals held that if a spouse disposes of community property in fraud of the other spouse's rights, the aggrieved spouse has a right of recourse first against the property or estate of the disposing spouse; and, if that proves to be of no avail, then the aggrieved spouse may pursue the proceeds to the extent of her community interest into the hands of the party to whom the funds have been conveyed.

Esther did not request findings of fact or conclusions of law. When findings of fact and conclusions of law are not properly requested and none are filed, it is implied that the trial court made all the necessary findings to support its judgment. Esther presented no evidence to challenge the court's implied finding Jose would not be able to satisfy any judgment Socorro obtained against him. . . .

Relying on Jackson v. Smith, 703 S.W.2d 791, 796 (Tex. App. — Dallas 1985, no writ), Esther contends she should only be liable for one-half of the transferred funds, *e.g.*, Socorro's one-half of the community. Esther confuses the division of a community estate in a probate action with the trial court's wide discretion to divide the marital estate upon divorce.

In *Jackson*, Sylvester Jackson purchased a $70,000 life insurance policy with community funds and named his sister, Betty Jackson, as the sole beneficiary. Eliza Smith, Jackson's common-law wife, claimed she was entitled to the proceeds, or at a minimum, one-half of the proceeds because Jackson had perpetrated a fraud on the community by designating his sister as beneficiary. The trial court agreed and awarded one-half of the policy proceeds to Eliza and one-half to Jackson's estate, less attorney's fees for the interpleaded insurance company.

The Dallas Court of Appeals reversed the one-half award to Jackson's estate and rendered judgment that Betty take these proceeds. The court held that where a surviving spouse establishes fraud on the community, that spouse may recover the one-half of the proceeds which represents that spouse's one-half interest in the community. The other one-half of the proceeds, representing the decedent spouse's community interest, is a gift to the designated beneficiary, and is unaffected by constructive fraud.

By contrast, in a divorce action, the entire community estate is "up for grabs," with the trial court empowered to make any division of the community property that is just and right, having due regard for the rights of each party. We find no merit to Esther's contention. . . .

In issue number two, Esther claims the trial court erred in awarding to Socorro the $26,400 held in the court's registry, the 1985 Mercedes Benz automobile, and the 1994 Dodge minivan. . . .

The Mercedes Benz was purchased by Jose in 1985 for $12,500. Jose testified Esther purchased the vehicle from him in 1990 for $5,000. As the trier of fact, the trial court was not required to believe this testimony. . . .

Esther claims the Hidden View house and the 1994 Dodge minivan were gifts to her and the minor children from Jose. Jose testified that he purchased the house and the minivan for Esther and his children. A spouse may make moderate gifts for just causes to persons outside the community. But a gift of community funds that is capricious, excessive, or arbitrary may be set aside as a constructive fraud on the other spouse.

The courts have long taken a dim view toward gifts by the husband to "strangers" of the marriage, "particularly of the female variety." Fanning v. Fanning, 828 S.W.2d 135, 148 (Tex. App.—Waco 1992), *aff'd in part, rev'd in part on other grounds*, 847 S.W.2d 225 (Tex. 1993). The same holds true for putative second wives when the first marriage remains undissolved. Money spent on another woman out of community property during the marriage requires an accounting to the community. This type of gift or expenditure amounts to fraud upon the community estate.

Jose spent community property funds of $164,456.23 as the down payment on the Hidden View house, as well as $149,200 in mortgage payments, and $17,000 on the minivan. Because the money used to purchase these gifts was community property, the community estate was defrauded. Moreover, it was Jose's burden as the disposing spouse, or Esther's burden as the donee, to prove the gifts were not capricious, excessive, or arbitrary. . . .

[Esther claims that Socorro cannot recover the house and minivan because they were given to the donor's wife, children, or natural objects of his bounty.] We thus consider whether the evidence established Esther was Jose's wife, or that Jose transferred the property to his children or a natural object of his bounty.

Despite Esther's statement that she has never been married, Jose testified he married Esther in 1983. Jose's testimony is supported by the record, which contains a Mexican "Act of Marriage" document certifying the August 19, 1983 marriage between Jose and Esther. We thus conclude that Esther and Jose were married in 1983.

. . . Jose and Esther's marriage is legally void under Texas law because Jose's marriage to Socorro had not been dissolved, [but that] does not preclude Esther's right to recovery if she can prove a putative marriage to Jose. *See* Davis v. Davis, 521 S.W.2d 603, 606 (Tex. 1975) (the effect of a putative marriage is to give the putative spouse who acted in good faith the same right in property acquired during the marital relationship as if he or she were a lawful spouse). A putative marriage is one that was entered into in good faith by at least one of the parties, but which is invalid by reason of an existing impediment on the part of one or both parties.

Jose testified that at the time of his marriage to Esther in 1983, Esther did not know he was married to Socorro. The testimony at this point is less than elucidating, but it appears that after the birth of their first child in 1984, Esther discovered Jose was married to Socorro. Thus, any putative marriage that may have existed terminated when Esther learned of Jose's undissolved marriage. All of the property in issue was purchased after the time when any putative marriage between Jose and Esther had already terminated.

Esther [claims] the house and the minivan were gifts to the minor children. While Jose did testify that the house and the minivan were gifts to Esther and the minor children, the children were not transferees of the property, nor was either piece of property titled in such a way as to implicate title in the minor children. Finally, we have found no authority, nor has appellant provided us with any authority holding a mistress or a lover is the natural object of a person's bounty. . . .

The trial court's judgment is *reformed* to reflect a joint and several liability judgment against Esther and Jose in the amount of $355,000. In all other respects the judgment is *affirmed.*

Notes and Questions

1. Jose testified that he made gifts not only to Esther, but also to their three children, but the court found insufficient evidence of gifts to the children. Suppose there was adequate proof of gifts to the children. Should Socorro still prevail, or can the children keep their gifts?

2. *Osuna* focuses on donative transfers of community property made by one spouse acting without the other spouse's consent. A spouse's unilateral sale of community property raises similar, but not identical, issues. With inter vivos gifts, there is a strong tendency to protect the innocent spouse by making the gift voidable. Generally, the donee cannot show a strong reliance interest; if the gift is overturned, the donee is usually no worse off than before the attempted gift was made. In contrast, when one spouse conveys community property in exchange for consideration, invalidation will often impose a substantial hardship on the purchaser. If the purchaser does not know that the transfer conflicts with the other spouse's community property rights, a bona fide purchaser problem arises. (Recall that in Chapter 2 we studied BFP principles in the context of personal property.) All community property states protect purchasers who buy community property from one spouse acting alone under some circumstances, but there is considerable variety as to what circumstances are necessary to gain the mantle of BFP.

Consider, for example, a California statute that addresses the purchase of land: "The sole lease, contract, mortgage, or deed of either spouse, holding the record title to community real property to a lessee, purchaser, or encumbrancer, in good faith without knowledge of the marriage relation, shall be presumed to be valid. . . ." Cal. Fam. Code §1102(c)(2). Suppose you're representing a person who is negotiating to buy Blackacre, a tract of land located in California. The seller is someone named Kristin Wilson. You learn that record title is in her name, but you know nothing about her, including her marital status. Based upon your careful reading of the statute reproduced above, what steps do you think you should take to minimize the risk that your client will encounter a community-property problem?

3. Suppose Jose and Socorro were domiciled in a state that followed common law marital property rights at all relevant times. What outcome and why?

C. PROPERTY RIGHTS OF UNMARRIED COUPLES

Traditional legal rules sharply distinguished between married and unmarried couples in the three areas of property management, survivorship rights in property, and distribution of property upon termination of the relationship. Today, while the marriage continues, spouses have shared rights of management and control over the property that they own together. A person who outlives his or her spouse has established property rights. At common law, tenancy by the entirety, dower, and curtesy protect surviving spouses. Today, when one spouse dies intestate, in common law states the survivor takes a statutory share of the decedent's estate (if there are surviving children, usually one-half or one-third; with no children, the entire estate). When the deceased spouse has a will, the survivor is a "forced heir" who can overturn the will if it fails to provide a statutorily specified minimum share of the estate. In community property states, a survivor's protection consists of retained ownership of his or her interest in community property. When marriage ends in divorce, the parties have substantial property rights in the wealth one or both accumulated during the marriage. This is true whether they live in a community property state or in a common law state that equitably distributes "marital property." In all three areas, strong presumptions in favor of marital property and community property support ownership claims made by spouses.

In contrast, unmarried couples have not had equivalent property rights in any of these areas of common management rights, survivor's rights, and rights upon voluntary termination of the relationship. Unmarried couples traditionally are treated the same as unrelated individuals regardless of the nature and character of their cohabitation. Indeed, some courts have struck down even voluntary contracts relating to property between unmarried cohabitants on the basis of public policy, focusing on the allegedly "illicit" nature of the relationship. The current diversity of family structures and living arrangements, accompanied by changing social attitudes, is transforming the traditional property law regime. Should property rights hinge so completely on whether opposite-sex couples chose to marry? Are further considerations raised by same-sex relationships, where the partners are not legally permitted to marry? The following two cases explore such questions.

■ **MARVIN v. MARVIN**
Supreme Court of California, 1976
557 P.2d 106

TOBRINER, Justice. During the past 15 years, there has been a substantial increase in the number of couples living together without marrying. Such nonmarital relationships lead to legal controversy when one partner dies or the couple separates. Courts of Appeal, faced with the task of determining property rights in such cases, have arrived at conflicting positions: two cases (In re Marriage of Cary, 109 Cal. Rptr. 862 (Cal. App. 1973); Estate of Atherley, 119 Cal. Rptr. 41 (Cal. App. 1975)) have held that the Family Law Act (Civ. Code §§4000 et seq.) requires division of the property according to community property principles, and one decision (Beckman v. Mayhew, 122 Cal. Rptr. 604 (Cal. App. 1975)) has rejected that holding. We take this opportunity to resolve that controversy and to declare the principles which should govern distribution of property acquired in a nonmarital relationship.

We conclude: (1) The provisions of the Family Law Act do not govern the distribution of property acquired during a nonmarital relationship; such a relationship remains subject solely to judicial decision. (2) The courts should enforce express contracts between nonmarital partners except to the extent that the contract is explicitly founded on the consideration of meretricious sexual services. (3) In the absence of an express contract, the courts should inquire into the conduct of the parties to determine whether that conduct demonstrates an implied contract, agreement of partnership or joint venture, or some other tacit understanding between the parties. The courts may also employ the doctrine of quantum meruit, or equitable remedies such as constructive or resulting trusts, when warranted by the facts of the case.

[Plaintiff Michelle Marvin and defendant Lee Marvin] lived together for seven years without marrying; all property acquired during this period was taken in defendant's name. When plaintiff sued to enforce a contract under which she was entitled to half the property and to support payments, the trial court granted judgment on the pleadings for defendant, thus leaving him with all property accumulated by the couple during their relationship. Since the trial court denied plaintiff a trial on the merits of her claim, its decision conflicts with the principles stated above, and must be reversed.

1. The Factual Setting of This Appeal

. . . Plaintiff avers that in October of 1964 she and defendant "entered into an oral agreement" that while "the parties lived together they would combine their efforts and earnings and would share equally any and all property accumulated as a result of their efforts whether individual or combined." Furthermore, they agreed to "hold themselves out to the general public as husband and wife" and that "plaintiff would further render her services as a companion, homemaker, housekeeper and cook to . . . defendant."

Shortly thereafter plaintiff agreed to "give up her lucrative career as an entertainer (and) singer" in order to "devote her full time to defendant . . . as a companion, homemaker, housekeeper and cook"; in return defendant agreed to "provide for all of plaintiff's financial support and needs for the rest of her life."

Plaintiff alleges that she lived with defendant from October of 1964 through May of 1970 and fulfilled her obligations under the agreement. During this period the parties as a result of their efforts and earnings acquired in defendant's name substantial real and personal property, including motion picture rights worth over $1 million. In May of 1970, however, defendant compelled plaintiff to leave his household. He continued to support plaintiff until November of 1971, but thereafter refused to provide further support.

On the basis of these allegations plaintiff asserts two causes of action. The first, for declaratory relief, asks the court to determine her contract and property rights; the second seeks to impose a constructive trust upon one-half of the property acquired during the course of the relationship.

2. Plaintiff's Complaint States a Cause of Action for Breach of an Express Contract

In Trutalli v. Meraviglia, 12 P.2d 430 (Cal. 1932), we established the principle that nonmarital partners may lawfully contract concerning the ownership of property acquired during the relationship. We reaffirmed this principle in Vallera v. Vallera, 134 P.2d 761, 763 (Cal. 1943), stating that "If a man and woman [who are not married] live together as husband and wife under an agreement to pool their earnings and share equally in their joint accumulations, equity will protect the interests of each in such property."

In the case before us plaintiff, basing her cause of action in contract upon these precedents, maintains that the trial court erred in denying her a trial on the merits of her contention. Although that court did not specify the ground for its conclusion that plaintiff's contractual allegations stated no cause of action, defendant offers some four theories to sustain the ruling; we proceed to examine them.

Defendant first and principally relies on the contention that the alleged contract is so closely related to the supposed "immoral" character of the relationship between plaintiff and himself that the enforcement of the contract would violate public policy. He points to cases asserting that a contract between nonmarital partners is unenforceable if it is "involved in" an illicit relationship, or made in "contemplation" of such a relationship. . . .

Although the past decisions hover over the issue in the somewhat wispy form of the figures of a Chagall painting, we can abstract from those decisions a clear and simple rule. The fact that a man and woman live together without marriage, and engage in a sexual relationship, does not in itself invalidate agreements between them relating to their earnings, property, or expenses. Neither is such an agreement invalid merely because the parties may have contemplated the creation or continuation of a nonmarital relationship when they entered into it. Agreements between nonmarital partners fail only to the extent that they rest upon a consideration of meretricious sexual services. Thus the rule asserted by defendant, that a contract fails if it is "involved in" or made "in contemplation" of a nonmarital relationship, cannot be reconciled with the decisions.

The . . . cases cited by defendant which have declined to enforce contracts between nonmarital partners involved consideration that was expressly founded upon illicit sexual services. In Hill v. Estate of Westbrook, 213 P.2d 727 (Cal. App. 1952), the woman promised to keep house for the man, to live with him as man and wife, and to bear his children; the man promised to provide for her in his will, but died without doing so. Reversing a judgment for the woman based on the reasonable value of her services, the Court of Appeal stated that "the action is predicated upon a claim which seeks, among other things, the reasonable value of living with decedent in meretricious relationship and bearing him two children. . . . The law does not award compensation for living with a man as a concubine and bearing him children. . . . As the judgment is, at least in part, for the value of the claimed services for which recovery cannot be had, it must be reversed." *Id.* at 730. Upon retrial, the trial court found that it could not sever the contract and place an independent value upon the legitimate services performed by claimant. We therefore affirmed a judgment for the estate. Hill v. Estate of Westbrook. 247 P.2d 19 (Cal. 1952). . . .

[A] standard which inquires whether an agreement is "involved" in or "contemplates" a nonmarital relationship is vague and unworkable. Virtually all agreements between nonmarital partners can be said to be "involved" in some sense in the fact of their mutual sexual relationship, or to "contemplate" the existence of that relationship. Thus defendant's proposed standards, if taken literally, might invalidate all agreements between nonmarital partners, a result no one favors. . . .

Defendant secondly relies upon the ground suggested by the trial court: that the 1964 contract violated public policy because it impaired the community property rights of Betty Marvin, defendant's lawful wife. Defendant points out that his earnings while living apart from his wife before rendition of the interlocutory decree were community property . . . and that defendant's agreement with plaintiff purported to transfer to her a half interest in that community property. But whether or not defendant's contract with plaintiff exceeded his authority as manager of the community property (*see* former Civ. Code §§169, 169.2), defendant's argument fails for the reason that an improper transfer of community property is not void ab initio, but merely voidable at the instance of the aggrieved spouse.

In the present case Betty Marvin, the aggrieved spouse, had the opportunity to assert her community property rights in the divorce action. The interlocutory and final decrees in that action fix and limit her interest. Enforcement of the contract between plaintiff and defendant against property awarded to defendant by the divorce decree will not impair any right of Betty's, and thus is not on that account violative of public policy.

[The court rejected defendant's final two theories.]

In summary, we base our opinion on the principle that adults who voluntarily live together and engage in sexual relations are nonetheless as competent as any other persons to contract respecting their earnings and property rights. Of course, they cannot lawfully contract to pay for the performance of sexual services, for such a contract is, in essence, an agreement for prostitution and unlawful for that reason. But they may agree to pool their earnings and to hold all property acquired during the relationship in accord with the law governing community property; conversely they may agree that each partner's earnings and the property acquired from those earnings remains the separate property of the earning partner. So long as the agreement does not rest upon illicit meretricious consideration, the parties may order their economic affairs as they choose, and no policy precludes the courts from enforcing such agreements.

3. PLAINTIFF'S COMPLAINT CAN BE AMENDED TO STATE A CAUSE OF ACTION FOUNDED UPON THEORIES OF IMPLIED CONTRACT OR EQUITABLE RELIEF

As we have noted, both causes of action in plaintiff's complaint allege an express contract; neither assert any basis for relief independent from the contract. In In re Marriage of Cary, supra, however, the Court of Appeal held that, in view of the policy of the Family Law Act, property accumulated by nonmarital partners in an actual family relationship should be divided equally. Upon examining the *Cary* opinion, the parties to the present case realized that plaintiff's alleged relationship with defendant might arguably support a cause of action independent of any express contract between the parties. The parties have therefore briefed and discussed the issue of the property rights of a nonmarital partner in the absence of an express contract. . . .

Both plaintiff and defendant stand in broad agreement that the law should be fashioned to carry out the reasonable expectations of the parties. Plaintiff, however, presents the following contentions: that the decisions prior to *Cary* rest upon implicit and erroneous notions of punishing a party for his or her guilt in entering into a nonmarital relationship, that such decisions result in an inequitable distribution of property accumulated during the relationship, and that *Cary* correctly held that the enactment of the Family Law Act in 1970 overturned those prior decisions. Defendant in response maintains that the prior decisions merely applied common law principles of contract and property to persons who have deliberately elected to remain outside the bounds of the community property system. . . .

[W]e note that the cases denying relief do not rest their refusal upon any theory of "punishing" a "guilty" partner. Indeed, to the extent that denial of relief "punishes" one partner, it necessarily rewards the other by permitting him to retain a disproportionate amount of the property. Concepts of "guilt" thus cannot justify an unequal division of property between two equally "guilty" persons.

Other reasons advanced in the decisions fare no better. The principal argument seems to be that "(e)quitable considerations arising from the reasonable expectation of . . . benefits attending the status of marriage . . . are not present (in a nonmarital relationship)." Vallera v. Vallera, *supra*, 134 P.2d at 763. But, although parties to a nonmarital relationship obviously cannot have based any expectations upon the belief that they were married, other expectations and equitable considerations remain. The parties may well expect that property will be divided in accord with the parties' own tacit understanding and that in the absence of such understanding the courts will fairly apportion property accumulated through mutual effort. We need not treat nonmarital partners as putatively married persons in order to apply principles of implied contract, or extend equitable remedies; we need to treat them only as we do any other unmarried persons.

The remaining arguments advanced from time to time to deny remedies to the nonmarital partners are of less moment. There is no more reason to presume that services are contributed as a gift than to presume that funds are contributed as a gift; in any event the better approach is to presume, as Justice Peters suggested, "that the parties intend to deal fairly with each other." Keene v. Keene, 371 P.2d 329, 339 (Cal. 1962) (dissenting opn.).

The argument that granting remedies to the nonmarital partners would discourage marriage must fail; as *Cary* pointed out, "with equal or greater force the point might be made that the pre-1970 rule was calculated to cause the income producing partner to avoid marriage and thus retain the benefit of all of his or her accumulated earnings." 109 Cal. Rptr. at 866. Although we recognize the well-established public policy to foster and promote the institution of marriage, perpetuation of judicial rules which result in an inequitable distribution of property accumulated during a nonmarital relationship is neither a just nor an effective way of carrying out that policy.

In summary, we believe that the prevalence of nonmarital relationships in modern society and the social acceptance of them, marks this as a time when our courts should by no means apply the doctrine of the unlawfulness of the so-called meretricious relationship to the instant case. As we have explained, the nonenforceability of agreements expressly providing for meretricious conduct rested upon the fact that such conduct, as the word suggests, pertained to and encompassed prostitution. To equate the nonmarital relationship of today to such a subject matter is to do violence to an accepted and wholly different practice.

We are aware that many young couples live together without the solemnization of marriage, in order to make sure that they can successfully later undertake marriage. This trial period, preliminary to marriage, serves as some assurance that the marriage will not subsequently end in dissolution to the harm of both parties. We are aware, as we have stated, of the pervasiveness of nonmarital relationships in other situations.

The mores of the society have indeed changed so radically in regard to cohabitation that we cannot impose a standard based on alleged moral considerations that have apparently been so widely abandoned by so many. Lest we be misunderstood, however, we take this occasion to point out that the structure of society itself largely depends upon the institution of marriage, and nothing we have said in this opinion should be taken to derogate from that institution. The joining of the man and woman in marriage is at once the most socially productive and individually fulfilling relationship that one can enjoy in the course of a lifetime.

We conclude that the judicial barriers that may stand in the way of a policy based upon the fulfillment of the reasonable expectations of the parties to a non-marital relationship should be removed. As we have explained, the courts now hold that express agreements will be enforced unless they rest on an unlawful meretricious consideration. We add that in the absence of an express agreement, the courts may look to a variety of other remedies in order to protect the parties' lawful expectations.[24]

The courts may inquire into the conduct of the parties to determine whether that conduct demonstrates an implied contract or implied agreement of partnership or joint venture, or some other tacit understanding between the parties. The courts may, when appropriate, employ principles of constructive trust. Finally, a nonmarital partner may recover in quantum meruit for the reasonable value of household services rendered less the reasonable value of support received if he can show that he rendered services with the expectation of monetary reward.[25]

Since we have determined that plaintiff's complaint states a cause of action for breach of an express contract, and, as we have explained, can be amended to state a cause of action independent of allegations of express contract,[26] we must conclude that the trial court erred in granting defendant a judgment on the pleadings.

The judgment is reversed and the cause remanded for further proceedings consistent with the views expressed herein.

CLARK, Justice, concurring and dissenting: The majority opinion properly permits recovery on the basis of either express or implied in fact agreement between the parties. These being the issues presented, their resolution requires reversal of the judgment. Here, the opinion should stop.

This court should not attempt to determine all anticipated rights, duties and remedies within every meretricious relationship—particularly in vague terms. Rather, these complex issues should be determined as each arises in a concrete case. . . .

The general sweep of the majority opinion raises but fails to answer several questions. First, because the Legislature specifically excluded some parties to a meretricious relationship from the equal division rule of Civil Code §4452, is this court now free to create an equal division rule? Second, upon termination of the relationship, is it equitable to impose the economic obligations of lawful spouses on meretricious parties when the latter may have rejected matrimony to avoid such obligations? Third, does not application of equitable principles—necessitating examination of the conduct of the parties—violate the spirit of the Family Law Act of 1969, designed to eliminate the bitterness and acrimony resulting from the former fault system in divorce? Fourth, will not application of equitable principles reimpose upon trial courts the unmanageable burden of arbitrating domestic disputes? Fifth, will not a quantum meruit system of compensation for services—discounted by benefits received—place meretricious spouses in a better position

---

24. We do not seek to resurrect the doctrine of common law marriage, which was abolished in California by statute in 1895. Thus we do not hold that plaintiff and defendant were "married," nor do we extend to plaintiff the rights which the Family Law Act grants valid or putative spouses; we hold only that she has the same rights to enforce contracts and to assert her equitable interest in property acquired through her effort as does any other unmarried person.

25. Our opinion does not preclude the evolution of additional equitable remedies to protect the expectations of the parties to a nonmarital relationship in cases in which existing remedies prove inadequate; the suitability of such remedies may be determined in later cases in light of the factual setting in which they arise.

26. We do not pass upon the question whether, in the absence of an express or implied contractual obligation, a party to a nonmarital relationship is entitled to support payments from the other party after the relationship terminates.

than lawful spouses? Sixth, if a quantum meruit system is to be allowed, does fairness not require inclusion of all services and all benefits regardless of how difficult the evaluation? . . .

By judicial overreach, the majority perform a nunc pro tunc marriage, dissolve it, and distribute its property on terms never contemplated by the parties, case law or the Legislature.

Notes and Questions

Lee Marvin and Michelle Triola at the Oscars, 1965

1. Lee Marvin met Michelle Triola, a professional singer and dancer, during the 1964 filming of *Ship of Fools*, in which she was a stand-in. In 1970, she legally changed her surname to Marvin, shortly before he broke off their relationship in order to marry his high-school sweetheart, Pamela Feeley. Long after Lee's death in 1987, Pamela published a biography. Pamela Marvin, *Lee: A Romance* (1999). Michelle also moved on. She has enjoyed a long-term relationship and happy marriage with Emmy Award–winning actor Dick Van Dyke, who is probably best known for his role in the popular 1960s television series, *The Dick Van Dyke Show*, and for co-starring in the 1964 movie, *Mary Poppins*. They live in Malibu near the beach house that she once occupied with Lee Marvin.

2. After remand, there was a long and involved trial, heavily covered by the local and national press. The parties' stories about their relationship varied markedly. The trial court ruled that Michelle had not proved an express or implied contract to share property. It also found no resulting trust or constructive trust covering Lee's assets. Moreover, it refused to award Michelle money because of her homemaking services, reasoning that their mutual efforts did not lead to the growth in Lee's wealth. However, the court awarded Michelle $104,000 for rehabilitative purposes, pointing to footnote 25 of the supreme court's opinion. After this victory, Michelle was quoted as saying, "If a man wants to leave a toothbrush at my house, he can damn well marry me." *Simpson's Contemporary Quotations* 1568 (1988). Lee appealed the $104,000 award and prevailed, with a 2-1 decision. Marvin v. Marvin, 176 Cal. Rptr. 555 (Ct. App. 1981). The majority noted that Michelle's complaint had not asked for rehabilitative relief, and stated that the trial court's finding of no express or implied contract was dispositive. The supreme court declined to review the case further.

3. Since *Marvin*, similar cases have arisen in many other states. The largest group of states have accepted the *Marvin* analysis. The second largest group accepts the express contract rationale only. A small number of states reject *Marvin* completely. A few states have legislative rules. For example, Minnesota Statute §513.075 provides a special statute of frauds for unmarried couples:

> If sexual relations between the parties are contemplated, a contract between a man and
> a woman who are living together in this state out of wedlock, or who are about to

commence living together in this state out of wedlock, is enforceable as to terms concerning the property and financial relations of the parties only if:
    (1) the contract is written and signed by the parties, and
    (2) enforcement is sought after termination of the relationship.

4. *Marvin* involves a person's claim to property for which title is held by the other person in the long-term relationship. Other issues arising in the context of unmarried relationships with property overtones include: (1) a suit for damages for the loss of consortium of a partner, (2) a suit for damages for the wrongful death of a partner, (3) assertion of homestead rights against the creditor of a partner, and (4) when a couple lives together before or after a marriage, the classification of property acquired pre- and post-marriage.

■ GORMLEY v. ROBERTSON
Court of Appeals of Washington, 2004
83 P.3d 1042

KATO, Judge. This appeal involves the division of property after the intimate domestic relationship ended between two single women, Lynn Gormley and Julia Robertson, who had cohabitated for some 10 years. The trial court applied the meretricious relationship doctrine to this same-sex couple in dividing their assets and liabilities. We affirm.

Between July 1988 and August 1998, Ms. Gormley and Dr. Robertson lived together. Both were lieutenant commanders in the Navy when they met. Dr. Robertson is a physician; Ms. Gormley is a nurse and administrator. They began their relationship having nearly equal incomes, but Dr. Robertson earned significantly more by the time it ended.

They pooled their resources and acquired property as well as debt. They had a joint banking account that was used to pay all monthly obligations, whether preexisting or incurred separately or jointly. . . .

In 1993, Ms. Gormley and Dr. Robertson bought a Yakima home that was put only in the doctor's name for convenience and financing. Payments were made from the joint account into which they both deposited their incomes. They used joint funds to improve, decorate, and furnish the home. The net equity in the home at the time of separation was $35,255. They spent at least $38,704 on improvements.

When they separated in 1998, a dispute over property arose. Seeking equitable relief based on constructive trust, implied partnership, joint tenancy, joint venture, conversion, implied contract, and joint acquisition, Ms. Gormley sued Dr. Robertson. Ms. Gormley was later permitted to add partition as another theory of recovery. . . . [T]he trial judge, Heather K. Van Nuys, . . . agreed with Ms. Gormley's position that the meretricious relationship doctrine applied to same-sex relationships. . . . The trial court denied Dr. Robertson's motion for reconsideration. She appeals.

Dr. Robertson contends the court erred by concluding the meretricious relationship doctrine was applicable to this same-sex couple. . . .

In Connell v. Francisco, 898 P.2d 831, 834 (Wash. 1995), the court stated that "[a] meretricious relationship is a stable, marital-like relationship where both parties cohabit with knowledge that a lawful marriage between them does not exist." Non-exclusive factors establishing a meretricious relationship include "continuous cohabitation, duration of the relationship, purpose of the relationship, pooling of resources and services for joint projects, and the intent of the parties." *Id.*

The trial court made detailed findings of fact reflecting its consideration of these factors. Each weighs in favor of finding a meretricious relationship. Since these findings are unchallenged, the next inquiry is whether the court's conclusion that a meretricious relationship existed is supported by them.

Had Ms. Gormley and Dr. Robertson not been a same-sex couple, the trial court could only conclude that a meretricious relationship existed between them. But because they were not, the issue squarely presented . . . is whether the meretricious relationship doctrine applies to same-sex couples.

Division Two of this court has held that "a same-sex relationship cannot be a meretricious relationship because such persons do not have a 'quasi-marital' relationship." *Vasquez v. Hawthorne*, 994 P.2d 240, 243 (Wash. Ct. App. 2000). Because persons of the same sex cannot legally marry, they are "not entitled to the rights and protections of a quasi-marriage, such as community property-like treatment." *Id.* But it is of no consequence to the cohabiting couple, same-sex or otherwise, whether they can legally marry. Indeed, one of the key elements of a meretricious relationship is knowledge by the partners that a *lawful* marriage between them does not exist.

Moreover, Division Two's reliance on "*Connell* and its predecessors," as indicating that a meretricious relationship can exist only between a man and a woman, is misplaced. *Id.* at 242-43. Those cases all addressed relationships between men and women simply because same-sex couples were not involved. Relying on this historical perspective not only ignores the present, but also makes too much of the past.

In refusing to find a meretricious relationship, Division Two also stated: "We find no legal basis for judicially extending the rights and protections of marriage to same-sex relationships. Such an extension of the law is for the Legislature to decide, not the courts." *Vasquez*, 994 P.2d at 243.

Whether same-sex couples can legally marry is for the legislature to decide. But the rule that courts must "'examine the [meretricious] relationship and the property accumulations and make a just and equitable disposition of the property'" is a judicial, not a legislative, extension of the rights and protections of marriage to intimate, unmarried cohabitants. *See* In re Marriage of Lindsey, 678 P.2d 328, 331 (Wash. 1984). We hold that the meretricious relationship doctrine should be extended to same-sex couples.

Dr. Robertson also contests certain aspects of the trial court's disposition of property. She assigns error to two of the court's findings.

We review findings of fact to determine whether they are supported by substantial evidence and, if so, whether the findings support the conclusions of law. Substantial evidence is "evidence in sufficient quantum to persuade a fair-minded person of the truth of the declared premise." Fred Hutchinson Cancer Research Ctr. v. Holman, 732 P.2d 974, 985 (Wash. 1987). Credibility is determined solely by the trier of fact.

Dr. Robertson contends substantial evidence does not support the court's findings . . . that $40,000 was spent from joint accounts on property retained by her and that she would be unjustly enriched if she were allowed to retain all the property and to be liable for only half of the credit card debt.[2]

---

2. If the meretricious relationship doctrine did not apply, the trial court indicated it would, in the alternative, make the same property division under the equitable theories of constructive trust and implied contract. Because the doctrine applies here, we need not address Dr. Robertson's claims relating to these alternative theories of relief. Rather, the trial court makes a just and equitable distribution of property acquired during the meretricious relationship by applying a community-property-like presumption.

The testimony and exhibits in the record show that Ms. Gormley and Dr. Robertson commingled their funds, made joint purchases, and incurred debt. The court's finding that they spent about $40,000 from joint accounts on property retained by Dr. Robertson was based primarily on evidence from Ms. Gormley. While there may be evidence to the contrary, credibility determinations are for the trial court. Permitting Dr. Robertson to retain property obtained by both of them for their joint use would unjustly benefit her at the expense of Ms. Gormley. The challenged findings are supported by substantial evidence.

Dr. Robertson asserts the court erred by awarding Ms. Gormley 30 percent of the equity in the home as well as 30 percent of the equitable lien on the home for improvements made to the property with joint funds. She argues the court's award resulted in a double recovery. We review a trial court's decision on property distribution for a manifest abuse of discretion.

The court found that Dr. Robertson and Ms. Gormley made mortgage payments on the Tieton Drive home from their joint checking account where they both deposited funds. It also found that the down payment on the home came from refinancing Dr. Robertson's car, which was also paid for with joint funds. The court found that the parties used joint funds to improve, decorate, and furnish the home. These findings are unchallenged.

"'Equity will create a lien where there is no valid lien at law and [one] is needed to prevent an injustice.'" In re Marriage of Sievers, 897 P.2d 388, 400 (Wash. Ct. App. 1995) (quoting N. Commercial Co. v. E.J. Hermann Co., 593 P.2d 1332, 1336 n.2 (Wash. Ct. App. 1979)). Denying Dr. Robertson's motion for reconsideration, the court stated in its memorandum opinion that it "did not include [the improvements] in finding the specific net equity of the home." CP at 10. The court further noted that Dr. Robertson would be "unjustly enriched if she is allowed to keep all of the improvements in the home without some reimbursement to [Ms. Gormley]." CP at 10.

Based on the unchallenged findings and its statement that improvements were not included in determining the equity, the court had a tenable basis for its decision. Furthermore, it exercised sound discretion in preventing unjust enrichment. The court did not err. . . .

The trial court is affirmed.

BROWN, Chief Judge, concurring. I disagree with the meretricious relationship rationale as the basis for the majority's decision. This case is best viewed as a property dispute filed as a civil suit, which it was, and decided in equity, not a domestic relations case. The parties were involved in a conceded 10-year, same-sex cohabitation relationship. With compassion for the parties and with the respect and dignity deserved by and accorded to all persons coming to courts for judicial dispute resolution, our duty remains to competently apply existing law to the facts presented and not venture into policy making best left to the legislature. In my view, based upon existing law, we should affirm based solely upon the facts and resulting equities between the parties, not the legal status of their relationship. . . .

Notes and Questions

1. The decision in *Gormley* illustrates both the application of marital property rights to unmarried, cohabiting couples and the operation of one state's community property rules. With respect to the former issue, the court cites a 1995

Washington State Supreme Court decision holding that, in the case of "meretricious" or marriage-like relationships, the property rights of unmarried couples will be treated like those of married couples. Connell v. Francisco, 898 P.2d 831 (Wash. 1995). As the *Gormley* court noted above, factors tending to determine if an unmarried relationship is meretricious or not include "continuous cohabitation, duration of the relationship, purpose of the relationship, pooling of resources and services for joint projects, and the intent of the parties." *Connell* involved the break-up of an opposite-sex couple and in that respect dealt with the type of situation at issue in *Marvin*. The *Connell* court ruled that property acquired during a meretricious relationship would be treated like community property, much as if the couple was married. *Gormley* carried the reasoning of *Connell* a step further by applying it to a same-sex couple.

2. In *Gormley*, the court found that Lynn Gormley and Julia Robertson had lived in a meretricious relationship for 10 years. During that period, they had pooled their resources and purchased a house together. Given that both Gormley and Robertson had paid for the house and made it their home, would it be fair for Dr. Robertson to keep the entire house and all its improvements simply because the house was solely in her name? Would this be fair in a marital relationship? Should it be different for a same-sex couple? When they bought the house together, what do you think that Gormley and Robertson intended should happen to it in the event their relationship ended? In resolving property disputes on the break-up of extramarital same-sex relationships, should courts strive for fairness between the parties or to carry out the parties' intentions, or should larger public policy considerations control?

3. Note that the Washington court awarded Gormley only 30 percent of the house and its improvements. This amount presumably represented Gormley's equitable share in the house and its improvements based on her contributions. Remember, Robertson is a doctor and Gormley is a nurse, so it should not be surprising that Robertson invested more money into the property. The same is often true for opposite-sex couples, where one of the partners makes more money than the other. Washington, like most community property states, provides for the equitable (rather than equal) division of community property upon the dissolution of a marriage, with the amounts of contribution being one factor in determining each person's equitable share. In fixing her share of a community-like property asset, the court treated Gormley like it would have treated a married person in a divorce action. The result would have been virtually the same in a common law property state that provides for the equitable division of marital property. In this respect, community and common law property states that use equitable division treat divorcing persons much the same. As noted earlier, some states (like California) provide for the equal division of community property upon a divorce — and if this approach had applied in Washington State, presumably Gormley would have received 50 percent of the house and its improvements. A similar result would follow in a common law property state that favors the equal division of marital property. Which approach is fairer for the parties involved in the termination of a marriage or meretricious relationship: equal or equitable division of community or marital property? Which approach better reflects the intentions of the parties during the marriage? In divorce actions, do non-wage-earning spouses believe that they should receive an equal division of properties purchased with funds contributed by wage-earning partners? Should they?

4. In 2004, when *Gormley* was decided, Washington State limited marriage to opposite-sex couples under a controversial 1998 state statute that was upheld as constitutional by the state's supreme court. Andersen v. King County, 138 P.3d 963 (Wash. 2006). By what legal authority does the *Gormley* court grant community-like property rights to same-sex couples?

5. Should same-sex couples have the right to marry and obtain the same property-based rights and obligations as opposite-sex married couples? Increasingly, they do. In 2001, the Netherlands became the first nation to authorize same-sex marriages. Since then, Belgium, Canada, Spain, and South Africa have done so, and dozens of countries have granted marriage-like rights to same-sex couples. During the 1990s, decisions by the high courts in Hawaii and Vermont interpreting their constitutions pushed those states toward granting marriage licenses to same-sex couples; Massachusetts followed suit by judicial decree in Goodridge v. Department of Public Health, 298 N.E.2d 941 (Mass. 2003).

These three decisions sparked prompt legislative responses in those and other states. In 1997, the Hawaii legislature passed a statute providing for inheritance rights, wrongful death actions, and ownership as tenants by the entirety for same-sex couples who register as "reciprocal beneficiaries." A year later, Hawaii voters responded to its judicial decision by passing a state constitutional amendment banning same-sex marriages. Since 2000, voters in dozens of other states have passed similar constitutional amendments, effectively limiting further judicial recognition of same-sex marriage under state constitutional law. Some of these constitutional amendments not only ban same-sex marriages but also bar the extension of marital-like legal rights, of the type contained in the Hawaii statute or recognized in *Gormley*, to same-sex partners.

During the early twenty-first century, however, the tide of public opinion appears to have turned on this issue. In 2000, the Vermont legislature passed the Civil Union Act, 15 Vt. Stat. §§1201-1207, extending to same-sex couples the same set of state-created property rights as apply to Vermont married couples. Subsequently, a number of states followed Vermont's lead in granting marriage-like legal rights to same-sex couples through civil unions. In 2004, pursuant to the ruling in *Goodridge*, Massachusetts became the first American state to grant marriage licenses to same-sex couples. Since 2004, eight other states, including Washington State where Gormley and Robinson lived, have joined Massachusetts in legalizing same-sex marriage. The first of these, Connecticut and Iowa, did so by judicial decree under their state constitutions. The next three, Vermont, New Hampshire, and New York, did so by legislation. The final three, Maine, Maryland, and Washington State, acted by voter-passed initiatives during the 2012 general elections.

At the federal level, in 1996 Congress enacted the Defense of Marriage Act, 1 U.S.C. §7, 28 U.S.C. §1738C. For federal purposes, it defines "marriage" as "only a legal union between one man and one woman as husband and wife." Opponents of same-sex marriage have feared that if one or more states allow such unions, all other states would have to respect marriages entered into in any one of those states. Same-sex couples seeking to marry could then obtain marriage licenses in such a state (subject only to its residency requirements, which are often minimal) and force their own states to recognize the marriages. The federal act provides that states are not required to give effect to same-sex relationships that are treated as marriages under the laws of other states. This provision arguably violates the Full Faith and Credit Clause of the U.S. Constitution. A number of lower federal courts have held that §3 of the Act, which denies federal benefits to same-sex couples, violates the U.S. Constitution. As of this book's publication, the Supreme Court has agreed to hear the issue but has not yet ruled.

9

Landlord and Tenant

A. THE NATURE OF LEASEHOLD ESTATES

A leasehold is a possessory estate; it's like the freehold estates we studied in Chapter 6 (fee simple, fee tail, and life estate) in that the tenant has the right to possess a specific parcel of real property. For historical reasons, our system of estates in land classifies a lease as a *non-freehold estate*, in contrast to the other "higher" freehold estates. In feudal England, an owner of a freehold, who had seisin, had a higher status than a tenant who owned a leasehold. At first, under early English law a leasehold was not an estate in land and was not even considered to be property. The lessee lacked protection against third persons, having merely contract rights enforceable against the lessor if the lessor committed a wrong. When the lessee died, rights to the leasehold weren't inheritable. Instead they passed, along with the decedent's other personal property, to the lessee's administrator or executor for the benefit of the next of kin. Based on these rules, English law referred to the leasehold by the hybrid term *chattel real,* "chattel" reflecting its legal character as personal property (like actual chattels) and "real" reflecting its physical character as land.

English and American law came to recognize four types of leasehold estates, distinguished by the duration of the tenant's right to possession:

Estate for years (also called *tenancy for years, term for years,* or *term of years*). The tenant has possession for a fixed period of time, agreed upon by the parties. At common law there is no maximum period, although some U.S. states limit the duration to a set number of years for some or all leases.

Periodic estate (also called *periodic tenancy* or *tenancy from [month] to [month]*). The tenant has possession for a fixed period of time, which repeats unless either party terminates the lease by giving notice of termination to the other party.

Estate at will (also called *tenancy at will*). The tenant has possession for no definite length of time, and either party can terminate the lease at any time.

Estate at sufferance (also called *tenancy at sufferance*). This estate only results when a tenant under one of the other three types of lease holds over (remains in possession without the landlord's consent). The estate at sufferance lasts indefinitely — until the tenant is evicted or surrenders possession or until the parties enter into a different type of tenancy.

Most but not all leases are bargained-for exchanges: in other words, contracts. The landlord transfers possession of the premises in exchange for rent. A landlord, however, can convey a leasehold without bargaining for rent or other consideration. A landowner can make a gift of a leasehold to a tenant.

Landlord-tenant law is complex. Some of that complexity arises because the norms governing disputes between landlords and tenants are found in a variety of sources. First, a written lease may purport to define the rights and obligations of the parties. Sometimes this provides the ultimate source of the norm used to resolve the dispute; often, however, there is no lease, or the lease is incomplete, ambiguous, or contains a provision that is unenforceable under applicable law. Second, the common law provides rules that govern disputes in the absence of an enforceable agreement to the contrary. Third, most states have adopted statutes touching the landlord-tenant relation. Sometimes the statutes codify the common law, but sometimes they displace or modify it. The statutory schemes are rarely comprehensive; even in states with landlord-tenant statutes, many disputes continue to be governed by common law. Fourth, to make matters more complex, local governments often enact ordinances that govern some leases and some disputes. These ordinances sometimes conflict with the common law or the statutes. Which control? And finally, some states have regulated some aspects of the landlord-tenant relationship in unfair trade practice statutes or regulations adopted to implement those statutes.

So, for example, if one were confronted with a dispute between a residential landlord and a tenant in Madison, Wisconsin, you would need to consult (1) the terms of the written lease (if there was one), (2) Chapter 704 (Landlord and Tenant) of the Wisconsin Statutes, (3) Chapter 32 of the Madison City Ordinances, and (4) Chapter 134 of the Administrative Rules of the Wisconsin Department of Agriculture, Trade and Consumer Protection adopted pursuant to Wisconsin Statute 100.20. Plus any judicial opinions construing those rules, as well as any judicial opinions constituting the common law — since the issue facing you might not be addressed by any of the provisions described in (1) through (4) above.

■ COOK v. UNIVERSITY PLAZA
Appellate Court of Illinois, 1981
427 N.E.2d 405

SEIDENFELD, Presiding Justice. In this appeal we consider the applicability of the statute providing payment of interest on security deposits to a tenant, Ill. Rev. Stat. 1979, ch. 74, pars. 91-93, to particular contracts. The parties to the agreements are the plaintiffs, the residents of University Plaza as a class, who entered into residence hall contracts with University Plaza and its general partners, defendants, a privately owned university dormitory which serves students of Northern Illinois University in DeKalb. Plaintiffs appeal from the dismissal of their class-action suit. The defendants' motion was sustained on the basis that the statute is inapplicable because no tenant-landlord relationship has been created by the contracts and thus that no cause of action was stated.

The individual contracts with the students are entitled "Residence Hall Contract Agreement." The introductory paragraph states that the agreement governs the use of the University Plaza facilities and services by the resident. In clause I the dormitory agrees to furnish accommodations and services, including basic furniture, carpeting and draperies, local telephone service, cleaning service, social and recreational facilities, and parking facilities. Clause III requires a $50 security deposit and spells out the rights that the resident has in that deposit. University

Plaza reserves the right to cancel the contract for default, although the resident has no right to cancel once it has accepted the agreement. If the resident has not vacated the premises at the end of seven days following a written notice of intent to cancel the contract, University Plaza may take possession of the premises and remove the resident. University Plaza provides meal service for the residents. It also reserves the right to make assignments of space, to authorize or deny room and roommate changes and to require the resident to move from one room to another. There is also a provision that the dormitory is closed and meals are not served during Thanksgiving and spring recess as well as during semester breaks; and that no one is allowed to remain in the residence hall during these stated periods or beyond the established academic year closing date.

Clause IV states:

Notwithstanding anything to the contrary which may herein be contained, expressly, impliedly or otherwise, it is specifically understood and agreed by and between the parties hereto, that it is not the intention of the parties hereto to create a landlord-tenant relationship, and that the intention hereof is strictly contractual in nature; for bed and board, ancillary service, the use of certain recreational facilities, and participation in student social programs promoted at University Plaza, all of which are for the most part in concert with others. The resident may not assign any rights hereunder and may not sublet the room assigned.

Whether a contract is a lease or a license is not to be determined from the language that the parties choose to call it but from the legal effect of its provisions. Illinois Central R.R. v. Michigan Central R.R., 152 N.E.2d 627, 632 (Ill. App. 1958). *See also* Holladay v. Chicago Arc Light & Power Co., 55 Ill. App. 463, 466 (1894).

In *Holladay*, a contract, referred [to] throughout as a lease of the right to run electric wires under the sidewalks of certain buildings, was held not to be a lease but a mere license. In reaching that conclusion, the court reasoned that an instrument which merely gives to another the right to "use premises for a specific purpose, the owner of the premises retaining the possession and control of the premises, confers no interest in the land and is not a lease, but a mere license." 55 Ill. App. at 466-67. In *Illinois Central R.R.*, the court held that an agreement between two railroads to share their track and railroad station rights was a license, not a lease, and concluded that where the railroad shared the use of the tracks and terminal areas there was no transfer of exclusive possession sufficient to create a lease. It noted that "a leasehold requires that the lessee's possession be more than merely coextensive with the lessor; it must be exclusive against the world and the lessor." 152 N.E.2d at 636-37. However, "there may be a reservation of a right to possession by the landlord for purposes not inconsistent with the privileges granted to the tenant." *Id.* at 634.

In In re Application of Rosewell, 387 N.E.2d 866 (Ill. App. 1979), the court considered whether agreements between the City of Chicago and certain individuals under which the individuals were permitted to operate city-owned parking garages or lots constituted leases or licenses. The court held that the essence of a lease was transfer of possession, *id.* at 869, while a license is "an agreement which merely entitles one party to use property subject to the management and control of the other party," *id.* at 870. Thus, it concluded that since the City retained the right to control how the parking lots were operated the agreement constituted a license, even though the City surrendered exclusive possession of the lots to the parking lot operators. In People v. Chicago Metro Car Rentals, Inc., 391 N.E.2d 42 (Ill. App.

1979), the issue was whether an agreement between the City of Chicago and a car rental agency, which permitted the agency to operate a rent-a-car business at O'Hare airport, constituted a lease or a license. In finding that the agreement constituted a lease the court noted that the document was written using traditional terms; that it contained all of the essential requirements of a lease, including a definite agreement as to the extent and bounds of the leased property; and that the agreement granted Metro exclusive possession of a designated service area and designated counter space amounting to a particular number of square feet, legally described and diagramed in the agreement. *Id.* at 45.

While the agreement before us contains certain aspects normally associated with leases, a definite and agreed term and a definite and agreed price of rental and manner of payment (*see Metro* at 45), we conclude that it lacks the essential requirement of being a definite agreement as to the extent and bounds of the property to be used. The fact that the students may be moved during the term from room to room at the will of the contracting party is the principal feature of the agreement which we find persuasive in our determination that the parties did not intend to enter into a landlord and tenant relationship since the agreement failed to pass a possessory interest in specific property.

The question remains as to whether the legislature intended the statute on security deposits to apply to dormitories which provide bed and board to students. Section 3 of the statute excludes only public housing units from the application of the act. Ill. Rev. Stat. 1979, ch. 74, par. 93. However, parties are only covered by the statute if the agreement between the residents and the dormitory can be considered a lease. We find nothing in either the legislative history of the act or in its terms which would support the view that the legislature intended to include security deposits paid by students in dormitories in which they reside without reference to whether their agreement is a license or a lease.

We would note that there appears to be no public policy which would prevent the legislature from enacting a statute which would require that interest be paid on deposits made by persons in the class of the plaintiffs or others similarly situated. However, we conclude that the legislature has not done so and that the remedy in these circumstances is within the legislative domain.

The judgment is therefore affirmed.

Notes and Questions

1. What result should follow if the dormitory owner and its residents use "lease" vocabulary consistently and have no express agreement on whether interest would be paid on the residents' deposits?

2. How relevant is the dormitory's contract right to move a student to another room? Does the following illustration from the Restatement support either party?

> *L* leases a described portion of a building to *T* for five years. The lease contains a provision that gives *L* the right to relocate *T* in the building at any time during the five-year period by giving him thirty days' notice, the relocation space to contain approximately the same number of square feet. This arrangement is one with respect to a space that is intended to have a fixed location for the duration of the lease. The fact that the fixed location may be varied within a predetermined area from time to time during the lease does not prevent the arrangement from creating a landlord-tenant relationship.

Restatement (Second) of Property, Landlord and Tenant §1.1, Illus. 1 (1977).

3. Should a guest at a hotel be considered a licensee or tenant? What about a guest who rents — perhaps a suite — for a week or a month at an apartment hotel? Consider the following Restatement illustration:

> *A* writes the *X* hotel requesting a reservation of a double room for himself and wife for arrival on July 1 and departure five days later. The *X* hotel confirms his reservation, but when *A* arrives at the hotel all rooms are occupied. Neither *A* nor the hotel contemplates that *A* would be entitled to remedies against another occupant of the room reserved for *A* for the recovery of possession of the room. Rather, *A* would look to the hotel management to provide *A* with a room. A shorthand way of expressing this conclusion is that the hotel guest is not given the right to "possession" of a particular hotel room. If the *X* hotel is an apartment hotel that makes space available on a basis that is comparable to the time arrangements made with regular apartment tenants, as well as on a transient basis, a conclusion may be justified that a landlord-tenant relationship is created as to all arrangements other than the ones made with transients.

Restatement (Second) of Property, Landlord and Tenant §1.2, illus. 1 (1977). Why does it matter to *A* and to *X* hotel whether they have entered into a lease or a license? Should the context of the dispute affect which label the court chooses to attach to their transaction?

■ PRESCOTT v. SMITS

Supreme Court of Vermont, 1985
505 A.2d 1211

HILL, Justice. This case asks us to determine the nature and duration of a tenancy created by entry under a lease agreement which is unenforceable under the Statute of Frauds. The superior court found that a year-to-year tenancy was created and adjudged the defendants liable for one year's rent less payments made. We affirm.

In early 1982, defendants-appellants, Dirk Smits and Kay Smits, approached plaintiffs-appellees, Richard Prescott and Nancy Prescott, and inquired about leasing the Prescotts' farm located in Panton, Vermont. The parties negotiated the lease agreement over a two-month period. Defendants, experienced dairy farmers, personally inspected and examined the property during the course of these negotiations. The parties eventually agreed that defendants would lease the farm for three years beginning on May 1, 1982. An annual rental of $14,400 was agreed upon, the rent to be paid in equal monthly installments.

Defendants moved themselves and their herd onto the farm in March of 1982, with plaintiffs' approval. During the summer months they made rental payments to plaintiffs totaling $2,600. The plaintiffs drew up a lease incorporating the durational and rental terms cited above. The defendants, however, objected to certain other provisions of the lease agreement and refused to sign the instrument.

Defendants experienced problems from the outset of their tenancy. In April and May, eight of their cows died; six other cows suffered from various forms of mastitis. When defendants complained that their water supply was inadequate, plaintiffs installed a new pump at their own expense.

Defendants vacated the farm in October of 1982, without giving plaintiffs prior notice. In November defendants harvested corn which they had planted on the farm and removed it from the property.

Plaintiffs began reasonable efforts to re-lease the property toward the end of 1982. In March of 1983, the farmhouse was re-leased for a monthly rental of $250. In May the farmland was re-leased for an annual rental of $4,500.

Plaintiffs brought this action for nonpayment of rent. Defendants counterclaimed for damages suffered because of plaintiffs' breach of their agreement to furnish defendants a farm in condition reasonably fit for the operation of a dairy farm.

By statute, to sustain an action at law an agreement to lease property for more than one year must be signed by the party to be charged therewith, or by his agent. 12 V.S.A. §181(5). All "[e]states or interests in lands, created or conveyed without an instrument in writing shall have the effect of estates at will only." 27 V.S.A. §302; *see* Barlow v. Wainwright, 22 Vt. 88, 91-92 (1849) (quoting former statute).

It is not disputed that an estate at will can be converted to a year-to-year tenancy. *See, e.g.,* Rich v. Bolton, 46 Vt. 84, 87 (1873); Silsby v. Allen, 43 Vt. 172, 177 (1870); *Barlow, supra,* 22 Vt. at 92. Defendants, citing *Barlow, supra,* and *Rich, supra,* however, maintain that such a conversion can only be effected where there is continued possession over a period of years and payment of annual rent. We disagree.

Entry and occupation under an invalid oral lease creates a tenancy which is either from year to year, from month to month, or strictly at will, depending on the circumstances of the case. *See* 3 G. Thompson, *Commentaries on the Modern Law of Real Property* §1021, at 42 (1980).

Perhaps the leading indicator of a year-to-year tenancy where the nature and duration of the tenancy is left undetermined by the lease agreement is an agreement to pay annual rent. *See Rich, supra,* 46 Vt. at 87. At trial defendants conceded they agreed to an annual rental term. Moreover, they went into possession and paid rent pursuant to that agreement. *See* 3 G. Thompson, *supra,* §1100, at 344 (where a tenant enters into possession and pays some aliquot part of an annual rental, general doctrine of tenancy from year-to-year is applicable).

The fact that the defendants lived on the farm for less than a year is not determinative. In *Silsby, supra,* 43 Vt. at 177, this Court expressly noted that "[i]t is not the length of time that the tenant holds and pays annual rent that works the conversion. It is wrought by the fact that the tenant enters and holds under a stipulation to pay annual rent, and pays accordingly." Nor is the form of the payments made controlling. Although the defendants here made payments which would be consistent with either a month-to-month or a year-to-year tenancy, the character of the lease agreement itself convinces us that the trial court's conclusion that a year-to-year tenancy was created should be affirmed.

In the normal residential rental transaction, parties typically agree to month-to-month tenancies. Farmers, on the other hand, operate on a yearly calendar; they use the property for six months to pasture their animals and grow their feed which then lasts them through the winter while the land is unproductive and virtually useless. Consequently, the year-to-year tenancy doctrine is more readily applicable in an agricultural lease setting; it is invoked for the protection of landlords as well as tenants. *See, e.g.,* Rhodes v. Sigler, 325 N.E.2d 381, 383 (Ill. App. 1975) (year-to-year tenancy arises where one is given possession under a parol agreement for indefinite term with annual reservations of rent — tenant farmers entitled to statutory notice of termination); *see also* Roseneau Foods, Inc. v. Coleman, 374 P.2d 87, 90 (Mont. 1962) (fact that the business conducted by the lessee fluctuated on a yearly basis held sufficient to overcome fact that rent was paid on a monthly basis and to create a year-to-year tenancy).

In sum, we hold that the agreement to pay annual rent, the payments made pursuant to that agreement and the character of the lease agreement converted the estate to a year-to-year tenancy, entitling both parties to six-month notice prior to termination. *See Silsby, supra,* 43 Vt. at 177 (when estate becomes converted to a year-to-year tenancy, six months' notice is necessary to terminate tenancy). Absent such notice, the defendants remained liable for the annual rent. . . .

Defendants' final claim is that the trial court erred in finding for the plaintiffs on defendants' counterclaim for damages resulting from plaintiffs' alleged breach of the lease agreement.

. . . The trial court in this case found that, after moving onto plaintiffs' farm, defendants' herd suffered a decrease in milk production. Defendants contend that the decrease was attributable to an inadequate water supply. We note, however, that eight of defendants' cows died and six other cows contracted various forms of mastitis. The court found that the potential causes of these misfortunes were many and that there was no basis in the evidence to determine the actual cause of the deaths, diseases or decrease in production. . . . Since the cause of the damages suffered was not established, the defendants' counterclaim must fail.

Affirmed.

Notes and Questions

1. The *Prescott* court decided that the parties had created a periodic estate — specifically, an estate from year to year. Most periodic estates (also called periodic tenancies) are annual (year-to-year), monthly (month-to-month), or weekly, but the parties can agree to any period. Either party can terminate a periodic tenancy by giving the other party advance notice. At common law, the notice must be given at least one period in advance; except, as *Prescott* indicates, six months' notice suffices for an annual tenancy. In addition, termination must take place at the end of a regular period.

2. Why did the court decide the Smits had a tenancy from year to year rather than a tenancy at will or a tenancy from month to month? What would have been their liability for rent under the latter alternatives? Suppose the Smits had signed the lease instrument prepared by the Prescotts. Then what sort of estate would they have owned, and what would have been their rent liability?

B. DISCRIMINATION IN THE SELECTION OF TENANTS

■ FAIR HOUSING ACT (TITLE VIII OF CIVIL RIGHTS ACT OF 1968)
42 U.S.C. §§3601-3619

§3601. *Declaration of policy*

It is the policy of the United States to provide, within constitutional limitations, for fair housing throughout the United States.

§3602. *Definitions*

As used in this subchapter . . .

(e) "To rent" includes to lease, to sublease, to let and otherwise to grant for a consideration the right to occupy premises not owned by the occupant. . . .

(h) "Handicap" means, with respect to a person —

(1) a physical or mental impairment which substantially limits one or more of such person's major life activities,

(2) a record of having such an impairment, or

(3) being regarded as having such an impairment,

but such term does not include current, illegal use of or addiction to a controlled substance (as defined in section 802 of Title 21). . . .

(k) "Familial status" means one or more individuals (who have not attained the age of 18 years) being domiciled with —

(1) a parent or another person having legal custody of such individual or individuals; or

(2) the designee of such parent or other person having such custody, with the written permission of such parent or other person.

The protections afforded against discrimination on the basis of familial status shall apply to any person who is pregnant or is in the process of securing legal custody of any individual who has not attained the age of 18 years.

§3604. *Discrimination in the sale or rental of housing and other prohibited practices*
. . . it shall be unlawful —

(a) To refuse to sell or rent after the making of a bona fide offer, or to refuse to negotiate for the sale or rental of, or otherwise make unavailable or deny, a dwelling to any person because of race, color, religion, sex, familial status, or national origin.

(b) To discriminate against any person in the terms, conditions, or privileges of sale or rental of a dwelling, or in the provision of services or facilities in connection therewith, because of race, color, religion, sex, familial status, or national origin.

(c) To make, print, or publish, or cause to be made, printed, or published any notice, statement, or advertisement, with respect to the sale or rental of a dwelling that indicates any preference, limitation, or discrimination based on race, color, religion, sex, handicap, familial status, or national origin, or an intention to make any such preference, limitation, or discrimination.

(d) To represent to any person because of race, color, religion, sex, handicap, familial status, or national origin that any dwelling is not available for inspection, sale, or rental when such dwelling is in fact so available.

(e) For profit, to induce or attempt to induce any person to sell or rent any dwelling by representations regarding the entry or prospective entry into the neighborhood of a person or persons of a particular race, color, religion, sex, handicap, familial status, or national origin.

(f) (1) To discriminate in the sale or rental, or to otherwise make unavailable or deny, a dwelling to any buyer or renter because of a handicap of —

(A) that buyer or renter,

(B) a person residing in or intending to reside in that dwelling after it is so sold, rented, or made available; or

(C) any person associated with that buyer or renter.

(2) To discriminate against any person in the terms, conditions, or privileges of sale or rental of a dwelling, or in the provision of services or facilities in connection with such dwelling, because of a handicap of —

(A) that person; or

(B) a person residing in or intending to reside in that dwelling after it is so sold, rented, or made available; or

(C) any person associated with that person. . . .

■ SULLIVAN v. HERNANDEZ

United States District Court for the District of Maryland, 2002
215 F. Supp. 2d 635

MOTZ, District Judge. In this action Harold and Carla Sullivan allege that they were unlawfully discriminated against on the basis of race and disability in violation of the Fair Housing Act, 42 U.S.C. §3601 et seq. ("FHA"), and the Civil Rights Act of 1866, 42 U.S.C. §1981 et seq. when their application for rental housing was rejected. They have brought suit against Jan Hernandez, Noah & Cummings Property Management, Inc. ("Noah & Cummings"), Susan Ronan, and Long and Foster Real Estate, Inc. ("Long and Foster"). Hernandez and Noah & Cummings joined Ronald and Maureen Carroll as third-party defendants. Discovery has been completed, and the defendants and the Carrolls have filed a joint motion for summary judgment. Plaintiffs have filed a cross-motion for summary judgment as to their claims for disability discrimination. For the reasons that follow, I will deny both motions.

I.

On December 31, 1998, the Sullivans, who are both African-American, met with Hernandez, an agent for Noah & Cummings, in order to discuss rental properties. After the Sullivans and Hernandez spoke, Hernandez took the Sullivans to view several properties. One property viewed by the Sullivans was 503 Curry Ford Road, owned by the Carrolls. After viewing this property, the Sullivans completed a rental application for it on December 31, 1998. Subsequently, Hernandez delivered the application to Susan Ronan, an agent for Long and Foster who listed the Carrolls' property. Ronan asserts that she did not receive the Sullivans' application until January 4, 1999.

A few days before Ronan allegedly received the Sullivans' application, Ronan received a rental application for the Carrolls' property from Partha Bagchi. Long and Foster personnel then obtained background information on the Sullivans and Bagchi, including credit reports, information about the rental history of the applicants, and information about the applicants' employment. Specifically, the reports indicated that (1) Bagchi's salary was $90,000 compared to the Sullivans' collective salary of approximately $50,000, (2) the Sullivans had a reserve in mutual funds and bank accounts totaling approximately $27,000, (3) there were two negative credit reports in Mrs. Sullivan's history, (4) Mrs. Sullivan had one prior bankruptcy, and (5) on one prior occasion Bagchi violated a rental lease by vacating a premises more than six months prior to the lease's expiration without landlord approval. On January 8, 1999, Ronan read the reports to Mr. Carroll.[1] After listening to these reports, the Carrolls chose to rent the home to Bagchi.

---

1. Due to the timing in processing, Ronan was only able to read an interim credit report for the Sullivans while the report for Bagchi was a final report.

II.

Courts have adapted the framework [of McDonnell Douglas Corp. v. Green, 411 U.S. 792 (1973)] to housing discrimination claims. *See, e.g.,* Mencer v. Princeton Square Apartments, 228 F.3d 631, 634 (6th Cir. 2000). Thus, in order to survive summary judgment, the Sullivans must allege sufficient facts to establish a prima facie case of housing discrimination. To establish a prima facie case of housing discrimination, the plaintiff must prove that: (1) he or she is a member of a statutorily protected class; (2) he or she applied for and was qualified to rent or purchase certain property or housing; (3) he or she was rejected; and (4) the housing or rental property remained available thereafter. *See Mencer*, 228 F.3d at 634-35. The first three elements are undisputed. The Sullivans are African-American. Additionally, the Sullivans applied to rent the Carroll's property, were qualified to rent the property, and their application was rejected.

The defendants . . . dispute the final element of a prima facie case. They contend that the Sullivans cannot establish that the rental property remained available because another application was accepted immediately after their application was rejected. That argument fails because it would allow a discriminating party to avoid a discrimination suit simply by accepting another application. The final element of a prima facie case does not require a plaintiff to establish that the property remained available indefinitely or for a long period. It simply requires a plaintiff to show that the property remained available immediately after the application in question was received. Here, the property was available when the Sullivans' application was received by the Carrolls and their real estate agent, Ronan, even though Bagchi's application was subsequently accepted. Thus, the Sullivans have established a prima facie case of housing discrimination.

The burden shifts to the defendants to offer a legitimate, non-discriminatory explanation for selecting Bagchi's application. In an affidavit submitted in support of defendants' summary judgment motion, Mr. Carroll states that he selected Bagchi's application because he believed that: (1) Bagchi had a stronger credit history than the Sullivans; (2) Bagchi had a greater income than the Sullivans; (3) several creditors reported that Mrs. Sullivan had not paid her debts; and (4) Mrs. Sullivan had declared bankruptcy. Although the Sullivans debate the merits of which applicant was better qualified financially, on its face Carroll's explanation is both reasonable and non-discriminatory.

Thus, the burden shifts back to the Sullivans to establish that the Carrolls' explanation is pretextual. A plaintiff may establish pretext by demonstrating that "the employer's proffered explanation is unworthy of credence." Reeves v. Sanderson Plumbing Products, Inc., 530 U.S. 133, 143 (2000). "Inconsistent post-hoc explanations" by an employer for its adverse action "is probative of pretext. . . ." Dennis v. Columbia Colleton Medical Center, Inc., 290 F.3d 639, 647 (4th Cir. 2002).

In this case, the Carrolls initially offered an explanation for selecting Bagchi's application over the Sullivans which is inconsistent with the more recent affidavit Mr. Carroll has submitted. In their answers to interrogatories, they cited three factors that led to their decision: Bagchi's financial and "fully qualified" status, the fact that Ronan recommended Bagchi's application, and the fact that Bagchi's application was received first.[2] When confronted with potential disputes over two of these factors, the Carrolls retreated and dwindled their explanation down to one factor: Bagchi's financial status.

A reasonable jury could find that the shift in the Carrolls' position was not incidental and raises a question concerning defendants' motivation. First, there is an inconsistency regarding Ronan's role in the decision to choose Bagchi's application. In their interrogatory answers, the Carrolls stated that they chose to enter into a lease with Mr. Bagchi because "Mr. Bagchi's application was recommended to us by our trusted real estate agent, Ms. Ronan." In contrast, in his current explanation, Mr. Carroll downplays Ronan's role in the decision. In fact, Mr. Carroll's recent affidavit, makes no reference to advice from Ronan. The reason for this change may be that defendants now realize that Ronan, but not the Carrolls, had reviewed the rental application, which included copies of the Sullivans' drivers' licenses. By detaching Ronan from the decision to choose Bagchi, the defendants are able to argue (and, in fact, do argue) that the decision to choose Bagchi could not have been discriminatory because Mr. Carroll made the decision without knowledge of the Sullivans' race.

Second, there is an inconsistency regarding the timing of the applications. In their interrogatory answers, the Carrolls stated that they chose Bagchi's application because it "was the first that [they] received." Mr. Carroll's later affidavit, however, makes no reference to the order in which the applications were received. This is significant because the evidence is contradictory concerning when Ronan received the Sullivans' application. Ronan testified that she did not receive the application from Hernandez until January 4, 1999. Hernandez, on the other hand, testified that she dropped the application off at Ronan's office on December 31, 1998. Again, an inconsistency is presented that could lead a reasonable jury to infer that the legitimate, nondiscriminatory explanation offered by the defendants is pretextual. Accordingly, I will deny the defendants' motion for summary judgment.

III.

I will now briefly address the Sullivans' contention that they should be granted summary judgment claim for disability discrimination. The Carrolls rejected the Sullivans' application, in part, because of Carla Sullivan's credit history and prior bankruptcy. This negative credit history was allegedly due to Carla Sullivan's disability. The Sullivans argue that simply because Mr. Carroll knew that the Sullivans' income was from disability payments, the defendants must be held per se liable for housing discrimination. They cite no authority for this proposition, and I find it entirely unpersuasive.

---

2. The Carrolls' answer to an interrogatory from third-party plaintiffs stated as follows:

> Ms. Ronan stated that the [Sullivan] application was not financially strong and that the [Sullivans] had previous financial problems. . . . Susan Ronan then recommended that the Carrolls select the first fully qualified applicant/application that she received, Mr. Bagchi. We chose to enter into a lease with Mr. Bagchi solely because a) Mr. Bagchi's application and offer to rent was the first that we received; b) Mr. Bagchi was fully qualified; c) Mr. Bagchi's application was recommended to us by our trusted real estate agent, Ms. Ronan; and d) Mr. Bagchi had a strong financial status and history.

Ordered that (1) Defendants'/Third-Party Defendants' motion for summary judgment is denied; and (2) Plaintiffs' motion for summary judgment is denied.

Notes and Questions

1. What is the purpose of the prima facie test applied in *Sullivan?* The FHA plainly prohibits intentional discrimination, that is, when the landlord's subjective motive is to refuse to rent based upon the protected status of the applicant. A number of lower federal courts have also held that proof of *disparate impact* suffices to establish unlawful discrimination, more often in the context of government defendants than private-sector defendants. The Supreme Court has not yet ruled on the issue.

2. The FHA is not the only federal statute that addresses housing discrimination. The Sullivans also pleaded that the defendants violated the Civil Rights Act of 1866. 42 U.S.C. §1982 provides that "All citizens of the United States shall have the same right, in every State and Territory, as is enjoyed by white citizens thereof to inherit, purchase, lease, sell, hold, and convey real and personal property." Why did Congress find it necessary to supplement that statute with the FHA? From the time of its enactment, it was well understood that the Act prohibited governmental discrimination in property transactions. Two months after President Johnson signed the Civil Rights Act of 1968 (which includes the FHA as Title VIII), the Supreme Court decided Jones v. Alfred H. Mayer Co., 392 U.S. 409 (1968), holding for the first time that §1982 barred private discrimination in the sale or rental of real property.

■ **FAIR HOUSING COUNCIL v. ROOMMATE.COM, LLC**
United States Court of Appeals for the Ninth Circuit, 2012
666 F.3d 1216

KOZINSKI, Chief Judge. There's no place like home. In the privacy of your own home, you can take off your coat, kick off your shoes, let your guard down and be completely yourself. While we usually share our homes only with friends and family, sometimes we need to take in a stranger to help pay the rent. When that happens, can the government limit whom we choose? Specifically, do the anti-discrimination provisions of the Fair Housing Act ("FHA") extend to the selection of roommates?

FACTS

Roommate.com, LLC ("Roommate") operates an internet-based business that helps roommates find each other. Roommate's website receives over 40,000 visits a day and roughly a million new postings for roommates are created each year. When users sign up, they must create a profile by answering a series of questions about their sex, sexual orientation and whether children will be living with them. An open-ended "Additional Comments" section lets users include information not prompted by the questionnaire. Users are asked to list their preferences for roommate characteristics, including sex, sexual orientation and familial status. Based on the profiles and preferences, Roommate matches users and provides them a list of housing-seekers or available rooms meeting their criteria. Users can also search available listings based on roommate characteristics, including sex, sexual orientation and familial status.

The Fair Housing Councils of San Fernando Valley and San Diego ("FHCs") sued Roommate in federal court, alleging that the website's questions requiring disclosure of sex, sexual orientation and familial status, and its sorting, steering and matching of users based on those characteristics, violate the Fair Housing Act ("FHA"), 42 U.S.C. §3601 et seq., and the California Fair Employment and Housing Act ("FEHA"), Cal. Gov't Code §12955.

The district court initially dismissed the claims, holding that Roommate was immune under section 230 of the Communications Decency Act ("CDA"), 47 U.S.C. §230. We reversed, holding that Roommate was protected by the CDA for publishing the "Additional Comments" section, but not for (1) posting questionnaires that required disclosure of sex, sexual orientation and familial status; (2) limiting the scope of searches by users' preferences on a roommate's sex, sexual orientation and familial status; and (3) a matching system that paired users based on those preferences. Fair Hous. Council v. Roommates.com, LLC, 521 F.3d 1157, 1166 (9th Cir. 2008) (en banc).

Our opinion was limited to CDA immunity and didn't reach whether the activities, in fact, violated the FHA. On remand, the district court held that Roommate's prompting of discriminatory preferences from users, matching users based on that information and publishing these preferences violated the FHA and FEHA, and enjoined Roommate from those activities. Roommate appeals the grant of summary judgment and permanent injunction, and also the district court's order awarding the FHCs $494,714.40 in attorney's fees. . . .

ANALYSIS

If the FHA extends to shared living situations, it's quite clear that what Roommate does amounts to a violation. The pivotal question is whether the FHA applies to roommates.

I

The FHA prohibits discrimination on the basis of "race, color, religion, sex, familial status, or national origin" in the "sale or rental *of a dwelling*." 42 U.S.C. §3604(b) (emphasis added). The FHA also makes it illegal to

> make, print, or publish, or cause to be made, printed, or published any notice, statement, or advertisement, with respect to the sale or rental *of a dwelling* that indicates any preference, limitation, or discrimination based on race, color, religion, sex, handicap, familial status, or national origin, or an intention to make any such preference, limitation, or discrimination.

Id. §3604(c) (emphasis added). The reach of the statute turns on the meaning of "dwelling."

The FHA defines "dwelling" as "any building, structure, or portion thereof which is occupied as, or designed or intended for occupancy as, a residence by one or more families." *Id.* §3602(b). A dwelling is thus a living unit designed or intended for occupancy by a family, meaning that it ordinarily has the elements generally associated with a family residence: sleeping spaces, bathroom and kitchen facilities, and common areas, such as living rooms, dens and hallways.

It would be difficult, though not impossible, to divide a single-family house or apartment into separate "dwellings" for purposes of the statute. Is a "dwelling" a bedroom plus a right to access common areas? What if roommates share a bedroom? Could a "dwelling" be a bottom bunk and half an armoire? It makes practical sense to interpret "dwelling" as an independent living unit and stop the FHA at the front door.

There's no indication that Congress intended to interfere with personal relationships *inside* the home. Congress wanted to address the problem of landlords discriminating in the sale and rental of housing, which deprived protected classes of housing opportunities. But a business transaction between a tenant and landlord is quite different from an arrangement between two people sharing the same living space. We seriously doubt Congress meant the FHA to apply to the latter. Consider, for example, the FHA's prohibition against sex discrimination. Could Congress, in the 1960s, really have meant that women must accept men as roommates? Telling women they may not lawfully exclude men from the list of acceptable roommates would be controversial today; it would have been scandalous in the 1960s.

While it's possible to read dwelling to mean sub-parts of a home or an apartment, doing so leads to awkward results. And applying the FHA to the selection of roommates almost certainly leads to results that defy mores prevalent when the statute was passed. Nonetheless, this interpretation is not wholly implausible and we would normally consider adopting it, given that the FHA is a remedial statute that we construe broadly. Therefore, we turn to constitutional concerns, which provide strong countervailing considerations.

II

The Supreme Court has recognized that "the freedom to enter into and carry on certain intimate or private relationships is a fundamental element of liberty protected by the Bill of Rights." Bd. of Dirs. of Rotary Int'l v. Rotary Club of Duarte, 481 U.S. 537, 545 (1987). . . . Courts have extended the right of intimate association to marriage, child bearing, child rearing and cohabitation with relatives. While the right protects only "highly personal relationships," IDK, Inc. v. Clark Cnty., 836 F.2d 1185, 1193 (9th Cir. 1988), the right isn't restricted exclusively to family, Bd. of Dirs. of Rotary Int'l, 481 U.S. at 545. The right to association also implies a right *not* to associate. Roberts v. U.S. Jaycees, 468 U.S. 609, 623 (1984).

To determine whether a particular relationship is protected by the right to intimate association we look to "size, purpose, selectivity, and whether others are excluded from critical aspects of the relationship." *Bd. of Dirs. of Rotary Int'l*, 481 U.S. at 546. The roommate relationship easily qualifies: People generally have very few roommates; they are selective in choosing roommates; and non-roommates are excluded from the critical aspects of the relationship, such as using the living spaces. Aside from immediate family or a romantic partner, it's hard to imagine a relationship more intimate than that between roommates, who share living rooms, dining rooms, kitchens, bathrooms, even bedrooms.

Because of a roommate's unfettered access to the home, choosing a roommate implicates significant privacy and safety considerations. The home is the center of our private lives. Roommates note our comings and goings, observe whom we bring back at night, hear what songs we sing in the shower, see us in various stages of undress and learn intimate details most of us prefer to keep private. Roommates also have access to our physical belongings and to our person. As the Supreme Court recognized, "[w]e are at our most vulnerable when we are asleep because we cannot monitor our own safety or the security of our belongings." Minnesota v. Olson, 495 U.S. 91, 99 (1990). Taking on a roommate means giving him full access to the space where we are most vulnerable.

Equally important, we are fully exposed to a roommate's belongings, activities, habits, proclivities and way of life. This could include matter we find offensive (pornography, religious materials, political propaganda); dangerous (tobacco, drugs, firearms); annoying (jazz, perfume, frequent overnight visitors, furry pets); habits that are incompatible with our lifestyle (early risers, messy cooks, bathroom hogs, clothing borrowers). When you invite others to share your living quarters, you risk becoming a suspect in whatever illegal activities they engage in.

Government regulation of an individual's ability to pick a roommate thus intrudes into the home, which "is entitled to special protection as the center of the private lives of our people." Minnesota v. Carter, 525 U.S. 83, 99 (1998) (Kennedy, J., concurring). "Liberty protects the person from unwarranted government intrusions into a dwelling or other private places. In our tradition the State is not omnipresent in the home." Lawrence v. Texas, 539 U.S. 558, 562 (2003). Holding that the FHA applies inside a home or apartment would allow the government to restrict our ability to choose roommates compatible with our lifestyles. This would be a serious invasion of privacy, autonomy and security.

For example, women will often look for female roommates because of modesty or security concerns. As roommates often share bathrooms and common areas, a girl may not want to walk around in her towel in front of a boy. She might also worry about unwanted sexual advances or becoming romantically involved with someone she must count on to pay the rent.

An orthodox Jew may want a roommate with similar beliefs and dietary restrictions, so he won't have to worry about finding honey-baked ham in the refrigerator next to the potato latkes. Non-Jewish roommates may not understand or faithfully follow all of the culinary rules, like the use of different silverware for dairy and meat products, or the prohibition against warming non-kosher food in a kosher microwave. Taking away the ability to choose roommates with similar dietary restrictions and religious convictions will substantially burden the observant Jew's ability to live his life and practice his religion faithfully. The same is true of individuals of other faiths that call for dietary restrictions or rituals inside the home.

The U.S. Department of Housing and Urban Development recently dismissed a complaint against a young woman for advertising, "I am looking for a female christian roommate," on her church bulletin board. In its Determination of No Reasonable Cause, HUD explained that "in light of the facts provided and after assessing the unique context of the advertisement and the roommate relationship involved . . . the Department defers to Constitutional considerations in reaching its conclusions." Fair Hous. Ctr. of W. Mich. v. Tricia, No. 05-10-1738-8 (Oct. 28, 2010).

It's a "well-established principle that statutes will be interpreted to avoid constitutional difficulties." Frisby v. Schultz, 487 U.S. 474, 483 (1988). . . . Reading "dwelling" to mean an independent housing unit is a fair interpretation of the text and consistent with congressional intent. Because the construction of "dwelling" to include shared living units raises substantial constitutional concerns, we adopt the narrower construction that excludes roommate selection from the reach of the FHA.

III

Because we find that the FHA doesn't apply to the sharing of living units, it follows that it's not unlawful to discriminate in selecting a roommate. As the underlying conduct is not unlawful, Roommate's facilitation of discriminatory roommate searches does not violate the FHA. While Roommate itself has no intimate association right, it is entitled to raise the constitutional claims of its users. *See* Craig v. Boren, 429 U.S. 190, 195 (1976). The injunction entered by the district court precludes Roommate's members from selecting roommates unfettered by government regulation. Roommate may therefore raise these claims on their behalf.

IV

The same constitutional concerns over the right to intimate association would arise if the California Fair Employment and Housing Act ("FEHA") were applied to roommates. Accordingly, we interpret "housing accommodation" in section 12955(c) of the FEHA to exclude the sharing of living units. Similarly to how the FHA defines "dwelling," the FEHA defines "housing accommodation" as "any building, structure, or portion thereof that is occupied as, or intended for occupancy as, a residence by one or more families." Cal. Gov. Code §12927(d). This ambiguous definition allows us to apply the canon of constitutional avoidance to find that the FEHA does not reach the selection of roommates.

In a 1995 amendment, the FEHA carved out from the definition of discrimination "the use of words stating or tending to imply that the housing being advertised is available only to persons of one sex," "[w]here the sharing of living areas in a single dwelling unit is involved." Cal. Gov. Code §12927(c)(2)(B). The concurrence infers from this 1995 exemption that the statute as passed in 1974 must have covered roommates. But the acts of a subsequent legislature tell us nothing definitive about the meaning of laws adopted by an earlier legislature. *See* Pension Benefit Guar. Corp. v. LTV Corp., 496 U.S. 633, 650 (1990) ("[S]ubsequent legislative history is a hazardous basis for inferring the intent of an earlier Congress."); *see also* Sullivan v. Finkelstein, 496 U.S. 617, 632 (1990) (Scalia, J., concurring) ("Arguments based on subsequent legislative history . . . should not be taken seriously, not even in a footnote."). The 1995 legislature may have been uncertain about whether the statute, as passed decades earlier, covered roommates, and wanted to remove any doubt that roommates could select each other by sex. But the amendment can shed no light on the meaning of "housing accommodation" in the FEHA, a statutory phrase it does not modify or reference. . . .

Because precluding individuals from selecting roommates based on their sex, sexual orientation and familial status raises substantial constitutional concerns, we interpret the FHA and FEHA as not applying to the sharing of living units. Therefore, we hold that Roommate's prompting, sorting and publishing of information to facilitate roommate selection is not forbidden by the FHA or FEHA. Accordingly, we vacate the district court's judgment and remand for entry of judgment for defendant. Because the FHCs are no longer prevailing, we vacate the district court's order for attorney's fees. . . .

IKUTA, Circuit Judge, concurring and dissenting. I concur in the majority's holding that the Fair Housing Act (FHA) does not apply to the sharing of living units. I write separately, however, to express my concern that our circuit's test for organizational standing cannot be reconciled with Supreme Court precedent.

Further, I respectfully dissent from Part IV of the majority decision, which applies its FHA analysis to the California Fair Employment and Housing Act (FEHA) claim of the two Fair Housing Councils. . . .

In addition to my concern about our standing inquiry, I must respectfully dissent from the majority's decision to "apply the canon of constitutional avoidance to find that FEHA does not reach the selection of roommates." . . . But this inter-pretive tool can be used only when a statute is ambiguous. . . .

. . . FEHA expressly defines "discrimination" as not including "the use of words stating or tending to imply that the housing being advertised is available only to persons of one sex," in a situation "[w]here the sharing of living areas in a single dwelling unit is involved." Cal. Gov. Code §12927(c)(2)(B). This language is not in the FHA. . . . FEHA's definition of "discrimination" in §12927(c)(2)(B) expresses the state legislature's intent to exempt sex-specific advertisements for shared living units in a single dwelling from the restrictions of FEHA, but not exempt advertisements that discriminate on the basis of other protected character-istics, such as race or religion.[3]

This plain-language reading of §12927(c)(2)(B) is confirmed by the decision of the California Fair Employment and Housing Commission in Dep't of Fair Emp't and Housing v. Larrick, FEHC Dec. No. 98-12, 1998 WL 750901 (July 22, 1998). *Larrick* involved two roommates who decided not to rent to a potential third room-mate because she was black. The Commission held that the "plain language" of FEHA applied to this shared living situation and prohibited the two roommates "from rejecting an applicant on the basis of race and color." *Id.* at *5. In arriving at this conclusion, the Commission stated that none of FEHA's exceptions were applicable, specifically noting that §12927(c)(2)(B) "allow[s] sex-specific (but not race-specific) advertisements for single dwellings with shared living areas." *Id.* at *6 n.2. . . .

Notes and Questions

1. When if ever should a person be liable for discrimination in the selection of a roommate or housemate? What different considerations are raised when the defendant is not the person who offers housing, but a third party such as Room-mate.com that provides advertising or matching services? As the opinion indicates, in an earlier round of the litigation, the Ninth Circuit sitting en banc considered Roommate.com's claim of immunity under the Communications Decency Act of 1996, which provides: "No provider or user of an interactive computer service shall be treated as the publisher or speaker of any information provided by another information content provider." 47 U.S.C. §230(c). The immunity does not apply if a person "is responsible, in whole or in part, for the creation or development of information provided through the Internet or any other interactive computer service." *Id.* §230(f)(3). The court denied immunity for Roommate.com's input

---

3. The majority contends that we can ignore this amendment to FEHA because the "acts of a subsequent legislature tell us nothing definitive about the meaning of laws adopted by an earlier legis-lature." But in determining whether a statute is ambiguous, we must construe the current version of the law, not what it used to be. *See* Red Lion Broad. Co. v. FCC, 395 U.S. 367, 380-81 (1969) (holding that a court must give "great weight" to amendments to a statute that clarify its proper construction). Once a duly enacted amendment clarifies a statute, it is no longer ambiguous, and we cannot treat it as such by pointing to its former ambiguity.

and search functions keyed to sex, sexual orientation, and familial status, but granted immunity for user content inputted in an "Additional Comments" section. Judge Kozinski, also author of the earlier majority opinion, explained, "The message to website operators is clear: If you don't encourage illegal content, or design your website to require users to input illegal content, you will be immune." Fair Hous. Council v. Roommates.com, LLC, 521 F.3d 1157, 1175 (9th Cir. 2008).

2. The FHA has five express exemptions: (1) a "single-family house" sold or rented by a person who owns no more than three such single-family houses; (2) "rooms or units in dwellings containing living quarters occupied or intended to be occupied by no more than four families living independently of each other, if the owner actually maintains and occupies one of such living quarters as his residence"; (3) religious organizations that give preference to persons of the same religion; (4) a "private club" that incidental to its primary purpose provides lodging to its members; and (5) housing specifically designed for older persons with respect to the protection of familial status. 42 U.S.C. §§3603(b), 3607(a), (b). The first two exemptions are limited to the decision to sell or rent; §3604(c) prohibits advertising that discloses an intent to discriminate. The second exemption is known as the "Mrs. Murphy exemption," named for a fictitious landlady invoked during congressional debates preceding enactment of the FHA. Senator Walter Mondale, cosponsor of the FHA, stated: "The sole intent of [the Mrs. Murphy exemption] is to exempt those who, by the direct personal nature of their activities, have a close personal relationship with their tenants." 114 Cong. Rec. 2495 (1968). When would a person seeking a roommate or housemate on Roommates.com, Craigslist, or a similar service be entitled to the Mrs. Murphy exemption? Does *Roommate.com* create a sixth exemption?

3. Are there other constitutional limits on the government's authority to regulate the selection of tenants by private landlords? In a number of cases, landlords have raised the right to the free exercise of religion when confronted by state or local laws forbidding discrimination based on marital status. For example, in Attorney General v. Desilets, 636 N.E.2d 233 (Mass. 1994), the defendants, two brothers, refused to rent an apartment to an unmarried couple because their Catholic beliefs taught that they should not facilitate sinful conduct. A Massachusetts agency concluded that this constituted unlawful discrimination under a state statute that prohibited a refusal to rent housing based upon marital status. The court held that application of the statute substantially burdened the defendants' rights to the free exercise of their religion guaranteed by the Massachusetts constitution. "[T]he government has placed a burden on the defendants that makes their exercise of religion more difficult and more costly. The statute affirmatively obliges the defendants to enter into a contract contrary to their religious beliefs and provides significant sanctions for its violation. Moreover, both their nonconformity to the law and any related publicity may stigmatize the defendants in the eyes of many and thus burden the exercise of the defendants' religion." The court, however, reversed and remanded a summary judgment for the defendants, holding that the state could enforce the statute if it demonstrated "a compelling interest in the elimination of discrimination in housing against an unmarried man and an unmarried woman who have a sexual relationship and wish to rent accommodations."

4. The Federal Housing Act does not bar discrimination based on sexual orientation, even though one might infer from *Roommate.com* that it does. Repeated efforts to extend the FHA's protections to sexual orientation have failed, but many states and cities have prohibited sexual orientation discrimination. In one of the few

cases involving such a law, the court held that Yeshiva University may have violated New York City's ordinance by excluding lesbian medical students from the school's married student housing. Levin v. Yeshiva University, 754 N.E.2d 1099 (N.Y. 2001). There is no similar provision in federal law despite repeated efforts to extend the FHA's protections to sexual orientation.

C. DELIVERY OF POSSESSION

■ DIEFFENBACH v. McINTYRE
Supreme Court of Oklahoma, 1952
254 P.2d 346

BINGAMAN, Justice. This action was brought by plaintiff Mildred E. McIntyre against the defendant Nevin J. Dieffenbach, seeking to recover rental paid, damages for repairs made upon a building leased by her from the defendant, and anticipated profits lost by her because of her removal from the building. The trial court submitted the cause to the jury as to the rental paid and cost of repairs, but refused to permit the introduction of evidence as to loss of anticipated profits. Defendant appeals from the judgment against him rendered on a verdict by the jury in favor of plaintiff, and plaintiff cross-appeals from the refusal of the court to permit her to introduce evidence as to loss of anticipated profits.

Undisputed facts are that plaintiff, prior to the time she leased the building from defendant, was operating a beauty parlor in one of the downtown buildings in Tulsa; that she was required to vacate the rooms used by her in said building on or before May 1, 1946, and that during the month of April she sought to find another place in which to conduct her beauty parlor. She got in touch with defendant, who was attorney in fact for his mother-in-law, who owned a building farther removed from the business section of Tulsa, and sought to lease a portion thereof from him for a term of years. The transaction finally resulted in her leasing the entire building, which consisted of four units of several rooms each, two upstairs and two downstairs. She installed her beauty parlor in one of the downstairs units, but upon failure to obtain the possession of the entire building removed therefrom to other quarters on or about the 1st of August, 1946.

Plaintiff testified that at or prior to the time she signed the lease on the building, which lease ran for a term of three years at a rental of $500 per month, she was assured by defendant that he had raised the rent on the other three units in the building from $50 to $150 per month, and had given thirty day notices requiring them to remove, and that they could not possibly remain there and pay the rental which he had fixed as the new rate on the property. Thereafter, she testified, he informed her that he could not give her possession until the 1st of June, and she made arrangements to stay in her old quarters for another month. On the 1st of June, when she was ready to move in, two of the units in the building were still occupied, and she hesitated to move in, but upon assurance from defendant to her attorney that he would obtain possession of the two occupied units on or before June 7th, she moved into the unit which she proposed to use as a beauty parlor. When the lease was signed she paid defendant one month's rent of $500, and she expended additional sums in fixing up the unit occupied by her. She testified that defendant failed to oust the tenants from the two units occupied by them, although one of them subsequently left, and that the occupant of the other unit offered her the regular $50 per month rental, but she refused to accept the same, telling them that arrangements for payments should be made with defendant. This unit was still occupied when she left the building and the tenants testified that they thereafter paid defendant the regular rental of $50 per month and were still occupying the unit and paying such rental at the time of the trial.

Plaintiff's attorney testified that when he found out the defendant could not deliver possession on the 1st of June, he talked to him with a view of revising the lease to include only a portion of the building, but that defendant assured him that he would have all of the tenants out by June 7th and that it would be all right for plaintiff to move in.

The defendant denied all these statements. Therefore the evidence being conflicting the question was properly submitted to the jury by the trial court and their verdict in favor of plaintiff was supported by competent evidence.

When plaintiff sought to introduce testimony as to the profits she made in her former location and the profits she made while in defendant's building, and the drop in her profits when she removed to another building, the trial court sustained defendant's objection thereto, and did not permit that testimony to go to the jury.

Defendant in his brief asserts that the major and paramount question for decision is whether as a matter of law the defendant, when he executed the lease of April 30th, transferred to the plaintiff the legal right to possession, and was under no further obligation, or whether he was obligated to go further and place the plaintiff in actual possession of the property on June 1st. In arguing this question he asserts that the lease transferred the legal right to possession to the plaintiff, which was all he was required to do; that the occupants holding over after the term of their rental periods had expired by reason of his notices to them were trespassers, or tenants at sufferance of plaintiff, and that he was not required to place the plaintiff in possession as against them. In support of this contention . . . he cites Brown v. International Land Co., 116 P. 799 (Okl. 1911); Holden v. Tidwell, 133 P. 54 (Okl. 1913), and other similar cases. We do not agree with this contention. An examination of the cases cited in support thereof discloses that they are not applicable to the fact situation herein involved. In none of them was the question of the failure of the lessor to place the lessee in actual possession at the beginning of the term involved, but rather they involved trespassing committed upon the property subsequent to the taking of possession thereof by the lessee.

Defendant calls attention to the fact that the so-called American rule as to the placing of a lessee in possession required only that he be placed in legal possession, while the other or English rule holds that there is an implied covenant to place the lessee in actual possession, see Hannan v. Dusch, 153 S.E. 824 (Va. 1930), and asserts that the American rule is generally prevalent in the United States. This state, among numerous others, has followed the other or so-called English rule, and holds that the lessor is required to place the lessee in actual possession of the property. King v. Coombs, 122 P. 181 (Okl. 1911); Flannagan v. Dickerson, 229 P. 552 (Okl. 1924). In these cases we recognized and adhered to the rule holding that the lease contained an implied obligation to place the lessee in actual possession. . . . [I]n Stewart v. Murphy, 148 P. 609 (Kan. 1915), it is stated that by the great weight of authority the covenant to put the lessee in possession at the beginning of the term is implied, citing numerous cases.

It follows that in the instant case the lessee was entitled to be put in possession of the entire building by the lessor on or before June 1, 1946, and the failure of the defendant to so place her in possession, or at least to place her in possession June 7, at which time he assured her attorney she would receive possession of the entire building, was a breach of the lease.

Defendant contends that the breach was only a partial breach since it did not interfere with the operation of the beauty parlor by plaintiff, but we think it was a complete breach, since it forced the plaintiff either to bring ouster proceedings against the tenants holding over, or to continue to pay $500 a month rent for a portion of the premises only.

[The trial court instructed the jury] that if they found by a preponderance of the evidence that plaintiff entered into possession of two units of the leased premises on June 1st, with the promise and agreement on the part of defendant that if she would take possession of said units on that date he would place her in possession of the remaining units on June 7th or 8th, and he failed to do so, the defendant committed an actionable breach of the contract and their verdict should be for plaintiff. By instruction No. 4, they were told that if they found for the plaintiff, her damages should be for the sum of $500, the first month's rental, admittedly paid by her to the defendant on April 30th, and also such additional damages as would compensate her for moving into the building and remodeling the part which she used for the beauty parlor, not to exceed the sum of $574.95, claimed by plaintiff for such expenses. Plaintiff contends that the true measure of damages due a tenant on failure of the landlord to deliver possession is the difference between the rental agreed upon and the actual rental value of the property, together with special damages incurred by the lessee or tenant in preparing to occupy the premises, citing Anderson v. Holdges, 100 P.2d 853 (Okl. 1940); Dills v. Calloway, 52 P.2d 707 (Okl. 1935), and other similar cases. However, in these cases the tenants had paid no rental and had not moved into the property in reliance upon any representation of defendant that the defendant would place them in the undisturbed possession thereof. . . . We . . . hold that the trial court properly instructed the jury. . . .

Plaintiff in her cross-appeal contends that the court erred in refusing to permit her to present to the jury for its consideration the profits made by her while operating in her previous location, the profits made by her while located in defendant's building, and the loss of profits occasioned by her removal therefrom. We are unable to agree with this contention. . . . She occupied the building of defendant only two months. . . . [I]n cases where the loss of anticipated profits is claimed as an element of damages, the business claimed to have been interrupted must be an established one, and it must be shown that it has been successfully conducted for such a length of time and has such a trade established that the profits therefrom are reasonably ascertainable. In our judgment the business of defendant, after her removal from her uptown location to defendant's building, had not been conducted for such length of time as to render it an established business, and the trial court properly refused to permit evidence of her claimed losses to go to the jury.

It follows that the judgment for plaintiff as rendered by the lower court must be and hereby is affirmed. . . .

Notes and Questions

1. Today, most states, like Oklahoma, apply the English rule for delivery of possession in the absence of an agreement of the parties to the contrary. The Restatement provides the following rule for delivery of possession:

Except to the extent the parties to the lease validly agree otherwise, there is a breach of the landlord's obligations if a third person is improperly in possession of the leased property on the date the tenant is entitled to possession and the landlord does not act promptly to remove the person and does not in fact remove him within a reasonable period of time. . . . During the period of time following the date the tenant is entitled to possession and before the time the landlord is in default, the tenant is entitled to appropriate relief from his obligations under the lease and is entitled to recover from the third person damages sustained by him during that period. Before or after the landlord's default the tenant may recover the possession of the leased property from the third person improperly in possession.

Restatement (Second) of Property, Landlord and Tenant §6.2 (1977). Does the Restatement adopt the American rule or the English rule? If a court applies the Restatement rule, who would prevail under the facts of *Dieffenbach*?

2. Should a state that generally follows the American rule for the delivery of possession change the rule to protect only residential tenants? Statutory law in many states substantially modifies the common law of landlord-tenant. This is especially true for residential tenancies. Traditional common law generally applies the same body of principles to all leases, regardless of their subject matter — industrial property, office or retail space, farmland, other rural land, single-family house, or residential apartment. Over the past four decades, law reform has substantially improved the position of residential tenants. This is one manifestation of the consumer protection movement, with residential leases becoming a field within consumer law. Courts have accomplished some of the reform of residential landlord-tenant law by changing the common law, but state legislatures have also enacted significant measures. Since 1972, 21 states have adopted the Uniform Residential Landlord and Tenant Act (URLTA). The URLTA comprehensively regulates residential tenancies, in many instances reversing or modifying common law rules. For delivery of possession, it provides: "At the commencement of the term a landlord shall deliver possession of the premises to the tenant. . . . The landlord may bring an action for possession against any person wrongfully in possession and may recover [damages against the holdover tenant]." URLTA §2.103.

D. CONDITION OF PREMISES

Traditional landlord-tenant law, focusing on the leasehold as an estate in land, viewed a leasing transaction as a conveyance of property. Thus, the law of conveyances generally defined the rights of landlord and tenant. During the twentieth century, landlord-tenant law evolved through the importation of contract law analysis. In a number of contexts, courts departed from traditional property rules by treating the lease as a contract that involves a continuing exchange of promises. Today, the lease is conceptualized as a hybrid — sometimes contract rules and sometimes property (conveyance) rules apply to resolve disputes between landlord and tenant.

A significant early step in the integration of contract law into landlord-tenant relations is the development of the covenant of quiet enjoyment. The covenant assures the tenant of his right to possession, as against the landlord and other persons for whom the landlord is treated as responsible. Many lease instruments have an express covenant of quiet enjoyment. Under early law, the tenant had to have an express covenant in order to have the right under the lease to quiet enjoyment. This rule treated leases the same as other conveyances of estates, for which the law refused to imply covenants in deeds of conveyance. Today, however, in almost all states the covenant is implied. Under contract law, implied promises are a staple, and thus the modern willingness to imply the covenant of quiet enjoyment represents a turn to contract principles. The doctrine of constructive eviction represented a further development in the direction of imposing contract-like obligations on the landlord not to interfere directly or indirectly with the tenant's reasonable use and enjoyment of the premises. More recently, the creation of the implied warranty of habitability constitutes an explicit extension of contract-law principles to the property rights of residential tenants. As you will see from the following three cases in this section, some of the tenant's remedies in this area also stem from contract law. This is particularly notable for the tenant's right to terminate the lease and the right to compensatory damages.

■ **SMITH v. McENANY**
Supreme Judicial Court of Massachusetts, 1897
48 N.E. 781

HOLMES, Justice. [Clara Smith brought] an action upon a lease for rent and for breach of a covenant to repair [against Thomas McEnany]. The defense is an eviction. The land is a lot in the city of Boston, the part concerned being covered by a shed which was used by the defendant to store wagons. The eviction relied on was the building of a permanent brick wall for a building on adjoining land belonging to the plaintiff's husband, which encroached 9 inches, by the plaintiff's admission, or, as her witness testified, from measurements, $13^{1}/_{2}$ inches, or, as the defendant said, 2 feet, for 34 feet along the back of the shed. The wall was built with the plaintiff's assent, and with knowledge that it encroached on the demised premises. The judge ruled that the defendant had a right to treat this as an eviction determining the lease. The plaintiff asked to have the ruling so qualified as to make the question depend upon whether the wall made the premises "uninhabitable for the purpose for which they were hired, materially changing the character and beneficial enjoyment thereof." This was refused, and the plaintiff excepted. . . .

The refusal was right. It is settled in this State, in accordance with the law of England, that a wrongful eviction of the tenant by the landlord from a part of the premises suspends the rent under the lease. The main reason which is given for the decisions is that the enjoyment of the whole consideration is the foundation of the debt and the condition of the covenant, and that the obligation to pay cannot be apportioned. Shumway v. Collins, 6 Gray 227, 232 (Mass. 1856); Leishman v. White, 1 Allen 489 (Mass. 1861); Royce v. Guggenheim, 106 Mass. 201, 202 (1870). It also is said that the landlord shall not apportion his own wrong, following an expression in some of the older English books. Royce v. Guggenheim, *supra.* But this does not so much explain the rule as suggest the limitation that there may be an apportionment when the eviction is by title paramount or when the lessor's entry is rightful. Fillebrown v. Hoar, 124 Mass. 580, 583 (1878); Christopher v. Austin, 11 N.Y. 216, 218 (1854); Co. Litt. 148b; Gilb. Rents, 151 et seq. It leaves open the question why the landlord may not show that his wrong extended only to a part of the premises. No doubt the question equally may be asked why the lease is construed to exclude apportionment, and it may be that this is partly due to the traditional doctrine that the rent issues out of the land, and that the whole rent is charged on every part of the land. Gilbert, Rents, 178, 179, gives this as one ground why the lessor shall not discharge any part from the burden and continue to charge the rest, coupled with considerations partly of a feudal nature. But the same view naturally would be taken if the question arose now for the first time. The land is hired as one whole. If by his own fault the landlord withdraws a part of it he cannot recover either on the lease or outside of it for the occupation of the residue. Leishman v. White, 1 Allen 489 (Mass. 1861).

It follows from the nature of the reason for the decisions which we have stated that, when the tenant proves a wrongful deforcement by the landlord from an appreciable part of the premises, no inquiry is open as to the greater or less importance of the parcel from which the tenant is deforced. Outside the rule de minimis, the degree of interference with the use and enjoyment of the premises is important only in the case of acts not physically excluding the tenant, but alleged to have an equally serious practical effect, just as the intent is important only in the case of acts not necessarily amounting to an entry and deforcement of the tenant. Skally v. Shute, 132 Mass. 367 (1882). The inquiry is for the purpose of settling whether the landlord's acts had the alleged effect; that is, whether the tenant is evicted from any portion of the land. If that is admitted, the rent is suspended because, by the terms of the instrument as construed, the tenant has made it an absolute condition that he should have the whole of the demised premises, at least as against willful interference on the landlord's part. . . .

We must repeat that we do not understand any question, except the one which we have dealt with, to be before us. An eviction like the present does not necessarily end the lease, Leishman v. White, 1 Allen 489, 490 (Mass. 1861), or other obligations of the tenant under it, such as the covenant to repair. Carrel v. Read, Cro. Eliz. 374; Newton v. Allin, 1 Q.B. 518.

Exceptions overruled.

Notes and Questions

1. A breach of the covenant of quiet enjoyment entitles the tenant to select among four contract remedies: injunctive relief, damages, lease termination, or rent withholding. The tenant may obtain an injunction ordering the landlord or the other person interfering with the tenant's possession to cease the offensive conduct. The tenant may collect damages, measured by the standard rules of contract law. Usually, the tenant may choose to terminate the lease because the landlord's interference will be considered to be a material breach. (In this classic decision, the legendary jurist Oliver Wendell Holmes is referring to termination by the tenant when he says that McEnany could treat the narrow encroachment "as an eviction determining the lease.")

The covenant of quiet enjoyment is said to be a *dependent covenant*. The tenant's duty to pay rent depends upon the landlord's performance of the covenant. Thus, McEnany had the right to withhold payment of rent for so long as the breach continued. The treatment of quiet enjoyment as a dependent covenant is in contrast to a general principle that lease covenants are independent. The doctrine of *independent covenants* means that a breach by one party of a covenant does not relieve the other party of the duty to perform. This traditional principle of landlord-tenant law predated the development of modern contract law and is contrary to the modern contract rule that allows a party to withhold performance upon a material breach by the other party.

2. An actual eviction by the landlord may be total or, as in *Smith*, partial. A partial eviction, like a total eviction, is a breach of quiet enjoyment, generally entitling the tenant to the same set of remedies. The only distinction concerns the operation of the remedy of rent withholding. *Smith* explains the traditional rule, which allows the tenant to remain in possession of the remainder of the premises and pay no rent whatsoever.

There are two alternative views, both of which are less generous to the tenant. The first, the Restatement view, calls for the partial abatement of rent, reducing the rent to "the amount of that proportion of the rent which the fair rental value after the event giving the right to abate bears to the fair rental value before the event." *Restatement (Second) of Property, Landlord and Tenant* §§6.1, 11.1 (1977).

The second alternative view allows the total abatement of rent for a partial eviction, but applies a higher threshold than *Smith*, asking whether the interference is "substantial." In Dussin Investment Company v. Bloxham, 157 Cal. Rptr. 646 (Ct. App. 1979), Bloxham rented a 14,000-square-foot tract of land including part of an office building at a monthly rent of $1,210. The landlord enlarged a storage area in the building, wrongly taking back 165 square feet of space. Bloxham claimed he owed no rent, but the court allowed an abatement of only $200 per month: "[I]n appropriate circumstances an actual, partial eviction of a tenant by a landlord will relieve the tenant from liability for future rents so long as the eviction continues even though the tenant remains in possession of the balance of the premises. However, the tenant's obligation to pay rent is not thus suspended unless the tenant has been actually evicted from a substantial portion of the demised premises. . . . [I]n determining the question of substantiality, the court may and should consider the extent of the interference with the tenant's use and enjoyment of the property. These conclusions are particularly appropriate where, as here, the eviction was not malicious or in bad faith but, rather, resulted from a tenable, though mistaken, interpretation of an ambiguous lease provision."

In Eastside Exhibition Corp. v. 210 East 86th Street Corp., 965 N.E.2d 246 (N.Y. 2012), the landlord installed cross-bracing between two existing steel support columns in a movie theatre, causing a change in the flow of patron foot traffic, and reduced the size of the leased premises by 12 square feet out of a total of over 15,000 square feet. Citing *Dussin* and other cases, the court refused to allow a full rental abatement. "Given the inherent inequity of a full rent abatement under the circumstances presented here and modern realities that a commercial lessee is free to negotiate appropriate lease terms, we see no need to apply a rule, derived from feudal concepts, that any intrusion — no matter how small — on the demised premises must result in full rent abatement. Rather, we recognize that there can be an intrusion so minimal that it does not prescribe such a harsh remedy. For an intrusion to be considered an actual partial eviction it must interfere in some, more than trivial, manner with the tenant's use and enjoyment of the premises." A dissenting judge criticized the majority for overruling "an easy to apply bright-line rule in favor of a new de minimis rule that affords no predictability of outcome." She also argued that "the new de minimis rule should not apply in this case or, for that matter, to any litigation arising out of commercial leases entered into *before* today's decision. Tenant, which justifiably relied on clear and long-standing New York law, now faces the prospect of paying landlord nine years' worth of rent (perhaps escrowed, perhaps not), presumably along with 9% interest, as a consequence of its confidence in our fidelity to the 'certainty of settled rules' governing property rights. Additionally, the 'concededly unaesthetic cross-bracing,' which creates the unbargained-for eyesore and obstruction, remains in place in the middle of the theater's 15-foot-wide lobby."

■ **BLACKETT v. OLANOFF**
Supreme Judicial Court of Massachusetts, 1976
358 N.E.2d 817

WILKINS, Justice. The defendant in each of these consolidated actions for rent successfully raised constructive eviction as a defense against the landlords' claim. The judge found that the tenants were "very substantially deprived" of quiet enjoyment of their leased premises "*for a substantial time*" (emphasis original). He ruled that the tenants' implied warranty of quiet enjoyment was violated by late evening and early morning music and disturbances coming from nearby premises which the landlords leased to others for use as a bar or cocktail lounge (lounge). The judge further found that, although the landlords did not intend to create the conditions, the landlords "had it within their control to correct the conditions which . . . amounted to a constructive eviction of each [tenant]." He also found that the landlords promised each tenant to correct the situation, that the landlords made some attempt to remedy the problem, but they were unsuccessful, and that each tenant vacated his apartment within a reasonable time. Judgment was entered for each tenant; the landlords appealed; and we transferred the appeals here. We affirm the judgments.

The landlords argue that they did not violate the tenants' implied covenant of quiet enjoyment because they are not chargeable with the noise from the lounge. The landlords do not challenge the judge's conclusion that the noise emanating from the lounge was sufficient to constitute a constructive eviction, if that noise could be attributed to the landlords.[3] Nor do the landlords seriously argue that a constructive eviction could not be found as matter of law because the lounge was not on the same premises as the tenants' apartments. *See* 1 *American Law of Property* §3.51, at 281 (A.J. Casner ed. 1952). The landlords' principal contention, based on the denial of certain requests for rulings, is that they are not responsible for the conduct of the proprietors, employees, and patrons of the lounge.

Our opinions concerning a constructive eviction by an alleged breach of an implied covenant of quiet enjoyment sometimes have stated that the landlord must perform some act with the intent of depriving the tenant of the enjoyment and occupation of the whole or part of the leased premises. *See* Katz v. Duffy, 158 N.E. 264, 264-65 (Mass. 1927), and cases cited. There are occasions, however, where a landlord has not intended to violate a tenant's rights, but there was nevertheless a breach of the landlord's covenant of quiet enjoyment which flowed as the natural and probable consequence of what the landlord did, what he failed to do, or what he permitted to be done. Charles E. Burt, Inc. v. Seven Grand Corp., 163 N.E.2d 4, 6

---

3. There was evidence that the lounge had amplified music (electric musical instruments and singing, at various times) which started at 9:30 P.M. and continued until 1:30 A.M. or 2 A.M., generally on Tuesdays through Sundays. The music could be heard through the granite walls of the residential tenants' building, and was described variously as unbelievably loud, incessant, raucous, and penetrating. The noise interfered with conversation and prevented sleep. There was also evidence of noise from patrons' yelling and fighting.

(Mass. 1959) (failure to supply light, heat, power, and elevator services); Westland Housing Corp. v. Scott, 44 N.E.2d 959, 963 (Mass. 1942) (intrusions of smoke and soot over a substantial period of time due to a defective boiler); Shindler v. Milden, 184 N.E. 673, 674 (Mass. 1933) (failure to install necessary heating system, as agreed); Case v. Minot, 33 N.E. 700, 701 (Mass. 1893) (landlord authorizing another lessee to obstruct the tenant's light and air, necessary for the beneficial enjoyment of the demised premises); Skally v. Shute, 132 Mass. 367, 370-371 (1882) (undermining of a leased building rendering it unfit for occupancy). Although some of our opinions have spoken of particular action or inaction by a landlord as showing a presumed intention to evict, the landlord's conduct, and not his intentions, is controlling. *See* Westland Housing Corp. v. Scott, *supra* at 963.

The judge was warranted in ruling that the landlords had it within their control to correct the condition which caused the tenants to vacate their apartments. The landlords introduced a commercial activity into an area where they leased premises for residential purposes. The lease for the lounge expressly provided that entertainment in the lounge had to be conducted so that it could not be heard outside the building and would not disturb the residents of the leased apartments. The potential threat to the occupants of the nearby apartments was apparent in the circumstances. The landlords complained to the tenants of the lounge after receiving numerous objections from residential tenants. From time to time, the pervading noise would abate in response to the landlord's complaints. We conclude that, as matter of law, the landlords had a right to control the objectionable noise coming from the lounge and that the judge was warranted in finding as a fact that the landlords could control the objectionable conditions.

This situation is different from the usual annoyance of one residential tenant by another, where traditionally the landlord has not been chargeable with the annoyance. *See* Katz v. Duffy, 158 N.E. 264 (Mass. 1927) (illegal sale of alcoholic beverages); DeWitt v. Pierson, 112 Mass. 8 (1873) (prostitution).[4] Here we have a case more like Case v. Minot, 33 N.E. 700 (Mass. 1893), where the landlord entered into a lease with one tenant which the landlord knew permitted that tenant to engage in activity which would interfere with the rights of another tenant. There, to be sure, the clash of tenants' rights was inevitable, if each pressed those rights. Here, although the clash of tenants' interests was only a known potentiality initially, experience demonstrated that a decibel level for the entertainment at the lounge,

---

4. The general, but not universal, rule in this country is that a landlord is not chargeable because one tenant is causing annoyance to another, A.H. Woods Theatre v. North American Union, 246 Ill. App. 521, 526-527 (1927) (music from one commercial tenant annoying another commercial tenant's employees), even where the annoying conduct would be a breach of the landlord's covenant of quiet enjoyment if the landlord were the miscreant. *See* Paterson v. Bridges, 75 So. 260, 261 (Ala. App. 1917); Thompson v. Harris, 452 P.2d 122, 126 (Ariz. App. 1969), and cases cited; 1 *American Law of Property* §3.53 (A.J. Casner ed. 1952). *Contra,* Kesner v. Consumers Co., 255 Ill. App. 216, 228-229 (1929) (storage of flammables constituting a nuisance); Bruckner v. Helfaer, 222 N.W. 790, 791 (Wis. 1929) (residential tenant not liable for rent where landlord, with ample notice, does not control another tenant's conduct).

The rule in New York appears to be that the landlord may not recover rent if he has had ample notice of the existence of conduct of one tenant which deprives another tenant of the beneficial enjoyment of his premises and the landlord does little or nothing to abate the nuisance. *See* Cohen v. Werner, 378 N.Y.S.2d 868 (N.Y. App. T. 1975); Rockrose Assocs. v. Peters, 366 N.Y.S.2d 567 (N.Y. Civ. Ct. 1975) (office lease). *But see* comments in Trustees of the Sailors' Snug Harbor in the City of New York v. Sugarman, 35 N.Y.S.2d 196, 198 (App. Div. 1942) (no nuisance).

A tenant with sufficient bargaining power may be able to obtain an agreement from the landlord to insert and to enforce regulatory restrictions in the leases of other, potentially offending, tenants. *See* E. Schwartz, *Lease Drafting in Massachusetts* §6.33 (1961).

acoustically acceptable to its patrons and hence commercially desirable to its proprietors, was intolerable for the residential tenants.

Because the disturbing condition was the natural and probable consequence of the landlords' permitting the lounge to operate where it did and because the landlords could control the actions at the lounge, they should not be entitled to collect rent for residential premises which were not reasonably habitable. Tenants such as these should not be left only with a claim against the proprietors of the noisome lounge. To the extent that our opinions suggest a distinction between nonfeasance by the landlord, which has been said to create no liability, P. Hall, *Massachusetts Law of Landlord and Tenant* §§90-91 (4th ed. 1949), and malfeasance by the landlord, we decline to perpetuate that distinction where the landlord creates a situation and has the right to control the objectionable conditions.

Judgments affirmed.

Notes and Questions

1. Not every interference with the tenant's possession and enjoyment breaches the covenant of quiet enjoyment. Whether the theory is actual eviction or constructive eviction, the landlord must in some sense be at fault. The landlord bears responsibility for the actions of:

(a) the landlord himself,
(b) the landlord's successors (persons who get title, authority, or other rights from the landlord), or
(c) paramount titleholders (persons who have better title to the premises than the landlord).

2. Recall that in Smith v. McEnany, Justice Holmes distinguished the eviction accomplished by the building of the brick wall from "eviction by title paramount." In *Blackett*, the commercial tenant also is not a paramount titleholder. The issue is the breadth of the second category—whether the commercial tenant should be considered a "landlord's successor" so as to make the landlord just as liable as if it were the noisemaker. Did the court reach the right result? Is it critical to the decision that the commercial lease expressly limited the noise level of the entertainment? Would it be possible for the tenants to win if the landlord, instead of leasing the commercial space, sold that space in fee simple to the lounge proprietor?

3. Can ethnic bias demonstrated by a property manager employed by the landlord constitute a constructive eviction? Yes, according to Gray v. Oxford Worldwide Group, Inc., 139 P.3d 267 (Utah Ct. App. 2006) (premises were used as a language school for Latinos; manager's conduct was "grossly insulting" and spoiled tenant's fiesta, a major community event held on premises).

4. To use the constructive eviction defense, the tenant must abandon the premises within a reasonable time after the interference begins. In *Blackett*, the court observes that the residential tenants left in time. Why has the law required abandonment? Imagine that you are counseling a tenant who may be able to prove the elements of constructive eviction, but is still in possession of the premises. Why might constructive eviction be an unattractive legal option? Should the law retain the abandonment requirement? The Restatement calls for abolition of the

abandonment requirement, *Restatement Second of Property, Landlord and Tenant* §6.1 (1977), a call courts have not yet heeded.

5. An interference with the tenant's right to possession may affect part, but not all, of the premises. Under traditional constructive eviction, if that interference is substantial enough, the tenant can choose to abandon the entire premises to obtain relief. For this type of fact pattern, a new theory of *partial constructive eviction* may give the tenant two advantages. First, it is easier to prove the interference is substantial because the focus is on the part of the premises that is alleged to be unusable, rather than the entire premises. Second, the tenant can satisfy the abandonment requirement by vacating just the part that is negatively affected. Partial constructive eviction is not yet well established. Several courts have endorsed partial constructive eviction, but others have rejected it. One of the authorities is Minjak Co. v. Randolph, 528 N.Y.S.2d 554 (App. Div. 1988), where the tenants used two-thirds of their space as a music studio and the other one-third as their residence. Due to the landlord's interference, they abandoned the music studio but remained in the residence. The court allowed their constructive eviction claim, stating "when the tenant is constructively evicted from a portion of the premises by the landlord's actions, he should not be obligated to pay the full rent."

■ JAVINS v. FIRST NATIONAL REALTY CORPORATION
United States Court of Appeals for the District of Columbia Circuit, 1970
428 F.2d 1071, cert. denied, 400 U.S. 925

J. SKELLY WRIGHT, Circuit Judge. These cases present the question whether housing code violations which arise during the term of a lease have any effect upon the tenant's obligation to pay rent. The Landlord and Tenant Branch of the District of Columbia Court of General Sessions ruled proof of such violations inadmissible when proffered as a defense to an eviction action for nonpayment of rent. The District of Columbia Court of Appeals upheld this ruling. Saunders v. First National Realty Corp., 245 A.2d 836 (D.C. Ct. App. 1968).

Because of the importance of the question presented, we granted appellants' petitions for leave to appeal. We now reverse and hold that a warranty of habitability, measured by the standards set out in the Housing Regulations for the District of Columbia, is implied by operation of law into leases of urban dwelling units covered by those Regulations and that breach of this warranty gives rise to the usual remedies for breach of contract.

I.

The facts revealed by the record are simple. By separate written leases, each of the appellants rented an apartment in a three-building apartment complex in Northwest Washington known as Clifton Terrace. The landlord, First National Realty Corporation, filed separate actions in the Landlord and Tenant Branch of the Court of General Sessions on April 8, 1966, seeking possession on the ground that each of the appellants had defaulted in the payment of rent due for the month of April. The tenants, appellants here, admitted that they had not paid the landlord any rent for April. However, they alleged numerous violations of the Housing Regulations as "an equitable defense or [a] claim by way of recoupment or set-off in an amount equal to the rent claim," as provided in the rules of the Court of General Sessions. They offered to prove

> [that] there are approximately 1500 violations of the Housing Regulations of the District of Columbia in the building at Clifton Terrace, where Defendant resides some affecting the premises of this Defendant directly, others indirectly, and all tending to establish a course of conduct of violation of the Housing Regulations to the damage of Defendants.

Settled Statement of Proceedings and Evidence, p. 2 (1966). Appellants conceded at trial, however, that this offer of proof reached only violations which had arisen since the term of the lease had commenced. The Court of General Sessions refused appellants' offer of proof and entered judgment for the landlord. The District of Columbia Court of Appeals affirmed, rejecting the argument made by appellants that the landlord was under a contractual duty to maintain the premises in compliance with the Housing Regulations. Saunders v. First National Realty Corp., *supra*, 245 A.2d at 838.

II.

Since, in traditional analysis, a lease was the conveyance of an interest in land, courts have usually utilized the special rules governing real property transactions to resolve controversies involving leases. However, as the Supreme Court has noted in another context, "the body of private property law . . . more than almost any other branch of law, has been shaped by distinctions whose validity is largely historical."[6] Courts have a duty to reappraise old doctrines in the light of the facts and values of contemporary life — particularly old common law doctrines which the courts themselves created and developed. As we have said before, "[The] continued vitality of the common law . . . depends upon its ability to reflect contemporary community values and ethics."[8]

The assumption of landlord-tenant law, derived from feudal property law, that a lease primarily conveyed to the tenant an interest in land, may have been reasonable in a rural, agrarian society; it may continue to be reasonable in some leases involving farming or commercial land. In these cases, the value of the lease to the tenant is the land itself. But in the case of the modern apartment dweller, the value of the lease is that it gives him a place to live. The city dweller who seeks to lease an apartment on the third floor of a tenement has little interest in the land 30 or 40 feet below, or even in the bare right to possession within the four walls of his apartment. When American city dwellers, both rich and poor, seek "shelter" today, they seek a well known package of goods and services[9] — a package which includes not merely walls and ceilings, but also adequate heat, light and ventilation, serviceable plumbing facilities, secure windows and doors, proper sanitation, and proper maintenance.

---

6. Jones v. United States, 362 U.S. 257, 266 (1960).

8. Whetzel v. Jess Fisher Management Co., 282 F.2d 943, 946 (D.C. Cir. 1960).

9. *See, e.g.*, National Commission on Urban Problems, *Building the American City* 9 (1968). The extensive standards set out in the Housing Regulations provide a good guide to community expectations.

Professor Powell summarizes the present state of the law:

> The complexities of city life, and the proliferated problems of modern society in general, have created new problems for lessors and lessees and these have been commonly handled by specific clauses inserted in leases. This growth in the number and detail of specific lease covenants has reintroduced into the law of estates for years a predominantly contractual ingredient. In practice, the law today concerning estates for years consists chiefly of rules determining the construction and effect of lease covenants.[10]

Ironically, however, the rules governing the construction and interpretation of "predominantly contractual" obligations in leases have too often remained rooted in old property law.

Some courts have realized that certain of the old rules of property law governing leases are inappropriate for today's transactions. In order to reach results more in accord with the legitimate expectations of the parties and the standards of the community, courts have been gradually introducing more modern precepts of contract law in interpreting leases. Proceeding piecemeal has, however, led to confusion where "decisions are frequently conflicting, not because of a healthy disagreement on social policy, but because of the lingering impact of rules whose policies are long since dead."[12]

In our judgment the trend toward treating leases as contracts is wise and well considered. Our holding in this case reflects a belief that leases of urban dwelling units should be interpreted and construed like any other contract.[13]

III.

Modern contract law has recognized that the buyer of goods and services in an industrialized society must rely upon the skill and honesty of the supplier to assure that goods and services purchased are of adequate quality. In interpreting most contracts, courts have sought to protect the legitimate expectations of the buyer and have steadily widened the seller's responsibility for the quality of goods and services through implied warranties of fitness and merchantability. Thus without any special agreement a merchant will be held to warrant that his goods are fit for the ordinary purposes for which such goods are used and that they are at least of reasonably average quality. Moreover, if the supplier has been notified that goods are required for a specific purpose, he will be held to warrant that any goods sold are fit for that purpose. These implied warranties have become widely accepted and well established features of the common law, supported by the overwhelming body of case law. Today most states as well as the District of Columbia have codified and

---

10. 2 R. Powell, *Real Property* ¶221[1] at 179 (1967).

12. Kessler, *The Protection of the Consumer Under Modern Sales Law*, 74 Yale L.J. 262, 263 (1964).

13. This approach does not deny the possible importance of the fact that land is involved in a transaction. The interpretation and construction of contracts between private parties has always required courts to be sensitive and responsive to myriad different factors. We believe contract doctrines allow courts to be properly sensitive to all relevant factors in interpreting lease obligations. We also intend no alteration of statutory or case law definitions of the term "real property" for purposes of statutes or decisions on recordation, descent, conveyancing, creditors' rights, etc. We contemplate only that contract law is to determine the rights and obligations of the parties to the lease agreement, as between themselves. The civil law has always viewed the lease as a contract, and in our judgment that perspective has proved superior to that of the common law. *See* 2 M. Planiol, *Treatise on the Civil Law* §1663 et seq. (1959); 11 La. Civil Code Art. 2669 (1952).

enacted these warranties into statute, as to the sale of goods, in the Uniform Commercial Code.

Implied warranties of quality have not been limited to cases involving sales. The consumer renting a chattel, paying for services, or buying a combination of goods and services must rely upon the skill and honesty of the supplier to at least the same extent as a purchaser of goods. Courts have not hesitated to find implied warranties of fitness and merchantability in such situations. In most areas product liability law has moved far beyond "mere" implied warranties running between two parties in privity with each other.

The rigid doctrines of real property law have tended to inhibit the application of implied warranties to transactions involving real estate. Now, however, courts have begun to hold sellers and developers of real property responsible for the quality of their product. For example, builders of new homes have recently been held liable to purchasers for improper construction on the ground that the builders had breached an implied warranty of fitness. In other cases courts have held builders of new homes liable for breach of an implied warranty that all local building regulations had been complied with. And following the developments in other areas, very recent decisions and commentary suggest the possible extension of liability to parties other than the immediate seller for improper construction of residential real estate.

Despite this trend in the sale of real estate, many courts have been unwilling to imply warranties of quality, specifically a warranty of habitability, into leases of apartments. Recent decisions have offered no convincing explanation for their refusal; rather they have relied without discussion upon the old common law rule that the lessor is not obligated to repair unless he covenants to do so in the written lease contract. However, the Supreme Courts of at least two states, in recent and well reasoned opinions, have held landlords to implied warranties of quality in housing leases. Lemle v. Breeden, 462 P.2d 470 (Haw. 1969); Reste Realty Corp. v. Cooper, 251 A.2d 268 (N.J. 1969). *See also* Pines v. Perssion, 111 N.W.2d 409 (Wis. 1961). In our judgment, the old no-repair rule cannot coexist with the obligations imposed on the landlord by a typical modern housing code, and must be abandoned in favor of an implied warranty of habitability.[29] In the District of Columbia, the standards of this warranty are set out in the Housing Regulations.

IV.

A.

In our judgment the common law itself must recognize the landlord's obligation to keep his premises in a habitable condition. This conclusion is compelled by three separate considerations. First, we believe that the old rule was based on certain factual assumptions which are no longer true; on its own terms, it can no longer be justified. Second, we believe that the consumer protection cases discussed above require that the old rule be abandoned in order to bring residential landlord-tenant law into harmony with the principles on which those cases rest. Third, we think that the nature of today's urban housing market also dictates abandonment of the old rule.

---

29. Although the present cases involve written leases, we think there is no particular significance in this fact. The landlord's warranty is implied in oral and written leases for all types of tenancies.

The common law rule absolving the lessor of all obligation to repair originated in the early Middle Ages.[30] Such a rule was perhaps well suited to an agrarian
economy; the land was more important[31] than whatever small living structure was
included in the leasehold, and the tenant farmer was fully capable of making
repairs himself.[32] These historical facts were the basis on which the common
law constructed its rule; they also provided the necessary prerequisites for its
application.[33]

Court decisions in the late 1800's began to recognize that the factual assumptions of the common law were no longer accurate in some cases. For example, the
common law, since it assumed that the land was the most important part of the
leasehold, required a tenant to pay rent even if any building on the land was
destroyed. Faced with such a rule and the ludicrous results it produced, in 1863
the New York Court of Appeals declined to hold that an upper story tenant was
obliged to continue paying rent after his apartment building burned down.[35] The
court simply pointed out that the urban tenant had no interest in the land, only in
the attached building.

Another line of cases created an exception to the no-repair rule for short term
leases of furnished dwellings. The Massachusetts Supreme Judicial Court, a court
not known for its willingness to depart from the common law, supported this exception, pointing out:

> [A] different rule should apply to one who hires a furnished room, or a furnished
> house, for a few days, or a few weeks or months. Its fitness for immediate use of a
> particular kind, as indicated by its appointments, is a far more important element
> entering into the contract than when there is a mere lease of real estate. One who
> lets for a short term a house provided with all furnishings and appointments for imme-
> diate residence may be supposed to contract in reference to a well-understood purpose
> of the hirer to use it as a habitation. . . . It would be unreasonable to hold, under such
> circumstances, that the landlord does not impliedly agree that what he is letting is a
> house suitable for occupation in its condition at the time.[37]

---

30. The rule was "settled" by 1485. 3 W. Holdsworth, *A History of English Law* 122-23 (6th ed. 1934).
The common law rule discussed in text originated in the even older rule prohibiting the tenant from
committing waste. The writ of waste expanded as the tenant's right to possession grew stronger. Eventually, in order to protect the landowner's reversionary interest, the tenant became obligated to make
repairs and liable to eviction and damages if he failed to do so. *Ibid.*

31. The land was so central to the original common law conception of a leasehold that rent was
viewed as "issuing" from the land: "[The] governing idea is that the land is bound to pay the rent. . . . We
may almost go to the length of saying that the land pays it through [the tenant's] hand." 2 F. Pollock &
F. Maitland, *The History of English Law* 131 (2d ed. 1923).

32. Many later judicial opinions have added another justification of the old common law rule. They
have invoked the timeworn cry of caveat emptor and argued that a lessee has the opportunity to inspect
the premises. On the basis of his inspection, the tenant must then take the premises "as is," according to
this reasoning. As an historical matter, the opportunity to inspect was not thought important when the
rule was first devised. *See* Note 30 *supra.* . . .

33. Even the old common law courts responded with a different rule for a landlord-tenant
relationship which did not conform to the model of the usual agrarian lease. Much more substantial
obligations were placed upon the keepers of inns (the only multiple dwelling houses known to the
common law). Their guests were interested solely in shelter and could not be expected to make their
own repairs. "The modern apartment dweller more closely resembles the guest in an inn than he resembles an agrarian tenant, but the law has not generally recognized the similarity." J. Levi, P. Hablutzel,
L. Rosenberg & J. White, *Model Residential Landlord-Tenant Code* 6-7 (Tent. Draft 1969).

35. Graves v. Berdan, 26 N.Y. 498 (1863).

37. Ingalls v. Hobbs, 31 N.E. 286 (Mass. 1892).

These as well as other similar cases[38] demonstrate that some courts began some time ago to question the common law's assumptions that the land was the most important feature of a leasehold and that the tenant could feasibly make any necessary repairs himself. Where those assumptions no longer reflect contemporary housing patterns, the courts have created exceptions to the general rule that landlords have no duty to keep their premises in repair.

It is overdue for courts to admit that these assumptions are no longer true with regard to all urban housing. Today's urban[39] tenants, the vast majority of whom live in multiple dwelling houses, are interested, not in the land, but solely in "a house suitable for occupation." Furthermore, today's city dweller usually has a single, specialized skill unrelated to maintenance work; he is unable to make repairs like the "jack-of-all-trades" farmer who was the common law's model of the lessee. Further, unlike his agrarian predecessor who often remained on one piece of land for his entire life, urban tenants today are more mobile than ever before. A tenant's tenure in a specific apartment will often not be sufficient to justify efforts at repairs. In addition, the increasing complexity of today's dwellings renders them much more difficult to repair than the structures of earlier times. In a multiple dwelling repair may require access to equipment and areas in the control of the landlord. Low and middle income tenants, even if they were interested in making repairs, would be unable to obtain any financing for major repairs since they have no long-term interest in the property.

Our approach to the common law of landlord and tenant ought to be aided by principles derived from the consumer protection cases referred to above. In a lease contract, a tenant seeks to purchase from his landlord shelter for a specified period of time. The landlord sells housing as a commercial businessman and has much greater opportunity, incentive and capacity to inspect and maintain the condition of his building. Moreover, the tenant must rely upon the skill and bona fides of his landlord at least as much as a car buyer must rely upon the car manufacturer. In dealing with major problems, such as heating, plumbing, electrical or structural defects, the tenant's position corresponds precisely with "the ordinary consumer who cannot be expected to have the knowledge or capacity or even the opportunity to make adequate inspection of mechanical instrumentalities, like automobiles, and to decide for himself whether they are reasonably fit for the designed purpose." Henningsen v. Bloomfield Motors, Inc., 161 A.2d 69, 78 (N.J. 1960).[42]

Since a lease contract specifies a particular period of time during which the tenant has a right to use his apartment for shelter, he may legitimately expect that the apartment will be fit for habitation for the time period for which it is rented. We

38. The cases developing the doctrines of "quiet enjoyment" and "constructive eviction" are the most important. *See* 2 R. Powell, *supra* Note 10, ¶225 [3]. *See also* Gladden v. Walker & Dunlop, 168 F.2d 321 (D.C. Cir. 1948) (landlord has duty to maintain portions of apartment "under his control" including plumbing, heating and electrical systems); J. D. Young Corp. v. McClintic, 26 S.W.2d 460 (Tex. Civ. App. 1930) (implied covenant of fitness in lease of building under construction); Steefel v. Rothschild, 72 N.E. 112 (N.Y. 1904) (duty to disclose latent defects).

39. In 1968 more than two thirds of America's people lived in the 228 largest metropolitan areas. Only 5.2% lived on farms. *The World Almanac 1970* at 251 (L. Long ed.). More than 98% of all housing starts in 1968 were non-farm. *Id.* at 313.

42. Nor should the average tenant be thought capable of "inspecting" plaster, floorboards, roofing, kitchen appliances, etc. To the extent, however, that some defects are obvious, the law must take note of the present housing shortage. Tenants may have no real alternative but to accept such housing with the expectation that the landlord will make necessary repairs. Where this is so, caveat emptor must of necessity be rejected.

point out that in the present cases there is no allegation that appellants' apartments were in poor condition or in violation of the housing code at the commencement of the leases.[43] Since the lessees continue to pay the same rent, they were entitled to expect that the landlord would continue to keep the premises in their beginning condition during the lease term. It is precisely such expectations that the law now recognizes as deserving of formal, legal protection.

Even beyond the rationale of traditional products liability law, the relationship of landlord and tenant suggests further compelling reasons for the law's protection of the tenants' legitimate expectations of quality. The inequality in bargaining power between landlord and tenant has been well documented.[44] Tenants have very little leverage to enforce demands for better housing. Various impediments to competition in the rental housing market, such as racial and class discrimination and standardized form leases, mean that landlords place tenants in a take it or leave it situation. The increasingly severe shortage of adequate housing further increases the landlord's bargaining power and escalates the need for maintaining and improving the existing stock. Finally, the findings by various studies of the social impact of bad housing has led to the realization that poor housing is detrimental to the whole society, not merely to the unlucky ones who must suffer the daily indignity of living in a slum.

Thus we are led by our inspection of the relevant legal principles and precedents to the conclusion that the old common law rule imposing an obligation upon the lessee to repair during the lease term was really never intended to apply to residential urban leaseholds. Contract principles established in other areas of the law provide a more rational framework for the apportionment of landlord-tenant responsibilities; they strongly suggest that a warranty of habitability be implied into all contracts for urban dwellings.

B.

We believe, in any event, that the District's housing code requires that a warranty of habitability be implied in the leases of all housing that it covers. The housing code — formally designated the Housing Regulations of the District of Columbia — was established and authorized by the Commissioners of the District of Columbia on August 11, 1955. Since that time, the code has been updated by numerous orders of the Commissioners. The 75 pages of the Regulations provide a comprehensive regulatory scheme setting forth in some detail: (a) the standards which housing in the District of Columbia must meet; (b) which party, the lessor or the lessee, must meet each standard; and (c) a system of inspections, notifications and criminal penalties. The Regulations themselves are silent on the question of private remedies.

Two previous decisions of this court, however, have held that the Housing Regulations create legal rights and duties enforceable in tort by private parties. In Whetzel v. Jess Fisher Management Co., 282 F.2d 943 (D.C. Cir. 1960), we followed the leading case of Altz v. Leiberson, 134 N.E. 703 (N.Y. 1922), in holding (1) that the housing code altered the common law rule and imposed a duty to repair upon the landlord, and (2) that a right of action accrued to a

---

43. In Brown v. Southall Realty Co., 237 A.2d 834 (D.C. Ct. App. 1968), the District of Columbia Court of Appeals held that unsafe and unsanitary conditions existing at the beginning of the tenancy and known to the landlord rendered any lease of those premises illegal and void.

44. See Edwards v. Habib, 397 F.2d 687, 701 (D.C. Cir. 1968); 2 R. Powell, *supra* Note 10, ¶221 [1] at 183; President's Committee on Urban Housing, *A Decent Home* 96 (1968).

tenant injured by the landlord's breach of this duty. As Judge Cardozo wrote in *Leiberson*:

> We may be sure that the framers of this statute, when regulating tenement life, had uppermost in thought the care of those who are unable to care for themselves. The Legislature must have known that unless repairs in the rooms of the poor were made by the landlord, they would not be made by any one. The duty imposed became commensurate with the need. The right to seek redress is not limited to the city or its officers. The right extends to all whom there was a purpose to protect.

134 N.E. at 704. Recently, in Kanelos v. Kettler, 406 F.2d 951, 953 (D.C. Cir. 1968), we reaffirmed our position in *Whetzel*, holding that "the Housing Regulations did impose maintenance obligations upon appellee [landlord] which he was not free to ignore."[52]

The District of Columbia Court of Appeals gave further effect to the Housing Regulations in Brown v. Southall Realty Co., 237 A.2d 834 (1968). There the landlord knew at the time the lease was signed that housing code violations existed which rendered the apartment "unsafe and unsanitary." Viewing the lease as a contract, the District of Columbia Court of Appeals held that the premises were let in violation of Sections 2304 and 2501 of the Regulations and that the lease, therefore, was void as an illegal contract. In the light of *Brown*, it is clear not only that the housing code creates privately enforceable duties as held in *Whetzel*, but that the basic validity of every housing contract depends upon substantial compliance with the housing code at the beginning of the lease term. The *Brown* court relied particularly upon Section 2501 of the Regulations which provides:

> Every premises accommodating one or more habitations shall be maintained and kept in repair so as to provide decent living accommodations for the occupants. This part of this Code contemplates more than mere basic repairs and maintenance to keep out the elements; its purpose is to include repairs and maintenance designed to make a premises or neighborhood healthy and safe.

By its terms, this section applies to maintenance and repair during the lease term. Under the *Brown* holding, serious failure to comply with this section before the lease term begins renders the contract void. We think it untenable to find that this section has no effect on the contract after it has been signed. To the contrary, by signing the lease the landlord has undertaken a continuing obligation to the tenant to maintain the premises in accordance with all applicable law.

This principle of implied warranty is well established. Courts often imply relevant law into contracts to provide a remedy for any damage caused by one party's illegal conduct. In a case closely analogous to the present ones, the Illinois Supreme Court held that a builder who constructed a house in violation of the Chicago building code had breached his contract with the buyer:

> [The] law existing at the time and place of the making of the contract is deemed a part of the contract, as though expressly referred to or incorporated in it. . . .

---

52. *Kanelos* and *Whetzel* have effectively overruled, on the basis of the enactment of the housing code, Bowles v. Mahoney, 202 F.2d 320 (D.C. Cir. 1952) (two-to-one decision, Judge Bazelon dissenting).

The rationale for this rule is that the parties to the contract would have expressed that which the law implies "had they not supposed that it was unnecessary to speak of it because the law provided for it." . . . Consequently, the courts, in construing the existing law as part of the express contract, are not reading into the contract provisions different from those expressed and intended by the parties, as defendants contend, but are merely construing the contract in accordance with the intent of the parties.[56]

We follow the Illinois court in holding that the housing code must be read into housing contracts — a holding also required by the purposes and the structure of the code itself.[57] The duties imposed by the Housing Regulations may not be waived or shifted by agreement if the Regulations specifically place the duty upon the lessor.[58]

Criminal penalties are provided if these duties are ignored. This regulatory structure was established by the Commissioners because, in their judgment, the grave conditions in the housing market required serious action. Yet official enforcement of the housing code has been far from uniformly effective. Innumerable studies have documented the desperate condition of rental housing in the District of Columbia and in the nation. In view of these circumstances, we think the conclusion reached by the Supreme Court of Wisconsin as to the effect of a housing code on the old common law rule cannot be avoided:

> [The] legislature has made a policy judgment — that it is socially (and politically) desirable to impose these duties on a property owner — which has rendered the old common law rule obsolete. To follow the old rule of no implied warranty of habitability in leases would, in our opinion, be inconsistent with the current legislative policy concerning housing standards.[60]

---

56. Schiro v. W. E. Gould & Co., 165 N.E.2d 286, 290 (Ill. 1960). As a general proposition, it is undoubtedly true that parties to a contract intend that applicable law will be complied with by both sides. We recognize, however, that reading statutory provisions into private contracts may have little factual support in the intentions of the particular parties now before us. But, for reasons of public policy, warranties are often implied into contracts by operation of law in order to meet generally prevailing standards of honesty and fair dealing. When the public policy has been enacted into law like the housing code, that policy will usually have deep roots in the expectations and intentions of most people. *See* Costigan, *Implied-in-Fact Contracts and Mutual Assent*, 33 Harv. L. Rev. 376, 383-85 (1920).

57. "The housing and sanitary codes, especially in light of Congress' explicit direction for their enactment, indicate a strong and pervasive congressional concern to secure for the city's slum dwellers decent, or at least safe and sanitary, places to live." Edwards v. Habib, *supra* Note 44, 397 F.2d at 700.

58. Any private agreement to shift the duties would be illegal and unenforceable. The precedents dealing with industrial safety statutes are directly in point:

> [The] only question remaining is whether the courts will enforce or recognize as against a servant an agreement express or implied on his part to waive the performance of a statutory duty of the master imposed for the protection of the servant, and in the interest of the public, and enforceable by criminal prosecution. We do not think they will. To do so would be to nullify the object of the statute.

Narramore v. Cleveland, C., C. & St. L. Ry. Co., 96 F. 298, 302 (6th Cir. 1899). *See* W. Prosser, *Torts* §67 at 468-469 (3d ed. 1964) and cases cited therein.

60. Pines v. Perssion, 111 N.W.2d 409, 412-13 (Wis. 1961).

We therefore hold that the Housing Regulations imply a warranty of habitability, measured by the standards which they set out, into leases of all housing that they cover.

V.

In the present cases, the landlord sued for possession for nonpayment of rent. Under contract principles,[61] however, the tenant's obligation to pay rent is dependent upon the landlord's performance of his obligations, including his warranty to maintain the premises in habitable condition. In order to determine whether any rent is owed to the landlord, the tenants must be given an opportunity to prove the housing code violations alleged as breach of the landlord's warranty.

At trial, the finder of fact must make two findings: (1) whether the alleged violations existed during the period for which past due rent is claimed, and (2) what portion, if any or all, of the tenant's obligation to pay rent was suspended by the landlord's breach. If no part of the tenant's rental obligation is found to have been suspended, then a judgment for possession may issue forthwith. On the other hand, if the jury determines that the entire rental obligation has been extinguished by the landlord's total breach, then the action for possession on the ground of nonpayment must fail.[64]

The jury may find that part of the tenant's rental obligation has been suspended but that part of the unpaid back rent is indeed owed to the landlord. In these circumstances, no judgment for possession should issue if the tenant agrees to pay the partial rent found to be due. If the tenant refuses to pay the partial amount, a judgment for possession may then be entered.

The judgment of the District of Columbia Court of Appeals is reversed and the cases are remanded for further proceedings consistent with this opinion.[67]

Circuit Judge Robb concurs in the result and in Parts IV-B and V of the opinion.

61. In extending all contract remedies for breach to the parties to a lease, we include an action for specific performance of the landlord's implied warranty of habitability.

64. As soon as the landlord made the necessary repairs rent would again become due. Our holding, of course, affects only eviction for nonpayment of rent. The landlord is free to seek eviction at the termination of the lease or on any other legal ground.

67. Appellants in the present cases offered to pay rent into the registry of the court during the present action. We think this is an excellent protective procedure. If the tenant defends against an action for possession on the basis of breach of the landlord's warranty of habitability, the trial court may require the tenant to make future rent payments into the registry of the court as they become due; such a procedure would be appropriate only while the tenant remains in possession. The escrowed money will, however, represent rent for the period between the time the landlord files suit and the time the case comes to trial. In the normal course of litigation, the only factual question at trial would be the condition of the apartment during the time the landlord alleged rent was due and not paid.

As a general rule, the escrowed money should be apportioned between the landlord and the tenant after trial on the basis of the finding of rent actually due for the period at issue in the suit. To insure fair apportionment, however, we think either party should be permitted to amend its complaint or answer at any time before trial, to allege a change in the condition of the apartment. In this event, the finder of fact should make a separate finding as to the condition of the apartment at the time at which the amendment was filed. This new finding will have no effect upon the original action; it will only affect the distribution of the escrowed rent paid after the filing of the amendment.

Notes and Questions

James Skelly Wright

1. Judge J. Skelly Wright had tremendous impact on the American law of landlord-tenant. *Javins* is one of a trilogy of major landlord-tenant opinions that he authored. In Edwards v. Habib, 397 F.2d 687, *cert. denied*, 393 U.S. 1016 (1969), Yvonne Edwards rented housing from Nathan Habib on a month-to-month basis. She soon complained to the city about sanitary code violations, and the resulting city inspection found 40 violations that the landlord was ordered to correct. Instead, Habib gave Edwards 30 days' notice to vacate the premises pursuant to the D.C. statute governing month-to-month tenancies. But Judge Wright explained that public policy and the interpretation of the D.C. housing and sanitary codes preclude an eviction for reporting violations of the housing code to the authorities. Then, in Robinson v. Diamond Housing Corp., 463 F.2d 853 (D.C. Cir. 1972), a landlord sued to evict a tenant who had stopped paying rent. The landlord gave Robinson 30 days' notice to vacate, claiming it would withdraw the dwelling unit from the market rather than make repairs. The court refused to allow the eviction to proceed so long as the motive was to retaliate against the tenant for challenging the conditions in the premises. Together *Edwards* and *Robinson* developed the retaliatory eviction doctrine, which most states have adopted in some form by statute or common law decision.

In 1982, Judge Wright reflected on his involvement in these cases in a letter to Professor Rabin, published in Edward R. Rabin, *The Revolution in Residential Landlord-Tenant Law: Causes and Consequences*, 69 Cornell L. Rev. 517, 549 (1984):

Why the revolution in landlord-tenant law is largely traceable to the 1960's rather than decades before I really cannot say with any degree of certainty. Unquestionably the Vietnam War and the civil rights movement of the 1960's did cause people to question existing institutions and authorities. And perhaps this inquisition reached the judiciary itself. Obviously, judges cannot be unaware of what all people know and feel.

With reference to your specific question, I was indeed influenced by the fact that, during the nationwide racial turmoil of the sixties and the unrest caused by the injustice of racially selective service in Vietnam, most of the tenants in Washington D.C. slums were poor and black and most of the landlords were rich and white. There is no doubt in my mind that these conditions played a subconscious role in influencing my landlord and tenant decisions.

I came to Washington in April 1962 after being born and raised in New Orleans, Louisiana for 51 years. I had never been exposed, either as a judge or as a lawyer, to the local practice of law which, of course, included landlord and tenant cases. I was Assistant U.S. Attorney, U.S. Attorney, and then U.S. District Court judge in New Orleans before I joined the U.S. Court of Appeals in Washington. It was my first exposure to landlord and tenant cases, the U.S. Court of Appeals here being a writ court to the local court system at the time. I didn't like what I saw, and I did what I could to ameliorate, if not eliminate, the injustice involved in the way many of the poor were required to live in the nation's capital.

I offer no apology for not following more closely the legal precedents which had cooperated in creating the conditions that I found unjust.

Sincerely,

s/J. Skelly Wright

2. Why is the warranty of habitability considered "revolutionary"? It goes beyond the covenant of quiet enjoyment, which protects tenants from actual eviction and constructive eviction. The warranty imposes an affirmative obligation on the landlord to maintain the premises. The covenant of quiet enjoyment does no such thing, and is consistent with the traditional caveat emptor regime. Moreover, to use constructive eviction, the tenant must abandon the premises, but there is no such requirement to invoke the warranty of habitability.

3. Almost all states now imply a warranty of habitability for residential leases. In many states, the warranty is common law or "judge made," as in *Javins*. In a number of states, the warranty instead comes from a statute. The scope of the warranty varies from state to state. *Javins* anchors the warranty to the local housing code. In other jurisdictions, habitability standards are not defined solely by housing codes. A substantial defect may violate the warranty, especially if it impairs health or safety, even if there is no housing code violation. The warranty can extend beyond defects in the structure itself. The failure to provide essential facilities or services can breach the warranty. *E.g.*, URLTA §2.104(a)(5) (landlord must provide for trash removal); Trentacost v. Brussel, 412 A.2d 436 (N.J. 1980) (absence of lock on entry door in common area of multi-family building breaches implied warranty; landlord must furnish reasonable safeguards to protect tenant from foreseeable criminal activity).

4. Is the warranty of habitability really a creature of contract law? If it is, shouldn't the parties be allowed to disclaim or modify the warranty? Most states, whether their warranty is judicially crafted or statutory, follow *Javins* to prohibit waiver. The Restatement, however, waffles. It permits agreements that modify the warranty and the remedies available to the tenant, provided the agreement is not "unconscionable or significantly against public policy." *Restatement (Second) of Property (Landlord Tenant)* §5.6 (1977).

5. Tenant remedies for breach of habitability are generally derived from contract law when the tenant's claim is for loss of use and enjoyment of the premises, rather than personal injury to the tenant or third persons. The available remedies, however, can vary considerably from state to state. Widely accepted remedies include the following:

- *Damages*, which can be measured several different ways: (1) fair rental value as repaired less fair rental value in the unrepaired condition; (2) agreed rent less fair rental value in the unrepaired condition; (3) a percentage reduction of the agreed rent, based upon the extent of the landlord's breach.
- *Termination* of the lease, accomplished by the tenant giving notice to the landlord while the premises are uninhabitable.
- *Specific performance*, whereby the landlord is compelled to make repairs or take other appropriate action to make the premises habitable.
- "*Repair and deduct*," whereby the tenant repairs the premises to make them habitable and deducts the cost from the rent. States recognizing this remedy require that the tenant first notify the landlord of the need for repairs and give him a reasonable period of time to make the repairs himself.
- *Rent withholding / rent abatement / rent escrow*. These actions, allowed by some courts, are procedural and are not substantively different than the damage remedies described above. If the tenant has the right to withhold or abate rent, this means that for the time being, while the habitability dispute is being adjudicated, the tenant may pay less than the agreed-upon rent (in some instances, the tenant pays no rent). Once a decision on the merits is

made, the landlord is able to collect all the accrued and unpaid rent, less the damages caused by the breach of the warranty of habitability. Rent escrow protects both parties from the risk that the other party will become insolvent after a decision is made on the merits of the tenant's habitability claim.

6. Commercial tenants have asked courts to imply a warranty of quality, analogous to the implied warranty of habitability. Should they prevail? The overwhelming majority of courts have rejected their pleas, reasoning that there are key differences between residential and commercial transactions: Housing codes do not apply to commercial premises, parties to commercial leases have relatively equal bargaining power, and commercial tenants have different expectations than residential ones. One exception is Davidow v. Inwood North Professional Group-Phase One, 747 S.W.2d 373 (Tex. 1988). Inwood rented medical office space to Dr. Davidow, promising to provide air conditioning, electricity, hot water, janitor and maintenance services, light fixtures, and security services. Shortly after moving in, he encountered the following problems: "The air conditioning did not work properly, often causing temperatures inside the office to rise above eighty-five degrees. The roof leaked whenever it rained, resulting in stained tiles and rotting, mildewed carpet. Patients were directed away from certain areas during rain so that they would not be dripped upon in the waiting room. Pests and rodents often infested the office. The hallways remained dark because hallway lights were unreplaced for months. Cleaning and maintenance were not provided. The parking lot was constantly filled with trash. Hot water was not provided, and on one occasion Dr. Davidow went without electricity for several days because Inwood failed to pay the electric bill. Several burglaries and various acts of vandalism occurred." Dr. Davidow finally vacated, and then Inwood sued him for unpaid rent. The court of appeals granted judgment to the landlord based upon the doctrine that covenants in leases are independent, but the supreme court reversed, holding that "there is an implied warranty of suitability by the landlord in a commercial lease that the premises are suitable for their intended commercial purpose. This warranty means that at the inception of the lease there are no latent defects in the facilities that are vital to the use of the premises for their intended commercial purpose and that these essential facilities will remain in a suitable condition."

7. As an alternative to recognition of an implied warranty of quality, under some facts commercial tenants can prevail if the state overturns the doctrine of independent covenants. In Wesson v. Leone Enterprises, 774 N.E.2d 611 (Mass. 2002), a commercial landlord breached its covenant to repair. After making a series of complaints, the tenant vacated the premises. The landlord brought action for rents for the remainder of the term. The tenant's constructive eviction defense failed because the leaks, although interfering with the tenant's business, did not make the premises untenantable. Nevertheless, the tenant won, the court holding: "we abandon the common-law rule of independent covenants in commercial leases in favor of the modern rule of mutually dependent covenants. . . . In applying the rule of mutually dependent covenants to the facts present in this case, we conclude that a landlord's failure to keep the roof of his building in good repair deprived the tenant of a substantial benefit significant to the purpose for which the lease was entered. Consequently, the tenant had the right to terminate the lease and recover reasonable relocation costs." How does this approach differ from *Davidow*? Would Dr. Davidow have prevailed under *Wesson* without the need for an implied warranty of suitability?

8. In *Javins*, Judge Wright extolled the utility of housing codes. The number of housing codes in the United States jumped from 56 in 1954 to 4,904 in 1968, thanks to the Workable Program Requirement of the federal Housing Act of 1954. Roger A. Cunningham, *The New Implied and Statutory Warranties of Habitability in Residential Leases: From Contract to Status*, 16 Urb. L. Ann. 3, 13-14 (1979). Housing codes are remarkably detailed. They contain standards for floors, walls, toilets, sinks, radiators, heat, running water, electricity, the permissible number of people per dwelling, and countless other details. They also contain general requirements that premises be kept in "reasonably good repair" or "safe, clean and fit for human habitation." But housing codes are only sporadically enforced. (For a notable exception, see City and County of San Francisco v. Sainez, 92 Cal. Rptr. 2d 418 (Ct. App. 2000) (approving a $663,000 fine against a landlord for repeated housing code violations).) There is also an ongoing academic debate about the efficacy of housing code enforcement. Judge Posner has argued that "housing code enforcement leads to a substantial reduction in the supply of low-income housing . . . coupled with a substantial rise in the price of the remaining supply." Richard Posner, *Economic Analysis of Law* 482-85 (6th ed. 2003). Professor Bruce Ackerman admits that "housing codes often contain obsolete or impractical requirements; successful code enforcement does not yield great political dividends for the incumbent administration; since code enforcement is such humdrum work, it does not often attract personnel of high quality; present methods of enforcing compliance with code requirements are woefully deficient; [and] finally, the poor often lack the political power to maintain a successful regulatory effort on their behalf." Bruce Ackerman, *Regulating Slum Housing Markets on Behalf of the Poor: Of Housing Codes, Housing Subsidies, and Income Distribution Policy*, 80 Yale L.J. 1093 (1971). Nonetheless, Ackerman contends that more aggressive housing code enforcement is justified as an efficient means of shifting resources from wealthy landlords to poor tenants. Landlords will lack the incentive to remove their properties from the housing market even if the costs of code improvement are imposed on them. In addition, housing advocates defend code enforcement as a means of improving both the quality and quantity of housing for the poor by pressuring negligent owners to sell their properties to tenants or community organizations.

The next case considers whether a landlord has a duty to keep premises, including common areas, reasonably safe from the threat of criminal violence. The case analyzes the issues using tort-law principles. Instead, can the problem be framed as one of contract law? Would it make a difference?

■ CASTANEDA v. OLSHER
Supreme Court of California, 2007
162 P.3d 610

WERDEGAR, Justice. Defendants George Olsher, Paule Olsher and P & G Enterprises (collectively Olsher) own a mobilehome park in which plaintiff Ernest Castaneda lived. Plaintiff was shot and injured while he was a bystander to a gang confrontation involving a resident of the mobilehome across the street from his. He sued Olsher contending Olsher had breached a duty not to rent to known gang members or to evict them when they harass other tenants. The superior court granted a defense motion for nonsuit after presentation of plaintiff's case, but the Court of Appeal reversed. . . .

Olsher has owned the Winterland-Westways mobilehome park in El Centro since at least 1991. Beverly Rogers and her son, Rodney Hicks, lived at and managed the 60-space park. On the night he was shot, November 9, 1996, plaintiff (who was 17 years old) lived in a mobilehome on space 10 with his grandmother and older sister.

The mobilehome on space 23, across the street from plaintiff's, was occupied by Paul Levario [the son of Carmen Levario, who rented space 23].

A former El Centro police officer who had specialized in studying and controlling local criminal gangs identified Paul Levario as a member of the Northside El Centro gang. According to the police report and an eyewitness, a fellow Northsider who was visiting Levario, Manuel Viloria, fired the shot that injured plaintiff.

On the night of his injury, plaintiff attended a party outside the mobilehome park. Sometime after 1:00 or 2:00 A.M., he drove home with three friends. Plaintiff went inside his mobilehome briefly to let his sister know they were there, while his friends waited in the car. A few minutes later, another car, with four young men in it, pulled up behind plaintiff's car. Around the same time, two young men came out of the mobilehome across the street and . . . started "exchanging words and gang slurs" with the men in the second car. . . . One of the men in the second car yelled, "Westside Centro, Westside Centro," while the men from the mobilehome called out, "Northside Centro." After a few minutes . . . "shots were fired." Plaintiff, who had reemerged from his home to his front porch area, was hit in the back.

Two or three months before the shooting, plaintiff's grandmother, Joyce Trow, complained to Rogers about people Trow thought looked like gang members hanging around the mobilehome park and breaking the bulbs in the outdoor lights. According to Trow, Rogers responded that there was "one more batch" moving in "right across from" Trow. When asked whether she could prevent this, Rogers said she could not: she had talked to George Olsher, but he had told her, "Go ahead and rent to them. Their money is as good as yours," or something to that effect.

Joyce Trow testified that for approximately two months before the shooting she saw people dressed like gang members congregating at the mobilehome across the street from hers. Her granddaughter (and plaintiff's sister), Diana Castaneda, encountered groups of four or five men, including the mobilehome owner's son, dressed in baggy pants and flannel shirts, drinking from 40-ounce bottles outside the mobilehome on space 23 over the month before plaintiff was shot. Because they whistled and hooted at her sometimes, she felt "a small amount of fear" and tried to avoid attracting their attention, covering herself up and walking quickly between her car and her home. Diana Castaneda told her grandmother about the incidents, and Trow testified she conveyed her granddaughter's complaint to Rogers. . . .

Another tenant, Monica Preciado-Langford, testified that when she walked with her small children past space 23, the "boys hanging out" there, who wore bandanas or Pendleton jackets, would sometimes kick their pit bull in the mouth to make it growl. Preciado-Langford asked the boys to stop, but they ignored her. She complained to Rogers about this group of boys, as well as about those at space 24, who were throwing rocks, and about lights that were broken at the park. . . .

Evidence was presented of two prior gunshot incidents related to the mobilehome park. In August 1995, a bullet — fired by an unknown shooter from a location estimated to be outside the mobilehome park — went through an occupied mobilehome, but did not hit anyone. In early 1996, during what Rodney Hicks, Rogers's son and assistant, was told was a gang confrontation, shots were fired on a property contiguous to the mobilehome park. A boy who lived at the park, seen trying to hide a gun after the shooting, was arrested that evening and never returned to the park; the management undertook efforts to evict his family. Rogers knew or was informed of both incidents.

Prior to the shooting that injured plaintiff, there had also been drug sales and apparent gang members at the mobilehome park. Rogers identified residents of four mobilehomes, other than the occupants of the mobilehome on space 23, whom she thought were members or aspiring members of gangs (including the boy arrested in the shooting incident on the property next to the park). Gang graffiti, including references to "Westside Centro," was seen regularly at the park. Rogers and Hicks painted it out "every day." Between 1993 and 1996, Hicks testified, he saw what he believed to be drug sales at the park "once or twice a week." . . .

Discussion

A landlord generally owes a tenant the duty, arising out of their special relationship, to take reasonable measures to secure areas under the landlord's control against foreseeable criminal acts of third parties. Delgado v. Trax Bar & Grill, 113 P.3d 1159, 1165 (Cal. 2005). In each case, however, the existence and scope of a property owner's duty to protect against third party crime is a question of law for the court to resolve. *Id.* at 1166-1167.

In determining a duty's existence and scope, our precedents call for consideration of several factors: "[T]he foreseeability of harm to the plaintiff, the degree of certainty that the plaintiff suffered injury, the closeness of the connection between the defendant's conduct and the injury suffered, the moral blame attached to the defendant's conduct, the policy of preventing future harm, the extent of the burden to the defendant and consequences to the community of imposing a duty to exercise care with resulting liability for breach, and the availability, cost, and prevalence of insurance for the risk involved." Rowland v. Christian, 443 P.2d 561, 564 (Cal. 1968). Foreseeability and the extent of the burden to the defendant are ordinarily the crucial considerations, but in a given case one or more of the other *Rowland* factors may be determinative of the duty analysis. *Delgado, supra* at 1166 n.15. . . .

We begin by identifying the specific action or actions plaintiff claims defendants were obliged to take to protect him from being shot.

As he did in the lower courts, plaintiff contends Olsher owed him a duty not to rent space 23 to the Levarios and, once having rented it, to evict them for disturbing and harassing other park residents. Asking rhetorically what Olsher should have done to protect him, plaintiff answers: "When told by Mrs. Rogers that a new bunch of gangsters wanted to move in across from Mrs. Trow, a reasonable person seeking to provide for the safety of his tenants, would just say 'no.'" Plaintiff argues that in light of the danger of violence that accompanies the presence of street gangs and illicit drug dealing, the shooting that injured him was sufficiently foreseeable to justify imposition of a duty to decline to rent to, or to evict, known gang members, duties he characterizes as placing only a "slight" burden on the landlord. Secondarily, plaintiff also contends that having rented to gang members and failed to evict them, Olsher should have hired trained security guards to suppress gang activity at the mobilehome park and should have improved and maintained the park's lighting. . . .

I. DUTY NOT TO RENT TO GANG MEMBERS

Plaintiff emphasizes the threat violent street gangs and associated illicit drug dealing pose to the safety of peaceful Californians and argues the extent of this danger warrants imposing a duty on landlords not to rent to gang members. We agree the threat is of the most serious dimensions and state policy urgently seeks its alleviation. The Legislature has said as much. . . . Street gang activity can often subject residents of an apartment building or mobilehome park to unacceptable levels of fear and risk. But we are not persuaded that imposing a duty on landlords to withhold rental units from those they believe to be gang members is a fair or workable solution to this problem, or one consistent with our state's public policy as a whole. Absent circumstances showing extraordinary foreseeability, we decline to recognize such a duty.

As defendants note, "Gang members do not . . . announce their gang affiliations on housing applications." If landlords regularly face liability for injuries gang members cause on the premises, they will tend to deny rental to anyone who might be a gang member or, even more broadly, to any family one of whose members might be in a gang. The result in many cases would be arbitrary discrimination on the basis of race, ethnicity, family composition, dress and appearance, or reputation. All of these are, in at least some circumstances, illegal and against public policy and could themselves subject the landlord to liability. *See* Gov. Code §§12920, 12955 (Fair Employment and Housing Act provisions stating policy against, and prohibiting, housing discrimination on the basis of race, ancestry or familial status, among other bases); Marina Point, Ltd. v. Wolfson, 640 P.2d 115 (Cal. 1982) (Unruh Civil Rights Act, Civ. Code §51, prohibits a landlord in a large housing complex from excluding families with children: the act "does not permit a business enterprise to exclude an entire class of individuals on the basis of a generalized prediction that the class 'as a whole' is more likely to commit misconduct than some other class of the public"); In re Cox, 474 P.2d 992 (Cal. 1970) (Unruh Civil Rights Act bars discrimination on the basis of unconventional dress and appearance); Orloff v. Los Angeles Turf Club, 227 P.2d 449 (Cal. 1951) (same as to reputation or suspicion of criminal tendencies: "mere suspicion based on past conduct and alleged reputed activities . . . or on conversations . . . with persons considered questionable" did not justify expulsion from a business establishment). Landlords would thus risk liability whichever choice they make, and families whose ethnicity, teenage children, or mode of dress or personal appearance could, to some, suggest a gang association would face an additional obstacle to finding housing.

Plaintiff maintains that when faced with a rental applicant who looks, dresses or talks like a gang member, a landlord should obtain the applicant's criminal record, which plaintiff asserts would be readily available through a commercial investigative service. But resting a duty not to rent to gang members on the availability of such screening would merely shift the trap for landlords to different ground. The landlord would face potential liability for personal injuries if he or she failed to seek out an applicant's criminal record, conducted an insufficiently searching inquiry, or misjudged the record as not reflecting a strong propensity for gang violence and such violence later ensued. In addition, liability for discrimination could arise if the landlord treated applicants differently, depending on their ethnicity, family composition, or appearance, either in deciding whether to obtain a criminal history or in deciding what prior convictions and arrests would disqualify an applicant. The alternative—obtaining full histories on all applicants and their families, and refusing to rent to anyone with arrests or convictions for any crime that could have involved a gang — would involve significant expense and delay for the landlord and unfairly deprive many Californians of housing. Nor is the proposed screening likely to be especially effective; juvenile court records, which are generally confidential by law (Welf. & Inst. Code §827), are presumably not available through the services plaintiff recommends, and even adult criminal records do not necessarily reflect the circumstances of the crime from which a landlord could reliably decide whether renting to the applicant poses a threat of gang violence. We decline to impose such a burdensome, dubiously effective and socially questionable obligation on landlords, at least absent circumstances making gang violence extraordinarily foreseeable.

In this case, plaintiff argues, we do not face any issue of the difficulty for land-lords in discerning gang membership, because Olsher knew — having been told by his manager — that the applicants for space 23 (the Levarios) were gang members. But the manager, Rogers, did not claim any particular certainty or expertise in her identification of gang members. She testified only that she "suspected" some of the young people residing in the mobilehome park were gang members, though she could not identify the gang or gangs; others she characterized as "wannabes," meaning they were not necessarily gang members but aspired to be associated with a gang. . . .

II. DUTY TO EVICT GANG MEMBER TENANTS

Plaintiff contends that having rented to the Levarios, Olsher was obliged to evict them once they began to harass and annoy other residents of the park. This asserted duty requires a different analysis of burden and foreseeability than above. A landlord ordinarily has more opportunity to judge the behavior of an existing tenant than of a rental applicant. In assessing the danger an existing tenant poses, the landlord can rely on his or her own observations or those of a property manager and, where the circumstances make these reliable, on complaints of the other tenants. The risk that landlords will feel compelled to make decisions on discriminatory bases, creating social costs as well as potential legal liability, is thus lessened.

On the other hand, undertaking eviction of a tenant cannot be considered a minimal burden. The expense of evicting a tenant is not necessarily trivial, and eviction typically results in the unit sitting vacant for some period. In some munic-ipalities — and, more to the present point, under the Mobilehome Residency Law — the landlord must provide, and may have to prove, cause for the eviction.[4] Finally, undertaking eviction of a hostile tenant, especially one involved in a violent street gang, could subject the landlord or property manager to retaliatory harass-ment or violence.

Not surprisingly in light of the burden involved, courts in this and other states have recognized a tort duty to evict a vicious or dangerous tenant only in cases where

---

4. As relevant to this case, the Mobilehome Residency Law permits termination of a tenancy for conduct that constitutes a "substantial annoyance" to other residents, Civ. Code §798.56, subd. (b), conviction of specified offenses occurring in the mobilehome park, *id.* subd. (c), and failure to comply with a reasonable rule included in the rental agreement, *id.* subd. (d). The park management must include in the notice of termination a statement of the reasons "with specific facts to permit determi-nation of the date, place, witnesses and circumstances" supporting the termination. Civ. Code §798.57. Under section 798.56, subdivision (d), moreover, the management must give the tenant notice and seven days to cure a rule violation or must have cited the tenant for the same violation three or more times in a 12-month period.

the tenant's behavior made violence toward neighbors or others on the premises highly foreseeable. . . .

We look, then, to the circumstances of this case to see if Olsher was on notice of facts making a gang shooting involving an occupant of the mobilehome on space 23 highly foreseeable. . . .

According to plaintiff's evidence, Olsher was aware of Rogers's belief that one or more members of the Levario family was in a gang; as we have explained, however, Olsher did not have a duty to refuse to rent to applicants his manager thought were gang members. The heightened foreseeability that would justify imposing a duty to evict the Levarios must be found, if anywhere, in their behavior as tenants, as reported to Olsher or his agent, Rogers. The evidence in this regard was that another park resident, Monica Preciado-Langford, had complained to Rogers that occupants of the mobilehome on space 23 or their guests had harassed her and her children by causing a pit bull to growl at them and that a person or persons she had been told lived at space 23 or 24, or both, had broken windows on her car. There was also evidence that four or five men at the mobilehome on space 23 whistled and hooted at plaintiff's sister, making her somewhat fearful, and that these incidents were reported to Rogers. Even coupled with Rogers's belief that the occupants of the mobilehome on space 23 were gang members, the possibility of gun violence established by this evidence does not rise to a level of heightened foreseeability necessary to impose a duty to evict. No one had reported that the Levarios or their guests had used, displayed or possessed a gun at the mobilehome park. Although Rogers suspected that members of the Levario family belonged to a gang, and told Olsher so, she did not identify the gang as Northside Centro. Thus, while Westside Centro graffiti might have suggested members of that group frequented the park, Olsher had no reason to expect a confrontation, involving the Levarios, between the two rival gangs.

In these circumstances, a shoot-out between two rival gangs was not highly foreseeable, and Olsher did not have a tort duty to prevent it by evicting the Levarios. "A landlord is not obliged to institute eviction proceedings whenever a tenant accuses another tenant of harassment." Morton v. Kirkland, 558 A.2d 693, 695 (D.C. 1989).

III. DUTY TO HIRE SECURITY GUARDS AND MAINTAIN BRIGHTER LIGHTING

At oral argument, plaintiff's attorney urged this court, as an alternative to the asserted landlord duties discussed above, to affirm the Court of Appeal's determination that Olsher had a duty to hire and deploy security guards to prevent gang violence in the mobilehome park and to maintain brighter lights in the common areas.

To establish the heightened foreseeability necessary to impose a heavily burdensome duty such as hiring security guards, we have explained, the plaintiff must show the existence of prior similar incidents on the premises or other sufficiently serious "indications of a reasonably foreseeable risk of violent criminal assaults." *Delgado, supra* at 1168. . . .

While insisting defendants should have hired security guards, plaintiff's counsel, at oral argument, also disavowed any claim that a guard would have been able to break up or quell the quickly developing late-night confrontation in which plaintiff was injured. Instead, counsel argued, the simple existence of guard patrols at the mobilehome park would likely have discouraged gangs from congregating there. Be that as it may, the injury in this case did not arise out of a public gang gathering. . . . Paul Levario and *one* other member of the Northside gang, Manuel Viloria, were *inside* the Levario home when the car with Westside gang members drove up and the confrontation began. Plaintiff presented no evidence to suggest that having security guards at the park would likely have deterred Levario from entertaining an individual guest inside his home, nor does common experience suggest any such an effect was likely. . . .

The same is true as to maintenance of the park's common-area lighting. While plaintiff's sister testified the street lights in the area of their mobilehome did not work or were inadequate, Christina Sandoval [one of plaintiff's friends] testified that during the argument leading up to the shooting she could see that one of the occupants of the mobilehome across the street had an object that looked like a gun, and she recognized the gunman from school. Given that the occupants of the mobilehome on space 23 were willing to engage in an armed confrontation with rival gang members where lighting allowed their weapon to be seen and themselves to be recognized, plaintiff simply has not shown that the absence of brighter lights was likely a substantial factor in producing the confrontation and ensuing gunshot. . . .

The judgment of the Court of Appeal is reversed.

KENNARD, Justice, dissenting. This is yet another case in which this court has had to grapple with the issue of a business owner's obligation to undertake efforts to protect others from the criminal acts of third parties. Instead of providing much-needed clarity, this court's decisions in this area have engendered confusion. The core of this confusion is the improper intermingling of two distinct concepts — duty, a question for the court, and breach of that duty, a question for the jury. In treating breach as if it were part of the duty analysis, and thus an issue of law for the trial court to decide, the court usurps the role of the jury as trier of fact.

Unlike the majority here, I would have the jury, not the court, decide whether defendant mobilehome park owners breached their duty to protect tenants from gang-related criminal acts. I agree, however, with the majority that under the multifactor test this court established in Rowland v. Christian, policy considerations support the conclusion that landlords have no duty to refuse to rent to individuals suspected of being members of a street gang. . . .

E. TENANT'S USE OF PREMISES

■ **STROUP v. CONANT**
Supreme Court of Oregon, 1974
520 P.2d 337

TONGUE, Justice. This is a suit to rescind a lease of space in a building in which the tenant undertook to operate the "Birds & Bees Adult Book Store." Plaintiff's complaint alleged that she was induced to enter into the lease in reliance upon the false representation by defendant that he intended to use the leased premises for the sale of watches, wallets, chains, novelties and a few books and magazines and imported items. Defendant appeals from a decree rescinding the lease. We affirm.

Defendant contends that there was no evidence of misrepresentation, reliance or damage. It thus becomes necessary to summarize the evidence, although not in completely unexpurgated form.

Defendant states in his brief that he informed plaintiff of his intent to sell "a variety of items," including magazines, "for adults only." Plaintiff, however, denies any such conversation. Plaintiff's son, who represented her in negotiating the lease, testified that defendant called him by telephone in response to a newspaper advertisement for lease of the premises, located on S.E. Division Street in Portland; that he asked defendant what his business was and was told that defendant intended to conduct "a variety type operation" and to sell watches, wallets, chains, trinkets and a few books and novelties, but did not say that he intended to operate an "adult book store" or to sell pornographic material.

Plaintiff's attorney then prepared a one-year lease, with an option to renew for one additional year. The lease provided, among other things, that the premises were to be used "for the sale of gifts, novelties, etc." Defendant then went to the lawyer's office and signed the lease. He was not present when plaintiff later signed the lease. The lease, as thus executed, was dated March 25, 1973.

On April 6, 1973, plaintiff's son received a telephone call from another tenant who operated a gun shop in the same building complaining that "you've ruined me" and informing him of the adult book store in the adjacent premises. Plaintiff testified that her son had reported to her that the premises had been rented for a variety and gift store and that she would not have signed the lease if she had known of defendant's intent to operate an adult book store on the premises. Upon visiting the premises, plaintiff's son found large signs in the store windows, and upon going inside he saw no watches, wallets, chains or novelties for sale, but only racks of pornographic magazines and books. He then called plaintiff's lawyer.

During the next few days one of the residents in the neighborhood, after going into the store and purchasing three magazines whose titles had best be left unstated, circulated a petition of "protest" upon which he secured 300 signatures in the neighborhood, which he described as "predominantly residential." The two other tenants in the building, the operators of a meat market and a paint store, also complained to plaintiff that the adjacent adult book store "spoils their business," and plaintiff was "deluged" with telephone calls.

On April 10, 1973, plaintiff's attorney wrote a letter to defendant charging him with violating the terms of the lease and demanding that he vacate the premises immediately. At that time, however, plaintiff did not tender the return of the first and last months' rent, as previously paid by defendant, claiming that she was entitled to that money.

On May 4, 1973, after defendant had apparently refused to move out, plaintiff filed a complaint seeking to rescind the lease and offering to "do complete equity and restore the status quo." Defendant filed a general denial and awaited trial, which was held on August 8, 1973.

Plaintiff then offered testimony of the foregoing facts. Defendant, in addition to testifying that he informed plaintiff by telephone of his intent to operate an adult book store (which she denied), stated that it "would be pretty hard to describe over a phone." He also testified that he didn't "have anything pornographic," and that although his literature was "devoted to various states or types of sexual activity . . . there is a lot of reading that is written by doctors." Defendant agreed, however, with the observation by the learned trial judge, that in talking about adult books he was "not talking about Charles Dickens or Thomas Wolfe." Upon examination of the pictorial "literature" offered in evidence it appears that this may well have been the understatement of this permissive age. Defendant also said that he exhibited moving pictures, presumably in "living color."

Based upon this record we have no hesitation in holding that there was ample basis to support the decision by this trial court in its decree rescinding this lease, dated September 17, 1973.

Even assuming that one who seeks to rent premises for the operation of such an "adult book store" and who does not disclose the nature of his intended operation may, by remaining silent, be able to acquire a binding lease from either an unsuspecting or a willing landlord, regardless of neighborhood protests, this is not such a case. . . .

There was ample evidence of misrepresentation by "half-truths and concealment of special knowledge" in this case, as well as reliance thereon by plaintiff, despite defendant's testimony to the contrary.

As for defendant's contention that plaintiff failed to show that she suffered any damage so as to entitle her to rescind the lease, we have previously held that proof of pecuniary damage is not a requirement for rescission. Furtado v. Gemmell, 408 P.2d 733 (Or. 1965). . . .

And if evidence of damage is required in such a case there was ample evidence that plaintiff suffered damage not only in the form of humiliation and embarrassment, but also by the potential loss of other tenants in the event that defendant's operation had continued. . . .

For these reasons we affirm the decree of the trial court.

Notes and Questions

1. Most written leases include express use restrictions. An apartment lease provides: "The leased premises shall be used only as, and for the purposes of, a private dwelling, excluding from any part thereof any use in connection with the practice of any profession, trade or craft." How does this clause apply to: (a) A computer technician starting a computer servicing and repair business, where he spends most of his time at clients' offices but does some work at home? (b) A seller of Amway products using a spare bedroom for storage of inventory, records, and related tasks? (c) An attorney bringing work home in a briefcase?

Suppose a tenant rents a house in a neighborhood that is primarily residential but has some professional businesses. The landlord previously rented the house to tenants who used it solely for residential purposes. May the tenant use it for business?

2. Compliance with laws is dealt with in some written leases. An apartment lease provides: "I agree not to use or permit the premises to be used for any illegal, or improper purposes, not to permit any disturbance, noise or annoyances whatsoever, detrimental to the inhabitants of the premises or to the reasonable comfort of the other inhabitants of this building or its neighbors." In the absence of such language, does the landlord have the right to complain that the tenant's use of the premises violates a law?

■ **BROWN v. DuBOIS**
Marion Municipal Court, Ohio, 1988
532 N.E.2d 223

ROGERS, Judge. This matter came before the court for trial on the complaint of the plaintiffs-landlords alleging that the defendants-tenants removed certain property from the leasehold upon termination of their lease. Plaintiffs allege that the items removed were fixtures and had become a part of the real estate and that the defendants had no right to remove them. The defendants in response denied that their removal of the property was improper.

Upon trial, the evidence demonstrated that the tenants had installed approximately five rooms of wall-to-wall carpet and certain track lighting appliances. It is uncontested that the defendants conducted a retail business in the premises and that the track lighting was used to highlight certain items on display for sale. Further, it is uncontested that the written lease between the parties was executed approximately on October 16, 1981, for a term of five years ending October 31, 1986, that the defendants vacated the property on or before October 31, 1986, and that the items in question were removed prior to that date. Also, the lease contains a specific provision granting the lessees the right to remove "trade fixtures."

The issue before the court is whether the track lighting appliances and wall-to-wall carpet are, in fact, fixtures or whether they have retained their identity as chattels or personalty.

> The term fixture itself, although always applied to articles of the nature of personal property which have been affixed to land, has been used with different significations, until it has become a term of ambiguous meaning. And this ambiguity which has attended the use of this word in various adjudications, and by different writers, has been productive of much of the uncertainty, which has perplexed investigations falling under this branch of the law. The term fixture has been used by various writers and in numerous reported decisions, as denoting personal chattels annexed to land which may be severed and removed against the will of the owner of the freehold, by the party who has annexed them, or his personal representatives. . . .

> There may be some propriety in this definition of the term when confined in its application to the relation of landlord and tenant, or tenant for life or years and remainderman or reversioner, to which several of the elementary authors, have chiefly confined their attention. But it does not appear to express the accurate meaning of the term in its general application. An article attached to the realty but which is removable against the will of the owner of the land, has not lost the nature and incidents of chattel property. It is still movable property, passes to the executor, and not to the heir, on the death of the owner, and may be taken on execution and sold as other chattels, etc. A removable fixture as a term of general application, is a solecism — a contradiction in words. There does not appear to be any necessity or propriety in classifying movable articles, which may be for temporary purposes somewhat attached to the land under any general denomination distinguishing them from other chattel property. . . .

> It is an ancient maxim of the law, that whatever becomes fixed to the realty, thereby becomes accessory to the freehold, and partakes of all its legal incidents and properties, and cannot be severed and removed without the consent of the owner. *Quic quid plantatur, solo, solo cedit*, is the language of antiquity in which the maxim has been expressed. The term *fixture*, in its ordinary signification, is expressive of the act of annexation, and denotes the change which has occurred in the nature and the legal incidents of the property; and it appears to be not only appropriate but necessary to distinguish this class of property from moveable property, possessing the nature and incidents of chattels. It is in this sense, that the term is used, in far the greater part of the adjudicated cases. . . . It is said that this rule has been greatly relaxed by exceptions to it, established in favor of trade, and also in favor of the tenant, as between landlord and tenant. And the attempt to establish the whole doctrine of fixtures upon these exceptions to the general rule, has occasioned much confusion and misunderstanding on this subject.

Teaff v. Hewitt, 1 Ohio St. 511, 524-25 (1853).

While the term "trade fixtures" may be a misnomer, precedent and usage have given us some standards by which to define the term.

> "Trade fixtures" are those which the tenant places on demised premises to promote the purpose of his occupation, and which he may remove during his term. In dealing with trade fixtures, the distinction to be observed is between the business which is carried on upon the premises, and the premises themselves. The former is personal in nature, and articles that are merely accessory to the business, and have been put upon the premises for this purpose, and not as accessions to the real estate, retain the personal character of the principal to which they belong and are subservient. But articles which have been annexed to the premises as accessory to it, whatever business may be carried on there, and not peculiarly for the benefit of the present business, which may be of temporary duration, become subservient to the realty and acquire its legal character.

50 *Ohio Jurisprudence 3d* (1984) 119-20, Fixtures, Section 21.

It is clear to the court that the track lighting appliances installed by the defendants were uniquely adapted to the purposes of their business and fit squarely within the usual connotation of the term "trade fixtures." At the time of the execution of the lease, the parties clearly evidenced their intention to allow the removal of such items and the defendants cannot be held liable for exercising their rights under the lease.

However, the issue of the right to remove carpet is not as clearly defined nor as easily resolved. Wall-to-wall carpeting has been held to be a fixture where it was cut to fit a dwelling and nailed or stapled into place. Merchants & Mechanics Fed. Sav. & Loan Assn. of Springfield v. Herald, 201 N.E.2d 237 (Ohio App. 1964); Exchange Leasing Corp. v. Finster N. Aegen, Inc., 218 N.E.2d 633 (Ohio App. 1966). Carpet may be said to be equally adaptable to either the unique purposes of the tenant, or to the structure in general regardless of the use to which it is put, thereby suggesting its installation renders it a fixture. However, even the above-cited cases suggest that the court should inquire further and consider additional factors such as the intention of the tenant and the possibility of windfall gain versus unfair deprivation.

The general rule has been stated that a tenant retains the right to remove articles which the tenant places in or on the leasehold during the term of the lease, which items were so placed to enhance the tenant's use or enjoyment of the premises. This rule applies not only to chattels which have retained their character as personalty, but also to chattels which would be classed as fixtures if emplaced by the owner of the leasehold property. While it is widely recognized that this rule applies to chattels installed for trade purposes, the rule also applies to articles which have been installed for purposes which are ornamental or merely enhanced comfort and convenience. *Teaff, supra.* Early cases established this rule based upon public policy for the encouragement of trade and the most profitable use of the leased premises. However, more recent decisions imply a contract for removal of such chattels under the doctrine of unjust enrichment and concern themselves with the intention of the parties as affected by the unique relationship of landlord and tenant and inferred from all other circumstances in the case. 50 *Ohio Jurisprudence 3d* (1984) 109, Fixtures, Section 14.

The landmark case of *Teaff, supra*, is still the foundation of the law in the state of Ohio, and in the country generally, as to when a chattel personal becomes a chattel real or a fixture. The *Teaff* court set forth the following standards at 529-30:

> . . . the united application of the following requisites will be found the safest criterion of a fixture:
> 1st. Actual annexation to the realty, or something appurtenant thereto.
> 2d. Appropriation to the use or purpose of that part of the realty with which it is connected.
> 3d. The intention of the party making the annexation, to make the article a permanent accession to the freehold — this intention being inferred from the *nature* of the article affixed, the *relation* and *situation* of *the party* making the annexation, the structure and mode of annexation, and the purpose or use for which the annexation has been made. (Emphasis *sic*.)

This general rule has been reviewed, examined, reaffirmed and refined by the Ohio Supreme Court. "We reaffirm that such a determination must be made in light of the particular facts of each case, taking into account such facts as the nature of the property; the manner in which it is annexed to the realty; the purpose for which annexation is made; the intention of the annexing party to make the property a part of the realty and dedicate it irrevocably to the realty for a particular use; the degree of difficulty and the extent of any economic loss involved in thereafter removing it from the realty; and the damage to the severed property which removal would cause." Masheter v. Boehm, 307 N.E.2d 533, 540 (Ohio 1974). The *Masheter* court indicated a desire to define a "proper rule of law, which provides that degree of flexibility and accommodation to circumstances necessary to ensure that . . . [the parties] will be dealt with fairly, with neither enjoying a windfall gain nor suffering unfair deprivation." *Masheter, supra* at 540.

Considering the evidence in the case at bar in light of the *Teaff* and *Masheter* standards, the court makes the following findings of fact: (1) that the carpeting at issue was securely attached to the realty by means of "tackless strips" which were nailed to the floor; (2) for the purpose of enhancing the appearance and comfort of the leased property; (3) there seemed to be little difficulty removing the carpet; (4) the plaintiffs failed to demonstrate any actual economic loss resulting from the removal although the removal caused some damage to the floors of the building; (5) that retention of the carpet by the lessors would allow them only a slight gain due to the age and use of the carpet; (6) and it would also appear from the evidence that neither party contemplated the retail establishment opening its doors to the public without some renovation, repair or covering of the original floors. Since the condition of the floors and the building in general was obvious, the court can reasonably infer from the parties' negotiations that the tenants intended to improve the premises in general and the floor in particular. This conclusion is further supported by the fact that plaintiffs agreed to expend up to $1,000 for repairs, and so stipulated in the written lease.

Consequently, the court has arrived at the following conclusions: (1) that the carpeting at issue was of a nature properly described as a chattel at time of purchase; (2) that it was susceptible of either continued existence as personalty, or of becoming a permanent fixture; (3) that the tenants intended the carpet as a permanent improvement to the property; (4) that lessors will receive no windfall because the gain was anticipated; (5) that upon installation said carpet became a fixture and, therefore, was not subject to removal by the tenants.

It remains then for the court to ascertain the damages suffered by the plaintiffs by the wrongful removal of the carpet. The complaint of the plaintiffs is couched in terms of conversion and the measure of damages "in an action for conversion is the value of the property at the time and place of the taking or conversion by the wrongdoer. . . ." *18 Ohio Jurisprudence 3d* (1980) 526, Conversion and Replevin, Section 54. Generally, where a market value is ascertainable it may be used as a standard for damages. Where no sufficient market exists on which to establish a value, the measure of damages for the conversion becomes the reasonable value of the property at the time of the conversion.

This court has received evidence of two measures of damage. The first was the plaintiffs' own opinion as to the value of the entire leasehold before and after the conversion resulting in a diminution in value of $2,000. The second measure offered to the court as evidence was testimony of the plaintiffs' witness, a professional carpet retailer and installer. This testimony related to replacement carpet including pad, labor and taxes for a total of $1,859.77. This estimate appeared to be based on similar goods and the witness further testified that reasonable life expectancy of the carpet removed would have been ten years.

While this court would have preferred to use as a starting point for determining damages the cost of the carpet to the tenant when installed in 1981, the court feels it is not unreasonable to consider the replacement value. After allowing a reasonable amount for inflation and five years' depreciation of carpet, the court estimates the value of the converted carpet at the time of removal in October 1986 as $925. Although the court recognizes that the method of determination used herein is not perfect, the court feels that it is as reasonable and as accurate a result as would have been obtained by submitting the same facts to a jury.

It is, therefore, ordered that judgment be entered for the plaintiffs against the defendants in the sum of $925.

Notes and Questions

1. In the past, residential tenants often received less protection with respect to their fixtures (sometimes called "domestic fixtures") than commercial tenants who installed trade fixtures. Today, most courts apply the same rules to both types of fixtures.

2. Sam rents an apartment for a term of one year and makes the following modifications: (1) hangs pictures in the living room; (2) installs a shelving unit on a wall in the bedroom, using metal brackets that are screwed into the wall; (3) installs his own chandelier in the dining room, storing the apartment's chandelier in a closet; (4) repaints the other bedroom light blue; and (5) adds Astroturf carpeting to the floor of the balcony porch, which he glues down. Which of these acts are permissible in the absence of the landlord's consent? How do the following alternative lease provisions change the common law rule?

    a. Residents may not remodel, structurally change apartment, or remove any fixture therefrom without the prior written consent of management.

    b. ALTERATIONS AND IMPROVEMENTS. Lessee agrees not to make any alterations to the premises without prior written consent of Management. Any alterations made by Lessee shall remain upon and be surrendered at termination of this agreement.

c. The lessee agrees that no alterations shall be made in said rented premises, nor signs put up or painted on walls, windows or other portions of said premises without first having obtained written consent of the lessor and further that if the lessor requires, such alterations, signs, etc. shall at termination of contract be removed at the expense of the lessee and any damage caused by the alteration or signs be paid for by lessee.

In general, which provision is better for landlords? For tenants?

■ **WHITE v. MOLYNEUX**
Supreme Court of Georgia, 1847
2 Ga. 124

NISBET, Justice. . . .

This was an action for rent, to which the defendant [Edward White] pleaded the destruction of the house rented, by fire. Upon motion the Court ordered the plea to be stricken out, and error is assigned upon that decision. We consider this question as conclusively settled in England and the United States, if authority can settle anything. It is well settled, that neither a court of law, nor of equity, will relieve against an express contract to pay rent upon the ground that the premises have been destroyed by fire, or the King's enemies, or any casualty whatever, unless there is an express stipulation to that effect. Inevitable accident will excuse a party from a penalty, but will not relieve him from his covenant to perform. 1 Dyer, 33a; 3 Kent, 468. . . .

By the law of Scotland, upon the hire of property, a loss or injury to that property, which is not occasioned by the fault or negligence of the hirer, falls upon the owner; and the lessee is entitled to an abatement of the rent in proportion to any partial destruction of the subject. 1 Bell's Com. 452. A similar doctrine prevails in Louisiana. Civil Code of Louisiana, art. 2667. And in France by the Code of Napoleon. Code Nap. art. 1722. Puffendorff considers this a plain principle of natural law, founded in eternal justice. Puff. book 5, ch. 6, sec. 2. By the Civil Law the Praetor would exempt the tenant from paying rent, or modify the obligation according to equity, when the property was destroyed by fire, inundation or violence, or the crops failed by bad seasons. Dig. 19, 2, 15, 2; Code, 4, 65, 8. In a case in England, Brown vs. Quitter, Lord Northman thought it very clear, that a man should not pay rent for what he cannot enjoy, if occasioned by an accident which he did not undertake to meet. Amb. R. 619. Indeed the Courts of Equity in England for a long time struggled against a contrary doctrine. *See* Harrison vs. North, 1 Ch. Cas. 83; Steel v. Wright, 1 T. R. 708, note. The question whether a Court of Equity would grant relief against a landlord's claim for rent has been set at rest in England, in Hare vs. Grove, 3 Anst. R. 687, and Holtzapffel v. Baker, 18 Ves. Jr. 115.

The reason in equity is, that in case of the destruction of the property, the loss of the rent must fall somewhere, and there is no more equity that the landlord should bear it than the tenant, when the tenant has expressly agreed to pay it, and when the landlord must bear the loss of the property destroyed. Equity considers the calamity mutual. She will not interfere to relieve against the express contract of the tenant. So that, notwithstanding the opinion of Puffendorff, the authority of the Civil Law, and even some adjudications in England and in this country, we consider the rule established as we at first laid it down.

As early as the reign of Henry VIII this question was mooted at law, and in the case of *Taverner* it was left unsettled. 1 Dyer's R. 55, 56. In the reign of Charles I, the Court of Kings' Bench held, that where the renter had been driven from the premises by public enemies, viz: Prince Rupert and his soldiers, he could not plead it in bar of the rent. Chancellor Kent, after reviewing the authorities, declares: "It is well settled that, upon an express contract to pay rent, the loss of the premises by fire, or inundation, or external violence, will not exempt the party from his obligation to pay rent." 3 John. R. 44; 3 Kent 466; 1 Dyer R. 33; 1 Story Com. secs. 101, 102.

The reasons upon which the decisions at law have gone are, that it is competent for a party, in his contract, to stipulate against payment in case of fire, or other casualty, or violence; and, having failed to do so, he cannot take advantage of his laches. The contract is an executed one; the tenant is in the position of a purchaser of the premises for the term; he is let into the possession, and the landlord has no right to enter or in any way molest him. And, as in all other express, unconditional contracts, both parties must abide by their solemn act.

The rule, too, is not without foundation in policy. It secures, on the part of the tenant, that carefulness and vigilance which is necessary to the safety of the owner's property whilst he is out of possession, and whilst it is under the absolute control of one who has only a temporary interest in it. If the destruction by fire would excuse the payment of rent, then might the tenant so far as pecuniary interest is concerned, become careless to protect it. The owner would be left to rely upon the tenant's sense of moral obligation, which unfortunately is not, in all men, so just or so strong as to constrain them to do right. Indeed there are men to be found base enough to burn down a house, to get rid of the payment of rent, if their interest might thereby be subserved. The contrary of this rule would therefore operate in restraint of renting. Let the judgment of the Court below be affirmed.

Notes and Questions

1. Ga. Code Ann. §44-7-15: "*Effect of destruction of tenement on obligation to pay rent.* The destruction of a tenement by fire or the loss of possession by any casualty not caused by the landlord or from a defect of his title shall not abate the rent contracted to be paid." This statute was enacted in 1863, 16 years after the decision in *White.* What effect does the statute have on the rule of decision in *White?*

2. Hurricane Katrina gave rise to a number of claims like that at issue in *White. See, e.g.,* Higbee Co. v. Greater Lakeside Corp., 2007 U.S. Dist. LEXIS 29438 (E.D. La. 2007) (granting in part and denying in part a motion for summary judgment filed by a department store seeking a rent abatement); Carrollton Central Plaza Assocs. v. Piccadilly Restaurants, LLC, 952 So. 2d 756 (La. Ct. App. 2007) (upholding the eviction of the owner of a restaurant destroyed by Katrina). Should the rule be any different when entire communities suffer the destruction of many buildings?

3. Courts continue to follow the common law rule that destruction of improvements on the leased premises does not alter the duty to pay rent. Modern courts, however, generally relieve the tenant from liability when the leased premises consist of only part of a building (such as one unit in a multitenant building). Less frequently, courts have relieved tenants when the improvements represent a high proportion of the value of the premises either on the basis of failure of consideration, impossibility of performance, or frustration of purpose. Moreover, some states have altered the common law rule by statute. Although the statutes vary

considerably they generally provide, in the absence of agreement to the contrary, for termination of the lease, or give the tenant the option to terminate the lease, upon the destruction of a substantial part of the premises.

4. Leases often include clauses that modify the implied terms governing destruction of all or part of the premises. Consider the following clauses. How do they alter the parties' common law rights with respect to casualty?

> a. If the property is rendered untenantable by fire, storm, earthquake, or other casualty, this agreement shall terminate as of the date of such destruction or damage and rental shall cease as of that date. Rent shall not abate in case of partial untenantability, and repairs will promptly be made.
>
> b. If premises are damaged by fire or casualty, at its option, management may terminate this lease upon notice to resident, or cause the damage to be repaired, in which event the rent shall be abated only for such time as the premises remain untenantable.

F. LANDLORD'S REMEDIES FOR TENANT BREACH

■ **HOLY PROPERTIES LIMITED, L.P. v. KENNETH COLE PRODUCTIONS, INC.**
Court of Appeal of New York, 1995
661 N.E.2d 694

SIMONS, Judge. In 1985, defendant Kenneth Cole Productions, Inc. entered into a written lease for premises in a commercial office building located at 29 West 57th Street in Manhattan. The term was to commence on January 1, 1985 and end on December 31, 1994. In December 1991, following a change of owners and an alleged deterioration in the level and quality of building services, defendant vacated the premises. Shortly thereafter, the new owner, plaintiff Holy Properties Limited, L.P., commenced a summary eviction proceeding against defendant for the nonpayment of rent. It obtained a judgment and warrant of eviction on May 19, 1992 and subsequently instituted this action seeking rent arrears and damages. At trial defendant asserted, as an affirmative defense, that plaintiff had failed to mitigate damages by deliberately failing to show or offer the premises to prospective replacement tenants. Supreme Court entered judgment for plaintiff, holding that defendant had breached the lease without cause and that plaintiff had no duty to mitigate damages. The Appellate Division affirmed.

The issue is whether, on these facts, the landlord had a duty to mitigate its damages after the tenant's abandonment of the premises and subsequent eviction.

The law imposes upon a party subjected to injury from breach of contract, the duty of making reasonable exertions to minimize the injury. Wilmot v. State of New York, 297 N.E.2d 90, 92 (N.Y. 1973). Leases are not subject to this general rule, however, for, unlike executory contracts, leases have been historically recognized as a present transfer of an estate in real property. *See* Becar v. Flues, 64 N.Y. 518, 520 (1876). Once the lease is executed, the lessee's obligation to pay rent is fixed according to its terms and a landlord is under no obligation or duty to the tenant to relet, or attempt to relet abandoned premises in order to minimize damages. 2 Rasch, *New York Landlord and Tenant* §26:22 (3d ed. 1988).

When defendant abandoned these premises prior to expiration of the lease, the landlord had three options: (1) it could do nothing and collect the full rent due under the lease, Becar v. Flues, *supra*, (2) it could accept the tenant's surrender, reenter the premises and relet them for its own account thereby releasing the tenant from further liability for rent, or (3) it could notify the tenant that it was entering and reletting the premises for the tenant's benefit. If the landlord relets the premises for the benefit of the tenant, the rent collected would be apportioned first to repay the landlord's expenses in reentering and reletting and then to pay the tenant's rent obligation. *See* lease para 18; Underhill v. Collins, 30 N.E. 576 (N.Y. 1892). Once the tenant abandoned the premises prior to the expiration of the lease, however, the landlord was within its rights under New York law to do nothing and collect the full rent due under the lease. *See Becar, supra.*

Defendant urges us to reject this settled law and adopt the contract rationale recognized by some courts in this State and elsewhere. We decline to do so. Parties who engage in transactions based on prevailing law must be able to rely on the stability of such precedents. In business transactions, particularly, the certainty of settled rules is often more important than whether the established rule is better than another or even whether it is the "correct" rule. *See* Maxton Bldrs. v. Lo Galbo, 502 N.E.2d 184, 188 (N.Y. 1986). This is perhaps true in real property more than any other area of the law, where established precedents are not lightly to be set aside. Heyert v. Orange & Rockland Utils., 218 N.E.2d 263, 267 (N.Y. 1966).

Defendant contends that even if it is liable for rent after abandoning the premises, plaintiff terminated the landlord-tenant relationship shortly thereafter by instituting summary proceedings. After the eviction, it maintains, its only liability was for contract damages, not rent, and under contract law the landlord had a duty to mitigate. Although an eviction terminates the landlord-tenant relationship, the parties to a lease are not foreclosed from contracting as they please. *See* International Publs. v. Matchabelli, 184 N.E. 51, 52 (N.Y. 1933); Mann v. Ferdinand Munch Brewery, 121 N.E. 746, 747 (N.Y. 1919). If the lease provides that the tenant shall be liable for rent after eviction, the provision is enforceable. *Id.*

In this case, the lease expressly provided that plaintiff was under no duty to mitigate damages and that upon defendant's abandonment of the premises or eviction, it would remain liable for all monetary obligations arising under the lease. *See* lease para 18.

Accordingly, the order of the Appellate Division should be affirmed, with costs.

■ **HINTON v. SEALANDER BROKERAGE CO.**
District of Columbia Court of Appeals, 2007
917 A.2d 95

Ferren, Senior Judge. This appeal presents an unusual, ostensibly inconsistent combination of circumstances: a landlord's wrongful, self-help eviction, followed by the tenant's holdover as a trespasser on the premises. The pro se tenant, Nokomis Hinton, filed an action in forma pauperis against her landlord, Sealander Brokerage Co., for allegedly locking her out of her single family rental house before she had been able to move out all her furniture and personal belongings.[1] The landlord then filed a counterclaim for unpaid rent attributable to the tenant's holding over by leaving property in the house after she had left. The trial judge ruled for the landlord on both the claim and the counterclaim. We vacate the judgment and remand the case for further proceedings.

I. BACKGROUND

The tenant filed her complaint on September 29, 2003, alleging that she had given the landlord a "30 day notice" that she was leaving the premises; that the landlord had changed the locks before her "30 day[s were] up" and that the landlord had denied her access to her "belongings" that remained in the house. She sought $16,000 in damages. . . . [A]fter a bench trial, the trial court ruled for the landlord on both the claim and the counterclaim and awarded money damages against the tenant totaling $7,808.30 (plus statutory interest from March 21, 2005) as compensation for storing the tenant's personal property on the premises for ten months ($7,000) and, thereafter, in a U-Haul storage facility ($808.30).

II. WRONGFUL EVICTION

. . . .

In order to establish wrongful eviction, a tenant must prove that the landlord performed "some act of a permanent character with the intention and effect of depriving the tenant of the enjoyment of the demised premises or a part thereof." International Comm'n on English in Liturgy v. Schwartz, 573 A.2d 1303, 1305 (D.C. 1990). "Whether the landlord performed an act with the intent to evict the tenant is a question of fact for the trial court." Id.[6] The law is clear in this jurisdiction, moreover, that a landlord is prohibited from using self-help to evict a tenant and must proceed instead by using the process provided by law. Mendes v. Johnson, 389 A.2d 781, 783-87 (D.C. 1978) (en banc) (landlord's common law right of self-help eviction by removing tenant's belongings from premises abrogated by exclusive statutory remedy mandating reliance on legal process). Nothing, however, precludes a landlord from securing a vacant unit to prevent theft and vandalism. See 14 DCMR §6800.3 (2006) ("[T]he owner of a vacant building is required to maintain the building . . . [by ensuring that] [d]oors, windows, areaways, and other openings are . . . secured against entry by . . . trespassers. . . .").

The tenant testified at trial that she had paid her rent through September 30; that she had sent the landlord "a notice of 30-day moveout . . . on the 3rd of

---

1. The tenancy at 1311 South Capitol St., S.W. was subsidized by the government under the Section 8 Housing Assistance Payments Program. See 42 U.S.C. §1437f (2001). See also D.C. Code §42-2851.06(c) (2001) ("The owner of a housing accommodation shall not refuse to rent a dwelling unit to a person because the person will provide his or her rental payment, in whole or in part, through a section 8 voucher."). Initially, of the tenant's $700 monthly rent, $492 was subsidized by Section 8 Housing Assistance Payments. By the end of the tenancy, however, the tenant was receiving a $700 subsidy covering her entire rent.

6. The "intention" criterion for a "wrongful" eviction is not a subjective one. The courts of this jurisdiction have said that "the law assumes that the landlord intends the natural and probable consequences of his acts. . . . Generally, whether the acts of the landlord have been done with intent to evict the tenant is a question of fact for the determination of the jury. But the question of actual intent arises only when the acts are such as do not of themselves afford a presumption of intent." Hughes v. Westchester Dev. Corp., 77 F.2d 550, 551 (D.C. Cir. 1935).

September"; that she had been moving out "constantly" from September 3 to September 20, 2003; that on the 20th she had found the landlord's locksmith "chang[ing] the locks on the door"; and that when she had asked the landlord's representative for a key so that she "could continue to move [her] things[,] . . . [h]e refused."

The landlord's representative told a different story. He acknowledged that the tenant's rent had been paid through September 30, 2003, but said that she had "never notified" him that she was leaving. He further testified that "approximately on the 26th of September" 2003, he learned from a former neighbor of the tenant that the house was vacant and "unsecured"—the "doors were open." He then testified that when he had gone right away to check on the property, "[i]t looked like someone had abandoned it, left it, and that somebody was ransacking." In particular, "[w]indows were broken, doors had been torn off the hinges[;] . . . it looked like someone was trying to, you know, maliciously damage the place." He found that the house still contained "many items" of personal property "in various states of [dis]array." . . . Accordingly, he said, in order to protect the tenant's property as well as the landlord's, he made arrangements with a locksmith "to put locks on the doors" three days later, September 29, 2003. Also on the 29th, the landlord's representative posted a notice on the front door of the house containing a phone number for the tenant to call in order to gain entry for removal of her belongings. The notice added that a "message has been left with your new landlord[;] we have no telephone number for you." The landlord's representative further testified that, on other occasions during the ensuing months, the landlord had informed the tenant that she "could pick up her things at any time." . . . "[B]ased upon the credibility of the witnesses," the trial judge ruled for the landlord in the wrongful eviction action.

The landlord's willingness to accommodate the tenant does not end the inquiry, however. The tenant has claimed an "illegal lock out." *See, e.g.*, Robinson v. Sarisky, 535 A.2d 901, 904-06 (D.C. 1988) (successful wrongful eviction action against tax sale purchaser who repeatedly boarded up property and changed locks despite notification that plaintiff was lawfully living in premises). The landlord admittedly installed new locks on September 26 and 29 and refused to give the tenant a new key, excluding her from freely entering the premises. The tenant, as a result, is claiming that the landlord did so before her lease expired. Further, she claims in effect that the landlord's withholding of the key amounted to a self-help eviction that violated the teaching of our en banc decision in *Mendes, supra*, limiting eviction to legal process. More specifically, three questions underlying the *Mendes* issue are presented here: (1) whether the landlord was entitled to install new locks on the premises without the tenant's participation; (2) if so, whether the landlord installed them (and refused to provide a key) at a time when the lease was still in effect, knowing that the tenant had not abandoned her personal property remaining on the premises; and, if so, (3) whether the lock change, when coupled with the landlord's willingness to open the premises for the tenant to remove her property, was action benign enough to foreclose a *Mendes* violation.

As to the first, the evidence indicates that, regardless of whether the tenant gave the landlord a thirty-day notice of intent to vacate, the tenant's rental house had become open, with door locks missing, inviting ransacking by others—which had already occurred. Upon learning of the situation, therefore, the landlord had a right, indeed a responsibility, under 14 DCMR §6800.3 to secure the premises, based on a reasonable, initial perception that the tenant had abandoned the house and her personal property, perhaps even damaging the premises herself while leaving. . . .

As to the second question, the record reveals that the landlord changed the locks and refused the tenant a key at a time when the lease was still in effect, knowing that the tenant had not abandoned the furniture and other belongings she had left in the house. . . .

. . . [T]he landlord understood on September 29 that the house was still occupied, constructively, by the tenant. Accordingly, having accepted rent through September 30 pursuant to the terms of the lease, the landlord is estopped to claim that the tenancy ended any sooner. And, having refused the tenant a key during the brief, two-day period (September 29-30) when the lease was still in effect, the landlord is further estopped to claim that the tenancy extended any later than September 30, the date through which the tenant claimed a right to occupy the premises.

We turn to the third, dispositive question under *Mendes*: the legal significance of the change in locks. It does not necessarily follow that the landlord's right to secure the vandalized house under lease to the tenant justified withholding a key for the new locks — a withholding the landlord acknowledges. The tenant's right to a key — to untrammeled entry — reflects a fundamental obligation of the landlord under any standard residential lease. Nonetheless, rather than allow the tenant free rein to haul away her belongings from the premises during the last two days of her tenancy, the landlord insisted on supervising her every entry, despite her having paid full rent through September 30. The landlord thus faced a choice: give the tenant a key or be willing to pay damages for excluding the tenant from the house for two days.

We accept the trial judge's findings crediting the landlord's representative's testimony but we must conclude, even so, that the judge erred as a matter of law in ruling that the tenant had not been evicted unlawfully. We are satisfied that, by constraining the tenant's right of entry for the two-day period while the lease was still in effect (September 29-30), the landlord intended to deprive the tenant of full use of the premises, see *supra* note 6, and exercised a kind of self-help proscribed by *Mendes, supra*. We conclude, accordingly, that the tenant is entitled to damages for that eviction to the extent provable.[14]

III. COUNTERCLAIM

We turn to the counterclaim. The landlord seeks recovery of unpaid rent for the period after the tenant moved out but left furniture and other personal property on the premises. As we have noted, by refusing to give the tenant a key to the house after the broken or missing locks had been replaced, the landlord evicted the tenant on September 29 while the lease was still in effect. As of the 29th, therefore, the tenant's obligation to pay rent ended, and she was entitled to damages from the landlord for ousting her before the lease terminated at midnight on September 30. Because she had left property in the house, however, she was still potentially liable to the landlord for damages for holding over.

---

14. We have noted that "the law presumes that some damages result from an unlawful eviction. Such damages are not limited to physical injury or property loss. This court long ago accepted the principle 'that a tenant who has been unlawfully evicted may recover for mental suffering, inconvenience and discomfort.'" *Robinson, supra*, 535 A.2d at 905. That said, "the damages in a particular wrongful eviction case may be 'small *or even nominal* in amount.'" Henson v. Prue, 810 A.2d 912, 915 (D.C. 2002).

When a landlord terminates a tenancy unlawfully, as in this case, the tenant has an election of remedies. She may either take legal action to reinstate the lease and obtain legal and equitable relief, as appropriate; or, as she did here, take action premised on an end of the lease by suing for damages. If, however, that wrongfully evicted tenant, in seeking damages, nonetheless remains in some way on the premises without acting to reinstate the lease, the landlord—despite evicting unlawfully—will retain the right, through setoff or counterclaim, to recover its own damages for the tenant's continued occupancy beyond the period reasonably necessary for her to remove her property after the landlord abruptly terminated the lease.

With this background in mind, we address the question whether the amount of personal property the tenant left behind was sufficient to generate liability for holding over. That is a question for the trier of fact to answer. We are satisfied—given the testimony and photographs revealing a list of over fifty items of significant value—that the trial judge did not err in finding that the tenant left enough property in the house for holdover liability, at least for the period after a reasonable time for removing her property had expired (an issue the judge did not address).

In ruling on the counterclaim, the trial judge determined that the tenant owed "$700 a month rent for a 10 month period" (October 2003-July 2004, the period the property remained in the house before it was moved to outside storage). Although the presumptive measure of damages, at least for continuous use of the premises, is the rent prescribed for the lease term, the judge erred in failing to come to grips with whether that presumptive value applied to the facts over that entire ten-month period. He characterized the $7,000 he ordered the tenant to pay for storage in the house simply as "rent," as though the lease were continuing, without converting the assessment to a damages analysis. The trial judge instead should have calculated the reasonable value for use of the premises during the tenant's holdover, beginning after the period reasonably required to allow the tenant to remove her property after the landlord's termination of her lease.

The tenant's holding over after September 30 did not give her rights as a statutory "tenant by sufferance" or as a tenant in limbo pending resolution of a dispute with the landlord over, say, alleged overcrowding or housing code violations. Rather, the actions of both parties brought termination of the lease—the landlord by withholding the key, the tenant by rejecting the lease and suing for damages. The question thus becomes: by the choice she made, did the tenant forfeit her right to insist on a key and instead create for herself an obligation to retrieve her property under reasonable conditions proposed by the key-holding landlord?

We conclude that the answer must be yes. . . .

. . . A key is not necessary to accomplish the tenant's retrieval of her property—assuming, as the trial judge's credibility findings require us to do, that the landlord stood ready at all reasonable times to open the house for the tenant to pick up her belongings. Accordingly, we do not perceive any reason why a tenant who repudiates the lease should be entitled to a key, as though the lease were still alive, rather than having to go along with a reasonable proposal by the landlord to facilitate retrieval of her property using the landlord's key. By her actions in holding over with her unremoved personal property, and in repudiating the lease, the tenant has no claim to any kind of tenancy, other than the bare right of entry to retrieve her belongings within a reasonable period of time after the lease was terminated. Aside from that brief period, for which the landlord has agreed to facilitate her retrieval by opening the door, she stands in no stronger relationship to the landlord than a trespasser who, by definition, has no right to a key.

IV. DAMAGES

That does not end the analysis, however. By claiming an "illegal withholding" of her property in addition to an "illegal lockout," the tenant can be said to have raised a mitigation defense. (Tenant claiming she informed landlord "[y]ou can't hold my things.") Essentially, the tenant maintains that the landlord could have reduced or eliminated its damages by giving her a key, permitting prompt retrieval of her property from the premises. The focus, therefore, shifts to the landlord's responsibility, if any, to mitigate damages while standing firm on its right — which we here sustain — to withhold the key after the lease ended.

Notwithstanding termination of a lease by a landlord's wrongful eviction, coupled with the tenant's election not to seek reinstatement, the terms of the lease may still govern damages; and, as a result, the contract principles requiring mitigation may apply.[31] For example, if a landlord specifically reserves the right to re-enter and re-let the premises upon termination of the lease while holding the tenant liable for damages, it is the landlord's "duty to make reasonable efforts to that end and thereby minimize his damages." McIntosh v. Gitomer, 120 A.2d 205, 206 (D.C. 1956). *See also* Lennon, *supra* note 31, 920 F.2d at 1000 ("Under District law . . . a lease provision giving the re-entering lessor a right to lost rent is construed as creating a right to damages, subject to the mitigation doctrine, *i.e.*, to a requirement that the lessor use 'reasonable efforts' to relet."). In this case, clause 12 of the lease provides that after termination of the lease the landlord "may, without notice, re-enter the said premises and remove . . . all contents." However, this lease provision (the validity of which we do not address) is premised on the landlord's *lawful* termination of the lease; literally, it does not apply in the context of an unlawful, self-help eviction.

In the absence of contractual provisions in the lease that dictate the respective liabilities of the landlord and tenant after a mutual effort to terminate, as in this case, general principles of property and tort law are available. Here, we have concluded that upon termination of the lease the tenant became a trespasser, entitling the landlord to damages for intrusion upon its property. With no governing contractual provision in the lease, therefore, we may draw on the doctrine of avoidable

---

31. Landlord and tenant jurisprudence on mitigation draws on principles of property law and contract law. Some courts have taken the position that a lease is a present transfer of an estate in real property, and thus that the well-established principle of mitigation from contract law does not apply. *See, e.g.*, Holy Properties Ltd., L.P. v. Kenneth Cole Prods., 661 N.E.2d 694 (N.Y. 1995). On the other hand, in line with the Restatement principle that the "landlord's obligations under the terminated lease . . . continue into the period in which the tenant holds over," except when those obligations are "clearly intended to prevail only during the period of the original lease," *Restatement (Second) of Property: Landlord and Tenant* §14.7, cmt. e, the U.S. Court of Appeals for the District of Columbia Circuit has found occasion to confirm that contract principles still can apply after termination of a "leasehold" interest in real property.

> In reality, the question of whether a contract "exists" after obligations to perform its covenants end, but a right to damages for breach survives, is highly metaphysical. But it is clear that a contract's provisions can define and provide remedies even after all obligations to perform under the contract have been discharged.

Lennon v. United States Theatre Corp., 920 F.2d 996, 999 (D.C. Cir. 1990). Thus, where there are specific post-termination damage provisions in the lease, the parties will continue to be bound by them.

consequences — the tort formulation for mitigation — for calculation of damages. "The avoidable consequences doctrine is that 'one injured by the tort of another is not entitled to recover damages for any harm that he could have avoided by the use of reasonable effort.'" Flowers v. District of Columbia, 478 A.2d 1073, 1077 (D.C. 1984) (quoting Restatement (Second) of Torts §918 (1979)). Surely, if a landlord must mitigate damages assessable against a holdover tenant when the landlord has terminated the lease lawfully, a landlord also must mitigate damages payable by a holdover — though technically trespassing — tenant when the landlord has terminated the lease unlawfully.

Although we have held that under the circumstances of this case the tenant was not entitled to a key after eviction, the court did not consider the landlord's own responsibility to mitigate damages, for example, by promptly moving the property to an outside storage facility and re-letting the premises, or by confining the tenant's property to an area of the house, such as the basement, that might have permitted attraction of a new tenant. There may, in other words, have been a way for the landlord to have handled the situation less expensively for the tenant than full rent over ten months while the tenant was persisting in her demand for a key. From this record, however, we cannot tell what, if any, reasonable possibilities for mitigation there were.

It follows, from the foregoing discussion, that the $7,000 in "rent" awarded on the counterclaim must be revisited in a "damages" analysis. This means that the trial judge will have to allocate responsibility over a ten-month period between a tenant who claimed to want her property but was insisting on a key to get it, and a landlord who refused to give the tenant a key and retained her property in the house, but stood willing to open the house, as needed, to permit removal of that property.

The court also awarded $808.30 to the landlord for the costs of eventually moving the tenant's property to the U-Haul storage facility. Such damages are appropriately awardable to the landlord.[34] It is possible, although not at all predictable, that in reevaluating the damages awardable to the landlord for storing the tenant's property at the house, the trial judge may find that the amount of damages awardable for off-site storage should be recalculated — a result that we find permissible but not required.

V. CONCLUSION

In sum, we vacate the judgment and remand the case for evaluation of damages payable to the tenant for her wrongful eviction, as well as for reconsideration of damages payable to the landlord for the tenant's holding over on the former rental premises by leaving her property there after her lease had expired. In particular, the trial judge shall consider the responsibility of each party to mitigate damages. We leave it to the judge to determine how much additional testimony and other evidence, if any, will be needed to resolve the matter. In view of the complex issues presented, we hope that the tenant will find counsel on remand. If she cannot afford to pay for a lawyer, we trust that the trial judge will acquaint her with legal services available from the law schools, the organized bar, and other nonprofit organizations.

Judgment vacated and case remanded.

---

34. Comedy v. Vito, 492 A.2d 276, 278 (D.C. 1985) ("When chattels left on the property by a former tenant interfere with the landlord's use of the property, the landlord is entitled to recover the cost of removal") (citing Restatement (Second) of Property: Landlord and Tenant §12.3 cmt. l).

Notes and Questions

1. What should Nokomis Hinton have done to avoid any liability to her landlord? What should Sealander Brokerage have done to avoid any liability to its tenant?

2. A number of states have decided to outlaw self-help repossession for residential leases, but allow it for other types of leases. *E.g.*, Rucker v. Wynn, 441 S.E.2d 417 (Ga. Ct. App. 1994) (after restaurant was closed and tenant was not present, lessor changed locks on doors pursuant to default clause authorizing landlord "to enter upon and rent the premises" to another tenant); Northeast Park Associates v. Northeast Ohio Harness, 521 N.E.2d 466 (Ohio Ct. App. 1987) (lessor repossessed horse racetrack, using security guards and changing locks on premises; lease authorized lessor, after giving notice of default and 10 days for lessee to cure default, to repossess "with or without process of law, and expel, remove or put out Lessee or any other person or persons occupying said premises"). Is this distinction sensible?

3. Footnote 1 of *Hinton* explains that the federal government paid most of Hinton's rent under the Section 8 program, yet a private landlord, not the government, rented the house to Hinton, managed the property, and made the decision to evict her. Established by Congress in 1974, Section 8 provides vouchers that give residents the freedom to use their subsidies in a wide range of private market housing. Supporters contend that the use of such subsidies instead of housing owned by the government helps the poor get access to better neighborhoods and reduces areas of concentrated poverty. The government limits the number of Section 8 vouchers, resulting in long waiting lists to obtain vouchers in most communities.

Vouchers developed as an alternative to public housing, begun in the 1930s as a New Deal initiative designed not only to provide housing for the working poor but also to create construction industry jobs. The federal government provides subsidies to local public housing authorities (PHAs), which develop and operate public housing communities. PHAs are chartered under the law of the state where the authority is located. Federal funding subjects PHAs to federal regulation, administered by the Department of Housing and Urban Development (HUD). Over the years, the nature of the public housing population has changed, with larger percentages of the residents having extremely low incomes. Increasingly, public housing has accommodated more disabled and elderly persons. Since the 1970s, Congress has reduced funding for public housing dramatically. As a consequence of chronic underfunding, many PHAs have delayed ordinary maintenance and diverted capital funds away from needed capital repairs, replacements, and improvements to pay for operations. Presently, there are approximately 1.2 million public housing units in the United States, down from a high point of over 1.4 million in the early 1990s, with continued shrinkage of about 10,000 units per year. Since the 1990s, the government has not funded any PHA construction projects that increase the net number of dwelling units. PHAs have been forced to maintain properties at a lower level and to curtail social service programs for their residents. In 2010, HUD Secretary Shaun Donovan testified before Congress that the public housing stock was nearing "a tipping point where its deterioration becomes rapid, increasingly expensive to remedy, and often irreversible."

Should the government be involved in providing housing? What does the government do that makes housing *less* affordable? What type of government assistance is best? Who should decide where affordable housing should be located?

G. TRANSFERS BY LANDLORD AND TENANT

As we have seen in other contexts in this course, transferability is a prime attribute of ownership property. The norm is that property is freely alienable, although there are examples of interests that are not alienable, but still may be considered property. (Can you think of examples?) In the landlord-tenant context, each party has an alienable interest if the relationship is a tenancy for years or a periodic tenancy. By definition, a tenancy at will rests upon the mutual assent of the original parties, and thus neither landlord nor tenant can transfer his interest to a third person. For tenancies for years and periodic tenancies, transfers by landlords and by tenants are very common. When a landlord sells the leased premises, the buyer normally acquires all of the landlord's rights under the lease and becomes the new landlord of the tenant. Often the transfer of the lease is documented using an *assignment of lease*. The following cases address transfers by tenants.

■ **JABER v. MILLER**
Supreme Court of Arkansas, 1951
239 S.W.2d 760

SMITH, Justice. This is a suit brought by Miller to obtain cancellation of fourteen promissory notes, each in the sum of $175, held by the appellant, Jaber. The plaintiff's theory is that these notes represent monthly rent upon a certain business building in Fort Smith for the period beginning January 1, 1950, and ending March 1, 1951. The building was destroyed by fire on December 3, 1949, and the plaintiff contends that his obligation to pay rent then terminated. The defendant contends that the notes were given not for rent but as deferred payments for the assignment of a lease formerly held by Jaber. The chancellor, in an opinion reflecting a careful study of the matter, concluded that the notes were intended to be rental payments and therefore should be canceled.

In 1945 Jaber rented the building from its owner for a five-year term beginning March 1, 1946, and ending March 1, 1951. The lease reserved a monthly rent of $200 and provided that the lease would terminate if the premises were destroyed by fire. Jaber conducted a rug shop in the building until 1949, when he sold his stock of merchandise at public auction and transferred the lease to Norber & Son. Whether this instrument of transfer is an assignment or a sublease is the pivotal issue in this case.

In form the document is an assignment rather than a sublease. It is entitled "Contract and Assignment." After reciting the existence of the five-year lease the instrument provides that Jaber "hereby transfers and assigns" to Norber & Son "the aforesaid lease contract . . . for the remainder of the term of said lease." It also provides that "in consideration of the sale and assignment of said lease contract" Norber & Son have paid Jaber $700 in cash and have executed five promissory notes for $700 each, due serially at specified four-month intervals. Norber & Son agree to pay to the owner of the property the stipulated rental of $200 a month, and Jaber reserves the right to retake possession if Norber & Son fail to pay the rent or the notes. The instrument contains no provision governing the rights of the parties in case the building is destroyed by fire.

Later on the plaintiff, Miller, obtained a transfer of the lease from Norber & Son. Miller, being unable to pay the $700 notes as they came due, arranged with

Jaber to divide the payments into monthly installments of $175 each. He and the Norbers accordingly executed the notes now in controversy, which Jaber accepted in substitution for those of the original notes that were still unpaid. When the premises burned Miller contended that Jaber's transfer to Norber & Son had been a sublease rather than an assignment and that the notes therefore represented rent. Miller now argues that, under the rule that a sublease terminates when the primary lease terminates, his sublease ended when the fire had the effect of terminating the original lease.

In most jurisdictions the question of whether an instrument is an assignment or a sublease is determined by principles applicable to feudal tenures. In a line of cases beginning in the year 1371 the English courts worked out the rules for distinguishing between an assignment and a sublease. *See* Ferrier, *Can There Be a Sublease for the Entire Term?*, 18 California L. Rev. 1 (1929). The doctrine established in England is quite simple: If the instrument purports to transfer the lessee's estate for the entire remainder of the term it is an assignment, regardless of its form or of the parties' intention. Conversely, if the instrument purports to transfer the lessee's estate for less than the entire term — even for a day less — it is a sublease, regardless of its form or of the parties' intention.

The arbitrary distinction drawn at common law is manifestly at variance with the usual conception of assignments and subleases. We think of an assignment as the outright transfer of all or part of an existing lease, the assignee stepping into the shoes of the assignor. A sublease, on the other hand, involves the creation of a new tenancy between the sublessor and the sublessee, so that the sublessor is both a tenant and a landlord. The common law distinction is logical only in the light of feudal property law.

In feudal times every one except the king held land by tenure from someone higher in the hierarchy of feudal ownership. "The king himself holds land which is in every sense his own; no one else has any proprietary right in it; but if we leave out of account this royal demesne, then every acre of land is 'held of' the king. The person whom we may call its owner, the person who has the right to use and abuse the land, to cultivate it or leave it uncultivated, to keep all others off it, holds the land of the king either immediately or mediately. In the simplest case he holds it immediately of the king; only the king and he have rights in it. But it well may happen that between him and the king there stand other persons; Z holds immediately of Y, who holds of X, who holds of V, who holds . . . of A, who holds of the king." Pollock and Maitland, *History of English Law* (2d Ed.), vol. I, p. 232. In feudal law each person owed duties, such as that of military service or the payment of rent, to his overlord. To enforce these duties the overlord had the remedy of distress, being the seizure of chattels found on the land.

It is evident that in feudal theory a person must himself have an estate in the land in order to maintain his place in the structure of ownership. Hence if a tenant transferred his entire term he parted with his interest in the property. The English courts therefore held that the transferee of the entire term held of the original lessor, that such a transferee was bound by the covenants in the original lease, and that he was entitled to enforce whatever duties that lease imposed upon the landlord. The intention of the parties had nothing to do with the matter; the sole question was whether the first lessee retained a reversion that enabled him to hold his place in the chain of ownership.

The injustice of these inflexible rules has often been pointed out. Suppose that A makes a lease to B for a certain rental. B then executes to C what both parties intend to be a sublease as that term is generally understood, but the sublease is for the entire term. If *C* in good faith pays his rent to *B*, as the contract requires, he does so at his peril. For the courts say that the contract is really an assignment, and therefore *C*'s primary obligation is to *A* if the latter elects to accept *C* as his tenant. Consequently *A* can collect the rent from the subtenant even though the sublessor has already been paid. For a fuller discussion of this possibility of double liability on the part of the subtenant *see* Darling, *Is a Sublease for the Residue of a Lessee's Term in Effect an Assignment?*, 16 American L. Rev. 16, 21.

Not only may the common law rule operate with injustice to the subtenant; it can be equally harsh upon the sublessor. Again suppose that *A* makes a lease to *B* for a certain rental. *B* then makes to *C* what *B* considers a profitable sublease for twice the original rent. But *B* makes the mistake of attempting to sublet for the entire term instead of retaining a reversion of a day. The instrument is therefore an assignment, and if the original landlord acquires the subtenant's rights there is a merger which prevents *B* from being able to collect the increased rent. That was the situation in Webb v. Russell, 100 Eng. Reprint 639 (1789). The court felt compelled to recognize the merger, but in doing so Lord Kenyon said: "It seems to me, with all the inclination which we have to support the action (and we have hitherto delayed giving judgment in the hopes of being able to find some ground on which the plaintiff's demand might be sustained), that it cannot be supported. The defence which is made is of a most unrighteous and unconscious nature; but unfortunately for the plaintiff the mode which she has taken to enforce her demand cannot be supported." Kent, in his Commentaries (14th Ed.), p.105, refers to this case as reaching an "inequitable result"; Williams and Eastwood, in their work on Real Property, p. 206, call it an "unpleasant result." Yet when the identical question arose in California the court felt bound to hold that the same distasteful merger had taken place. Smiley v. Van Winkle, 6 Cal. 605 (1856).

A decided majority of the American courts have adopted the English doctrine in its entirety. Tiffany, *Landlord & Tenant*, §151. A minority of our courts have made timid but praiseworthy attempts to soften the harshness of the common law rule. In several jurisdictions the courts follow the intention of the parties in controversies between the sublessor and the sublessee, thus preserving the inequities of feudal times only when the original landlord is concerned. Johnson v. Moxley, 113 So. 656 (Ala. 1927); Saling v. Flesch, 277 P. 612 (Mont. 1929); Mausert v. Feigenspan, 63 A. 610 (N.J. 1906); Hobbs v. Cawley, 299 P. 1073 (N.M. 1931).

In other jurisdictions the courts have gone as far as possible to find something that might be said to constitute a reversion in what the parties intended to be a sublease. In some States, notably Massachusetts, it has been held that if the sublessor reserves a right of re-entry for nonpayment of rent this is a sufficient reversionary estate to make the instrument a sublease. Dunlap v. Bullard, 131 Mass. 161 (1881); Davis v. Vidal, 151 S.W. 290 (Tex. 1912). But even these decisions have been criticized on the ground that at common law a right of re-entry was a mere chose in action instead of a reversionary estate. *See*, for example, Tiffany, *supra*, §151.

The appellee urges us to follow the Massachusetts rule and to hold that since Jaber reserved rights of re-entry his transfer to Norber & Son was a sublease. We are not in sympathy with this view. It may be true that a right of re-entry for condition broken has now attained the status of an estate in Arkansas. *See* Moore v. Sharpe, 121 S.W. 341 (Ark. 1909); Core, *Transmissibility of Certain Contingent Future Interests*, 5 Ark. L. Rev. 111. Even so, the Massachusetts rule was adopted to carry out the intention of parties who thought they were making a sublease rather than an assignment. Here the instrument is in form an assignment, and it would be an obvious perversion of the rule to apply it as a means of defeating intention. . . .

In this state of the law we do not feel compelled to adhere to an unjust rule which was logical only in the days of feudalism. The execution of leases is a very practical matter that occurs a hundred times a day without legal assistance. The layman appreciates the common sense distinction between a sublease and an assignment, but he would not even suspect the existence of the common law distinction. As Darling, *supra*, puts it: "Every one knows that a tenant may in turn let to others, and the latter thereby assumes no obligations to the owner of the property; but who would guess that this could only be done for a time falling short by something — a day or an hour is sufficient — of the whole term? And who, not familiar with the subject of feudal tenures, could give a reason why it is held to be so?" It was of such a situation that Holmes was thinking when he said: "It is revolting to have no better reason for a rule than that so it was laid down in the time of Henry IV. It is still more revolting if the grounds upon which it was laid down have vanished long since, and the rule simply persists from blind imitation of the past." *The Path of the Law*, 10 Harv. L. Rev. 457, 469. The rule now in question was laid down some years before the reign of Henry IV.

The English distinction between an assignment and a sublease is not a rule of property in the sense that titles or property rights depend upon its continued existence. A lawyer trained in common law technicalities can prepare either instrument without fear that it will be construed to be the other. But for the less skilled lawyer or for the layman the common law rule is simply a trap that leads to hardship and injustice by refusing to permit the parties to accomplish the result they seek.

For these reasons we adopt as the rule in this State the principle that the intention of the parties is to govern in determining whether an instrument is an assignment or a sublease. If, for example, a tenant has leased an apartment for a year and is compelled to move to another city, we know of no reason why he should not be able to sublease it for a higher rent without needlessly retaining a reversion for the last day of the term. The duration of the primary term, as compared to the length of the sublease, may in some instances be a factor in arriving at the parties' intention, but we do not think it should be the sole consideration. Pennsylvania Min. Co. v. Bailey, 161 S.W. 200 (Ark. 1913), to the extent that it is contrary to this opinion, is overruled.

In the case at bar it cannot be doubted that the parties intended an assignment and not a sublease. The document is so entitled. All its language is that of an assignment rather than that of a sublease. The consideration is stated to be in payment for the lease and not in satisfaction of a tenant's debt to his landlord. The deferred payments are evidenced by promissory notes, which are not ordinarily given by one making a lease. From the appellee's point of view it is unfortunate that the assignment makes no provision for the contingency of a fire, but the appellant's position is certainly not without equity. Jaber sold his merchandise at public auction, and doubtless at reduced prices, in order to vacate the premises for his assignees. Whether he would have taken the same course had the contract provided for a cancellation of the deferred payments in case of a fire we have no way of knowing. A decision either way works a hardship on the losing party. In this situation we do not feel called upon to supply a provision in the assignment which might have been, but was not, demanded by the assignees.

Reversed.

Notes and Questions

1. As *Jaber* indicates, the law insists that any transfer of possession by a tenant must be either an assignment or a sublease. Just as for the law of freehold estates, pigeonholing is required. There is no hybrid category or third choice. Difficulties arise when the parties do not select a "pure sublease" or a "pure assignment." Instead, they agree to terms having characteristics of both. For a pure sublease, there are two leases. Under the sublease, the subtenant pays rent (subrent) to the original tenant; and the original tenant continues to pay the rent under the prime lease to the original landlord. The original landlord and the subtenant have no direct relationship — not one of contract law, and not one of property law. For a pure assignment on the other hand, the assignee pays the rent directly to the landlord. The assignor/original tenant drops out of the picture, and no longer owns any property interest (although he may still owe contractual duties to the landlord, as explained below). The landlord and assignee have a property relationship, and as the next case indicates, may have a contract relationship. In *Jaber*, what fact made the transfer by the original tenant something other than a "pure assignment"?

2. Is the intent test announced by *Jaber* superior to the traditional view that characterizes the transfer based upon the presence or absence of a reversionary interest? Do you think the parties in *Jaber* employed attorneys to represent them in planning and documenting the transfers? What if anything does the court assume about the role of counsel in such transactions? If, as *Jaber* indicates, intent is the key, precisely what intent should matter? Does the context matter? Did the parties have any actual intent as to what should happen if fire destroyed the leased premises? Did they know that the sublease-assignment distinction would decide who bears the risk of loss from fire?

3. When a leasehold is assigned, the assignee becomes personally liable to pay the rent to the landlord. This is said to follow from *privity of estate*, an expression with a historical pedigree grounded in medieval land tenure, which means both landlord and assignee own linked estates in the same real property. An assignment, however, does not relieve the original tenant/assignor from liability to pay the rent. The assignor is relieved from liability only if the landlord expressly agrees to a release of liability. If the assignee fails to pay, the landlord can sue both parties to collect the unpaid rent. The assignor is considered a *surety*. This means that the assignee is primarily liable and the assignor is secondarily liable; if the landlord forces the assignor to pay, the assignor has a cause of action against the assignee to recover that amount.

Leasehold assignments can be structured two ways: a "simple assignment" or an "assignment with an assumption." If the assignor simply assigns the leasehold to the assignee, the assignee's liability under privity of estate lasts so long as the assignee continues to own the leasehold. If the assignee makes a further assignment to another person, that second assignee takes on "privity of estate," and the first assignee is no longer liable for the rent.

Conversely, an assignment with an assumption means that the assignee expressly promises the assignor that he will pay the rent to the landlord and, typically, will perform other leasehold covenants. This creates what is called *privity of contract* between landlord and assignee. Liability based on that privity of contract remains after any further assignment made by the assignee. An assuming assignee is treated just like the original tenant. He becomes a surety, with secondary personal liability to the landlord if the new assignee defaults. For a case that extensively analyzes the rules governing the liability of successive leasehold assignees, *see* A.D. Julliard & Co. v. American Woolen Co., 32 A.2d 800 (R.I. 1943) (refusing to follow a minority position followed by Texas courts that made all assignees liable as sureties, regardless of an assumption agreement; and rejecting the landlord's argument that a solvent assignee who intentionally assigns to a marginally capitalized entity has engaged in misconduct and ought to remain liable for rents).

4. Similar liability issues are raised when the landlord transfers all or part of his interest. When a landlord sells rental property, typically the landlord executes two separate documents: a deed to convey fee simple title to the buyer, and an assignment of lease(s) to transfer the landlord's interest in the leases. The parties' sale contract should expressly address these points and specify whether the assignor shall have any continuing rights or liabilities under the leases. When the landlord conveys the property and the parties do not expressly address the lease, privity of estate steps in to fill the gap. The grantee acquires the property subject to the lease, with the benefit and the burden of those lease covenants that "run with the land." For example, the grantee will become obligated on the covenant of habitability (for a residential lease) and will have the right to collect the rent.

On the other hand, those lease covenants that are considered "personal" remain the obligation of the original landlord, the grantor. The landlord's duty to return the security deposit is often considered personal. These landlord-tenant rules are one branch of the law of servitudes (real covenants and equitable servitudes), to be considered more fully later in this course.

■ KENDALL v. ERNEST PESTANA, INC.

Supreme Court of California, 1985
709 P.2d 837

BROUSSARD, Justice. This case concerns the effect of a provision in a commercial lease[1] that the lessee may not assign the lease or sublet the premises without the lessor's prior written consent. The question we address is whether, in the absence of a provision that such consent will not be unreasonably withheld, a lessor may unreasonably and arbitrarily withhold his or her consent to an assignment.[2] This is a question of first impression in this court.

I.

. . . .

. . . The lease at issue is for 14,400 square feet of hangar space at the San Jose Municipal Airport. The City of San Jose, as owner of the property, leased it to Irving and Janice Perlitch, who in turn assigned their interest to respondent Ernest Pestana, Inc. Prior to assigning their interest to respondent, the Perlitches entered into a 25-year sublease with one Robert Bixler commencing on January 1, 1970. The sublease covered an original five-year term plus four 5-year options to renew. The

---

1. We are presented only with a commercial lease and therefore do not address the question whether residential leases are controlled by the principles articulated in this opinion.

2. Since the present case involves an assignment rather than a sublease, we will speak primarily in terms of assignments. However, our holding applies equally to subleases. . . .

rental rate was to be increased every 10 years in the same proportion as rents increased on the master lease from the City of San Jose. The premises were to be used by Bixler for the purpose of conducting an airplane maintenance business.

Bixler conducted such a business under the name "Flight Services" until, in 1981, he agreed to sell the business to appellants Jack Kendall, Grady O'Hara and Vicki O'Hara. The proposed sale included the business and the equipment, inventory and improvements on the property, together with the existing lease. The proposed assignees had a stronger financial statement and greater net worth than the current lessee, Bixler, and they were willing to be bound by the terms of the lease.

The lease provided that written consent of the lessor was required before the lessee could assign his interest, and that failure to obtain such consent rendered the lease voidable at the option of the lessor.[5] Accordingly, Bixler requested consent from the Perlitches' successor-in-interest, respondent Ernest Pestana, Inc. Respondent refused to consent to the assignment and maintained that it had an absolute right arbitrarily to refuse any such request. The complaint recites that respondent demanded "increased rent and other more onerous terms" as a condition of consenting to Bixler's transfer of interest.

The proposed assignees brought suit for declaratory and injunctive relief and damages seeking, inter alia, a declaration "that the refusal of Ernest Pestana, Inc. to consent to the assignment of the lease is unreasonable and is an unlawful restraint on the freedom of alienation. . . ." The trial court sustained a demurrer to the complaint without leave to amend and this appeal followed.

II.

The law generally favors free alienability of property, and California follows the common law rule that a leasehold interest is freely alienable. *See* Kassan v. Stout, 507 P.2d 87, 89 (Cal. 1973). Contractual restrictions on the alienability of leasehold interests are, however, permitted. *See id.* "Such restrictions are justified as reasonable protection of the interests of the lessor as to who shall possess and manage property in which he has a reversionary interest and from which he is deriving income." Schoshinski, *American Law of Landlord and Tenant* §8:15, at pp. 578-579 (1980). *See also* 2 *Powell on Real Property* ¶246[1], at p. 372.97.

The common law's hostility toward restraints on alienation has caused such restraints on leasehold interests to be strictly construed against the lessor. . . .

Nevertheless, a majority of jurisdictions have long adhered to the rule that where a lease contains an approval clause (a clause stating that the lease cannot be assigned without the prior consent of the lessor), the lessor may arbitrarily refuse to approve a proposed assignee no matter how suitable the assignee appears to be and no matter how unreasonable the lessor's objection. *See, e.g.,* B & R Oil Co., Inc. v.

---

5. Paragraph 13 of the sublease between the Perlitches and Bixler provides: "Lessee shall not assign this lease, or any interest therein, and shall not sublet the said premises or any part thereof, or any right or privilege appurtenant thereto, or suffer any other person (the agents and servants of Lessee excepted) to occupy or use said premises, or any portion thereof, without written consent of Lessor first had and obtained, and a consent to one assignment, subletting, occupation or use by any other person, shall not be deemed to be a consent to any subsequent assignment, subletting, occupation or use by another person. Any such assignment or subletting without this consent shall be void, and shall, at the option of Lessor, terminate this lease. This lease shall not, nor shall any interest therein, be assignable, as to the interest of lessee, by operation of alaw [sic], without the written consent of Lessor."

Ray's Mobile Homes, Inc., 422 A.2d 1267 (Vt. 1980); Dress Shirt Sales, Inc. v. Hotel Martinique Associates, 190 N.E.2d 10 (N.Y. 1963); Jacobs v. Klawans, 169 A.2d 677 (Md. 1961); Segre v. Ring, 170 A.2d 265 (N.H. 1961); Gruman v. Investors Diversified Services, 78 N.W.2d 377 (Minn. 1956). The harsh consequences of this rule have often been avoided through application of the doctrines of waiver and estoppel, under which the lessor may be found to have waived (or be estopped from asserting) the right to refuse consent to assignment.

The traditional majority rule has come under steady attack in recent years. A growing minority of jurisdictions now hold that where a lease provides for assignment only with the prior consent of the lessor, such consent may be withheld *only where the lessor has a commercially reasonable objection to the assignment*, even in the absence of a provision in the lease stating that consent to assignment will not be unreasonably withheld.

For the reasons discussed below, we conclude that the minority rule is the preferable position. . . .

III.

The impetus for change in the majority rule has come from two directions, reflecting the dual nature of a lease as a conveyance of a leasehold interest and a contract. *See* Medico-Dental etc. Co. v. Horton & Converse, 132 P.2d 457, 462 (Cal. 1942). The policy against restraints on alienation pertains to leases in their nature as *conveyances*. . . .

One commentator explains as follows:

> The common-law hostility to restraints on alienation had a large exception with respect to estates for years. A lessor could prohibit the lessee from transferring the estate for years to whatever extent he might desire. It was believed that the objectives served by allowing such restraints outweighed the social evils implicit in the restraints, in that they gave to the lessor a needed control over the person entrusted with the lessor's property and to whom he must look for the performance of the covenants contained in the lease. Whether this reasoning retains full validity can well be doubted. Relationships between lessor and lessee have tended to become more and more impersonal. Courts have considerably lessened the effectiveness of restraint clauses by strict construction and liberal applications of the doctrine of waiver. With the shortage of housing and, in many places, of commercial space as well, the allowance of lease clauses forbidding assignments and subleases is beginning to be curtailed by statutes.

2 Powell, *supra*, ¶246[1], at pp. 372.97-372.98.

The *Restatement Second of Property* adopts the minority rule on the validity of approval clauses in leases: "A restraint on alienation without the consent of the landlord of a tenant's interest in leased property is valid, *but the landlord's consent to an alienation by the tenant cannot be withheld unreasonably,* unless a freely negotiated provision in the lease gives the landlord an absolute right to withhold consent." *Rest. 2d Property*, §15.2(2) (1977), italics added.[14] A comment to the section explains: "The landlord may have an understandable concern about certain personal qualities of a tenant, particularly his reputation for meeting his financial obligations.

---

14. This case does not present the question of the validity of a clause absolutely prohibiting assignment, or granting absolute discretion over assignment to the lessor. We note that under the Restatement rule such a provision would be valid if freely negotiated.

The preservation of the values that go into the personal selection of the tenant justifies upholding a provision in the lease that curtails the right of the tenant to put anyone else in his place by transferring his interest, but this justification does not go to the point of allowing the landlord arbitrarily and without reason to refuse to allow the tenant to transfer an interest in leased property." *Id.*, com. a. Under the Restatement rule, the lessor's interest in the character of his or her tenant is protected by the lessor's right to object to a proposed assignee on reasonable commercial grounds. *See id.*, reporter's note 7 at pp. 112-13. The lessor's interests are also protected by the fact that the original lessee remains liable to the lessor as a surety even if the lessor consents to the assignment and the assignee expressly assumes the obligations of the lease. Peiser v. Mettler, 328 P.2d 953, 957 (Cal. 1958).

The second impetus for change in the majority rule comes from the nature of a lease as a *contract*. . . . "[W]here a contract confers on one party a discretionary power affecting the rights of the other, a duty is imposed to exercise that discretion in good faith and in accordance with fair dealing." Cal. Lettuce Growers v. Union Sugar Co., 289 P.2d 785, 791 (Cal. 1955). Here the lessor retains the discretionary power to approve or disapprove an assignee proposed by the other party to the contract; this discretionary power should therefore be exercised in accordance with commercially reasonable standards. . . .

Under the minority rule, the determination whether a lessor's refusal to consent was reasonable is a question of fact. Some of the factors that the trier of fact may properly consider in applying the standards of good faith and commercial reasonableness are: financial responsibility of the proposed assignee; suitability of the use for the particular property; legality of the proposed use; need for alteration of the premises; and nature of the occupancy, *i.e.*, office, factory, clinic, etc. *See* Fernandez v. Vasquez, 397 So. 2d 1171, 1174 (Fla. App. 1981); Cohen v. Ratinoff, 195 Cal. Rptr. 84, 89 (Ct. App. 1983); Rest. 2d Property, §15.2, reporter's note 7 at pp. 112-13; 1 *Friedman on Leases* (1974) §7.304c.

Denying consent solely on the basis of personal taste, convenience or sensibility is not commercially reasonable. Broad & Branford Place Corp. v. J. J. Hockenjos Co., 39 A.2d 80, 82 (N.J. 1944); Fernandez v. Vasquez, *supra*, 397 So. 2d at 1174; *Rest. 2d Property*, §15.2, reporter's note 7 at pp. 112-113. Nor is it reasonable to deny consent "in order that the landlord may charge a higher rent than originally contracted for." Schweiso v. Williams, 198 Cal. Rptr. 238, 240 (Ct. App. 1984). This is because the lessor's desire for a better bargain than contracted for has nothing to do with the permissible purposes of the restraint on alienation — to protect the lessor's interest in the preservation of the property and the performance of the lease covenants. . . .

In contrast to the policy reasons advanced in favor of the minority rule, the majority rule has traditionally been justified on three grounds. Respondent raises a fourth argument in its favor as well. None of these do we find compelling.

First, it is said that a lease is a conveyance of an interest in real property, and that the lessor, having exercised a personal choice in the selection of a tenant and provided that no substitute shall be acceptable without prior consent, is under no obligation to look to anyone but the lessee for the rent. . . .

A lessor's freedom at common law to look to no one but the lessee for the rent has, however, been undermined by the adoption in California of a rule that lessors — like all other contracting parties — have a duty to mitigate damages upon the lessee's abandonment of the property by seeking a substitute lessee. *See* Civ. Code, §1951.2. Furthermore, the values that go into the personal selection of a lessee are preserved under the minority rule in the lessor's right to refuse consent to assignment on any commercially reasonable grounds. Such grounds include not only the obvious objections to an assignee's financial stability or proposed use of the premises, but a variety of other commercially reasonable objections as well. *See, e.g.,* Arrington v. Walter E. Heller International Corp., 333 N.E.2d 50 (Ill. App. 1975) (desire to have only one "lead tenant" in order to preserve "image of the building" as tenant's international headquarters); Warmack v. Merchants Nat. Bank of Fort Smith, 612 S.W.2d 733 (Ark. 1981) (desire for good "tenant mix" in shopping center); List v. Dahnke, 638 P.2d 824 (Colo. App. 1981) (lessor's refusal to consent to assignment of lease by one restaurateur to another was reasonable where lessor believed proposed specialty restaurant would not succeed at that location). The lessor's interests are further protected by the fact that the original lessee remains a guarantor of the performance of the assignee.

The second justification advanced in support of the majority rule is that an approval clause is an unambiguous reservation of absolute discretion in the lessor over assignments of the lease. The lessee could have bargained for the addition of a reasonableness clause to the lease (*i.e.,* "consent to assignment will not be unreasonably withheld"). The lessee having failed to do so, the law should not rewrite the parties' contract for them. *See* Gruman v. Investors Diversified Services, *supra,* 78 N.W.2d at 381-82.

Numerous authorities have taken a different view of the meaning and effect of an approval clause in a lease, indicating that the clause is not "clear and unambiguous," as respondent suggests. . . . [T]he court in Gamble v. New Orleans Housing Mart, Inc., 154 So. 2d 625 (La. App. 1963), stated:

> Here the lessee is simply not permitted to sublet without the written consent of the lessor. This does not *prohibit* or *interdict* subleasing. To the contrary, it permits subleasing provided only that the lessee first obtain the written consent of the lessor. *It suggests or connotes that, when the lessee obtains a subtenant acceptable or satisfactory to the lessor, he may sublet.* . . . Otherwise the provision simply would prohibit subleasing.

Id. at 627, final italics added. . . .

In light of the interpretations given to approval clauses in the cases cited above, and in light of the increasing number of jurisdictions that have adopted the minority rule in the last 15 years, the assertion that an approval clause "clearly and unambiguously" grants the lessor absolute discretion over assignments is untenable. It is not a rewriting of a contract, as respondent suggests, to recognize the obligations imposed by the duty of good faith and fair dealing, which duty is implied by law in every contract.

The third justification advanced in support of the majority rule is essentially based on the doctrine of stare decisis. It is argued that the courts should not depart from the common law majority rule because "many leases now in effect covering a substantial amount of real property and creating valuable property rights were carefully prepared by competent counsel in reliance upon the majority viewpoint." Gruman v. Investors Diversified Services, *supra,* 78 N.W.2d at 381. As pointed out above, however, the majority viewpoint has been far from universally held and has never been adopted by this court. Moreover, the trend in favor of the minority rule should come as no surprise to observers of the changing state of real property law in the 20th century. The minority rule is part of an increasing recognition of the contractual nature of leases and the implications in terms of contractual duties that flow therefrom. . . .

A final argument in favor of the majority rule is advanced by respondent and stated as follows: "Both tradition and sound public policy dictate that the lessor has a right, under circumstances such as these, to realize the increased value of his property." Respondent essentially argues that any increase in the market value of real property during the term of a lease properly belongs to the lessor, not the lessee. We reject this assertion. . . .

Respondent here is trying to get *more* than it bargained for in the lease. A lessor is free to build periodic rent increases into a lease, as the lessor did here. Any increased value of the property beyond this "belongs" to the lessor only in the sense . . . that the lessor's reversionary estate will benefit from it upon the expiration of the lease. We must therefore reject respondent's argument in this regard.[17]

IV.

In conclusion, both the policy against restraints on alienation and the implied contractual duty of good faith and fair dealing militate in favor of adoption of the rule that where a commercial lease provides for assignment only with the prior consent of the lessor, such consent may be withheld only where the lessor has a commercially reasonable objection to the assignee or the proposed use. Under this rule, appellants have stated a cause of action against respondent Ernest Pestana, Inc.

The order sustaining the demurrer to the complaint . . . is reversed.

LUCAS, Justice. I respectfully dissent. In my view we should follow the weight of authority which, as acknowledged by the majority herein, allows the commercial lessor to withhold his consent to an assignment or sublease arbitrarily or without reasonable cause. The majority's contrary ruling, requiring a "commercially reasonable objection" to the assignment, can only result in a proliferation of unnecessary litigation. . . .

MOSK, Justice, concurred [with Lucas].

Notes and Questions

1. In states following *Kendall* and in other states when the lease expressly provides that the landlord will not unreasonably withhold consent, it is often hard to decide whether a particular landlord's refusal to consent is reasonable. Courts have often struggled in making such determinations. Which of the following landlord objections do you believe are meritorious? Does the validity of the objection depend at all on the nature of the property?

- Transferee has a blemished credit history.
- Transferee has no credit history (or is under age 25).
- Transferee smokes cigarettes.

17. Amicus Pillsbury, Madison & Sutro request that we make clear that, "whatever principle governs in the absence of express lease provisions, nothing bars the parties to commercial lease transactions from making their own arrangements respecting the allocation of appreciated rentals if there is a transfer of the leasehold." This principle we affirm; we merely hold that the clause in the instant lease established no such arrangement.

- Transferee was convicted of a felony.
- Transferor is in default at time of proposal.
- Term of sublease is too short.
- Term of sublease is too long (sublandlord retains reversion of one day).
- Subtenant will pay too much (or too little) subrent.
- Transfer will be sublease and landlord prefers assignment.
- Transfer will be assignment and landlord prefers sublease.
- Transferee is an assignee who will not agree to assume obligations of prime lease.
- For retail lease, transferee will change use from bookstore to coffee shop.
- For residential lease, transferee will use premises as vacation home rather than principal residence.

2. In 1989, the California legislature responded to *Kendall* by enacting the following provisions:

> Cal. Civil Code §1995.230. *Prohibition of transfer.* A restriction on transfer of a tenant's interest in a lease may absolutely prohibit transfer.
>
> Cal. Civil Code §1995.240. *Express standards or conditions of transfer.* A restriction on transfer of a tenant's interest in a lease may provide that the transfer is subject to any express standard or condition, including, but not limited to, a provision that the landlord is entitled to some or all of any consideration the tenant receives from a transferee in excess of the rent under the lease.
>
> Cal. Civil Code §1995.250. *Consent of landlord; requirements.* A restriction on transfer of a tenant's interest in a lease may require the landlord's consent for transfer subject to any express standard or condition for giving or withholding consent, including, but not limited to, either of the following:
>
> (a) The landlord's consent may not be unreasonably withheld.
> (b) The landlord's consent may be withheld subject to express standards or conditions.
>
> Cal. Civil Code §1995.260. *Unreasonably withheld consent; burden of proof.* If a restriction on transfer of the tenant's interest in a lease requires the landlord's consent for transfer but provides no standard for giving or withholding consent, the restriction on transfer shall be construed to include an implied standard that the landlord's consent may not be unreasonably withheld. Whether the landlord's consent has been unreasonably withheld in a particular case is a question of fact on which the tenant has the burden of proof. The tenant may satisfy the burden of proof by showing that, in response to the tenant's written request for a statement of reasons for withholding consent, the landlord has failed, within a reasonable time, to state in writing a reasonable objection to the transfer.

To what extent does the statute codify *Kendall?* To what extent does it modify or supplement *Kendall?*

3. How important is the retention of "settled rules" of property law? Recall the court's observations in *Holy Properties.* Was the *Kendall* majority right to reject the landlord's *stare decisis* argument that judicial imposition of a reasonableness standard would improperly interfere with landlords' expectations? The legislature, as part of its 1989 response, mandated that *Kendall* not apply retroactively to commercial leases, stating: "Until the case of *Kendall* . . . and its predecessor, Cohen v. Ratinoff, 195 Cal. Rptr. 84 (Ct. App. 1983), the parties to commercial

real property leases could reasonably rely on the law of the state to provide that if a lease restriction requires the landlord's consent for transfer of the tenant's interest in the lease but provides no standard for giving or withholding consent, the landlord's consent may be unreasonably withheld." Cal. Civ. Code §1995.270(a)(3).

4. Suppose tenant proposes an assignee or subtenant, landlord refuses to consent, and tenant then abandons the premises? Must landlord mitigate damages by renting to the prospect he just turned down? What if the transaction takes place in a state, such as New York (*see Holy Properties*), that doesn't generally require landlords to mitigate upon abandonment? California regulates the interplay by allowing a landlord to collect rent after a tenant abandons only if the tenant has the right to sublet or assign, subject only to reasonable limitations or to the landlord's consent, not to be unreasonably withheld. Cal. Civ. Code §1951.4.

10
Real Estate Transfers

This chapter provides a short introduction to real property sales, conveyances, and titles. In most law schools, detailed examination of the process of selling and buying real estate is left for an upper-level course, often called *Real Estate Transactions*. In this chapter, we emphasize the typical residential transaction (buying a home), but you should bear in mind that there are many similarities between that relatively simple transaction and commercial real estate transactions. The structure of the transaction, its stages, and the governing law are generally the same for both.

The typical sales transaction is divisible into four distinct stages, as reflected by the following timeline:

The chronology reflected by the four stages is highly significant, both transactionally and legally. The parties' activities with respect to the property and the transaction hinge upon which stage they are in. Likewise, their legal rights and obligations are heavily influenced by their passage through the stages.

Pre-contract stage. Prior to entering into a contract of sale and purchase, Seller and Buyer are busy making plans and seeking information. Once a homeowner decides to sell his property, he is immediately faced with a critical decision. Will he hire a real estate broker or try to sell his home without one, hoping to improve his bottom line by saving part or all of the broker's commission? A standard commission is 5 to 7 percent of the sales price. Most home sellers end up hiring a broker to take advantage of the broker's marketing expertise and their representation. Often a key consideration is the broker's access to the local multiple listing service (MLS), through which all potential homebuyers in the community can quickly learn that the seller's home is for sale. Potential buyers contact a brokerage firm to obtain information about houses on the market and to visit those that seem most promising. This costs a buyer nothing even though a broker often expends significant effort to locate the "right" house at the "right" price for that buyer, as brokers look only to commissions paid by sellers for compensation. Even those relatively rare buyers who purchase houses not listed with brokers usually also "comparison shop" by contacting a broker to canvass the market of listed properties.

When Buyer identifies a home he wants to purchase, he submits a written offer to purchase to Seller. This step initiates negotiation on price and other terms of a prospective contract. If Seller has listed the house with a broker, Broker transmits the offer to Seller for consideration. Under the MLS system, it makes no appreciable difference to the dynamics of the transaction if Buyer, to look at houses, has contacted a different brokerage firm than the one employed by Seller. Then two brokers (the *listing broker* hired by Seller, and the *selling broker* contacted by Buyer) are involved in contract preparation and negotiation. The traditional practice is that both brokers represent Seller, with the selling broker compensated by splitting the commission paid by Seller to the listing broker. But a broker may agree to represent Buyer, and over the years, the percentage of homebuyers who hire buyers' brokers has risen steadily. This is partially due to market specialization, with many brokers choosing to concentrate on buyer representation and advertise their services as such.

Executory contract stage. When Seller accepts Buyer's offer, with or without further negotiations or counter-offers, a binding contract results. The executory contract stage lasts from the moment of contract formation until closing; when at closing the parties perform their promises, the contract is said to be "executed" and thus no longer executory. The contract is of paramount importance, serving as a blueprint for the final three stages of the transaction. A good contract explicitly addresses a host of risks and legal concerns, laying out the parties' rights and obligations and establishing conditions to each party's duty to perform. It's customary for a buyer to make a deposit, generally called *earnest money*, when the contract is signed. The amount is negotiable and can vary widely according to local practice. Typically, the range is from 2 to 10 percent of the price.

At this point, it's critical to observe that in the typical home transaction in all states, the only real estate professionals who have been involved are one or more brokers. Neither Seller nor Buyer has hired an attorney to represent them. During the pre-contract stage, Seller signed a standard-form broker's listing agreement, prepared by the brokerage firm or a brokers' trade association, loaded with pro-broker, anti-seller terms. Both parties signed a standard-form contract of sale and purchase, unilaterally selected by Broker. Although the typical contract is several pages in length, they probably paid no attention to any of the terms except price, anticipated closing date, and (sometimes) what items of personal property will stay with the house. In many communities, brokers lead the parties to use standard-form contracts prepared by brokers' trade associations, which have the dominant orientation of shoring up the brokers' right to collect the commission at the expense of both parties. In other communities, form contracts sanctioned by bar associations are regularly employed. A competent real estate attorney, employed by either Seller or Buyer, would virtually never use a standard-form contract without making major modifications to a number of the provisions. Yet the very large majority of home sellers and buyers fail to hire an attorney to represent their interests; those who consider the issue at all usually conclude that an attorney's fee is a wasted expense — other professionals can handle all aspects of the transaction, and nothing will go legally wrong. In some eastern states, it is customary for Seller or Buyer to hire an attorney after they have entered into the contract. At this point in time, with all the contract terms set, there is much less that the attorney can do to reduce the client's risk and protect his expectations than he could have done had he been employed earlier. Nationally, in most home sales, no attorney is ever involved; and in most cases when there is an attorney, that person surfaces late in the executory contract period and serves only as counsel for the mortgage lender, refusing to represent Seller or Buyer.

This executory contract stage usually lasts for one to three months; this is much longer than is typical for contracts to purchase assets other than real estate. A person who contracts to buy an automobile, a computer system, jewelry, or securities will almost always complete the transaction within days of reaching agreement. Often, contracting, payment, and delivery are close to instantaneous. The significant time period between entering into a real estate contract and closing is unusual. This interval has great impact on the dynamics of the transaction, and has given rise to a number of special legal rules for real estate contracts. There are good reasons for the significant time lag between contracting and closing. Seller must make preparations to move to another residence. Buyer will also make preparations to move, and has a number of other chores as well. Real estate contracts have a number of conditions, which must be satisfied prior to closing. Buyer must apply for a mortgage loan, for very seldom do buyers pay all cash for a house. Professional inspections of the house and its systems are usually conducted. A title search of the property, completed prior to closing, is also necessary.

Closing stage. Assuming the mortgage loan application, inspections, and title work have gone smoothly, closing (sometimes called *settlement*) is scheduled. At closing, the parties consummate their exchange, Buyer paying the price and Seller conveying the property by warranty deed. The parties check the other side's performance and confirm that all contract conditions are satisfied. A document called the *closing statement* reflects payment of the purchase price and shows the expenses of both parties incurred with respect to the transaction. Most expenses are paid "through closing," with Seller's expenses deducted from the price and Buyer paying funds into closing for his expenses. The mortgage lender funds its loan at closing, thereby enabling payment of the balance of the price to Seller. If, as is usually the case, Seller has an existing mortgage on the property, arrangements are made for using part of the price to pay off that mortgage loan. Buyer gets the right to possession of the house at the completion of closing, unless the parties have otherwise agreed.

The traditional real estate closing, still widely employed in many parts of the country, is a face-to-face meeting attended by the parties and a number of professionals, including one or more brokers. The closing ceremony, conducted by a *closing officer* (a title company employee, lender's employee, or an attorney), lasts an hour or two, during which time both parties sign a blizzard of papers. Closing details vary considerably from state to state. In a number of communities, the typical closing is an *escrow closing* rather than a face-to-face closing. With an escrow closing, Seller, Buyer, and Lender separately submit documents and money to an *escrow agent*, who holds all the items until the submissions are complete and all closing requirements are satisfied.

Post-closing stage. After the completion of closing, whether or not accomplished through escrow, the parties enter the final post-closing stage. With most closings, there are some post-closing tasks related to the sale, including completion of work involving documents. The deed and mortgage instrument are recorded immediately after closing, with the original deed sent to Buyer. Title insurance policies are issued only after closing, following recordation of documents. After closing, if all goes well Seller and Buyer will have no further contact (or if they do, it will be social in nature, rather than a discussion or dispute with legal aspects). Of course, in the real world, all transactional stories don't have idyllic endings. Most often, it's Buyer and not Seller who makes a complaint after closing. The problems that come up most frequently involve physical condition of the property, with Buyer asserting that something, such as an improvement or an appliance, has a defect or is not as represented. Not infrequently, title problems also surface for the first time after closing. On occasion, the parties agree to defer a particular performance until after closing, in which event the timeliness or quality of that performance can become an issue. For example, Seller may have promised to replace a malfunctioning garage door opener.

A. CONTRACTS OF SALE

Contracts for the sale of real property have a number of distinctive features. The contract must adequately describe the land and any other property that is to be conveyed. Among other things, it should address the title search process, the quality of title and how it is to be documented, the buyer's right to inspect the property, payment of the price including provisions for the buyer to obtain mortgage financing, time for performance of both parties' obligations, and remedies for both parties. When the contract fails to handle such matters with express provisions, the law implies terms to fill in the gaps. The law of real estate contracts is a vast subject matter. In this section, we focus on only two of their peculiarities: the statute of frauds requirement of a writing, and the doctrine of equitable conversion.

■   **STERLING v. TAYLOR**
Supreme Court of California, 2007
152 P.3d 420

CORRIGAN, Justice. The statute of frauds provides that certain contracts "are invalid, unless they, or some note or memorandum thereof, are in writing and subscribed by the party to be charged. . . ." Civ. Code §1624. In this case, the Court of Appeal held that a memorandum regarding the sale of several apartment buildings was sufficient to satisfy the statute of frauds. Defendants contend the court improperly considered extrinsic evidence to resolve uncertainties in the terms identifying the seller, the property, and the price.

We reverse, but not because the court consulted extrinsic evidence. Extrinsic evidence has long been held admissible to clarify the terms of a memorandum for purposes of the statute of frauds. Statements to the contrary appear in some cases, but we disapprove them. A memorandum serves only an evidentiary function under the statute. If the writing includes the essential terms of the parties' agreement, there is no bar to the admission of relevant extrinsic evidence to explain or clarify those terms. The memorandum, viewed in light of the evidence, must be sufficient to demonstrate with reasonable certainty the terms to which the parties agreed to be bound. Here, plaintiffs attempt to enforce a price term that lacks the certainty required by the statute of frauds.

I. FACTUAL AND PROCEDURAL BACKGROUND

In January 2000, defendant Lawrence N. Taylor and plaintiff Donald Sterling discussed the sale of three apartment buildings in Santa Monica owned by the Santa Monica Collection partnership (SMC). Defendant was a general partner in SMC. Plaintiff and defendant, both experienced real estate investors, met on March 13, 2000, and discussed a series of transactions including the purchase of the SMC properties. At this meeting, plaintiff drafted a handwritten memorandum entitled "Contract for Sale of Real Property."

The memorandum encompasses the sale of five properties; only the SMC properties are involved here. They are identified in the memorandum as "808 4th St.," "843 4th St.," and "1251 14th St.," with an aggregate price term of "approx. 10.468 × gross income[,] estimated income 1.600.000, Price $16,750.00." Although defendant had given plaintiff rent rolls showing the income from the properties, neither man brought these documents to the March 13 meeting. Plaintiff dated and initialed the memorandum as "Buyer," but the line he provided for "Seller" was left blank. Plaintiff contends the omission was inadvertent. Defendant, however, asserts he did not sign the document because he needed approval from a majority of SMC's limited partners. . . .

On April 4, 2000, defendant sent plaintiff three formal purchase agreements with escrow instructions, identifying the properties by their legal descriptions. SMC was named as the seller and the Sterling Family Trust as the buyer. The price terms totalled $16,750,000. Defendant signed the agreements as a general partner of SMC. Plaintiff refused to sign. Defendant claims plaintiff telephoned on April 28, saying the purchase price was unacceptable. Plaintiff asserts that after reviewing the rent rolls, he determined the actual rental income from the SMC buildings was $1,375,404, not $1,600,000 as estimated on the March 13 memorandum. Plaintiff claims he tried to have defendant correct the escrow instructions, but defendant did not return his calls. Plaintiff wanted to lower the price to $14,404,841, based on the actual rental income figure and the 10.468 multiplier noted in the memorandum.

Plaintiff did not ask for the $16,750.00 purchase price stated in the memorandum. He admits that he "accidentally left off one zero" when he wrote down that figure. Defendant also acknowledges that the price recorded on the memorandum was meant to be $16,750,000.

[In March 2001, the trustees of the Sterling Family Trust sued Taylor, SMC, and related entities, alleging breach of a written contract to sell the properties for a total price of $14,404,841. Defendants sought summary judgment, claiming that the alleged contract violated the statute of frauds because it established no agreement on price. The trial court granted summary judgment, ruling that the price term was too uncertain to be enforced and the writings did not comply with the statute of frauds. The Court of Appeal reversed, holding that defendants' evidence raised a triable issue as to whether the parties had agreed on a formula for determining the purchase price.]

II. DISCUSSION

Defendants contend the Court of Appeal improperly considered extrinsic evidence to establish essential contract terms. They insist the statute of frauds requires a memorandum that, standing alone, supplies all material elements of the contract. Plaintiffs, on the other hand, argue that extrinsic evidence is routinely admitted for the purpose of determining whether memoranda comply with the statute of frauds.

Both sides of this debate find support in California case law, sometimes in the same opinion. Part A of our discussion explains that plaintiffs' view is correct. The statute of frauds does not preclude the admission of evidence in any form; it imposes a writing requirement, but not a comprehensive one. In part B, however, we conclude that defendants are nevertheless entitled to judgment. The Court of Appeal properly considered the parties' extrinsic evidence, but erroneously deemed it legally sufficient under the statute of frauds to establish the price sought by plaintiffs.

A. THE MEMORANDUM REQUIREMENT OF THE STATUTE OF FRAUDS

The statute of frauds does not require a written contract; a "note or memorandum . . . subscribed by the party to be charged" is adequate. Civ. Code §1624(a). In Crowley v. Modern Faucet Mfg. Co., 282 P.2d 33, 35 (Cal. 1955), we observed that "a written memorandum is not identical with a written contract; it is merely evidence of it and usually does not contain all of the terms." Indeed, in most instances it is not even necessary that the parties intended the memorandum to serve a contractual purpose.

A memorandum satisfies the statute of frauds if it identifies the subject of the parties' agreement, shows that they made a contract, and states the essential contract terms with reasonable certainty. Only the essential terms must be stated, "'details or particulars' need not [be]. What is essential depends on the agreement and its context and also on the subsequent conduct of the parties. . . ." *Rest. 2d Contracts* §131, com. g (1981).

This court recently observed that the writing requirement of the statute of frauds "'serves only to prevent the contract from being unenforceable' [citation]; it does not necessarily establish the terms of the parties' contract." Casa Herrera, Inc. v. Beydoun, 83 P.3d 497, 503 (Cal. 2004). Unlike the parol evidence rule, which "determines the enforceable and incontrovertible terms of an integrated written agreement," the statute of frauds "merely serve[s] an evidentiary purpose." *Id.* As the drafters of the Second Restatement of Contracts explained:

> The primary purpose of the Statute is evidentiary, to require reliable evidence of the existence and terms of the contract and to prevent enforcement through fraud or perjury of contracts never in fact made. The contents of the writing must be such as to make successful fraud unlikely, but the possibility need not be excluded that some other subject matter or person than those intended will also fall within the words of the writing. Where only an evidentiary purpose is served, *the requirement of a memorandum is read in the light of the dispute which arises and the admissions of the party to be charged*; there is no need for evidence on points not in dispute.

Rest. 2d Contracts §131, com. c, italics added.

Thus, when ambiguous terms in a memorandum are disputed, extrinsic evidence is admissible to resolve the uncertainty. Extrinsic evidence can also support reformation of a memorandum to correct a mistake.

Because the memorandum itself must include the essential contractual terms, it is clear that extrinsic evidence cannot *supply* those required terms. It can, however, be used to *explain* essential terms that were understood by the parties but would otherwise be unintelligible to others. . . .

To clarify the law on this point, we disapprove the statements in California cases barring consideration of extrinsic evidence to determine the sufficiency of a memorandum under the statute of frauds. The purposes of the statute are not served by such a rigid rule, which has never been a consistent feature of the common law. Corbin observes:

> Judicial dicta abound to the effect that the writing must contain all of the "essential terms and conditions" of the contract, and it is often said that these must be so clear as to be understood "without any aid from parol testimony." But the long course of judicial decision shows that "essential terms and conditions" is itself a term of considerable flexibility and that the courts do not in fact blind themselves by excluding parol testimony when it is a necessary aid to understanding. . . .
>
> Some confusion is attributable to a failure to keep clearly in mind the purpose of the statute and the informal character of the evidence that the actual words of the statute require; some is no doubt due to differences in the attitude of the judges as to the beneficence of the statute and the wisdom of its existence. Further, there are differences in the strictness of judicial requirements as to the contents of the memorandum. It is believed that sometimes these apparent differences can be explained by the degree of doubt existing in the court's mind as to the actual making and performance of the alleged contract. The better and the more disinterested is the oral testimony offered by the plaintiff, the more convincing the corroboration that is found in the surrounding circumstances, and the more limited the disputed issue because of admissions made by the defendant, the less that should be and is required of the written memorandum.

4 *Corbin on Contracts* §22.2, at 706-07, 709 (rev. ed. 1997; fns. omitted). . . .

We emphasize that a memorandum of the parties' agreement is *controlling* evidence under the statute of frauds. Thus, extrinsic evidence cannot be employed to prove an agreement at odds with the terms of the memorandum. This point was made in Beazell v. Schrader, 381 P.2d 390 (Cal. 1963). There, the plaintiff sought to recover a 5 percent real estate broker's commission under an oral agreement. The escrow instructions, which specified a 1.25 percent commission, were the "memorandum" on which the plaintiff relied to comply with the statute. However, he contended the instructions incorrectly reflected the parties' actual agreement, as shown by extrinsic evidence. The *Beazell* court rejected this argument, holding that under the statute of frauds, "the parol agreement of which the writing is a memorandum must be one whose terms are consistent with the terms of the memorandum." *Id.* at 393. Thus, in determining whether extrinsic evidence provides the certainty required by the statute, courts must bear in mind that the evidence cannot contradict the terms of the writing.

B. THE SUFFICIENCY OF THIS MEMORANDUM

As noted above, it is a question of law whether a memorandum, considered in light of the circumstances surrounding its making, complies with the statute of frauds. Accordingly, the issue is generally amenable to resolution by summary judgment. We independently review the record to determine whether a triable issue of fact might defeat the statute of frauds defense in this case.

A memorandum of a contract for the sale of real property must identify the buyer, the seller, the price, and the property. Defendants contend the memorandum drafted by plaintiff Sterling fails to adequately specify the seller, the property, or the price. . . .

As defendants forthrightly conceded in the trial court, "[t]he problem here is the price term." The Court of Appeal concluded that the lines in the memorandum stating "approx. 10.468 × gross income[,] estimated income 1.600.000, Price $16,750.00" were ambiguous, given the use of the modifier "approx." before the multiplier, the omitted zero in the price, and the uncertain meaning of "gross income." The court then considered Sterling's testimony that "approx." was meant to modify the total price, not the multiplier; that the missing zero was merely an error; and that "gross income" was used by the parties to refer to actual gross annual income. It decided that this evidence, if accepted by the trier of fact, could establish an agreement to determine the price based on a formula, which would be binding under Carver v. Teitsworth, 2 Cal. Rptr. 2d 446, 450 (Ct. App. 1991). In *Carver*, a bid for either a specified price or $1,000 over any higher bid was deemed sufficiently certain. . . .

The Court of Appeal erred by deeming Sterling's testimony sufficient to establish his interpretation of the memorandum for purposes of the statute of frauds. Had Taylor testified that the parties meant to leave the price open to determination based on a rental income figure that was yet to be determined, this would be a different case. Then, the "admissions of the party to be charged" might have supported a reasonably certain price term derived from a negotiated formula. *Rest. 2d Contracts* §131, com. c. Here, however, Taylor insists the price was meant to be $16,750,000, and Sterling agrees that was the number he intended to write down, underlined, as the "Price."

$16,750,000 is clearly an approximate product of the formula specified in the memorandum, applied to the income figure stated there. On the other hand, Sterling's asserted price of $14,404,841 cannot reasonably be considered an approximation of $16,750,000. It is instead an approximate product of the formula applied to an actual income figure not found in the memorandum. The writing does not include the term "actual gross income," nor does it state that the price term will vary depending on proof or later agreement regarding the actual rental income from the buildings. In effect, Sterling would employ only the first part of the price term ("approx. 10.468 × gross income") and ignore the last parts ("estimated income 1.600.000, Price $16,750.00"). He would hold Taylor to a price that is 10.468 times the actual rental income figure gleaned from the rent rolls, but only "approximately" so because of Sterling's computational errors.

Thus, two competing interpretations of the memorandum were before the court. Taylor's is consistent with the figures provided in the memorandum, requiring only the correction of the price by reference to undisputed extrinsic evidence. Sterling's price is not stated in the memorandum, and depends on extrinsic evidence in the form of his own testimony, disputed by Taylor, that the parties intended to apply the formula to actual gross rental income instead of the estimated income noted in the memorandum. Even if the trier of fact were to accept Sterling's version of the parties' negotiations, the price he seeks is not reflected in the memorandum; indeed, it is inconsistent with the price term that appears in the memorandum. Under these circumstances, we conclude the evidence is insufficient to establish Sterling's price term with the reasonable certainty required by the statute of frauds.

The statute of frauds demands written evidence that reflects the parties' mutual understanding of the essential terms of their agreement, when viewed in light of the transaction at issue and the dispute before the court. The writing requirement is intended to permit the enforcement of agreements actually reached, but "to prevent enforcement through fraud or perjury of contracts never in fact made." *Rest. 2d Contracts*, §131, com. c, p. 335. The sufficiency of a memorandum to fulfill this purpose may depend on the quality of the extrinsic evidence offered to explain its terms. . . . Here . . . the extrinsic evidence offered by plaintiffs is at odds with the writing, which states a specific price and does not indicate that the parties contemplated any change based on actual rental income. Therefore, the evidence is insufficient to show with reasonable certainty that the parties understood and agreed to the price alleged by plaintiffs. The price terms stated in the memorandum, considered together with the extrinsic evidence of the contemplated price, leave a degree of doubt that the statute of frauds does not tolerate. The trial court properly granted defendants summary judgment.

III. DISPOSITION

The judgment of the Court of Appeal is reversed with directions to affirm the trial court judgment in its entirety.

KENNARD, Justice, concurring and dissenting, joined by Justice WERDEGAR. I agree with the majority that extrinsic evidence is admissible to resolve the meaning of an ambiguity in a written memorandum required by the statute of frauds as evidence of an agreement, and that conflicts in the evidence are for the trier of fact to resolve. The majority, however, goes astray when it takes it upon itself to resolve an existing conflict in the evidence. In my view, the ambiguity in the language of the memorandum at issue should be resolved by the trier of fact. . . .

Notes and Questions

1. What did the parties agree to do? How do we know? Could Sterling have insisted upon the sale of the property for $16,750, instead of $16,750,000?

2. The *essential terms* required by the statute of frauds to be in a writing are (1) the names of the parties, (2) a description of the land, and (3) an intent to sell and buy the land. Courts have differed as to the treatment of price or other consideration. In many states, it is an essential term; however, other states will imply a reasonable price if the evidence shows that the parties failed to agree upon a price but nevertheless intended to be bound. Although the norm in real estate contracts is for the parties both to sign a single writing, the essential terms do not have to be set forth in a single writing. Multiple writings can comprise the statutorily mandated "note or memorandum."

3. Notwithstanding the statute of frauds, some oral contracts for the sale of land are enforceable. Under the doctrine of *part performance*, courts protect buyers who demonstrate substantial reliance upon an oral contract. Generally, the buyer must have taken possession under the oral contract and, in most states, changed his position further by paying some or all of the price or improving or repairing the property. As a substitute for, or alternative to, part performance, some states use the closely related *equitable estoppel* doctrine. Part performance focuses on the nature of the buyer's acts of reliance, while equitable estoppel tends to focus more on the actions of the seller in allowing the buyer to change his position. In addition, some states recognize a third, closely related theory — *promissory estoppel*. Almost always it's

a buyer who succeeds in using one of these theories to enforce an oral contract. Seller enforcement against a buyer is extremely rare.

4. The vocabulary of traditional statutes of frauds dates back to the English seventeenth-century model and on their face require a "writing." These state statutes are largely still on the books today. How should modern courts in the computer age interpret them? Congress passed the "E-sign Act" in 2000, authorizing electronic signatures in any transaction in or affecting interstate commerce. Electronic Signatures in Global and National Commerce Act, 15 U.S.C. §§7001 to 7031. Transactions include contracts for the sale of real and personal property. The Act preempts any state law to the contrary. Thus, it is possible to contract to sell or buy real estate online through the use of e-mail or web page interaction.

■   **BRUSH GROCERY KART, INC. v. SURE FINE MARKET, INC.**
Supreme Court of Colorado, 2002
47 P.3d 680

COATS, Justice. . . .

In October 1992 Brush Grocery Kart, Inc. and Sure Fine Market, Inc. entered into a five-year "Lease with Renewal Provisions and Option to Purchase" for real property, including a building to be operated by Brush as a grocery store. Under the contract's purchase option provision, any time during the last six months of the lease, Brush could elect to purchase the property at a price equal to the average of the appraisals of an expert designated by each party.

Shortly before expiration of the lease, Brush notified Sure Fine of its desire to purchase the property and begin the process of determining a sale price. Although each party offered an appraisal, the parties were unable to agree on a final price by the time the lease expired. Brush then vacated the premises, returned all keys to Sure Fine, and advised Sure Fine that it would discontinue its casualty insurance covering the property during the lease. Brush also filed suit, alleging that Sure Fine failed to negotiate the price term in good faith and asking for the appointment of a special master to determine the purchase price. Sure Fine agreed to the appointment of a special master and counterclaimed, alleging that Brush negotiated the price term in bad faith and was therefore the breaching party.

During litigation over the price term, the property was substantially damaged during a hail storm. With neither party carrying casualty insurance, each asserted that the other was liable for the damage. The issue was added to the litigation at a stipulated amount of $60,000. The court appointed a special master pursuant to C.R.C.P. 53 and accepted his appraised value of $375,000. The court then found that under the doctrine of equitable conversion, Brush was the equitable owner of the property and bore the risk of loss. It therefore declined to abate the purchase price or award damages to Brush for the loss.

Brush appealed the loss allocation, and the court of appeals affirmed on similar grounds. . . . Noting that allocation of the risk of loss in circumstances where the vendee is not in possession had not previously been addressed by an appellate court in this jurisdiction, the court of appeals went on to conclude that a "bright line rule" allocating the risk of loss to the vendee, without regard to possession, would best inform the parties of their rights and obligations under a contract for the sale of land. . . .

III. The Risk of Casualty Loss in the Absence of Statutory Authority

In the absence of statutory authority, the rights, powers, duties, and liabilities arising out of a contract for the sale of land have frequently been derived by reference to the theory of equitable conversion. People v. Alexander, 663 P.2d 1024, 1030 n.6 (Colo. 1983) (quoting III *American Law of Property* §11.22, at 62-63 (A. Casner ed. 1974)). This theory or doctrine . . . is based on equitable principles that permit the vendee to be considered the equitable owner of the land and debtor for the purchase money and the vendor to be regarded as a secured creditor. *Alexander*, 663 P.2d at 1030 n.6. The changes in rights and liabilities that occur upon the making of the contract result from the equitable right to specific performance. *Id.* Even with regard to third parties, the theory has been relied on to determine, for example, the devolution, upon death, of the rights and liabilities of each party with respect to the land, *see* Chain O'Mines v. Williamson, 72 P.2d 265, 266 (Colo. 1937), and to ascertain the powers of creditors of each party to reach the land in payment of their claims. *Alexander*, 663 P.2d at 1030 n.6.

The assignment of the risk of casualty loss in the executory period of contracts for the sale of real property varies greatly throughout the jurisdictions of this country. What appears to yet be a slim majority of states, *see* Randy R. Koenders, Annotation, *Risk of Loss by Casualty Pending Contract for Conveyance of Real Property Modern Cases*, 85 A.L.R.4th 233 (2001), places the risk of loss on the vendee from the moment of contracting, on the rationale that once an equitable conversion takes place, the vendee must be treated as owner for all purposes. *See* Skelly Oil v. Ashmore, 365 S.W.2d 582, 588 (Mo. 1963) (criticizing this approach). Once the vendee becomes the equitable owner, he therefore becomes responsible for the condition of the property, despite not having a present right of occupancy or control. In sharp contrast, a handful of other states reject the allocation of casualty loss risk as a consequence of the theory of equitable conversion and follow the equally rigid "Massachusetts Rule," under which the seller continues to bear the risk until actual transfer of the title, absent an express agreement to the contrary. *See, e.g., Skelly Oil*, 365 S.W.2d at 588-89. A substantial and growing number of jurisdictions, however, base the legal consequences of no-fault casualty loss on the right to possession of the property at the time the loss occurs. Koenders, *supra*, §§6, 7. This view has found expression in the Uniform Vendor and Purchaser Risk Act,[2] and while a number of states have adopted some variation of the Uniform Act, others have arrived at a similar position through the interpretations of their courts. *See, e.g.*, Lucenti v. Cayuga Apartments, 399 N.E.2d 918, 923-24 (N.Y. 1979).

---

2. Under the Uniform Vendor and Purchaser Risk Act §1, 14 U.L.A. 471 (1968) ("Risk of Loss"):

Any contract hereafter made in this State for the purchase and sale of realty shall be interpreted as including an agreement that the parties shall have the following rights and duties, unless the contract expressly provides otherwise:

(a) If, when neither the legal title nor the possession of the subject matter of the contract has been transferred, all or a material part thereof is destroyed without fault of the purchaser or is taken by eminent domain, the vendor cannot enforce the contract, and the purchaser is entitled to recover any portion of the price that he has paid;

(b) If, when either the legal title or the possession of the subject matter of the contract has been transferred, all or any part thereof is destroyed without fault of the vendor or is taken by eminent domain, the purchaser is not thereby relieved from a duty to pay the price, nor is he entitled to recover any portion thereof that he has paid.

This court has applied the theory of equitable conversion in limited circumstances affecting title, *see* Konecny v. von Gunten, 379 P.2d 158 (Colo. 1963) (finding vendors incapable of unilaterally changing their tenancy in common to joint tenancy during the executory period of the contract because their interest had been equitably converted into a mere security interest and the vendee's interest into realty), and refused to apply it in some circumstances, *see Chain O'Mines*, 72 P.2d 265 (holding that even if the doctrine applies to option contracts, no conversion would take place until the option were exercised by the party having the right of election). . . . It has never before, however, expressly relied on the theory of equitable conversion alone as allocating the risk of casualty loss to a vendee. . . .

Those jurisdictions that indiscriminately include the risk of casualty loss among the incidents or "attributes" of equitable ownership do so largely in reliance on ancient authority or by considering it necessary for consistent application of the theory of equitable conversion. *See Skelly Oil*, 365 S.W.2d at 592 (Stockman, J. dissenting) (quoting 4 Williston, *Contracts* §929, at 2607: "Only the hoary age and frequent repetition of the maxim prevents a general recognition of its absurdity."); *see also* Paine v. Meller, 31 Eng. Rep. 1088 (1801). Under virtually any accepted understanding of the theory, however, equitable conversion is not viewed as entitling the purchaser to every significant right of ownership, and particularly not the right of possession. As a matter of both logic and equity, the obligation to maintain property in its physical condition follows the right to have actual possession and control rather than a legal right to force conveyance of the property through specific performance at some future date. *See* 17 Samuel Williston, *A Treatise on the Law of Contracts* §50:46, at 457-58 (Richard A. Lord ed., 4th ed. 1990) ("it is wiser to have the party in possession of the property care for it at his peril, rather than at the peril of another").

The equitable conversion theory is literally stood on its head by imposing on a vendee, solely because of his right to specific performance, the risk that the vendor will be unable to specifically perform when the time comes because of an accidental casualty loss. It is counterintuitive, at the very least, that merely contracting for the sale of real property should not only relieve the vendor of his responsibility to maintain the property until execution but also impose a duty on the vendee to perform despite the intervention of a material, no-fault casualty loss preventing him from ever receiving the benefit of his bargain. Such an extension of the theory of equitable conversion to casualty loss has never been recognized by this jurisdiction, and it is neither necessary nor justified solely for the sake of consistency. . . .

Furthermore, where a vendee is entitled to rescind as a result of casualty loss, the vendee should generally also be entitled to partial specific performance of the contract with an abatement in the purchase price reflecting the loss. Where the damage is ascertainable, permitting partial specific performance with a price abatement allows courts as nearly as possible to fulfill the expectations of the parties expressed in the contract, while leaving each in a position that is equitable relative to the other. . . .

Here, Brush was clearly not in possession of the property as the equitable owner. Even if the doctrine of equitable conversion applies to the option contract between Brush and Sure Fine and could be said to have converted Brush's interest to an equitable ownership of the property at the time Brush exercised its option to purchase, *see Chain O'Mines*, 72 P.2d at 266, neither party considered the contract for sale to entitle Brush to possession. Brush was, in fact, not in possession of the property, and the record indicates that Sure Fine considered itself to hold the right of use and occupancy and gave notice that it would consider Brush a holdover tenant if it continued to occupy the premises other than by continuing to lease the property. The casualty loss was ascertainable and in fact stipulated by the parties, and neither party challenged the district court's enforcement of the contract except with regard to its allocation of the casualty loss. Both the court of appeals and the district court therefore erred in finding that the doctrine of equitable conversion required Brush to bear the loss caused by hail damage.

IV. CONCLUSION

Where Brush was not an equitable owner in possession at the time of the casualty loss, it was entitled to rescind its contract with Sure Fine. At least under the circumstances of this case, where Brush chose to go forward with the contract under a stipulation as to loss from the hail damage, it was also entitled to specific performance with an abatement of the purchase price equal to the casualty loss. The judgment of the court of appeals is therefore reversed and the case is remanded for further proceedings consistent with this opinion.

Notes and Questions

1. The core idea of equitable conversion is that Buyer acquires a property right, called *equitable title*, the moment the contract is signed. Prior to closing, when Seller signs and delivers the deed of conveyance, Seller has *legal title*. It is said that the equitable title is the real or beneficial ownership, and the legal title represents only Seller's interest in getting paid the purchase price. Legal title is retained as security (like collateral) to ensure Seller will be paid. As *Brush Grocery Kart* demonstrates, one important application of equitable conversion is to shift the risk of loss from casualty to Buyer, at least under some circumstances.

Standard written real estate contracts, prepared by attorneys, bar associations, or brokers, almost always have an express provision addressing risk of loss from casualty, which modifies the state's default rule, whether it is the traditional rule rejected by *Brush Grocery Kart* or some variation. An informed buyer will virtually never agree to undertake the risk of loss from casualty prior to the earlier of closing (when title is conveyed) or taking possession. Does the combination of these two facts mean the *Brush Grocery Kart* court was right or wrong in changing (or refusing to recognize) the traditional rule?

Most casualties are insurable, and the parties should consider who will insure any improvements, and in what amounts, while their contract is executory. Both Seller and Buyer have insurable interests. Obviously, they should coordinate their insurance responsibilities with their agreement as to who bears the risk of an insurable loss. Usually the simplest arrangement is for Seller to keep his existing insurance coverage until closing. The parties' agreement as to insurance will be set forth in a well-drafted contract, but many standard-form contracts ignore the issue. Then, when parties are not represented by attorneys in drafting their contract, insurance issues are often unaddressed or poorly addressed.

2. The equitable conversion concept has importance beyond the allocation of casualty losses. Under its logic, what should happen if some event other than a casualty causes a dramatic drop in value (or increase in value) of the property after the contract is signed? Suppose an endangered species is discovered on the

tract, making the land far less valuable for commercial development due to the restrictions of the federal Endangered Species Act. Who should bear this *legal risk of loss*? Suppose the land quadruples in value because nearby seismic tests reveal that valuable minerals lie underneath the surface. Seller seeks to rescind on the basis of unanticipated circumstances. Should he prevail?

In some respects, the equitable conversion doctrine means that Seller and Buyer are co-owners of the property while the contract is executory. Each has some sticks in the "bundle of sticks"; each has property rights, which can be held, insured, or transferred by sale, assignment, mortgage, devise, or inheritance.

Equitable conversion also affects the *characterization* of the parties' ownership as between real and personal property in a way most laypersons wouldn't expect. The court in *Brush Grocery Kart* mentions that the theory has affected devolution on a party's death and creditor's lien rights. Buyer, the equitable owner, has the benefits and burdens of ownership and thus owns *real property*. Seller conversely owns personal property because he owns the right to receive money (legal title represents security for the unpaid price). Based on this characterization, what should happen if, after a contract for the sale of Blackacre is signed but before closing, Seller dies, devising "all of my real property to *X* and all of my personal property to *Y*"? If Buyer dies having a will with the identical devise? What if, while Blackacre is under contract, Creditor obtains a judgment lien on all the real property owned by Seller; or by Buyer?

B. PROPERTY QUALITY

■   DONNELLY v. TAYLOR
Court of Common Pleas of Ohio, 2002
786 N.E.2d 119, aff'd, 2003 WL 356316 (Ohio Ct. App. 2003)

KIMBLER, Judge. Mr. and Mrs. Patrick Donnelly filed a complaint against Mr. and Mrs. Loren Taylor alleging three causes of action. One was for breach of contract, one was for loss of enjoyment, and the other was for fraud and misrepresentation. . . .

In the fall of 1999, Mr. and Mrs. Taylor listed their house for sale. The house was located in Lodi, Ohio, on Prospect Street. The listing agency was Padgett Young in Lodi, Ohio. The house was purchased by Mr. and Mrs. Donnelly. The Donnellys never talked directly to the Taylors. All of their conversations went through either the real estate agent or the Taylors' son.

The parties executed the purchase agreement on October 14, 1999. The agreement contained the following clause: "In the absence of written notice of any deficiency, from Purchaser prior to closing, Purchaser understands that they will take the property in an 'as is' condition."

Following the execution of the purchase agreement, the house was inspected by a V.A. inspector, but the Donnellys decided not to have the house inspected by anyone other than the V.A. except for a termite inspection. The termite inspection was done and did not reveal any termite infestation.

After all inspections, the Donnellys took possession of the house. Approximately two weeks after their possession began, they started to hear noises in the walls of the house. The noises were heard during the night but not during the day.

They called out a pest-control service. The employee of the pest-control service told them they had either mice or squirrels in their home. The pest-control service attempted to catch the suspected rodents by setting out traps but failed to catch any.

In January to early February, there was a warm spell. It was during that warm spell that Mrs. Donnelly found a bat on the floor of a shower in the basement. She called for her husband. They removed the bat and notified the pest-control service. The pest-control service informed them that the house had bats living in the walls.

Sometime after the discovery of the bat in the shower, their daughter came to them and told them there was a cricket in her room. The Donnellys, who had not told her about the bats, went upstairs to her room. They heard scratching in the walls, screeching from the walls, and the sound that their daughter described as sounding like crickets.

At that point, they sent their daughter to stay with her grandparents for the night. They started "bat watches" to locate the bats. They located several small holes near the roof line, but they did not think the holes were big enough to allow bats in and out.

They then had another pest-control expert come out and look for the bats. The expert, Mr. Jameson, told them that bats can come in and out of a hole the size of a dime. He located several holes that he thought were being used by the bats and started sealing them up. His plan was to seal all the holes but one, thus forcing the bats to use that hole to enter and leave the roof area.

The remaining hole was screened in with a screening that allows the bats to leave, but not return, through the hole. This happens because the screening is designed to let them crawl down the screen and then drop, which is how bats take off, but when they come back they run into the screens.

Mr. Jameson then sealed up all the holes but one. He sealed that one after waiting several days. The interval allowed the bats to leave the house. Unfortunately, some bats were still in the house, and they tried to escape by going down into the basement. A live bat was found in the basement, and dead bats were found in the sump pump and the drains in the basement.

Although Mr. Jameson believed that dead bats were probably in the walls of the house, the Donnellys have not yet paid his company to remove the dead bats or remove the bat droppings that are in the attic and the walls of the house.

The Taylors filed affidavits claiming that they had no knowledge of the existence of the bats. They filled out a disclosure form, which, although it asks about wood-boring insects, does not ask about bats. There is a part, though, that asks about knowledge of any other material defects. The Taylors did not list anything on the blanks provided in that part of the form.

The Donnellys found pieces of foil in the registers of the forced-air heating system, which they assume were placed there to make noise to keep the bats out of the vents. They also found a boarded-up fireplace when they looked at the house prior to purchasing and, when they inquired, were told by the real estate agent that the Taylors never used the fireplace. They also found boards nailed up in the basement. . . .

HOLDING

The Donnellys have not shown that there is a material issue of fact regarding whether the Taylors actively misrepresented or actively concealed the presence of the bats in the house, and therefore summary judgment is granted to the Taylors.

(This holding and the discussion below assume that the bats and their droppings are a defect in the condition of the premises.) . . .

With respect to latent defects, Ohio follows the doctrine of caveat emptor if the defect is one that is discoverable by a reasonable inspection, there is an unimpeded opportunity to inspect the premises, and there is no fraud by the sellers. Layman v. Binns, 519 N.E.2d 642 (Ohio 1988).

If, however, the defect is not discoverable by reasonable inspection or opportunity to inspect is impeded by the sellers, then the doctrine does not apply, assuming that the contract does not contain an "as is" provision. The doctrine also does not apply if there is fraudulent misrepresentation or concealment by the sellers even though they allowed inspection or an opportunity to inspect.

Where the contract contains an "as is" clause, the sellers have no duty to disclose latent defects, even though they are aware of them, but they may not actively misrepresent the condition of the property or actively conceal the defects. Kaye v. Buehrle, 457 N.E.2d 373 (Ohio App. 1983). Put another way, fraud "trumps" an "as is" clause, and the purchasers may proceed with a lawsuit.

The question then becomes what happens when you have a latent defect that is not discoverable by a reasonable inspection, no fraud on the part of the sellers, and the contract contains an "as is" clause?

This court believes that in such a case the "as is" clause shifts the risk of the nondisclosure (perhaps a better term might be "nondiscovery") of the defect to the purchasers. In such a case, the existence of an "as is" clause puts the parties back in the position of caveat emptor. . . .

Therefore, the Donnellys cannot recover for breach of contract, absent fraud, for any latent defects in the property. In this case, that means that the Taylors are entitled to a summary judgment on the Donnellys' cause of action for breach of contract.

An "as is" provision in a real estate contract means that the purchasers have to establish that the sellers actively engaged in either a misrepresentation or a concealment of a latent defect. In this case, since the Donnellys never talked to the Taylors about the house until after the discovery of the bats, there is no evidence of any misrepresentation by the Taylors of the condition of the property.

The Donnellys argue that since, according to their expert, the bats were in the house for approximately two to three years prior to October 1999, and since the bats made noises that were heard by the Donnellys after they purchased the house, the Taylors must have been aware of the existence of the bats. In support of this contention, the Donnellys point to the existence of the foil in the vents and the boards in the basement to further show that the Donnellys knew of the bat colony.

Since the contract contained an "as is" clause, however, it is not enough to show that the Taylors knew of the existence of the bats. The Donnellys have to show that the Taylors took steps to actively conceal the bats from the Donnellys. The Donnellys fail to show how the foil in the registers and the boards in the basement stopped them from knowing of the bats' existence. They also fail to show any other steps taken by the Taylors to conceal the bats' existence. . . .

Notes and Questions

1. Traditionally, the caveat emptor doctrine defined Buyer's rights with respect to property quality. *Donnelly* reflects the classic view of caveat emptor. The doctrine

sends a strong message to buyers. Buyer bears the risk of defects he discovers after closing. He can seek to minimize this risk in two ways — by making inspections, and by bargaining for Seller to give express representations and warranties. Although Buyer should personally inspect the property, getting property inspections from professionals is essential. Recall that the buyer in *Donnelly* obtained a termite inspection. That was not sufficient, however, to inform the buyer about the presence of bats. Few buyers have the expertise to assess the condition of components such as the electrical system, the heating and air conditioning system, the plumbing, and the roof and foundation.

2. Caveat emptor has never been airtight. As the *Donnelly* opinion states, a buyer can recover for fraudulent misrepresentation or active concealment of the defect. In addition, over the past century many states have softened the caveat emptor doctrine in order to protect buyers in a broader range of cases. In many states, the present rules excuse the seller from having to disclose patent defects (those discoverable by a buyer who inspects with reasonable diligence), but do not excuse the seller from having to disclose latent defects. Indeed, according to the *Donnelly* court, Ohio law would have applied this distinction but for the fact that the parties included an "as is" clause in their contract. Suppose they had no such clause? Do you agree with the court that the presence of bats was a latent defect? Can you fashion an argument that it was patent? Is the latent defect/patent defect line a useful, flexible standard; or does it leave too much room for variation in decision making?

The classic caveat emptor doctrine did not distinguish between patent and latent defects — the buyer took subject to all of them, unless he bargained for special protection or unless seller committed fraud. Under that classic view, an "as is" clause in a real estate contract is not highly significant. It merely restates or codifies the default rule.

3. Statutes require sellers to disclose some types of information about their property. A statutory duty to disclose, when it exists, of course overrides caveat emptor. Requirements come from federal, state, and local laws. Federal laws require disclosure of lead paint and lead pipes. Some states require disclosures about whether the property was ever flooded. Most states, beginning with California in 1985, have passed statutes requiring the sellers of used housing to fill out and deliver property disclosure forms, listing all known material defects under a range of specified categories. Ohio passed such an act in 1992. Ohio Stat. §5302.30. The *Donnelly* opinion states that the Taylors gave the Donnellys the statutorily required disclosure form, which did not mention bats. In many states, buyers have successfully sued sellers for failing to list defects on the disclosure form. It appears, however, that the Donnellys did not include breach of statutory duty as one of their causes of action.

■ **REED v. KING**

Court of Appeal of California, 1983
193 Cal. Rptr. 130

BLEASE, Justice. In the sale of a house, must the seller disclose it was the site of a multiple murder? Dorris Reed purchased a house from Robert King. Neither King nor his real estate agents (the other named defendants) told Reed that a woman and her four children were murdered there ten years earlier. However, it seems "truth will come to light; murder cannot be hid long." Shakespeare, *Merchant of Venice*, Act

II, Scene II. Reed learned of the gruesome episode from a neighbor after the sale. She sues seeking rescission and damages. King and the real estate agent defendants successfully demurred to her first amended complaint for failure to state a cause of action. Reed appeals the ensuing judgment of dismissal. We will reverse the judgment.

FACTS

We take all issuable facts pled in Reed's complaint as true. *See* 3 Witkin, *Cal. Procedure* (2d ed. 1971) Pleading, §800. King and his real estate agent knew about the murders and knew the event materially affected the market value of the house when they listed it for sale. They represented to Reed the premises were in good condition and fit for an "elderly lady" living alone. They did not disclose the fact of the murders. At some point King asked a neighbor not to inform Reed of that event. Nonetheless, after Reed moved in neighbors informed her no one was interested in purchasing the house because of the stigma. Reed paid $76,000, but the house is only worth $65,000 because of its past. . . .

DISCUSSION

. . . .

In general, a seller of real property has a duty to disclose:

> where the seller knows of facts *materially* affecting the value or desirability of the property which are known or accessible only to him and also knows that such facts are not known to, or within the reach of the diligent attention and observation of the buyer, the seller is under a duty to disclose them to the buyer. (Emphasis added)

Lingsch v. Savage, 29 Cal. Rptr. 201, 204 (Ct. App. 1963). This broad statement of duty has led one commentator to conclude: "The ancient maxim caveat emptor ('let the buyer beware.') has little or no application to California real estate transactions." 1 Miller and Starr, *Current Law of Cal. Real Estate* §1:80 (rev. ed. 1975). . . .

Numerous cases have found non-disclosure of physical defects and legal impediments to use of real property are material. *See* 1 Miller and Starr, *supra*, §1:81. However, to our knowledge, no prior real estate sale case has faced an issue of non-disclosure of the kind presented here. Should this variety of ill-repute be required to be disclosed? Is this a circumstance where "non-disclosure of the fact amounts to a failure to act in good faith and in accordance with reasonable standards of fair dealing?" *Rest. 2d Contracts* §161(b).

The paramount argument against an affirmative conclusion is it permits the camel's nose of unrestrained irrationality admission to the tent. If such an "irrational" consideration is permitted as a basis of rescission the stability of all conveyances will be seriously undermined. Any fact that might disquiet the enjoyment of some segment of the buying public may be seized upon by a disgruntled purchaser to void a bargain. In our view, keeping this genie in the bottle is not as difficult a task as these arguments assume. We do not view a decision allowing Reed to survive a demurrer in these unusual circumstances as endorsing the materiality of facts predicating peripheral, insubstantial, or fancied harms.

The murder of innocents is highly unusual in its potential for so disturbing buyers they may be unable to reside in a home where it has occurred. This fact may foreseeably deprive a buyer of the intended use of the purchase. Murder is not such a common occurrence that *buyers* should be charged with anticipating and discovering this disquieting possibility. Accordingly, the fact is not one for which a duty of inquiry and discovery can sensibly be imposed upon the buyer.

Reed alleges the fact of the murders has a quantifiable effect on the market value of the premises. We cannot say this allegation is inherently wrong and, in the pleading posture of the case, we assume it to be true. If information known or accessible only to the seller has a significant and measurable effect on market value and, as is alleged here, the seller is aware of this effect, we see no principled basis for making the duty to disclose turn upon the character of the information. Physical usefulness is not and never has been the sole criterion of valuation. Stamp collections and gold speculation would be insane activities if utilitarian considerations were the sole measure of value. *See also* Civ. Code §3355 (deprivation of property of peculiar value to owner); Annot., 12 A.L.R.2d 902 (1950) (measure of damages for conversion or loss of, or damage to, personal property having no market value).

Reputation and history can have a significant effect on the value of realty. "George Washington slept here" is worth something, however physically inconsequential that consideration may be. Ill-repute or "bad will" conversely may depress the value of property. Failure to disclose such a negative fact where it will have a foreseeably depressing effect on income expected to be generated by a business is tortious. *See Rest. 2d Torts* §551, illus. 11. Some cases have held that *unreasonable* fears of the potential buying public that a gas or oil pipeline may rupture may depress the market value of land and entitle the owner to incremental compensation in eminent domain. *See* Annot., *Eminent Domain: Elements and measure of compensation for oil or gas pipeline through private property,* 38 A.L.R.2d 788, 801-04 (1954).

Whether Reed will be able to prove her allegation the decade-old multiple murder has a significant effect on market value we cannot determine. If she is able to do so by competent evidence she is entitled to a favorable ruling on the issues of materiality and duty to disclose. Her demonstration of objective tangible harm would still the concern that permitting her to go forward will open the floodgates to rescission on subjective and idiosyncratic grounds.

A more troublesome question would arise if a buyer in similar circumstances were unable to plead or establish a significant and quantifiable effect on market value. However, this question is not presented in the posture of this case. Reed has not alleged the fact of the murders has rendered the premises useless to her as a residence. As currently pled, the gravamen of her case is pecuniary harm. We decline to speculate on the abstract alternative.

The judgment is reversed.

■ STAMBOVSKY v. ACKLEY
Supreme Court of New York, Appellate Division, 1991
572 N.Y.S.2d 672

RUBIN, Justice. Plaintiff, to his horror, discovered that the house he had recently contracted to purchase was widely reputed to be possessed by poltergeists, reportedly seen by defendant seller and members of her family on numerous occasions over the last nine years. Plaintiff promptly commenced this action seeking rescission of the contract of sale. Supreme Court reluctantly dismissed the complaint, holding that plaintiff has no remedy at law in this jurisdiction.

The unusual facts of this case, as disclosed by the record, clearly warrant a grant of equitable relief to the buyer who, as a resident of New York City, cannot be expected to have any familiarity with the folklore of the Village of Nyack. Not being a "local," plaintiff could not readily learn that the home he had contracted to purchase is haunted. Whether the source of the spectral apparitions seen by defendant seller are parapsychic or psychogenic, having reported their presence in both a national publication ("Readers' Digest") and the local press (in 1977 and 1982, respectively), defendant is estopped to deny their existence and, as a matter of law, the house is haunted. More to the point, however, no divination is required to conclude that it is defendant's promotional efforts in publicizing her close encounters with these spirits which fostered the home's reputation in the community. In 1989, the house was included in a five-home walking tour of Nyack and described in a November 27th newspaper article as "a riverfront Victorian (with ghost)." The impact of the reputation thus created goes to the very essence of the bargain between the parties, greatly impairing both the value of the property and its potential for resale. . . .

While I agree with Supreme Court that the real estate broker, as agent for the seller, is under no duty to disclose to a potential buyer the phantasmal reputation of the premises and that, in his pursuit of a legal remedy for fraudulent misrepresentation against the seller, plaintiff hasn't a ghost of a chance, I am nevertheless moved by the spirit of equity to allow the buyer to seek rescission of the contract of sale and recovery of his down payment. New York law fails to recognize any remedy for damages incurred as a result of the seller's mere silence, applying instead the strict rule of caveat emptor. Therefore, the theoretical basis for granting relief, even under the extraordinary facts of this case, is elusive if not ephemeral.

"Pity me not but lend thy serious hearing to what I shall unfold." William Shakespeare, *Hamlet*, Act I, Scene V (Ghost).

From the perspective of a person in the position of plaintiff herein, a very practical problem arises with respect to the discovery of a paranormal phenomenon: "Who you gonna call?" as the title song to the movie "Ghostbusters" asks. Applying the strict rule of caveat emptor to a contract involving a house possessed by poltergeists conjures up visions of a psychic or medium routinely accompanying the structural engineer and Terminix man on an inspection of every home subject to a contract of sale. It portends that the prudent attorney will establish an escrow account lest the subject of the transaction come back to haunt him and his client — or pray that his malpractice insurance coverage extends to supernatural disasters. In the interest of avoiding such untenable consequences, the notion that a haunting is a condition which can and should be ascertained upon reasonable inspection of the premises is a hobgoblin which should be exorcised from the body of legal precedent and laid quietly to rest.

It has been suggested by a leading authority that the ancient rule which holds that mere non-disclosure does not constitute actionable misrepresentation "finds proper application in cases where the fact undisclosed is patent, or the plaintiff has equal opportunities for obtaining information which he may be expected to utilize, or the defendant has no reason to think that he is acting under any misapprehension." Prosser, *Law of Torts* §106, at 696 (4th ed., 1971). However, with respect to transactions in real estate, New York adheres to the doctrine of caveat emptor and imposes no duty upon the vendor to disclose any information concerning the premises unless there is a confidential or fiduciary relationship between the parties or some conduct on the part of the seller which constitutes "active concealment." *See* 17 East 80th Realty Corp. v. 68th Associates, 569 N.Y.S.2d 647 (App. Div. 1991) (dummy ventilation system constructed by seller); Haberman v. Greenspan, 368 N.Y.S.2d 717 (Sup. Ct. 1975) (foundation cracks covered by seller). Normally, some affirmative misrepresentation or partial disclosure is required to impose upon the seller a duty to communicate undisclosed conditions affecting the premises.

Caveat emptor is not so all-encompassing a doctrine of common law as to render every act of non-disclosure immune from redress, whether legal or equitable.

> In regard to the necessity of giving information which has not been asked, the rule differs somewhat at law and in equity, and while the law courts would permit no recovery of *damages* against a vendor, because of mere concealment of facts *under certain circumstances*, yet if the vendee refused to complete the contract because of the concealment of a material fact on the part of the other, equity would refuse to compel him so to do, because equity only compels the specific performance of a contract which is fair and open, and in regard to which all material matters known to each have been communicated to the other.

Rothmiller v. Stein, 38 N.E. 718, 721 (N.Y. 1894) (emphasis added). . . . Where fairness and common sense dictate that an exception should be created, the evolution of the law should not be stifled by rigid application of a legal maxim.

The doctrine of caveat emptor requires that a buyer act prudently to assess the fitness and value of his purchase and operates to bar the purchaser who fails to exercise due care from seeking the equitable remedy of rescission. . . . It should be apparent, however, that the most meticulous inspection and the search would not reveal the presence of poltergeists at the premises or unearth the property's ghoulish reputation in the community. Therefore, there is no sound policy reason to deny plaintiff relief for failing to discover a state of affairs which the most prudent purchaser would not be expected to even contemplate. *See* Da Silva v. Musso, 428 N.E.2d 382, 386 (N.Y. 1981). . . .

Where a condition which has been created by the seller materially impairs the value of the contract and is peculiarly within the knowledge of the seller or unlikely to be discovered by a prudent purchaser exercising due care with respect to the subject transaction, nondisclosure constitutes a basis for rescission as a matter of equity. Any other outcome places upon the buyer not merely the obligation to exercise care in his purchase but rather to be omniscient with respect to any fact which may affect the bargain. No practical purpose is served by imposing such a burden upon a purchaser. To the contrary, it encourages predatory business practice and offends the principle that equity will suffer no wrong to be without a remedy.

Defendant's contention that the contract of sale, particularly the merger or "as is" clause, bars recovery of the buyer's deposit is unavailing. . . . [A] fair reading of the merger clause reveals that it expressly disclaims only representations made with respect to the physical condition of the premises and merely makes general reference to representations concerning "any other matter or things affecting or relating to the aforesaid premises." As broad as this language may be, a reasonable interpretation is that its effect is limited to tangible or physical matters and does not extend to paranormal phenomena. Finally, if the language of the contract is to be construed as broadly as defendant urges to encompass the presence of poltergeists in the house, it cannot be said that she has delivered the premises "vacant" in accordance with her obligation under the provisions of the contract rider. . . .

In the case at bar, defendant seller deliberately fostered the public belief that her home was possessed. Having undertaken to inform the public at large, to whom she has no legal relationship, about the supernatural occurrences on her property, she may be said to owe no less a duty to her contract vendee. It has been remarked that the occasional modern cases which permit a seller to take unfair advantage of a buyer's ignorance so long as he is not actively misled are "singularly unappetizing." Prosser, *Law of Torts* §106, at 696 (4th ed. 1971). Where, as here, the seller not only takes unfair advantage of the buyer's ignorance but has created and perpetuated a condition about which he is unlikely to even inquire, enforcement of the contract (in whole or in part) is offensive to the court's sense of equity. Application of the remedy of rescission, within the bounds of the narrow exception to the doctrine of caveat emptor set forth herein, is entirely appropriate to relieve the unwitting purchaser from the consequences of a most unnatural bargain.

Accordingly, the judgment of the Supreme Court, New York County . . . should be modified . . . and the first cause of action seeking rescission of the contract reinstated, without costs.

SMITH, Justice, dissenting. I would affirm the dismissal of the complaint by the motion court. . . .

> It is settled law in New York that the seller of real property is under no duty to speak when the parties deal at arm's length. The mere silence of the seller, without some act or conduct which deceived the purchaser, does not amount to a concealment that is actionable as a fraud. The buyer has the duty to satisfy himself as to the quality of his bargain pursuant to the doctrine of caveat emptor, which in New York State still applies to real estate transactions.

London v. Courduff, 529 N.Y.S.2d 874, 875 (App. Div.), *app. dism'd*, 534 N.E.2d 332 (N.Y. 1988).

Notes and Questions

1. How would the Donnellys have fared if the bat-infested house they bought was located in California, with their transaction governed by the common law rules described in *Reed?* Ohio law, as reflected by *Donnelly*, and California law, as reflected by *Reed*, are at or near the opposite ends of a spectrum in terms of pro-seller and pro-buyer orientation. Many states occupy an intermediate position, departing from caveat emptor but stopping short of a duty to disclose all material defects known to the seller and not the buyer. Can you interpret *Stambovsky* as occupying an intermediate position?

2. Although the risk of physical defects should be a paramount concern for the buyer, *Reed* and *Stambovsky* illustrate how many other factors can have a substantial impact on property value. Intangibles stemming from the surrounding community matter a great deal: the quality of the school system, neighborhood safety/crime levels, proximity to parks and recreational amenities, access to transportation corridors, plus many other considerations. Although much litigation between sellers

and buyers focuses on the physical quality of the property under contract, disputes over intangibles also arise. *See, e.g.*, Capiccioni v. Brennan Naperville, Inc., 791 N.E.2d 553 (Ill. App. Ct. 2003) (buyers have cause of action for negligent misrepresentation against seller's real estate broker when sales brochure incorrectly stated house was in one school district when in fact it was in another).

Reed and *Stambovsky* deal with one type of intangible that has become known as *stigma*, whereby the property is said to have a psychological defect. Do you agree with the risk allocation effected by the decisions in *Reed* and *Stambovsky*? Such decisions have prompted intervention by many legislatures, readjusting the law back toward caveat emptor. Stigma nondisclosure statutes generally relieve Seller and Broker from liability for failure to disclose certain stigmatizing events; however, the immunity does not apply if Seller or Broker makes an affirmative misrepresentation. Although the statutes vary considerably, typically they shield disclosure of homicide, suicide, other felonies, and the infection of occupants with AIDS or HIV virus. *See* Stuart C. Edmiston, Comment, *Secrets Worth Keeping: Toward a Principled Basis for Stigmatized Property Disclosure Statutes*, 58 UCLA L. Rev. 281 (2010). Cal. Civ. Code §1710.2, enacted in 1986, provides:

> (a) No cause of action arises against an owner of real property or his or her agent, or any agent of a transferee of real property, for the failure to disclose to the transferee the occurrence of an occupant's death upon the real property or the manner of death where the death has occurred more than three years prior to the date the transferee offers to purchase, lease, or rent the real property, or that an occupant of that property was afflicted with, or died from, Human T-Lymphotropic Virus Type III/Lymphadeno-pathy-Associated Virus.

3. With respect to quality issues, new housing is treated differently from used housing and other real estate. Rarely does caveat emptor apply. In almost all states, buyers of new homes have express or implied warranties of quality. Beginning in the 1960s, courts implied warranties of habitability, rejecting caveat emptor when a buyer was confronted by a latent defect that made their new house uninhabitable, unsafe, or had a major effect on value. Today, a number of states have statutory warranties, which either replace or are in lieu of the implied warranties. Today, most homebuilders give their buyers express warranties, similar in detail and scope to what a buyer of a new automobile obtains. Many builders issue their own warranties, but standardized warranties issued by a third-party insurer are usually a superior form of protection. Many buyers of new homes obtain third-party warranties. The federal government requires a third-party warranty when the buyer obtains a mortgage loan insured by the Federal Housing Authority (FHA) or the Department of Veterans' Affairs (VA). Usually, the seller disclaims all implied warranties, and offers only the express warranty. The same practice obtains for the sale of new goods, whereby sellers routinely give express warranties and disclaim the UCC implied warranties of merchantability and fitness for a particular purpose.

C. RECORDING SYSTEM

Common law priority. All states maintain public records that reflect ownership claims to land. To understand the recording system, it is important to have a firm grasp on how the common law resolves competing claims. At common law, the basic rule is "first in time, first in right."

Example 1. A delivers a deed conveying Blackacre to B on June 1. A delivers a deed conveying Blackacre to C on June 5. B owns Blackacre, though C might have a claim against A.

For grantees under deeds, the respective dates of delivery rather than the date of execution (signing) control.

Example 2. A signs a deed conveying Blackacre to B on July 1 and delivers that deed to B on July 5. A signs a deed conveying Blackacre to C on July 2 and delivers that deed to C on July 3. C now owns Blackacre.

The common law rule also applies to equitable interests.

Example 3. A contracts to sell Greenacre to B on August 1. A contracts to sell Greenacre to C on August 3. B has equitable title to Greenacre under the doctrine of equitable conversion. B's right as purchaser is prior (superior) to C's because it is first in time.

The common law recognizes one exception to letting time decide priorities. If the "first in time" claim was an equitable claim and a bona fide purchaser (BFP) acquired legal title without notice of the earlier claim, the BFP wins. The rationale is that, since both grantees have an equity but only one has legal title, the legal title should control to break the tie.

Example 4. A contracts to sell Greenacre to B on August 1. A contracts to sell Greenacre to C on August 3. Pursuant to the latter contract, on August 25 C pays the purchase price in exchange for A's delivery of a deed to Greenacre. At the closing on August 25, C did not have notice of B's interest in Greenacre. C now owns Greenacre; B has no right to Greenacre (only an action for damages against A).

Recording process. All states have recording acts, which provide a public system for the retention and searching of instruments that affect title to land. To qualify for recording, a deed or other instrument must be acknowledged. Notary publics acknowledge most instruments (the instrument is said to be "notarized"), but other public officials such as judges may acknowledge a signature. A deed that is not acknowledged, or is defectively acknowledged, is valid between the parties, but is not entitled to be recorded.

To record a deed or other instrument, a person takes the original to a public office in the county where the land is situated and pays a filing fee. The recorder's office makes a copy or image of the original, adds the item to the public records, and enters references for it in the index system. The degree to which the records are computerized varies widely from state to state, and often within states from county to county.

Functions of recording system. The recording system has two basic functions: title assurance and priority ranking. The recording system provides a method for determining who owns any tract of land. The filed instruments are public records, open to examination by anyone. As part of the process of buying land, a purchaser will hire someone (usually an attorney or another title professional) to check the public records to confirm Seller's claim of good title. The search may reveal any number of title defects: for example, outstanding mortgages or tax liens, easements, future interests, cotenancy shares; or in the worst case, that Seller has no record title at all.

The second basic function of the recording system is to establish relative priorities among successive transfers, which do not directly conflict. "Priority" means the law determines who among various claimants has the superior, prior interest.

Example 5. A mortgages Blueacre to M to secure payment of A's debt to M, and A leases Blueacre to T for five years. The recording system determines whether M's mortgage or T's lease is prior. If M's mortgage is prior, foreclosure under that mortgage cuts off (eliminates) T's leasehold. If T's lease is prior, the mortgage covers only A's interest as landlord. Thus, M's foreclosure will result in the sale of the landlord's estate to satisfy A's debt, without affecting T's leasehold.

Title search process. The basic process for searching title has four common steps. First, the title examiner must discover the *chain of title.* Every parcel of land has a chain of title, the first link being the sovereign and the last link being the present owner. The best possible title search traces title back to the sovereign, reconstructing the entire chain of title. In most states, this is not done for most title searches. Due to custom, sometimes backed by state bar title standards or by legislation, the search typically goes back a set period such as 50 years, resulting in a chain of title that begins with the last private owner to acquire title prior to the specified period.

After finding the chain of title, the searcher's second step is to look for *adverse recorded transfers* by the present owner and by all prior owners in the chain of title. To find these adverse transfers, the searcher checks the records of deeds and other instruments in the county where the land is located. An adverse transfer may upset the apparent chain of title by showing that a prior owner conveyed the land twice or that the apparent present owner has conveyed to someone else. Other adverse transfers, such as mortgages or easements, do not jeopardize the conclusion that the apparent present owner actually owns the estate.

The searcher's third step is to read carefully all recorded instruments found in steps one and two. Deeds in the chain may contain mortgages, leases, exceptions, covenants, or other matters. Formalities of all recorded instruments, such as the parties' names, the land descriptions, and acknowledgments, must be examined. The searcher may find that some of the adverse transfers do not presently affect title. An old mortgage may have been satisfied, with a recorded release signed by the lender. The term of a recorded lease may have expired. In many states, if a recorded instrument refers to unrecorded rights, the searcher has a duty of inquiry.

The fourth and last step is for the searcher to consult other records, in addition to recorded instruments, for adverse interests. These sources vary from state to state, but commonly include bankruptcy filings, tax liens, judgment liens, and mechanics' liens.

Indexing systems. With thousands of recorded instruments on file even in small counties, an index system is essential to find the relevant documents for a title search. Most states have only *name indexes* (often called "grantor-grantee" indexes), which display, in alphabetical order, names of parties to the deeds and other instruments. The searcher uses the name indexes to construct a chain of title for the land by working back from the present owner. After the searcher constructs a chain of title, of sufficient length, then he uses the grantor indexes to check for the presence of adverse record transfers by each owner.

Some states have *tract indexes* in addition to or in lieu of name indexes. A tract index divides all the land in the county into parcels and organizes deeds and other instruments according to the parcel or parcels they affect. Tract indexes are much better and easier to use than name indexes, but most states do not have them due to the high cost of converting from name indexes to tract indexes, the greater skill required for recording office employees to manage a tract system, and the relative unimportance of the public records in many communities where private title insurance companies and abstract companies do most of the title work and maintain their own sets of records.

Types of recording acts. Recording statutes modify the common law "first in time" rule by granting certain subsequent takers of interests priority over earlier unrecorded interests. The statutes expand the common law rule that a subsequent legal BFP cuts off a prior equity. Recording acts do not completely displace common law priority rules. For this reason, the common law rules remain important today. First in time, first in right still applies unless the second taker can show entitlement as a BFP under a recording act. A valid title or lien, at law, is never cut off by a subsequent transfer, except under a recording act. There are three basic types of recordings acts, which specify when the subsequent taker defeats the prior taker.

(1) Under a race statute (sometimes called a "pure race" statute), the first person to record their instrument wins. Only three states, Delaware, Louisiana, and North Carolina, have a race statute as their general recording act. Several states use a race approach for certain specialized types of conveyances. Ohio, for example, has a pure race system for mortgages. The North Carolina statute provides:

> No (i) conveyance of land, or (ii) contract to convey, or (iii) option to convey, or (iv) lease of land for more than three years shall be valid to pass any property interest as against lien creditors or purchasers for a valuable consideration from the donor, bargainor or lessor, but from the time of registration thereof in the county where the land lies.

N.C. Gen. Stat. §47-18(a). To become a BFP under this statute, does the subsequent grantee have to pay value for the conveyance?

(2) Under a notice statute, a subsequent purchaser who takes without notice of the prior unrecorded interest wins. The Texas statute provides:

> (a) A conveyance of real property or an interest in real property or a mortgage or deed of trust is void as to a creditor or to a subsequent purchaser for a valuable consideration without notice unless the instrument has been acknowledged, sworn to, or proved and filed for record as required by law.
> (b) The unrecorded instrument is binding on a party to the instrument, on the party's heirs, and on a subsequent purchaser who does not pay a valuable consideration or who has notice of the instrument.

Tex. Prop. Code §13.001. Does this statute make it harder or easier for a person to become a BFP, compared to the North Carolina statute?

(3) A race-notice statute is a hybrid of the race and notice types of recording acts. The subsequent purchaser must both record first (as under a race statute) and take without notice of the prior interest (as under a notice statute). Thus, the race-notice statute makes it harder for BFPs to prevail than either a race statute or a notice statute. Roughly one-half the states have notice acts and the other half have race-notice acts. The California statute provides:

> Every conveyance of real property or an estate of years therein, other than a lease for a term not exceeding one year, is void as against any subsequent purchaser or mortgagee of the same property, or any part thereof, in good faith and for a valuable consideration, whose conveyance is first duly recorded. . . .

Cal. Civ. Code §1214. Of the three types of recording acts, which one do you believe is superior? Which one is most efficient? Which is fairest?

Meaning of notice. Under both the notice and race-notice statutes, it is critical to determine when a person has "notice" of an earlier unrecorded claim. Notice is evaluated at the time the grantee pays value. There are three types of notice:

Actual Notice. The purchaser who has actual knowledge of the prior interest is disqualified. This is a state of mind test.

Constructive Notice. The purchaser is charged with notice of all recorded interests — everything that a proper search of the public records should reveal.

Inquiry Notice. The purchaser who knows facts that suggest that someone might have an unrecorded interest has a duty to inquire further. The purchaser is charged with whatever information that inquiry would have revealed. The most important aspect of inquiry notice is a duty to inspect the land; the purchaser generally takes subject to the rights of parties in possession and other unrecorded interests that are visible from inspection.

Importance of searching and prompt recording. In real estate practice, the similarities among the types of recording acts matter more than the differences. Whatever the type of act, there are two powerful incentives for parties to use the recording system. First, when a person contracts to buy land, a search of the land records is essential prior to paying value. Otherwise, the purchaser's expectations of good title will be frustrated by prior recorded interests that are unknown to the purchaser and not disclosed by the seller. Second, as soon as a purchaser acquires an interest in land, he should record his instrument. Otherwise, there is the risk that the seller, who still has record title, will transfer a competing interest to a BFP, who will trump the prior purchaser. Therefore, in all states it is standard operating practice for purchasers to order a search of the records before closing and to record promptly after closing.

■ **CARUSO v. PARKOS**
Supreme Court of Nebraska, 2002
637 N.W.2d 351

GERRARD, Justice. This is a quiet title action relating to certain real property in Valley County, Nebraska. Prior to June 20, 1997, the property was owned by Virginia M. Parkos and two of her children, Susan Caruso and Carol Nattress. Virginia held an undivided five-sevenths interest in the property, while Carol and Susan each held a one-seventh interest in the property.

In April 1997, Carol approached Virginia about receiving an early inheritance to pay for Carol's medical expenses. The proposal was that Virginia would convey her five-sevenths interest in the property to Carol and Susan and that Susan would then obtain a loan to pay Carol $50,000 for Carol's share of the property, thus providing Carol with the money to pay for needed medical care. Carol and Susan contacted Curtis Sikyta, Virginia's attorney, regarding preparation of a deed. A warranty deed was prepared and signed by Virginia on June 20, and the deed was provided to Sikyta for recording. Another deed, conveying Carol's interest in the property to Susan, was executed on June 26 and returned to Sikyta for recording. The deeds, however, were not promptly recorded by Sikyta's office.

On October 27, 1997, Virginia executed and delivered a warranty deed to her son James D. Parkos, purporting to convey the same property that was the subject of the June 20 and 26 deeds. The October 27 deed was recorded with the Valley County register of deeds on October 29. Thereafter, Susan contacted the register of deeds regarding her loan application process and was informed that the only deed on file with respect to the subject property was the deed conveying the property from Virginia to James. Susan contacted Sikyta, who, on November 14, recorded the June 20 and 26 deeds.

Procedural History

Susan filed a quiet title action in the district court against Virginia and James, alleging that both Virginia and James had been aware of the June 20, 1997, conveyance at the time that the October 27 deed was executed and that there was no consideration given at the execution of the October 27 deed. James denied the allegations and further alleged that the June 20 deed was never delivered, that the June 20 deed was given without consideration and was not intended to be a gift, and that Susan made misrepresentations to Virginia that induced Virginia to sign the June 20 deed.

James filed a motion for summary judgment which was overruled, and the case proceeded to trial. The primary witnesses to testify at trial were Sikyta, Carol, Susan, and James; Virginia neither appeared as a party nor testified. After trial, the district court determined that Virginia was competent when she executed the June 20, 1997, deed, that there was consideration given for the conveyance, and that the deed had been delivered to Sikyta, who was acting as an escrow agent. The district court further determined that James had knowledge of the June 20 deed prior to his receipt and recording of the October 27 deed. Consequently, the district court quieted title to the subject property in Susan. James appeals. . . .

Delivery of June 20 Deed

James first assigns that the district court erred in determining that there had been delivery of the June 20, 1997, deed. It is essential to the validity of a deed that there be a delivery, and the burden of proof rests upon the party asserting delivery to establish it by a preponderance of the evidence. Brtek v. Cihal, 515 N.W.2d 628 (Neb. 1994).

To constitute a valid delivery of a deed, there must be an intent on the part of the grantor that the deed shall operate as a muniment of title to take effect presently. *Id.* The essential fact to render delivery effective is always that the deed itself has left the control of the grantor, who has reserved no right to recall it, and it has passed to the grantee. *Id.* No particular acts or words are necessary to constitute delivery of a deed; anything done by the grantor from which it is apparent that a delivery was intended, either by words or acts, or both combined, is sufficient. *Id.* Whether a deed or other instrument conveying an interest in property has been delivered is largely a question of intent to be determined by the facts and circumstances of the particular case. *Id.*

The essential question, then, is whether Virginia, at the June 20, 1997, meeting with Carol, Susan, and Sikyta, intended her execution of the deed and presentation of the deed to Sikyta for recording to presently transfer title of the property. The evidence presented at trial supports the district court's conclusion that Virginia did intend to transfer title on June 20.

Sikyta testified that he discussed the transaction at length with Virginia and that Virginia indicated that she intended to transfer the property so that Carol could obtain needed surgery. Sikyta further testified that the deed was given to him without restrictions and that everyone at the meeting, including Virginia, told him to take the deed and record it. Sikyta testified that he was not instructed to retain the deed for any reason. Carol and Susan's testimony corroborated Sikyta's account of the June 20, 1997, meeting.

Furthermore, Sikyta testified regarding a telephone call on December 3, 1997, in which he spoke to Virginia. Sikyta testified that Virginia told Sikyta that she had wanted to convey the property on June 20, but that she had since changed her mind and wanted James to have it. Sikyta testified that in a conversation with Virginia in February 1998, Virginia again stated that she had intended to convey the property on June 20, 1997, but later had reservations. However, where a grantor has conveyed his or her property, he or she cannot subsequently, by withdrawing or destroying the deed, or by other acts indicating a subsequent change of intention, affect the transaction thus completed. . . .

[In] the instant case, the delivery of the deed to Sikyta rather than to Carol or Susan does not defeat the delivery, as the evidence indicated that the deed was presented to Sikyta for the specific purpose of having the deed recorded. The vital inquiry is whether the grantor intended a complete transfer — whether the grantor parted with dominion over the instrument with the intention of relinquishing all dominion over it and making it presently operative as a conveyance of title to the land. Brtek v. Cihal, 515 N.W.2d 628 (Neb. 1994). Given the undisputed testimony that Sikyta was instructed, at the June 20, 1997, meeting, to take the deed and have it recorded, we conclude, on our de novo review, that Susan met her burden of proving by a preponderance of the evidence that the June 20 deed was validly delivered. *See id.*

James contends that the delivery was not effective because it was conditional on the payment, by Carol and Susan, of Sikyta's legal fees for the transaction. The delivery by the grantor of a deed to a third person to hold until the happening of a contingency does not operate as a delivery. Action Realty Co., Inc. v. Miller, 215 N.W.2d 629 (Neb. 1974). The evidence does indicate that Virginia insisted that Carol and Susan were to pay the legal and filing fees, and a letter from Sikyta to Carol regarding the fees may have implied that both deeds were being held pending payment of those fees.

However, Sikyta testified at the trial that the implication of that letter was a mistake and that retention of the deeds until the fees were paid was not part of the agreement with Virginia, Carol, and Susan. Sikyta testified that the sole reason for the delay in filing the deeds was a clerical error in his office and that he was not instructed to hold the deeds for any reason. Furthermore, the intent of the grantor is the controlling factor, and there is no indication in the record that Virginia intended for the conveyance of the land to be conditional or that Virginia, on June 20, 1997, intended anything other than that the conveyance be immediately effective. James' first assignment of error is without merit.

James' second assignment of error also relates to the delivery of the June 20, 1997, deed. James contends that the delivery was ineffective because Sikyta was Virginia's attorney and thus Virginia's agent, not an "escrow agent" as found by the district court. James argues that Sikyta was incapable of acting as an escrow agent because he was counsel to one of the parties and, thus, could not act as a third party. *See* Baye v. Airlite Plastics Co., 618 N.W.2d 145 (Neb. 2000).

However, Sikyta testified that he considered himself to be acting as an agent of Carol and Susan for the limited purpose of filing the deed and thus an "escrow agent" for filing purposes. There is support in our law for an attorney of one party to a transaction being able to act as an escrow agent for that transaction. *See* Pike v.

Triska, 84 N.W.2d 311 (Neb. 1957). In any event, the issue here is not propriety, but the intent of the grantor. There is no indication in the record that the deed was given to Sikyta in order to permit Virginia to retain control over the deed, and in fact substantial evidence exists to the contrary. As such, we find James' argument, and his second assignment of error, to be without merit.

UNDUE INFLUENCE

James argues that the June 20, 1997, deed should be set aside as the result of undue influence on the part of Carol and Susan. . . . The elements necessary to be established to warrant the rejection of a written instrument on the ground of undue influence are (1) that the person who executed the instrument was subject to undue influence, (2) that there was opportunity to exercise undue influence, (3) that there was a disposition to exercise undue influence for an improper purpose, and (4) that the result was clearly the effect of such undue influence. Miller v. Westwood, 472 N.W.2d 903 (Neb. 1991).

In this regard, the testimony of Sikyta regarding the June 20, 1997, meeting is particularly illuminating and representative of the entire record:

> [O]ne of the first responses I had was I had asked [Virginia] if she understood, in transferring this land, that she would be giving up the full use of it and she responded yes. I asked her if she understood that when this land went out of her possession that meant she would no longer have the income off of it. She stated yes. I asked her if she was sure she wanted to transfer it to the girls. Her first response was I think so or something to that effect. And so I persisted about what do you mean by you think so. Well, yes, I do. And, you know, there was several exchanges of that nature. I told her that I think so was not good enough. That I needed to know if she really intended to transfer and she said yes. I asked her if anyone was putting her under any pressure to do that. She said no. I asked her if there was a reason why she wanted to transfer it and she said, yes, it was the only way that Carol could have her surgery, so she wanted to do it for Carol's benefit. There was several other questions of that nature, but generally that's the line it took.

James' argument is that Carol and Susan misled Virginia regarding their motives for proposing the conveyances. However, James presented no evidence that directly supports this argument. . . .

The court, in examining the matter of whether a deed was procured by undue influence, is not concerned with the rightness of the conveyance but only with whether it was the voluntary act of the grantor. *Westwood, supra.* While the record is clear that Carol and Susan proposed the conveyance and persuaded Virginia to agree to the conveyance, it is not mere influence that makes a conveyance unlawful, but undue influence as established in the law. *See Westwood, supra.* Although there is evidence that Virginia wavered on her decision months after the transaction, there is simply no clear and convincing evidence that Virginia was subject to undue influence on or around June 20, 1997, the date of the conveyance of the deed. James' third assignment of error is without merit.

NOTICE TO JAMES OF JUNE 20 DEED

James' final assignment of error is that the district court erred in determining that James had notice of the June 20, 1997, deed prior to his receipt and recording of the October 27 deed. James argues that he is a subsequent purchaser in good faith without notice entitled to the protection of Neb. Rev. Stat. §76-238 (Reissue 1996), which provides:

> All deeds, mortgages and other instruments of writing which are required to be or which under the laws of this state may be recorded, shall take effect and be in force from and after the time of delivering the same to the register of deeds for recording, and not before, as to all creditors and subsequent purchasers in good faith without notice; and all such deeds, mortgages and other instruments shall be adjudged void as to all such creditors and subsequent purchasers without notice whose deeds, mortgages or other instruments shall be first recorded; *Provided*, that such deeds, mortgages and other instruments shall be valid between the parties. (Emphasis in original.)

A good faith purchaser of land is one who purchases for valuable consideration without notice of any suspicious circumstances which would put a prudent person on inquiry. How v. Baker, 388 N.W.2d 462 (Neb. 1986); Mader v. Kallos, 365 N.W.2d 408 (Neb. 1985). The burden of proof is upon a litigant who alleges that he or she is a good faith purchaser to prove that he or she purchased the property for value and without notice. *How, supra*; *Mader, supra*. This burden includes proving that the litigant was without notice, actual or constructive, of another's rights or interest in the land. *Mader, supra.*

James testified that he prepared the October 27, 1997, deed and related documents himself, without counsel. James claimed that the October 27 deed was part of a transaction in which he was given title to several of Virginia's real properties in exchange for taking care of Virginia on a daily basis. Leaving aside the question whether James' care was "valuable consideration" for the conveyances, *see id.*, the record is replete with evidence that James had actual notice of the June 20 deed prior to receiving and recording the October 27 deed.

Carol, Susan, and James all testified regarding a "family meeting" that was held in May 1997, which included Virginia and her children Carol, Susan, James, and Tammy Parkos, as well as Tammy's husband. Carol, Susan, and James all agreed that the subject of the meeting was the proposed conveyance that is the subject of this dispute and that Carol and Susan were in favor of the transaction, while James and Tammy opposed it. James' account differs from that of Carol and Susan with respect to Virginia's participation in the meeting. Carol and Susan each testified that at the family meeting, Virginia decided that she wanted to convey the property to Carol and Susan. James claimed that at the family meeting, Virginia opposed the conveyance to Carol and Susan, but James acknowledged that he had not mentioned this fact in his prior deposition. Nonetheless, James' own testimony regarding this meeting could be held to reveal a notice of suspicious circumstances which would put a prudent person on inquiry regarding the subsequent transaction. *See How, supra*; *Mader, supra.*

Beyond that, however, several witnesses testified to conversations with James after June 20, 1997, in which James indicated his awareness of the June 20 conveyance. Sikyta testified regarding a telephone conversation on December 3 in which James admitted that James had known about the June 20 deed prior to recording the October 27 deed. Sikyta testified that in a later meeting, in February 1998, James changed his story and claimed that while he had known in October 1997 of the plan to convey the property to Carol and Susan, he did not know that it had actually been accomplished. Even if the latter conversation reflected James' actual knowledge, however, that would still constitute sufficient notice to place him on inquiry regarding the June 20 transaction. *See id.*

Moreover, Carol testified to a conversation with James in August 1997 in which James allegedly told Carol to "give back" the subject property. Susan testified that she had spoken to James on July 7 and that James had congratulated her on obtaining the property and asked if he could borrow money off the remaining credit for the property. Susan also testified regarding another conversation with James in mid-August, in which James said that Virginia could not afford nursing home care because "you girls have her income, her farm." Susan further testified that James again acknowledged his awareness of the conveyance in a conversation on August 28.

In James' testimony, he asserted simply that he did not know about the June 20, 1997, deed when he received and recorded the October 27 deed. James did not deny the conversations testified to by Sikyta, Carol, and Susan; instead, James merely denied any recollection of any of those conversations.

The overwhelming weight of the evidence supports the district court's conclusion that James was aware of the June 20, 1997, deed prior to the October 27 conveyance. The district court, which had the opportunity to hear and observe the witnesses, did not accept James' version of the facts, and we consider and give weight to this in our de novo review. *See* Jeffrey Lake Dev. v. Central Neb. Pub. Power, 633 N.W.2d 102 (Neb. 2001). After reviewing the record, we conclude, as did the district court, that James did not sustain his burden of proving he was a subsequent purchaser in good faith without notice with respect to the October 27 conveyance. James' final assignment of error is without merit.

Conclusion

Susan met her burden of showing a valid delivery of the June 20, 1997, deed, and James did not meet his burden of showing that the June 20 deed was the result of undue influence or that he was a subsequent purchaser in good faith without notice. Thus, title to the subject property passed from Virginia on June 20, and the October 27 deed purporting to convey the same property is a nullity. James' assignments of error having no merit, we affirm the judgment of the district court quieting title to the subject property in Susan.

Notes and Questions

1. *Caruso* illustrates two reasons why a deed, which appears valid on its face when a person examines it, may be defective. First, a deed is *void* (it has no effect whatsoever) unless delivered by the grantor to the grantee. Satisfaction of the delivery requirement is almost never an issue for sales of real estate, but for alleged gifts the issue frequently arises. Second, a deed procured by undue influence is *voidable*. This means a court may set it aside at the instance of the grantor.

2. James Caruso claimed he was a BFP. What type of recording act does Nebraska have? What requirement did James fail to satisfy?

3. Did James pay *value* as required by the Nebraska statute? Issues of measurement and timing arise. As to measure, the value must be more than nominal. It needn't be as much as the fair market value of the property, however. The value requirement is intended to disqualify a donee from claiming the protection of the

recording act. (Why do this?) Courts require that the value be "substantial," but they have not quantified the requirement in numerical terms.

As to timing, the general rule is that a purchaser is not a BFP until he transfers the value to the seller. Thus, a promise not yet performed is not value for this purpose. Consider a person who has contracted to buy property, but before closing learns of an earlier unrecorded interest. This buyer is not yet a BFP, and thus must seek to rescind her contract if the seller is unable or unwilling to cure the title problem represented by the unrecorded interest.

■ MidCOUNTRY BANK v. KRUEGER
Supreme Court of Minnesota, 2010
782 N.W.2d 238

ANDERSON, G. BARRY, Justice. At issue in this appeal is whether a mortgage was "properly recorded" under Minn. Stat. §507.32 (2008), thereby giving constructive notice to a subsequent purchaser of land and a mortgagee.

Respondent MidCountry Bank brought an action in district court to foreclose a mortgage on property owned by appellant Cherolyn Hinshaw (the "Hinshaw property"). . . .

. . . On March 21, 2000, Frederick and Nancy Krueger purchased the Hinshaw property in Belle Plaine, Minnesota. Four years later, the Kruegers obtained a loan from MidCountry to purchase two different parcels of land (the "Krueger properties") and to build a house on the acquired property.

To provide security for the loan, the Kruegers executed and delivered a mortgage to MidCountry that encumbered not only the Krueger properties but also the Hinshaw property purchased four years earlier. On May 19, 2004, the deed to the Krueger properties and the MidCountry mortgage were delivered to the Scott County Recorder's Office to be recorded.

RECORDING PROCESS

The Scott County Recorder provided deposition testimony concerning the process for recording real-property instruments. Scott County uses the TriMin computer system to electronically store all official property records. The day after a document is delivered to the recorder's office to be recorded, a label is placed on the document showing the date, time of receipt, and the document number to fulfill the requirements of Minn. Stat. §386.41 (2008). After the labeling procedure is complete, information about the document is entered into the TriMin system, beginning with the names of the grantor and grantee, the date of the document, and the legal description of the property contained in the document.

When a deed and a mortgage are brought in together to be recorded, such as here, the recorder will "clone" the legal description from the first document entered into the system, and apply that legal description to the second document so that the information does not have to be reentered. The recorder assumes that the legal descriptions are the same for the bundled documents. After the recorder enters the information into the system, the documents are scanned so that an image of each document is available on the TriMin system. Scott County has been scanning real estate documents presented for recording since approximately 1991. The public can access the records at the recorder's office or via the county recorder's website. But the information contained on the county recorder's website is only for reference purposes and is not considered the official record for county property recording purposes. In addition, images of documents that may have a Social Security number are not available on the website due to privacy concerns. Images of such documents are, however, available on the county recorder's official in-house system.

Minnesota Statutes §§386.03-.05 and 386.32 (2008) require a county to maintain a grantor-grantee index, a consecutive index, and a tract index. The TriMin system satisfies these requirements because it is searchable by (1) grantor-grantee name (the grantor-grantee index), (2) tract/legal description (the tract index), and (3) document number. If a search is conducted by the name of the grantor or grantee, any document under the grantor or grantee name will be listed. The search also displays the type of instrument, the document number, the date it was recorded, and a brief legal description of the property. On the county recorder's official in-house system, users of the system have several options that allow them to review specific information, such as the legal description of property and images of documents.[5]

SCOTT COUNTY RECORDER'S OFFICE AND THE MIDCOUNTRY MORTGAGE

When the deed to the Krueger properties and the MidCountry mortgage were delivered to the Scott County Recorder's Office to be recorded, the deed and the mortgage were labeled as received on May 19, 2004, and were marked as document numbers A657035 and A657036, respectively. The deed to the Krueger properties was entered into the TriMin system prior to the MidCountry mortgage. But because the deed transferred only the two Krueger properties, the deed only contained the legal descriptions of those two Krueger properties. Only those two descriptions were entered into the TriMin system as being related to that document. The next document was the MidCountry mortgage, and the recorder's office cloned the legal descriptions from the deed for the legal descriptions in the TriMin system for the mortgage. Because the legal descriptions in the deed referenced the two Krueger properties and only those legal descriptions were cloned for the mortgage, the only way that the TriMin system showed the mortgage as encumbering the third property—the Hinshaw property—was by the imaged copy of page three of the mortgage, which stated that it encumbered the Hinshaw property in addition to the Krueger properties.

KRUEGERS' CONVEYANCE OF THE HINSHAW PROPERTY TO HINSHAW AND FORECLOSURE

Two years after the MidCountry mortgage was delivered to the Scott County Recorder's Office to be recorded, the Kruegers conveyed the Hinshaw property to Hinshaw, but without any recorded documentary disclosure of the mortgage to MidCountry.[6] Hinshaw executed a mortgage on the property and delivered it to

---

5. For instance, a user of the in-house system has the option of placing an "X" next to a document in order to enter into a document number inquiry screen to view additional information. From there, a user can push the "F8" key to view more specific information about the legal description of the land, or the "F13" key to view an image of the document.

6. The Kruegers apparently did not disclose to Hinshaw that the Hinshaw property was still encumbered by the MidCountry mortgage, and did not obtain a satisfaction, release, or consent from MidCountry.

[appellant PHH Home Loans]. . . . The Kruegers defaulted on the MidCountry mortgage, which encumbered not only the Krueger properties, but also the Hinshaw property. MidCountry brought an action in district court to foreclose on the Krueger properties and the Hinshaw property. . . .

The licensed abstracter that had conducted title examinations of the Hinshaw property prior to Hinshaw's purchase of the Hinshaw property from the Kruegers testified, as part of the foreclosure discovery process, that she had performed two title examinations prior to the sale of the Hinshaw property. She had performed those searches by using the tract index (*i.e.*, searched by entering the legal description of the property), and those searches did not indicate that the MidCountry mortgage was recorded against the Hinshaw property. She did not check the grantor-grantee index (*i.e.*, did not search by grantor or grantee name), because she testified that she does not routinely check that index when performing title examinations, but will if requested. . . .

. . . [The district] court held that the [MidCountry] mortgage was not properly recorded, and granted summary judgment in favor of Hinshaw and PHH because neither could be charged with actual, implied, or constructive notice of the Mid-Country mortgage.

MidCountry appealed and the court of appeals reversed, [concluding that the MidCountry mortgage was properly recorded]. . . . We granted review. . . .

The Minnesota Recording Act gives priority to those who purchase property in good faith, for valuable consideration, and who first record their interests, by providing that

> [e]very conveyance of real estate shall be recorded in the office of the county recorder of the county where such real estate is situated; and every such conveyance not so recorded shall be void as against any subsequent purchaser in good faith and for a valuable consideration of the same real estate . . . whose conveyance is first duly recorded.

Minn. Stat. §507.34 (2008). . . . The only dispute here is whether Hinshaw and PHH had constructive notice of the MidCountry mortgage as a matter of law. . . .

B.

We turn next to Hinshaw and PHH's contention that proper recording requires proper indexing, and that Minn. Stat. §§386.03-.05 and 386.32 establish the requirements for proper recording. Minnesota Statutes chapter 386 requires that a county recorder's office keep (1) a *grantor-grantee reception index* that includes the date and time an instrument was received to be recorded, the names of the grantor and grantee, where the land is situated, the instrument number, and the type of instrument; (2) a *consecutive index* of all records showing the number of the instrument consecutively and the time of its reception . . . and (3) a *tract index* that includes the legal description of the affected land. . . .

Hinshaw and PHH argue that these statutes require the indexes to record the legal descriptions of property affected by a recorded instrument. They contend that Scott County's indexing system failed to do this, and thus the system did not show that the Hinshaw property was encumbered by the MidCountry mortgage. They maintain that even though the document number appeared in the grantor-grantee index under the Krueger name, the TriMin system did not list the description of the Hinshaw property in connection with the mortgage. According to Hinshaw and

PHH, the indexing system failed to provide the "where situated" information required under Minn. Stat. ch. 386, making the MidCountry mortgage not properly recorded. . . .

[We] note that the MidCountry mortgage was not listed in the tract index as encumbering the Hinshaw property. Additionally, if a title searcher looked under the mortgage's document number A657036 in the document number inquiry screen and pressed the "F8" key, the legal descriptions of the Krueger properties were listed, but not the Hinshaw property. Based on these omissions, the mortgage did not meet all of the indexing requirements of sections 386.03-.05 and 386.32. On the other hand, it did meet some of the requirements. Most importantly, the mortgage was listed in the historically primary grantor-grantee index under the names of both Frederick Krueger and Nancy Krueger. Further, the index provided information about the nature of the instrument (*i.e.*, that the document was a mortgage), the mortgage's document number, and the date it was recorded. The "where situated" or legal description column gave the general location of the land as "Belle Plaine." Given the limited amount of space available for the column in the grantor-grantee index screen, it would have been impossible to provide there the full legal description of all the properties the MidCountry mortgage encumbered.[11]

An index is intended to be a springboard in helping the record searcher find the word-for-word record of the document that is on file with the county recorder's office as required by Minn. Stat. §386.19 (2008). The MidCountry mortgage was listed in the grantor-grantee index under both of the Kruegers' names, and was described as situated in "Belle Plaine." The title searcher could have typed an "X" by the listing for the mortgage and entered into a document number inquiry screen that contained additional information about the mortgage. While viewing that screen, a title searcher could have viewed an image of the MidCountry mortgage and found on page three that it encumbered the Hinshaw property. Because the mortgage was listed in the grantor-grantee index under the Kruegers' names with a description of the land as located in "Belle Plaine," and there was an image of the document itself, which provided the correct legal description of each property that the mortgage encumbered, we conclude that the mortgage was properly recorded. Although the mortgage was properly recorded, it was imperfectly indexed; one screen revealed the mortgage while another screen showed the legal description of the Krueger properties and nothing for the Hinshaw property. . . .

We conclude that the indexes are the starting point for a subsequent purchaser or title examiner, and that Hinshaw and PHH are charged with notice of the facts contained in the MidCountry mortgage itself because the mortgage was indexed in the grantor-grantee index under the correct names (the Kruegers) and an image of the document itself was available through the grantor-grantee index. We are not dealing with a misindexed document (*e.g.*, a document indexed under the wrong grantor's or grantee's name), nor are we dealing with an unindexed document (i.e., a document that was not indexed at all). Instead, the mortgage here was indexed, although imperfectly. But we do not consider "properly recorded" as coterminous with "properly indexed." Rather, "properly recorded" requires a reference in the

---

11. A screen print of the grantor-grantee index indicates that only 12 spaces are available in the "where situated" or legal description column. The legal description of all three of the properties encumbered by the MidCountry mortgage would take approximately 300 spaces.

indexes sufficient to locate the document and a record of the document itself, and that between the indexes and the record, there is sufficient evidence that the document pertains to the property. Here, the MidCountry mortgage was listed in the grantor-grantee index, and an image of the document was available via this index. In spite of the incomplete legal description of the encumbered property in the index, the contents of the mortgage itself were available and compensated for the deficiencies in the indexes for constructive notice purposes. Therefore, although the mortgage may have been imperfectly indexed, it was "properly recorded." Because we conclude that the MidCountry mortgage was properly recorded, Hinshaw and PHH are charged with constructive notice of its existence, and therefore were not good faith purchasers.

C.

Hinshaw and PHH cite cases from other jurisdictions in an effort to show that an instrument must be properly indexed in order to be considered properly recorded for constructive notice purposes. *E.g.*, Noyes v. Horr, 13 Iowa 570 (1862); Hanson v. Zoller, 187 N.W.2d 47 (N.D. 1971). But these cases are from states that have different recording statutes, different indexing systems, and different case law precedent. Further, courts in other jurisdictions have rejected Hinshaw and PHH's position. *See, e.g.*, First Citizens Nat'l Bank v. Sherwood, 583 Pa. 466, 879 A.2d 178 (2005). Looking to other jurisdictions for guidance is not instructive here.

D.

Hinshaw and PHH also raise a policy argument in support of their position. They contend that if they are charged with constructive notice and are required to read the entire record, including the terms of the MidCountry mortgage imaged into an electronic system, then subsequent purchasers cannot rely on the recording and indexing performed by county recorders. Instead, purchasers would have to assume that the recording indexes are inaccurate and must read the full text of every document referenced in any index. They argue that this inefficiently places the risk of loss on subsequent purchasers when the risk of loss should be placed on the party seeking to have an instrument recorded with the county recorder's office because only that party would know what and where to check, and how to identify a problem. Further, Hinshaw and PHH argue that by not equating proper indexing with proper recording, title examinations will be more burdensome and real estate closings will be more expensive.

We understand Hinshaw and PHH's policy argument, but think it is overstated. Reviewing the legal descriptions contained in a mortgage that is indexed under the names of the grantor and grantee is not overly burdensome, nor is checking documents that potentially relate to the property at issue. The electronic storing of real property records significantly reduces the burden of searching in comparison with the burden that existed prior to electronic access to county property records. Our conclusion that the MidCountry mortgage was properly recorded for constructive notice purposes merely affirms what we believe the rule has been in this state for over 90 years: purchasers are presumed to have read and are charged with constructive notice of the entire record, including information contained in the indexes and the contents of the recorded document itself if it appears in the grantor-grantee index under the correct name.[14]

Because we hold that the MidCountry mortgage was properly recorded, thereby charging Hinshaw and PHH with constructive notice, MidCountry's mortgage takes priority over Hinshaw's and PHH's interests in the Hinshaw property. Accordingly, we affirm the court of appeals. . . .

Notes and Questions

1. Public land records in the United States date back to the eighteenth century, and not surprisingly their nature has changed dramatically over that period of time. One constant is that the recorder's office returns the original instrument to the grantee or to the person who files the instrument. Why this should be the case is not clear, but it reflects the pre-Revolutionary English practice, when there was no public recording system and landowners kept and preserved deeds and other instruments constituting the chain of title (called *muniments of title*), treating them as property to be passed on to heirs and purchasers. Prior to the invention of photocopying in the twentieth century, an office employee copied the instrument by handwriting into the public records. Today, scanning technology, as described in *MidCountry Bank*, is becoming the norm, although many recording offices still use "old fashioned" photocopier machines instead of creating digital images.

2. Land title records, like all of our information, have become increasingly computerized. Soon traditional title searches, accomplished by traveling to the recorder's office and studying only pieces of paper, will no longer take place in any U.S. jurisdiction. In addition to mastering the search tools of the electronic system, the electronic searcher must fully understand the organization of the underlying land title records, including the details of the indexing system. Knowledge of the underlying recording system and the search engine enables you to do an accurate and complete search and also informs you of the types of errors and risks that may arise for any particular search. The scope of the electronic records matters a great deal. Just as for paper records, the electronic records generally are not comprehensive, so it will be necessary to consult other sets of relevant records. Note that the court in *MidCountry Bank* indicates that certain document images are not available at the Scott County website, and can only be viewed by going to the recorder's physical office to use the "in-house system." In addition, in many communities, the electronic records only go back a given number of years, whereas the county's paper records usually go back to the beginning of the polity, making it possible to search

---

14. The requirement that a subsequent purchaser and title abstracter must examine the records of the instrument themselves and a subsequent purchaser is imputed with notice of the instrument's contents appears to continue today in Minnesota. For example, the Legislature established the Minnesota Electronic Real Estate Recording Task Force "to study and make recommendations for the establishment of a system for the electronic filing and recording of real estate documents." Act of Apr. 14, 2000, ch. 391, §1, 2000 Minn. Laws 500, 500-01. The Electronic Real Estate Recording Task Force prepared and submitted a report in 2001 to the Legislature, as required by the Act of Apr. 14, 2000; in the report, the task force noted the continued connection between the indexes and the transcription of the original document (which is now an electronic or imaged copy of the document) in an electronic records system: "The copy of the document and both indexes are public records, so anyone who wants to know who currently owns a particular parcel of property, or wishes to trace its history of ownership, may do so by searching the indexes and *then examining the documents* located through the search." Elec. Real Estate Recording Task Force, *Workplan Report to the Legislature* 13 (Jan. 15, 2001) (emphasis added). . . .

title back to the sovereign. Also no matter how complete and diligent the title search, there are certain title risks that are impossible to discover from the records, such as forged deeds, fraudulent transactions, unrecorded interests, and improperly recorded interests. Consequently, after completing a title search it is important to manage the risk of error with some form of title assurance. Who ultimately bore the loss in *MidCountry Bank*? The opinion does not mention whether Hinshaw and PHH Home Loans obtained title insurance, but if so, the title insurer would have compensated them for the loss caused by MidCountry's foreclosure, and the insurer would have been the real party in interest in the litigation.

3. A majority of states including Minnesota have adopted the Uniform Real Property Electronic Recording Act (URPERA), which authorizes electronic signatures, filing, recording, and storage. As of 2011, over 625 counties in 37 states plus the District of Columbia have adopted some form of eRecording technology. In most states, the use of eRecording technology varies county by county. Colorado, the District of Columbia, and Hawaii have 100 percent coverage. Given advances in technology, are county governments still the proper entities to accept and maintain electronic land records?

As is true for other types of digital information technology, one challenge is the selection of software and technical standards. URPERA provides a legal framework for generating and recording electronic documents. The Property Records Industry Association (PRIA), pursuant to an alliance with the Mortgage Industry Standards Maintenance Organization (MISMO), has developed and revised the Extensible Markup Language (XML) standards to define an electronic vocabulary for eRecording. The goal is to produce a single reference model that allows the recording industry to achieve increased accuracy, reduced cost, and quicker processing of real estate instruments.

■ RAUB v. GENERAL INCOME SPONSORS OF IOWA, INC.
Supreme Court of Iowa, 1970
176 N.W.2d 216

LeGrand, Justice. This de novo appeal of two consolidated cases involves an attempt by Jessie O. Raub to set aside a deed to her homestead allegedly obtained from her by fraud and to declare invalid two mortgages which the grantee of that deed later placed on the property. The trial court entered a decree declaring the deed void and providing that neither mortgage was a lien on her property.

This appeal is by First National Bank of Fort Dodge, Iowa, holder of the first mortgage, and by Manson State Bank of Manson, Iowa, holder of the second mortgage. General Income Sponsors of Iowa, Inc., the grantee in the controversial deed, does not appeal. . . .

As already mentioned, General Income Sponsors of Iowa, Inc. does not appeal. The decree holding that its warranty deed was obtained from plaintiff by fraud is therefore a finality. Indeed the evidence is overwhelming that plaintiff was the unfortunate victim of gross fraud practiced upon her by Clark Barczewski and Joseph Huffman, officers and agents of General Income Sponsors of Iowa, Inc., over a period of more than three years during which they bilked her of some $33,000 for which she now has nothing. These unscrupulous men, having once ingratiated themselves with plaintiff, did not rest until they had taken virtually all she had saved. She testified she is now "financially drained."

Plaintiff was employed at Geo. A. Hormel & Co. for a number of years. She had only a ninth grade education but was not without some experience in business affairs. She had bought and sold several pieces of real estate. She knew what a warranty deed was and understood the legal effect of such an instrument. She was hard-working and frugal and had accumulated substantial savings and investments when she first met Barczewski and Huffman in 1963. She also owned her own home, upon which there was then a small mortgage.

She sought these men out to help her sell stock she owned in Allied Fund of New York. Her dealings thereafter were principally with Mr. Barczewski although she also had some contact with Mr. Huffman. Upon Barczewski's advice she sold her Allied Fund holdings and invested the proceeds in two other corporations suggested by him. For some time she received small dividends from at least one of these corporations.

Plaintiff was interested in providing for her eventual retirement. She was then 58 years old and expected to work only a few more years. She talked with Barczewski about her plans, and he advised her concerning what course her investments should take. Within a short time he had her complete trust and confidence. She formed a close personal association with him and his wife. They visited back and forth. She made a will naming him as her executor. Little by little he prevailed upon her to place all her money in stock of General Income Sponsors of Iowa, Inc., about which she knew nothing. He told her this was a company he and Mr. Huffman were starting and she should "get it all in General Income Sponsors." By a series of transactions from February to October (1965) she gave Barczewski $10,000 for stock in that corporation. On December 2, 1965, plaintiff executed and delivered to General Income Sponsors of Iowa, Inc. a warranty deed to her homestead, which by then had been cleared of its existing mortgage, in return for which she was to receive an additional $14,000 in company stock. Although she asked for the stock certificate several times, apparently she never received it. The warranty deed was recorded December 20, 1965. Thereafter plaintiff remained in possession of the real estate as a tenant, paying $70 a month rent from December, 1965, through August, 1966. The rent was paid to Mr. Barczewski on behalf of General Income Sponsors of Iowa, Inc.

On September 17, 1966, the defendant, First National Bank of Fort Dodge, took a mortgage on this property from General Income Sponsors in the amount of $6,000. The mortgage was promptly recorded. On October 25, 1966, the Manson State Bank placed a second mortgage on the real estate to secure payment of $10,350. This mortgage was recorded on November 7, 1966.

During all this time plaintiff still reposed great trust and confidence in Mr. Barczewski. Although she was being systematically swindled, she did not suspect this until early in 1967 when an officer of the First National Bank called to tell her future rent payments should be made there. She then consulted her attorney and investigation quickly disclosed the perfidy which had been practiced upon her.

As we understand defendants' argument, they concede plaintiff's warranty deed of December 2, 1965, was obtained by fraud and was properly set aside by the trial court. However, they assert they are nevertheless entitled to enforce the liens of their mortgages because they qualify as bona fide purchasers.

I.

A bona fide purchaser is one who takes a conveyance of real estate in good faith from the holder of legal title, paying a valuable consideration for it without notice of outstanding equities. . . .

We have held a mortgagee is regarded the same as a purchaser for this purpose. Brunsdon v. Brunsdon, 200 N.W. 823, 829 (Iowa 1924).

II.

In considering the status of defendants, no serious dispute exists except as to good faith and notice of outstanding equities. The evidence clearly establishes both mortgages were taken from the legal title holder, General Income Sponsors of Iowa, Inc., and each defendant paid valuable consideration for its mortgage.

The critical question is: did defendants have notice, either actual or constructive, that their mortgagor's title had been obtained by fraud? The trial court found, and we agree, that the defendant banks, as well as plaintiff, were the victims of Barczewski's fraud. However, this does not answer the question. There may still be notice to defendants if circumstances are shown which would lead a reasonably prudent person to investigate the possible existence of outstanding rights hostile to the grantor's title. . . .

A consideration of this problem requires us to determine, first, if plaintiff's possession of the property after she had conveyed it away imparted notice of her present claim; and, second, apart from that, were there any other circumstances which should have put a reasonably prudent person on notice to investigate concerning outstanding equities. We discuss these in reverse order.

III.

One who asserts he is a bona fide purchaser must prove his good faith; and good faith is lacking if he knew or, as a reasonably prudent person, should have known others made claims hostile to his grantor's title. . . .

Although the trial court found the defendants, too, had been victimized by the fraud of Barczewski and Huffman, it also found the defendants should have known of the fraud by which plaintiff had been induced to transfer her property to General Income Sponsors.

We have searched the record carefully and can find no evidence to charge defendants with such knowledge or to put them on notice to make inquiry.

There was nothing about the mortgage transactions to arouse defendants' suspicions as to the conditions under which the mortgagor's title had been obtained. They were dealing with the holder of legal title, whose deed had been recorded. The record showed payment of adequate consideration. Plaintiff herself testifies she had been paid $14,000 for property reasonably worth $12,500. True it *now* appears payment was made in worthless stock, but there was nothing *then* to cause defendants to suspect this. Nor can it be said that an owner's application to borrow money on the security of his property is a suspicious circumstance. . . .

IV.

Even if this is true, however, plaintiff asserts that, since she was the occupant of the real estate at the time of the mortgages, the banks were obliged to investigate her occupancy. Having failed to do so, she argues, they are now charged with notice that the deed to her property had been obtained by fraud.

To put it another way: Did the plaintiff's possession of the real estate in question after the execution and delivery of the warranty deed in question import notice to defendants of her present claim?

Although the question there involved was different, Bartels v. Hennessey Bros., Inc., 164 N.W.2d 87 (Iowa 1969), has something to say on this subject. At page 91, we said,

> Absent express notice given, a land purchaser generally has three established sources of information to which he should turn for ascertainment of existing rights in any property he proposes to buy: (1) the records in the county recorder's office where basic rights involved are recorded; (2) other public records, to discover existence of rights not always disclosed in the county recorder's office, *i.e.,* judgments, liens and taxes; and (3) an inspection of the land itself, to determine by observation any rights which may exist apart from our recording system by virtue of occupancy, use or otherwise.

It is apparent only the third item of this list is material here, and we now direct our attention to deciding if, under the circumstances of this case, the defendants had notice of plaintiff's claim because of her occupancy of the property.

We follow the rule that possession of land by one other than the grantor is ordinarily sufficient to put parties on inquiry as to the rights of the party in possession. Clark v. Chapman, 239 N.W. 797, 802 (Iowa 1931).

However, there is a general exception to this rule which we also observe: possession by the grantor of a recorded deed does not impart such notice. This is because occupancy, to impart notice, must be hostile to or inconsistent with that of the holder of legal title. Booth v. Cady, 257 N.W. 802, 804 (Iowa 1934). We have held the occupancy by one who has conveyed his title, at least for a reasonable period, is not inconsistent with the rights of the person to whom he has conveyed. Koon v. Tramel, 32 N.W. 243, 245 (Iowa 1887).

We are forced to the conclusion that plaintiff's possession of the property following her warranty deed did not impart notice to defendants that she claimed any right or interest therein.

V.

Perhaps we could stop our discussion here, but we desire to comment briefly to show it would be of no benefit to plaintiff even if we had held defendants were obligated to investigate her occupancy of the premises.

Defendants would then be bound only by such knowledge as that investigation would probably have disclosed. Clark v. Chapman, 239 N.W. 797, 801 (Iowa 1931).

Investigation by defendants would have disclosed nothing to indicate the fraud upon which plaintiff now relies. Her testimony shows she intended to convey her entire interest in the home by the warranty deed of December 2, 1965. At the time the mortgages were given plaintiff was paying rent as a tenant and made no claim to the property. She did not then know the deed had been obtained from her by fraud. She was still completely convinced of Barczewski's loyalty, so much so that she had named him as her executor shortly before that time. She testified she trusted both men "beyond September or October of 1966."

If an investigation had been made, it would have disclosed simply that plaintiff had conveyed her property by warranty deed to General Income Sponsors of Iowa, Inc.; that she continued to occupy the property as a tenant; that she was paying $70 a month rent; and that she claimed no ownership interest in the property. . . .

VI.

. . . .

The trial court [found that the mortgages to First National Bank and Manson State Bank were void and should be stricken from the record.] We reverse that . . . judgment and hold [each] mortgage . . . is a valid and enforceable lien on plaintiff's property. . . .

We fully recognize plaintiff has lost her life savings through fraud of Barczewski and Huffman. We further recognize she is probably without redress against them. The corporation is now apparently defunct. Huffman has plead guilty to a charge of obtaining money under false pretenses. Barczewski has been indicted on a similar charge. At the time this case was tried, he had not been apprehended to stand trial.

These are tragic circumstances brought about by the trust and confidence which plaintiff mistakenly reposed in Barczewski and Huffman. We agree with the trial court that this was an outrageous scheme unscrupulously carried out until plaintiff was completely impoverished. While we would like to rescue her from the consequences of her own folly, we cannot do so by improperly shifting the loss to defendants simply because they are better able to stand it.

The decree of the trial court is accordingly affirmed in part and reversed in part.

All Justices concur except MASON, who dissents, and UHLENHOPP, who takes no part.

Notes and Questions

1. As *Raub* explains, a subsequent purchaser is charged with notice of the rights of anyone in possession of the land being purchased. This means a prudent purchaser must inspect the land and question anyone, other than the seller, who appears to be a possessor of all or part of the land. Courts have fashioned several exceptions to this general rule. One prime exception is when possession is consistent with record title. For example, consider a buyer who contracts to buy rental property from the landlord. If the tenant's lease is recorded, the tenant's possession is consistent with record title, and buyer need not ask the tenant what rights he is claiming. Buyer may assume the recorded lease discloses the nature and full extent of the tenant's rights. Conversely, if the tenant's lease is not recorded, possession and record title are not consistent. Buyer is on inquiry notice that the tenant possessor has an unrecorded interest. Buyer may choose to trust the landlord/seller accurately to describe the tenant's rights, but Buyer does this at his peril. Buyer is not a BFP if the seller told him the tenant has a month-to-month lease, but the tenant really has a term for years.

In *Raub*, General Income Sponsors had record title when the two banks made their mortgage loans. Thus, it appears that Jessie Raub's possession of her house was inconsistent with record title, and the banks should have had a duty of inquiry. In a number of states this would be the outcome, but there is a split of authority on the question. Iowa and some other states have a special rule when the possessor is the grantor in the last deed in the chain of title, and the new transfer takes place a reasonably short period after the possessor's conveyance. The rationale is that, although the norm is for a grantee to take possession upon delivery of the deed, it's not unusual for the parties to agree that the grantor can stay in possession for a limited time period. Under this view, a grantor's retained possession is consistent with record title for a reasonable period, but not indefinitely.

2. *Raub* also explains that Jessie should lose for another reason — inquiring of possessors is excused if the facts conclusively show that inquiry would not have revealed the unrecorded interest. Jessie owned the right to rescind (the deed she signed was voidable due to the grantee's fraud), but she was unaware of the fraud at the time the banks made their mortgage loans. What does the court presume Jessie would have said if a bank representative had knocked on her door in September or October 1966 and asked her about her occupancy rights?

3. A recording act only protects a BFP against an off-the-record interest that is capable of being recorded. Recording acts define what instruments should be recorded. Their scope varies from state to state, but in every state there are some interests in land that are not required to be recorded. There are two types of nonrecordable interests: those that cannot be created by instrument, such as claims of adverse possession, prescriptive easements, and marital property rights; and instruments that are not eligible for recording, such as short-term leases. The consequence of having nonrecordable rights in land is that a purchaser is bound by them, even though their existence is not ascertainable by a search of the records. Often a prudent purchaser can detect these nonrecorded interests by inspecting the land (for example, the adverse possessor may have remained in open, visible possession after expiration of the limitations period), but this is not always the case.

11

Private Land Use Restrictions

A. EASEMENTS, PROFITS, AND LICENSES

Property owners enter into a wide variety of private-law arrangements that address the use of land. Two neighbors may agree to build a fence together along their boundary and thereafter maintain it. One owner may desire access across a neighbor's lot, either by foot or motor vehicle, to reach a public street or a lake. A group of neighbors may build a swimming pool for their joint use, each agreeing to pay their share of the costs of construction and operation. A hunter may bargain for rights to hunt on another person's rural tract. Property law contains several devices that facilitate such agreements. The estates system (including defeasible estates, concurrent ownership, and leases) sometimes provides useful tools, but it is not well suited for many such transactions. The other mechanisms are easements, profits, covenants, and licenses. Collectively, the first three legal creatures are known as *servitudes*. Generally, an *easement* is the right to make a specific limited use of land possessed by someone else; a *profit* (more fully called a *profit à prendre*) is the right to remove something of value (like timber or fish) from another's land; and a *covenant* restricts a person's use of his land. Profits are often viewed as a subcategory of easements. A *license* is usually an interest of lesser importance than a servitude because generally it is nontransferable and is revocable by the landowner. The related functions performed by servitudes have led to calls to create a single integrated interest rather than three distinct ones. Indeed, the latest Restatement moves in this direction, although it retains some distinctions. *See Restatement of Property (Servitudes)* §1.1, cmt. a (explaining that servitude "is the generic term that describes legal devices private parties can use to create rights and obligations that run with the land"). But most states persist in the use of separate terminology, so in this chapter we first consider easements and then turn to covenants.

Easements and other servitudes provide a means by which a person can obtain the right to use someone else's land or surrender a right to use her own land in a specified way. Why would a person want to gain, or lose, such a right? And why do such private agreements proliferate? Most of the land use decisions that are the subject of easements and covenants may also be made the subject of governmental action. Nuisance law offers a judicial remedy for landowners who suffer from substantial interferences with the use of their land. Zoning and other government regulations (described in Chapter 12) address many of the same issues, but they rely upon legislation or administrative action instead of private decisions. Perhaps the most fundamental question raised by this chapter is whether — or more likely, in what circumstances — such private devices are better equipped to govern land use decisions than their legislative or administrative alternatives.

The terminology of easements and profits is an artifact of their early history, which has persisted through the centuries. History thus explains more than common sense. For example, a profit à prendre was originally designed to allow feudal tenants to conduct activities such as fishing or picking apples on land that they did not own, and it (barely) survives as a separate interest today only because of the circumstances of its creation centuries ago. Easements, like the estates in land, evolved with the common law in response to changing uses of land in England from medieval times through the nineteenth century. Easements were unnecessary when most land was held in common; they became invaluable once land was partitioned into discrete private holdings. Today, easements are an important feature of property law. They provide a nonpossessory right to use land that is otherwise owned by someone else. (Thus, you cannot have an easement across your own land.) The rights granted by an easement are not *exclusive* unless the conveyance makes them so, which explains the large number of cases in which the easement holder and the landowner complain about conflicting uses. An easement may have any *duration* agreed to by the parties; it may be perpetual, for a term of years, or for the lifetime of the holder; and it may be *defeasible*.

1. Express Creation and Scope

■ **HAGAN v. DELAWARE ANGLERS' & GUNNERS' CLUB**
Court of Chancery of Delaware, 1995
655 A.2d 292

BERGER, Justice. This is an action brought by plaintiffs, Harriet L. Hagan and Charles T. Blaisdell, to enforce their alleged right to fish in Shallcross Lake. Defendant, Delaware Anglers' and Gunners' Club, is a Delaware corporation that owns the land under the lake, as well as certain of the property surrounding it. Plaintiffs claim that they are entitled to fish in the lake on either of two grounds. First, they say that the lake is open to the public because the creek that was dammed up to form the lake was a navigable body of water. Alternatively, plaintiffs claim the benefit of a reservation of rights included in the original deed pursuant to which defendant obtained title to the lake. [The original deed from Mary Shallcross to defendant reserved to Shallcross, her heirs, assigns and tenants, the right to fish in the lake. Plaintiffs, owners of nearby property, acquired their property through a chain of title that traces back to Mary Shallcross.] . . .

. . . Shallcross Lake was formed as a mill pond in the mid-1700's, by the erection of a dam on a branch of Drawyers Creek. The lake is fed by springs, rainfall, water run off from adjacent lands, and two small streams. [The court held that plaintiffs had no public fishing rights based on a finding that if the dam were removed, neither the creek nor the land under the lake would be navigable for boats.]

With respect to plaintiffs' claimed deed rights, the question is whether the reservation of fishing rights by Mary Shallcross was appurtenant or in gross. If the profit à prendre is appurtenant, it passes automatically with the property; if it is in gross, it is a personal right and will not automatically pass with the property. Whether a profit is "appurtenant or in gross is controlled mainly by the nature of the right and the intention of the parties creating it, and must be determined by the fair interpretation of the grant or reservation creating [it], aided if necessary by the situation of the property and the surrounding circumstances." 28 C.J.S. Easements §4 (1941). Where a profit à prendre exists independent of claimant's ownership of land, as in the case where one is granted the exclusive right to remove timber or hunt and fish on the property of another, it is generally a profit in gross. Oakley Valley Stone, Inc. v. Alastra, 715 P.2d 935, 937 (Idaho 1985). Here, plaintiffs offered no evidence to suggest that the parties intended Mary Shallcross's reservation of fishing rights to pass with her property. Shallcross testified that there was no discussion of fishing rights when he and his brother sold the property following his mother's death. There was also nothing in Mary Shallcross's estate filings to suggest that she viewed the fishing rights as an asset capable of being transferred. Based upon the foregoing, I conclude that the reservation of fishing rights in Mary Shallcross's deed was a profit a prendre in gross that did not convey any rights to successive landowners.

Having found that Shallcross Lake is not navigable in fact and that plaintiffs have no fishing rights by virtue of their deeds, I need not reach defendant's counterclaim based upon adverse possession. Judgment is entered in favor of defendant.

■ LEABO v. LENINSKI

Supreme Court of Connecticut, 1981
438 A.2d 1153

BOGDANSKI, Associate Justice. This appeal is from an action brought by the plaintiffs seeking to quiet title and to enjoin the defendant from opening a beach for public use, and for damages. After the issues were found for the plaintiffs the defendant appealed.

On the appeal, the defendant maintains that the court erred (1) in the criteria it applied in determining the plaintiffs' easement rights; (2) in finding irreparable injury; (3) in concluding that the policy of public access to beaches did not affect the rights and duties of the parties; and (4) in concluding that the defendant acted with malice.

. . . In 1959, the Guilford zoning commission approved a subdivision plan of certain property owned by the estate of George T. Sperry located in the Sachem's Head section of Guilford. The subdivision consisted of six lots situated northerly of Falcon Road and a small piece of rocky shore, known as the "Second Piece," located southerly of Falcon Road. Falcon Road runs east and west along the beach on Long Island Sound and westerly of a proposed private road to be known as Walden Hill Road. The estate also owned additional property not included in the subdivision plan. That property consisted of a 2.23 acre parcel located on the easterly side of Walden Hill Road and a small beach, approximately 1300 square feet in area, located southerly of Falcon Road and easterly of the "Second Piece."

The estate sold the six lots, Walden Hill Road and the "Second Piece" to Falcon, Inc. The deed granted Falcon, its successors and assigns, the "right to use the beach located easterly of the second piece hereinbefore described for the purpose of bathing only." Falcon later sold the six lots and the "Second Piece" to various individuals. Each deed from Falcon contained the following language: "[t]ogether with the right to use in common with others, for the purpose of bathing only, the beach located easterly of the Second Piece." . . . The plaintiffs are successors in title to the grantees of Falcon.

On November 22, 1975, the defendant purchased the 2.23 acre parcel from the successor in title of the Sperry estate. . . . Located on the 2.23 acre parcel were four cottages. The defendant obtained a permit to improve one of the cottages but, after he had incurred much expense in improvements, the Guilford zoning authorities revoked the permit and ordered him to desist and to restore the cottage to its original condition.

The defendant then painted the cottage red, white and blue simulating the American flag and posted large signs announcing the opening of the beach for public use. The Guilford zoning commission sought a temporary injunction claiming that these actions violated the zoning ordinance. The trial court denied the request for the injunction seeking to close the beach on the ground that serious questions of law were involved in this dispute, the resolution of which should await a trial on the merits. . . . The defendant thereafter purchased Walden Hill Road and began to widen it in order to provide accommodations for the vehicles which the public would use to get to the beach.

The plaintiffs brought the present action claiming that in opening the beach to public use, the defendant caused material interference with their easement rights. They sought an injunction and compensatory and punitive damages. The court granted injunctive relief and punitive damages but denied compensatory damages because of insufficient evidence.

The first issue for determination is whether the plaintiffs' easements are appurtenant or in gross. "This question is to be resolved by seeking the intent of the parties as expressed in the deed, and this intent is to be ascertained by reading the words of the deed in the light of the attendant circumstances." Birdsey v. Kosienski, 101 A.2d 274, 277 (Conn. 1953). If the easement makes no mention of the heirs and assigns of the grantee, a presumption is created that the intent of the parties was that merely a personal right of way was reserved. This presumption, however, is not conclusive. A reservation will be interpreted as creating a permanent easement if, from all the surrounding circumstances, it appears that that was the intention of the parties. *Id.* at 277.

"One circumstance which must be given great weight in the ascertainment of the intent of the parties is that the easement is of value to the dominant tenement itself. If it is of value to the property to which it is appurtenant and will continue to be of value whoever may own the property, that is strong evidence that the parties intended a permanent easement." Birdsey v. Kosienski, *supra* at 277. In its decision, the court found that the evidence clearly established that the plaintiffs' easements enhance the value of the property and that such enhancement was implied by the subdivision's character as a waterfront development.

Also significant is whether the owner of the servient estate recognized the right of the subsequent owners of the dominant estate to exercise the easement. Birdsey v. Kosienski, *supra.* As to this aspect the court found that prior to the defendant's acquisition in 1975, only the owners of the lots in the subdivision and their guests used the beach; that the beach was not open to the public, and that the defendant's predecessors in title did not object to such limited use. The court thereafter concluded that the language bearing on the easements clearly indicated that they are to run with the land owned by the plaintiffs and that this intention is further supported by all the surrounding circumstances. We agree. The court further determined that the action of the defendant in opening the beach to the public constituted an irreparable injury for which there was no adequate remedy at law and that the plaintiffs were entitled to injunctive relief. . . .

The record reveals that there was ample evidence to show that the plaintiffs were disturbed or obstructed in the exercise of their right to use their beach easements. The contention that the impact of the public using the beach was minimal is contradicted by the defendant's own testimony. He admitted stating that "thousands have come" to the beach since he opened it; that "we had more than 500 people last year after the high school prom"; that "busloads of kids. . . pulled up one day . . . used the beach"; that if there was not enough parking, he was going to "shuttle the people from downtown Guilford" to the beach; that he had purchased the Walden Hill Road piece to provide "parking for 2000 bikes and 200 cars" for people using the beach; that his efforts to make the beach public were so successful that he boasted the beach is "open. Everybody knows. No signs are needed anymore, everybody just comes down there and uses it."

Considering the limited size of the beach, it becomes apparent that the above evidence supports the court's conclusion of irreparable injury. A beach easement is more than a mere right of access; it involves the more sensitive rights of recreational use, enjoyment and pleasure implied in the reasonable use of the easement. Thus, in Young v. Scofero, 127 N.Y.S.2d 196 (Sup. Ct. 1954), the court enjoined a beach owner's attempt to alter physically a beach subject to lot owners' easements holding that such a change constituted an unreasonable interference with the easement rights. . . .

While it is true that title to the area between the mean low tide and mean high tide lines, covered by the daily flow of tides (the wet sand area, also called the foreshore or tideland) remains in the state; Shorefront Park Improvement Assn. v. King, 253 A.2d 29, 33 (Conn. 1968); the fact remains that the present case does not involve public access to the wet sand area but to the privately owned dry sand area above the mean high water line.

We are not unmindful of the broader implications of public access to beaches and that General Statutes §22a-92(a)(6) evinces a policy to encourage public access to the waters of Long Island Sound. "As the nation's shoreline undergoes continuing development, and as public demand for access to beach recreational areas increases, the age-old problem of guaranteeing public beach access becomes ever more critical. Our beaches are disappearing, both literally, through the processes of erosion, and figuratively, behind rows of fences and 'No Trespassing, Private Beach' signs. . . . More detrimental to public beach recreation is the growth of private control over sand beaches." Maloney, *Public Beach Access: A Guaranteed Place to Spread Your Towel,* 29 Fla. L. Rev. 853 (1977).

Nevertheless, we must point out that while other jurisdictions have recognized public access to the dry sand beaches, they have done so on theories which do not apply to the present case. *E.g.* Gion v. City of Santa Cruz, 465 P.2d 50 (Cal. 1970) (implied dedication); State ex rel. Thornton v. Hay, 254 Or. 584, 462 P.2d 671 (1969) (custom theory); Seaway Co. v. Attorney General, 375 S.W.2d 923 (Tex. Civ. App.1964) (dedication and prescriptive easement). . . .

There is no error.

Notes and Questions

1. Most easements and profits are created by an express writing, as in *Hagan* and *Leabo*. As we'll see later in this chapter, others are implied under legal rules applicable to certain well-established categories. The creation of an express easement must satisfy the statute of frauds. The writing that achieves such compliance may either embody an *express grant* of the right to use the land or an *express reservation*, which allows a grantor who conveys an estate to continue to use the conveyed land. Notice that in *Hagan*, Mary Shallcross, the original owner of the lake (named not surprisingly "Shallcross Lake") and surrounding land, made a reservation when she conveyed the lake to the anglers' and gunners' club. In *Leabo*, was there a grant or reservation?

2. As *Hagan* and *Leabo* indicate, an easement or profit may be *appurtenant* or *in gross*. Both are alike in that the owner's rights must be exercised on specific land; this burdened land is known as the *servient tenement* or *servient estate*. For an *appurtenant easement* (or profit), the easement rights are attached to the *dominant tenement* or *dominant estate*. Necessarily, then, each appurtenant easement involves two parcels of land and two landowners. An *easement in gross* benefits the owner without regard to that person's ownership of any other property. There is no dominant tenement.

3. The writing that creates an easement or profit should expressly indicate whether the interest is appurtenant or in gross. If the former, the writing should carefully and properly describe both parcels of land — the servient and dominant estates. If the latter, the writing must describe the servient estate. As *Hagan* and *Leabo* indicate, often the author of the easement language does not make the intention sufficiently clear. Then courts must apply rules of construction to determine whether the interest is appurtenant or in gross. In *Hagan*, the court held that the reservation of a profit to fish by "Mary Shallcross, her heirs, assigns and tenants" was in gross. Yet in *Leabo* the court held that the grant of an easement for "bathing" on the beach was appurtenant, despite the lack of a reference to the grantee's heirs and assigns. Are the two decisions reconcilable? The plaintiffs in *Hagan* would have won if the court labeled the interest an appurtenant profit. The plaintiffs in *Leabo* would have lost if the court labeled the interest an easement in gross. Do you understand why?

4. The second major issue in *Leabo* concerns use of the servient estate by the servient owner. Leninski has fee simple absolute title to the small beach, and he owns the nearby four cottages. Why did the court conclude that he cannot open the beach to the public? After the decision, what uses if any can he make of *his* beach? Conflicts between the easement owner's use and the servient owner's use are fertile ground for litigation. Consider two examples. In Blalock v. Conzelman, 751 So. 2d 2 (Ala. 1999), a landowner wanted to build a circular driveway on land that he owned but that was subject to "an easement for ingress and egress to" the neighboring residential property. The holder of the easement protested that the driveway would require the cutting of century-old oak trees, growing within the boundaries of the easement, that he had carefully nurtured and that provided "beauty and shade" to his property. But the majority of the court held the right to access did not encompass a right to preserve vegetation on the easement. In another case — Louis W. Epstein Family Partnership v. Kmart Corp., 13 F.3d 762 (3d Cir. 1994) — the parties contested the scope of an express easement that guaranteed public access to property containing a Levitz furniture store. The court explained that the "owner of the

servient estate may make continued use of the area the easement covers so long as the use does not 'substantially interfere' with the easement's purpose." Applying that rule, the court held that Kmart violated the easement when its traffic flow plan for a new store severely limited access to the existing Levitz store, but that Levitz did not have a right to keep up a sign that had been standing along the adjacent frontage road since 1963.

■ ESTATE OF THOMSON v. WADE
Court of Appeals of New York, 1987
509 N.E.2d 309

PER CURIAM. Plaintiff, executrix of the estate of A. Graham Thomson, and defendant, Judith Wade, own adjoining parcels of land on the St. Lawrence River in the Village of Alexandria Bay. Plaintiff's property, on which a motel has been built, is known as the annex parcel and fronts on the river. Defendant owns the unimproved inland parcel, which is adjacent to plaintiff's and borders the public road. Plaintiff claims an easement over defendant's parcel to the public road. Both parcels were previously owned by Edward John Noble, who, in 1945, separately conveyed them to different parties. Although Noble had always used defendant's parcel to gain access to the public road from the annex parcel, in transferring the annex parcel to plaintiff's predecessor-in-interest, he did not convey an express easement appurtenant over defendant's parcel for the benefit of the annex parcel. When Noble subsequently conveyed defendant's parcel to defendant's predecessor-in-interest, however, he "excepted and reserved" to himself personally, and to plaintiff's predecessor-in-interest, a right-of-way across defendant's parcel. In the ensuing years, members of the public generally, and the various owners of the annex parcel, including plaintiff who purchased the parcel in 1954, used this right-of-way over defendant's land to reach the public road or the waterfront. When, in 1978, plaintiff erected a 50-room motel on the annex parcel, threatening an increase in traffic across defendant's property, defendant immediately sought to bar plaintiff's use of her property to benefit the annex parcel. Plaintiff thereafter acquired from Noble's successor-in-interest, the Noble Foundation, a quitclaim deed to the right-of-way over defendant's property that Noble had reserved to himself.

In this declaratory judgment action, plaintiff claims title to an easement over defendant's property by express grant, relying not on its own deed to the annex parcel, but on the purported intent of Noble that the annex parcel benefit from an easement over defendant's property, as evidenced by his conveyance of defendant's parcel subject to a right-of-way in himself and in plaintiff's predecessor-in-interest. Plaintiff also relies on the express conveyance of Noble's personal right-of-way in the quitclaim deed from the Noble Foundation. The Appellate Division concluded that no express easement was created here, 499 N.Y.S.2d 541. We agree.

It is axiomatic that Noble could not create an easement benefiting land which he did not own. *See* 3 Powell, *Real Property, Easements by Express Conveyance,* ¶407. Thus, having already conveyed the annex parcel, he could not "reserve" in the deed to defendant's predecessor-in-interest an easement appurtenant to the annex parcel for the benefit of plaintiff's predecessor-in-interest. The long-accepted rule in this State holds that a deed with a reservation or exception by the grantor in favor of a third party, a so-called "stranger to the deed," does not create a valid interest in favor of that third party. *See* Tuscarora Club v. Brown, 109 N.E. 597 (N.Y. 1915). Plaintiff invites us to abandon this rule and adopt the minority view which would recognize an interest reserved or excepted in favor of a stranger to the deed, if such was the clearly discernible intent of the grantor. *See, e.g.,* Willard v. First Church of Christ, 498 P.2d 987 (Cal. 1972).

Although application of the stranger-to-the-deed rule may, at times, frustrate a grantor's intent, any such frustration can readily be avoided by the direct convey-ance of an easement of record from the grantor to the third party. The overriding considerations of the "public policy favoring certainty in title to real property, both to protect bona fide purchasers and to avoid conflicts of ownership, which may engender needless litigation," Matter of Violi, 482 N.E.2d 29, 32 (N.Y. 1985), per-suade us to decline to depart from our settled rule. We have previously noted that in this area of law, "where it can reasonably be assumed that settled rules are necessary and necessarily relied upon, stability and adherence to precedent are generally more important than a better or even a 'correct' rule of law." Matter of Eckart, 348 N.E.2d 905, 908 (N.Y. 1976). Consequently, we hold here that any right-of-way reserved to plaintiff's predecessor-in-interest in the defendant's deed was ineffective to create an express easement in plaintiff's favor.

Additionally, inasmuch as the right-of-way reserved to Noble personally was not shown to be commercial in nature, the Appellate Division correctly determined that it could not be transferred to plaintiff in the quitclaim deed by the Noble Founda-tion. *See* Saratoga State Waters Corp. v. Pratt, 125 N.E. 834, 839 (N.Y. 1920). Thus, neither the reservation of an easement in gross in Noble, nor the reservation of a right-of-way in plaintiff's predecessor-in-interest, entitles plaintiff to an express ease-ment across defendant's property. . . .

Accordingly, the order of the Appellate Division should be affirmed, with costs.

Notes and Questions

1. Most easements are two-party transactions, with a grantor and a grantee. Despite *Estate of Thomson* and the court's reference to the California case of *Willard* as representing "the minority view," the modern trend is to allow the creation of easements for third parties. One example is Uhes v. Blake, 892 P.2d 439 (Colo. Ct. App. 1995), which allowed a third-party easement because (1) Colorado had never adopted the traditional rule, (2) the distinction between reservations and excep-tions is of decreasing importance, (3) primacy should always be given to the intent of the parties to a deed, and (4) the Restatement approves of easements for third parties.

2. In *Estate of Thomson*, the plaintiff's second theory was based on Noble's trans-fer by quitclaim deed of the right-of-way easement that Noble had reserved for himself. Why did this fail? Most easements are transferable to third parties. The benefit and the burden of an appurtenant easement transfers automatically with the conveyance of the dominant estate. American courts have long debated whether an easement in gross is transferable by conveyance, devise, or inheritance. The modern rule allows the assignment of most such easements if that is what the parties intended. In the absence of clear language in the easement document, the intent to allow transfer is usually inferred when the easement is given for a commercial purpose. Conversely, such intent is seldom inferred when the easement in gross is for the personal use or enjoyment of its owner.

■ WINDHAM LAND TRUST v. JEFFORDS

Supreme Judicial Court of Maine, 2009
967 A.2d 690

ALEXANDER, Justice. Russell I. Jeffords and Susan A. Poulin (the Owners) appeal from a summary judgment entered in, and a permanent injunction issued by, the Superior Court (Cumberland County, Cole, J.) in favor of the Windham Land Trust . . . .

The Owners hold title to 100 acres of land in Gray known as the Freeman Farm. The Owners purchased the Freeman Farm in 2004 from a couple who had previously acquired the property from the Estate of George L. Freeman. There are no deed restrictions on the front fifteen acres of the Freeman Farm, which contain farm buildings and the Owners' residence. The rear eighty-five acres (the Protected Parcel) are subject to a conservation easement (Conservation Easement).

The Conservation Easement covering the rear eighty-five acres of the property was created in 2003 when the Freeman Estate donated the Conservation Easement to the Windham Land Trust, an entity described in the Internal Revenue Code, 26 U.S.C. §501(c)(3) (2009). The Conservation Easement deed placed restrictions on the purposes for which the grantor, and its transferees, assignees, and successors-in-interest, could use the Protected Parcel. . . . The Owners expressly agreed to be bound by the Conservation Easement when they acquired the Freeman Farm.

The Protected Parcel is woodland through which several logging roads or trails run. The Owners originally planned to hold country music festivals on the front fifteen acres, hoping to attract 1000 attendees, and to allow these attendees to camp on the Protected Parcel. The Owners also planned to operate a campground on the Protected Parcel for which they obtained a State permit for thirty-six tent and trailer campsites. The Owners assert that they no longer plan to operate a campground, admitting that such a use is prohibited by the Conservation Easement. The Owners now plan to use the logging roads for wagon rides and horse-drawn sleigh rides, hiking, snowshoeing, and Nordic skiing, and to use a pond on the Protected Parcel for fishing and ice skating, all made available to "their paying guests." The Owners have stated that, if they cannot use the Protected Parcel for these commercial purposes, "they will not be able to generate income needed to maintain the trails and pond from these activities, either as separate charitable events or as part of larger events on the unprotected 15 acres such as weddings."

The Owners claim that, in late 2005 and mid-2006, when they were formulating their planned uses of the Protected Parcel, the Trust's attorney told them that the Conservation Easement deed does not prohibit earning money from activities permitted under the deed and that the then-proposed campsites would not violate the deed. The Owners contend that they relied to their detriment upon the statements by the Trust's attorney in preparing their 2007 financial plan. . . .

The Trust filed a three-count complaint against the Owners on March 23, 2007, alleging that the Owners' use of the Protected Parcel for commercial purposes interfered with the Trust's Conservation Easement and seeking a declaratory judgment and injunctive relief against the Owners. The Owners filed a two-count counterclaim. . . .

. . . The court granted the [Trust's] motion for summary judgment, concluding that the Conservation Easement does not permit commercial use of the Protected Parcel as intended by the Owners. The court also permanently enjoined the

Owners from "any collateral use of the Easement Parcel, recreation or otherwise by patrons or attendees of permitted commercial activities on the Front Parcel." The Owners filed this appeal. . . .

1. WHETHER THE COURT ERRED IN FINDING THAT THE OWNERS' PROPOSED USES OF THE PROTECTED PARCEL DO NOT COMPLY WITH THE TERMS OF THE CONSERVATION EASEMENT

The Owners argue that the commercial activities they now propose to offer to the paying public are within the scope of allowable uses under the Conservation Easement, will cause no harm to the Protected Parcel, and that, even if their proposed use for the Protected Parcel would constitute a "commercial use," the Conservation Easement does not prohibit commercial uses and the grantors of the easement intended such uses. . . .

The deed states that the Conservation Easement's "dominant purpose" is:

> [T]o preserve and protect in perpetuity the natural, open space, scenic, aesthetic and ecological features and values of the Property while not limiting the Grantor's power to utilize the property for residential recreational purposes. In so doing, it is the purpose of this Easement to foster responsible conservation practices while permitting Grantor to engage in certain recreational uses on the Property.

The deed also states that "[t]he Property shall be used by the [Owners] only for residential recreational purposes, and maintenance or access related to such purposes, together with conservation purposes and for the proper management of its forest resources." Further, the deed states that the Conservation Easement is intended to "prevent any non-residential use, non-recreational use or development which would conflict with [the land's] natural, scenic condition, except as provided" in the deed and that the Protected Parcel is intended to provide "a place of recreation and of natural solitude." The key issue for analysis is to determine whether the term "residential recreational purposes" encompasses the uses proposed by the Owners.

We note at the outset that, despite the parties' attempts to define "residential" by contrasting it to "commercial," the word "commercial" does not appear in the Conservation Easement. We do not, therefore, attempt to define "commercial" for purposes of interpreting "residential recreational purposes."

The terms "residential recreational purposes" and "non-residential use" are not defined in the deed. . . . We apply the common, everyday understanding of the word "residential," which is "of or relating to residence or residences." Webster's New Collegiate Dictionary 977 (1979). The definition of "residence" is understood to include:

> 1a: the act or fact of dwelling in a place for some time; b: the act or fact of living or regularly staying at or in some place for the discharge of a duty or the enjoyment of a benefit; 2a(1): the place where one actually lives as distinguished from his domicile or a place of temporary sojourn. *Id.*

The meaning of "residential recreational purposes," therefore, refers, unambiguously, to recreational activities associated with those who are regularly living at that locale. Thus, the deed's several references to "residential recreational purposes" indicate the parties' intent to restrict the use of the Protected Parcel to the residents of the front fifteen acres for their recreational purposes, and to preclude the income-producing or -generating uses proposed by the Owners.

The Owners' several arguments in favor of a contrary conclusion are not persuasive. First, the deed occasionally refers to "recreational use" (without the "residential" modifier) and to the Owners' right of "general enjoyment" on the Protected Parcel. However, when those terms are read in the context of the deed as a whole, it is evident that the parties intended the more specific term, "residential recreational purposes" to trump any more general terms.

Second, the Owners argue that the deed's reference to the legal duties of the Owner and the Trust with respect to "members of the general public" who may enter the Protected Parcel "for recreational purposes" can only refer to an intent to allow the Owners to "open the Protected [Parcel] to the general public for a fee." We disagree. This provision merely reiterates our statutory law limiting landowner liability for recreational uses, see 14 M.R.S. §159-A(2) (2008), and acknowledges Maine's open lands tradition, allowing public access to wilderness lands for recreational use. This section of the deed does not undermine a conclusion that, as a matter of law, the deed prohibits the Owners from engaging in the types of activities they propose.

We can, without resort to extrinsic evidence, derive from the deed's language the intent of the parties to limit use of the Protected Parcel to "residential recreational purposes" and to preclude the activities now proposed by the Owners. The Conservation Easement may be an imperfectly drafted document. However, even if we were to conclude that the document was sufficiently ambiguous to require a court to look to extrinsic evidence to glean the parties' intent in drafting the deed, the Owners failed to demonstrate that such evidence exists. . . .

Accordingly, the language of the deed is sufficiently clear for us to conclude that the intent of the parties to that document was to prohibit use of the Protected Parcel for the income-generating purposes proposed by the Owners and that the Owners failed to show the existence of a genuine issue of material fact in this regard. . . .

As to their equitable estoppel argument, the Owners . . . assert that the Trust's attorney told them more than a year after they purchased the Freeman Farm that he thought their proposed activities on the Protected Parcel would not violate the Conservation Easement and that the Owners relied on his statements in developing their "2007 financial plan." Assuming for purposes of this discussion that this is true, the Owners have not shown any detrimental reliance given that they purchased the Freeman Farm long before the alleged conversation with the Trust's attorney; they purchased the land fully aware of the Conservation Easement; and they admit that, but for a few activities associated with charitable events held on the front fifteen-acre parcel, they have not gone forward with any of their proposed activities on the Protected Parcel.

Because there are no genuine disputes of material fact, the court did not err in granting a summary judgment in favor of the Trust and the State. . . .

The entry is: Judgment affirmed.

Notes and Questions

1. *Windham Land Trust* explores yet another easement classification. An *affirmative easement* creates a right to make a physical entry upon the servient

tenement. A *negative easement* allows the holder to restrict the servient possessor from using her land in an otherwise permissible way. Affirmative easements are far more common, in part because the limitations on land use that can be accomplished by negative easements are instead addressed by covenants. The common law recognized only a limited number of negative easements; today, most negative easements are the creature of state statutes, as in *Windham Land Trust*.

2. Conservation easements have become the most common form of negative easements. Nearly nine million acres were subject to conservation easements in 2010, an almost four-fold increase since 2000. Land Trust Alliance, 2010 National Land Trust Census Report 6, available at http://www.landtrustalliance.org/land-trusts/land-trust-census/national-land-trust-census-2010/2010-final-report. Proponents of conservation easements tout their many virtues. They are attractive to conservation groups like the Nature Conservancy, which relies upon such easements to protect ecosystems around the world. A study of the use of conservation easements to establish the Ice Age National Scenic Trail through Wisconsin's glacial landscape identified three primary benefits: (1) the flexibility given to landowners and to the conservation foundations that obtain the easements, (2) the generation of additional funding by purchasing land in fee, then selling it while reserving an easement, and (3) avoiding the expense and time necessary to comply with local zoning and subdivision regulations. Christine Thisted, "Easements and Public Access on the Ice Age National Scenic Trail," in *Protecting the Land: Conservation Easements Past, Present, and Future* 347-48 (Julie Ann Gustanski & Roderick H. Squires eds., 2000). Landowners benefit from conservation easements as well. A landowner may want to protect the environment. Less altruistically, a landowner may be seeking a tax benefit. The landowner may want to avoid property tax on higher valued uses (*e.g.*, subdivisions) so that she can continue a lower valued use (*e.g.*, farming or ranching). A landowner may also desire the tax deduction that can be gained by granting a conservation easement on land for which they retain title. That deduction may come grudgingly. In Strasburg v. Commissioner, T.C. Memo 2000-94 (Tax Ct. 2000), the owner of "a spectacular piece of property" surrounded by the Gallatin National Forest on three sides conveyed a 320-acre open space easement to the Montana Land Reliance. The IRS valued the easement as worth $275,000 (after originally saying it was worth nothing), while the owner claimed it was worth $1,080,000. The court held that it was worth $800,000 and refused to order the landowner to pay a penalty for a slight error.

But not everyone sees conservation easements as an environmental or property law panacea. The Ice Age Scenic Trail study noted that "the need for persistent monitoring" was "[w]ithout a doubt, the biggest drawback to using easements to secure access" to the trail. Collecting adequate funds to manage and defend an easement poses a further challenge. Another writer observed that many westerners "perceive conservation easements as a provider of tax shelters for the rich who have recently dedicated trophy ranches." Heidi Anderson et al., "Conservation Easements in the Tenth Circuit," in *Protecting the Land, supra* at 429. A more sustained argument against conservation easements appears in Julia D. Mahoney, *Perpetual Restrictions on Land and the Problem of the Future*, 88 Va. L. Rev. 739 (2002). According to Professor Mahoney, conservation easements are troublesome because they are so much more difficult to modify or eliminate than governmental environmental regulations. In addition, increased reliance upon conservation easements "may further the interests of members of the present generation at the expense of future generations." Professor Mahoney objects that conservation easements are "based upon two widely held but erroneous assumptions":

> The first assumption is that today's landowners, together with the institutions that purchase conservation servitudes and accept them for donation, are capable of making long-term land preservation decisions, and that they can and should identify particular parcels of land as deserving of perpetual protection. Acceptance of this assumption leads to the belief that the present generation has the right, or perhaps even the duty, to engage in long-range conservation planning through the imposition of conservation easements that spell out (often in considerable detail) permissible land uses. In other words, the ability of the present generation to predict the needs and preferences of future generations is so good that the present generation should save their descendants trouble and transaction costs by making a substantial number of land use decisions for them. All available evidence, however, indicates that our competence does not extend that far.
>
> The second assumption is that the present generation represents nature's last or near-to-last chance, because once land is developed, it will never or almost never go back to being undeveloped. Under this supposition, the only way to ensure that future generations have a sufficient supply of undeveloped land is to preserve as much land as possible today, and to construct legal institutions to make it hard to reverse decisions not to develop. But this inference, too, appears to be incorrect, due both to the lack of long-term effects of much land development and to the instability of the categories of "development" and "preservation."

Id. at 744-45. In the words of George Orwell, "Each generation imagines itself to be more intelligent than the one that went before it, and wiser than the one that comes after it." *Id.* at 740 (quoting 4 *The Collected Essays, Journalism and Letters of George Orwell* 51 (Sonia Orwell & Ian Angus eds., 1968)).

3. Agricultural easements have become much more common, too. An agricultural easement seeks to keep land in agricultural use. The person or organization seeking to maintain the agricultural use buys the easement, paying the difference of value between urban development uses and agricultural uses. "About 1,100,000 farmland acres nationwide have been put under easements at an approximate cost of $2.3 billion." American Farmland Trust, *A National View of Agricultural Easement Programs*, http://www.farmland.org/resources/national-view/default.asp. States fund these easements in a number of different ways, and the 1996 federal farm bill authorized $35 million for that purpose. Still, there are many more farmers seeking such easements than there is money available to pay for them.

■ **M.P.M. BUILDERS, LLC v. DWYER**
Supreme Judicial Court of Massachusetts, 2004
809 N.E.2d 1053

COWIN, Justice. We are asked to decide whether the owner of a servient estate may change the location of an easement without the consent of the easement holder. We conclude that, subject to certain limitations, described below, the servient estate owner may do so.

The essential facts are not in dispute. The defendant, Leslie Dwyer, owns a parcel of land in Raynham abutting property owned by the plaintiff, M.P.M. Builders, L.L.C. (M.P.M.). Dwyer purchased his parcel in 1941, and, in the deed, he was also conveyed an easement, a "right of way along the cartway to Pine Street," across M.P.M.'s land. The cartway branches so that it provides Dwyer access to his property at three separate points. The deed describes the location of the easement and contains no language concerning its relocation.

In July, 2002, M.P.M. received municipal approval for a plan to subdivide and develop its property into seven house lots. Because Dwyer's easement cuts across and interferes with construction on three of M.P.M.'s planned lots, M.P.M. offered to construct two new access easements to Dwyer's property. The proposed easements would continue to provide unrestricted access from the public street (Pine Street) to Dwyer's parcel in the same general areas as the existing cartway. The relocation of the easement would allow unimpeded construction by M.P.M. on its three house lots. M.P.M. has agreed to clear and construct the new access ways, at its own expense, so "that they are as convenient [for the defendant] as the existing cartway." Dwyer objected to the proposed easement relocation, "preferring to maintain [his] right of way in the same place that it has been and has been used by [him] for the past 62 years."

[The trial judge] entered summary judgment against M.P.M., and dismissed the case. . . .

The parties disagree whether our common law permits the servient estate owner to relocate an easement without the easement holder's consent. Dwyer, citing language in our cases, contends that, once the location of an easement has been defined, it cannot be changed except by agreement of the parties. *See, e.g.*, Anderson v. DeVries, 93 N.E.2d 251, 255 (Mass. 1950). On the other hand, relying principally on the Appeals Court's decision in Lowell v. Piper, 575 N.E.2d 1159 (Mass. App. Ct. 1991), M.P.M. claims that our common law permits the servient estate owner to relocate an easement as long as such relocation would not materially increase the cost of, or inconvenience to, the easement holder's use of the easement for its intended purpose. M.P.M. urges us to clarify the law by expressly adopting the modern rule proposed by the American Law Institute in the *Restatement (Third) of Property (Servitudes)* §4.8(3) (2000).

This section provides that:

> Unless expressly denied by the terms of an easement, as defined in §1.2, the owner of the servient estate is entitled to make reasonable changes in the location or dimensions of an easement, at the servient owner's expense, to permit normal use or development of the servient estate, but only if the changes do not (a) significantly lessen the utility of the easement, (b) increase the burdens on the owner of the easement in its use and enjoyment, or (c) frustrate the purpose for which the easement was created.

Section 4.8(3) is a default rule, to apply only in the absence of an express prohibition against relocation in the instrument creating the easement and only to changes made by the servient, not the dominant, estate owner.[4] *Id.* It "is designed to permit development of the servient estate to the extent it can be accomplished without unduly interfering with the legitimate interests of the easement holder." *Id.* at comment f, at 563. Section 4.8(3) maximizes the over-all property utility by increasing the value of the servient estate without diminishing the value of the

---

4. We previously have concluded that the dominant estate owner, that is, the easement holder, may not unilaterally relocate an easement. *See* Kesseler v. Bowditch, 111 N.E. 887, 888 (Mass. 1916); Jennison v. Walker, 77 Mass. 423 (1858). According to the Restatement, many jurisdictions have erroneously expanded that sensible restriction into one that prevents the owner of the servient estate from relocating the easement without the consent of the easement holder. *Restatement (Third) of Property (Servitudes)* §4.8(3) comment f, at 563 (2000).

dominant estate; minimizes the cost associated with an easement by reducing the risk that the easement will prevent future beneficial development of the servient estate; and encourages the use of easements. *See id.*; Roaring Fork Club, L.P. v. St. Jude's Co., 36 P.3d 1229, 1236 (Colo. 2001). Regardless of what heretofore has been the common law, we conclude that §4.8(3) of the Restatement is a sensible development in the law and now adopt it as the law of the Commonwealth. . . .

Dwyer urges us to reject the Restatement approach. He argues that adoption of §4.8(3) will devalue easements, create uncertainty in property interests, and lead to an increase in litigation over property rights.[5] Our adoption of §4.8(3) will neither devalue easements nor place property interests in an uncertain status. An easement is by definition a limited, nonpossessory interest in realty. The owner of the servient estate is in possession of the estate burdened by the easement. An easement is created to serve a particular objective, not to grant the easement holder the power to veto other uses of the servient estate that do not interfere with that purpose.

The limitations embodied in §4.8(3) ensure a relocated easement will continue to serve the purpose for which it was created. So long as the easement continues to serve its intended purpose, reasonably altering the location of the easement does not destroy the value of it. For the same reason, a relocated easement is not any less certain as a property interest. The only uncertainty generated by §4.8(3) is in the easement's location. A rule that permits the easement holder to prevent any reasonable changes in the location of an easement would render an access easement virtually a possessory interest rather than what it is, merely a right of way. *See* Lowell v. Piper, 575 N.E.2d 1159, 1162 (Mass. App. Ct. 1991). Finally, parties retain the freedom to contract for greater certainty as to the easement's location by incorporating consent requirements into their agreement. . . .

Although Dwyer may be correct that increased litigation could result as a consequence of adopting §4.8(3), we do not reject desirable developments in the law solely because such developments may result in disputes spurring litigation. Section 4.8(3) "imposes upon the easement holder the burden and risk of bringing suit against an unreasonable relocation," but this "far surpasses in utility and fairness the traditional rule that left the servient land owner remediless against an unreasonable easement holder." Roaring Fork Club, L.P. v. St. Jude's Co., *supra* at 1237, quoting Note, *Balancing the Equities: Is Missouri Adopting a Progressive Rule for Relocation of Easements?*, 61 Mo. L. Rev. 1039, 1060 (1996). We trust that, over time, uncertainties will diminish and litigation will subside as easement holders realize that in some circumstances unilateral changes to an easement, paid for by the servient estate owner, will be enforced by courts. Dominant and servient estate owners will have an incentive to negotiate a result rather than having a court impose one on them.[6]

We return to the facts of this case. The Land Court judge ruled correctly under existing law. But we conclude that §4.8(3) of the Restatement best complies with

---

5. Dwyer correctly states that the majority of jurisdictions require mutual consent to change the location of an easement. *See Restatement (Third) of Property (Servitudes), supra* at comment f, at 563; Note, *The Right of Owners of Servient Estates to Relocate Easements Unilaterally*, 109 Harv. L. Rev. 1693, 1694 (1996). However, most of these decisions were issued prior to the publication of the Restatement (Third) of Property (Servitudes) (2000). Of the State appellate courts that have addressed the issue since §4.8(3) was drafted, four have adopted, or referred with approval to, the rule in some form. We have found only two State appellate courts that have expressly rejected it. *See* Herren v. Pettengill, 538 S.E.2d 735 (Ga. 2000); MacMeekin v. Low Income Hous. Inst., 45 P.3d 570 (Wash. App. 2002).

6. In his amicus brief, the Attorney General, asks that, should we adopt §4.8(3) of the Restatement, we carve an exception for public easements on a private party's land. We do not address this proposition as it is not an issue in this case.

present-day realities. The deed creating Dwyer's easement does not expressly prohibit relocation. Therefore, M.P.M. may relocate the easement at its own expense if the proposed change in location does not significantly lessen the utility of the easement, increase the burdens on Dwyer's use and enjoyment of the easement, or frustrate the purpose for which the easement was created. M.P.M. shall pay for all the costs of relocating the easement.

Because we cannot determine from the present record whether the proposed relocation of the easement meets the aforementioned criteria, we vacate the judgment and remand the case to the Land Court for further proceedings consistent with this opinion.

Notes and Questions

1. Once an easement is located on the ground, the law traditionally has required the consent of both parties to relocate the easement. *M.P.M. Builders* departs from this rule when the servient owner seeks to relocate the easement. Should the court also allow the owner of the easement to relocate the easement, without the servient owner's consent, subject to limitations that are parallel to those expressed in Restatement §4.8(3)?

2. Are all easements subject to relocation, or only a right-of-way easement such as in *M.P.M. Builders*? For example, consider the conservation easement discussed in *Windham Land Trust.* Should the owner of the servient estate have the unilateral right to relocate the conservation easement by imposing the easement on similar land and thus permitting commercial use of the initially encumbered land?

■ **CHRISTENSEN v. CITY OF POCATELLO**
Supreme Court of Idaho, 2005
124 P.3d 1008

JONES, Justice. The Christensens and Fairchilds initiated this action to prevent the City of Pocatello from extending its Portneuf Greenway, a biking and walking path, over an unopened road and an easement, both of which traverse their property. The City counterclaimed, seeking an order allowing it to proceed with the Greenway extension. After deciding some of the issues on summary judgment and conducting a bench trial on other issues, the district court ruled in favor of the City, issuing an order allowing the City to proceed with its plans. We affirm in part and reverse in part.

Harper Road was platted and dedicated as a public city road in 1946 but has never been opened or used as such. It runs from Bannock Highway on the west, through property owned by the Christensens and another party, terminating at the west boundary of a parcel that was owned by the Fairchilds at the commencement of the action but subsequently acquired by the Christensens. The latter parcel will be referred to as the Fairchild property. The east terminus of Harper Road abuts the Fairchild property at about the mid-point of its west side. A "roadway and utility" easement encumbers the west 30 feet of the Fairchild property. The north end of the easement abuts a piece of land owned by the City and known as the "Sewer Lagoon" property, located to the north of the Fairchild property. The easement was created in 1974 when Western National Corporation deeded the Fairchild property to

Calvin and Marie Mercer, reserving the easement in order to provide access to the Sewer Lagoon property from Cree Avenue, located to the south of the Fairchild property. When the easement was created, Western National owned the dominant Sewer Lagoon property. That property was deeded to the City later in 1974, but the City has not used the easement for many years. . . .

In a letter to the Christensens, the City announced its intent to expand the Greenway onto Harper Road and the easement, thus connecting Harper Road, the easement, and the Sewer Lagoon property with the rest of the Greenway, but the Christensens and Fairchilds objected. They filed a complaint in November 2000, seeking declaratory relief and an injunction preventing the City from using the road and easement as intended. Specifically, the Christensens alleged . . . (4) the City's proposed use is not consistent with that permitted on a public road. The Fairchilds alleged the easement is a private easement and that the public's use of it as part of the Greenway would unlawfully increase the burden on their servient property. . . .

We must decide on appeal (1) whether the City may extend the Greenway across the easement; and (2) whether the City has the authority to open Harper Road and limit traffic on it to pedestrians and bicyclists for use as part of the Greenway. . . .

If made part of the Greenway, the easement will allow foot and bicycle traffic between Harper Road, the Sewer Lagoon property, and the rest of the Greenway. Thus, the easement, originally intended to provide ingress and egress between Cree Avenue and the Sewer Lagoon property, will become part of a thoroughfare. This, say the Christensens, cannot be allowed, since easements appurtenant to land cannot serve parcels other than the dominant estate.[2] The district court acknowledged that the easement would serve other stretches of the Greenway not part of the dominant parcel, but wrote that the nature of this access was "too attenuated as a matter of law to constitute an improper use of an easement. . . ."

While we have addressed in different contexts the rules applicable to a changed or increased use of an easement, *see* Abbott v. Nampa Sch. Dist. 131, 808 P.2d 1289, 1293 (Idaho 1991), we have not dealt with the question presented here — whether an easement may be used to benefit property other than the identified dominant parcel. The authoritative sources for the Christensens' theory are the *Restatement (Third) of Property: Servitudes* and a decision of the Arizona Court of Appeals. According to the Restatement, "[u]nless the terms of the servitude . . . provide otherwise, an appurtenant easement or profit may not be used for the benefit of property other than the dominant estate." *Restatement (Third) of Property: Servitudes* §4.11. "The rationale," as explained in comment b. to this provision, is "that use to serve other property is not within the intended purpose of the servitude." *Id.* at cmt. b. Another purpose of the rule is to "avoid otherwise difficult litigation over the question whether increased use unreasonably increases the burden on the servient estate." *Id.* Thus, where one seeks to use an easement appurtenant to an identified dominant estate to serve a parcel other than that dominant estate, it is impermissible as a matter of law and the factual inquiry regarding increased use is not conducted.

In DND Neffson Co. v. Galleria Partners, 745 P.2d 206 (Ariz. Ct. App. 1987), the panel affirmed an order enjoining a shopping mall owner from using an easement to access property that was not part of the dominant parcel served by the easement.

---

2. The Christensens seem to have abandoned any argument that the change in use will create an impermissible burden on the servient estate based on the volume of use. While it was a contested issue at the district court, none of the Christensens' brief is dedicated to that argument. Accordingly, we will not address the issue.

The shopping mall developer's plan would have allowed mallgoers to use the easement to access the dominant parcel and, from there, access a parcel adjacent to the dominant parcel. . . . The court thought it irrelevant that the actual burden on the easement would not be known until the mall was completed. The court wrote that "[a]n easement can be overburdened either by overuse or by *improper* use." *Id.* at 207 (emphasis added.)

Many other jurisdictions follow the Restatement rule. . . .

Under the City's plan, the easement will be used to serve property other than the dominant estate — the easement will benefit properties along and west of Harper Road, which were not part of the original dominant estate. Pedestrians and bicyclists coming from properties located along Harper Road and to the west will be able to gain access to the easement at about the midpoint of its west boundary on the Fairchild property and traverse to the Sewer Lagoon property, as well as to properties located along the Greenway beyond the southeasterly boundary of the dominant parcel. There was no evidence demonstrating that the easement and dominant parcel were ever accessed via Harper Road. The City admitted in its answer that the easement provided the only access to the dominant parcel and conceded at oral argument that Harper Road was not used to access the easement.

Moreover, the proposed change in use of the easement, from a virtually unused ingress/egress easement serving a specific dominant parcel, to part of a thoroughfare open to the public for recreation purposes, is not consistent with the purpose of the easement. *See Restatement (Third) of Property: Servitudes* §4.11 cmt. b. Indeed, it is fundamentally different. The proposed change does not involve recreators using the easement to travel from Cree Avenue to the dominant parcel to frolic in a park or run around a track and then return to Cree Avenue on the same easement. Counsel for the Christensens conceded they could not complain if this were the City's plan. In sum, we cannot find any intent that the easement was intended to serve the purpose proposed by the City.

In light of the foregoing, we believe the facts of this case are an appropriate set on which to adopt §4.11 of the Restatement. The principle expressed therein prevents the City from using the easement to benefit parcels other than the dominant parcel. Thus, the easement may not be used to serve Harper Road or property beyond the dominant parcel.

The City, however, contends there is no need to adopt the Restatement since, it believes, our caselaw addresses the issue. According to the City, it can change the use of the easement to reflect the changed use on the dominant estate. They rely on a portion of *Abbott*, which provides that

> an easement granted or reserved in general terms, without any limitations as to its use, is one of unlimited reasonable use. It is not restricted to use merely for such purposes of the dominant estate as are reasonably required at the time of the grant or reservation, but the right may be exercised by the dominant owner for those purposes to which *that estate* may be subsequently devoted. Thus, there may be an increase in the volume and kind of use for such an easement during the course of its enjoyment.

Abbott v. Nampa Sch. Dist. No. 131, 808 P.2d at 1293 (quoting 25 Am. Jur. 2d *Easements and Licenses* §74 (1966)) (emphasis added). The City's reliance on this statement is misplaced. This statement speaks only to the changed use on "that estate," *i.e.*, the dominant parcel; it does not endorse a change in use that involves the easement serving parcels *other than* the dominant parcel.

[The court held that the City has the power to open Harper Road only for pedestrians and bicyclists, keeping the road closed for motor vehicles.]

The City proposes an impermissible expansion of the use and purpose for which the easement was created. Accordingly, the district court's ruling with respect to the easement is reversed. The district court's judgment is otherwise affirmed. No fees, no costs.

Notes and Questions

1. The City of Pocatello wants to use its "roadway and utility easement" for bikers and walkers. The Christensens are not arguing that this character or volume of traffic will interfere with their use and enjoyment of their neighboring land, compared to the City's concededly permissible use for motor vehicle traffic to access "Sewer Lagoon" (see footnote 2 of the opinion). So why did the Christensens win? Is the court's bright-line rule appropriate?

2. Easements often last for decades and even centuries after their creation. Changing land use patterns produce questions about the scope of old easements created decades before. The flexible rule argued for by the City, drawn from the *Abbott* case, allows for "unlimited reasonable use" including "an increase in the volume and kind of use." This rule is well accepted, provided the owner of an appurtenant easement stays within the bounds of the servient estate and uses the easement in ways that benefit only the dominant estate. For example, Shooting Point, L.L.C. v. Wescoat, 576 S.E.2d 497 (Va. 2003), involved a road easement created in 1974 across a 176-acre tract when "both the servient estate and the dominant estate were used primarily for agricultural and recreational purposes." Normally, an appurtenant easement is *divisible*; subdivision of the dominant estate allows multiple owners to use the easement. In 1999, however, the owner of the servient estate objected to the increased traffic across his land that would result if a new owner of the dominant estate was allowed to build a proposed subdivision with 18 residential lots of five acres each. The court held that the substantially increased use of the easement was permissible because it resulted in "only an increase in degree of burden, not an imposition of an additional burden, on the servient estate."

2. Non-Express Creation

■ **THOMPSON v. E.I.G. PALACE MALL, LLC**
Supreme Court of South Dakota, 2003
657 N.W.2d 300

KONENKAMP, Justice. The owners of a restaurant sought a judgment declaring that they had the right to use an adjacent mall parking lot for customer parking and truck deliveries. The trial court granted summary judgment to the mall owner. Because there are genuine issues of material fact on the question of an implied easement for access by delivery trucks, we reverse and remand that question for trial. In all other respects, we affirm.

BACKGROUND

The plaintiffs are the owners of Fanny Horner's Eating Establishment in Mitchell, South Dakota. The restaurant lies adjacent to the Palace Mall parking lot owned by E.I.G. Palace Mall, LLC. In their complaint, the plaintiff restaurant owners sought a judgment recognizing that they had a prescriptive right to use part of the mall parking lot for customer parking and for entrance and exit to the restaurant property. If successful, this suit would halt the intended development of the mall parking lot. The mall owner had contracted to sell a portion of the lot to C.S.K. Auto, which planned to build an auto parts store on the property.

At one time, Paul Bjornsen owned both the restaurant and mall properties. While Bjornsen owned the restaurant, the mall parking lot was purportedly used by restaurant patrons and delivery trucks. He deeded the restaurant property to the present owners on November 14, 1974.

Because customer and delivery truck use of the mall parking lot has continued since they purchased the restaurant, the plaintiffs claim that they have occupied the mall parking lot property for more than twenty years and have established open and notorious use and possession for purposes of customer parking, as well as for ingress and egress. They have represented to their patrons that they have the authority to park in the mall parking lot. The plaintiffs claim that an additional overlay of pavement was made on the mall parking lot, with the exception of the area claimed by the plaintiffs. The mall owner contends that the use of the mall's parking lot by the general public, including the restaurant customers, was permitted because it was not adverse to the mall's interests.

At the hearing on the mall owner's motion for summary judgment, the plaintiffs argued that they had an implied easement and not just a prescriptive right as averred in their complaint. The circuit court considered both theories and granted summary judgment to the mall owner, concluding that the plaintiffs had neither a prescriptive nor an implied easement. The court noted that the restaurant has a separate means of street access and available parking on both sides of the restaurant, which does not require the use of the mall property. In this appeal, the plaintiffs' question whether the circuit court properly granted summary judgment to the mall owner on the plaintiffs' claims for (1) a prescriptive easement, and (2) an implied easement.

1. PRESCRIPTIVE EASEMENT

Generally, a prescriptive easement occurs from a use of another's land adverse to the owner of that land or the owner's interest in the land against which a servitude is sought. *See Restatement of Property (Third)* §2.16, Servitudes Created By Prescription; *cf.* Black's Law Dictionary 1183 (6th ed. 1991). To prove a prescriptive easement, one must show an "open, continued, and unmolested use of the land in the possession of another for the statutory period . . . of 20 years." Steiner v. County of Marshall, 568 N.W.2d 627, 631 (S.D. 1997); Wolff v. South Dakota Game, Fish & Parks Dep't, 544 N.W.2d 531, 536 n.5 (S.D. 1996).

In addition, for a prescriptive easement to exist, a party seeking the easement must use the property in a manner that is hostile or adverse to the owner. Bartels v. Anaconda Co., 304 N.W.2d 108, 110 (S.D. 1981). A prescriptive easement is much like a claim of ownership by adverse possession, except that with the former the adverse user acquires only an easement and not title. *Wolff*, 544 N.W.2d at 536 n.5. Under South Dakota statutes, the sole test for adverse possession has been said to be "physical exclusion of all others under a claim of right." *Bartels*, 304 N.W.2d at 110. Thus, a use that is merely permissive and not adverse to the interests of the property owner will not become a prescriptive easement.

The party asserting a prescriptive right makes a prima facie case by showing an open and continuous use of another's land with the owner's knowledge, creating a presumption that such use is adverse and under a claim of right. Kougl v. Curry, 44

N.W.2d 114, 117 (S.D. 1950). The presumption of a grant arises from proof of an uninterrupted adverse use for the prescriptive period. *Id.* However, the presumption of a prescriptive right may be rebutted by proof that the use was by permission or not under a claim of right. *Id.*

The plaintiffs alleged that they acquired prescriptive rights to the mall parking lot because restaurant patrons parked there and large delivery trucks used the mall lot as a means to make deliveries to the restaurant. The mall owner replies that the restaurant patrons and delivery trucks servicing Fanny Horner used the parking lot permissively: they were allowed to use the lot the same as other members of the general public.

In Greenco, Inc. v. May, 506 N.E.2d 42 (Ind. Ct. App. 1987), an Indiana court addressed a similar dispute. There, the owner of a restaurant adjacent to a commercial parking lot used by restaurant customers sought a prescriptive easement for customer parking and for ingress and egress. The court ruled that members of "the general public cannot, by routine and regular use, create a prescriptive easement on behalf of a landholder." *Id.* at 46. A permissive use, the court reasoned, "can never ripen into an easement, regardless of how long the use is continued." *Id.* (citation omitted). Here, likewise, the owner merely acquiesced in the use of the lot by members of the general public, who were permitted to use the lot and did so of their own volition. The plaintiffs established no claim of right from which the mall owner could have acquired notice of the adverse claim. Therefore, the trial court properly granted summary judgment to the mall owner on the plaintiffs' claim for a prescriptive easement.

2. IMPLIED EASEMENT

The common law recognizes two types of implied easements: easements by necessity and easements implied from prior use. An easement by necessity can occur when a grantor conveys to another an inner portion of land surrounded by lands owned by the grantor or the grantor and others. Unless a contrary intent is manifest, the landlocked grantee will be entitled to have a right-of-way across the retained land of the grantor for ingress and egress. Conversely, an easement is implied by necessity in a deed when the owner retains the inner portion, but conveys to another a surrounding parcel. 2 *American Law of Property* §8.38 (A.J. Casner ed. 1952); 3 R. Powell, *The Law of Real Property* §410 (P. Rohan ed. 1987).

An easement implied from prior use arises when an owner of an entire tract of land or of two or more adjoining tracts, uses one tract, or a part of it, so that one part derives from another a benefit or advantage of an apparent, continuous, and permanent nature, and the owner later conveys part of the property without mention being made of these uses. Unless there is an express agreement to the contrary, the conveyance imparts a grant with the benefits and burdens existing at the time of the conveyance, even when such grant is not reserved or specified in the deed. 3 R. Powell, *The Law of Real Property* §411 (P. Rohan ed. 1987).

While the plaintiffs did not specifically plead an implied easement by prior use in their complaint, it is apparent from their arguments in circuit court and in this Court that such an easement is what they seek. Our prior cases have not mentioned the distinction between easements by necessity and easements by prior use. In either instance, the party claiming the existence of an implied easement must show that it is necessary, though the requisite degree of necessity is not as high when an easement by prior use is sought. *Compare* the *Restatement of Property (Third)* §2.15, Servitudes Created By Necessity, cmt d. (necessary rights include those essential to enjoyment of the property and those necessary to make effective use of the property) *with* the *Restatement of Property (Third)* §2.12, Servitudes Implied From Prior Use (continuance of prior use need only be "reasonably necessary"). *See* Homes Development Co. v. Simmons, 70 N.W.2d 527, 530 (S.D. 1955) (easement was "essential" to the beneficial enjoyment of the land).

To establish an easement by implication from prior use, the claimant must show that (1) the relevant parcels of land had been in unitary ownership; (2) the use giving rise to the easement was in existence at the time of the conveyance dividing ownership of the property; (3) the use had been so long continued and so obvious as to show that it was meant to be permanent; and (4) at the time of the severance, the easement was necessary for the proper and reasonable enjoyment of the dominant tract. Peterson v. Beck, 537 N.W.2d 375, 378 (S.D. 1995); Homes Development Co., 70 N.W.2d at 530; R. Cunningham, W. Stoebuck & D. Whitman, *The Law of Property* §8.4 (1984). In this case, the only inarguable element of the four is the first one. A single owner had title to both the restaurant and mall properties when the claimed uses began. In the summary judgment proceeding the court fixed its attention on the fourth element, concluding that none of the claimed uses were necessary. We will examine each claimed use.

As to whether an implied easement arose for use of the mall parking area for customers, the circuit court ruled that the plaintiffs submitted inadequate proof on whether continuance of such use was reasonably necessary to the enjoyment of the restaurant property. The court noted that the restaurant has its own parking lot and separate street access. Allowing cars, tour busses, and other large vehicles to park in the mall lot was more convenient than necessary, even if some of the larger vehicles could not park in the restaurant lot. At the least, a claimant must establish something more than mere convenience. Jon W. Bruce and James W. Ely, Jr., *The Law of Easements & Licenses* in Land §4:10 (citations omitted). We affirm the court's ruling that the plaintiffs failed to establish an implied easement for their customer parking on the mall lot.

On the other hand, looking at the evidence in a light most favorable to the owners of the restaurant, as we are required to do, we conclude that the circuit court was premature in ruling on the question whether an implied easement for delivery truck access existed. One of the plaintiffs stated in his affidavit opposing summary judgment that "the only access for delivery trucks and big vehicles that Fanny Horners has is the [mall] parking lot, which has been continually, since 1972, used for customer parking. That the delivery trucks must use the parking lot, as they are unable to have access to the property through the driveway which is at the south end of the premises."

The Illinois Supreme Court confronted a similar issue in Granite Properties Ltd. P'ship v. Manns, 512 N.E.2d 1230 (Ill. 1987). There, a grantor deeded a parcel of undeveloped land to a grantee, retaining two parcels located on either side of the deeded land. In the retained parcels were a shopping center and an apartment complex. The grantor claimed two easements over the grantee's property: a driveway at the rear of the shopping center used for deliveries, and a driveway allowing the only access to a parking lot at the rear of the apartment complex. In upholding the grantor's claims, the court held that the evidence supported the creation of easements by implication. The court noted that the driveways had been in use since the properties were developed and were permanent, thus their prior uses had been apparent, and those uses were reasonably necessary to the beneficial use of the grantor's property. It would have been particularly difficult and disruptive for semi trailer trucks to make deliveries anyplace other than where they had always made them.

In this case, of course, we have only disputed assertions concerning the necessity of using the mall parking lot for access by large delivery trucks during the time when the same person owned both the restaurant and mall property. The circuit court concluded that because vehicles could use the restaurant's street access, the mall parking lot access was unnecessary. However, according to the plaintiffs, the south entrance to the restaurant property will not permit large delivery trucks access for unloading. Thus we have a disputed issue of fact, which must be resolved by the trier of fact.

Affirmed in part, reversed in part, and remanded.

Notes and Questions

1. Why should the law ever imply an easement? It could always require express creation. If the law recognizes implied easements, should the party seeking an implied easement have to pay for that right?

2. Today, prescriptive easements are typically justified, as a matter of theory, by analogy to adverse possession rules. Historically, they had a different justification: a "lost grant" theory, which English courts developed and then fictionalized. Today, there are two ways to establish an easement by prescription. The first method simply requires the satisfaction of the requirements of adverse possession: The use must be actual, adverse, open and notorious, and continuous and uninterrupted for the statutorily required period. The adversity and openness requirements tend to be more difficult to apply to easements than to adverse possession of a fee simple estate. Some states have addressed the issue by statute. *E.g.*, Cal. Civ. Code §1008 (providing that an easement by prescription cannot arise if a landowner posts signs indicating that any use is permissive). The second method for establishing an easement by prescription, described as "a failed express creation theory," applies when "a use . . . is made pursuant to the terms of an intended but imperfectly created servitude, or the enjoyment of the benefit of an intended but imperfectly created servitude." *Restatement of Property (Servitudes)* §2.16.

3. The other two easements discussed in *Thompson* (easement implied from prior use and easement by necessity) can arise only if a tract of land is subdivided into two or more parts. Courts have split over the extent of necessity required for both of these types of easements. For the easement implied from prior use, the Restatement eschews strict necessity, offering a flexible standard that asks whether "the parties had reasonable grounds to expect that the conveyance would not terminate the right to continue the prior use." As factors to consider, it identifies the extent of the prior use, its necessity, the awareness of the parties, and a use for underground utilities. Restatement, *supra*, §2.12. The next case focuses on the standards for implying an easement by necessity.

■ **SCHWAB v. TIMMONS**
Supreme Court of Wisconsin, 1999
589 N.W.2d 1

WILCOX, Justice. The petitioners, James and Katherine Schwab and Dorice McCormick ("petitioners"), seek review of a decision affirming the circuit court's dismissal of their declaratory judgment action requesting an easement by necessity or by implication for both ingress and egress and utilities over the properties owned by the respondents in order to gain access to their landlocked parcels located in Door County. The circuit court, as affirmed by the court of appeals, concluded that the historical circumstances in this case do not fit the typical situation from which ways of necessity are implied and that even if they did, the easement would not have survived because it was not recorded.

On appeal, the petitioners claim they are entitled to an easement by necessity or by implication over the respondents' properties; or in the alternative, they seek an expansion of the common law in this state to recognize an easement by necessity where property is landlocked due to geographical barriers and due to the actions of the common owner and grantor, in this case the United States. We conclude that the petitioners have failed to establish entitlement to an easement by implication or by necessity either because of actions by the federal government or by geographical barriers. Not only were the parcels at issue not landlocked at the time of conveyance, but the petitioners themselves created their landlocked parcels when they conveyed away their highway access. We refuse to turn 100-plus years of Wisconsin common law on its head to accommodate such actions. Accordingly, we affirm the court of appeals.

I.

The petitioners and the respondents all own property that is located on Green Bay in the Village of Ephraim in Door County. The properties are situated between the waters of Green Bay on the west and a bluff ranging in height from 37 to 60 feet on the east. The following is a diagram of the properties (lots and parcels) involved.

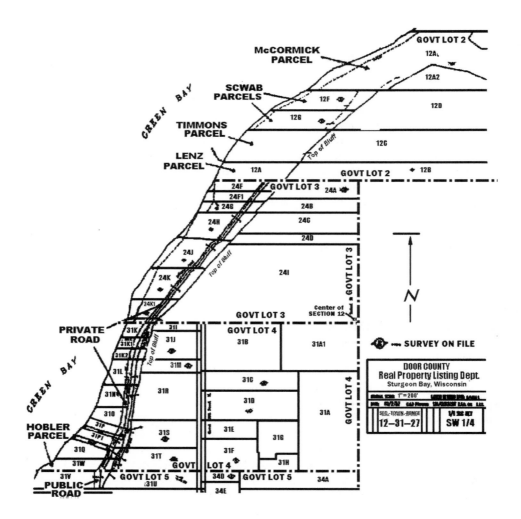

. . . Prior to 1854, the property involved was owned by the United States and was divided into three lots: Lot 2, the northernmost lot; Lot 3; and Lot 4, the southernmost lot. In 1854, the United States granted by patent Lot 4 to Ingebret Torgerson, but retained Lots 2 and 3. At the time that Lot 4 was severed from Lots 2 and 3, the United States did not retain a right-of-way through Lot 4 to get to Lots 2 and 3. At oral argument, it was explained that at the time of this conveyance by the United States, the eastern boundary of the lots extended to the east to what is now a public roadway. The lots were comprised of property both above and below the bluff with access to a public roadway from above. In 1882, the United States granted Lots 2 and 3 to Halvor Anderson.

At some point after the United States granted the lots, they were further subdivided into parcels.[1] After 1854, Lots 2, 3, and 4 were never fully owned by one person or entity, except that some unspecified parcels within Lots 2, 3, and 4 were owned by Malcolm and Margaret Vail during the years 1950 to 1963.

The petitioners' parcels are located in Lot 2, the northernmost lot. McCormick owns the northernmost parcel and the Schwabs own two adjacent parcels directly south of McCormick. Together the properties comprise over 1,200 feet of frontage and over nine acres of property. Directly south of the Schwabs' parcels is a parcel owned by the Timmons within Lot 2, followed to the south by a parcel owned by the Lenzes, also in Lot 2; all of the remaining respondents' parcels follow sequentially to the south, located in Lots 3 and 4, with the parcel owned by Hobler being the southernmost parcel located at the southern boundary of Lot 4.

It was indicated at oral argument that the current eastern boundary line, the bluff line, which produced parcels above and below the bluff was created at various unknown times. The Schwabs' parcels were originally purchased by James' parents in the 1940s and were later gifted to James in 1965 and 1974. At purchase, the Schwabs' parcels extended east from the waters of Green Bay to property above the bluff where there was access to a public roadway and a house. Some time after the 1974 inheritance, the Schwabs conveyed the property above the bluff to James' relatives and retained the parcel below. McCormick also inherited her parcel, which originally included land above and below the bluff with highway access from above, and she conveyed the property above the bluff to a third party, retaining the parcel below.

As they currently stand, both of the petitioners' parcels are bordered by water on the [west] and the bluff on the [east]. Because their properties are between the lake and the bluff, the petitioners claim their only access is over the land to the south, owned by the respondents, for which they do not have a right-of-way.

A private road runs north from Hobler's parcel across all of the respondents' properties, terminating on the Lenz parcel. Timmons also has the right to use the private road. This is the road that the petitioners are seeking to extend for their use. Negotiations for an agreement to extend the road have failed.

In 1988, the petitioners petitioned the Village of Ephraim, pursuant to Wis. Stat. §80.13 (1985-86), to extend a public road — North Shore Drive — to the private road beginning at the Hobler property northward over all of the respondents' properties to McCormick's property. Section 80.13 allows a landowner to request the local government, in its discretion, to construct a public roadway at the

---

1. Throughout this decision, our use of "lots" pertains to Lots 2, 3, and 4, which were originally conveyed by the United States to Torgerson and Anderson. We shall designate the subdivided land from Lots 2, 3, and 4, which is now owned by McCormick, the Schwabs, and the respondents, as "parcels."

petitioning landowners' expense. The Village of Ephraim board, however, declined the request, finding that extending the road was not in the public's interest.

[The petitioners then brought this declaratory judgment action seeking an easement by necessity or by implication to gain access to their land. The circuit court granted the motions to dismiss, and the court of appeals summarily affirmed.]

III.

The petitioners claim an easement by implication or by necessity over the respondents' properties. . . .

Easements by implication and by necessity are similar, but legally distinguishable, concepts. Since the early 1900s, the public policy in Wisconsin has strongly opposed the implication of covenants of conveyance, *i.e.*, easements.

An easement by implication arises when there has been a "separation of title, a use before separation took place which continued so long and was so obvious or manifest as to show that it was meant to be permanent, and it must appear that the easement is necessary to the beneficial enjoyment of the land granted or retained." Bullis v. Schmidt, 93 N.W.2d 476, 479 (Wis. 1958) (quoting 1 Thompson, *Real Property* §390 at 630 (perm. ed.)). Implied easements may only be created when the necessity for the easement is "so clear and absolute that without the easement the grantee cannot enjoy the use of the property granted to him for the purposes to which similar property is customarily devoted." *Bullis*, 93 N.W.2d at 480.

The petitioners have failed to establish a claim for an easement by implication. While a landlocked parcel may satisfy the necessity element, it is apparent from the amended complaint that the private road the petitioners seek to extend does not and has never extended to the petitioners' properties. They have failed to allege that any use by the United States was so obvious, manifest or continuous as to show that it was meant to be permanent.

Instead, the petitioners claim their parcels are landlocked and the use and enjoyment of their property is permanently and substantially impaired without having access to their property. This claim is more akin to an easement by necessity.

An easement of necessity "arises where an owner severs a landlocked portion of his or her property by conveying such parcel to another." Ludke v. Egan, 274 N.W.2d 641, 645 (Wis. 1979). To establish an easement by necessity, a party must show common ownership of the two parcels prior to severance of the landlocked parcel, and that the owner of the now landlocked parcel cannot access a public roadway from his or her own property. If this can be demonstrated, an easement by necessity will be implied over the land retained by the grantor.

The petitioners argue that the United States ownership of all three lots prior to 1854 satisfies the common ownership requirement—a question never before addressed by this court. We conclude that we need not reach that issue because even if the United States' possession of the three lots could constitute common ownership, the petitioners have conceded that neither Lot 2 nor Lot 3 were landlocked when the United States conveyed Lot 4. Rather, at the time of conveyance, the eastern boundary of the lots was above and east of the bluff (the current boundary line). Access to a public roadway was possible above the bluff. A party may only avail himself or herself of an easement by necessity when the common owner severs a landlocked portion of the property and the owner of the landlocked portion cannot access a public roadway. Because the United States never severed a landlocked portion of its property that was inaccessible from a public roadway, the petitioners have failed to establish the elements for an easement by necessity.

Nevertheless, petitioners insist that the property was effectively landlocked because of the geographical barriers inhibiting access. As the petitioners see it, their land was landlocked because the land to the south was owned by an individual, the land to the east and north was bordered by a cliff and rocky terrain, and the land to the west was bordered by the waters of Green Bay. They cite Sorenson v. Czinger, 852 P.2d 1124 (Wash. Ct. App. 1992), and Teich v. Haby, 408 S.W.2d 562 (Tex. Civ. App. 1966), in support of their position.

Wisconsin courts have never before recognized geographical barriers alone as circumstances warranting an easement by necessity. In fact, case law suggests otherwise. This court stated in Backhausen v. Mayer, 234 N.W. 904, 905 (Wis. 1931), that a way of necessity is not merely one of convenience, and "the law will not imply such a way where it has provided another method for obtaining the same at a reasonable expense to the landowner."

While the petitioners have provided evidence that the cost of building a road over the bluff would cost approximately $700,000 — an unreasonable expense, it is apparent that they consider other methods of access — a stairway, an elevator — unacceptable. Petitioners narrowly focus on vehicular access to the lake itself as the only possible way to enjoy this property. Certainly it may be more convenient for the petitioners to seek an extension of the private road to their parcels rather than travel across the property above the bluff and navigate the bluff, but that in itself does not create the right to an easement by necessity. A grantor is not landlocked when he or she has difficulty getting from his or her land to a public road as long as he or she can get from his or her land to a public road. *See Ludke*, 274 N.W.2d at 645. *See also* Sicchio v. Alvey, 103 N.W.2d 544 (Wis. 1960) (access to building at front, even though rear entry was used, does not allow for right-of-way by necessity to rear entry of store).

In this case, the petitioners had access to a public road, albeit not ideal or the most convenient access, which they sold off. Thus, the petitioners' current ownership of landlocked property resulted not from a grant of property to them but by their own acts in conveying away their highway access. They were not unwitting purchasers of landlocked property (stemming from the United States 1854 sale).

An easement by necessity only exists where an owner sells a landlocked parcel to another, in which case the law will recognize a way of necessity in the grantee over the land retained by the grantor. Rock Lake Estates Unit Owners Ass'n v. Township of Lake Mills, 536 N.W.2d 415 (Wis. Ct. App. 1995). The petitioners in this case are the grantors, not the grantees, and as in *Rock Lake Estates*, the conveyances which resulted in their landlocked property were made by the petitioners when they sold off the property above the bluff. We conclude that it would be contrary to this state's policy against encumbrances for this court to award an easement to the petitioners over parcels of unrelated third parties under these circumstances.

Finally, the petitioners assert that without an easement their property will be virtually useless because they will have no way to get to it. Thus, the petitioners renew their request for a "drastic" expansion of the law, arguing that there is no rational basis for landlocked property. The petitioners suggest that this court set forth a "reasonable use" test that balances the equities by weighing the competing interests of the need and benefit to allow access by easement to develop otherwise useless land versus the detriment such a burden may place on other property to use an existing road. The petitioners insist that the benefit and policy towards development far outweigh any anticipated costs to the burdened property.

In order to adopt the petitioners' proposal, we would have to ignore not only long-standing precedent in this state, but also well-established public policy as illustrated in our recording and conveyance statutes. Long ago this court recognized:

> It is so easy, in conveying a defined piece of land, to express either any limitations intended to be reserved over it, or to be conveyed with it over other land, that the necessity of raising any such grant or reservation by implication is hardly apparent. Courts of equity can afford relief where the grant is not of that understood by both parties to be conveyed, or so understood by one by inducement of the other. Such rights outside the limits of one's proper title seriously derogate from the policy of both our registry statutes and our statute against implication of convenants in conveyances. That policy is that a buyer of land may rely on the public records as information of all the conveyances, and upon the words of the instruments for all rights thereunder.

Miller v. Hoeschler, 105 N.W. 790, 792 (Wis. 1905).

More recently in Kordecki v. Rizzo, 317 N.W.2d 479, 483 n.5 (Wis. 1982), this court reiterated that a purchaser of real estate has three sources of information from which to learn of rights to the land he or she is about to purchase: (1) reviewing the chain of title; (2) searching other public records that may reveal other non-recorded rights, such as judgments or liens; and (3) inspecting the land itself. These sources may be irrelevant under the petitioners' proposal if someone with a landlocked piece of property desired a right-of-way through another person's property "in the interest of development."

The petitioners are effectively asking this court to sanction hidden easements. An easement which in this case was not created by, but was, according to petitioners, clearly intended by the United States at conveyance. . . .

In sum, we conclude that the petitioners have failed to establish entitlement to an easement by implication or by necessity either because of actions by the United States or by geographical barriers. We further reject the petitioners' public policy arguments for placing development of landlocked parcels above all other interests. For these reasons, we conclude that the petitioners have failed to state a claim upon which relief can be granted. Accordingly, we affirm the court of appeals' decision dismissing the petitioners' declaratory judgment action.

Notes and Questions

1. Would the petitioners have fared any better before the South Dakota Supreme Court that decided *Thompson*?

2. Some states have addressed claimed rights of necessity by statute. *See, e.g.*, Tenn. Code Ann. §54-14-102(a) ("Any person owning any lands, ingress or egress to and from which is cut off or obstructed entirely from a public road or highway by the intervening lands of another, or who has no adequate and convenient outlet from such lands to a public road in the state, by reason of the intervening lands of another, is given the right to have an easement or right-of-way condemned and set aside for the benefit of such lands over and across such intervening lands or property."). What are the advantages of that approach? Why is it not more popular?

3. The federal government faces unique questions about easements that it seeks, or easements that it must acknowledge across public land. For example, the federal government encouraged the construction of transcontinental railroads during the nineteenth century by giving alternate sections of land to the railroad companies. The resulting land ownership patterns resemble a checkerboard in which the railroads (and their successors) own the squares of one color while the government owns the squares of the other color. Not surprisingly, it becomes difficult to travel from one of your squares to another without crossing land owned by someone else. Yet claims of right to cross another's land have produced conflicting answers. In Leo Sheep Co. v. United States, 440 U.S. 668 (1979), the Court held that the government did not retain an easement across the land that it gave to the railroads, so the government would have to use its eminent domain power to secure such a right. By contrast, the Ninth Circuit has found that the railroads hold a statutory right to cross Forest Service land owned by the federal government. Montana Wilderness Ass'n v. United States Forest Service, 655 F.2d 951 (9th Cir. 1981), *cert. denied*, 455 U.S. 989 (1982).

■ **MARRONE v. WASHINGTON JOCKEY CLUB**
Supreme Court of the United States, 1913
227 U.S. 633

HOLMES, Justice. This is an action of trespass for forcibly preventing the plaintiff from entering the Bennings Race Track in this District after he had bought a ticket of admission, and for doing the same thing, or turning him out, on the following day, just after he had dropped his ticket into the box. There was also a count charging that the defendants conspired to destroy the plaintiff's reputation, and that they excluded him on the charge of having "doped" or drugged a horse entered by him for a race a few days before, in pursuance of such conspiracy. But as no evidence of a conspiracy was introduced, and as no more force was used than was necessary to prevent the plaintiff from entering upon the race track, the argument hardly went beyond an attempt to overthrow the rule commonly accepted in this country from the English cases, and adopted below, that such tickets do not create a right in rem. Wood v. Leadbitter, 13 Mees. & W. 838.

We see no reason for declining to follow the commonly accepted rule. The fact that the purchase of the ticket made a contract is not enough. A contract binds the person of the maker, but does not create an interest in the property that it may concern, unless it also operates as a conveyance. The ticket was not a conveyance of an interest in the race track, not only because it was not under seal, but because by common understanding it did not purport to have that effect. There would be obvious inconveniences if it were construed otherwise. But if it did not create such an interest, that is to say, a right in rem, valid against the landowner and third persons, the holder had no right to enforce specific performance by self-help. His only right was to sue upon the contract for the breach. It is true that if the contract were incidental to a right of property either in the land or in goods upon the land, there might be an irrevocable right of entry; but when the contract stands by itself, it must be either a conveyance or a license, subject to be revoked.

Judgment affirmed.

■ KIENZLE v. MYERS

Court of Appeals of Ohio, 2006
853 N.E.2d 1203

SINGER, Presiding Judge. This is an appeal from a summary judgment issued by the Wood County Court of Common Pleas in a property dispute. Because we conclude that a property owner's reasonable reliance on an adjacent owner's permission for use ripened into an easement by estoppel, we reverse in part and affirm in part.

Jo An Van Duyne, formerly known as Smart, and Ruth Bauer were friends and neighbors on adjoining property on West River Road in Perrysburg. In 1981, following construction of a public sewer line along West River Road, both Van Duyne and Bauer were required by law to connect to the public system.

For Bauer, a direct connection to the River Road sewer line meant that her driveway would have to be excavated, at substantial cost and inconvenience. The two women talked and reached an accommodation. They agreed that Bauer would install her sewer through a 96-foot-long trench from her home to Van Duyne's property, where it would share a 207-foot trench with Van Duyne's connector line to the street. Because of the hilly topography of the area, the pipes were buried at a depth of five and one-half feet. Each party bore her own tap and assessment fees. It is not clear from the record as to whether there was any sharing of excavation or installation costs for the sewer line.

In 1982, Jo An Van Duyne's daughter and son-in-law, Susan S. and David W. Kienzle, moved into her River Road property. In 1987, appellee, Susan S. Kienzle Trust, acquired the property. In 1989, appellants, Michael P. and Joan Myers, acquired the Bauer property.

On November 5, 2003, counsel for the Kienzles sent a letter to appellants advising them that the Kienzles had "decided to terminate the revocable license" by which appellants' sewer pipe crossed the Kienzle property. The letter directed appellants to "make other arrangements" within 30 days. Subsequent letters from David Kienzle threatened to "cap" the sewer line absent certain concessions.

On March 26, 2004, appellee sued appellants, seeking to quiet title with respect to appellants' "encroachment" across appellee's property and to enjoin further trespass, as well as damages. Appellants answered, denying an encroachment on appellee's property, maintaining that they possessed an easement, an easement by estoppel, or a prescriptive easement for the sewer line. Appellants also filed a counterclaim, seeking . . . damages from the Kienzles for cutting vegetation on appellants' property.

Following discovery, appellee was granted partial summary judgment. The trial court rejected appellants' assertion that their use of appellee's property was by easement. . . .

Easements may be created by express grant, by implication, by prescription, or by estoppel. An express easement must be part of a deed or lease or other conveyance. . . . An easement by implication needs a unity, then severance, of ownership of an estate. A prescriptive easement may arise if use is open, notorious, continuous, and adverse under a claim of right for 21 years. A permissive use can never ripen into a prescriptive easement.

Here, there is no conveyance or statutory compliance. There is also no unity, then severance, of estates. Consequently, there can be no express or implied easement. Moreover, the unrefuted affidavit of appellee's predecessor in interest, Jo An Van Duyne, states that she gave appellants' predecessor, Ruth Bauer, permission to share the sewer trench at issue. Thus, there can be no prescriptive easement.

An easement by estoppel may be found when an owner of property misleads or causes another in any way to change the other's position to his or her prejudice. Monroe Bowling Lanes v. Woodsfield Livestock Sales, 244 N.E.2d 762 (Ohio Ct. App. 1969). "Where an owner of land, without objection, permits another to expend money in reliance upon a supposed easement, when in justice and equity the former ought to have disclaimed his conflicting rights, he is estopped to deny the easement." *Id.* at 765-66.

A more modern, and slightly broader, statement of the doctrine is contained in *Restatement (Third) of Property (Servitudes)* §2.10 (2000):

> If injustice can be avoided only by establishment of a servitude, the owner or occupier of land is estopped to deny the existence of a servitude burdening the land when: (1) the owner or occupier permitted another to use that land under circumstances in which it was reasonable to foresee that the user would substantially change position believing that the permission would not be revoked, and the user did substantially change position in reasonable reliance on that belief. . . .

According to the commentary accompanying Section 2.10(1), the rule "covers the situation where a land owner or occupier gives permission to another to use the land, but does not characterize the permission as an easement or profit, and does not expressly state the duration of the permission."

In this matter, the trial court [stated]:

> . . . Under common law, an easement claimant must establish reasonable reliance upon a representation, resulting in actual prejudice. In this case, it is undisputed that the construction of the sewer pipe was with Van Duyne's permission. There is no evidence of misrepresentation. There is also no evidence of prejudice. Bauer actually received a benefit by not having to destroy her driveway. Defendants produced evidence showing that Bauer secured permits and spent money for the construction of the sewer pipe. The Court does not find actual prejudice from such facts. Bauer would have made those expenditures, regardless of the location of the sewer line. . . .

We disagree with the trial court's analysis. There is no requirement for an easement by estoppel in the common law that a property owner must mislead or misrepresent. The rule simply states that if an owner misleads *or causes another in any way* to change his or her position to that party's prejudice, the owner is estopped from denying the existence of an easement. *Monroe Bowling Lanes*, 244 N.E.2d at 765. While permissive use may prevent an easement by prescription from arising, in another context an owner's grant of permission for land use may act as an inducement for another to act, especially when the permission granted is for an act not easily undone. . . .

In the present matter, Jo An Van Duyne gave Ruth Bauer permission to install her sewer line in the same trench as Van Duyne's. There was testimony in the damage phase that plastic sewer lines have a 50-year expected lifespan. It can be reasonably inferred that neither party anticipated that burying a sewer pipe in a five and one-half foot deep trench would be a transient or temporary event. Thus, Van Duyne's permission reasonably induced appellants' predecessor in interest to change her position.

The trial court also refused to find prejudice in that Bauer would have had to pay for the construction of the sewer pipe even had she located it on her own property. Again, we disagree with this analysis. "Prejudice," in this context, is used as a synonym for "detriment." That is, Bauer relied upon Van Duyne's permission to her prejudice or detriment. This may be shown not only by the expenditures of funds but by the forbearance of some right to which one might otherwise be entitled.

While it is true that, in any event, Bauer would have had to spend money to connect to the public sewer, it is also true that but for Van Duyne's acquiescence to Bauer's use of her property, Bauer would have linked to the sewer wholly on her own property. Thus, Bauer's decision to cross Van Duyne's land constituted a change in position which placed her access to the public sewer out of her control. As the present lawsuit suggests, this decision disadvantaged Bauer. . . .

Judgment affirmed in part and reversed in part, and cause remanded.

Notes and Questions

1. *Marrone* and *Kienzle* both address the same general question: When a landowner allows a person to enter her land for a limited purpose and the right of entry is not documented by a formal instrument, should the landowner have the right to change her mind? How much strength is left in the landowner's right to exclude after she has made an initial decision *to include*? Another context, which we studied earlier in Chapter 9, concerns limits on a landlord's traditional power to terminate a periodic tenancy or refuse to renew a lease for any reason at all.

2. *Marrone* is widely accepted in the United States, but is it sound? How broadly should it apply? Suppose an opera theater terminates a customer's season tickets, refunding the purchase price, in order to reallocate them to a new patron who is willing to make a large donation. Sports venues regularly sell the rights to use luxury skyboxes and suites under long-term contracts. Do they create licenses that are revocable at will? Consider an English case decided shortly after *Marrone*. In Hurst v. Picture Theatres, Ltd., [1915] 1 K.B. 1, Hurst entered the theater and sat in an unreserved seat. The proprietors insisted that he leave, claiming he had not paid for a ticket. He refused to leave. The doorkeeper, in the presence of a policeman, took "hold of the plaintiff [Hurst] under the arms, lifted him out of his seat. The plaintiff then walked quietly out." Hurst brought an action for assault and false imprisonment, obtaining a jury verdict for £150. The Court of Appeals affirmed in a 2-1 decision.

> Buckley, L.J. [T]he licence was a licence to enter the building and see the spectacle from its commencement until its termination [and] there was included in that contract a contract not to revoke the licence until the play had run to its termination. [Defendants] broke that contract and it was a tort on their part to remove him. They committed an assault upon him in law. It was not of a violent kind, because, like a wise man, the plaintiff gave way to superior force and left the theatre. They sought to justify the assault by saying that they were entitled to remove him because he had not paid. He had

paid, the jury have so found. Failing on that question of fact, they say that they were entitled to remove him because his licence was revocable. In my opinion, it was not. . . . [I]t was for the jury to give him such a sum as was right for the assault which was committed upon him, and for the serious indignity to a gentleman of being seized and treated in this way in a place of public resort.

3. In *Kienzle*, the Kienzles claimed that Bauer's permission to locate the sewer pipe on her property was a license and that they had the right to revoke that license. Normally a license is revocable, but as an alternative method of analysis, a court holding for the Kienzles could invoke the doctrine of *irrevocable license.* Would this change in terminology have any effect upon the "bundle of rights" held by the user? Courts often use the two terms interchangeably, but arguably there may be some situations in which they are not complete functional equivalents.

3. Termination

■ PRESEAULT v. UNITED STATES
United States Court of Appeals for the Federal Circuit (en banc), 1996
100 F.3d 1525

PLAGER, Circuit Judge. . . .

[The Rails-to-Trails Act, 16 U.S.C. §1247(d), enacted in 1983, endorses the practice of *rail banking.* The Act authorizes public and private entities to convert discontinued rail corridors into recreational trails as an "interim use." Interim trail use "shall not be treated, for purposes of any law or rule of law, as an abandonment of the use of such rights-of-way for railroad purposes." The Act provides for "future reactivation of rail service" if demand for rail transport increases in the future. *Id.*]

In brief, the issue in this case is whether the conversion, under the authority of the Rails-to-Trails Act and by order of the Interstate Commerce Commission, of a long unused railroad right-of-way to a public recreational hiking and biking trail constituted a taking of the property of the owners of the underlying fee simple estate. . . .

The Preseaults own a fee simple interest in a tract of land near the shore of Lake Champlain in Burlington, Vermont, on which they have a home. This tract of land is made up of several previously separate properties, the identities of which date back to before the turn of the century. The dispute centers on three parcels within this tract, areas over which the original railroad right-of-way ran. The areas are designated by the trial court as Parcels A, B, and C. Two of those parcels, A and B, derive from the old Barker Estate property. The third parcel, C, is part of what was the larger Manwell property.

The Rutland-Canadian Railroad Company, a corporation organized under the laws of Vermont, acquired in 1899 the rights-of-way at issue on Parcels A, B, and C, over which it laid its rails and operated its railroad. Over time the ownership interests of the Rutland-Canadian passed into the hands of several successor railroads with different names; except as it may be necessary to differentiate among them, they will be referred to collectively as the Railroad.

Meanwhile, ownership of the properties over which the rights-of-way ran passed through the hands of successors in interest, eventually arriving in the hands of the Preseaults. A map of the Preseault tract, showing the various parcels and the areas subject to the railroad's rights-of-way, appears in 27 Fed. Cl. at 72, and is reproduced here for the benefit of the reader:

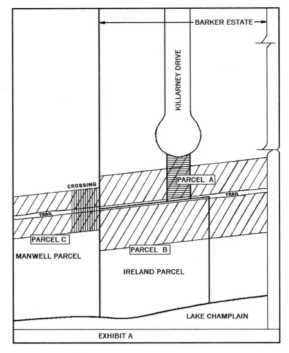

The map contained on page 1532 of the court's opinion

C. THE PROPERTY INTERESTS

. . . .

The determinative issues in the case, then, are three: (1) who owned the strips of land involved, specifically did the Railroad by the 1899 transfers acquire only easements, or did it obtain fee simple estates; (2) if the Railroad acquired only easements, were the terms of the easements limited to use for railroad purposes, or did they include future use as public recreational trails; and (3) even if the grants of the Railroad's easements were broad enough to encompass recreational trails, had these easements terminated prior to the alleged taking so that the property owners at that time held fee simples unencumbered by the easements. . . .

. . . With regard to the two parcels, A and B, derived from the Barker Estate, the trial judge examined, as have we, the document referred to as a "Commissioner's Award," dated September 2, 1899, as well as the relevant cases and statutes of Vermont. The Commissioner's Award, which is the only document that memorializes the event, is unlike a deed in that it does not contain the usual premises (the clause describing the parties to and purposes of the transaction) or habendum clause (defining the extent of the ownership interest conveyed). Usually in a deed the habendum clause would define the exact interest to be conveyed, whether a fee simple or a lesser interest, although the premises clause sometimes serves as well.

Here, the Commissioner's Award simply confirms that "the Rutland-Canadian Railroad Company . . . for the purposes of its railroad has located, entered upon and occupied lands owned by [the Barkers] . . . described as follows [and here follows a metes and bounds description of the strip of land]." The document then states that the owners of the land and the Railroad have not agreed as to the damages to be paid to the owners, that upon application by the Railroad three disinterested commissioners were appointed by the Supreme Court of Vermont, and that "according to the provisions of the Act incorporating said Company and the Statutes of the State of Vermont" the commissioners "appraise and determine the damage to the said owners of said land occasioned by such location, entry and occupation by the said Company" to be a stated sum.

It is clear from the relevant documents and statutes that the actions of the Railroad in this case fall under well-established Vermont laws and procedures for acquisition of rights-of-way by companies incorporated for railroad purposes. In her opinion, the trial judge concluded that, in the context of the Vermont procedure for commissioners' awards for railroad rights-of-way, and in light of the Vermont case law, cited and discussed in the trial court's opinion, "the portion of the right-of-way consisting of the parcel of land condemned from the Barker Estate and taken by commissioner's award is indisputably an easement under the law of the State of Vermont." 24 Cl. Ct. at 827. . . .

[For] the third parcel, C, [the] operative instrument is a warranty deed, dated August 2, 1899, from Frederick and Mary Manwell to the Railroad. The deed contains the usual habendum clause found in a warranty deed, and purports to convey the described strip of land to the grantee railroad "[t]o have and to hold the above granted and bargained premises . . . unto it the said grantee, its successors and assigns forever, to its and their own proper use, benefit and behoof forever." The deed further warrants that the grantors have "a good, indefeasible estate, in fee simple, and have good right to bargain and sell the same in manner and form as above written. . . ." In short, the deed appears to be the standard form used to convey a fee simple title from a grantor to a grantee. . . .

At trial, the Preseaults argued that, although the Manwell deed purports to grant a fee simple, the deed was given following survey and location of the right-of-way and therefore it should be construed as conveying only an easement in accordance with Vermont railroad law. The Government responded that, while it was true that survey and location of the railroad's right-of-way had occurred, no "formal" eminent domain proceedings had taken place, and therefore the deed should be taken at its face as a conveyance in fee simple. Each side cited Vermont cases to support its position. The trial court, after reviewing and discussing at length the cases and other relevant materials, concluded that "[u]nder well-settled Vermont law, the property interests in the parcel . . . conveyed following survey and location by warranty deed, amounted to [an] easement." 24 Cl. Ct. at 830.

Our independent review of the state of Vermont law on this issue leads us to conclude, despite some uncertainties in the matter, that the trial court is correct. Part of the problem is that the Vermont cases that seem most on point are quite old. Assuming the Vermont courts would follow its precedents, a fair assumption, the probable outcome is that, despite the apparent terms of the deed indicating a transfer in fee, the legal effect was to convey only an easement. Two cases, from among others, will illustrate why.

In Hill v. Western Vermont Railroad, 32 Vt. 68 (1859), the railroad had a contract with one Josiah Burton to purchase some land for railroad purposes. The bond, or contract, entered into before the railroad had surveyed their right-of-way called for Burton to convey such lands "as shall be required" for the company's road. Plaintiff, a creditor of the railroad, attempted to levy on a part of the land potentially subject to the contract. The railroad defended against the levy by arguing that the tract at issue was not needed by the railroad for its purposes, and thus Burton could not have been made to sell it to the railroad. Since, it was argued, the claimed land was not subject to contract enforcement, it was not subject to the levying creditor.

The Vermont Supreme Court held for the railroad. The court observed that railroads acquire needed land either by order of a designated public body (through the exercise of eminent domain) or by consent of the landowner, although even in the latter case "the proceeding is, in some sense, compulsory." *Id.* at 75. . . .

Thus it is that a railroad that proceeds to acquire a right-of-way for its road acquires only that estate, typically an easement, necessary for its limited purposes, and that the act of survey and location is the operative determinant, and not the particular form of transfer, if any. Here, the evidence is that the Railroad had obtained a survey and location of its right-of-way, after which the Manwell deed was executed confirming and memorializing the Railroad's action. On balance it would seem that . . . the proceeding retained its eminent domain flavor, and the railroad acquired only that which it needed, an easement for its roadway. Nothing the Government points to or that we can find in the later cases would seem to undermine that view of the case; the trial court's conclusion that the estate conveyed was an easement is affirmed.

We thus conclude that fee simple title to all three parcels in dispute remained with their original owners, subject only to the burden of the easements in favor of the Railroad. Those titles passed through various hands, coming to rest eventually in the hands of the Preseaults, where they lay in 1986 when the public recreational trail was created by the Government's action. . . .

D. THE SCOPE OF THE RAILROAD'S EASEMENT

We turn then to the question of whether the easements granted to the Railroad, to which the Preseaults' title was subject, are sufficiently broad in their scope so that the use of the easements for a public recreational trail is not a violation of the Preseaults' rights as owners of the underlying fee estate. Both the Government and the State argue that under the doctrine of "shifting public use" the scope of the original easements, admittedly limited to railroad purposes, is properly construed today to include other public purposes as well, and that these other public purposes include a public recreational hiking and biking trail. Under that theory of the case, the establishment in 1986 of such a trail would be within the scope of the easements presumably now in the State's hands, and therefore the Preseaults would have no complaint. On the other hand, if the Government's use of the land for a recreational trail is not within the scope of the easements, then that use would constitute an unauthorized invasion of the land to which the Preseaults hold title. The argument on this issue assumes that the easements were still in existence in 1986, and for purposes of this part of the discussion we assume they were. . . .

The general rule does not preclude the scope of an easement being adjusted in the face of changing times *to serve the original purpose*, so long as the change is consistent with the terms of the original grant:

> It is often said that the parties are to be presumed to have contemplated such a scope for the created easement as would reasonably serve the purposes of the

grant. . . . This presumption often allows an expansion of use of the easement, but does not permit a change in use not reasonably foreseeable at the time of establishment of the easement.

Richard R. Powell, 3 *Powell on Real Property* §34.12[2] (Patrick J. Rohan ed., 1996). . . .

When the easements here were granted to the Preseaults' predecessors in title at the turn of the century, specifically for transportation of goods and persons via railroad, could it be said that the parties contemplated that a century later the easements would be used for recreational hiking and biking trails, or that it was necessary to so construe them in order to give the grantee railroad that for which it bargained? We think not. Although a public recreational trail could be described as a roadway for the transportation of persons, the nature of the usage is clearly different. In the one case, the grantee is a commercial enterprise using the easement in its business, the transport of goods and people for compensation. In the other, the easement belongs to the public, and is open for use for recreational purposes, which happens to involve people engaged in exercise or recreation on foot or on bicycles. It is difficult to imagine that either party to the original transfers had anything remotely in mind that would resemble a public recreational trail.

Furthermore, there are differences in the degree and nature of the burden imposed on the servient estate. It is one thing to have occasional railroad trains crossing one's land. Noisy though they may be, they are limited in location, in number, and in frequency of occurrence. Particularly is this so on a relatively remote spur. When used for public recreational purposes, however, in a region that is environmentally attractive, the burden imposed by the use of the easement is at the whim of many individuals, and, as the record attests, has been impossible to contain in numbers or to keep strictly within the parameters of the easement. As the Bruce & Ely treatise noted, "an easement created to serve a particular purpose ends when the underlying purpose no longer exists," Jon. W. Bruce and James W. Ely, Jr., *The Law of Easements and Licenses in Land* ¶10.03[1], at 10-12 (rev. ed. 1995), and "when an easement for railway purposes is found, it is generally considered to end when it is no longer used for the stated purposes," *id.* ¶1.06[2][d], at 1-48. . . .

Most state courts that have been faced with the question of whether conversion to a nature trail falls within the scope of an original railroad easement have held that it does not. . . . A few courts, under the particular terms of an easement or in light of a special statute, have held otherwise. . . . For reasons peculiar to the particular circumstances, these few cases depart from the well established common law rules governing easements, and carry little persuasive authority. . . .

E. ABANDONMENT

Even assuming for sake of argument that the Government and the State are correct and that the so-called "doctrine of shifting public use" is available to permit reading the original conveyances in the manner for which they argue, there remains yet a further obstacle to the Government's successful defense. The Preseaults contend that under Vermont law the original easements were abandoned, and thus extinguished, in 1975. If that is so, the State could not, over ten years later in 1986, have re-established the easement even for the narrow purposes provided in the original conveyances without payment of the just compensation required by the Constitution. *See, e.g.,* Loretto v. Teleprompter Manhattan CATV Corp., 458 U.S.

419, 441 (1982). It follows that if the State could not in 1986 use the parcels for railroad purposes without that use constituting a taking, then it surely could not claim the right to use the property for other purposes free of Constitutional requirements. *See* Preseault v. United States, 24 Cl. Ct. 818, 835 (1992) (concluding that a "shifting public use" doctrine could not apply because of discontinuity of use of the easement by State between 1975 and 1985). . . .

Typically the grant under which such rights-of-way are created does not specify a termination date. The usual way in which such an easement ends is by abandonment, which causes the easement to be extinguished by operation of law. *See generally Restatement of Property* §504. Upon an act of abandonment, the then owner of the fee estate, the "burdened" estate, is relieved of the burden of the easement. In most jurisdictions, including Vermont, this happens automatically when abandonment of the easement occurs.

Vermont law recognizes the well-established proposition that easements, like other property interests, are not extinguished by simple non-use. As was said in Nelson v. Bacon, 32 A.2d 140, 146 (Vt. 1943), "one who acquires title to an easement in this manner [by deed in that case] has the same right of property therein as an owner of the fee and it is not necessary that he should make use of his right in order to maintain his title." Thus in cases involving a passageway through an adjoining building (*Nelson*), or a shared driveway, Sabins v. McAllister, 76 A.2d 106 (Vt. 1950), the claimed easement was not extinguished merely because the owner had not made use of it regularly.

Something more is needed. The Vermont Supreme Court in *Nelson* summarized the rule in this way: "In order to establish an abandonment there must be in addition to nonuser, acts by the owner of the dominant tenement conclusively and unequivocally manifesting *either* a present intent to relinquish the easement *or* a purpose inconsistent with its future existence." *Nelson*, 32 A.2d at 146 (emphasis added). The record here establishes that these easements, along with the other assets of the railroad, came into the hands of the State of Vermont in the 1960s. The State then leased them to an entity called the Vermont Railway, which operated trains over them. In 1970, the Vermont Railway ceased active transport operations on the line which included the right-of-way over the parcels at issue, and used the line only to store railroad cars. In 1975 the Railroad removed all of the railroad equipment, including switches and tracks, from the portion of the right-of-way running over the three parcels of land now owned by the Preseaults. In light of these facts, the trial court concluded that under Vermont law this amounted to an abandonment of the easements, and adjudged that the easements were extinguished as a matter of law in 1975. . . .

In the 1985 proceedings before the ICC, the State of Vermont and Vermont Railway . . . sought approval from the ICC for a 30-year lease with the City of Burlington, indicating that the State fully recognized that railroad operations had ceased on the easement, and that none were contemplated in the foreseeable future. Although events occurring after 1975 cannot change the consequences of the facts then in place, these later declarations confirm the conclusion that the purpose of the Railroad's actions leading up to the track removal in 1975 was to abandon this stretch of rail line.

The Government and the State argue that there are facts inconsistent with that determination, but we are not persuaded that any of them significantly undercut the trial court's conclusion. For example, when the Vermont Railway removed its tracks in 1975, it did not remove the two bridges or any of the culverts on the line, all of which remained "substantially intact." That is not surprising. The Railroad was under no obligation to restore the former easement to its original condition. Tearing out existing structures would simply add to its costs, whereas the rails that were taken up could be used for repairs of defective rails elsewhere on the line. It is further argued that, since the rail line continues to operate to a point approximately one and one-third miles south of the Preseaults' property, it is possible to restore the line to full operation. The fact that restoration of the northern portion of the line would be technically feasible tells us little. The question is not what is technically possible to do in the future, but what was done in the past.

Almost immediately after the tracks were removed, members of the public began crossing over the easement. Perhaps illustrating the difficulty in getting government paperwork to catch up with reality, or perhaps indicating that revenue collectors do not give up easily, the State of Vermont and Vermont Railway, as they had done before the removal of the tracks, continued to collect fees under various license and crossing agreements from persons wishing to establish fixed crossings. In January 1976, the Preseaults executed a crossing agreement with the Vermont Railway which gave the Preseaults permission to cross the right-of-way. In March 1976, the Preseaults entered into a license agreement with the State and the Vermont Railway to locate a driveway and underground utility service across the railroad right-of-way. As late as 1991, 985 Associates (through Paul Preseault) paid a $10 license fee to "Vermont Railroad" (sic), presumably pursuant to one of the 1976 agreements. The Preseaults paid "under protest." Much of this activity suggests that, initially at least, the adjacent property owners decided it was cheaper to pay a nominal license fee to the State than to litigate the question of whether the State had the right to extract the fee. In view of all the contrary evidence of physical abandonment, we find this behavior by the State's revenue collectors unconvincing as persuasive evidence of a purpose or intent not to abandon the use of the right-of-way for actual railroad purposes.

One uncontrovertible piece of evidence in favor of abandonment is that, in the years following the shutting down of the line in 1970 and the 1975 removal of the tracks, no move has been made by the State or by the Railroad to reinstitute service over the line, or to undertake replacement of the removed tracks and other infrastructure necessary to return the line to service. The declarations in the 1985 lease between the State of Vermont, Vermont Railway, and the City of Burlington, which refer to the possible resumption of railroad operations at some undefined time in the future are of course self-serving and not indicative of the facts and circumstances in 1975. . . .

[The court reversed and remanded after concluding that "the occupation of the Preseaults' property by the City of Burlington under the authority of the Federal Government constituted a taking of their property for which the Constitution requires that just compensation be paid."]

RADER, Circuit Judge, concurring, with whom LOURIE, Circuit Judge, joins. . . . The vague notion that the State may at some time in the future return the property to the use for which it was originally granted, does not override its present use of that property inconsistent with the easement. That conversion demands compensation. . . .

CLEVENGER, Circuit Judge, dissenting, joined by Judges MICHEL and SCHALL. . . . [Because] the State has not abandoned its easements, the Preseaults can only show ownership of the servient tenements. No argument has been made that the current use of the easements imposes a greater burden on the servient tenement than would be imposed were the State to use the easements for railroad purposes.

Notes and Questions

1. Easements can be terminated in a variety of ways. An easement of a specified duration *expires* at the conclusion of that time. Both parties can expressly *consent* to release the servient tenement from the easement. Ordinarily, the easement owner will give a release in exchange for an acceptable payment. Sometimes the owner will relinquish the easement without compensation. An easement automatically ends by *merger* if the same person now owns the dominant tenement and the servient tenement. An easement can terminate by *prescription* if the servient owner uses the land adversely to the dominant owner for a sufficient period. An easement ceases through *forfeiture* if the dominant owner abuses the easement in a way that cannot be solved by an injunction, or upon a failed attempt to convert an easement appurtenant into an easement in gross. An easement terminates by *estoppel* if the servient tenement owner relies upon the statements of the easement owner. Or the government can terminate an easement by *condemnation* if it exercises its eminent domain power to obtain the easement. Two other means of termination depend upon the manner in which an easement was created. An easement by estoppel ends if, due to changed circumstances, fairness no longer requires the easement to continue. An easement by necessity ends once the necessity ends. For example, an easement will no longer be necessary when a new road serves the dominant tenement.

The abandonment claim in *Preseault* succeeded because the easement owner acted in a way that demonstrated it would not use the easement again. The Restatement lists about a half dozen additional cases finding the abandonment of railroad easements, often in the context of an attempt to create a public trail. *Restatement (Third) of Property: Servitudes*, §7.4, at 363-64 (2000). Yet in Grantwood Village v. Missouri Pac. R.R. Co., 95 F.3d 654 (8th Cir. 1996), the court held that a railroad had not abandoned its interest in a right-of-way and that it could transfer its interest to a trails organization, so the village's use of the property as a parkway and a bird sanctuary was subject to that easement.

2. In May 2001, a federal jury ordered the government to pay the Preseaults $234,000 plus 15 years' interest as compensation for the deprivation of their property rights. One year later, the Court of Federal Claims awarded an additional $894,855 in attorney's fees. Preseault v. Vermont, 52 Fed. Cl. 667 (2002). Even so, Paul Preseault complained that "no amount of money can make up for the invasion of our privacy by a paved and heavily-trafficked bicycle and roller-blade path next to our front door, and nothing can compensate for the years it took to get to this result." The case generated a passionate debate within Vermont. A property rights activist contended that "the outcome should be a mighty reproach to the government officials who ran up a huge taxpayer-paid legal bill trying to deprive one Vermonter of his rights." John McClaughry, *Property Seizure Case a Warning to State Officials*, Burlington Free Press, July 23, 2001. But the former President of Vermont Railway applauded state officials who "recognize the value of existing transportation infrastructure and are willing to fight for its preservation, despite the shrill protests of those who decline to look beyond short-term gain." John R. Pennington, *Few Tears*

for "Victimized Landowner" Near Path, Burlington Free Press, Aug. 10, 2001. The Rails-to-Trails Act has given rise to a high volume of inverse condemnation litigation. One example is Howard v. United States, 964 N.E.2d 779 (Ind. 2012), holding that under Indiana law railbanking and interim trail use are not within the scope of railroad easements and that the doctrine of "shifting public use" does not justify trail use.

B. COVENANTS

The need for covenants arises out of concerns about how someone else is using their land. You want your neighbors to cut their grass, rake their leaves, and shovel their snow. Or you may want your neighbor to keep the big oak tree in the front yard or to maintain the Colonial architecture that characterizes your neighborhood. Alternately, you may want to make sure that your neighbors do not build a gas station on their property, or leave up their Christmas decorations all year round, or operate a store out of their home. What are the advantages of covenants in achieving these goals? What other ways are there to achieve such goals besides covenants?

■ NEPONSIT PROPERTY OWNERS' ASSOCIATION v. EMIGRANT INDUSTRIAL SAVINGS BANK
Court of Appeals of New York, 1938
15 N.E.2d 793

LEHMAN, Judge. The plaintiff, as assignee of Neponsit Realty Company, has brought this action to foreclose a lien upon land which the defendant owns. The lien, it is alleged, arises from a covenant, condition or charge contained in a deed of conveyance of the land from Neponsit Realty Company to a predecessor in title of the defendant. The defendant purchased the land at a judicial sale. The referee's deed to the defendant and every deed in the defendant's chain of title since the conveyance of the land by Neponsit Realty Company purports to convey the property subject to the covenant, condition or charge contained in the original deed. . . .

. . . Upon this appeal the defendant contends that the land which it owns is not subject to any lien or charge which the plaintiff may enforce. . . .

[I]n January, 1911, Neponsit Realty Company, as owner of a tract of land in Queens county, caused to be filed in the office of the clerk of the county a map of the land. The tract was developed for a strictly residential community, and Neponsit Realty Company conveyed lots in the tract to purchasers, describing such lots by reference to the filed map and to roads and streets shown thereon. In 1917, Neponsit Realty Company conveyed the land now owned by the defendant to Robert Oldner Deyer and his wife by deed which contained the covenant upon which the plaintiff's cause of action is based.

That covenant provides:

And the party of the second part for the party of the second part and the heirs, successors and assigns of the party of the second part further covenants that the property conveyed by this deed shall be subject to an annual charge in such an amount as will be fixed by the party of the first part, its successors and assigns, not, however exceeding in any year the sum of four ($4.00) Dollars per lot 20x100 feet. The assigns of the party of the first part may include a Property Owners' Association which may hereafter be organized for the purposes referred to in this paragraph, and in case such association is organized the sums in this paragraph provided for shall be payable to such association. The party of the second part for the party of the second part and the heirs, successors and assigns of the party of the second part covenants that they will pay this charge to the party of the first part, its successors and assigns on the first day of May in each and every year, and further covenants that said charge shall on said date in each year become a lien on the land and shall continue to be such lien until fully paid. Such charge shall be payable to the party of the first part or its successors or assigns, and shall be devoted to the maintenance of the roads, paths, parks, beach, sewers and such other public purposes as shall from time to time be determined by the party of the first part, its successors or assigns. And the party of the second part by the acceptance of this deed hereby expressly vests in the party of the first part, its successors and assigns, the right and power to bring all actions against the owner of the premises hereby conveyed or any part thereof for the collection of such charge and to enforce the aforesaid lien therefor.

These covenants shall run with the land and shall be construed as real covenants running with the land until January 31st, 1940, when they shall cease and determine. . . .

There can be no doubt that Neponsit Realty Company intended that the covenant should run with the land and should be enforceable by a property owners association against every owner of property in the residential tract which the realty company was then developing. The language of the covenant admits of no other construction. Regardless of the intention of the parties, a covenant will run with the land and will be enforceable against a subsequent purchaser of the land at the suit of one who claims the benefit of the covenant, only if the covenant complies with certain legal requirements. These requirements rest upon ancient rules and precedents. The age-old essentials of a real covenant, aside from the form of the covenant, may be summarily formulated as follows: (1) It must appear that grantor and grantee intended that the covenant should run with the land; (2) it must appear that the covenant is one "touching" or "concerning" the land with which it runs; (3) it must appear that there is "privity of estate" between the promisee or party claiming the benefit of the covenant and the right to enforce it, and the promisor or party who rests under the burden of the covenant. *Clark on Covenants and Interests Running with Land*, p. 74. Although the deeds of Neponsit Realty Company conveying lots in the tract it developed "contained a provision to the effect that the covenants ran with the land, such provision in the absence of the other legal requirements is insufficient to accomplish such a purpose." Morgan Lake Co. v. New York, N. H. & H. R. R. Co., 186 N.E. 685, 686 (N.Y. 1933). . . .

The covenant in this case is intended to create a charge or obligation to pay a fixed sum of money to be "devoted to the maintenance of the roads, paths, parks, beach, sewers and such other public purposes as shall from time to time be determined by the party of the first part [the grantor], its successors or assigns." It is an affirmative covenant to pay money for use in connection with, but not upon, the land which it is said is subject to the burden of the covenant. Does such a covenant "touch" or "concern" the land? These terms are not part of a statutory definition, a limitation placed by the State upon the power of the courts to enforce covenants intended to run with the land by the parties who entered into the covenants.

Rather they are words used by courts in England in old cases to describe a limitation which the courts themselves created or to formulate a test which the courts have devised and which the courts voluntarily apply. *Cf.* Spencer's Case, 77 Eng. Rep. 72 (1583). In truth such a description or test so formulated is too vague to be of much assistance and judges and academic scholars alike have struggled, not with entire success, to formulate a test at once more satisfactory and more accurate. "It has been found impossible to state any absolute tests to determine what covenants touch and concern land and what do not. The question is one for the court to determine in the exercise of its best judgment upon the facts of each case." Clark, *op. cit.* p. 76.

It has been often said that a covenant to pay a sum of money is a personal affirmative covenant which usually does not concern or touch the land. Such statements are based upon English decisions which hold in effect that only covenants, which compel the covenanter to submit to some *restriction on the use* of his property, touch or concern the land, and that the burden of a covenant which requires the covenanter to do an affirmative act, even on his own land, for the benefit of the owner of a "dominant" estate, does not run with his land. Miller v. Clary, 103 N.E. 1114 (N.Y. 1913). In that case the court pointed out that in many jurisdictions of this country the narrow English rule has been criticized and a more liberal and flexible rule has been substituted. In this State the courts have not gone so far. We have not abandoned the historic distinction drawn by the English courts. So this court has recently said: "Subject to a few exceptions not important at this time, there is now in this state a settled rule of law that a covenant to do an affirmative act, as distinguished from a covenant merely negative in effect, does not run with the land so as to charge the burden of performance on a subsequent grantee [citing cases]. This is so though the burden of such a covenant is laid upon the very parcel which is the subject-matter of the conveyance." Guaranty Trust Co. v. New York & Queens County Ry., 170 N.E. 887, 892 (N.Y. 1930, opinion by Cardozo, Ch. J.).

Both in that case and in the case of Miller v. Clary, *supra*, the court pointed out that there were some exceptions or limitations in the application of the general rule. Some promises to pay money have been enforced, as covenants running with the land, against subsequent holders of the land who took with notice of the covenant. *Cf.* Greenfarb v. R. S. K. Realty Corp., 175 N.E. 649 (N.Y. 1931). It may be difficult to classify these exceptions or to formulate a test of whether a particular covenant to pay money or to perform some other act falls within the general rule that ordinarily an affirmative covenant is a personal and not a real covenant, or falls outside the limitations placed upon the general rule. At least it must "touch" or "concern" the land in a substantial degree, and though it may be inexpedient and perhaps impossible to formulate a rigid test or definition which will be entirely satisfactory or which can be applied mechanically in all cases, we should at least be able to state the problem and find a reasonable method of approach to it. It has been suggested that a covenant which runs with the land must affect the legal relations — the advantages and the burdens — of the parties to the covenant, as owners of particular parcels of land and not merely as members of the community in general, such as taxpayers or owners of other land. Clark, *op. cit.* p.76. *Cf.* Professor Bigelow's article on *The Contents of Covenants in Leases,* 12 Mich. L. Rev. 639. That method of approach has the merit of realism. The test is based on the effect of the covenant rather than on technical distinctions. Does the covenant impose, on the one hand, a burden upon an interest in land, which on the other hand increases the value of a different interest in the same or related land?

Even though we accept that approach and test, it still remains true that whether a particular covenant is sufficiently connected with the use of land to run with the land, must be in many cases a question of degree. A promise to pay for something to be done in connection with the promisor's land does not differ essentially from a promise by the promisor to do the thing himself, and both promises constitute, in a substantial sense, a restriction upon the owner's right to use the land, and a burden upon the legal interest of the owner. On the other hand, a covenant to perform or pay for the performance of an affirmative act disconnected with the use of the land cannot ordinarily touch or concern the land in any substantial degree. Thus, unless we exalt technical form over substance, the distinction between covenants which run with land and covenants which are personal, must depend upon the effect of the covenant on the legal rights which otherwise would flow from ownership of land and which are connected with the land. The problem then is: Does the covenant in purpose and effect substantially alter these rights? . . .

Looking at the problem presented in this case from the same point of view and stressing the intent and substantial effect of the covenant rather than its form, it seems clear that the covenant may properly be said to touch and concern the land of the defendant and its burden should run with the land. True, it calls for payment of a sum of money to be expended for "public purposes" upon land other than the land conveyed by Neponsit Realty Company to plaintiff's predecessor in title. By that conveyance the grantee, however, obtained not only title to particular lots, but an easement or right of common enjoyment with other property owners in roads, beaches, public parks or spaces and improvements in the same tract. For full enjoyment in common by the defendant and other property owners of these easements or rights, the roads and public places must be maintained. In order that the burden of maintaining public improvements should rest upon the land benefited by the improvements, the grantor exacted from the grantee of the land with its appurtenant easement or right of enjoyment a covenant that the burden of paying the cost should be inseparably attached to the land which enjoys the benefit. It is plain that any distinction or definition which would exclude such a covenant from the classification of covenants which "touch" or "concern" the land would be based on form and not on substance.

Another difficulty remains. Though between the grantor and the grantee there was privity of estate, the covenant provides that its benefit shall run to the assigns of the grantor who "may include a Property Owners' Association which may hereafter be organized for the purposes referred to in this paragraph." The plaintiff has been organized to receive the sums payable by the property owners and to expend them for the benefit of such owners. Various definitions have been formulated of "privity of estate" in connection with covenants that run with the land, but none of such definitions seems to cover the relationship between the plaintiff and the defendant in this case. The plaintiff has not succeeded to the ownership of any property of the grantor. It does not appear that it ever had title to the streets or public places upon which charges which are payable to it must be expended. It does not appear that it owns any other property in the residential tract to which any easement or right of enjoyment in such property is appurtenant. It is created solely to act as the assignee of the benefit of the covenant, and it has no interest of its own in the enforcement of the covenant.

The arguments that under such circumstances the plaintiff has no right of action to enforce a covenant running with the land are all based upon a distinction between the corporate property owners association and the property owners for whose benefit the association has been formed. If that distinction may be ignored, then the basis of the arguments is destroyed. . . .

The corporate plaintiff has been formed as a convenient instrument by which the property owners may advance their common interests. We do not ignore the corporate form when we recognize that the Neponsit Property Owners' Association, Inc., is acting as the agent or representative of the Neponsit property owners. . . . Only blind adherence to an ancient formula devised to meet entirely different conditions could constrain the court to hold that a corporation formed as a medium for the enjoyment of common rights of property owners owns no property which would benefit by enforcement of common rights and has no cause of action in equity to enforce the covenant upon which such common rights depend. Every reason which in other circumstances may justify the ancient formula may be urged in support of the conclusion that the formula should not be applied in this case. In substance if not in form the covenant is a restrictive covenant which touches and concerns the defendant's land, and in substance, if not in form, there is privity of estate between the plaintiff and the defendant. . . .

The order should be affirmed, with costs. . . .

Notes and Questions

1. The *Neponsit* court identified three criteria that must be satisfied for a real covenant imposing an affirmative benefit to run with the land: (1) the parties must *intend* that result, (2) the covenant must *touch and concern* the land, and (3) the subsequent grantees of the original parties must be in *privity of estate*. The *Neponsit* court wrestled with the touch and concern requirement, which has generated an ongoing debate. Its basic justification posits that there is no reason for requiring a future landowner to honor a promise that relates to the original landowner, not to the land itself. It has been criticized, though, as unpredictable in application and unfair to contracting parties. The Restatement favors the replacement of the touch and concern requirement with a more generalized inquiry into the consistency of the agreement with public policy. *See Restatement (Third) of Property: Servitudes* §3.2 (2000). Some states have adopted that approach, but most states continue to adhere to the formal touch and concern requirement.

Negative covenants, which restrict land use, almost always satisfy the test because they directly affect the possible uses of the land, and thus its value. As *Neponsit* demonstrates, *affirmative covenants* are more problematic. The cases holding that the touch and concern requirement was not satisfied include: In re El Paso Refinery, LP, 302 F.3d 343 (5th Cir. 2002), which held that a promise to indemnify for environmental cleanup costs was a mere personal covenant; In re Ormond Beach Assocs. Ltd. Partnership, 184 F.3d 143 (2d Cir. 1999), where the Second Circuit held that a subsequent purchaser did not have to pay the original owner's mortgage because the promise to pay the mortgage does not touch and concern the land; Paloma Investment Ltd. Partnership v. Jenkins, 978 P.2d 110, 115-16 (Ariz. Ct. App. 1998), which held that a provision in a water rights agreement that the prevailing party in any dispute was entitled to attorney's fees did not touch and concern the land; and Mullendore Theatres, Inc. v. Growth Realty Investors Co., 691 P.2d 970 (Wash. Ct. App. 1984), which determined that a landlord's covenant to refund a tenant's security deposit does not touch and concern the land. By contrast, another court has held that a covenant to pay attorney's fees is enforceable based in part upon a state statute prescribing which covenants run with the land. Prairie Hills Water & Dev. Co. v. Gross, 653 N.W.2d 745 (S.D. 2002). Courts have also split on whether the duty to pay membership dues for recreational facilities run with the land. Should such covenants be enforceable against future landowners, or not?

2. *Neponsit* also addresses *privity of estate*, which has two elements that must be considered in every case dealing with a covenant that is alleged to run with the land. The *Neponsit* court stated that "between the grantor and the grantee there was privity of estate" before it considered the status of the property owners' association. This is what modern authorities call *horizontal privity*. This term refers to the relationship between the original parties to the covenant at the time that they entered into the covenant. The original English view equated horizontal privity with tenure. With the elimination of many forms of English tenure and diminished significance for remaining forms, as a practical matter this strict view of privity confined real covenants to leases. Most U.S. states, including New York by the time of *Neponsit*, have liberalized their definition of tenure. Thus, horizontal privity exists when "the transaction of which the promise is a part includes a transfer of an interest either in the land benefited by or in the land burdened by the performance of the promise." *Restatement of Property* §534(a) (1944). The "transaction" involving the original parties can be contained in more than one document. *See* Sonoma Development, Inc. v. Miller, 515 S.E.2d 577, 580 (Va. 1999) (holding that horizontal privity had been established when the covenant was contained in one document and the land conveyance was accomplished through another document drafted at the same time). A better understanding of the meaning of horizontal privity is offered by examples of the kinds of relationships that may establish it:

- Conveyance of land ("deed privity") — if the covenant was agreed to when one party conveyed the property to the other, then every state (except Massachusetts) holds that horizontal privity is established.
- Leases — if the covenant was agreed to when the parties entered into a lease, then horizontal privity is established.
- Co-ownership interests — if the covenant was agreed to when the parties jointly owned the property, then most states hold that horizontal privity is established.
- Easements — if the covenant was agreed to at a time when one party held an easement over the other party's land, then most states hold that horizontal privity is established.
- A mere agreement — if the parties agreed to the covenant at a time when they did not have any other property relationship, then horizontal privity does not exist.

For real covenants, states have three different views of the need to establish horizontal privity: (1) horizontal privity is required for the benefit to run and for the burden to run; (2) horizontal privity is required for the burden to run, but not for the benefit to run; and (3) horizontal privity is not required for the benefit to run or for the burden to run. The precise requirements vary by jurisdiction, with many courts insisting that more of the criteria be satisfied in order for the burden of an agreement to run with the land, while those criteria are relaxed if the question is whether the benefit of the agreement runs with the land.

3. The *Neponsit* court's discussion of whether the property owners' association has standing to enforce the covenant to pay assessments deals with *vertical privity*.

This term refers to the relationship between one of the covenanting parties and its successor in interest. For a real covenant, the successor must acquire the covenantor's entire estate for the burden to be enforceable against it. In other words, vertical privity exists when the fee simple owner conveys the fee simple to another party, but not if the owner of the fee conveys only a life estate. Vertical privity is the same idea that prevented consumers from suing product manufacturers in tort law until Judge Cardozo's opinion in MacPherson v. Buick Motor Co., 111 N.E. 1050 (N.Y. 1916). Note the difference from easements, where any *possessor* of the servient tenement must honor the easement. We now turn to the famous English case that had the effect of reforming the law of real covenants by inventing an interest known as the *equitable servitude.*

■   **TULK v. MOXHAY**
    Court of Chancery, England, 1848
    41 Eng. Rep. 1143

In the year 1808 the Plaintiff, being then the owner in fee of the vacant piece of ground in Leicester Square, as well as of several of the houses forming the Square, sold the piece of ground by the description of "Leicester Square garden or pleasure ground, with the equestrian statue then standing in the centre thereof, and the iron railing and stone work round the same," to one Elms in fee: and the deed of conveyance contained a covenant by Elms, for himself, his heirs, and assigns, with the Plaintiff, his heirs, executors, and administrators, "that Elms, his heirs, and assigns should, and would from time to time, and at all times thereafter at his and their own costs and charges, keep and maintain the said piece of ground and square garden, and the iron railing round the same in its then form, and in sufficient and proper repair as a square garden and pleasure ground, in an open state, uncovered with any buildings, in neat and ornamental order; and that it should be lawful for the inhabitants of Leicester Square, tenants of the Plaintiff, on payment of a reasonable rent for the same, to have keys at their own expense and the privilege of admission therewith at any time or times into the said square garden and pleasure ground."

The piece of land so conveyed passed by divers mesne conveyances into the hands of the Defendant, whose purchase deed contained no similar covenant with this vendor: but he admitted that he had purchased with notice of the covenant in the deed of 1808.

The Defendant having manifested an intention to alter the character of the square garden, and asserted a right if he thought fit, to build upon it, the Plaintiff, who still remained owner of several houses in the square, filed this bill for an injunction; and an injunction was granted by the Master of the Rolls to restrain the Defendant from converting or using the piece of ground and square garden, and the iron railing round the same, to or for any other purpose than as a square garden and pleasure ground in an open state, and uncovered with buildings.

On a motion, now made, to discharge that order,

Mr. R. Palmer, for the Defendant, contended that the covenant did not run with the land, so as to be binding at law upon a purchaser from the covenantor, and he relied on the dictum of Lord Brougham C. in Keppell v. Bailey, 2 M. & K. 547 (1834), to the effect that notice of such a covenant did not give a Court of Equity jurisdiction to enforce it by injunction against such purchaser, inasmuch as "the knowledge by an assignee of an estate, that this assignor had assumed to bind others than the law authorised him to affect by his contract — had attempted to create a burthen upon property which was inconsistent with the nature of that property, and unknown to the principles of the law — could not bind such assignee by affecting his conscience." In applying that doctrine to the present case, he drew a distinction between a formal covenant as this was, and a contract existing in mere agreement, and requiring some further act to carry it into effect; contending that executory contracts of the latter description were alone such as were binding in equity upon purchasers with notice; for that where the contract between the parties was executed in the form of a covenant, their mutual rights and liabilities were determined by the legal operation of that instrument, and that if a Court of Equity were to give a more extended operation to such covenant, it would be giving the party that for which he had never contracted. . . .

The LORD CHANCELLOR [Cottenham], (without calling upon the other side). That the Court has jurisdiction to enforce a contract between the owner of land and his neighbour purchasing a part of it, that the latter shall either use or abstain from using the land purchased in a particular way, is what I never knew disputed. Here there is no question about the contract: the owner of certain houses in the square sells the land adjoining, with a covenant from the purchaser not to use it for any other purpose than as a square garden. And it is now contended, not that the vendee could violate that contract, but that he might sell the piece of land, and that the purchaser from him may violate it without this Court having any power to interfere. If that were so, it would be impossible for an owner of land to sell part of it without incurring the risk of rendering what he retains worthless. It is said that, the covenant being one which does not run with the land, this Court cannot enforce it; but the question is, not whether the covenant runs with the land, but whether a party shall be permitted to use the land in a manner inconsistent with the contract entered into by his vendor, and with notice of which he purchased. Of course, the price would be affected by the covenant, and nothing could be more inequitable than that the original purchaser should be able to sell the property the next day for a greater price, in consideration of the assignee being allowed to escape from the liability which he had himself undertaken.

That the question does not depend upon whether the covenant runs with the land is evident from this, that if there was a mere agreement and no covenant, this Court would enforce it against a party purchasing with notice of it; for if an equity is attached to the property by the owner, no one purchasing with notice of that equity can stand in a different situation from the party from whom he purchased. There are not only cases before the Vice-Chancellor of England, in which he considered that doctrine as not in dispute; but looking at the ground on which Lord Eldon disposed of the case of The Duke of Bedford v. The Trustees of the British Museum (2 My. & K. 552), it is impossible to suppose that he entertained any doubt of it. In the case of Mann v. Stephens before me, I never intended to make the injunction depend upon the result of the action: nor does the order imply it. The motion was, to discharge an order for the commitment of the Defendant for an alleged breach of the injunction, and also to dissolve the injunction. I upheld the injunction, but discharged the order of commitment, on the ground that it was not clearly proved that any breach had been committed; but there being a doubt whether part of the premises on which the Defendant was proceeding to build was locally situated within what was called the Dell, on which alone he had under the covenant a right to build at all, and the Plaintiff insisting that it was not, I thought the pendency of the suit ought not to prejudice the Plaintiff in his right to bring an action in which he thought he had such right, and, therefore, I give him liberty to do so.

With respect to the observations of Lord Brougham in Keppell v. Bailey, he never could have meant to lay down that this Court would not enforce an equity attached to land by the owner, unless under such circumstances as would maintain an action at law. If that be the result of his observations, I can only say that I cannot coincide with it.

I think the cases cited before the Vice-Chancellor and this decision of the Master of the Rolls perfectly right, and, therefore, that this motion must be refused, with costs.

Notes and Questions

1. Prior to *Tulk*, the only covenants that ran with estates in land were *real covenants*. As we discussed in connection with *Neponsit*, for the burden of a real covenant to run with the land, privity of estate between the contracting parties was essential. Under the English view of privity, Tulk and Elms were not in privity of estate. *Tulk* proved extremely influential, leading to the recognition of a new type of covenant: the *equitable servitude*. Horizontal privity of estate is not required for an equitable servitude. A very long time ago, the distinction between a real covenant and an equitable servitude had remedial consequences because courts of equity did not award damages and courts of law did not issue injunctions. In modern U.S. law, the distinction between real covenants and equitable servitudes is virtually never important. The procedural integration of law and equity has eviscerated remedial distinctions, and notice to the successors of the covenantor is required for real covenants, just as it is for equitable servitudes, due to the U.S. recording acts. Academic commentators have long proposed collapsing the categories, and the Restatement agrees. *Restatement (Third) of Property: Servitudes* §8.2 cmt. a (2000) (covenants "may be enforced by any appropriate remedy, whether the remedy is traditionally classified as legal or equitable").

2. The other elements developed for real covenants apply to equitable servitudes. The original contracting parties must have intended that the covenant bind and benefit successors. The substance of the promise must touch and concern the land. Vertical privity (the relationship between the original parties and their successors) is required for an equitable servitude to run, but courts have loosened the definition. In equity, a successor to the burdened land who acquires a lesser estate than the original party sometimes is bound by a covenant (*e.g.*, the promisor owns a fee simple and rents the property to a tenant). Similarly, a successor to the benefited land with a lesser estate sometimes may enforce the covenant.

■ SHAFF v. LEYLAND

Supreme Court of New Hampshire, 2006
914 A.2d 1240

HICKS, Justice. The respondent, Edith W. Leyland, appeals an order of the Superior Court granting summary judgment to the petitioner, Margaret A. Shaff, on the basis that the respondent lacked standing to enforce a restrictive covenant contained in a warranty deed. We affirm.

The trial court found the following facts. In the 1960s, the respondent acquired approximately seventy-five acres along Mont Vernon Road in Amherst, where she lived in the only house located on the property. Beginning with the sale of her home in 1975, the respondent sold portions of this land to various parties. In 1985, she conveyed approximately twenty-three acres to the petitioner by a warranty deed that contained the following restrictive covenant:

> The above described premises are conveyed subject to the restriction, which shall run with the land, that the Grantees, their heirs and assigns shall construct on said premises only a colonial-type residence having a market value of at least One Hundred Thousand Dollars ($100,000).

The respondent did not reserve a right of enforcement in the deed. In 1998, she conveyed the last 11.6 acres of the original seventy-five acre parcel. The respondent currently owns no real estate near the original seventy-five acre parcel or in the town of Amherst.

The petitioner sought a declaratory judgment that the restrictive covenant does not limit the number of homes to be built on her property. She moved for summary judgment, requesting that the trial court determine as a matter of law that the respondent lacks standing to object to the relief she sought. Noting that "the respondent does not dispute that she currently owns no land in Amherst . . . that benefits from the Restrictive Covenant," the trial court entered summary judgment for the petitioner because "the respondent will suffer no legal injury" if the restrictive covenant is extinguished and thus she lacks standing to enforce it. . . .

Because the issue is one of first impression in New Hampshire, the trial court looked to the law of other jurisdictions. It applied the majority rule that "[i]f an individual does not own the property that is benefited by th[e] restrictive covenant, he or she has not suffered a legal injury," and therefore does not have standing to enforce the restriction. The trial court found this rule to be "consistent with New Hampshire law concerning restrictive covenants and standing." . . .

The benefit and the burden of a covenant are subject to two general classifications — "appurtenant" and "in gross" — which themselves are subject to further classification as "personal" or "running with the land." *Restatement (Third) of Property: Servitudes* §1.5 comment a. at 31 (2000). . . . Covenants appurtenant and covenants in gross can be personal or can run with the land. *Id.* §1.5(3). "Running with the land means that the benefit or burden passes automatically to successors. . . ." *Id.* comment a. at 31. "'Personal' means that a servitude benefit or burden is not transferable and does not run with land." *Id.* §1.5(3).

Since the common law has not always recognized covenants in gross, it does not distinguish between covenants appurtenant or covenants in gross with regard to a party's standing. *Id.* §8.1 comment a. at 474-75. Thus, the common law requires that a person own land that benefits from the restriction in order to have standing to enforce it: "Where a person no longer has any land in the vicinity which might be affected by the disregard of a covenant, he or she cannot enforce the restrictions." 20 Am. Jur. 2d Covenants, Etc. §244 (2005). . . .

The petitioner urges us to affirm the common law rule relied upon by the trial court, and rule that the respondent lacks standing to enforce the covenant because she no longer owns property benefited by the restriction. The respondent argues that we should adopt the view of the *Restatement (Third) of Property*, which eliminates the requirement of an ownership interest in benefited property in order to have standing to enforce a covenant in gross, instead requiring only that a holder "establish a legitimate interest in enforcing [it]." *Restatement (Third) Property: Servitudes* §8.1. Adoption of this view would change the common law standing requirement for covenants in gross, but not for covenants appurtenant. *Id.* comment a. at 474-75. In her brief, the respondent assumes that the covenant at issue is held in gross and therefore our adoption of the Restatement view would give her standing to seek enforcement of the covenant.

The trial court did not determine which type of covenant is at issue in this case. The petitioner asserted during oral argument that the classification of the covenant is not properly before us. The record shows that the issue was before the trial court and was raised in the respondent's notice of appeal. . . .

The general rule of construction favors appurtenant servitudes over servitudes in gross. *Cf.* Burcky v. Knowles, 413 A.2d 585, 588 (N.H. 1980). Further, "[r]estrictions in a deed will be regarded as for the personal benefit of the grantor unless a contrary intention appears, and the burden of showing that they constitute covenants running with the land is upon the party claiming the benefit of the restriction." Stegall v. Housing Authority of City of Charlotte, 178 S.E.2d 824, 828 (N.C. 1971). . . .

. . . The restrictive covenant contained in the deed to the petitioner expressly states that the burden "shall run with the land" but expresses no intent regarding the benefit of the covenant or the type of covenant conveyed. At the time she conveyed the twenty-three acres and created the restrictive covenant, the respondent owned acreage in the immediate area. Applying the principles discussed above, we conclude that the restrictive covenant was created to personally benefit the respondent as the owner of land that benefited from enforcement of the restriction. Had the respondent wished to hold the covenant in gross, regardless of whether or not she owned land in the area, she could have included language to that effect. Therefore, we hold that the restrictive covenant at issue is appurtenant, and that the respondent held the benefit personally. Accordingly, the respondent does not have standing to enforce the covenant because she no longer owns land that benefits from it. . . .

The respondent lastly argues that she has standing to enforce the restrictive covenant under principles of contract law. While we recognize that a covenant constitutes an agreement between parties, Arnold v. Chandler, 428 A.2d 1235, 1237 (N.H. 1981), this fact does not lead us to repudiate the common law's well-developed and widely recognized standing rules regarding the enforceability of servitudes.

Affirmed.

Notes and Questions

1. English common law treated easements and covenants the same — it did not permit the creation of easements in gross, real covenants in gross, or equitable servitudes in gross. Long ago American law began to recognize easements in gross, gradually increasing the legal protections afforded such easements. American law was much slower to recognize covenants in gross. In many states, they are still

prohibited. The Restatement, however, calls for the general recognition of covenants in gross that run with the land.

> *Creation of Benefits in Gross and Third-Party Beneficiaries.* The benefit of a servitude may be created to be held in gross, or as an appurtenance to another interest in property. . . .

Restatement (Third) of Property: Servitudes §2.6(1) (2000). The comments explain:

> a. Historical note. Early law prohibited the creation of servitude benefits in gross and the creation of servitude benefits in persons who were not immediate parties to the transaction. The origin of the prohibitions is obscure, but they survived into modern times even though they appear to serve little function. English law adopted the prohibition on benefits in gross from Roman law, but applied it only to easements and equitable servitudes. American law recognizes easements in gross, but has retained remnants of the prohibition against interests in gross with respect to covenants. . . .
>
> d. Benefits in gross are freely permitted. Under the rule stated in this section, benefits of affirmative and negative covenants, as well as of easements and profits, can be held in gross. Benefits in gross are useful in a variety of transactions in which burdens running with land are desired, and are permitted whether the servitude is a covenant, an easement, or a profit. To the extent that benefits in gross cause greater problems than appurtenant benefits in locating the persons who are able to negotiate modification or termination of the servitudes, those problems are dealt with by doctrines governing modification and termination of servitudes, rather than by the ancient method of prohibiting their creation. . . .

2. In *Shaff,* the original promisee sued the original promisor and lost. Suppose instead that the covenant had not referred to the grantee's "heirs and assigns" or included a statement that the restriction "shall run with the land." It only said: "The above described premises are conveyed subject to the restriction that the Grantees shall construct on said premises only a colonial-type residence having a market value of at least One Hundred Thousand Dollars ($100,000)." Would this change make the restriction a covenant in gross? If so, would Leyland (the original promisee) have won?

3. Suppose Shaff (the original promisor) had sold the property before building a residence. Would the promise to build a colonial-type residence worth at least $100,000 be enforceable against Shaff's purchaser?

■ **FONG v. HASHIMOTO**
Supreme Court of Hawai'i, 2000
994 P.2d 500

KLEIN, Justice. [The Alewa Heights subdivision — also known as the "Fogarty Subdivision" for the common grantor of the lots, Edward Fogarty — consists of 15 lots overlooking the ocean on the east side of Oahu. Lots 4 and 5 are adjacent lots located to the left as one enters the subdivision, and they are owned by Dale and Linda Fong (the Junior Fongs) and Leonard and Ellen Fong (the Senior Fongs) respectively. Lot 11, owned by the Hashimotos, is located across the street from and at a lower elevation than Lots 4 and 5 on the "makai" (Hawaiian for ocean) side of the road. The properties command a stunning view of the ocean, Diamond Head, and the Ewa plains.

In March 1940, Fogarty entered into an unrecorded agreement to sell Lot 4. Pursuant to that agreement, the Ais obtained Lot 4 from Fogarty's estate in 1944 with a deed that contained a covenant prohibiting buildings near the boundary of the lot. The Ais conveyed Lot 4 to the Junior Fongs through a recorded deed in 1944.

In April 1940, Fogarty conveyed Lot 5 to the Howells pursuant to a deed that did not mention any height or view restrictions, but that contained a provision prohibiting any buildings near the boundary of the lot. The Senior Fongs obtained Lot 5 from the Howells by recorded deed in 1968.

In April 1941, Fogarty entered into an unrecorded agreement to sell Lot 11 to the De Canios, who then obtained the property from the administrators of Fogarty's estate in 1943. The deed conveying Lot 11 contained several restrictive covenants:

> AND the Grantees, in consideration of the premises and of One Dollar ($1.00) received to their satisfaction from the Grantors, do hereby for themselves and their assigns, and the survivor of them and his or her heirs and assigns, covenant and agree with the Grantors and their successors and assigns, as follows:
>
> 1. That *at no time shall any building or structure or any part thereof be erected or placed or allowed to remain on the hereinabove described premises of more than one (1) story in height,* nor within fifteen (15) feet of the property boundary line on the 20-foot road right-of-way adjoining said premises, nor within five (5) feet of the property boundary line on the 15-foot road right-of-way adjoining said premises.
>
> 2. That no deed, lease, mortgage or other conveyance of the premises hereby conveyed will be made unless the same shall in each case contain the same restrictive covenants, including this covenant, either expressly or by appropriate reference, nor unless or until the grantee, lessee, mortgagee, or other person thereunder shall join therein and bind himself, his heirs and assigns to require the same covenants on the part of any grantee, lessee, mortgagee, or other person under any deed, lease, mortgage or other conveyance made by him.
>
> 3. That the foregoing covenants *shall run with the land hereby conveyed and shall also apply to and be equally binding upon the legal representatives and successors in interest of the parties hereto,* whether or not expressly contained in any deed or other instrument whereby any title to or interest in said property is obtained.

(Emphases added.)

In 1943, the De Canios conveyed Lot 11 to the Mendoncas with a deed containing the same covenants. Three years later, the Mendoncas conveyed Lot 11 to the Hashimotos pursuant to a deed stating that the conveyance was subject to "the covenants and building restrictions relative to the use of said land as set forth in [the De Canio-Mendonca deed]." Lot 11 remains within the Hashimoto family.

Lot 11 and the two lots next to it are the only properties in the Fogarty Subdivision that have a one-story height restriction in their deeds. The subdivision map filed with the City and County of Honolulu in 1938 shows a building setback for the lots abutting the private road, but that map does not indicate any height restrictions.

The Hashimotos began building a two-story home on Lot 11 in January 1995. The Fongs protested that the covenants prohibited the construction of a two-story home and that their view of the ocean would be blocked by such a home. In the ensuing lawsuit, the circuit court ruled in favor of the Hashimotos. On appeal, the Intermediate Court of Appeals (ICA) held that there was a common plan for the

Fogarty Subdivision that allowed the Fongs to enforce the height restriction as an equitable servitude, so the Fongs were entitled to injunctive relief to prevent the Hashimotos from building the second story of their home. Fong v. Hashimoto, 994 P.2d 569 (Haw. Ct. App. 1998).]

A. THE "ONE-STORY IN HEIGHT" RESTRICTION IS UNENFORCEABLE

Because of this court's recent decision in Hiner v. Hoffman, 977 P.2d 878 (Haw. 1999) (holding that a "two-story in height" restriction was ambiguous and therefore unenforceable), the restriction over the Hashimotos' Lot 11, worded as a "one-story in height" restriction, is likewise ambiguous, and therefore unenforceable.

Furthermore, we granted certiorari to correct the ICA's analysis with respect to the possibility of an equitable servitude over the Hashimotos' Lot 11 and the lack of a creation of a legally enforceable restrictive covenant by the common grantor.

B. THERE IS NO COMMON SCHEME OR PLAN TO SUPPORT AN EQUITABLE SERVITUDE IN FAVOR OF THE FONGS

The ICA determined that the height restriction placed in the deed to the Hashimotos' Lot 11 was enforceable, by the Fongs, as an equitable servitude because the height restriction was part of a common scheme or plan created by Fogarty. However, restrictions on only three of the fifteen lots in the subdivision do not constitute a clear "common scheme or plan." Olson v. Albert, 523 A.2d 585, 588 (Me. 1987) (restrictions in four of sixteen subdivided lots were insufficient to establish a common scheme). A common grantor may establish a general scheme by conveying the majority of his subdivided lots subject to a restriction that reflects the general scheme.

As the evidence in this case reveals, Fogarty conveyed only three of the fifteen lots in the subdivision with a height restriction. There was also a fourth lot, similarly situated to the three burdened lots, that was not restricted. Moreover, the conveyances and restrictions were generated in a piecemeal fashion, not evidencing a "common scheme or plan." If Fogarty's original intent was to create a subdivision with universal height restrictions, he could have provided for such restrictions at the same time that he provided for setback restrictions. However, Fogarty chose not to describe height restrictions on the plat map filed with the City and County of Honolulu in 1938.

A general building scheme may be defined as one under which a tract of land is divided into building lots, to be sold to purchasers by deeds containing uniform restrictions. The courts will only discern such a scheme from a plan of lots and sales where all the deeds from the common grantor for the lots making up any particular neighborhood group of common benefit therefrom are made subject to the common covenant. In the instant case, there was no uniformity throughout the subdivision as to height restrictions because twelve of the fifteen lots in the subdivision were not subjected to a height restriction. Therefore, there was no "common scheme or plan" to support the enforcement of the height restriction, by the Fongs, as an equitable servitude.

C. A RESTRICTIVE COVENANT ENFORCEABLE AT LAW WAS NOT CREATED

The ICA held that an agreement of sale vendor's mere legal interest in an upslope lot is sufficient to impose a height restriction over a downslope lot favoring the upslope lot or lots. We disagree with the ICA's proposition and emphasize that, as a matter of law, a restrictive covenant burdening a down-slope lot for the benefit of an upslope lot is not enforceable at law when either (1) the deeds to the affected lots do not contain a recitation establishing which lot or lots are to be benefitted or burdened by the restriction or (2) the common grantor simply does not have a sufficient interest in the affected properties to create an enforceable restrictive covenant with respect to the benefitted lots. . . .

[A]lthough the Hashimotos had notice that their lot was restricted, their deed did not contain any reference to the dominant parcel or parcels, a required element of a real covenant.

Moreover, Fogarty did not even have the right to create an enforceable restrictive covenant benefitting Lots 4 or 5. On April 4, 1940, the Senior Fongs' Lot 5 was conveyed by deed to the Howells, more than a year before Fogarty entered into an agreement of sale for the Hashimotos' Lot 11. Put simply, Fogarty retained absolutely no interest in the Senior Fongs' Lot 5 at the time that the height restriction over Lot 11 was created. Therefore, . . . it was not possible for the Fongs' Lot 5 to be the beneficiary of the height restriction over Lot 11. . . .

[W]e vacate the ICA's decision and affirm the circuit court's judgment dissolving the TRO and granting the Hashimotos' motion to dismiss on the basis that a "one-story in height" restriction is ambiguous, and as such, is unenforceable.

NAKAYAMA, Justice, with whom RAMIL, Justice joins, concurring and dissenting. I concur in Parts B. and C. of the majority opinion. However, for the reasons expressed in my dissent in Hiner v. Hoffman, 977 P.2d 878, 886 (Haw. 1999), I do not agree that the restrictive language in this case is ambiguous and unenforceable. I further note that the Hashimotos never disputed that their house was anything but two stories in height and never raised the issue of ambiguity until, during the pendency of this appeal, this court issued the *Hiner* decision.

The view from the Fongs' house once the Hashimotos completed their new home

Notes and Questions

1. The Fongs' first theory was the creation of a *reciprocal negative easement*. Generally, covenants must be express and set forth in a writing that complies with the statute of frauds. The one exception is the reciprocal negative easement, also known as an *implied equitable servitude*. This interest arises when an owner of two or more related lots sells one lot with restrictions to benefit the retained lot, so the servitude becomes mutual. In the leading case of Sanborn v. McLean, 206 N.W. 496 (Mich. 1925), the general plan for the Green Lawn subdivision in Detroit restricted the use of the land to residential purposes. Fifty-three of the 91 lots contained an express provision to that effect. But John McLean owned one of the 48 lots without such a provision, and he began to build a gas station on his property. The court prohibited him from doing so because the original owners who subdivided the land intended to impose a scheme of restrictions that could be enforced by the purchasers of any lot and their successors. McLean was found to have had notice of that scheme because of the general plan and the fact that all of the other buildings in the subdivision were residential. An even clearer case for a reciprocal negative easement occurred in Forster v. Hall, 576 S.E.2d 746 (Va. 2003), where the original owner conveyed 105 of the 113 lots in a subdivision with a covenant prohibiting mobile homes. The court held that the fact that 93 percent of the lots contained the covenant, along with a general scheme of development to enhance the marketability of the lots by excluding mobile homes, resulted in the creation of a reciprocal negative easement imposed upon all lots in the subdivision. (Also, unlike the treatment of "single-story" in *Fong*, the Virginia Supreme Court rejected a claim that "mobile home" was too ambiguous to be enforceable.) The Fongs' second theory was that the Hashimotos were bound by an express covenant set forth in the 1941 deed from Fogarty to De Canios. Why did the court reject this argument?

2. In *Fong*, the court relied upon its decision in Hiner v. Hoffman, 977 P.2d 878 (Haw. 1999), for the conclusion that the covenant was ambiguous. In *Hiner*, the court held that a covenant's failure "to prescribe, in feet or by some other numerical measure, the maximum 'height' of a 'story' renders the language of the covenant ambiguous. . . . [W]ithout such a definition, the 'height restriction' . . . is meaningless." *Id.* at 881. The majority cited cases decided in six other states that reached the same result. *Id.* at 883. The dissent, however, charged that the court's decision "saves one story of a single house, but betrays years of reliance by the Hoffmans' neighbors and the larger Pacific Palisades community on the covenant's plain language and increases uncertainty and litigation with respect to other plainly worded covenants." *Id.* at 886 (Nakayama, J., dissenting).

Single-story covenants are not the only ones whose meaning has produced litigation. Consider the restriction on the use of property for a "single-family home," the most common covenant in the United States. Can someone provide day care in a home burdened by such a covenant? How about a home office? The courts are split on whether group homes for former convicts, recovering alcohol and drug addicts, or AIDS patients qualify as single-family homes (with federal discrimination law often affecting the permissibility of such restrictions as well).

3. Suppose that the court had concluded that the Hashimotos were prohibited from building a two-story house, but that the house was already completed. What remedy would be appropriate?

■ NAHRSTEDT v. LAKESIDE VILLAGE CONDOMINIUM ASSOCIATION

Supreme Court of California, 1994
878 P.2d 1275

KENNARD, Justice. A homeowner in a 530-unit condominium complex sued to prevent the homeowners association from enforcing a restriction against keeping cats, dogs, and other animals in the condominium development. The owner asserted that the restriction, which was contained in the project's declaration recorded by the condominium project's developer, was "unreasonable" as applied to her because she kept her three cats indoors and because her cats were "noiseless" and "created no nuisance." Agreeing with the premise underlying the owner's complaint, the Court of Appeal concluded that the homeowners association could enforce the restriction only upon proof that plaintiff's cats would be likely to interfere with the right of other homeowners "to the peaceful and quiet enjoyment of their property." . . .

[T]he narrow issue here is whether a pet restriction that is contained in the recorded declaration of a condominium complex is enforceable against the challenge of a homeowner. As we shall explain, the Legislature, in Civil Code section 1354, has required that courts enforce the covenants, conditions and restrictions contained in the recorded declaration of a common interest development "unless unreasonable."

Because a stable and predictable living environment is crucial to the success of condominiums and other common interest residential developments, and because recorded use restrictions are a primary means of ensuring this stability and predictability, the Legislature in section 1354 has afforded such restrictions a presumption of validity and has required of challengers that they demonstrate the restriction's "unreasonableness" by the deferential standard applicable to equitable servitudes. Under this standard established by the Legislature, enforcement of a restriction does not depend upon the conduct of a particular condominium owner. Rather, the restriction must be uniformly enforced in the condominium development to which it was intended to apply unless the plaintiff owner can show that the burdens it imposes on affected properties so substantially outweigh the benefits of the restriction that it should not be enforced against any owner. Here, the Court of Appeal did not apply this standard in deciding that plaintiff had stated a claim for declaratory relief. Accordingly, we reverse the judgment of the Court of Appeal and remand for further proceedings consistent with the views expressed in this opinion.

I.

Lakeside Village is a large condominium development in Culver City, Los Angeles County. It consists of 530 units spread throughout 12 separate 3-story buildings. The residents share common lobbies and hallways, in addition to laundry and trash facilities.

The Lakeside Village project is subject to certain covenants, conditions and restrictions (hereafter CC&R's) that were included in the developer's declaration recorded with the Los Angeles County Recorder on April 17, 1978, at the inception of the development project. Ownership of a unit includes membership in the project's homeowners association, the Lakeside Village Condominium Association (hereafter Association), the body that enforces the project's CC&R's, including the pet restriction, which provides in relevant part: "No animals (which shall mean dogs and cats), livestock, reptiles or poultry shall be kept in any unit."[3]

In January 1988, plaintiff Natore Nahrstedt purchased a Lakeside Village condominium and moved in with her three cats. When the Association learned of the cats' presence, it demanded their removal and assessed fines against Nahrstedt for each successive month that she remained in violation of the condominium project's pet restriction.

Nahrstedt then brought this lawsuit against the Association, its officers, and two of its employees, asking the trial court to invalidate the assessments, to enjoin future assessments, to award damages for violation of her privacy when the Association "peered" into her condominium unit, to award damages for infliction of emotional distress, and to declare the pet restriction "unreasonable" as applied to indoor cats (such as hers) that are not allowed free run of the project's common areas. Nahrstedt also alleged she did not know of the pet restriction when she bought her condominium. The complaint incorporated by reference the grant deed, the declaration of CC&R's, and the condominium plan for the Lakeside Village condominium project.

The Association demurred to the complaint. In its supporting points and authorities, the Association argued that the pet restriction furthers the collective "health, happiness and peace of mind" of persons living in close proximity within the Lakeside Village condominium development, and therefore is reasonable as a matter of law. The trial court sustained the demurrer as to each cause of action and dismissed Nahrstedt's complaint. Nahrstedt appealed. . . .

II.

Today, condominiums, cooperatives, and planned-unit developments with homeowners associations have become a widely accepted form of real property ownership. These ownership arrangements are known as "common interest" developments. The owner not only enjoys many of the traditional advantages associated with individual ownership of real property, but also acquires an interest in common with others in the amenities and facilities included in the project. It is this hybrid nature of property rights that largely accounts for the popularity of these new and innovative forms of ownership in the 20th century. . . .

Use restrictions are an inherent part of any common interest development and are crucial to the stable, planned environment of any shared ownership arrangement. The viability of shared ownership of improved real property rests on the existence of extensive reciprocal servitudes, together with the ability of each co-owner to prevent the property's partition.

The restrictions on the use of property in any common interest development may limit activities conducted in the common areas as well as in the confines of the home itself. Commonly, use restrictions preclude alteration of building exteriors, limit the number of persons that can occupy each unit, and place limitations on — or prohibit altogether — the keeping of pets.

Restrictions on property use are not the only characteristic of common interest ownership. Ordinarily, such ownership also entails mandatory membership in an owners association, which, through an elected board of directors, is empowered to

---

3. The CC&R's permit residents to keep "domestic fish and birds."

enforce any use restrictions contained in the project's declaration or master deed and to enact new rules governing the use and occupancy of property within the project. Because of its considerable power in managing and regulating a common interest development, the governing board of an owners association must guard against the potential for the abuse of that power. As Professor Natelson observes, owners associations "can be a powerful force for good or for ill" in their members' lives. Natelson, Consent, Coercion, and "Reasonableness" [in *Private Law: The Special Case of the Property Owners Association* (1990) 51 Ohio St. L.J. 41, 43]. Therefore, anyone who buys a unit in a common interest development with knowledge of its owners association's discretionary power accepts "the risk that the power may be used in a way that benefits the commonality but harms the individual." *Id.* at 67. Generally, courts will uphold decisions made by the governing board of an owners association so long as they represent good faith efforts to further the purposes of the common interest development, are consistent with the development's governing documents, and comply with public policy.

Thus, subordination of individual property rights to the collective judgment of the owners association together with restrictions on the use of real property comprise the chief attributes of owning property in a common interest development. . . .

Notwithstanding the limitations on personal autonomy that are inherent in the concept of shared ownership of residential property, common interest developments have increased in popularity in recent years, in part because they generally provide a more affordable alternative to ownership of a single-family home.

One significant factor in the continued popularity of the common interest form of property ownership is the ability of homeowners to enforce restrictive CC&R's against other owners (including future purchasers) of project units. Generally, however, such enforcement is possible only if the restriction that is sought to be enforced meets the requirements of equitable servitudes or of covenants running with the land. . . .

When restrictions limiting the use of property within a common interest development satisfy the requirements of covenants running with the land or of equitable servitudes, what standard or test governs their enforceability? . . .

In Hidden Harbour Estates v. Basso, 393 So. 2d 637 (Fla. Dist. Ct. App. 1981), the Florida court distinguished two categories of use restrictions: use restrictions set forth in the declaration or master deed of the condominium project itself, and rules promulgated by the governing board of the condominium owners association or the board's interpretation of a rule. *Id.* at 639. The latter category of use restrictions, the court said, should be subject to a "reasonableness" test, so as to "somewhat fetter the discretion of the board of directors." *Id.* at 640. Such a standard, the court explained, best assures that governing boards will "enact rules and make decisions that are reasonably related to the promotion of the health, happiness and peace of mind" of the project owners, considered collectively. *Ibid.*

By contrast, restrictions contained in the declaration or master deed of the condominium complex, the Florida court concluded, should not be evaluated under a "reasonableness" standard. Hidden Harbour Estates v. Basso, *supra*, 393 So. 2d at 639-40. Rather, such use restrictions are "clothed with a very strong presumption of validity" and should be upheld even if they exhibit some degree of unreasonableness. *Id.* at 639, 640. Nonenforcement would be proper only if such restrictions were arbitrary or in violation of public policy or some fundamental constitutional right. *Id.* at 639-40. . . .

III.

In California, common interest developments are subject to the provisions of the Davis-Stirling Common Interest Development Act (hereafter Davis-Stirling Act or Act) §1350 et seq. . . . From the authorities discussed above [including the Act, decisions from other states, and the Restatement], we distill these principles: An equitable servitude will be enforced unless it violates public policy; it bears no rational relationship to the protection, preservation, operation or purpose of the affected land; or it otherwise imposes burdens on the affected land that are so disproportionate to the restriction's beneficial effects that the restriction should not be enforced.

With these principles of equitable servitude law to guide us, we now turn to section 1354 [of the Davis-Stirling Act, which provides that] use restrictions for a common interest development that are set forth in the recorded declaration are "enforceable equitable servitudes, unless unreasonable." In other words, such restrictions should be enforced unless they are wholly arbitrary, violate a fundamental public policy, or impose a burden on the use of affected land that far outweighs any benefit. . . .

When courts accord a presumption of validity to all such recorded use restrictions and measure them against deferential standards of equitable servitude law, it discourages lawsuits by owners of individual units seeking personal exemptions from the restrictions. This also promotes stability and predictability in two ways. It provides substantial assurance to prospective condominium purchasers that they may rely with confidence on the promises embodied in the project's recorded CC&R's. And it protects all owners in the planned development from unanticipated increases in association fees to fund the defense of legal challenges to recorded restrictions.

How courts enforce recorded use restrictions affects not only those who have made their homes in planned developments, but also the owners associations charged with the fiduciary obligation to enforce those restrictions. When courts treat recorded use restrictions as presumptively valid, and place on the challenger the burden of proving the restriction "unreasonable" under the deferential standards applicable to equitable servitudes, associations can proceed to enforce reasonable restrictive covenants without fear that their actions will embroil them in costly and prolonged legal proceedings. Of course, when an association determines that a unit owner has violated a use restriction, the association must do so in good faith, not in an arbitrary or capricious manner, and its enforcement procedures must be fair and applied uniformly.

There is an additional beneficiary of legal rules that are protective of recorded use restrictions: the judicial system. Fewer lawsuits challenging such restrictions will be brought, and those that are filed may be disposed of more expeditiously, if the rules courts use in evaluating such restrictions are clear, simple, and not subject to exceptions based on the peculiar circumstances or hardships of individual residents in condominiums and other shared-ownership developments. . . .

The salutary effect of enforcing written instruments and the statutes that apply to them is particularly true in the case of the declaration of a common interest development. As we have discussed, common interest developments are a more intensive and efficient form of land use that greatly benefits society and expands opportunities for home ownership. In turn, however, a common interest development creates a community of property owners living in close proximity to each other, typically much closer than if each owned his or her separate plot of land. This proximity is feasible, and units in a common interest development are marketable, largely because the recorded declaration of CC&R's assures owners of a stable and predictable environment. . . .

Enforcing the CC&R's contained in a recorded declaration only after protracted case-by-case litigation would impose substantial litigation costs on the owners through their homeowners association, which would have to defend not only against owners contesting the application of the CC&R's to them, but also against owners contesting any case-by-case exceptions the homeowners association might make. In short, it is difficult to imagine what could more disrupt the harmony of a common interest development than the course proposed by the dissent. . . .

V.

Under the holding we adopt today, the reasonableness or unreasonableness of a condominium use restriction that the Legislature has made subject to section 1354 is to be determined *not* by reference to facts that are specific to the objecting homeowner, but by reference to the common interest development as a whole. As we have explained, when, as here, a restriction is contained in the declaration of the common interest development and is recorded with the county recorder, the restriction is presumed to be reasonable and will be enforced uniformly against all residents of the common interest development *unless* the restriction is arbitrary, imposes burdens on the use of lands it affects that substantially outweigh the restriction's benefits to the development's residents, or violates a fundamental public policy. . . .

We conclude, as a matter of law, that the recorded pet restriction of the Lakeside Village condominium development prohibiting cats or dogs but allowing some other pets is not arbitrary, but is rationally related to health, sanitation and noise concerns legitimately held by residents of a high-density condominium project such as Lakeside Village, which includes 530 units in 12 separate 3-story buildings.

Nahrstedt's complaint alleges no facts that could possibly support a finding that the burden of the restriction on the affected property is so disproportionate to its benefit that the restriction is unreasonable and should not be enforced. Also, the complaint's allegations center on Nahrstedt and her cats (that she keeps them inside her condominium unit and that they do not bother her neighbors), without any reference to the effect on the condominium development as a whole, thus rendering the allegations legally insufficient to overcome section 1354's presumption of the restriction's validity.

Nahrstedt's complaint does contend that the restriction violates her right to privacy under the California Constitution, article I, section 1. According to Nahrstedt, this state constitutional provision (enacted by voter initiative in 1972) guarantees her the right to keep cats in her Lakeside Village condominium notwithstanding the existence of a restriction in the development's originating documents recorded with the county recorder specifically disallowing cats or dogs in the condominium project. Because a land-use restriction in violation of a state constitutional provision presumably would conflict with public policy, we construe Nahrstedt's contention as a claim that the Lakeside Village pet restriction violates a fundamental public policy and for that reason cannot be enforced. As we have pointed out earlier, courts will not enforce a land use restriction that violates a fundamental public policy. The pertinent question, therefore, is whether the privacy provision in our state Constitution implicitly guarantees condominium owners or residents the right to keep cats or dogs as household pets. We conclude that California's Constitution confers no such right. . . .

ARABIAN, Justice, dissenting. "There are two means of refuge from the misery of life: music and cats."[1]

I respectfully dissent. While technical merit may commend the majority's analysis, its application to the facts presented reflects a narrow, indeed chary, view of the law that eschews the human spirit in favor of arbitrary efficiency. In my view, the resolution of this case well illustrates the conventional wisdom, and fundamental truth, of the Spanish proverb, "It is better to be a mouse in a cat's mouth than a man in a lawyer's hands."

As explained below, I find the provision known as the "pet restriction" contained in the covenants, conditions, and restrictions (CC&R's) governing the Lakeside Village project patently arbitrary and unreasonable within the meaning of Civil Code section 1354. Beyond dispute, human beings have long enjoyed an abiding and cherished association with their household animals. Given the substantial benefits derived from pet ownership, the undue burden on the use of property imposed on condominium owners who can maintain pets within the confines of their units without creating a nuisance or disturbing the quiet enjoyment of others substantially outweighs whatever meager utility the restriction may serve in the abstract. It certainly does not promote "health, happiness [or] peace of mind" commensurate with its tariff on the quality of life for those who value the companionship of animals. Worse, it contributes to the fraying of our social fabric.[3] . . .

Notes and Questions

1. Residential communities containing private covenants governed by homeowners' associations are becoming increasingly popular in the United States. According to the Community Associations Institute (CAI), the number of such associations jumped from 500 in 1965 to 323,600 in 2012. Nearly half of the new homes built in major metropolitan areas are part of community associations, with 63.4 million Americans now living in such communities.

2. Consider the summary of the covenants governing the Round Rock Ranch neighborhood in suburban Austin, Texas:

- Any new or altered building, fence, wall, or other structure needs written approval by at least [one or two] members of the Architectural Control committee.
- If an owner does not maintain the premises in a neat and orderly manner, the Homeowners Association can hire someone to repair, maintain, and

---

1. Albert Schweitzer.

3. The majority imply that if enough owners find the restriction too oppressive, they can act collectively to alter or rescind it. However, realistically speaking, implementing this alternative would only serve to exacerbate the divisiveness rampant in our society and to which the majority decision itself contributes.

restore the Lot and exterior of the buildings and any other improvements erected thereon, at the expense of the owner.

- No noxious or offensive activity shall be carried on upon any Lot, nor shall anything be thereon which may become an annoyance or nuisance to the neighborhood.
- No structure of a temporary character, mobile home, trailer, derelict, junk, or motor vehicle without a current license tag, or any tent, shack, barn, or other outbuilding which exceeds 6 feet in height, 8 feet in width, or 10 feet in length shall be permitted to remain on any lot at any time.
- No signs of any character shall be allowed on any lot, except a sign of not more than five feet square advertising the property for sale or rent.
- No garbage or waste shall be kept except in sanitary containers. All trash cans shall be kept in a clean and sanitary condition and screened or hidden from view.
- No hedges or shrubs above three feet on street corners. Trees which block the street intersection sightlines are not permitted.
- No animals, livestock, or poultry of any kind shall be raised, bred, or kept on any Lot except that dogs, cats, or other household pets may be kept, provided they are not kept, bred, or maintained for any commercial purpose, and provided that never more than three mature animals are kept on one lot at any one time.
- No truck larger than a three-quarter ton pickup, bus, motor home, or trailer shall be parked in the street, on the driveway, or on any portion of the Lot so as to be visible from the street or any adjoining Lot.
- No unsightly storage shall be permitted on any Lot.
- No boat, trucks, or unsightly vehicles shall be stored for the purpose of repair on any Lot, except in enclosed garages or storage facilities protected from the view of the public and other residences.
- The owner shall keep grass, weeds and vegetation in a neat and attractive condition.

This summary, along with a form that can be downloaded to provide confidential reports of violations, is available at http://roundrockranch.com/HOA.html.

3. Reliance upon private covenants is becoming more controversial even as they become more popular. One objection accuses private residential communities of facilitating a class divide. As the late Senator Paul Wellstone once remarked, "You have one America with the economic resources to purchase the security of gated communities, living in gated communities, and you have another America that is beset by the decay of some of our very important social institutions which we have to rebuild if we are to rebuild communities, libraries, hospitals, and schools." 144 Cong. Rec. S16 (daily ed. Jan. 27, 1998). Another objection bemoans the loss of community generated by homeowners' associations and the enforcement of private covenants. Professor Paula Franzese insists that "the predicates for successful community building are apt to be stifled, if not obliterated, by the sort of restrictiveness and attendant preoccupation with compliance that is inherent in the traditional [common interest community] model." Paula A. Franzese, *Does It Take a Village? Privatization, Patterns of Restrictiveness and the Demise of Community*, 47 Vill. L. Rev. 553, 558-59 (2002). She advocates instead "more participatory structures that redistribute and decentralize authority." *Id.* at 591. Yet she acknowledges the results of a CAI study that reported that 75 percent of the residents of communities with

homeowners' associations are satisfied. *Id.* at 559. How can you explain those results? Would *you* want to live in Lakeside Village, or in Austin's Round Rock neighborhood?

4. Claims similar to that raised in *Nahrstedt* have met a similar fate in other states. Ridgewood Homeowners Ass'n v. Mignacca, 813 A.2d 965 (R.I. 2003), involved the fate of "Sonny," the prize-winning miniature horse purchased by David and Cathy Mignacca in 2001 for the therapeutic needs of their son Christian. The City of Cranston Zoning Code required them to own 10 acres of land to be able to raise and keep animals, but the Mignaccas obtained a zoning variance (about which more in Chapter 12) that enabled them to keep Sonny on their property. But their subdivision's homeowners' association complained that Sonny's presence violated a covenant against animals except for two dogs and two cats. (The association added that the Mignaccas violated their covenants by keeping "three dogs, four ducks, and two rabbits on their property, as well as a boat, a go-cart, five all-terrain vehicles, an industrial dumpster, an industrial loader, and a fence erected without the association's approval.") The trial court found the covenant ambiguous, but the Supreme Court disagreed. Moreover, the Supreme Court held that occasional violations of the covenant by other community residents did not foreclose the association from acting against the Mignaccas' horse. The court advised that "enforcing a restrictive covenant is important to all who are burdened and benefited by the restriction. For precisely that reason, plaintiffs seeking to enforce restrictive covenants need not establish money damages or any other hardship to receive equitable relief."

5. Legislative action provides an alternative to judicial scrutiny of covenants. In 2000, the California legislature heeded Justice Arabian's recommendation in dissent in *Nahrstedt* and enacted a statute requiring common interest developments to allow residents to keep at least one pet in their home. *See* Cal. Civ. Code §1360.5. Another California statute prohibits covenants that limit the display of the American flag. Cal. Civ. Code §1353.5.

■ RIVER HEIGHTS ASSOCIATES LIMITED PARTNERSHIP v. BATTEN

Supreme Court of Virginia, 2004
591 S.E.2d 683

CARRICO, Senior Justice. In a bill of complaint for declaratory judgment, Alice Batten and other owners of lots in the Carrsbrook Subdivision in Albemarle County (collectively, Batten) sought a declaration favoring the enforceability of restrictive covenants prohibiting commercial use of four unimproved lots in the same subdivision [owned by two entities].

Although the entities just listed hold title to the four lots in question, the briefs describe Wendell W. Wood and his wife, Marlene C. Wood, as the beneficial owners of the lots. While the Woods were not named as defendants below and are not parties to this appeal, the appellants in the case are referred to collectively in the briefs as "Wood," and we will follow the same practice. . . .

In a section styled "Affirmative Defenses," Wood contended that Batten had failed to state a cause of action upon which relief could be granted, that the restrictive covenant was unenforceable, and that the covenant did not apply to his property. Wood also contended that he had no knowledge of the covenant.

Carrsbrook Subdivision is located on the eastern side of U.S. Route 29 between the northern city limits of Charlottesville and the Rivanna River. The four lots here in dispute are located at the western edge of the subdivision and are the only lots with frontage on U.S. Route 29.

The restrictive covenants were established in a deed dated May 6, 1959, from Norman Kelsey and wife to Charles W. Hurt (the Kelsey-Hurt deed), which conveyed an unsubdivided 40-acre portion of "the land known as 'Carrsbrook.'" The conveyance was made subject to "certain restrictions . . . which shall be considered as covenants running with the land." Only one of the restrictions is pertinent here: "The property is to be used for residential purposes only and no rooming house, boarding house, tourist home, or any other type of commercial enterprise, or any church, hospital, asylum, or charitable institution shall be operated thereon" (the restrictive covenant).

In October 1960, Section C of Carrsbrook was subdivided into 19 lots, all made "subject to the restrictive covenants applicable to Carrsbrook Subdivision of record." . . .

In 1969, Albemarle County adopted its first comprehensive zoning ordinance. The lots in question were zoned to a depth of 200 feet from Route 29 in a B-1 classification, a commercial district in which residential use is prohibited. This zoning classification was continued in a comprehensive rezoning in 1980, with the result that presently the lots in question are zoned for commercial use but are subject to the restrictive covenant prohibiting such use.

When Carrsbrook Subdivision was created in 1959, Route 29 was a two-lane road with residences and small businesses located on each side of the road. In the area where the lots in question are located, Route 29 is today an eight- to ten-lane road that is highly developed commercially on both sides with shopping centers, hotels, restaurants, automobile dealerships, and other types of businesses. No residential uses have been implemented along Route 29 since 1959. There have been no changes within the Carrsbrook Subdivision other than the aging of homes and the maturing of trees.

At the conclusion of an *ore tenus* hearing, the trial court held that the restrictive covenant against commercial use did apply to the four lots in question and that the covenant was enforceable. The court entered a final decree declaring the covenant enforceable and enjoining the use or operation of the lots in violation of the covenant, including developing the lots commercially in the future. We awarded Wood this appeal. . . .

. . . Batten's bill of complaint alleged Wendell Wood had met with members of the Carrsbrook Subdivision and "indicated that he intended to commercially develop the properties at issue [and] he spoke of developing a commercial three (3) story office building with related parking facilities." Further, the amended bill alleged that Richard E. Carter, an attorney, had written Wendell Wood a letter stating that the "properties [in question] were bound by restrictive covenants and could not be used commercially." In response, Wendell Wood told the attorney "that he did not believe the restrictions applied to his property and that it was his express intention to develop any of the properties he owned on Route 29 as commercial property and that he wanted to make sure that there was no mistake as to his intentions." . . .

Wood claimed he did not know of the restrictions or thought they would expire in twenty years. However, the very deed by which Wood acquired title to Lots 2C and 2D specifically provided that the lots were subject, without any time limitation, (1) to the restrictions set forth in the Kelsey-Hurt deed of 1959, which included the non-commercial use restriction, and (2) the restrictions set forth in "an instrument with the plat of Subdivision of Section C, Carrsbrook," the plat containing, of course, the restriction denying Lots 2C and 2D access to Route 29 if developed residentially. But, whether Wood actually knew of the existence of the restrictions or their length, his fate is to be determined by what he should have known, harsh though the result might be. . . .

CHANGE OF CONDITIONS

In his remaining assignment of error, Wood alleges that "[t]he trial court erred in failing to remove the residential restrictive covenant as to all four lots (Lots 1E, 1C, 2C, and 2D) in light of the overwhelming evidence that established a change of conditions so radical as practically to destroy the essential objects and purposes of the restriction."

Wood stresses the changes, outlined *supra*, that have taken place in the Route 29 corridor since Carrsbrook Subdivision was created in 1959, *viz.*, the previous two-lane road with residences and small businesses strung along each side has become a heavily traveled eight- to ten-lane thoroughfare lined on each side with shopping centers, hotels, restaurants, automobile dealerships, and other types of businesses. Further, Wood also stresses the fact that "no residential houses have been built or used from the city limits of Charlottesville to the South Rivanna River on either the east or west side of Route 29 in the last thirty years."[9]

The test for determining whether changed conditions warrant the nullification of a restrictive covenant was enunciated in Deitrick v. Leadbetter, 8 S.E.2d 276, 279 (Va. 1940), as follows: "No hard and fast rule can be laid down as to when changed conditions have defeated the purpose of restrictions, but it can be safely asserted the changes must be so radical as practically to destroy the essential objects and purposes of the agreement."

Wood takes the trial court to task, saying that the court "ignored the radical changes that have occurred in and around the subject properties since 1959, but rather focused myopically on whether or not there have been changes within the *interior* of the Subdivision." This is an unfair representation of what the trial court ruled in this case.

In a letter opinion, the trial court wrote: "[Wood has] failed to prove that radical changes *both in and around the neighborhood* have occurred such that the purpose of the restrictive covenant is destroyed" (emphasis added). Thus, it is clear the court did not focus upon conditions in Carrsbrook Subdivision alone but on conditions "around the neighborhood" as a whole.

This is in accord with Virginia law. In Booker v. Old Dominion Land Co., 49 S.E.2d 314 (Va. 1948), relief was sought from a restrictive covenant prohibiting commercial uses of residential lots in a subdivision. It was alleged that there had

---

9. Wood also stresses the zoning changes that have occurred along both sides of Route 29 since the restrictive covenant was created. However, in Ault v. Shipley, 52 S.E.2d 56, 58 (Va. 1949), this Court said that "a zoning law cannot constitutionally relieve land within the district covered by it from lawful restrictive covenants affecting its use for business purposes."

been a change of conditions so radical as to destroy the essential objectives and purposes of the covenant. These changes included the operation of a nearby zipper factory, the conversion of one of the lots into a hard-surfaced road leading to the factory, the widening of the road on which all the lots abutted from a two-lane roadway, carrying a small amount of traffic, to a heavily traveled four-lane federal highway, the construction nearby of a large shopping center, and the presence of a skating rink across the road from one of the lots. *Id.* at 317.

The trial court refused to remove the restrictive covenant. This Court affirmed. We said that "if a radical change takes place *in the whole neighborhood* so as to defeat the purpose of the restrictions and render their enforcement inequitable and oppressive, equity will not compel observance of them by injunction." *Id.* at 317.

Wood seemingly would have the rule the other way — ignore the circumstances within the property protected by a restrictive covenant and focus only upon the surrounding area. However, common sense tells us that when the issue is whether a restrictive covenant still serves its intended purpose and that purpose is to protect the lots in a particular subdivision from commercial uses, the conditions existing within the subdivision must be examined along with those existing in the surrounding area in order to determine the issue fairly. To ignore the conditions within the subdivision and to hold the covenant unenforceable solely because of changed conditions elsewhere would deny the lot owners the protection to which they are entitled according to a solemn covenant voluntarily made, and that would be grossly unfair.

What is required, therefore, is a leveling exercise in which fair consideration is given both to conditions in the subdivision and those in the surrounding area. Here, the facts are that there have been no changes within Carrsbrook Subdivision other than the aging of homes and the maturing of trees but there have been substantial changes within the surrounding area. After giving fair consideration to both situations, we are of opinion the changes are not so radical as to defeat the purpose of the covenant.

Finally, Wood cites Chesterfield Meadows Shopping Center Associates, L.P. v. Smith, 568 S.E.2d 676 (Va. 2002). That case involved a covenant that restricted the use of one piece of property to protect a historic home located on other property across the road. Later, the historic home was moved to a different location and, in the meantime, the surrounding area had been transformed into a thriving commercial area. This Court affirmed the trial court's nullification of the covenant, holding that such a radical change satisfied the standard articulated in *Booker* and its progeny. *Id.* at 680. However, *Chesterfield Meadows* is inapposite. Lacking here is a radical change like moving a historic home from its protected location, which negates the very purpose of the restrictive covenant.

For the reasons assigned, the judgment of the trial court will be affirmed.

Notes and Questions

1. *River Heights* analyzes the most common affirmative defense to the enforcement of a covenant, known as the *doctrine of changed conditions*. This applies when the character of the neighborhood has changed since the covenant was made so that the benefits of the covenants cannot be substantially realized. The policy rationale for refusing to enforce a covenant because of changed conditions asserts that "the potentially unlimited duration of servitudes creates substantial risks that, absent

mechanisms for nonconsensual modification and termination, obsolete servitudes will interfere with desirable uses of land." *Restatement (Third) of Property: Servitudes* §7.13, cmt. a (2000). How can those risks be avoided? Should the party benefiting from a covenant that the courts will not enforce be compensated?

2. There are other affirmative defenses, which when successful have the effect of either terminating the covenant or precluding its enforcement under particular circumstances. They include waiver, laches, estoppel, abandonment, prescription, unclean hands by the enforcer's own prior breach, and acquiescence as to other breaches. Covenants may also be terminated by the expiration of the specific duration in covenant itself, the merger of the benefited and burdened land, or a release by the benefited party.

3. The most famous judicial refusal to enforce a covenant as unconstitutional occurred in Shelley v. Kraemer, 334 U.S. 1 (1948). *Shelley* involved two consolidated cases arising from Missouri and Michigan. In the Missouri case, 30 of 39 owners of 47 of the 57 lots fronting Labadie Avenue in St. Louis signed an agreement in 1911 providing that for 55 years the property shall not be "occupied by any person not of the Caucasian race," and not by any "people of the Negro or Mongolian Race." Five of the nine owners who did not sign were African American, and African Americans had occupied one lot since 1882. In 1945, J.D. & Ethel Lee Shelley—who were African Americans—bought the property without knowledge of the covenant. Louis and Fern Kraemer then brought suit to prevent the Shelleys from taking possession of the property and to divest title from them. The Missouri Supreme Court opined that "[a]greements restricting property from being transferred to or occupied by negroes have been consistently upheld by the courts of this state as one which the parties have a right to make and which is not contrary to public policy." To hold that the judicial enforcement of such covenants violates the Fourteenth Amendment "would be to deny the parties to such an agreement one of the fundamental privileges of citizenship, access to the courts." The court thus ordered the trial court to grant the relief requested by the Kraemers. Kraemer v. Shelley, 198 S.W.2d 679 (Mo. 1946).

In the Michigan case, Ferguson and his wife executed a contract in 1934 providing that their Detroit property "shall not be used or occupied by any person or persons except those of the Caucasian race" until 1960, provided that the restriction shall not be effective unless at least 80 percent of the nearby properties were subject to a similar restriction. The 80-percent requirement was satisfied. Then, in 1944, the property was transferred to Orsel & Minnie McGhee, "who were found by the trial court to be Negroes"—the racial status of the McGhees was a contested issue at trial, with the testimony of the neighbors used to support the finding that the McGhees were not whites. The Michigan Supreme Court perceived the case as presenting a conflict between the state public policies against race discrimination and for the enforcement of restrictions on land use. It did not find any constitutional prohibition against the enforcement of the covenant, so it affirmed the trial court's order enjoining the McGhees from using or occupying the premises and directing them to move within 90 days. Sipes v. McGhee, 25 N.W.2d 638 (Mich. 1947).

The United States Supreme Court unanimously reversed. It reasoned that the Fourteenth Amendment protects the right to acquire, enjoy, own, and dispose of property from any discriminatory state action. The restrictive covenants themselves did not violate the Fourteenth Amendment's Equal Protection Clause, but the enforcement of the agreements by the state courts did. State courts are subject to the Fourteenth Amendment, and "but for the active intervention of the state courts, supported by the full panoply of state power, petitioners would have been free to occupy the properties in question without restraint."

C. NUISANCE LAW

■ **BIGLANE v. UNDER THE HILL CORPORATION**
Supreme Court of Mississippi, 2007
949 So. 2d 9

DIAZ, Justice. In this case we [consider whether] the noise coming from a local saloon . . . constituted a private nuisance to the residents of an apartment next door. . . .

FACTS

"No spot on the American continent ever bore a viler name" wrote one historian about the section of Natchez that was closest to the mighty Mississippi River. Edith Wyatt Moore, *Natchez Under-The-Hill* 7 (1958). The spot gained its name from the bluffs of loess which the river carved through easily, creating an "upper" Natchez and the one called "under-the-Hill." "Early travelers described it variously as a gambler's paradise, a sink-hole of iniquity and a resort of the damned," likely because "legitimate business houses and firms lined the streets but . . . were far outnumbered by gambling dens, saloons, houses of ill repute," not to mention the presence of pirates and slave-traders — or the possibility that the rule of code duello might be invoked at any time. *Id.* at 7-9.

"For the size of it, there is not, perhaps in the world, a more profligate place," said one visitor, while another called it "hell on earth, with bells attached." David G. Sansing, *Natchez: An Illustrated History* 65 (1992). At one point "[s]treet brawling in Natchez became so prevalent that [Spanish Mayor Manuel] Gayoso issued a ban on knives and other metal weapons," to little effect. *Id.* at 46.

Straddling the uncertain area between crumbling cliffs and the wild river, Natchez Under-the-Hill suffered many natural disasters, and "[s]ome claim that the Great River, in revenge against the place that shamed its name, altered its course, widened its banks and gobbled up much of that awful place." *Id.* at 66. Indeed, the "fine mansions and patrician elegance" of the upper city "soon eclipsed the fame of Natchez's lower half, though both found an easy journey into lore and legend." *Id.* at 48.

Time and great changes in technology eliminated the necessity of Natchez as a port, as the riverboats gave way to steam-powered locomotives, which in turn gave way under the advent of automobiles and airplanes. "It was the area's infamous past, however, that eventually saved it and secured its future," as the growing tourist industry brought those persons who "could not resist the pull of the landing's past, the power of its legends or the magic of its name: Natchez Under-the-Hill." *Id.* at 164. Tourists began to flock to Silver Street — the only remaining portion of Under-the-Hill — in much the same way they began pilgrimages to sprawling and majestic homes such as Rosalie, the stately mansion used as a headquarters for the Union forces in the Civil War; Longwood, the legendarily-unfinished octagon house; and the Burn, used as a hospital during the War, with its towering spiral staircase.

Onto this stage strode the two families who take center stage in the case at hand. In 1967 Nancy and James Biglane purchased a dilapidated building at 27 Silver Street that had been built in the 1840s, and opened the lower portion of the building as a gift shop in 1978. In 1973, Andre Farish, Sr., and Paul O'Malley purchased the building directly next door, at 25 Silver Street, which had been built in the 1830s; in 1975 they opened the Natchez Under the Hill Saloon. Eventually the Saloon would come to be run by the children of Mr. Farish, Melissa and Andre, Jr.

The Saloon would establish itself proudly as a welcoming haven for locals and visitors alike, and maintained its presence on 25 Silver Street as other businesses came and went. The Biglanes began converting the upper floors of 27 Silver Street into a large apartment, which they moved into in 2002.

Despite installing insulated walls and windows, locating their bedroom on the side of the building away from the Saloon, and placing their air conditioner unit on the side nearest the Saloon, the Biglanes quickly realized they had a problem: the raucous nature of the Saloon kept them wide awake at night.

Specifically, it was live music, a hallmark of the Saloon. During the summertime the un-air conditioned Under the Hill opened its windows and doors to lessen the heat inside, and music echoed up and down Silver Street. While the music was easier on Mr. Biglane, who had lost his hearing over the years, it was particularly difficult on Mrs. Biglane, who was frustrated by the constant rock and roll, conversation, and the clack of pool balls.

The Biglanes contacted the Saloon and asked that the music be turned down, and it was: Mr. Farish got rid of Groove Line, the band that seemed to trouble the Biglanes the most, and installed thick windows to block noise. He also purchased a sound meter by which bands could measure their output in decibels, and forbade them from going over a certain point. . . .

[The Biglanes brought a complaint.] The trial court heard multiple witnesses who testified to a dazzling array of subjects, including a historian who described the origins and evolution of under-the-Hill and a doctor with an expertise in sound who played loud music in court to replicate the alleged decibel levels of Under the Hill. The trial court ultimately rendered a highly detailed and intricately reasoned opinion and order that ran to 17 pages.

The chancellor determined that Under the Hill was a private nuisance to the Biglanes, and enjoined the Saloon from leaving open any doors or windows when music was playing, and ordered it to prevent patrons from loitering in the streets. . . .

[The Saloon appealed] arguing that its business was not a private nuisance. . . .

I. Is the Under the Hill Saloon a Private Nuisance to the Biglanes?

The Biglanes asserted that the Saloon was a private nuisance. "A private nuisance is a nontrespassory invasion of another's interest in the use and enjoyment of his property." Leaf River Forest Prods., Inc. v. Ferguson, 662 So. 2d 648, 662 (Miss. 1995). "One landowner may not use his land so as to unreasonably annoy, inconvenience, or harm others." Id. (internal quotations and citation omitted).

An entity is subject to liability for a private nuisance only when its conduct is a legal cause of an invasion of another's interest in the private use and enjoyment of land and that invasion is either (a) intentional and unreasonable, or

(b) unintentional but otherwise provides the basis for a cause of action for negligent or reckless conduct or for abnormally dangerous conditions or activities. *Id.*

The trial court proceeded under the first path of liability—whether the conduct complained of was intentional and unreasonable. After reviewing the evidence presented at trial, the chancellor found ample evidence that the Biglanes frequently could not use or enjoy their property—significantly, that Mrs. Biglane often slept away from the apartment on weekends to avoid the noise and that she could not have her grandchildren over on the weekends because of the noise. The audiologist who testified for the Biglanes concluded that the noise levels were excessive and unreasonable, although he also conceded that he had never measured the noise levels in the couple's bedroom. This problem was exacerbated during the summer months, when the un-airconditioned Saloon left its doors and windows open to defray the oppressive Natchez heat.

The Saloon did offer a witness who lived in back of the establishment who said he never had any problems with the noise, but the chancellor held that he was not an impartial witness, since he was testifying for his landlord.

Ultimately the trial court weighed the fact that the Biglanes knew or should have known that there was going to be some sort of noise associated with living "within five feet of a well established saloon which provides live music on the weekends."

We have examined similar issues before. An important Mississippi case regarding private nuisance based on the actions of a neighbor is Alfred Jacobshagen Co. v. Dockery, 139 So. 2d 632 (Miss. 1962). In that case a group of residents in Byram were overwhelmed by the "repulsive" odors of a nearby rendering plant. *Id.* at 632-33.

The general rule is that "[a] business, although in itself lawful, which impregnates the atmosphere with disagreeable and offensive odors and stenches, may become a nuisance to those occupying property in the vicinity, where such obnoxious smells result in a material injury to such owners." *Id.* at 634. This same rule extends to a situation where a lawful business injects loud music into the surrounding neighborhoods. . . .

Accordingly, even a lawful business—which the Under the Hill Saloon certainly is[1]—"may become . . . a nuisance" by interfering with its neighbors' enjoyment of their property." *Id.* We recognize that "[each private nuisance] case must be decided upon its own peculiar facts, taking into consideration the location and the surrounding circumstances." *Id.* Ultimately, "[i]t is not necessary that other property owners should be driven from their dwellings," because "[i]t is enough that the enjoyment of life and property is rendered materially uncomfortable and annoying." *Id.*

In *Dockery* we deferred greatly to the chancery court and determined that it "had the power to enjoin such future operations of the rendering plant as constituted in fact a nuisance," and that it also "had the lesser power to permit continued operation of the plant, subject to certain stated conditions and requirements." 139 So. 2d at 634; *see also* Lambert v. Matthews, 757 So. 2d 1066, 1068 (Miss. Ct. App. 2000) (chancery court's limitation on farmowners "from keeping more than two

---

1. In 1963 the City of Natchez zoned the area encompassing Silver Street as a "WD district," or a waterfront development district; the ordinance is still in place today. It explicitly authorized "as of right" the use of dwelling homes such as the Biglanes' and businesses like Under the Hill. The ordinance noted that "[i]t is intended that [the WD district] be reserved for active uses which animate the waterfront and take advantage of their proximity to the waterfront. Such uses should be oriented toward the enjoyment of tourists and citizens of the community." . . .

roosters on their property at any time" was affirmed as a proper equitable response to private nuisance caused by the crowing of the birds).

In the case at hand, the trial court exercised its power to permit continued operation of the Saloon while setting conditions to its future operation. Namely, it found that the Saloon could not "operat[e] its business with its doors and windows opened during any time that amplified music is being played inside the saloon." . . .

From a review of the record it is clear that the chancery court balanced the interests between the Biglanes and the Saloon in a quest for an equitable remedy that allowed the couple to enjoy their private apartment and while protecting a popular business and tourist attraction from over-regulation. *See also Lambert,* 757 So. 2d at 1071 ("Equity should adjust the remedy to the need in a nuisance case"). Accordingly, we agree that the Saloon was a private nuisance to the Biglanes and affirm the trial court's equitable conditions placed upon its continued operation. . . .

Notes and Questions

1. Should it matter that the Biglanes converted their building into a residence long after their neighbor opened the Saloon? Courts sometimes apply a "coming to the nuisance" doctrine when a newcomer to a community raises a nuisance challenge to a preexisting activity. This affirmative defense has intrinsic appeal. It comports with the familiar property principle of "first in time, first in right." It seems unfair to shut down a long-standing activity when the plaintiff could have avoided the harm by simply not buying the property or commencing the use that has turned out to be incompatible with the defendant's use. Moreover, the plaintiff may have purchased the property at a price that was discounted due to its proximity to the defendant's property, in which case granting a remedy for nuisance might amount to a windfall. Yet the "coming to the nuisance" defense often fails. In most instances, courts are unwilling to find that a newcomer must suffer a continuing nuisance or compensate persons responsible for a preexisting nuisance simply because those persons were there first. As the Florida Supreme Court explained nearly 50 years ago, the coming to the nuisance doctrine "is out of place in modern societies where people often have no real choices as to whether or not they will reside in an area adulterated by air pollution," and the doctrine wrongly "permits a defendant to condemn surrounding land to endure a perpetual nuisance simply because he was in the area first." Lawrence v. Eastern Airlines, Inc., 81 So. 2d 632, 634 (Fla. 1955).

2. Nuisance law offers a common law vehicle for addressing many problems that are increasingly the subject of zoning laws or government land use regulation. The *Biglane* court observes in footnote 1 of its opinion that the Saloon was in full compliance with the City of Natchez zoning ordinance, a point undoubtedly emphasized in the litigation by counsel for the Saloon. Should zoning compliance immunize a business from nuisance liability? Conversely, how much weight should be given in nuisance litigation to the fact that a defendant, such as a polluting factory, is violating a zoning ordinance or an environmental law such as the federal Clean Air Act? Nuisance law often overlaps with the enactments of legislatures and executive agencies, and thus offers an opportunity to consider the relative institutional merits of addressing problematic land uses through each kind of legal device.

3. Almost every nuisance case involves two owners of land. Indeed, Prosser went so far as to say that *all* nuisance cases involve two competing landowners. That is a bit of an exaggeration. It is true that a nuisance exists only where one's use or enjoyment of land is injured. Thus, for example, one cannot claim a nuisance when someone wrongfully fails to endorse a check. *See* Mahogany Run Condominium Ass'n v. ICG Realty Mgmt. Corp., 1999 U.S. Dist. LEXIS 2005 (D.V.I. Feb. 16, 1999). There are a few old cases that found a nuisance unrelated to any land use — *see, e.g.,* Carroll v. New York Pie Baking Co., 213 N.Y.S. 533 (Sup. Ct. 1926) (holding that a cockroach baked in a pie constituted a nuisance) — but such cases must be treated as an aberration "if 'nuisance' is to have any meaning at all." W. Page Keeton et al., *Prosser and Keeton on Torts* 618 (5th ed. 1984). But it is not necessarily true that the party interfering with the land use must be a landowner, too. Can you think of an example of a nuisance that does not arise out of someone's use of his land?

It is not necessary to own property in fee simple in order to pursue a nuisance claim. Renters, owners of easements, and owners of reversionary interests can bring suit if an activity interferes with their current interest in the land. By contrast, a holder of a license to enter property and any other person who does not have an actual property interest in the land will not be able to pursue a private nuisance claim.

4. Ronald Coase offers another perspective on these disputes between neighbors. According to Coase, the harm in each case is reciprocal: The Saloon harmed the Biglanes by interfering with their enjoyment of their residence, but it is equally true that the Biglanes harmed the Saloon by restricting its operation. Ronald Coase, *The Problems of Social Cost*, 3 J.L. & Econ. 1 (1960). What are the implications of that observation? How should the law determine which neighbor has a right to engage in their preferred activity and which one does not? How would you decide the following cases: (1) a school district wants to build a minor league baseball stadium, but the residential neighbors object to the noise, lights, traffic and stray baseballs; (2) dairy farmers object to a cemetery because it is depressing and because it could contaminate the groundwater; (3) an oceanfront hotel that attracts many business conventions objects to a nightclub across the street whose noise disturbs the hotel's guests? How would each case be decided according to the test set forth in *Biglane*? To what extent should considerations of efficiency govern nuisance decision making?

■ **PRAH v. MARETTI**
Supreme Court of Wisconsin, 1982
321 N.W.2d 182

ABRAHAMSON, J. This appeal . . . present[s] an issue of first impression, namely, whether an owner of a solar-heated residence states a claim upon which relief can be granted when he asserts that his neighbor's proposed construction of a residence (which conforms to existing deed restrictions and local ordinances) interferes with his access to an unobstructed path for sunlight across the neighbor's property. This case thus involves a conflict between one landowner (Glenn Prah, the plaintiff) interested in unobstructed access to sunlight across adjoining property as a natural source of energy and an adjoining landowner (Richard D. Maretti, the defendant) interested in the development of his land.

The circuit court concluded that the plaintiff presented no claim upon which relief could be granted and granted summary judgment for the defendant. We reverse the judgment of the circuit court and remand the cause to the circuit court for further proceedings. . . .

We consider first whether the complaint states a claim for relief based on common law private nuisance. This state has long recognized that an owner of land does not have an absolute or unlimited right to use the land in a way which injures the rights of others. The rights of neighboring landowners are relative; the uses by one must not unreasonably impair the uses or enjoyment of the other. When one landowner's use of his or her property unreasonably interferes with another's enjoyment of his or her property, that use is said to be a private nuisance.

The private nuisance doctrine has traditionally been employed in this state to balance the conflicting rights of landowners, and this court has recently adopted the analysis of private nuisance set forth in the *Restatement (Second) of Torts*. The Restatement defines private nuisance as "a nontrespassory invasion of another's interest in the private use and enjoyment of land." *Restatement (Second) of Torts* §821D (1977). The phrase "interest in the private use and enjoyment of land" as used in sec. 821D is broadly defined to include any disturbance of the enjoyment of property. The comment in the Restatement describes the landowner's interest protected by private nuisance law as follows:

> "The phrase 'interest in the use and enjoyment of land' is used in this Restatement in a broad sense. It comprehends not only the interests that a person may have in the actual present use of land for residential, agricultural, commercial, industrial and other purposes, but also his interests in having the present use value of the land unimpaired by changes in its physical condition. Thus the destruction of trees on vacant land is as much an invasion of the owner's interest in its use and enjoyment as is the destruction of crops or flowers that he is growing on the land for his present use. 'Interest in use and enjoyment' also comprehends the pleasure, comfort and enjoyment that a person normally derives from the occupancy of land. Freedom from discomfort and annoyance while using land is often as important to a person as freedom from physical interruption with his use or freedom from detrimental change in the physical condition of the land itself." *Restatement (Second) of Torts* §821D, Comment b, p. 101 (1977).

Although the defendant's obstruction of the plaintiff's access to sunlight appears to fall within the Restatement's broad concept of a private nuisance as a nontrespassory invasion of another's interest in the private use and enjoyment of land, the defendant asserts that he has a right to develop his property in compliance with statutes, ordinances and private covenants without regard to the effect of such development upon the plaintiff's access to sunlight. In essence, the defendant is asking this court to hold that the private nuisance doctrine is not applicable in the instant case and that his right to develop his land is a right which is per se superior to his neighbor's interest in access to sunlight. This position is expressed in the maxim "cujus est solum, ejus est usque ad coelum et ad infernos," that is, the owner of land owns up to the sky and down to the center of the earth. The rights of the surface owner are, however, not unlimited. U.S. v. Causby, 328 U.S. 256, 260-61 (1946). . . .

This court's reluctance in the nineteenth and early part of the twentieth century to provide broader protection for a landowner's access to sunlight was premised on three policy considerations. First, the right of landowners to use their property as they wished, as long as they did not cause physical damage to a neighbor, was jealously guarded.

Second, sunlight was valued only for aesthetic enjoyment or as illumination. Since artificial light could be used for illumination, loss of sunlight was at most a personal annoyance which was given little, if any, weight by society.

Third, society had a significant interest in not restricting or impeding land development. This court repeatedly emphasized that in the growth period of the nineteenth and early twentieth centuries change is to be expected and is essential to property and that recognition of a right to sunlight would hinder property development. The court expressed this concept as follows:

> As the city grows, large grounds appurtenant to residences must be cut up to supply more residences. . . . The cistern, the outhouse, the cesspool, and the private drain must disappear in deference to the public waterworks and sewer; the terrace and the garden, to the need for more complete occupancy. . . . Strict limitation [on the recognition of easements of light and air over adjacent premises is] in accord with the popular conception upon which real estate has been and is daily being conveyed in Wisconsin and to be essential to easy and rapid development at least of our municipalities. Miller v. Hoeschler, 105 N.W. 790, 791, 792 (1905).

Considering these three policies, this court concluded that in the absence of an express agreement granting access to sunlight, a landowner's obstruction of another's access to sunlight was not actionable. These three policies are no longer fully accepted or applicable. They reflect factual circumstances and social priorities that are now obsolete.

First, society has increasingly regulated the use of land by the landowner for the general welfare. Euclid v. Ambler Realty Co., 272 U.S. 365 (1926).

Second, access to sunlight has taken on a new significance in recent years. In this case the plaintiff seeks to protect access to sunlight, not for aesthetic reasons or as a source of illumination but as a source of energy. Access to sunlight as an energy source is of significance both to the landowner who invests in solar collectors and to a society which has an interest in developing alternative sources of energy.

Third, the policy of favoring unhindered private development in an expanding economy is no longer in harmony with the realities of our society. The need for easy and rapid development is not as great today as it once was, while our perception of the value of sunlight as a source of energy has increased significantly. . . .

Private nuisance law, the law traditionally used to adjudicate conflicts between private landowners, has the flexibility to protect both a landowner's right of access to sunlight and another landowner's right to develop land. Private nuisance law is better suited to regulate access to sunlight in modern society and is more in harmony with legislative policy and the prior decisions of this court than is an inflexible doctrine of non-recognition of any interest in access to sunlight across adjoining land.

We therefore hold that private nuisance law, that is, the reasonable use doctrine as set forth in the Restatement, is applicable to the instant case. Recognition of a nuisance claim for unreasonable obstruction of access to sunlight will not prevent land development or unduly hinder the use of adjoining land. It will promote the reasonable use and enjoyment of land in a manner suitable to the 1980's. That obstruction of access to light might be found to constitute a nuisance in certain circumstances does not mean that it will be or must be found to constitute a nuisance under all circumstances. The result in each case depends on whether the conduct complained of is unreasonable.

Accordingly we hold that the plaintiff in this case has stated a claim under which relief can be granted. Nonetheless we do not determine whether the plaintiff in this case is entitled to relief. In order to be entitled to relief the plaintiff must prove the elements required to establish actionable nuisance, and the conduct of the defendant herein must be judged by the reasonable use doctrine.

[I]t appears that the circuit court recognized that the common law private nuisance doctrine was applicable but concluded that defendant's conduct was not unreasonable. The circuit court apparently attempted to balance the utility of the defendant's conduct with the gravity of the harm. *Restatement (Second) of Torts* §826 (1977).[16] The defendant urges us to accept the circuit court's balance as adequate. We decline to do so.

The circuit court concluded that because the defendant's proposed house was in conformity with zoning regulations, building codes and deed restrictions, the defendant's use of the land was reasonable. This court has concluded that a landowner's compliance with zoning laws does not automatically bar a nuisance claim. Compliance with the law "is not the controlling factor, though it is, of course, entitled to some weight." Bie v. Ingersoll, 135 N.W.2d 250, 253 (Wis. 1965). The circuit court also concluded that the plaintiff could have avoided any harm by locating his own house in a better place. Again, plaintiff's ability to avoid the harm is a relevant but not a conclusive factor. *See Restatement (Second) of Torts* §§826, 827, 828 (1977).

Furthermore, our examination of the record leads us to conclude that the record does not furnish an adequate basis for the circuit court to apply the proper legal principles on summary judgment. The application of the reasonable use standard in nuisance cases normally requires a full exposition of all underlying facts and circumstances. Too little is known in this case of such matters as the extent of the harm to the plaintiff, the suitability of solar heat in that neighborhood, the

---

16. The factors involved in determining the gravity of the harm caused by the conduct complained of are set out in sec. 827 of the Restatement as follows:

Sec. 827. Gravity of Harm — Factors Involved.
In determining the gravity of the harm from an intentional invasion of another's interest in the use and enjoyment of land, the following factors are important:
   (a) The extent of the harm involved;
   (b) the character of the harm involved;
   (c) the social value that the law attaches to the type of use or enjoyment invaded;
   (d) the suitability of the particular use or enjoyment invaded to the character of the locality; and
   (e) the burden on the person harmed of avoiding the harm.

The factors involved in determining the utility of conduct complained of are set out in sec. 828 of the Restatement as follows:

Sec. 828. Utility of Conduct — Factors Involved.
In determining the utility of conduct that causes an intentional invasion of another's interest in the use and enjoyment of land, the following factors are important:
   (a) the social value that the law attaches to the primary purpose of the conduct;
   (b) the suitability of the conduct to the character of the locality; and
   (c) the impracticability of preventing or avoiding the invasion.

availability of remedies to the plaintiff, and the costs to the defendant of avoiding the harm. Summary judgment is not an appropriate procedural vehicle in this case when the circuit court must weigh evidence which has not been presented at trial.

Because the plaintiff has stated a claim of common law private nuisance upon which relief can be granted, the judgment of the circuit court must be reversed.

CALLOW, J., dissenting. . . .

I would submit that any policy decisions in this area are best left for the legislature. . . . I would concur with these observations of the trial judge: "While temptation lingers for the court to declare by judicial fiat what is right and what should be done, under the facts in this case, such action under our form of constitutional government where the three branches each have their defined jurisdiction and power, would be an intrusion of judicial egoism over legislative passivity." . . .

I conclude that plaintiff's solar heating system is an unusually sensitive use. In other words, the defendant's proposed construction of his home, under ordinary circumstances, would not interfere with the use and enjoyment of the usual person's property. *See* Prosser, *Law of Torts* §87 at 578-79 (4th ed. 1971). "The plaintiff cannot, by devoting his own land to an unusually sensitive use, such as a drive-in motion picture theater easily affected by light, make a nuisance out of conduct of the adjoining defendant which would otherwise be harmless." *Id.* at 579. . . .

Notes and Questions

In *Prah*, Justice Abrahamson emphasized that evolving social policies favored the treatment of interferences with solar access as a nuisance. Do you agree? Consider Sher v. Leiderman, 226 Cal. Rptr. 698 (Ct. App. 1986), where the court rejected a claim that a neighbor's growing trees constituted a nuisance because they interfered with a landowner's solar energy collector and also created a "gloomy atmosphere" inside the landowner's home. The court noted that "[t]hough the Solar Age may indeed be upon us, it is not so easily conceded that individual property rights are no longer important policy considerations." *Prah* had discounted individual property rights because "society has increasingly regulated the use of land by the landowner for the general welfare," citing Euclid v. Ambler Realty Co., 272 U.S. 365 (1926), the leading case on zoning that appears below in Chapter 12. But the court in *Sher* responded that "expanded use of the police power and eminent domain only supports the conclusion that society has increasingly seen fit to regulate private land use for the public health, safety, morals, or welfare. The case before us concerns the imposition of restrictions for land use for a private benefit, a far different proposition in our view." Echoing Justice Callow's dissent in *Prah*, the *Sher* court concluded that "it is solely within the province of the Legislature to gauge the relative importance of social policies and decide whether to effect a change in the law." The California legislature had already acted in this field by enacting the Solar Shade Control Act, which prohibits a property owner from allowing a tree to shade more than 10 percent of a neighbor's solar collector between 10:00 A.M. and 2:00 P.M.

■ **WERNKE v. HALAS**
   Court of Appeals of Indiana, 1992
   600 N.E.2d 117

BAKER, Judge. America's wise and thoughtful poet laureate, Robert Frost, once wrote that "good fences make good neighbors." R. Frost, *Mending Wall* (1914), in E. Lathem, *Poetry of Robert Frost* 33-34 (1979). Lamentably, not everyone has read Frost.

In this private nuisance action, defendant-appellant Roland Wernke challenges the trial court's grant of summary judgment in favor of Wernke's neighbors, plaintiff-appellees John and Karen Halas. Wernke also appeals the trial court's subsequent award of compensatory damages, punitive damages, and attorney fees.

. . . Wernke . . . and the Halases are next door neighbors, with abutting side yards. The Peacock family owns the other lot abutting Wernke's property. In 1990, after a period of mounting neighborhood tension over the fate of a tree growing astride the common Wernke-Halas-Peacock boundary, and during which the parties complained about the appearance and maintenance of each other's land, Wernke built a privacy fence facing the Halas property. The fence is constructed of vertically placed boards, and the parties agree it is no more than six feet tall. On the side of the fence facing the Halases, Wernke placed some vinyl strips and a license plate over some of the cracks between the boards. He also attached a section of orange plastic construction fencing to the Halas side of the fence. The orange fencing ran almost the length of the board fence and was approximately five feet tall.

Wernke placed support posts sunken in concrete at regular intervals along the fence line. One day, as Wernke's work on the fence was progressing, vandals scrawled "Fuck J.H.," "Fuck R.P.," and "D. Head" into the wet concrete of a support post. No part of the concrete, the post, or the fence as a whole encroached upon any of Wernke's neighbors' property.

Prior to Wernke's erection of the fence, the Peacocks nailed a toilet seat to a tree facing Wernke's yard. The Peacocks removed the seat after several months, and Wernke, in a display of equal taste, set up his own toilet seat, mounting the seat and its lid on a piece of plywood placed atop a post overlooking his neighbors' land. A brown spot, alleged by the Halases to represent human excrement, was painted on the plywood within the ring inscribed by the seat. Like the fence, the toilet rested entirely on Wernke's property.

The Halases filed suit in September 1990, alleging the toilet and the fence with all its accoutrements, including the graffiti, constituted nuisances. On the advice of his attorney, Wernke removed the license plate from the fence, and the toilet and graffiti prior to the hearing on the Halases' motion for summary judgment. After the summary judgment hearing, the judge found as a matter of law that the toilet, the graffiti, and the fence constituted a nuisance. He therefore ordered the orange fencing and the vinyl strips removed, and Wernke complied.

Several weeks after summary judgment was entered, the court held a damages hearing. The Halases were awarded $5,600 for the loss in the rental value of their property during the period the graffiti, the toilet and the objectionable portions of the fence were visible, $2,400 for the discomfort and annoyance they suffered, $5,000 in punitive damages, and $3,937 in attorney fees. . . .

EXISTENCE OF NUISANCE

. . . Nuisances may be either public or private. A public nuisance is one which affects an entire neighborhood or community, while a private nuisance affects only a single person or a determinate number of people. The essence of a private nuisance is the use of property to the detriment of the use and enjoyment of another's property.

Both public and private nuisances are further subdivided into nuisances *per se*, or nuisances at law, and nuisances *per accidens*, or nuisances in fact. "A nuisance *per se*, as the term implies, is that which is a nuisance in itself, and which, therefore, cannot be so conducted or maintained as to be lawfully carried on or permitted to exist." Windfall Manufacturing Co. v. Patterson, 47 N.E. 2, 4 (Ind. 1897). Thus, for example, a house of prostitution and an obstruction that encroaches on the right-of-way of a public highway are nuisances *per se*. *Id. See also* Town of Rome City v. King, 450 N.E.2d 72 (Ind. App. 1983) (blocked highway). On the other hand, an otherwise lawful use may become a nuisance *per accidens* by virtue of the circumstances surrounding the use.

Logically, therefore, the determination that something is a nuisance *per se* is a question of law for the court, and the determination of "whether that which is not in itself a nuisance is a nuisance in fact" is a question for the jury or the judge as trier of fact. Shatto v. McNulty, 509 N.E.2d 897, 899 (Ind. App. 1987). . . .

The essence of these holdings is unmistakable and straightforward. The conclusion that something is a *per accidens* nuisance is a conclusion to be reached only after a full review of the material facts. Summary judgment, which by definition is meant to resolve only with those cases lacking material factual disputes, is therefore rarely appropriate in *per accidens* nuisance cases. . . .

THE FENCE

In Indiana, at common law, a landowner had no nuisance claim against an adjacent landowner for erection of a fence that did not encroach on the landowner's property. Giller v. West, 69 N.E. 548, 549-50 (Ind. 1904). The rule applied regardless of the adjacent landowner's motive in erecting the fence and regardless of the ugliness of the fence. *Id.* "The law does not require that . . . fences shall be constructed of fine materials, or that they shall be attractive in appearance." *Id.* at 549.

Five years after *Giller*, in 1909, the legislature modified the common law. Ind. Code 32-10-10-1 provides "[a]ny fence or other structure in the nature of a fence unnecessarily exceeding six feet (6′) in height, maliciously erected or maintained for the purpose of annoying the owners or occupants of adjoining property, shall be deemed a nuisance." Ind. Code 32-10-10-2 provides affected landowners with a cause of action for damages and abatement as for any other nuisance. . . .

The fence here, as the parties agree, is no more than six feet tall. Therefore, regardless of how unsightly the fence may be, with its attached vinyl strips, license plate, and orange construction site fencing, it cannot be a nuisance. *Giller, supra.* . . .

THE TOILET

In Indiana, a plaintiff who has proved a *per accidens* nuisance may recover aesthetic damages. Rust v. Guinn, 429 N.E.2d 299 (Ind. App 1981). These are damages for the "annoyance, discomfort, and inconvenience" caused by the nuisance. *Id.* at 304. It does not follow, however, that a use or structure may constitute a nuisance merely on the basis of displeasing aesthetics.

On the contrary, it is well-settled throughout this country that, standing alone, unsightliness, or lack of aesthetic virtue, does not constitute a private nuisance.[5] Haehlen v. Wilson, 54 P.2d 62 (Cal. Ct. App. 1936); Allison v. Smith, 695 P.2d 791 (Colo. App. 1984); Mathewson v. Primeau, 395 P.2d 183 (Wash. 1964).[6] Instead, aesthetics are the province of restrictive covenants, *see* Adult Group Properties, Ltd. v. Imler, 505 N.E.2d 459 (Ind. App. 1987) (upholding architectural restrictive covenants), and this is as it should be.

Aesthetic values are inherently subjective; if landowners in a given neighborhood or development wish to contract among themselves for the appearance of their homes, the courts stand ready, within well-settled limits, to provide enforcement. It would require a great leap of logic, however, to say that courts themselves should be the arbiters of proper aesthetics and good taste, and it is a leap we are unwilling to make. As the Colorado Supreme Court eloquently stated, "[i]n our populous society, the courts cannot be available to enjoin an activity solely because it causes some aesthetic discomfort or annoyance. Given our myriad and disparate tastes, life styles, mores, and attitudes, the availability of a judicial remedy for such complaints would cause inexorable confusion." Green v. Castle Concrete Co., 509 P.2d 588, 591 (Colo. 1973).

In the present case, the evidence concerning the toilet seat is undisputed. The seat and lid are affixed to a piece of blue plywood with a painted brown spot. The plywood is framed and attached to a pole roughly 10 feet tall facing out of Wernke's yard. Wernke claimed the entire contraption was a bird house, and indeed, three small boxes with holes suitable for birds surround the frame. It may be the ugliest bird house in Indiana, or it may merely be a toilet seat on a post. The distinction is irrelevant, however; Wernke's tasteless decoration is merely an aesthetic annoyance, and we are not engaged in the incommodious task of judging aesthetics. The trial court erroneously entered summary judgment for the Halases on this issue, and again, because the evidence is undisputed, Wernke, not the Halases, is entitled to judgment as a matter of law.

THE GRAFFITI

Like the toilet, the graffiti is unattractive and vulgar. Nonetheless, it is not a nuisance. The law, especially in nuisance cases, when rights to the free use of property are concerned, does not deal in trifles, and "mere annoyance or inconvenience will not support an action for a nuisance because the damages resulting therefrom are deemed *damnum absque injuria* in recognition of the fact life is not perfect." Sherk v. Indiana Waste Systems, Inc., 495 N.E.2d 815, 818 (Ind. App. 1986).

Here, even if we were to ignore our summary judgment standard and view the evidence in the light most favorable to the Halases, the graffiti is a non-actionable

---

5. The rule may well be different for public nuisances. *See Restatement (Second) of Torts* §821B, Comment e at 91 (1977).

6. If unsightliness is coupled with additional harms, however, such as pollution or a physical invasion, a private nuisance may be established. *See Allison, supra.* Moreover, even without additional harms, a large amount of refuse, such as that associated with junkyards and salvage operations, may so essentially interfere with the comfortable enjoyment of life and property that it constitutes a nuisance. *See, e.g., Allison, supra* at 794, and cases cited therein.

trifle. The inscriptions "Fuck J.H.," "Fuck R.P.," and "D. Head"[7] are engraved in areas of concrete, no more than two feet in diameter, which surround the ground level bases of two of Wernke's fenceposts. The fenceposts themselves are located at least several inches over the property line onto Wernke's property *beyond* the Halases' own chain link fence, and the letters comprising the inscriptions are only three to four inches tall. In short, the graffiti is almost invisible from the Halases' yard, and it is not the appearance of the graffiti, but rather knowledge of its presence, that causes annoyance. Annoyance does not constitute a nuisance, and the Halases can no more claim nuisance because they know Wernke has offensive inscriptions in his yard than they could if they knew Wernke had an offensive color scheme in his bathroom.

Moreover, freedom of expression is at issue here, and although the language is offensive and vulgar, it is a "bedrock principle underlying the First Amendment that the government may not prohibit the expression of an idea simply because society finds the idea itself offensive or disagreeable." Texas v. Johnson, 491 U.S. 397, 414 (1989).[8] The graffiti simply is not a nuisance. . . .

The trial court erred in granting summary judgment to the Halases for all three alleged nuisances. Because there is no genuine issue of material fact, the summary judgment in favor of the Halases on all counts is reversed, and summary judgment is ordered for Wernke. The award of attorney fees was error, and is therefore also reversed.

Notes and Questions

1. As *Wernke* explains, nuisance fact patterns can be divided into three groups. First, certain activities are castigated as a *nuisance per se*, which is an activity pursued by a possessor or user of land that is *always* considered wrongful (*i.e.*, there is nuisance liability), without inquiry into the particular facts bearing on how the defendant conducts the activity or the nature and extent of the harm to the plaintiff. Second, there are activities that *sometimes* may be nuisances, depending on the facts and circumstances. The *Wernke* court identifies this as nuisance *per accidens*, also known as *nuisance in fact*. Last, some activities are *never* considered nuisances, even if a neighbor is really irritated and may be able to prove economic harm. The rule applied in *Wernke*—the *doctrine of aesthetic nuisance*—is one example. This is a rule of nuisance immunity. A landowner is privileged to do certain things on her property without undertaking the risk of nuisance liability to a neighbor.

2. The *doctrine of aesthetic nuisance* is well entrenched in American law, but some jurisdictions have modified or rejected the rule. One example is Rattigan v. Wile, 841 N.E.2d 680 (Mass. 2006), where a homeowner, disappointed because he lost litigation with his neighbor, put stacks of construction debris and unusual objects,

---

7. The record does not reveal the meaning of "D. Head," but the context of the phrase and the posture of the case leave little doubt it is not a complimentary phrase.

8. We are not confronted with, and therefore leave for another day, the question of whether some language may be presented so invasively to the privacy of the home that it could constitute an abatable nuisance within the confines of the First Amendment to the United States Constitution. *See, e.g.*, Frisby v. Schultz, 487 U.S. 474 (1988) (upholding ban on targeted residential picketing that intruded upon residential privacy); F.C.C. v. Pacifica Foundation, 438 U.S. 726 (1978) (upholding ban on offensive radio broadcasts that invade the privacy of the home); Rowan v. Post Office Dep't, 397 U.S. 728 (1970) (upholding ban on offensive mailings); Kovacs v. Cooper, 336 U.S. 77 (1949) (upholding ban on noisy sound trucks that could be heard within homes).

including a "gigantic, red, metal ocean freight container," near their common boundary. He also placed portable toilets near the boundary, where odors interfered with use of the neighbor's swimming pool. He frequently landed his helicopter near the boundary. The helicopter created loud noise and occasionally threw debris on the homeowner's property. The homeowner sued for nuisance, obtaining an injunction and recovering damages of over $400,000 plus interest. The trial judge found that the neighbor located the objects near the boundary only for the purpose of annoying and offending the homeowner. The appellate court affirmed, stating that "activities on one's property that create or maintain unreasonable aesthetic conditions for neighbors are actionable as a private nuisance."

■ **DOWDELL v. BLOOMQUIST**
Supreme Court of Rhode Island, 2004
847 A.2d 827

FLAHERTY, Justice. "Tree at my window, window tree, My sash is lowered when night comes on; But let there never be curtain drawn Between you and me." Robert Frost.

In the matter before us, four western arborvitae trees are at the plaintiff's window. Sadly, however, the curtains between the neighboring parties have long since been drawn, forever dividing what was once an amicable relationship between them. The fate of the offending trees now hangs in the balance.

The plaintiff, Cheryl Dowdell, brought this action in Superior Court alleging that the defendant, Peter Bloomquist, planted four western arborvitae trees on his Charlestown property solely to exact revenge against her, to retaliate by blocking her view, and in violation of the spite fence statute, G.L. 1956 §34-10-20.[1] She sought legal and equitable relief. After considering the testimony and evidence presented at a nonjury trial, the presiding Superior Court justice found that the trees were planted to satisfy defendant's malicious intent, not his pretextual desire for privacy, and that defendant had violated §34-10-20. The trial justice granted plaintiff injunctive relief. We affirm the judgment of the trial justice.

The facts pertinent to this appeal are as follows. The parties' homes are on adjoining lots in a subdivision of Charlestown, each approximately one acre in size. Dowdell's home sits at a higher elevation than Bloomquist's and has a distant view of the ocean over the Bloomquist property. In June 2000, defendant acquired the home from his mother, Lorraine Bloomquist. Prior to that time, the Dowdell family had an amicable relationship with defendant's mother. Change was in the wind in the fall of 2000, however, when defendant petitioned for a zoning variance from the Charlestown zoning board seeking permission to build a second-story addition to his home. The plaintiff expressed concern about the petition, anxious that the addition would compromise her view of the Atlantic Ocean. For six months the

---

1. General Laws 1956 §34-10-20 provides as follows:

Spite fences. A fence or other structure in the nature of a fence which unnecessarily exceeds six feet (6′) in height and is maliciously erected or maintained for the purpose of annoying the owners or occupants of adjoining property, shall be deemed a private nuisance, and any owner or occupant who is injured, either in the comfort or enjoyment of his or her estate thereby, may have an action to recover damages for the injury.

parties argued before the Charlestown Zoning Board of Review as to the merits of the addition. As a result, the relationship between the neighbors became less than friendly. . . . In May, one day after the zoning board closed its hearing on defendant's variance request,[4] defendant began planting the four western arborvitae trees that now stand in a row bordering the property line.[5] Although the forty-foot-high trees enabled little light to pass into Dowdell's second- and third-story picture windows, testimony at trial evidenced that the vegetation was not a bar to the unkind words between the neighbors. . . .

This is the first occasion this Court has had to address the issue of whether a row of trees may be considered a fence within the meaning of the spite fence statute, §34-10-20. We believe the trial justice properly referred to the definition of "lawful fences" found in §34-10-1 to understand the simple meaning and legislative intent behind its use of the word "fence." Based upon the language of §34-10-1, a fence clearly includes a hedge. And based upon the expert testimony relied on by the trial justice, a row of western arborvitae trees may constitute a hedge. However, even if the trees were not a hedge per se, the spite fence statute refers to "[a] fence or other structure in the nature of a fence." The trial justice considered the proximity of the four trees that touched one another, and the broad span of sixty feet across which they spread, and rationally interpreted that the trees were a fence. . . . We are not alone in this assessment. Recently, a California appellate court found a row of evergreen trees to be a fence within the meaning of the California spite fence statute. Wilson v. Handley, 119 Cal. Rptr. 2d 263 (Ct. App. 2002). . . .

FLANDERS, Justice, concurring in part and dissenting in part. Although I concur with that portion of the majority opinion affirming the Superior Court's finding that the spite-fence statute, G.L.1956 §34-10-20, applies to this case, I would hold that the Superior Court did not have the power to issue an injunction in favor of the plaintiff for the defendant's violation of that statute because it provides only for "an action to recover damages." Thus, I conclude that the trial justice erred in awarding injunctive relief because the applicable rules of statutory construction require us to strictly construe statutes such as this one — granting rights and remedies not recognized at common law — and to refrain from inferring causes of action and statutory remedies that are not contained in the express language of the statute. . . .

Notes and Questions

1. Why should it matter if Bloomquist put in the row of trees out of spite, or because he wanted more privacy, or perhaps simply because he liked western arborvitae trees? Do you agree that Bloomquist's row of four trees is "a fence or

---

4. The Zoning Board of Review of the Town of Charlestown subsequently granted defendant's dimensional variance request. Although Dowdell appealed the decision to the Superior Court, it was affirmed in March 2003.

5. The western arborvitae were planted directly behind a row of eastern arborvitae already existing on the Dowdell property near its boundary with the Bloomquist land. According to expert testimony at trial, the eastern arborvitae are smaller trees, growing to a height of eight to eleven feet. In contrast, the western arborvitae are capable of growing to a height of seventy feet. Although the Dowdell trees are in excess of six feet, there are no allegations that they were ever placed out of spite and these trees are not the subject of the instant matter. However, the trial justice noted that the Dowdell trees already offered sufficient privacy between the Dowdell and Bloomquist properties and cited this as one reason why he considered defendant's purported privacy motive to be a subterfuge for malicious intent.

other structure in the nature of a fence" within the meaning of the Rhode Island spite fence statute? Could the court have held for the neighbor, Dowdell, apart from the statute? In *Wernke* the court discussed the Indiana spite fence statute, enacted in 1909, and in *Dowdell* the court applied the Rhode Island spite fence statute, coincidentally enacted the same year. During that time period many state legislatures passed spite fence laws, in reaction to judicial rulings like the one described in *Wernke* (Giller v. West from 1904), which announced an immunity rule, regardless of motive, provided the fence builder does not trespass (*i.e.,* the fence is located completely on defendant's real estate). The common law decisions were (and are) split. Some courts, as far back as the nineteenth century, held that a fence built for the sole purpose of cutting off a neighbor's air and light was a private nuisance.

2. If trees planted for the purpose of revenge or mere hostility to a neighbor qualify as nuisances, how much further should the doctrine extend? Suppose a landowner builds a house that is much more expensive than her neighbor's for the purpose of making her envious. Could a landowner's inaction (say, failing to maintain her property) ever be a "spite nuisance"?

■ MARK v. OREGON

Court of Appeals of Oregon, 1999
974 P.2d 716

WARREN, Presiding Judge. Plaintiffs have lived on Sauvie Island since June 1990. They bought their land, which is surrounded by the Sauvie Island Wildlife Area (wildlife area), in February 1990. The portion of the wildlife area near where they live is a popular location for public nudity to an extent that, plaintiffs assert, constitutes both a private and a public nuisance. Defendant Division of State Lands (State Lands) owns the wildlife area, which it leases to defendant Department of Fish and Wildlife (Fish and Wildlife). In this case, plaintiffs seek compensation for the effects of the nudity on their land and an injunction restraining defendants from allowing public nudity in the wildlife area. They also assert a claim in inverse condemnation on the ground that the effect of the nudity on the value of their land constitutes a taking for which they are entitled to just compensation. . . . [T]he trial court determined that defendants are immune from liability under the Oregon Tort Claims Act because they were exercising a discretionary function and that plaintiffs had not stated a claim for inverse condemnation. It therefore dismissed both the original and amended complaints. We reverse on the injunction claims and otherwise affirm.

. . . Defendants own, manage, and control the wildlife area, with the statutory purpose of developing it to provide wildlife management, wildlife-oriented recreation, and public hunting. The wildlife area contains several miles of undeveloped beaches along the Columbia River that attract public use for non-wildlife related activities. An increasing number of those users engage in open public nudity, which is not wildlife-oriented recreation. Defendants estimate the total number of yearly visits for that purpose to be in the thousands. Many of those users "parade naked throughout the year all over the wildlife area, including the roads and bushes, and on, around and in view of plaintiffs' and others' private residences."

The activities of the nude users have created a situation where plaintiffs, other local residents, and visitors to the area are helpless to prevent "continuous and oftentimes daily exposure" to full adult nudity. Plaintiffs and their family, friends, and guests have been forced to witness adult nudity and "repeated acts of depravity, illegality and lewdness" because of their location adjacent to defendants' lands. Plaintiffs, other residents, and other members of the public have reported those facts to defendants and informed them of the harm that results from the public nudity and related activities.

According to plaintiffs, defendants have the authority, obligation, and duty to control the activities of the public in the wildlife area in a way reasonably calculated to prevent harm to the rights and safety of adjacent landowners and the public in general and to the value of surrounding private property. Defendants have knowingly and intentionally failed to exercise that control in a way calculated to prohibit or reasonably restrict public nudity, resulting in harm to plaintiffs and their property. The harm to plaintiffs is that their use of their property and their social life have been restricted by their reluctance to expose themselves, family, friends, and guests to public nudity and open sexual activity, that they are fearful for their safety due to their proximity to the nude beach activities, that they are embarrassed, offended and angered by coming in contact with nude adult behavior, that their right to go for a walk and enjoy the public beaches adjacent to their home has been restricted by harassment from nude sunbathers, and that those things have greatly diminished the value of their property. . . .

The doctrines of public nuisance and private nuisance have different origins and protect different interests. However, many of the governing rules are the same, and we will therefore treat the claims together. A public nuisance is the invasion of a right that is common to all members of the public. Because the primary responsibility for preventing public nuisances is with the public authorities, a private action to enforce that right requires proof that the plaintiff suffered an injury distinct from the injury that the public as a whole suffered. A private nuisance is an unreasonable non-trespassory interference with another's private use and enjoyment of land. The right to recover is in the person whose land is harmed.

Undesired exposure to sexual activity, such as the presence of a neighboring house of prostitution, is one of the traditional grounds for finding either a public or a private nuisance. *See* Prosser and Keeton on the *Law of Torts*, 5th ed. (W. Page Keeton, ed. 1984), §87 at 620, §90 at 644; 66 C.J.S. 796, *Nuisances* §45. In Blagen v. Smith, 56 P. 292 (Or. 1899), the plaintiffs owned manufacturing and other businesses near the waterfront just north of Burnside Street in Portland. The defendant built cheap wooden buildings, called "cribs," on a neighboring lot, with the apparent purpose of renting them to prostitutes. The plaintiffs sought an injunction to prevent him from doing so on the ground that that use constituted a public nuisance. The evidence indicated, among other things, that a prostitute inside one of the buildings, "in undress uniform," would negotiate with a group of potential customers who were standing outside.

The Supreme Court noted that other courts held that keeping a house of ill fame was a private nuisance when it rendered the premises of a neighbor "unfit for comfortable or respectable occupation and enjoyment[.]" The plaintiffs, however, sought an injunction on the ground that the "cribs" were a public nuisance, something that the Supreme Court accepted without question. The issue, thus, was whether the plaintiffs were entitled to enjoin that public nuisance.

To do so they had to prove that the effect of the nuisance on them was different in kind from that suffered by the public as a whole. The court held that it was different:

> All property in a city is affected by the maintenance of a bawdy house, just in proportion to its contiguity thereto, and the damage which such property sustains, while differing in degree, does not differ in kind; and, such being the case, the owner of any such property affected in the same general way as other property therein could not successfully invoke equitable relief to enjoin its continuance. *But where, by reason of the proximity of such property to the public nuisance, disgusting scenes and sounds shock the sense of those whose property, or the enjoyment thereof, is affected thereby, the injury sustained is necessarily different in kind from that suffered by the public at large. Id.* at 296 (emphasis added).

We have not found any Oregon case that indicates that nudity in itself, with no clear sexual component, constitutes a nuisance. On the one hand, public nudity is not illegal unless it occurs with the intent of arousing the sexual desire of either the actor or another person. On the other hand, an activity that is otherwise legal may still constitute a nuisance. Otherwise, among other things, there would have been no need to provide that farming and forestry practices conducted on land zoned for farm or forestry use outside an urban growth boundary do not give rise to an action for nuisance. *See* ORS 30.930 through ORS 30.947. The allegations in plaintiffs' original complaint are not limited to mere nudity but would support proof of uncontrolled and intrusive nudity occurring on the area immediately around their property. Whether a particular activity is a nuisance is primarily a factual question that requires applying well-established criteria. Although the question is the effect of the challenged activity on an ordinary person, and although the law does not protect the delicate, *see* Amphitheaters, Inc. v. Portland Meadows, 198 P.2d 847 (1948), plaintiff's allegations would allow finding that the nudity constituted a nuisance.

Plaintiffs also allege that they have been exposed not merely to nudity but also to a variety of sexual activity. A court could find that the routine use of defendants' land for public sexual activity was a public nuisance. Plaintiffs' allegations would also allow proof that, because of the proximity of their land to the intrusive nudity and the sexual activity, those things have affected their property or their enjoyment of it. If so, plaintiffs' injury would be different in kind from that of the public at large, and they would be entitled to sue to enjoin the public nuisance. The same facts would support a finding that the intrusive nudity and sexual activity impair their use and enjoyment of their land; they would thus constitute a private nuisance for which they could seek damages or an injunction.

That these actions on defendants' land may constitute a nuisance does not, in itself, create a claim against defendants. . . . [P]laintiffs' complaint is that defendants do not prevent third parties from engaging in public nudity and sexual activity on defendants' lands. That raises the question of whether a court can hold defendants responsible for the acts of third parties when those third parties' actions on defendants' land may constitute a nuisance.

The Restatement suggests that, in order to be liable for the acts of third parties that create a nuisance on their land, defendants must both (1) know that the activity is being carried on and will involve an unreasonable risk of causing the nuisance and (2) consent to the activity or fail to exercise reasonable care to prevent it. *Restatement (Second), Torts* §838 (1979). . . .

Plaintiffs allege that defendants have the authority to exercise control over the behavior of the members of the public who congregate in the wildlife area and that defendants, either knowingly and intentionally, or with reckless disregard for the rights and safety of the public, failed to exercise control over nudity in the wildlife area. That is sufficient to allege that defendants are responsible for the actions of the public under the criteria of section 838. . . .

[Plaintiffs' amended complaint] focused on a management plan that defendants adopted in 1993 in order to regulate nudity in the wildlife area. Plaintiffs first attack the underlying decision to regulate and control public nudity rather than to attempt to eliminate it. That approach, they allege, conflicts with defendants' mission to permit only wildlife-related activities in the wildlife area. Plaintiffs then describe the plan as, among other things, distinguishing between "clothing optional" and "clothed" areas, providing for buffer areas between the clothing optional area and private lands, and prohibiting any use of those buffer areas during the warmer months. The plan also contains provisions concerning signs and other matters that were intended to discourage or eliminate public nudity outside of the designated nude beach area. . . .

Plaintiffs and other residents are helpless to prevent "continuous and oftentimes daily exposure" to nudity. They allege that defendants are negligent by failing to develop a plan that is adequate to control, discourage, or eliminate nudity, by failing adequately to implement the plan that they did adopt, and by failing to consider the effect that nude recreation would have on plaintiffs' interests in their private property, thus breaching a nondiscretionary duty to plaintiffs under ORS 496.138. . . .

Whether plaintiffs' amended complaint states a claim for a public or private nuisance is a closer issue than is their original complaint. It is less clear from the amended complaint that plaintiffs' land has been affected by sexual activity rather than simple nudity, and it now appears that defendants are in fact attempting to reduce the impact of public nudity on plaintiffs. As plaintiffs describe the plan, if implemented it will eliminate the effect of intrusive nudity on their land, thus ending any private nuisance. It will similarly end the special injury to plaintiffs from any public nuisance.

Plaintiffs' continuing claims must be based on their allegation that defendants are failing to implement the plan adequately. Under section 838 of the Restatement, they must also show that defendants' failure to implement the plan is the result of their lack of reasonable care. A number of plaintiffs' concerns, such as embarrassment at coming in contact with public nudity or their fear for their safety because of their proximity to the nude beach, are things that they share in common with the public at large and thus cannot support a claim for a public nuisance. Those things are also not directly related to the use and enjoyment of plaintiffs' land and therefore do not support a claim for a private nuisance. Plaintiffs' reliance on ORS 496.138 to establish that defendants have a duty to them as property owners to prevent nudity and limit the use of the wildlife area to wildlife-related uses is unavailing. As we discuss below, the statute sets forth the general duty of the State Fish and Wildlife Commission to implement state policies for the management of wildlife. Nothing in the statement of the Commission's responsibilities creates any private rights.

We conclude, despite these concerns, that the amended complaint states a claim for both a public and private nuisance, because its allegations could be read to include those things that we found sufficient in the original complaint and because it alleges that defendants have failed to implement the management plan. That conclusion means that plaintiffs are entitled to pursue their injunction claims.

The essence of plaintiffs' claim for damages is that defendants had a non-discretionary duty to exercise their authority over the wildlife area to reduce or eliminate nudity and its effects. . . . However, [under the Oregon statutes Fish and Wildlife] has discretion about whether to regulate nude recreation in the wildlife area and, if so, how to regulate it. That is the essence of discretionary immunity under [the state Tort Claims Act]. . . .

Reversed and remanded on claims for injunctive relief for private and public nuisance; otherwise affirmed.

EDMONDS, Judge, dissenting. The majority holds that plaintiffs have properly pled a claim for nuisance against the defendant agencies but that the agencies are immune from liability for damages. . . .

In my view, the duty of a state agency to exercise discretion to prevent harm to adjoining lands from activities on land under its control is nondiscretionary under the statute. It is like the duty of a public body to exercise discretion to prevent harm from a known dangerous condition such as the existence of a dam on a river typically used by boaters or the duty to exercise discretion to maintain traffic signals so that motorists will not be misled and injured when they use a public intersection. [The statute] affords no immunity from damages in this case. . . .

Notes and Questions

1. On remand, the trial court held that "a private nuisance exists as to regular intrusive nudity which is visible from plaintiffs' property," and "as to the numerous episodes of illegal sexual conduct occurring on defendant's property which is observable from plaintiffs' property." Mark v. Oregon, 84 P.3d 155, 161 (Or. App. 2004) (quoting the trial court's unpublished letter opinion). The Court of Appeals affirmed that decision, too. The court emphasized that "[h]undreds, and perhaps thousands, of naked adults engaged in various activities on defendants' property in plain view of plaintiffs' property. At least a dozen times a year, plaintiffs or their guests saw adults engaged in explicit sexual conduct on defendants' property and, occasionally, on plaintiffs' property." Id. at 162. The court further held that the record failed to show that the use of the wildlife area was — or should have been — known to the plaintiffs when they brought the property. And the court affirmed the terms of the trial court's injunction, which ordered the state to "adequately staff the area in and around plaintiffs' property to adequately police compliance," to "establish a buffer of sufficient length to avoid viewing of nude sunbathers on Collins Beach from plaintiffs' real property," and to "sufficiently sign the North boundary." Id. at 165.

2. A host of older cases found immoral conduct to be a private nuisance or a public nuisance that could be challenged by neighboring landowners. The cases involved houses of prostitution, saloons, illegal liquor establishments, unlicensed prize fights, massage parlors, an unmarried couple living next door, and gambling houses. Most of the recent moral nuisance cases have been brought by the state against a public nuisance, rather than by a landowner objecting to a neighbor's immoral activities. See Masterson v. Arkansas ex rel. Bryant, 949 S.W.2d 63 (Ark.

1997) (enjoining the operation of two commercial bingo halls as public nuisances); Ohio ex rel. Montgomery v. Pakrats Motorcycle Club, Inc., 693 N.E.2d 310 (Ohio App. 1997) (holding that an annual party that attracted as many as 8,000 people and at which public sex occurred in front of children was a public nuisance). The nature of the harm in such cases is discussed in John Copeland Nagle, *Moral Nuisances*, 50 Emory L.J. 265, 269 n.18 (2001).

3. In *Mark*, the court cited Amphitheaters, Inc. v. Portland Meadows, 198 P.2d 847 (Or. 1948), for the proposition that "the law does not protect the delicate." In *Amphitheaters*, two landowners began construction on projects on their neighboring land north of Portland. One landowner was building a horse race track equipped for night racing; the other landowner was building a drive-in theater. The drive-in sued, but the court held that the lighted race track was not a nuisance. The court explained that "whether a particular annoyance or inconvenience is sufficient to constitute a nuisance depends upon its effect upon an ordinarily reasonable man, that is, a normal person of ordinary habits and sensibilities." It added that the drive-in's suit fell within the rule that "a man cannot increase the liabilities of his neighbor by applying his own property to special and delicate uses, whether for business or pleasure." This nuisance law principle is in contrast with the general rule in other torts cases, in which a defendant cannot escape liability simply because an injury resulted from the plaintiff's particular sensibilities. Why should the law be different in nuisance cases? Alternately, should the question of the sensibilities of the plaintiff be addressed differently when the alleged nuisance is immoral conduct rather than environmental contamination, noise, or odors?

4. A remedial issue raised by *Mark* is whether to award the nuisance victim injunctive relief or damages. In the famous case of Spur Industries Inc. v. Del E. Webb Development Co., 494 P.2d 700 (Ariz. 1972), a developer placed a retirement community near cattle feedlots. The feedlot operator had begun its operations many years before the Phoenix metropolitan area began expanding in the direction of the feedlot. To protect the residents, the court ordered the feedlots to close, but adopted an innovative remedy, conditioning relief on the developer's payment of the costs of closing or relocating the feedlots.

Spur Industries is often paired with Boomer v. Atlantic Cement Co., 257 N.E.2d 870 (N.Y. 1970), where the court issued an injunction against a polluting cement plant, but provided that the injunction would be lifted if the plant paid the permanent damages suffered by the neighbors. Judge Jasen dissented in *Boomer* because he would have made the injunction permanent lest the cement plant be given a right to pollute the air. Together, *Spur Industries* and *Boomer* illustrate the possible remedies described by Professors Calabresi and Melamed in their landmark article, *Property Rules, Liability Rules, and Inalienability: One View of the Cathedral*, excerpted in Chapter 1. Their scheme identifies four possible results:

	Plaintiff wins	**Defendant wins**
Property rule	*Boomer* dissent	Not a nuisance
Liability rule	*Boomer* majority	*Spur Industries*

Consider how each rule works. First, *the plaintiff can be protected by a property rule.* That is the traditional New York rule advocated by Judge Jasen in dissent in *Boomer*. It is also illustrated by McClung v. North Bend Coal & Coke Co., 1 Ohio Dec. 187

(Ohio Ct. Common Pleas 1892), where the court issued an injunction against a coking operation that destroyed more than 200 evergreen trees and impaired the health of people on the ancestral estate of President William Henry Harrison. Second, *the defendant can be protected by a property rule.* In other words, that is a holding of no liability. It is also exemplified by right-to-farm statutes that protect agricultural operations from nuisance liability. *See, e.g.,* Mich. Comp. Laws Ann. §§286.471-.474. Third, *the plaintiff can be protected by a liability rule.* That is the holding produced by the majority in *Boomer.* It is also seen in Madison v. Ducktown Sulphur, Copper & Iron Co., 83 S.W. 658 (Tenn. 1904), which held that landowners whose trees and crops were destroyed by copper smelter could not enjoin the operation of the smelter, and instead could only obtain damages. Fourth, *the defendant can be protected by a liability rule.* That is the holding in *Spur*— and no other reported case.

12

Government Land Use Restrictions

A. ZONING

■ **VILLAGE OF EUCLID v. AMBLER REALTY COMPANY**
Supreme Court of the United States, 1926
272 U.S. 365

SUTHERLAND, Justice. The Village of Euclid is an Ohio municipal corporation. It adjoins and practically is a suburb of the City of Cleveland. Its estimated population is between 5,000 and 10,000, and its area from twelve to fourteen square miles, the greater part of which is farm lands or unimproved acreage. It lies, roughly, in the form of a parallelogram measuring approximately three and one-half miles each way. East and west it is traversed by three principal highways: Euclid Avenue, through the southerly border, St. Clair Avenue, through the central portion, and Lake Shore Boulevard, through the northerly border in close proximity to the shore of Lake Erie. The Nickel Plate railroad lies from 1,500 to 1,800 feet north of Euclid Avenue, and the Lake Shore railroad 1,600 feet farther to the north. The three highways and the two railroads are substantially parallel.

Appellee is the owner of a tract of land containing 68 acres, situated in the westerly end of the village, abutting on Euclid Avenue to the south and the Nickel Plate railroad to the north. Adjoining this tract, both on the east and on the west, there have been laid out restricted residential plats upon which residences have been erected.

On November 13, 1922, an ordinance was adopted by the Village Council establishing a comprehensive zoning plan for regulating and restricting the location of trades, industries, apartment houses, two-family houses, single family houses, etc., the lot area to be built upon, the size and height of buildings, etc.

The entire area of the village is divided by the ordinance into six classes of use districts, denominated U-1 to U-6, inclusive; three classes of height districts, denominated H-1 to H-3, inclusive; and four classes of area districts, denominated A-1 to A-4, inclusive. The use districts are classified in respect of the buildings which may be erected within their respective limits, as follows: U-1 is restricted to single family dwellings, public parks, water towers and reservoirs, suburban and interurban electric railway passenger stations and rights of way, and farming, non-commercial greenhouse nurseries and truck gardening; U-2 is extended to include two-family dwellings; U-3 is further extended to include apartment houses, hotels, churches, schools, public libraries, museums, private clubs, community center buildings, hospitals, sanitariums, public playgrounds and recreation buildings, and a city hall and courthouse; U-4 is further extended to include banks, offices, studios, telephone exchanges, fire and police stations, restaurants, theatres and moving picture shows, retail stores and shops, sales offices, sample rooms, wholesale stores for hardware, drugs and groceries, stations for gasoline and oil (not exceeding 1,000 gallons storage) and for ice delivery, skating rinks and dance halls, electric substations, job and newspaper printing, public garages for motor vehicles, stables and wagon sheds (not exceeding five horses, wagons or motor trucks) and distributing stations for central store and commercial enterprises; U-5 is further extended to include billboards and advertising signs (if permitted), warehouses, ice and ice cream manufacturing and cold storage plants, bottling works, milk bottling and central distribution stations, laundries, carpet cleaning, dry cleaning and dyeing establishments, blacksmith, horseshoeing, wagon and motor vehicle repair shops, freight stations, street car barns, stables and wagon sheds (for more than five horses, wagons or motor trucks), and wholesale produce markets and salesrooms; U-6 is further extended to include plants for sewage disposal and for producing gas, garbage and refuse incineration, scrap iron, junk, scrap paper and rag storage, aviation fields, cemeteries, crematories, penal and correctional institutions, insane and feeble minded institutions, storage of oil and gasoline (not to exceed 25,000 gallons), and manufacturing and industrial operations of any kind other than, and any public utility not included in, a class U-1, U-2, U-3, U-4 or U-5 use. There is a seventh class of uses which is prohibited altogether.

Class U-1 is the only district in which buildings are restricted to those enumerated. In the other classes the uses are cumulative; that is to say, uses in class U-2 include those enumerated in the preceding class, U-1; class U-3 includes uses enumerated in the preceding classes, U-2 and U-1; and so on. In addition to the enumerated uses, the ordinance provides for accessory uses, that is, for uses customarily incident to the principal use, such as private garages. Many regulations are provided in respect of such accessory uses.

The height districts are classified as follows: In class H-1, buildings are limited to a height of two and one-half stories or thirty-five feet; in class H-2, to four stories or fifty feet; in class H-3, to eighty feet. To all of these, certain exceptions are made, as in the case of church spires, water tanks, etc.

The classification of area districts is: In A-1 districts, dwellings or apartment houses to accommodate more than one family must have at least 5,000 square feet for interior lots and at least 4,000 square feet for corner lots; in A-2 districts, the area must be at least 2,500 square feet for interior lots, and 2,000 square feet for corner lots; in A-3 districts, the limits are 1,250 and 1,000 square feet, respectively; in A-4 districts, the limits are 900 and 700 square feet, respectively. The ordinance contains, in great variety and detail, provisions in respect of width of lots, front, side and rear yards, and other matters, including restrictions and regulations as to the use of billboards, signboards and advertising signs. . . .

Appellee's tract of land comes under U-2, U-3 and U-6. The first strip of 620 feet immediately north of Euclid Avenue falls in class U-2, the next 130 feet to the north, in U-3, and the remainder in U-6. The uses of the first 620 feet, therefore, do not include apartment houses, hotels, churches, schools, or other public and semi-public buildings, or other uses enumerated in respect of U-3 to U-6, inclusive. The uses of the next 130 feet include all of these, but exclude industries, theatres, banks, shops, and the various other uses set forth in respect of U-4 to U-6, inclusive.

Annexed to the ordinance, and made a part of it, is a zone map, showing the location and limits of the various use, height and area districts, from which it appears that the three classes overlap one another; that is to say, for example, both U-5 and U-6 use districts are in A-4 area districts, but the former is in H-2 and the latter in H-3 height districts. The plan is a complicated one and can be better understood by an inspection of the map, though it does not seem necessary to reproduce it for present purposes.

The lands lying between the two railroads for the entire length of the village area and extending some distance on either side to the north and south, having an average width of about 1,600 feet, are left open, with slight exceptions, for industrial and all other uses. This includes the larger part of appellee's tract. Approximately one-sixth of the area of the entire village is included in U-5 and U-6 use districts. That part of the village lying south of Euclid Avenue is principally in U-1 districts. The lands lying north of Euclid Avenue and bordering on the long strip just described are included in U-1, U-2, U-3 and U-4 districts, principally in U-2.

The enforcement of the ordinance is entrusted to the inspector of buildings, under rules and regulations of the board of zoning appeals. Meetings of the board are public, and minutes of its proceedings are kept. It is authorized to adopt rules and regulations to carry into effect provisions of the ordinance. Decisions of the inspector of buildings may be appealed to the board by any person claiming to be adversely affected by any such decision. The board is given power in specific cases of practical difficulty or unnecessary hardship to interpret the ordinance in harmony with its general purpose and intent, so that the public health, safety and general welfare may be secure and substantial justice done. Penalties are prescribed for violations, and it is provided that the various provisions are to be regarded as independent and the holding of any provision to be unconstitutional, void or ineffective shall not affect any of the others.

The ordinance is assailed on the grounds that it is in derogation of §1 of the Fourteenth Amendment to the Federal Constitution in that it deprives appellee of liberty and property without due process of law and denies it the equal protection of the law, and that it offends against certain provisions of the Constitution of the State of Ohio. The prayer of the bill is for an injunction restraining the enforcement of the ordinance and all attempts to impose or maintain as to appellee's property any of the restrictions, limitations or conditions. The court below held the ordinance to be unconstitutional and void, and enjoined its enforcement. 297 Fed. 307.

Before proceeding to a consideration of the case, it is necessary to determine the scope of the inquiry. The bill alleges that the tract of land in question is vacant and has been held for years for the purpose of selling and developing it for industrial uses, for which it is especially adapted, being immediately in the path of progressive industrial development; that for such uses it has a market value of about $10,000 per acre, but if the use be limited to residential purposes the market value is not in excess of $2,500 per acre; that the first 200 feet of the parcel back from Euclid Avenue, if unrestricted in respect of use, has a value of $150 per front foot, but if limited to residential uses, and ordinary mercantile business be excluded therefrom, its value is not in excess of $50 per front foot.

It is specifically averred that the ordinance attempts to restrict and control the lawful uses of appellee's land so as to confiscate and destroy a great part of its value; that it is being enforced in accordance with its terms; that prospective buyers of land for industrial, commercial and residential uses in the metropolitan district of Cleveland are deterred from buying any part of this land because of the existence of the ordinance and the necessity thereby entailed of conducting burdensome and expensive litigation in order to vindicate the right to use the land for lawful and legitimate purposes; that the ordinance constitutes a cloud upon the land, reduces and destroys its value, and has the effect of diverting the normal industrial, commercial and residential development thereof to other and less favorable locations.

The record goes no farther than to show, as the lower court found, that the normal, and reasonably to be expected, use and development of that part of appellee's land adjoining Euclid Avenue is for general trade and commercial purposes, particularly retail stores and like establishments, and that the normal, and reasonably to be expected, use and development of the residue of the land is for industrial and trade purposes. Whatever injury is inflicted by the mere existence and threatened enforcement of the ordinance is due to restrictions in respect of these and similar uses; to which perhaps should be added — if not included in the foregoing — restrictions in respect of apartment houses. Specifically, there is nothing in the record to suggest that any damage results from the presence in the ordinance of those restrictions relating to churches, schools, libraries and other public and semi-public buildings. It is neither alleged nor proved that there is, or may be, a demand for any part of appellee's land for any of the last named uses; and we cannot assume the existence of facts which would justify an injunction upon this record in respect of this class of restrictions. For present purposes the provisions of the ordinance in respect of these uses may, therefore, be put aside as unnecessary to be considered. It is also unnecessary to consider the effect of the restrictions in respect of U-1 districts, since none of appellee's land falls within that class.

We proceed, then, to a consideration of those provisions of the ordinance to which the case as it is made relates, first disposing of a preliminary matter.

A motion was made in the court below to dismiss the bill on the ground that, because complainant [appellee] had made no effort to obtain a building permit or apply to the zoning board of appeals for relief as it might have done under the terms of the ordinance, the suit was premature. The motion was properly overruled. The effect of the allegations of the bill is that the ordinance of its own force operates greatly to reduce the value of appellee's lands and destroy their marketability for industrial, commercial and residential uses; and the attack is directed, not against any specific provision or provisions, but against the ordinance as an entirety. Assuming the premises, the existence and maintenance of the ordinance, in effect, constitutes a present invasion of appellee's property rights and a threat to continue it. Under these circumstances, the equitable jurisdiction is clear. . . .

Building zone laws are of modern origin. They began in this country about twenty-five years ago. Until recent years, urban life was comparatively simple; but with the great increase and concentration of population, problems have developed, and constantly are developing, which require, and will continue to require, additional restrictions in respect of the use and occupation of private lands in urban communities. Regulations, the wisdom, necessity and validity of which, as applied to existing conditions, are so apparent that they are now uniformly sustained, a century ago, or even half a century ago, probably would have been rejected as arbitrary and oppressive. Such regulations are sustained, under the complex conditions of our day, for reasons analogous to those which justify traffic regulations, which, before the advent of automobiles and rapid transit street railways, would have been condemned as fatally arbitrary and unreasonable. And in this there is no inconsistency, for while the meaning of constitutional guaranties never varies, the scope of their application must expand or contract to meet the new and different conditions which are constantly coming within the field of their operation. In a changing world, it is impossible that it should be otherwise. But although a degree of elasticity is thus imparted, not to the *meaning*, but to the *application* of constitutional principles, statutes and ordinances, which, after giving due weight to the new conditions, are found clearly not to conform to the Constitution, of course, must fall.

The ordinance now under review, and all similar laws and regulations, must find their justification in some aspect of the police power, asserted for the public welfare. The line which in this field separates the legitimate from the illegitimate assumption of power is not capable of precise delimitation. It varies with circumstances and conditions. A regulatory zoning ordinance, which would be clearly valid as applied to the great cities, might be clearly invalid as applied to rural communities. In solving doubts, the maxim *sic utere tuo ut alienum non laedas*, which lies at the foundation of so much of the common law of nuisances, ordinarily will furnish a fairly helpful clue. And the law of nuisances, likewise, may be consulted, not for the purpose of controlling, but for the helpful aid of its analogies in the process of ascertaining the scope of, the power. Thus the question whether the power exists to forbid the erection of a building of a particular kind or for a particular use, like the question whether a particular thing is a nuisance, is to be determined, not by an abstract consideration of the building or of the thing considered apart, but by considering it in connection with the circumstances and the locality. A nuisance may be merely a right thing in the wrong place, like a pig in the parlor instead of the barnyard. If the validity of the legislative classification for zoning purposes be fairly debatable, the legislative judgment must be allowed to control.

There is no serious difference of opinion in respect of the validity of laws and regulations fixing the height of buildings within reasonable limits, the character of materials and methods of construction, and the adjoining area which must be left open, in order to minimize the danger of fire or collapse, the evils of over-crowding, and the like, and excluding from residential sections offensive trades, industries and structures likely to create nuisances.

Here, however, the exclusion is in general terms of all industrial establishments, and it may thereby happen that not only offensive or dangerous industries will be excluded, but those which are neither offensive nor dangerous will share the same fate. But this is no more than happens in respect of many practice-forbidding laws which this Court has upheld although drawn in general terms so as to include individual cases that may turn out to be innocuous in themselves. The inclusion of a reasonable margin to ensure effective enforcement will not put upon a law, otherwise valid, the stamp of invalidity. Such laws may also find their justification in the fact that, in some fields, the bad fades into the good by such insensible degrees that the two are not capable of being readily distinguished and separated in terms of legislation. In the light of these considerations, we are not prepared to say that the end in view was not sufficient to justify the general rule of the ordinance, although some industries of an innocent character might fall within the proscribed class. It cannot be said that the ordinance in this respect "passes the bounds of reason and assumes the character of a merely arbitrary fiat." Purity Extract Co. v. Lynch, 226 U.S. 192, 204 (1912). Moreover, the restrictive provisions of the ordinance in this particular may be sustained upon the principles applicable to the broader exclusion from residential districts of all business and trade structures, presently to be discussed.

It is said that the Village of Euclid is a mere suburb of the City of Cleveland; that the industrial development of that city has now reached and in some degree extended into the village and, in the obvious course of things, will soon absorb the entire area for industrial enterprises; that the effect of the ordinance is to divert this natural development elsewhere with the consequent loss of increased values to the owners of the lands within the village borders. But the village, though physically a suburb of Cleveland, is politically a separate municipality, with powers of its own and authority to govern itself as it sees fit within the limits of the organic law of its creation and the State and Federal Constitutions. Its governing authorities, presumably representing a majority of its inhabitants and voicing their will, have determined, not that industrial development shall cease at its boundaries, but that the course of such development shall proceed within definitely fixed lines. If it be a proper exercise of the police power to relegate industrial establishments to localities separated from residential sections, it is not easy to find a sufficient reason for denying the power because the effect of its exercise is to divert an industrial flow from the course which it would follow to the injury of the residential public if left alone, to another course where such injury will be obviated. It is not meant by this, however, to exclude the possibility of cases where the general public interest would so far outweigh the interest of the municipality that the municipality would not be allowed to stand in the way.

We find no difficulty in sustaining restrictions of the kind thus far reviewed. The serious question in the case arises over the provisions of the ordinance excluding from residential districts, apartment houses, business houses, retail stores and shops, and other like establishments. This question involves the validity of what is really the crux of the more recent zoning legislation, namely, the creation and maintenance of residential districts, from which business and trade of every sort, including hotels and apartment houses, are excluded. Upon that question, this Court has not thus far spoken. The decisions of the state courts are numerous and conflicting; but those which broadly sustain the power greatly outnumber those which deny altogether or narrowly limit it; and it is very apparent that there is a constantly increasing tendency in the direction of the broader view. . . .

The matter of zoning has received much attention at the hands of commissions and experts, and the results of their investigations have been set forth in comprehensive reports. These reports, which bear every evidence of painstaking consideration, concur in the view that the segregation of residential, business, and industrial buildings will make it easier to provide fire apparatus suitable for the character and intensity of the development in each section; that it will increase the safety and security of home life; greatly tend to prevent street accidents, especially to children, by reducing the traffic and resulting confusion in residential sections; decrease noise and other conditions which produce or intensify nervous disorders; preserve a more favorable environment in which to rear children, etc. With particular reference to apartment houses, it is pointed out that the development of detached house sections is greatly retarded by the coming of apartment houses, which has sometimes resulted in destroying the entire section for private house purposes; that in such sections very often the apartment house is a mere parasite, constructed in order to take advantage of the open spaces and attractive surroundings created by the residential character of the district. Moreover, the coming of one apartment house is followed by others, interfering by their height and bulk with the free circulation of air and monopolizing the rays of the sun which otherwise would fall upon the smaller homes, and bringing, as their necessary accompaniments, the disturbing noises incident to increased traffic and business, and the occupation, by means of moving and parked automobiles, of larger portions of the streets, thus detracting from their safety and depriving children of the privilege of quiet and open spaces for play, enjoyed by those in more favored localities, until, finally, the residential character of the neighborhood and its desirability as a place of detached residences are utterly destroyed. Under these circumstances, apartment houses, which in a different environment would be not only entirely unobjectionable but highly desirable, come very near to being nuisances.

If these reasons, thus summarized, do not demonstrate the wisdom or sound policy in all respects of those restrictions which we have indicated as pertinent to the inquiry, at least, the reasons are sufficiently cogent to preclude us from saying, as it must be said before the ordinance can be declared unconstitutional, that such provisions are clearly arbitrary and unreasonable, having no substantial relation to the public health, safety, morals, or general welfare.

It is true that when, if ever, the provisions set forth in the ordinance in tedious and minute detail, come to be concretely applied to particular premises, including those of the appellee, or to particular conditions, or to be considered in connection with specific complaints, some of them, or even many of them, may be found to be clearly arbitrary and unreasonable. But where the equitable remedy of injunction is sought, as it is here, not upon the ground of a present infringement or denial of a specific right, or of a particular injury in process of actual execution, but upon the broad ground that the mere existence and threatened enforcement of the ordinance, by materially and adversely affecting values and curtailing the opportunities of the market, constitute a present and irreparable injury, the court will not scrutinize its provisions, sentence by sentence, to ascertain by a process of piecemeal dissection whether there may be, here and there, provisions of a minor character, or relating to matters of administration, or not shown to contribute to the injury complained of, which, if attacked separately, might not withstand the test of constitutionality. In respect of such provisions, of which specific complaint is not made, it cannot be said that the landowner has suffered or is threatened with an injury which entitles him to challenge their constitutionality. . . .

The relief sought here is of the same character, namely, an injunction against the enforcement of any of the restrictions, limitations or conditions of the ordinance. And the gravamen of the complaint is that a portion of the land of the appellee cannot be sold for certain enumerated uses because of the general and broad restraints of the ordinance. What would be the effect of a restraint imposed by one or more of the innumerable provisions of the ordinance, considered apart, upon the value or marketability of the lands is neither disclosed by the bill nor by the evidence, and we are afforded no basis, apart from mere speculation, upon which to rest a conclusion that it or they would have any appreciable effect upon those matters. Under these circumstances, therefore, it is enough for us to determine, as we do, that the ordinance in its general scope and dominant features, so far as its provisions are here involved, is a valid exercise of authority, leaving other provisions to be dealt with as cases arise directly involving them. . . .

Decree reversed.

Justice VAN DEVANTER, Justice McREYNOLDS, and Justice BUTLER, dissent [without an opinion].

Notes and Questions

1. *A zoning problem.* Zoning law is an effort to arrange the use of land in a manner that provides the greatest benefit to the public. But even if you have the power to

decide which land can be used in which ways, it is not easy to locate each use in a place that is consistent with every other use. For example, the map set forth below contains 12 zones of land, and 12 different uses of the land are listed beneath the map. How would you best arrange each of the 12 uses in the 12 zones on the map?

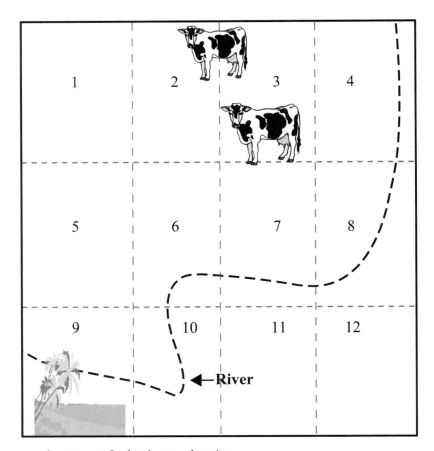

Apartments for low-income housing
Church for 2,500 people
Factory to manufacture car parts
Gambling casino
Hospital
Landfill
Mall with 200 stores
Office building 25 stories high
Park with playgrounds, lighted tennis courts, and lighted ball fields
Residential subdivision for single-family homes
School for 2,500 high school students
Wildlife refuge

2. Zoning developed in the twentieth century as private agreements and judicial doctrines failed to control the growth of large cities. Nuisance law was viewed as too reactive and too expensive to enforce. Covenants worked only in new subdivisions and other instances involving an original common owner. Earlier legislation

focused on specific activities — like laundries, taverns, and slaughterhouses — that were treated like nuisances if they were located in the wrong place. The first general attempt at zoning occurred in Los Angeles, where the city divided itself into zones between 1909 and 1915. New York followed by enacting comprehensive zoning in 1916 after an advisory committee concluded that "there is too much at stake to permit a habit of thought as to private property rights to stand in the way of a plan that is essential to the health, order and welfare of the entire city and to the conservation of property values." Many other cities enacted similar zoning laws during the next decade. Today, most American cities have zoning laws.

3. The zoning approved in *Euclid* is usually portrayed as the victory of community planning over unbridled individualism. But there is an alternative, more sinister version of that history. Professor Richard Chused asserts that it was possible for Justice Sutherland, "without ever mentioning race, immigration, or tenement houses, to call upon other code words that had the same impact." Richard S. Chused, Euclid's *Historical Imagery*, 51 Case W. Res. L. Rev. 597, 614 (2001). Chused explains that Euclid Avenue — otherwise known as "Millionaire's Avenue" because of the mansions that lined the street heading toward Cleveland — "had begun to fall upon hard times. Some of its mansions had given way to gas stations or other uses, and a few had turned into apartments." *Id.* at 603. Euclid Avenue was also home to James Metzenbaum, the village counsel and the author of the zoning ordinance. Moreover, the district judge who struck down the ordinance explicitly analogized the case to Buchanan v. Worley, 245 U.S. 60 (1917), which had struck down a city ordinance that prohibited "colored" people from occupying certain houses. And the Supreme Court brief filed by the head of the National Conference on City Planning emphasized that houses needed to be separated from apartments because "[t]he man who seeks to place the home for his children in an orderly neighborhood, with some open space and light and fresh air and quiet, is not motivated so much by considerations of taste or beauty as by the assumption that his children are likely to grow mentally, physically and morally more healthful in such a neighborhood than in a disorderly, noisy, slovenly, blighted and slum-like district. This assumption is indubitably correct." Chused, *supra* at 612 (quoting the brief).

The standard account of *Euclid* must also account for the aftermath of the Supreme Court's decision. In 1941, the land at issue in the case was rezoned to accommodate a one million square foot General Motors factory that manufactured aircraft engines and landing gear during World War II. The factory switched to auto bodies after the war, and then to seats and trim for Cadillacs and other GM cars in 1970. Then, in 1994, General Motors closed the plant. "Surprisingly for the community that put zoning on the map, the huge plant's immediate surroundings today are a potpourri of residential, commercial, and industrial uses. Modest bungalows and high-rise apartments, including some subsidized developments, are intermingled in the streets that stretch north from Euclid Avenue to the railroad lines that bisect the city." Ruth Eckdish Knack, *Return to* Euclid, Planning, Nov. 1996.

4. *Euclid* did not end the constitutional challenges to zoning laws. Indeed, two years later the Supreme Court held in Nectow v. City of Cambridge, 277 U.S. 183 (1928), that a particular application of a zoning ordinance was unconstitutional because it lacked a substantial relation to public health, morals, safety, or welfare. But since then due process objections to zoning laws have rarely succeeded. For example, consider Board of County Commissioners of Teton County, Wyoming v. Crow, 65 P.3d 720 (Wyo. 2003), which rejected both a facial and as-applied

constitutional challenge to Teton County's maximum lot size provision. Instead, takings challenges of the sort described in Chapter 14 have become more common.

5. The academic debate over need for and effects of zoning persists despite its nearly universal acceptance in the United States. Opponents of zoning regard it as *unnecessary*, because the market and private agreements will produce the optimum land use decisions; *inefficient*, because it encourages suburban sprawl and forces low-income residents to travel farther to work; *expensive*, because of the costs of maintaining an administrative bureaucracy and paying lawyers to secure compliance; *inequitable*, because it can be manipulated more easily by those with wealth and power; *hostile to private property rights*, for the reasons rejected in *Euclid*; and *discriminatory*, as witnessed by the complaints of exclusionary zoning discussed below in Section B of this chapter. Proponents of zoning respond that it avoids conflicting uses that are not remedied by other laws, stimulates municipal economic growth, corrects for market distortions favoring the wealthy, is flexible in actual application, is successful in preserving communities, and is consistent with democratic norms by encouraging public participation in land use decisions for the larger community. Who is more persuasive?

6. Consider the following sign:

Why would a city — even a small city with a population of slightly more than 1,000 people — highlight its commitment to zoning as the single feature to announce to anyone entering town?

■ SNAKE RIVER BREWING COMPANY v. TOWN OF JACKSON
Supreme Court of Wyoming, 2002
39 P.3d 397

Voigt, Justice. In 1993, Snake River Brewing Company, Inc. (Snake River) obtained from the Town of Jackson (the Town) a building permit for a restaurant and micro-brewery. Snake River then invested approximately $1,768,000.00 in the project. The zoning ordinances in effect at the time allowed Snake River to choose from three methods of providing patron parking: on-site, off-site, and fee in-lieu-of parking. Snake River chose a combination of on-site parking and off-site leased parking. The Town approved this arrangement. In 1995, the Town amended its zoning ordinances so that Snake River's property was no longer in the area approved for payment of a fee in-lieu-of parking. In 1996, the Town approved an expansion of Snake River's project, and Snake River eventually invested another $1,000,000.00 or so in the business. In 1998, Snake River's parking lease became, in its opinion, cost-prohibitive, so it searched for other alternatives, including paying the fee in-lieu-of parking. The Town has taken the position that Snake River abandoned the fee in-lieu-of parking choice by not adopting it initially in 1993, or within twelve months of issuance of the building permit, and that Snake River has now abandoned the off-site choice by not renewing its parking lease for twelve months.

Snake River has appealed the district court's order granting summary judgment to the Town in a declaratory judgment action. Finding that summary judgment should have been granted to Snake River, rather than the Town, we reverse. . . .

PLANNING AND ZONING

Since the concept of a "non-conforming use" must be understood within the context of planning and zoning law, it may be helpful first to define those general terms:

> Planning may range in scope from a study of the parking needs of a community, followed by a proposed solution, to a comprehensive plan for the development of an entire municipality, or even a region which includes several municipalities. It is a generic term, and not a word of art unless its dimensions are marked out by a statute or ordinance.

1 Kenneth H. Young, *Anderson's American Law of Zoning* §1.03 at 7 (4th ed. 1996). Municipal planning in Wyoming has as its goal the development of a "master plan for the physical development of the municipality." Wyo. Stat. Ann. §15-1-503(a) (LexisNexis 2001). "The plan shall be made for the general purpose of guiding and accomplishing a coordinated, adjusted and harmonious development of the municipality which will best promote the general welfare as well as efficiency and economy in the process of development." Wyo. Stat. Ann. §15-1-504 (LexisNexis 2001). "Planning, therefore, is more than a suggested pattern of land use; it involves the planning of all the usual public improvements and services which go into making up the community." Ford v. Board of County Com'rs of Converse County, 924 P.2d 91, 95 (Wyo. 1996).

Zoning is a planning tool that must be used in accordance with a comprehensive plan.

> Comprehensive zoning consists of the division of the whole territory of a municipality into districts, and the imposition of restrictions upon the use of land in such districts. . . . [Zoning regulations] permit a municipality to apply constant and consistent pressure upon landowners to the end that land use will be guided by the community plan and the public interest.

1 Young, *supra*, §1.13 at 20 (footnote omitted). Municipal zoning in Wyoming contemplates the division of a town into districts, with uniform regulations within each district. We have described zoning as "the process that a community employs to legally control the use which may be made of property and the physical configuration of development upon the tracts of land located within its jurisdiction." *Ford*, 924 P.2d at 94. Zoning ordinances may regulate both the nature of the land usage and the physical dimension of uses, including height, setbacks, and minimum areas. The comprehensive plan is the policy statement; the zoning ordinances are what have the force and effect of law.

When a zoning ordinance goes into effect, almost invariably there will be existing buildings or uses that do not meet the new regulations for the zoning district in which they are located. Such buildings or uses are called "non-conforming uses."

> A non-conforming use is a use which, although it does not conform with existing zoning regulations, existed lawfully prior to the enactment of the zoning regulations. These uses are permitted to continue, although technically in violation of the current zoning regulations, until they are abandoned. An exception of this kind is commonly referred to as a "grandfather" exception.

River Springs Ltd. Liability Co. v. Board of County Com'rs of County of Teton, 899 P.2d 1329, 1334 (Wyo. 1995).

"When a zoning ordinance is enacted, it cannot outlaw previously existing nonconforming uses." Snake River Venture v. Board of County Com'rs, Teton County, 616 P.2d 744, 750 (Wyo. 1980). This right to continue a non-conforming use is a vested property right, protected by statute, and by both federal and state constitutions. Wyoming's county and municipal zoning statutes both protect vested property rights, although in different ways. Wyo. Stat. Ann. §18-5-207 (LexisNexis 2001) simply forbids counties from enacting zoning regulations that prohibit existing uses. Wyo. Stat. Ann. §15-1-601(d)(iv), on the other hand, renders invalid any municipal zoning regulation that constitutes an unconstitutional taking without compensation. This Court has also noted that the doctrine of equitable estoppel plays a role in denying the authority to outlaw a grandfathered use. *Snake River Venture*, 616 P.2d at 750. "The concept of vested rights is a judicial construct designed to provide individual relief in zoning cases involving egregious statutory or bureaucratic inequities." Ebzery v. City of Sheridan, 982 P.2d 1251, 1257 (Wyo. 1999).

Because zoning ordinances are in derogation of the common law, and because they operate to deprive property owners of a use thereof that would otherwise be lawful, the general rule is to construe zoning ordinances strictly in favor of the property owner. This rule does not, however, hold true for non-conforming uses which thwart the public policies behind comprehensive plans. Consequently, courts narrowly construe the right to continue a non-conforming use.

The right to continue a non-conforming use exists only so long as the use, itself, continues to exist. Four principal methods of termination of a non-conforming use have been recognized: (1) abandonment; (2) discontinuance or non-use for a prescribed period; (3) amortization; and (4) voluntary or involuntary destruction. Neither amortization nor destruction is at issue in the instant case. However, both abandonment and discontinuance must be addressed because, although they are distinct theories, both are mentioned in the Town's zoning ordinance:

> If a nonconforming use is operationally *discontinued or abandoned for a period of more than twelve (12) consecutive months, whether or not* the equipment or furniture are removed, or *there is an intention to resume such activity in the future,* such use may not be reestablished or resumed, and any subsequent use shall conform to the provisions specified by these Land Development Regulations. When government action, a natural disaster, or any other action not considered a willful act of the owner or occupant can be documented as the reason for discontinuance or abandonment, such time of discontinuance or

abandonment shall not be calculated for the purpose of this Section. Regardless of the reason for discontinuance or abandonment, the period for reestablishing the non-conforming use may be extended by the Town Council for just cause.

Town of Jackson Land Development Regulations, §7160 (emphasis added).

Historically, abandonment of a non-conforming use has been said to occur upon the concurrence of two factors: an intention to abandon and some overt act or failure to act that implies the owner's renunciation of the use. Abandonment has been equated with waiver, that is, "'the voluntary intentional relinquishment of a known right.'" 4 E.C. Yokley, *Zoning Law and Practice* §22-13, at 93 (4th ed. 1979). The burden of proving an abandonment, which is a question of fact, lies with the party asserting abandonment.

Where a statute or ordinance provides for loss of the right to a non-conforming use upon non-use or discontinuance for a prescribed period of time, the party asserting the discontinuance need not prove intent to abandon as part of a *prima facie* case. However, there are two views as to the legal effect of the simple passage of time:

> Many jurisdictions provide easier routes for terminating a nonconforming use on the basis of nonuse. Some jurisdictions impose a presumption of intent to abandon a nonconforming use upon the running of a certain period of nonuse. Thus, all a challenger need show to make out a prima facie case in such a jurisdiction is nonuse for the designated period. Still, the owner of the nonconforming use could come back with evidence to rebut the presumption. A number of jurisdictions have taken a more aggressive stance by allowing zoning authorities to do away with the intent issue altogether upon the running of a certain period of nonuse. In these jurisdictions, termination is automatic once nonuse over the discontinuance period is proved.

8A McQuillin, *supra*, §25.191 at 68-69 (footnotes omitted). . . .

DISCUSSION

In this action, the Town seeks a judicial declaration that, because Snake River chose to provide a combination of on-site parking and off-site leased parking, Snake River's right to pay a fee in-lieu-of providing on-site parking was not grandfathered as part of its non-conforming use. Alternatively, if this Court finds that the choice of paying the fee in-lieu-of parking was part of the non-conforming use, then the Town argues that such right was abandoned when Snake River failed to pay the fee within twelve months of receiving its building permit. Finally, the Town's position is that the passage of twelve months after Snake River's off-site parking lease expired has also resulted in abandonment or discontinuance of that use.

Snake River responds, first, with the contention that what was grandfathered as part of the non-conforming use was the option available under the old code Section 18.38.040, not just the one choice of off-site leased parking. Second, Snake River argues that its conduct, including its attempt to negotiate a reasonable lease or purchase of the parking lot, and its pursuit of the fee in-lieu-of parking alternative indicates it did not intend to abandon its rights.

We agree with the district court that there are no genuine issues of material fact in this case. We do not, however, agree that the Town is entitled to judgment as a matter of law. The district court ruled in favor of the Town on the ground that there is no vested right to a potential use of property; to be grandfathered, there must be an actual use at the time the new zoning ordinance comes into effect. While this premise is true, we do not find that it controls the decision in this case.

The concept of vested rights is applied to non-conforming uses to protect property owners' investments in their property. For that reason, where substantial funds have not yet been expended on a proposed use, that proposed use is not considered to be a non-conforming use. The district court relied on this theory in ruling against Snake River, concluding that since Snake River had not paid the fee in-lieu-of parking, that choice was not part of the grandfathered non-conforming use. We disagree.

The Snake River Brewing Company

As this case has been presented, the relevant inquiry is the extent of the vested right grandfathered as a legally non-conforming use.[7] The answer lies in an analysis of what is an appropriate exercise of a municipality's police powers. We have long held that a municipality may, through the exercise of its police power, regulate property usage without paying compensation, so long as the purpose of the regulation is to protect the public "'health, safety, morals and general welfare,'" and the means used to implement the regulation are reasonable. *Sun Ridge Development, Inc. v. City of Cheyenne*, 787 P.2d 583, 589-90 (Wyo. 1990). As mentioned above, Wyoming's municipal zoning statutes specifically recognize that zoning regulations may not "constitute[] an unconstitutional taking without compensation." Wyo. Stat. Ann. §15-1-601(d)(iv).

There is no precise test available to determine reasonableness; rather, each case must be judged on its own facts. The Wyoming State Legislature has specifically

---

7. Because the parties have presented this question solely in terms of a non-conforming use, we will not address the issue of whether an "accessory use," such as parking, can become the basis for establishment of a non-conforming use. The primary use of Snake River's property as a restaurant and microbrewery is not a use that once was lawful and now is unlawful. It was and is lawful. In that sense, it is not a non-conforming use. The parties have, however, treated it thus, and we will follow their lead for purposes of this case.

authorized municipalities to design plans to "lessen congestion in the streets," which certainly extends to the authority to regulate business parking. Wyo. Stat. Ann. §15-1-601(d)(i)(A). The primary question presented in the instant case is whether the Town's interpretation of its zoning regulations unreasonably will deprive Snake River of a substantial portion of the value of its property. In answering such questions, courts often compare the gain or benefit to the public to the seriousness of the injury or loss to the owner. The test has also been stated as whether enforcement of the new ordinance would render "valueless substantial improvements or businesses built up over the years [or] cause serious financial harm to the property owner." People v. Miller, 106 N.E.2d 34, 36 (N.Y. 1952). . . .

We conclude that the only reasonable interpretation of the Town's zoning ordinances is that all three choices under the parking option remained available to Snake River as part of its non-conforming use. No reasonable town official would have intended the ordinances to require a property owner to gamble his investment on the single hope that an off-site leased parking arrangement would exist indefinitely in the future. The only reasonable interpretation of the ordinances is that expensive improvements could be made to the property with the assurance that the owner would be able to provide patron parking in the future, even if off-site leased parking later became unavailable due to cost, through one of the other methods allowed under the zoning ordinances. The continuation of Snake River's non-conforming use "carries with it all the incidents of that use which appertained to it" under the original zoning ordinances. Abbadessa v. Board of Zoning Appeals of City of New Haven, 54 A.2d 675, 678 (Conn. 1947). When the Town approved this project in 1993, there was insufficient space on Snake River's property to provide on-site patron parking. Both Snake River and the Town knew that, in the future, parking would have to be accommodated off-site or through payment of the fee in-lieu-of parking.

We also conclude, both in the context of equitable estoppel and in the context of the reasonable exercise of its police power, that the Town may not enforce its new zoning ordinances so as to deprive Snake River of a substantial portion of the value of its investment in its property. Under the circumstances of this case, a strict construction of the ordinances is appropriate to protect the right of Snake River to make lawful use of its property. The Town amended the zoning ordinances to take Snake River out of the fee in-lieu-of zone after Snake River relied on the existing ordinances and the Town's approval of the project. The new fee in-lieu-of zone ends in the alley directly behind Snake River's property, so allowing fee in-lieu-of parking will not be an aberration in the area. There is nothing in the record showing that the benefit to the Town from excluding Snake River is equal to the damage caused Snake River from the exclusion. It would violate Wyo. Stat. Ann. §15-1-601(d)(iv) to declare now that the parking options are no longer available to Snake River; the result would be to "render valueless" Snake River's substantial business investment.

On the final issue, we conclude that Snake River never showed any intent to abandon its non-conforming use. Discontinuance of the leased parking arrangement, one of the "incidents" of that use, was caused by economic conditions beyond its control. The primary use of the premises as a restaurant and a micro-brewery was never discontinued, and various solutions to the accessory parking use were sought. There simply was no discontinuance, and certainly no abandonment, of the primary use of Snake River's premises.

The decision of the district court is reversed and the case is remanded with instructions to enter summary judgment in favor of Snake River. We have made no decision herein as to the amount of any fee in-lieu-of parking that may be owed to the Town as that issue is not now before this Court.

Notes and Questions

1. *Snake River Brewing Company* illustrates the challenge of imposing zoning laws upon areas in which a variety of different land uses already exist. This is a common problem because many areas are already developed before a zoning law is enacted. Several general rules have been developed to address existing uses that do not conform to the new zoning law. First, the right to the existing use runs with the land. Second, the right to the use may end if it is abandoned or if an act of God destroys it. Third, the right to the use does not include a right to expand the use or change to a different use, but minor changes to the same use may be permissible. Whether a use is sufficiently like the original use has generated lots of litigation. *See, e.g.,* Motel 6 Operating Ltd. P'ship v. City of Flagstaff, 991 P.2d 272 (Ariz. Ct. App. 1999) (holding that a city must allow a Motel 6 to make reasonable changes such as updating its sign to reflect a new corporate logo); Baxter v. City of Preston, 768 P.2d 1340 (Idaho 1989) (disallowing a change from the seasonal grazing of livestock to a feed lot that operated year-round); Granger v. Board of Adjustment, 44 N.W.2d 399 (Iowa 1950) (allowing a brick and frame commercial building to be changed to concrete and steel); Russell v. Flathead County, 67 P.3d 182 (Mont. 2003) (holding that the previous use of property to repair a dairy's farm equipment did not authorize a new owner to repair heavy equipment there); Belleville v. Parrillo's, Inc., 416 A.2d 388 (N.J. 1980) (disallowing a change from a restaurant to a disco). Another rule provides that the right to repair a nonconforming use may be limited. Repairs may be allowed, but not alteration or construction. For example, in Mossman v. City of Columbus, 449 N.W.2d 214 (Neb. 1989), the court disallowed the replacement of a mobile home.

2. An alternative approach to the nonconforming use problem establishes an amortization period after which the use must conform to the zoning law. Such a period responds to the judicial concern that an immediate prohibition on an existing use would constitute a governmental taking of property, triggering the just compensation requirement. An amortization period is thus designed to allow the use for a duration that is sufficient for landowners to realize their investments as the value depreciates. The statutory amortization periods have ranged from one year to 30 years, and courts have struck down and upheld periods at both ends as being sufficient, or not. The factors to be considered in judging a reasonable amortization period include the nature of the use, the amount invested in the use, the number of improvements, the public harm from the use, the character of the neighborhood, the time needed to actually amortize the investment, the time needed to amortize the investment for tax purposes, the time needed to completely depreciate the property, the number of nonconforming uses of that type, and the availability of variances from the general zoning plan.

■ **WATERGATE WEST, INC. v. DISTRICT OF COLUMBIA BOARD OF ZONING ADJUSTMENT**
District of Columbia Court of Appeals, 2003
815 A.2d 762

TERRY, Associate Judge. Watergate West, Inc. ("Watergate"), seeks review of an order in which the Board of Zoning Adjustment ("BZA") affirmed the decision of the Zoning Administrator to approve a certificate of occupancy for George Washington University ("GWU") to use a former hotel as a dormitory for some of its students. The site of the building is an R-5-E ("high density") residential zoning district. *See* 11 DCMR §105.1 (a)(5)(E) (1995). . . . Watergate argues that the Zoning Administrator and the BZA failed to give effect to the District of Columbia Comprehensive Plan ("the Plan"), which, in Watergate's view, prohibits GWU from using the building as a dormitory. We affirm.

I.

In May 1999 GWU purchased the former Howard Johnson Hotel at 2601 Virginia Avenue, N.W., with plans to convert it into a dormitory for 388 students. A few days later, GWU applied to the Department of Consumer and Regulatory Affairs for a certificate of occupancy.

During the processing of this application, Advisory Neighborhood Commission 2-A ("ANC 2-A") wrote a letter to the Acting Zoning Administrator, Armando Lourenco, asking whether GWU needed to obtain a special exception before converting the hotel into a dormitory. The Administrator replied that a dormitory was a matter-of-right use in the R-5-E district where the building was located. The BZA, in turn, informed ANC 2-A of its right to appeal the Zoning Administrator's determination. The certificate of occupancy was issued on July 28, 1999. Both Watergate and ANC 2-A appealed to the BZA on August 2.

At a hearing before the BZA a few months later, Mr. Lourenco testified about the basis for his decision. He said:

> There are two issues, I believe, that the Board needs to consider here. The first one is whether or not the decision of considering this site as a site where, as a matter of right, you can establish that the dormitory was correct. And that of course is intertwined with the issue of the campus plan. And the second issue is whether or not that decision is consistent, as the law requires, with the comprehensive plan.
>
> And I believe the answer to those two questions can only be yes.

. . . Mr. Lourenco also made clear that he did consider the Comprehensive Plan while processing GWU's application for a certificate of occupancy. He explained that the relevant provisions of the Plan sought to prevent GWU from converting existing permanent residential housing into dormitories. However, because the building at issue was a former hotel, *i.e.,* was not and had never been permanent residential housing, these provisions did not apply to GWU's application. To the contrary, Mr. Lourenco reasoned, GWU's use of the building as a dormitory would help to relieve pressure on other housing stock in the area, and thus it furthered the stated goals of the Plan. . . .

The BZA affirmed the Administrator's approval of GWU's application for a certificate of occupancy. It held that . . . despite amendments to the Comprehensive Plan, this court's decision in Tenley & Cleveland Park Emergency Committee v. District of Columbia Board of Zoning Adjustment ("*TACPEC*"), 550 A.2d 331 (D.C. 1988), *cert. denied,* 489 U.S. 1082 (1989), which held that the Plan was not self-executing, still prevailed: "The Zoning Commission is the body having exclusive jurisdiction over amendments to the Zoning Regulations. It would be improper for the Zoning Administrator to read the Comprehensive Plan to require an action not provided for in the Zoning Regulations." Nevertheless, the BZA recognized that the

Administrator had considered the Plan and concluded that his "determination that the dormitory was consistent with the Plan [was] a reasonable interpretation of the intent of the Plan. . . ."

II.

Watergate asserts that the BZA and the Administrator misconstrued the applicable regulations in concluding that GWU was entitled as a matter of right to use the former hotel as a dormitory. Watergate also argues that the Administrator and the BZA failed to follow the Comprehensive Plan, which, in Watergate's view, prohibits GWU from using property outside its campus area for student accommodations.

[The court first rejected Watergate's contention that the BZA improperly interpreted the zoning regulations by allowing GWU to use the hotel as a dormitory as a matter of right without obtaining a special exception.]

III.

Watergate also argues that the Administrator's decision to issue a certificate of occupancy for an off-campus dormitory was inconsistent with the Comprehensive Plan. It maintains that the Plan is enforceable independently of the zoning regulations, even though this court held in *TACPEC* that the Plan "is not self-executing," 550 A.2d at 337, that the Zoning Commission has exclusive authority to amend the zoning regulations, and that the Zoning Administrator has no authority to enforce the Plan independent of the regulations. Watergate takes the position that the Council of the District of Columbia has since overruled the holding in *TACPEC* by amending the Plan.

The Comprehensive Plan was first enacted on April 10, 1984; the land use element of the Plan was enacted almost a year later, on March 16, 1985. In 1986 the Tenley and Cleveland Park Emergency Committee ("TACPEC") challenged a projected real estate development on Wisconsin Avenue, contending that the Plan required a moratorium on any development inconsistent with its provisions, regardless of whether that use was permitted as a matter of right under the zoning regulations. We rejected TACPEC's argument, holding that "the Zoning Commission is the exclusive agency vested with responsibility for assuring that the zoning regulations are not inconsistent with the Comprehensive Plan. . . ." *TACPEC*, 550 A.2d at 341. We further held that "the Comprehensive Plan is not self-executing, and contrary to TACPEC's contention, this statutory language plainly does not evince any legislative intent to impose a moratorium on development in the District." *Id.* at 337.

Watergate contends that amendments made by the Council in 1994, *see* section 112.6 of the Plan, 46 D.C. Register 1462-1463 (1999), have overruled the holding in *TACPEC*, so that the Plan now has independent force above and beyond the zoning regulations. This case, however, does not require us to decide whether the Council has overruled *TACPEC*. Watergate's argument rests on two incorrect assumptions: first, that the Zoning Administrator did not consider the Plan, and second, that the issuance of the certificate of occupancy for use of the former hotel as a dormitory was inconsistent with the Plan. On the contrary, not only did the Administrator consider the Plan, but he, as well as the BZA, rationally concluded that GWU's application did not contravene its provisions. Since the Zoning Administrator considered and correctly applied the relevant provisions of the Plan, the post-1994 status of *TACPEC* is irrelevant.

Mr. Lourenco testified at the BZA hearing that he considered the provisions of the Plan cited by Watergate but that his reading of them supported granting GWU's application to turn the hotel into a dormitory. The BZA agreed, holding that the Administrator's "determination that the dormitory was consistent with the Plan [was] a reasonable interpretation of the intent of the Plan, which addresses generally the pressure on the housing stock occasioned by conversions to dormitories."

Watergate responds that the Plan not only focuses on the problem of GWU's conversion of housing stock into dormitories, but also requires that GWU alleviate this problem by building *all* dormitories on campus. We are not persuaded. There is nothing whatsoever in the Plan that would require GWU to build all of its dormitories on campus. In any event, we are fully satisfied that the BZA was correct when it ruled that Watergate and the ANC "have not demonstrated that the conversion of a hotel to a dormitory is inconsistent with the Comprehensive Plan."

In so holding we agree with the Administrator's and the BZA's conclusion that the central concern of the Plan, as far as GWU is concerned, is to alleviate the diminution of housing stock outside GWU's campus boundaries. *See* section 1358.1 of the Plan, 46 D.C. Register 1775 (1999), which states that GWU "must continue to construct student dormitories to alleviate the pressure on the housing stock outside the boundaries of the campus plan." Because the building at issue in this case, a former hotel, was never permanent residential housing at any point in its history, its conversion to a dormitory had no effect whatever on the local housing stock. Thus we conclude that the Administrator and the BZA rationally determined that GWU's application to use the building as a dormitory was consistent with the underlying policy of the Plan.

Watergate further contends that the BZA failed to address the Comprehensive Plan issue "in the manner required for issues raised by the ANC." The BZA specifically noted, however, that "in addressing the issues raised by [Watergate], the Board has also addressed the ANC's issues, since the ANC's resolution was virtually identical to [Watergate's] statement." The record shows that this comment is accurate. *See, e.g.,* Foggy Bottom Ass'n v. District of Columbia Board of Zoning Adjustment, 791 A.2d 64, 77 (D.C. 2002) (holding that BZA gave sufficient consideration to "the issues and concerns raised by the ANC, which for the most part echoed the issues and concerns raised by the [petitioner]"). The mere fact that the BZA did not agree with the ANC's interpretation of the Plan does not mean that the BZA failed to give the ANC's views "great weight." *See Levy,* 570 A.2d at 746. We hold that the BZA considered all of the ANC's concerns with more than sufficient particularity to satisfy the "great weight" requirement. . . .

Notes and Questions

1. The Standard State Zoning Enabling Act, developed in 1922, has served as a model for state laws describing how the zoning process proceeds. Those laws empower local governments to establish zoning districts, detail the procedures to be followed in developing and modifying a locality's zoning, and create the administrative offices responsible for implementing the system. Section 3 of the model act provides for a comprehensive plan to achieve the health, safety, welfare, and economic purposes of zoning regulations. The comprehensive plan is the local

government's statement of objectives and standards for development. A typical plan consists of maps, charts, and descriptive text. A comprehensive plan can change as specific zoning regulations change. As *Watergate West* shows, judicial review of the consistency of particular zoning regulations with the comprehensive plan is relatively lax. While there are some instances of courts invalidating a zoning regulation as contrary to the comprehensive plan, most courts do not insist upon much adherence to any planning process. Instead, they only require that zoning decisions be reasonable and impartial. Some states now require local zoning ordinances to be "consistent with" the plan, not "in accordance" with the plan, but the practical distinction between the two tests remains uncertain.

2. The former Howard Johnson's hotel at issue in *Watergate West* enjoys its own place in American history. On June 17, 1972, Room 723 of the hotel was occupied by lookouts who watched the burglary being conducted by agents of President Richard Nixon's reelection campaign of the Democratic National Committee offices in the Watergate building across the street. The failure of the lookouts to alert the burglars of the impending arrival of the police, and the subsequent arrest of those CIA-connected burglars, began the scandal that culminated in Nixon's resignation two years later. By the 1990s, Howard Johnson's seized upon that notoriety by decorating Room 723 with Nixon-era political memorabilia and charging $135 per night to stay there. Once George Washington University acquired the building, it dedicated the entire seventh floor to house students who wrote essays describing how their parents' views of government were changed by the Watergate scandal. *See* Patrice Gaines, *A Look at History from Room 723; Watergate View Lures Students*, Wash. Post, Aug. 21, 1999, at B1.

3. *Watergate West* is just one example of the controversies surrounding George Washington University's efforts to provide housing for its students within the city. The university lost one of those battles just days after prevailing in *Watergate West*. In 2002, the BZA responded to concerns about "'the livability and residential character' of the Foggy Bottom neighborhood" by requiring the university to house 70 percent of its undergraduates on campus or outside of the adjacent Foggy Bottom area. The university immediately filed a constitutional challenge to the BZA's action, insisting that the action infringed upon its First Amendment right to academic freedom. The university also cited a previous judicial proclamation that "a university — even a law school — is not to be presumed, for the purposes of the Zoning Regulations, to be the land use equivalent of the bubonic plague." Glenbrook Rd. Ass'n v. D.C. Bd. of Zoning Adjustment, 605 A.2d 22, 32 (D.C. 1992). But the federal courts rejected the claim, noting that "the university cites no case giving universities any special status vis-à-vis neutral, generally applicable zoning and land-use regulations of the standard externality-constraining type." George Washington Univ. v. District of Columbia, 318 F.3d 203, 212 (D.C. Cir. 2003).

4. The crush of students into inexpensive housing around universities often clashes with the residential density requirements and conventional-family orientation of typical urban zoning ordinances. This can raise constitutional issues where the ordinance restricts certain areas to single "family" homes. In Village of Belle Terre v. Boraas, 416 U.S. 1 (1974), six unrelated college students challenged a municipal zoning ordinance that limited land use to one family dwelling. Family was defined as "one or more persons related by blood, adoption, or marriage, living and cooking together as a single housekeeping unit, exclusive of household servants." The Supreme Court upheld the ordinance, with Justice Douglas explaining that "[a] quiet place where yards are wide, people few, and motor vehicles restricted

are legitimate guidelines in a land-use project addressed to family needs." The police power, he added, permits "zones where family values, youth values, and the blessings of quiet seclusion and clean air make the area a sanctuary for people." Justice Marshall was the lone dissenter, insisting that strict scrutiny should have applied because the classification violates the students' fundamental rights of association and privacy guaranteed by the First and Fourteenth Amendments. A few state courts have agreed with Justice Marshall when construing their own constitutions. *See* State v. Baker, 405 A.2d 368 (N.J. 1979) (invalidating a Plainfield ordinance defining family because the goal of preserving the family character of a neighborhood could be achieved by much less restrictive means); McMinn v. Town of Oyster Bay, 488 N.E.2d 1240 (N.Y. 1985) (holding that an ordinance like that upheld in *Belle Terre* violated the state due process clause because occupancy restrictions based on biological or legal relationships had no reasonable tie to the city's quality of life objectives). But most states have approved zoning restrictions like those upheld in *Belle Terre*.

5. What qualifies as a "family" for purposes of zoning regulations presents another vexing issue. In Moore v. City of East Cleveland, 431 U.S. 494 (1977), Inez Moore lived with her son and two grandsons who were not brothers in violation of a city ordinance that defined family to include no more than one set of grandchildren. The U.S. Supreme Court held 5-4 that the ordinance violated the constitutional requirement of substantive due process because it wrongfully regulated the structure of family. Another common issue is presented where group homes for ex-convicts or recovering drug addicts, AIDS patients, or alcoholics are involved. City of Cleburne v. Cleburne Living Center, Inc., 473 U.S. 432 (1985), held that a city's refusal to grant a special use permit to allow construction of a group home for the mentally retarded violated the Constitution's Equal Protection Clause because special use permits were not required for hospitals and nursing homes.

The federal Fair Housing Act (FHA) serves as an added limit on municipal zoning of group homes. For example, in the summer of 1990, Oxford House opened Oxford House-Edmonds, a group home in Edmonds, Washington, for 10 to 12 adults recovering from alcoholism and drug addiction. The house was in a neighborhood zoned for single-family residences, which the city zoning code defines as applying to an unlimited number of people "related by genetics, adoption, or marriage," or five or fewer unrelated people. Oxford House argued that the zoning law contradicted §3607(b)(1) of the FHA, which limits municipal land use regulations of group homes generally but exempts "any reasonable local, State or Federal restrictions regarding the maximum number of occupants permitted to occupy a dwelling." The Supreme Court agreed with Oxford House. Justice Ginsburg distinguished between permissible maximum occupancy restrictions and impermissible land use restrictions. Land use restrictions are designed to segregate permissible uses, and since one such use is single-family homes, "family" must be defined. Maximum occupancy restrictions, by contrast, are designed to protect health and safety from overcrowding, so they limit the total number of people per building. Rules designed to prevent overcrowding are within the FHA exemption, but rules designed to preserve the family character of a neighborhood are not; the Edmonds zoning code was a classic example of an impermissible land use restriction because it allowed *any* number of related people to live together. City of Edmonds v. Oxford House, Inc., 514 U.S. 725 (1995).

■ COCHRAN v. FAIRFAX COUNTY BOARD OF ZONING APPEALS

Supreme Court of Virginia, 2004
594 S.E.2d 571

RUSSELL, Senior Justice. These three cases involve decisions by local boards of zoning appeals (collectively and individually, BZA) upon applications for variances from the local zoning ordinances. Although the facts and proceedings differ in each case, and will be discussed separately, the governing principles of law are the same. We therefore consider and decide the cases in a single opinion.

THE FAIRFAX CASE

Michael R. Bratti was the owner of a tract of land containing approximately 20,470 square feet, in the McLean area of Fairfax County. The property was zoned R-2, a residential classification permitting two dwelling units per acre, and was improved by a home in which Bratti had resided for eight years. The zoning ordinance required side yard setbacks of at least 15 feet from the property lines. Bratti's existing home fit well within the setbacks.

Bratti filed an application with the BZA for four variances. He proposed to demolish his existing home and erect a much larger house on the site. The proposed structure would come within 13 feet of the northerly property line, rather than the 15 feet required by the ordinance, and would be further extended into the setback area by three exterior chimneys which would extend beyond the northerly wall of the house. The proposed house would be 71 feet wide and 76 feet from front to back. The proposed encroachment into the side yard setback would extend the entire 76 foot depth of the house.

It was undisputed that Bratti's proposed house could be built upon the existing lot without any need for a variance by simply moving it two feet to the south, plus the additional distance required by the chimneys. Bratti explained to the Board, however, that he desired to have a "side-load" garage on the south side of his house and that a reduction of two feet of open space on the south side would make it inconvenient for vehicles to turn into the garage. The present house had a "front-load" garage which opened directly toward the street. When it was pointed out to Bratti that he could avoid this problem by reconfiguring his proposed house to contain a "front-load" garage, he responded that such a house would have less "curb appeal" than the design he proposed.

If the house were built in its proposed location, but reduced in size by two feet to comply with the zoning ordinance, there would be a resulting loss of 152 square feet of living space. The topography of the lot was such that it rose 42 feet vertically throughout its 198-foot depth from the street to the rear property line. However, there were two relatively level areas shown on the plans for the proposed dwelling, one in front of the house and one in the rear. It was conceded that an additional 152 square feet of living space could have been constructed in either of these areas, but Bratti explained that he wanted to use the level area in front of the house as a play area for children and for additional parking, and that he was unwilling to encroach upon the level area in the rear because he desired to use it as a large outdoor courtyard which he said was "the central idea in the house."

The proposed dwelling had two stories. A third story could have been added as a matter of right, without variances. Bratti conceded that this could easily be done and would more than accommodate the 152 square feet lost by compliance with the zoning ordinance, but that it would be aesthetically undesirable, causing the house to appear to be a "towering structure" as seen from the street.

Over the opposition of a number of neighbors, the BZA granted all four variances. The BZA made findings of fact, including the following: "3. The lot suffers from severe topographical conditions which the applicant has worked hard to accommodate. . . . 5. The requests are modest." This was followed by a conclusion of law "that the applicant has satisfied the Board that physical conditions as listed above exist which under a strict interpretation of the Zoning Ordinance would result in practical difficulty or unnecessary hardship that would deprive the user of all reasonable use of the land and/or buildings involved."

The objecting neighbors petitioned the circuit court for certiorari. The Board of Supervisors of Fairfax County obtained leave of court to enter the case as an additional petitioner, opposing the variances. The court, after a hearing, affirmed the decision of the BZA and entered an order dismissing the petition for writ of certiorari. The objecting neighbors and the Board of Supervisors brought this appeal.

THE PULASKI CASE

Jack D. Nunley and Diana M. Nunley owned a corner lot in the Town of Pulaski that contained .6248 acre. The lot was bounded by public streets on three sides. A street 40 feet wide ran along the front of the property and the intersection of that street with a street approximately 30 feet wide formed the southeastern corner of the lot. The 30-foot street ran northward from the intersection, forming the eastern boundary of the lot, and then curved to the west to form the lot's northern boundary. The curvature was gradual, having a radius of 34.53 feet. This curve formed the northeasterly corner of the lot.

The property was zoned R-1, a residential classification which contained a special provision relating to corner lots: "The side yard on the side facing the side street shall be at least 15 feet from both main and accessory structures." Town of Pulaski, Va., Zoning Ordinance, art. IV §2.6.2 (2002).

The Nunleys petitioned the BZA for a variance from the required 15-foot set back to zero feet, in order to construct a garage at the northeast corner of the lot, the northeast corner of which would be placed tangent to the curving property line. There was no existing garage on the property, and the Nunleys explained that placing a garage in this location would provide the easiest access to the street. The topography of the lot was difficult, the curve along the 30-foot street lying at a considerable elevation above the floor level of the existing house. The garage could be constructed closer to the house without the need for a variance, but this would require construction of a ramp that would add considerably to the expense of the project. Also, the Nunleys explained, there was a stone retaining wall, five feet in height, behind the house that would be weakened or destroyed if the garage were to be built closer to the house.

Neighbors objected, pointing out to the BZA that the construction of the garage so close to the corner would create a blind area that would be dangerous for traffic coming around the curve on the 30-foot street. They also complained that it would be an "eyesore" and would destroy existing vegetation.

The BZA had some difficulty with the question whether the Nunleys' request involved a "hardship" as required by law. The BZA held four meetings to discuss the question and obtained an opinion from the town attorney. The BZA eventually granted the Nunleys a modified variance, permitting an accessory structure no closer than five feet from the northern projected boundary and no closer than 15 feet from the eastern projected boundary of the property. The modified variance also provided that construction should not "alter or destroy the aesthetic looks of existing vegetation bordering the northern projected boundary" of the property.

Virginia C. MacNeal, a neighbor who had objected to the variance before the BZA, filed a petition for certiorari in the circuit court. The court, in a letter opinion, affirmed the decision of the BZA and denied the petition for certiorari. Virginia C. MacNeal brought this appeal.

THE VIRGINIA BEACH CASE

Jack and Rebecca Pennington owned a 1.25-acre parcel of land in a subdivision known as Avalon Terrace, in the City of Virginia Beach. The property was improved by their home, in which they had lived for many years, and a detached garage containing 528 square feet which they had built in 1972. The property was zoned R-10, a single-family residential classification permitting four dwelling units per acre. The ordinance contained a limitation on "accessory structures" by requiring that they "do not exceed five hundred (500) square feet of floor area or twenty (20) percent of the floor area of the principal structure, whichever is greater." The size of the Penningtons' home was such that the 500 square-foot limitation applied to their property.

The Penningtons applied to the BZA for a variance permitting accessory structures containing a total of 816 square feet, in lieu of the 500-square foot limitation. They explained that the purpose of the request was to permit the construction of a storage shed, 12 by 24 feet, adjacent to the garage, and also to bring into conformity the 28 square feet by which the existing garage exceeded the limitation imposed by the zoning ordinance.

The Penningtons could have built the storage shed as an appendage or as an addition to the existing house without the need for any variance, but their representative explained to the BZA that their lot was so large that the shed would be nearly invisible from the street and would have no impact upon neighboring properties. He contended that the obvious purpose of the size limitation on accessory structures, as contained in the ordinance, was to inhibit the erection of large, unsightly outbuildings on small lots. He pointed out that the Penningtons' lot was so large that four dwelling sites could be carved out of it, and that therefore the impact of a small additional outbuilding would be minimal and would not contravene the spirit of the zoning ordinance. He also pointed out that a number of the neighbors were related to the Penningtons and that no neighbors had any objection to their request.

The zoning administrator of the City of Virginia Beach opposed the request, pointing out that there was no need for a variance because the desired storage shed could be built as an appurtenance to the existing house. The zoning administrator had no objection to a variance to the extent of the 28 square feet needed to bring the existing garage into conformity with the zoning ordinance. The BZA granted the variance to bring the garage into conformity, but denied the remainder of the Penningtons' request on the ground that no "hardship" existed.

The Penningtons filed a petition for certiorari in the circuit court. At a hearing on the petition, counsel for the Penningtons asserted a claim of hardship that had not been presented to the BZA: Mr. Pennington was seriously ill and disabled. His wife had full-time employment, was the "bread-winner" of the family and was therefore unable to care for him during the day. The Penningtons' daughter, who had recently graduated from college, had returned to live with the Penningtons and assist in the care of her father. The storage shed was needed as a place to store her belongings. The court ruled that a hardship existed, overruled the decision of the BZA and granted the Penningtons' requested variance. The BZA brought this appeal.

ANALYSIS

Zoning is a valid exercise of the police power of the Commonwealth. Zoning ordinances, of necessity, regulate land use uniformly within large districts. It is impracticable to tailor such ordinances to meet the condition of each individual parcel within the district. The size, shape, topography or other conditions affecting such a parcel may, if the zoning ordinance is applied to it as written, render it relatively useless. Thus, a zoning ordinance, valid on its face, might be unconstitutional as applied to an individual parcel, in violation of Article 1, §11 of the Constitution of Virginia.

> Because a facially valid zoning ordinance may prove unconstitutional in application to a particular landowner, some device is needed to protect landowners' rights without destroying the viability of zoning ordinances. The variance traditionally has been designed to serve this function. In this role, the variance aptly has been called an "escape hatch" or "escape valve." A statute may, of course, authorize variances in cases where an ordinance's application to particular property is not unconstitutional. However, the language used in Va. Code §15.2-2309(2) to define "unnecessary hardship" clearly indicates that the General Assembly intended that variances be granted *only in cases where application of zoning restrictions would appear to be constitutionally impermissible.*

Packer v. Hornsby, 267 S.E.2d 140, 142 (1980) (emphasis added).

Therefore, the BZA has authority to grant variances only to avoid an unconstitutional result. We said in Commonwealth v. County Utilities Corp., 290 S.E.2d 867, 872 (1982) (emphasis added):

> All citizens hold property subject to the proper exercise of police power for the common good. Even where such an exercise results in substantial diminution of property values, an owner has no right to compensation therefor. Hadacheck v. Sebastian, 239 U.S. 394 (1915). In Penn Central Transportation Co. v. City of New York, 438 U.S. 104 (1978), the Supreme Court held that no taking occurs in the circumstances unless the regulation interferes with all reasonable beneficial uses of the property, taken as a whole.

. . . The General Assembly has prescribed . . . standards regulating the authority of the BZA to grant variances by enacting Va. Code §15.2-2309(2) which provides, in pertinent part:

> Boards of zoning appeals shall have the following powers and duties: . . .
> (2) To authorize . . . such variance as defined in §15.2-2201 from the terms of the ordinance as will not be contrary to the public interest, when, owing to special conditions a literal enforcement of the provisions will result in unnecessary hardship; . . . as follows: . . . where by reason of exceptional topographic conditions or other

extraordinary situation or condition of the piece of property . . . the strict application of the terms of the ordinance would effectively prohibit or unreasonably restrict the utilization of the property or where the board is satisfied, upon the evidence heard by it, that the granting of the variance will alleviate a clearly demonstrable hardship approaching confiscation, as distinguished from a special privilege or convenience sought by the applicant. . . .

Adhering to the rule in *Packer*, we construe the statutory terms "effectively prohibit or unreasonably restrict the utilization of the property," "unnecessary hardship" and "undue hardship" in that light and hold that the BZA has no authority to grant a variance unless the effect of the zoning ordinance, as applied to the piece of property under consideration, would, in the absence of a variance, "interfere with all reasonable beneficial uses of the property, taken as a whole." *County Utilities Corp.*, 290 S.E.2d at 872.

CONCLUSION

Notwithstanding the presumption of correctness to which the decision of the BZA is entitled, each of the present cases fails to meet the foregoing standard. The proposed house in Fairfax could have been reconfigured or moved two feet to the south, avoiding the need for a variance. Indeed, the project could simply have been abandoned and the existing use continued in effect. The proposed garage in Pulaski could have been moved to another location on the lot, or the project abandoned. The shed in Virginia Beach could have been built as an addition to the existing house, or the project abandoned. Without any variances, each of the properties retained substantial beneficial uses and substantial value. The effect of the respective zoning ordinances upon them in no sense "interfere[d] with all reasonable beneficial uses of the property, taken as a whole."

Compelling reasons were presented in favor of each of the applications for variances: The desires of the owners, supported by careful planning to minimize harmful effects to neighboring properties; probable aesthetic improvements to the neighborhood as a whole, together with a probable increase in the local tax base; greatly increased expense to the owners if the plans were reconfigured to meet the requirements of the zoning ordinances; lack of opposition, or even support of the application by neighbors; and serious personal need, by the owners, for the proposed modification.

When the impact of the zoning ordinance is so severe as to meet the foregoing standard, the BZA becomes vested with wide discretion in tailoring a variance that will alleviate the "hardship" while remaining "in harmony with the intended spirit and purpose of the ordinance." Va. Code §15.2-2309(2). Factors such as those advanced in support of the variances in these cases are appropriate for consideration by the BZA in a case that falls within that discretionary power, but they are immaterial in a case in which the BZA has no authority to act. The threshold question for the BZA in considering an application for a variance as well as for a court reviewing its decision, is whether the effect of the zoning ordinance upon the property under consideration, as it stands, interferes with "all reasonable beneficial uses of the property, taken as a whole." If the answer is in the negative, the BZA has no authority to go further.

For these reasons, we will reverse the judgments of the circuit courts in each of the cases, vacate the resolutions of the Boards of Zoning Appeals of the County of

Fairfax and the Town of Pulaski, respectively, reinstate the resolution of the Board of Zoning Appeals of the City of Virginia Beach, and enter final judgments here.

Notes and Questions

1. *Variance* applications are ubiquitous, with landowners seeking relief from zoning regulations on nearly every conceivable basis. These requests often succeed, sometimes conditioned upon a landowner's taking steps — for example, the installation of lighting or fencing — that minimize the effects upon the neighbors. The issuance of variances raises problems of its own, for by definition every variance moves away from the zoning plan that the legislature determined best for the community. Thus, New York's renowned Chief Judge Benjamin N. Cardozo once described a zoning board's power to issue variances as "easily abused." People ex rel. Fordham Manor Reformed Church v. Walsh, 155 N.E. 575, 578 (N.Y. 1927). As the decision in *Cochran* suggests, courts are much more likely to reverse the issuance of a variance than the denial of a variance. But not all states are as strict as Virginia in reviewing the issuance of variances. *See, e.g.*, Rousseau v. Zoning Board of Appeals, 764 N.W.2d 130 (Neb. Ct. App. 2009) (upholding a variance that reduced building setback and on-site parking requirements because an applicant need not show a violation of a fundamental right and because courts should defer to the decisions of local zoning boards).

2. Nearly every state empowers a local zoning board to issue variances in certain circumstances. Virginia is representative of most states in limiting the board's authority to grant variances to cases where application of the zoning ordinance to a particular landowner causes *unnecessary hardship*. Although zoning boards often apply this standard loosely, courts tend to interpret it quite strictly, as did the Virginia Supreme Court in *Cochran*. Typically, courts will deny a variance where the hardship is self-imposed, sometimes taking the position that simply buying land with knowledge of its physical restrictions involves self-inflicted hardship so as to preclude a variance. The law in some states imposes a looser *practical difficulties* standard on local zoning boards in granting variances. *E.g.*, Ind. Code §36-7-4-918.5. This standard typically requires the owner to show that application of the zoning ordinance to a particular parcel would cause significant economic injury.

The owners in *Cochran* sought *area variances*, which give relief from requirements such as setback lines, minimum or maximum building size, or building height. It is generally easier to obtain an area variance than a *use variance*, which allows the owner to make a use that is otherwise prohibited in the zone (such as opening a store in a residential zone). Indeed, some states bar use variances altogether. *See* Cal. Gov't Code §65906 (ban enacted 1970).

3. Variances are just one of the mechanisms for introducing administrative flexibility into the zoning process. A *special exception* (also known as a *conditional use*) is a use permitted by the ordinance in a district where it is not necessarily incompatible, but where it might cause harm if its location is not monitored. Accordingly, the use may be authorized only upon special approval by the board in individual cases rather than as a matter of right. In *Watergate West* (reproduced above at page 712), the neighbors claimed that George Washington University needed to obtain a special exception before it could convert a hotel into a dormitory, but the court held that an exception was not necessary because a dormitory was allowed in that zone as a matter of right. Examples of when a special exception may

be required include a hospital to be located in a residential area or a gas station to be placed in a light commercial district. To cite another example, the city of Seattle authorizes special exceptions for oversized signs in commercial and downtown zones if the sign represents an affirmative attempt to improve the aesthetics of the area and if it meets certain criteria related to compatibility with the area, such as adding "interest to the street level environment," helping pedestrians and motorists, and being integrated into the existing infrastructure. Seattle Municipal Code §23.55.040. In each instance, the zoning law permits such uses, but only upon an administrative review to confirm that the use is entitled to a special exception. The theory underlying special exceptions is that certain uses are entirely appropriate and not necessarily incompatible with the basic uses of a zone, but not at every location in the district or without any conditions.

■ **RODGERS v. VILLAGE OF TARRYTOWN**
Court of Appeals of New York, 1951
96 N.E.2d 731

FULD, Judge. This appeal, here by our permission, involves the validity of two amendments to the General Zoning Ordinance of the Village of Tarrytown, a suburban area in the County of Westchester, within twenty-five miles of New York City.

Some years ago, Tarrytown enacted a General Zoning Ordinance dividing the village into seven district or zones: Residence A for single family dwellings, Residence B for two-family dwellings, Residence C for multiple dwellings and apartment houses, three business districts and an industrial zone. In 1947 and 1948, the board of trustees, the village's legislative body, passed the two amendatory ordinances here under attack.

The 1947 ordinance creates "A new district or class of zone . . . [to] be called 'Residence B-B,'" in which, besides one- and two-family dwellings, buildings for multiple occupancy of fifteen or fewer families were permitted. The boundaries of the new type district were not delineated in the ordinance but were to be "fixed by amendment of the official village building zone map, at such times in the future as such district or class of zone is applied, to properties in this village." The village planning board was empowered to approve such amendments and, in case such approval was withheld, the board of trustees was authorized to grant it by appropriate resolution. In addition, the ordinance erected exacting standards of size and physical layouts for Residence B-B zones: a minimum of ten acres of land and a maximum building height of three stores were mandated; set-back and spacing requirements for structures were carefully prescribed; and no more than 15% of the ground area of the plot was to be occupied by buildings.

A year and a half after the 1947 amendment was enacted, defendant Elizabeth Rubin sought to have her property, consisting of almost ten and a half acres in the Residence A district, placed in a Residence B-B classification. After repeated modification of her plans to meet suggestions of the village planning board, that body gave its approval, and, several months later, in December of 1948, the board of trustees, also approving, passed the second ordinance here under attack. In essence, it provides that the Residence B-B district "is hereby applied to the [Rubin] property . . . and the district or zone of said property is hereby changed to 'Residence B-B' and the official Building Zone Map of the Village of Tarrytown is hereby amended accordingly [by specification of the various parcels and plots involved]."

Plaintiff, who owns a residence on a six acre plot about a hundred yards from Rubin's property, brought this action to have the two amendments declared invalid and to enjoin defendant Rubin from constructing multiple dwellings on her property. The courts below, adjudging the amendments valid and the action of the trustees proper, dismissed the complaint. We agree with their determination.

While stability and regularity are undoubtedly essential to the operation of zoning plans, zoning is by no means static. Changed or changing conditions call for changed plans, and persons who own property in a particular zone or use district enjoy no eternally vested right to that classification if the public interest demands otherwise. Accordingly, the power of a village to amend its basic zoning ordinance in such a way as reasonably to promote the general welfare cannot be questioned. Just as clearly, decision as to how a community shall be zoned or rezoned, as to how various properties shall be classified or reclassified, rests with the local legislative body; its judgment and determination will be conclusive, beyond interference from the courts, unless shown to be arbitrary, and the burden of establishing such arbitrariness is imposed upon him who asserts it. . . .

By that test, the propriety of the decision here made is not even debatable. In other words, viewing the rezoning in the case before us, as it must be viewed, in the light of the area involved and the present and reasonably foreseeable needs of the community, the conclusion is inescapable that what was done not only accorded with sound zoning principles, not only complied with every requirement of law, but was accomplished in a proper, careful and reasonable manner.

The Tarrytown board of trustees was entitled to find that there was a real need for additional housing facilities; that the creation of Residence B-B districts for garden apartment developments would prevent young families, unable to find accommodations in the village, from moving elsewhere; would attract business to the community; would lighten the tax load of the small home owner, increasingly burdened by the shrinkage of tax revenues resulting from the depreciated value of large estates and the transfer of many such estates to tax exempt institutions; and would develop otherwise unmarketable and decaying property.

The village's zoning aim being clear, the choice of methods to accomplish it lay with the board. Two such methods were at hand. It could amend the General Zoning Ordinance so as to permit garden apartments on any plot of ten acres or more in Residence A and B zones (the zones more restricted) or it could amend that Ordinance so as to invite owners of ten or more acres, who wished to build garden apartments on their properties, to apply for a Residence B-B classification. The board chose to adopt the latter procedure. . . . Whether we would have made the same choice is not the issue; it is sufficient that the board's decision was neither arbitrary nor unreasonable.

As to the requirement that the applicant own a plot of at least ten acres, we find nothing therein unfair to plaintiff or other owners of smaller parcels. The board undoubtedly found, as it was privileged to find, that garden apartments would blend more attractively and harmoniously with the community setting, would impose less of a burden upon village facilities, if placed upon larger tracts of land rather than scattered about in smaller units. Obviously, some definite acreage had to be chosen, and, so far as the record before us reveals, the choice of ten acres as a minimum plot was well within the range of an unassailable legislative judgment. . . .

The charge of illegal "spot zoning" — leveled at the creation of a Residence B-B district and the reclassification of defendant's property — is without substance. Defined as the process of singling out a small parcel of land for a use classification totally different from that of the surrounding area, for the benefit of the owner of such property and to the detriment of other owners, "spot zoning" is the very antithesis of planned zoning. If, therefore, an ordinance is enacted in accordance with a comprehensive zoning plan, it is not "spot zoning," even though it (1) singles out and affects but one small plot. Thus, the relevant inquiry is not whether the particular zoning under attack consists of areas fixed within larger areas of different use, but whether it was accomplished for the benefit of individual owners rather than pursuant to a comprehensive plan for the general welfare of the community. Having already noted our conclusion that the ordinances were enacted to promote a comprehensive zoning plan, it is perhaps unnecessary to add that the record negates any claim that they were designed solely for the advantage of defendant or any other particular owner. Quite apart from the circumstance that defendant did not seek the benefit of the 1947 amendment until eighteen months after its passage, the all-significant fact is that that amendment applied to the entire territory of the village and accorded each and every owner of ten or more acres identical rights and privileges.

By the same token, there is no basis for the argument that "what has been done by the board of trustees" constitutes a device for "the granting of a variance," [as charged by the dissent]. As we have already shown, the village's zoning aim, the statute's purpose, was not to aid the individual owner but to permit the development of the property for the general welfare of the entire community. That being so, the board of trustees followed approved procedure by changing the General Zoning Ordinance itself. Accordingly, when the board was called upon to consider the reclassification of the Rubin property under the 1947 amendment, it was concerned, not with any issue of hardship, but only with the question of whether the property constituted a desirable location for a garden apartment.

We turn finally to the contention that the 1947 ordinance is invalid because, in proclaiming a Residence B-B district, it set no boundaries for the new district and made no changes on the building zone map. The short answer is that, since the ordinance merely prescribed specifications for a new use district, there was no need for it to do either the one or the other. . . .

The judgment of the Appellate Division should be affirmed, with costs.

Conway, Judge, dissenting, in opinion in which Judge Desmond concurs. The decision here made gives judicial sanction to a novel and unprecedented device whereby the board of trustees of a village may, in the exercise of its discretion, authorize the erection of multiple family dwellings on property, located wholly within established districts theretofore uniformly zoned for use as one- or two-family dwellings, by the simple expedient of declaring, upon the application of individuals owning a certain acreage, that henceforth such property shall constitute a new and separate zoning district. The device may have much to commend it in the way of administrative convenience, but it most assuredly is not "zoning," as that term has previously been understood. We think the action of the board of trustees of the village of Tarrytown is unauthorized by the Village Law of this State, which is the sole source of the board's power to act. Moreover, we feel that the board's action, here approved, is completely at odds with all sound zoning theory and practice, and may well prove to be the opening wedge in the destruction of effective and efficient zoning in this State. . . .

. . . Essentially and basically, what has been done by the board of trustees in the instant case is to permit a nonconforming use in an established zone. Heretofore, such action has always been referred to as the granting of a "variance," yet the board has here sought to cloak its ultimate objective under the label and form of "rezoning." In order to protect and preserve our zoning systems from the frequent and inevitable attacks of interested parties who seek to avoid zoning laws for their own purposes, this court has imposed strict and severe limitations upon the granting of variances. . . . It cannot be denied that the individual respondent here would never have been able to secure a variance permitting the erection of multiple family dwellings in Residence A or B districts. . . . Nevertheless, the identical result has here been reached by denominating the action of the board as "rezoning." . . . That, we submit, is truly exalting form over substance.

. . . [A] person purchasing property in Tarrytown in a Residence A or B district to bring up his children now has no way of knowing whether the property next to his may or may not become the site of a multiple family dwelling with the attendant increases in population, traffic dangers, commerce and congestion. . . .

Notes and Questions

1. Just as *Euclid* served as the landmark case for authorizing Euclidean zoning, *Tarrytown* became a seminal case for opening the door to various forms of non-Euclidean zoning. In residential zones, Euclidean zoning seeks to spread out houses through setback, frontage, and yard-size requirements. This approach became popular with suburbanites early in the twentieth century and remains so in many places. During the mid-twentieth century, and increasingly in the early twenty-first century, suburban and urban dwellers grew more interested in inhabiting neighborhoods with a mix of cluster housing and open spaces. In some cases, neighborhood businesses, such as coffee shops and grocery stores, can enhance the mix. Such neighborhoods are commonly located on the suburban fringe of larger cities, but occasionally can serve as a means of revitalizing older urban areas. They typically have a unifying theme, such as having the visual characteristics of a Victorian village. *Tarrytown* anticipated this development with its authorization of what became known as cluster zoning and floating zones, both of which jettison traditional principles of Euclidean zoning.

2. Rather than impose restrictions on each individual residential lot or parcel, residential cluster zoning limits a subdivision's overall density of residential units. This leaves a developer free to create a mix of clustered housing and open spaces while still meeting overall density goals, as in the garden apartment development at issue in *Tarrytown*. By clustering residential units, the developer can save money on layout and site preparation while preserving attractive natural features. The result can be more affordable or more desirable housing. A cluster zoning ordinance typically will mandate a specific minimum area for such subdivisions, such as the 10-acre minimum at issue in this case. *Planned Unit Developments* (or PUDs) represent a logical evolution from the concept of cluster zoning. Whereas cluster zoning loosens the area requirements for residential units so as to allow a mix of housing types and open spaces, PUDs relax both area and use requirements so as to admit some non-residential uses, such as retail shops and even professional offices, into the mix as part of a designed neighborhood.

3. In its experiment with non-Euclidean zoning, *Tarrytown* also utilized the concept of a *floating zone*. As originally adopted, its Residential B-B zone was a floating zone. Such a zone is defined for a particular use (clustered residences in this

case) and later applied to particular land (such as Elizabeth Rubin's 10-acre plot) by amending the zoning ordinance. The zone is "floating" in that, although the city or town has authorized its creation, it has not specified where the zone is located. Landowners then submit an application for rezoning along with detailed plans about their proposed development. In *Tarrytown*, the applicant repeatedly modified her development plans to address concerns raised by city planners before her rezoning application was granted. Urban planners view floating zones as an effective means to control the location and impact of large-scale commercial, residential, and industrial developments. They are widely used in virtually all states.

4. In *Tarrytown*, the court defended the proposed 10-acre Residence B-B zone from the charge of *spot zoning*, which judges look upon with disfavor and commonly strike down. Spot zoning is the treatment of an island of land differently than adjacent properties. That differential treatment is typically favorable, though sometimes the spot of land is treated less favorably than neighboring property. Concerns that spot zoning results from political pressure or even bribes have prompted some courts to invalidate the resulting change when a small parcel is singled out for special and privileged treatment, when doing so is either for the benefit of the landowner rather that the public generally or not in accord with the comprehensive plan. In this respect, one case from Florida noted:

> The Dade County Commission rezoned a tiny, 0.23 acre tract in the middle of a West Dade area known as "Horse Country" from AU (Agricultural Use) to BU-3 (Business Use-3) solely and admittedly so the owner could operate a feed store—which is forbidden in an AU zone, but permitted (along with many other uses) in BU-3. No other BU zoning is anywhere close. On the face of it, the rezoning resolution embodies, to the nth degree, all the evils of spot zoning . . . which have been universally proscribed.

Bird-Kendall Homeowners Ass'n v. Metropolitan Dade County Comm'rs, 695 So. 2d 908, 909 (Fla. Dist. Ct. App. 1997). Despite their general acceptance, floating zones remain subject to attack as spot zoning in individual cases.

5. As a further enhancement of their zoning authority, many cities have enacted *subdivision controls*, which are ordinances that seek to assure adequate services, streets, and other infrastructure by establishing standards and procedures for subdividing land for residential development. As the court explained in Gardner v. Baltimore Mayor & City Council, 969 F.2d 63, 66-67 (4th Cir. 1992):

> Land use controls over subdivisions . . . date from the late nineteenth century. The original statutes took the form of land platting legislation and were intended to provide a more efficient method of conveying property. *See* D. Hagman & J. Juergensmeyer, *Urban Planning and Land Development Control Law* §7.2, at 191 (2d ed. 1986). Before subdivision control, land was sold by reference to metes and bounds, an unreliable system that often resulted in confusion and overlapping titles. Subdivision regulations avoided these problems by requiring land developers to record in the local records office a "plat," or map, of the property. The plat, which contained precise dimensions, subdivided the land into blocks and lots and indicated the location of roads and parks. Once the plat was recorded, individual lots could then be conveyed by reference to the lot, block, and plat name, thereby avoiding the confusion inherent in the metes and bounds system.
>
> Beginning in the 1920s, subdivision control became not only a mechanism to simplify the conveyance of individual lots, [but] also a means through which localities could regulate urban and suburban development through comprehensive planning.

Localities began to use subdivision regulations to prevent the construction of new streets that were not well aligned with existing roads. Subdivision control also functioned to ensure that development did not result in platted lots of unusable sizes that remained vacant, or in the splitting of large holdings suited for industrial or agricultural uses into numerous parcels that a private person could not reassemble.

Following the Second World War, localities used subdivision control to implement more extensive substantive regulation. With the expansion of suburban areas, subdivision regulation turned to ensuring the provision of adequate local governmental facilities and services.

Thus, such regulation mandated the construction of parks and other recreational facilities as well as schools for area residents. Comprehensive planning also became concerned with structuring development to avoid serious off-site drainage problems and to avert the negative impact of development on the local environment. Subdivision regulation also became a mechanism to ensure that streets were properly constructed and were sufficiently wide for anticipated traffic. Finally, localities required each lot to have adequate access to public services and utilities, such as water, sewage, gas, electricity, telephone, and cable television.

Finally, the imposition of *impact fees* (or exactions) to pay for such services and to mitigate the burdens on the larger community is an increasingly common tool, albeit one that presents constitutional takings problems, as discussed below in Chapter 14.

■ **H.H.B., L.L.C. v. D & F, L.L.C.**
Supreme Court of Alabama, 2002
843 So. 2d 116

PER CURIAM. . . .

H.H.B., L.L.C., is a limited liability company, whose owners are accountants. D & F, L.L.C., is a limited liability company, whose owners are the principals of The Mitchell Company, a real-estate company, and other real-estate companies in Mobile. D & F owns a 1.7-acre corner parcel of property located at the intersection of Dauphin Street, North Florida Street, and Woodruff Street in Mobile ("the subject property"). The building in which H.H.B. is located is across North Florida Street from the subject property. All of the property in the immediate neighborhood is zoned, as defined in the zoning ordinance of the City of Mobile, R-1 (One-Family Residential Districts) or B-1 (Buffer Business Districts). D & F intends to build a 10,000-square-foot CVS retail discount store with 60 parking places on the subject property. In order to do so, however, D & F must have the zoning designation of the subject property changed to B-2 (Neighborhood Business Districts).

Woodruff Street is exclusively residential. Dauphin Street and North Florida Street are a mixture of residential areas and buffer-business areas. Buffer businesses are by definition those businesses in which permitted uses are uses of a semicommercial nature, such as professional offices and studios. The subject property previously consisted of eight lots, almost all of which have been zoned for the past 50 years as either R-1 or B-1. During the 1960s, a drugstore occupied the corner site for several years. Before D & F acquired the property, three residences and a building used as a real-estate office were situated on it. The subject property has since been cleared and all buildings removed.

In order to obtain a zoning change, an applicant must first obtain the approval of the Mobile City Planning Commission, followed by the approval of the Mobile

City Council. D & F began its efforts to obtain B-2 zoning in 1999. It withdrew its first two applications after they were submitted to the planning commission, but before the city council considered the matter. D & F submitted its third application to the planning commission in August 2000. Between the filing of the second and third applications, D & F voluntarily incorporated numerous changes to its plans and restrictions on otherwise acceptable B-2 uses in an effort to accommodate the concerns of residents of the neighborhood. Those changes and restrictions included eliminating any use that could be made of the property under B-2 zoning except for a drugstore, designing a building that would be architecturally compatible with the neighborhood's surrounding buildings, not allowing the sale of beer and wine, not providing outside telephones, restricting dumpster pickups to daylight hours, and constructing a brick wall behind the store. Despite D & F's efforts, however, the planning commission's staff recommended to the commission, as it had with the first two applications, that it deny the third application. In spite of its staff's recommendation, the planning commission, in September 2000, voted 6-2 to recommend to the city council that it approve D & F's application to change the subject property's zoning designation to B-2. The planning commission's recommendation was subject to the conditions and restrictions D & F had voluntarily attached to its application. The proposed amendment to the zoning ordinance to effectuate the zoning change for the subject property was presented to the city council in October 2000. Although the council members voted 4-3 to approve the amendment to the zoning ordinance, §11-44C-28, Ala. Code 1975, requires a "supermajority" of the city council before an ordinance can be adopted, which meant that five votes were required in order for the amendment to the zoning ordinance to become effective; the amendment was therefore denied. In December 2000, D & F appealed the denial of the zoning-ordinance amendment to the Mobile Circuit Court. [The court held that the City's decision not to amend the zoning ordinance to change the zoning of the subject property to B-2 was arbitrary and capricious as applied to D & F, that keeping the subject property zoned R-1 and B-1 bore no substantial relationship to the health, safety, morals, or general welfare of the City, and that the City's decision not to rezone was not fairly debatable because D & F was not seeking to change the basic use of the property.]

Zoning

Judicial review of municipal decisions regarding zoning ordinances is severely limited. In American Petroleum Equipment & Construction, Inc. v. Fancher, 708 So. 2d 129 (Ala. 1997), this Court discussed the standard of review that both the trial court and this Court must apply in reviewing those decisions.

It is settled law that the Alabama Legislature has delegated to municipal legislative bodies, such as city councils, the power and authority to enact zoning ordinances. Section 11-52-76, Ala. Code [1975], provides that "the legislative body of such municipality shall provide for the manner in which such [zoning] regulations and restrictions and the boundaries of such districts shall be determined, established and enforced." The power to amend, supplement, or change zoning ordinances "as may be necessary" from "time to time" is also delegated to municipal legislative bodies. Id. See BP Oil Co. v. Jefferson County, 571 So. 2d 1026, 1028 (Ala. 1990), citing Village of Euclid, Ohio v. Ambler Realty Co., 272 U.S. 365 (1926).

In Homewood Citizens Association v. City of Homewood, 548 So. 2d 142 (Ala. 1989), this Court discussed the law applicable to a court's review of a city's action in zoning cases, stating that "when a municipal body acts either to adopt or to amend a zoning ordinance, it acts in a legislative capacity and the scope of judicial review of such action is quite restricted." The restrictions on this Court's review of the validity of a zoning ordinance have been explained as follows:

> Zoning is a legislative matter, and, as a general proposition, the exercise of the zoning power should not be subjected to judicial interference unless clearly necessary. *In enacting or amending zoning legislation, the local authorities are vested with broad discretion, and, in cases where the validity of a zoning ordinance is fairly debatable, the court cannot substitute its judgment for that of the legislative authority. If there is a rational and justifiable basis for the enactment and it does not violate any state statute or positive constitutional guaranty, the wisdom of the zoning regulation is a matter exclusively for legislative determination.*
>
> In accordance with these principles, it has been stated that the courts should not interfere with the exercise of the zoning power and hold a zoning enactment invalid, unless the enactment, in whole or in relation to any particular property, is shown to be clearly arbitrary, capricious, or unreasonable, having no substantial relation to the public health, safety, or welfare, or . . . plainly contrary to the zoning laws.

Homewood Citizens Association, 548 So. 2d at 143. The Court further stated in Homewood Citizens Association that "the burden is upon the party seeking relief from an ordinance to show that the ordinance was not a fairly debatable issue before the municipal governing body." 548 So. 2d at 144.

708 So. 2d at 131 (emphasis added). The Court went on in *American Petroleum* to discuss the "fairly debatable" rule.

> The "fairly debatable" rule concerns the application of a zoning classification to a specific parcel of property. Byrd Companies v. Jefferson County, 445 So. 2d 239, 247 (Ala. 1983). "*[I]f the application of a zoning classification to a specific parcel of property is reasonably subject to disagreement, that is, if its application is fairly debatable, then the application of the ordinance by the zoning authority should not be disturbed by the courts.*" *Id.* Thus, if the zoning ordinance is "subject to controversy or contention" or "open to question or dispute," it is "fairly debatable" and should not be disturbed by the courts.

708 So. 2d at 131 (emphasis added).

Under the highly deferential standard we must apply in this case, we cannot say that a rezoning request that received a split vote by the planning commission and a split vote by the city council was not reasonably subject to disagreement, that is, not fairly debatable. The trial court determined that the city council's decision was not fairly debatable because D & F was not seeking to change the basic use of the subject property from that of a drugstore. The record reflects, however, that the "drugstore" that occupied the site in the 1960s was of the "mom-and-pop" variety, not the large retail establishments that exist today. The record in this case demonstrates that the question whether to zone the subject property B-2 instead of B-1 was certainly "subject to controversy or contention" or "open to question or dispute," especially as it relates to a change from a small, family-run apothecary to a modern, broad-based retail facility such as is before the Court in this case. Therefore, the city council's decision should not be disturbed by a court. Because D & F's application to amend the zoning ordinance to designate the subject property as B-2 was fairly debatable, we hold that the city council's decision not to rezone the subject property had a reasonable relationship to the health, safety, morals, or general welfare of the community and that the trial court erred in finding its decision to deny rezoning to be arbitrary and capricious. We reverse the judgment, and remand the case for the trial court to enter an order affirming the decision of the city council.

JOHNSTONE, J., dissenting. . . . Section IX.A.1.b. of the Zoning Ordinance of the City of Mobile allows zoning amendments like the one sought by D & F if "changed or changing conditions in a particular area, or in the planning region generally, make a change in the ordinance necessary and desirable." In essence, the trial court, upon evidence *ore tenus*, found that the conditions in the particular area at issue in this case had changed to such an extent and in such a way that the application of the existing B-1 classification, as distinguished from the proposed B-2 classification, to the D & F property would no longer bear a substantial relationship to the health, safety, morals, or general welfare of the City, that no fairly debatable rationale supported the denial of the zoning amendment, and that, therefore, the denial constituted an impermissible arbitrary and capricious act by the City. The record contains superabundant evidence to support this finding.

The nature and extent of change in the particular area is a factual issue to be decided by the fact-finder. Fact-findings based on evidence *ore tenus* are not to "'be disturbed on appeal unless they are palpably wrong, manifestly unjust, or without supporting evidence.'" Samek v. Sanders, 788 So. 2d 872, 876 (Ala. 2000) (quoting McCoy v. McCoy, 549 So. 2d 53, 57 (Ala. 1989)). The correctness of the fact-findings by the trial court in the case now before us is buttressed by the prior six-to-two vote of the planning commission in favor of recommending adoption of the zoning amendment sought by D & F and the four-to-three vote (albeit legally insufficient) of the city council in favor of adopting the amendment. Because the record supports a factual basis sufficient to support the legal conclusions by the trial court necessary to its judgment granting zoning relief to D & F, that judgment should be affirmed.

Notes and Questions

1. When all else fails, change the law. That is a common tactic employed by property owners whose desired activities are prohibited by the zoning regulations, who are unable to secure a variance or other administrative relief, and who cannot persuade the courts that the result is unconstitutional or contrary to a federal or state statute. Actually, property owners often seek to amend the zoning regulations long before they have exhausted their administrative and judicial appeals. Early zoning advocates have been proven naive in their belief that few changes in the ordinances would be necessary once a city's zoning plan was implemented. Every state zoning enabling act empowers a locality to amend its zoning regulations, though such changes must often be approved by a supermajority. Zoning amendments may also be enacted by popular initiative instead of by the local legislative body.

2. Not every state follows *H.H.B.*'s deferential standard of judicial review for zoning amendments. Fasano v. Board of County Commissioners of Washington County, 507 P.2d 23 (Or. 1973), announced a more stringent approach to judicial review because it viewed zoning amendments as an adjudicative act rather than a legislative act and so subject to an arbitrary and capricious standard of review. Few

states follow the *Fasano* approach, but the question continues to generate substantial debate.

3. *Conditional zoning* and *contract zoning* offer further planning tools for local governments. Under both approaches, the government rezones property subject to the petitioning landowner meeting certain requirements. For example, an Ohio condominium developer was issued a conditional zoning certificate provided that he could meet numerous conditions related to compliance with Ohio condominium law, including the development of roads and satisfaction of bonding requirements; federal environmental approval to build on wetlands; compliance with the minimum land requirements; reduction of the number of units in the development; responsibility for erosion and sedimentation control; and board approval for a final site plan review. Silver v. Franklin Township Bd. of Zoning Appeals, 966 F.2d 1031, 1032 (6th Cir. 1992).

Conditional zoning does not involve any commitments by the local government, whereas contract zoning involves an enforceable reciprocal agreement with the local government. These actions are generally sustained despite fears of undue influence undermining the comprehensive plan. As one court has explained, "Conditional zoning, once roundly condemned, appears to be in the ascendency. In Maryland, the concept has evolved indirectly through the use of various zoning devices such as planned developments, and has found at least limited favor with the state legislature. *See* Article 66B, §§4.01(b), permitting a county or municipal corporation to impose certain conditions at the time of zoning or rezoning land, under certain circumstances." Mayor & Council of Rockville v. Rylyns Enters., 814 A.2d 469, 487 (Md. 2002). Maryland is one of several states with statutes that expressly permit conditional rezoning, while special exceptions are the most common alternative in jurisdictions where conditional or contract zoning is prohibited.

B. GROWTH CONTROLS

■ CONSTRUCTION INDUSTRY ASSOCIATION OF SONOMA COUNTY v. CITY OF PETALUMA

United States Court of Appeals for the Ninth Circuit, 1975
522 F.2d 897, cert. denied, 424 U.S. 934 (1976)

CHOY, Circuit Judge. The City of Petaluma (the City) appeals from a district court decision voiding as unconstitutional certain aspects of its five-year housing and zoning plan. We reverse.

STATEMENT OF FACTS

The City is located in southern Sonoma County, about 40 miles north of San Francisco. In the 1950's and 1960's, Petaluma was a relatively self-sufficient town. It experienced a steady population growth from 10,315 in 1950 to 24,870 in 1970. Eventually, the City was drawn into the Bay Area metropolitan housing market as people working in San Francisco and San Rafael became willing to commute longer distances to secure relatively inexpensive housing available there. By November 1972, according to unofficial figures, Petaluma's population was at 30,500, a dramatic increase of almost 25 percent in little over two years.

The increase in the City's population, not surprisingly, is reflected in the increase in the number of its housing units. From 1964 to 1971, the following number of residential housing units were completed:

1964	270	1968	379
1965	440	1969	358
1966	321	1970	591
1967	234	1971	891

In 1970 and 1971, the years of the most rapid growth, demand for housing in the City was even greater than above indicated. Taking 1970 and 1971 together, builders won approval of a total of 2,000 permits although only 1,482 were actually completed by the end of 1971.

Alarmed by the accelerated rate of growth in 1970 and 1971, the demand for even more housing, and the sprawl of the City eastward, the City adopted a temporary freeze on development in early 1971. The construction and zoning change moratorium was intended to give the City Council and the City planners an opportunity to study the housing and zoning situation and to develop short and long range plans. The Council made specific findings with respect to housing patterns and availability in Petaluma, including the following: That from 1960-1970 housing had been in almost unvarying 6,000 square-foot lots laid out in regular grid patterns; that there was a density of approximately 4.5 housing units per acre in the single-family home areas; that during 1960-1970, 88 percent of housing permits issued were for single-family detached homes; that in 1970, 83 percent of Petaluma's housing was single-family dwellings; that the bulk of recent development (largely single-family homes) occurred in the eastern portion of the City, causing a large deficiency in moderately priced multi-family and apartment units on the east side.

To correct the imbalance between single-family and multi-family dwellings, curb the sprawl of the City on the east, and retard the accelerating growth of the City, the Council in 1972 adopted several resolutions, which collectively are called the "Petaluma Plan" (the Plan).

The Plan, on its face limited to a five-year period (1972-1977), fixes a housing development growth rate not to exceed 500 dwelling units per year. Each dwelling unit represents approximately three people. The 500-unit figure is somewhat misleading, however, because it applies only to housing units (hereinafter referred to as "development-units") that are part of projects involving five units or more. Thus, the 500-unit figure does not reflect any housing and population growth due to construction of single-family homes or even four-unit apartment buildings not part of any larger project.

The Plan also positions a 200-foot-wide "greenbelt" around the City, to serve as a boundary for urban expansion for at least five years, and with respect to the east and north sides of the City, for perhaps ten to fifteen years. One of the most innovative features of the Plan is the Residential Development Control System, which provides procedures and criteria for the award of the annual 500 development-unit permits. At the heart of the allocation procedure is an intricate point system, whereby a builder accumulates points for conformity by his projects with the City's general plan and environmental design plans, for good architectural design, and for providing low and moderate income dwelling units and various recreational facilities. The Plan further directs that allocations of building permits are to be divided as evenly as feasible between the west and east sections of the City and between single-family dwellings and multiple residential units (including rental units), that the sections of the City closest to the center are to be developed first in order to cause "infilling" of vacant area, and that 8 to 12 percent of the housing units approved be for low and moderate income persons.

In a provision of the Plan, intended to maintain the close-in rural space outside and surrounding Petaluma, the City solicited Sonoma County to establish stringent subdivision and appropriate acreage parcel controls for the areas outside the urban extension line of the City and to limit severely further residential infilling.

PURPOSE OF THE PLAN

The purpose of the Plan is much disputed in this case. According to general statements in the Plan itself, the Plan was devised to ensure that "development in the next five years, will take place in a reasonable, orderly, attractive manner, rather than in a completely haphazard and unattractive manner." The controversial 500-unit limitation on residential development-units was adopted by the City "in order to protect its small town character and surrounding open space."[5] The other features of the Plan were designed to encourage an east-west balance in development, to provide for variety in densities and building types and wide ranges in prices and rents, to ensure infilling of close-in vacant areas, and to prevent the sprawl of the City to the east and north. The Builders Association of Sonoma County (the Association) argues and the district court found, however, that the Plan was primarily enacted "to limit Petaluma's demographic and market growth rate in housing and in the immigration of new residents." 375 F. Supp. 574, 576.

MARKET DEMAND AND EFFECT OF THE PLAN

In 1970 and 1971, housing permits were allotted at the rate of 1,000 annually, and there was no indication that without some governmental control on growth consumer demand would subside or even remain at the 1,000-unit per year level. Thus, if Petaluma had imposed a flat 500-unit limitation on *all* residential housing, the effect of the Plan would clearly be to retard to a substantial degree the natural growth rate of the City. Petaluma, however, did not apply the 500-unit limitation across the board, but instead exempted all projects of four units or less. Because appellees failed to introduce any evidence whatsoever as to the number of exempt units expected to be built during the five-year period, the effect of the 500 *development-unit* limitation on the natural growth in housing is uncertain. For purposes of this decision, however, we will assume that the 500 development-unit growth rate is in fact below the reasonably anticipated market demand for such units and that absent the Petaluma Plan, the City would grow at a faster rate.

According to undisputed expert testimony at trial, if the Plan (limiting housing starts to approximately 6 percent of existing housing stock each year) were to be adopted by municipalities throughout the region, the impact on the housing market would be substantial. For the decade 1970 to 1980, the shortfall in needed housing in the region would be about 105,000 units (or 25 percent of the units

---

5. After the appellees initiated this suit, the City attempted to show that the Plan was implemented to prevent the overtaxing of available water and sewage facilities. We find it unnecessary, however, to consider the claim that sewage and water problems justified implementation of the Plan.

needed). Further, the aggregate effect of a proliferation of the Plan throughout the San Francisco region would be a decline in regional housing stock quality, a loss of the mobility of current and prospective residents and a deterioration in the quality and choice of housing available to income earners with real incomes of $14,000 per year or less. If, however, the Plan were considered by itself and with respect to Petaluma only, there is no evidence to suggest that there would be a deterioration in the quality and choice of housing available there to persons in the lower and middle income brackets. Actually, the Plan increases the availability of multi-family units (owner-occupied and rental units) and low-income units that were rarely constructed in the pre-Plan days.

COURT PROCEEDINGS

Two landowners (the Landowners) and the Association instituted this suit under 28 U.S.C. §§1331, 1343 and 42 U.S.C. §1983 against the City and its officers and council members, claiming that the Petaluma Plan was unconstitutional. The district court ruled that certain aspects of the Plan unconstitutionally denied the right to travel insofar as they tended "to limit the natural population growth of the area." 375 F. Supp. 574 at 588. The court enjoined the City and its agents from implementing the unconstitutional elements of the Plan, but the order was stayed by Justice Douglas pending this appeal. [The Ninth Circuit refused to consider the constitutional right to travel claim because the plaintiffs lacked standing to assert it.]

SUBSTANTIVE DUE PROCESS

Appellees claim that the Plan is arbitrary and unreasonable and, thus, violative of the due process clause of the Fourteenth Amendment. According to appellees, the Plan is nothing more than an exclusionary zoning device,[10] designed solely to insulate Petaluma from the urban complex in which it finds itself. The Association and the Landowners reject, as falling outside the scope of any legitimate governmental interest, the City's avowed purposes in implementing the Plan — the preservation of Petaluma's small town character and the avoidance of the social and environmental problems caused by an uncontrolled growth rate.

In attacking the validity of the Plan, appellees rely heavily on the district court's finding that the express purpose and the actual effect of the Plan is to exclude substantial numbers of people who would otherwise elect to move to the City. The existence of an exclusionary purpose and effect reflects, however, only *one* side of the zoning regulation. Practically all zoning restrictions have as a purpose and effect the *exclusion* of some activity or type of structure or a certain density of inhabitants. And in reviewing the reasonableness of a zoning ordinance, our inquiry does not terminate with a finding that it is for an exclusionary purpose. We must

---

10. "Exclusionary zoning" is a phrase popularly used to describe suburban zoning regulations that have the effect, if not also the purpose, of preventing the migration of low- and middle-income persons. Since a large percentage of racial minorities fall within the low- and middle-income brackets, exclusionary zoning regulations may also effectively wall out racial minorities.

Most court challenges to and comment upon so-called exclusionary zoning focus on such traditional zoning devices as height limitations, minimum square footage and minimum lot size requirements, and the prohibition of multi-family dwellings or mobile homes. The Petaluma Plan is unique in that although it assertedly slows the growth rate it replaces the past pattern of single-family detached homes with an assortment of housing units, varying in price and design.

determine further whether the *exclusion* bears any rational relationship to a *legitimate state interest.* If it does not, then the zoning regulation is invalid. If, on the other hand, a legitimate state interest is furthered by the zoning regulation, we must defer to the legislative act. Being neither a super legislature nor a zoning board of appeal, a federal court is without authority to weigh and reappraise the factors considered or ignored by the legislative body in passing the challenged zoning regulation.[12] The reasonableness, not the wisdom, of the Petaluma Plan is at issue in this suit.

It is well settled that zoning regulations "must find their justification in some aspect of the police power, asserted for the public welfare." Village of Euclid v. Ambler Realty Co., 272 U.S. 365, 387 (1926). The concept of the public welfare, however, is not limited to the regulation of noxious activities or dangerous structures. As the Court stated in Berman v. Parker, 348 U.S. 26, 33 (1954):

> The concept of the public welfare is broad and inclusive. The values it represents are spiritual as well as physical, aesthetic as well as monetary. It is within the power of the legislature to determine that the community should be beautiful as well as healthy, spacious as well as clean, well-balanced as well as carefully patrolled.

(Citations omitted.) *Accord,* Village of Belle Terre v. Boraas, 416 U.S. 1, 6, 9 (1974). . . . [16]

Although we assume that some persons desirous of living in Petaluma will be excluded under the housing permit limitation and that, thus, the Plan may frustrate some legitimate regional housing needs, the Plan is not arbitrary or unreasonable. We agree with appellees that unlike the situation in the past most municipalities today are neither isolated nor wholly independent from neighboring municipalities and that, consequently, unilateral land use decisions by one local entity affect the needs and resources of an entire region. *See, e.g.,* Golden v. Planning Board of Town of Ramapo, 285 N.E.2d 291 (N.Y), *appeal dismissed,* 409 U.S. 1003 (1972); National Land & Investment Co. v. Kohn, 215 A.2d 597 (Pa. 1965); Note, *Phased Zoning: Regulation of the Tempo and Sequence of Land Development,* 26 Stan. L. Rev. 585, 605

---

12. Appellees' brief is unnecessarily oversize (125 pages) mainly because it is rife with quotations from writers on regional planning, economic regulation and sociological policies and themes. These types of considerations are more appropriate for legislative bodies than for courts.

16. Although appellees have attempted to align their business interests in attacking the Plan with legitimate housing needs of the urban poor and racial minorities, the Association has not alleged nor can it allege, based on the record in this case, that the Plan has the purpose and effect of excluding poor persons and racial minorities. Contrary to the picture painted by appellees, the Petaluma Plan is "inclusionary" to the extent that it offers new opportunities, previously unavailable, to minorities and low- and moderate-income persons. Under the pre-Plan system, single-family, middle-income housing dominated the Petaluma market, and as a result low- and moderate-income persons were unable to secure housing in the area. The Plan radically changes the previous building pattern and requires that housing permits be evenly divided between single-family and multi-family units and that approximately eight to twelve percent of the units be constructed specifically for low- and moderate-income persons.

In stark contrast, each of the exclusionary zoning regulations invalidated by state courts in recent years impeded the ability of low and moderate income persons to purchase or rent housing in the locality. *See, e.g.,* Southern Burlington County NAACP v. Township of Mount Laurel, 67 N.J. 151, 336 A.2d 713 (1975) (zoned exclusively for single-family, detached dwellings and multi-family dwellings designed for middle and upper income persons); Oakwood at Madison, Inc. v. Township of Madison, 283 A.2d 353 (N.J. Super. 1971) (minimum one or two acre requirement and severe limitation on multi-family units); Appeal of Kit-Mar Builders, Inc., 268 A.2d 765 (Pa. 1970) (two to three acre minimum lot size); Appeal of Girsh, 263 A.2d 395 (Pa. 1970) (prohibition of apartment buildings); National Land & Investment Co. v. Kohn, 215 A.2d 597 (Pa. 1965) (4 acre minimum lot); Board of County Supervisors of Fairfax County v. Carper, 107 S.E.2d 390 (Va. 1959) (rezoning to minimum two acre lots with the effect of keeping poor in another section of municipality).

(1974). It does not necessarily follow, however, that the *due process* rights of builders and landowners are violated merely because a local entity exercises in its own self-interest the police power lawfully delegated to it by the state. If the present system of delegated zoning power does not effectively serve the state interest in furthering the general welfare of the region or entire state, it is the state legislature's and not the federal courts' role to intervene and adjust the system. As stated *supra*, the federal court is not a super zoning board and should not be called on to mark the point at which legitimate local interests in promoting the welfare of the community are outweighed by legitimate regional interests.

We conclude therefore that . . . the concept of the public welfare is sufficiently broad to uphold Petaluma's desire to preserve its small town character, its open spaces and low density of population, and to grow at an orderly and deliberate pace.[17]

[The court also held that "since the local regulation here is rationally related to the social and environmental welfare of the community and does not discriminate against interstate commerce or operate to disrupt its required uniformity, appellees' claim that the Plan unreasonably burdens commerce must fail."]

Notes and Questions

1. How is the Petaluma Plan different from the laws at issue in *Euclid, Tarrytown,* and other zoning cases? How is it like them?

2. One year later and one state to the north, the state legislature enacted the Oregon Comprehensive Land Use Planning Act of 1973. That Act created a Land Conservation and Development Commission charged with creating statewide goals with citizen input. The resulting state plan identified three key goals: requiring urban areas to define growth boundaries around their perimeters to prevent sprawl and to preserve farmland, providing adequate housing of all types within the boundary, and preventing urban encroachment on natural resources. The state plan required all Oregon municipalities and counties to prepare and adopt comprehensive plans consistent with state goals.

Portland adopted a plan in 1979 that governed 24 cities in 4 counties. The plan established an outer perimeter beyond which no development was allowed until 2000, and an inner perimeter outside of which development could be forbidden until the land inside had been fully developed. Originally, the plan was designed to encourage building in the 35 percent of the land that was vacant inside the boundaries. But Metro, the regional planning authority, declined to expand the boundary

---

17. Our decision upholding the Plan as not in violation of the appellees' due process rights should not be read as a permanent endorsement of the Plan. In a few years the City itself for good reason may abandon the Plan or the state may decide to alter its laws delegating its zoning power to the local authorities; or to meet legitimate regional needs, regional zoning authorities may be established. *See, e.g.,* Cal. Gov. Code §§66600 et seq. (San Francisco Bay Conservation and Development Commission); Cal. Gov. Code §§66801, 67000 et seq. (Tahoe Regional Planning Agency); Public Resources Code §§27000 et seq. (California Coastal Zone Conservation Commission). To be sure, housing needs in metropolitan areas like the San Francisco Bay Area are pressing and the needs are not being met by present methods of supplying housing. However, the federal court is not the proper forum for resolving these problems. The controversy stirred up by the present litigation, as indicated by the number and variety of *amici* on each side, and the complex economic, political and social factors involved in this case are compelling evidence that resolution of the important housing and environmental issues raised here is exclusively the domain of the legislature.

as 2000 drew near and as land within the boundary was filled in. Instead, Metro mandated much higher population densities within the boundary. These steps have produced several results. Portland is widely viewed as a very liveable city. But housing prices rose 61.5 percent between 1990 and 1995 — compared to the national median of 18.2 percent — and many poor and minority residents could no longer afford to live in the city. Moreover, open space is disappearing within the boundary. Yet the plan remains popular both in Oregon, where four popular referendums to repeal the law have failed, and in other jurisdictions that are drawing upon Portland's experience in their own struggles to control sprawl.

3. Although the court rejected their charge, challengers of the Petaluma Plan asserted that it was exclusionary. *Exclusionary zoning* refers to governmental land use restrictions that serve to exclude particular types of people or kinds of lawful activity. Under the federal Fair Housing Act and various state constitution provisions, for example, courts have stuck down local zoning ordinances that serve to exclude low-income or minority groups. For classic cases in this area, see Village of Arlington Heights v. Metropolitan Housing Authority, 429 U.S. 252 (1977) (Fair Housing Act), and Southern Burlington County NAACP v. Township of Mount Laurel, 67 N.J. 151 (1975) (New Jersey state constitution). Charges of exclusionary zoning are also leveled against local zoning ordinances in other contexts, such as when they effectively preclude churches from residential areas or so-called X-rated businesses from a community altogether. It may seem strange to discuss houses of worship and places of adult entertainment in the same breath, but both have been the targets of zoning restrictions due to the number and type of people they attract at odd hours from outside the community and, in some cases, the locally unpopular nature of their activities. Further, their defenders often claim special protection under the First Amendment of the Constitution: churches, temples, and mosques under the Free Exercise Clause; porn shops and adult theaters under the Free Speech Clause.

4. In 2000, Congress addressed concerns about municipal restrictions on religious land uses by passing the Religious Land Use and Institutionalized Persons Act, 42 U.S.C. §2000cc (RLUIPA). This statute provides that any government regulation of the land use of religious bodies must serve a compelling state interest and employ the least restrictive means of serving that interest. *Id.* §2000cc(2)(b). It also prohibits government land use discrimination against any institution on the basis of religion or religious denomination. *Id.* §2000cc(2)(b). Before RLUIPA, the courts were split on the validity of zoning laws that excluded churches or other religious uses from residential areas. Most cases forbade the exclusion of houses of worship from residential areas on the grounds that such facilities further public morals and the general welfare. A minority view applied the usual presumption of the constitutionality of zoning. *E.g.*, Mount Elliott Cemetery Ass'n v. City of Troy, 171 F.3d 398 (6th Cir. 1999) (city's refusal to rezone residential property for use as a Catholic cemetery did not deny the church its constitutional rights to the free exercise of religion and it did not constitute exclusionary zoning prohibited by state law).

5. The leading case involving the zoning of adult businesses is City of Renton v. Playtime Theatres, Inc., 475 U.S. 41 (1986). In April 1981, Renton, Washington enacted an ordinance that prohibited an adult theater from locating within one mile of any residential zone, residential dwelling, church, park, or school, which would have effectively barred them from the city. Less than one year later, with the intent of showing full-length adult films, Playtime Theatres, Inc. and Sea-First Properties, Inc. purchased two existing theaters in an area of downtown Renton where

adult theaters were prohibited. The theater owners sought an injunction against the enforcement of the ordinance, and the city council responded by reducing the distance to 1,000 feet, which narrowly limited where adult theaters could locate. The Supreme Court upheld the ordinance as a valid restriction on the time, place, and manner of speech. The Court explained that the city's "predominant" intent was to prevent crime, protect retail trade, maintain property values, and preserve the quality of life — not simply to suppress unpopular speech. In this sense, the case was like Young v. American Mini Theatres, Inc., 427 U.S. 50 (1976), which upheld a Detroit zoning ordinance that effectively disbursed adult theaters by prohibited them within 1,000 feet of certain uses or 500 feet of a residential zone. Cities are thus permitted to use zoning to either disperse adult theaters (like Detroit) or concentrate them (like Renton) so long as they make some allowance for them. Renton satisfied that requirement because it allowed adult theaters on 520 acres (or 5 percent of the city's land) within the city, even though a prospective theater would have to convince the current owners to sell their property. Since *Renton*, courts have reached differing conclusions regarding claims that adult businesses were improperly precluded by zoning ordinances.

6. The population of Petaluma grew to 56,000 in 2002, about twice the number of people as when the growth controls were approved 30 years before. Residential growth has been more stable than during the late 1960s, dropping below the 500 units per year cap. "Downtown has very slowly morphed into a trendy shopping and nightlife district. A niche of the telecommunications industry has made its home in southern Sonoma County, and Petaluma received applications for about 2 million square feet of office space in only 18 months. . . . Yet Petaluma remains well-connected to its rural roots. Pastures and open space surround the city. Two creameries operate in town. Tall feed silos that hover over downtown are still in use." Paul Shigley, *Petaluma Marks 30 Years of Growth Control*, 17 California Planning & Development Report 4 (2002). The only significant change in the law occurred in 1998, when voters approved an urban growth boundary similar to the plan adopted by Portland.

7. Does it matter who decides whether to impose growth controls? On election day 2000, voters in Arizona and Colorado rejected ballot initiatives to impose growth controls even as many local growth controls received popular approval. Reflecting on that disparity, Professor Nicole Garnett asks, "Why would an electorate that expresses overwhelming concern about sprawl vote to raise taxes to conserve open space and to impose local growth controls, but reject proposals designed to address suburban sprawl through comprehensive, regional growth management?" She offers three possible answers:

> First, not all of the members of the coalitions that formed to defeat Amendment 24 [in Colorado] and Proposition 202 [in Arizona] had the same interests at stake in the outcome of initiatives proposing conservation measures or local growth controls. For example, while developers, who represented the primary financiers of the "NO" campaigns, might not have believed they had as much at stake with respect to local growth control measures, they may have believed they could have channeled their new developments elsewhere. Thus, they may have lacked the incentive to work as hard to defeat local measures.
>
> Second, enlarging the geographic scope of the regulatory proposal may change how voters evaluate the costs and benefits of growth controls. Building upon the prediction that growth controls drive up housing prices, a number of academics have

suggested that growth controls benefit existing homeowners and hurt prospective home-owners. Existing homeowners can charge prospective homeowners the premium that they gain when the government limits new development. Of course, an existing homeowner who wishes to reap the benefit of this premium is usually also a prospective homeowner; she generally plans to sell her home and purchase a new one. In order for the existing home-owner to reap the full benefit of the premium, therefore, she must be able to sell her home within the controlled area and move to a home outside of it, where she will not have to pay a similar growth control imposed premium. Regional or statewide growth controls make it much more difficult to profit from the growth control premium. If an existing homeowner must leave the state in order to avoid paying the growth control premium on a new home, her costs of exit are much higher than if she can move one town over. She might have to change jobs, leave family and friends, and make other lifestyle changes. Thus, increasing the scope of the proposed controls may lead more residents to vote as prospective homeowners, who worry about the price effects of growth controls, instead of as existing homeowners, who stand to benefit from increases in property values.

Finally, the American psyche may also explain these results. Kenneth Jackson's insightful history of suburbia illustrates that a detached, suburban home has long formed the centerpiece of the American Dream. Contemporary public opinion polls illustrate that this remains the case. Americans consider a single-family suburban home their "ideal," and they are willing to make significant financial sacrifices, and commute long distances, to live in one. In Colorado and Arizona, opponents successfully appealed to our psychological fixation on home ownership. When they told voters that comprehensive growth controls might place this cornerstone of the American Dream out of reach, voters responded by overwhelmingly rejecting the controls.

Nicole Stelle Garnett, *Trouble Preserving Paradise?*, 87 Cornell L. Rev. 158, 176-79 (2001).

C. REGULATING PARTICULAR USES OF LAND

■ CITY OF NEW ORLEANS v. PERGAMENT

Supreme Court of Louisiana, 1941
5 So. 2d 129

O'NIELL, Chief Justice. The defendant has a gasoline filling station in the old section of New Orleans called the Vieux Carre. He was prosecuted in the recorder's court on a charge of violating a municipal ordinance, by displaying on his premises a large advertising sign without the permission of the Vieux Carre Commission, and contrary to the provisions of section 6 of Ordinance No. 14,538 C.C.S., as amended by Ordinance No. 15,085 C.C.S. He filed a demurrer and motion to quash the affidavit, on the ground that the ordinance if applied to his place of business would be arbitrary, unreasonable and oppressive, and would deprive him of his property without due process of law, and deny to him the equal protection of the laws. He pleaded also in his demurrer that the city had no authority to enact such an ordinance with reference to buildings like that in which he conducted his business, and particularly that such authority was not conferred by the constitutional amend-ment adopted pursuant to Act 139 of 1936, and designated as Section 22A of Article XIV of the Constitution. In this connection he avers that the only purpose of the amendment was to enable the municipal council to preserve for the public the architectural and historical worth of the ancient buildings in the Vieux Carre, and that his place of business, being a modern structure, having no architectural or historical worth, is not subject to the provisions of the constitutional amendment. . . .

The Recorder in whose court the prosecution was instituted withheld his judgment on the demurrer, or referred it to the merits of the case, as he expressed it, and after hearing the evidence sustained the demurrer and dismissed the prosecution. The city has appealed from the decision.

The constitutional amendment which was adopted pursuant to the provisions of Act 139 of 1936, and which is Section 22A of Article XIV of the Constitution, authorized the municipal council of New Orleans to establish the commission known as the Vieux Carre Commission, the members of which are appointed by the Mayor. The purpose of the amendment is stated in these three paragraphs:

> The said [Vieux Carre] Commission shall have for its purpose the preservation of such buildings in the Vieux Carre section of the City of New Orleans as, in the opinion of said Commission, shall be deemed to have architectural and historical value, and which buildings should be preserved for the benefit of the people of the City of New Orleans and the State of Louisiana, and to that end the Commission shall be given such powers and duties as the Commission Council of the City of New Orleans shall deem fit and necessary.
>
> Hereafter and for the public welfare and in order that the quaint and distinctive character of the Vieux Carre section of the City of New Orleans may not be injuriously affected, and in order that the value to the community of those buildings having architectural and historical worth may not be impaired, and in order that a reasonable degree of control may be exercised over the architecture of private and semi-public buildings erected on or abutting the public streets of said Vieux Carre section, whenever any application is made for a permit for the erection of any new building or whenever any application is made for a permit for alterations or additions to any existing building, any portion of which is to front on any public street in the Vieux Carre section, the plans therefor, so far as they relate to the appearance, color, texture of materials and architectural design of the exterior thereof shall be submitted, by the owner, to the Vieux Carre Commission and the said Commission shall report promptly to the Commission Council its recommendations, including such changes, if any, as in its judgment are necessary, and the said Commission Council shall take such action as shall, in its judgment, effect reasonable compliance with such recommendation, or to prevent any violation thereof.
>
> The Commission Council of the City of New Orleans may, by ordinance or otherwise, carry the above and foregoing provisions into effect.

The Vieux Carre Commission was created by Ordinance No. 14,538 C.C.S., which was amended by Ordinance No. 15,085 C.C.S. The sixth section of the ordinance is the one which forbids the proprietor of any building in the Vieux Carre to maintain a display sign, or advertising sign, without first obtaining a permit from the Vieux Carre Commission. The ordinance prescribes the maximum size and the details of the various kinds of advertising signs which may be displayed. The maximum area of any sign or signboard allowed to be displayed in the Vieux Carre, according to the ordinance, is 8 square feet if only one side or surface of the sign is displayed, or 16 square feet if both sides are displayed. The sign or signboard which the defendant in this case is displaying in violation of the ordinance has an area of 560 square feet. The lower part of the sign measures 24 feet in width and 20 feet in height, above which is an extension 12 feet wide and having an area of 80 square feet. The size of the sign therefore is far above the ordinary, and above the maximum size allowed by the ordinance. The defendant's offense is not only that he failed to obtain or apply for permission of the Vieux Carre Commission to erect the sign but also that the size of the sign exceeds the maximum size allowed by the ordinance, and hence could not be permitted by the commission.

The ordinance might be deemed violative of the equal protection clause in the Fourteenth Amendment if the ordinance undertook to confer upon the Vieux Carre Commission the authority to grant or withhold permits arbitrarily, or without prescribing uniform requirements or standards which all persons similarly situated should be obliged to comply with. But the ordinance does prescribe such uniform requirements or standards. And there is nothing arbitrary or discriminating in forbidding the proprietor of a modern building, as well as the proprietor of one of the ancient landmarks, in the Vieux Carre to display an unusually large sign upon his premises. The purpose of the ordinance is not only to preserve the old buildings themselves, but to preserve the antiquity of the whole French and Spanish quarter, the tout ensemble, so to speak, by defending this relic against iconoclasm or vandalism. Preventing or prohibiting eyesores in such a locality is within the police power and within the scope of this municipal ordinance. The preservation of the Vieux Carre as it was originally is a benefit to the inhabitants of New Orleans generally, not only for the sentimental value of this show place but for its commercial value as well, because it attracts tourists and conventions to the city, and is in fact a justification for the slogan, America's most interesting city. . . .

[The court also concluded that the municipal council had the state law authority to enact the ordinance.]

Notes and Questions

1. Most cities and many states have historic preservation laws like the one at issue in *City of New Orleans*. Such laws may protect an entire neighborhood like the Vieux Carre, or they may protect individual buildings or other structures. The general approach is to first identify which places are deemed historic and then prohibit any activities that would alter or destroy those places. (The federal statute establishes a national list of historic places that is found at http://www.cr.nps.gov/nr/, but it does not regulate the use of private property even if it is on the list.) Like certain zoning laws, historic preservation laws are justified by the idea that aesthetics alone is a legitimate purpose for governmental regulation. Unlike zoning laws, historic preservation laws focus on the value of particular existing buildings or neighborhoods, rather than what new uses of land should be permitted.

2. Historic preservation laws have featured in leading constitutional law cases. In Penn Central Transportation Co. v. New York City, 438 U.S. 104 (1978) (reprinted below in Chapter 14), the Court held that the application of New York City's Landmarks Preservation Law to prevent the construction of an office tower on top of the historic Grand Central Terminal did not constitute a governmental taking of property within the meaning of the Fifth Amendment. Also, in City of Boerne v. Flores, 521 U.S. 507 (1997), the Court held that the federal Religious Freedom Restoration Act exceeded the power of Congress to protect the freedom of religion from state laws, and so rejected the complaint of a San Antonio church that wanted to renovate its historic building. The controversies exemplified by *Penn Central* and *City of Boerne* continue to surface in the governmental regulation of historic places.

■ PRIMECO PERSONAL COMMUNICATIONS v. CITY OF MEQUON

United States Court of Appeals for the Seventh Circuit, 2003
352 F.3d 1147

POSNER, Circuit Judge. One of the concerns that led up to the enactment of the Telecommunications Act of 1996, 47 U.S.C. §§151 *et seq.*, was that zoning decisions by local governments were unreasonably retarding the growth of cellphone and other wireless services. Congress decided not to preempt local regulation entirely, but instead (so far as bears on this case) to require that the denial by a zoning board or other state or local government body of a permit to construct "personal wireless service facilities," such as an antenna high enough to be in the line of sight of cellphone users, as required for cellphone service, "shall be in writing and supported by substantial evidence contained in a written record." §332(c)(7)(B)(iii). . . . But Congress did not prescribe a standard to guide the local authorities' determination whether to grant a permit.

Turned down by the planning commission of the City of Mequon, a suburb of Milwaukee, and on appeal by the City's board of zoning appeals (without opinion, so that the only written record of the evidence and reasoning supporting denial is the transcript of the planning commission's deliberations), for a permit to build an antenna in its preferred location, Verizon sued the City in the federal district court in Milwaukee. . . . The district judge granted summary judgment for Verizon and ordered Mequon to issue the permit. The City has appealed. . . .

. . . [T]he question in this case comes down to whether the Mequon planning commission was clearly in error to turn down Verizon's application, in light of the evidence that had been placed before the commission.

A reasonable decision whether to approve the construction of an antenna for cellphone communications requires balancing two considerations. The first is the contribution that the antenna will make to the availability of cellphone service. The second is the aesthetic or other harm that the antenna will cause. The unsightliness of the antenna and the adverse effect on property values that is caused by its unsightliness are the most common concerns. . . . But adverse environmental effects are properly considered also, and even safety effects: fear of adverse health effects from electromagnetic radiation is excluded as a factor, 47 U.S.C. §332(c)(7)(B)(iv), but not, for example, concern that the antenna might obstruct vision or topple over in a strong wind. . . .

Verizon was having trouble providing cellphone service along a stretch of a busy street called Mequon Road. A nearby church in an area zoned institutional, though largely residential, was willing for a price that Verizon was willing to pay to allow an antenna to be built in the church's backyard. The antenna would be 70 feet high and 9.5 inches in diameter (originally it was to be both higher and thicker, but its dimensions were changed in an unsuccessful bid to make it more palatable to the planning commission). To reduce its unsightliness, it would be disguised as a flagpole.

The planning commission hired a reputable telecommunications consulting firm to analyze the issue of availability of service. The firm reported that the antenna would increase Verizon's coverage of the area along Mequon Road from 37 percent of the area to 95 percent. Two alternative locations, one a high school and the other a country club, both of which the planning commissioners preferred to the church's backyard, were analyzed but were adjudged unsuitable. This was less because they would give Verizon coverage of only 72 percent of the Mequon Road area than because their proximity to other Verizon antennas would interfere with the service provided from those antennas. . . .

Against the impact on Verizon's coverage the commission set aesthetic considerations. But no evidence or reasoned analysis can be found in the transcript of the commission's meetings, and except for the commission's letter turning down Verizon's application on the ground that alternative locations for its antenna were available (which is not denied — the issue is how inferior they are), that transcript is the only record of the basis for the commission's decision. We know that the church in the backyard of which Verizon wants to put its antenna is located in an area in which institutional land uses are permitted, though apparently residential uses predominate; but that is all we know, except the dimensions of the "flagpole" that Verizon wants to build. We are not told the height of any of the structures in the area, not even that of the church, which for all we know is 70 feet high or higher. We are not told why a 70-foot "light pole" — the disguise for the antenna that the commission suggested be used for the alternative site at the high school — would be less unsightly than the flagpole in the churchyard, or visible to fewer people. . . .

The commissioners invoked a preference for "collocation" (also and more illuminatingly spelled "co-location") — that is, for placing a new antenna in an existing telecommunications tower or other structure of the requisite height and capacity, such as a church steeple. Fair enough. But it is undisputed that Verizon had no suitable collocation opportunity. And the preference for collocation comes into play only when erecting an antenna in a new location is objectionable because of unsightliness or some other factor, and we have seen that there is no evidence that Verizon's proposed flagpole would if erected in the churchyard be considered unsightly by the neighbors or have any other adverse consequences. . . .

Since the problem with the commission's decision is not that the evidence shows that it was wrong but that the record contains insufficient evidence to have enabled the commission to make a responsible decision, it might seem that we should remand the case to the commission for further evidentiary proceedings. But the City has not requested such relief, and so the district court was right to order that the permit be issued. . . .

Affirmed.

Notes and Questions

1. Cell phone towers pose a dilemma for land use regulators. On the one hand, they have become one of the most frequent targets of "visual pollution" complaints raised by local residents who object to the sight of a structure looming over their neighborhood. As National Public Radio's beloved correspondent Noah Adams reported in November 2004, "Americans everywhere from Manhattan to Hollywood take their cell phones for granted, but in many parts of the country where scenery is cherished, cell phone towers have been called visual pollution." *Day to Day* (National Public Radio, Nov. 22, 2004); *see also* AT&T Wireless PCS v. City Council of Virginia Beach, 155 F.3d 423, 427 (4th Cir. 1998) (describing the "visual pollution" complaint against cell phone towers). Residents sometimes insist that cell phone towers present health and safety risks as well, but the primary objection to such towers is aesthetic, which in turn leads to claims of reduced property values.

On the other hand, the prevention of the aesthetic harms of cell phone towers is difficult because people want cell phones, and they want them to work as we move from one area to another. Cell phone providers satisfy these popular desires by designing a honeycomb of cells, each containing a tower that transmits the radio signals necessary for communication via cell phone.

Congress intervened to recalibrate the balance between local zoning control over cell towers and the general demand for cell phone coverage in the Telecommunications Act of 1996 (TCA). The Act mostly deals with the deregulated telephone service, but buried in §332(c)(7) is a provision expressing a concern that local zoning decisions were creating a patchwork of requirements that impeded the development of national wireless communications while acknowledging legitimate local concerns about the location of cell phone towers. The section tries to balance these interests by imposing several substantive and procedural requirements for local zoning regulation of cell phone towers. For example, denial of permission to build a tower must be in writing, supported by "substantial evidence in a written record," and neither "unreasonably discriminate" among providers nor effectively prohibit personal wireless services. 42 U.S.C. §332(c)(7)(B).

2. Municipal zoning officials, constrained by federal law but also vested with local authority, have been encouraged to identify those places in their community where cell phone towers would produce the least aesthetic harms, rather than trying to ban such towers altogether. Many cities have adopted ordinances that specify the possible sites for towers in order of preference. Providers responded to the incentives created by the TCA by researching the propriety of possible sites for cell phone towers rather than simply choosing a site and then trying to force local officials to approve it. An approach that ignores the availability of sites that would satisfy coverage needs while minimizing aesthetic harms can doom a provider's TCA claim. Another strategy is to eliminate the aesthetic stigma usually associated with cell phone towers. The standard image of a tower has been replaced by towers disguised as flag poles, church steeples, light poles, chimneys, trees, cacti, or bird nests. Towers have also been attached to existing structures, such as church steeples, buildings, electricity poles, and clock towers.

3. Beyond zoning and immune from attack under TCA, developers can use private land use covenants and servitudes to exclude cell phone towers. The first reported case to enforce a restrictive covenant to exclude a cell phone tower arose on land in Westchester County, New York, that was subject to a covenant prohibiting anything besides a single-family home. The New York Court of Appeals rejected the provider's claims that the enforcement of the covenant would violate the TCA or generalized interests in public policy. The court reached that result even though the tower had already been built, and thus the court's decision ordered the removal of the tower within "'a reasonable period of time.'" Chambers v. Old Stone Hill Road Assocs., 806 N.E.2d 979 (N.Y. 2004). *See also* Burke v. Voicestream Wireless Corp. II, 87 P.3d 81 (Ariz. Ct. App. 2004) (enforcing a covenant that prohibited a cell phone tower built on a church).

4. The law has long struggled with the regulation of aesthetics. Although advancing no evidence in support of its concern, aesthetic considerations apparently turned the Mequon planning commission against the cell phone tower. Preferred or objectionable architectural styles, colors, and signs have elicited similar zoning disputes in other communities. At first, many courts held that aesthetic concerns alone do not justify zoning, but courts today are more likely (though still not certain) to approve such regulations. The New Jersey courts vividly illustrate the dramatic change. In City of Passaic v. Paterson Bill, Posting, Advertising & Sign Painting Co., 62 A. 267, 268 (N.J. 1905), the court held that "aesthetic

considerations are a matter of luxury and indulgence rather than necessity" and are thus beyond the police power. Seventy-five years later, though, the same court held that "considerations of aesthetics in municipal land use planning are no longer a matter of luxury or indulgence. . . . The development and preservation of natural resources and clean, salubrious neighborhoods contribute to psychological well-being as well as stimulate a sense of civic pride." State v. Miller, 416 A.2d 821, 824 (N.J. 1980).

■ **SIERRA CLUB v. VAN ANTWERP**
United States Court of Appeals for the District of Columbia Circuit, 2011
661 F.3d 1147

WILLIAMS, Senior Circuit Judge. In 2007 the U.S. Army Corps of Engineers issued a permit authorizing the discharge of dredge and fill material into specified wetlands outside Tampa, Florida; it thereby enabled construction of a large mall. A number of firms are involved on the permittee's side in these appeals, but we will simplify by referring to them all, as well as the project, as "CCTC," standing for "Cypress Creek Town Center." Three environmental groups (collectively referred to as the "Sierra Club") brought suit in district court [alleging that the issuance of the permit violated the Clean Water Act (CWA) and the Endangered Species Act (ESA). The district court granted summary judgment for the Corps.]

Because CCTC proposed to discharge dredge and fill material into wetlands classified as "waters of the United States," it was required to secure a permit from the Corps under §404 of the CWA, 33 U.S.C. §§1311(a), 1362(7). The Corps originally issued the permit in 2007, allowing CCTC to discharge such material into about 54 acres of wetlands. In exchange, the Corps required various conservation measures, including the preservation, creation, or enhancement of wetlands on about 13 acres of the project site and nearly 120 acres offsite. . . .

CWA. The governing regulations bar the Corps from granting a CWA fill permit when "[t]here is a practicable alternative to the proposed discharge that would have less adverse effect on the aquatic ecosystem." 40 C.F.R. §230.12(a)(3)(i). . . . The Sierra Club contended (and contends here) that in fact there were practicable alternatives — other sites, or alternative ways of using the CCTC site — having less adverse effect. The Corps rejected these claims. Resolution of the practicability issue turns on four subissues: (1) use of the site's fair market value as its cost, rather than CCTC's (lower) out-of-pocket cost; (2) failure on the Corps's part to update the fair market value in its second look at the permit (which took place after the onset of the global financial meltdown in 2008); (3) the Corps's use of 8% as the minimum rate of return necessary for an alternative to be considered practicable; and (4) CCTC's intention to provide more parking per 1000 square feet of retail space than is provided on average, locally and indeed nationally.

For any given minimum rate of return, assumption of a lower cost for the site will tend to render "practicable" less intensive uses, *i.e.*, uses inflicting less ecological damage. This fact drives the Sierra Club's argument for acquisition cost, which in this case happened to be lower than fair market value. But the Sierra Club's contention that the regulation required the Corps to use the developer's acquisition cost is ill-founded.

First, as a matter of simple language, opportunity cost (the value the owner could realize by a current sale) is a well-recognized form of cost. This is obviously true in economics, and the practicability test, though certainly neither a cost-benefit test nor an efficiency test, nonetheless encompasses economic factors. And courts have recognized opportunity cost as a variant of "cost." Thus, the Supreme Court, in upholding the Federal Communications Commission's decision to set certain rates "on a forward-looking basis untied to [the providers'] investment," cited opportunity cost by way of analogy. Verizon v. FCC, 535 U.S. 467, 475, 499 n.17 (2002). Second, the regulations' evaluation of alternatives requires consideration of cost on *both* sides of the comparison, and the cost of an alternative project site would presumably be that site's market value. The comparison would be meaningful only if the Corps used the same metric for all options. Third, 40 C.F.R. §230.10(a)(2), in directing consideration of "cost," can sensibly (perhaps most sensibly, but we need not so decide) mean *the cost of proceeding* with the project as planned; for this, clearly, the relevant measure of the developer's land cost is what it foregoes by proceeding (rather than selling the land and realizing its market value). Fourth, whereas use of opportunity cost minimizes subjective, applicant-specific factors, reliance on the developer's acquisition cost would create the odd possibility that an alternative practicable for one applicant would be impracticable for another. Finally (and this is really a variation of the fourth point), to use out-of-pocket cost would create an anomaly: An applicant with a low acquisition cost could resell the site at market value and thereby enable a successor developer to refute practicability claims that had been fatal for the seller. Accordingly, we have no difficulty whatever deferring to the Corps's reasonable choice to use the land's market value, rather than the developer's acquisition cost.

[The Corps suspended the permit in 2008 because of unauthorized discharges of turbid water, updated plans, and data related to mitigation and stormwater management, and] reinstated the permit in 2009, after land values had fallen sharply, especially in the so-called "sand" states, including Florida. . . . [The] Corps's decision to update ecological but not economic data appears reasonable in light of the Corps's reasons for reexamining the original permit. . . .

The Sierra Club also attacks the Corps's acceptance of the applicant's contentions that an 8% rate of return was necessary to secure financing and that the planned project configuration was the only way to achieve that return. The Sierra Club claims that the record does not support use of an 8% rate; assumption of a lower required rate of return, of course, would tend to increase the range of practicable alternatives.

The CCTC submitted several reports, including one prepared by Ernst & Young, that examined the rates of return expected from comparable projects in the Tampa area. These reports produced estimates ranging from 7.6% to 10.06%. The Ernst & Young report concluded that a 7.6% return would be a "reasonable rate to expect" for the project when completed, but the project was subject to "a number of development risk factors" since it had not yet been completed. The report stressed the need for a "spread" between the rate of return on a project still under development and the rate of return on a "stabilized operating property." . . . We think the record plainly supports the Corps's use of an interest rate at the low end of the range that was in evidence, and with its modest excess over the very lowest figures plainly justifiable.

The last of the practicability issues relates to the project's planned number of parking spaces — a serious matter because parking accounts for such a large share of the mall's surface. The Sierra Club argues that "CCTC would have more parking than any existing comparable mall in the Tampa area." The record does not make it clear exactly how many parking spaces CCTC is expected to have, but gives a range of 5.13 to 6.59 parking spaces per 1,000 square feet of retail space, and the Sierra Club estimates the overall ratio as being 5.4. CCTC submitted various items of evidence on the point: On one hand it provided developer guidelines from Target, Costco, and Kohls that required 5, 5.5, and 6 spaces, respectively, per 1,000 square feet of retail space, and on the other, it also submitted letters from other Florida developers stating that retail tenants "typically" have "4.5 to 5" parking spaces per 1,000 square feet of retail space.

In fact both sides agree that CCTC's parking ratio exceeds that of nearby malls. But CCTC defends its above-average ratio by pointing to the above-average proportion of restaurants in its project. While the Sierra Club does not contest the restaurant-parking link, it argues that there is no reason for so many restaurants. CCTC, in turn, seeks to justify the high proportion by saying that it aims to create more than a traditional mall. Whereas traditional malls use 4.8% of their square footage for restaurants, "lifestyle centers" use 11.3%; CCTC, a self-described "town center," is between these two figures at 8.08%.

Given the nature of Sierra Club's arguments to the agency on this point, the Corps's acceptance of CCTC's parking ratio was not arbitrary or capricious in light of the practicability regulations. Those require the Corps to evaluate the practicability of alternatives "in light of overall project purposes." 40 C.F.R. §230.10(a)(2). . . .

The Sierra Club observed in a letter to the Corps that even if "town center" malls feature more restaurants than traditional malls, that fact "does not clearly demonstrate that reduced parking is impracticable." We do not think this observation was enough to impose on the Corps the task of evaluating the practicability of non-"town center" alternatives. . . . Accordingly, the Corps was not arbitrary (or in violation of the CWA) in accepting CCTC's conception of the mall's design, including its relatively high proportion of restaurant space, and hence in finding that fewer parking spaces did not represent a practicable, less environmentally damaging, means to satisfy that purpose. . . .

ESA. . . . The Sierra Club also argues that the district court erred by upholding the Corps's determination that formal consultation under the ESA was not required. The ESA requires that federal agencies "insure that any action authorized, funded, or carried out by such agency . . . is not likely to jeopardize the continued existence of any endangered species or threatened species or result in the destruction or adverse modification of habitat." 16 U.S.C. §1536(a)(2). Regulations promulgated under the ESA provide that "[e]ach Federal agency shall review its actions at the earliest possible time to determine whether any action may affect listed species or critical habitat. If such a determination is made, formal consultation [with the Fish and Wildlife Service (FWS)] is required." 50 C.F.R. §402.14(a). The regulations create an exception to that obligation where, as a result of informal consultation, the "Federal agency determines, with the written concurrence of the Director [of the FWS], that the proposed action is not likely to adversely affect any listed species or critical habitat." *Id.* §402.14(b). After issuing its first public notice in October 2005, the Corps engaged in informal consultation with the FWS, [which "concurred with the Corps's determination that the proposed project was not likely to adversely affect the wood stork nor any other species listed under the ESA"]. Accordingly, the Corps did not undertake formal consultation; as a technical matter, it is the Corps's dispensing with formal consultation to which the Sierra Club objects.

The Sierra Club argues that the Corps's determination was erroneous because the project may have adverse effects on habitat used by both the indigo snake and wood stork. . . .

As to the wood stork, the Corps's conclusions rested on the project's mitigation measures, which will bring about a net *gain* of wood stork foraging habitat. During informal consultation, the FWS determined that 16.22 acres of "potential wood stork habitat" existed on the site pre-construction and that with mitigation 21.35 acres would exist post-construction, resulting in a net gain. But the Sierra Club argues that the government did not "address *near term* adverse impacts on breeding colonies while off-site mitigation is being implemented." The Corps's answer here was to rely on the mitigation plan's "more than a one-to-one replacement ratio to compensate for the temporal lag between the loss of a wetland's foraging value and when the new resource achieves that value." We certainly cannot say that as a general matter a roughly 33% net quantitative gain in habitat offsets a non-trivial "temporal lag"; in an extreme case no members of the species would make it through to enjoy the replacement area. But here the FWS found that the lost habitat, although "within the core foraging areas [*i.e.*, within 13 miles] of five wood stork breeding colonies," was not within the "primary or secondary zone" of any colonies. Given the relatively marginal role of the lost habitat, it does not seem arbitrary or in contravention of its statutory mandate for the Corps to find that the mitigation's more than "one-to-one replacement ratio" made up for the temporary deprivation.

For the indigo snake, the Corps's 2007 mitigation plan concluded that "[i]nadequate habitat for maintenance of eastern indigo snakes exists on the impact site in its *predevelopment* state." But conservation guidelines submitted in CCTC's own application noted that the snake is "especially vulnerable" to habitat "fragmentation" because of the snake's large range. Nevertheless, the Corps and FWS did not address the fragmentation risk. After the permit was suspended in 2008, the Corps's new public notice said that it would "reinitiate informal consultation with the [FWS] regarding the issues addressed in this public notice."

In this renewed proceeding, the Sierra Club submitted two declarations related to the eastern indigo snake. The first declarant, a local Sierra Club member, wrote that he had seen an eastern indigo snake on the project site in May 2007. The second declaration was from Dr. Kenneth Dodd, a herpetologist who as Staff Herpetologist for the Office of Endangered Species in the FWS had been "primarily responsible for the listing of the" eastern indigo snake as threatened under the ESA. Dr. Dodd asserted that the project site was an important "wildlife corridor" linking protected areas to the north and south. He noted that "movements over large areas of fragmented habitats expose Eastern Indigo Snakes to increased road mortality," and that "the more edge there is in relation to protected habitat [*i.e.*, ratio of perimeter to surface area], the less likely large snakes can be maintained." He claimed more broadly that the Corps had failed to consider how the project would adversely affect the snake through "fragmentation" of its "habitat in lands near the site as a result of impacts to the site and the wildlife corridor connecting these lands."

. . . Given Dr. Dodd's expertise and experience, and the seeming logic of his analysis, as well as CCTC's own acknowledgment of the snake's vulnerability to fragmentation risk, we think his comment qualifies as the sort of "relevant and significant" public comment to which an agency must respond, lest its action be arbitrary and capricious. *See* Cape Cod Hospital v. Sebelius, 630 F.3d 203, 211 (D.C. Cir. 2011). Accordingly, we must remand for further explanation by the Corps of its determination that the project was "not likely to adversely affect" the indigo snake. We do not reach the issue of whether formal consultation is required, but the Corps must make some determination on the issue of habitat fragmentation. . . .

Notes and Questions

1. Many environmental laws protect lands on which society places particular value. Wetlands and the habitat of rare animals are two such places, as illustrated in *Sierra Club*. Section 404 of the federal Clean Water Act (CWA) protects wetlands by requiring landowners to obtain a permit before any development takes place. Why did the court hold that CCTC satisfied §404's criteria for issuing a permit?

2. The federal Endangered Species Act (ESA) contains two provisions that can regulate land use. Section 7 of the ESA, as applied in *Sierra Club*, requires federal agencies to consult with the U.S. Fish and Wildlife Service (FWS) before funding or permitting any activity that would affect a species that has been listed as endangered or threatened, and it further prohibits any federal agency from taking any action that would jeopardize the survival of any species or its designated critical habitat. Section 9 of the ESA makes it illegal to "take" a protected species, and the Supreme Court has upheld an administrative regulation that treats some habitat destruction as a prohibited *take*. Babbitt v. Sweet Home Chapter of Communities for a Great Oregon, 515 U.S. 687 (1995). Accordingly, the FWS lists those land use activities that it views as permissible, and those that are not, whenever the agency lists a new species as endangered. For example, when the FWS listed the Carson wandering skipper — a butterfly found only along the border between Nevada and California near Carson City — the agency explained that the ESA prohibited "[a]ctivities (*e.g.*, habitat conversion, urban and residential development, gas and geothermal exploration and development, excessive livestock grazing, farming, road and trail construction, water development, recreation, and unauthorized application of herbicides and pesticides in violation of label restrictions) that directly or indirectly result in the death or injury of adult Carson wandering skippers, or their pupae, larvae or eggs, or that modify Carson wandering skipper habitat and significantly affect their essential behavioral patterns including breeding, foraging, sheltering, or other life functions that result in death or physical injuries to skippers." Endangered and Threatened Wildlife and Plants; Determination of Endangered Status for the Carson Wandering Skipper, 67 Fed. Reg. 51,116, 51,128 (2002). A landowner can proceed with a proposed development only if she receives an incidental take permit, which often involves the preparation of a habitat conservation plan in which the landowner sets aside some land for the species in order to gain permission to develop another part of the land. Nonetheless, the ESA continues to generate passionate opposition, especially in Western states where rare species and rapid human development are both common. *See generally* John Copeland Nagle & J.B. Ruhl, *The Law of Biodiversity and Ecosystem Management* 245-96 (2002) (describing the application of the ESA to land use activities).

3. Similarly, many state and local laws directly regulate conduct that would harm wetlands, wildlife habitat, and other environmentally important lands. In re Killington, Ltd., 616 A.2d 241 (Vt. 1992), illustrates this approach. The Vermont Environmental Appeals Board denied a building permit to the Killington ski resort because the project would have threatened the food supply of nearby black bears in violation of a state statute prohibiting projects that "will destroy or significantly imperil necessary wildlife habitat or any endangered species." The state supreme court agreed and upheld the denial.

■ LEWIS OPERATING CORP. v. UNITED STATES

United States District Court for the Central District of California, 2007
533 F. Supp. 2d 1041

WRIGHT, District Judge. Plaintiffs have brought this suit against the United States to recover approximately $3.2 million in costs that Plaintiffs allegedly incurred in cleaning up a World War II airplane crash site that Plaintiffs discovered on their property in Chino, California. Plaintiffs argue that the United States bears all cleanup costs under section 107 of the Comprehensive Environmental Response, Compensation and Liability Act of 1980 ("CERCLA") on the basis that Plaintiffs qualify as "innocent landowners." . . .

On October 13, 1943, a United States Army Air Force aircraft crashed on land located near the southwest corner of Kimball and Grove Avenues in Chino, California ("Crash Site"). The Crash Site is approximately 3000 square feet in area.

In 2002, an affiliate of the Plaintiffs, Lewis-STG Chelsea, LLC, purchased approximately 136 acres of property, which included the Crash Site area, in Chino, California ("the Property"). Plaintiffs purchased the land to develop it into a commercial and residential development. In 2000, prior to purchasing the Property, Plaintiffs hired an environmental consulting company to conduct a site investigation and report on the Property. The pre-purchase review of the Property did not uncover any evidence of contamination.

In early December 2003, Plaintiffs' contractor, Titan Engineering, was grading portions of the Property for development by removing 10,000 cubic yards of soils from land which included the Crash Site and putting the soils into Fill Site A. Fill Site A is approximately 3.2 acres. On December 5, 2003, the contractors reported finding .50 caliber machine gun rounds in Fill Site A. After the discovery of the munitions, operations were immediately halted and the area was cordoned off. Plaintiff Lewis contacted local authorities, which caused the City of Ontario Fire Department Bomb Squad to inspect the premises and remove all visible ordnance from the Crash Site. Plaintiffs then sought proposals from private contractors to clear munitions from Fill Site A.

On December 10, 2003, contractor Titan resumed excavations of the Crash Site. The soils from the December 10th excavation were placed in an area referred to as Fill Site B. Fill Site B is a 2.9-acre parcel, which contained an estimated 38,000 cubic yards of fill. Throughout December other munitions were unearthed in Fill Site A.

In January 2004, Plaintiffs contacted the United States Army Corps of Engineers ("Corps") for help cleaning up the Crash Site. After assessing Plaintiffs' possible eligibility for the Formerly Used Defense Sites program, the Corps ultimately decided not to conduct the removal of any of the remnants of the airplane crash from the Property. On January 23, 2004, Plaintiffs met with the Department of Toxic Substances Control, School Property Evaluation and Cleanup Division ("DTSC") to discuss an investigation and cleanup of munitions. In addition to the Crash Site, and Fill Sites A and B, DTSC identified Fill Site C as an area of potential concern insofar as Fill Site C, a 10-acre parcel, included soils taken from the haul road that was used prior to the Titan's unearthing munitions from Fill Site A on December 5, 2003.

On April 29, 2007, DTSC sent a letter to Plaintiffs approving a work plan to remediate approximately 10,000 cubic yards of soil in Fill Site A that originated from the Crash Site. The approval letter did not address the removal of soils from Fill Sites B and C, or from the original Crash Site. Eventually, DTSC investigated and removed all ordnance and explosives ("OE") with regard to Fill Sites A, B, and C and the Crash Site. In total, 46,442 tons of soil were processed through a soil screening plant and 163 OE and suspect-OE were recovered. On December 29, 2004, the removal process was completed. . . .

ANALYSIS

"CERCLA sets forth a comprehensive scheme for the cleanup of hazardous waste sites, and imposes liability for cleanup costs on the parties responsible for the release or potential release of hazardous substances into the environment." Pakootas v. Teck Cominco Metals, Ltd., 452 F.3d 1066, 1072 (9th Cir. 2006).

CERCLA Section 107(a)(4)(A) authorizes the United States, as well as certain other entities and persons, to seek recovery of appropriate response costs from four categories of "covered persons," referred to as "potentially responsible parties" or "PRPs." The four categories of PRPs are: (1) owners and operators of facilities at which hazardous substances are located; (2) past owners and operators of such facilities at the time hazardous substances were disposed of; (3) persons who arranged for disposal or treatment of hazardous substances; and (4) certain transporters of hazardous substances to the site. 42 U.S.C. §9607(a)(1)-(4).

Even if a party is considered an otherwise liable PRP, that party may assert a variety of defenses to liability. Most relevant here is the so-called "innocent landowner" defense under Section 107(b) of CERCLA. In order to prevail on an "innocent landowner" defense, the party seeking to establish such defense must prove by a preponderance of the evidence:

(1) that another party was the "sole cause" of the *release* of hazardous substances and the damages caused thereby; (2) that the other, responsible party did not cause the release in connection with a contractual, employment, or agency relationship with the [plaintiffs]; and (3) that the [plaintiffs] exercised due care and guarded against the foreseeable acts or omissions of the responsible party. Westfarm Assocs. Ltd. Partnership v. Washington Suburban Sanitary Com'n, 66 F.3d 669, 682 (4th Cir. 1995) (emphasis added).

Here, there is no dispute that Plaintiffs should be considered PRPs unless they can establish that they meet the requirements for the "innocent landowner" defense. If so, they are immune from liability. Therefore, the only question here is whether Plaintiffs qualify as "innocent landowners."

At first glance it would appear that Plaintiffs easily meet the definition of innocent landowners. Plaintiffs properly inspected the property before they purchased it. And, it appears that Plaintiffs exercised due care in cleaning up the contaminated land. Therefore, Plaintiffs would be considered innocent landowners *if* the only clean-up area at issue was the Crash Site. However, as the United States points out, Plaintiffs spread the contaminated soil from the Crash Site to Fill Sites A, B, and C. Thus, the original 3000 square feet Crash Site area was spread over 16.1 acres of land. It is not a stretch to say that sifting through 16.1 acres compared to 3000 square feet of soil would greatly increase the time, effort, and expense involved in the clean-up process. Therefore, the analysis here turns on the application of the first element of the "innocent landowner" defense. . . .

. . . In Carson Harbor Village, Ltd. v. Unocal Corp., 270 F.3d 863, 871 (9th Cir. 2001), the Ninth Circuit examined whether a previous landowner could be considered a PRP when the previous owner did not actively participate in the disposal of pollutants, but rather, the pollutants only passively migrated throughout the soil while the previous owner owned the land. . . . Ultimately, the court in *Carson Harbor* held that a previous owner cannot become a PRP simply because there is passive soil migration on the land. Otherwise, as the court noted, there would never be a use for the "innocent landowner" defense. *Id.* at 883-84.

However, and more important to the instant case, the court in *Carson Harbor* clearly distinguished passive movement of contamination from the active movement that was addressed in *Kaiser Aluminum & Chem. Corp. v. Catellus Dev. Corp.*, 976 F.2d 1338 (9th Cir. 1992). The court noted that the term "release," as it is used in the "innocent landowner" statute, includes the term "disposal." *Id.* at 882. Then, the court noted that the term "disposal" includes moving soil throughout a development site and thus spreading the contaminated soil. . . . *Id.* at 876. Therefore, if a landowner actively spreads contaminated soil from one area of a development site to another, as was done here, that landowner has "released" contaminants onto the land.

At oral argument, Plaintiffs' counsel alleged that the test for the "innocent land-owner" defense should include a "knowledge" or "discovery" element (*i.e.* if a party has not discovered that it is moving contaminated soil, that party is still an innocent land-owner). However, knowledge [is] not part of the test. . . . Plaintiffs in the instant case actively moved contaminated soil from the Crash Site to Fill Sites A, B, and C. . . .

In sum, Defendants here were not the "sole cause" of the "release" of hazard-ous substances, because Plaintiffs *actively* spread contaminated soil from a 3000 square feet Crash Site to more than 16 acres. Therefore, because Plaintiffs have failed to meet the first prong of the "innocent landowner" defense, they will be considered PRPs for purposes of contribution. The Court's holding today does not determine the extent of Plaintiffs' liability, or even if Plaintiffs will be liable at all. The Court's finding simply means that further factual inquiry must be made to determine if Plaintiffs should contribute to the clean-up costs now that it is clear that the "innocent landowner" defense does not apply. . . .

Notes and Questions

1. Is it fair to hold the plaintiffs responsible for cleaning up contamination that they did not cause? Why would Congress have intended that result?

2. Many CERCLA cases involve multiple, even hundreds, of responsible parties. Most courts have held that CERCLA liability is joint and several, which means that solvent parties must assume the costs attributable to companies that have gone bankrupt or otherwise disappeared. Joint and several liability can only be avoided if a court apportions liability according to traditional tort law principles. *See* Burlington Northern & Santa Fe Railway Co. v. United States, 556 U.S. 599 (2009). A court must then allocate the remaining costs among the jointly and severally liable parties, usually employing a list of factors suggested by then Representative Al Gore during the congressional debate over CERCLA. Those factors include the amount of the hazardous waste each party introduced to the site, the toxicity of that waste, the involvement of the parties in generating or disposing of that waste, the degree of care exercised by each party, and cooperation with governmental officials. See H.R. 7020, 96th Cong., 2d Sess. (1980). How would you apply those factors to the cleanup of the Crash Site?

3. Besides hazardous wastes, what is the worst thing that you could discover on your land?

13
Natural Resources

Land is more than dirt or a place to build something. Many people value land because of the things that occur naturally on the land. That includes stands of trees, valuable minerals, native wildlife, wind, scenic vistas, bodies of water, and even rocks that can be used for commercial purposes. Generally, ownership of the land carries with it ownership of the resources that it contains and its natural attributes, but there are numerous exceptions to this principle. We will consider three such exceptions in this chapter. First, water is subject to discrete legal regimes that vary depending upon the area of the country and the placement of the water. Second, property rights may be divided between the owners of mineral rights and the owners of the overlying land surface. Third, the rights to resources on public lands (*i.e.*, owned by the government) are allocated pursuant to statutory and administrative procedures that mandate environmental studies and citizen participation. These ways in which the law structures rights in natural resources add to the understanding of land ownership that we have gained in the previous chapters, and that we will continue to explore in the final following chapter.

A. WATER

Water is ubiquitous. Except where it's not. Seventy percent of the earth's surface is covered by water; only 30 percent is land. Yet land has long been the focus of property law. That is beginning to change, though, as societies around the world find it necessary to compete for limited supplies of water. The world's water is abundant but unevenly distributed. Water law in the United States reflects the fact that water is abundant in the east but scarce in much of the west.

As you consider how the law treats water, consider the remarks of Professor Carol Rose, a leading scholar of both property and environmental law:

> If water were our chief symbol of property, we might think of property rights . . . in a quite different way. We might think of rights literally and figuratively as more fluid and less fenced in; we might think of property as entailing less of the awesome Blackstonian power of exclusion and more of the qualities of flexibility, reasonableness and moderation, attentiveness to others, and cooperative solutions to common problems.

Carol Rose, *Property as the Keystone Right?*, 71 Notre Dame L. Rev. 329, 351 (1996).

■ **TOWN OF OYSTER BAY v. COMMANDER OIL CORPORATION**
Court of Appeals of New York, 2001
759 N.E.2d 1233

KAYE, Chief Judge. Does a riparian owner have the right to conduct "maintenance" dredging of public underwater lands? We conclude that a riparian owner may dredge if dredging is necessary to preserve reasonable access to navigable water and does not unreasonably interfere with the rights of the underwater owner. Because the courts below did not apply this standard, we reverse the Appellate Division order permanently enjoining the dredging, and remit the matter to Supreme Court for proceedings consistent with this opinion.

I.

Since 1929, defendant Commander Oil Corporation has owned and operated a petroleum storage facility on land adjacent to Oyster Bay Harbor in Nassau County. Commander stores gasoline, diesel fuel and home heating oil at the facility. Plaintiff Town owns the underwater land in the harbor. In 1952, replacing a previous pier, Commander built the pier that currently extends from its land into the harbor. Barges dock at this pier while the oil they carry is pumped through pipes to storage tanks.

Barges have mainly docked at the "west basin," the larger and deeper of the two basins adjoining the pier. Both the east and west basins become shallower as they accumulate silt deposited by a creek that borders Commander's property to the south, and a sand spit to the south and west. Storm water runoff systems maintained by the Town and by the State of New York contribute to the silt deposits from these sources.

In 1966, owing to the accumulation of silt, Commander felt it necessary to dredge both basins in order to maintain adequate depth for its barges. Commander performed this dredging with the Town's permission, under a lease effective between 1960 and 1985. Commander also had the permission of the United States Army Corps of Engineers, as set forth in a letter in 1966 and permits issued in 1970 and 1975, authorizing it to dredge ultimately to a depth of 14 feet below mean low water. The letter, and the permits, made clear that they conveyed no property rights and authorized no impairment to private property rights.

After the last permit and the lease expired in 1985, Commander did not seek to dredge for a decade. By 1995, the east basin was as shallow as one foot deep in places, while the west basin ranged from 4 to 14 feet. Nevertheless, Commander was still docking well over 100 barges a year at the facility, and traffic continued at this rate at least into 1998.

When Commander sought to dredge, it did not ask the Town for permission, but applied to State and Federal agencies. Granting Commander's application, the State Department of Environmental Conservation issued a permit effective March 20, 1995. The permit authorized Commander to "maintenance dredge" to a depth of 14 feet, subject to various conditions calculated to minimize the effect of the dredging on vegetated tidal wetlands, spawning shellfish and other environmental concerns. The permit stated that it did not "authorize the impairment of any rights, title, or interest in real or personal property held or vested in a person not a party to the permit."

One month later, the State Department of State (DOS) issued a Consistency Certification Concurrence, concurring in Commander's certification that maintenance dredging was consistent with the Long Island Sound Coastal Management

Program. The DOS concurrence contained three conditions. The first reduced the square footage of dredging of the east basin, in order to avoid affecting a neighboring sand spit. The second required installation of a silt curtain during dredging, in order to avoid silting the open water of Oyster Bay. "Because of questions regarding the need for using the east basin," the third condition was that Commander "receive permission from the owner of the underwater lands, which may be the Town of Oyster Bay, to occupy and use the underwater lands." The Army Corps of Engineers has not ruled on Commander's application. . . .

In September 1996 the Town sued Commander . . . in Supreme Court, seeking to enjoin Commander from dredging. . . .

Supreme Court thereafter denied the Town's application for a permanent injunction, finding that "in its natural condition prior to dredging and the augmented deposit of silt attributable to the Town and State storm water runoff systems both basins of the dock were usable for tying up barges and offloading oil." 677 N.Y.S.2d 746, 750 (1998). . . .

On the Town's appeal, the Appellate Division . . . reversed and . . . granted the Town a permanent injunction. The court did not question Supreme Court's key factual finding, which the Appellate Division paraphrased as a finding that dredging was "*reasonably necessary to restore the basins to their natural condition and to maintain a level of access to navigation similar to that which existed when Commander originally constructed its dock.*" 700 N.Y.S.2d 47, 49 (1999) (emphasis added). The Appellate Division held, however, that an upland owner "has no riparian right to dredge public underwater lands in the absence of the public owner's permission." *Id.* The court further noted that granting such a "right would limit the Town's ability, as public trustee of the underwater lands, to balance the many diverse and competing interests in the coastal resource for the benefit of the public." *Id.* . . .

II.

We begin analysis by reviewing settled principles of law. First, Commander has the rights of a riparian owner. Strictly speaking, Commander is a littoral owner, one whose land is bounded by the seashore. A true riparian owner owns land along a river. But this distinction is vestigial; we have long used "riparian" to describe owners like Commander. *See, e.g.*, Tiffany v. Town of Oyster Bay, 136 N.E. 224 (N.Y. 1922).

Riparian owners generally are entitled to access to water for navigation, fishing and other such uses. Although *Tiffany* and several other authorities most pertinent to this appeal are comparatively old cases, as we have recently suggested riparian owners still enjoy "their full panoply of rights." Adirondack League Club v. Sierra Club, 706 N.E.2d 1192 (N.Y. 1998). Accordingly, Commander, like any riparian owner, has the right of access to navigable water, and the right to make this access a practical reality by building a pier, or "wharfing out." *See* Trustees of Town of Brookhaven v. Smith, 80 N.E. 665, 669 (N.Y. 1907).

Second, the Town owns the underwater land beneath Oyster Bay by virtue of a colonial patent. The Town holds the land in "trust for the public good," and, as such, has long enjoyed rights "general in their character, as yet not defined with accuracy beyond the ownership and regulation of oyster beds and some general aid to commerce, navigation, fishing or bathing." *Tiffany, supra*, 136 N.E. at 225. In keeping with this public trust, legislation authorizes the Town Board to lease the Town's common lands, including the foreshore, for oyster culture and other uses, and requires the Town Board to hold a hearing when it receives applications from prospective lessees. Nassau County Civil Divisions Act, L 1939, ch 273, §§320.0-323.0. Commander does not approach the Town, however, as a prospective lessee, but as a riparian owner enjoying property rights distinct from and not subordinate to those of the Town.

Finally, as a logical implication of the foregoing, neither the Town nor Commander may exercise its rights in a manner unreasonably intrusive upon the other's rights. The Town's rights "are at all times subject to the public rights and to the right of the riparian owner to access to the water." *Tiffany, supra,* 136 N.E. at 225. Conversely, the riparian owner's right of access is not "absolute, but qualified by other rights in the owner" of the submerged land; the riparian owner's rights "cannot be enlarged at will or according to his convenience or necessity." Hedges v. West Shore R.R. 44 N.E. 691, 694 (N.Y. 1896).

Thus, neither the riparian owner nor the underwater landowner has an unfettered veto over reasonable land uses necessary to the other's acknowledged rights, and where the rights conflict the courts must strike the correct balance.

In contending that dredging is simply impermissible, the Town relies heavily on *Hedges,* where we concluded that the riparian owners' right of access to navigable water did not encompass the right to dig a canal from their brickyard out across submerged lands owned by a railroad (under a grant from the public owner) and into the Hudson River. The Town urges that the right to dredge therefore is distinct from the right of access to navigable water and, if granted to Commander, would represent an unprecedented expansion of the rights of a riparian owner.

We do not believe, however, that *Hedges* requires dredging to be treated differently from other means of exercising riparian rights of access. *Hedges* holds that a riparian owner has no unqualified right to expand its access by dredging in a manner that would seriously impair the underwater landowner's rights. In other words, the riparian owner may not adopt "an artificial mode of navigating . . . destructive" of the public owner's rights. *Id.* at 694. Under *Hedges,* then, the Town would be entitled to an injunction only if it could demonstrate that Commander's dredging would destroy, or seriously impair, its rights as owner of the underwater land.

Commander contends that it would dredge merely to preserve reasonable access, and that it may do so even under *Hedges.* While we assumed in *Hedges* that the riparian owner could not complain while "the natural condition of things is left practically unchanged," *id.* at 694, Commander contends that here it is the Town, with its storm water runoff system, that has changed the foreshore from its "natural condition." Several other cases suggest that when the public owner itself causes a diminution of the riparian owner's access, the *Hedges* calculus changes.

For instance, as we have noted, the right to wharf out upheld in *Brookhaven* seems to imply "that the town could not fill in and reclaim such [underwater] land and so deprive" the riparian owner of its use. *See* People ex rel. Palmer v. Travis, 119 N.E. 437, 442 (N.Y. 1918). In *Tiffany,* similarly, we observed that the public owner could not "fill in, occupy and obstruct with buildings the foreshore under the pretext of providing for the public enjoyment, so as to interfere with the rights of owners of the upland, although they may still be able to reach the water." *Tiffany, supra,* 136 N.E. at 226. If a public owner cannot actively fill the foreshore in order to construct buildings, it would seem equally improper for the Town passively to fill Commander's basins with runoff while prohibiting dredging.

Additionally, we have held that a riparian owner's rights include title to accreted land — land previously underwater, which had emerged due to soil deposits — because this was the only way to preserve the right of access. If a riparian owner may take title to previously underwater land that is fully accreted in order to maintain access, it would seem to follow that the same owner could dredge deposited underwater land that blocks access, especially where the soil or silt has been deposited by the underwater landowner.

In sum, well over a century of common law adjudication has established the riparian owner's right to reasonable access, and nothing in these cases would preclude Commander from dredging to preserve such access, if the court was satisfied that dredging was necessary and did not unreasonably interfere with the rights of the Town. Because this standard was not applied below, we reverse and remit the matter to Supreme Court to strike the appropriate balance. . . .

We underscore that in reversing, we do not hold that, as a riparian owner, Commander has a general right to dredge or a particular right to dredge to maintain the prior depth of the basins. . . .

Notes and Questions

1. New York, like most eastern states, employs the *riparian* doctrine to allocate rights to use water. A partial list of the rights of riparian landowners includes access to the water, use of the water for navigation, an unobstructed view of the water, withdrawals of water, accretions and relictions to the property, the flow of the stream, fishing, building a wharf, pure water, the prevention of erosion, and the right *not* to use the water. What riparian right is Commander asserting? What riparian right is the Town asserting?

2. Disputes between riparian owners are often resolved by the principle that riparian owners have a right to reasonable use of the water so long as that use does not injure other reasonable uses. For example, in Sandusky Portland Cement Co. v. Dixon Pure Ice Co., 251 F. 506 (7th Cir. 1918), an ice producer and a cement factory were located on opposite sides of a river. The cement factory took water from the river to cool its machinery, and then it returned the warmed water to the river, where it melted the ice fields used by the ice producer. The court upheld a damage award for the ice producer. Was the factory's use of the river unreasonable? Was the ice producer's?

■ BOARD OF COUNTY COMMISSIONERS v. PARK COUNTY SPORTSMEN'S RANCH, LLP
Supreme Court of Colorado, 2002
45 P.3d 693

HOBBS, Justice. In this appeal from a judgment of the District Court for Water Division No. 1 (Water Court), Plaintiffs-Appellants, the Park County Board of County Commissioners, James B. Gardner, and Amanda Woodbury (Landowners) claimed in a declaratory judgment action that the applicant for a conditional water right, Park County Sportsmen's Ranch, LLP (PCSR) has "no right to occupy the space beneath the lands of the Plaintiffs to store water or other substances on or below the surface of the lands. Any such placement or storage of water on or below the surface constitutes a trespass for which the Defendant may be liable for damages." For this proposition, the Landowners rely upon the common-law property doctrine "Cujus est solum ejus est usque ad coelum et ad inferos"[2] (cujus doctrine). . . .

The Water Court determined that: (1) artificial recharge activities involving the movement of underground water into, from, or through aquifers underlying surface lands of the Landowners would not constitute a trespass; and (2) PCSR's proposed project would not require the Landowners' consent or condemnation and the payment of just compensation . . . because the project did not involve the construction of any facilities on or in the Landowners' properties. We agree with the Water Court and uphold its judgment.

I.

The Landowners and PCSR own property in South Park, Colorado, a high mountain valley approximately seventy-five miles southwest of Denver. PCSR filed with the Water Court an application for a conditional water rights decree and plan for augmentation and exchange involving extraction from and recharge of water into the South Park formation for augmentation, storage, and beneficial use. The South Park formation is a natural geological structure containing aquifers PCSR intends to utilize in connection with its project.

PCSR owns 2,307 acres of land in South Park. As part of its conditional water rights application and plan for augmentation and exchange, PCSR claimed the right to occupy saturated and unsaturated portions of the South Park formation for water extraction, augmentation, and storage as part of a water project it calls the South Park Conjunctive Use Project intended for City of Aurora municipal use. Project features would include twenty-six wells to withdraw water from the South Park formation and six surface reservoirs for artificially recharging the aquifers. PCSR's application did not propose to locate any of the project's recharge and extraction features on the Landowners' properties.

We have previously determined that the aquifers of the South Platte formation are tributary to the natural stream and projects affecting them are subject to Colorado's prior appropriation law. *See* Park County Sportsmen's Ranch v. Bargas, 986 P.2d 262, 275 (Colo. 1999). PCSR's Water Court application sought a decree for aquifer water extraction, recharge, augmentation, exchange, and storage activities, identifying two "Reservoir Zones" within the South Platte formation in connection with its claimed "conditional underground storage rights," each zone having a volume of 70,000 acre-feet of water for a total of 140,000 acre-feet extending under approximately 115 square miles of land. . . .

B. LANDOWNERS' TRESPASS CLAIM

. . . .

On appeal, the Landowners take no exception to the passage of augmentation water through the aquifers underlying their lands. They also concede that PCSR's proposed project does not involve the construction of any facilities on or within their properties. However, they contend that use of the aquifers for "storage" of PCSR's artificially recharged water within their properties would constitute a trespass. This novel proposition has attracted several amicus briefs arguing that

---

2. This phrase translates to mean: "To whomsoever the soil belongs, he owns also to the sky and to the depths." *See* Norman W. Thorson, *Storing Water Underground: What's the Aqui-Fer?*, 57 Neb. L. Rev. 581, 588 (1978).

artificial recharge, augmentation, and storage of water in aquifers are authorized by Colorado law and do not require the consent of overlying landowners, unless the project facilities are located on or within the overlying landowners' properties.

To support their theory, the Landowners invoke our decisions in Walpole v. State Board of Land Commissioners, 163 P. 848 (Colo. 1917) and Wolfley v. Lebanon Mining Co., 4 Colo. 112 (1878). The Landowners invoke *Walpole* and *Wolfley* for the assertion that their "fee ownership includes the space underneath the land" and therefore they have a right to withhold consent and require compensation for PCSR's project. In *Walpole*, we invalidated a State Land Board mineral reservation the Board had made in the course of selling and conveying title to a parcel of school trust land property. In holding under the law existing at that time that the Board had authority only to convey the entire fee interest, we said: "Land has an indefinite extent upward and downward from the surface of earth, and therefore includes whatever may be erected upon it, and whatever may lie in a direct line between the surface and the center of the earth." *Walpole*, 163 P. at 849-50. In *Wolfley*, we said: "At common law a grant of land carries with it all that lies beneath the surface down to the center of the earth." *Wolfley*, 4 Colo. at 114.

The Water Court found that "Plaintiffs have not alleged that their use, benefit and enjoyment of the estate will be invaded or compromised in any way." The Landowners simply assert that common-law principles entitle them to control the storage space in aquifers underneath the surface of their lands and grant them a remedy in trespass against migration of PCSR's water laterally into their property. The Ohio Supreme Court has rejected a very similar contention in Chance v. BP Chemicals, Inc., 670 N.E.2d 985 (Ohio 1996). In that case, a property owner claimed that the migration of injected liquid into portions of a very deep aquifer underlying its property constituted a trespass. Determining that the injectate mixed with "waters of the state" in the aquifer, the Ohio Supreme Court rejected the property owner's claim of ownership and trespass based on the cujus doctrine. It stated:

> Our analysis above concerning the native brine illustrates that appellants do not enjoy absolute ownership of waters of the state below their properties, and therefore underscores that their subsurface ownership rights are limited. As the discussion in *Willoughby Hills*[9] makes evident, ownership rights in today's world are not so clear-cut as they were before the advent of airplanes and injection wells.
>
> Consequently, we do not accept appellants' assertion of absolute ownership of everything below the surface of their properties. Just as a property owner must accept some limitations on the ownership rights extending above the surface of the property, we find that there are also limitations on property owners' subsurface rights. We therefore extend the reasoning of *Willoughby Hills*, that absolute ownership of air rights is a doctrine which "has no place in the modern world," to apply as well to ownership of subsurface rights.

Chance, 670 N.E.2d at 992.

We find the Ohio Supreme Court's discussion of state waters and limitations upon absolute subsurface ownership rights to be of particular significance to the case before us, in light of Colorado's strong constitutional, statutory, and case law

---

9. *See* Willoughby Hills v. Corrigan, 278 N.E.2d 658, 664 (Ohio 1972) (stating that "the doctrine of the common law, that the ownership of land extends to the periphery of the universe, has no place in the modern world") (citing United States v. Causby, 328 U.S. 256 (1946)).

holding all water in Colorado to be a public resource and allowing holders of water rights decrees the right of passage for their appropriated water through and within the natural surface and subsurface water-bearing formations. . . .

D. STATUTORY AUTHORIZATION FOR CONJUNCTIVE USE PROJECTS

When parties have use rights to water they have captured, possessed, and controlled, they may place that water into an aquifer by artificial recharge and enjoy the benefit of that water as part of their decreed water use rights, if the aquifer can accommodate the recharged water without injury to decreed senior water rights.

This authority resides in a number of statutory sections that implement the "Colorado Doctrine," which is that all water in the state is a public resource dedicated to the beneficial use of public and private agencies, as prescribed by law. *See* Chatfield E. Well Co. v. Chatfield E. Prop. Owners Ass'n, 956 P.2d 1260, 1268 (Colo. 1998).

Sections 37-92-305(9)(b) and (c) [10 Colo. Rev. Stat. (2001)] provide that the Water Court may issue a conditional decree for storage of water in underground aquifers if the applicant can and will lawfully capture, possess, and control water for beneficial use which it then artificially recharges into the aquifer. Section 37-87-101(1) provides that the right to store water of a natural stream is a right of appropriation in order of priority, and section 37-87-101(2) provides that underground aquifers can be used for storage of water that the applicant artificially recharges into the aquifer pursuant to a decreed right. . . .

Construing the General Assembly's wording and intent and effectuating evident legislative purposes, we determine that the General Assembly has authorized the issuance of decrees for artificial recharge and storage of water in an aquifer when the decree holder lawfully captures, possesses, and controls water and then places it into the aquifer for subsequent beneficial use. The applicant bears the burden of demonstrating that the aquifer is capable of being utilized for the recharge and storage of the applicant's water without impairment to the decreed water rights of senior surface or ground water users who depend upon the aquifer for supply. . . .

E. WATER USE RIGHTS AND LAND OWNERSHIP RIGHTS UNDER COLORADO LAW

Colorado law differs fundamentally from the English common law it replaced. The English case of Acton v. Blundell, 152 Eng. Rep. 1223 (1843), set forth the common-law rule of surface streams and ground water, based on Roman precedent. Enjoyment of the flowing surface stream was a riparian right of property owners whose land abutted the stream:

> The rule of law which governs the enjoyment of a stream flowing in its natural course over the surface of land belonging to different proprietors is well established; each proprietor of the land has a right to the advantage of the stream flowing in its natural course over his land, to use the same as he pleases, for any purposes of his own, not inconsistent with a similar right in the proprietors of the land above or below; so that, neither can any proprietor above diminish the quantity or injure the quality of the water which would otherwise naturally descend, nor can any proprietor below throw back the water without the license for the grant of the proprietor above.

Acton, 152 Eng. Rep. at 1233. In contrast to the surface stream, so the court declared, ground water moves "through the hidden veins of the earth beneath its surface; no man can tell what changes these underground sources have undergone in the progress of time." *Id.* The court then held that ground water was not governed by the law that applies to rivers and flowing streams; rather, it was subject to the cujus doctrine. The court asserted that ground water:

> falls within that principle, which gives to the owner of the soil all that lies beneath his surface; that the land immediately below is his property, whether it is solid rock, or porous ground, or venous earth, or part soil, part water; that the person who owns the surface may dig therein, and apply all that is there found to his own purposes at his free will and pleasure; and that if, in the exercise of such right, he intercepts or drains off the water collected from underground springs in his neighbor's well, this inconvenience to his neighbor falls within the description of damnum absque injuria, which cannot become the ground of an action.

Id. at 1235.

Advancing the national agenda of settling the public domain required abandonment of the pre-existing common-law rules of property ownership in regard to water and water use rights. Reducing the public land and water to possession and ownership was a preoccupation of territorial and state law from the outset. A new law of custom and usage in regard to water use rights and land ownership rights, the "Colorado Doctrine," arose from "imperative necessity" in the western region. This new doctrine established that: (1) water is a public resource, dedicated to the beneficial use of public agencies and private persons wherever they might make beneficial use of the water under use rights established as prescribed by law; (2) the right of water use includes the right to cross the lands of others to place water into, occupy and convey water through, and withdraw water from the natural water bearing formations within the state in the exercise of a water use right; and (3) the natural water bearing formations may be used for the transport and retention of appropriated water. This new common law established a property-rights-based allocation and administration system which promotes multiple use of a finite resource for beneficial purposes. Empire Lodge Homeowners' Ass'n v. Moyer, 39 P.3d 1139, 1146-47 (Colo. 2001).

When first announcing the Colorado Doctrine, we said that "rules respecting the tenure of private property must yield to the physical laws of nature, whenever such laws exert a controlling influence." Yunker v. Nichols, 1 Colo. 551, 553 (1872) (Hallett, C.J.).

> When the lands of this territory were derived from the general government, they were subject to the law of nature, which holds them barren until awakened to fertility by nourishing streams of water, and the purchasers could have no benefit from the grant without the right to irrigate them. It may be said, that all lands are held in subordination to the dominant right of others, who must necessarily pass over them to obtain a supply of water to irrigate their own lands, and this servitude arises, not by grant, but by operation of law.

Yunker, 1 Colo. at 555. . . .

Accordingly, by reason of Colorado's constitution, statutes, and case precedent, neither surface water, nor ground water, nor the use rights thereto, nor the water-bearing capacity of natural formations belong to a landowner as a stick in the property rights bundle. Section 37-87-103, 10 C.R.S. (2001), for example, codifies this longstanding aspect of the Colorado Doctrine. It provides that water appropriated by means of a reservoir impoundment and then released for travel to its place of beneficial use shall enjoy the right of passage through the natural formation in the administration of water use rights. . . .

F. ACCOMMODATION OF WATER USE RIGHTS AND LAND OWNERSHIP RIGHTS

Upon adoption of Colorado's constitution, the state struck an accommodation between two kinds of property interests — water use rights and land rights — by requiring the owners of water use rights to obtain the consent of, or pay just compensation to, owners of land in, upon, or across which the water right holders constructed dams, reservoirs, ditches, canals, flumes, or other manmade facilities for the diversion, conveyance, or storage of water. *See* Colo. Const. art. XVI, §7; Colo. Const. art. II, §§14 & 15; §37-86-102, 10 C.R.S. (2001).

But, this requirement does not extend to vesting in landowners the right to prevent access to the water source or require compensation for the water use right holder's employment of the natural water bearing surface and subsurface formations on or within the landowners' properties for the movement of its appropriated water. Our decision in State v. Southwestern Colo. Water Conservation Dist., 671 P.2d 1294 (Colo. 1983), reaffirming the Colorado Doctrine, is adverse to the Landowners' property right and just compensation claims in this regard. . . .

Of particular significance to the case before us, we held in *Southwestern* that: (1) federal patents to land did not include water; (2) ground water is not a mineral under the federal mining laws or Colorado law; (3) federal statutes as interpreted by the United States Supreme Court recognize Colorado's authority to adopt its own system for the use of all waters within the state in accordance with the needs of its citizens, subject to the prohibitions against interference with federal reserved rights, with interstate commerce, and with the navigability of any navigable waters; (4) the right of prior appropriation applies under Colorado law to waters of the natural stream, including surface water and tributary ground water; (5) the property rights of landowners do not include the right to control the use of water in the ground, whatever the character of that water; and (6) the General Assembly has plenary control over the use and disposition of ground water that is not part of the natural stream.

Despite our holding in *Southwestern*, the Landowners claim a common-law property right to require consent or just compensation for an easement to use the subsurface estate for artificial recharge and storage of water in aquifers extending through their properties, asserting that "fee ownership includes the space underneath the land" which the water occupies. The Landowners rely on *Walpole* and *Wolfley* for this proposition, but these are mineral cases which are clearly distinguishable from water cases, as we held in *Southwestern*.

In deference to the laws of nature, which we held to be foundational in *Yunker v. Nichols*, Colorado law does not recognize a land ownership right by which the Landowners can claim control of the aquifers as part of their bundle of sticks. To the contrary, "as knowledge of the science of hydrology advanced, it became clear that natural streams are surface manifestations of extensive tributary systems, including underground water in stream basins," Three Bells Ranch Assocs. v. Cache La Poudre Water Users Ass'n, 758 P.2d 164, 170 (Colo. 1988), and passage of appropriated water through the natural streams is part of the Colorado law of water use rights.

However, Article XVI, section 7 does subject the construction of artificial water facilities on another's land to the payment of just compensation and grants a right of private condemnation for the construction of such waterworks:

> All persons and corporations shall have the right of way across public, private and corporate lands for the construction of ditches, canals and flumes for the purpose of conveying water for domestic purposes, for the irrigation of agricultural lands, and for mining and manufacturing purposes, and for drainage, upon payment of just compensation.

Colo. Const. art. XVI, §7. Contrary to the Landowners' argument that use of their subsurface estate is different from use of their surface estate — over which appropriators may transport water in natural stream channels without payment of compensation — Colorado holds no distinction between surface water and ground water, tributary or non-tributary, in regard to the right and ability of the holders of decreed water rights to employ the natural water bearing formations in the exercise of those rights. Colorado's common law and statutory law in this regard rests on the bedrock of: (1) the plenary authority Congress recognized in the states and territories for the establishment and exercise of water use rights; (2) the election of Congress to patent land separately from water, so that the states and territories could legislate in regard to water and water rights as they deemed fit; and (3) Colorado's choice to include all water wherever it resides or travels through the natural formations as a public resource held open and available for the establishment of use rights as prescribed by law.

In sum, the holders of water use rights may employ underground as well as surface water bearing formations in the state for the placement of water into, occupation of water in, conveyance of water through, and withdrawal of water from the natural water bearing formations in the exercise of water use rights.

We reject the Landowners' claim that the cujus doctrine provides them with a property right to require consent for artificial recharge and storage of water in aquifers that extend through their land. Water is not a mineral. The law of minerals and property ownership we relied on in *Walpole* and *Wolfley* is inapplicable to water and water use rights.[32]

G. CONDEMNATION FOR CONSTRUCTED WATERWORKS

[The court also rejected "the Landowners' contention that certain statutory provisions, in combination with Article II, sections 14 and 15 of the Colorado Constitution, evidence legislative intent to require consent or the payment of just compensation for the right of storage occupancy in aquifers extending through the Landowners' properties."]

Justice KOURLIS specially concurring in part and dissenting in part, joined by Justice COATS. . . .

Although I agree with the basic premise that conjunctive use is anticipated and that underground storage of water is legislatively permitted, without any blanket

---

32. We decline to extend principles of mineral law to water law in Colorado for additional reasons. Ownership of oil and gas is a private right closely tied to property ownership; it logically follows that the right to ownership, extraction, and storage of mineral resources would remain sticks in the property owner's bundle of sticks. Water is a public resource, and any rights to it are usufructary. Mineral law is a special body of law derived from special circumstances.

need for overlying landowner approval, I read the statutes to pose as many questions as they answer. . . .

[A]lthough I agree that the Landowners here made an insufficient showing to defeat summary judgment, I do not dismiss their claims of ownership in the absolutist manner in which the majority does. I could envision a circumstance in which there would be a segregated underground storage cavern, unrelated to the aquifer and self-contained — as to which overlying landowners would retain ownership interests. It is clear in the law that landowners retain the right to the physical ownership of their properties, absent reservations, easements, or other reductions in the "bundle of sticks." The legislature has specified that "land" should be defined broadly to include a coextensive meaning with "the terms 'land,' 'tenements,' and 'hereditaments' and as embracing all mining claims and other claims, and chattels real." §38-30-150, 10 C.R.S. (2001). For as long as Colorado has been a state, this court has recognized that "land has an indefinite extent upward and downward from the surface of earth, and therefore includes whatever may be erected upon it, and whatever may lie in a direct line between the surface and the center of the earth." Walpole v. State Bd. of Land Comm'rs, 163 P. 848, 849-50 (1917) ("Land is the soil of the earth, and includes everything . . . buried beneath it. . . . A grant of lands therefore, without any qualification, conveys not only the soil, but everything which is attached to it, or which constitutes a part of it, the buildings, mines, trees, growing crops, etc."). . . .

Courts around the nation have also held that the owner of a mineral estate (or where the estates are unsevered, the owner of the surface estate) also owns the empty space created by the removal of the minerals and any use of that space constitutes trespass. 6 American Law of Mining §203.01[3] (Rocky Mountain Mineral Law Foundation 2d ed., 2001).

Some courts, in early jurisprudence, addressed ownership based on theories of adverse possession and location of entrance and exit. Those courts reached the conclusion that, where severance has not occurred, the portion of the subterranean cavern underneath a surface owner's land belongs entirely to the surface owner. E.g., Marengo Cave Co. v. Ross, 10 N.E.2d 917, 922-23 (Ind. 1937) (holding that when dealing with an underground cavity, absent severance of the mineral estate, a landowner's title extends from the surface of the earth downward to all land and caverns underlying the surface); Edwards v. Sims, 24 S.W.2d 619, 620 (Ky. 1929) ("The owner of realty, unless there has been a division of the estate, is entitled to the free and unfettered control of his own land above, upon and beneath the surface. So, whatever is in a direct line between the surface of the land and the center of the earth belongs to the owner of the surface."); City of Kingston v. Knaust, 733 N.Y.S.2d 771, 773 (N.Y. App. Div. 2001) (reconfirming the long-established principle that a conveyance of real property encompasses all subterranean rights including ownership of mines, caves, and caverns).

Hence, although a landowner does not own a moving creek or river — be it on the surface or underground, the landowner may own subterranean caverns and caves under his land. I could envision circumstances in which overlying landowners might well have the right to demand compensation for the use of underground facilities used for storage of water and would not preclude consideration of such a case by operation of today's judgment. . . .

Notes and Questions

1. *Park County Sportsmen's Ranch* involves the interplay of three distinct property regimes: land ownership, prior appropriation, and groundwater law. Under *prior appropriation,* the first party to claim water receives the right to use that amount. Land ownership is unnecessary to assert a claim. Instead, a claimant must demonstrate an *intent* to apply the water to a beneficial use, an actual *diversion* of water from a natural source, and application of the water to a *beneficial use* within a reasonable time. The law recognizes a wide range of beneficial uses, including domestic, municipal, irrigation, agricultural, industrial, stock watering, power, mining, recreation, fish and wildlife, groundwater recharge, navigation, transportation, water quality, pollution abatement, and frost protection. Water rights are then distributed among all appropriations according to a "first in time, first in right" formula, which results in state courts overseeing massive proceedings to adjudicate the date of each claim. More recent appropriators face the risk of not receiving any water during drought years once all of the available water has been claimed by users with earlier appropriation dates.

2. Colorado is one of nine Western states to rely upon a prior appropriation approach to allocating water rights. Why is prior appropriation attractive to Western states, while Eastern states rely upon the riparian doctrine?

3. The third legal regime at issue in *Park County Sportsmen's Ranch* governs *groundwater.* States throughout the nation employ at least three distinct systems for allocating rights to groundwater. The absolute ownership doctrine provides that a landowner has an unlimited right to withdraw any water found beneath the owned land. The correlative rights doctrine provides that landowners have a right to a reasonable share of the total supply of the groundwater based upon the proportion of land owned. Prior appropriation may also apply to groundwater. Each system specifies rules for liability, limits on pumping, restrictions on the pollution of groundwater, and the relationship between groundwater and surface water. Why is groundwater subject to different rules than other things that are found underground, such as natural gas, coal, caves, or antique coins?

4. Combining the three regimes, the *Park County Sportsmen's Ranch* court had to decide whether PCSR could take both surface water that it could use thanks to prior appropriation and groundwater that it pumped from under its land, and then store that water beneath the land of the landowners. Why did the landowners believe that they could prevent such storage? Why did the court allow it?

5. Note that the dispute was initially adjudicated by Colorado's "Water Court." Why should there be a special court to decide claims to water rights? Should there be analogous courts to decide other kind of property disputes, such as those involving competing land uses, ownership of personal property, or the extent of intellectual property rights?

B. OIL, GAS, AND MINERALS

Some natural resources are found below the surface of the ground. Yet the law governing oil, gas, and minerals is much different from that governing other things that are found underground, such as groundwater, caves, or lost jewels. Why should there be a separate body of law — indeed, a body of law far more extensive than we can cover here — for oil, gas, and minerals? What principles animate the legal treatment of such resources?

■ **ELLIFF v. TEXON DRILLING CO.**
Supreme Court of Texas, 1948
210 S.W.2d 558

FOLLEY, Justice. This is a suit by the petitioners, Mrs. Mabel Elliff, Frank Elliff, and Charles C. Elliff, against the respondents, Texon Drilling Company, a Texas corporation, Texon Royalty Company, a Texas corporation, Texon Royalty Company, a Delaware corporation, and John L. Sullivan, for damages resulting from a "blowout" gas well drilled by respondents in the Agua Dulce Field in Nueces County.

The petitioners owned the surface and certain royalty interests in 3054.9 acres of land in Nueces County, upon which there was a producing well known as Elliff No. 1. They owned all the mineral estate underlying the west 1500 acres of the tract, and an undivided one-half interest in the mineral estate underlying the east 1554.9 acres. Both tracts were subject to oil and gas leases, and therefore their royalty interest in the west 1500 acres was one-eighth of the oil or gas, and in the east 1554.9 acres was one-sixteenth of the oil and gas.

It was alleged that these lands overlaid approximately fifty per cent of a huge reservoir of gas and distillate and that the remainder of the reservoir was under the lands owned by Mrs. Clara Driscoll, adjoining the lands of petitioners on the east. Prior to November 1936, respondents were engaged in the drilling of Driscoll-Sevier No. 2 as an offset well at a location 466 feet east of petitioners' east line. On the date stated, when respondents had reached a depth of approximately 6838 feet, the well blew out, caught fire and cratered. Attempts to control it were unsuccessful, and huge quantities of gas, distillate and some oil were blown into the air, dissipating large quantities from the reservoir into which the offset well was drilled. When the Driscoll-Sevier No. 2 well blew out, the fissure or opening in the ground around the well gradually increased until it enveloped and destroyed Elliff No. 1. The latter well also blew out, cratered, caught fire and burned for several years. Two water wells on petitioners' land became involved in the cratering and each of them blew out. Certain damages also resulted to the surface of petitioners' lands and to their cattle thereon. The cratering process and the eruption continued until large quantities of gas and distillate were drained from under petitioners' land and escaped into the air, all of which was alleged to be the direct and proximate result of the negligence of respondents in permitting their well to blow out. The extent of the emissions from the Driscoll-Sevier No. 2 and Elliff No. 1, and the two water wells on petitioners' lands, was shown at various times during the several years between the blowout in November 1936, and the time of the trial in June 1946. There was also expert testimony from petroleum engineers showing the extent of the losses from the underground reservoir, which computations extended from the date of the blowout only up to June 1938. It was indicated that it was not feasible to calculate the losses subsequent thereto, although lesser emissions of gas continued even up to the time of the trial. All the evidence with reference to the damages included all losses from the reservoir beneath petitioners' land without regard to whether they were wasted and dissipated from above the Driscoll land or from petitioners' land.

The jury found that respondents were negligent in failing to use drilling mud of sufficient weight in drilling their well, and that such negligence was the proximate cause of the well blowing out. . . .

On the findings of the jury the trial court rendered judgment for petitioners for $154,518.19, which included $148,548.19 for the gas and distillate, and $5,970 for damages to the land and cattle. The Court of Civil Appeals reversed the judgment and remanded the cause. 210 S.W.2d 553.

The reversal by the Court of Civil Appeals rests upon [the ground] that since substantially all of the gas and distillate which was drained from under petitioners' lands was lost through respondents' blowout well, petitioners could not recover because under the law of capture they had lost all property rights in the gas or distillate which had migrated from their lands. . . .

[O]ur attention will be confined to the sole question as to whether the law of capture absolves respondents of any liability for the negligent waste or destruction of petitioners' gas and distillate, though substantially all of such waste or destruction occurred after the minerals had been drained from beneath petitioners' lands.

We do not regard as authoritative the three decisions by the Supreme Court of Louisiana to the effect that an adjoining owner is without right of action for gas wasted from the common pool by his neighbor, because in that state only qualified ownership of oil and gas is recognized, no absolute ownership of minerals in place exists, and the unqualified rule is that under the law of capture the minerals belong exclusively to the one that produces them. Louisiana Gas & Fuel Co. v. White Bros., 103 So. 23 (La. 1925); McCoy v. Arkansas Natural Gas Co., 143 So. 383 (La.), *cert. denied*, 287 U.S. 661 (1932); McCoy v. Arkansas Natural Gas Co., 165 So. 632 (La. 1936). Moreover, from an examination of those cases it will be seen that the decisions rested in part on the theory that "the loss complained of was, manifestly, more a matter of uncertainty and speculation than of fact or estimate." In the more recent trend of the decisions of our state, with the growth and development of scientific knowledge of oil and gas, it is now recognized "that when an oil field has been fairly tested and developed, experts can determine approximately the amount of oil and gas in place in a common pool, and can also equitably determine the amount of oil and gas recoverable by the owner of each tract of land under certain operating conditions." Brown v. Humble Oil & Refining Co., 83 S.W.2d 935, 940 (Tex. 1935).

In Texas, and in other jurisdictions, a different rule exists as to ownership. In our state the landowner is regarded as having absolute title in severalty to the oil and gas in place beneath his land. Lemar v. Garner, 50 S.W.2d 769 (Tex. 1932). The only qualification of that rule of ownership is that it must be considered in connection with the law of capture and is subject to police regulations. Brown v. Humble Oil & Refining Co., *supra*. The oil and gas beneath the soil are considered a part of the realty. Each owner of land owns separately, distinctly and exclusively all the oil and gas under his land and is accorded the usual remedies against trespassers who appropriate the minerals or destroy their market value.

The conflict in the decisions of the various states with reference to the character of ownership is traceable to some extent to the divergent views entertained by the courts, particularly in the earlier cases, as to the nature and migratory character of oil and gas in the soil. 31A Tex. Jur. 24, Sec. 5. In the absence of common law precedent, and owing to the lack of scientific information as to the movement of these minerals, some of the courts have sought by analogy to compare oil and gas to other types of property such as wild animals, birds, subterranean waters and other migratory things, with reference to which the common law had established rules denying any character of ownership prior to capture. However, as was said by Professor A. W. Walker, Jr., of the School of Law of the University of Texas: "There is no oil or gas producing state today which follows the wild-animal analogy to its logical conclusion that the landowner has no property interest in the oil and gas in place." 16 Tex. L. Rev. 370, 371. In the light of modern scientific knowledge these early analogies have been disproven, and courts generally have come to recognize that oil and gas, as commonly found in underground reservoirs, are securely entrapped in a static condition in the original pool, and, ordinarily, so remain until disturbed by penetrations from the surface. It is further established, nevertheless, that these minerals will migrate across property lines towards any low pressure area created by production from the common pool. This migratory character of oil and gas has given rise to the so-called rule or law of capture. That rule simply is that the owner of a tract of land acquires title to the oil or gas which he produces from wells on his land, though part of the oil or gas may have migrated from adjoining lands. He may thus appropriate the oil and gas that have flowed from adjacent lands without the consent of the owner of those lands, and without incurring liability to him for drainage. The non-liability is based upon the theory that after the drainage the title or property interest of the former owner is gone. This rule, at first blush, would seem to conflict with the view of absolute ownership of the minerals in place, but it was otherwise decided in the early case of Stephens County v. Mid-Kansas Oil & Gas Co., 254 S.W. 290 (Tex. 1923). Mr. Justice Greenwood there stated, 254 S.W. at 292:

> The objection lacks substantial foundation that gas or oil in a certain tract of land cannot be owned in place, because subject to appropriation, without the consent of the owner of the tract, through drainage from wells on adjacent lands. If the owners of adjacent lands have the right to appropriate, without liability, the gas and oil underlying their neighbor's land, then their neighbor has the correlative right to appropriate, through like methods of drainage, the gas and oil underlying the tracts adjacent to his own.

Thus it is seen that, notwithstanding the fact that oil and gas beneath the surface are subject both to capture and administrative regulation, the fundamental rule of absolute ownership of the minerals in place is not affected in our state. In recognition of such ownership, our courts, in decisions involving well-spacing regulations of our Railroad Commission, have frequently announced the sound view that each landowner should be afforded the opportunity to produce his fair share of the recoverable oil and gas beneath his land, which is but another way of recognizing the existence of correlative rights between the various landowners over a common reservoir of oil or gas.

It must be conceded that under the law of capture there is no liability for reasonable and legitimate drainage from the common pool. The landowner is privileged to sink as many wells as he desires upon his tract of land and extract therefrom and appropriate all the oil and gas that he may produce, so long as he operates within the spirit and purpose of conservation statutes and orders of the Railroad Commission. These laws and regulations are designed to afford each owner a reasonable opportunity to produce his proportionate part of the oil and gas from the entire pool and to prevent operating practices injurious to the common reservoir. In this manner, if all operators exercise the same degree of skill and diligence, each owner will recover in most instances his fair share of the oil and gas. This reasonable opportunity to produce his fair share of the oil and gas is the landowner's common law right under our theory of absolute ownership of the minerals in place. But from the very nature of this theory the right of each land holder is qualified, and is limited to legitimate operations. Each owner whose land overlies the basin has a like interest, and each must of necessity exercise his right with some regard to the rights of others. No owner should be permitted to carry on his operations in reckless or lawless irresponsibility, but must submit to such limitations as are necessary to enable each to get his own. Hague v. Wheeler, 27 A. 714, 717 (Pa. 1893).

While we are cognizant of the fact that there is a certain amount of reasonable and necessary waste incident to the production of oil and gas to which the non-liability rule must also apply, we do not think this immunity should be extended so as to include the negligent waste or destruction of the oil and gas.

In 1 Summers, *Oil and Gas*, Perm. Ed., §63 correlative rights of owners of land in a common source of supply of oil and gas are discussed and described in the following language:

> These existing property relations, called correlative rights of the owners of land in the common source of supply, were not created by the statute, but held to exist because of the peculiar physical facts of oil and gas. The term "correlative rights" is merely a convenient method of indicating that each owner of land in a common source of supply of oil and gas has legal privileges as against other owners of land therein to take oil or gas therefrom by lawful operations conducted on his own land; that each such owner has duties to the other owners not to exercise his privileges of taking so as to injure the common source of supply; and that each such owner has rights that other owners not exercise their privileges of taking so as to injure the common source of supply.

In 85 A.L.R. 1156, in discussing the case of Hague v. Wheeler, *supra*, the annotator states:

> . . . The fact that the owner of the land has a right to take and to use gas and oil, even to the diminution or exhaustion of the supply under his neighbor's land, does not give him the right to waste the gas. His property in the gas underlying his land consists of the right to appropriate the same, and permitting the gas to escape into the air is not an appropriation thereof in the proper sense of the term.

In like manner, the negligent waste and destruction of petitioners' gas and distillate was neither a legitimate drainage of the minerals from beneath their lands nor a lawful or reasonable appropriation of them. Consequently, the petitioners did not lose their right, title and interest in them under the law of capture. At the time of their removal they belonged to petitioners, and their wrongful dissipation deprived these owners of the right and opportunity to produce them. That right is forever lost, the same cannot be restored, and petitioners are without an adequate legal remedy unless we allow a recovery under the same common law which governs other actions for damages and under which the property rights in oil and gas are vested. This remedy should not be denied.

In common with others who are familiar with the nature of oil and gas and the risks involved in their production, the respondents had knowledge that a failure to use due care in drilling their well might result in a blowout with the consequent waste and dissipation of the oil, gas and distillate from the common reservoir. In the conduct of one's business or in the use and exploitation of one's property, the law imposes upon all persons the duty to exercise ordinary care to avoid injury or damage to the property of others. Thus under the common law, and independent of the conservation statutes, the respondents were legally bound to use due care to avoid the negligent waste or destruction of the minerals imbedded in petitioners' oil and gas-bearing strata. This common-law duty the respondents failed to discharge. For that omission they should be required to respond in such damages as will reasonably compensate the injured parties for the loss sustained as the proximate result of the negligent conduct. The fact that the major portion of the gas and distillate escaped from the well on respondents' premises is immaterial. Irrespective of the opening from which the minerals escaped, they belonged to the petitioners and the loss was the same. They would not have been dissipated at any opening except for the wrongful conduct of the respondents. Being responsible for the loss they are in no position to deny liability because the gas and distillate did not escape through the surface of petitioners' lands.

We are therefore of the opinion the Court of Civil Appeals erred in holding that under the law of capture the petitioners cannot recover for the damages resulting from the wrongful drainage of the gas and distillate from beneath their lands. . . . [T]he judgment of the Court of Civil Appeals is reversed and the cause remanded to that court for consideration of [assignments of error with respect to the measure of damages].

"We got a great buy on the apartment, but, unfortunately, it didn't include the mineral rights."

Notes and Questions

1. Most nations of the world presently treat minerals in place underground as a common resource, owned by the nation as a whole and thus subject to control and

development in the public interest. In those nations, land ownership consists of surface ownership, together with whatever airspace and support rights are necessary to enjoy the surface, with no private right to extract mineral wealth. The United States, in contrast, fully applies the institution of private property to mineral resources, as well as all other components of subsurface geology. The *ad coelum* doctrine reflects the general principle that surface owners have the full right to develop (or leave in place) all underlying deposits and resources, subject only to legal rules that regulate exploration and development in order to protect various societal interests. Why should there be an exception for migratory resources, such as oil and gas, to the general rule that all underground things belong to the surface owner?

2. Many law schools, especially in oil- and gas-producing states, have upper-level courses in oil and gas law. In addition, oil and gas law (relating to privately and publicly owned land) is often explored in other more general courses such as natural resources, public lands, and energy law. Oil and gas property rights can be bundled and subdivided many different ways. The general categories are mineral interests, royalties, and leasehold estates.

3. The owner of a mineral estate has the right to explore the land, in the hope of finding oil, gas, or other valuable minerals. Courts have recognized liability for *geophysical trespass* when a person enters upon the surface of land to conduct sub-surface exploration. Traditional exploration consists of physical penetration by borings or test wells. Modern three-dimensional (3D) seismic technology has revolutionized the process of oil and gas exploration. The information gained through 3D surveying is much more accurate and extensive than that rendered by earlier two-dimensional seismic surveying. Should trespass liability attach when an explorer collects seismic data from a neighboring parcel without the consent of a mineral owner of that parcel? *See* Owen Anderson, *Geophysical "Trespass" Revisited*, 5 Tex. Wesleyan L. Rev. 137 (1999) (arguing such exploration should be privileged by a rule of capture to promote increased energy production).

4. Oil production is controversial wherever it is proposed: in northern Alaska, in the Gulf of Mexico, off-shore in California. Yet importing oil from overseas raises its own serious concerns, and even sources of renewable energy raise environmental objections. *See, e.g.*, Quechan Tribe of the Fort Yuma Indian Reservation v. United States DOI, 755 F. Supp. 2d 1104 (S.D. Cal. 2010) (blocking construction of a proposed solar energy project because of the possible destruction of ancient Native American cultural sites); Zimmerman v. Bd. of County Comm'rs, 218 P.3d 400 (Kan. 2009) (upholding a county zoning law prohibiting large wind farms because of aesthetic concerns). How should property law generally, and the management of public lands in particular, resolve these disputes?

■ CONTINENTAL RESOURCES OF ILLINOIS, INC. v. ILLINOIS METHANE, LLC

Appellate Court of Illinois, Fifth District, 2006
847 N.E.2d 897

Donovan, Justice. Plaintiff, Continental Resources of Illinois, Inc. (Continental), brought an action against defendants, Illinois Methane, LLC (Illinois Methane), and DeMier Oil Company (DeMier), alleging that, pursuant to certain oil and gas leases, it has the exclusive right to explore, drill, and produce the coalbed methane gas that is being produced by defendants. . . . The circuit court of Franklin County dismissed Continental's complaint for a failure to state a cause of action because Continental did not have any right to produce coalbed methane under the conventional oil and gas leases it controlled. The court further found that, under the mineral-production principle known as the rule of capture, the complaint did not state a cause of action for the drainage of gas. Continental appeals the dismissal of its complaint. . . .

While the ownership of and the right to develop coalbed methane gas are questions of first impression in Illinois, courts in other jurisdictions have struggled with these issues for more than a decade. A review of these cases reveals a split of authority. Many of the cases have resolved the issues by resorting to interpreting or looking to the intent of the original leases and/or grants. *See* Carbon County v. Union Reserve Coal Co., 898 P.2d 680 (Mont. 1995); Newman v. RAG Wyoming Land Co., 53 P.3d 540 (Wyo. 2002); *see also* Amoco Production Co. v. Southern Ute Indian Tribe, 526 U.S. 865 (1999). Others have relied upon the general property laws of their respective states with respect to the production of all "minerals" and the manner in which coal is mined in that particular jurisdiction. *See* NCNB Texas National Bank, N.A. v. West, 631 So. 2d 212 (Ala. 1993); United States Steel Corp. v. Hoge, 468 A.2d 1380 (Pa. 1983). No one answer is right for every state and/or every lease or grant. While cases from other states are helpful, we must make our own determinations based on Illinois law. And, in order to make those determinations, we also must consider fully the natural characteristics of coalbed methane gas and the methods, rights, and obligations of mining and extraction in general. We begin with a basic description of coalbed methane gas and the methods for its extraction.

The process by which organic material becomes coal is known as coalification. The coalification process generates gases, one of which is coalbed methane. There are three states of coalbed methane gas: (1) free gas within the cleats and matrixes of the coal, (2) gas dissolved in water in the coal pores, and (3) gas adsorbed onto the solid surface of the coal. When the pressure on the coal is reduced, the forces that hold the coalbed methane to the coal are reduced and coalbed methane is released from the coal.

Historically, coalbed methane gas was considered a "dangerous waste product of coal mining." *Amoco Production Co.*, 526 U.S. at 871. Technological developments in the 1980s and changes in federal law made the commercial development of coalbed methane gas possible. The extraction of coalbed methane gas is generally accomplished by one of three methods: vertical degasification wells, horizontal boreholes, or gob wells. Vertical degasification wells are drilled from the surface into an unmined coal seam. Horizontal boreholes are bored into the coal seam from a point within the coal mine itself. Gob wells, relating to longwall mining, are drilled from the surface to an area near the coal seam. During the longwall mining method, a machine grinds progressively into the wall of coal to tear away the coal. As the machine grinds further and further into the wall, it leaves behind it a void into which the ceiling of the mine collapses, creating a gob of rubble in which the coalbed gas collects. The collapse of the ceiling of the mine also leaves the overlying strata unsupported, and gravity causes it to subside and to fracture, thereby releasing more gas. Gas from the gob can then travel upward into noncoal strata as well.

In Illinois, mineral rights may be severed from surface rights and conveyed separately. Oil and gas in place are minerals, but because of their fugacious qualities, they are incapable of ownership distinct from the soil. They belong to the owner of the land only so long as they remain under the land, and if the owner makes a grant of them to another, it is a grant only of the gas and oil that the grantee takes from the land. Oil and gas are incapable of ownership until actually found and produced. This principle is the basis for the rule of capture. Under the rule of capture, gas that migrates from one property to another is subject to recovery and possession by the holder of the gas estate on the property to which the gas migrates. Because coalbed gas is similar to and migrates in the same manner as other natural gas, there is no reason that the rule of capture and the laws governing the ownership of migratory natural gas should not apply to coalbed methane gas as well. With these principles in mind, we turn to Continental's arguments on appeal.

Continental first alleges that oil and gas leases granting the right to produce all gases include the right to produce coalbed methane gas as well. As shown, coalbed methane gas is distinct, and the answer is not that simple. Each side has presented cogent arguments why coalbed gas should be declared the property of that particular side. Notable arguments include the fact that coalbed gas has practically the same chemical composition as natural gas with only very small percentages of other ingredients. On the other side, coalbed gas is a by-product of coal and has a natural and unique affinity for coal. The coal owner cannot mine the coal without removing the coalbed gas because it poses the perils of explosion and asphyxiation. In addition, coal owners need to control the production of coalbed gas in order to maintain the safety of the mines and the value of the coal seams.

Given the status of this case and the leases and land interests involved, we need not determine to whom the coalbed methane gas belongs in the absolute. We first note that the leases at issue here deny Continental the right to produce coalbed methane from a coal seam or void. The leases specifically require the lessee to permanently case and cement all holes drilled through coal seams or mine workings. The reservation of the right to drill through the coal does not include the right to drill into the coal and develop coalbed methane. We further note that the conveyance of coal as a distinct property also includes the bundle of property rights included within the coal, such as the rights incident and necessary to the recovery of the coal. If oil and gas leases included the right to develop coalbed methane, they then would also carry an implied right to invade the coal seams and stimulate them in a fashion that could make it more dangerous or difficult to later produce the coal. Oil and gas producers have no direct interest in coal mine safety, and therefore coalbed methane gas historically has been completely controlled by whoever controlled the coal. We believe this to be a wise and just result. The control of coalbed methane gas should not change simply by virtue of its increased value. We further conclude that the bundle of property rights associated with the coal estate also includes the right to reduce to possession any gas trapped within the coal itself so long as the gas remains within that coal until the time of its capture.

Continental argues that the coalbed methane found in mine voids, however, should not be treated the same as that found in coal seams or active mines. It is true that natural gas produced and reduced to possession is personal property. And gas injected into underground, defined, and controlled reservoirs belongs to whoever produced or bought the gas and transported it to those reservoirs. Coalbed methane gas found in mine voids has never been produced or reduced to possession by someone above the ground and therefore is not personal property. The coalbed methane gas in those voids is there as a result of natural deadsorption or deabsorption from the coal formations and mine workings. Given that Illinois also follows the container space doctrine, a doctrine which states that the holder of coal rights also holds the rights to the void after the coal is mined, coalbed methane gas found in the mine voids must therefore still be a part of the coal estate, subject to the rule of capture.

We therefore conclude that coalbed methane gas found in coal seams and/or in mine voids is controlled by the coal estate. Under the rule of capture, coalbed methane gas cannot be owned until it is reduced to possession. Consequently, Continental does not and cannot own the coalbed methane gas at issue here. We further conclude that defendants' production of coalbed methane gas from wells located outside Continental's lands is not a violation of Continental's rights. For these reasons, even after viewing the facts and evidence in the light most favorable to Continental, we agree with the trial court that Continental failed to state a cause of action. Clearly, there is no set of facts that can be proved under these pleadings entitling Continental to the relief it seeks. We therefore find no error in the dismissal of Continental's complaint and affirm the judgment of the circuit court of Franklin County.

Notes and Questions

1. Why is "no one answer" to the coalbed methane problem "right for every state"? What characteristics of the coalbed methane gas in this case persuade the court that the gas is owned by the owner of the coal?

2. Natural gas is often stored in the ground, in depleted reservoirs near population centers, until it is needed for consumption. Programs to reinject natural gas, produced elsewhere, for storage purposes have raised two related legal problems. First, does the reinjecting owner lose title (or risk losing title) to the reinjected gas? Second, who has the right to reinject hydrocarbons when the reservoir is owned by more than one person? In Hammonds v. Central Kentucky Gas Co., 75 S.W.2d 204 (Ky. 1934), the company brought in natural gas from other fields and injected it into a vacated underground reservoir. The gas company leased most of the field of approximately 15,000 acres, but Hammonds, the owner of 54 acres of unleased land in the field, sued in trespass for damages. The company won the case, but received bad news along with the good news. The court, per Commissioner Stanley, stated: "If one capture a fox in a forest and turn it loose in another, or if he catch a fish and put it back in the stream at another point, has he not done with that migratory, common property just what the appellee has done with the gas in this case? Did the company not lose its exclusive property in the gas when it restored the substance to its natural habitat? . . . [I]f in fact the gas turned loose in the earth wandered into the plaintiff's land, the defendant is not liable to her for the value of the use of her property, for the company ceased to be the exclusive owner of the whole of the gas — it again became mineral ferae naturae."

Subsequently, some courts followed *Hammonds*, but most courts and several state legislatures rejected its wild animal analogy. Texas American Energy Corp. v. Citizens Fidelity Bank & Trust Co., 736 S.W.2d 25 (Ky. 1987). In a declaratory judgment action between a natural gas company and its secured lender, the court held that reinjected natural gas remains personal property (*i.e.*, "goods") for purposes of Article 9 of the Uniform Commercial Code. Accordingly, the court stated that stored gas cannot be encumbered by a real estate mortgage. The court quoted extensively from decisions in New York and Texas that spurned *Hammonds*: "'[T]he storage gas in question has not escaped from its owners. On the contrary, it is very much in possession of the storage companies, being within a well-defined storage field. . . . Deferring to the analogy of animals *ferae naturae* under the circumstances of this case would no more divest a storage company of title to stored gas than a zookeeper in Pittsburgh to title to an escaped elephant. . . . Gas is an inanimate, diminishing non-reproductive substance lacking any free will of its own, and instead of running wild at large as animals do, is subject to be moved solely by pressure or mechanical means.'" Thus, the court stated "*Hammonds* should be narrowly construed or limited. . . . [W]hen previously extracted oil or gas is subsequently stored in underground reservoirs capable of being defined with certainty and the integrity of said reservoirs is capable of being maintained, title to such oil and gas is not lost and said minerals do not become subject to the rights of the owners of the surface above the storage fields."

C. PUBLIC LANDS

The U.S. government owns 650 million acres of land, or about 28 percent of the nation's total. During the nineteenth century, the government claimed ownership of much of this land through a series of major territorial expansions, particularly those attributable to: the 1803 Louisiana Purchase from France; the Oregon Treaty with Great Britain in 1846; conquests, purchases, and annexations from Mexico during the late 1840s and early 1850s; and the 1867 Alaskan Purchase from Russia. In many cases, however, these formal acquisitions from foreign governments needed to be sealed though military actions and forced treaties with the Native American nations, tribes, or residents possessing the land itself. Most federal public land is concentrated in Alaska and western states, where federal ownership constitutes nearly one-third of all lands. The management of this land and the resources that it contains raises ongoing property law issues.

■ **PUBLIC LANDS FOR THE PEOPLE, INC. v. UNITED STATES DEPARTMENT OF AGRICULTURE**
United States Court of Appeals for the Ninth Circuit, 2012
697 F.3d 1192

McKEOWN, Circuit Judge. The Wild West has long conjured up images of prospectors with pack mules and pickaxes foraging for gold. The oft-romanticized ways of the Wild West eventually modernized and gave way to prospecting with the aid of motor vehicles and heavy machinery. The United States Forest Service (the "Forest Service"), an arm of the Department of Agriculture, recently limited the use of motor vehicles to certain roads in the century-old Eldorado National Forest ("ENF"). Concerned about the impact of the limitation on their activities, a group of miners and prospectors challenged the Forest Service's decision. The district court dismissed the complaint, and we affirm.

BACKGROUND

Beginning in 2005, the Forest Service published a Notice of Intent to propose prohibitions on motor vehicle use in the ENF, held public meetings, and circulated for public comment a draft environmental impact statement on proposed travel management in the ENF. The Final Environmental Impact Statement ("FEIS"), issued in March 2008, recognized that if prohibitions on motor vehicle use were adopted, miners and prospectors would need to obtain permission, through a Notice of Intent or Plan of Operations, to use motor vehicles in areas where no such permission restriction existed before. The FEIS noted the effect of 36 C.F.R. §228, which requires miners to obtain pre-authorization when conducting certain operations:

> Individuals or companies that conduct prospecting and exploration activities are not usually required to obtain a permit or other form of authorization, pursuant to 36 CFR 228, but must comply with other Forest rules and regulations. Access associated with mineral development activities, such as for an active mine, is commonly dealt with through a Plan of Operations or Notice of Intent, pursuant to 36 CFR 228.

The FEIS explicitly acknowledged that, because mining and prospecting are "facilitated by the use of public wheeled motor vehicles for access and hauling of equipment," restrictions on motorized vehicle use in areas with likely mineral resources "may have the affect [sic] of reducing access for prospecting or exploration, with the subsequent effect of a reduction of discovery of new mineral resource commodities."

In April 2008, the Forest Service issued a decision limiting motor vehicle use in the ENF to certain roads and trails and prohibiting public wheeled motor vehicle cross-country travel (the "2008 Decision"). The 2008 Decision specifically limits motor vehicle use by the public to "1,002 miles of ML-2 roads and 210 miles of trails," while concurrently disallowing motor vehicle use on 502,000 acres of previously open forest land. . . .

Appellants ("the Miners") are seven individuals who wish to use motor vehicles to pursue mining or prospecting activities in the ENF, and Public Lands for the People, Inc., an association of miners and prospectors. Some of the individuals claim existing mining rights within the ENF, while others simply anticipate prospecting for minerals. . . .

The Miners claim that the Forest Service is without authority to restrict their motor vehicle use and that the Forest Service "acted arbitrarily and capriciously by requiring that entry onto roads and rights of way previously open, and now closed due to the [2008 Decision], requires a Notice of Intent or Plan of Operations pursuant to 36 C.F.R. §228.4(a) in order to prospect and/or access a valid Federal mining claim and mineral estate." The district court held that the Miners failed to establish standing and, alternatively, that they failed to state a claim upon which relief could be granted because the Secretary of Agriculture had the authority to impose the road restrictions and reasonably interpreted a Forest Service regulation pertaining to "public roads."

ANALYSIS

I. STANDING

[Some of the Miners] have suffered an injury in fact because they can no longer access their mining claims via motor vehicles without first filing a Notice of Intent or Plan of Operations. . . . [Thus,] the Miners have standing to pursue this action.

II. FOREST SERVICE AUTHORITY

We now turn to the Miners' claim that the Forest Service lacks authority to restrict motor vehicles use in the ENF. The Forest Service's extensive statutory authority dooms this challenge. Over a century ago, Congress granted the Forest Service broad authority to regulate access to mining claims on National Forest Service lands. The Organic Administration Act of 1897 gives the Secretary of Agriculture authority "to promulgate rules and regulations to protect the national forest lands from destruction and depredation." Clouser v. Espy, 42 F.3d 1522, 1529 (9th Cir. 1994); see 16 U.S.C. §551. Although nothing prohibits an individual from entering "national forests for all proper and lawful purposes, including that of prospecting, locating, and developing the mineral resources thereof," he "must comply with the rules and regulations covering such national forests." Id. §478.

Consistent with this statutory scheme, the Secretary of Agriculture "may adopt reasonable rules and regulations which do not impermissibly encroach upon the right to the use and enjoyment of . . . claims for mining purposes." United States v. Weiss, 642 F.2d 296, 299 (9th Cir. 1981). . . .

The Forest Supervisor's Record of Decision illustrates the balancing undertaken by the Forest Service:

> The designated system of routes will provide for diverse public wheeled motor vehicle opportunities, provide routes that enhance wheeled motor vehicle recreation, and provide access to dispersed recreation. In prohibiting wheeled motor vehicle use off of designated routes, the Forest is minimizing damage to Forest resources, minimizing harassment of wildlife and limiting conflict between wheeled motor vehicle use and other recreation opportunities.

Among other factors, the Forest Service considered "impacts from motor vehicle use on quiet recreation opportunities" and "impacts to wildlife, water quality, air quality, and other resources." Its goal "was to allow a diversity of highway and non-highway classes of public wheeled motor vehicle use on ML-2 roads, while still reducing environmental impacts." The 2008 Decision struck a balance between competing interests by allowing motor vehicle use by the public on "1,002 miles of ML-2 native surfaced roads" while prohibiting other vehicular access. Contrary to the Miners' allegations, the 2008 Decision is not an indirect prohibition on mining operations masquerading as an access regulation, and its access restrictions aren't unreasonable.

The Miners claim that a web of statutes creates a national policy that protects self-initiation and encourages prospecting and mining on federal lands by limiting the Forest Service's authority to regulate motor vehicle access on National Forest Service lands. The Miners' argument understates the Forest Service's legitimate authority to regulate access. Although the Miners list a litany of statutes, they do not point to any specific statutory language that strips the Secretary of Agriculture of his authority to regulate motor vehicle use.

We conclude that none of the statutes cited by the Miners cabin the Secretary's authority with respect to vehicular access. No statutory provision gives the Miners an unfettered right to access their mining claims via motor vehicles. See, e.g., 30 U.S.C. §22: "All valuable mineral deposits in lands belonging to the United States . . . shall be free and open to exploration . . . by citizens of the United States . . . under regulations prescribed by law . . . ." (emphasis added).

The only specific argument the Miners make is that 16 U.S.C. §472 restricts the Secretary's discretion because the "Secretary of the Department of Agriculture shall execute or cause to be executed all laws affecting public lands . . . excepting such laws as affect the surveying, prospecting, locating, appropriating, entering, relinquishing, reconveying, certifying, or patenting of any of such lands." The Miners claim that the 2008 Decision impinges upon possessory rights in their mining claims by imposing access regulations that have "the same effect as prohibition under the guise of time consuming delay causing regulations." But the Secretary of Agriculture has long had the authority to restrict motorized access to specified areas of national forests, including to mining claims. *See Clouser*, 42 F.3d at 1530. . . .

III. FOREST SERVICE INTERPRETATION

Anticipating the shortcomings of their challenge to the Forest Service's authority, the Miners claim that 36 C.F.R. §228.4(a) creates an exception to the 2008 Decision. Section 228.4(a)(1)(i) provides that a Notice of Intent to operate is not required for "Operations which will be limited to the use of vehicles on existing public roads or roads used and maintained for National Forest System purposes." Reasoning that the 2008 Decision does not change the "public" character of previously "public roads," the Miners posit that they need not seek pre-authorization for motor vehicle use on such "public" roads in the ENF.

Although the concept of a "public road" may seem obvious, the definition is not immediately clear. The Forest Service urges that its 2008 Decision, which limited motor vehicle use to certain roads, rendered all other roads within the ENF "non-public" because those roads now fall outside the Forest Service Manual's definition of "public road." The Manual defines a "public road" as:

> 1. Available, except during scheduled periods, extreme weather, or emergency conditions; 2. Passable by four-wheel standard passenger cars; and 3. Open to the general public for use without restrictive gates, prohibitive signs, or regulation other than restrictions based on size, weight, or class of registration.

The Miners accuse the Forest Service of "aggressively redefining" the meaning of "public road."

We give wide deference to an agency's reasonable interpretation of its own regulation. "[W]here an agency interprets its own regulation, even if through an informal process, its interpretation of an ambiguous regulation is controlling . . . unless 'plainly erroneous or inconsistent with the regulation.'" Bassiri v. Xerox Corp., 463 F.3d 927, 930 (9th Cir. 2006). The Forest Service's definition of "public roads"—roads open to motor vehicle use by the general public—is reasonable because "public" is commonly defined as "[o]pen or available for all to use, share, or enjoy." *Black's Law Dictionary* 1348 (9th ed. 2009). Given the many restrictions placed on their use, the roads restricted by the 2008 Decision are no longer public roads. The Miners' alternative definition does not render the Forest Service's definition plainly erroneous or inconsistent with the regulation. . . .

Notes and Questions

1. In *Public Lands for the People*, the court upheld a government decision that pleased one group while disappointing another. Such conflicting interests are ubiquitous in public land management. Some ranchers without extensive landholdings

of their own complain that grazing restrictions on public lands are driving them out of business while other ranchers with extensive landholdings counter that granting expanded grazing rights to their competitors gives those competitors an unfair advantage. Oil companies insist that national security and American consumers alike would benefit if exploration was allowed in the Arctic National Wildlife Refuge while environmentalists dispute these claims. Some recreational users (particular owners of snowmobiles, four-wheel drive vehicles, and dirt bikes) object to limits on motorized vehicles while other recreational users (especially hikers, backpackers, and campers) fight any further encroachment of off-road vehicles. Developers in expanding Western cities like Las Vegas accuse federal land managers of limiting urban growth while their critics complain that there is already too much urban sprawl and that ready access to open land is what makes Western living so desirable in the first place. Environmentalists insist that federal land use decisions too often benefit corporate economic interests while their critics complain that civil servants in the Departments of Agriculture and the Interior, which oversee federal land policy, have an anti-development bias. How should the law reconcile these conflicting demands and concerns?

2. During the nineteenth century, the federal government reduced its holding in Western lands through policies of selling farm and ranch land to settlers at low prices, giving vast tracts of land to corporations as incentives for the construction of railroads in undeveloped regions, awarding lands to fund so-called land grant state universities, and transferring ownership rights to the holders of mining claims on public lands. The twentieth century brought a conservation movement that sought to keep environmentally valuable lands in public ownership, and the twenty-first century has already yielded debates about whether the federal government should acquire additional lands. *See* H.R. Rep. No. 107-758, Pt. 1 (2002) (analyzing the proposed Conservation and Reinvestment Act (CARA), which would authorize the federal government to spend $900 million annually for environmentally valuable lands). Even so, the mere ownership of so much land in Western states, particularly Alaska, by the federal government is a source of resentment among many Westerners who complain about land use decisions made in distant Washington.

3. Federal lands are classified in numerous distinct ways that result in the application of different land use rules by different federal agencies:

National parks are managed by the National Park Service within the Department of the Interior. Yellowstone became the world's first national park in 1872, and by 2003 there were 379 different national parks areas containing 83.6 million acres within the overall system. The National Park Service Organic Act states that the purpose of the parks "is to conserve the scenery and natural and historic objects and the wild life therein and to provide for the enjoyment of the same in such manner and by such means as will leave them unimpaired for the enjoyment of future generations." 16 U.S.C. §1. Most national parks are also governed by individualized statutes that provide more specific management directions.

National wildlife refuges encompass over 93 million acres of land and are managed by the Fish and Wildlife Service, which is an agency within the Department of the Interior. Use and management of the refuges were subject to many individualized laws until 1966, and most recently the enactment of the National Wildlife Refuge System Improvement Act in 1997 has provided more regularized standards. The 1997 organic statute treats the conservation of wildlife, plants, and their habitats as the highest priority use, followed by "wildlife-dependent recreational uses" such as hunting, fishing, wildlife observation and photography, and environmental education, with "all other uses" such as oil production, logging, grazing, and other recreation receiving lowest priority.

National forests are managed by the Forest Service within the Department of Agriculture. There are 155 national forests encompassing 191 million acres of land. Generally, the Forest Service must seek to accommodate "multiple uses" of national forests, though some forests are governed by special rules. A variety of other classifications (including national grasslands, wild and scenic rivers, national trails, and national marine sanctuaries) apply to a smaller collection of federal lands. The remaining 262 million acres of federal lands that are not otherwise designated are managed by the Bureau of Land Management in the Department of the Interior pursuant to the Federal Land Policy and Management Act of 1976.

■ **WILDERNESS WATCH v. MAINELLA**
   United States Court of Appeals for the Eleventh Circuit, 2004
   375 F.3d 1085

BARKETT, Circuit Judge. Wilderness Watch appeals the grant of summary judgment to the National Park Service on its complaint seeking to enjoin the Park Service's practice of using motor vehicles to transport visitors across the designated wilderness area on Cumberland Island, Georgia. Wilderness Watch asserts that this practice violates the Wilderness Act, 16 U.S.C. §§1131-36. . . .

Mindful of our "increasing population, accompanied by expanding settlement and growing mechanization," Congress passed the 1964 Wilderness Act in order to preserve and protect certain lands "in their natural condition" and thus "secure for present and future generations the benefits of wilderness." 16 U.S.C. §1131(a). The Act recognized the value of preserving "an area where the earth and its community of life are untrammeled by man, where man himself is a visitor who does not remain." *Id.* §1131(c). Congress therefore directed that designated wilderness areas "shall be administered for the use and enjoyment of the American people in such manner as will leave them unimpaired for future use and enjoyment as wilderness, and so as to provide for the protection of these areas, the preservation of their wilderness character, and for the gathering and dissemination of information regarding their use and enjoyment as wilderness." *Id.* §1131(a).

Cumberland Island, which features some of the last remaining undeveloped land on the barrier islands along the Atlantic coast of the United States, was declared by Congress to be a National Seashore in 1972. Ten years later, Congress designated as wilderness or potential wilderness[2] some 19,000 acres, including most of the northern three-fifths of the island. . . . Today, visitors to Cumberland Island must leave their vehicles on the mainland and travel to the island by boat.

---

2. Potential wilderness areas contain certain temporary conditions that do not conform to the Wilderness Act. They are to receive full wilderness designation when the Secretary of the Interior determines that "uses prohibited by the Wilderness Act have ceased." P.L. 97-250 §2(a). Park Service policy "is to treat potential wilderness in exactly the same manner as wilderness." R. at 2-17 Ex. 1 (declaration of Cumberland Island Superintendent Arthur Frederick).

First African Baptist Church on Cumberland Island, part of the island's historic district, built in the 1930s and the site of the September 1996 wedding of John F. Kennedy, Jr. and Carolyn Bessette

In addition to wilderness area, Park Service land includes several buildings and facilities on the southern end of the island as well as two historical areas on the northern and western coasts: Plum Orchard, just outside the wilderness boundary, and the Settlement, located in potential wilderness area.[3] Historically, these two locations have been reached via the "Main Road," a one-lane dirt road that has also been designated as part of the wilderness and potential wilderness areas.

Once federal land has been designated as wilderness, the Wilderness Act places severe restrictions on commercial activities, roads, motorized vehicles, motorized transport, and structures within the area, subject to very narrow exceptions and existing private rights. Specifically, the relevant section provides:

> Except as specifically provided for in this chapter, and subject to existing private rights, there shall be no commercial enterprise and no permanent road within any wilderness area designated by this chapter and, except as necessary to meet minimum requirements for the administration of the area for the purpose of this chapter (including measures required in emergencies involving the health and safety of persons within the area), there shall be no temporary road, no use of motor vehicles, motorized equipment or motorboats, no landing of aircraft, no other form of mechanical transport, and no structure or installation within any such area.

16 U.S.C. §1133(c). Thus, aside from exceptions not relevant here, the statute permits the use of motor vehicles and transport only "as necessary to meet minimum requirements for the administration of the area for the purpose of this chapter." *Id.*

Following the wilderness designation, the Park Service continued to use the existing one-lane dirt road to access the historical areas. Motorized transportation

---

3. Plum Orchard, a mansion complex commissioned by Thomas Carnegie in the late nineteenth century, lies some two-and-one-half miles from the wilderness boundary on the western coast. The Settlement, the remnants of an area occupied by a group of freed slaves after the Civil War, lies another six miles north of Plum Orchard.

on Cumberland Island became a controversial issue in the 1990s, as the federal government sought to obtain remaining private tracts on the island and various groups called for greater public access to and support of the historical sites. An informal group of environmental organizations, historical societies, and local residents met several times in an attempt to discuss and ultimately to influence Park Service policy. Jack Kingston, the representative to Congress from the district including Cumberland, introduced legislation that would have removed the wilderness designation from the roads leading to the historical sites. This bill died in committee in 1998, but later that year the Park Service convened the first of two meetings with many of the same interested parties in an attempt to negotiate a solution to the conflict over its policies. In February 1999 the Park Service agreed to provide regular public access to Plum Orchard and the Settlement via Park Service motor vehicles until boat service could be established.

The Park Service claimed that it needed motorized access to the historical areas in order to "meet its obligations to restore, maintain, preserve and curate the historic resources . . . and permit visitor access and interpretation." R. at 4-46-559, 562. The Service also claimed that permitting tourists to "piggyback" along on Park Service personnel trips to these locations would yield "no net increase in impact," — that is, the number of trips and overall impact on the area would be no greater than if the Park Service were simply meeting its statutory obligations. *Id.* For the first two months, the Park Service used vehicles that held four passengers, but the agency soon acquired a fifteen-person van in order to accommodate larger numbers of visitors. The Park Service offered trips to Plum Orchard three times per week and to the Settlement once per month. Although the Park Service had not previously visited the sites on a regular schedule, the agency decided to establish a regular schedule in order to accommodate the transportation of visitors. . . .

The Park Service . . . claims that the Act allows land designated as wilderness to be devoted to multiple purposes, citing as authority 16 U.S.C. §1133(b), which provides that "wilderness areas shall be devoted to the public purposes of recreational, scenic, scientific, educational, conservation, and historical use." Thus, the Park Service argues, because it has a separate duty to preserve the historical structures at the Settlement, the "preservation of historic structures in wilderness (or, as here, potential wilderness) is in fact administration to further the purposes of the Wilderness Act." Appellees' Br. at 32. . . .

As an initial matter, we cannot agree with the Park Service that the preservation of historical structures furthers the goals of the Wilderness Act. The Park Service's responsibilities for the historic preservation of Plum Orchard and the Settlement derive, not from the Wilderness Act, but rather from the National Historic Preservation Act (NHPA), 16 U.S.C. §461, et seq. The NHPA requires agencies to "assume responsibility for the preservation of historic properties" they control. *Id.* §470h-2(a)(1). Plum Orchard and the historic district containing the Settlement have both been listed in the National Register of Historic Places. . . .

The agency's obligations under the Wilderness Act are quite different. The Wilderness Act defines wilderness as "undeveloped Federal land retaining its primeval character and influence, without permanent improvements or human habitation." 16 U.S.C. §1131(c). A wilderness area should "generally appear to have been affected primarily by the forces of nature, with the imprint of man's work substantially unnoticeable." *Id.* Another section of the Act explicitly states that, except as necessary for minimal administrative needs that require occasional vehicle use, "there shall be . . . no structure or installation within any such [wilderness] area." 16 U.S.C. §1133(c). As the Park Service notes, Section 1133(b) mentions "historical use" along with "recreational, scenic, scientific, educational, [and] conservation" uses. However, this list tracks the definition of wilderness areas in §1131(c), which describes "a primitive and unconfined type of recreation" and "ecological, geological, or other features of scientific, educational, scenic, or historical value." 16 U.S.C. §1131(c). Given the consistent evocation of "untrammeled" and "natural" areas, the previous pairing of "historical" with "ecological" and "geological" features, and the explicit prohibition on structures, the only reasonable reading of "historical use" in the Wilderness Act refers to natural, rather than man-made, features. . . .

This appeal turns not on the preservation of historical structures but on the decision to provide motorized public access to them across designated wilderness areas. The Wilderness Act bars the use of motor vehicles in these areas "except as necessary to meet minimum requirements for the administration of the area for the purpose of this chapter [the Wilderness Act]." 16 U.S.C. §1133(c). The Park Service's decision to "administer" the Settlement using a fifteen-passenger van filled with tourists simply cannot be construed as "necessary" to meet the "minimum requirements" for administering the area "for the purpose of [the Wilderness Act]." 16 U.S.C. §1133(c). . . . In no ordinary sense of the word can the transportation of fifteen people through wilderness area be "necessary" to administer the area for the purpose of the Wilderness Act.

The Park Service argues that these trips affect the wilderness no more than would a standard Park Service vehicle with no additional passengers. Thus, the agency argues that the "use of motor vehicles" remains the same as what would be minimally necessary for administration. There are several problems with this interpretation. Most obviously, it still runs counter to the plain meaning of the provision. Under an ordinary, common-sense reading, people "use" motor vehicles when they ride in the Park Service van, thereby increasing the "use of motor vehicles" beyond the minimum necessary for administration of the Wilderness Act. The Park Service wishes to define the term based on the number of vehicles used rather than on the number of people using them, but even so, the acquisition and use of a large passenger van for transporting tourists cannot reasonably be squeezed into the phrase "necessary to meet minimum requirements" of administration. The language in this subsection is quite categorical, providing for "*no* motor vehicle use" except "as necessary" and labels this a "*prohibition.*" 16 U.S.C. §1133(c) (emphasis added). Moreover, the same subsection provides that there shall be "no other form of mechanical transport" beyond what is necessary for administration of the Wilderness Act. *Id.* A passenger van certainly provides more "transport" than would a Park Service vehicle without extra passengers.

In addition, the overall purpose and structure of the statute argue against the agency interpretation. The prohibition on motor vehicle "use" in the Wilderness Act stems from more than just its potential for physical impact on the environment. The Act seeks to preserve wilderness areas "in their natural condition" for their "use and enjoyment as *wilderness.*" 16 U.S.C. §1131(a) (emphasis added). The Act promotes the benefits of wilderness "for the American people," especially the "opportunities for a primitive and unconfined type of recreation." *Id.* §1131(c). Thus, the statute seeks to provide the opportunity for a primitive wilderness experience as much as to protect the wilderness lands themselves from physical harm. Use of a passenger van changes the wilderness experience, not only for the actual passengers, but also for any other persons they happen to pass (more so than would be the case upon meeting a lone park ranger in a jeep). Of course, there is nothing wrong with appreciating natural beauty from inside a passenger van, and many other categories of public land administered by the federal government appropriately offer this opportunity. It simply is not the type of "use and enjoyment" promoted by the Wilderness Act. . . .

We recognize the difficult position of the Park Service in this case. Faced with competing demands from different constituencies in both Congress and the general public, the agency attempted to find a compromise that would satisfy all interested parties and potentially stave off legislative changes to the status of the Cumberland Island wilderness area. Although this goal is laudable, the statute limits motor vehicle use and transport to what is "necessary to meet minimum requirements for the administration of the area." The compromise on public transportation reached in this case cannot be squared with the language of the Wilderness Act.

Reversed.

Notes and Questions

1. Should there be a Red Lobster seafood restaurant or a Club Med resort on Cumberland Island? Who should decide on the uses of public lands: Congress acting on behalf of the people, the market operating in accord with economic laws, or some other visible or invisible hand?

2. The Wilderness Act, passed by Congress and signed by President Johnson in 1964 with broad bipartisan support, requires the federal land management agency — here, the National Park Service — to "preserve the wilderness character" of a designated wilderness area. 16 U.S.C. §1133(b). Does the Wilderness Act presume that some property should not be used by humans, or does it instead presume that wilderness is a desirable form of property use that benefits humans? In this respect, Henry David Thoreau famously wrote, "In wildness is the preservation of the World." Henry David Thoreau, *Walking*, Atlantic Monthly, 1862, *reprinted in Walden and Other Writings of Henry David Thoreau* 597, 613 (Brooks Atkinson ed., 1950). More recently, novelist and nature writer Wendell Berry noted, "We have never known what we were doing because we have never known what we were *un*doing. We cannot know what we are doing until we know what nature would be doing if we were doing nothing." Wendell Berry, *Preserving Wildness*, in *Home Economics: Fourteen Essays by Wendell Berry* 137, 147 (1987). Expressing a widely held sentiment of the type that presumably inspired the Wilderness Act, essayist Edward Hoagland commented, "The swan song sounded by the wilderness grows ever fainter, ever more constricted, until only sharp ears can catch it at all. It fades to a nearly inaudible level, and yet there never is going to be any one time when we can say right *now* it is gone." Edward Hoagland, *Hailing the Elusory Mountain Lion*, in *Hoagland on Nature: Essays* 35, 35 (2003).

3. The Wilderness Act prohibits any "commercial enterprise" within a designated wilderness area. The Ninth Circuit construed the scope of that prohibition in two cases. In Wilderness Society v. FWS, 353 F.3d 1051 (9th Cir. 2003) (en banc), two environmental groups challenged a project by which the Cook Inlet Aquaculture Association (CIAA) added six million sockeye salmon fry to Tustumena Lake each year. Tustumena Lake is the largest freshwater lake within the Kenai wilderness area southwest of Anchorage, and the project was designed to enhance commercial fishing operations in the area. CIAA emphasized its non-profit status and the fact

that the fishing occurred outside the wilderness area. Conceding that "this fish-stocking program is nothing like building a McDonald's restaurant or a Wal-Mart store on the shores of Tustumena Lake," the court nevertheless held that it was "literally a project related to commerce." *Id.* at 1061-62. Further, it was not "aimed at preserving a threatened salmon run" or otherwise "furthering the goals of the Wilderness Act." *Id.* at 1062-63. Rather, the court noted, "The primary purpose of the Enhancement Project is to advance commercial interests of Cook Inlet fishermen by swelling the salmon runs from which they will eventually make their catch," *id.* at 1064. Thus, the court concluded, "The primary effect of the Enhancement Project is to aid commercial enterprise of fishermen." *Id.* at 1065.

High Sierra Hikers Ass'n v. Blackwell, 390 F.3d 630 (9th Cir. 2004), involved the Forest Service's issuance of use permits to commercial horse and mule outfitters within the John Muir and Ansel Adams wilderness areas. High Sierra Hikers Association complained that such commercial activities violated the Wilderness Act. The general prohibition on commercial enterprises in wilderness contains an exception "to the extent necessary for activities which are proper for realizing the recreational or other wilderness purposes of the areas." 16 U.S.C. §1133(d)(5). Even though the court recognized, "Commercial packstock operators provide the public with the opportunity to take guided trips into the wilderness areas, transport equipment for backcountry visitors, and enable access for people who would otherwise not be able to hike in those areas," it held that the Forest Service failed to limit the packstock operations to the extent necessary. "At best, when the Forest Service simply continued preexisting permit levels, it failed to balance the impact that the level of commercial activity was having on the wilderness character of the land. At worst, the Forest Service elevated recreational activity over the long-term preservation of the wilderness character of the land," the court noted. *Id.* at 892, 903-04. It thus remanded the case "to the district court for a determination of appropriate relief under the Wilderness Act, including whether remediation of any degradation that has already occurred is appropriate." *Id.* at 905. What should the district court order?

4. Cumberland Island is one of few pieces of wilderness or semi-wilderness left on the intensely developed Atlantic coast of the United States. A larger public controversy rages over the use of federally owned wilderness land on the much less developed Arctic coast of Alaska. "The Arctic National Wildlife Refuge is one of the great untouched lands remaining in America and on the northern continent. Its ecological value is unlike any other in the Nation and in the world." 148 Cong. Rec. S2774 (daily ed. Apr. 17, 2002) (remarks of Sen. Kerry). The Arctic National Wildlife Refuge (ANWR) is home to a herd of approximately 160,000 free-range caribou; 45 other species of land and marine mammals, including grizzly, polar, and black bears, wolves, muskox, and moose; up to 180 species of birds, many of them migratory waterfowl; and a variety of other animals and plants. It is also the apparent site of some of the largest undeveloped oil deposits in the United States. The supposed presence of commercially valuable oil deposits under this wilderness has made it the subject of ongoing battles in Congress. Since the 1980s, Republicans have introduced bills to open ANWR to exploration and development. The House has passed 12 such bills, most recently in February 2012, but none has resulted in legislation. The only bill also to make it through the Senate was vetoed by President Clinton in 1995.

Although betraying fundamentally differing attitudes toward environmental protection and economic development, much of the actual debate over ANWR presents wholly contradictory portrayals of the refuge, the possible effects on it of oil drilling, and the extent of its potential contribution to decreasing national dependence on foreign sources for oil. Opponents of drilling tend to see ANWR as a pristine wilderness and its abundant wildlife as vulnerable in the face of oil drilling and extraction. Further, they cite figures suggesting that oil from ANWR would do little to solve the nation's energy woes. In contrast, proponents of drilling see ANWR as a bleak and uninhabited place whose wildlife could easily adapt to the presence of environmentally friendly drilling operations. They see tapping its oil as one small but significant part of a larger national energy policy. The status quo favors the opponents of drilling because existing law prohibits oil development in ANWR. Despite President Bush's appeals, Congress has been unwilling to change the law.

5. After the Eleventh Circuit's decision in *Wilderness Watch*, Representative Kingston persevered in his efforts to remove the Main Road from the Cumberland Island wilderness area. He finally succeeded in adding a rider to the omnibus federal appropriations bill in December 2004, which excluded the Main Road, two smaller roads, and a historic district from the wilderness area and directed the Park Service to authorize visitor tours of the historic sites on the island. In 2011, the Park Service began offering what it calls the "Lands and Legacies" tour, costing $15 per person and lasting five to six hours. *See* Mary Landers, *New tour motors through the wilderness of Cumberland Island*, Savannah Morning News, Aug. 20, 2011.

14
Takings

The government is always buying property. Roads, parks, and government offices depend upon the government acquiring the necessary land. The government also procures military equipment, office supplies, computer software, and lots of personal property. Most of the time the government, just like any private party, simply negotiates to buy property from a willing seller. But sometimes the government wants to buy property that the owner does not want to sell. And sometimes the government's actions substantially impair the utility and value of property to its owner even when the government does not buy that property.

An owner's challenge to government action that affects private property often falls under the general category of "takings," per the Fifth Amendment's command that the government must satisfy certain conditions to be able to "take" property. Takings has become an extraordinarily controversial — and equally complicated — problem of equitable policy and constitutional interpretation. Generally, takings raises four questions. Why should the government have the power to take someone's property? What constitutes the government's taking of someone's property? Why should the government have to pay for that property? How much should the government have to pay for it?

A. THE POWER OF EMINENT DOMAIN

■ KELO v. CITY OF NEW LONDON
Supreme Court of the United States, 2005
545 U.S. 469

STEVENS, Justice. In 2000, the city of New London approved a development plan that, in the words of the Supreme Court of Connecticut, was "projected to create in excess of 1,000 jobs, to increase tax and other revenues, and to revitalize an economically distressed city, including its downtown and waterfront areas." Kelo v. City of New London, 843 A.2d 500, 507 (Conn. 2004). In assembling the land needed for this project, the city's development agent has purchased property from willing sellers and proposes to use the power of eminent domain to acquire the remainder of the property from unwilling owners in exchange for just compensation. The question presented is whether the city's proposed disposition of this property qualifies as a "public use" within the meaning of the Takings Clause of the Fifth Amendment to the Constitution.[1]

I.

The city of New London (hereinafter City) sits at the junction of the Thames River and the Long Island Sound in southeastern Connecticut. Decades of economic decline led a state agency in 1990 to designate the City a "distressed municipality." In 1996, the Federal Government closed the Naval Undersea Warfare Center, which had been located in the Fort Trumbull area of the City and had employed over 1,500 people. In 1998, the City's unemployment rate was nearly double that of the State, and its population of just under 24,000 residents was at its lowest since 1920.

These conditions prompted state and local officials to target New London, and particularly its Fort Trumbull area, for economic revitalization. To this end, respondent New London Development Corporation (NLDC), a private nonprofit entity established some years earlier to assist the City in planning economic development, was reactivated. In January 1998, the State authorized a $5.35 million bond issue to support the NLDC's planning activities and a $10 million bond issue toward the creation of a Fort Trumbull State Park. In February, the pharmaceutical company Pfizer Inc. announced that it would build a $300 million research facility on a site immediately adjacent to Fort Trumbull; local planners hoped that Pfizer would draw new business to the area, thereby serving as a catalyst to the area's rejuvenation. After receiving initial approval from the city council, the NLDC continued its planning activities and held a series of neighborhood meetings to educate the public about the process. In May, the city council authorized the NLDC to formally submit its plans to the relevant state agencies for review. Upon obtaining state-level approval, the NLDC finalized an integrated development plan focused on 90 acres of the Fort Trumbull area. . . .

The city council approved the plan in January 2000, and designated the NLDC as its development agent in charge of implementation. *See* Conn. Gen. Stat. §8-188 (2005). The city council also authorized the NLDC to purchase property or to acquire property by exercising eminent domain in the City's name. §8-193. The NLDC successfully negotiated the purchase of most of the real estate in the 90-acre area, but its negotiations with petitioners failed. As a consequence, in November 2000, the NLDC initiated the condemnation proceedings that gave rise to this case.

II.

Petitioner Susette Kelo has lived in the Fort Trumbull area since 1997. She has made extensive improvements to her house, which she prizes for its water view. Petitioner Wilhelmina Dery was born in her Fort Trumbull house in 1918 and has lived there her entire life. Her husband Charles (also a petitioner) has lived in the house since they married some 60 years ago. In all, the nine petitioners own 15 properties in Fort Trumbull — 4 in parcel 3 of the development plan and 11 in

---

1. "[N]or shall private property be taken for public use, without just compensation." U.S. Const., Amdt. 5. That Clause is made applicable to the States by the Fourteenth Amendment. *See* Chicago, B. & Q.R. Co. v. Chicago, 166 U.S. 226 (1897).

parcel 4A. Ten of the parcels are occupied by the owner or a family member; the other five are held as investment properties. There is no allegation that any of these properties is blighted or otherwise in poor condition; rather, they were condemned only because they happen to be located in the development area.

In December 2000, petitioners brought this action in the New London Superior Court. They claimed, among other things, that the taking of their properties would violate the "public use" restriction in the Fifth Amendment. After a 7-day bench trial, the Superior Court granted a permanent restraining order prohibiting the taking of the properties located in parcel 4A (park or marina support). It, however, denied petitioners relief as to the properties located in parcel 3 (office space).

After the Superior Court ruled, both sides took appeals to the Supreme Court of Connecticut. That court held, over a dissent [by a 4-3 vote], that all of the City's proposed takings were valid. . . .

III.

Two polar propositions are perfectly clear. On the one hand, it has long been accepted that the sovereign may not take the property of *A* for the sole purpose of transferring it to another private party *B*, even though *A* is paid just compensation. On the other hand, it is equally clear that a State may transfer property from one private party to another if future "use by the public" is the purpose of the taking; the condemnation of land for a railroad with common-carrier duties is a familiar example. Neither of these propositions, however, determines the disposition of this case. . . .

. . . [T]his is not a case in which the City is planning to open the condemned land — at least not in its entirety — to use by the general public. Nor will the private lessees of the land in any sense be required to operate like common carriers, making their services available to all comers. But although such a projected use would be sufficient to satisfy the public use requirement, this "Court long ago rejected any literal requirement that condemned property be put into use for the general public." Hawaii Housing Authority v. Midkiff, 467 U.S. 229, 244 (1984). Indeed, while many state courts in the mid-19th century endorsed "use by the public" as the proper definition of public use, that narrow view steadily eroded over time. Not only was the "use by the public" test difficult to administer (*e.g.*, what proportion of the public need have access to the property? at what price?), but it proved to be impractical given the diverse and always evolving needs of society. Accordingly, when this Court began applying the Fifth Amendment to the States at the close of the 19th century, it embraced the broader and more natural interpretation of public use as "public purpose." . . .

The disposition of this case therefore turns on the question whether the City's development plan serves a "public purpose." Without exception, our cases have defined that concept broadly, reflecting our longstanding policy of deference to legislative judgments in this field.

In Berman v. Parker, 348 U.S. 26 (1954), this Court upheld a redevelopment plan targeting a blighted area of Washington, D.C., in which most of the housing for the area's 5,000 inhabitants was beyond repair. Under the plan, the area would be condemned and part of it utilized for the construction of streets, schools, and other public facilities. The remainder of the land would be leased or sold to private parties for the purpose of redevelopment, including the construction of low-cost housing. . . .

In *Midkiff*, the Court considered a Hawaii statute whereby fee title was taken from lessors and transferred to lessees (for just compensation) in order to reduce the concentration of land ownership. We unanimously upheld the statute and rejected the Ninth Circuit's view that it was "a naked attempt on the part of the state of Hawaii to take the property of *A* and transfer it to *B* solely for *B*'s private use and benefit." 467 U.S. at 235. Reaffirming *Berman*'s deferential approach to legislative judgments in this field, we concluded that the State's purpose of eliminating the "social and economic evils of a land oligopoly" qualified as a valid public use. *Id.* at 241-242. Our opinion also rejected the contention that the mere fact that the State immediately transferred the properties to private individuals upon condemnation somehow diminished the public character of the taking. "[I]t is only the taking's purpose, and not its mechanics," we explained, that matters in determining public use. *Id.* at 244.

In that same Term we decided another public use case that arose in a purely economic context. In Ruckelshaus v. Monsanto Co., 467 U.S. 986 (1984), the Court dealt with provisions of the Federal Insecticide, Fungicide, and Rodenticide Act under which the Environmental Protection Agency could consider the data (including trade secrets) submitted by a prior pesticide applicant in evaluating a subsequent application, so long as the second applicant paid just compensation for the data. We acknowledged that the "most direct beneficiaries" of these provisions were the subsequent applicants, *id.* at 1014, but we nevertheless upheld the statute under *Berman* and *Midkiff.* We found sufficient Congress' belief that sparing applicants the cost of time-consuming research eliminated a significant barrier to entry in the pesticide market and thereby enhanced competition. *Id.* at 1015. . . .

IV.

Those who govern the City were not confronted with the need to remove blight in the Fort Trumbull area, but their determination that the area was sufficiently distressed to justify a program of economic rejuvenation is entitled to our deference. The City has carefully formulated an economic development plan that it believes will provide appreciable benefits to the community, including — but by no means limited to — new jobs and increased tax revenue. As with other exercises in urban planning and development, the City is endeavoring to coordinate a variety of commercial, residential, and recreational uses of land, with the hope that they will form a whole greater than the sum of its parts. To effectuate this plan, the City has invoked a state statute that specifically authorizes the use of eminent domain to promote economic development. Given the comprehensive character of the plan, the thorough deliberation that preceded its adoption, and the limited scope of our review, it is appropriate for us, as it was in *Berman*, to resolve the challenges of the individual owners, not on a piecemeal basis, but rather in light of the entire plan. Because that plan unquestionably serves a public purpose, the takings challenged here satisfy the public use requirement of the Fifth Amendment.

To avoid this result, petitioners urge us to adopt a new bright-line rule that economic development does not qualify as a public use. Putting aside the unpersuasive suggestion that the City's plan will provide only purely economic benefits, neither precedent nor logic supports petitioners' proposal. Promoting economic development is a traditional and long accepted function of government. There is, moreover, no principled way of distinguishing economic development from the other public purposes that we have recognized. . . .

Petitioners contend that using eminent domain for economic development impermissibly blurs the boundary between public and private takings. Again, our cases foreclose this objection. Quite simply, the government's pursuit of a public purpose will often benefit individual private parties. . . . Our rejection of [petitioners'] contention [in *Berman*] has particular relevance to the instant case: "The public end may be as well or better served through an agency of private enterprise than through a department of government—or so the Congress might conclude. We cannot say that public ownership is the sole method of promoting the public purposes of community redevelopment projects." 348 U.S. at 33-34.

It is further argued that without a bright-line rule nothing would stop a city from transferring citizen *A*'s property to citizen *B* for the sole reason that citizen *B* will put the property to a more productive use and thus pay more taxes. Such a one-to-one transfer of property, executed outside the confines of an integrated development plan, is not presented in this case. While such an unusual exercise of government power would certainly raise a suspicion that a private purpose was afoot, the hypothetical cases posited by petitioners can be confronted if and when they arise. They do not warrant the crafting of an artificial restriction on the concept of public use.[19] . . .

In affirming the City's authority to take petitioners' properties, we do not minimize the hardship that condemnations may entail, notwithstanding the payment of just compensation. We emphasize that nothing in our opinion precludes any State from placing further restrictions on its exercise of the takings power. Indeed, many States already impose "public use" requirements that are stricter than the federal baseline. Some of these requirements have been established as a matter of state constitutional law,[22] while others are expressed in state eminent domain statutes that carefully limit the grounds upon which takings may be exercised.[23] As the submissions of the parties and their *amici* make clear, the necessity and wisdom of using eminent domain to promote economic development are certainly matters of legitimate public debate. . . .

The judgment of the Supreme Court of Connecticut is affirmed.

Justice O'CONNOR, with whom THE CHIEF JUSTICE, Justice SCALIA, and Justice THOMAS join, dissenting: Over two centuries ago, just after the Bill of Rights was ratified, Justice Chase wrote:

An act of the Legislature (for I cannot call it a law) contrary to the great first principles of the social compact, cannot be considered a rightful exercise of legislative authority. . . . A few instances will suffice to explain what I mean. . . . [A] law that takes property from *A* and gives it to *B*: It is against all reason and justice, for a people to entrust a Legislature with such powers; and, therefore, it cannot be presumed that they have done it.

19. A parade of horribles is especially unpersuasive in this context, since the Takings Clause largely "operates as a conditional limitation, permitting the government to do what it wants so long as it pays the charge." Eastern Enterprises v. Apfel, 524 U.S. 498, 545 (1998) (Kennedy, J., concurring). . . .

22. *See, e.g.*, County of Wayne v. Hathcock, 684 N.W.2d 765 (Mich. 2004).

23. Under California law, for instance, a city may only take land for economic development purposes in blighted areas. Cal. Health & Safety Code Ann. §§33030-33037 (West 1997).

Calder v. Bull, 3 Dall. 386, 388 (1798). Today the Court abandons this long-held, basic limitation on government power. Under the banner of economic development, all private property is now vulnerable to being taken and transferred to another private owner, so long as it might be upgraded — *i.e.*, given to an owner who will use it in a way that the legislature deems more beneficial to the public — in the process. To reason, as the Court does, that the incidental public benefits resulting from the subsequent ordinary use of private property render economic development takings "for public use" is to wash out any distinction between private and public use of property — and thereby effectively to delete the words "for public use" from the Takings Clause of the Fifth Amendment. Accordingly I respectfully dissent. . . .

Justice THOMAS dissenting: Long ago, William Blackstone wrote that "the law of the land . . . postpone[s] even public necessity to the sacred and inviolable rights of private property." 1 *Commentaries on the Laws of England* 134-135 (1765). The Framers embodied that principle in the Constitution, allowing the government to take property not for "public necessity," but instead for "public use." Amdt. 5. Defying this understanding, the Court replaces the Public Use Clause with a "'[P]ublic [P]urpose'" Clause, (or perhaps the "Diverse and Always Evolving Needs of Society" Clause, a restriction that is satisfied, the Court instructs, so long as the purpose is "legitimate" and the means "not irrational." This deferential shift in phraseology enables the Court to hold, against all common sense, that a costly urban-renewal project whose stated purpose is a vague promise of new jobs and increased tax revenue, but which is also suspiciously agreeable to the Pfizer Corporation, is for a "public use."

I cannot agree. If such "economic development" takings are for a "public use," any taking is, and the Court has erased the Public Use Clause from our Constitution, as Justice O'Connor powerfully argues in dissent. I do not believe that this Court can eliminate liberties expressly enumerated in the Constitution and therefore join her dissenting opinion. Regrettably, however, the Court's error runs deeper than this. Today's decision is simply the latest in a string of our cases construing the Public Use Clause to be a virtual nullity, without the slightest nod to its original meaning. In my view, the Public Use Clause, originally understood, is a meaningful limit on the government's eminent domain power. Our cases have strayed from the Clause's original meaning, and I would reconsider them. . . .

The Court relies almost exclusively on this Court's prior cases to derive today's far-reaching, and dangerous, result. But the principles this Court should employ to dispose of this case are found in the Public Use Clause itself. . . . When faced with a clash of constitutional principle and a line of unreasoned cases wholly divorced from the text, history, and structure of our founding document, we should not hesitate to resolve the tension in favor of the Constitution's original meaning. . . .

Notes and Questions

1. When the government uses its power of eminent domain to acquire property, the legal action is referred to a *condemnation*. Why should the government have the power to condemn property for its fair market value? What if the government was required to obtain property by paying a willing seller, just like everyone else? The various explanations for the power of eminent domain include the necessity of

preventing monopolies and holdouts, original government ownership of all property prior to possession by individual citizens, and inherent attributes of sovereignty. Are any of those answers sufficient to justify New London's condemnation of Susette Kelo's home?

2. Although governments and quasi-governmental entities regularly condemn real estate and occasionally condemn intellectual and other personal property, the power of eminent domain power is rarely used to obtain a going private business. Even during major wars, such as the Civil War and World War II, when prosecution of the war depended upon the production of essential military equipment and supplies, the government contracted with private industries instead of simply taking the necessary companies. Perhaps the most famous government effort to seize private businesses — President Truman's executive order taking over the steel industry to assure necessary production during the Korean War — resulted in a Supreme Court decision holding that Truman had exceeded his constitutional war powers as president. Youngstown Sheet & Tube Co. v. Sawyer, 343 U.S. 579 (1952). Why would the government be reluctant to condemn going businesses that could be turned to public uses?

3. The critical public-policy issue raised in *Kelo* is whether New London's effort to obtain land for a publicly planned but privately owned redevelopment project satisfied the public use requirement. Why is the government's eminent domain power limited to "public uses"? What constitutes a "public use"? Historically, two conceptions of public use have competed for legal acceptance. The broad view asks if there is a benefit to the public from the taking. It focuses upon the ends, not the means, of the government's taking. The broad view thus makes the understanding of public use coextensive with the police power. By contrast, the narrow view requires an actual use by the public or a public right to use the property that has been taken. That view focuses upon the means, not the ends, of the taking. As *Kelo* indicates, the current Supreme Court test adopts the broad view but, as the following decision from Michigan illustrates, cases challenging attempted takings as contrary to the public use requirement persist, particularly under state constitutional or statutory law.

■ **COUNTY OF WAYNE v. HATHCOCK**
Supreme Court of Michigan, 2004
684 N.W.2d 765

YOUNG, Justice. We are presented again with a clash of two bedrock principles of our legal tradition: the sacrosanct right of individuals to dominion over their private property, on the one hand and, on the other, the state's authority to condemn private property for the commonwealth. In this case, Wayne County would use the power of eminent domain to condemn defendants' real properties for the construction of a 1,300-acre business and technology park. This proposed commercial center is intended to reinvigorate the struggling economy of southeastern Michigan by attracting businesses, particularly those involved in developing new technologies, to the area.

Defendants argue that this exercise of the power of eminent domain is neither authorized by statute nor permitted under article 10 of the 1963 Michigan Constitution, which requires that any condemnation of private property advance a "public use." Both the Wayne Circuit Court and the Court of Appeals rejected these arguments — compelled, in no small measure, by this Court's opinion in Poletown Neighborhood Council v. Detroit, 304 N.W.2d 455 (Mich. 1981). . . .

This dispute has its roots in recent renovations of Metropolitan Airport. The county's $2 billion construction program produced a new terminal and jet runway and, consequently, raised concerns that noise from increased air traffic would plague neighboring landowners. In an effort to obviate such problems, the county, funded by a partial grant of $21 million from the Federal Aviation Administration, began a program of purchasing neighboring properties through voluntary sales. . . .

Wayne County's agreement with the FAA provided that any properties acquired through the noise abatement program were to be put to economically productive use. . . . Thus, the "Pinnacle Project" was born.

The Pinnacle Project calls for the construction of a state-of-the-art business and technology park in a 1,300-acre area adjacent to Metropolitan Airport. The county avers that the Pinnacle Project will create thousands of jobs, and tens of millions of dollars in tax revenue, while broadening the County's tax base from predominantly industrial to a mixture of industrial, service and technology. The Pinnacle Project will enhance the image of the County in the development community, aiding in its transformation from a high industrial area, to that of an arena ready to meet the needs of the 21st century. This cutting-edge development will attract national and international businesses, leading to accelerated economic growth and revenue enhancement. . . .

Having acquired over one thousand acres, the county determined that an additional forty-six parcels distributed in a checkerboard fashion throughout the project area were needed for the business and technology park. The county apparently determined that further efforts to negotiate additional voluntary sales would be futile and decided instead to invoke the power of eminent domain. Thus, on July 12, 2000, the Wayne County Commission adopted a Resolution of Necessity and Declaration of Taking (Resolution of Necessity) authorizing the acquisition of the remaining three hundred acres needed for the Pinnacle Project.

The remaining properties were appraised as required by the Uniform Condemnation Procedures Act and the county issued written offers based on these appraisals to the property owners. Twenty-seven more property owners accepted these offers and sold their parcels to the county. But according to the county's estimates, nineteen additional parcels were still needed for the Pinnacle Project. These properties, owned by [Edward Hathcock and the other] defendants, are the subject of the present condemnation actions. . . .

Art. 10, §2 of Michigan's 1963 Constitution provides that "[p]rivate property shall not be taken for public use without just compensation therefor being first made or secured in a manner prescribed by law." Defendants contend that the proposed condemnations are not "for public use," and therefore are not within constitutional bounds. Accordingly, our analysis must now focus on the "public use" requirement of art. 10, §2. . . .

When our Constitution was ratified in 1963, it was well-established in this Court's eminent domain jurisprudence that the constitutional "public use" requirement was not an absolute bar against the transfer of condemned property to private entities. It was equally clear, however, that the constitutional "public use" requirement worked to prohibit the state from transferring condemned property to private entities for a private use. Thus, this Court's eminent domain jurisprudence — at least that portion concerning the reasons for which the state may condemn private property — has focused largely on the area between these poles.

Justice Ryan's *Poletown* dissent accurately describes the factors that distinguish takings in the former category from those in the latter according to our pre-1963 eminent domain jurisprudence. Accordingly, we conclude that the transfer of condemned property is a "public use" when it possesses one of the three characteristics in our pre-1963 case law identified by Justice Ryan.

First, condemnations in which private land was constitutionally transferred by the condemning authority to a private entity involved "public necessity of the extreme sort otherwise impracticable." *Poletown*, 304 N.W.2d at 478 (Ryan J., dissenting). The "necessity" that Justice Ryan identified in our pre-1963 case law is a specific kind of need: "[T]he exercise of eminent domain for private corporations has been limited to those enterprises generating public benefits whose very *existence* depends on the use of land that can be assembled only by the coordination central government alone is capable of achieving." *Id.* (emphasis in original). Justice Ryan listed "highways, railroads, canals, and other instrumentalities of commerce" as examples of this brand of necessity. *Id.* A corporation constructing a railroad, for example, must lay track so that it forms a more or less straight path from point *A* to point *B*. If a property owner between points *A* and *B* holds out — say, for example, by refusing to sell his land for any amount less than fifty times its appraised value — the construction of the railroad is halted unless and until the railroad accedes to the property owner's demands. And if owners of adjoining properties receive word of the original property owner's windfall, they too will refuse to sell. . . .

Second, this Court has found that the transfer of condemned property to a private entity is consistent with the constitution's "public use" requirement when the private entity remains accountable to the public in its use of that property. . . . As Justice Ryan observed:

> [T]his Court disapproved condemnation that would have facilitated the generation of water power by a private corporation because the power company "will own, lease, use, and control" the water power. In addition, [we] warned, "Land cannot be taken, under the exercise of the power of eminent domain, unless, after it is taken, it will be devoted to the use of the public, *independent of the will of the corporation taking it.*"

Id. at 479 (emphasis in original), *quoting* Berrien Springs Water Power Co. v. Berrien Circuit Judge, 94 N.W. 379, 380-81 (Mich. 1903).

In contrast, we concluded in Lakehead Pipe Line Co. v. Dehn, 64 N.W.2d 903 (Mich. 1954), that the state retained sufficient control of a petroleum pipeline constructed by the plaintiff on condemned property. We noted specifically that the plaintiff had "pledged itself to transport in intrastate commerce," that plaintiff's pipeline was used pursuant to directions from the Michigan Public Service Commission, and that the state would be able to enforce those obligations, should the need arise. *Id.* at 912. Thus, in the common understanding of those sophisticated in the law at the time of ratification, the "public use" requirement would have allowed for the transfer of condemned property to a private entity when the public retained a measure of control over the property.

Finally, condemned land may be transferred to a private entity when the selection of the land to be condemned is itself based on public concern. In Justice Ryan's words, the property must be selected on the basis of "facts of independent public significance," meaning that the underlying purposes for resorting to condemnation, rather than the subsequent use of condemned land, must satisfy the Constitution's public use requirement. *Poletown*, 304 N.W.2d at 480 (Ryan, J., dissenting).

The primary example of a condemnation in this vein is found in In re Slum Clearance, 50 N.W.2d 340 (Mich. 1951), a 1951 decision from this Court. In that case, we considered the constitutionality of Detroit's condemnation of blighted housing and its subsequent resale of those properties to private persons. The city's controlling purpose in condemning the properties was to remove unfit housing and thereby advance public health and safety; subsequent resale of the land cleared of blight was "incidental" to this goal. We concluded, therefore, that the condemnation was indeed a "public use," despite the fact that the condemned properties would inevitably be put to private use. *Slum Clearance* turned on the fact that the act of condemnation itself, rather than the use to which the condemned land eventually would be put, was a public use. *Id.* at 343. Thus, as Justice Ryan observed, the condemnation was a "public use" because the land was selected on the basis of "facts of independent public significance" — namely, the need to remedy urban blight for the sake of public health and safety. *Poletown*, 304 N.W.2d at 480 (Ryan, J., dissenting). . . .

The exercise of eminent domain at issue here — the condemnation of defendants' properties for the Pinnacle Project and the subsequent transfer of those properties to private entities — implicates none of the saving elements noted by our pre-1963 eminent domain jurisprudence.

The Pinnacle Project's business and technology park is certainly not an enterprise "whose very *existence* depends on the use of land that can be assembled only by the coordination central government alone is capable of achieving." *Id.* at 478 (Ryan, J., dissenting). To the contrary, the landscape of our country is flecked with shopping centers, office parks, clusters of hotels, and centers of entertainment and commerce. We do not believe, and plaintiff does not contend, that these constellations required the exercise of eminent domain or any other form of collective public action for their formation.

Second, the Pinnacle Project is not subject to public oversight to ensure that the property continues to be used for the commonwealth after being sold to private entities. Rather, plaintiff intends for the private entities purchasing defendants' properties to pursue their own financial welfare with the single-mindedness expected of any profit-making enterprise. The public benefit arising from the Pinnacle Project is an epiphenomenon of the eventual property owners' collective attempts at profit maximization. No formal mechanisms exist to ensure that the businesses that would occupy what are now defendants' properties will continue to contribute to the health of the local economy.

Finally, there is nothing about the act of condemning defendants' properties that serves the public good in this case. The only public benefits cited by plaintiff arise after the lands are acquired by the government and put to private use. Thus, the present case is quite unlike *Slum Clearance* because there are no facts of independent public significance (such as the need to promote health and safety) that might justify the condemnation of defendants' lands.

We can only conclude, therefore, that no one sophisticated in the law at the 1963 Constitution's ratification would have understood "public use" to permit the condemnation of defendants' properties for the construction of a business and technology park owned by private entities. Therefore, the condemnations proposed in this case are unconstitutional under art. 10, §2.

Indeed, the only support for plaintiff's position in our eminent domain jurisprudence is the majority opinion in *Poletown*. In that opinion per curiam, a majority of this Court concluded that our Constitution permitted the Detroit Economic Development Corporation to condemn private residential properties in order to convey those properties to a private corporation for the construction of an assembly plant. . . .

Because *Poletown*'s conception of a public use — that of "alleviating unemployment and revitalizing the economic base of the community" — has no support in the Court's eminent domain jurisprudence before the Constitution's ratification, its interpretation of "public use" in art. 10, §2 cannot reflect the common understanding of that phrase among those sophisticated in the law at ratification. Consequently, the *Poletown* analysis provides no legitimate support for the condemnations proposed in this case and, for the reasons stated above, is overruled.

We conclude that the condemnations proposed in this case do not pass constitutional muster because they do not advance a public use as required by Const. 1963, art. 10, §2. Accordingly, this case is remanded to the Wayne Circuit Court for entry of summary disposition in defendants' favor. . . .

Notes and Questions

1. Why does the use of land by private enterprises for economic redevelopment under a plan instigated and approved by the government constitute a "public use" in Connecticut but not in Michigan?

2. In *County of Wayne*, the Michigan Supreme Court overruled *Poletown*, one of the most famous (or infamous) state takings decisions. *Poletown* approved the condemnation of a working-class residential neighborhood for the purpose of clearing the land and conveying it to General Motors as a site for constructing an automobile assembly plant. In its decision, the court stated (304 N.W.2d at 457, 458, 459):

> This case raises a question of paramount importance to the future welfare of this state and its residents: Can a municipality use the power of eminent domain granted to it by the Economic Development Corporations Act to condemn property for transfer to a private corporation to build a plant to promote industry and commerce, thereby adding jobs and taxes to the economic base of the municipality and state? . . .
>
> There is no dispute about the law. All agree that condemnation for a public use or purpose is permitted. All agree that condemnation for a private use or purpose is forbidden. Similarly, condemnation for a private use cannot be authorized whatever its incidental public benefit and condemnation for a public purpose cannot be forbidden whatever the incidental private gain. The heart of this dispute is whether the proposed condemnation is for the primary benefit of the public or the private user. . . .
>
> In the court below, the plaintiffs-appellants challenged the necessity for the taking of the land for the proposed project. In this regard the city presented substantial evidence of the severe economic conditions facing the residents of the city and state, the need for new industrial development to revitalize local industries, the economic boost the proposed project would provide, and the lack of other adequate available sites to implement the project. . . .
>
> The power of eminent domain is to be used in this instance primarily to accomplish the essential public purposes of alleviating unemployment and revitalizing the economic base of the community. The benefit to a private interest is merely incidental.
>
> Our determination that this project falls within the public purpose, as stated by the Legislature, does not mean that every condemnation proposed by an economic

development corporation will meet with similar acceptance simply because it may provide some jobs or add to the industrial or commercial base. If the public benefit was not so clear and significant, we would hesitate to sanction approval of such a project.

Why didn't General Motors buy the land itself? Why was the city of Detroit willing to use its powers of eminent domain to acquire the land for GM? Why might local residents displaced by the new GM plant be suspicious of the city's motives? Why might the Michigan Supreme Court view this development as critical for the region's economic future at the time?

3. Either through state supreme court interpretations of state constitutional provisions, as in *County of Wayne,* or state statutes directly addressing the issue, most states enforce a narrow interpretation of public use. For example, Texas Gov't Code §2206.001 (enacted 2005) states in part:

A government or private entity may not take private property through the use of eminent domain if the taking:

(1) confers a private benefit on a particular private party through the use of the property;
(2) is for a public use that is merely a pretext to confer a private benefit on a particular private party; or
(3) is for economic development purposes, unless the economic development is a secondary purpose resulting from municipal community development or municipal urban renewal activities to eliminate an existing affirmative harm on society from slum or blighted areas under [certain statutes].

Why might the authors of this statute have singled out economic development projects for specific limitation? Why might they exempt projects in slum or blighted areas from this limitation? Should the determination of what constitutes a "blighted area" be made by the court, the municipality, or property owners in that area? Is there a risk of class or racial factors affecting such a decision?

■ UNITED STATES v. 564.54 ACRES OF LAND
Supreme Court of the United States, 1979
441 U.S. 506

MARSHALL, Justice. At issue in this case is the proper measure of compensation when the Government condemns property owned by a private nonprofit organization and operated for a public purpose. In particular, we must decide whether the Just Compensation Clause of the Fifth Amendment requires payment of replacement cost rather than fair market value of the property taken.

I.

Respondent, the Southeastern Pennsylvania Synod of the Lutheran Church in America, operates three nonprofit summer camps along the Delaware River. In June 1970, the United States initiated a condemnation proceeding to acquire respondent's land for a public recreational project. Before trial, the Government offered to pay respondent $485,400 as the fair market value of its property. Respondent rejected the offer and demanded approximately $5.8 million, the asserted cost of developing functionally equivalent substitute facilities at a new site. This substantial award was necessary, respondent contended, because the new facilities would be subject to financially burdensome regulations from which existing facilities were exempt under grandfather provisions.

[A jury determined that the respondent was not entitled to compensation for "substitute facilities," or replacement cost, and awarded $740,000 as the fair market value of the property. The Third Circuit reversed because it believed that the jury should have been instructed that compensation for substitute facilities would be appropriate if the facility provided "a benefit to the community" that would "not be as fully provided after the facility" was taken.]

II.

A.

In giving content to the just compensation requirement of the Fifth Amendment, this Court has sought to put the owner of condemned property "in as good a position pecuniarily as if his property had not been taken." Olson v. United States, 292 U.S. 246, 255 (1934). However, this principle of indemnity has not been given its full and literal force. Because of serious practical difficulties in assessing the worth an individual places on particular property at a given time, we have recognized the need for a relatively objective working rule. The Court therefore has employed the concept of fair market value to determine the condemnee's loss. Under this standard, the owner is entitled to receive "what a willing buyer would pay in cash to a willing seller" at the time of the taking. United States v. Miller, 317 U.S. 369, 374 (1943).

Although the market-value standard is a useful and generally sufficient tool for ascertaining the compensation required to make the owner whole, the Court has acknowledged that such an award does not necessarily compensate for all values an owner may derive from his property. Thus, we have held that fair market value does not include the special value of property to the owner arising from its adaptability to his particular use. As Mr. Justice Frankfurter wrote for the Court in Kimball Laundry Co. v. United States, 338 U.S. 1, 5 (1949):

> The value of property springs from subjective needs and attitudes; its value to the owner may therefore differ widely from its value to the taker. Most things, however, have a general demand which gives them a value transferable from one owner to another. As opposed to such personal and variant standards as value to the particular owner whose property has been taken, this transferable value has an external validity which makes it a fair measure of public obligation to compensate the loss incurred by an owner as a result of the taking of his property for public use. In view, however, of the liability of all property to condemnation for the common good, loss to the owner of nontransferable values deriving from his unique need for property or idiosyncratic attachment to it, like loss due to an exercise of the police power, is properly treated as part of the burden of common citizenship.

In short, the concept of fair market value has been chosen to strike a fair "balance between the public's need and the claimant's loss" upon condemnation of property for a public purpose. United States v. Toronto, Hamilton & Buffalo Nav. Co., 338 U.S. 396, 402 (1949).

But while the indemnity principle must yield to some extent before the need for a practical general rule, this Court has refused to designate market value as the sole measure of just compensation. For there are situations where this standard is inappropriate. As we held in United States v. Commodities Trading Corp., 339 U.S. 121, 123 (1950):

> [When] market value has been too difficult to find, or when its application would result in manifest injustice to owner or public, courts have fashioned and applied other standards. . . . Whatever the circumstances under which such constitutional questions arise, the dominant consideration always remains the same: What compensation is "just" both to an owner whose property is taken and to the public that must pay the bill?

Hence, we must determine whether application of the fair-market-value standard here would be impracticable or whether an award of market value would diverge so substantially from the indemnity principle as to violate the Fifth Amendment.

B.

The instances in which market value is too difficult to ascertain generally involve property of a type so infrequently traded that we cannot predict whether the prices previously paid, assuming there have been prior sales, would be repeated in a sale of the condemned property. This might be the case, for example, with respect to public facilities such as roads or sewers. But respondent's property does not fall in this category. There was a market for camps, albeit not an extremely active one. The Government's expert witness presented evidence concerning 11 recent sales of comparable facilities in the vicinity, and estimated that respondent's camps could have been sold within six months to a year after they were offered for sale. Indeed, respondent's own expert testified that he had prepared an appraisal of the camps' fair market value as of the date of the taking. And the Court of Appeals implicitly acknowledged that the market value of nonprofit property is ordinarily ascertainable since application of the court's "ready market" criterion requires assessment of fair market value. Thus, it seems clear that respondent's property had a readily discernible market value. The only remaining inquiry is whether such an award would impermissibly deviate from the indemnity principle.

Emphasizing that the primary value of the condemned property lies in the use to which it is put, respondent argues that compensating only for market value would be unjust in the present context. Because new facilities would bear financial burdens imposed by regulations to which the existing camps were not subject, an award of market value would preclude continuation of respondent's use. Respondent therefore concludes that such a recovery would be insufficient to indemnify for its loss.

However, it is not at all unusual that property uniquely adapted to the owner's use has a market value on condemnation which falls far short of enabling the owner to preserve that use. Such a situation may often arise, for example, where a family home has been built to the owner's tastes, but is old and deteriorated, or where property, like respondent's camps, is exempt from regulations applicable to new facilities. Yet the Court has previously determined that nontransferable values arising from the owner's unique need for the property are not compensable, and has found that this divergence from full indemnification does not violate the Fifth Amendment.

We are unable to discern why a different result should obtain here. That respondent is a nonprofit organization may provide some basis for distinguishing it from business enterprises, since the uses to which commercial property is put can often be valued in terms of the capitalized earnings produced. But there is no reason to treat respondent differently from the many private homeowners and other non-commercial property owners who neither derive earnings from their property nor hold it for investment purposes. Unless the Just Compensation Clause mandates a Government subsidy for nonprofit organizations, a proposition we find patently implausible, respondent's nonprofit status does not require us to reject application of the fair-market-value standard.

Nor is it relevant in this case whether respondent's camps were reasonably necessary to the public welfare. In condemnations of property owned by public entities, lower courts have applied the reasonable-necessity standard to determine if the entity has an obligation to continue providing the facilities taken. United States v. Certain Property in Borough of Manhattan, 403 F.2d 800 (CA2 1968). This duty may be legally compelled or arise from necessity; "the distinction has little practical significance in public condemnation." *Id.* at 803. If the condemnee has such a duty to replace the property, these courts have reasoned that only an award of the costs of developing requisite substitute facilities will compensate for the loss.

Whatever the merits of this reasoning with respect to public entities, it does not advance analysis here. For respondent is under no legal or factual obligation to replace the camps, regardless of their social worth. As a private entity, respondent is free to allocate its resources to serve its own institutional objectives, which may or may not correspond with community needs. Awarding replacement cost on the theory that respondent would continue to operate the camps for a public purpose would thus provide a windfall if substitute facilities were never acquired, or if acquired, were later sold or converted to another use.

Finally, that the camps may have benefited the community does not warrant compensating respondent differently from other private owners. The community benefit which the camps conferred might provide an indication of the public's loss upon condemnation of the property. But we cannot accept the Court of Appeals' conclusion that this loss is relevant to assessing the compensation due a private entity. . . . Respondent did not hold its property as the public's trustee and thus is not entitled to be indemnified for the public's loss. Moreover, many condemnees use their property in a manner that confers a benefit on the community, and there is no sound basis for considering this factor only in condemnations of property owned by nonprofit organizations. And to make the measure of compensation depend on a jury's subjective estimation of whether a particular use "benefits" the community would conflict with this Court's efforts to develop relatively objective valuation standards.

In sum, we find no circumstances here that require suspension of the normal rules for determining just compensation. Respondent, like other private owners, is not entitled to recover for nontransferable values arising from its unique need for the property. To the extent denial of such an award departs from the indemnity principle, it is justified by the necessity for a workable measure of valuation. Allowing respondent the fair market value of its property is thus consistent with the "basic equitable principles of fairness," United States v. Fuller, 409 U.S. 488, 490 (1973), underlying the Just Compensation Clause.

The judgment of the Court of Appeals is reversed.

Notes and Questions

1. Why should the government have to pay for property that it needs? A variety of policy arguments have been advanced for the compensation requirement,

including a distrust of the legislature and concern for individual rights, preventing the government from overusing the power to take property, protecting against the exploitation of relatively powerless groups and individuals, ensuring that everyone shares equally in the cost of government, and an unadorned moral imperative. Which of those arguments is most persuasive? What would happen if none of those arguments succeeded and the government could acquire property without compensating the owner? These questions are purely academic, of course, because the Fifth Amendment establishes a constitutional duty to pay "just compensation," and similar provisions exist in the constitutions of every state except North Carolina.

2. *564.54 Acres of Land* demonstrates that "just compensation" will not always make a property owner whole. As Judge Posner explained, many property owners "value their property at more than its market value (*i.e.*, it is not for sale)" due to "relocation costs, sentimental attachments, or the special suitability of the property for their particular (perhaps idiosyncratic) needs." Coniston Corp. v. Village of Hoffman Estates, 844 F.2d 461, 464 (7th Cir. 1988). Nor does a compensation award account for the costs of the transaction itself, such as attorney's fees. *See, e.g.*, State v. Armstrong, 779 So. 2d 1211 (Ala. 2000) (reversing a jury's award of attorney's fees in an eminent domain case). Remember the *Preseault* case in Chapter 11: It took the Preseaults over 20 years to obtain any compensation for the government's taking of an easement over their property, and even then they did not recover their attorney's fees or receive anything for the invasion of their privacy. Is Justice Frankfurter convincing in the portion of *Kimball Laundry* quoted in *564.54 Acres of Land* in which he defends the failure to pay such compensation?

3. *564.54 Acres of Land* also shows that the government and a private owner often disagree about the appropriate amount of compensation for property even when both sides acknowledge that compensation is determined by fair market value. Traditional real estate appraisal techniques, including the sale price of similar properties and actual rental values, are employed in an effort to identify the fair market value. Frequently, each side will retain realtors or appraisers who serve as dueling experts, with the court forced to decide the matter based on wildly conflicting opinions.

4. In United States v. 50 Acres of Land, 469 U.S. 24 (1984), the Supreme Court closed a question left open in *564.54 Acres of Land* by holding that, like a private or non-profit entity, a public entity is only entitled to compensation based on ascertainable market value, and not the replacement cost of a substitute facility, even if the replacement of the condemned facility was necessary.

B. WHAT CONSTITUTES A "TAKING"?

Most eminent domain disputes skip the threshold question of whether the government has taken private property in the first place. Instead, they usually involve the public use of the property or the appropriate amount of just compensation. That is understandable in the paradigmatic case where the government seeks to obtain a fee simple interest in land so that it can build a highway or facilitate urban redevelopment. In many other instances, the dispute concerns whether the government has acted in a way that triggers a compensation requirement at all, given that the private owner retains title to the property. That is the problem of *regulatory takings*: When does government regulation or similar action constitute a taking of property?

A takings quiz. Which of the following 10 property owners are deserving of compensation by the government?

1. In 1972, Donna Developer bought 50 acres of beachfront property in the Florida Keys. The contract according to which she purchased the land stated that "development of the property is subject to environmental regulations." In 1973, Congress enacted the Endangered Species Act, which restricts the development of land that serves as habitat for species that are listed as endangered or threatened. In 1990, Developer submitted plans to develop a marina and 100 beachfront condominiums on her property. Just before she received all of the necessary government approvals for the development, two animals that live on her property—the Keys marsh rabbit and the silver rice rat—were listed as endangered species by the federal government. As a result, federal regulators will only allow Developer to build 25 condominiums on her property, and no marina.

2. In 1899, the Jones Brewery opened a $2 million factory on the outskirts of South Bend. The factory steadily expanded over the next 20 years as beer sales increased. Then Congress enacted the Volstead Act, which implemented the Eighteenth Amendment and prohibited the manufacture of alcoholic beverages. The Jones Brewery had to close its factory.

3. The Washington Metro is expanding its existing subway line out of Washington into Silver Spring, Maryland. The construction project is expected to take 10 months. During the project, Georgia Avenue—a major commercial strip on the border of Washington and Silver Spring—will be closed to all vehicle traffic. Thai Gourmet, a restaurant that perennially ranks among the most popular eateries in the region, estimates that it will lose 80 percent of its business. As a result, the restaurant will have to close for the duration of the construction project.

4. With much fanfare, the Pharmaceutical Company of New Jersey (PCNJ) announces that it has developed a drug that can cure AIDS. With less fanfare, PCNJ obtains a patent on the drug. Doctors, hospitals, and other medical providers are excited about the new drug until they learn that PCNJ plans to sell it for $5,000 per month per patient. PCNJ refuses to bow to the public pressure to charge less for the drug, so the state health department begins to produce the drug itself in violation of PCNJ's patent.

5. During the American military action against Iraq in 2003, an errant cruise missile fired from the U.S.S. *Tennessee* destroyed a water bottling plant outside of Baghdad. The owner of the plant has a friend who works for a law firm in Washington. With that friend's legal assistance, the owner sues the U.S. government to obtain compensation for the plant.

6. Don Developer bought 250 acres of southern New Jersey swampland in 1958. Within 10 years, he had subdivided 200 acres of the property and built a variety of residential homes and retail stores. In 1993, Developer submitted plans to construct additional residential and commercial buildings on the remaining 50 acres. The state Department of Environmental Protection (DEP) viewed the land as protected wetlands, so it agreed to permit development on 12.5 acres only if Developer agreed to preserve the other 37.5 acres as wetlands. Then when Developer applied for a permit from the *federal* government, DEP exercised its veto power to block the project.

7. In June 1986, Roy Rancher bought 100 acres of Montana rangeland and 250 sheep to graze on that land. Soon thereafter, six of his sheep were killed by grizzly

bears that the federal government had reintroduced to the area in an effort to preserve the grizzly from extinction. Rancher wanted to shoot the grizzlies when they attacked his sheep, but he was advised by federal officials that he would be subject to criminal fines if he did so.

8. Gladys Gardener owns a small commercial nursery that supplies plants to homeowners in her neighborhood. The city of Campbell wants to encourage the development of businesses that generate additional property taxes to pay for the increased demand for municipal services. So the city purchased the land next to Gardener's property and gave it free of charge to Olivia Office, who built a 30-story commercial tower that houses several health care providers, technology companies, and law firms that have just moved to the city. Meanwhile, plants can no longer grow in Gardener's nursery because the new building blocks the sun during much of the day.

9. Larry Landlord owns an apartment building in Chicago. In 1988, in an effort to aid the new cable television industry, the Chicago City Council authorized cable operators to install their equipment on the outside of any building within the city. The local cable operator attached a small box containing cable wiring to the outside of Landlord's building. Landlord objected, but he was unable to have the box removed because of the authority that had been enacted into law by the city council.

10. Becky Biker owns a small bicycle shop in Daytona Beach, Florida. Sales have increased in recent years, so she wants to expand her shop. She needs the approval of the Daytona Beach city zoning board because the shop is in a floodplain. The zoning board is willing to approve her expansion plans, but only if she gives the city a 15-foot-wide strip of land behind her shop so that the town can build a hiking and biking trail.

1. The Bright Line of Physical Takings

■ LORETTO v. TELEPROMPTER MANHATTAN CATV CORP.
Supreme Court of the United States, 1982
458 U.S. 419

MARSHALL, Justice. This case presents the question whether a minor but permanent physical occupation of an owner's property authorized by government constitutes a "taking" of property for which just compensation is due under the Fifth and Fourteenth Amendments of the Constitution. New York law provides that a landlord must permit a cable television company to install its cable facilities upon his property. N.Y. Exec. Law §828(1) (McKinney Supp. 1981-1982). In this case, the cable installation occupied portions of appellant's roof and the side of her building. The New York Court of Appeals ruled that this appropriation does not amount to a taking. 423 N.E.2d 320 (1981). Because we conclude that such a physical occupation of property is a taking, we reverse.

I.

Appellant Jean Loretto purchased a five-story apartment building located at 303 West 105th Street, New York City, in 1971. The previous owner had granted appellees Teleprompter Corp. and Teleprompter Manhattan CATV (collectively Teleprompter) permission to install a cable on the building and the exclusive privilege of furnishing cable television (CATV) services to the tenants. . . .

Prior to 1973, Teleprompter routinely obtained authorization for its installations from property owners along the cable's route, compensating the owners at the standard rate of 5% of the gross revenues that Teleprompter realized from the particular property. To facilitate tenant access to CATV, the State of New York enacted §828 of the Executive Law, effective January 1, 1973. Section 828 provides that a landlord may not "interfere with the installation of cable television facilities upon his property or premises," and may not demand payment from any tenant for permitting CATV, or demand payment from any CATV company "in excess of any amount which the [State Commission on Cable Television] shall, by regulation, determine to be reasonable." The landlord may, however, require the CATV company or the tenant to bear the cost of installation and to indemnify for any damage caused by the installation. Pursuant to §828(1)(b), the State Commission has ruled that a one-time $1 payment is the normal fee to which a landlord is entitled. . . .

Appellant did not discover the existence of the cable until after she had purchased the building. She brought a class action against Teleprompter in 1976 on behalf of all owners of real property in the State on which Teleprompter has placed CATV components, alleging that Teleprompter's installation was a trespass and, insofar as it relied on §828, a taking without just compensation. She requested damages and injunctive relief. . . .

II.

The Court of Appeals determined that §828 serves the legitimate public purpose of "rapid development of and maximum penetration by a means of communication which has important educational and community aspects," 423 N.E.2d at 329, and thus is within the State's police power. We have no reason to question that determination. It is a separate question, however, whether an otherwise valid regulation so frustrates property rights that compensation must be paid. We conclude that a permanent physical occupation authorized by government is a taking without regard to the public interests that it may serve. Our constitutional history confirms the rule, recent cases do not question it, and the purposes of the Takings Clause compel its retention. . . .

As Penn Central Transportation Co. v. New York City, 438 U.S. 104 (1978), affirms, the Court has often upheld substantial regulation of an owner's use of his own property where deemed necessary to promote the public interest. At the same time, we have long considered a physical intrusion by government to be a property restriction of an unusually serious character for purposes of the Takings Clause. Our cases further establish that when the physical intrusion reaches the extreme form of a permanent physical occupation, a taking has occurred. In such a case, "the character of the government action," *id.* at 124, not only is an important factor in resolving whether the action works a taking but also is determinative.

When faced with a constitutional challenge to a permanent physical occupation of real property, this Court has invariably found a taking. As early as 1872, in Pumpelly v. Green Bay Co., 13 Wall. (80 U.S.) 166 (1872), this Court held that the defendant's construction, pursuant to state authority, of a dam which permanently flooded plaintiff's property constituted a taking. A unanimous Court stated, without qualification, that "where real estate is actually invaded by superinduced additions of water, earth, sand, or other material, or by having any artificial structure placed on it, so as to effectually destroy or impair its usefulness, it is a taking, within the meaning of the Constitution." *Id.* at 181. . . .

The historical rule that a permanent physical occupation of another's property is a taking has more than tradition to commend it. Such an appropriation is perhaps the most serious form of invasion of an owner's property interests. To borrow a metaphor, the government does not simply take a single "strand" from the "bundle" of property rights: it chops through the bundle, taking a slice of every strand.

Property rights in a physical thing have been described as the rights "to possess, use and dispose of it." United States v. General Motors Corp., 323 U.S. 373, 378 (1945). To the extent that the government permanently occupies physical property, it effectively destroys *each* of these rights. First, the owner has no right to possess the occupied space himself, and also has no power to exclude the occupier from possession and use of the space. The power to exclude has traditionally been considered one of the most treasured strands in an owner's bundle of property rights. Second, the permanent physical occupation of property forever denies the owner any power to control the use of the property; he not only cannot exclude others, but can make no nonpossessory use of the property. Although deprivation of the right to use and obtain a profit from property is not, in every case, independently sufficient to establish a taking, it is clearly relevant. Finally, even though the owner may retain the bare legal right to dispose of the occupied space by transfer or sale, the permanent occupation of that space by a stranger will ordinarily empty the right of any value, since the purchaser will also be unable to make any use of the property. . . .

The traditional rule also avoids otherwise difficult line-drawing problems. Few would disagree that if the State required landlords to permit third parties to install swimming pools on the landlords' rooftops for the convenience of the tenants, the requirement would be a taking. If the cable installation here occupied as much space, again, few would disagree that the occupation would be a taking. But constitutional protection for the rights of private property cannot be made to depend on the size of the area permanently occupied.[13] Indeed, it is possible that in the future, additional cable installations that more significantly restrict a landlord's use of the roof of his building will be made. Section 828 requires a landlord to permit such multiple installations.

Finally, whether a permanent physical occupation has occurred presents relatively few problems of proof. The placement of a fixed structure on land or real property is an obvious fact that will rarely be subject to dispute. Once the fact of occupation is shown, of course, a court should consider the *extent* of the occupation as one relevant factor in determining the compensation due. For that reason, moreover, there is less need to consider the extent of the occupation in determining whether there is a taking in the first instance. . . .

---

13. In United States v. Causby, 328 U.S. 256 (1946), the Court approvingly cited Butler v. Frontier Telephone Co., 79 N.E. 716 (N.Y. 1906), holding that ejectment would lie where a telephone wire was strung across the plaintiff's property without touching the soil. The Court quoted the following language:

[A]n owner is entitled to the absolute and undisturbed possession of every part of his premises, including the space above, as much as a mine beneath. If the wire had been a huge cable, several inches thick and but a foot above the ground, there would have been a difference in degree, but not in principle. Expand the wire into a beam supported by posts standing upon abutting lots without touching the surface of plaintiff's land, and the difference would still be one of degree only. Enlarge the beam into a bridge, and yet space only would be occupied. Erect a house upon the bridge, and the air above the surface of the land would alone be disturbed.

328 U.S. at 265 n.10, *quoting* Butler v. Frontier Telephone Co., 79 N.E. at 718.

III.

. . . .

. . . [O]ur conclusion that §828 works a taking of a portion of appellant's property does not presuppose that the fee which many landlords had obtained from Teleprompter prior to the law's enactment is a proper measure of the value of the property taken. The issue of the amount of compensation that is due, on which we express no opinion, is a matter for the state courts to consider on remand.

The judgment of the New York Court of Appeals is reversed, and the case is remanded for further proceedings not inconsistent with this opinion.

Justice BLACKMUN, with whom Justice BRENNAN and Justice WHITE join, dissenting. . . .

In a curiously anachronistic decision, the Court today acknowledges its historical disavowal of set formulae in almost the same breath as it constructs a rigid *per se* takings rule: "a permanent physical occupation authorized by government is a taking without regard to the public interests that it may serve." . . .

In the end, what troubles me most about today's decision is that it represents an archaic judicial response to a modern social problem. Cable television is a new and growing, but somewhat controversial, communications medium. *See* Brief for New York State Cable Television Association as Amicus Curiae 6-7 (about 25% of American homes with televisions — approximately 20 million families — currently subscribe to cable television, with the penetration rate expected to double by 1990). The New York Legislature not only recognized, but also responded to, this technological advance by enacting a statute that sought carefully to balance the interests of all private parties. . . .

Notes and Questions

1. On remand, how should the state courts compute the amount of compensation due for the physical takings involved in dropping a television cable less than one-half inch in diameter down the front of Jean Loretto's five-story apartment building? Should it matter that the cable provides television reception for Loretto's tenants and thus may enhance the value of the apartment building? Should the fee that Teleprompter actually paid to many landlords prior to the law's enactment serve as evidence of the proper measure of the value of the property taken? Is there any reasonable way to determine market value in this case; and, if not, would that effectively render meaningless a judicial finding of a taking?

2. For purposes of federal constitutional law, how should courts define when private property is "taken" for public use? Should the term simply mean what it meant in 1791, when the states ratified the Fifth Amendment? Should it mean what the Supreme Court has said it means in the Court's past decisions? Should "taken" mean what people (or lawyers) currently understand the term to mean? Should all of these and perhaps other definitions be considered by the courts? Although these definitions tend to converge in many specific instances of physical takings, *Loretto* suggests that this does not necessarily happen in every case. In the era when the Bill of Rights was written and ratified, for example, courts simply did not face the issue of takings in the context of the installation on private property of television, telephone, Ethernet, or electrical wires. These definitions for "taken" can diverge sharply in

cases of regulatory takings, however, and fuel bitter legal disputes. The following subsection samples the mix of leading decisions in this controversial area of constitutional law.

2. The Gray Area of Regulatory Takings

■ HADACHECK v. SEBASTIAN
Supreme Court of the United States, 1915
239 U.S. 394

McKENNA, Justice. *Habeas corpus* prosecuted in the Supreme Court of the State of California for the discharge of plaintiff in error from the custody of defendant in error, Chief of Police of the City of Los Angeles.

Plaintiff in error, to whom we shall refer as petitioner, was convicted of a misdemeanor for the violation of an ordinance of the City of Los Angeles which makes it unlawful for any person to establish or operate a brick yard or brick kiln, or any establishment, factory or place for the manufacture or burning of brick within described limits in the city. Sentence was pronounced against him and he was committed to the custody of defendant in error as Chief of Police of the City of Los Angeles.

Being so in custody he filed a petition in the Supreme Court of the State for a writ of *habeas corpus*. The writ was issued. Subsequently defendant in error made a return thereto supported by affidavits, to which petitioner made sworn reply. The court rendered judgment discharging the writ and remanding petitioner to custody. The Chief Justice of the court then granted this writ of error.

The petition sets forth the reason for resorting to *habeas corpus* and that petitioner is the owner of a tract of land within the limits described in the ordinance upon which tract of land there is a very valuable bed of clay, of great value for the manufacture of brick of a fine quality, worth to him not less than $100,000 per acre or about $800,000 for the entire tract for brick-making purposes, and not exceeding $60,000 for residential purposes or for any purpose other than the manufacture of brick. That he has made excavations of considerable depth and covering a very large area of the property and that on account thereof the land cannot be utilized for residential purposes or any purpose other than that for which it is now used. That he purchased the land because of such bed of clay and for the purpose of manufacturing brick; that it was at the time of purchase outside of the limits of the city and distant from dwellings and other habitations and that he did not expect or believe, nor did other owners of property in the vicinity expect or believe, that the territory would be annexed to the city. That he has erected expensive machinery for the manufacture of bricks of fine quality which have been and are being used for building purposes in and about the city.

That if the ordinance be declared valid he will be compelled to entirely abandon his business and will be deprived of the use of his property.

That the manufacture of brick must necessarily be carried on where suitable clay is found and the clay cannot be transported to some other location, and, besides, the clay upon his property is particularly fine and clay of as good quality cannot be found in any other place within the city where the same can be utilized for the manufacture of brick. That within the prohibited district there is one other brick yard besides that of plaintiff in error.

That there is no reason for the prohibition of the business; that its maintenance cannot be and is not in the nature of a nuisance as defined in §3479 of the Civil Code of the State, and cannot be dangerous or detrimental to health or the morals or safety or peace or welfare or convenience of the people of the district or city.

That the business is so conducted as not to be in any way or degree a nuisance; no noises arise therefrom, and no noxious odors, and that by the use of certain means (which are described) provided and the situation of the brick yard an extremely small amount of smoke is emitted from any kiln and what is emitted is so dissipated that it is not a nuisance nor in any manner detrimental to health or comfort. That during the seven years which the brick yard has been conducted no complaint has been made of it, and no attempt has ever been made to regulate it.

That the city embraces 107.62 square miles in area and 75% of it is devoted to residential purposes; that the district described in the ordinance includes only about three square miles, is sparsely settled and contains large tracts of unsubdivided and unoccupied land; and that the boundaries of the district were determined for the sole and specific purpose of prohibiting and suppressing the business of petitioner and that of the other brick yard.

That there are and were at the time of the adoption of the ordinance in other districts of the city thickly built up with residences brick yards maintained more detrimental to the inhabitants of the city. That a petition was filed, signed by several hundred persons, representing such brick yards to be a nuisance and no ordinance or regulation was passed in regard to such petition and the brick yards are operated without hindrance or molestation. That other brick yards are permitted to be maintained without prohibition or regulation.

That no ordinance or regulation of any kind has been passed at any time regulating or attempting to regulate brick yards or inquiry made whether they could be maintained without being a nuisance or detrimental to health.

That the ordinance does not state a public offense and is in violation of the constitution of the State and the Fourteenth Amendment to the Constitution of the United States.

That the business of petitioner is a lawful one, none of the materials used in it are combustible, the machinery is of the most approved pattern and its conduct will not create a nuisance.

There is an allegation that the ordinance if enforced fosters and will foster a monopoly and protects and will protect other persons engaged in the manufacture of brick in the city, and discriminates and will discriminate against petitioner in favor of such other persons who are his competitors, and will prevent him from entering into competition with them.

The petition, after almost every paragraph, charges a deprivation of property, the taking of property without compensation, and that the ordinance is in consequence invalid.

We have given this outline of the petition as it presents petitioner's contentions, with the circumstances (which we deem most material) that give color and emphasis to them.

But there are substantial traverses made by the return to the writ, among others, a denial of the charge that the ordinance was arbitrarily directed against the business of petitioner, and it is alleged that there is another district in which brick yards are prohibited.

There was a denial of the allegations that the brick yard was conducted or could be conducted sanitarily or was not offensive to health. And there were affidavits supporting the denials. In these it was alleged that the fumes, gases, smoke, soot, steam and dust arising from petitioner's brick-making plant have from time to time caused sickness and serious discomfort to those living in the vicinity.

There was no specific denial of the value of the property or that it contained deposits of clay or that the latter could not be removed and manufactured into brick elsewhere. There was, however, a general denial that the enforcement of the ordinance would "entirely deprive petitioner of his property and the use thereof." . . .

The [state supreme] court, on the evidence, rejected the contention that the ordinance was not in good faith enacted as a police measure and that it was intended to discriminate against petitioner or that it was actuated by any motive of injuring him as an individual. . . .

We think the conclusion of the court is justified by the evidence and makes it unnecessary to review the many cases cited by petitioner in which it is decided that the police power of a state cannot be arbitrarily exercised. The principle is familiar, but in any given case it must plainly appear to apply. It is to be remembered that we are dealing with one of the most essential powers of government, one that is the least limitable. It may, indeed, seem harsh in its exercise, usually is on some individual, but the imperative necessity for its existence precludes any limitation upon it when not exerted arbitrarily. A vested interest cannot be asserted against it because of conditions once obtaining. Chicago & Alton R.R. v. Tranbarger, 238 U.S. 67, 78 (1915). To so hold would preclude development and fix a city forever in its primitive conditions. There must be progress, and if in its march private interests are in the way they must yield to the good of the community. The logical result of petitioner's contention would seem to be that a city could not be formed or enlarged against the resistance of an occupant of the ground and that if it grows at all it can only grow as the environment of the occupations that are usually banished to the purlieus.

The police power and to what extent it may be exerted we have recently illustrated in Reinman v. Little Rock, 237 U.S. 171 (1915). The circumstances of the case were very much like those of the case at bar and give reply to the contentions of petitioner, especially that which asserts that a necessary and lawful occupation that is not a nuisance *per se* cannot be made so by legislative declaration. There was a like investment in property, encouraged by the then conditions; a like reduction of value and deprivation of property was asserted against the validity of the ordinance there considered; a like assertion of an arbitrary exercise of the power of prohibition. Against all of these contentions, and causing the rejection of them all, was adduced the police power. There was a prohibition of a business, lawful in itself, there as here. It was a livery stable there; a brick yard here. They differ in particulars, but they are alike in that which cause and justify prohibition in defined localities — that is, the effect upon the health and comfort of the community.

The ordinance passed upon prohibited the conduct of the business within a certain defined area in Little Rock, Arkansas. This court said of it: granting that the business was not a nuisance *per se*, it was clearly within the police power of the State to regulate it, "and to that end to declare that in particular circumstances and in particular localities a livery stable shall be deemed a nuisance in fact and in law." And the only limitation upon the power was stated to be that the power could not be exerted arbitrarily or with unjust discrimination. There was a citation of cases. We think the present case is within the ruling thus declared.

There is a distinction between Reinman v. Little Rock and the case at bar. There a particular business was prohibited which was not affixed to or dependent upon its locality; it could be conducted elsewhere. Here, it is contended, the latter condition does not exist, and it is alleged that the manufacture of brick must necessarily be carried on where suitable clay is found and that the clay on petitioner's property cannot be transported to some other locality. This is not urged as a physical impossibility but only, counsel say, that such transportation and the transportation of the bricks to places where they could be used in construction work would be prohibitive "from a financial standpoint." But upon the evidence the Supreme Court considered the case, as we understand its opinion, from the standpoint of the offensive effects of the operation of a brick yard and not from the deprivation of the deposits of clay, and distinguished *Ex parte Kelso*, 82 P. 241 (Cal. 1905), wherein the court declared invalid an ordinance absolutely prohibiting the maintenance or operation of a rock or stone quarry within a certain portion of the city and county of San Francisco. The court there said that the effect of the ordinance was "to absolutely deprive the owners of real property within such limits of a valuable right incident to their ownership, viz., the right to extract therefrom such rock and stone as they might find it to their advantage to dispose of." The court expressed the view that the removal could be regulated but that "an absolute prohibition of such removal under the circumstances," could not be upheld.

In the present case there is no prohibition of the removal of the brick clay; only a prohibition within the designated locality of its manufacture into bricks. And to this feature of the ordinance our opinion is addressed. Whether other questions would arise if the ordinance were broader, and opinion on such questions, we reserve. . . .

Notes and Questions

1. What constitutional violation does Hadacheck allege? What remedy does he seek?

2. Justice McKenna cited Reinman v. Little Rock, 237 U.S. 171 (1915), as a precedent for the ability of Los Angeles to outlaw Hadacheck's business without violating the Takings Clause. Two earlier cases provide additional support for that holding. In Mugler v. Kansas, 123 U.S. 623 (1887), the Court held that a Kansas constitutional provision stating that "the manufacture and sale of intoxicating liquors shall be forever prohibited in this State, except for medical, scientific, and mechanical purposes," did not constitute a taking of Peter Mugler's beer brewery because the state could deem it a public nuisance. Then, in Powell v. Pennsylvania, 127 U.S. 678 (1888), Pennsylvania enacted "an act for the protection of dairymen, and to prevent deception in sales of butter and cheese" that prohibited the manufacture or use of "articles or substances in semblance or imitation of butter or cheese, not the legitimate product of the dairy, and not made exclusively of milk or cream, but into which oil, lard, or fat, not produced from milk or cream, entered as a component part, or into which melted butter or any oil thereof had been introduced to take the place of cream." In short, the state banned oleomargarine. The Court upheld the ban.

3. Recall that we have already encountered other claims that government restrictions on the use of property constitute a taking. In United States v. Causby (reprinted above in Chapter 3), the Supreme Court held that the federal government must pay for taking an easement across the airspace of a farm next to a military airbase. Likewise, City of Palm Springs v. Living Desert Reserve (reprinted in Chapter 6) held that the city had to compensate a landowner who held a future

interest in land taken by the city. Preseault v. United States (reprinted in Chapter 11) found a taking when the state re-created an easement that had already been abandoned. And in Village of Euclid v. Amber Realty Corp. (reprinted in Chapter 12) the Supreme Court held that a municipal zoning ordinance did not take the property of those landowners who could no longer use their property as they desired. How do those cases compare to Hadacheck's claims?

■ PENNSYLVANIA COAL COMPANY v. MAHON

Supreme Court of the United States, 1922
260 U.S. 393

HOLMES, Justice. This is a bill in equity brought by the defendants in error to prevent the Pennsylvania Coal Company from mining under their property in such way as to remove the supports and cause a subsidence of the surface and of their house. The bill sets out a deed executed by the Coal Company in 1878, under which the plaintiffs claim. The deed conveys the surface, but in express terms reserves the right to remove all the coal under the same, and the grantee takes the premises with the risk, and waives all claim for damages that may arise from mining out the coal. But the plaintiffs say that whatever may have been the Coal Company's rights, they were taken away by an Act of Pennsylvania, approved May 27, 1921, P.L. 1198, commonly known there as the Kohler Act. The Court of Common Pleas found that if not restrained the defendant would cause the damage to prevent which the bill was brought, but denied an injunction, holding that the statute if applied to this case would be unconstitutional. On appeal the Supreme Court of the State agreed that the defendant had contract and property rights protected by the Constitution of the United States, but held that the statute was a legitimate exercise of the police power and directed a decree for the plaintiffs. A writ of error was granted bringing the case to this Court.

The statute forbids the mining of anthracite coal in such way as to cause the subsidence of, among other things, any structure used as a human habitation, with certain exceptions, including among them land where the surface is owned by the owner of the underlying coal and is distant more than one hundred and fifty feet from any improved property belonging to any other person. As applied to this case the statute is admitted to destroy previously existing rights of property and contract. The question is whether the police power can be stretched so far.

Government hardly could go on if to some extent values incident to property could not be diminished without paying for every such change in the general law. As long recognized, some values are enjoyed under an implied limitation and must yield to the police power. But obviously the implied limitation must have its limits, or the contract and due process clauses are gone. One fact for consideration in determining such limits is the extent of the diminution. When it reaches a certain magnitude, in most if not in all cases there must be an exercise of eminent domain and compensation to sustain the act. So the question depends upon the particular facts. The greatest weight is given to the judgment of the legislature, but it always is open to interested parties to contend that the legislature has gone beyond its constitutional power.

This is the case of a single private house. No doubt there is a public interest even in this, as there is in every purchase and sale and in all that happens within the commonwealth. Some existing rights may be modified even in such a case. Rideout v. Knox, 19 N.E. 390 (Mass. 1889). But usually in ordinary private affairs the public interest does not warrant much of this kind of interference. A source of damage to such a house is not a public nuisance even if similar damage is inflicted on others in different places. The damage is not common or public. Wesson v. Washburn Iron Co., 13 Allen 95, 103 (Mass. 1866). The extent of the public interest is shown by the statute to be limited, since the statute ordinarily does not apply to land when the surface is owned by the owner of the coal. Furthermore, it is not justified as a protection of personal safety. That could be provided for by notice. Indeed the very foundation of this bill is that the defendant gave timely notice of its intent to mine under the house. On the other hand the extent of the taking is great. It purports to abolish what is recognized in Pennsylvania as an estate in land — a very valuable estate — and what is declared by the Court below to be a contract hitherto binding the plaintiffs. If we were called upon to deal with the plaintiffs' position alone, we should think it clear that the statute does not disclose a public interest sufficient to warrant so extensive a destruction of the defendant's constitutionally protected rights.

But the case has been treated as one in which the general validity of the act should be discussed. The Attorney General of the State, the City of Scranton, and the representatives of other extensive interests were allowed to take part in the argument below and have submitted their contentions here. It seems, therefore, to be our duty to go farther in the statement of our opinion, in order that it may be known at once, and that further suits should not be brought in vain.

It is our opinion that the act cannot be sustained as an exercise of the police power, so far as it affects the mining of coal under streets or cities in places where the right to mine such coal has been reserved. As said in a Pennsylvania case, "For practical purposes, the right to coal consists in the right to mine it." Commonwealth v. Clearview Coal Co., 100 A. 820, 820 (Pa. 1917). What makes the right to mine coal valuable is that it can be exercised with profit. To make it commercially impracticable to mine certain coal has very nearly the same effect for constitutional purposes as appropriating or destroying it. This we think that we are warranted in assuming that the statute does.

It is true that in Plymouth Coal Co. v. Pennsylvania, 232 U.S. 531 (1914), it was held competent for the legislature to require a pillar of coal to be left along the line of adjoining property, that, with the pillar on the other side of the line, would be a barrier sufficient for the safety of the employees of either mine in case the other should be abandoned and allowed to fill with water. But that was a requirement for the safety of employees invited into the mine, and secured an average reciprocity of advantage that has been recognized as a justification of various laws.

The rights of the public in a street purchased or laid out by eminent domain are those that it has paid for. If in any case its representatives have been so shortsighted as to acquire only surface rights without the right of support, we see no more authority for supplying the latter without compensation than there was for taking the right of way in the first place and refusing to pay for it because the public wanted it very much. The protection of private property in the Fifth Amendment presupposes that it is wanted for public use, but provides that it shall not be taken for such use without compensation. A similar assumption is made in the decisions upon the Fourteenth Amendment. Hairston v. Danville & Western Ry. Co., 208 U.S. 598, 605 (1908). When this seemingly absolute protection is found to be qualified by the police power, the natural tendency of human nature is to extend the qualification more and more until at last private property disappears. But that cannot be accomplished in this way under the Constitution of the United States.

The general rule at least is, that while property may be regulated to a certain extent, if regulation goes too far it will be recognized as a taking. It may be doubted how far exceptional cases, like the blowing up of a house to stop a conflagration, go — and if they go beyond the general rule, whether they do not stand as much upon tradition as upon principle. Bowditch v. Boston, 101 U.S. 16 (1879). In general it is not plain that a man's misfortunes or necessities will justify his shifting the damages to his neighbor's shoulders. Spade v. Lynn & Boston R.R., 52 N.E. 747, 747 (Mass. 1899). We are in danger of forgetting that a strong public desire to improve the public condition is not enough to warrant achieving the desire by a shorter cut than the constitutional way of paying for the change. As we already have said, this is a question of degree — and therefore cannot be disposed of by general propositions. But we regard this as going beyond any of the cases decided by this Court. The late decisions upon laws dealing with the congestion of Washington and New York, caused by the war, dealt with laws intended to meet a temporary emergency and providing for compensation determined to be reasonable by an impartial board. They went to the verge of the law but fell far short of the present act. Block v. Hirsh, 256 U.S. 135 (1921); Marcus Brown Holding Co. v. Feldman, 256 U.S. 170 (1921); Levy Leasing Co. v. Siegel, 258 U.S. 242 (1922).

We assume, of course, that the statute was passed upon the conviction that an exigency existed that would warrant it, and we assume that an exigency exists that would warrant the exercise of eminent domain. But the question at bottom is upon whom the loss of the changes desired should fall. So far as private persons or communities have seen fit to take the risk of acquiring only surface rights, we cannot see that the fact that their risk has become a danger warrants the giving to them greater rights than they bought.

Decree reversed.

BRANDEIS, Justice, dissenting. The Kohler Act prohibits, under certain conditions, the mining of anthracite coal within the limits of a city in such a manner or to such an extent "as to cause the . . . subsidence of any dwelling or other structure used as a human habitation, or any factory, store, or other industrial or mercantile establishment in which human labor is employed." Coal in place is land; and the right of the owner to use his land is not absolute. He may not so use it as to create a public nuisance; and uses, once harmless, may, owing to changed conditions, seriously threaten the public welfare. Whenever they do, the legislature has power to prohibit such uses without paying compensation; and the power to prohibit extends alike to the manner, the character and the purpose of the use. Are we justified in declaring that the Legislature of Pennsylvania has, in restricting the right to mine anthracite, exercised this power so arbitrarily as to violate the Fourteenth Amendment?

Every restriction upon the use of property imposed in the exercise of the police power deprives the owner of some right theretofore enjoyed, and is, in that sense, an abridgment by the State of rights in property without making compensation. But restriction imposed to protect the public health, safety or morals from dangers threatened is not a taking. The restriction here in question is merely the prohibition of a noxious use. The property so restricted remains in the possession of its owner. The State does not appropriate it or make any use of it. The State merely prevents the owner from making a use which interferes with paramount rights of the public. Whenever the use prohibited ceases to be noxious, as it may because of further change in local or social conditions, the restriction will have to be removed and the owner will again be free to enjoy his property as heretofore.

The restriction upon the use of this property cannot, of course, be lawfully imposed, unless its purpose is to protect the public. But the purpose of a restriction does not cease to be public, because incidentally some private persons may thereby receive gratuitously valuable special benefits. Thus, owners of low buildings may obtain, through statutory restrictions upon the height of neighboring structures, benefits equivalent to an easement of light and air. Welch v. Swasey, 214 U.S. 91 (1909). Furthermore, a restriction, though imposed for a public purpose, will not be lawful, unless the restriction is an appropriate means to the public end. But to keep coal in place is surely an appropriate means of preventing subsidence of the surface; and ordinarily it is the only available means. Restriction upon use does not become inappropriate as a means, merely because it deprives the owner of the only use to which the property can then be profitably put. The liquor and the oleomargarine cases settled that. Mugler v. Kansas, 123 U.S. 623, 668, 669 (1887); Powell v. Pennsylvania, 127 U.S. 678, 682 (1888). *See also* Hadacheck v. Los Angeles, 239 U.S. 394 (1915). Nor is a restriction imposed through exercise of the police power inappropriate as a means, merely because the same end might be effected through exercise of the power of eminent domain, or otherwise at public expense. Every restriction upon the height of buildings might be secured through acquiring by eminent domain the right of each owner to build above the limiting height; but it is settled that the State need not resort to that power. *Compare* Laurel Hill Cemetery v. San Francisco, 216 U.S. 358 (1910); Missouri Pacific Ry. v. Omaha, 235 U.S. 121 (1914). If by mining anthracite coal the owner would necessarily unloose poisonous gasses, I suppose no one would doubt the power of the State to prevent the mining, without buying his coal fields. And why may not the State, likewise, without paying compensation, prohibit one from digging so deep or excavating so near the surface, as to expose the community to like dangers? In the latter case, as in the former, carrying on the business would be a public nuisance.

It is said that one fact for consideration in determining whether the limits of the police power have been exceeded is the extent of the resulting diminution in value; and that here the restriction destroys existing rights of property and contract. But values are relative. If we are to consider the value of the coal kept in place by the restriction, we should compare it with the value of all other parts of the land. That is, with the value not of the coal alone, but with the value of the whole property. The rights of an owner as against the public are not increased by dividing the interests in his property into surface and subsoil. The sum of the rights in the parts cannot be greater than the rights in the whole. The estate of an owner in land is grandiloquently described as extending *ab orco usque ad coelum*. But I suppose no one would contend that by selling his interest above one hundred feet from the surface he could prevent the State from limiting, by the police power, the height of structures in a city. And why should a sale of underground rights bar the State's power? For aught that appears the value of the coal kept in place by the restriction may be negligible as compared with the value of the whole property, or even as compared with that part of it which is represented by the coal remaining in place and which may be extracted despite the statute. Ordinarily a police regulation, general in operation, will not be held void as to a particular property, although proof is offered that owing to conditions peculiar to it the restriction could not reasonably be applied. *See* Powell v. Pennsylvania, 127 U.S. 678, 681, 684 (1888); Murphy v. California, 225 U.S. 623, 629 (1912). But even if the particular facts are to govern, the statute should, in my opinion, be upheld in this case. For the defendant has failed to adduce any evidence from which it appears that to restrict its mining operations was an unreasonable exercise of the police power. *Compare* Reinman v. Little Rock, 237 U.S. 171, 177, 180 (1915); Pierce Oil Corporation v. City of Hope, 248 U.S. 498, 500 (1919). Where the surface and the coal belong to the same person, self-interest would ordinarily prevent mining to such an extent as to cause a subsidence. It was, doubtless, for this reason that the legislature, estimating the degrees of danger, deemed statutory restriction unnecessary for the public safety under such conditions.

It is said that this is a case of a single dwelling house; that the restriction upon mining abolishes a valuable estate hitherto secured by a contract with the plaintiffs; and that the restriction upon mining cannot be justified as a protection of personal safety, since that could be provided for by notice. The propriety of deferring a good deal to tribunals on the spot has been repeatedly recognized. May we say that notice would afford adequate protection of the public safety where the legislature and the highest court of the State, which greater knowledge of local conditions, have declared, in effect, that it would not? If public safety is imperiled, surely neither grant, nor contract, can prevail against the exercise of the police power. The rule that the State's power to take appropriate measures to guard the safety of all who may be within its jurisdiction may not be bargained away was applied to compel carriers to establish grade crossings at their own expense, despite contracts to the contrary; and, likewise, to supersede, by an employers' liability act, the provision of a charter exempting a railroad from liability for death of employees, since the civil liability was deemed a matter of public concern, and not a mere private right. Nor can existing contracts between private individuals preclude exercise of the police power. "One whose rights, such as they are, are subject to state restriction, cannot remove them from the power of the State by making a contract about them." Hudson County Water Co. v. McCarter, 209 U.S. 349, 357 (1908). The fact that this suit is brought by a private person is, of course, immaterial to protect the community through invoking the aid, as litigant, of interested private citizens is not a novelty in our law. That it may be done in Pennsylvania was decided by its Supreme Court in this case. And it is for a State to say how its public policy shall be enforced.

This case involves only mining which causes subsidence of a dwelling house. But the Kohler Act contains provisions in addition to that quoted above; and as to these, also, an opinion is expressed. These provisions deal with mining under cities to such an extent as to cause subsidence of—

(a) Any public building or any structure customarily used by the public as a place of resort, assemblage, or amusement, including, but not being limited to, churches, schools, hospitals, theatres, hotels, and railroad stations.

(b) Any street, road, bridge, or other public passageway, dedicated to public use or habitually used by the public.

(c) Any track, roadbed, right of way, pipe, conduit, wire, or other facility, used in the service of the public by any municipal corporation or public service company as defined by the Public Service Company Law.

A prohibition of mining which causes subsidence of such structures and facilities is obviously enacted for a public purpose; and it seems, likewise, clear that mere notice of intention to mine would not in this connection secure the public safety. Yet it is said that these provisions of the act cannot be sustained as an exercise of the police power where the right to mine such coal has been reserved. The conclusion seems to rest upon the assumption that in order to justify such exercise of the police power there must be "an average reciprocity of advantage" as between the owner of the property restricted and the rest of the community; and that here such reciprocity is absent. Reciprocity of advantage is an important consideration, and may even be an essential, where the State's power is exercised for the purpose of conferring benefits upon the property of a neighborhood, as in drainage projects, Wurts v. Hoagland, 114 U.S. 606 (1885); Fallbrook Irrigation District v. Bradley, 164 U.S. 112 (1896); or upon adjoining owners, as by party wall provisions, Jackman v. Rosenbaum Co., 260 U.S. 22, 31 (1922). But where the police power is exercised, not to confer benefits upon property owners, but to protect the public from detriment and danger, there is, in my opinion, no room for considering reciprocity of advantage. There was no reciprocal advantage to the owner prohibited from using his oil tanks in 248 U.S. 498; his brickyard, in 239 U.S. 394; his livery stable, in 237 U.S. 171; his billiard hall, in 225 U.S. 623; his oleomargarine factory, in 127 U.S. 678; his brewery, in 123 U.S. 623; unless it be the advantage of living and doing business in a civilized community. That reciprocal advantage is given by the act to the coal operators.

Notes and Questions

1. There is an ongoing historical debate about the existence of regulatory takings claims before *Mahon*. Dean William Treanor's scholarship claims that *Mahon* represented a watershed between the previous rule that denied compensation to property owners affected by government regulations and the modern pressure for such compensation. Treanor argues that the original understanding was that the Takings Clause "required compensation when the federal government physically took private property, but not when government regulations limited the ways in which property could be used." William Michael Treanor, *The Original Understanding of the Takings Clause and the Political Process*, 95 Colum. L. Rev. 782 (1995). John Hart's review of colonial land use regulation agrees that "[m]any land use laws of the founding era imposed severe economic burdens, yet compensation for such losses was never paid." John F. Hart, *Land Use Law in the Early Republic and the Original Meaning of the Takings Clause*, 94 Nw. U. L. Rev. 1099, 1101 (2000). But Professor Kris Kobach argues that compensation for regulatory takings began neither when the Takings Clause was drafted nor when *Mahon* was decided in 1922, but rather in nineteenth-century state court decisions. According to Kobach, "By 1861, numerous courts required compensation when property remained in the possession of its owner but the state restricted usage rights or diminished the property's value." Kris W. Kobach, *The Origins of Regulatory Takings: Setting the Record Straight*, 1996 Utah L. Rev. 1211, 1213.

2. The careful and entertaining research of Professor William Fischel indicates that the Kohler Act was one of two statutes drafted by Philip Mattes, the Scranton city solicitor, to address the city's coal subsidence problem. Labor relations had proven far more difficult than subsidence for local coal companies, but several well-publicized subsidence episodes yielded the voluntary agreement of the companies to pay to repair dwellings damaged by mining. Then another major subsidence occurred in 1919 that wrecked sewer, gas, and water lines, sidewalks, and whole rows of buildings. An investigation revealed that the Peoples Coal Company had been deliberately robbing the pillars of coals designed to prevent subsidence, in violation of both the voluntary agreement and a court injunction. Two company officials were jailed, but the company was judgment-proof and did not pay for the repairs. The

state legislature responded by enacting both the Kohler Act and a statute taxing the anthracite coal that came only from Pennsylvania, and especially Scranton. *Mahon* invalidated the Kohler Act, but the Supreme Court upheld the tax. Despite winning in *Mahon*, the coal companies continued to compensate landowners for subsidence with an eye toward favorable public relations. William A. Fischel, *Regulatory Takings: Law, Economics, and Politics* 24-42 (1995).

3. Pennsylvania's coal subsidence problem returned to the Supreme Court in 1978. The latest state statute invalidated express contractual waivers of surface support rights, finding instead that the surface owner retained a right to support that would be violated by the failure to prevent subsidence. This time the Court declined to find a taking, sounding much more like Justice Brandeis but distinguishing *Mahon* on the facts of the different statutes. Keystone Bituminous Coal Ass'n v. DeBenedictis, 480 U.S. 470 (1987) (5-4 vote).

■ PENN CENTRAL TRANSPORTATION CO. v. NEW YORK CITY
Supreme Court of the United States, 1978
438 U.S. 104

BRENNAN, Justice. The question presented is whether a city may, as part of a comprehensive program to preserve historic landmarks and historic districts, place restrictions on the development of individual historic landmarks — in addition to those imposed by applicable zoning ordinances — without effecting a "taking" requiring the payment of "just compensation." Specifically, we must decide whether the application of New York City's Landmarks Preservation Law to the parcel of land occupied by Grand Central Terminal has "taken" its owners' property in violation of the Fifth and Fourteenth Amendments.

I.

Over the past 50 years, all 50 States and over 500 municipalities have enacted laws to encourage or require the preservation of buildings and areas with historic or aesthetic importance. . . . The New York City law is typical of many urban landmark laws in that its primary method of achieving its goals is not by acquisitions of historic properties,[6] but rather by involving public entities in land-use decisions affecting these properties and providing services, standards, controls, and incentives that will encourage preservation by private owners and users. While the law does place special restrictions on landmark properties as a necessary feature to the attainment of its larger objectives, the major theme of the law is to ensure the owners of any such properties both a "reasonable return" on their investments and maximum latitude to use their parcels for purposes not inconsistent with the preservation goals. . . .

Final designation as a landmark results in restrictions upon the property owner's options concerning use of the landmark site. First, the law imposes a duty upon the owner to keep the exterior features of the building "in good repair" to assure that the law's objectives not be defeated by the landmark's falling into a state of

---

6. The consensus is that widespread public ownership of historic properties in urban settings is neither feasible nor wise. Public ownership reduces the tax base, burdens the public budget with costs of acquisitions and maintenance, and results in the preservation of public buildings as museums and similar facilities, rather than as economically productive features of the urban scene.

irremediable disrepair. Second, the [Landmarks Preservation] Commission must approve in advance any proposal to alter the exterior architectural features of the landmark or to construct any exterior improvement on the landmark site, thus ensuring that decisions concerning construction on the landmark site are made with due consideration of both the public interest in the maintenance of the structure and the landowner's interest in use of the property. [The law also provides three distinct procedures by which an owner can make a request to alter a landmark site, and it provides transferable development rights that owners can use to allow greater development on other nearby properties that they own.]

This case involves the application of New York City's Landmarks Preservation Law to Grand Central Terminal (Terminal). The Terminal, which is owned by the Penn Central Transportation Co. and its affiliates (Penn Central), is one of New York City's most famous buildings. Opened in 1913, it is regarded not only as providing an ingenious engineering solution to the problems presented by urban railroad stations, but also as a magnificent example of the French beaux-arts style.

The Terminal is located in midtown Manhattan. Its south facade faces 42nd Street and that street's intersection with Park Avenue. At street level, the Terminal is bounded on the west by Vanderbilt Avenue, on the east by the Commodore Hotel, and on the north by the Pan-American Building. Although a 20-story office tower, to have been located above the Terminal, was part of the original design, the planned tower was never constructed. The Terminal itself is an eight-story structure which Penn Central uses as a railroad station and in which it rents space not needed for railroad purposes to a variety of commercial interests. The Terminal is one of a number of properties owned by appellant Penn Central in this area of midtown Manhattan. The others include the Barclay, Biltmore, Commodore, Roosevelt, and Waldorf-Astoria Hotels, the Pan-American Building and other office buildings along Park Avenue, and the Yale Club. At least eight of these are eligible to be recipients of development rights afforded the Terminal by virtue of landmark designation.

[One year after the Terminal was designated as an historic landmark in 1967, Penn Central applied to the Commission for permission to construct a 55-story office building on top of the Terminal. The Commission denied the request, describing the proposed tower as "nothing more than an aesthetic joke" that "would reduce the Landmark itself to the status of a curiosity." Penn Central then sued the City alleging that the refusal to permit the addition constituted a taking of its property for which it was entitled to just compensation under the Fifth Amendment. The trial court ruled for Penn Central, but the Appellate Division and the Court of Appeals held that the City's actions did not constitute a taking.]

II.

. . . .

. . . The question of what constitutes a "taking" for purposes of the Fifth Amendment has proved to be a problem of considerable difficulty. While this Court has recognized that the "Fifth Amendment's guarantee . . . [is] designed to bar Government from forcing some people alone to bear public burdens which, in all fairness and justice, should be borne by the public as a whole," Armstrong v. United States, 364 U.S. 40, 49 (1960), this Court, quite simply, has been unable to develop any "set formula" for determining when "justice and fairness" require that economic injuries caused by public action be compensated by the government, rather than remain disproportionately concentrated on a few persons.

Indeed, we have frequently observed that whether a particular restriction will be rendered invalid by the government's failure to pay for any losses proximately caused by it depends largely "upon the particular circumstances [in that] case." United States v. Central Eureka Mining Co., 357 U.S. 155, 168 (1958).

In engaging in these essentially ad hoc, factual inquiries, the Court's decisions have identified several factors that have particular significance. The economic impact of the regulation on the claimant and, particularly, the extent to which the regulation has interfered with distinct investment-backed expectations are, of course, relevant considerations. So, too, is the character of the governmental action. A "taking" may more readily be found when the interference with property can be characterized as a physical invasion by government, *see, e.g.*, United States v. Causby, 328 U.S. 256 (1946), than when interference arises from some public program adjusting the benefits and burdens of economic life to promote the common good.

"Government hardly could go on if to some extent values incident to property could not be diminished without paying for every such change in the general law," Pennsylvania Coal Co. v. Mahon, 260 U.S. 393, 413 (1922), and this Court has accordingly recognized, in a wide variety of contexts, that government may execute laws or programs that adversely affect recognized economic values. Exercises of the taxing power are one obvious example. A second are the decisions in which this Court has dismissed "taking" challenges on the ground that, while the challenged government action caused economic harm, it did not interfere with interests that were sufficiently bound up with the reasonable expectations of the claimant to constitute "property" for Fifth Amendment purposes.

More importantly for the present case, in instances in which a state tribunal reasonably concluded that "the health, safety, morals, or general welfare" would be promoted by prohibiting particular contemplated uses of land, this Court has upheld land-use regulations that destroyed or adversely affected recognized real property interests. *See* Nectow v. Cambridge, 277 U.S. 183, 188 (1928). Zoning laws are, of course, the classic example, *see* Euclid v. Ambler Realty Co., 272 U.S. 365 (1926) (prohibition of industrial use), which have been viewed as permissible governmental action even when prohibiting the most beneficial use of the property. . . .

Unlike the governmental acts in [*Causby, Hadacheck,* and other previous cases], the New York City law does not interfere in any way with the present uses of the Terminal. Its designation as a landmark not only permits but contemplates that appellants may continue to use the property precisely as it has been used for the past 65 years: as a railroad terminal containing office space and concessions. So the law does not interfere with what must be regarded as Penn Central's primary expectation concerning the use of the parcel. More importantly, on this record, we must regard the New York City law as permitting Penn Central not only to profit from the Terminal but also to obtain a "reasonable return" on its investment.

Appellants, moreover, exaggerate the effect of the law on their ability to make use of the air rights above the Terminal in two respects. First, it simply cannot be maintained, on this record, that appellants have been prohibited from occupying *any* portion of the airspace above the Terminal. While the Commission's actions in denying applications to construct an office building in excess of 50 stories above the Terminal may indicate that it will refuse to issue a certificate of appropriateness for any comparably sized structure, nothing the Commission has said or done suggests an intention to prohibit *any* construction above the Terminal. The Commission's report emphasized that whether any construction would be allowed depended upon whether the proposed addition "would harmonize in scale, material, and character with [the Terminal]." Since appellants have not sought approval for the construction of a smaller structure, we do not know that appellants will be denied any use of any portion of the airspace above the Terminal.

Second, to the extent appellants have been denied the right to build above the Terminal, it is not literally accurate to say that they have been denied *all* use of even those pre-existing air rights. Their ability to use these rights has not been abrogated; they are made transferable to at least eight parcels in the vicinity of the Terminal, one or two of which have been found suitable for the construction of new office buildings. Although appellants and others have argued that New York City's transferable development-rights program is far from ideal, the New York courts here supportably found that, at least in the case of the Terminal, the rights afforded are valuable. While these rights may well not have constituted "just compensation" if a "taking" had occurred, the rights nevertheless undoubtedly mitigate whatever financial burdens the law has imposed on appellants and, for that reason, are to be taken into account in considering the impact of regulation.

On this record, we conclude that the application of New York City's Landmarks Law has not effected a "taking" of appellants' property. The restrictions imposed are substantially related to the promotion of the general welfare and not only permit reasonable beneficial use of the landmark site but also afford appellants opportunities further to enhance not only the Terminal site proper but also other properties. . . .

Justice REHNQUIST, with whom THE CHIEF JUSTICE and Justice STEVENS join, dissenting. Of the over one million buildings and structures in the city of New York, appellees have singled out 400 for designation as official landmarks. The owner of a building might initially be pleased that his property has been chosen by a distinguished committee of architects, historians, and city planners for such a singular distinction. But he may well discover, as appellant Penn Central Transportation Co. did here, that the landmark designation imposes upon him a substantial cost, with little or no offsetting benefit except for the honor of the designation. . . .

Only in the most superficial sense of the word can this case be said to involve "zoning." Typical zoning restrictions may, it is true, so limit the prospective uses of a piece of property as to diminish the value of that property in the abstract because it may not be used for the forbidden purposes. But any such abstract decrease in value will more than likely be at least partially offset by an increase in value which flows from similar restrictions as to use on neighboring properties. All property owners in a designated area are placed under the same restrictions, not only for the benefit of the municipality as a whole but also for the common benefit of one another. In the words of Mr. Justice Holmes, speaking for the Court in Pennsylvania Coal Co. v. Mahon, 260 U.S. 393, 415 (1922), there is "an average reciprocity of advantage." . . .

Notes and Questions

1. Note how the relevant factors listed by Justice Brennan in *Penn Central* differ from the factors cited by Justice Holmes in *Mahon*. Professors David Dana and Thomas Merrill observe that "the most obvious explanation is that each of the three factors that were downplayed in *Penn Central*—whether the regulation targets a noxious use of property, secures an average reciprocity of advantage, and

abrogates a recognized property right—inconveniently suggested that the preservation order should have been deemed a taking." David A. Dana & Thomas W. Merrill, *Property: Takings* 130 (2002). Is there a more charitable explanation? Which factors should be most helpful in identifying a taking?

2. What do the three listed factors actually mean? How would you apply them to the 10 questions listed in the takings quiz above at page 805?

3. Justice Brennan cites taxes as an "obvious" example of laws that do not constitute a taking. There are no cases holding that a tax is a taking. But why not? Does a taking occur when the property taken by the government is money? The Supreme Court has held that the right to earn interest on deposits constitutes private property for purposes of the Takings Clause. Phillips v. Washington Legal Found., 524 U.S. 156 (1998). Likewise, in Eastern Enterprises v. Apfel, 524 U.S. 498 (1998), four justices in the majority concluded that the federal government had taken the property of coal companies by holding them retroactively liable for the health care costs of retired workers. The four dissenting justices denied the applicability of the Takings Clause, as did Justice Kennedy in his concurrence that provided the majority with its fifth vote. As he explained, "The Coal Act does not appropriate, transfer, or encumber an estate in land (*e.g.*, a lien on particular piece of property), a valuable interest in intangible (*e.g.*, intellectual property), or even a bank account or accrued interest. The law simply imposes an obligation to perform an act, the payment of benefits. . . . To call this sort of governmental action a taking as a matter of constitutional interpretation is both imprecise, and with all due respect, unwise." *Id.* at 540 (Kennedy, J., concurring in the judgment and dissenting in part). Justice Kennedy instead viewed the statute's imposition of retroactive liability as unconstitutional under the Due Process Clause.

■ **LUCAS v. SOUTH CAROLINA COASTAL COUNCIL**
Supreme Court of the United States, 1992
505 U.S. 1003

SCALIA, Justice. In 1986, petitioner David H. Lucas paid $975,000 for two residential lots on the Isle of Palms in Charleston County, South Carolina, on which he intended to build single-family homes. In 1988, however, the South Carolina Legislature enacted the Beachfront Management Act, S.C. Code Ann. §48-39-250 et seq. (Supp. 1990), which had the direct effect of barring petitioner from erecting any permanent habitable structures on his two parcels. *See* §48-39-290(A). A state trial court found that this prohibition rendered Lucas's parcels "valueless." . . .

South Carolina's expressed interest in intensively managing development activities in the so-called "coastal zone" dates from 1977 when, in the aftermath of Congress's passage of the federal Coastal Zone Management Act of 1972, 16 U.S.C. §1451 et seq., the legislature enacted a Coastal Zone Management Act of its own. In its original form, the South Carolina Act required owners of coastal zone land that qualified as a "critical area" (defined in the legislation to include beaches and immediately adjacent sand dunes, §48-39-10(J)) to obtain a permit from the newly created South Carolina Coastal Council (Council) (respondent here) prior to committing the land to a "use other than the use the critical area was devoted to on [September 28, 1977]." §48-39-130(A).

In the late 1970's, Lucas and others began extensive residential development of the Isle of Palms, a barrier island situated eastward of the city of Charleston. Toward the close of the development cycle for one residential subdivision known as "Beachwood East," Lucas in 1986 purchased the two lots at issue in this litigation for his own account. No portion of the lots, which were located approximately 300 feet from the beach, qualified as a "critical area" under the 1977 Act; accordingly, at the time Lucas acquired these parcels, he was not legally obliged to obtain a permit from the Council in advance of any development activity. His intention with respect to the lots was to do what the owners of the immediately adjacent parcels had already done: erect single-family residences. He commissioned architectural drawings for this purpose.

The Beachfront Management Act brought Lucas's plans to an abrupt end. Under that 1988 legislation, the Council was directed to establish a "baseline" connecting the landward-most "point[s] of erosion . . . during the past forty years" in the region of the Isle of Palms that includes Lucas's lots. S.C. Code Ann. §48-39-280(A)(2) (Supp. 1988). In action not challenged here, the Council fixed this baseline landward of Lucas's parcels. . . .

. . . [O]ur decision in Pennsylvania Coal Co. v. Mahon offered little insight into when, and under what circumstances, a given regulation would be seen as going "too far" for purposes of the Fifth Amendment. In 70-odd years of succeeding "regulatory takings" jurisprudence, we have generally eschewed any "'set formula'" for determining how far is too far, preferring to "engage in . . . essentially ad hoc, factual inquiries." Penn Central Transportation Co. v. New York City, 438 U.S. 104, 124 (1978) (quoting Goldblatt v. Hempstead, 369 U.S. 590, 594 (1962)). We have, however, described at least two discrete categories of regulatory action as compensable without case-specific inquiry into the public interest advanced in support of the restraint. The first encompasses regulations that compel the property owner to suffer a physical "invasion" of his property. In general (at least with regard to permanent invasions), no matter how minute the intrusion, and no matter how weighty the public purpose behind it, we have required compensation. For example, in Loretto v. Teleprompter Manhattan CATV Corp., 458 U.S. 419 (1982), we determined that New York's law requiring landlords to allow television cable companies to emplace cable facilities in their apartment buildings constituted a taking, *id.* at 435-440, even though the facilities occupied at most only $1\frac{1}{2}$ cubic feet of the landlords' property, *see id.* at 438 n.16.

The second situation in which we have found categorical treatment appropriate is where regulation denies all economically beneficial or productive use of land. As we have said on numerous occasions, the Fifth Amendment is violated when land-use regulation "does not substantially advance legitimate state interests *or denies an owner economically viable use of his land.*" Agins v. City of Tiburon, 447 U.S. 255, 260 (1980) (citations omitted) (emphasis added).[7]

---

7. Regrettably, the rhetorical force of our "deprivation of all economically feasible use" rule is greater than its precision, since the rule does not make clear the "property interest" against which the loss of value is to be measured. When, for example, a regulation requires a developer to leave 90% of a rural tract in its natural state, it is unclear whether we would analyze the situation as one in which the owner has been deprived of all economically beneficial use of the burdened portion of the tract, or as one in which the owner has suffered a mere diminution in value of the tract as a whole. (For an extreme — and, we think, unsupportable — view of the relevant calculus, *see* Penn Central Transportation Co. v. New York City, 366 N.E.2d 1271, 1276-1277 (N.Y. 1977), *aff'd,* 438 U.S. 104 (1978), where the state court examined the diminution in a particular parcel's value produced by a municipal ordinance in light of total value of the takings claimant's other holdings in the vicinity.) Unsurprisingly, this uncertainty regarding the composition of the denominator in our "deprivation" fraction has produced inconsistent pronouncements by the Court. . . .

We have never set forth the justification for this rule. Perhaps it is simply, as Justice Brennan suggested, that total deprivation of beneficial use is, from the land-owner's point of view, the equivalent of a physical appropriation. *See* San Diego Gas & Electric Co. v. City of San Diego, 450 U.S. 621, 652 (1980) (dissenting opinion). "For what is the land but the profits thereof?" 1 E. Coke, *Institutes*, ch. 1, §1 (1st Am. ed. 1812). Surely, at least, in the extraordinary circumstance when *no* productive or economically beneficial use of land is permitted, it is less realistic to indulge our usual assumption that the legislature is simply "adjusting the benefits and burdens of economic life," *Penn Central Transportation Co.*, 438 U.S. at 124, in a manner that secures an "average reciprocity of advantage" to everyone concerned, *Mahon*, 260 U.S. at 415. And the *functional* basis for permitting the government, by regulation, to affect property values without compensation — that "Government hardly could go on if to some extent values incident to property could not be diminished without paying for every such change in the general law," *id.* at 413 — does not apply to the relatively rare situations where the government has deprived a landowner of all economically beneficial uses.

On the other side of the balance, affirmatively supporting a compensation requirement, is the fact that regulations that leave the owner of land without economically beneficial or productive options for its use — typically, as here, by requiring land to be left substantially in its natural state — carry with them a height-ened risk that private property is being pressed into some form of public service under the guise of mitigating serious public harm. *See, e.g.*, Annicelli v. South Kings-town, 463 A.2d 133, 140-141 (R.I. 1983) (prohibition on construction adjacent to beach justified on twin grounds of safety and "conservation of open space"); Morris County Land Improvement Co. v. Parsippany-Troy Hills Township, 193 A.2d 232, 240 (N.J. 1963) (prohibition on filling marshlands imposed in order to preserve region as water detention basin and create wildlife refuge). As Justice Brennan explained: "From the government's point of view, the benefits flowing to the public from preservation of open space through regulation may be equally great as from creating a wildlife refuge through formal condemnation or increasing electricity production through a dam project that floods private property." San Diego Gas & Elec. Co., *supra* at 652 (dissenting opinion). The many statutes on the books, both state and federal, that provide for the use of eminent domain to impose servitudes on private scenic lands preventing developmental uses, or to acquire such lands altogether, suggest the practical equivalence in this setting of negative regulation and appropriation.

We think, in short, that there are good reasons for our frequently expressed belief that when the owner of real property has been called upon to sacrifice *all* economically beneficial uses in the name of the common good, that is, to leave his property economically idle, he has suffered a taking. . . .

Where the State seeks to sustain regulation that deprives land of all econom-ically beneficial use, we think it may resist compensation only if the logically antecedent inquiry into the nature of the owner's estate shows that the proscribed use interests were not part of his title to begin with. This accords, we think, with our "takings" jurisprudence, which has traditionally been guided by the understandings of our citizens regarding the content of, and the State's power over, the "bundle of rights" that they acquire when they obtain title to property. It seems to us that the property owner necessarily expects the uses of his property to be restricted, from time to time, by various measures newly enacted by the State in legitimate exercise of its police powers; "as long recognized, some values are enjoyed under an implied limitation and must yield to the police power." *Mahon*, 260 U.S. at 413. And in the case of personal property, by reason of the State's traditionally high degree of control over commercial dealings, he ought to be aware of the possibility that new regulation might even render his property economically worthless (at least if the property's only economically productive use is sale or manufacture for sale). *See* Andrus v. Allard, 444 U.S. 51, 66-67 (1979) (prohibition on sale of eagle feathers). In the case of land, however, we think the notion pressed by the Council that title is somehow held subject to the "implied limitation" that the State may subsequently eliminate all economically valuable use is inconsistent with the historical compact recorded in the Takings Clause that has become part of our constitutional culture.

Where "permanent physical occupation" of land is concerned, we have refused to allow the government to decree it anew (without compensation), no matter how weighty the asserted "public interests" involved, Loretto v. Teleprompter Manhattan CATV Corp., 458 U.S. at 426 — though we assuredly *would* permit the government to assert a permanent easement that was a pre-existing limitation upon the landowner's title. We believe similar treatment must be accorded confiscatory regulations, *i.e.*, regulations that prohibit all economically beneficial use of land: Any limitation so severe cannot be newly legislated or decreed (without compensation), but must inhere in the title itself, in the restrictions that background principles of the State's law of property and nuisance already place upon land ownership. A law or decree with such an effect must, in other words, do no more than duplicate the result that could have been achieved in the courts — by adjacent landowners (or other uniquely affected persons) under the State's law of private nuisance, or by the State under its complementary power to abate nuisances that affect the public generally, or otherwise. . . .

The "total taking" inquiry we require today will ordinarily entail (as the application of state nuisance law ordinarily entails) analysis of, among other things, the degree of harm to public lands and resources, or adjacent private property, posed by the claimant's proposed activities, *see, e.g., Restatement (Second) of Torts* §§826, 827, the social value of the claimant's activities and their suitability to the locality in question, *see, e.g., id.* §§828(a) and (b), 831, and the relative ease with which the alleged harm can be avoided through measures taken by the claimant and the government (or adjacent private landowners) alike, *see, e.g., id.* §§827(e), 828(c), 830. The fact that a particular use has long been engaged in by similarly situated owners ordinarily imports a lack of any common-law prohibition (though changed circumstances or new knowledge may make what was previously permissible no longer so. So also does the fact that other landowners, similarly situated, are permitted to continue the use denied to the claimant.

It seems unlikely that common-law principles would have prevented the erection of any habitable or productive improvements on petitioner's land; they rarely support prohibition of the "essential use" of land. The question, however, is one of state law to be dealt with on remand. We emphasize that to win its case South Carolina must do more than proffer the legislature's declaration that the uses Lucas desires are inconsistent with the public interest, or the conclusory assertion that they violate a common-law maxim such as *sic utere tuo ut alienum non laedas*. As we have said, a "State, by *ipse dixit*, may not transform private property into public property without compensation. . . ." Webb's Fabulous Pharmacies, Inc. v. Beckwith, 449 U.S. 155, 164 (1980). Instead, as it would be required to do if it sought to restrain Lucas in a common-law action for public nuisance, South Carolina must identify background principles of nuisance and property law that prohibit the uses he now intends in the circumstances in which the property is presently found. Only on this showing can the State fairly claim that, in proscribing all such beneficial uses, the Beachfront Management Act is taking nothing.

Justice STEVENS, dissenting. . . . Like many bright-line rules, the categorical rule established in this case is only "categorical" for a page or two in the U.S. Reports. No sooner does the Court state that "total regulatory takings must be compensated," than it quickly establishes an exception to that rule.

The exception provides that a regulation that renders property valueless is not a taking if it prohibits uses of property that were not "previously permissible under relevant property and nuisance principles." The Court thus rejects the basic holding in Mugler v. Kansas, 123 U.S. 623 (1887). There we held that a statewide statute that prohibited the owner of a brewery from making alcoholic beverages did not effect a taking, even though the use of the property had been perfectly lawful and caused no public harm before the statute was enacted. . . . Under our reasoning in *Mugler*, a State's decision to prohibit or to regulate certain uses of property is not a compensable taking just because the particular uses were previously lawful. Under the Court's opinion today, however, if a State should decide to prohibit the manufacture of asbestos, cigarettes, or concealable firearms, for example, it must be prepared to pay for the adverse economic consequences of its decision. One must wonder if government will be able to "go on" effectively if it must risk compensation "for every such change in the general law." *Mahon*, 260 U.S. at 413.

The Court's holding today effectively freezes the State's common law, denying the legislature much of its traditional power to revise the law governing the rights and uses of property. . . . Arresting the development of the common law is not only a departure from our prior decisions; it is also profoundly unwise. The human condition is one of constant learning and evolution—both moral and practical. Legislatures implement that new learning; in doing so they must often revise the definition of property and the rights of property owners. Thus, when the Nation came to understand that slavery was morally wrong and mandated the emancipation of all slaves, it, in effect, redefined "property." On a lesser scale, our ongoing self-education produces similar changes in the rights of property owners: New appreciation of the significance of endangered species, the importance of wetlands, and the vulnerability of coastal lands shapes our evolving understandings of property rights.

Of course, some legislative redefinitions of property will effect a taking and must be compensated—but it certainly cannot be the case that every movement away from common law does so. There is no reason, and less sense, in such an absolute rule. We live in a world in which changes in the economy and the environment occur with increasing frequency and importance. If it was wise a century ago to allow government "the largest legislative discretion" to deal with "the special exigencies of the moment," *Mugler*, 123 U.S. at 669, it is imperative to do so today. The rule that should govern a decision in a case of this kind should focus on the future, not the past.

Notes and Questions

1. Justice Kennedy concurred in the judgment in *Lucas* because he believed that the state should not be limited to the common law of nuisance, but should also be

able to enact new regulatory initiatives in response to changing conditions. In other words, "[t]he Takings Clause does not require a static body of state property law; it protects private expectations to ensure private investment." Justice Blackmun's dissent accused the Court of "launching a missile to kill a mouse." Justice Souter would have dismissed the writ of certiorari as improvidently granted because of the questionable determination of a total deprivation of value.

On remand, the South Carolina Supreme Court held that there was no common law basis by which the state could restrain Lucas's desired use of his land, so it remanded to the state circuit court for a determination of the actual damages Lucas sustained. The state then bought the two lots from Lucas for $850,000 and paid him another $725,000 in interest, attorney's fees, and costs. Faced with those costs, the state sold the lots to a construction company.

2. *Lucas* left many questions unanswered. The Court answered two of them in 2001 when it held that property owners are not barred from pursuing takings claims simply because they acquired the subject property after a regulatory law was adopted or took effect and that the government cannot leave a "token interest" in order to avoid the duty to compensate a property owner. Palazzolo v. Rhode Island, 533 U.S. 606 (2001). *Palazzolo* addressed but did not answer a further question highlighted by *Lucas* of what constitutes the entire property for purposes of finding a total taking: the so-called *denominator problem.* Like *Lucas, Palazzolo* involved property affected by state wetlands regulation but, unlike *Lucas*, the regulation did not apply to the petitioner's entire parcel, which covered roughly 36 acres on the Rhode Island seacoast. Indeed, the petitioner accepted the lower court's finding that the unregulated, 18-acre, upland part of the property retained $200,000 in development value but claimed that the regulated, 18-acre, wetland portion of the parcel had lost its entire $3,150,000 value due to the state's denial of development permits. Referring to the petitioner's claim of a total regulatory taking of all value by the state's action, Justice Kennedy wrote for the Court (*id.* at 631-32):

> In his brief submitted to us petitioner attempts to revive this part of his claim by reframing it. He argues, for the first time, that the upland parcel is distinct from the wetlands portions, so he should be permitted to assert a deprivation limited to the latter. This contention asks us to examine the difficult, persisting question of what is the proper denominator in the takings fraction. Some of our cases indicate that the extent of deprivation effected by a regulatory action is measured against the value of the parcel as a whole, *see, e.g.*, Keystone Bituminous Coal Assn. v. DeBenedictis, 480 U.S. 470 (1987); but we have at times expressed discomfort with the logic of this rule, *see Lucas*, 505 U.S. 1003, 1016-1017 n.7, a sentiment echoed by some commentators, *see, e.g.*, Epstein, *Takings: Descent and Resurrection*, 1987 S. Ct. Rev. 1, 16-17 (1987); Fee, *Unearthing the Denominator in Regulatory Takings Claims*, 61 U. Chi. L. Rev. 1535 (1994). Whatever the merits of these criticisms, we will not explore the point here. Petitioner did not press the argument in the state courts, and the issue was not presented in the petition for certiorari. The case comes to us on the premise that petitioner's entire parcel serves as the basis for his takings claim, and, so framed, the total deprivation argument fails.

3. The *Lucas* majority opinion assumes the stability of the common law, provoking criticism from Justice Stevens. Almost all takings claims are directed to legislative or executive action. When if ever might *judicial action* unconstitutionally take property rights? In Stop the Beach Renourishment, Inc. v. Florida Dep't of Envtl. Protection, 130 S. Ct. 2592 (2010), oceanfront landowners challenged a government beach renourishment program, which would create fixed boundary lines

between the privately owned tracts and newly restored beaches. The owners alleged an infringement of their riparian rights to receive title to accretions (imperceptibly slow addition of sand) and to have their property remain in contact with the public waters. Traditional common law provides for a migrating or "floating" boundary between private tracts and the public beach, which adjusts to accretion and erosion. Overruling a lower court, the Florida Supreme Court held that the government program did not infringe their property rights. Before the U.S. Supreme Court, the owners claimed that the state court effected a "judicial taking" of their property rights. The Court affirmed, holding unanimously that the state judicial decision was not a taking because it did not violate established property rights. However, a four-justice plurality opinion written by Justice Scalia declared that, in an appropriate case, a judicial departure from established property law could violate the Takings Clause. This position is controversial, and the subject of "judicial takings" is certain to receive further attention from courts.

■ **TAHOE-SIERRA PRESERVATION COUNCIL, INC. v. TAHOE REGIONAL PLANNING AGENCY**
Supreme Court of the United States, 2002
535 U.S. 302

STEVENS, Justice. The question presented is whether a moratorium on development imposed during the process of devising a comprehensive land-use plan constitutes a *per se* taking of property requiring compensation under the Takings Clause of the United States Constitution. This case actually involves two moratoria ordered by respondent Tahoe Regional Planning Agency (TRPA) to maintain the status quo while studying the impact of development on Lake Tahoe and designing a strategy for environmentally sound growth. . . . All agree that Lake Tahoe is "uniquely beautiful," Tahoe-Sierra Preservation Council, Inc. v. Tahoe Reg'l Planning Agency, 34 F. Supp. 2d 1226, 1230 (Nev. 1999), that President Clinton was right to call it a "'national treasure that must be protected and preserved,'" *ibid.*, and that Mark Twain aptly described the clarity of its waters as "'not *merely* transparent, but dazzlingly, brilliantly so,'" *ibid.* (emphasis added) (quoting M. Twain, *Roughing It* 174-75 (1872)).

Lake Tahoe's exceptional clarity is attributed to the absence of algae that obscures the waters of most other lakes. Historically, the lack of nitrogen and phosphorous, which nourish the growth of algae, has ensured the transparency of its waters. Unfortunately, the lake's pristine state has deteriorated rapidly over the past 40 years; increased land development in the Lake Tahoe Basin (Basin) has threatened the "'noble sheet of blue water'" beloved by Twain and countless others. 34 F. Supp. 2d at 1230. As the District Court found, "dramatic decreases in clarity first began to be noted in the 1950's/early 1960's, shortly after development at the lake began in earnest." *Id.* at 1231. The lake's unsurpassed beauty, it seems, is the wellspring of its undoing.

[Beginning in the 1960s, Congress, the U.S. Forest Service (manager of the national forests), the States of Nevada and California, and numerous county and municipal governments acted to protect the water quality in Lake Tahoe. These efforts culminated in the TRPA's enactment of two moratoria that effectively prohibited all construction on sensitive lands in California and on all "Stream Environment Zones" (SEZ) lands in the entire Basin for 32 months, and on sensitive lands in Nevada (other than SEZ lands) for eight months. The moratoria were challenged by the Tahoe Sierra Preservation Council, a non-profit membership corporation representing about 2,000 owners of both improved and unimproved parcels of real estate in the Basin, and a class of some 400 individual owners of vacant lots located either on SEZ lands or in other sensitive lands. The plaintiffs had purchased their properties before enactment of the moratoria primarily for the purpose of constructing "at a time of their choosing" a single-family home "to serve as a permanent, retirement or vacation residence" with the understanding that such construction was authorized provided that "they complied with all reasonable requirements for building." The District Court found no taking under the *Penn Central* factors due to the temporary nature of the regulations, the testimony that the "average holding time of a lot in the Tahoe area between lot purchase and home construction is twenty-five years," and the failure of petitioners to offer specific evidence of harm; however, it concluded that the moratoria constituted a "categorical" taking under *Lucas*. The plaintiffs did not appeal the rejection of its *Penn Central* claim, but the TRPA appealed the district court's finding of a taking under *Lucas*. The Ninth Circuit reversed, distinguishing *Lucas* as applying to the "relatively rare" case in which a regulation denies all productive use of an entire parcel, whereas the moratoria involve only a "temporal slice" of the fee interest.]

The text of the Fifth Amendment itself provides a basis for drawing a distinction between physical takings and regulatory takings. Its plain language requires the payment of compensation whenever the government acquires private property for a public purpose, whether the acquisition is the result of a condemnation proceeding or a physical appropriation. But the Constitution contains no comparable reference to regulations that prohibit a property owner from making certain uses of her private property. Our jurisprudence involving condemnations and physical takings is as old as the Republic and, for the most part, involves the straightforward application of *per se* rules. Our regulatory takings jurisprudence, in contrast, is of more recent vintage and is characterized by "essentially ad hoc, factual inquiries," *Penn Central*, 438 U.S. at 124, designed to allow "careful examination and weighing of all the relevant circumstances." Palazzolo v. Rhode Island, 533 U.S. 606, 636 (2001) (O'Connor, J., concurring). . . .

This longstanding distinction between acquisitions of property for public use, on the one hand, and regulations prohibiting private uses, on the other, makes it inappropriate to treat cases involving physical takings as controlling precedents for the evaluation of a claim that there has been a "regulatory taking," and vice versa. For the same reason that we do not ask whether a physical appropriation advances a substantial government interest or whether it deprives the owner of all economically valuable use, we do not apply our precedent from the physical takings context to regulatory takings claims. Land-use regulations are ubiquitous and most of them impact property values in some tangential way — often in completely unanticipated ways. Treating them all as *per se* takings would transform government regulation into a luxury few governments could afford. By contrast, physical appropriations are relatively rare, easily identified, and usually represent a greater affront to individual property rights. . . .

Certainly, our holding that the permanent "obliteration of the value" of a fee simple estate constitutes a categorical taking does not answer the question whether a regulation prohibiting any economic use of land for a 32-month period has the same legal effect. Petitioners seek to bring this case under the rule announced in *Lucas* by arguing that we can effectively sever a 32-month segment from the remainder of each landowner's fee simple estate, and then ask whether that segment has been taken in its entirety by the moratoria. Of course, defining the property interest taken in terms of the very regulation being challenged is circular. With property so divided, every delay would become a total ban; the moratorium and the normal permit process alike would constitute categorical takings. Petitioners' "conceptual severance" argument is unavailing because it ignores *Penn Central*'s admonition that in regulatory takings cases we must focus on "the parcel as a whole." 438 U.S. at 130-131. We have consistently rejected such an approach to the "denominator" question. Thus, the District Court erred when it disaggregated petitioners' property into temporal segments corresponding to the regulations at issue and then analyzed whether petitioners were deprived of all economically viable use during each period. The starting point for the court's analysis should have been to ask whether there was a total taking of the entire parcel; if not, then *Penn Central* was the proper framework.

Neither *Lucas* . . . nor any of our other regulatory takings cases compels us to accept petitioners' categorical submission. In fact, these cases make clear that the categorical rule in *Lucas* was carved out for the "extraordinary case" in which a regulation permanently deprives property of all value; the default rule remains that, in the regulatory taking context, we require a more fact-specific inquiry. Nevertheless, we will consider whether the interest in protecting individual property owners from bearing public burdens "which, in all fairness and justice, should be borne by the public as a whole," Armstrong v. United States, 364 U.S. at 49, justifies creating a new rule for these circumstances. . . .

Considerations of "fairness and justice" arguably could support the conclusion that TRPA's moratoria were takings of petitioners' property based on any of seven different theories. First, even though we have not previously done so, we might now announce a categorical rule that, in the interest of fairness and justice, compensation is required whenever government temporarily deprives an owner of all economically viable use of her property. Second, we could craft a narrower rule that would cover all temporary land-use restrictions except those "normal delays in obtaining building permits, changes in zoning ordinances, variances, and the like." . . . Third, we could adopt a rule like the one suggested by an *amicus* supporting petitioners that would "allow a short fixed period for deliberations to take place without compensation — say maximum one year — after which the just compensation requirements" would "kick in." Fourth, with the benefit of hindsight, we might characterize the successive actions of TRPA as a "series of rolling moratoria" that were the functional equivalent of a permanent taking. Fifth, were it not for the findings of the District Court that TRPA acted diligently and in good faith, we might have concluded that the agency was stalling in order to avoid promulgating the environmental threshold carrying capacities and regional plan mandated by the 1980 [Tahoe Regional Planning Compact entered into by California and Nevada]. Sixth, apart from the District Court's finding that TRPA's actions represented a proportional response to a serious risk of harm to the lake, petitioners might have argued that the moratoria did not substantially advance a legitimate state interest. Finally, if petitioners had challenged the application of the moratoria to their individual parcels, instead of making a facial challenge, some of them might have prevailed under a *Penn Central* analysis.

With respect to the [last three theories, which are the only ones properly before the Court], the ultimate constitutional question is whether the concepts of "fairness and justice" that underlie the Takings Clause will be better served by one of these categorical rules or by a *Penn Central* inquiry into all of the relevant circumstances in particular cases. From that perspective, the extreme categorical rule that any deprivation of all economic use, no matter how brief, constitutes a compensable taking surely cannot be sustained. Petitioners' broad submission would apply to numerous "normal delays in obtaining building permits, changes in zoning ordinances, variances, and the like," 482 U.S. at 321, as well as to orders temporarily prohibiting access to crime scenes, businesses that violate health codes, fire-damaged buildings, or other areas that we cannot now foresee. Such a rule would undoubtedly require changes in numerous practices that have long been considered permissible exercises of the police power. As Justice Holmes warned in *Mahon*, "government hardly could go on if to some extent values incident to property could not be diminished without paying for every such change in the general law." 260 U.S. at 413. A rule that required compensation for every delay in the use of property would render routine government processes prohibitively expensive or encourage hasty decisionmaking. Such an important change in the law should be the product of legislative rulemaking rather than adjudication.

More importantly, for reasons set out at some length by Justice O'Connor in her concurring opinion in Palazzolo v. Rhode Island, 533 U.S. at 636 (2001), we are persuaded that the better approach to claims that a regulation has effected a temporary taking "requires careful examination and weighing of all the relevant circumstances." . . . In rejecting petitioners' *per se* rule, we do not hold that the temporary nature of a land-use restriction precludes finding that it effects a taking; we simply recognize that it should not be given exclusive significance one way or the other. . . .

The interest in facilitating informed decisionmaking by regulatory agencies counsels against adopting a *per se* rule that would impose such severe costs on their deliberations. Otherwise, the financial constraints of compensating property owners during a moratorium may force officials to rush through the planning process or to abandon the practice altogether. To the extent that communities are forced to abandon using moratoria, landowners will have incentives to develop their property quickly before a comprehensive plan can be enacted, thereby fostering inefficient and ill-conceived growth. . . . We conclude, therefore, that the interest in "fairness and justice" will be best served by relying on the familiar *Penn Central* approach when deciding cases like this, rather than by attempting to craft a new categorical rule.

[Chief Justice Rehnquist's dissenting opinion, joined by Justices Scalia and Thomas, is omitted.]

Justice Thomas, with whom Justice Scalia joins, dissenting. . . . A taking is exactly what occurred in this case. No one seriously doubts that the land use regulations at issue rendered petitioners' land unsusceptible of *any* economically beneficial use. This was true at the inception of the moratorium, and it remains true today. These individuals and families were deprived of the opportunity to build single-family homes as permanent, retirement, or vacation residences on land upon which such construction was authorized when purchased. The Court assures them that "a temporary prohibition on economic use" cannot be a taking because "logically . . . the property will recover value as soon as the prohibition is lifted." But the "logical" assurance that a "temporary restriction . . . merely causes a diminution in value," is cold comfort to the property owners in this case or any other. After all, "*in the long run* we are all dead." John Maynard Keynes, *Monetary Reform* 88 (1924). . . .

Notes and Questions

1. Law professor and former law school basketball player Richard Lazarus, who represented some of the parties defending the moratorium in the Supreme Court, describes Lake Tahoe as "a classic environmental commons, all too reminiscent of [the type of dysfunctional situations identified in] Garret Hardin's famed essay, The Tragedy of the Commons." Richard J. Lazarus, *Celebrating Tahoe-Sierra*, 33 Envtl. L. 1, 4 (2003). Thinking back to the excerpt from Hardin's influential essay in Chapter 1, is there merit to Lazarus' analogy or it is simply a lawyer's argument on behalf of his clients?

2. The TRPA finally issued its promised regulations while the Supreme Court was deciding the challenge to the moratoria. The regulations included a "Scenic Review Ordinance," which uses a "Contrast/Visual Magnitude Rating system . . . which numerically scores a house's scenic impact, as viewed from the Lake towards its shore, based upon certain pre-determined traits. Basic traits of the proposed structure result in an objective color-contrast score. Examples of these basic traits are a structure's color, the percentage of a structure's perimeter which is visible, and the articulation and surface texture of a structure's facade. A high color contrast score translates into more visible square footage allowed. Conversely, a low color contrast score results in less visible square footage allowed." Committee for Reasonable Regulation of Lake Tahoe v. Tahoe Regional Planning Agency, 365 F. Supp. 2d 1146, 1148 (D. Nev. 2005). Does the ordinance result in a taking? *See id.* at 1161-65 (holding that an association of landowners lacked standing to bring the takings claim).

■ **PHILIP MORRIS, INC. v. REILLY**
United States Court of Appeals for the First Circuit, 2002
312 F.3d 24

TORRUELLA, Circuit Judge. Unquestionably, tobacco is subject to heavy regulation by federal and state governments. This case concerns one attempt, by Massachusetts, to further regulate tobacco products by requiring tobacco companies to submit to Massachusetts the ingredient lists for all cigarettes, snuffs, and chewing tobaccos sold in the state. For each brand, the manufacturer must list, by relative amount, all ingredients besides tobacco, water, or reconstituted tobacco sheet. Mass. Gen. Laws ch. 94, §307B (2002). Currently, the appellees, a group of tobacco companies, treat these ingredient lists as trade secrets and either do not disclose brand-specific information at all or do not disclose it without some guarantee of confidentiality.

The tobacco companies brought suit claiming that the Massachusetts statute, which allows the public disclosure of these ingredient lists whenever such disclosure "could reduce risks to public health," Mass. Gen. Laws ch. 94, §307B, creates an unconstitutional taking. [The district court found a taking, a divided panel of the First Circuit reversed, then the First Circuit agreed to rehear the case *en banc.*]

The Supreme Court has distinguished between two branches of Takings Clause cases: physical takings and regulatory takings. *See* Tahoe-Sierra Pres. Council, Inc. v. Tahoe Reg'l Planning Agency, 535 U.S. 302 (2002) (distinguishing "between acquisitions of property for public uses . . . and regulations prohibiting private uses"). A physical taking occurs either when there is a condemnation or a physical appropriation of property. Generally, courts apply "straightforward" *per se* rules when addressing physical takings. *Id.* A regulatory taking transpires when some significant restriction is placed upon an owner's use of his property for which "justice and fairness" require that compensation be given. Goldblatt v. Hempstead, 369 U.S. 590, 594 (1962); *accord* Penn. Coal Co. v. Mahon, 260 U.S. 393, 415 (1922) ("The general rule at least is that while property may be regulated to a certain extent, if that regulation goes too far it will be recognized as a taking."). For the most part, courts apply a three-part "ad hoc, factual inquiry" to evaluate whether a regulatory taking has occurred: (1) what is the economic impact of the regulation; (2) whether the government action interferes with reasonable investment-backed expectations; and (3) what is the character of the government action. Penn Central Transportation Co. v. New York City, 438 U.S. 104, 124 (1978). However, the Supreme Court has developed at least one *per se* rule in the regulatory takings sphere. *See Tahoe-Sierra*, 122 S. Ct. at 1480. When a regulation denies all economically beneficial or productive uses of land, it is a taking. Lucas v. S.C. Coastal Council, 505 U.S. 1003, 1015 (1992).

Here, there is an alleged taking of intellectual property — trade secrets. The Supreme Court has addressed an alleged taking of trade secrets only once, in Ruckelshaus v. Monsanto Co., 467 U.S. 986 (1984). There, the Court simply applied the multi-factored regulatory takings analysis enunciated in *Penn Central*. . . . Before proceeding to the *Penn Central* analysis, I note that the tobacco companies argue that the *Lucas per se* rule governs this case. The decision in and reasoning behind *Lucas* certainly raise some interesting questions about the constitutionality of the Disclosure Act. However, I am uncomfortable with the suggestion that we simply import that *per se* rule into this case. *Lucas* dealt with real, not personal, property, and the Court cautioned that the value of personal property could be wiped out without triggering the strictures of the Takings Clause. 505 U.S. at 1027-28. . . . Since I interpret *Monsanto* to require courts to apply the *Penn Central* framework in cases like ours, I now proceed with that analysis.

I. Reasonable Investment-Backed Expectations

Despite the importance of reasonable investment-backed expectations under the *Penn Central* framework, the courts have struggled to adequately define this term. Some very general contours are clear. Courts protect only reasonable expectations. Ideally, the relevant inquiry should recognize that not every investment deserves protection and that some investors inevitably will be disappointed. However, beyond the general landscape, there is a paucity of clear landmarks that can be used to navigate the terrain. Some recent decisions have added specific details, *see, e.g.*, Palazzolo v. Rhode Island, 533 U.S. 606, 627 (2001) (holding that whether property is acquired before or after a regulation is enacted does not completely determine the owner's reasonable investment-backed expectations), but many areas are still uncharted. As I proceed into this quagmire, the first guidepost is *Monsanto*.

Monsanto answered a challenge to disclosures by the EPA of data which had been submitted under the Federal Insecticide, Fungicide, and Rodenticide Act ("FIFRA"). 7 U.S.C. §§136-136y. FIFRA was enacted in 1947, amended in 1972, and amended again in 1978, each time offering different protections to submitted data. Monsanto challenged disclosures of data which had been submitted under each of these schemes, and the Court looked at the protections provided by each scheme to determine whether applicants had a reasonable investment-backed expectation that their trade secrets would remain secret. . . . Monsanto preserved its trade secrets because there was a promise of confidentiality. The tobacco companies will lose their trade secrets because there is no similar promise here. Therefore, a slightly different question is posed by the current case. In *Monsanto*, the question was whether the government could disclose trade secrets it had previously agreed to keep secret. Here, the question is whether Massachusetts can force the tobacco companies to cede their trade secrets.

To answer that question I must look at the tobacco companies' reasonable investment-backed expectations that they can maintain the integrity of their trade secrets. The fact that the Disclosure Act has been enacted is not dispositive because, as discussed above, Massachusetts cannot simply redefine property rights without regard to previously existing protections. *See* Webb's Fabulous Pharmacies v. Beckwith, 449 U.S. 155, 164 (1980); *cf. Palazzolo*, 533 U.S. at 627 (holding that enactment of a regulation inhibiting development before a purchaser acquires his property does not alone negate the purchaser's reasonable investment-backed expectations because otherwise "a State would be allowed, in effect, to put an expiration date on the Takings Clause"). I must examine the tobacco companies' reasonable investment-backed expectations "in light of the whole of our legal tradition," *Lucas*, 505 U.S. at 1035 (Kennedy, J., concurring), not just in light of the provisions of the Disclosure Act.

. . . While the federal government and other states worry about the health effects of tobacco additives, none of their regimes requires the publication of brand-specific ingredient lists. They either do not require brand-specific disclosures, or they grant the tobacco companies protections against public disclosure of ingredient lists submitted to the states. Furthermore, regulations governing other products recognize the difference between requiring accurate labeling and protecting secret formulas. For example, the Food, Drug, and Cosmetic Act allows additives to be grouped as "spices, flavoring, and coloring" without specifically identifying the individual ingredients. 21 U.S.C. §343(i)(2). This allows many manufacturers to maintain their secret formulas.

Given this complex background and the fact that Massachusetts has long protected trade secrets, I cannot hold that the tobacco companies have no reasonable investment-backed expectation that their ingredient lists will remain secret. Therefore, I proceed to the other elements of the *Penn Central* inquiry.

II. ECONOMIC IMPACT

In contrast to reasonable investment-backed expectations, the law regarding economic impact is fairly straightforward. The inquiry is whether the regulation "impair[s] the value or use of [the] property" according to the owners' general use of their property. Pruneyard Shopping Ctr. v. Robins, 447 U.S. 74, 83 (1980). Not only is the use to which the property owner puts her property important, but the economic impact needs to be considered in the context of other laws and regulatory schemes.

The evidence presented here is similarly straightforward. The appellees' have spent millions of dollars developing the formulas for different brands. The evidence shows that public disclosure of the appellees' ingredient lists, even in part, will make it much easier to reverse engineer those formulas. If competitors can obtain these formulas, they can replicate appellees' products, undermining the value of appellees' brands. Some of those brands, such as Marlboro, are worth billions of dollars. While it is impossible to predict the exact economic impact that the Disclosure Act will have, it is potentially tremendous.

III. CHARACTER OF THE GOVERNMENT ACTION

In this last section, I delve into how the Disclosure Act regulates and what that regulation does to the tobacco companies' trade secrets. As mentioned above, the tobacco companies believe that the Disclosure Act regulations are so egregious that they rise to the level of a *per se* taking. They ground this claim on the fact that the Disclosure Act gives Massachusetts the right to publish the ingredient lists. The Act, in essence, prevents the tobacco companies from excluding others from their trade secrets, destroying their essential attribute. It also, allegedly, destroys the entire value of the trade secrets. I now address those arguments in full. However, I will also balance the effects of the Disclosure Act against Massachusetts' interests. *See* Keystone Bituminous Coal Ass'n v. DeBenedictis, 480 U.S. 470, 488 (1987) (considering the state's asserted interests in "health, the environment, and the fiscal integrity of the area"). Here, the asserted state interest is the promotion of public health.

I begin with the tobacco companies' argument that they will lose the right to exclude others from their trade secrets and, consequently, their trade secrets will lose all value. It appears paradigmatic that these assertions are true. In *Monsanto*, the Supreme Court recognized that, "if an individual discloses his trade secret to others who are under no obligation to protect the confidentiality of the information, or otherwise publicly discloses the secret, his property right is extinguished." 467 U.S. at 1002. That is exactly what happens here. The Disclosure Act requires the tobacco companies to share their trade secrets with Massachusetts, which is under no obligation to keep the information secret. In fact, the Disclosure Act spells out the terms under which Massachusetts will publish those trade secrets. It thus provides specific notice to the tobacco companies that Massachusetts need not respect their property rights. Therefore, if the tobacco companies comply with the requirements of the Disclosure Act, their property right will be extinguished. In the future, should a competitor use published data, the tobacco companies will have no ability to enforce their rights. Similarly, the value of the trade secrets will be lost because their value lies in the ability of the tobacco companies to exclude others. The Disclosure Act essentially destroys the tobacco companies' trade secrets. . . .

I simply am not convinced that the Disclosure Act, particularly the provisions about which the tobacco companies complain, really helps to promote public health. The Disclosure Act allows for full disclosure of the ingredient lists when doing so "could" further public health. This places an extremely low burden on Massachusetts. Frankly, for a state to be able to completely destroy valuable trade secrets, it should be required to show more than a possible beneficial effect. The tremendous individual loss is simply not justified by such a speculative public gain. Furthermore, it is not at all clear that protecting the overall integrity of the tobacco companies' ingredient lists will interfere with Massachusetts' goal of promoting public health. I note that the tobacco companies comply, without complaint, with regimes which require them to make confidential disclosure of brand-specific, ingredient information, *see* Tex. Health & Safety Code Ann. §§161.351-55, or which require public disclosures when specific ingredients are used, *see* Minn. Stat. §461.17. There is no evidence that suggests that regimes similar to those adopted by Texas and Minnesota, or some combination thereof, would not achieve the goals which appellants claim underlie the requirements of the Disclosure Act. . . .

IV. Conclusion — Regulatory Takings Analysis

As I conclude my analysis of the *Penn Central* factors, I first note that there is no formula as to how to weigh the importance of the various factors. As has been clear from the preceding discussion, different factors can be dispositive.

Here, the tobacco companies have at least some reasonable investment-backed expectation that their trade secrets will remain secret and the economic impact of that revelation is likely to be great. These factors, alone, may not be sufficient to raise this case to the level of an unconstitutional taking. However, the character of the government action determines the case. The Disclosure Act causes the tobacco companies to lose their trade secrets, entirely, and appellants advance no convincing public policy rationale to justify the taking itself. Instead, they point to a general, laudable goal which cannot justify the specific action of which the tobacco companies complain. . . .

For the reasons discussed above, I find that the Disclosure Act violates the Takings Clause. Therefore, I affirm the district court's judgment.

Selya, Circuit Judge, concurring in the judgment. . . . Simply put, I see no principled reason to refrain from extending *per se* takings analysis to alleged takings of trade secrets. Indeed, the Supreme Court hinted at this result when it observed that the term "property" in the Takings Clause is meant in its "more accurate sense to denote the group of rights inhering in the citizen's relation to the physical thing" as opposed to its "vulgar and untechnical sense of the physical thing" itself. *Monsanto*, 467 U.S. at 1003. . . .

The Court further elucidated the conceptual nature of rights in physical property in Tahoe-Sierra Preservation Council, Inc. v. Tahoe Regional Planning Agency, 535 U.S. 302 (2002). There, the Court reasoned that an "interest in real property is defined by the metes and bounds that describe its geographic dimensions and the term of years that describes the temporal aspect of the owner's interest." *Id.* at 1484. Realistically, however, such "property" exists principally in the minds of legal theorists; to the archetypical landowner, such concepts are meaningless unless and until the integrity of her rights are challenged. In my view, this illustrates that property rights, in general, consist largely of legal fictions, and exist only to the extent that they are recognized and enforceable in court — and that verity holds true whether the subject matter they encompass is corporeal or conceptual.

This point is further supported by comparing the valuation of real and intellectual property. The basis of value for both is the owner's right to exclude (relative to others' demand for access). For example, it is obvious that, other things being equal, ten acres of undeveloped land in rural Maine is not as valuable as ten acres of undeveloped land in midtown Manhattan. If the physical thing itself were the basis of value, these tracts of equal size and topographical characteristics should be worth the same. The value differential results from the fact that people are willing to pay a higher price for access to Manhattan. *Cf. The Executive's Book of Quotations* 168 (Oxford Univ. Press 1994) citing the "long-standing real estate principle" of "location, location, location." So too trade secrets: if I have a secret formula for, say, prune juice, people presumably will not be willing to pay as high a price for the secret as they would for a secret recipe for making Marlboro cigarettes.

In short, the value of trade secrets, like the value of land, is inextricably tied to both the demand of others for access and the legal enforceability of the owner's right to exclude. In either case, if the right to exclude is diminished, the value decreases. And in either case, if the sovereign effectively deprives the owner of the right to exclude, the value is destroyed — and the Constitution requires just compensation. Limiting *per se* takings analysis to cases involving real property is a crude boundary with no compelling basis in the law. We should not be hesitant to take the next logical step when justice demands it. . . .

LIPEZ, Circuit Judge, dissenting. . . .

The tobacco companies mount only a facial challenge to the Disclosure Act. Thus, they must show that the "mere enactment of the [Disclosure Act] constituted a taking." Tahoe-Sierra Pres. Council, Inc. v. Tahoe Reg'l Planning Agency, 535 U.S. 302, 318 (2002). The test is a stringent one, and the tobacco companies "face an uphill battle." *Id.* at 320. . .

The tobacco companies have not met that burden here. As Judge Torruella's opinion indicates, the constitutionality of any given disclosure under the Act depends on how much — and what sort of — ingredient information is made public. The question of what information will be publicized cannot be answered by reference to the terms of the Act and its implementing regulations, which indicate only that Massachusetts may disclose some of the information it receives. Thus, there is nothing unconstitutional about the Act itself. What matters is how it is applied in each individual case. . . .

Notes and Questions

1. The government has numerous reasons for obtaining intellectual property. It may need to use a patented manufacturing process to produce a new missile. It may want to use a copyrighted book to train new government employees. It may want to disclose a company's trade secrets so that the public can properly evaluate health and safety concerns. It may even seek to exploit an existing trademark. *See, e.g.,* Ringling Bros.-Barnum & Bailey Combined Shows, Inc. v. Utah Div. of Travel Dev., 955 F. Supp. 605 (E.D. Va. 1997) (unsuccessful suit challenging a state tourist agency's use of the slogan "The Greatest Snow on Earth"). Congress anticipated these events by enacting a statute that governs federal government takings of intellectual property. According to 28 U.S.C. §1498, the owner of a patent or a copyright that is used by the federal government without permission is entitled to "reasonable and entire compensation."

"The application of the Takings Clause to intellectual property — trademarks, copyrights and patents — has not yet been seriously tested in the courts." David A. Dana & Thomas W. Merrill, *Property: Takings* 233 (2002). The leading case remains James v. Campbell, 104 U.S. 356 (1881), where the plaintiff charged a local postmaster with the unauthorized use of his patented stamping machine. The Court had "no doubt" that "the government of the United States when it grants letters-patent for a new invention or discovery in the arts, confers upon the patentee an exclusive property in the patented invention which cannot be appropriated or used by the government itself, without just compensation, any more than it can appropriate or use without compensation land which has been patented to a private purchaser." The Court added that "[m]any inventions relate to subjects which can only be properly used by the government, such as explosive shells, rams, and submarine batteries attached to armed vessels. If it could use such inventions without compensation, the inventors could get no return at all for their discoveries and experiments." *Id.* at 357-58. The Court held, though, that the postmaster did not infringe the plaintiff's patent because the two machines were sufficiently different.

2. The liability of *states* for infringements of patent, trademark, and copyright violations was called into question in the aftermath of Seminole Tribe of Fla. v. Florida, 517 U.S. 44 (1996). In that case the Court held that the Eleventh Amendment to the Constitution limited congressional power to abrogate states' sovereign immunity. In follow-up cases, the Court extended the logic of the ruling to federal intellectual property statutes. (Florida Prepaid Postsecondary Expense Board v. College Savings Bank, 527 U.S. 627 (1999), with respect to the patent statute and College Savings Bank v. Florida Prepaid Postsecondary Expense Board, 527 U.S. 666 (1999), with respect to the trademark statute. Most assume states are similarly immune with respect to copyright claims. *See* Peter Bray, *After* College Savings v. Florida Prepaid, *Are States Subject to Suit for Copyright Infringement?*, 36 Hous. L. Rev. 1531 (1999).) Essentially, the Supreme Court has ruled that states have not clearly waived their sovereign immunity with respect to claims based on the federal intellectual property statutes. The intricacies of the differences between damage liability and vulnerability for injunctive relief, and the liability of state employees as opposed to the liability of the states themselves, is beyond the scope of these materials. For now, just realize that there are limits on the enforcement of federal intellectual property laws against states.

■ **DOLAN v. CITY OF TIGARD**
  Supreme Court of the United States, 1994
  512 U.S. 374

REHNQUIST, Chief Justice. Petitioner challenges the decision of the Oregon Supreme Court which held that the city of Tigard could condition the approval of her building permit on the dedication of a portion of her property for flood control and traffic improvements. 854 P.2d 437 (1993). We granted certiorari to resolve a question left open by our decision in Nollan v. California Coastal Comm'n, 483 U.S. 825 (1987), of what is the required degree of connection between the exactions imposed by the city and the projected impacts of the proposed development.

I.

The State of Oregon enacted a comprehensive land use management program in 1973. Ore. Rev. Stat. §§197.005-197.860 (1991). The program required all Oregon cities and counties to adopt new comprehensive land use plans that were consistent with the statewide planning goals. The plans are implemented by land use regulations which are part of an integrated hierarchy of legally binding goals, plans, and regulations. Pursuant to the State's requirements, the city of Tigard, a community of some 30,000 residents on the southwest edge of Portland, developed a comprehensive plan and codified it in its Community Development Code (CDC). The CDC requires property owners in the area zoned Central Business District to comply with a 15% open space and landscaping requirement, which limits total site coverage, including all structures and paved parking, to 85% of the parcel. After the completion of a transportation study that identified congestion in the Central Business District as a particular problem, the city adopted a plan for a pedestrian/bicycle pathway intended to encourage alternatives to automobile transportation for short trips. The CDC requires that new development facilitate this plan by dedicating land for pedestrian pathways where provided for in the pedestrian/bicycle pathway plan.

The city also adopted a Master Drainage Plan (Drainage Plan). The Drainage Plan noted that flooding occurred in several areas along Fanno Creek, including areas near petitioner's property. The Drainage Plan also established that the increase in impervious surfaces associated with continued urbanization would exacerbate these flooding problems. To combat these risks, the Drainage Plan suggested a series of improvements to the Fanno Creek Basin, including channel excavation in the area next to petitioner's property. Other recommendations included ensuring that the floodplain remains free of structures and that it be preserved as greenways to minimize flood damage to structures. The Drainage Plan concluded that the cost of these improvements should be shared based on both direct and indirect benefits, with property owners along the waterways paying more due to the direct benefit that they would receive. . . .

Petitioner Florence Dolan owns a plumbing and electric supply store located on Main Street in the Central Business District of the city. The store covers approximately 9,700 square feet on the eastern side of a 1.67-acre parcel, which includes a gravel parking lot. Fanno Creek flows through the southwestern corner of the lot and along its western boundary. The year-round flow of the creek renders the area within the creek's 100-year floodplain virtually unusable for commercial development. The city's comprehensive plan includes the Fanno Creek floodplain as part of the city's greenway system.

Petitioner applied to the city for a permit to redevelop the site. Her proposed plans called for nearly doubling the size of the store to 17,600 square feet and paving a 39-space parking lot. The existing store, located on the opposite side of the parcel, would be razed in sections as construction progressed on the new building. In the second phase of the project, petitioner proposed to build an additional structure on the northeast side of the site for complementary businesses and to provide more parking. The proposed expansion and intensified use are consistent with the city's zoning scheme in the Central Business District.

The City Planning Commission (Commission) granted petitioner's permit application subject to conditions imposed by the city's CDC. The . . . Commission required that petitioner dedicate the portion of her property lying within the 100-year floodplain for improvement of a storm drainage system along Fanno Creek and that she dedicate an additional 15-foot strip of land adjacent to the floodplain as a pedestrian/bicycle pathway. The dedication required by that condition encompasses approximately 7,000 square feet, or roughly 10% of the property. In accordance with city practice, petitioner could rely on the dedicated property to meet the 15% open space and landscaping requirement mandated by the city's zoning scheme. The city would bear the cost of maintaining a landscaped buffer between the dedicated area and the new store.

Petitioner requested variances from the CDC standards. Variances are granted only where it can be shown that, owing to special circumstances related to a specific piece of the land, the literal interpretation of the applicable zoning provisions would cause "an undue or unnecessary hardship" unless the variance is granted. Rather than posing alternative mitigating measures to offset the expected impacts of her proposed development, as allowed under the CDC, petitioner simply argued that her proposed development would not conflict with the policies of the comprehensive plan. The Commission denied the request.

The Commission made a series of findings concerning the relationship between the dedicated conditions and the projected impacts of petitioner's project. First, the Commission noted that "it is reasonable to assume that customers and employees of the future uses of this site could utilize a pedestrian/bicycle pathway adjacent to this development for their transportation and recreational needs." The Commission noted that the site plan has provided for bicycle parking in a rack in front of the proposed building and "it is reasonable to expect that some of the users of the bicycle parking provided for by the site plan will use the pathway adjacent to Fanno Creek if it is constructed." In addition, the Commission found that creation of a convenient, safe pedestrian/bicycle pathway system as an alternative means of transportation "could offset some of the traffic demand on [nearby] streets and lessen the increase in traffic congestion."

The Commission went on to note that the required floodplain dedication would be reasonably related to petitioner's request to intensify the use of the site given the increase in the impervious surface. The Commission stated that the "anticipated increased storm water flow from the subject property to an already strained creek and drainage basin can only add to the public need to manage the stream channel and floodplain for drainage purposes." Based on this anticipated increased storm water flow, the Commission concluded that "the requirement of dedication of the floodplain area on the site is related to the applicant's plan to intensify development on the site." The Tigard City Council approved the Commission's final order, subject to one minor modification; the city council reassigned the responsibility for surveying and marking the floodplain area from petitioner to the city's engineering department.

Petitioner appealed to the Land Use Board of Appeals (LUBA) on the ground that the city's dedication requirements were not related to the proposed development, and, therefore, those requirements constituted an uncompensated taking of her property under the Fifth Amendment. [LUBA rejected Petitioner's claim, as did the Oregon Court of Appeals and the Oregon Supreme Court.]

II.

The Takings Clause of the Fifth Amendment of the United States Constitution, made applicable to the States through the Fourteenth Amendment, provides: "Nor shall private property be taken for public use, without just compensation." One of the principal purposes of the Takings Clause is "to bar Government from forcing some people alone to bear public burdens which, in all fairness and justice, should be borne by the public as a whole." Armstrong v. United States, 364 U.S. 40, 49 (1960). Without question, had the city simply required petitioner to dedicate a strip of land along Fanno Creek for public use, rather than conditioning the grant of her permit to redevelop her property on such a dedication, a taking would have occurred. Such public access would deprive petitioner of the right to exclude others, "one of the most essential sticks in the bundle of rights that are commonly characterized as property."

On the other side of the ledger, the authority of state and local governments to engage in land use planning has been sustained against constitutional challenge as long ago as our decision in Village of Euclid v. Ambler Realty Co., 272 U.S. 365 (1926). "Government hardly could go on if to some extent values incident to property could not be diminished without paying for every such change in the general law." Pennsylvania Coal Co. v. Mahon, 260 U.S. 393, 413 (1922). A land use regulation does not effect a taking if it "substantially advances legitimate state interests" and does not "deny an owner economically viable use of his land." Agins v. City of Tiburon, 447 U.S. 255, 260 (1980).

The sort of land use regulations discussed in the cases just cited, however, differ in two relevant particulars from the present case. First, they involved essentially legislative determinations classifying entire areas of the city, whereas here the city made an adjudicative decision to condition petitioner's application for a building permit on an individual parcel. Second, the conditions imposed were not simply a limitation on the use petitioner might make of her own parcel, but a requirement that she deed portions of the property to the city. In *Nollan, supra,* we held that governmental authority to exact such a condition was circumscribed by the Fifth and Fourteenth Amendments. Under the well-settled doctrine of "unconstitutional conditions," the government may not require a person to give up a constitutional right — here the right to receive just compensation when property is taken for a public use — in exchange for a discretionary benefit conferred by the government where the benefit sought has little or no relationship to the property.

Petitioner contends that the city has forced her to choose between the building permit and her right under the Fifth Amendment to just compensation for the public easements. Petitioner does not quarrel with the city's authority to exact some forms of dedication as a condition for the grant of a building permit, but challenges the showing made by the city to justify these exactions. She argues that the city has identified "no special benefits" conferred on her, and has not identified any "special quantifiable burdens" created by her new store that would justify the particular dedications required from her which are not required from the public at large.

III.

In evaluating petitioner's claim, we must first determine whether the "essential nexus" exists between the "legitimate state interest" and the permit condition exacted by the city. *Nollan,* 483 U.S. at 837. If we find that a nexus exists, we must then decide the required degree of connection between the exactions and the projected impact of the proposed development. We were not required to reach this question in *Nollan,* because we concluded that the connection did not meet even the loosest standard. Here, however, we must decide this question.

A.

We addressed the essential nexus question in *Nollan.* The California Coastal Commission demanded a lateral public easement across the Nollans' beachfront lot in exchange for a permit to demolish an existing bungalow and replace it with a three-bedroom house. The public easement was designed to connect two public beaches that were separated by the Nollans' property. The Coastal Commission had asserted that the public easement condition was imposed to promote the legitimate state interest of diminishing the "blockage of the view of the ocean" caused by construction of the larger house.

We agreed that the Coastal Commission's concern with protecting visual access to the ocean constituted a legitimate public interest. We also agreed that the permit condition would have been constitutional "even if it consisted of the requirement that the Nollans provide a viewing spot on their property for passersby with whose sighting of the ocean their new house would interfere." *Id.* at 836. We resolved, however, that the Coastal Commission's regulatory authority was set completely adrift from its constitutional moorings when it claimed that a nexus existed between visual access to the ocean and a permit condition requiring lateral public access along the Nollans' beachfront lot. How enhancing the public's ability to "traverse to and along the shorefront" served the same governmental purpose of "visual access to the ocean" from the roadway was beyond our ability to countenance. The absence of a nexus left the Coastal Commission in the position of simply trying to obtain an easement through gimmickry, which converted a valid regulation of land use into "an out-and-out plan of extortion." *Ibid.*

No such gimmicks are associated with the permit conditions imposed by the city in this case. Undoubtedly, the prevention of flooding along Fanno Creek and the reduction of traffic congestion in the Central Business District qualify as the type of legitimate public purposes we have upheld. *Agins,* 447 U.S. at 260-262. It seems equally obvious that a nexus exists between preventing flooding along Fanno Creek and limiting development within the creek's 100-year floodplain. Petitioner proposes to double the size of her retail store and to pave her now-gravel parking lot, thereby expanding the impervious surface on the property and increasing the amount of storm water runoff into Fanno Creek.

The same may be said for the city's attempt to reduce traffic congestion by providing for alternative means of transportation. In theory, a pedestrian/bicycle pathway provides a useful alternative means of transportation for workers and shoppers: "Pedestrians and bicyclists occupying dedicated spaces for walking and/or bicycling . . . remove potential vehicles from streets, resulting in an overall improvement in total transportation system flow." A. Nelson, *Public Provision of Pedestrian and Bicycle Access Ways: Public Policy Rationale and the Nature of Private Benefits* 11, Center for Planning Development, Georgia Institute of Technology, Working Paper Series (Jan. 1994).

B.

The second part of our analysis requires us to determine whether the degree of the exactions demanded by the city's permit conditions bears the required relationship to the projected impact of petitioner's proposed development. *Nollan, supra,* at 834, *quoting* Penn Central Transp. Co. v. New York City, 438 U.S. 104, 127 (1978) ("[A] use restriction may constitute a 'taking' if not reasonably necessary to the effectuation of a substantial government purpose"). Here the Oregon Supreme Court deferred to what it termed the "city's unchallenged factual findings" supporting the dedication conditions and found them to be reasonably related to the impact of the expansion of petitioner's business.

The city required that petitioner dedicate "to the City as Greenway all portions of the site that fall within the existing 100-year floodplain [of Fanno Creek] . . . and all property 15 feet above [the floodplain] boundary." In addition, the city demanded that the retail store be designed so as not to intrude into the greenway area. The city relies on the Commission's rather tentative findings that increased storm water flow from petitioner's property "can only add to the public need to manage the [floodplain] for drainage purposes" to support its conclusion that the "requirement of dedication of the floodplain area on the site is related to the applicant's plan to intensify development on the site." The city made the following specific findings relevant to the pedestrian/bicycle pathway:

> In addition, the proposed expanded use of this site is anticipated to generate additional vehicular traffic thereby increasing congestion on nearby collector and arterial streets. Creation of a convenient, safe pedestrian/bicycle pathway system as an alternative means of transportation could offset some of the traffic demand on these nearby streets and lessen the increase in traffic congestion.

The question for us is whether these findings are constitutionally sufficient to justify the conditions imposed by the city on petitioner's building permit. Since state courts have been dealing with this question a good deal longer than we have, we turn to representative decisions made by them. . . . In some States, very generalized statements as to the necessary connection between the required dedication and the proposed development seem to suffice. . . . Other state courts require a very exacting correspondence, described as the "specific and uniquely attributable" test. . . . A number of state courts have taken an intermediate position, requiring the municipality to show a "reasonable relationship" between the required dedication and the impact of the proposed development.

We think the "reasonable relationship" test adopted by a majority of the state courts is closer to the federal constitutional norm than either of those previously discussed. But we do not adopt it as such, partly because the term "reasonable relationship" seems confusingly similar to the term "rational basis" which describes the minimal level of scrutiny under the Equal Protection Clause of the Fourteenth Amendment. We think a term such as "rough proportionality" best encapsulates what we hold to be the requirement of the Fifth Amendment. No precise mathematical calculation is required, but the city must make some sort of individualized determination that the required dedication is related both in nature and extent to the impact of the proposed development.

It is axiomatic that increasing the amount of impervious surface will increase the quantity and rate of storm water flow from petitioner's property. Therefore, keeping the floodplain open and free from development would likely confine the pressures on Fanno Creek created by petitioner's development. In fact, because petitioner's property lies within the Central Business District, the CDC already required that petitioner leave 15% of it as open space and the undeveloped floodplain would have nearly satisfied that requirement. But the city demanded more — it not only wanted petitioner not to build in the floodplain, but it also wanted petitioner's property along Fanno Creek for its greenway system. The city has never said why a public greenway, as opposed to a private one, was required in the interest of flood control. . . . We conclude that the findings upon which the city relies do not show the required reasonable relationship between the floodplain easement and the petitioner's proposed new building.

With respect to the pedestrian/bicycle pathway, we have no doubt that the city was correct in finding that the larger retail sales facility proposed by petitioner will increase traffic on the streets of the Central Business District. The city estimates that the proposed development would generate roughly 435 additional trips per day. Dedications for streets, sidewalks, and other public ways are generally reasonable exactions to avoid excessive congestion from a proposed property use. But on the record before us, the city has not met its burden of demonstrating that the additional number of vehicle and bicycle trips generated by petitioner's development reasonably relate to the city's requirement for a dedication of the pedestrian/bicycle pathway easement. The city simply found that the creation of the pathway "could offset some of the traffic demand . . . and lessen the increase in traffic congestion."

As Justice Peterson of the Supreme Court of Oregon explained in his dissenting opinion, however, "the findings of fact that the bicycle pathway system '*could* offset some of the traffic demand' is a far cry from a finding that the bicycle pathway system *will*, or is *likely to*, offset some of the traffic demand." 854 P.2d at 447 (emphasis in original). No precise mathematical calculation is required, but the city must make some effort to quantify its findings in support of the dedication for the pedestrian/bicycle pathway beyond the conclusory statement that it could offset some of the traffic demand generated.

IV.

Cities have long engaged in the commendable task of land use planning, made necessary by increasing urbanization, particularly in metropolitan areas such as Portland. The city's goals of reducing flooding hazards and traffic congestion, and providing for public greenways, are laudable, but there are outer limits to how this may be done. "A strong public desire to improve the public condition [will not] warrant achieving the desire by a shorter cut than the constitutional way of paying for the change." *Pennsylvania Coal*, 260 U.S. at 416. . . .

Dolan's store after the expansion

Justice Stevens, with whom Justices Blackmun and Ginsburg join, dissenting. . . .

In our changing world one thing is certain: uncertainty will characterize predictions about the impact of new urban developments on the risks of floods, earthquakes, traffic congestion, or environmental harms. When there is doubt concerning the magnitude of those impacts, the public interest in averting them must outweigh the private interest of the commercial entrepreneur. If the government can demonstrate that the conditions it has imposed in a land use permit are rational, impartial and conducive to fulfilling the aims of a valid land use plan, a strong presumption of validity should attach to those conditions. The burden of demonstrating that those conditions have unreasonably impaired the economic value of the proposed improvement belongs squarely on the shoulders of the party challenging the state action's constitutionality. That allocation of burdens has served us well in the past. The Court has stumbled badly today by reversing it. . . .

[Justice Souter's dissenting opinion is omitted.]

Notes and Questions

1. *Dolan* and *Nollan* both involved exactions of land. Impact fees are a device by which governments exact money from prospective developers, as noted in Chapter 12. In Ehrlich v. City of Culver City, 911 P.2d 429 (Cal. 1996), for example, the city sought a $280,000 recreation fee and a $33,300 fee to provide art in public places. The court held that while *Dolan* and *Nollan* apply to nonpossessory exactions, the art in public places fee satisfied the Supreme Court's tests, while the validity of the recreation fee would depend upon the determination on remand of the city's interest. The tests were also applied in Benchmark Land Co. v. City of Battle Ground, 49 F.3d 860 (Wash. 2002), where a city ordinance required a developer to finance improvements to adjacent roads that did not actually service the development. The court found a taking because there was no rough proportionality between the need to improve the roads and the minimal traffic on those roads that would be generated by the development. In another case, Krupp v. Breckenridge Sanitation Dist., 19 P.2d 687 (Colo. 2001), the court held that a sewer service fee is not subject to *Dolan* and *Nollan*.

2. City of Monterrey v. Del Monte Dunes, Ltd., 526 U.S. 687 (1999), indicates that the *Dolan* proportionality test applies only to exactions of land or money, not to regulatory takings generally. Should the Court insist upon compensation when a regulation is not roughly proportional to the state's interest? And what other implications might *Dolan* have? Consider that Judge O'Scannlain has suggested that "the underlying thrust of the *Nollan-Lucas-Dolan* decisions — increasing scrutiny of regulations to determine if they go 'too far' (enough to require compensation) — is inconsistent with *Midkiff*'s sweeping deference" to legislative and executive findings of public use. Richardson v. City and County of Honolulu, 124 F.3d 1150, 1167 (9th Cir. 1997) (O'Scannlain, J., concurring in part and dissenting in part).

3. A handful of states have constitutional provisions requiring the government to pay compensation for "damaging" someone's property. *See, e.g.,* Colo. Const. art. II, §15 (stating that "[p]rivate property shall not be taken or damaged, for public or private use, without just compensation"). How do those provisions differ from "takings" clauses?

4. In recent years, over two-thirds of the states have enacted some form of property rights protection legislation dealing with compensation for regulatory takings. Although many of these statutes did not fundamentally change standards for government compensation of property owners impacted by government actions, others did. For example, a 1995 Florida statute mandates compensation whenever a property owner is "inordinately burdened" by a government action. Fla. Stat. §70.001. In Texas, the Private Real Property Rights Preservation Act authorizes compensation of private landowners when certain government actions reduce the value of a parcel of land by more than 25 percent. Tex. Gov't Code Ann. §2007.001 (enacted 1995). Another statute approved by Oregon voters in 2000 would have required the payment of compensation equal to the reduction in value caused by all new government regulations except "historically and commonly recognized nuisance laws." Measure 7 to amend Or. Const. art. I, §18. That statute, however, was invalidated by a state court because it failed to comply with the state constitutional requirements for enacting initiatives. League of Oregon Cities v. State, 56 P.3d 892 (Or. 2002).

5. Takings legislation reflects a desire to provide clear rules concerning when the government should compensate owners whose property suffers from governmental actions. Are such clear rules desirable? Professors David Dana and Thomas Merrill describe the affirmative answer: "Categorical rules designed to produce consistent outcomes under readily identifiable states of fact can be seen as a strategy for reducing legal risk, and hence reducing demoralization costs." David A. Dana & Thomas W. Merrill, *Property: Takings* 91 (2002). Professor Marc Poirier advances the contrary answer. He first makes a "fundamental societal limitation claim" that "it is in fact impossible to be altogether precise about property and the treatment of it in regulatory takings scenarios." Marc R. Poirier, *The Virtue of Vagueness in Takings Doctrine*, 24 Cardozo L. Rev. 93, 132 (2002). More positively, Poirier posits that "a muddy takings doctrine . . . forces people to negotiate with each other as though they were members of the same community, [and] can foster behavior and eventually beliefs that do in fact reproduce community." *Id.* at 153. Thus "a vague takings doctrine . . . urges that, although surprises and bad things happen, we will all try to be fair and to make it right." *Id.* at 191.

6. Takings legislation is also premised upon particular understandings of the very idea of property. So, more generally, are all debates about takings. Sometimes that is explicit. *See, e.g.*, Paul J. Otterstedt, *A Natural Rights Approach to Regulatory Takings*, 7 Tex. Rev. L. & Pol. 25 (2002) (articulating an approach to regulatory takings premised upon natural law). More often, claims about takings presume certain views about property that claimants fail to express or even fully recognize. How is the answer to the takings question affected by the preferred theory of property selected among those described in Chapter 1?

Table of Cases

Index